Computer Networks

Third Edition

Other bestselling titles by Andrew S. Tanenbaum:

Operating Systems: Design and Implementation, 2nd edition

This now-classic text on operating systems is the only book covering both the principles of operating systems and their application to a real system. All the traditional operating systems topics are covered in detail. In addition, the principles are carefully illustrated by MINIX, a free UNIX-like operating system for personal computers. The second edition, which is expected in late 1996, will deal with the new POSIX-based MINIX 2.0 system. As with the first edition, the book will include a listing of the MINIX source code. New to the second edition is a free CD-ROM in each book containing the complete MINIX system (binary and source code).

Modern Operating Systems

This bestselling text presents the basics of both single processor and distributed computer systems. Tanenbaum covers traditional topics including processes, memory management, and files systems as well as key issues in distributed systems including the client-server model, remote procedure call, threads and distributed files servers. This practical guide uses UNIX, MS-DOS, Mach and Amoeba to illustrate operating system concepts.

Distributed Operating Systems

This text covers the fundamental concepts of distributed operating systems. Key topics include communication and synchronization, processes and processors, distributed shared memory, distributed file systems, and distributed real-time systems. The principles of distributed computing are illustrated in four detailed case studies using Mach, Amoeba, Chorus and DCE operating environments.

Structured Computer Organization, 3rd edition

This leading text looks at computer architecture as a series of levels. At the bottom is the hardware: transistors, gates, registers, adders, and other circuits. Then comes the microprogramming level. After that is the conventional machine level, with its ADD, MOVE, JUMP, and other instructions. On top of that is the operating system, which adds new facilities such as file management and virtual memory. The final chapter deals with two advanced topics: parallel computers and the design of RISC machines.

Computer Networks

Third Edition

Andrew S. Tanenbaum

Vrije Universiteit
Amsterdam, The Netherlands

For book and bookstore information

http://www.prenhall.com

Prentice Hall PTR
Upper Saddle River, New Jersey 07458

Library of Congress Cataloging in Publication Data

Tanenbaum, Andrew S. 1944-.
    Computer networks / Andrew S. Tanenbaum. -- 3rd ed.
       p.   cm.
    Includes bibliographical references and index.
    ISBN 0-13-349945-6
    1.Computer networks. I. Title.
TK5105.5.T36 1996   96-4121
004.6--dc20   CIP

Editorial/production manager: *Camille Trentacoste*
Interior design and composition: *Andrew S. Tanenbaum*
Cover design director: *Jerry Votta*
Cover designer: *Don Martinetti, DM Graphics, Inc.*
Cover concept: *Andrew S. Tanenbaum, from an idea by Marilyn Tremaine*
Interior graphics: *Hadel Studio*
Manufacturing manager: *Alexis R. Heydt*
Acquisitions editor: *Mary Franz*
Editorial Assistant: *Noreen Regina*

 © 1996 by Prentice Hall PTR
Prentice-Hall, Inc.
A Simon & Schuster Company
Upper Saddle River, New Jersey 07458

The publisher offers discounts on this book when ordered in bulk quantities. For more information, contact:
Corporate Sales Department, Prentice Hall PTR, One Lake Street, Upper Saddle River, NJ 07458.
Phone: (800) 382-3419; Fax: (201) 236-7141. E-mail: corpsales@prenhall.com

Printed in the United States of America
10 9 8 7 6 5 4 3 2

ISBN 0-13-349945-6

Prentice-Hall International (UK) Limited, *London*
Prentice-Hall of Australia Pty. Limited, *Sydney*
Prentice-Hall Canada Inc., *Toronto*
Prentice-Hall Hispanoamericana, S.A., *Mexico*
Prentice-Hall of India Private Limited, *New Delhi*
Prentice-Hall of Japan, Inc., *Tokyo*
Simon & Schuster Asia Pte. Ltd., *Singapore*
Editora Prentice-Hall do Brasil, Ltda., *Rio de Janeiro*

To Suzanne, Barbara, Marvin, and Little Bram

CONTENTS

3 THE DATA LINK LAYER 175

5 THE NETWORK LAYER 339

6 THE TRANSPORT LAYER   479

PREFACE

This book is now in its third edition. Each edition has corresponded to a different phase in the way computer networks were used. When the first edition appeared in 1980, networks were an academic curiosity. When the second edition appeared in 1988, networks were used by universities and large businesses. When the third edition appeared in 1996, computer networks, especially the worldwide Internet, had become a daily reality for millions of people.

Furthermore, the networking hardware and software have completely changed since the second edition appeared. In 1988, nearly all networks were based on copper wire. Now, many are based on fiber optics or wireless communication. Proprietary networks, such as SNA, have become far less important than public networks, especially the Internet. The OSI protocols have quietly vanished, and the TCP/IP protocol suite has become dominant. In fact, so much has changed, the book has almost been rewritten from scratch.

Although Chap. 1 has the same introductory function as it did in the second edition, the contents have been completely revised and brought up to date. For example, instead of basing the book on the seven-layer OSI model, a five-layer hybrid model (shown in Fig. 1-21) is now used and introduced in Chap. 1. While not exactly identical to the TCP/IP model, it is much closer to the TCP/IP model in spirit than it is to the OSI model used in the second edition. Also, the new running examples used throughout the book—the Internet and ATM networks— are introduced here, along with some gigabit networks and other popular networks.

In Chap. 2, the focus has moved from copper wire to fiber optics and wireless communication, since these are the technologies of the future. The telephone system has become almost entirely digital in the past decade, so the material on it has been largely rewritten, with new material on broadband ISDN added. The material on cellular radio has been greatly expanded, and new material on low-orbit satellites has been added to the chapter.

The order of discussion of the data link layer and the MAC sublayer has been reversed, since experience with students shows that they understand the MAC sublayer better after they have studied the data link layer. The example protocols there have been kept, as they have proven very popular, but they have been rewritten in C. New material on the Internet and ATM data link layers has been added.

The MAC sublayer principles of Chap. 4. have been revised to reflect new protocols, including wavelength division multiplexing, wireless LANs, and digital radio. The discussion of bridges has been revised, and new material has been added on high-speed LANs.

Most of the routing algorithms of Chap. 5 have been replaced by more modern ones, including distance vector and link state routing. The sections on congestion control have been completely redone, and material on the running examples, the Internet and ATM is all new.

Chap. 6 is still about the transport layer, but here, too, major changes have occurred, primarily, the addition of a large amount of new material about the Internet, ATM, and network performance.

Chap. 7, on the application layer, is now the longest chapter in the book. The material on network security has been doubled in length, and new material has been added on DNS, SNMP, email, USENET, the World Wide Web, HTML, Java, multimedia, video on demand, and the MBone.

Of the 395 figures in the third edition, 276 (70 percent) are completely new and some of the others have been revised. Of the 371 references to the literature, 282 (76 percent) are to books and papers that have appeared since the second edition was published. Of these, over 100 are to works published in 1995 and 1996 alone. All in all, probably 75 percent of the entire book is brand new, and parts of the remaining 25 percent have been heavily revised. Since this is effectively a new book, the cover was redesigned to avoid confusion with the second edition.

Computer books are full of acronyms. This one is no exception. By the time you are finished reading this one, all of the following should ring a bell: AAL, AMPS, ARP, ASN, ATM, BGP, CDMA, CDPD, CSMA, DQDB, DNS, FAQ, FDM, FTP, FTTC, FTTH, GSM, HDLC, HEC, HIPPI, IAB, ICMP, IDEA, IETF, IPv6, ISO, ITU, LATA, MAC, MACA, MAN, MIB, MIME, NAP, NNTP, NSA, NSAP, OSI, OSPF, PCM, PCN, PCS, PEM, PGP, PPP, PSTN, PTT, PVC, QAM, RARP, RFC, RSA, SABME, SAP, SAR, SDH, SDLC, SHA, SMI, SNA, SNMP, SNRME, SPX, TCP, UDP, VHF, VLF, VSAT, WARC, WDM, WWV, and WWW. But don't worry. Each one will be carefully defined before it is used.

To help instructors using this book as a text for course, the author has prepared three teaching aids:

- A problem solutions manual.

- PostScript files containing all the figures (for making overhead sheets).

- A simulator (written in C) for the example protocols of Chap. 3.

The solutions manual is available from Prentice Hall (but only to instructors). The file with the figures and the simulator are available via the World Wide Web. To get them, please see the author's home page: *http://www.cs.vu.nl/~ast/* .

The book was typeset in Times Roman using Troff, which, after all these years, is still the only way to go. While Troff is not as trendy as WYSIWYG systems, the reader is invited to compare the typesetting quality of this book with books produced by WYSIWYG systems. My only concession to PCs and desktop publishing is that for the first time, the art was produced using Adobe Illustrator, instead of being drawn on paper. Also for the first time, the book was produced entirely electronically. The PostScript output from Troff was sent over the Internet to the printer, where the film for making the offset plates was produced. No intermediate paper copy was printed and photographed, as is normally done.

Many people helped me during the course of the third edition. I would especially like to thank Chase Bailey, Saniya Ben Hassen, Nathaniel Borenstein, Ron Cocchi, Dave Crocker, Wiebren de Jonge, Carl Ellison, M. Rasit Eskicioglu, John Evans, Mario Gerla, Mike Goguen, Paul Green, Dick Grune, Wayne Hathaway, Franz Hauck, Jack Holtzman, Gerard Holzmann, Philip Homburg, Peter Honeyman, Raj Jain, Dave Johnson, Charlie Kaufman, Vinay Kumar, Jorg Liebeherr, Paul Mockapetris, Carol Orange, Craig Partridge, Charlie Perkins, Thomas Powell, Greg Sharp, Anne Steegstra, George Swallow, Mark Taylor, Peter van der Linden, Hans van Staveren, Maarten van Steen, Kees Verstoep, Stephen Walters, Michael Weintraub, Joseph Wilkes, and Stephen Wolff. Special thanks go to Radia Perlman for many helpful suggestions. My students have also helped in many ways. I would like to single out Martijn Bot, Wilbert de Graaf, Flavio del Pomo, and Arnold de Wit for their assistance.

My editor at Prentice Hall, Mary Franz, provided me with more reading material than I had consumed in the previous 10 years. She was also helpful in numerous other ways, small, medium, large, and jumbo. My production editor, Camille Trentacoste, taught me about people of snow, 8-up flats, fax [sic], and other important items, while performing yeoperson's service with a Picky Author and a tight schedule.

Finally, we come to the most important people. Suzanne, Barbara, Marvin, and even little Bram, have been through this routine before. They endure it with infinite patience and good grace. Thank you.

ANDREW S. TANENBAUM

1

INTRODUCTION

Each of the past three centuries has been dominated by a single technology. The 18th Century was the time of the great mechanical systems accompanying the Industrial Revolution. The 19th Century was the age of the steam engine. During the 20th Century, the key technology has been information gathering, processing, and distribution. Among other developments, we have seen the installation of worldwide telephone networks, the invention of radio and television, the birth and unprecedented growth of the computer industry, and the launching of communication satellites.

Due to rapid technological progress, these areas are rapidly converging, and the differences between collecting, transporting, storing, and processing information are quickly disappearing. Organizations with hundreds of offices spread over a wide geographical area routinely expect to be able to examine the current status of even their most remote outpost at the push of a button. As our ability to gather, process, and distribute information grows, the demand for even more sophisticated information processing grows even faster.

Although the computer industry is young compared to other industries (e.g., automobiles and air transportation), computers have made spectacular progress in a short time. During the first two decades of their existence, computer systems were highly centralized, usually within a single large room. Not infrequently, this room had glass walls, through which visitors could gawk at the great electronic wonder inside. A medium-size company or university might have had one or two computers, while large institutions had at most a few dozen. The idea that within 20 years equally powerful computers smaller than postage stamps would be mass produced by the millions was pure science fiction.

The merging of computers and communications has had a profound influence on the way computer systems are organized. The concept of the "computer center" as a room with a large computer to which users bring their work for processing is now totally obsolete. The old model of a single computer serving all of the organization's computational needs has been replaced by one in which a large number of separate but interconnected computers do the job. These systems are called **computer networks**. The design and organization of these networks are the subjects of this book.

Throughout the book we will use the term "computer network" to mean an *interconnected* collection of *autonomous* computers. Two computers are said to be interconnected if they are able to exchange information. The connection need not be via a copper wire; fiber optics, microwaves, and communication satellites can also be used. By requiring the computers to be autonomous, we wish to exclude from our definition systems in which there is a clear master/slave relation. If one computer can forcibly start, stop, or control another one, the computers are not autonomous. A system with one control unit and many slaves is not a network; nor is a large computer with remote printers and terminals.

There is considerable confusion in the literature between a computer network and a **distributed system**. The key distinction is that in a distributed system, the existence of multiple autonomous computers is transparent (i.e., not visible) to the user. He[†] can type a command to run a program, and it runs. It is up to the operating system to select the best processor, find and transport all the input files to that processor, and put the results in the appropriate place.

In other words, the user of a distributed system is not aware that there are multiple processors; it looks like a virtual uniprocessor. Allocation of jobs to processors and files to disks, movement of files between where they are stored and where they are needed, and all other system functions must be automatic.

With a network, users must *explicitly* log onto one machine, *explicitly* submit jobs remotely, *explicitly* move files around and generally handle all the network management personally. With a distributed system, nothing has to be done explicitly; it is all automatically done by the system without the users' knowledge.

In effect, a distributed system is a software system built on top of a network. The software gives it a high degree of cohesiveness and transparency. Thus the distinction between a network and a distributed system lies with the software (especially the operating system), rather than with the hardware.

Nevertheless, there is considerable overlap between the two subjects. For example, both distributed systems and computer networks need to move files around. The difference lies in who invokes the movement, the system or the user.

† "He" should be read as "he or she" throughout this book.

Although this book primarily focuses on networks, many of the topics are also important in distributed systems. For more information about distributed systems, see (Coulouris et al., 1994; Mullender, 1993; and Tanenbaum, 1995).

1.1. USES OF COMPUTER NETWORKS

Before we start to examine the technical issues in detail, it is worth devoting some time to pointing out why people are interested in computer networks and what they can be used for.

1.1.1. Networks for Companies

Many organizations have a substantial number of computers in operation, often located far apart. For example, a company with many factories may have a computer at each location to keep track of inventories, monitor productivity, and do the local payroll. Initially, each of these computers may have worked in isolation from the others, but at some point, management may have decided to connect them to be able to extract and correlate information about the entire company.

Put in slightly more general form, the issue here is **resource sharing**, and the goal is to make all programs, equipment, and especially data available to anyone on the network without regard to the physical location of the resource and the user. In other words, the mere fact that a user happens to be 1000 km away from his data should not prevent him from using the data as though they were local. This goal may be summarized by saying that it is an attempt to end the "tyranny of geography."

A second goal is to provide **high reliability** by having alternative sources of supply. For example, all files could be replicated on two or three machines, so if one of them is unavailable (due to a hardware failure), the other copies could be used. In addition, the presence of multiple CPUs means that if one goes down, the others may be able to take over its work, although at reduced performance. For military, banking, air traffic control, nuclear reactor safety, and many other applications, the ability to continue operating in the face of hardware problems is of utmost importance.

Another goal is **saving money**. Small computers have a much better price/performance ratio than large ones. Mainframes (room-size computers) are roughly a factor of ten faster than personal computers, but they cost a thousand times more. This imbalance has caused many systems designers to build systems consisting of personal computers, one per user, with data kept on one or more shared **file server** machines. In this model, the users are called **clients**, and the whole arrangement is called the **client-server model**. It is illustrated in Fig. 1-1.

In the client-server model, communication generally takes the form of a request message from the client to the server asking for some work to be done.

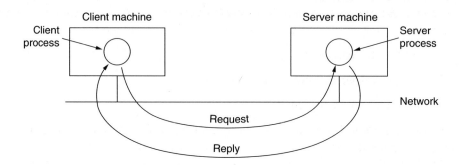

Fig. 1-1. The client-server model.

The server then does the work and sends back the reply. Usually, there are many clients using a small number of servers.

Another networking goal is scalability, the ability to increase system performance gradually as the workload grows just by adding more processors. With centralized mainframes, when the system is full, it must be replaced by a larger one, usually at great expense and even greater disruption to the users. With the client-server model, new clients and new servers can be added as needed.

Yet another goal of setting up a computer network has little to do with technology at all. A computer network can provide a powerful **communication medium** among widely separated employees. Using a network, it is easy for two or more people who live far apart to write a report together. When one worker makes a change to an on-line document, the others can see the change immediately, instead of waiting several days for a letter. Such a speedup makes cooperation among far-flung groups of people easy where it previously had been impossible. In the long run, the use of networks to enhance human-to-human communication will probably prove more important than technical goals such as improved reliability.

1.1.2. Networks for People

The motivations given above for building computer networks are all essentially economic and technological in nature. If sufficiently large and powerful mainframes were available at acceptable prices, most companies would simply choose to keep all their data on them and give employees terminals connected to them. In the 1970s and early 1980s, most companies operated this way. Computer networks only became popular when networks of personal computers offered a huge price/performance advantage over mainframes.

Starting in the 1990s, computer networks began to start delivering services to private individuals at home. These services and the motivations for using them are quite different than the "corporate efficiency" model described in the previous section. Below we will sketch three of the more exciting ones that are starting to happen:

1. Access to remote information.

2. Person-to-person communication.

3. Interactive entertainment.

Access to remote information will come in many forms. One area in which it is already happening is access to financial institutions. Many people pay their bills, manage their bank accounts, and handle their investments electronically. Home shopping is also becoming popular, with the ability to inspect the on-line catalogs of thousands of companies. Some of these catalogs will soon provide the ability to get an instant video on any product by just clicking on the product's name.

Newspapers will go on-line and be personalized. It will be possible to tell the newspaper that you want everything about corrupt politicians, big fires, scandals involving celebrities, and epidemics, but no football, thank you. At night while you sleep, the newspaper will be downloaded to your computer's disk or printed on your laser printer. On a small scale, this service already exists. The next step beyond newspapers (plus magazines and scientific journals) is the on-line digital library. Depending on the cost, size, and weight of book-sized notebook computers, printed books may become obsolete. Skeptics should take note of the effect the printing press had on the medieval illuminated manuscript.

Another application that falls in this category is access to information systems like the current World Wide Web, which contains information about the arts, business, cooking, government, health, history, hobbies, recreation, science, sports, travel, and too many other topics to even mention.

All of the above applications involve interactions between a person and a remote database. The second broad category of network use will be person-to-person interactions, basically the 21st Century's answer to the 19th Century's telephone. Electronic mail or **email** is already widely used by millions of people and will soon routinely contain audio and video as well as text. Smell in messages will take a bit longer to perfect.

Real-time email will allow remote users to communicate with no delay, possibly seeing and hearing each other as well. This technology makes it possible to have virtual meetings, called **videoconference**, among far-flung people. It is sometimes said that transportation and communication are having a race, and whichever wins will make the other obsolete. Virtual meetings could be used for remote school, getting medical opinions from distant specialists, and numerous other applications.

Worldwide newsgroups, with discussions on every conceivable topic are already commonplace among a select group of people, and this will grow to include the population at large. These discussions, in which one person posts a message and all the other subscribers to the newsgroup can read it, run the gamut from humorous to impassioned.

Our third category is entertainment, which is a huge and growing industry. The killer application here (the one that may drive all the rest) is video on demand. A decade or so hence, it may be possible to select any movie or television program ever made, in any country, and have it displayed on your screen instantly. New films may become interactive, where the user is occasionally prompted for the story direction (should MacBeth murder Duncan or just bide his time?) with alternative scenarios provided for all cases. Live television may also become interactive, with the audience participating in quiz shows, choosing among contestants, and so on.

On the other hand, maybe the killer application will not be video on demand. Maybe it will be game playing. Already we have multiperson real-time simulation games, like hide-and-seek in a virtual dungeon, and flight simulators with the players on one team trying to shoot down the players on the opposing team. If done with goggles and 3-dimensional real-time, photographic-quality moving images, we have a kind of worldwide shared virtual reality.

In short, the ability to merge information, communication, and entertainment will surely give rise to a massive new industry based on computer networking.

1.1.3. Social Issues

The widespread introduction of networking will introduce new social, ethical, political problems (Laudon, 1995). Let us just briefly mention a few of them; a thorough study would require a full book, at least. A popular feature of many networks are newsgroups or bulletin boards where people can exchange messages with like-minded individuals. As long as the subjects are restricted to technical topics or hobbies like gardening, not too many problems will arise.

The trouble comes when newsgroups are set up on topics that people actually care about, like politics, religion, or sex. Views posted to such groups may be deeply offensive to some people. Furthermore, messages need not be limited to text. High-resolution color photographs and even short video clips can now easily be transmitted over computer networks. Some people take a live-and-let-live view, but others feel that posting certain material (e.g., child pornography) is simply unacceptable. Thus the debate rages.

People have sued network operators, claiming that they are responsible for the contents of what they carry, just as newspapers and magazines are. The inevitable response is that a network is like a telephone company or the post office and cannot be expected to police what its users say. Stronger yet, having network operators censor messages would probably cause them to delete everything with even the slightest possibility of their being sued, and thus violate their users' rights to free speech. It is probably safe to say that this debate will go on for a while.

Another fun area is employee rights versus employer rights. Many people read and write email at work. Some employers have claimed the right to read and possibly censor employee messages, including messages sent from a home terminal after work. Not all employees agree with this (Sipior and Ward, 1995).

Even if employers have power over employees, does this relationship also govern universities and students? How about high schools and students? In 1994, Carnegie-Mellon University decided to turn off the incoming message stream for several newsgroups dealing with sex because the university felt the material was inappropriate for minors (i.e., those few students under 18). The fallout from this event will take years to settle.

Computer networks offer the potential for sending anonymous messages. In some situations, this capability may be desirable. For example, it provides a way for students, soldiers, employees, and citizens to blow the whistle on illegal behavior on the part of professors, officers, superiors, and politicians without fear of reprisals. On the other hand, in the United States and most other democracies, the law specifically permits an accused person the right to confront and challenge his accuser in court. Anonymous accusations cannot be used as evidence.

In short, computer networks, like the printing press 500 years ago, allow ordinary citizens to distribute their views in different ways and to different audiences than were previously possible. This new-found freedom brings with it many unsolved social, political, and moral issues. The solution to these problems is left as an exercise for the reader.

1.2. NETWORK HARDWARE

It is now time to turn our attention from the applications and social aspects of networking to the technical issues involved in network design. There is no generally accepted taxonomy into which all computer networks fit, but two dimensions stand out as important: transmission technology and scale. We will now examine each of these in turn.

Broadly speaking, there are two types of transmission technology:

1. Broadcast networks.

2. Point-to-point networks.

Broadcast networks have a single communication channel that is shared by all the machines on the network. Short messages, called **packets** in certain contexts, sent by any machine are received by all the others. An address field within the packet specifies for whom it is intended. Upon receiving a packet, a machine checks the address field. If the packet is intended for itself, it processes the packet; if the packet is intended for some other machine, it is just ignored.

As an analogy, consider someone standing at the end of a corridor with many rooms off it and shouting "Watson, come here. I want you." Although the packet may actually be received (heard) by many people, only Watson responds. The others just ignore it. Another example is an airport announcement asking all flight 644 passengers to report to gate 12.

Broadcast systems generally also allow the possibility of addressing a packet to *all* destinations by using a special code in the address field. When a packet with this code is transmitted, it is received and processed by every machine on the network. This mode of operation is called **broadcasting**. Some broadcast systems also support transmission to a subset of the machines, something known as **multicasting**. One possible scheme is to reserve one bit to indicate multicasting. The remaining $n - 1$ address bits can hold a group number. Each machine can "subscribe" to any or all of the groups. When a packet is sent to a certain group, it is delivered to all machines subscribing to that group.

In contrast, **point-to-point** networks consist of many connections between individual pairs of machines. To go from the source to the destination, a packet on this type of network may have to first visit one or more intermediate machines. Often multiple routes, of different lengths are possible, so routing algorithms play an important role in point-to-point networks. As a general rule (although there are many exceptions), smaller, geographically localized networks tend to use broadcasting, whereas larger networks usually are point-to-point.

Interprocessor distance	Processors located in same	Example
0.1 m	Circuit board	Data flow machine
1 m	System	Multicomputer
10 m	Room	
100 m	Building	Local area network
1 km	Campus	
10 km	City	Metropolitan area network
100 km	Country	
1,000 km	Continent	Wide area network
10,000 km	Planet	The internet

Fig. 1-2. Classification of interconnected processors by scale.

An alternative criterion for classifying networks is their scale. In Fig. 1-2 we give a classification of multiple processor systems arranged by their physical size. At the top are **data flow machines**, highly parallel computers with many functional units all working on the same program. Next come the **multicomputers**, systems that communicate by sending messages over very short, very fast buses. Beyond the multicomputers are the true networks, computers that communicate by exchanging messages over longer cables. These can be divided into local, metropolitan, and wide area networks. Finally, the connection of two or more networks is called an internetwork. The worldwide Internet is a well-known example of an internetwork. Distance is important as a classification metric because different techniques are used at different scales. In this book we will be concerned with only the true networks and their interconnection. Below we give a brief introduction to the subject of network hardware.

1.2.1. Local Area Networks

Local area networks, generally called **LANs**, are privately-owned networks within a single building or campus of up to a few kilometers in size. They are widely used to connect personal computers and workstations in company offices and factories to share resources (e.g., printers) and exchange information. LANs are distinguished from other kinds of networks by three characteristics: (1) their size, (2) their transmission technology, and (3) their topology.

LANs are restricted in size, which means that the worst-case transmission time is bounded and known in advance. Knowing this bound makes it possible to use certain kinds of designs that would not otherwise be possible. It also simplifies network management.

LANs often use a transmission technology consisting of a single cable to which all the machines are attached, like the telephone company party lines once used in rural areas. Traditional LANs run at speeds of 10 to 100 Mbps, have low delay (tens of microseconds), and make very few errors. Newer LANs may operate at higher speeds, up to hundreds of megabits/sec. In this book, we will adhere to tradition and measure line speeds in megabits/sec (Mbps), not megabytes/sec (MB/sec). A megabit is 1,000,000 bits, not 1,048,576 (2^{20}) bits.

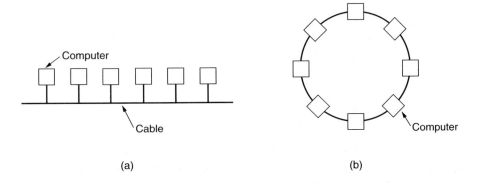

(a) (b)

Fig. 1-3. Two broadcast networks. (a) Bus. (b) Ring.

Various topologies are possible for broadcast LANs. Figure 1-3 shows two of them. In a bus (i.e., a linear cable) network, at any instant one machine is the master and is allowed to transmit. All other machines are required to refrain from sending. An arbitration mechanism is needed to resolve conflicts when two or more machines want to transmit simultaneously. The arbitration mechanism may be centralized or distributed. IEEE 802.3, popularly called **Ethernet**^{TM}, for example, is a bus-based broadcast network with decentralized control operating at 10 or 100 Mbps. Computers on an Ethernet can transmit whenever they want to; if two or more packets collide, each computer just waits a random time and tries again later.

A second type of broadcast system is the ring. In a ring, each bit propagates around on its own, not waiting for the rest of the packet to which it belongs. Typically, each bit circumnavigates the entire ring in the time it takes to transmit a few bits, often before the complete packet has even been transmitted. Like all other broadcast systems, some rule is needed for arbitrating simultaneous accesses to the ring. Various methods are in use and will be discussed later in this book. IEEE 802.5 (the IBM token ring), is a popular ring-based LAN operating at 4 and 16 Mbps.

Broadcast networks can be further divided into static and dynamic, depending on how the channel is allocated. A typical static allocation would be to divide up time into discrete intervals and run a round robin algorithm, allowing each machine to broadcast only when its time slot comes up. Static allocation wastes channel capacity when a machine has nothing to say during its allocated slot, so most systems attempt to allocate the channel dynamically (i.e., on demand).

Dynamic allocation methods for a common channel are either centralized or decentralized. In the centralized channel allocation method, there is a single entity, for example a bus arbitration unit, which determines who goes next. It might do this by accepting requests and making a decision according to some internal algorithm. In the decentralized channel allocation method, there is no central entity; each machine must decide for itself whether or not to transmit. You might think that this always leads to chaos, but it does not. Later we will study many algorithms designed to bring order out of the potential chaos.

The other kind of LAN is built using point-to-point lines. Individual lines connect a specific machine with another specific machine. Such a LAN is really a miniature wide area network. We will look at these later.

1.2.2. Metropolitan Area Networks

A **metropolitan area network**, or **MAN** (plural: MANs, not MEN) is basically a bigger version of a LAN and normally uses similar technology. It might cover a group of nearby corporate offices or a city and might be either private or public. A MAN can support both data and voice, and might even be related to the local cable television network. A MAN just has one or two cables and does not contain switching elements, which shunt packets over one of several potential output lines. Not having to switch simplifies the design.

The main reason for even distinguishing MANs as a special category is that a standard has been adopted for them, and this standard is now being implemented. It is called **DQDB (Distributed Queue Dual Bus)** or for people who prefer numbers to letters, 802.6 (the number of the IEEE standard that defines it). DQDB consists of two unidirectional buses (cables) to which all the computers are connected, as shown in Fig. 1-4. Each bus has a head-end, a device that initiates transmission activity. Traffic that is destined for a computer to the right of the sender uses the upper bus. Traffic to the left uses the lower one.

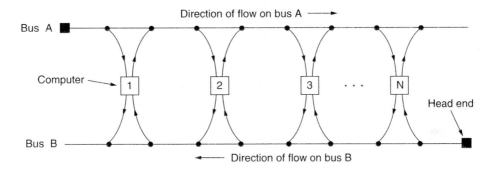

Fig. 1-4. Architecture of the DQDB metropolitan area network.

A key aspect of a MAN is that there is a broadcast medium (for 802.6, two cables) to which all the computers are attached. This greatly simplifies the design compared to other kinds of networks. We will discuss DQDB in more detail in Chap. 4.

1.2.3. Wide Area Networks

A **wide area network**, or **WAN**, spans a large geographical area, often a country or continent. It contains a collection of machines intended for running user (i.e., application) programs. We will follow traditional usage and call these machines **hosts**. The term **end system** is sometimes also used in the literature. The hosts are connected by a **communication subnet**, or just **subnet** for short. The job of the subnet is to carry messages from host to host, just as the telephone system carries words from speaker to listener. By separating the pure communication aspects of the network (the subnet) from the application aspects (the hosts), the complete network design is greatly simplified.

In most wide area networks, the subnet consists of two distinct components: transmission lines and switching elements. Transmission lines (also called **circuits**, **channels**, or **trunks**) move bits between machines.

The switching elements are specialized computers used to connect two or more transmission lines. When data arrive on an incoming line, the switching element must choose an outgoing line to forward them on. Unfortunately, there is no standard terminology used to name these computers. They are variously called **packet switching nodes**, **intermediate systems**, and **data switching exchanges**, among other things. As a generic term for the switching computers, we will use the word **router**, but the reader should be aware that no consensus on terminology exists here. In this model, shown in Fig. 1-5, each host is generally connected to a LAN on which a router is present, although in some cases a host can be connected directly to a router. The collection of communication lines and routers (but not the hosts) form the subnet.

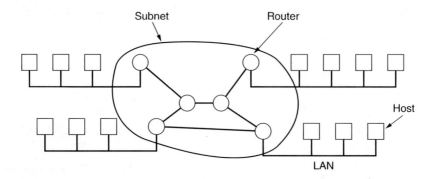

Fig. 1-5. Relation between hosts and the subnet.

An aside about the term "subnet" is worth making. Originally, its only meaning was the collection of routers and communication lines that moved packets from the source host to the destination host. However, some years later, it also acquired a second meaning in conjunction with network addressing (which we will discuss in Chap. 5). Hence the term has a certain ambiguity about it. Unfortunately, no widely-used alternative exists for its initial meaning, so with some hesitation we will use it in both senses. From the context, it will always be clear which is meant.

In most WANs, the network contains numerous cables or telephone lines, each one connecting a pair of routers. If two routers that do not share a cable nevertheless wish to communicate, they must do this indirectly, via other routers. When a packet is sent from one router to another via one or more intermediate routers, the packet is received at each intermediate router in its entirety, stored there until the required output line is free, and then forwarded. A subnet using this principle is called a **point-to-point**, **store-and-forward**, or **packet-switched** subnet. Nearly all wide area networks (except those using satellites) have store-and-forward subnets. When the packets are small and all the same size, they are often called **cells**.

When a point-to-point subnet is used, an important design issue is what the router interconnection topology should look like. Figure 1-6 shows several possible topologies. Local networks that were designed as such usually have a symmetric topology. In contrast, wide area networks typically have irregular topologies.

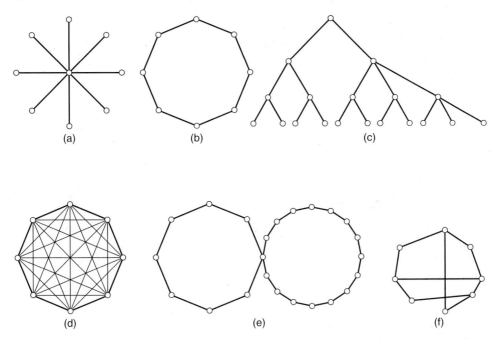

Fig. 1-6. Some possible topologies for a point-to-point subnet. (a) Star. (b) Ring. (c) Tree. (d) Complete. (e) Intersecting rings. (f) Irregular.

A second possibility for a WAN is a satellite or ground radio system. Each router has an antenna through which it can send and receive. All routers can hear the output *from* the satellite, and in some cases they can also hear the upward transmissions of their fellow routers *to* the satellite as well. Sometimes the routers are connected to a substantial point-to-point subnet, with only some of them having a satellite antenna. Satellite networks are inherently broadcast and are most useful when the broadcast property is important.

1.2.4. Wireless Networks

Mobile computers, such as notebook computers and personal digital assistants (PDAs), are the fastest-growing segment of the computer industry. Many of the owners of these computers have desktop machines on LANs and WANs back at the office and want to be connected to their home base even when away from home or en route. Since having a wired connection is impossible in cars and air-planes, there is a lot of interest in wireless networks. In this section we will briefly introduce this topic. (Note: by section, we mean those portions of the book with a three-part number such as 1.2.4.)

Actually, digital wireless communication is not a new idea. As early as 1901, the Italian physicist Guglielmo Marconi demonstrated a ship-to-shore wireless telegraph using Morse Code (dots and dashes are binary, after all). Modern digital wireless systems have better performance, but the basic idea is the same. Additional information about these systems can be found in (Garg and Wilkes, 1996; and Pahlavan et al., 1995).

Wireless networks have many uses. A common one is the portable office. People on the road often want to use their portable electronic equipment to send and receive telephone calls, faxes, and electronic mail, read remote files, login on remote machines, and so on, and do this from anywhere on land, sea, or air.

Wireless networks are of great value to fleets of trucks, taxis, buses, and repairpersons for keeping in contact with home. Another use is for rescue workers at disaster sites (fires, floods, earthquakes, etc.) where the telephone system has been destroyed. Computers there can send messages, keep records, and so on.

Finally, wireless networks are important to the military. If you have to be able to fight a war anywhere on earth on short notice, counting on using the local networking infrastructure is probably not a good idea. It is better to bring your own.

Although wireless networking and mobile computing are often related, they are not identical, as Fig. 1-7 shows. Portable computers are sometimes wired. For example, if a traveler plugs a portable computer into the telephone jack in a hotel, we have mobility without a wireless network. Another example is someone carrying a portable computer along as he inspects a train for technical problems. Here a long cord can trail along behind (vacuum cleaner model).

Wireless	Mobile	Applications
No	No	Stationary workstations in offices
No	Yes	Using a portable in a hotel; train maintenance
Yes	No	LANs in older, unwired buildings
Yes	Yes	Portable office; PDA for store inventory

Fig. 1-7. Combinations of wireless networks and mobile computing.

On the other hand, some wireless computers are not portable. An important example here is a company that owns an older building that does not have network cabling installed and wants to connect its computers. Installing a wireless LAN may require little more than buying a small box with some electronics and setting up some antennas. This solution may be cheaper than wiring the building.

Although wireless LANs are easy to install, they also have some disadvantages. Typically they have a capacity of 1–2 Mbps, which is much slower than wired LANs. The error rates are often much higher, too, and the transmissions from different computers can interfere with one another.

But of course, there are also the true mobile, wireless applications, ranging from the portable office to people walking around a store with a PDA doing inventory. At many busy airports, car rental return clerks work out in the parking lot with wireless portable computers. They type in the license plate number of returning cars, and their portable, which has a built-in printer, calls the main computer, gets the rental information, and prints out the bill on the spot. True mobile computing is discussed further in (Forman and Zahorjan, 1994).

Wireless networks come in many forms. Some universities are already installing antennas all over campus to allow students to sit under the trees and consult the library's card catalog. Here the computers communicate directly with the wireless LAN in digital form. Another possibility is using a cellular (i.e., portable) telephone with a traditional analog modem. Direct digital cellular service, called **CDPD** (**Cellular Digital Packet Data**) is becoming available in many cities. We will study it in Chap. 4.

Finally, it is possible to have different combinations of wired and wireless networking. For example, in Fig. 1-8(a), we depict an airplane with a number of people using modems and seat-back telephones to call the office. Each call is independent of the other ones. A much more efficient option, however, is the flying LAN of Fig. 1-8(b). Here each seat comes equipped with an Ethernet connector into which passengers can plug their computers. A single router on the aircraft maintains a radio link with some router on the ground, changing routers as it flies along. This configuration is just a traditional LAN, except that its connection to the outside world happens to be a radio link instead of a hardwired line.

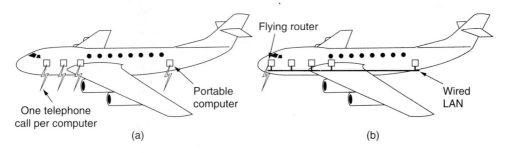

Fig. 1-8. (a) Individual mobile computers. (b) A flying LAN.

While many people believe that wireless portable computers are the wave of the future, at least one dissenting voice has been heard. Bob Metcalfe, the inventor of Ethernet, has written: "Mobile wireless computers are like mobile pipeless bathrooms—portapotties. They will be common on vehicles, and at construction sites, and rock concerts. My advice is to wire up your home and stay there" (Metcalfe, 1995). Will most people follow Metcalfe's advice? Time will tell.

1.2.5. Internetworks

Many networks exist in the world, often with different hardware and software. People connected to one network often want to communicate with people attached to a different one. This desire requires connecting together different, and frequently incompatible networks, sometimes by using machines called **gateways** to make the connection and provide the necessary translation, both in terms of hardware and software. A collection of interconnected networks is called an **internetwork** or just **internet**.

A common form of internet is a collection of LANs connected by a WAN. In fact, if we were to replace the label "subnet" in Fig. 1-5 by "WAN," nothing else in the figure would have to change. The only real distinction between a subnet and a WAN in this case is whether or not hosts are present. If the system within the closed curve contains only routers, it is a subnet. If it contains both routers and hosts with their own users, it is a WAN.

To avoid confusion, please note that the word "internet" will always be used in this book in a generic sense. In contrast, the **Internet** (note uppercase I) means a specific worldwide internet that is widely used to connect universities, government offices, companies, and of late, private individuals. We will have much to say about both internets and the Internet later in this book.

Subnets, networks, and internetworks are often confused. Subnet makes the most sense in the context of a wide area network, where it refers to the collection of routers and communication lines owned by the network operator, for example, companies like America Online and CompuServe. As an analogy, the telephone system consists of telephone switching offices connected to each other by high-speed lines, and to houses and businesses by low-speed lines. These lines and equipment, owned and managed by the telephone company, form the subnet of the telephone system. The telephones themselves (the hosts in this analogy) are not part of the subnet. The combination of a subnet and its hosts forms a network. In the case of a LAN, the cable and the hosts form the network. There really is no subnet.

An internetwork is formed when distinct networks are connected together. In our view, connecting a LAN and a WAN or connecting two LANs forms an internetwork, but there is little agreement in the industry over terminology in this area.

1.3. NETWORK SOFTWARE

The first computer networks were designed with the hardware as the main concern and the software as an afterthought. This strategy no longer works. Network software is now highly structured. In the following sections we examine the software structuring technique in some detail. The method described here forms the keystone of the entire book and will occur repeatedly later on.

1.3.1. Protocol Hierarchies

To reduce their design complexity, most networks are organized as a series of **layers** or **levels**, each one built upon the one below it. The number of layers, the name of each layer, the contents of each layer, and the function of each layer differ from network to network. However, in all networks, the purpose of each layer is to offer certain services to the higher layers, shielding those layers from the details of how the offered services are actually implemented.

Layer n on one machine carries on a conversation with layer n on another machine. The rules and conventions used in this conversation are collectively known as the layer n **protocol**. Basically, a protocol is an agreement between the communicating parties on how communication is to proceed. As an analogy, when a woman is introduced to a man, she may choose to stick out her hand. He, in turn, may decide either to shake it or kiss it, depending, for example, on whether she is an American lawyer at a business meeting or a European princess at a formal ball. Violating the protocol will make communication more difficult, if not impossible.

A five-layer network is illustrated in Fig. 1-9. The entities comprising the corresponding layers on different machines are called **peers**. In other words, it is the peers that communicate using the protocol.

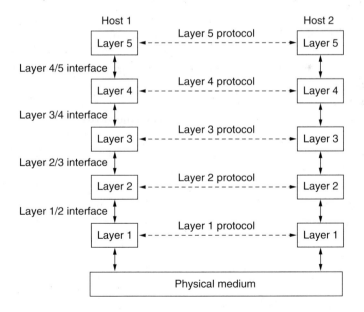

Fig. 1-9. Layers, protocols, and interfaces.

In reality, no data are directly transferred from layer n on one machine to layer n on another machine. Instead, each layer passes data and control information to the layer immediately below it, until the lowest layer is reached. Below layer 1 is the **physical medium** through which actual communication occurs. In Fig. 1-9, virtual communication is shown by dotted lines and physical communication by solid lines.

Between each pair of adjacent layers there is an **interface**. The interface defines which primitive operations and services the lower layer offers to the upper one. When network designers decide how many layers to include in a network and what each one should do, one of the most important considerations is defining clean interfaces between the layers. Doing so, in turn, requires that each layer perform a specific collection of well-understood functions. In addition to minimizing the amount of information that must be passed between layers, clean-cut interfaces also make it simpler to replace the implementation of one layer with a completely different implementation (e.g., all the telephone lines are replaced by satellite channels), because all that is required of the new implementation is that it offers exactly the same set of services to its upstairs neighbor as the old implementation did.

A set of layers and protocols is called a **network architecture**. The specification of an architecture must contain enough information to allow an implementer to write the program or build the hardware for each layer so that it will correctly obey the appropriate protocol. Neither the details of the implementation nor the specification of the interfaces are part of the architecture because these are hidden away inside the machines and not visible from the outside. It is not even necessary that the interfaces on all machines in a network be the same, provided that each machine can correctly use all the protocols. A list of protocols used by a certain system, one protocol per layer, is called a **protocol stack**. The subjects of network architectures, protocol stacks, and the protocols themselves are the principal topics of this book.

An analogy may help explain the idea of multilayer communication. Imagine two philosophers (peer processes in layer 3), one of whom speaks Urdu and English and one of whom speaks Chinese and French. Since they have no common language, they each engage a translator (peer processes at layer 2), each of whom in turn contacts a secretary (peer processes in layer 1). Philosopher 1 wishes to convey his affection for *oryctolagus cuniculus* to his peer. To do so, he passes a message (in English) across the 2/3 interface, to his translator, saying "I like rabbits," as illustrated in Fig. 1-10. The translators have agreed on a neutral language, Dutch, so the message is converted to "Ik hou van konijnen." The choice of language is the layer 2 protocol and is up to the layer 2 peer processes.

The translator then gives the message to a secretary for transmission, by, for example, fax (the layer 1 protocol). When the message arrives, it is translated into French and passed across the 2/3 interface to philosopher 2. Note that each protocol is completely independent of the other ones as long as the interfaces are not changed. The translators can switch from Dutch to say, Finnish, at will, provided that they both agree, and neither changes his interface with either layer 1 or

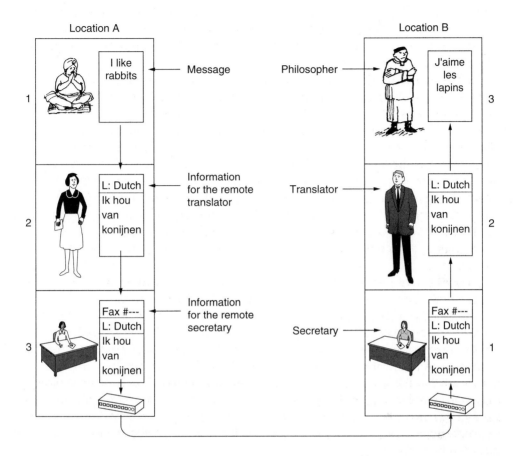

Fig. 1-10. The philosopher-translator-secretary architecture.

layer 3. Similarly the secretaries can switch from fax to email, or telephone without disturbing (or even informing) the other layers. Each process may add some information intended only for its peer. This information is not passed upward to the layer above.

Now consider a more technical example: how to provide communication to the top layer of the five-layer network in Fig. 1-11. A message, M, is produced by an application process running in layer 5 and given to layer 4 for transmission. Layer 4 puts a **header** in front of the message to identify the message and passes the result to layer 3. The header includes control information, such as sequence numbers, to allow layer 4 on the destination machine to deliver messages in the right order if the lower layers do not maintain sequence. In some layers, headers also contain sizes, times, and other control fields.

In many networks, there is no limit to the size of messages transmitted in the layer 4 protocol, but there is nearly always a limit imposed by the layer 3 protocol. Consequently, layer 3 must break up the incoming messages into smaller

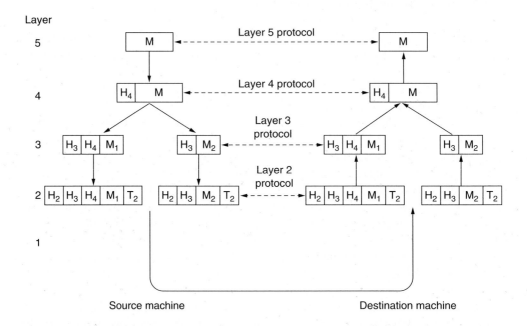

Fig. 1-11. Example information flow supporting virtual communication in layer 5.

units, packets, prepending a layer 3 header to each packet. In this example, M is split into two parts, M_1 and M_2.

Layer 3 decides which of the outgoing lines to use and passes the packets to layer 2. Layer 2 adds not only a header to each piece, but also a trailer, and gives the resulting unit to layer 1 for physical transmission. At the receiving machine the message moves upward, from layer to layer, with headers being stripped off as it progresses. None of the headers for layers below n are passed up to layer n.

The important thing to understand about Fig. 1-11 is the relation between the virtual and actual communication and the difference between protocols and interfaces. The peer processes in layer 4, for example, conceptually think of their communication as being "horizontal," using the layer 4 protocol. Each one is likely to have a procedure called something like *SendToOtherSide* and *GetFromOtherSide*, even though these procedures actually communicate with lower layers across the 3/4 interface, not with the other side.

The peer process abstraction is crucial to all network design. Using it, the unmanageable task of designing the complete network can be broken into several smaller, manageable, design problems, namely the design of the individual layers.

Although Section 1-3 is called "Network Software," it is worth pointing out that the lower layers of a protocol hierarchy are frequently implemented in hardware or firmware. Nevertheless, complex protocol algorithms are involved, even if they are embedded (in whole or in part) in hardware.

1.3.2. Design Issues for the Layers

Some of the key design issues that occur in computer networking are present in several layers. Below, we will briefly mention some of the more important ones.

Every layer needs a mechanism for identifying senders and receivers. Since a network normally has many computers, some of which have multiple processes, a means is needed for a process on one machine to specify with whom it wants to talk. As a consequence of having multiple destinations, some form of addressing is needed in order to specify a specific destination.

Another set of design decisions concerns the rules for data transfer. In some systems, data only travel in one direction (**simplex communication**). In others they can travel in either direction, but not simultaneously (**half-duplex communication**). In still others they travel in both directions at once (**full-duplex communication**). The protocol must also determine how many logical channels the connection corresponds to, and what their priorities are. Many networks provide at least two logical channels per connection, one for normal data and one for urgent data.

Error control is an important issue because physical communication circuits are not perfect. Many error-detecting and error-correcting codes are known, but both ends of the connection must agree on which one is being used. In addition, the receiver must have some way of telling the sender which messages have been correctly received and which have not.

Not all communication channels preserve the order of messages sent on them. To deal with a possible loss of sequencing, the protocol must make explicit provision for the receiver to allow the pieces to be put back together properly. An obvious solution is to number the pieces, but this solution still leaves open the question of what should be done with pieces that arrive out of order.

An issue that occurs at every level is how to keep a fast sender from swamping a slow receiver with data. Various solutions have been proposed and will be discussed later. Some of them involve some kind of feedback from the receiver to the sender, either directly or indirectly, about the receiver's current situation. Others limit the sender to an agreed upon transmission rate.

Another problem that must be solved at several levels is the inability of all processes to accept arbitrarily long messages. This property leads to mechanisms for disassembling, transmitting, and then reassembling messages. A related issue is what to do when processes insist upon transmitting data in units that are so small that sending each one separately is inefficient. Here the solution is to gather together several small messages heading toward a common destination into a single large message and dismember the large message at the other side.

When it is inconvenient or expensive to set up a separate connection for each pair of communicating processes, the underlying layer may decide to use the same connection for multiple, unrelated conversations. As long as this multiplexing and demultiplexing is done transparently, it can be used by any layer. Multiplexing is needed in the physical layer, for example, where all the traffic for all connections has to be sent over at most a few physical circuits.

When there are multiple paths between source and destination, a route must be chosen. Sometimes this decision must be split over two or more layers. For example, to send data from London to Rome, a high-level decision might have to be made to go via France or Germany based on their respective privacy laws, and a low-level decision might have to be made to choose one of the many available circuits based on the current traffic load.

1.3.3. Interfaces and Services

The function of each layer is to provide services to the layer above it. In this section we will look at precisely what a service is in more detail, but first we will give some terminology.

The active elements in each layer are often called **entities**. An entity can be a software entity (such as a process), or a hardware entity (such as an intelligent I/O chip). Entities in the same layer on different machines are called **peer entities**. The entities in layer n implement a service used by layer $n + 1$. In this case layer n is called the **service provider** and layer $n + 1$ is called the **service user**. Layer n may use the services of layer $n - 1$ in order to provide its service. It may offer several classes of service, for example, fast, expensive communication and slow, cheap communication.

Services are available at **SAP**s (**Service Access Points**), The layer n SAPs are the places where layer $n + 1$ can access the services offered. Each SAP has an address that uniquely identifies it. To make this point clearer, the SAPs in the telephone system are the sockets into which modular telephones can be plugged, and the SAP addresses are the telephone numbers of these sockets. To call someone, you must know the callee's SAP address. Similarly, in the postal system, the SAP addresses are street addresses and post office box numbers. To send a letter, you must know the addressee's SAP address.

In order for two layers to exchange information, there has to be an agreed upon set of rules about the interface. At a typical interface, the layer $n + 1$ entity passes an **IDU** (**Interface Data Unit**) to the layer n entity through the SAP as shown in Fig. 1-12. The IDU consists of an **SDU** (**Service Data Unit**) and some control information. The SDU is the information passed across the network to the peer entity and then up to layer $n + 1$. The control information is needed to help the lower layer do its job (e.g., the number of bytes in the SDU) but is not part of the data itself.

In order to transfer the SDU, the layer n entity may have to fragment it into several pieces, each of which is given a header and sent as a separate **PDU** (**Protocol Data Unit**) such as a packet. The PDU headers are used by the peer entities

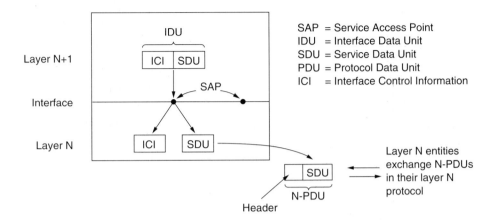

Fig. 1-12. Relation between layers at an interface.

to carry out their peer protocol. They identify which PDUs contain data and which contain control information, provide sequence numbers and counts, and so on.

1.3.4. Connection-Oriented and Connectionless Services

Layers can offer two different types of service to the layers above them: connection-oriented and connectionless. In this section we will look at these two types and examine the differences between them.

Connection-oriented service is modeled after the telephone system. To talk to someone, you pick up the phone, dial the number, talk, and then hang up. Similarly, to use a connection-oriented network service, the service user first establishes a connection, uses the connection, and then releases the connection. The essential aspect of a connection is that it acts like a tube: the sender pushes objects (bits) in at one end, and the receiver takes them out in the same order at the other end.

In contrast, **connectionless service** is modeled after the postal system. Each message (letter) carries the full destination address, and each one is routed through the system independent of all the others. Normally, when two messages are sent to the same destination, the first one sent will be the first one to arrive. However, it is possible that the first one sent can be delayed so that the second one arrives first. With a connection-oriented service this is impossible.

Each service can be characterized by a **quality of service**. Some services are reliable in the sense that they never lose data. Usually, a reliable service is implemented by having the receiver acknowledge the receipt of each message, so the sender is sure that it arrived. The acknowledgement process introduces overhead and delays, which are often worth it but are sometimes undesirable.

A typical situation in which a reliable connection-oriented service is appropriate is file transfer. The owner of the file wants to be sure that all the bits arrive correctly and in the same order they were sent. Very few file transfer customers would prefer a service that occasionally scrambles or loses a few bits, even if it is much faster.

Reliable connection-oriented service has two minor variations: message sequences and byte streams. In the former, the message boundaries are preserved. When two 1-KB messages are sent, they arrive as two distinct 1-KB messages, never as one 2-KB message. (Note: KB means kilobytes; kb means kilobits.) In the latter, the connection is simply a stream of bytes, with no message boundaries. When 2K bytes arrive at the receiver, there is no way to tell if they were sent as one 2-KB message, two 1-KB messages, or 2048 1-byte messages. If the pages of a book are sent over a network to a phototypesetter as separate messages, it might be important to preserve the message boundaries. On the other hand, with a terminal logging into a remote timesharing system, a byte stream from the terminal to the computer is all that is needed.

As mentioned above, for some applications, the delays introduced by acknowledgements are unacceptable. One such application is digitized voice traffic. It is preferable for telephone users to hear a bit of noise on the line or a garbled word from time to time than to introduce a delay to wait for acknowledgements. Similarly, when transmitting a video film, having a few pixels wrong is no problem, but having the film jerk along as the flow stops to correct errors is very irritating.

Not all applications require connections. For example, as electronic mail becomes more common, can electronic junk mail be far behind? The electronic junk mail sender probably does not want to go to the trouble of setting up and later tearing down a connection just to send one item. Nor is 100 percent reliable delivery essential, especially if it costs more. All that is needed is a way to send a single message that has a high probability of arrival, but no guarantee. Unreliable (meaning not acknowledged) connectionless service is often called **datagram service**, in analogy with telegram service, which also does not provide an acknowledgement back to the sender.

In other situations, the convenience of not having to establish a connection to send one short message is desired, but reliability is essential. The **acknowledged datagram service** can be provided for these applications. It is like sending a registered letter and requesting a return receipt. When the receipt comes back, the sender is absolutely sure that the letter was delivered to the intended party and not lost along the way.

Still another service is the **request-reply service**. In this service the sender transmits a single datagram containing a request; the reply contains the answer. For example, a query to the local library asking where Uighur is spoken falls into this category. Request-reply is commonly used to implement communication in the client-server model: the client issues a request and the server responds to it. Figure 1-13 summarizes the types of services discussed above.

	Service	Example
Connection-oriented	Reliable message stream	Sequence of pages
	Reliable byte stream	Remote login
	Unreliable connection	Digitized voice
Connection-less	Unreliable datagram	Electronic junk mail
	Acknowledged datagram	Registered mail
	Request-reply	Database query

Fig. 1-13. Six different types of service.

1.3.5. Service Primitives

A service is formally specified by a set of **primitives** (operations) available to a user or other entity to access the service. These primitives tell the service to perform some action or report on an action taken by a peer entity. One way to classify the service primitives is to divide them into four classes as shown in Fig. 1-14.

Primitive	Meaning
Request	An entity wants the service to do some work
Indication	An entity is to be informed about an event
Response	An entity wants to respond to an event
Confirm	The response to an earlier request has come back

Fig. 1-14. Four classes of service primitives.

To illustrate the uses of the primitives, consider how a connection is established and released. The initiating entity does a CONNECT.request which results in a packet being sent. The receiver then gets a CONNECT.indication announcing that an entity somewhere wants to set up a connection to it. The entity getting the CONNECT.indication then uses the CONNECT.response primitive to tell whether it wants to accept or reject the proposed connection. Either way, the entity issuing the initial CONNECT.request finds out what happened via a CONNECT.confirm primitive.

Primitives can have parameters, and most of them do. The parameters to a CONNECT.request might specify the machine to connect to, the type of service desired, and the maximum message size to be used on the connection. The parameters to a CONNECT.indication might contain the caller's identity, the type of service desired, and the proposed maximum message size. If the called entity did not agree to the proposed maximum message size, it could make a counterproposal in its *response* primitive, which would be made available to the original caller in the *confirm*. The details of this **negotiation** are part of the protocol. For example, in the case of two conflicting proposals about maximum message size, the protocol might specify that the smaller value is always chosen.

As an aside on terminology, we will carefully avoid the terms "open a connection" and "close a connection" because to electrical engineers, an "open circuit" is one with a gap or break in it. Electricity can only flow over "closed circuits." Computer scientists would never agree to having information flow over a closed circuit. To keep both camps pacified, we will use the terms "establish a connection" and "release a connection."

Services can be either **confirmed** or **unconfirmed**. In a confirmed service, there is a *request*, an *indication*, a *response*, and a *confirm*. In an unconfirmed service, there is just a *request* and an *indication*. CONNECT is always a confirmed service because the remote peer must agree to establish a connection. Data transfer, on the other hand, can be either confirmed or unconfirmed, depending on whether or not the sender needs an acknowledgement. Both kinds of services are used in networks.

To make the concept of a service more concrete, let us consider as an example a simple connection-oriented service with eight service primitives as follows:

1. CONNECT.request – Request a connection to be established.

2. CONNECT.indication – Signal the called party.

3. CONNECT.response – Used by the callee to accept/reject calls.

4. CONNECT.confirm – Tell the caller whether the call was accepted.

5. DATA.request – Request that data be sent.

6. DATA.indication – Signal the arrival of data.

7. DISCONNECT.request – Request that a connection be released.

8. DISCONNECT.indication – Signal the peer about the request.

In this example, CONNECT is a confirmed service (an explicit response is required), whereas DISCONNECT is unconfirmed (no response).

It may be helpful to make an analogy with the telephone system to see how these primitives are used. For this analogy, consider the steps required to call Aunt Millie on the telephone and invite her to your house for tea.

1. CONNECT.request – Dial Aunt Millie's phone number.

2. CONNECT.indication – Her phone rings.

3. CONNECT.response – She picks up the phone.

4. CONNECT.confirm – You hear the ringing stop.

5. DATA.request – You invite her to tea.

6. DATA.indication – She hears your invitation.

7. DATA.request – She says she would be delighted to come.

8. DATA.indication – You hear her acceptance.

9. DISCONNECT.request – You hang up the phone.

10. DISCONNECT.indication – She hears it and hangs up too.

Figure 1-15 shows this same sequence of steps as a series of service primitives, including the final confirmation of disconnection. Each step involves an interaction between two layers on one of the computers. Each *request* or *response* causes an *indication* or *confirm* at the other side a little later. In this example, the service users (you and Aunt Millie) are in layer $N + 1$ and the service provider (the telephone system) is in layer N.

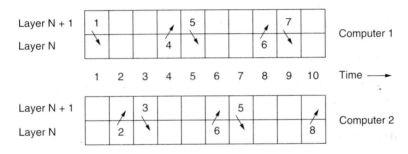

Fig. 1-15. How a computer would invite its Aunt Millie to tea. The numbers near the tail end of each arrow refer to the eight service primitives discussed in this section.

1.3.6. The Relationship of Services to Protocols

Services and protocols are distinct concepts, although they are frequently confused. This distinction is so important, however, that we emphasize it again here. A *service* is a set of primitives (operations) that a layer provides to the layer above it. The service defines what operations the layer is prepared to perform on behalf of its users, but it says nothing at all about how these operations are implemented. A service relates to an interface between two layers, with the lower layer being the service provider and the upper layer being the service user.

A *protocol*, in contrast, is a set of rules governing the format and meaning of the frames, packets, or messages that are exchanged by the peer entities within a layer. Entities use protocols in order to implement their service definitions. They are free to change their protocols at will, provided they do not change the service visible to their users. In this way, the service and the protocol are completely decoupled.

An analogy with programming languages is worth making. A service is like an abstract data type or an object in an object-oriented language. It defines operations that can be performed on an object but does not specify how these operations are implemented. A protocol relates to the *implementation* of the service and as such is not visible to the user of the service.

Many older protocols did not distinguish the service from the protocol. In effect, a typical layer might have had a service primitive SEND PACKET with the user providing a pointer to a fully assembled packet. This arrangement meant that all changes to the protocol were immediately visible to the users. Most network designers now regard such a design as a serious blunder.

1.4. REFERENCE MODELS

Now that we have discussed layered networks in the abstract, it is time to look at some examples. In the next two sections we will discuss two important network architectures, the OSI reference model and the TCP/IP reference model.

1.4.1. The OSI Reference Model

The OSI model is shown in Fig. 1-16 (minus the physical medium). This model is based on a proposal developed by the International Standards Organization (ISO) as a first step toward international standardization of the protocols used in the various layers (Day and Zimmermann, 1983). The model is called the **ISO OSI (Open Systems Interconnection) Reference Model** because it deals with connecting open systems—that is, systems that are open for communication with other systems. We will usually just call it the OSI model for short.

The OSI model has seven layers. The principles that were applied to arrive at the seven layers are as follows:

1. A layer should be created where a different level of abstraction is needed.

2. Each layer should perform a well defined function.

3. The function of each layer should be chosen with an eye toward defining internationally standardized protocols.

4. The layer boundaries should be chosen to minimize the information flow across the interfaces.

5. The number of layers should be large enough that distinct functions need not be thrown together in the same layer out of necessity, and small enough that the architecture does not become unwieldy.

Below we will discuss each layer of the model in turn, starting at the bottom layer. Note that the OSI model itself is not a network architecture because it does not specify the exact services and protocols to be used in each layer. It just tells what each layer should do. However, ISO has also produced standards for all the layers, although these are not part of the reference model itself. Each one has been published as a separate international standard.

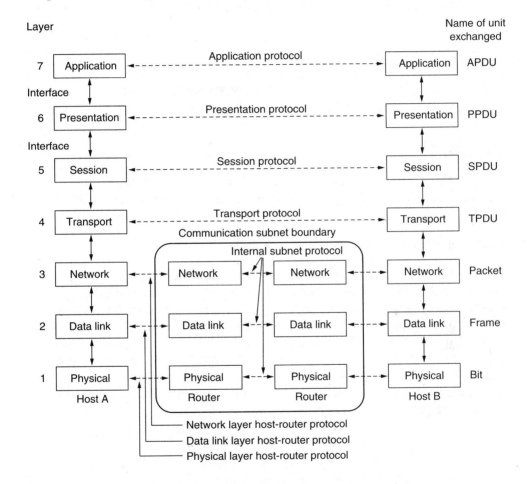

Fig. 1-16. The OSI reference model.

The Physical Layer

The **physical layer** is concerned with transmitting raw bits over a communication channel. The design issues have to do with making sure that when one side sends a 1 bit, it is received by the other side as a 1 bit, not as a 0 bit. Typical questions here are how many volts should be used to represent a 1 and how many for a 0, how many microseconds a bit lasts, whether transmission may proceed simultaneously in both directions, how the initial connection is established and how it is torn down when both sides are finished, and how many pins the network connector has and what each pin is used for. The design issues here largely deal with mechanical, electrical, and procedural interfaces, and the physical transmission medium, which lies below the physical layer.

The Data Link Layer

The main task of the **data link layer** is to take a raw transmission facility and transform it into a line that appears free of undetected transmission errors to the network layer. It accomplishes this task by having the sender break the input data up into **data frames** (typically a few hundred or a few thousand bytes), transmit the frames sequentially, and process the **acknowledgement frames** sent back by the receiver. Since the physical layer merely accepts and transmits a stream of bits without any regard to meaning or structure, it is up to the data link layer to create and recognize frame boundaries. This can be accomplished by attaching special bit patterns to the beginning and end of the frame. If these bit patterns can accidentally occur in the data, special care must be taken to make sure these patterns are not incorrectly interpreted as frame delimiters.

A noise burst on the line can destroy a frame completely. In this case, the data link layer software on the source machine can retransmit the frame. However, multiple transmissions of the same frame introduce the possibility of duplicate frames. A duplicate frame could be sent if the acknowledgement frame from the receiver back to the sender were lost. It is up to this layer to solve the problems caused by damaged, lost, and duplicate frames. The data link layer may offer several different service classes to the network layer, each of a different quality and with a different price.

Another issue that arises in the data link layer (and most of the higher layers as well) is how to keep a fast transmitter from drowning a slow receiver in data. Some traffic regulation mechanism must be employed to let the transmitter know how much buffer space the receiver has at the moment. Frequently, this flow regulation and the error handling are integrated.

If the line can be used to transmit data in both directions, this introduces a new complication that the data link layer software must deal with. The problem is that the acknowledgement frames for A to B traffic compete for the use of the line with data frames for the B to A traffic. A clever solution (piggybacking) has been devised; we will discuss it in detail later.

Broadcast networks have an additional issue in the data link layer: how to control access to the shared channel. A special sublayer of the data link layer, the medium access sublayer, deals with this problem.

The Network Layer

The **network layer** is concerned with controlling the operation of the subnet. A key design issue is determining how packets are routed from source to destination. Routes can be based on static tables that are "wired into" the network and rarely changed. They can also be determined at the start of each conversation, for example a terminal session. Finally, they can be highly dynamic, being determined anew for each packet, to reflect the current network load.

If too many packets are present in the subnet at the same time, they will get in each other's way, forming bottlenecks. The control of such congestion also belongs to the network layer.

Since the operators of the subnet may well expect remuneration for their efforts, there is often some accounting function built into the network layer. At the very least, the software must count how many packets or characters or bits are sent by each customer, to produce billing information. When a packet crosses a national border, with different rates on each side, the accounting can become complicated.

When a packet has to travel from one network to another to get to its destination, many problems can arise. The addressing used by the second network may be different from the first one. The second one may not accept the packet at all because it is too large. The protocols may differ, and so on. It is up to the network layer to overcome all these problems to allow heterogeneous networks to be interconnected.

In broadcast networks, the routing problem is simple, so the network layer is often thin or even nonexistent.

The Transport Layer

The basic function of the **transport layer** is to accept data from the session layer, split it up into smaller units if need be, pass these to the network layer, and ensure that the pieces all arrive correctly at the other end. Furthermore, all this must be done efficiently, and in a way that isolates the upper layers from the inevitable changes in the hardware technology.

Under normal conditions, the transport layer creates a distinct network connection for each transport connection required by the session layer. If the transport connection requires a high throughput, however, the transport layer might create multiple network connections, dividing the data among the network connections to improve throughput. On the other hand, if creating or maintaining a network connection is expensive, the transport layer might multiplex several transport connections onto the same network connection to reduce the cost. In all cases, the transport layer is required to make the multiplexing transparent to the session layer.

The transport layer also determines what type of service to provide the session layer, and ultimately, the users of the network. The most popular type of transport connection is an error-free point-to-point channel that delivers messages or bytes in the order in which they were sent. However, other possible kinds of transport service are transport of isolated messages with no guarantee about the order of delivery, and broadcasting of messages to multiple destinations. The type of service is determined when the connection is established.

The transport layer is a true end-to-end layer, from source to destination. In other words, a program on the source machine carries on a conversation with a similar program on the destination machine, using the message headers and control messages. In the lower layers, the protocols are between each machine and its immediate neighbors, and not by the ultimate source and destination machines, which may be separated by many routers. The difference between layers 1 through 3, which are chained, and layers 4 through 7, which are end-to-end, is illustrated in Fig. 1-16.

Many hosts are multiprogrammed, which implies that multiple connections will be entering and leaving each host. There needs to be some way to tell which message belongs to which connection. The transport header (H_4 in Fig. 1-11) is one place this information can be put.

In addition to multiplexing several message streams onto one channel, the transport layer must take care of establishing and deleting connections across the network. This requires some kind of naming mechanism, so that a process on one machine has a way of describing with whom it wishes to converse. There must also be a mechanism to regulate the flow of information, so that a fast host cannot overrun a slow one. Such a mechanism is called **flow control** and plays a key role in the transport layer (also in other layers). Flow control between hosts is distinct from flow control between routers, although we will later see that similar principles apply to both.

The Session Layer

The session layer allows users on different machines to establish **sessions** between them. A session allows ordinary data transport, as does the transport layer, but it also provides enhanced services useful in some applications. A session might be used to allow a user to log into a remote timesharing system or to transfer a file between two machines.

One of the services of the session layer is to manage dialogue control. Sessions can allow traffic to go in both directions at the same time, or in only one direction at a time. If traffic can only go one way at a time (analogous to a single railroad track), the session layer can help keep track of whose turn it is.

A related session service is **token management**. For some protocols, it is essential that both sides do not attempt the same operation at the same time. To manage these activities, the session layer provides tokens that can be exchanged. Only the side holding the token may perform the critical operation.

Another session service is **synchronization**. Consider the problems that might occur when trying to do a 2-hour file transfer between two machines with a 1-hour mean time between crashes. After each transfer was aborted, the whole transfer would have to start over again and would probably fail again the next time as well. To eliminate this problem, the session layer provides a way to insert checkpoints into the data stream, so that after a crash, only the data transferred after the last checkpoint have to be repeated.

The Presentation Layer

The **presentation layer** performs certain functions that are requested sufficiently often to warrant finding a general solution for them, rather than letting each user solve the problems. In particular, unlike all the lower layers, which are just interested in moving bits reliably from here to there, the presentation layer is concerned with the syntax and semantics of the information transmitted.

A typical example of a presentation service is encoding data in a standard agreed upon way. Most user programs do not exchange random binary bit strings. They exchange things such as people's names, dates, amounts of money, and invoices. These items are represented as character strings, integers, floating-point numbers, and data structures composed of several simpler items. Different computers have different codes for representing character strings (e.g., ASCII and Unicode), integers (e.g., one's complement and two's complement), and so on. In order to make it possible for computers with different representations to communicate, the data structures to be exchanged can be defined in an abstract way, along with a standard encoding to be used "on the wire." The presentation layer manages these abstract data structures and converts from the representation used inside the computer to the network standard representation and back.

The Application Layer

The **application layer** contains a variety of protocols that are commonly needed. For example, there are hundreds of incompatible terminal types in the world. Consider the plight of a full screen editor that is supposed to work over a network with many different terminal types, each with different screen layouts, escape sequences for inserting and deleting text, moving the cursor, etc.

One way to solve this problem is to define an abstract **network virtual terminal** that editors and other programs can be written to deal with. To handle each terminal type, a piece of software must be written to map the functions of the network virtual terminal onto the real terminal. For example, when the editor moves the virtual terminal's cursor to the upper left-hand corner of the screen, this software must issue the proper command sequence to the real terminal to get its cursor there too. All the virtual terminal software is in the application layer.

Another application layer function is file transfer. Different file systems have different file naming conventions, different ways of representing text lines, and so on. Transferring a file between two different systems requires handling these and other incompatibilities. This work, too, belongs to the application layer, as do electronic mail, remote job entry, directory lookup, and various other general-purpose and special-purpose facilities.

Data Transmission in the OSI Model

Figure 1-17 shows an example of how data can be transmitted using the OSI model. The sending process has some data it wants to send to the receiving process. It gives the data to the application layer, which then attaches the application header, *AH* (which may be null), to the front of it and gives the resulting item to the presentation layer.

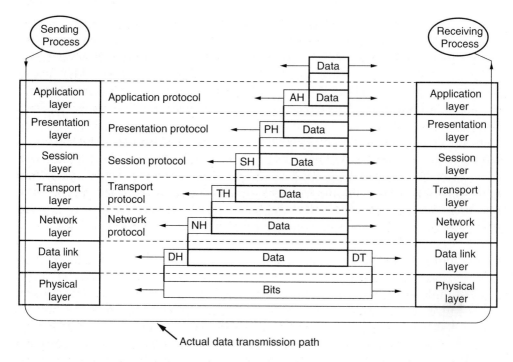

Fig. 1-17. An example of how the OSI model is used. Some of the headers may be null. (Source: H.C. Folts. Used with permission.)

The presentation layer may transform this item in various ways and possibly add a header to the front, giving the result to the session layer. It is important to realize that the presentation layer is not aware of which portion of the data given to it by the application layer is *AH*, if any, and which is true user data.

This process is repeated until the data reach the physical layer, where they are actually transmitted to the receiving machine. On that machine the various headers are stripped off one by one as the message propagates up the layers until it finally arrives at the receiving process.

The key idea throughout is that although actual data transmission is vertical in Fig. 1-17, each layer is programmed as though it were horizontal. When the sending transport layer, for example, gets a message from the session layer, it attaches a transport header and sends it to the receiving transport layer. From its point of view, the fact that it must actually hand the message to the network layer on its own machine is an unimportant technicality. As an analogy, when a Tagalog-speaking diplomat is addressing the United Nations, he thinks of himself as addressing the other assembled diplomats. That, in fact, he is really only speaking to his translator is seen as a technical detail.

1.4.2. The TCP/IP Reference Model

Let us now turn from the OSI reference model to the reference model used in the grandparent of all computer networks, the ARPANET, and its successor, the worldwide Internet. Although we will give a brief history of the ARPANET later, it is useful to mention a few key aspects of it now. The ARPANET was a research network sponsored by the DoD (U.S. Department of Defense). It eventually connected hundreds of universities and government installations using leased telephone lines. When satellite and radio networks were added later, the existing protocols had trouble interworking with them, so a new reference architecture was needed. Thus the ability to connect multiple networks together in a seamless way was one of the major design goals from the very beginning. This architecture later became known as the **TCP/IP Reference Model**, after its two primary protocols. It was first defined in (Cerf and Kahn, 1974). A later perspective is given in (Leiner et al., 1985). The design philosophy behind the model is discussed in (Clark, 1988).

Given the DoD's worry that some of its precious hosts, routers, and internetwork gateways might get blown to pieces at a moment's notice, another major goal was that the network be able to survive loss of subnet hardware, with existing conversations not being broken off. In other words, DoD wanted connections to remain intact as long as the source and destination machines were functioning, even if some of the machines or transmission lines in between were suddenly put out of operation. Furthermore, a flexible architecture was needed, since applications with divergent requirements were envisioned, ranging from transferring files to real-time speech transmission.

The Internet Layer

All these requirements led to the choice of a packet-switching network based on a connectionless internetwork layer. This layer, called the **internet layer**, is the linchpin that holds the whole architecture together. Its job is to permit hosts to inject packets into any network and have them travel independently to the destination (potentially on a different network). They may even arrive in a different order than they were sent, in which case it is the job of higher layers to rearrange them, if in-order delivery is desired. Note that "internet" is used here in a generic sense, even though this layer is present in the Internet.

The analogy here is with the (snail) mail system. A person can drop a sequence of international letters into a mail box in one country, and with a little luck, most of them will be delivered to the correct address in the destination country. Probably the letters will travel through one or more international mail gateways along the way, but this is transparent to the users. Furthermore, that each country (i.e., each network) has its own stamps, preferred envelope sizes, and delivery rules is hidden from the users.

The internet layer defines an official packet format and protocol called **IP** (**Internet Protocol**). The job of the internet layer is to deliver IP packets where they are supposed to go. Packet routing is clearly the major issue here, as is avoiding congestion. For these reasons, it is reasonable to say that the TCP/IP internet layer is very similar in functionality to the OSI network layer. Figure 1-18 shows this correspondence.

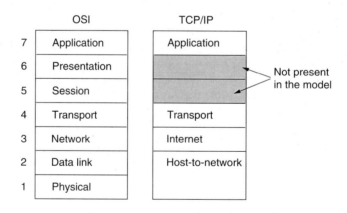

Fig. 1-18. The TCP/IP reference model.

The Transport Layer

The layer above the internet layer in the TCP/IP model is now usually called the **transport layer**. It is designed to allow peer entities on the source and destination hosts to carry on a conversation, the same as in the OSI transport layer. Two end-to-end protocols have been defined here. The first one, **TCP** (**Transmission Control Protocol**) is a reliable connection-oriented protocol that allows a byte stream originating on one machine to be delivered without error on any other machine in the internet. It fragments the incoming byte stream into discrete messages and passes each one onto the internet layer. At the destination, the receiving TCP process reassembles the received messages into the output stream. TCP also handles flow control to make sure a fast sender cannot swamp a slow receiver with more messages than it can handle.

The second protocol in this layer, **UDP** (**User Datagram Protocol**), is an unreliable, connectionless protocol for applications that do not want TCP's sequencing or flow control and wish to provide their own. It is also widely used for one-shot, client-server type request-reply queries and applications in which prompt delivery is more important than accurate delivery, such as transmitting speech or video. The relation of IP, TCP, and UDP is shown in Fig. 1-19. Since the model was developed, IP has been implemented on many other networks.

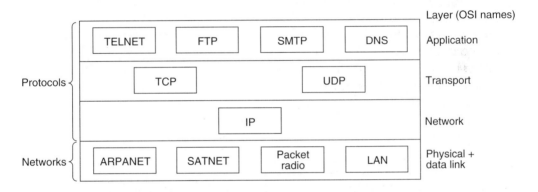

Fig. 1-19. Protocols and networks in the TCP/IP model initially.

The Application Layer

The TCP/IP model does not have session or presentation layers. No need for them was perceived, so they were not included. Experience with the OSI model has proven this view correct: they are of little use to most applications.

On top of the transport layer is the **application layer**. It contains all the higher-level protocols. The early ones included virtual terminal (TELNET), file transfer (FTP), and electronic mail (SMTP), as shown in Fig. 1-19. The virtual terminal protocol allows a user on one machine to log into a distant machine and work there. The file transfer protocol provides a way to move data efficiently from one machine to another. Electronic mail was originally just a kind of file transfer, but later a specialized protocol was developed for it. Many other protocols have been added to these over the years, such as the Domain Name Service (DNS) for mapping host names onto their network addresses, NNTP, the protocol used for moving news articles around, and HTTP, the protocol used for fetching pages on the World Wide Wide, and many others.

The Host-to-Network Layer

Below the internet layer is a great void. The TCP/IP reference model does not really say much about what happens here, except to point out that the host has to connect to the network using some protocol so it can send IP packets over it. This protocol is not defined and varies from host to host and network to network. Books and papers about the TCP/IP model rarely discuss it.

1.4.3. A Comparison of the OSI and TCP Reference Models

The OSI and TCP/IP reference models have much in common. Both are based on the concept of a stack of independent protocols. Also, the functionality of the layers is roughly similar. For example, in both models the layers up through and including the transport layer are there to provide an end-to-end network-independent transport service to processes wishing to communicate. These layers form the transport provider. Again in both models, the layers above transport are application-oriented users of the transport service.

Despite these fundamental similarities, the two models also have many differences. In this section we will focus on the key differences between the two reference models. It is important to note that we are comparing the *reference models* here, not the corresponding *protocol stacks*. The protocols themselves will be discussed later. For an entire book comparing and contrasting TCP/IP and OSI, see (Piscitello and Chapin, 1993).

Three concepts are central to the OSI model:

1. Services

2. Interfaces

3. Protocols

Probably the biggest contribution of the OSI model is to make the distinction between these three concepts explicit. Each layer performs some services for the layer above it. The *service* definition tells what the layer does, not how entities above it access it or how the layer works.

A layer's *interface* tells the processes above it how to access it. It specifies what the parameters are and what results to expect. It, too, says nothing about how the layer works inside.

Finally, the peer *protocols* used in a layer are the layer's own business. It can use any protocols it wants to, as long as it gets the job done (i.e., provides the offered services). It can also change them at will without affecting software in higher layers.

These ideas fit very nicely with modern ideas about object-oriented programming. An object, like a layer, has a set of methods (operations) that processes outside the object can invoke. The semantics of these methods define the set of services that the object offers. The methods' parameters and results form the object's interface. The code internal to the object is its protocol and is not visible or of any concern outside the object.

The TCP/IP model did not originally clearly distinguish between service, interface, and protocol, although people have tried to retrofit it after the fact to make it more OSI-like. For example, the only real services offered by the internet layer are SEND IP PACKET and RECEIVE IP PACKET.

As a consequence, the protocols in the OSI model are better hidden than in the TCP/IP model and can be replaced relatively easily as the technology changes. Being able to make such changes is one of the main purposes of having layered protocols in the first place.

The OSI reference model was devised *before* the protocols were invented. This ordering means that the model was not biased toward one particular set of protocols, which made it quite general. The down side of this ordering is that the designers did not have much experience with the subject and did not have a good idea of which functionality to put in which layer.

For example, the data link layer originally dealt only with point-to-point networks. When broadcast networks came around, a new sublayer had to be hacked into the model. When people started to build real networks using the OSI model and existing protocols, it was discovered that they did not match the required service specifications (wonder of wonders), so convergence sublayers had to be grafted onto the model to provide a place for papering over the differences. Finally, the committee originally expected that each country would have one network, run by the government and using the OSI protocols, so no thought was given to internetworking. To make a long story short, things did not turn out that way.

With the TCP/IP the reverse was true: the protocols came first, and the model was really just a description of the existing protocols. There was no problem with the protocols fitting the model. They fit perfectly. The only trouble was that the *model* did not fit any other protocol stacks. Consequently, it was not especially useful for describing other non-TCP/IP networks.

Turning from philosophical matters to more specific ones, an obvious difference between the two models is the number of layers: the OSI model has seven layers and the TCP/IP has four layers. Both have (inter)network, transport, and application layers, but the other layers are different.

Another difference is in the area of connectionless versus connection-oriented communication. The OSI model supports both connectionless and connection-oriented communication in the network layer, but only connection-oriented communication in the transport layer, where it counts (because the transport service is visible to the users). The TCP/IP model has only one mode in the network layer (connectionless) but supports both modes in the transport layer, giving the users a choice. This choice is especially important for simple request-response protocols.

1.4.4. A Critique of the OSI Model and Protocols

Neither the OSI model and its protocols nor the TCP/IP model and its protocols are perfect. Quite a bit of criticism can be, and has been, directed at both of them. In this section and the next one, we will look at some of these criticisms. We will begin with OSI and examine TCP/IP afterward.

At the time the second edition of this book was published (1989), it appeared to most experts in the field that the OSI model and its protocols were going to take over the world and push everything else out of their way. This did not happen. Why? A look back at some of the lessons may be useful. These lessons can be summarized as:

1. Bad timing.

2. Bad technology.

3. Bad implementations.

4. Bad politics.

Bad Timing

First let us look at reason one: bad timing. The time at which a standard is established is absolutely critical to its success. David Clark of M.I.T. has a theory of standards that he calls the *apocalypse of the two elephants*, and which is illustrated in Fig. 1-20.

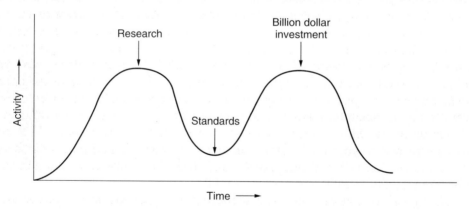

Fig. 1-20. The apocalypse of the two elephants.

This figure shows the amount of activity surrounding a new subject. When the subject is first discovered, there is a burst of research activity in the form of discussions, papers, and meetings. After a while this subsides, corporations discover the subject, and the billion-dollar wave of investment hits.

It is essential that the standards be written in the trough between the two "elephants." If they are written too early, before the research is finished, the subject may still be poorly understood, which leads to bad standards. If they are written too late, so many companies may have already made major investments in different ways of doing things that the standards are effectively ignored. If the interval between the two elephants is very short (because everyone is in a hurry to get started), the people developing the standards may get crushed.

It now appears that the standard OSI protocols got crushed. The competing TCP/IP protocols were already in widespread use by research universities by the time the OSI protocols appeared. While the billion-dollar wave of investment had not yet hit, the academic market was large enough that many vendors had begun cautiously offering TCP/IP products. When OSI came around, they did not want to support a second protocol stack until they were forced to, so there were no initial offerings. With every company waiting for every other company to go first, no company went first and OSI never happened.

Bad Technology

The second reason that OSI never caught on is that both the model and the protocols are flawed. Most discussions of the seven-layer model give the impression that the number and contents of the layers eventually chosen were the only way, or at least the obvious way. This is far from true. The session layer has little use in most applications, and the presentation layer is nearly empty. In fact, the British proposal to ISO only had five layers, not seven. In contrast to the session and presentation layers, the data link and network layers are so full that subsequent work has split them into multiple sublayers, each with different functions.

Although hardly anyone ever admits it in public, the real reason that the OSI model has seven layers is that at the time it was designed, IBM had a proprietary seven-layer protocol called **SNA**^{TM} (**Systems Network Architecture**). At that time, IBM so dominated the computer industry that everyone else, including telephone companies, competing computer companies, and even major governments, were scared to death that IBM would use its market clout to effectively force everybody to use SNA, which it could change whenever it wished. The idea behind OSI was to produce an IBM-like reference model and protocol stack that would become the world standard, and controlled not by one company, but by a neutral organization, ISO.

The OSI model, along with the associated service definitions and protocols, is extraordinarily complex. When piled up, the printed standards occupy a significant fraction of a meter of paper. They are also difficult to implement and inefficient in operation. In this context, a riddle posed by Paul Mockapetris and cited in (Rose, 1993) comes to mind:

Q: What do you get when you cross a mobster with an international standard?
A: Someone who makes you an offer you can't understand.

In addition to being incomprehensible, another problem with OSI is that some functions, such as addressing, flow control, and error control reappear again and again in each layer. Saltzer et al. (1984), for example, have pointed out that to be effective, error control must be done in the highest layer, so that repeating it over and over in each of the lower layers is often unnecessary and inefficient.

Another issue is that the decision to place certain features in particular layers is not always obvious. The virtual terminal handling (now in the application layer) was in the presentation layer during much of the development of the standard. It was moved to the application layer because the committee had trouble deciding what the presentation layer was good for. Data security and encryption were so controversial that no one could agree which layer to put them in, so they were left out altogether. Network management was also omitted from the model for similar reasons.

Another criticism of the original standard is that it completely ignored connectionless services and connectionless protocols, even though most local area networks work that way. Subsequent addenda (known in the software world as bug fixes) corrected this problem.

Perhaps the most serious criticism is that the model is dominated by a communications mentality. The relationship of computing to communications is barely mentioned anywhere, and some of the choices made are wholly inappropriate to the way computers and software work. As an example, consider the OSI primitives, listed in Fig. 1-14. In particular, think carefully about the primitives and how one might use them in a programming language.

The CONNECT.request primitive is simple. One can imagine a library procedure, *connect*, that programs can call to establish a connection. Now think about CONNECT.indication. When a message arrives, the destination process has to be signaled. In effect, it has to get an interrupt—hardly an appropriate concept for programs written in any modern high-level language. Of course, in the lowest layer, an indication (interrupt) does occur.

If the program were expecting an incoming call, it could call a library procedure *receive* to block itself. But if this were the case, why was *receive* not the primitive instead of *indication*? *Receive* is clearly oriented toward the way computers work, whereas *indication* is equally clearly oriented toward the way telephones work. Computers are different from telephones. Telephones ring. Computers do not ring. In short, the semantic model of an interrupt-driven system is conceptually a poor idea and totally at odds with all modern ideas of structured programming. This and similar problems are discussed by Langsford (1984).

Bad Implementations

Given the enormous complexity of the model and the protocols, it will come as no surprise that the initial implementations were huge, unwieldy, and slow. Everyone who tried them got burned. It did not take long for people to associate

"OSI" with "poor quality." While the products got better in the course of time, the image stuck.

In contrast, one of the first implementations of TCP/IP was part of Berkeley UNIX® and was quite good (not to mention, free). People began using it quickly, which led to a large user community, which led to improvements, which led to an even larger community. Here the spiral was upward instead of downward.

Bad Politics

On account of the initial implementation, many people, especially in academia, thought of TCP/IP as part of UNIX, and UNIX in the 1980s in academia was not unlike parenthood (then incorrectly called motherhood) and apple pie.

OSI, on the other hand, was thought to be the creature of the European telecommunication ministries, the European Community, and later the U.S. Government. This belief was only partly true, but the very idea of a bunch of government bureaucrats trying to shove a technically inferior standard down the throats of the poor researchers and programmers down in the trenches actually developing computer networks did not help much. Some people viewed this development in the same light as IBM announcing in the 1960s that PL/I was the language of the future, or DoD correcting this later by announcing that it was actually Ada®.

Despite the fact that the OSI model and protocols have been less than a resounding success, there are still a few organizations interested in it, mostly European PTTs that still have a monopoly on telecommunication. Consequently a feeble effort has been made to update OSI, resulting in a revised model published in 1994. For what was changed (little) and what should have been changed (a lot), see (Day, 1995).

1.4.5. A Critique of the TCP/IP Reference Model

The TCP/IP model and protocols have their problems too. First, the model does not clearly distinguish the concepts of service, interface, and protocol. Good software engineering practice requires differentiating between the specification and the implementation, something that OSI does very carefully, and TCP/IP does not. Consequently, the TCP/IP model is not much of a guide for designing new networks using new technologies.

Second, the TCP/IP model is not at all general and is poorly suited to describing any protocol stack other than TCP/IP. Trying to describe SNA using the TCP/IP model would be nearly impossible, for example.

Third, the host-to-network layer is not really a layer at all in the normal sense that the term is used in the context of layered protocols. It is an interface (between the network and data link layers). The distinction between an interface and a layer is a crucial one and one should not be sloppy about it.

Fourth, the TCP/IP model does not distinguish (or even mention) the physical and data link layers. These are completely different. The physical layer has to do with the transmission characteristics of copper wire, fiber optics, and wireless communication. The data link layer's job is to delimit the start and end of frames and get them from one side to the other with the desired degree of reliability. A proper model should include both as separate layers. The TCP/IP model does not do this.

Finally, although the IP and TCP protocols were carefully thought out, and well implemented, many of the other protocols were ad hoc, generally produced by a couple of graduate students hacking away until they got tired. The protocol implementations were then distributed free, which resulted in their becoming widely used, deeply entrenched, and thus hard to replace. Some of them are a bit of an embarrassment now. The virtual terminal protocol, TELNET, for example, was designed for a ten-character per second mechanical Teletype terminal. It knows nothing of graphical user interfaces and mice. Nevertheless, 25 years later, it is still in widespread use.

In summary, despite its problems, the OSI *model* (minus the session and presentation layers) has proven to be exceptionally useful for discussing computer networks. In contrast, the OSI *protocols* have not become popular. The reverse is true of TCP/IP: the *model* is practically nonexistent, but the *protocols* are widely used. Since computer scientists like to have their cake and eat it, too, in this book we will use a modified OSI model but concentrate primarily on the TCP/IP and related protocols, as well as newer ones such as SMDS, frame relay, SONET, and ATM. In effect, we will use the hybrid model of Fig. 1-21 as the framework for this book.

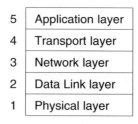

Fig. 1-21. The hybrid reference model to be used in this book.

1.5. EXAMPLE NETWORKS

Numerous networks are currently operating around the world. Some of these are public networks run by common carriers or PTTs, others are research networks, yet others are cooperative networks run by their users, and still others are commercial or corporate networks. In the following sections we will take a look at a few current and historical networks to get an idea of what they are (or were) like and how they differ from one another.

Networks differ in their history, administration, facilities offered, technical design, and user communities. The history and administration can vary from a network carefully planned by a single organization with a well-defined goal, to an ad hoc collection of machines that have been connected to one another over the years without any master plan or central administration at all. The facilities available range from arbitrary process-to-process communication to electronic mail, file transfer, remote login, and remote execution. The technical designs can differ in the transmission media used, the naming and routing algorithms employed, the number and contents of the layers present, and the protocols used. Finally, the user community can vary from a single corporation to all the academic computer scientists in the industrialized world.

In the following sections we will look at a few examples. These are the popular commercial LAN networking package, Novell NetWare®, the worldwide Internet (including its predecessors, the ARPANET and NSFNET), and the first gigabit networks.

1.5.1. Novell NetWare

The most popular network system in the PC world is **Novell NetWare**. It was designed to be used by companies downsizing from a mainframe to a network of PCs. In such systems, each user has a desktop PC functioning as a client. In addition, some number of powerful PCs operate as servers, providing file services, database services, and other services to a collection of clients. In other words, Novell NetWare is based on the client-server model.

NetWare uses a proprietary protocol stack illustrated in Fig. 1-22. It is based on the old Xerox Network System, XNS^{TM} but with various modifications. Novell NetWare predates OSI and is not based on it. If anything, it looks more like TCP/IP than like OSI.

Layer			
Application	SAP	File server	. . .
Transport	NCP		SPX
Network	IPX		
Data link	Ethernet	Token ring	ARCnet
Physical	Ethernet	Token ring	ARCnet

Fig. 1-22. The Novell NetWare reference model.

The physical and data link layers can be chosen from among various industry standards, including Ethernet, IBM token ring, and ARCnet. The network layer runs an unreliable connectionless internetwork protocol called **IPX** (**Internet Packet eXchange**). It passes packets transparently from source to destination, even if the source and destination are on different networks. IPX is functionally similar to IP, except that it uses 12-byte addresses instead of 4-byte addresses. The wisdom of this choice will become apparent in Chap. 5.

Above IPX comes a connection-oriented transport protocol called **NCP** (**Network Core Protocol**). NCP also provides various other services besides user data transport and is really the heart of NetWare. A second protocol, **SPX** (**Sequenced Packet eXchange**), is also available, but provides only transport. TCP is another option. Applications can choose any of them. The file system uses NCP and Lotus Notes® uses SPX, for example. The session and presentation layers do not exist. Various application protocols are present in the application layer.

As in TCP/IP, the key to the entire architecture is the internet datagram packet on top of which everything else is built. The format of an IPX packet is shown in Fig. 1-23. The *Checksum* field is rarely used, since the underlying data link layer also provides a checksum. The *Packet length* field tells how long the entire packet is, header plus data. The *Transport control* field counts how many networks the packet has traversed. When this exceeds a maximum, the packet is discarded. The *Packet type* field is used to mark various control packets. The two addresses each contain a 32-bit network number, a 48-bit machine number (the 802 LAN address), and 16-bit local address (socket) on that machine. Finally, we have the data, which occupy the rest of the packet, with the maximum size being determined by the underlying network.

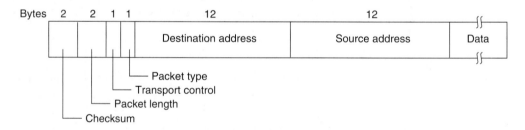

Fig. 1-23. A Novell NetWare IPX packet.

About once a minute, each server broadcasts a packet giving its address and telling what services it offers. These broadcasts use the **SAP** (**Service Advertising Protocol**) protocol. The packets are seen and collected by special agent processes running on the router machines. The agents use the information contained in them to construct databases of which servers are running where.

When a client machine is booted, it broadcasts a request asking where the nearest server is. The agent on the local router machine sees this request, looks in its database of servers, and matches up the request with the best server. The choice of server to use is then sent back to the client. The client can now establish an NCP connection with the server. Using this connection, the client and server negotiate the maximum packet size. From this point on, the client can access the file system and other services using this connection. It can also query the server's database to look for other (more distant) servers.

1.5.2. The ARPANET

Let us now switch gears from LANs to WANs. In the mid-1960s, at the height of the Cold War, the DoD wanted a command and control network that could survive a nuclear war. Traditional circuit-switched telephone networks were considered too vulnerable, since the loss of one line or switch would certainly terminate all conversations using them and might even partition the network. To solve this problem, DoD turned to its research arm, ARPA (later DARPA, now ARPA again), the (periodically Defense) Advanced Research Projects Agency.

ARPA was created in response to the Soviet Union's launching Sputnik in 1957 and had the mission of advancing technology that might be useful to the military. ARPA had no scientists or laboratories, in fact, it had nothing more than an office and a small (by Pentagon standards) budget. It did its work by issuing grants and contracts to universities and companies whose ideas looked promising to it.

Several early grants went to universities for investigating the then-radical idea of packet switching, something that had been suggested by Paul Baran in a series of RAND Corporation reports published in the early 1960s. After some discussions with various experts, ARPA decided that the network the DoD needed should be a packet-switched network, consisting of a subnet and host computers.

The subnet would consist of minicomputers called **IMP**s (**Interface Message Processors**) connected by transmission lines. For high reliability, each IMP would be connected to at least two other IMPs. The subnet was to be a datagram subnet, so if some lines and IMPs were destroyed, messages could be automatically rerouted along alternative paths.

Each node of the network was to consist of an IMP and a host, in the same room, connected by a short wire. A host could send messages of up to 8063 bits to its IMP, which would then break these up into packets of at most 1008 bits and forward them independently toward the destination. Each packet was received in its entirety before being forwarded, so the subnet was the first electronic store-and-forward packet-switching network.

ARPA then put out a tender for building the subnet. Twelve companies bid for it. After evaluating all the proposals, ARPA selected BBN, a consulting firm in Cambridge, Massachusetts, and in December 1968, awarded it a contract to build the subnet and write the subnet software. BBN chose to use specially modified Honeywell DDP-316 minicomputers with 12K 16-bit words of core memory as the IMPs. The IMPs did not have disks, since moving parts were considered unreliable. The IMPs were interconnected by 56-kbps lines leased from telephone companies.

The software was split into two parts: subnet and host. The subnet software consisted of the IMP end of the host-IMP connection, the IMP-IMP protocol, and a source IMP to destination IMP protocol designed to improve reliability. The original ARPANET design is shown in Fig. 1-24.

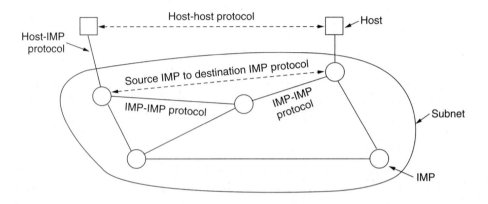

Fig. 1-24. The original ARPANET design.

Outside the subnet, software was also needed, namely, the host end of the host-IMP connection, the host-host protocol, and the application software. It soon became clear that BBN felt that when it had accepted a message on a host-IMP wire and placed it on the host-IMP wire at the destination, its job was done.

To deal with problem of host software, Larry Roberts of ARPA convened a meeting of network researchers, mostly graduate students, at Snowbird, Utah, in the summer of 1969. The graduate students expected some network expert to explain the design of the network and its software to them and then to assign each of them the job of writing part of it. They were astounded when there was no network expert and no grand design. They had to figure out what to do on their own.

Nevertheless, somehow an experimental network went on the air in December 1969 with four nodes, at UCLA, UCSB, SRI, and the University of Utah. These four were chosen because all had a large number of ARPA contracts, and all had different and completely incompatible host computers (just to make it more fun). The network grew quickly as more IMPs were delivered and installed; it soon spanned the United States. Figure 1-25 shows how rapidly the ARPANET grew in the first 3 years.

Later the IMP software was changed to allow terminals to connect directly to a special IMP, called a **TIP** (**Terminal Interface Processor**), without having to go through a host. Subsequent changes included having multiple hosts per IMP (to save money), hosts talking to multiple IMPs (to protect against IMP failures),

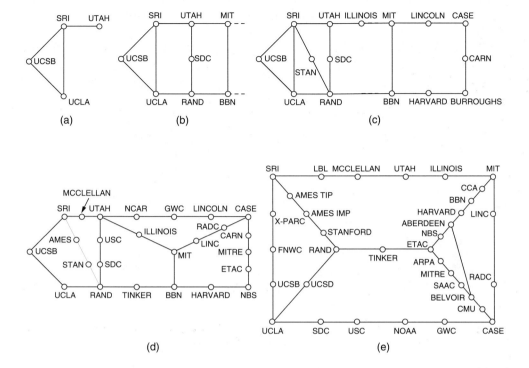

Fig. 1-25. Growth of the ARPANET. (a) Dec. 1969. (b) July 1970. (c) March 1971. (d) April 1972. (e) Sept. 1972.

and hosts and IMPs separated by a large distance (to accommodate hosts far from the subnet).

In addition to helping the fledgling ARPANET grow, ARPA also funded research on satellite networks and mobile packet radio networks. In one famous demonstration, a truck driving around in California used the packet radio network to send messages to SRI, which were then forwarded over the ARPANET to the East Coast, where they were shipped to University College in London over the satellite network. This allowed a researcher in the truck to use a computer in London while driving around in California.

This experiment also demonstrated that the existing ARPANET protocols were not suitable for running over multiple networks. This observation led to more research on protocols, culminating with the invention of the TCP/IP model and protocols (Cerf and Kahn, 1974). TCP/IP was specifically designed to handle communication over internetworks, something becoming increasingly important as more and more networks were being hooked up to the ARPANET.

To encourage adoption of these new protocols, ARPA awarded several contracts to BBN and the University of California at Berkeley to integrate them into Berkeley UNIX. Researchers at Berkeley developed a convenient program interface to the network (sockets) and wrote many application, utility, and management programs to make networking easier.

The timing was perfect. Many universities had just acquired a second or third VAX computer and a LAN to connect them, but they had no networking software. When 4.2BSD came along, with TCP/IP, sockets, and many network utilities, the complete package was adopted immediately. Furthermore, with TCP/IP, it was easy for the LANs to connect to the ARPANET, and many did.

By 1983, the ARPANET was stable and successful, with over 200 IMPs and hundreds of hosts. At this point, ARPA turned the management of the network over to the Defense Communications Agency (DCA), to run it as an operational network. The first thing DCA did was to separate the military portion (about 160 IMPs, of which 110 in the United States and 50 abroad) into a separate subnet, **MILNET**, with stringent gateways between MILNET and the remaining research subnet.

During the 1980s, additional networks, especially LANs, were connected to the ARPANET. As the scale increased, finding hosts became increasingly expensive, so **DNS** (**Domain Naming System**) was created to organize machines into domains and map host names onto IP addresses. Since then, DNS has become a generalized, distributed database system for storing a variety of information related to naming. We will study it in detail in Chap. 7.

By 1990, the ARPANET had been overtaken by newer networks that it itself had spawned, so it was shut down and dismantled, but it lives on in the hearts and minds of network researchers everywhere. MILNET continues to operate, however.

1.5.3. NSFNET

By the late 1970s, NSF (the U.S. National Science Foundation) saw the enormous impact the ARPANET was having on university research, allowing scientists across the country to share data and collaborate on research projects. However, to get on the ARPANET, a university had to have a research contract with the DoD, which many did not have. This lack of universal access prompted NSF to set up a virtual network, **CSNET**, centered around a single machine at BBN that supported dial-up lines and had connections to the ARPANET and other networks. Using CSNET, academic researchers could call up and leave email for other people to pick up later. It was simple, but it worked.

By 1984 NSF began designing a high-speed successor to the ARPANET that would be open to all university research groups. To have something concrete to start with, NSF decided to build a backbone network to connect its six supercomputer centers, in San Diego, Boulder, Champaign, Pittsburgh, Ithaca, and Princeton. Each supercomputer was given a little brother, consisting of an LSI-11 microcomputer called a **fuzzball**. The fuzzballs were connected with 56 kbps leased lines and formed the subnet, the same hardware technology as the

ARPANET used. The software technology was different however: the fuzzballs spoke TCP/IP right from the start, making it the first TCP/IP WAN.

NSF also funded some (eventually about 20) regional networks that connected to the backbone to allow users at thousands of universities, research labs, libraries, and museums to access any of the supercomputers and to communicate with one another. The complete network, including the backbone and the regional networks, was called **NSFNET**. It connected to the ARPANET through a link between an IMP and a fuzzball in the Carnegie-Mellon machine room. The first NSFNET backbone is illustrated in Fig. 1-26.

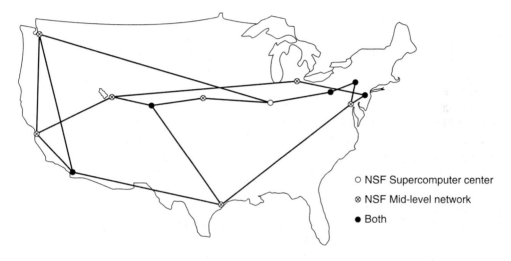

O NSF Supercomputer center

⊗ NSF Mid-level network

● Both

Fig. 1-26. The NSFNET backbone in 1988.

NSFNET was an instantaneous success and was overloaded from the word go. NSF immediately began planning its successor and awarded a contract to the Michigan-based MERIT consortium to run it. Fiber optic channels at 448 kbps were leased from MCI to provide the version 2 backbone. IBM RS6000s were used as routers. This, too, was soon overwhelmed, and by 1990, the second backbone was upgraded to 1.5 Mbps.

As growth continued, NSF realized that the government could not continue financing networking forever. Furthermore, commercial organizations wanted to join but were forbidden by NSF's charter from using networks NSF paid for. Consequently, NSF encouraged MERIT, MCI, and IBM to form a nonprofit corporation, **ANS (Advanced Networks and Services)** as a step along the road to commercialization. In 1990, ANS took over NSFNET and upgraded the 1.5-Mbps links to 45 Mbps to form **ANSNET**.

In December 1991, the U.S. Congress passed a bill authorizing **NREN**, the **National Research and Educational Network**, the research successor to NSFNET, only running at gigabits speeds. The goal was a national network running at 3 Gbps before the millenium. This network is to act as a prototype for the much-discussed information superhighway.

By 1995, the NSFNET backbone was no longer needed to interconnect the NSF regional networks because numerous companies were running commercial IP networks. When ANSNET was sold to America Online in 1995, the NSF regional networks had to go out and buy commercial IP service to interconnect.

To ease the transition and make sure every regional network could communicate with every other regional network, NSF awarded contracts to four different network operators to establish a **NAP** (**Network Access Point**). These operators were PacBell (San Francisco), Ameritech (Chicago), MFS (Washington, D.C.), and Sprint (New York City, where for NAP purposes, Pennsauken, N.J. counts as New York City). Every network operator that wanted to provide backbone service to the NSF regional networks had to connect to all the NAPs. This arrangement meant that a packet originating on any regional network had a choice of backbone carriers to get from its NAP to the destination's NAP. Consequently, the backbone carriers were forced to compete for the regional networks' business on the basis of service and price, which was the idea, of course. In addition to the NSF NAPs, various government NAPs (e.g., FIX-E, FIX-W, MAE-East and MAE-West) and commercial NAPs (e.g., CIX) have also been created, so the concept of a single default backbone was replaced by a commercially-driven competitive infrastructure.

Other countries and regions are also building networks comparable to NSFNET. In Europe, for example, EBONE is an IP backbone for research organizations and EuropaNET is a more commercially oriented network. Both connect numerous cities in Europe with 2-Mbps lines. Upgrades to 34 Mbps are in progress. Each country in Europe has one or more national networks, which are roughly comparable to the NSF regional networks.

1.5.4. The Internet

The number of networks, machines, and users connected to the ARPANET grew rapidly after TCP/IP became the only official protocol on Jan. 1, 1983. When NSFNET and the ARPANET were interconnected, the growth became exponential. Many regional networks joined up, and connections were made to networks in Canada, Europe, and the Pacific.

Sometime in the mid-1980s, people began viewing the collection of networks as an internet, and later as the Internet, although there was no official dedication with some politician breaking a bottle of champagne over a fuzzball.

Growth continued exponentially, and by 1990 the Internet had grown to 3000 networks and 200,000 computers. In 1992, the one millionth host was attached. By 1995, there were multiple backbones, hundreds of mid-level (i.e., regional) networks, tens of thousands of LANs, millions of hosts, and tens of millions of users. The size doubles approximately every year (Paxson, 1994).

Much of the growth comes from connecting existing networks to the Internet. In the past these have included SPAN, NASA's space physics network, HEPNET, a high energy physics network, BITNET, IBM's mainframe network, EARN, a European academic network now widely used in Eastern Europe, and many others. Numerous transatlantic links are in use, running from 64 kbps to 2 Mbps.

The glue that holds the Internet together is the TCP/IP reference model and TCP/IP protocol stack. TCP/IP makes universal service possible and can be compared to the telephone system or the adoption of standard gauge by the railroads in the 19th Century.

What does it actually mean to be on the Internet? Our definition is that a machine is on the Internet if it runs the TCP/IP protocol stack, has an IP address, and has the ability to send IP packets to all the other machines on the Internet. The mere ability to send and receive electronic mail is not enough, since email is gatewayed to many networks outside the Internet. However, the issue is clouded somewhat by the fact that many personal computers have the ability to call up an Internet service provider using a modem, be assigned a temporary IP address, and send IP packets to other Internet hosts. It make sense to regard such machines as being on the Internet for as long as they are connected to the service provider's router.

With exponential growth, the old informal way of running the Internet no longer works. In January 1992, the **Internet Society** was set up, to promote the use of the Internet and perhaps eventually take over managing it.

Traditionally, the Internet had four main applications, as follows:

1. **Email**. The ability to compose, send, and receive electronic mail has been around since the early days of the ARPANET and is enormously popular. Many people get dozens of messages a day and consider it their primary way of interacting with the outside world, far outdistancing the telephone and snail mail. Email programs are available on virtually every kind of computer these days.

2. **News**. Newsgroups are specialized forums in which users with a common interest can exchange messages. Thousands of newsgroups exist, on technical and nontechnical topics, including computers, science, recreation, and politics. Each newsgroup has its own etiquette, style, and customs, and woe be to anyone violating them.

3. **Remote login**. Using the Telnet, Rlogin, or other programs, users anywhere on the Internet can log into any other machine on which they have an account.

4. **File transfer**. Using the FTP program, it is possible to copy files from one machine on the Internet to another. Vast numbers of articles, databases, and other information are available this way.

Up until the early 1990s, the Internet was largely populated by academic, government, and industrial researchers. One new application, the **WWW** (**World Wide Web**) changed all that and brought millions of new, nonacademic users to the net. This application, invented by CERN physicist Tim Berners-Lee, did not change any of the underlying facilities but made them easier to use. Together with the Mosaic viewer, written at the National Center for Supercomputer Applications, the WWW made it possible for a site to set up a number of pages of information containing text, pictures, sound, and even video, with embedded links to other pages. By clicking on a link, the user is suddenly transported to the page pointed to by that link. For example, many companies have a home page with entries pointing to other pages for product information, price lists, sales, technical support, communication with employees, stockholder information, and much more.

Numerous other kinds of pages have come into existence in a very short time, including maps, stock market tables, library card catalogs, recorded radio programs, and even a page pointing to the complete text of many books whose copyrights have expired (Mark Twain, Charles Dickens, etc.). Many people also have personal pages (home pages).

In the first year after Mosaic was released, the number of WWW servers grew from 100 to 7000. Enormous growth will undoubtedly continue for years to come, and will probably be the force driving the technology and use of the Internet into the next millenium.

Many books have been written about the Internet and its protocols. For more information, see (Black, 1995; Carl-Mitchell and Quarterman, 1993; Comer, 1995; and Santifaller, 1994).

1.5.5. Gigabit Testbeds

The Internet backbones operate at megabit speeds, so for people who want to push the technological envelope, the next step is gigabit networking. With each increase in network bandwidth, new applications become possible, and gigabit networks are no exception. In this section we will first say a few words about gigabit applications, mention two of them, and then list some example gigabit testbeds that have been built.

Gigabit networks provide better bandwidth than megabit networks, but not always much better delay. For example, sending a 1-kbit packet from New York to San Francisco at 1 Mbps takes 1 msec to pump the bits out and 20 msec for the transcontinental delay, for a total of 21 msec. A 1-Gbps network can reduce this to 20.001 msec. While the bits go out faster, the transcontinental delay remains the same, since the speed of light in optical fiber (or copper wire) is about 200,000 km/sec, independent of the data rate. Thus for wide area applications in which low delay is critical, going to higher speeds may not help much. Fortunately, for some applications, bandwidth is what counts, and these are the applications for which gigabit networks will make a big difference.

One application is telemedicine. Many people think that a way to reduce medical costs is to reintroduce family doctors and family clinics on a large scale, so everyone has convenient access to first line medical care. When a serious medical problem occurs, the family doctor can order lab tests and medical imaging, such as X-rays, CAT scans, and MRI scans. The test results and images can then be sent electronically to a specialist who then makes the diagnosis.

Doctors are generally unwilling to make diagnoses from computer images unless the quality of the transmitted image is as good as the original image. This requirement means images will probably need 4K × 4K pixels, with 8 bits per pixel (black and white images) or 24 bits per pixel (color images). Since many tests require up to 100 images (e.g., different cross sections of the organ in question), a single series for one patient can generate 40 gigabits. Moving images (e.g., a beating heart) generate even more data. Compression can help some but doctors are leary of it because the most efficient algorithms reduce image quality. Furthermore, all the images must be stored for years but may need to be retrieved at a moment's notice in the event of a medical emergency. Hospitals do not want to become computer centers, so off-site storage combined with high-bandwidth electronic retrieval is essential.

Another gigabit application is the virtual meeting. Each meeting room contains a spherical camera and one or more people. The bit streams from each of the cameras are combined electronically to give the illusion that everyone is in the same room. Each person sees this image using virtual reality goggles. In this way meetings can happen without travel, but again, the data rates required are stupendous.

Starting in 1989, ARPA and NSF jointly agreed to finance a number of university-industry gigabit testbeds, later as part of the NREN project. In some of these, the data rate in each direction was 622 Mbps, so only by counting the data going in both directions do you get a gigabit. This kind of gigabit is sometimes called a "government gigabit." (Some cynics call it a gigabit after taxes.) Below we will briefly mention the first five projects. They have done their job and been shut down, but deserve some credit as pioneers, in the same way the ARPANET does.

1. **Aurora** was a testbed linking four sites in the Northeast: M.I.T., the University of Pennsylvania, IBM's T.J. Watson Lab, and Bellcore (Morristown, N.J.) at 622 Mbps using fiber optics provided by MCI, Bell Atlantic, and NYNEX. Aurora was largely designed to help debug Bellcore's Sunshine switch and IBM's (proprietary) plaNET switch using parallel networks. Research issues included switching technology, gigabit protocols, routing, network control, distributed virtual memory, and collaboration using videoconferencing. For more information, see (Clark et al., 1993).

2. **Blanca** was originally a research project called XUNET involving AT&T Bell Labs, Berkeley, and the University of Wisconsin. In 1990 it added some new sites (LBL, Cray Research, and the University of Illinois) and acquired NSF/ARPA funding. Some of it ran at 622 Mbps, but other parts ran at lower speeds. Blanca was the only nationwide testbed; the rest were regional. Consequently, much of the research was concerned with the effects of speed-of-light delay. The interest here was in protocols, especially network control protocols, host interfaces, and gigabit applications such as medical imaging, meteorological modeling, and radio astronomy. For more information, see (Catlett, 1992; and Fraser, 1993).

3. **CASA** was aimed at doing research on supercomputer applications, especially those in which part of the problem ran best on one kind of supercomputer (e.g., a Cray vector supercomputer) and part ran best on a different kind of supercomputer (e.g., a parallel supercomputer). The applications investigated included geology (analyzing Landsat images), climate modeling, and understanding chemical reactions. It operated in California and New Mexico and connected Los Alamos, Cal Tech, JPL, and the San Diego Supercomputer Center.

4. **Nectar** differed from the three testbeds given above in that it was an experimental gigabit MAN running from CMU to the Pittsburgh Supercomputer Center. The designers were interested in applications involving chemical process flowsheeting and operations research, as well as the tools for debugging them.

5. **VISTAnet** was a small gigabit testbed operated in Research Triangle Park, North Carolina, and connecting the University of North Carolina, North Carolina State University, and MCNC. The interest here was in a prototype for a public switched gigabit network with switches having hundreds of gigabit lines, meaning that the switches had to be capable of processing terabits/sec. The scientific research focused on using 3D images to plan radiation therapy for cancer patients, with the oncologist being able to vary the beam parameters and instantaneously see the radiation dosages being delivered to the tumor and surrounding tissue (Ransom, 1992).

1.6. EXAMPLE DATA COMMUNICATION SERVICES

Telephone companies and others have begun to offer networking services to any organization that wishes to subscribe. The subnet is owned by the network operator, providing communication service for the customers' hosts and terminals.

Such a system is called a **public network**. It is analogous to, and often a part of, the public telephone system. We already briefly looked at one new service, DQDB, in Fig. 1-4. In the following sections we will study four other example services, SMDS, X.25, frame relay, and broadband ISDN.

1.6.1. SMDS—Switched Multimegabit Data Service

The first service we will look at, **SMDS (Switched Multimegabit Data Service)**, was designed to connect together multiple LANs, typically at the branch offices and factories of a single company. It was designed by Bellcore in the 1980s and deployed in the early 1990s by regional and a few long distance carriers. The goal was to produce a high-speed data service and get it out into the world with a minimum of fuss. SMDS is the first broadband (i.e., high-speed) switched service offered to the public.

To see a situation in which SMDS would be useful, consider a company with four offices in four different cities, each with its own LAN. The company would like to connect all the LANs, so that packets can go from one LAN to another. One solution would be to lease six high-speed lines and fully connect the LANs as shown in Fig. 1-27(a). Such a solution is certainly possible, but expensive.

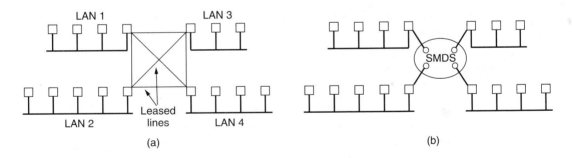

Fig. 1-27. (a) Four LANs interconnected with leased lines. (b) Interconnection using SMDS.

An alternative solution is to use SMDS, as shown in Fig. 1-27(b). The SMDS network acts like a high-speed LAN backbone, allowing packets from any LAN to flow to any other LAN. Between the LANs, in the customer's offices, and the SMDS network, in the telephone company's offices, is a (short) access line leased from the telephone company. Usually, this line is a MAN and uses DQDB, but other options may also be available.

Whereas most telephone company services are designed for continuous traffic, SMDS is designed to handle bursty traffic. In other words, once in a while a packet has to be carried from one LAN to another quickly, but much of the time there is no LAN to LAN traffic. The leased line solution of Fig. 1-27(a) has the problem of high monthly bills; once installed, the customer has to pay for the lines whether or not they are used continuously. For intermittent traffic, leased lines are an expensive solution, and SMDS is priced to compete with them. With n LANs, a fully connected leased line network requires leasing $n(n - 1)/2$ possibly long (i.e., expensive) lines, whereas SMDS only requires leasing n short access lines to the nearest SMDS router.

Since the goal of SMDS is to carry LAN to LAN traffic, it must be fast enough to do the job. The standard speed is 45 Mbps, although sometimes lower speed options are available. MANs can also operate at 45 Mbps, but they are not switched, that is, to connect four LANs using a MAN, the telephone company would have to run a single wire from LAN 1 to LAN 2 to LAN 3 to LAN 4, which is only possible if they are in the same city. With SMDS, each LAN connects to a telephone company switch which routes packets through the SMDS network as needed to reach the destination, possibly traversing multiple switches in the process.

The basic SMDS service is a simple connectionless packet delivery service. The packet format is shown in Fig. 1-28. It has three fields: the destination (where the packet is to go to), the source (who sent it), and a variable length payload field for up to 9188 bytes of user data. The machine on the sending LAN that is connected to the access line puts the packet on the access line, and SMDS makes a best effort attempt to deliver it to the correct destination. No guarantee is given.

Fig. 1-28. The SMDS packet format.

The source and destination addresses consist of a 4-bit code followed by a telephone number of up to 15 decimal digits. Each digit is coded in a separate 4-bit field. The telephone numbers contain country code, area code, and subscriber number, so the service could eventually be offered internationally. It was thought that having decimal telephone numbers as network addresses would make the new offering seem familiar to nervous users.

When a packet arrives at the SMDS network, the first router checks to make sure that the source address corresponds to the incoming line, to prevent billing fraud. If the address is incorrect, the packet is simply discarded. If it is correct, the packet is sent along toward its destination.

A useful SMDS feature is broadcasting. The customer can specify a list of SMDS telephone numbers, and be assigned a special number for the whole list. Any packet sent to that number is delivered to all members on that list. The National Association of Securities Dealers uses this feature of MCI's SMDS service to broadcast new stock prices to all of its 5000 members.

An additional user feature is address screening, on both outgoing and incoming packets. With outgoing screening, the customer can give a list of telephone numbers and specify that no packets may be sent to any other addresses. With incoming screening, only packets from certain pre-arranged telephone numbers will be accepted. When both features are enabled, the user can effectively build a private network with no SMDS connections to the outside world. For companies with confidential data, this feature is highly valuable.

The payload can contain any byte sequence the user wishes, up to 9188 bytes. SMDS does not look at it. It can contain an Ethernet packet, an IBM token ring packet, an IP packet, or anything else. Whatever is present in the payload field is moved without modification from the source LAN to the destination LAN.

SMDS handles bursty traffic as follows. The router connected to each access line contains a counter that is incremented at a constant rate, say once every 10 μsec. When a packet arrives at the router, a check is made to see if the counter is greater than the packet length, in bytes. If it is, the packet is sent without delay and the counter is decremented by the packet length. If the packet length is greater than the counter, the packet is discarded.

In effect, with a tick every 10 μsec the user may send at an *average* rate of 100,000 bytes/sec, but the burst rate may be much higher. If, for example, the line has been idle for 10 msec, the counter will be 1000, and the user will be allowed to send a 1-kilobyte burst at the full 45 Mbps, so it will be transmitted in about 180 μsec. With a 100,000 byte/sec leased line, the same kilobyte would take 10 msec. Thus SMDS offers short delays for widely spaced independent data bursts, as long as the average rate remains below the agreed upon value. This mechanism provides fast response when needed but prevents users from using up more bandwidth than they have agreed to pay for.

1.6.2. X.25 Networks

Many older public networks, especially outside the United States, follow a standard called **X.25**. It was developed during the 1970s by CCITT to provide an interface between public packet-switched networks and their customers.

The physical layer protocol, called **X.21**, specifies the physical, electrical, and procedural interface between the host and the network. Very few public networks actually support this standard, because it requires digital, rather than analog signaling on the telephone lines. As an interim measure, an analog interface similar to the familiar RS-232 standard was defined.

The data link layer standard has a number of (slightly incompatible) variations. They all are designed to deal with transmission errors on the telephone line between the user's equipment (host or terminal) and the public network (router).

The network layer protocol deals with addressing, flow control, delivery confirmation, interrupts, and related issues. Basically, it allows the user to establish virtual circuits and then send packets of up to 128 bytes on them. These packets are delivered reliably and in order. Most X.25 networks work at speeds up to 64 kbps, which makes them obsolete for many purposes. Nevertheless, they are still widespread, so readers should be aware of their existence.

X.25 is connection-oriented and supports both switched virtual circuits and permanent ones. A **switched virtual circuit** is created when one computer sends a packet to the network asking to make a call to a remote computer. Once established, packets can be sent over the connection, always arriving in order. X.25 provides flow control, to make sure a fast sender cannot swamp a slow or busy receiver.

A **permanent virtual circuit** is used the same way as a switched one, but it is set up in advance by agreement between the customer and the carrier. It is always present, and no call setup is required to use it. It is analogous to a leased line.

Because the world is still full of terminals that do not speak X.25, another set of standards was defined that describes how an ordinary (nonintelligent) terminal communicates with an X.25 public network. In effect, the user or network operator installs a "black box" to which these terminals can connect. The black box is called a **PAD** (**Packet Assembler Disassembler**), and its function is described in a document known as **X.3**. A standard protocol has been defined between the terminal and the PAD, called **X.28**; another standard protocol exists between the PAD and the network, called **X.29**. Together, these three recommendations are often called **triple X**.

1.6.3. Frame Relay

Frame relay is a service for people who want an absolute bare-bones connection-oriented way to move bits from A to B at reasonable speed and low cost (Smith, 1993). Its existence is due to changes in technology over the past two decades. Twenty years ago, communication using telephone lines was slow, analog, and unreliable, and computers were slow and expensive. As a result, complex protocols were required to mask errors, and the users' computers were too expensive to have them do this work.

The situation has changed radically. Leased telephone lines are now fast, digital, and reliable, and computers are fast and inexpensive. This suggests the use of simple protocols, with most of the work being done by the users' computers, rather than by the network. It is this environment that frame relay addresses.

Frame relay can best be thought of as a virtual leased line. The customer leases a permanent virtual circuit between two points and can then send frames (i.e., packets) of up to 1600 bytes between them. It is also possible to lease permanent virtual circuits between a given site and multiple other sites, so each frame carries a 10-bit number telling which virtual circuit to use.

The difference between an actual leased line and a virtual leased line is that with an actual one, the user can send traffic all day long at the maximum speed. With a virtual one, data bursts may be sent at full speed, but the long-term average usage must be below a predetermined level. In return, the carrier charges much less for a virtual line than a physical one.

In addition to competing with leased lines, frame relay also competes with X.25 permanent virtual circuits, except that it operates at higher speeds, usually 1.5 Mbps, and provides fewer features.

Frame relay provides a minimal service, primarily a way to determine the start and end of each frame, and detection of transmission errors. If a bad frame is received, the frame relay service simply discards it. It is up to the user to discover that a frame is missing and take the necessary action to recover. Unlike X.25, frame relay does not provide acknowledgements or normal flow control. It does have a bit in the header, however, which one end of a connection can set to indicate to the other end that problems exist. The use of this bit is up to the users.

1.6.4. Broadband ISDN and ATM

Even if the above services become popular, the telephone companies are still faced with a far more fundamental problem: multiple networks. POTS (Plain Old Telephone Service) and Telex use the old circuit-switched network. Each of the new data services such as SMDS and frame relay uses its own packet-switching network. DQDB is different from these, and the internal telephone company call management network (SSN 7) is yet another network. Maintaining all these separate networks is a major headache, and there is another network, cable television, that the telephone companies do not control and would like to.

The perceived solution is to invent a single new network for the future that will replace the entire telephone system and all the specialized networks with a single integrated network for all kinds of information transfer. This new network will have a huge data rate compared to all existing networks and services and will make it possible to offer a large variety of new services. This is not a small project, and it is certainly not going to happen overnight, but it is now under way.

The new wide area service is called **B-ISDN (Broadband Integrated Services Digital Network)**. It will offer video on demand, live television from many sources, full motion multimedia electronic mail, CD-quality music, LAN interconnection, high-speed data transport for science and industry and many other services that have not yet even been thought of, all over the telephone line.

The underlying technology that makes B-ISDN possible is called **ATM (Asynchronous Transfer Mode)** because it is not synchronous (tied to a master clock), as most long distance telephone lines are. Note that the acronym ATM here has nothing to do with the Automated Teller Machines many banks provide (although an ATM machine can use an ATM network to talk to its bank).

A great deal of work has already been done on ATM and on the B-ISDN system that uses it, although there is more ahead. For more information on this subject, see (Fischer et al., 1994; Gasman, 1994; Goralski, 1995; Kim et al., 1994; Kyas, 1995; McDysan and Spohn, 1995; and Stallings, 1995a).

The basic idea behind ATM is to transmit all information in small, fixed-size packets called **cells**. The cells are 53 bytes long, of which 5 bytes are header and 48 bytes are payload, as shown in Fig. 1-29. ATM is both a technology (hidden from the users) and potentially a service (visible to the users). Sometimes the service is called **cell relay**, as an analogy to frame relay.

Bytes 5   48

| Header | User data |

Fig. 1-29. An ATM cell.

The use of a cell-switching technology is a gigantic break with the 100-year old tradition of circuit switching (establishing a copper path) within the telephone system. There are a variety of reasons why cell switching was chosen, among them are the following. First, cell switching is highly flexible and can handle both constant rate traffic (audio, video) and variable rate traffic (data) easily. Second, at the very high speeds envisioned (gigabits per second are within reach), digital switching of cells is easier than using traditional multiplexing techniques, especially using fiber optics. Third, for television distribution, broadcasting is essential; cell switching can provide this and circuit switching cannot.

ATM networks are connection-oriented. Making a call requires first sending a message to set up the connection. After that, subsequent cells all follow the same path to the destination. Cell delivery is not guaranteed, but their order is. If cells 1 and 2 are sent in that order, then if both arrive, they will arrive in that order, never first 2 then 1.

ATM networks are organized like traditional WANs, with lines and switches (routers). The intended speeds for ATM networks are 155 Mbps and 622 Mbps, with the possibility of gigabit speeds later. The 155-Mbps speed was chosen because this is about what is needed to transmit high definition television. The exact choice of 155.52 Mbps was made for compatibility with AT&T's SONET transmission system. The 622 Mbps speed was chosen so four 155-Mbps channels could be sent over it. By now it should be clear why some of the gigabit testbeds operated at 622 Mbps: they used ATM.

When ATM was proposed, virtually all the discussion (i.e., the hype) was about video on demand to every home and replacing the telephone system, as described above. Since then, other developments have become important. Many organizations have run out of bandwidth on their campus or building-wide LANs and are being forced to go to some kind of switched system that has more bandwidth than does a single LAN. Also, in client-server computing, some applications need the ability to talk to certain servers at high speed. ATM is certainly a major candidate for both of these applications. Nevertheless, it is a bit of a letdown to go from a goal of trying to replace the entire low-speed analog telephone system with a high-speed digital one to a goal of trying connect all the Ethernets on campus. LAN interconnection using ATM is discussed in (Kavak, 1995; Newman, 1994; and Truong et al., 1995).

It is also worth pointing out that different organizations involved in ATM have different (financial) interests. The long-distance telephone carriers and PTTs are mostly interested in using ATM to upgrade the telephone system and compete with the cable TV companies in electronic video distribution. The computer vendors see campus ATM LANs as the big moneymaker (for them). All these competing interests do not make the ongoing standardization process any easier, faster, or more coherent. Also, politics and power within the organization standardizing ATM (The ATM Forum) have considerable influence on where ATM is going.

The B-ISDN ATM Reference Model

Let us now turn back to the technology of ATM, especially as used in the (future) telephone system. Broadband ISDN using ATM has its own reference model, different from the OSI model and also different from the TCP/IP model. This model is shown in Fig. 1-30. It consists of three layers, the physical, ATM, and ATM adaptation layers, plus whatever the users want to put on top of that.

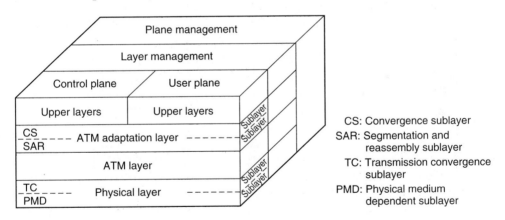

Fig. 1-30. The B-ISDN ATM reference model.

The physical layer deals with the physical medium: voltages, bit timing, and various other issues. ATM does not prescribe a particular set of rules, but instead says that ATM cells may be sent on a wire or fiber by themselves, but they may also be packaged inside the payload of other carrier systems. In other words, ATM has been designed to be independent of the transmission medium.

The **ATM layer** deals with cells and cell transport. It defines the layout of a cell and tells what the header fields mean. It also deals with establishment and release of virtual circuits. Congestion control is also located here.

Because most applications do not want to work directly with cells (although some may), a layer above the ATM layer has been defined that allows users to send packets larger than a cell. The ATM interface segments these packets, transmits the cells individually, and reassembles them at the other end. This layer is the **AAL (ATM Adaptation Layer)**.

Unlike the earlier two-dimensional reference models, the ATM model is defined as being three-dimensional, as shown in Fig. 1-30. The **user plane** deals with data transport, flow control, error correction, and other user functions. In contrast, the **control plane** is concerned with connection management. The layer and plane management functions relate to resource management and interlayer coordination.

The physical and AAL layers are each divided into two sublayers, one at the bottom that does the work and a convergence sublayer on top that provides the proper interface to the layer above it. The functions of the layers and sublayers are given in Fig. 1-31.

OSI layer	ATM layer	ATM sublayer	Functionality
3/4	AAL	CS	Providing the standard interface (convergence)
		SAR	Segmentation and reassembly
2/3	ATM		Flow control Cell header generation/extraction Virtual circuit/path management Cell multiplexing/demultiplexing
2	Physical	TC	Cell rate decoupling Header checksum generation and verification Cell generation Packing/unpacking cells from the enclosing envelope Frame generation
1		PMD	Bit timing Physical network access

Fig. 1-31. The ATM layers and sublayers, and their functions.

The **PMD (Physical Medium Dependent)** sublayer interfaces to the actual cable. It moves the bits on and off and handles the bit timing. For different carriers and cables, this layer will be different.

The other sublayer of the physical layer is the **TC (Transmission Convergence)** sublayer. When cells are transmitted, the TC layer sends them as a string of bits to the PMD layer. Doing this is easy. At the other end, the TC sublayer gets a pure incoming bit stream from the PMD sublayer. Its job is to convert this bit stream into a cell stream for the ATM layer. It handles all the issues related to telling where cells begin and end in the bit stream. In the ATM model, this functionality is in the physical layer. In the OSI model and in pretty much all other networks, the job of framing, that is, turning a raw bit stream into a sequence of frames or cells, is the data link layer's task. For that reason we will discuss it in this book along with the data link layer, not with the physical layer.

As we mentioned earlier, the ATM layer manages cells, including their generation and transport. Most of the interesting aspects of ATM are located here. It is a mixture of the OSI data link and network layers, but it is not split into sublayers.

The AAL layer is split into a **SAR (Segmentation And Reassembly)** sublayer and a **CS (Convergence Sublayer)**. The lower sublayer breaks packets up into cells on the transmission side and puts them back together again at the destination. The upper sublayer makes it possible to have ATM systems offer different kinds of services to different applications (e.g., file transfer and video on demand have different requirements concerning error handling, timing, etc.).

Perspective on ATM

To a considerable extent, ATM is a project invented by the telephone industry because after Ethernet was widely installed, the computer industry never rallied around any higher-speed network technology to make it standard. The telephone companies filled this vacuum with ATM, although in October 1991, many computer vendors joined with the telephone companies to set up the **ATM Forum**, an industry group that will guide the future of ATM.

Although ATM promises the ability to deliver information anywhere at speeds soon to exceed 1 Gbps, delivering on this promise will not be easy. ATM is basically high-speed packet-switching, a technology the telephone companies have little experience with. What they do have, is a massive investment in a different technology (circuit switching) that is in concept unchanged since the days of Alexander Graham Bell. Needless to say, this transition will not happen quickly, all the more so because it is a revolutionary change rather than an evolutionary one, and revolutions never go smoothly.

The economics of installing ATM worldwide also have to be considered. A substantial fraction of the existing telephone system will have to be replaced. Who will pay for this? How much will consumers be willing to pay to get a movie on demand electronically, when they can get one at the local video store for a couple of dollars? Finally, the question of where many of the advanced services are provided is crucial. If they are provided by the network, the telephone companies will profit from them. If they are provided by computers attached to the network, the manufacturers and operators of these devices make the profits. The users may not care, but the telephone companies and computer vendors certainly do, and this will surely affect their interest in making ATM happen.

1.6.5. Comparison of Services

The reader may be wondering why so many incompatible and overlapping services exist, including DQDB, SMDS, X.25, frame relay, ATM, and more. The underlying reason is the 1984 decision to break up AT&T and foster competition in the telecommunications industry. Different companies with different interests and technologies are now free to offer whatever services they think there is a demand for, and many of them are doing this with a vengeance.

To recap some of the services we have touched on in this chapter, DQDB is an unswitched MAN technology that allows 53-byte cells (of which 44 are payload) to be sent down long wires within a city. SMDS is a switched datagram technology for sending datagrams anywhere in a network at 45 Mbps. X.25 is an older connection-oriented networking technology for transmitting small variable-sized packets at 64 kbps. Frame relay is a service that provides virtual leased lines at speeds around 1.5 Mbps. Finally, ATM is designed to replace the entire circuit-switched telephone system with cell switching and be able to handle data and television as well. Some differences between these competitors are summarized in Fig. 1-32.

Issue	DQDB	SMDS	X.25	Frame Relay	ATM AAL
Connection oriented	Yes	No	Yes	Yes	Yes
Normal speed (Mbps)	45	45	.064	1.5	155
Switched	No	Yes	Yes	No	Yes
Fixed-size payload	Yes	No	No	No	No
Max payload	44	9188	128	1600	Variable
Permanent VCs	No	No	Yes	Yes	Yes
Multicasting	No	Yes	No	No	Yes

Fig. 1-32. Different networking services.

1.7. NETWORK STANDARDIZATION

Many network vendors and suppliers exist, each with their own ideas of how things should be done. Without coordination, there would be complete chaos, and users would be able to get nothing done. The only way out is to agree upon some network standards.

Not only do standards allow different computers to communicate, but they also increase the market for products adhering to the standard, which leads to mass production, economies of scale in manufacturing, VLSI implementations, and other benefits that decrease price and further increase acceptance. In the following sections we will take a quick look at the important, but little-known, world of international standardization.

Standards fall into two categories: de facto and de jure. **De facto** (Latin for "from the fact") standards are those that have just happened, without any formal plan. The IBM PC and its successors are de facto standards for small office computers because dozens of manufacturers have chosen to copy IBM's machines very closely. UNIX is the de facto standard for operating systems in university computer science departments.

De jure (Latin for "by law") standards, in contrast, are formal, legal standards adopted by some authorized standardization body. International standardization authorities are generally divided into two classes: those established by treaty among national governments, and voluntary, nontreaty organizations. In the area of computer network standards, there are several organizations of each type, which are discussed below.

1.7.1. Who's Who in the Telecommunications World

The legal status of the world's telephone companies varies considerably from country to country. At one extreme is the United States, which has 1500 separate, privately owned telephone companies. Before it was broken up in 1984, AT&T, at that time the world's largest corporation, completely dominated the scene. It provided telephone service to about 80 percent of America's telephones, spread throughout half of its geographical area, with all the other companies combined servicing the remaining (mostly rural) customers. Since the breakup, AT&T continues to provide long-distance service, although now in competition with other companies. The seven Regional Bell Operating Companies that were split off from AT&T and 1500 independents provide local and cellular telephone service. Some of these independents, such as GTE, are very large companies.

Companies in the United States that provide communication services to the public are called **common carriers**. Their offerings and prices are described by a document called a **tariff**, which must be approved by the Federal Communications Commission for the interstate and international traffic, and by the state public utilities commissions for intrastate traffic.

At the other extreme are countries in which the national government has a complete monopoly on all communication, including the mail, telegraph, telephone, and often radio and television as well. Most of the world falls in this category. In some cases the telecommunication authority is a nationalized company, and in others it is simply a branch of the government, usually known as the **PTT** (**Post, Telegraph & Telephone** administration). Worldwide, the trend is toward liberalization and competition and away from government monopoly.

With all these different suppliers of services, there is clearly a need to provide compatibility on a worldwide scale to ensure that people (and computers) in one country can call their counterparts in another one. Actually, this need has existed for a long time. In 1865, representatives from many European governments met to form the predecessor to today's **ITU (International Telecommunication Union)**. ITU's job was standardizing international telecommunications, which in those days meant telegraphy. Even then it was clear that if half the countries used Morse code and the other half used some other code, there was going to be a problem. When the telephone was put into international service, ITU took over the job of standardizing telephony as well. In 1947, ITU became an agency of the United Nations.

ITU has three main sectors:

1. Radiocommunications Sector (ITU-R).

2. Telecommunications Standardization Sector (ITU-T).

3. Development Sector (ITU-D).

ITU-R is concerned with allocating radio frequencies worldwide to the competing interest groups. We will be primarily concerned with ITU-T, which is concerned with telephone and data communication systems. From 1956 to 1993, ITU-T was known as **CCITT**, an acronym for its French name: Comité Consultatif International Télégraphique et Téléphonique. On March 1, 1993, CCITT was reorganized to make it less bureaucratic and renamed to reflect its new role. Both ITU-T and CCITT issued recommendations in the area of telephone and data communications. One still frequently runs into CCITT recommendations, such as CCITT X.25, although since 1993 recommendations bear the ITU-T label.

ITU-T has five classes of members:

1. Administrations (national PTTs).

2. Recognized private operators (e.g., AT&T, MCI, British Telecom).

3. Regional telecommunications organizations (e.g., the European ETSI).

4. Telecommunications vendors and scientific organizations.

5. Other interested organizations (e.g., banking and airline networks).

ITU-T has about 200 administrations, 100 private operators, and several hundred other members. Only administrations may vote, but all members may participate in ITU-T's work. Since the United States does not have a PTT, somebody else had to represent it in ITU-T. This task fell to the State Department, probably on the grounds that ITU-T had to do with foreign countries, the State Department's specialty.

ITU-T's task is to make technical recommendations about telephone, telegraph, and data communication interfaces. These often become internationally recognized standards, for example, V.24 (also known as EIA RS-232 in the United States), which specifies the placement and meaning of the various pins on the connector used by most asynchronous terminals.

It should be noted that ITU-T recommendations are technically only suggestions that governments can adopt or ignore, as they wish. In practice, a country that wishes to adopt a different telephone standard than the rest of the world is free to do so, but at the price of cutting itself off from everyone else. This might work for Albania, but elsewhere it would be a real problem. The fiction of calling ITU-T standards "recommendations" was and is necessary to keep nationalist forces in many countries placated.

The real work of ITU-T is done in Study Groups, often as large as 400 people. To make it possible to get anything at all done, the Study Groups are divided into Working Parties, which are in turn divided into Expert Teams, which are in turn divided into ad hoc groups. Once a bureaucracy, always a bureaucracy.

Despite all this, ITU-T actually gets things done. Its current output runs to about 5000 pages of recommendations a year. The members chip in to cover ITU's costs. Big, rich countries are supposed to pay up to 30 contributory units a year; small, poor ones can get away with 1/16 of a contributory unit (a contributory unit is about 250,000 dollars). It is a testimony to ITU-T's value that pretty much everyone pays their fair share, even though contributions are completely voluntary.

As telecommunications completes the transition started in the 1980s from being entirely national to being entirely global, standards will become increasingly important, and more and more organizations will want to become involved in setting them. For more information about ITU, see (Irmer, 1994).

1.7.2. Who's Who in the International Standards World

International standards are produced by **ISO (International Standards Organization**[†]), a voluntary, nontreaty organization founded in 1946. Its members are the national standards organizations of the 89 member countries. These members include ANSI (U.S.), BSI (Great Britain), AFNOR (France), DIN (Germany), and 85 others.

ISO issues standards on a vast number of subjects, ranging from nuts and bolts (literally) to telephone pole coatings. Over 5000 standards have been issued, including the OSI standards. ISO has almost 200 Technical Committees, numbered in the order of their creation, each dealing with a specific subject. TC1 deals with the nuts and bolts (standardizing screw thread pitches). TC97 deals with computers and information processing. Each TC has subcommittees (SCs) divided into working groups (WGs).

The real work is done largely in the WGs by over 100,000 volunteers

---

† For the purist, ISO's true name is the International Organization for Standardization.

worldwide. Many of these "volunteers" are assigned to work on ISO matters by their employers, whose products are being standardized. Others are government officials keen on having their country's way of doing things become the international standard. Academic experts also are active in many of the WGs.

On issues of telecommunication standards, ISO and ITU-T often cooperate (ISO is a member of ITU-T) to avoid the irony of two official and mutually incompatible international standards.

The U.S. representative in ISO is **ANSI (American National Standards Institute**), which despite its name, is a private, nongovernmental, nonprofit organization. Its members are manufacturers, common carriers, and other interested parties. ANSI standards are frequently adopted by ISO as international standards.

The procedure used by ISO for adopting standards is designed to achieve as broad a consensus as possible. The process begins when one of the national standards organizations feels the need for an international standard in some area. A working group is then formed to come up with a **CD (Committee Draft**). The CD is then circulated to all the member bodies, which get 6 months to criticize it. If a substantial majority approves, a revised document, called a **DIS (Draft International Standard**) is produced and circulated for comments and voting. Based on the results of this round, the final text of the **IS (International Standard**) is prepared, approved, and published. In areas of great controversy, a CD or DIS may have to go through several versions before acquiring enough votes, and the whole process can take years.

NIST (National Institute of Standards and Technology) is an agency of the U.S. Dept. of Commerce. It was formerly known as the National Bureau of Standards. It issues standards that are mandatory for purchases made by the U.S. Government, except for those of the Department of Defense, which has its own standards.

Another major player in the standards world is **IEEE (Institute of Electrical and Electronics Engineers**), the largest professional organization in the world. In addition to publishing scores of journals and running numerous conferences each year, IEEE has a standardization group that develops standards in the area of electrical engineering and computing. IEEE's 802 standard for local area networks is the key standard for LANs. It has subsequently been taken over by ISO as the basis for ISO 8802.

1.7.3. Who's Who in the Internet Standards World

The worldwide Internet has its own standardization mechanisms, very different from those of ITU-T and ISO. The difference can be crudely summed up by saying that the people who come to ITU or ISO standardization meetings wear suits. The people who come to Internet standardization meetings wear either jeans or military uniforms.

ITU-T and ISO meetings are populated by corporate officials and government civil servants for whom standardization is their job. They regard standardization as a good thing and devote their lives to it. Internet people, on the other hand, definitely prefer anarchy as a matter of principle, but sometimes agreement is needed to make things work. Thus standards, however regrettable, are occasionally needed.

When the ARPANET was set up, DoD created an informal committee to oversee it. In 1983, the committee was renamed the **IAB** (**Internet Activities Board**) and given a slighter broader mission, namely, to keep the researchers involved with the ARPANET and Internet pointed more-or-less in the same direction, an activity not unlike herding cats. The meaning of the acronym "IAB" was later changed to **Internet Architecture Board.**

Each of the approximately ten members of the IAB headed a task force on some issue of importance. The IAB met several times a year to discuss results and give feedback to the DoD and NSF, which were providing most of the funding at this time. When a standard was needed (e.g., a new routing algorithm), the IAB members would thrash it out and then announce the change so the graduate students who were the heart of the software effort could implement it. Communication was done by a series of technical reports called **RFCs** (**Request For Comments**). RFCs are stored on-line and can be fetched by anyone interested in them. They are numbered in chronological order of creation. Close to 2000 now exist.

By 1989, the Internet had grown so large that this highly informal style no longer worked. Many vendors by then offered TCP/IP products and did not want to change them just because ten researchers had thought of a better idea. In the summer of 1989, the IAB was reorganized again. The researchers were moved to the **IRTF** (**Internet Research Task Force**), which was made subsidiary to IAB, along with the **IETF** (**Internet Engineering Task Force**). The IAB was repopulated with people representing a broader range of organizations than just the research community. It was initially a self-perpetuating group, with members serving for a 2-year term, and new members being appointed by the old ones. Later, the **Internet Society** was created, populated by people interested in the Internet. The Internet Society is thus in a sense comparable to ACM or IEEE. It is governed by elected trustees who appoint the IAB members.

The idea of this split was to have the IRTF concentrate on long-term research, while the IETF dealt with short-term engineering issues. The IETF was divided up into working groups, each with a specific problem to solve. The chairmen of these working groups initially met together as a steering committee to direct the engineering effort. The working group topics include new applications, user information, OSI integration, routing and addressing, security, network management, and standards. Eventually, so many working groups were formed (more than 70) that they were grouped into areas, and the area chairmen met as the steering committee.

In addition, a more formal standardization process was adopted, patterned after ISOs. To become a **Proposed Standard**, the basic idea must be completely explained in an RFC and have sufficient interest in the community to warrant consideration. To advance to the **Draft Standard** stage, there must be a working implementation that has been thoroughly tested by at least two independent sites for 4 months. If the IAB is convinced that the idea is sound and the software works, it can declare the RFC to be an Internet Standard. Some Internet Standards have become DoD standards (MIL-STD), making them mandatory for DoD suppliers. David Clark once made a now-famous remark about Internet standardization consisting of "rough consensus and running code."

1.8. OUTLINE OF THE REST OF THE BOOK

This book discusses both the principles and practice of computer networking. Most chapters start with a discussion of the relevant principles, followed by a number of examples that illustrate these principles. Two networks are used as running examples throughout the text: the Internet and ATM networks. In a way, the two are complementary: ATM is mostly concerned with the lower layers, and the Internet is mostly concerned with upper layers. In the future, the Internet may run largely on an ATM backbone, so both of them may coexist. Other examples will be given where relevant.

The book is structured according to the hybrid model of Fig. 1-21. Starting with Chap. 2, we begin working our way up the protocol hierarchy beginning at the bottom. The second chapter provides some background in the field of data communication. It covers analog and digital transmission, multiplexing, switching, and the telephone system, past current, and future. This material is concerned with the physical layer, although we cover only the architectural rather than the hardware aspects. Several examples of the physical layer are also discussed, such as SONET and cellular radio.

Chap. 3 discusses the data link layer and its protocols by means of a number of increasingly complex examples. The analysis of these protocols is also covered. After that, some important real-world protocols are discussed, including HDLC (used in low- and medium-speed networks), SLIP, and PPP (used in the Internet), and ATM (used in B-ISDN).

Chap. 4 concerns the medium access sublayer, which is part of the data link layer. The basic question it deals with is how to determine who may use the network next when the network consists of a single shared channel, as in most LANs and some satellite networks. Many examples are given from the areas of LANs, fiber optic networks, and satellite networks. Bridges, which are used to connect LANs together, are also discussed here.

Chap. 5 deals with the network layer, especially routing, congestion control, and internetworking. It discusses both static and dynamic routing algorithms. Broadcast routing is also covered. The effect of poor routing, congestion, is discussed in some detail. Connecting heterogeneous networks together to form internetworks leads to numerous problems that are discussed here. The network layers in the Internet and ATM networks are given extensive coverage.

Chap. 6 deals with the transport layer. Much of the emphasis is on connection-oriented protocols, since many applications need these. An example transport service and its implementation are discussed in detail. Both the Internet transport protocols (TCP and UDP) and the ATM transport protocols (AAL 1-5) are covered in detail.

The OSI session and presentation layers are not discussed in this book as they are not widely used for anything.

Chapter 7 deals with the application layer, its protocols and applications. Among the applications covered are security, naming, electronic mail, net news, network management, the World Wide Web, and multimedia.

Chap. 8 contains an annotated list of suggested readings arranged by chapter. It is intended to help those readers who would like to pursue their study of networking further. The chapter also has an alphabetical bibliography of all references cited in this book.

1.9. SUMMARY

Computer networks can be used for numerous services, both for companies and for individuals. For companies, networks of personal computers using shared servers often provide flexibility and a good price/performance ratio. For individuals, networks offer access to a variety of information and entertainment resources.

Roughly speaking, networks can be divided up into LANs, MANs, WANs, and internetworks, each with their own characteristics, technologies, speeds, and niches. LANs cover a building, MANs cover a city, and WANs cover a country or continent. LANs and MANs are unswitched (i.e., do not have routers); WANs are switched.

Network software consists of protocols, or rules by which processes can communicate. Protocols can be either connectionless or connection-oriented. Most networks support protocol hierarchies, with each layer providing services to the layers above it and insulating them from the details of the protocols used in the lower layers. Protocol stacks are typically based either on the OSI model or the TCP/IP model. Both of these have network, transport, and application layers, but they differ on the other layers.

Well-known networks have included Novell's NetWare, the ARPANET (now defunct), NSFNET, the Internet, and various gigabit testbeds. Network services have included DQDB, SMDS, X.25, frame relay, and broadband ISDN. All of these are available commercially, from a variety of suppliers. The marketplace will determine which ones will survive and which ones will not.

PROBLEMS

1. In the future, when everyone has a home terminal connected to a computer network, instant public referendums on important pending legislation will become possible. Ultimately, existing legislatures could be eliminated, to let the will of the people be expressed directly. The positive aspects of such a direct democracy are fairly obvious; discuss some of the negative aspects.

2. An alternative to a LAN is simply a big timesharing system with terminals for all users. Give two advantages of a client-server system using a LAN.

3. A collection of five routers is to be connected in a point-to-point subnet. Between each pair of routers, the designers may put a high-speed line, a medium-speed line, a low-speed line, or no line. If it takes 100 ms of computer time to generate and inspect each topology, how long will it take to inspect all of them to find the one that best matches the expected load?

4. A group of $2^n - 1$ routers are interconnected in a centralized binary tree, with a router at each tree node. Router i communicates with router j by sending a message to the root of the tree. The root then sends the message back down to j. Derive an approximate expression for the mean number of hops per message for large n, assuming that all router pairs are equally likely.

5. A disadvantage of a broadcast subnet is the capacity wasted due to multiple hosts attempting to access the channel at the same time. As a simplistic example, suppose that time is divided into discrete slots, with each of the n hosts attempting to use the channel with probability p during each slot. What fraction of the slots are wasted due to collisions?

6. What are the SAP addresses in FM radio broadcasting?

7. What is the principal difference between connectionless communication and connection-oriented communication?

8. Two networks each provide reliable connection-oriented service. One of them offers a reliable byte stream and the other offers a reliable message stream. Are these identical? If so, why is the distinction made? If not, give an example of how they differ.

9. What is the difference between a confirmed service and an unconfirmed service? For each of the following, tell whether it might be a confirmed service, an unconfirmed service, both, or neither.
   (a) Connection establishment.
   (b) Data transmission.
   (c) Connection release.

10. What does "negotiation" mean when discussing network protocols? Give an example of it.

11. What are two reasons for using layered protocols?

12. List two ways in which the OSI reference model and the TCP/IP reference model are the same. Now list two ways in which they differ.

13. The president of the Specialty Paint Corp. gets the idea to work together with a local beer brewer for the purpose of producing an invisible beer can (as an anti-litter measure). The president tells her legal department to look into it, and they in turn ask engineering for help. As a result, the chief engineer calls his counterpart at the other company to discuss the technical aspects of the project. The engineers then report back to their respective legal departments, which then confer by telephone to arrange the legal aspects. Finally, the two corporate presidents discuss the financial side of the deal. Is this an example of a multilayer protocol in the sense of the OSI model?

14. In most networks, the data link layer handles transmission errors by requesting damaged frames to be retransmitted. If the probability of a frame's being damaged is p, what is the mean number of transmissions required to send a frame if acknowledgements are never lost?

15. Which of the OSI layers handles each of the following:
    (a) Breaking the transmitted bit stream into frames.
    (b) Determining which route through the subnet to use.

16. Do TPDUs encapsulate packets or the other way around? Discuss.

17. A system has an n-layer protocol hierarchy. Applications generate messages of length M bytes. At each of the layers, an h-byte header is added. What fraction of the network bandwidth is filled with headers?

18. What is the main difference between TCP and UDP?

19. Does the Novell NetWare architecture look more like X.25 or like the Internet? Explain your answer.

20. The Internet is roughly doubling in size every 18 months. Although no one really knows for sure, one estimate put the number of hosts on it at 7 million in January 1996. Use these data to compute the expected number of Internet hosts in the year 2008.

21. Why was SMDS designed as a connectionless network and frame relay as a connection-oriented one?

22. Imagine that you have trained your St. Bernard, Bernie, to carry a box of three 8mm Exabyte tapes instead of a flask of brandy. (When your disk fills up, you consider that an emergency.) These tapes each contain 7 gigabytes. The dog can travel to your side, wherever you may be, at 18 km/hour. For what range of distances does Bernie have a higher data rate than a 155-Mbps ATM line?

23. When transferring a file between two computers, (at least) two acknowledgement strategies are possible. In the first one, the file is chopped up into packets, which are individually acknowledged by the receiver, but the file transfer as a whole is not acknowledged. In the second one, the packets are not acknowledged individually, but the entire file is acknowledged when it arrives. Discuss these two approaches.

24. Imagine that the SMDS packet of Fig. 1-28 were to be incorporated in OSI protocol hierarchy. In which layer would it appear?

25. Give an advantage and a disadvantage of frame relay over a leased telephone line.

26. Why does ATM use small, fixed-length cells?

27. List two advantages and two disadvantages of having international standards for network protocols.

28. When a system has a permanent part and a removable part, such as a diskette drive and the diskette, it is important that the system be standardized, so that different companies can make both the permanent and removable parts and have everything work together. Give three examples outside the computer industry where such international standards exist. Now give three areas outside the computer industry where they do not exist.

2

THE PHYSICAL LAYER

In this chapter we will look at the lowest layer depicted in the hierarchy of Fig. 1-21. We will begin with a theoretical analysis of data transmission, only to discover that Mother (Parent?) Nature puts some limits on what can be sent over a channel.

Then we will cover transmission media, both guided (copper wire and fiber optics) and unguided (wireless). This material will provide background information on the key transmission technologies used in modern networks.

The remainder of the chapter is devoted to examples of communication systems that use these underlying transmission media. We will start with the telephone system, looking at three different versions: the current (partly) analog system, a potential digital system for the near future (N-ISDN), and a likely digital system for the distant future (ATM). Then we will look at two wireless systems, cellular radio and communication satellites.

2.1. THE THEORETICAL BASIS FOR DATA COMMUNICATION

Information can be transmitted on wires by varying some physical property such as voltage or current. By representing the value of this voltage or current as a single-valued function of time, $f(t)$, we can model the behavior of the signal and analyze it mathematically. This analysis is the subject of the following sections.

2.1.1. Fourier Analysis

In the early 19th Century, the French mathematician Jean-Baptiste Fourier proved that any reasonably behaved periodic function, $g(t)$, with period T can be constructed by summing a (possibly infinite) number of sines and cosines:

$$g(t) = \frac{1}{2}c + \sum_{n=1}^{\infty} a_n \sin(2\pi nft) + \sum_{n=1}^{\infty} b_n \cos(2\pi nft) \tag{2-1}$$

where $f = 1/T$ is the fundamental frequency and a_n and b_n are the sine and cosine amplitudes of the nth **harmonics** (terms). Such a decomposition is called a **Fourier series**. From the Fourier series, the function can be reconstructed; that is, if the period, T, is known and the amplitudes are given, the original function of time can be found by performing the sums of Eq. (2-1).

A data signal that has a finite duration (which all of them do) can be handled by just imagining that it repeats the entire pattern over and over forever (i.e., the interval from T to $2T$ is the same as from 0 to T, etc.).

The a_n amplitudes can be computed for any given $g(t)$ by multiplying both sides of Eq. (2-1) by $\sin(2\pi kft)$ and then integrating from 0 to T. Since

$$\int_0^T \sin(2\pi kft)\,\sin(2\pi nft)\,dt = \begin{cases} 0 \text{ for } k \neq n \\ T/2 \text{ for } k = n \end{cases}$$

only one term of the summation survives: a_n. The b_n summation vanishes completely. Similarly, by multiplying Eq. (2-1) by $\cos(2\pi kft)$ and integrating between 0 and T, we can derive b_n. By just integrating both sides of the equation as it stands, c can be found. The results of performing these operations are as follows:

$$a_n = \frac{2}{T}\int_0^T g(t)\sin(2\pi nft)\,dt \qquad b_n = \frac{2}{T}\int_0^T g(t)\cos(2\pi nft)\,dt \qquad c = \frac{2}{T}\int_0^T g(t)\,dt$$

2.1.2. Bandwidth-Limited Signals

To see what all this has to do with data communication, let us consider a specific example: the transmission of the ASCII character "b" encoded in an 8-bit byte. The bit pattern that is to be transmitted is 01100010. The left-hand part of Fig. 2-1(a) shows the voltage output by the transmitting computer. The Fourier analysis of this signal yields the coefficients:

$$a_n = \frac{1}{\pi n}[\cos(\pi n/4) - \cos(3\pi n/4) + \cos(6\pi n/4) - \cos(7\pi n/4)]$$

$$b_n = \frac{1}{\pi n}[\sin(3\pi n/4) - \sin(\pi n/4) + \sin(7\pi n/4) - \sin(6\pi n/4)]$$

$$c = 3/8$$

The root-mean-square amplitudes, $\sqrt{a_n^2 + b_n^2}$, for the first few terms are shown on the right-hand side of Fig. 2-1(a). These values are of interest because their squares are proportional to the energy transmitted at the corresponding frequency.

No transmission facility can transmit signals without losing some power in the process. If all the Fourier components were equally diminished, the resulting signal would be reduced in amplitude but not distorted [i.e., it would have the same nice squared-off shape as Fig. 2-1(a)]. Unfortunately, all transmission facilities diminish different Fourier components by different amounts, thus introducing distortion. Usually, the amplitudes are transmitted undiminished from 0 up to some frequency f_c [measured in cycles/sec or Hertz (Hz)] with all frequencies above this cutoff frequency strongly attenuated. In some cases this is a physical property of the transmission medium, and in other cases a filter is intentionally introduced into the circuit to limit the amount of (scarce) bandwidth available to each customer.

Now let us consider how the signal of Fig. 2-1(a) would look if the bandwidth were so low that only the lowest frequencies were transmitted [i.e., the function were being approximated by the first few terms of Eq. (2-1)]. Figure 2-1(b) shows the signal that results from a channel that allows only the first harmonic (the fundamental, f) to pass through. Similarly, Fig. 2-1(c)-(e) show the spectra and reconstructed functions for higher bandwidth channels.

The time T required to transmit the character depends on both the encoding method and the signaling speed [the number of times per second that the signal changes its value (e.g., its voltage)]. The number of changes per second is measured in **baud**. A b baud line does not necessarily transmit b bits/sec, since each signal might convey several bits. If the voltages 0, 1, 2, 3, 4, 5, 6, and 7 were used, each signal value could be used to convey 3 bits, so the bit rate would be three times the baud rate. In our example, only 0s and 1s are being used as signal levels, so the bit rate is equal to the baud rate.

Given a bit rate of b bits/sec, the time required to send 8 bits (for example) is $8/b$ sec, so the frequency of the first harmonic is $b/8$ Hz. An ordinary telephone line, often called a **voice-grade line**, has an artificially introduced cutoff frequency near 3000 Hz. This restriction means that the number of the highest harmonic passed through is $3000/(b/8)$ or $24,000/b$, roughly (the cutoff is not sharp).

For some data rates, the numbers work out as shown in Fig. 2-2. From these numbers, it is clear that trying to send at 9600 bps over a voice-grade telephone line will transform Fig. 2-1(a) into something looking like Fig. 2-1(c), making accurate reception of the original binary bit stream tricky. It should be obvious that at data rates much higher than 38.4 kbps there is no hope at all for *binary* signals, even if the transmission facility is completely noiseless. In other words, limiting the bandwidth limits the data rate, even for perfect channels. However, sophisticated coding schemes that use several voltage levels do exist and can achieve higher data rates. We will discuss these later in this chapter.

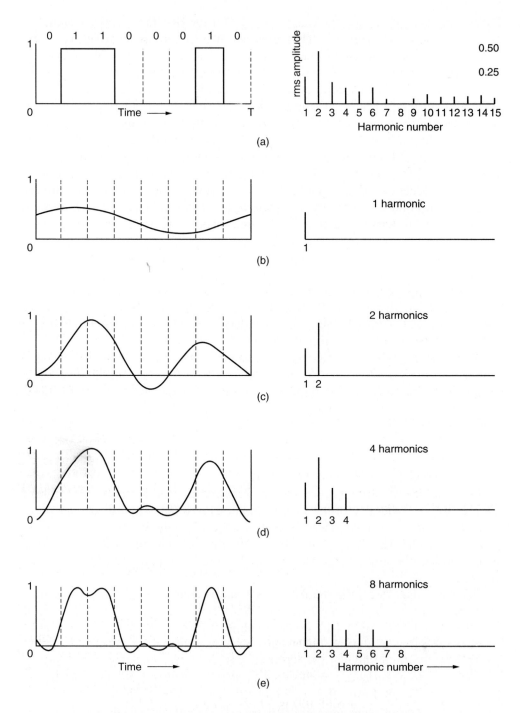

Fig. 2-1. (a) A binary signal and its root-mean-square Fourier amplitudes. (b)-(e) Successive approximations to the original signal.

Bps	T (msec)	First harmonic (Hz)	# Harmonics sent
300	26.67	37.5	80
600	13.33	75	40
1200	6.67	150	20
2400	3.33	300	10
4800	1.67	600	5
9600	0.83	1200	2
19200	0.42	2400	1
38400	0.21	4800	0

Fig. 2-2. Relation between data rate and harmonics.

2.1.3. The Maximum Data Rate of a Channel

As early as 1924, H. Nyquist realized the existence of this fundamental limit and derived an equation expressing the maximum data rate for a finite bandwidth noiseless channel. In 1948, Claude Shannon carried Nyquist's work further and extended it to the case of a channel subject to random (that is, thermodynamic) noise (Shannon, 1948). We will just briefly summarize their now classical results here.

Nyquist proved that if an arbitrary signal has been run through a low-pass filter of bandwidth H, the filtered signal can be completely reconstructed by making only $2H$ (exact) samples per second. Sampling the line faster than $2H$ times per second is pointless because the higher frequency components that such sampling could recover have already been filtered out. If the signal consists of V discrete levels, Nyquist's theorem states:

$$\text{maximum data rate} = 2H \log_2 V \text{ bits/sec}$$

For example, a noiseless 3-kHz channel cannot transmit binary (i.e., two-level) signals at a rate exceeding 6000 bps.

So far we have considered only noiseless channels. If random noise is present, the situation deteriorates rapidly. The amount of thermal noise present is measured by the ratio of the signal power to the noise power, called the **signal-to-noise ratio**. If we denote the signal power by S and the noise power by N, the signal-to-noise ratio is S/N. Usually, the ratio itself is not quoted; instead, the quantity $10 \log_{10} S/N$ is given. These units are called **decibels** (dB). An S/N ratio of 10 is 10 dB, a ratio of 100 is 20 dB, a ratio of 1000 is 30 dB and so on. The manufacturers of stereo amplifiers often characterize the bandwidth (frequency range) over which their product is linear by giving the 3-dB frequency on each end. These are the points at which the amplification factor has been approximately halved.

Shannon's major result is that the maximum data rate of a noisy channel whose bandwidth is H Hz, and whose signal-to-noise ratio is S/N, is given by

$$\text{maximum number of bits/sec} = H \log_2 (1 + S/N)$$

For example, a channel of 3000-Hz bandwidth, and a signal to thermal noise ratio of 30 dB (typical parameters of the analog part of the telephone system) can never transmit much more than 30,000 bps, no matter how many or few signal levels are used and no matter how often or how infrequent samples are taken. Shannon's result was derived using information-theory arguments and applies to any channel subject to Gaussian (thermal) noise. Counterexamples should be treated in the same category as perpetual motion machines. It should be noted, however, that this is only an upper bound and real systems rarely achieve it.

2.2. TRANSMISSION MEDIA

The purpose of the physical layer is to transport a raw bit stream from one machine to another. Various physical media can be used for the actual transmission. Each one has its own niche in terms of bandwidth, delay, cost, and ease of installation and maintenance. Media are roughly grouped into guided media, such as copper wire and fiber optics, and unguided media, such as radio and lasers through the air. We will look at these in this section and the next one.

2.2.1. Magnetic Media

One of the most common ways to transport data from one computer to another is to write them onto magnetic tape or floppy disks, physically transport the tape or disks to the destination machine, and read them back in again. While this method is not as sophisticated as using a geosynchronous communication satellite, it is often much more cost effective, especially for applications in which high bandwidth or cost per bit transported is the key factor.

A simple calculation will make this point clear. An industry standard 8-mm video tape (e.g., Exabyte) can hold 7 gigabytes. A box $50 \times 50 \times 50$ cm can hold about 1000 of these tapes, for a total capacity of 7000 gigabytes. A box of tapes can be delivered anywhere in the United States in 24 hours by Federal Express and other companies. The effective bandwidth of this transmission is 56 gigabits/86400 sec or 648 Mbps, which is slightly better than the high-speed version of ATM (622 Mbps). If the destination is only an hour away by road, the bandwidth is increased to over 15 Gbps.

For a bank with gigabytes of data to be backed up daily on a second machine (so the bank can continue to function even in the face of a major flood or earthquake) it is likely that no other transmission technology can even begin to approach magnetic tape for performance.

If we now look at cost, we get a similar picture. The cost of 1000 video tapes is perhaps 5000 dollars when bought in bulk. A video tape can be reused at least ten times, so the tape cost is maybe 500 dollars. Add to this another 200 dollars for shipping, and we have a cost of roughly 700 dollars to ship 7000 gigabytes. This amounts to 10 cents per gigabyte. No network carrier on earth can compete with that. The moral of the story is:

> *Never underestimate the bandwidth of a station wagon full of tapes*
> *hurtling down the highway.*

2.2.2. Twisted Pair

Although the bandwidth characteristics of magnetic tape are excellent, the delay characteristics are poor. Transmission time is measured in minutes or hours, not milliseconds. For many applications an on-line connection is needed. The oldest and still most common transmission medium is **twisted pair**. A twisted pair consists of two insulated copper wires, typically about 1 mm thick. The wires are twisted together in a helical form, just like a DNA molecule. The purpose of twisting the wires is to reduce electrical interference from similar pairs close by. (Two parallel wires constitute a simple antenna; a twisted pair does not.)

The most common application of the twisted pair is the telephone system. Nearly all telephones are connected to the telephone company office by a twisted pair. Twisted pairs can run several kilometers without amplification, but for longer distances, repeaters are needed. When many twisted pairs run in parallel for a substantial distance, such as all the wires coming from an apartment building to the telephone company office, they are bundled together and encased in a protective sheath. The pairs in these bundles would interfere with one another if it were not for the twisting. In parts of the world where telephone lines run on poles above ground, it is common to see bundles several centimeters in diameter.

Twisted pairs can be used for either analog or digital transmission. The bandwidth depends on the thickness of the wire and the distance traveled, but several megabits/sec can be achieved for a few kilometers in many cases. Due to their adequate performance and low cost, twisted pairs are widely used and are likely to remain so for years to come.

Twisted pair cabling comes in several varieties, two of which are important for computer networks. **Category 3** twisted pairs consist of two insulated wires gently twisted together. Four such pairs are typically grouped together in a plastic sheath for protection and to keep the eight wires together. Prior to about 1988, most office buildings had one category 3 cable running from a central **wiring closet** on each floor into each office. This scheme allowed up to four regular telephones or two multiline telephones in each office to connect to the telephone company equipment in the wiring closet.

Starting around 1988, the more advanced **category 5** twisted pairs were introduced. They are similar to category 3 pairs, but with more twists per centimeter and Teflon insulation, which results in less crosstalk and a better quality signal over longer distances, making them more suitable for high-speed computer communication. Both of these wiring types are often referred to as **UTP** (**Unshielded Twisted Pair**), to contrast them with the bulky, expensive, shielded twisted pair cables IBM introduced in the early 1980s, but which have not proven popular outside of IBM installations.

2.2.3. Baseband Coaxial Cable

Another common transmission medium is the **coaxial cable** (known to its many friends as just "coax"). It has better shielding than twisted pairs, so it can span longer distances at higher speeds. Two kinds of coaxial cable are widely used. One kind, 50-ohm cable, is commonly used for digital transmission and is the subject of this section. The other kind, 75-ohm cable, is commonly used for analog transmission and will be described in the next section. This distinction is based on historical, rather than technical, factors (e.g., early dipole antennas had an impedance of 300 ohms, and it was easy to build 4:1 impedance matching transformers).

A coaxial cable consists of a stiff copper wire as the core, surrounded by an insulating material. The insulator is encased by a cylindrical conductor, often as a closely woven braided mesh. The outer conductor is covered in a protective plastic sheath. A cutaway view of a coaxial cable is shown in Fig. 2-3.

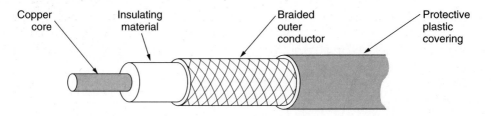

Fig. 2-3. A coaxial cable.

The construction and shielding of the coaxial cable give it a good combination of high bandwidth and excellent noise immunity. The bandwidth possible depends on the cable length. For 1-km cables, a data rate of 1 to 2 Gbps is feasible. Longer cables can also be used, but only at lower data rates or with periodic amplifiers. Coaxial cables used to be widely used within the telephone system but have now largely been replaced by fiber optics on long-haul routes. In the United States alone, 1000 km of fiber is installed every day (counting a 100-km bundle with 10 strands of fiber as 1000 km). Sprint is already 100 percent fiber, and the other major carriers are rapidly approaching that. Coax is still widely used for cable television and some local area networks, however.

2.2.4. Broadband Coaxial Cable

The other kind of coaxial cable system uses analog transmission on standard cable television cabling. It is called **broadband**. Although the term "broadband" comes from the telephone world, where it refers to anything wider than 4 kHz, in the computer networking world "broadband cable" means any cable network using analog transmission (see Cooper, 1986).

Since broadband networks use standard cable television technology, the cables can be used up to 300 MHz (and often up to 450 MHz) and can run for nearly 100 km due to the analog signaling, which is much less critical than digital signaling. To transmit digital signals on an analog network, each interface must contain electronics to convert the outgoing bit stream to an analog signal, and the incoming analog signal to a bit stream. Depending on the type of these electronics, 1 bps may occupy roughly 1 Hz of bandwidth. At higher frequencies, many bits per Hz are possible using advanced modulation techniques.

Broadband systems are divided up into multiple channels, frequently the 6-Mhz channels used for television broadcasting. Each channel can be used for analog television, CD-quality audio (1.4 Mbps), or a digital bit stream at, say, 3 Mbps, independent of the others. Television and data can be mixed on one cable.

One key difference between baseband and broadband is that broadband systems typically cover a large area and therefore need analog amplifiers to strengthen the signal periodically. These amplifiers can only transmit signals in one direction, so a computer outputting a packet will not be able to reach computers "upstream" from it if an amplifier lies between them. To get around this problem, two types of broadband systems have been developed: dual cable and single cable systems.

Dual cable systems have two identical cables running in parallel, next to each other. To transmit data, a computer outputs the data onto cable 1, which runs to a device called the **head-end** at the root of the cable tree. The head-end then transfers the signal to cable 2 for transmission back down the tree. All computers transmit on cable 1 and receive on cable 2. A dual cable system is shown in Fig. 2-4(a).

The other scheme allocates different frequency bands for inbound and outbound communication on a single cable [see Fig. 2-4(b)]. The low-frequency band is used for communication from the computers to the head-end, which then shifts the signal to the high-frequency band and rebroadcasts it. In the **subsplit** system, frequencies from 5 to 30 MHz are used for inbound traffic, and frequencies from 40 to 300 MHz are used for outbound traffic.

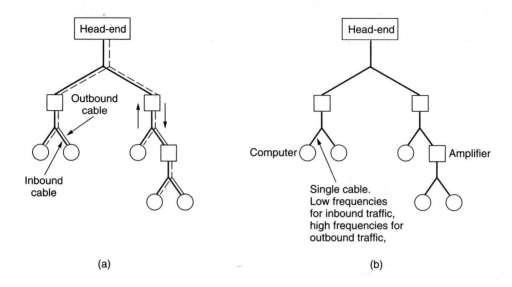

Fig. 2-4. Broadband networks. (a) Dual cable. (b) Single cable.

In the **midsplit** system, the inbound band is 5 to 116 MHz and the outbound band is 168 MHz to 300 MHz. The choice of these frequency bands is historical, having to do with how the U.S. Federal Communications Commission has assigned frequencies for television broadcasting, for which broadband was designed. Both split systems require an active head-end that accepts inbound signals on one band and rebroadcasts them on another. These techniques and frequencies were developed for cable television and have been taken over for networking without modification due to the availability of reliable and relatively inexpensive hardware.

Broadband can be used in various ways. Some computer pairs may be given a permanent channel for their exclusive use. Other computers may be able to request a channel for a temporary connection on a control channel, and then switch their frequencies to that channel for the duration of the connection. Still another arrangement is to have all the computers compete for access to a single channel or a group of channels, using techniques to be covered in Chap. 4.

Technically, broadband cable is inferior to baseband (i.e., single channel) cable for sending digital data but has the advantage that a huge amount of it is already in place. In the Netherlands, for example, 90 percent of all homes have a cable TV connection. In the United States, a TV cable runs past 80 percent of all homes. About 60 percent of these actually have a cable connection. With the competition between telephone companies and cable TV companies already in full swing, we can expect cable TV systems to begin operating as MANs and offering telephone and other services more and more often. For more information about using cable TV as a computer network, see (Karshmer and Thomas, 1992).

2.2.5. Fiber Optics

Many people in the computer industry take enormous pride in how fast computer technology is improving. In the 1970s, a fast computer (e.g., CDC 6600) could execute an instruction in 100 nsec. Twenty years later, a fast Cray computer could execute an instruction in 1 nsec, a factor of 10 improvement per decade. Not too bad.

In the same period, data communication went from 56 kbps (the ARPANET) to 1 Gbps (modern optical communication), a gain of more than a factor of 100 per decade, while at the same time the error rate went from 10^{-5} per bit to almost zero.

Furthermore, single CPUs are beginning to approach physical limits, such as speed of light and heat dissipation problems. In contrast, with *current* fiber technology, the achievable bandwidth is certainly in excess of 50,000 Gbps (50 Tbps) and many people are looking very hard for better materials. The current practical signaling limit of about 1 Gbps is due to our inability to convert between electrical and optical signals any faster. In the laboratory, 100 Gbps is feasible on short runs. A speed of 1 terabit/sec is only a few years down the road. Fully optical systems, including getting into and out of the computer, are within reach (Miki, 1994a).

In the race between computing and communication, communication won. The full implications of essentially infinite bandwidth (although not at zero cost) have not yet sunk in to a generation of computer scientists and engineers taught to think in terms of the low Nyquist and Shannon limits imposed by copper wire. The new conventional wisdom should be that all computers are hopelessly slow, and networks should try to avoid computation at all costs, no matter how much bandwidth that wastes. In this section we will study fiber optics to see how that transmission technology works.

An optical transmission system has three components: the light source, the transmission medium, and the detector. Conventionally, a pulse of light indicates a 1 bit and the absence of light indicates a zero bit. The transmission medium is an ultra-thin fiber of glass. The detector generates an electrical pulse when light falls on it. By attaching a light source to one end of an optical fiber and a detector to the other, we have a unidirectional data transmission system that accepts an electrical signal, converts and transmits it by light pulses, and then reconverts the output to an electrical signal at the receiving end.

This transmission system would leak light and be useless in practice except for an interesting principle of physics. When a light ray passes from one medium to another, for example, from fused silica to air, the ray is refracted (bent) at the silica/air boundary as shown in Fig. 2-5. Here we see a light ray incident on the boundary at an angle α_1 emerging at an angle β_1. The amount of refraction depends on the properties of the two media (in particular, their indices of refraction). For angles of incidence above a certain critical value, the light is refracted back into the silica; none of it escapes into the air. Thus a light ray incident at or above the critical angle is trapped inside the fiber, as shown in Fig. 2-5(b), and can propagate for many kilometers with virtually no loss.

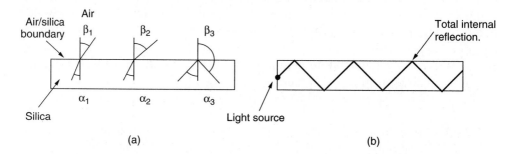

Fig. 2-5. (a) Three examples of a light ray from inside a silica fiber impinging on the air/silica boundary at different angles. (b) Light trapped by total internal reflection.

The sketch of Fig. 2-5(b) shows only one trapped ray, but since any light ray incident on the boundary above the critical angle will be reflected internally, many different rays will be bouncing around at different angles. Each ray is said to have a different **mode** so a fiber having this property is called a **multimode fiber**.

However, if the fiber's diameter is reduced to a few wavelengths of light, the fiber acts like a wave guide, and the light can only propagate in a straight line, without bouncing, yielding a **single-mode fiber**. Single mode fibers are more expensive but can be used for longer distances. Currently available single-mode fibers can transmit data at several Gbps for 30 km. Even higher data rates have been achieved in the laboratory for shorter distances. Experiments have shown that powerful lasers can drive a fiber 100 km long without repeaters, although at lower speeds. Research on erbium-doped fibers promises even longer runs without repeaters.

Transmission of Light through Fiber

Optical fibers are made of glass, which, in turn, is made from sand, an inexpensive raw material available in unlimited amounts. Glass making was known to the ancient Egyptians, but their glass had to be no more than 1 mm thick or the light could not shine through. Glass transparent enough to be useful for windows was developed during the Renaissance. The glass used for modern optical fibers is so transparent that if the oceans were full of it instead of water, the seabed would as visible from the surface as the ground is from an airplane on a clear day.

The attenuation of light through glass depends on the wavelength of the light.

For the kind of glass used in fibers, the attenuation is shown in Fig. 2-6 in decibels per linear kilometer of fiber. The attenuation in decibels is given by the formula

$$\text{Attenuation in decibels} = 10 \log_{10} \frac{\text{transmitted power}}{\text{received power}}$$

For example, a factor of two loss gives an attenuation of $10 \log_{10} 2 = 3$ dB. The figure shows the near infrared part of the spectrum, which is what is used in practice. Visible light has slightly shorter wavelengths, from 0.4 to 0.7 microns (1 micron is 10^{-6} meters).

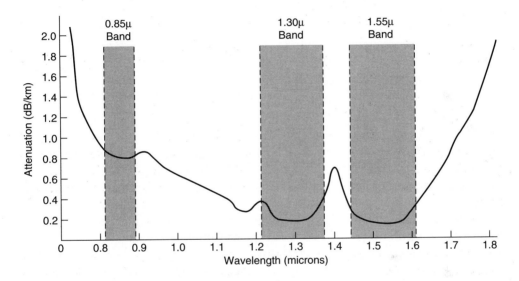

Fig. 2-6. Attenuation of light through fiber in the infrared region.

Three wavelength bands are used for communication. They are centered at 0.85, 1.30, and 1.55 microns, respectively. The latter two have good attenuation properties (less than 5 percent loss per kilometer). The 0.85 micron band has higher attenuation, but the nice property that at that wavelength, the lasers and electronics can be made from the same material (gallium arsenide). All three bands are 25,000 to 30,000 GHz wide.

Light pulses sent down a fiber spread out in length as they propagate. This spreading is called **dispersion**. The amount of it is wavelength dependent. One way to keep these spread-out pulses from overlapping is to increase the distance between them, but this can only be done by reducing the signaling rate. Fortunately, it has been discovered that by making the pulses in a special shape related to the reciprocal of the hyperbolic cosine, all the dispersion effects cancel out, and it may be possible to send pulses for thousands of kilometers without appreciable shape distortion. These pulses are called **solitons**. A considerable amount of research is going on to take solitons out of the lab and into the field.

Fiber Cables

Fiber optic cables are similar to coax, except without the braid. Figure 2-7(a) shows a single fiber viewed from the side. At the center is the glass core through which the light propagates. In multimode fibers, the core is 50 microns in diameter, about the thickness of a human hair. In single-mode fibers the core is 8 to 10 microns.

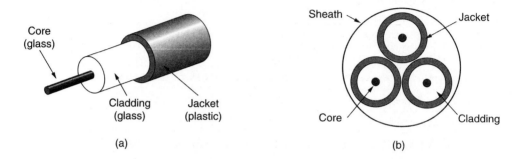

Core
(glass)

Cladding
(glass)

Jacket
(plastic)

(a)

Sheath

Jacket

Core

Cladding

(b)

Fig. 2-7. (a) Side view of a single fiber. (b) End view of a sheath with three fibers.

The core is surrounded by a glass cladding with a lower index of refraction than the core, to keep all the light in the core. Next comes a thin plastic jacket to protect the cladding. Fibers are typically grouped together in bundles, protected by an outer sheath. Figure 2-7(b) shows a sheath with three fibers.

Terrestrial fiber sheaths are normally laid in the ground within a meter of the surface, where they are occasionally subject to attacks by backhoes or gophers. Near the shore, transoceanic fiber sheaths are buried in trenches by a kind of seaplow. In deep water, they just lie on the bottom, where they can be snagged by fishing trawlers or eaten by sharks.

Fibers can be connected in three different ways. First, they can terminate in connectors and be plugged into fiber sockets. Connectors lose about 10 to 20 percent of the light, but they make it easy to reconfigure systems.

Second, they can be spliced mechanically. Mechanical splices just lay the two carefully cut ends next to each other in a special sleeve and clamp them in place. Alignment can be improved by passing light through the junction and then making small adjustments to maximize the signal. Mechanical splices take trained personnel about 5 minutes, and result in a 10 percent light loss.

Third, two pieces of fiber can be fused (melted) to form a solid connection. A fusion splice is almost as good as a single drawn fiber, but even here, a small amount of attenuation occurs. For all three kinds of splices, reflections can occur at the point of the splice, and the reflected energy can interfere with the signal.

Two kinds of light sources can be used to do the signaling, LEDs (Light Emitting Diodes) and semiconductor lasers. They have different properties, as shown in Fig. 2-8. They can be tuned in wavelength by inserting Fabry-Perot or Mach-Zehnder interferometers between the source and the fiber. Fabry-Perot interferometers are simple resonant cavities consisting of two parallel mirrors. The light is incident perpendicularly to the mirrors. The length of the cavity selects out those wavelengths that fit inside an integral number of times. Mach-Zehnder interferometers separate the light into two beams. The two beams travel slightly different distances. They are recombined at the end and are in phase for only certain wavelengths.

Item	LED	Semiconductor laser
Data rate	Low	High
Mode	Multimode	Multimode or single mode
Distance	Short	Long
Lifetime	Long life	Short life
Temperature sensitivity	Minor	Substantial
Cost	Low cost	Expensive

Fig. 2-8. A comparison of semiconductor diodes and LEDs as light sources.

The receiving end of an optical fiber consists of a photodiode, which gives off an electrical pulse when struck by light. The typical response time of a photodiode is 1 nsec, which limits data rates to about 1 Gbps. Thermal noise is also an issue, so a pulse of light must carry enough energy to be detected. By making the pulses powerful enough, the error rate can be made arbitrarily small.

Fiber Optic Networks

Fiber optics can be used for LANs as well as for long-haul transmission, although tapping onto it is more complex than connecting to an Ethernet. One way around the problem is to realize that a ring network is really just a collection of point-to-point links, as shown in Fig. 2-9. The interface at each computer passes the light pulse stream through to the next link and also serves as a T junction to allow the computer to send and accept messages.

Two types of interfaces are used. A passive interface consists of two taps fused onto the main fiber. One tap has an LED or laser diode at the end of it (for transmitting), and the other has a photodiode (for receiving). The tap itself is completely passive and is thus extremely reliable because a broken LED or photodiode does not break the ring. It just takes one computer off-line.

The other interface type, shown in Fig. 2-9, is the **active repeater**. The incoming light is converted to an electrical signal, regenerated to full strength if it

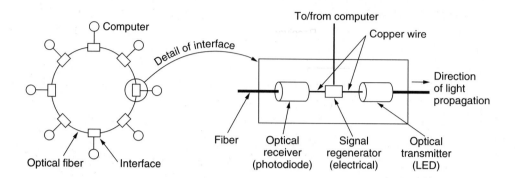

Fig. 2-9. A fiber optic ring with active repeaters.

has been weakened, and retransmitted as light. The interface with the computer is an ordinary copper wire that comes into the signal regenerator. Purely optical repeaters are now being used, too. These devices do not require the optical to electrical to optical conversions, which means they can operate at extremely high bandwidths.

If an active repeater fails, the ring is broken and the network goes down. On the other hand, since the signal is regenerated at each interface, the individual computer-to-computer links can be kilometers long, with virtually no limit on the total size of the ring. The passive interfaces lose light at each junction, so the number of computers and total ring length are greatly restricted.

A ring topology is not the only way to build a LAN using fiber optics. It is also possible to have hardware broadcasting using the **passive star** construction of Fig. 2-10. In this design, each interface has a fiber running from its transmitter to a silica cylinder, with the incoming fibers fused to one end of the cylinder. Similarly, fibers fused to the other end of the cylinder are run to each of the receivers. Whenever an interface emits a light pulse, it is diffused inside the passive star to illuminate all the receivers, thus achieving broadcast. In effect, the passive star combines all the incoming signals and transmits the merged result out on all lines. Since the incoming energy is divided among all the outgoing lines, the number of nodes in the network is limited by the sensitivity of the photodiodes.

Comparison of Fiber Optics and Copper Wire

It is instructive to compare fiber to copper. Fiber has many advantages. To start with, it can handle much higher bandwidths than copper. This alone would require its use in high-end networks. Due to the low attenuation, repeaters are needed only about every 30 km on long lines, versus about every 5 km for copper, a substantial cost saving. Fiber also has the advantage of not being affected by

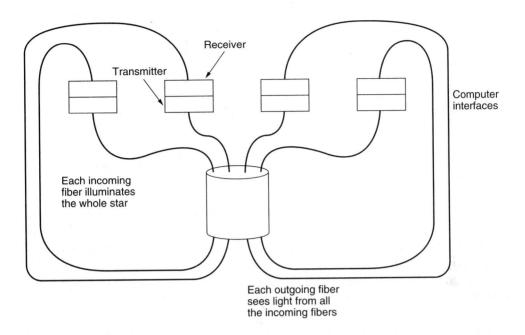

Fig. 2-10. A passive star connection in a fiber optics network.

power surges, electromagnetic interference, or power failures. Nor is it affected by corrosive chemicals in the air, making it ideal for harsh factory environments.

Oddly enough, telephone companies like fiber for a different reason: it is thin and lightweight. Many existing cable ducts are completely full, so there is no room to add new capacity. Removing all the copper and replacing it by fibers empties up the ducts, and the copper has excellent resale value to copper refiners who see it as very high grade ore. Also fiber is lighter than copper. One thousand twisted pairs 1 km long weigh 8000 kg. Two fibers have more capacity and weigh only 100 kg, which greatly reduces the need for expensive mechanical support systems that must be maintained. For new routes, fiber wins hands down due to its much lower installation cost.

Finally, fibers do not leak light and are quite difficult to tap. This gives them excellent security against potential wiretappers.

The reason that fiber is better than copper is inherent in the underlying physics. When electrons move in a wire, they affect one another and are themselves affected by electrons outside the wire. Photons in a fiber do not affect one another (they have no electric charge) and are not affected by stray photons outside the fiber.

On the downside, fiber is an unfamiliar technology requiring skills most engineers do not have. Since optical transmission is inherently unidirectional, two-way communication requires either two fibers or two frequency bands on one fiber. Finally, fiber interfaces cost more than electrical interfaces. Nevertheless, the future of all fixed data communication for distances of more than a few meters is clearly with fiber. For a detailed discussion of all aspects of fiber optic networks, see (Green, 1993).

2.3. WIRELESS TRANSMISSION

Our age has given rise to information junkies: people who need to be on-line all the time. For these mobile users, twisted pair, coax, and fiber optics are of no use. They need to get their hits of data for their laptop, notebook, shirt pocket, palmtop, or wristwatch computers without being tethered to the terrestrial communication infrastructure. For these users, wireless communication is the answer. In this section we will look at wireless communication in general, as it has many other important applications besides providing connectivity to users who want to read their email in airplanes.

Some people even believe that the future holds only two kinds of communication: fiber and wireless. All fixed (i.e., nonmobile) computers, telephones, faxes, and so on will be by fiber, and all mobile ones will use wireless.

However wireless also has advantages for even fixed devices in some circumstances. For example, if running a fiber to a building is difficult due to the terrain (mountains, jungles, swamps, etc.) wireless may be preferable. It is noteworthy that modern wireless digital communication began in the Hawaiian Islands, where large chunks of Pacific Ocean separated the users and the telephone system was inadequate.

2.3.1. The Electromagnetic Spectrum

When electrons move, they create electromagnetic waves that can propagate through free space (even in a vacuum). These waves were predicted by the British physicist James Clerk Maxwell in 1865 and first produced and observed by the German physicist Heinrich Hertz in 1887. The number of oscillations per second of an electromagnetic wave is called its **frequency**, f, and is measured in **Hz** (in honor of Heinrich Hertz). The distance between two consecutive maxima (or minima) is called the **wavelength**, which is universally designated by the Greek letter λ (lambda).

By attaching an antenna of the appropriate size to an electrical circuit, the electromagnetic waves can be broadcast efficiently and received by a receiver some distance away. All wireless communication is based on this principle.

In vacuum, all electromagnetic waves travel at the same speed, no matter what their frequency. This speed, usually called the **speed of light**, c, is approximately 3×10^8 m/sec, or about 1 foot (30 cm) per nanosecond. In copper or fiber the speed slows to about 2/3 of this value and becomes slightly frequency dependent. The speed of light is the ultimate speed limit. No object or signal can ever move faster than it.

The fundamental relation between f, λ, and c (in vacuum) is

$$\lambda f = c \tag{2-2}$$

Since c is a constant, if we know f we can find λ and vice versa. For example, 1-MHz waves are about 300 meters long and 1-cm waves have a frequency of 30 GHz.

The electromagnetic spectrum is shown in Fig. 2-11. The radio, microwave, infrared, and visible light portions of the spectrum can all be used for transmitting information by modulating the amplitude, frequency, or phase of the waves. Ultraviolet light, X-rays, and gamma rays would be even better, due to their higher frequencies, but they are hard to produce and modulate, do not propagate well through buildings, and are dangerous to living things. The bands listed at the bottom of Fig. 2-11 are the official ITU names and are based on the wavelengths, so the LF band goes from 1 km to 10 km (approximately 30 kHz to 300 kHz). The terms LF, MF, and HF refer to low, medium, and high frequency, respectively. Clearly, when the names were assigned, nobody expected to go above 10 MHz, so the higher bands were later named the Very, Ultra, Super, Extremely, and Tremendously High Frequency bands. Beyond that there are no names, but Incredibly, Astonishingly, and Prodigiously high frequency (IHF, AHF, and PHF) would sound nice.

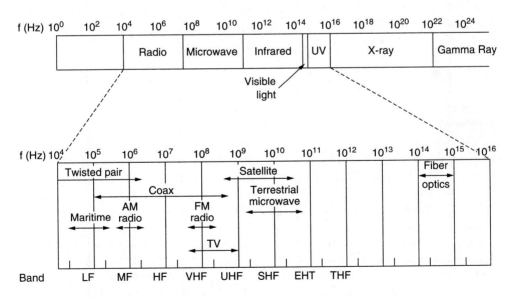

Fig. 2-11. The electromagnetic spectrum and its uses for communication.

The amount of information that an electromagnetic wave can carry is related to its bandwidth. With current technology, it is possible to encode a few bits per Hertz at low frequencies, but often as many as 40 under certain conditions at high frequencies, so a cable with a 500 MHz bandwidth can carry several gigabits/sec. From Fig. 2-11 it should now be obvious why networking people like fiber optics so much.

If we solve Eq. (2-2) for f and differentiate with respect to λ we get

$$\frac{df}{d\lambda} = -\frac{c}{\lambda^2}$$

If we now go to finite differences instead of differentials and only look at absolute values, we get

$$\Delta f = \frac{c \Delta \lambda}{\lambda^2} \tag{2-3}$$

Thus given the width of a wavelength band, $\Delta \lambda$, we can compute the corresponding frequency band, Δf, and from that the data rate the band can produce. The wider the band, the higher the data rate. As an example, consider the 1.30-micron band of Fig. 2-6. Here we have $\lambda = 1.3 \times 10^{-6}$ and $\Delta \lambda = 0.17 \times 10^{-6}$, so Δf is about 30 THz.

To prevent total chaos, there are national and international agreements about who gets to use which frequencies. Since everyone wants a higher data rate, everyone wants more spectrum. In the United States, the FCC allocates spectrum for AM and FM radio, television, and cellular phones, as well as for telephone companies, police, maritime, navigation, military, government, and many other competing users. Worldwide, an agency of ITU-R (WARC) does this work. In the meeting in Spain in 1991, for example, WARC allocated some spectrum to hand-held personal communicators. Unfortunately, the FCC, which is not bound by WARC's recommendations, chose a different piece (because the people in the United States who had the band WARC chose did not want to give it up and had enough political clout to prevent that). Consequently, personal communicators built for the U.S. market will not work in Europe or Asia, and vice versa.

Most transmissions use a narrow frequency band (i.e., $\Delta f / f \ll 1$) to get the best reception (many watts/Hz). However, in some cases, the transmitter hops from frequency to frequency in a regular pattern or the transmissions are intentionally spread out over a wide frequency band. This technique is called **spread spectrum** (Kohno et al., 1995). It is popular for military communication because it makes transmissions hard to detect and next to impossible to jam. Frequency hopping is not of much interest to us (other than to note that it was co-invented by the movie actress Hedy Lamarr). True spread spectrum, sometimes called **direct sequence spread spectrum**, is gaining popularity in the commercial world, and we will come back to it in Chap. 4. For a fascinating and detailed history of spread spectrum communication, see (Scholtz, 1982).

For the moment, we will assume that all transmissions use a narrow frequency band. We will now discuss how the various parts of the spectrum are used, starting with radio.

2.3.2. Radio Transmission

Radio waves are easy to generate, can travel long distances, and penetrate buildings easily, so they are widely used for communication, both indoors and outdoors. Radio waves also are omnidirectional, meaning that they travel in all directions from the source, so that the transmitter and receiver do not have to be carefully aligned physically.

Sometimes omnidirectional radio is good, but sometimes it is bad. In the 1970s, General Motors decided to equip its new Cadillacs with computer-controlled antilock brakes. When the driver stepped on the brake pedal, the computer pulsed the brakes on and off instead of locking them on hard. One fine day an Ohio Highway Patrolman began using his new mobile radio to call headquarters, and suddenly the Cadillac next to him began behaving like a bucking bronco. When the officer pulled the car over, the driver claimed that he had done nothing and that the car had gone crazy.

Eventually, a pattern began to emerge: Cadillacs would sometimes go berserk, but only on major highways in Ohio and then only when the Highway Patrol was watching. For a long, long time General Motors could not understand why Cadillacs worked fine in all the other states, and also on minor roads in Ohio. Only after a considerable amount of searching did they discover that the Cadillac's wiring made a fine antenna for the frequency the Ohio Highway Patrol's new radio system used.

The properties of radio waves are frequency dependent. At low frequencies, radio waves pass through obstacles well, but the power falls off sharply with distance from the source, roughly as $1/r^3$ in air. At high frequencies, radio waves tend to travel in straight lines and bounce off obstacles. They are also absorbed by rain. At all frequencies, radio waves are subject to interference from motors and other electrical equipment.

Due to radio's ability to travel long distances, interference between users is a problem. For this reason, all governments tightly license the user of radio transmitters, with one exception (discussed below).

In the VLF, LF, and MF bands, radio waves follow the ground, as illustrated in Fig. 2-12(a). These waves can be detected for perhaps 1000 km at the lower frequencies, less at the higher ones. AM radio broadcasting uses the MF band, which is why Boston AM radio stations cannot be heard easily in New York. Radio waves in these bands easily pass through buildings, which is why portable radios work indoors. The main problem with using these bands for data communication is the relative low bandwidth they offer [see Eq. (2-2)].

In the HF and VHF bands, the ground waves tend to be absorbed by the earth.

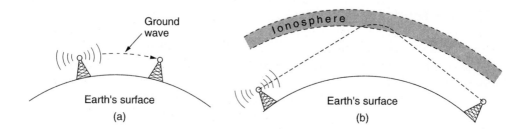

Fig. 2-12. (a) In the VLF, VF, and MF bands, radio waves follow the curvature of the earth. (b) In the HF they bounce off the ionosphere.

However, the waves that reach the ionosphere, a layer of charged particles circling the earth at a height of 100 to 500 km, are refracted by it and sent back to earth, as shown in Fig. 2-12(b). Under certain atmospheric conditions, the signals may bounce several times. Amateur radio operators (hams) use these bands to talk long distance. The military also communicates in the HF and VHF bands.

2.3.3. Microwave Transmission

Above 100 MHz, the waves travel in straight lines and can therefore be narrowly focused. Concentrating all the energy into a small beam using a parabolic antenna (like the familiar satellite TV dish) gives a much higher signal to noise ratio, but the transmitting and receiving antennas must be accurately aligned with each other. In addition, this directionality allows multiple transmitters lined up in a row to communicate with multiple receivers in a row without interference. Before fiber optics, for decades these microwaves formed the heart of the long-distance telephone transmission system. In fact, the long-distance carrier MCI's name first stood for Microwave Communications, Inc., because its entire system was originally built on microwave towers (it has since upgraded major portions of its network to fiber).

Since the microwaves travel in a straight line, if the towers are too far apart, the earth will get in the way (think about a San Francisco to Amsterdam link). Consequently, repeaters are needed periodically. The higher the towers are, the further apart they can be. The distance between repeaters goes up very roughly with the square root of the tower height. For 100-m high towers, repeaters can be spaced 80 km apart.

Unlike radio waves at lower frequencies, microwaves do not pass through buildings well. In addition, even though the beam may be well focused at the transmitter, there is still some divergence in space. Some waves may be refracted off low-lying atmospheric layers and may take slightly longer to arrive than direct waves. The delayed waves may arrive out of phase with the direct wave and thus cancel the signal. This effect is called **multipath fading** and is often a serious problem. It is weather and frequency dependent. Some operators keep 10 percent of their channels idle as spares to switch on when multipath fading wipes out some frequency band temporarily.

The demand for more and more spectrum works to keep improving the technology so transmissions can use still higher frequencies. Bands up to 10 GHz are now in routine use, but at about 8 GHz a new problem sets in: absorption by water. These waves are only a few centimeters long and are absorbed by rain. This effect would be fine if one were planning to build a huge outdoor microwave oven, but for communication, it is a severe problem. As with multipath fading, the only solution is to shut off links that are being rained on and route around them.

In summary, microwave communication is so widely used for long-distance telephone communication, cellular telephones, television distribution, and other uses, that a severe shortage of spectrum has developed. It has several significant advantages over fiber. The main one is that no right of way is needed, and by buying a small plot of ground every 50 km and putting a microwave tower on it, one can bypass the telephone system and communicate directly. This is how MCI managed to get started as a new long-distance telephone company so quickly. (Sprint went a different route: it was formed by the Southern Pacific Railroad, which already owned a large amount of right of way, and just buried fiber next to the tracks.)

Microwave is also relatively inexpensive. Putting up two simple towers (maybe just big poles with four guy wires) and putting antennas on each one may be cheaper than burying 50 km of fiber through a congested urban area or up over a mountain, and it may also be cheaper than leasing the telephone company's fiber, especially if the telephone company has not yet even fully paid for the copper it ripped out when it put in the fiber.

In addition to being used for long-distance transmission, microwaves have another important use, namely, the **Industrial/Scientific/Medical** bands. These bands form the one exception to the licensing rule: transmitters using these bands do not require government licensing. One band is allocated worldwide: 2.400–2.484 GHz. In addition, in the United States and Canada, bands also exist from 902–928 MHz and from 5.725–5.850 GHz. These bands are used for cordless telephones, garage door openers, wireless hi-fi speakers, security gates, etc. The 900-MHz band works best but is crowded and equipment using it may only be operated in North America. The higher bands require more expensive electronics and are subject to interference from microwave ovens and radar installations. Nevertheless, these bands are popular for various forms of short-range wireless networking because they avoid the problems associated with licensing.

2.3.4. Infrared and Millimeter Waves

Unguided infrared and millimeter waves are widely used for short-range communication. The remote controls used on televisions, VCRs, and stereos all use infrared communication. They are relatively directional, cheap, and easy to build, but have a major drawback: they do not pass through solid objects (try standing between your remote control and your television and see if it still works). In general, as we go from long-wave radio toward visible light, the waves behave more and more like light and less and less like radio.

On the other hand, the fact that infrared waves do not pass through solid walls well is also a plus. It means that an infrared system in one room of a building will not interfere with a similar system in adjacent rooms. Furthermore, security of infrared systems against eavesdropping is better than that of radio systems precisely for this reason. For these reasons, no government license is needed to operate an infrared system, in contrast to radio systems, which must be licensed.

These properties have made infrared an interesting candidate for indoor wireless LANs. For example, the computers and offices in a building can be equipped with relatively unfocused (i.e., somewhat omnidirectional) infrared transmitters and receivers. In this way, portable computers with infrared capability can be on the local LAN without having to physically connect to it. When several people show up for a meeting with their portables, they can just sit down in the conference room and be fully connected, without having to plug in. Infrared communication cannot be used outdoors because the sun shines as brightly in the infrared as in the visible spectrum. For more information about infrared communication, see (Adams et al., 1993; and Bantz and Bauchot, 1994).

2.3.5. Lightwave Transmission

Unguided optical signaling has been in use for centuries. Paul Revere used binary optical signaling from the Old North Church just prior to his famous ride. A more modern application is to connect the LANs in two buildings via lasers mounted on their rooftops. Coherent optical signaling using lasers is inherently unidirectional, so each building needs its own laser and its own photodetector. This scheme offers very high bandwidth and very low cost. It is also relatively easy to install, and, unlike microwave, does not require an FCC license.

The laser's strength, a very narrow beam, is also its weakness here. Aiming a laser beam 1 mm wide at a target 1 mm wide 500 meters away requires the marksmanship of a latter-day Annie Oakley. Usually, lenses are put into the system to defocus the beam slightly.

A disadvantage is that laser beams cannot penetrate rain or thick fog, but they normally work well on sunny days. However, the author once attended a conference at a modern hotel in Europe at which the conference organizers thoughtfully provided a room full of terminals for the attendees to read their email during boring presentations. Since the local PTT was unwilling to install a large number of telephone lines for just 3 days, the organizers put a laser on the roof and aimed it at their university's computer science building a few kilometers away. They tested it the night before the conference and it worked perfectly. At 9 a.m. the next morning, on a bright sunny day, the link failed completely and stayed down all day. That evening, the organizers tested it again very carefully, and once again it worked absolutely perfectly. The pattern repeated itself for two more days consistently.

After the conference, the organizers discovered the problem. Heat from the sun during the daytime caused convection currents to rise up from the roof of the building, as shown in Fig. 2-13. This turbulent air diverted the beam and made it dance around the detector. Atmospheric "seeing" like this makes the stars twinkle (which is why astronomers put their telescopes on the tops of mountains—to get above as much of the atmosphere as possible). It is also responsible for shimmering roads on a hot day and the wavy images when looking out above a hot radiator.

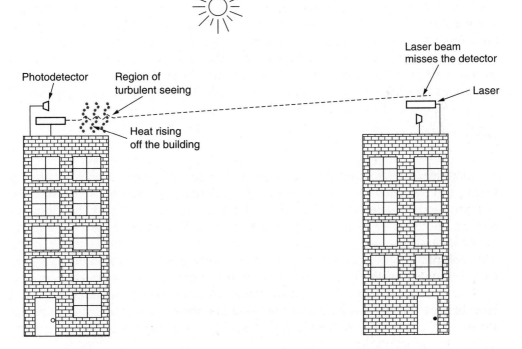

Fig. 2-13. Convection currents can interfere with laser communication systems. A bidirectional system, with two lasers, is pictured here.

2.4. THE TELEPHONE SYSTEM

When two computers owned by the same company or organization and located close to each other need to communicate, it is often easiest just to run a cable between them. LANs work this way. However, when the distances are large, or there are many computers, or the cables would have to pass through a public road or other public right of way, the costs of running private cables are usually prohibitive. Furthermore, in just about every country in the world, stringing private transmission lines across (or underneath) public property is also illegal. Consequently, the network designers must rely upon the existing telecommunication facilities.

These facilities, especially the **PSTN**, (**Public Switched Telephone Network**), were usually designed many years ago, with a completely different goal in mind: transmitting the human voice in a more or less recognizable form. Their suitability for use in computer-computer communication is often marginal at best, but the situation is rapidly changing with the introduction of fiber optics and digital technology. In any event, the telephone system is so tightly intertwined with (wide area) computer networks, that it is worth devoting considerable time studying it.

To see the order of magnitude of the problem, let us make a rough but illustrative comparison of the properties of a typical computer-computer connection via a local cable and via a dial-up telephone line. A cable running between two computers can transfer data at memory speeds, typically 10^7 to 10^8 bps. The error rate is usually so low that it is hard to measure, but one error per day would be considered poor at most installations. One error per day at these speeds is equivalent to one error per 10^{12} or 10^{13} bits sent.

In contrast, a dial-up line has a maximum data rate on the order of 10^4 bps and an error rate of roughly 1 per 10^5 bits sent, varying somewhat with the age of the telephone switching equipment involved. The combined bit rate times error rate performance of a local cable is thus 11 orders of magnitude better than a voice-grade telephone line. To make an analogy in the field of transportation, the ratio of the cost of the entire Apollo project, which landed men on the moon, to the cost of a bus ride downtown is about 11 orders of magnitude (in 1965 dollars: 40 billion to 0.40).

The trouble, of course, is that computer systems designers are used to working with computer systems, and when suddenly confronted with another system whose performance (from their point of view) is 11 orders of magnitude worse, it is not surprising that much time and effort have been devoted to trying to figure out how to use it efficiently. On the other hand, the telephone companies have made massive strides in the past decade in upgrading equipment and improving service in certain areas. In the following sections we will describe the telephone system and show what it used to be and where it is going. For additional information about the innards of the telephone system see (Bellamy, 1991).

2.4.1. Structure of the Telephone System

When Alexander Graham Bell patented the telephone in 1876 (just a few hours ahead of his rival, Elisha Gray), there was an enormous demand for his new invention. The initial market was for the sale of telephones, which came in pairs. It was up to the customer to string a single wire between them. The electrons returned through the earth. If a telephone owner wanted to talk to *n* other telephone owners, separate wires had to be strung to all *n* houses. Within a year, the cities were covered with wires passing over houses and trees in a wild jumble. It became immediately obvious that the model of connecting every telephone to every other telephone, as shown in Fig. 2-14(a) was not going to work.

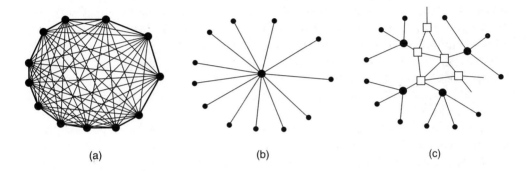

(a)   (b)   (c)

Fig. 2-14. (a) Fully interconnected network. (b) Centralized switch. (c) Two-level hierarchy.

To his credit, Bell saw this and formed the Bell Telephone Company, which opened its first switching office (in New Haven, Connecticut) in 1878. The company ran a wire to each customer's house or office. To make a call, the customer would crank the phone to make a ringing sound in the telephone company office to attract the attention of an operator, who would then manually connect the caller to the callee using a jumper cable. The model of a single switching office is illustrated in Fig. 2-14(b).

Pretty soon, Bell System switching offices were springing up everywhere and people wanted to make long-distance calls between cities, so the Bell system began to connect the switching offices. The original problem soon returned: to connect every switching office to every other switching office by means of a wire between them quickly became unmanageable, so second-level switching offices were invented, After a while, multiple second-level offices were needed, as shown in Fig. 2-14(c). Eventually, the hierarchy grew to five levels.

By 1890, the three major parts of the telephone system were in place: the switching offices, the wires between the customers and the switching offices (by now balanced, insulated, twisted pairs instead of open wires with an earth return), and the long-distance connections between the switching offices. While there have been improvements in all three areas since then, the basic Bell System model has remained essentially intact for over 100 years. For a short technical history of the telephone system, see (Hawley, 1991).

At present, the telephone system is organized as a highly redundant, multilevel hierarchy. The following description is highly simplified but gives the essential flavor nevertheless. Each telephone has two copper wires coming out of it that go directly to the telephone company's nearest **end office** (also called a **local central office**). The distance is typically 1 to 10 km, being smaller in cities than in rural areas.

In the United States alone there are about 19,000 end offices. The concatenation of the area code and the first three digits of the telephone number uniquely specify an end office, which is why the rate structure uses this information. The two-wire connections between each subscriber's telephone and the end office are known in the trade as the **local loop**. If the world's local loops were stretched out end to end, they would extend to the moon and back 1000 times.

At one time, 80 percent of AT&T's capital value was the copper in the local loops. AT&T was then, in effect, the world's largest copper mine. Fortunately, this fact was not widely known in the investment community. Had it been known, some corporate raider might have bought AT&T, terminated all telephone service in the United States, ripped out all the wire, and sold the wire to a copper refiner to get a quick payback.

If a subscriber attached to a given end office calls another subscriber attached to the same end office, the switching mechanism within the office sets up a direct electrical connection between the two local loops. This connection remains intact for the duration of the call.

If the called telephone is attached to another end office, a different procedure has to be used. Each end office has a number of outgoing lines to one or more nearby switching centers, called **toll offices** (or if they are within the same local area, **tandem offices**). These lines are called **toll connecting trunks**. If both the caller's and callee's end offices happen to have a toll connecting trunk to the same toll office (a likely occurrence if they are relatively close by), the connection may be established within the toll office. A telephone network consisting only of telephones (the small dots), end offices (the large dots) and toll offices (the squares) is shown in Fig. 2-14(c).

If the caller and callee do not have a toll office in common, the path will have to be established somewhere higher up in the hierarchy. There are primary, sectional, and regional offices that form a network by which the toll offices are connected. The toll, primary, sectional, and regional exchanges communicate with each other via high bandwidth **intertoll trunks** (also called **interoffice trunks**). The number of different kinds of switching centers and their topology (e.g., may two sectional offices have a direct connection or must they go through a regional office?) varies from country to country depending on its telephone density. Figure 2-15 shows how a medium-distance connection might be routed.

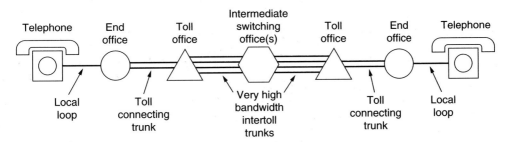

Fig. 2-15. Typical circuit route for a medium-distance call.

A variety of transmission media are used for telecommunication. Local loops consist of twisted pairs nowadays, although in the early days of telephony, uninsulated wires spaced 25 cm apart on telephone poles were common. Between switching offices, coaxial cables, microwaves, and especially fiber optics are widely used.

In the past, signaling throughout the telephone system was analog, with the actual voice signal being transmitted as an electrical voltage from source to destination. With the advent of digital electronics and computers, digital signaling has become possible. In this system, only two voltages are allowed, for example −5 volts and +5 volts.

This scheme has a number of advantages over analog signaling. First is that although the attenuation and distortion are more severe when sending two-level signals than when using modems, it is easy to calculate how far a signal can propagate and still be recognizable. A digital regenerator can be inserted into the line there, to restore the signal to its original value, since there are only two possibilities. A digital signal can pass through an arbitrary number of regenerators with no loss in signal and thus travel long distances with no information loss. In contrast, analog signals always suffer some information loss when amplified, and this loss is cumulative. The net result is that digital transmission can be made to have a low error rate.

A second advantage of digital transmission is that voice, data, music, and images (e.g., television, fax, and video) can be interspersed to make more efficient use of the circuits and equipment. Another advantage is that much higher data rates are possible using existing lines.

A third advantage is that digital transmission is much cheaper than analog transmission, since it is not necessary to accurately reproduce an analog waveform after it has passed through potentially hundreds of amplifiers on a transcontinental call. Being able to correctly distinguish a 0 from a 1 is enough.

Finally, maintenance of a digital system is easier than maintenance of an analog one. A transmitted bit is either received correctly or not, making it simpler to track down problems.

Consequently, all the long-distance trunks within the telephone system are rapidly being converted to digital. The old system used analog transmission over copper wires; the new one uses digital transmission over optical fibers.

In summary, the telephone system consists of three major components:

1. Local loops (twisted pairs, analog signaling).

2. Trunks (fiber optics or microwave, mostly digital).

3. Switching offices.

After a short digression on the politics of telephones, we will come back to each of these three components in some detail. For the local loop, we will be concerned with how to send digital data over it (quick answer: use a modem). For the long-haul trunks, the main issue is how to collect multiple calls together and send them together. This subject is called multiplexing, and we will study three different ways to do it. Finally, there are two fundamentally different ways of doing switching, so we will look at both of these.

2.4.2. The Politics of Telephones

For decades prior to 1984, the Bell System provided both local and long distance service throughout most of the United States. In the 1970s, the U.S. government came to believe that this was an illegal monopoly and sued to break it up. The government won, and on Jan. 1, 1984, AT&T was broken up into AT&T Long Lines, 23 **BOCs** (**Bell Operating Companies**), and a few other pieces. The 23 BOCs were grouped together into seven regional BOCs (RBOCs) to make them economically viable. The entire nature of telecommunication in the United States was changed overnight by court order (*not* by an act of Congress).

The exact details of the divestiture were described in the so-called **MFJ** (**Modified Final Judgment**), an oxymoron if ever there was one (if the judgment could be modified, it clearly was not final). This event led to increased competition, better service, and lower prices to consumers and businesses. Many other countries are now considering introducing competition along similar lines.

To make it clear who could do what, the United States was divided up into about 160 **LATAs** (**Local Access and Transport Areas**). Very roughly, a LATA is about as big as the area covered by one area code. Within a LATA, there is normally one **LEC** (**Local Exchange Carrier**) that has a monopoly on traditional telephone service within the LATA. The most important LECs are the BOCs, although some LATAs contain one or more of the 1500 independent telephone companies operating as LECs. In geographically large LATAs (mostly in the West), the LEC may handle long distance calls within its own LATA but may not handle calls going to a different LATA.

All inter-LATA traffic is handled by a different kind of company, an **IXC** (**IntereXchange Carrier**). Originally, AT&T Long Lines was the only serious IXC, but now MCI and Sprint are well-established competitors in the IXC business. One of the concerns at the breakup was to ensure that all the IXCs would be treated equally in terms of line quality, tariffs, and the number of digits their customers would have to dial to use them. The way this is handled is illustrated in Fig. 2-16. Here we see three example LATAs, each with several end offices. LATAs 2 and 3 also have a small hierarchy with tandem offices (intra-LATA toll offices).

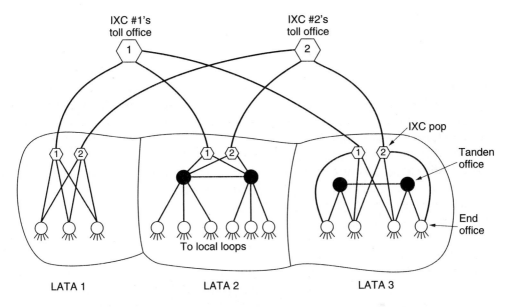

Fig. 2-16. The relationship of LATAs, LECs, and IXCs. All the circles are LEC switching offices. Each hexagon belongs to the IXC whose number is in it.

Any IXC that wishes to handle calls originating in a LATA can build a switching office called a **POP (Point of Presence)** there. The LEC is required to connect each IXC to every end office, either directly, as in LATAs 1 and 3, or indirectly, as in LATA 2. Furthermore, the terms of the connection, both technical and financial, must be identical for all IXCs. In this way, a subscriber in, say, LATA 1, can choose which IXC to use for calling subscribers in LATA 3.

As part of the MFJ, the IXCs were forbidden to offer local telephone service and the LECs were forbidden to offer inter-LATA telephone service, although both were free to enter other businesses, such as operating fried chicken restaurants. In 1984, that was a fairly unambiguous statement. Unfortunately, technology has a way of making the law obsolete. Neither cable television nor cellular phones were covered by the agreement. As cable television went from one way to two way, and cellular phones exploded in popularity, both LECs and IXCs began buying up or merging with cable and cellular operators.

By 1995, Congress saw that trying to maintain a distinction between the various kinds of companies was no longer tenable and drafted a bill to allow cable TV

companies, local telephone companies, long distance carriers, and cellular operators to enter one another's businesses. The idea was that any company could then
offer its customers a single integrated package containing cable TV, telephone,
and information services, and that different companies would compete on service
and price. The bill was enacted into law in February 1996. As a result, the U.S.
telecommunications landscape is currently undergoing a radical restructuring.

2.4.3. The Local Loop

For the past 100 years, analog transmission has dominated all communication.
In particular, the telephone system was originally based entirely on analog signaling. While the long-distance trunks are now largely digital in the more advanced
countries, the local loops are still analog and are likely to remain so for at least a
decade or two, due to the enormous cost of converting them. Consequently, when
a computer wishes to send digital data over a dial-up line, the data must first be
converted to analog form by a modem for transmission over the local loop, then
converted to digital form for transmission over the long-haul trunks, then back to
analog over the local loop at the receiving end, and finally back to digital by
another modem for storage in the destination computer. This arrangement is
shown in Fig. 2-17.

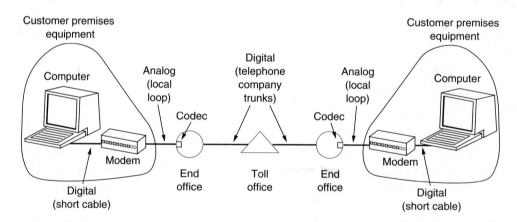

Fig. 2-17. The use of both analog and digital transmission for a computer to
computer call. Conversion is done by the modems and codecs.

While this situation is not exactly ideal, such is life for the time being, and
students of networking should have some understanding of both analog and digital
transmission, as well as how the conversions back and forth work. For leased
lines it is possible to go digital from start to finish, but these are expensive and are
only useful for building intracompany private networks.

In the following sections we will look briefly at what is wrong with analog transmission and examine how modems make it possible to transmit digital data over analog circuits. We will also look at two common modem interfaces, RS-232-C and RS-449.

Transmission Impairments

Analog signaling consists of varying a voltage with time to represent an information stream. If transmission media were perfect, the receiver would receive exactly the same signal that the transmitter sent. Unfortunately, media are not perfect, so the received signal is not the same as the transmitted signal. For digital data, this difference can lead to errors.

Transmission lines suffer from three major problems: attenuation, delay distortion, and noise. **Attenuation** is the loss of energy as the signal propagates outward. On guided media (e.g., wires and optical fibers), the signal falls off logarithmically with the distance. The loss is expressed in decibels per kilometer. The amount of energy lost depends on the frequency. To see the effect of this frequency dependence, imagine a signal not as a simple waveform, but as a series of Fourier components. Each component is attenuated by a different amount, which results in a different Fourier spectrum at the receiver, and hence a different signal.

If the attenuation is too much, the receiver may not be able to detect the signal at all, or the signal may fall below the noise level. In many cases, the attenuation properties of a medium are known, so amplifiers can be put in to try to compensate for the frequency-dependent attenuation. The approach helps but can never restore the signal exactly back to its original shape.

The second transmission impairment is **delay distortion**. It is caused by the fact that different Fourier components travel at different speeds. For digital data, fast components from one bit may catch up and overtake slow components from the bit ahead, mixing the two bits and increasing the probability of incorrect reception.

The third impairment is **noise**, which is unwanted energy from sources other than the transmitter. Thermal noise is caused by the random motion of the electrons in a wire and is unavoidable. Cross talk is caused by inductive coupling between two wires that are close to each other. Sometimes when talking on the telephone, you can hear another conversation in the background. That is cross talk. Finally, there is impulse noise, caused by spikes on the power line or other causes. For digital data, impulse noise can wipe out one or more bits.

Modems

Due to the problems just discussed, especially the fact that both attenuation and propagation speed are frequency dependent, it is undesirable to have a wide range of frequencies in the signal. Unfortunately, square waves, as in digital data, have a wide spectrum and thus are subject to strong attenuation and delay distortion. These effects make baseband (DC) signaling unsuitable except at slow speeds and over short distances.

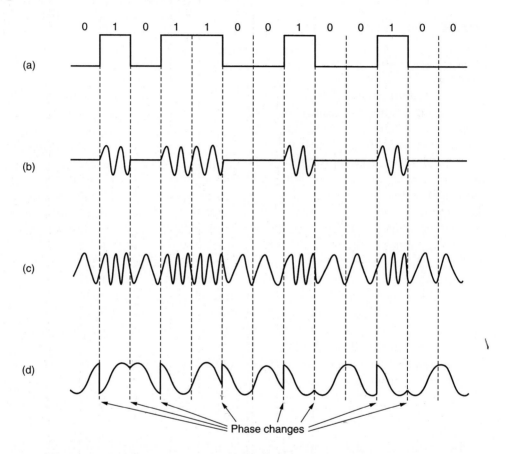

Fig. 2-18. (a) A binary signal. (b) Amplitude modulation. (c) Frequency modulation. (d) Phase modulation.

To get around the problems associated with DC signaling, especially on telephone lines, AC signaling is used. A continuous tone in the 1000- to 2000-Hz range, called a **sine wave carrier** is introduced. Its amplitude, frequency, or phase can be modulated to transmit information. In **amplitude modulation**, two different voltage levels are used to represent 0 and 1, respectively. In **frequency modulation**, also known as **frequency shift keying**, two (or more) different tones are used. In the simplest form of **phase modulation**, the carrier wave is systematically shifted 45, 135, 225, or 315 degrees at uniformly spaced intervals. Each phase shift transmits 2 bits of information. Figure 2-18 illustrates the three forms of modulation. A device that accepts a serial stream of bits as input and produces a modulated carrier as output (or vice versa) is called a **modem** (for modulator-demodulator). The modem is inserted between the (digital) computer and the (analog) telephone system.

To go to higher and higher speeds, it is not possible to just keep increasing the sampling rate. The Nyquist theorem says that even with a perfect 3000-Hz line (which a dial-up telephone is decidedly not), there is no point in sampling faster than 6000 Hz. Thus all research on faster modems is focused on getting more bits per sample (i.e., per baud).

Most advanced modems use a combination of modulation techniques to transmit multiple bits per baud. In Fig. 2-19(a), we see dots at 0, 90, 180, and 270 degrees, with two amplitude levels per phase shift. Amplitude is indicated by the distance from the origin. In Fig. 2-19(b) we see a different modulation scheme, in which 16 different combinations of amplitude and phase shift are used. Thus Fig. 2-19(a) has eight valid combinations and can be used to transmit 3 bits per baud. In contrast, Fig. 2-19(b) has 16 valid combinations and can thus be used to transmit 4 bits per baud. The scheme of Fig. 2-19(b) when used to transmit 9600 bps over a 2400-baud line is called **QAM** (**Quadrature Amplitude Modulation**).

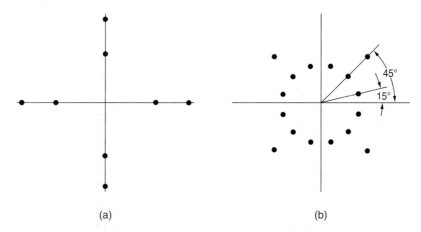

(a)   (b)

Fig. 2-19. (a) 3 bits/baud modulation. (b) 4 bits/baud modulation.

Diagrams such as those of Fig. 2-19, which show the legal combinations of amplitude and phase, are called **constellation patterns**. Each high-speed modem standard has its own constellation pattern and can talk only to other modems that use the same one (although most modems can emulate all the slower ones). The ITU V.32 9600 bps modem standard uses the constellation pattern of Fig. 2-19(b), for example.

The next step above 9600 bps is 14,400 bps. It is called **V.32 bis**. This speed is achieved by transmitting 6 bits per sample at 2400 baud. Its constellation pattern has 64 points. Fax modems use this speed to transmit pages that have been scanned in as bit maps. After V.32 bis comes **V.34**, which runs at 28,800 bps.

With so many points in the constellation pattern, even a small amout of noise in the detected amplitude or phase can result in an error, and potentially 6 bad bits. To reduce the chance of getting an error, many modems add a parity bit, giving 128 points in the constellation pattern. The coding of the points is carefully done to maximize the chance of detecting errors. The coding that does this is called **trellis coding**.

A completely different approach to high-speed transmission is to divide the available 3000-Hz spectrum into 512 tiny bands and transmit at, say, 20 bps in each one. This scheme requires a substantial processor inside the modem, but has the advantage of being able to disable frequency bands that are too noisy. Modems that use this approach normally have V.32 or V.34 capability as well, so they can talk to standard modems.

Many modems now have compression and error correction built into the modems. The big advantage of this approach is that these features improve the effective data rate without requiring any changes to existing software. One popular compression scheme is **MNP 5**, which uses run-length encoding to squeeze out runs of identical bytes. Fax modems also use run-length encoding, since runs of 0s (blank paper) are very common. Another scheme is **V.42 bis**, which uses a Ziv-Lempel compression algorithm also used in Compress and other programs (Ziv and Lempel, 1977).

Even when modems are used, another problem can occur on telephone lines: echoes. On a long line, when the signal gets to the final destination, some of the energy may be reflected back, analogous to acoustic echos in the mountains. As an illustration of electromagnetic echoes, try shining a flashlight from a darkened room through a closed window at night. You will see a reflection of the flashlight in the window (i.e., some of the energy has been reflected at the air-glass junction and sent back toward you). The same thing happens on transmission lines, especially at the point where the local loop terminates in the end office.

The effect of the echo is that a person speaking on the telephone hears his own words after a short delay. Psychological studies have shown that this is annoying to many people, often making them stutter or become confused. To eliminate the problem of echoes, echo suppressors are installed on lines longer than 2000 km. (On short lines the echoes come back so fast that people are not bothered by them.) An **echo suppressor** is a device that detects human speech coming from one end of the connection and suppresses all signals going the other way. It is basically an amplifier than can be switched on and off by a control signal produced by a speech detection circuit.

When the first person stops talking and the second begins, the echo suppressor switches directions. A good echo suppressor can reverse in 2 to 5 msec. While it is functioning, however, information can only travel in one direction; echoes cannot get back to the sender. Figure 2-20(a) shows the state of the echo suppressors while A is talking to B. Figure 2-20(b) shows the state after B has started talking.

The echo suppressors have several properties that are undesirable for data

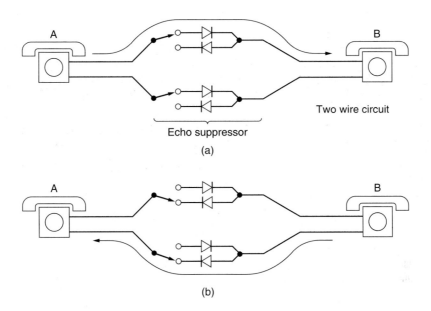

A

B

Two wire circuit

Echo suppressor

(a)

A

B

(b)

Fig. 2-20. (a) *A* talking to *B*. (b) *B* talking to *A*.

communication. First, it they were not present, it would be possible to transmit in both directions at the same time by using a different frequency band for each direction. This approach is called **full-duplex** transmission. With echo suppressors, full-duplex transmission is impossible. The alternative is **half-duplex** transmission, in which communication can go either way, but only one at a time. A single railroad track is half-duplex. Even if half-duplex transmission is adequate, it is a nuisance because the time required to switch directions can be substantial. Furthermore, the echo suppressors are designed to reverse upon detecting human speech, not digital data.

To alleviate these problems, an escape hatch has been provided on telephone circuits with echo suppressors. When the echo suppressors hear a pure tone at 2100 Hz, they shut down and remain shut down as long as a carrier is present. This arrangement is one of the many examples of **in-band signaling**, so called because the control signals that activate and deactivate internal control functions lie within the band accessible to the user. In general the trend is away from in-band signaling, to prevent users from interfering with the operation of the system itself. In the United States, most of the in-band signaling is gone, but in other countries it still exists.

An alternative to echo suppressors are **echo cancelers.** These are circuits that simulate the echo, estimate how much it is, and subtract it from the signal delivered, without the need for mechanical relays. When echo cancelers are used, full-duplex operation is possible. For this reason, echo cancelers are rapidly replacing echo suppressors in the United States and other large countries.

RS-232-C and RS-449

The interface between the computer or terminal and the modem is an example of a physical layer protocol. It must specify in detail the mechanical, electrical, functional, and procedural interface. We will now look closely at two well-known physical layer standards: RS-232-C and its successor, RS-449.

Let us start with **RS-232-C**, the third revision of the original RS-232 standard. The standard was drawn up by the Electronic Industries Association, a trade organization of electronics manufacturers, and is properly referred to as EIA RS-232-C. The international version is given in CCITT recommendation **V.24**, which is similar but differs slightly on some of the rarely used circuits. In the standards, the terminal or computer is officially called a **DTE (Data Terminal Equipment)** and the modem is officially called a **DCE (Data Circuit-Terminating Equipment)**.

The mechanical specification is for a 25-pin connector 47.04 ± .13 mm wide (screw center to screw center), with all the other dimensions equally well specified. The top row has pins numbered 1 to 13 (left to right); the bottom row has pins numbered 14 to 25 (also left to right).

The electrical specification for RS-232-C is that a voltage more negative than −3 volts is a binary 1 and a voltage more positive than +4 volts is a binary 0. Data rates up to 20 kbps are permitted, as are cables up to 15 meters.

The functional specification tells which circuits are connected to each of the 25 pins, and what they mean. Figure 2-21 shows 9 pins that are nearly always implemented. The remaining ones are frequently omitted. When the terminal or computer is powered up, it asserts (i.e., sets to a logical 1) Data Terminal Ready (pin 20). When the modem is powered up, it asserts Data Set Ready (pin 6). When the modem detects a carrier on the telephone line, it asserts Carrier Detect (pin 8). Request to Send (pin 4) indicates that the terminal wants to send data. Clear to Send (pin 5) means that the modem is prepared to accept data. Data are transmitted on the Transmit circuit (pin 2) and received on the Receive circuit (pin 3).

Other circuits are provided for selecting the data rate, testing the modem, clocking the data, detecting ringing signals, and sending data in the reverse direction on a secondary channel. They are hardly ever used in practice.

The procedural specification is the protocol, that is, the legal sequence of events. The protocol is based on action-reaction pairs. When the terminal asserts Request to Send, for example, the modem replies with Clear to Send, if it is able to accept data. Similar action-reaction pairs exist for other circuits as well.

It commonly occurs that two computers must be connected using RS-232-C. Since neither one is a modem, there is an interface problem. This problem is solved by connecting them with a device called a **null modem**, which connects the transmit line of one machine to the receive line of the other. It also crosses some of the other lines in a similar way. A null modem looks like a short cable.

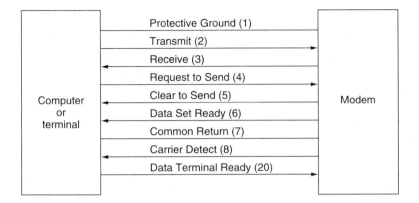

Fig. 2-21. Some of the principal RS-232-C circuits. The pin numbers are given in parentheses.

RS-232-C has been around for years. Gradually, the limitation of the data rate to not more than 20 kbps and the 15-meter maximum cable length have become increasingly annoying. EIA had a long debate about whether to try to have a new standard that was compatible with the old one (but technically not very advanced) or a new and incompatible one that would meet all needs for years to come. They eventually compromised by choosing both.

The new standard, called **RS-449**, is actually three standards in one. The mechanical, functional, and procedural interfaces are given in RS-449, but the electrical interface is given by two different standards. The first of these, **RS-423-A**, is similar to RS-232-C in that all its circuits share a common ground. This technique is called **unbalanced transmission**. The second electrical standard, **RS-422-A**, in contrast, uses **balanced transmission**, in which each of the main circuits requires two wires, with no common ground. As a result, RS-422-A can be used at speeds up to 2 Mbps over 60-meter cables.

The circuits used in RS-449 are shown in Fig. 2-22. Several new circuits not present in RS-232-C have been added. In particular, circuits for testing the modem both locally and remotely were included. Due to the inclusion of a number of two-wire circuits (when RS-422-A is used), more pins are needed in the new standard, so the familiar 25-pin connector was dropped. In its place is a 37-pin connector and a 9-pin connector. The 9-pin connector is required only if the second (reverse) channel is being used.

Fiber in the Local Loop

For advanced future services, such as video on demand, the 3-kHz channel currently used will not do. Discussions about what to do about this tend to focus on two solutions. The straightforward one—running a fiber from the end office

RS-232-C			CCITT V .24			RS-449		
Code	Pin	Circuit	Code	Pin	Circuit	Code	Pin	Circuit
AA	1	Protective ground	101	1	Protective ground	_	1	
AB	7	Signal ground	102	7	Signal ground	SG	19	Signal ground
						SC	37	Send common
						RC	20	Receive common
BA	2	Transmitted data	103	2	Transmitted data	SD	4, 22	Send data
BB	3	Received data	104	3	Received data	RD	6, 24	Receive data
CA	4	Request to send	105	4	Request to send	RS	7, 25	Request to send
CB	5	Clear to send	106	5	Ready for sending	CS	9, 27	Clear to send
CC	6	Data set ready	107	6	Data set ready	DM	11, 29	Data mode
CD	20	Data terminal ready	108	20	Data terminal ready	TR	12, 30	Terminal ready
CE	22	Ring indicator	125	22	Calling indicator	IC	15	Incoming call
CF	8	Line detector	109	8	Line detector	RR	13, 31	Receiver ready
CG	21	Signal quality	110	21	Signal quality	SQ	33	Signal quality
CH	23	DTE rate	111	23	DTE rate	SR	16	Signaling rate
CI	18	DCE rate	112	18	DCE rate	SI	2	Signaling indicators
						IS	28	Terminal in service
			136		New signal	NS	34	New signal
			126	11	Select frequency	SF	16	Select frequency
DA	24	DTE timing	113	24	DTE timing	TT	17, 25	Terminal timing
DB	15	DCE timing	114	15	DCE timing	ST	5, 23	Send timing
DD	17	Receiver timing	115	17	Receiver timing	RT	8, 26	Receive timing
SBA	14	Transmitted data	118	14	Transmitted data	SSD	3	Send data
SBB	16	Received data	119	16	Received data	SRD	4	Receive data
SCA	19	Request to send	120	19	Line signal	SRS	7	Request to send
SCB	13	Clear to send	121	13	Channel ready	SCS	8	Clear to send
SCF	12	Line detector	122	12	Line detector	SRR	2	Receiver ready
						LL	10	Local loopback
						RL	14	Remote loopback
						TM	18	Test mode
						SS	32	Select standby
						SB	36	Standby indicator

(The SBA–SCF rows are bracketed as "Secondary Channel".)

Fig. 2-22. Comparison of RS-232-C, V.24, and RS-449.

into everyone's house is called **FTTH** (**Fiber To The Home**). This solution fits in well with the current system but will not be economically feasible for decades. It is simply too expensive.

An alternative solution that is much cheaper is **FTTC** (**Fiber To The Curb**). In this model, the telephone company runs an optical fiber from each end office into each neighborhood (the curb) that it serves (Paff, 1995). The fiber is terminated in a junction box that all the local loops enter. Since the local loops are now much shorter (perhaps 100 meters instead of 3 km), they can be run at higher speeds, probably around 1 Mbps, which is just enough for compressed video. This design is shown in Fig. 2-23(a).

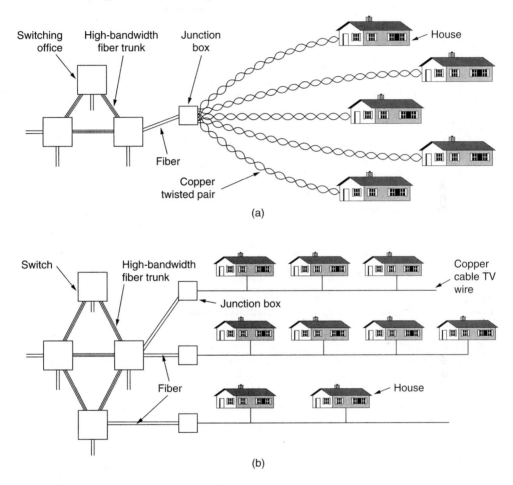

Fig. 2-23. Fiber to the curb. (a) Using the telephone network. (b) Using the cable TV network.

In this manner, multiple videos (or other information channels) can pour down the fiber at high speed and be split over the twisted pairs at the end. By sharing a 1-Gbps fiber over 100 to 1000 customers, the cost per customer can be reduced, and considerably higher bandwidth can be provided than now. Going appreciably above 1 Mbps for long distances with the existing twisted pairs is impossible. Thus in the long term, all the twisted pairs will have to be replaced by fiber. Whether the intermediate solution of FTTC should be used for the time being or

FTTH should be the goal from the beginning is a matter of some debate within the telephone industry.

An alternative design using the existing cable TV infrastructure is shown in Fig. 2-23(b). Here a multidrop cable is used instead of the point-to-point system characteristic of the telephone system. It is likely that both Fig. 2-23(a) and Fig. 2-23(b) will coexist in the future, as telephone companies and cable TV operators become direct competitors for voice, data, and possibly even television service. For more information about this topic, see (Cook and Stern, 1994; Miki, 1994b; and Mochida, 1994).

2.4.4. Trunks and Multiplexing

Economies of scale play an important role in the telephone system. It costs essentially the same amount of money to install and maintain a high-bandwidth trunk as a low-bandwidth trunk between two switching offices (i.e., the costs come from having to dig the trench and not from the copper wire or optical fiber). Consequently, telephone companies have developed elaborate schemes for multiplexing many conversations over a single physical trunk. These multiplexing schemes can be divided into two basic categories: **FDM** (**Frequency Division Multiplexing**), and **TDM** (**Time Division Multiplexing**). In FDM the frequency spectrum is divided among the logical channels, with each user having exclusive possession of some frequency band. In TDM the users take turns (in a round robin), each one periodically getting the entire bandwidth for a little burst of time.

AM radio broadcasting provides illustrations of both kinds of multiplexing. The allocated spectrum is about 1 MHz, roughly 500 to 1500 kHz. Different frequencies are allocated to different logical channels (stations), each operating in a portion of the spectrum, with the interchannel separation great enough to prevent interference. This system is an example of frequency division multiplexing. In addition (in some countries), the individual stations have two logical subchannels: music and advertising. These two alternate in time on the same frequency, first a burst of music, then a burst of advertising, then more music, and so on. This situation is time division multiplexing.

Below we will examine frequency division multiplexing. After that we will see how FDM can be applied to fiber optics (wavelength division multiplexing). Then we will turn to TDM, and end with an advanced TDM system used for fiber optics (SONET).

Frequency Division Multiplexing

Figure 2-24 shows how three voice-grade telephone channels are multiplexed using FDM. Filters limit the usable bandwidth to about 3000 Hz per voice-grade channel. When many channels are multiplexed together, 4000 Hz is allocated to each channel to keep them well separated. First the voice channels are raised in frequency, each by a different amount. Then they can be combined, because no two channels now occupy the same portion of the spectrum. Notice that even though there are gaps (guard bands) between the channels, there is some overlap between adjacent channels, because the filters do not have sharp edges. This overlap means that a strong spike at the edge of one channel will be felt in the adjacent one as nonthermal noise.

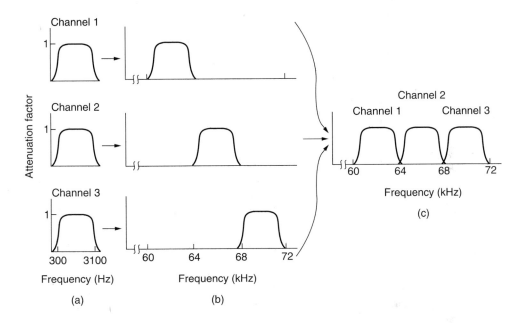

Fig. 2-24. Frequency division multiplexing. (a) The original bandwidths. (b) The bandwidths raised in frequency. (c) The multiplexed channel.

The FDM schemes used around the world are to some degree standardized. A widespread standard is 12 4000-Hz voice channels (3000 Hz for the user, plus two guard bands of 500 Hz each) multiplexed into the 60 to 108 kHz band. This unit is called a **group.** The 12- to 60-kHz band is sometimes used for another group. Many carriers offer a 48- to 56-kbps leased line service to customers, based on the group. Five groups (60 voice channels) can be multiplexed to form a **super-group**. The next unit is the **mastergroup**, which is five supergroups (CCITT standard) or ten supergroups (Bell system). Other standards up to 230,000 voice channels also exist.

Wavelength Division Multiplexing

For fiber optic channels, a variation of frequency division multiplexing is used. It is called **WDM (Wavelength Division Multiplexing)**. A simple way of achieving FDM on fibers is depicted in Fig. 2-25. Here two fibers come together at a prism (or more likely, a diffraction grating), each with its energy in a different band. The two beams are passed through the prism or grating, and combined onto a single shared fiber for transmission to a distant destination, where they are split again.

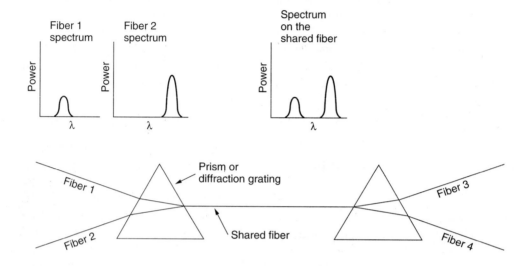

Fig. 2-25. Wavelength division multiplexing.

There is really nothing new here. As long as each channel has its own frequency range, and all the ranges are disjoint, they can be multiplexed together on the long-haul fiber. The only difference with electrical FDM is that an optical system using a diffraction grating is completely passive, and thus highly reliable.

It should be noted that the reason WDM is popular is that the energy on a single fiber is typically only a few gigahertz wide because it is currently impossible to convert between electrical and optical media any faster. Since the bandwidth of a single fiber band is about 25,000 GHz (see Fig. 2-6), there is great potential for multiplexing many channels together over long-haul routes. A necessary condition, however, is that the incoming channels use different frequencies.

A potential application of WDM is in the FTTC systems described earlier. Initially, a telephone company could run a single fiber from an end office to a neighborhood junction box where it met up with twisted pairs from the houses. Years later, when the cost of fiber is lower and the demand for it is higher, the twisted pairs can be replaced by fiber and all the local loops joined onto the fiber running to the end office using WDM.

In the example of Fig. 2-25, we have a fixed wavelength system. Bits from fiber 1 go to fiber 3, and bits from fiber 2 go to fiber 4. It is not possible to have bits go from fiber 1 to fiber 4. However, it is also possible to build WDM systems that are switched. In such a device, there are many input fibers and many output fibers, and the data from any input fiber can go to any output fiber. Typically, the coupler is a passive star, with the light from every input fiber illuminating the star. Although spreading the energy over n outputs dilutes it by a factor n, such systems are practical for hundreds of channels.

Of course, if the light from one of the incoming fibers is at 1.50206 microns and potentially might have to go to any output fiber, all the output fibers need tunable filters so the selected one can set itself to 1.50206 microns. Such optical tunable filters can be built from Fabry-Perot or Mach-Zehnder interferometers. Alternatively, the input fibers could be tunable and the output ones fixed. Having both be tunable is an unnecessary expense and is rarely worth it.

Time Division Multiplexing

Although FDM is still used over copper wires or microwave channels, it requires analog circuitry and is not amenable to being done by a computer. In contrast, TDM can be handled entirely by digital electronics, so it has become far more widespread in recent years. Unfortunately, it can only be used for digital data. Since the local loops produce analog signals, a conversion is needed from analog to digital in the end office, where all the individual local loops come together to be combined onto outgoing trunks. We will now look at how multiple analog voice signals are digitized and combined onto a single outgoing digital trunk. (Remember that computer data sent over a modem are also analog when they get to the end office.)

The analog signals are digitized in the end office by a device called a **codec** (coder-decoder), producing a 7- or 8-bit number (see Fig. 2-17). The codec makes 8000 samples per second (125 μsec/sample) because the Nyquist theorem says that this is sufficient to capture all the information from the 4-kHz telephone channel bandwidth. At a lower sampling rate, information would be lost; at a higher one, no extra information would be gained. This technique is called **PCM (Pulse Code Modulation)**. PCM forms the heart of the modern telephone system. As a consequence, virtually all time intervals within the telephone system are multiples of 125 μsec.

When digital transmission began emerging as a feasible technology, CCITT was unable to reach agreement on an international standard for PCM. Consequently, there are now a variety of incompatible schemes in use in different countries around the world. International hookups between incompatible countries require (often expensive) "black boxes" to convert the originating country's system to that of the receiving country.

One method that is in widespread use in North America and Japan is the T1 carrier, depicted in Fig. 2-26. (Technically speaking, the format is called DS1 and the carrier is called T1, but we will not make that subtle distinction here.) The T1 carrier consists of 24 voice channels multiplexed together. Usually, the analog signals are sampled on a round-robin basis with the resulting analog stream being fed to the codec rather than having 24 separate codecs and then merging the digital output. Each of the 24 channels, in turn, gets to insert 8 bits into the output stream. Seven bits are data, and one is for control, yielding $7 \times 8000 = 56,000$ bps of data, and $1 \times 8000 = 8000$ bps of signaling information per channel.

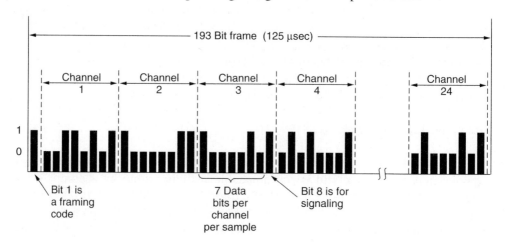

Fig. 2-26. The T1 carrier (1.544 Mbps).

A frame consists of $24 \times 8 = 192$ bits, plus one extra bit for framing, yielding 193 bits every 125 µsec. This gives a gross data rate of 1.544 Mbps. The 193rd bit is used for frame synchronization. It takes on the pattern 0101010101 . . . . Normally, the receiver keeps checking this bit to make sure that it has not lost synchronization. If it does get out of sync, the receiver can scan for this pattern to get resynchronized. Analog customers cannot generate the bit pattern at all, because it corresponds to a sine wave at 4000 Hz, which would be filtered out. Digital customers can, of course, generate this pattern, but the odds are against its being present when the frame slips. When a T1 system is being used entirely for data, only 23 of the channels are used for data. The 24th one is used for a special synchronization pattern, to allow faster recovery in the event that the frame slips.

When CCITT finally did reach agreement, they felt that 8000 bps of signaling information was far too much, so its 1.544-Mbps standard is based upon an 8- rather than a 7-bit data item; that is, the analog signal is quantized into 256 rather than 128 discrete levels. Two (incompatible) variations are provided. In **common-channel signaling**, the extra bit (which is attached onto the rear rather than the front of the 193 bit frame) takes on the values 10101010 . . . in the odd frames and contains signaling information for all the channels in the even frames.

In the other variation, **channel associated signaling**, each channel has its own private signaling subchannel. A private subchannel is arranged by allocating one of the eight user bits in every sixth frame for signaling purposes, so five out of six samples are 8 bits wide, and the other one is only 7 bits wide. CCITT also has a recommendation for a PCM carrier at 2.048 Mbps called **E1**. This carrier has 32 8-bit data samples packed into the basic 125-μsec frame. Thirty of the channels are used for information and two are used for signaling. Each group of four frames provides 64 signaling bits, half of which are used for channel associated signaling and half of which are used for frame synchronization or are reserved for each country to use as it wishes. Outside North America and Japan, the 2.048-Mbps carrier is in widespread use.

Once the voice signal has been digitized, it is tempting to try to use statistical techniques to reduce the number of bits needed per channel. These techniques are appropriate not only to encoding speech, but to the digitization of any analog signal. All of the compaction methods are based upon the principle that the signal changes relatively slowly compared to the sampling frequency, so that much of the information in the 7- or 8-bit digital level is redundant.

One method, called **differential pulse code modulation**, consists of outputting not the digitized amplitude, but the difference between the current value and the previous one. Since jumps of ±16 or more on a scale of 128 are unlikely, 5 bits should suffice instead of 7. If the signal does occasionally jump wildly, the encoding logic may require several sampling periods to "catch up." For speech, the error introduced can be ignored.

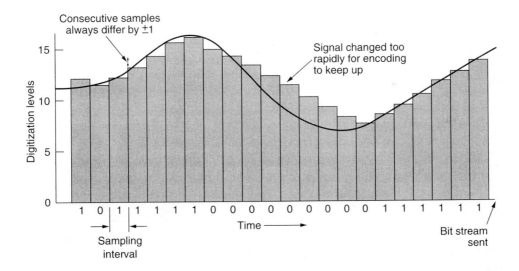

Fig. 2-27. Delta modulation.

A variation of this compaction method requires each sampled value to differ from its predecessor by either +1 or −1. A single bit is transmitted, telling whether the new sample is above or below the previous one. This technique, called **delta modulation**, is illustrated in Fig. 2-27. Like all compaction techniques that assume small level changes between consecutive samples, delta encoding can get into trouble if the signal changes too fast, as shown in the figure. When this happens, information is lost.

An improvement to differential PCM is to extrapolate the previous few values to predict the next value and then to encode the difference between the actual signal and the predicted one. The transmitter and receiver must use the same prediction algorithm, of course. Such schemes are called **predictive encoding**. They are useful because they reduce the size of the numbers to be encoded, hence the number of bits to be sent.

Although PCM is widely used on interoffice trunks, the computer user gets relatively little benefit from it if all data must be sent to the end office in the form of a modulated analog sine wave at 28.8 kbps. It would be nice if the carrier would attach the local loop directly to the PCM trunk system, so that the computer could output digital data directly onto the local loop at 1.544 or 2.048 Mbps. Unfortunately, the local loops cannot run at these speeds for very far.

Time division multiplexing allows multiple T1 carriers to be multiplexed into higher-order carriers. Figure 2-28 shows how this can be done. At the left we see four T1 channels being multiplexed onto one T2 channel. The multiplexing at T2 and above is done bit for bit, rather than byte for byte with the 24 voice channels that make up a T1 frame. Four T1 streams at 1.544 Mbps should generate 6.176 Mbps, but T2 is actually 6.312 Mbps. The extra bits are used for framing and recovery, in case the carrier slips.

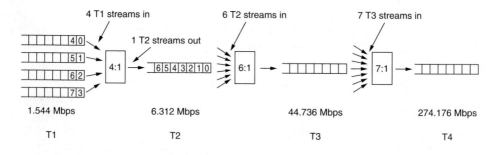

Fig. 2-28. Multiplexing T1 streams onto higher carriers.

At the next level, six T2 streams are combined bitwise to form a T3 stream. Then seven T3 streams are joined to form a T4 stream. At each step a small amount of overhead is added for framing and recovery.

Just as there is little agreement on the basic carrier between the United States and the rest of the world, there is equally little agreement on how it is to be multiplexed into higher bandwidth carriers. The U.S. scheme of stepping up by 4, 6, and 7 did not strike everyone else as the way to go, so the CCITT standard calls for multiplexing four streams onto one stream at each level. Also, the framing and recovery data are different. The CCITT hierarchy for 32, 128, 512, 2048, and 8192 channels runs at speeds of 2.048, 8.848, 34.304, 139.264, and 565.148 Mbps.

SONET/SDH

In the early days of fiber optics, every telephone company had its own proprietary optical TDM system. After AT&T was broken up in 1984, local telephone companies had to connect to multiple long-distance carriers, all with different optical TDM systems, so the need for standardization became obvious. In 1985, Bellcore, the RBOCs research arm, began working on a standard, called **SONET (Synchronous Optical NETwork)**. Later, CCITT joined the effort, which resulted in a SONET standard and a set of parallel CCITT recommendations (G.707, G.708, and G.709) in 1989. The CCITT recommendations are called **SDH (Synchronous Digital Hierarchy)** but differ from SONET only in minor ways. Virtually all the long-distance telephone traffic in the United States, and much of it elsewhere now uses trunks running SONET in the physical layer. As SONET chips become cheaper, SONET interface boards for computers may become more widespread, so it may become easier for companies to plug their computers directly into the heart of the telephone network over specially conditioned leased lines. Below we will discuss the goals and design of SONET briefly. For additional information see (Bellamy, 1991; and Omidyar and Aldridge, 1993).

The SONET design had four major goals. First and foremost, SONET had to make it possible for different carriers to interwork. Achieving this goal required defining a common signaling standard with respect to wavelength, timing, framing structure, and other issues.

Second, some means was needed to unify the U.S., European, and Japanese digital systems, all of which were based on 64-kbps PCM channels, but all of which combined them in different (and incompatible) ways.

Third, SONET had to provide a way to multiplex multiple digital channels together. At the time SONET was devised, the highest speed digital carrier actually used widely in the United States was T3, at 44.736 Mbps. T4 was defined, but not used much, and nothing was even defined above T4 speed. Part of SONET's mission was to continue the hierarchy to gigabits/sec and beyond. A standard way to multiplex slower channels into one SONET channel was also needed.

Fourth, SONET had to provide support for operations, administration, and maintenance (OAM). Previous systems did not do this very well.

An early decision was to make SONET a traditional TDM system, with the entire bandwidth of the fiber devoted to one channel containing time slots for the various subchannels. As such, SONET is a synchronous system. It is controlled by a master clock with an accuracy of about 1 part in 10^9. Bits on a SONET line are sent out at extremely precise intervals, controlled by the master clock.

When cell switching was later proposed to be the basis of broadband ISDN, the fact that it permitted irregular cell arrivals got it labeled as *asynchronous transfer mode* (i.e., ATM) to contrast it to the synchronous operation of SONET.

A SONET system consists of switches, multiplexers, and repeaters, all connected by fiber. A path from a source to destination with one intermediate multiplexer and one intermediate repeater is shown in Fig. 2-29. In SONET terminology, a fiber going directly from any device to any other device, with nothing in between, is called a **section**. A run between two multiplexers (possibly with one or more repeaters in the middle) is called a **line**. Finally, the connection between the source and destination (possibly with one or more multiplexers and repeaters) is called a **path**. The SONET topology can be a mesh, but is often a dual ring.

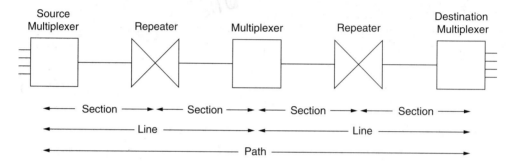

Fig. 2-29. A SONET path.

The basic SONET frame is a block of 810 bytes put out every 125 μsec. Since SONET is synchronous, frames are emitted whether or not there are any useful data to send. Having 8000 frames/sec exactly matches the sampling rate of the PCM channels used in all digital telephony systems.

The 810-byte SONET frames are best described as a rectangle of bytes, 90 columns wide by 9 rows high. Thus $8 \times 810 = 6480$ bits are transmitted 8000 times per second, for a gross data rate of 51.84 Mbps. This is the basic SONET channel and is called **STS-1 (Synchronous Transport Signal-1)**. All SONET trunks are a multiple of STS-1.

The first three columns of each frame are reserved for system management information, as illustrated in Fig. 2-30. The first three rows contain the section overhead; the next six contain the line overhead. The section overhead is generated and checked at the start and end of each section, whereas the line overhead is generated and checked at the start and end of each line.

The remaining 87 columns hold $87 \times 9 \times 8 \times 8000 = 50.112$ Mbps of user data. However, the user data, called the **SPE (Synchronous Payload Envelope)** do not always begin in row 1, column 4. The SPE can begin anywhere within the frame. A pointer to the first byte is contained in the first row of the line overhead. The first column of the SPE is the path overhead (i.e., header for the end-to-end path sublayer protocol).

The ability to allow the SPE to begin anywhere within the SONET frame, and even to span two frames, as shown in Fig. 2-30, gives added flexibility to the

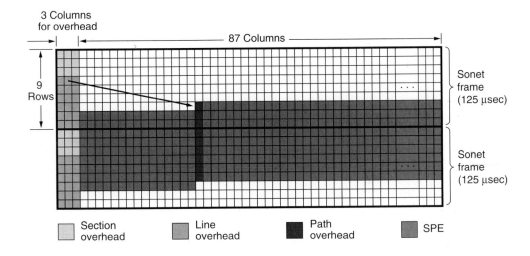

Fig. 2-30. Two back-to-back SONET frames.

system. For example, if a payload arrives at the source while a dummy SONET frame is being constructed, it can be inserted into the current frame, instead of being held until the start of the next one. This feature is also useful when the payload does not fit exactly in one frame, as in the case of a sequence of 53-byte ATM cells. The first row of the line overhead can then point to the start of the first full cell, to provide synchronization.

The section, line, and path overheads contain a profusion of bytes used for operations, administration, and maintenance. Since each byte occurs 8000 times per second, it represents a PCM channel. Three of these are, in fact, used to provide voice channels for section, line, and path maintenance personnel. Other bytes are used for framing, parity, error monitoring, IDs, clocking, synchronization, and other functions. Bellamy (1991) describes all the fields in detail.

The multiplexing of multiple data streams, called **tributaries**, plays an important role in SONET. Multiplexing is illustrated in Fig. 2-31. On the left, we start with various low-speed input streams, which are converted to the basic STS-1 SONET rate, in most cases by adding filler to round up to 51.84 Mbps. Next, three STS-1 tributaries are multiplexed onto one 155.52-Mbps STS-3 output stream. This stream, in turn, is multiplexed with three others onto a final output stream having 12 times the capacity of the STS-1 stream. At this point the signal is scrambled, to prevent long runs of 0s or 1s from interfering with the clocking, and converted from an electrical to an optical signal.

Multiplexing is done byte for byte. For example, when three STS-1 tributaries at 51.84 Mbps are merged into one STS-3 stream at 155.52 Mbps, the multiplexer first outputs 1 byte from tributary 1, then 1 from tributary 2, and finally 1 from tributary 3, before going back to 1. The STS-3 figure analogous to Fig. 2-30

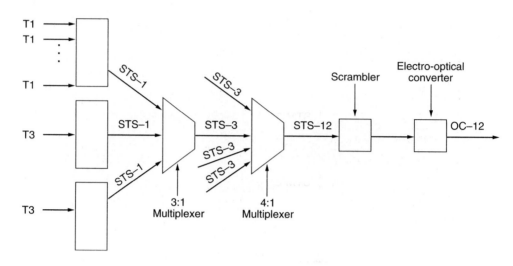

Fig. 2-31. Multiplexing in SONET.

shows (from left to right) columns from tributaries 1, 2, and 3, in that order, then another triple, and so on, out to column 270. One of these 270 × 9 byte frames is sent every 125 μsec, giving the 155.52-Mbps data rate.

The SONET multiplexing hierarchy is shown in Fig. 2-32. Rates from STS-1 to STS-48 have been defined. The optical carrier corresponding to STS-*n* is called OC-*n* but is bit-for-bit the same except for the scrambling shown in Fig. 2-31. The SDH names are different, and they start at OC-3 because CCITT-based systems do not have a rate near 51.84 Mbps. The OC-9 carrier is present because it closely matches the speed of a major high-speed trunk used in Japan. OC-18 and OC-36 will be used in Japan in the future. The gross data rate includes all the overhead. The SPE data rate excludes the line and section overhead. The user data rate excludes all overhead and only counts the 86 columns available for the payload.

As an aside, when a carrier, such as OC-3, is not multiplexed, but carries the data from only a single source, the letter *c* (for concatenated) is appended to the designation, so OC-3 indicates a 155.52-Mbps carrier consisting of three separate OC-1 carriers, but OC-3c indicates a data stream from a single source at 155.52 Mbps. The three OC-1 streams within an OC-3c stream are interleaved by column, first column 1 from stream 1, then column 1 from stream 2, then column 1 from stream 3, followed by column 2 from stream 1, and so on, leading to a frame 270 columns wide and 9 rows deep.

The amount of actual user data in an OC-3c stream is slightly higher than in an OC-3 stream (149.760 Mbps versus 148.608 Mbps) because the path overhead column is included inside the SPE only once, instead of the three times it would be with three independent OC-1 streams. In other words, 260 of the 270 columns

SONET		SDH	Data rate (Mbps)		
Electrical	**Optical**	**Optical**	**Gross**	**SPE**	**User**
STS-1	OC-1		51.84	50.112	49.536
STS-3	OC-3	STM-1	155.52	150.336	148.608
STS-9	OC-9	STM-3	466.56	451.008	445.824
STS-12	OC-12	STM-4	622.08	601.344	594.432
STS-18	OC-18	STM-6	933.12	902.016	891.648
STS-24	OC-24	STM-8	1244.16	1202.688	1188.864
STS-36	OC-36	STM-12	1866.24	1804.032	1783.296
STS-48	OC-48	STM-16	2488.32	2405.376	2377.728

Fig. 2-32. SONET and SDH multiplex rates.

are available for user data in OC-3c, whereas only 258 columns are available for user data in OC-3. Higher-order concatenated frames (e.g., OC-12c) also exist.

By now it should be clear why ATM runs at 155 Mbps: the intention is to carry ATM cells over SONET OC-3c trunks. It should also be clear that the widely quoted 155-Mbps figure is the gross rate, including the SONET overhead. Furthermore, somewhere along the way somebody incorrectly rounded 155.52 Mbps to 155 Mbps instead of 156 Mbps, and now everyone else does it wrong, too.

The SONET physical layer is divided up into four sublayers, as shown in Fig. 2-33. The lowest sublayer is the **photonic sublayer**. It is concerned with specifying the physical properties of the light and fiber to be used.

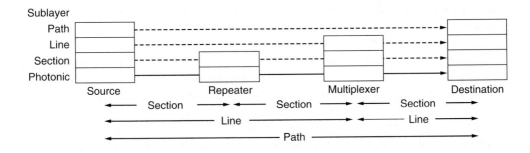

Fig. 2-33. The SONET architecture.

The three remaining sublayers correspond to the sections, lines, and paths. The section sublayer handles a single point-to-point fiber run, generating a standard frame at one end and processing it at the other. Sections can start and end at repeaters, which just amplify and regenerate the bits, but do not change or process them in any way.

The line sublayer is concerned with multiplexing multiple tributaries onto a single line and demultiplexing them at the other end. To the line sublayer, the repeaters are transparent. When a multiplexer puts out bits on a fiber, it expects them to arrive at the next multiplexer unchanged, no matter how many repeaters are used in between. The protocol in the line sublayer is thus between two multiplexers and deals with issues such as how many inputs are being multiplexed together and how. In contrast, the path sublayer and protocol deal with end-to-end issues.

2.4.5. Switching

From the point of view of the average telephone engineer, the phone system is divided into two parts: outside plant (the local loops and trunks, since they are outside the switching offices), and inside plant (the switches). We have just looked at outside plant. Now it is time to examine inside plant.

Two different switching techniques are used inside the telephone system: circuit switching and packet switching. We will give a brief introduction to each of them below. Then we will go into circuit switching in detail, because that is how the current telephone system works. Later in the chapter we will go into packet switching in detail in the context of the next generation telephone system, broadband ISDN.

Circuit Switching

When you or your computer places a telephone call, the switching equipment within the telephone system seeks out a physical "copper" (including fiber and radio) path all the way from your telephone to the receiver's telephone. This technique is called **circuit switching** and is shown schematically in Fig. 2-34(a). Each of the six rectangles represents a carrier switching office (end office, toll office, etc.). In this example, each office has three incoming lines and three outgoing lines. When a call passes through a switching office, a physical connection is (conceptually) established between the line on which the call came in and one of the output lines, as shown by the dotted lines.

In the early days of the telephone, the connection was made by having the operator plug a jumper cable into the input and output sockets. In fact, there is a surprising little story associated with the invention of automatic circuit switching equipment. It was invented by a 19th Century undertaker named Almon B. Strowger. Shortly after the telephone was invented, when someone died, one of the survivors would call the town operator and say: "Please connect me to an undertaker." Unfortunately for Mr. Strowger, there were two undertakers in his town, and the other one's wife was the town telephone operator. He quickly saw that either he was going to have to invent automatic telephone switching equipment or he was going to go out of business. He chose the first option. For nearly 100 years, the circuit switching equipment used worldwide was known as Strowger gear. (History does not record whether the now-unemployed switchboard operator got a job as an information operator, answering questions such as: What is the phone number of an undertaker?

The model shown in Fig. 2-34(a) is highly simplified of course, because parts of the "copper" path between the two telephones may, in fact, be microwave links onto which thousands of calls are multiplexed. Nevertheless, the basic idea is valid: once a call has been set up, a dedicated path between both ends exists and will continue to exist until the call is finished.

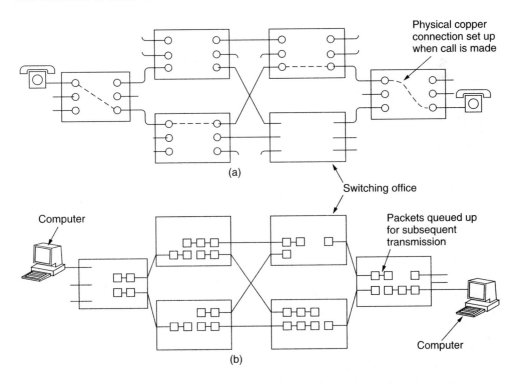

Fig. 2-34. (a) Circuit switching. (b) Packet switching.

An important property of circuit switching is the need to set up an end-to-end path *before* any data can be sent. The elapsed time between the end of dialing and the start of ringing can easily be 10 sec, more on long-distance or international calls. During this time interval, the telephone system is hunting for a copper path, as shown in Fig. 2-35(a). Note that before data transmission can even begin, the call request signal must propagate all the way to the destination, and be acknowledged. For many computer applications (e.g., point-of-sale credit verification), long setup times are undesirable.

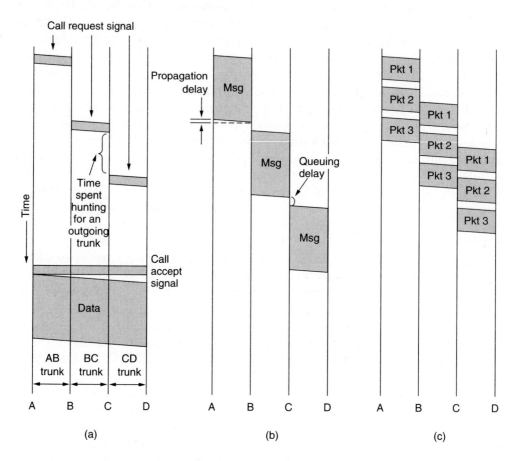

Fig. 2-35. Timing of events in (a) circuit switching, (b) message switching, (c) packet switching.

As a consequence of the copper path between the calling parties, once the setup has been completed, the only delay for data is the propagation time for the electromagnetic signal, about 5 msec per 1000 km. Also as a consequence of the established path, there is no danger of congestion—that is, once the call has been put through, you never get busy signals, although you might get one before the connection has been established due to lack of switching or trunk capacity.

An alternative switching strategy is **message switching**, shown in Fig. 2-35(b). When this form of switching is used, no physical copper path is established in advance between sender and receiver. Instead, when the sender has a block of data to be sent, it is stored in the first switching office (i.e., router) and then forwarded later, one hop at a time. Each block is received in its entirety, inspected for errors, and then retransmitted. A network using this technique is called a **store-and-forward** network, as mentioned in Chap. 1.

The first electromechanical telecommunication systems used message switching, namely for telegrams. The message was punched on paper tape off-line at the sending office, and then read in and transmitted over a communication line to the next office along the way, where it was punched out on paper tape. An operator there tore the tape off and read it in on one of the many tape readers, one per outgoing trunk. Such a switching office was called a **torn tape office**.

With message switching, there is no limit on block size, which means that routers (in a modern system) must have disks to buffer long blocks. It also means that a single block may tie up a router-router line for minutes, rendering message switching useless for interactive traffic. To get around these problems, **packet switching** was invented. Packet-switching networks place a tight upper limit on block size, allowing packets to be buffered in router main memory instead of on disk. By making sure that no user can monopolize any transmission line very long (milliseconds), packet-switching networks are well suited to handling interactive traffic. A further advantage of packet switching over message switching is shown in Fig. 2-35(b) and (c): the first packet of a multipacket message can be forwarded before the second one has fully arrived, reducing delay and improving throughput. For these reasons, computer networks are usually packet switched, occasionally circuit switched, but never message switched.

Circuit switching and packet switching differ in many respects. The key difference is that circuit switching statically reserves the required bandwidth in advance, whereas packet switching acquires and releases it as it is needed. With circuit switching, any unused bandwidth on an allocated circuit is just wasted. With packet switching it may be utilized by other packets from unrelated sources going to unrelated destinations, because circuits are never dedicated. However, just because no circuits are dedicated, a sudden surge of input traffic may overwhelm a router, exceeding its storage capacity and causing it to lose packets.

In contrast, with circuit switching, when packet switching is used, it is straightforward for the routers to provide speed and code conversion. Also, they can provide error correction to some extent. In some packet-switched networks, however, packets may be delivered in the wrong order to the destination. Reordering of packets can never happen with circuit switching.

Another difference is that circuit switching is completely transparent. The sender and receiver can use any bit rate, format, or framing method they want to. The carrier does not know or care. With packet switching, the carrier determines the basic parameters. A rough analogy is a road versus a railroad. In the former, the user determines the size, speed, and nature of the vehicle; in the latter, the carrier does. It is this transparency that allows voice, data, and fax to coexist within the phone system.

A final difference between circuit and packet switching is the charging algorithm. Packet carriers usually base their charge on both the number of bytes (or packets) carried and the connect time. Furthermore, transmission distance usually does not matter, except perhaps internationally. With circuit switching, the charge is based on the distance and time only, not the traffic. The differences are summarized in Fig. 2-36.

Item	Circuit-switched	Packet-switched
Dedicated "copper" path	Yes	No
Bandwidth available	Fixed	Dynamic
Potentially wasted bandwidth	Yes	No
Store-and-forward transmission	No	Yes
Each packet follows the same route	Yes	No
Call setup	Required	Not needed
When can congestion occur	At setup time	On every packet
Charging	Per minute	Per packet

Fig. 2-36. A comparison of circuit-switched and packet-switched networks.

Both circuit switching and packet switching are so important, we will come back to them shortly and describe the various technologies used in detail.

The Switch Hierarchy

It is worth saying a few words about how the routing between switches is done within the current circuit-switched telephone system. We will describe the AT&T system here, but other companies and countries use the same general principles. The telephone system has five classes of switching offices, as illustrated in Fig. 2-37. There are 10 regional switching offices, and these are fully interconnected by 45 high-bandwidth fiber optic trunks. Below the regional offices are 67 sectional offices, 230 primary offices, 1300 toll offices, and 19,000 end offices. The lower four levels were originally connected as a tree.

Calls are generally connected at the lowest possible level. Thus if a subscriber connected to end office 1 calls another subscriber connected to end office 1, the call will be completed in that office. However, a call from a customer attached to end office 1 in Fig. 2-37 to a customer attached to end office 2 will have to go toll office 1. However, a call from end office 1 to end office 4 will have to go up to primary office 1, and so on. With a pure tree, there is only one minimal route, and that would normally be taken.

During years of operation, the telephone companies noticed that some routes were busier than others. For example, there were many calls from New York to Los Angeles. Rather than go all the way up the hierarchy, they simply installed **direct trunks** for the busy routes. A few of these are shown in Fig. 2-37 as

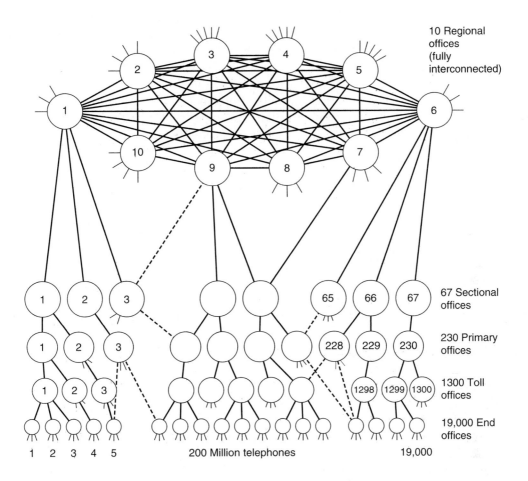

Fig. 2-37. The AT&T telephone hierarchy. The dashed lines are direct trunks.

dashed lines. As a consequence, many calls can now be routed along many paths. The actual route chosen is generally the most direct one, but if the necessary trunks along it are full, an alternative is chosen. This complex routing is now possible because a switching machine, like the AT&T 5 ESS, is in fact just a general purpose computer with a large amount of very specialized I/O equipment.

Crossbar Switches

Let us now turn from how calls are routed among switches to how individual switches actually work inside. Several kinds of switches are (or were) common within the telephone system. The simplest kind is the **crossbar switch** (also called a **crosspoint switch),** shown in Fig. 2-38. In a switch with n input lines and n output lines (i.e., n full duplex lines), the crossbar switch has n^2

intersections, called **crosspoints**, where an input and an output line may be connected by a semiconductor switch, as shown in Fig. 2-38(a). In Fig. 2-38(b) we see an example in which line 0 is connected to line 4, line 1 is connected to line 7, and line 2 is connected to line 6. Lines 3 and 5 are not connected. All the bits that arrive at the switch from line 4, for example, are immediately sent out of the switch on line 0. Thus the crossbar switch implements circuit switching by making a direct electrical connection, just like the jumper cables in the first-generation switches, only automatically and within microseconds.

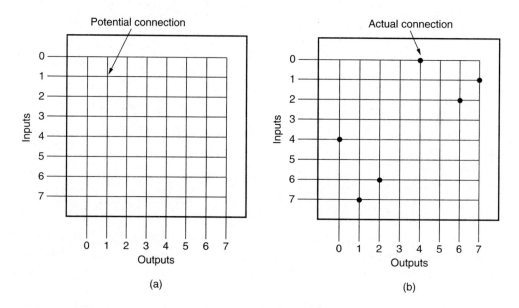

Fig. 2-38. (a) A crossbar switch with no connections. (b) A crossbar switch with three connections set up: 0 with 4, 1 with 7, and 2 with 6.

The problem with a crossbar switch is that the number of crossbars grows as the square of the number of lines into the switch. If we assume that all lines are full duplex and that there are no self-connections, only the crosspoints above the diagonal are needed. Still, $n(n-1)/2$ crosspoints are needed. For $n = 1000$, we need 499,500 crosspoints. While building a VLSI chip with this number of transistor switches is possible, having 1000 pins on the chip is not. Thus a single crossbar switch is only useful for relatively small end offices.

Space Division Switches

By splitting the crossbar switch into small chunks and interconnecting them, it is possible to build multistage switches with many fewer crosspoints. These are called **space division switches**. Two configurations are illustrated in Fig. 2-39.

To keep our example simple, we will consider only three-stage switches, but

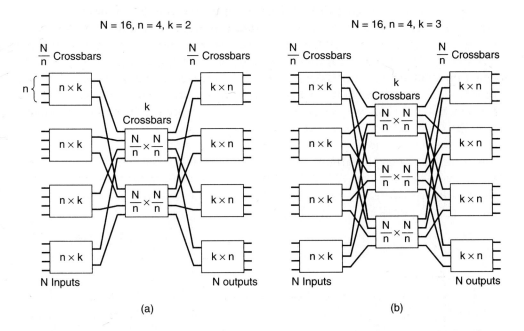

Fig. 2-39. Two space division switches with different parameters.

switches with more stages are also possible. In these examples, we have a total of N inputs and N outputs. Instead of building a single $N \times N$ crossbar, we build the switch out of smaller rectangular crossbars. In the first stage, each crossbar has n inputs, so we need N/n of them to handle all N incoming lines.

The second stage has k crossbars, each with N/n inputs and N/n outputs. The third stage is a repeat of the first stage, but reversed left to right. Each intermediate crossbar is connected to each input crossbar and each output crossbar. Consequently, it is possible to connect every input to every output using either the first intermediate crossbar in Fig. 2-39(a) or using the second one. In fact, there are two disjoint paths from each input to each output, depending which intermediate crossbar is chosen. In Fig. 2-39(b) there are three paths for each input/output pair. With k intermediate stages (k is a design parameter), there are k disjoint paths.

Let us now compute the number of crosspoints needed for a three-stage switch. In the first stage, there are N/n crossbars, each with nk crosspoints, for a total of Nk. In the second stage, there are k crossbars, each with $(N/n)^2$ crosspoints. The third stage is the same as the first. Adding up the three stages, we get

$$\text{Number of crosspoints} = 2kN + k(N/n)^2$$

For $N = 1000$, $n = 50$ and $k = 10$, we need only 24,000 crosspoints instead of the 499,500 required by a 1000×1000 single-stage crossbar.

Unfortunately, as usual, there is no free lunch. The switch can block. Consider Fig. 2-39(a) again. Stage 2 has eight inputs, so a maximum of eight calls can be connected at once. When call nine comes by, it will have to get a busy signal, even though the destination is available. The switch of Fig. 2-39(b) is better, handling a maximum of 12 calls instead of 8, but it uses more crosspoints. Sometimes when making a phone call you may have gotten a busy signal before you finished dialing. This was probably caused by blocking part way through the network.

It should be obvious that the larger k is, the more expensive the switch and the lower the blocking probability. In 1953, Clos showed that when $k = 2n - 1$, the switch will never block (Clos, 1953). Other researchers have analyzed calling patterns in great detail to construct switches that theoretically can block but do so only rarely in practice.

Time Division Switches

A completely different kind of switch is the **time division switch**, shown in Fig. 2-40. With time division switching, the n input lines are scanned in sequence to build up an input frame with n slots. Each slot has k bits. For T1 switches, the slots are 8 bits, with 8000 frames processed per second.

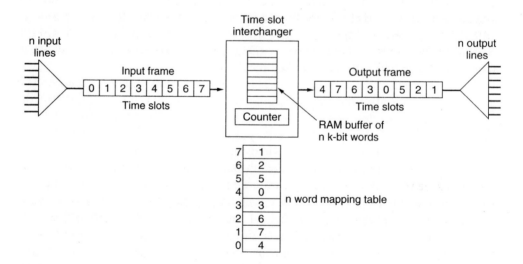

Fig. 2-40. A time division switch.

The heart of the time division switch is the **time slot interchanger**, which accepts input frames and produces output frames in which the time slots have been reordered. In Fig. 2-40, input slot 4 is output first, then slot 7, and so on. Finally, the output frame is demultiplexed, with output slot 0 (input slot 4) going to line 0, and so on. In essence, the switch has moved a byte from input line 4 to output line 0, another byte from input line 7 to output line 1, and so on. Viewed from the outside, the whole arrangement is a circuit switch, even though there are no physical connections.

The time slot interchanger works as follows: When an input frame is ready to be processed, each slot (i.e., each byte in the input frame) is written into a RAM buffer inside the interchanger. The slots are written in order, so buffer word i contains slot i.

After all the slots of the input frame have been stored in the buffer, the output frame is constructed by reading out the words again, but in a different order. A counter goes from 0 to $n - 1$. At step j, the contents of word j of a mapping table is read out and used to address the RAM table. Thus if word 0 of the mapping table contains a 4, word 4 of the RAM buffer will be read out first, and the first slot of the output frame will be slot 4 of the input frame. Thus the contents of the mapping table determine which permutation of the input frame will be generated as the output frame, and thus which input line is connected to which output line.

Time division switches use tables that are linear in the number of lines, rather than quadratic, but they have another limitation. It is necessary to store n slots in the buffer RAM and then read them out again within one frame period of 125 µsec. If each of these memory accesses takes T microsec, the time needed to process a frame is $2nT$ microsec, so we have $2nT = 125$ or $n = 125/2T$. For a memory with 100-nsec cycle time, we can support at most 625 lines. We can also turn this relation around and use it to determine the required memory cycle to support a given number of lines. As with a crossbar switch, it is possible to devise multistage switches that split the work up into several parts and then combine the results in order to handle larger numbers of lines.

2.5. NARROWBAND ISDN

For more than a century, the primary international telecommunication infrastructure has been the public circuit-switched telephone system. This system was designed for analog voice transmission and is inadequate for modern communication needs. Anticipating considerable user demand for an end-to-end digital service (i.e., not like Fig. 2-17 which is part digital and part analog), the world's telephone companies and PTTs got together in 1984 under the auspices of CCITT and agreed to build a new, fully digital, circuit-switched telephone system by the early part of the 21st Century. This new system, called **ISDN** (**Integrated Services Digital Network**), has as its primary goal the integration of voice and nonvoice services. It is already available in many locations and its use is growing slowly. In the following sections we will describe what it does and how it works. For further information, see (Dagdeviren et al., 1994; and Kessler, 1993).

2.5.1. ISDN Services

The key ISDN service will continue to be voice, although many enhanced features will be added. For example, many corporate managers have an intercom button on their telephone that rings their secretaries instantly (no call setup time). One ISDN feature is telephones with multiple buttons for instant call setup to arbitrary telephones anywhere in the world. Another feature is telephones that display the caller's telephone number, name, and address on a display while ringing. A more sophisticated version of this feature allows the telephone to be connected to a computer, so that the caller's database record is displayed on the screen as the call comes in. For example, a stockbroker could arrange that when she answers the telephone, the caller's portfolio is already on the screen along with the current prices of all the caller's stocks. Other advanced voice services include call forwarding and conference calls worldwide.

Advanced nonvoice services are remote electricity meter reading, and on-line medical, burglar, and smoke alarms that automatically call the hospital, police, or fire department, respectively, and give their address to speed up response.

2.5.2. ISDN System Architecture

It is now time to look at the ISDN architecture in detail, particularly the customer's equipment and the interface between the customer and the telephone company or PTT. The key idea behind ISDN is that of the **digital bit pipe**, a conceptual pipe between the customer and the carrier through which bits flow. Whether the bits originated from a digital telephone, a digital terminal, a digital facsimile machine, or some other device is irrelevant. All that matters is that bits can flow through the pipe in both directions.

The digital bit pipe can, and normally does, support multiple independent channels by time division multiplexing of the bit stream. The exact format of the bit stream and its multiplexing is a carefully defined part of the interface specification for the digital bit pipe. Two principal standards for the bit pipe have been developed, a low bandwidth standard for home use and a higher bandwidth standard for business use that supports multiple channels that are identical to the home use channel. Furthermore, businesses may have multiple bit pipes if they need additional capacity beyond what the standard business pipe can provide.

In Fig. 2-41(a) we see the normal configuration for a home or small business. The carrier places a network terminating device, **NT1**, on the customer's premises and connects it to the ISDN exchange in the carrier's office, several kilometers away, using the twisted pair that was previously used to connect to the telephone. The NT1 box has a connector on it into which a passive bus cable can be inserted. Up to eight ISDN telephones, terminals, alarms, and other devices can be connected to the cable, similar to the way devices are connected to a LAN. From the customer's point of view, the network boundary is the connector on NT1.

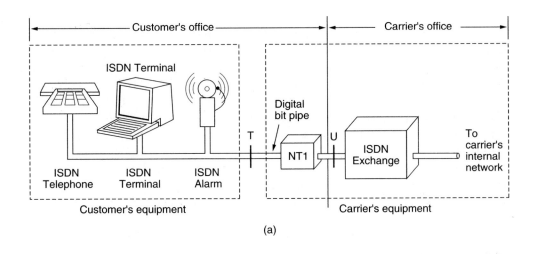

(a)

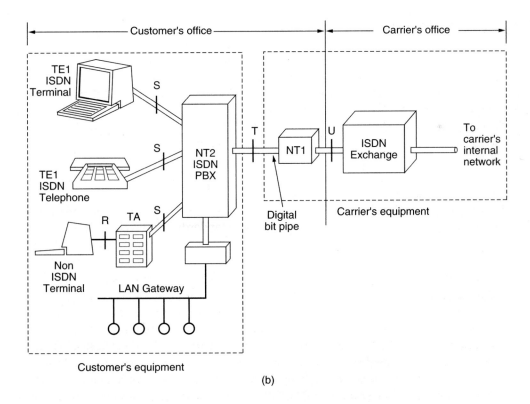

(b)

Fig. 2-41. (a) Example ISDN system for home use. (b) Example ISDN system with a PBX for use in large businesses.

For large businesses, the model of Fig. 2-41(a) is inadequate because it is common to have more telephone conversations going on simultaneously than the bus can handle. Therefore, the model of Fig. 2-41(b) is used. In this model we find a device, **NT2**, called a **PBX (Private Branch eXchange)**, connected to NT1 and providing the real interface for telephones, terminals and other equipment. An ISDN PBX is not very different conceptually from an ISDN switch, although it is usually smaller and cannot handle as many conversations at the same time.

CCITT defined four **reference points**, called **R**, **S**, **T**, and **U**, between the various devices. These are marked in Fig. 2-41. The U reference point is the connection between the ISDN exchange in the carrier's office and NT1. At present it is a two-wire copper twisted pair, but at some time in the future it may be replaced by fiber optics. The T reference point is what the connector on NT1 provides to the customer. The S reference point is the interface between the ISDN PBX and the ISDN terminals. The R reference point is the connection between the terminal adapter and non-ISDN terminals. Many different kinds of interfaces will be used at R.

2.5.3. The ISDN Interface

The ISDN bit pipe supports multiple channels interleaved by time division multiplexing. Several channel types have been standardized:

A - 4-kHz analog telephone channel
B - 64-kbps digital PCM channel for voice or data
C - 8- or-16 kbps digital channel
D - 16-kbps digital channel for out-of-band signaling
E - 64-kbps digital channel for internal ISDN signaling
H - 384-, 1536-, or 1920-kbps digital channel

It was not CCITT's intention to allow an arbitrary combination of channels on the digital bit pipe. Three combinations have been standardized so far:

1. **Basic rate**: 2B + 1D

2. **Primary rate**: 23B + 1D (U.S. and Japan) or 30B + 1D (Europe)

3. **Hybrid**: 1A + 1C

The basic rate and primary rate channels are illustrated in Fig. 2-42.

The basic rate should be viewed as a replacement for **POTS (Plain Old Telephone Service)** for home or small business use. Each of the 64-kbps B channels can handle a single PCM voice channel with 8-bit samples made 8000 times a second (note that 64 kbps means 64,000 here, not 65,536). Signaling is on a separate 16-kbps D channel, so the full 64 kbps are available to the user (as in the CCITT 2.048-Mbps system and unlike the U.S. and Japanese T1 system).

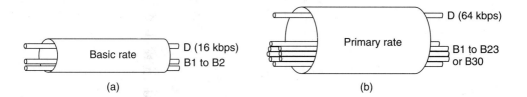

Fig. 2-42. (a) Basic rate digital pipe. (b) Primary rate digital pipe.

Because ISDN is so focused on 64-kbps channels, we refer to it as **N-ISDN** (**Narrowband ISDN**), to contrast it with broadband ISDN (ATM) to be discussed later.

The primary rate interface is intended for use at the T reference point for businesses with a PBX. It has 23 B channels and 1 D channel (at 64 kbps) in the United States and Japan and 30 B channels and 1 D channel (at 64 kbps) in Europe. The 23B + 1D choice was made to allow an ISDN frame fit nicely on AT&T's T1 system. The 30B + 1D choice was made to allow an ISDN frame fit nicely in CCITT's 2.048 Mbps system. The 32nd time slot in the CCITT system is used for framing and general network maintenance. Note that the amount of D channel per B channel in the primary rate is much less than in the basic rate, as it is not expected that there will be much telemetry or low bandwidth packet data there.

2.5.4. Perspective on N-ISDN

N-ISDN was a massive attempt to replace the analog telephone system with a digital one suitable for both voice and nonvoice traffic. Achieving worldwide agreement on the interface standard for the basic rate was supposed to lead to a large user demand for ISDN equipment, thus leading to mass production, economies of scale, and inexpensive VLSI ISDN chips. Unfortunately, the standardization process took years and the technology in this area moved very rapidly, so that once the standard was finally agreed upon, it was obsolete.

For home use, the largest demand for new services will undoubtedly be for video on demand. Unfortunately, the ISDN basic rate lacks the necessary bandwidth by two orders of magnitude. For business use, the situation is even bleaker. Currently available LANs offer at least 10 Mbps and are now being replaced by 100-Mbps LANs. Offering 64-kbps service to businesses in the 1980s was a serious proposition. In the 1990s, it is a joke.

Oddly enough, ISDN may yet be saved, but by a totally unexpected application: Internet access. Various companies now sell ISDN adaptors that combine the 2B + D channels into a single 144-kbps digital channel. Many Internet service providers also support these adaptors. The result is that people can access the

Internet over a 144-kbps fully digital link, instead of a 28.8-kbps analog modem link. For many Internet users, gaining a factor of five for downloading World Wide Web pages full of graphics is a service worth having. While B-ISDN at 155 Mbps is even better, N-ISDN at 144 kbps is here now for an affordable price, and that may be its main niche for the next few years.

2.6. BROADBAND ISDN AND ATM

When CCITT finally figured out that narrowband ISDN was not going to set the world on fire, it tried to think of a new service that might. The result was **broadband ISDN (B-ISDN)**, basically a digital virtual circuit for moving fixed-size packets (cells) from source to destination at 155 Mbps (really 156 Mbps, as mentioned earlier). Since this data rate is even enough for (uncompressed) HDTV, it is likely to satisfy even the biggest bandwidth hogs for at least a few years.

Whereas narrowband ISDN was a timid first step into the digital age, broadband ISDN is a bold leap into the unknown. The benefits are enormous, such as a bandwidth increase over narrowband ISDN by a factor of 2500, but the challenges are equally huge (Armbruster, 1995).

To start with, broadband ISDN is based on ATM technology, and as we discussed briefly in Chap. 1, ATM is fundamentally a packet-switching technology, not a circuit-switching technology (although it can emulate circuit switching fairly well). In contrast, both the existing PSTN and narrowband ISDN are circuit-switching technologies. An enormous amount of engineering experience in circuit switching will be rendered obsolete by this change. Going from circuit switching to packet switching is truly a paradigm shift.

As if that were not enough, broadband ISDN cannot be sent over existing twisted pair wiring for any substantial distance. This means that introducing it will require ripping out most of the local loops and putting in either category 5 twisted pair or fiber (Stephens and Banwell, 1995). Furthermore, space division and time division switches cannot be used for packet switching. They will all have to be replaced by new switches based on different principles and running at much higher speeds. The only things that can be salvaged are the wide area fiber trunks.

In short, throwing out 100 years' accumulated knowledge plus an investment in both inside plant and outside plant worth many hundreds of billions of dollars is not exactly a small step to be taken lightly. Nevertheless, it is clear to the telephone companies that if they do not do it, the cable television companies, thinking about video on demand, probably will. While it is likely that both the existing PSTN and narrowband ISDN will be around for a decade or perhaps even longer, the long-term future probably lies with ATM, so we will study it in great detail in this book, starting with the physical layer in this chapter.

2.6.1. Virtual Circuits versus Circuit Switching

The basic broadband ISDN service is a compromise between pure circuit switching and pure packet switching. The actual service offered is connection oriented, but it is implemented internally with packet switching, not circuit switching. Two kinds of connections are offered: permanent virtual circuits and switched virtual circuits. **Permanent virtual circuits** are requested by the customer manually (e.g., by sending a fax to the carrier) and typically remain in place for months or years. **Switched virtual circuits** are like telephone calls: they are set up dynamically as needed and potentially torn down immediately afterward.

In a circuit-switching network, making a connection actually means a physical path is established from the source to the destination through the network, certainly when space division switches are used. (With time division switches, the concept of "a physical path" is already getting a little fuzzy around the edges.) In a virtual circuit network, like ATM, when a circuit is established, what really happens is that the route is chosen from source to destination, and all the switches (i.e., routers) along the way make table entries so they can route any packets on that virtual circuit. They also have the opportunity to reserve resources for the new circuit. Figure 2-43 shows a single virtual circuit from host H_1 to host H_5 via switches (routers) A, E, C, and D.

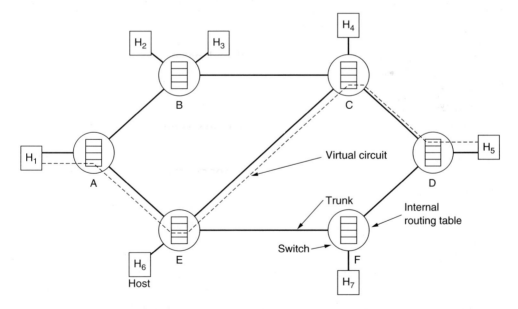

Fig. 2-43. The dotted line shows a virtual circuit. It is simply defined by table entries inside the switches.

When a packet comes along, the switch inspects the packet's header to find out which virtual circuit it belongs to. Then it looks up that virtual circuit in its tables to determine which communication line to send on. We will examine this process in more detail in Chap. 5.

The meaning of the permanent virtual circuit between H_1 and H_5 in Fig. 2-43 should now be clear. It is an agreement between the customer and the carrier that the switches will always hold table entries for a particular destination, even if there has been no traffic for months. Clearly, such an agreement costs resources (certainly table space inside the switches and possibly reserved bandwidth and buffers as well) so there is always a monthly charge per permanent virtual circuit. The advantage over a switched virtual circuit is that there is no setup time. Packets can move instantly. For some applications, such as credit card verification, saving a few seconds on each transaction may easily be worth the cost.

In contrast, a leased line from H_1 to H_5 in a circuit-switched network with the topology of Fig. 2-43 and space division switches would actually hold the crosspoints closed for months and would actually reserve bandwidth on the trunks permanently, either as FDM bands or as time slots (a leased "line" can be multihop if no direct line is available). Such an arrangement is obviously far more wasteful of resources when it is idle than a virtual circuit.

2.6.2. Transmission in ATM Networks

As we have pointed out before, ATM stands for *Asynchronous* Transfer Mode. This mode can be contrasted with the synchronous T1 carrier illustrated in Fig. 2-44(a). One T1 frame is generated precisely every 125 μsec. This rate is governed by a master clock. Slot k of each frame contains 1 byte of data from the same source. T1 is synchronous.

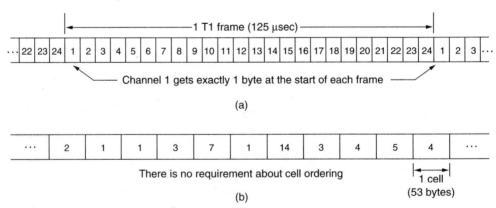

Fig. 2-44. (a) Synchronous transmission mode. (b) Asynchronous transmission mode.

ATM, in contrast, has no requirement that cells rigidly alternate among the various sources. Fig. 2-44(b) shows cells on a line from various sources, with no particular pattern. Cells arrive randomly from different sources.

Furthermore, it is not even required that the stream of cells coming out of a computer be continuous. Gaps between the data cells are possible. Such gaps are filled by special idle cells.

ATM does not standardize the format for transmitting cells. Rather, it specifies that just sending individual cells is allowed but also specifies that cells may be encased in a carrier such as T1, T3, SONET, or FDDI (a fiber optic LAN). For these examples, standards exist telling how cells are packed into the frames these systems provide.

In the original ATM standard, the primary rate was 155.52 Mbps, with an additional rate at four times that speed (622.08 Mbps). These rates were chosen to be compatible with SONET, the framing standard used on fiber optic links throughout the telephone system. ATM over T3 (44.736 Mbps) and FDDI (100 Mbps) is also foreseen.

The transmission medium for ATM is normally fiber optics, but for runs under 100 meters, coax or category 5 twisted pair are also acceptable. Fiber runs can be many kilometers. Each link goes between a computer and an ATM switch, or between two ATM switches. In other words, all ATM links are point-to-point (unlike LANs, which have many senders and receivers on the same cable). Multicasting is achieved by having a cell enter a switch on one line and exit it on multiple lines. Each point-to-point link is unidirectional. For full-duplex operation, two parallel links are needed, one for traffic each way.

The ATM **Physical Medium Dependent** sublayer is concerned with getting the bits on and off the wire. Different hardware is needed for different cables and fibers, depending on the speed and line encoding. The purpose of the transmission convergence sublayer is to provide a uniform interface to the ATM layer in both directions. Outbound, the ATM layer provides a sequence of cells, and the PMD sublayer encodes them as necessary and pushes them out the door as a bit stream.

Inbound, the PMD sublayer takes the incoming bits from the network and delivers a bit stream to the TC sublayer. The cell boundaries are not marked in any way. It is up to the TC sublayer to somehow figure out how to tell where one cell ends and the next one begins. This job is not only difficult, it is theoretically impossible. Thus the TC sublayer clearly has its work cut out for it. Because the TC sublayer is doing cell framing, it is a data link function, so we will discuss it in Chap. 3. For additional information about the ATM physical layer, see (Rao and Hatamian, 1995).

2.6.3. ATM Switches

Many ATM cell switch designs have been described in the literature. Some of these have been implemented and tested. In this section we will give a brief introduction to the principles of ATM cell switch design and illustrate these with a few examples. For more information, see (De Prycker 1993; Garcia-Haro and

Jajszczyk, 1994; Handel et al., 1994; and Partridge, 1994). For an ATM switch optimized for running IP over ATM, see (Parulkar et al., 1995).

The general model for an ATM cell switch is shown in Fig. 2-45. It has some number of input lines and some number of output lines, almost always the same number (because the lines are bidirectional). ATM switches are generally synchronous in the sense of during a cycle, one cell is taken from each input line (if one is present), passed into the internal **switching fabric**, and eventually transmitted on the appropriate output line.

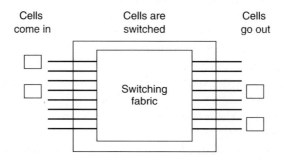

Fig. 2-45. A generic ATM switch.

Switches may be pipelined, that is, it may take several cycles before an incoming cell appears on its output line. Cells actually arrive on the input lines asynchronously, so there is a master clock that marks the beginning of a cycle. Any cell fully arrived when the clock ticks is eligible for switching during that cycle. A cell not fully arrived has to wait until the next cycle.

Cells arrive at ATM speed, normally about 150 Mbps. This works out to slightly over 360,000 cells/sec, which means that the cycle time of the switch has to be about 2.7 μsec. A commercial switch might have anywhere from 16 to 1024 input lines, which means that it must be prepared to accept and start switching a batch of 16 to 1024 cells every 2.7 μsec. At 622 Mbps, a new batch of cells is injected into the switching fabric about every 700 nsec. The fact that the cells are fixed length and short (53 bytes) makes it possible to build such switches. With longer variable-length packets, high-speed switching would be more complex, which is why ATM uses short fixed-length cells.

All ATM switches have two common goals:

1. Switch all cells with as low a discard rate as possible.

2. Never reorder the cells on a virtual circuit.

Goal 1 says that it is permitted to drop cells in emergencies, but that the loss rate should be as small as possible. A loss rate of 1 cell in 10^{12} is probably acceptable. On a large switch, this loss rate is about 1 or 2 cells per hour. Goal 2 says that cells arriving on a virtual circuit in a certain order must also depart in that order, with no exceptions, ever. This constraint makes switch design considerably more difficult, but it is required by the ATM standard.

A problem that occurs in all ATM switches is what to do if the cells arriving at two or more input lines want to go to the same output port in the same cycle. Solving this problem is one of the key issues in the design of all ATM switches. One nonsolution is to pick one cell to deliver and discard the rest. Since this algorithm violates goal 1, we cannot use it.

Our next attempt is to provide a queue for each input line. If two or more cells conflict, one of them is chosen for delivery, and the rest are held for the next cycle. The choice can be made at random, or cyclically, but should not exhibit systematic bias in favor of, for example, the lowest-numbered line to avoid giving lines with low numbers better service than lines with high numbers. Figure 2-46(a) depicts the situation at the start of cycle 1, in which cells have arrived on all four input lines, destined for output lines 2, 0, 2, and 1, respectively. Because there is a conflict for line 2, only one of the cells can be chosen. Suppose that it is the one on input line 0. At the start of cycle 1, shown in Fig. 2-46(b), three cells have been output, but the cell on line 2 has been held, and two more cells have arrived. Only at the start of cycle 4, shown in Fig. 2-46(d), have all the cells cleared the switch.

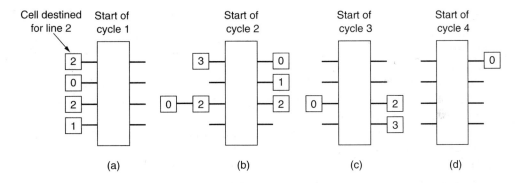

Fig. 2-46. Input queueing at an ATM switch.

The problem with input queueing is that when a cell has to be held up, it blocks the progress of any cells behind it, even if they could otherwise be switched. This effect is called **head-of-line blocking**. It is somewhat more complicated than shown here, since in a switch with 1024 input lines, conflicts may not be noticed until the cells are actually through the switch and fighting over the output line. Keeping a cell on its input queue until a signal comes back saying it made it through the switch requires extra logic, a reverse signaling path, and more delay. What is sometimes done is to put the losing cells on a recirculating bus that sends them back to the input side, but the switch has to be careful where it puts them, to avoid delivering cells from the same virtual circuit out of order.

An alternative design, one that does not exhibit head-of-line blocking does the queueing on the output side, as shown in Fig. 2-47. Here we have the same cell arrival pattern, but now when two cells want to go to the same output line in the same cycle, both are passed through the switch. One of them is put on the output line, and the other is queued on the output line, as shown in Fig. 2-47(b). Here it takes only three cycles, instead of four, to switch all the packets. Karol et al. (1987) have shown that output queueing is generally more efficient than input queueing.

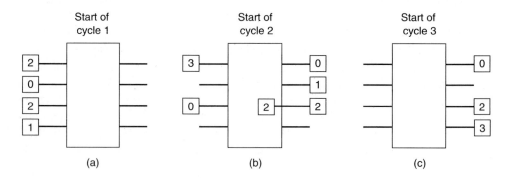

Fig. 2-47. Output queueing at an ATM switch.

The Knockout Switch

Let us now look more carefully at one ATM switch design that uses output queueing. It is called the **knockout switch** (Yeh et al., 1987) and is illustrated in Fig. 2-48 for eight input lines and eight output lines. Each input line is connected to a bus on which incoming cells are broadcast in the cycle they arrive. Having only one bus driver per bus simplifies the design and timing considerably.

For each arriving cell, hardware inspects the cell's header to find its virtual circuit information, looks that up in the routing tables (see Fig. 2-43), and enables the correct crosspoint. The cell then travels along its bus until it gets to the enabled crosspoint, at which time it heads south toward its output line. It is possible for multiple cells, in fact even all of them, to go to the same output line. It is also possible for a cell to be multicast to several output lines by just enabling several crosspoints on its broadcast bus.

The simplest way to handle collisions would be to simply buffer all cells at the output side. However, for a switch with 1024 input lines, in the worst case 1024 output buffers would be needed. In practice, this situation is very unlikely to occur, so a reasonable optimization is to provide far fewer output buffers, say n.

In the unlikely event that more cells arrive in one cycle than can be handled, the concentrator on each line selects out n cells for queueing, discarding the rest. The concentrator is a clever circuit for making this selection in a fair way, using

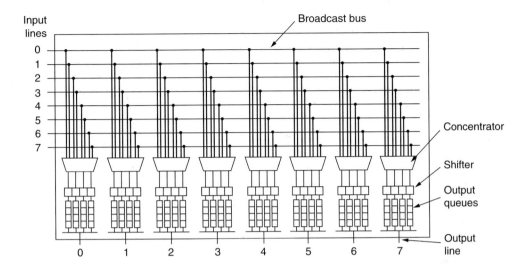

Fig. 2-48. A simplified diagram of the knockout switch.

an elimination (knockout) tournament similar to the quarter finals, semifinals, and finals in many sports tournaments.

Conceptually, all the selected cells go into a single output queue (unless it is full, in which case cells are discarded). However, actually getting all the cells into a single queue in the allotted time is not feasible, so the output queue is simulated by multiple queues. The selected cells go into a shifter, which then distributes them uniformly over n output queues using a token to keep track of which queue goes next, in order to maintain sequencing within each virtual circuit. By varying n, the designers can trade switch cost off against expected cell loss rate.

The Batcher-Banyan Switch

The problem with the knockout switch is that it is basically a crossbar switch, so the number of crosspoints is quadratic in the number of lines. Just as this factor proved to be a problem with circuit switching, it is also a problem with packet switching. The solution for circuit switching was space division switching, which vastly reduced the number of crosspoints, at the cost of requiring a multistage switch. A similar solution is available for packet switching.

This solution is called the **Batcher-banyan switch**. Like knockout switches, Batcher-banyan switches are synchronous, accepting a set of cells (zero or one per input line) on each cycle. Even a simple Batcher-banyan is more complicated than the space division switches of Fig. 2-39, so we will introduce it step by step. In Fig. 2-49(a) we have an 8×8 three-stage banyan switch, so called because its wiring is said to resemble the roots of a banyan tree. In all banyan switches, only one path exists from each input line to each output line. Routing is done by looking up the output line for each cell (based on the virtual circuit information and tables). This 3-bit binary number is then put in front of the cell, as it will be used for routing through the switch.

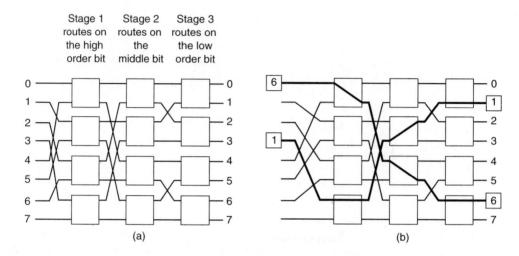

Fig. 2-49. (a) A banyan switch with eight input lines and eight output lines. (b) The routes that two cells take through the banyan switch.

Each of the 12 switching elements in the banyan switch has two inputs and two outputs. When a cell arrives at a switching element, 1 bit of the output line number is inspected, and based on that, the cell is routed either to port 0 (the upper one) or port 1 (the lower one). In the event of a collision, one cell is routed and one is discarded.

A banyan switch parses the output line number from left to right, so stage 1 examines the leftmost (i.e., high-order) bit, stage 2 examines the middle bit, and stage 3 examines the rightmost (i.e., low-order) bit. In Fig. 2-49(b) we have two cells present: a cell on input line 0 heading for output line 6, and a cell on input line 3 heading for output line 1. For the first cell, the binary output address is 110, so it passes through the three stages using the lower, lower, and upper ports, respectively, as shown. Similarly, the other cell, labeled 001 in binary, uses the upper, upper, and lower ports, respectively.

Unfortunately, a collision occurs in a banyan switch when two incoming cells want to exit a switching element via the same port at the same time. A series of such collisions is illustrated in Fig. 2-50(a). In stage 1, the collisions involve the cells heading for the following pairs of output lines: (5, 7), (0, 3), (6, 4), and (2, 1). Suppose that these collisions are resolved in favor of 5, 0, 4, and 1. In the second stage we get collisions between (0, 1) and (5, 4). Here we let 1 and 5 win, and they are then routed to the correct output lines.

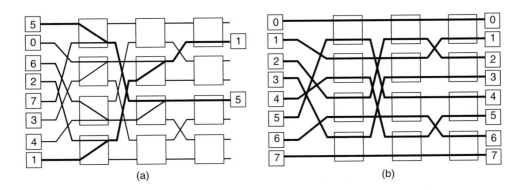

Fig. 2-50. (a) Cells colliding in a banyan switch. (b) Collision-free routing through a banyan switch.

Now look at Fig. 2-50(b). All eight cells get through with no collisions. The conclusion is: depending on the input, the banyan switch can do a good job or a bad job of routing.

The idea behind the Batcher-banyan switch is to put a switch in front of the banyan switch to permute the cells into a configuration that the banyan switch can handle without loss. For example, if the incoming cells are sorted by destination and presented on input lines 0, 2, 4, 6, 1, 3, 5, and 7, in that order as far as necessary (depending on how many cells there are), then the banyan switch does not lose cells.

To sort the incoming cells we can use a Batcher switch, invented by K.E. Batcher (1968). Like the banyan and knockout switches, it too is synchronous and works with discrete cycles. A Batcher switch is built up of 2×2 switching elements, but these work differently than those in the banyan switch. When a switching element receives two cells, it compares their output addresses numerically (thus not just 1 bit) and routes the higher one on the port in the direction of the arrow, and the lower one the other way. If there is only one cell, it goes to the port opposite the way the arrow is pointing.

A Batcher switch for eight lines is depicted on the left in Fig. 2-51. Stage 1 sorts the incoming cells pairwise. The next two stages do a four-way merge. The final three stages do an eight-way merge. In general, for n lines, the complexity of a Batcher switch grows like $n\log^2 n$. When k cells are present on the input lines, the Batcher switch puts the cells in sort order on the first k output lines.

After exiting the Batcher switch, the cells undergo a shuffle and are then injected into a banyan switch. The final result is that every cell appears on the correct output line at the far end of the banyan switch.

An example of how the combined Batcher-banyan switching fabric works is given in Fig. 2-52. Here cells are present on input lines 2, 3, 4, and 5, headed for output lines 6, 5, 1, and 4, respectively. Initially, cells for 5 and 6 enter the same

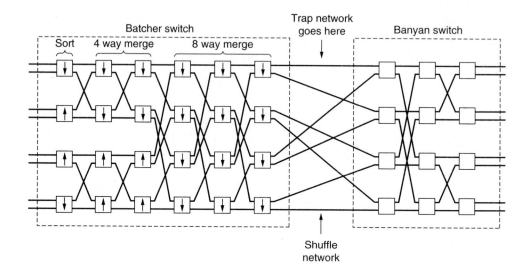

Fig. 2-51. The switching fabric for a Batcher-banyan switch.

switching element. Cell 6 has a higher address, so it exits in the direction of the arrow; cell 5 goes the other way. Here no exchange occurs. With cells 1 and 4, an exchange occurs, with cell 4 entering from the bottom but leaving from the top. The heavy lines show the paths all the way through to the end.

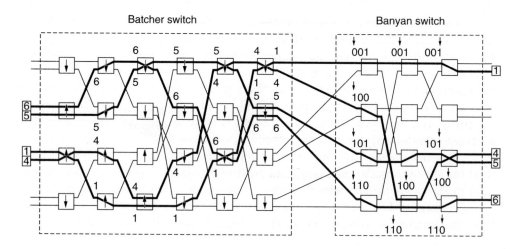

Fig. 2-52. An example with four cells using the Batcher-banyan switch.

Note that at the end of the Batcher switch, the four cells are stacked up at the top, in order. They are then run through a shuffle network and injected into the banyan switch, which is able to process them without collisions.

In principle, the Batcher-banyan switch makes a fine ATM switch, but there are two complications that we have ignored: output line collisions and multicasting. If two or more cells are aimed at the same output line, the Batcher-banyan switch cannot handle them, so we have to go back to some kind of buffering. One way to solve this problem is by inserting a trap network between the Batcher switch and the banyan switch. The job of the trap network is to filter out duplicates and recirculate them for subsequent cycles, all the while maintaining the order of cells on a virtual circuit. (By now it should be clear that the ordering requirement is much more of a problem than it might have at first appeared.) Commercial switches also have to handle multicast.

The first Batcher-banyan ATM switch was designed by Huang and Knauer (1984). It was called Starlite. Then came Moonshine (Hui, 1987) and Sunshine (Giacopelli et al., 1991). You have to admit that these folks have a sense of humor. Starlite, Moonshine, and Sunshine differ primarily in the trap circuit and how they handle multicast.

2.7. CELLULAR RADIO

The traditional telephone system (even when broadband ISDN is fully operational) will still not be able to satisfy a growing group of users: people on the go. Consequently, there is increasing competition from a system that uses radio waves instead of wires and fibers for communication. This system will play an increasingly important role in the networking of notebook computers, shirt-pocket telephones, and personal digital assistants in the coming years. In the following sections we will examine satellite paging, cordless telephones, cellular telephones, and similar technologies. These systems are now merging, producing portable computers capable of sending and receiving phone calls, faxes, and email, as well as looking up information in remote databases, and doing this anywhere on earth.

Such devices are already creating a huge market. Many companies in the computer, telephone, satellite, and other industries want a piece of the action. The result is a chaotic market, with numerous overlapping and incompatible products and services, all rapidly changing, and typically different in every country as well. Nevertheless, the descriptions given below should provide at least a basic knowledge of the underlying technologies. For more information, see (Bates, 1994; Goodman, 1991; Macario, 1993; Padgett et al., 1995; and Seybold, 1994).

2.7.1. Paging Systems

The first paging systems used loudspeakers within a single building. In a hospital it is common to hear announcements on the public address system like: Will Dr. Suzanne Johnson please call extension 4321? Nowadays, people who want to be paged wear small beepers, usually with tiny screens for displaying short incoming messages.

A person wanting to page a beeper wearer can then call the beeper company and enter a security code, the beeper number, and the number the beeper wearer is to call (or another short message). The computer receiving the request then transmits it over land lines to a hilltop antenna, which either broadcasts the page directly (for local paging), or sends it to an overhead satellite (for long-distance paging), which then rebroadcasts it. When the beeper detects its unique number in the incoming radio stream, it beeps and displays the number to be called. It is also possible to page a group of people simultaneously with a single phone call.

The most advanced beeper systems plug directly into a computer and can receive not just a telephone number, but a longer message. The computer can then process the data as they come in. For example, a company could keep the price lists in its salespeoples' portable computers up to date using this form of paging.

Most current paging systems have the property that they are one-way systems, from a single computer out to a large number of receivers. There is no problem about who will speak next, and no contention among many competing users for a small number of channels as there is only one sender in the whole system.

Paging systems require little bandwidth since each message requires only a single burst of perhaps 30 bytes. At this data rate, a 1-Mbps satellite channel can handle over 240,000 pages per minute. The older paging systems run at various frequencies in the 150–174 MHz band. Most of the modern ones run in the 930–932 MHz band. Figure 2-53(a) shows the one-way nature of a paging system, with all communication being outbound at a single frequency. We will later see how this mode contrasts with mobile telephones, which are two way and use two frequencies per call, with different frequency pairs used for different calls, as depicted in Fig. 2-53(b). These differences make the paging system much simpler and less expensive to operate.

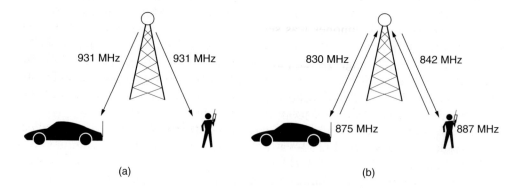

Fig. 2-53. (a) Paging systems are one way. (b) Mobile telephones are two way.

2.7.2. Cordless Telephones

Cordless telephones started as a way to allow people to walk around the house while on the phone. A cordless telephone consists of two parts: a base station and a telephone. These are always sold together. The base station has a standard phone jack at the back so it can be connected (by a wire) to the telephone system. The telephone communicates with the base station by low-power radio. The range is typically 100 to 300 meters.

Because early cordless telephones were only expected to communicate with their own base stations, there was no need for standardization. Some of the cheaper models used a fixed frequency, selected at the factory. If, by accident, your cordless phone happened to use the same frequency as your neighbor's, each of you could listen in on one another's calls. More expensive models avoided this problem by allowing the user to select the transmission frequency.

The first generation of cordless telephones, known as CT-1 in the United States and CEPT-1 in Europe, were entirely analog. They could, and often did, cause interference with radios and televisions. The poor reception and lack of security led the industry to develop a digital standard, CT-2, which originated in England. The first CT-2 devices could make calls, but not receive them, but as soon as the first one was sold, the manufacturer received some negative feedback and the system was quickly redesigned. Like the CT-1 version, each telephone had to be within a few hundred meters of its own base station, making it useful around the house or office, but useless in cars or when walking around town.

In 1992, a third generation, CT-3 or DECT, was introduced, which supported roaming over base stations. This technology is beginning to approach cellular telephones, which we will now describe.

2.7.3. Analog Cellular Telephones

Mobile radiotelephones were used sporadically for maritime and military communication during the early decades of the 20th Century. In 1946, the first system for car-based telephones was set up in St. Louis. This system used a single large transmitter on top of a tall building and had a single channel, used for both sending and receiving. To talk, the user had to push a button that enabled the transmitter and disabled the receiver. Such systems, known as **push-to-talk systems**, were installed in several cities beginning in the late 1950s. CB-radio, taxis, and police cars on television programs often use this technology.

In the 1960s, **IMTS (Improved Mobile Telephone System)** was installed. It, too, used a high-powered (200-watt) transmitter, on top of a hill, but now had two frequencies, one for sending and one for receiving, so the push-to-talk button was no longer needed. Since all communication from the mobile telephones went inbound on a different channel than the telephones listened to, the mobile users could not hear each other (unlike the push-to-talk system used in taxis).

IMTS supported 23 channels spread out from 150 MHz to 450 MHz. Due to the small number of channels, users often had to wait a long time before getting a dial tone. Also, due to the large power of the hilltop transmitter, adjacent systems had to be several hundred kilometers apart to avoid interference. All in all, the system was impractical due to the limited capacity.

Advanced Mobile Phone System

All that changed with **AMPS (Advanced Mobile Phone System)**, invented by Bell Labs and first installed in the United States in 1982. It is also used in England, where it is called TACS, and in Japan, where it is called MCS-L1. In AMPS, a geographic region is divided up into **cells**, typically 10 to 20 km across, each using some set of frequencies. The key idea that gives AMPS far more capacity than all previous systems is using relatively small cells, and reusing transmission frequencies in nearby (but not adjacent) cells. Whereas an IMTS system 100 km across can have one call on each frequency, an AMPS system might have 100 10-km cells in the same area and be able to have 5 to 10 calls on each frequency, in widely separated cells. Furthermore, smaller cells mean less power is needed, which leads to smaller and cheaper devices. Hand-held telephones put out 0.6 watts; transmitters in cars are typically 3 watts, the maximum allowed by the FCC.

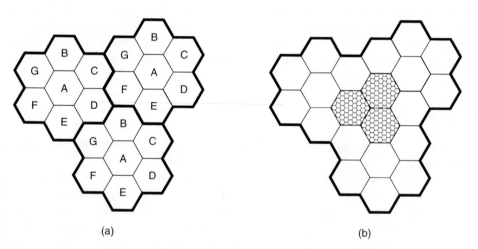

(a)   (b)

Fig. 2-54. (a) Frequencies are not reused in adjacent cells. (b) To add more users, smaller cells can be used.

The idea of frequency reuse is illustrated in Fig. 2-54(a). The cells are normally roughly circular, but they are easier to model as hexagons. In Fig. 2-54(a), the cells are all the same size. They are grouped together in units of seven cells. Each letter indicates a group of frequencies. Notice that for each frequency set, there is a buffer about two cells wide where that frequency is not reused, providing for good separation and low interference.

Finding locations high in the air to place base station antennas is a major issue. This problem has led some telecommunication carriers to forge alliances with the Roman Catholic Church, since the latter owns a substantial number of exalted potential antenna sites worldwide, all conveniently under a single management.

In an area where the number of users has grown to the point where the system is overloaded, the power is reduced and the overloaded cells are split into smaller cells to permit more frequency reuse, as shown in Fig. 2-54(b). How big the cells should be is a complex matter, and is treated in (Hac, 1995).

At the center of each cell is a base station to which all the telephones in the cell transmit. The base station consists of a computer and transmitter/receiver connected to an antenna. In a small system, all the base stations are connected to a single device called an **MTSO** (**Mobile Telephone Switching Office**) or **MSC** (**Mobile Switching Center**). In a larger one, several MTSOs may be needed, all of which are connected to a second-level MTSO, and so on. The MTSOs are essentially end offices as in the telephone system, and are, in fact, connected to at least one telephone system end office. The MTSOs communicate with the base stations, each other, and the PSTN using a packet switching network.

At any instant, each mobile telephone is logically in one specific cell and under the control of that cell's base station. When a mobile telephone leaves a cell, its base station notices the telephone's signal fading away and asks all the surrounding base stations how much power they are getting from it. The base station then transfers ownership to the cell getting the strongest signal, that is, the cell where the telephone is now located. The telephone is then informed of its new boss, and if a call is in progress, it will be asked to switch to a new channel (because the old one is not reused in any of the adjacent cells). This process is called **handoff** and takes about 300 msec. Channel assignment is done by the MTSO, which is the nerve center of the system. The base stations are really just radio relays.

Channels

The AMPS system uses 832 full-duplex channels, each consisting of a pair of simplex channels. There are 832 simplex transmission channels from 824 to 849 MHz, and 832 simplex receive channels from 869 to 894 MHz. Each of these simplex channels is 30 kHz wide. Thus AMPS uses FDM to separate the channels.

In the 800-MHz band, radio waves are about 40 cm long and travel in straight lines. They are absorbed by trees and plants and bounce off the ground and buildings. It is possible that a signal sent by a mobile telephone will reach the base station by the direct path, but also slightly later after bouncing off the ground or a building. This may lead to an echo effect or signal distortion. Sometimes, it is even possible to hear a distant conversation that has bounced several times.

In the United States, the 832 channels in each city are allocated by the FCC. Of these, half are assigned to the local telephone company, the **wireline carrier** or **B-side carrier**. The other half are assigned to a new entrant in the cellular business, the **A-side carrier**. The idea is to make sure there are at least two competing cellular suppliers, to promote competition and lower prices.

However, the distinction between a telephone company and a cellular phone company is now blurred, since most telephone companies have a cellular partner, and in 1994 AT&T merged with McCaw Cellular, the largest cellular operator. It frequently occurs that a company is an A-side carrier in some markets and a B-side carrier in others. Additional mixing occurs because a carrier may sell or trade any or all of its 416 channel licenses.

The 832 channels are divided into four categories:

1. Control (base to mobile) to manage the system.

2. Paging (base to mobile) to alert mobile users to calls for them.

3. Access (bidirectional) for call setup and channel assignment.

4. Data (bidirectional) for voice, fax, or data.

Twenty-one of the channels are reserved for control, and these are wired into a PROM in each telephone. Since the same frequencies cannot be reused in nearby cells, the actual number of voice channels available per cell is much smaller than 832, typically about 45.

Call Management

Each mobile telephone in AMPS has a 32-bit serial number and 10-digit telephone number in its PROM. The telephone number is represented as a 3-digit area code, in 10 bits, and a 7-digit subscriber number, in 24 bits. When a phone is switched on, it scans a preprogrammed list of 21 control channels to find the most powerful signal. Mobile phones are preset to scan for A-side only, B-side only, A-side preferred, or B-side preferred, depending on which service(s) the customer has subscribed to. From the control channel, it learns the numbers of the paging and access channels.

The phone then broadcasts its 32-bit serial number and 34-bit telephone number. Like all the control information in AMPS, this packet is sent in digital form, multiple times, and with an error-correcting code, even though the voice channels themselves are analog.

When the base station hears the announcement, it tells the MTSO, which records the existence of its new customer and also informs the customer's home

MTSO of his current location. During normal operation, the mobile telephone reregisters about once every 15 minutes.

To make a call, a mobile user switches on the phone, enters the number to be called on the keypad, and hits the SEND button. The phone then sends the number to be called and its own identity on the access channel. If a collision occurs there, it tries again later. When the base station gets the request, it informs the MTSO. If the caller is a customer of the MTSO's company (or one of its partners), the MTSO looks for an idle channel for the call. If one is found, the channel number is sent back on the control channel. The mobile phone then automatically switches to the selected voice channel and waits until the called party picks up the phone.

Incoming calls work differently. To start with, all idle phones continuously listen to the paging channel to detect messages directed at them. When a call is placed to a mobile phone (either from a fixed phone or another mobile phone), a packet is sent to the callee's home MTSO to find out where it is. A packet is then sent to the base station in its current cell, which then sends a broadcast on the paging channel of the form: "Unit 14, are you there?" The called phone then responds with "Yes" on the control channel. The base then says something like: "Unit 14, call for you on channel 3." At this point, the called phone switches to channel 3 and starts making ringing sounds.

Security Issues

Analog cellular phones are totally insecure. Anyone with an all-band radio receiver (scanner) can tune in and hear everything going on in a cell. Princess Di and her lover were once caught this way, which resulted in worldwide headlines. Since most cellular users do not realize how insecure the system is, they often give out credit card numbers and other once-confidential information this way.

Another major problem is theft of air time. With an all-band receiver attached to a computer, a thief can monitor the control channel and record the 32-bit serial number and 34-bit telephone numbers of all the mobile telephones it hears. By just driving around for a couple of hours, he can build up a large database. The thief can then pick a number and use it for his calls. This trick will work until the victim gets the bill, weeks later, at which time the thief just picks a new number.

Some thieves offer a low-cost telephone service by making calls for their customers using stolen numbers. Others reprogram mobile telephones with stolen numbers and sell them as phones that can make free calls.

Some of these problems could be solved by encryption, but then the police could not easily perform "wiretaps" on wireless criminals. This subject is very controversial and is discussed in more detail in Chap. 7.

Another issue in the general area of security is vandalism and damage to antennas and base stations. All these problems are quite severe and add up to hundreds of millions of dollars a year in losses for the cellular industry.

2.7.4. Digital Cellular Telephones

First generation cellular systems were analog. The second generation is digital. In the United States there was basically only one system: AMPS. When it was time for digital, three or four competitors emerged, and a struggle for survival began. It now appears that two systems will survive. The first one is backward compatible with the AMPS frequency allocation scheme and is specified in standards known as IS-54 and IS-135. The other is based on direct sequence spread spectrum and is specified in standard IS-95.

IS-54 is dual mode (analog and digital) and uses the same 30-kHz channels that AMPs does. It packs 48.6 kbps in each channel and shares it among three simultaneous users. Each user gets 13 kbps; the rest is control and timing overhead. Cells, base stations, and MTSOs work the same as in AMPS. Only the digital signaling and digital voice encoding is different. The IS-95 system is quite novel. We will discuss it when we get to channel allocation in Chap. 4.

In Europe, the reverse process happened. Five different analog systems were in use, in different countries, so someone with a British phone could not use it in France, and so on. This experience led the European PTTs to agree on a common digital system, called **GSM (Global Systems for Mobile communications)**, which was deployed before any of the competing American systems. The Japanese system is different from all of the above.

Since the European systems were all different, it was simplest to make them pure digital operating in a new frequency band (1.8 GHz), in addition to retrofitting the 900-MHz band where possible. GSM uses both FDM and TDM. The available spectrum is broken up into 50 200-kHz bands. Within each band TDM is used to multiplex multiple users.

Some GSM telephones use smart cards, that is, credit card sized devices containing a CPU. The serial number and telephone number are contained there, not in the telephone, making for better physical security (stealing the phone without the card will not get you the number). Encryption is also used. We will discuss GSM in Chap. 4.

2.7.5. Personal Communications Services

The holy grail of the telephone world is a small cordless phone that you can use around the house and take with you anywhere in the world. It should respond to the same telephone number, no matter where it is, so people only have one telephone number (with AMPS, your home phone and your mobile phone have different numbers). This system is currently under vigorous development (Lipper and Rumsewicz, 1994). In the United States it is called **PCS (Personal Communications Services)**. Everywhere else it is called **PCN (Personal Communications Network)**. In the world of telephony, the United States has something of a tradition of marching to a different drummer than everyone else. Fortunately, most of the technical details are the same.

PCS will use cellular technology, but with microcells, perhaps 50 to 100 meters wide. This allows very low power (1/4 watt), which makes it possible to build very small, light phones. On the other hand, it requires many more cells than the 20-km AMPS cells. If we assume that a microcell is 1/200th the diameter of an AMPS cell, 40,000 times as many cells are required to cover the same area. Even if these microcells are much cheaper than AMPS cells, it is clear that building a complete PCS system from scratch will require a far more massive investment in infrastructure than did AMPS. Some telephone companies have realized that their telephone poles are excellent places to put the toaster-sized base stations, since the poles and wires already exist, thus greatly reducing the installation costs. These small base stations are sometimes called **telepoints**. How many to install and where to put them is a complicated issue (Steele et al., 1995a, 1995b).

The U.S. government (specifically, the FCC) is using PCS to make money out of thin air. In 1994–95 it auctioned off licenses to use the PCS spectrum (1.7 to 2.3 GHz). The auction raised 7.7 billion dollars for the government. This auction replaced the previous system of awarding frequency bands by lottery, thus eliminating the practice of companies with no interest in telecommunication entering the lottery. Any such company winning a frequency could instantly sell it to one of the losers for millions of dollars.

Unfortunately, there is no such thing as a free lunch, not even for the government. The 1.7- to 2.3-GHz band is already completely allocated to other users. These users will be given spectrum elsewhere and told to move there. The trouble is, antenna size depends on frequency, so this forced frequency reallocation will require a multibillion dollar investment in antennas, transmitters, etc. to be thrown away. Hordes of lobbyists are roaming around Washington with suggestions as to who should pay for all this. The net result is that PCS may not be widely deployed in this millenium. For a more rational way to deal with the spectrum, see (Youssef et al., 1995).

2.8. COMMUNICATION SATELLITES

In the 1950s and early 1960s, people tried to set up communication systems by bouncing signals off metallized weather balloons. Unfortunately, the received signals were too weak to be of any practical use. Then the U.S. Navy noticed a kind of permanent weather balloon in the sky—the moon—and built an operational system for ship-to-shore communication by bouncing signals off it.

Further progress in the celestial communication field had to wait until the first communication satellite was launched in 1962. The key difference between an artificial satellite and a real one is that the artificial one can amplify the signals before sending them back, turning a strange curiosity into a powerful communication system.

Communication satellites have some interesting properties that make them attractive for many applications. A communication satellite can be thought of as a big microwave repeater in the sky. It contains several **transponders**, each of which listens to some portion of the spectrum, amplifies the incoming signal, and then rebroadcasts it at another frequency, to avoid interference with the incoming signal. The downward beams can be broad, covering a substantial fraction of the earth's surface, or narrow, covering an area only hundreds of kilometers in diameter.

2.8.1. Geosynchronous Satellites

According to Kepler's law, the orbital period of a satellite varies as the orbital radius to the 3/2 power. Near the surface of the earth, the period is about 90 min. Communication satellites at such low altitudes are problematic because they are within sight of any given ground station for only a short time interval.

However, at an altitude of approximately 36,000 km above the equator, the satellite period is $24^{\dagger}$ hours, so it revolves at the same rate as the earth under it. An observer looking at a satellite in a circular equatorial orbit sees the satellite hang in a fixed spot in the sky, apparently motionless. Having the satellite be fixed in the sky is extremely desirable, because otherwise an expensive steerable antenna would be needed to track it.

With current technology, it is unwise to have satellites spaced much closer than 2 degrees in the 360-degree equatorial plane, to avoid interference. With a spacing of 2 degrees, there can only be 360/2 = 180 geosynchronous communication satellites in the sky at once. Some of these orbit slots are reserved for other classes of users (e.g., television broadcasting, government and military use, etc.).

Fortunately, satellites using different parts of the spectrum do not compete, so each of the 180 possible satellites could have several data streams going up and down simultaneously. Alternatively, two or more satellites could occupy one orbit slot if they operate at different frequencies.

To prevent total chaos in the sky, there have been international agreements about who may use which orbit slots and frequencies. The main commercial bands are listed in Fig. 2-55. The C band was the first to be designated for commercial satellite traffic. Two frequency ranges are assigned in it, the lower one for downlink traffic (from the satellite) and the upper one for uplink traffic (to the satellite). For a full-duplex connection one channel each way is required. These bands are already overcrowded because they are also used by the common carriers for terrestrial microwave links.

The next highest band available to commercial telecommunication carriers is

---

† For the purist, the rotation rate is the sidereal day: 23 hours 56 minutes 4.09 seconds.

Band	Frequencies	Downlink (GHz)	Uplink (GHz)	Problems
C	4/6	3.7–4.2	5.925–6.425	Terrestrial interference
Ku	11/14	11.7–12.2	14.0–14.5	Rain
Ka	20/30	17.7–21.7	27.5–30.5	Rain; equipment cost

Fig. 2-55. The principal satellite bands.

the Ku band. This band is not (yet) congested, and at these frequencies satellites can be spaced as close as 1 degree. However, another problem exists: rain. Water is an excellent absorber of these short microwaves. Fortunately, heavy storms are usually localized, so by using several widely separated ground stations instead of just one, the problem can be circumvented at the price of extra antennas, extra cables, and extra electronics to switch rapidly between stations. Bandwidth has also been allocated in the Ka band for commercial satellite traffic, but the equipment needed to use them is still expensive. In addition to these commercial bands, many government and military bands also exist.

A typical satellite has 12–20 transponders, each with a 36–50-MHz bandwidth. A 50-Mbps transponder can be used to encode a single 50-Mbps data stream, 800 64-kbps digital voice channels, or various other combinations. Furthermore, two transponders can use different polarizations of the signal, so they can use the same frequency range without interfering. In the earliest satellites, the division of the transponders into channels was static, by splitting the bandwidth up into fixed frequency bands (FDM). Nowadays, time division multiplexing is also used due to its greater flexibility.

The first satellites had a single spatial beam that illuminated the entire earth. With the enormous decline in the price, size, and power requirements of microelectronics, a much more sophisticated broadcasting strategy has become possible. Each satellite is equipped with multiple antennas and multiple transponders. Each downward beam can be focused on a small geographical area, so multiple upward and downward transmissions can take place simultaneously. These so-called **spot beams** are typically elliptically shaped, and can be as small as a few hundred km in diameter. A communication satellite for the United States would typically have one wide beam for the contiguous 48 states, plus spot beams for Alaska and Hawaii.

A new development in the communication satellite world is the development of low-cost microstations, sometimes called **VSATs (Very Small Aperture Terminals)** (Ivancic et al., 1994). These tiny terminals have 1-meter antennas and can put out about 1 watt of power. The uplink is generally good for 19.2 kbps, but the downlink is more, often 512 kbps. In many VSAT systems, the microstations do not have enough power to communicate directly with one another (via the satellite, of course). Instead, a special ground station, the **hub**, with a large, high-gain antenna is needed to relay traffic between VSATs, as shown in Fig. 2-56. In this mode of operation, either the sender or the receiver has a large antenna and a powerful amplifier. The trade-off is a longer delay in return for having cheaper end-user stations.

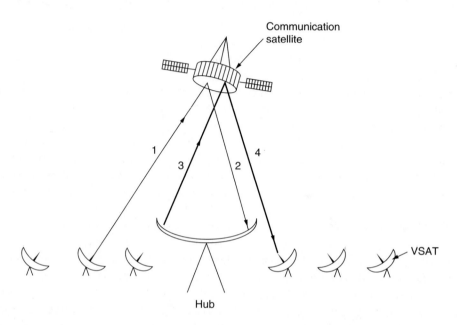

Fig. 2-56. VSATs using a hub.

Communication satellites have several properties that are radically different from terrestrial point-to-point links. To begin with, even though signals to and from a satellite travel at the speed of light (nearly 300,000 km/sec), the large round-trip distance introduces a substantial delay. Depending on the distance between the user and the ground station, and the elevation of the satellite above the horizon, the end-to-end transit time is between 250 and 300 msec. A typical value is 270 msec (540 msec for a VSAT system with a hub).

For comparison purposes, terrestrial microwave links have a propagation delay of roughly 3 μsec/km and coaxial cable or fiber optic links have a delay of approximately 5 μsec/km (electromagnetic signals travel faster in air than in solid materials).

Another important property of satellites is that they are inherently broadcast media. It does not cost more to send a message to thousands of stations within a transponder's footprint than it does to one. For some applications, this property is very useful. Even when broadcasting can be simulated using point-to-point line, satellite broadcasting may be much cheaper. On the other hand, from a security and privacy point of view, satellites are a complete disaster: everybody can hear everything. Encryption is essential when security is required.

Satellites also have the property that the cost of transmitting a message is independent of the distance traversed. A call across the ocean costs no more to service than a call across the street. Satellites also have excellent error rates and can be deployed almost instantly, a major consideration for military communication.

2.8.2. Low-Orbit Satellites

For the first 30 years of the satellite era, low-orbit satellites were rarely used for communication because they zip into and out of view so quickly. In 1990, Motorola broke new ground by filing an application with the FCC asking for permission to launch 77 low-orbit satellites for the Iridium project (element 77 is iridium). The plan was later revised to use only 66 satellites, so the project should have been renamed Dysprosium (element 66), but that probably sounded too much like a disease. The idea was that as soon as one satellite went out of view, another would replace it. This proposal set off a feeding frenzy among other communication companies. All of a sudden, everyone wanted to launch a chain of low-orbit satellites. We will briefly describe the Iridium system here, but the others are similar.

The basic goal of Iridium is to provide worldwide telecommunication service using hand-held devices that communicate directly with the Iridium satellites. It provides voice, data, paging, fax, and navigation service everywhere on earth. This service competes head-on with PCS/PCN and makes the latter unnecessary.

It uses ideas from cellular radio, but with a twist. Normally, the cells are fixed, but the users are mobile. Here, each satellite has a substantial number of spot beams that scan the earth as the satellite moves. Thus both the cells and the users are mobile in this system, but the handover techniques used for cellular radio are equally applicable to the case of the cell leaving the user as to the case of the user leaving the cell.

The satellites are to be positioned at an altitude of 750 km, in circular polar orbits. They would be arranged in north-south necklaces, with one satellite every 32 degrees of latitude. With six satellite necklaces, the entire earth would be covered, as suggested by Fig. 2-57(a). People not knowing much about chemistry can think of this arrangement as a very, very big dysprosium atom, with the earth as the nucleus and the satellites as the electrons.

Each satellite would have a maximum of 48 spot beams, with a total of 1628 cells over the surface of the earth, as shown in Fig. 2-57(b). Frequencies could be reused two cells away, as with conventional cellular radio. Each cell would have 174 full-duplex channels, for a total of 283,272 channels worldwide. Some of these would be for paging and navigation, which require hardly any bandwidth at all. (The paging devices envisioned would display two lines of alphanumeric text.)

The uplinks and downlinks would operate in the L band, at 1.6 GHz, making

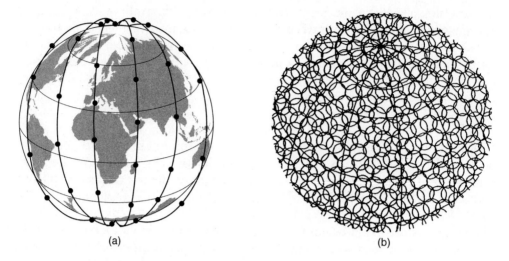

(a)   (b)

Fig. 2-57. (a) The Iridium satellites form six necklaces around the earth.
(b) 1628 moving cells cover the earth.

it possible to communicate with a satellite using a small battery-powered device. Messages received by one satellite but destined for a remote one would be relayed among the satellites in the Ka band. Sufficient bandwidth is available in outer space for the intersatellite links. The limiting factor would be the uplink/downlink segments. Motorola estimates that 200 MHz would be sufficient for the whole system.

The projected cost to the end user is about 3 dollars per minute. If this technology can provide universal service anywhere on earth for that price, it is unlikely that the project will die for lack of customers. Business and other travelers who want to be in touch all the time, even in undeveloped areas, will sign up in droves. However, in developed areas, Iridium will face stiff competition from PCS/PCN with their toaster-on-a-pole telepoints.

2.8.3. Satellites versus Fiber

A comparison between satellite communication and terrestrial communication is instructive. As recently as 20 years ago, a case could be made that the future of communication lay with communication satellites. After all, the telephone system had changed little in the past 100 years and showed no signs of changing in the next 100 years. This glacial movement was caused in no small part by the regulatory environment in which the telephone companies were expected to provide good voice service at reasonable prices (which they did), and in return got a guaranteed profit on their investment. For people with data to transmit, 1200-bps modems were available. That was pretty much all there was.

The introduction of competition in 1984 in the United States and somewhat later in Europe changed all that radically. Telephone companies began replacing their long-haul networks with fiber and introduced high-bandwidth services like SMDS and B-ISDN. They also stopped their long-time practice of charging artificially high prices to long-distance users to subsidize local service.

All of a sudden, terrestrial fiber connections looked like the long-term winner. Nevertheless, communication satellites have some major niche markets that fiber does not (and sometimes, cannot) address. We will now look at a few of these.

While a single fiber has, in principle, more potential bandwidth than all the satellites ever launched, this bandwidth is not available to most users. The fibers that are now being installed are used within the telephone system to handle many long distance calls at once, not to provide individual users with high bandwidth. Furthermore, few users even have access to a fiber channel because the trusty old twisted pair local loop is in the way. Calling up the local telephone company end office at 28.8 kbps will never give more bandwidth than 28.8 kbps, no matter how wide the intermediate link is. With satellites, it is practical for a user to erect an antenna on the roof of the building and completely bypass the telephone system. For many users, bypassing the local loop is a substantial motivation.

For users who (sometimes) need 40 or 50 Mbps, an option is leasing a (44.736-Mbps) T3 carrier. However, this is an expensive undertaking. If that bandwidth is only needed intermittently, SMDS may be a suitable solution, but it is not available everywhere, and satellite service is.

A second niche is for mobile communication. Many people nowadays want to communicate while jogging, driving, sailing, and flying. Terrestrial fiber optic links are of no use to them, but satellite links potentially are. It is possible, however, that a combination of cellular radio and fiber will do an adequate job for most users (but probably not for those airborne or at sea).

A third niche is for situations in which broadcasting is essential. A message sent by satellite can be received by thousands of ground stations at once. For example, an organization transmitting a stream of stock, bond, or commodity prices to thousands of dealers might find a satellite system much cheaper than simulating broadcasting on the ground.

A fourth niche is for communication in places with hostile terrain or a poorly developed terrestrial infrastructure. Indonesia, for example, has its own satellite for domestic telephone traffic. Launching one satellite was much easier than stringing thousands of undersea cables among all the islands in the archipelago.

A fifth niche market for satellites is where obtaining the right of way for laying fiber is difficult or unduly expensive. Sixth, when rapid deployment is critical, as in military communication systems in time of war, satellites win easily.

In short, it looks like the mainstream communication of the future will be terrestrial fiber optics combined with cellular radio, but for some specialized uses, satellites are better. However, there is one caveat that applies to all of this: economics. Although fiber offers more bandwidth, it is certainly possible that terrestrial and satellite communication will compete aggressively on price. If advances in technology radically reduce the cost of deploying a satellite (e.g., some future space shuttle can toss out dozens of satellites on one launch), or low-orbit satellites catch on, it is not certain that fiber will win in all markets.

2.9. SUMMARY

The physical layer is the basis of all networks. Nature imposes two fundamental limits on al channels, and these determine their bandwidth. These limits are the Nyquist limit, which deals with noiseless channels, and the Shannon limit, for noisy channels.

Transmission media can be guided or unguided. The principle guided media are twisted pair, coaxial cable, and fiber optics. Unguided media include radio, microwaves, infrared, and lasers through the air.

A key element in most wide area networks is the telephone system. Its main components are the local loops, trunks, and switches. Local loops are analog, twisted pair circuits, which require modems for transmitting digital data. Trunks are digital, and can be multiplexed in several ways, including FDM, TDM, and WDM. The switches include crossbars, space division switches, and time division switches. Both circuit switching and packet switching are important.

In the future, the telephone system will be digital from end to end and will carry both voice and nonvoice traffic over the same lines. Two variants of this new system, known as ISDN, are being introduced. Narrowband ISDN is a circuit-switched digital system that is an incremental improvement over the current system. In contrast, broadband ISDN represents a paradigm shift, since it is based on cell switching ATM technology. Various kinds of ATM switches exist, including the knockout switch and the Batcher-banyan switch.

For mobile applications, the hard-wired telephone system is not suitable. Alternatives to the telephone system include cellular radio and communication satellites. Cellular radio is now widely used for portable telephones but will soon be common for data traffic as well. The current generation of cellular systems (e.g., AMPS) are analog, but the next generation (e.g., PCS/PCN) will be fully digital. Traditional communication satellites are geosynchronous, but there is now much interest in low-orbit satellite systems such as Iridium.

PROBLEMS

1. Compute the Fourier coefficients for the function $f(t) = t$ $(0 \leq t \leq 1)$.

2. A noiseless 4-kHz channel is sampled every 1 msec. What is the maximum data rate?

3. Television channels are 6 MHz wide. How many bits/sec can be sent if four-level digital signals are used? Assume a noiseless channel.

4. If a binary signal is sent over a 3-kHz channel whose signal-to-noise ratio is 20 dB, what is the maximum achievable data rate?

5. What signal-to-noise ratio is needed to put a T1 carrier on a 50-kHz line?

6. What is the difference between a passive star and an active repeater in a fiber optic network?

7. How much bandwidth is there in 0.1 micron of spectrum at a wavelength of 1 micron?

8. It is desired to send a sequence of computer screen images over an optical fiber. The screen is 480×640 pixels, each pixel being 24 bits. There are 60 screen images per second. How much bandwidth is needed, and how many microns of wavelength are needed for this band at 1.30 microns?

9. Is the Nyquist theorem true for optical fiber, or only for copper wire?

10. In Fig. 2-6 the lefthand band is narrower than the others. Why?

11. Radio antennas often work best when the diameter of the antenna is equal to the wavelength of the radio wave. Reasonable antennas range from 1 cm to 5 meters in diameter. What frequency range does this cover?

12. Multipath fading is maximized when the two beams arrive 180 degrees out of phase. How much of a path difference is required to maximize the fading for a 50 km long 1 GHz microwave link?

13. A laser beam 1 mm wide is aimed at a detector 1 mm wide 100 m away on the roof of a building. How much of an angular diversion (in degrees) does the laser have to have before it misses the detector?

14. A simple telephone system consists of two end offices and a single toll office to which each end office is connected by a 1-MHz full-duplex trunk. The average telephone is used to make four calls per 8-hour workday. The mean call duration is 6 min. Ten percent of the calls are long-distance (i.e., pass through the toll office). What is the maximum number of telephones an end office can support? (Assume 4 kHz per circuit.)

15. A regional telephone company has 10 million subscribers. Each of their telephones is connected to a central office by a copper twisted pair. The average length of these twisted pairs is 10 km. How much is the copper in the local loops worth? Assume that the cross section of each strand is a circle 1 mm in diameter, the specific gravity of copper is 9.0, and that copper sells for 3 dollars per kilogram.

16. The cost of a powerful microprocessor has dropped to the point where it is now possible to include one in each modem. How does that affect the handling of telephone line errors?

17. A modem constellation diagram similar to Fig. 2-19 has data points at the following coordinates: $(1, 1)$, $(1, -1)$, $(-1, 1)$, and $(-1, -1)$. How many bps can a modem with these parameters achieve at 1200 baud?

18. A modem constellation diagram similar to Fig. 2-19 has data points at $(0, 1)$ and $(0, 2)$. Does the modem use phase modulation or amplitude modulation?

19. Does FTTH fit into the telephone company model of end offices, toll offices, and so on, or does the model have to be changed in a fundamental way? Explain your answer.

20. At the low end, the telephone system is star shaped, with all the local loops in a neighborhood converging on an end office. In contrast, cable television consists of a single long cable snaking its way past all the houses in the same neighborhood. Suppose that a future TV cable were 10 Gbps fiber instead of copper. Could it be used to simulate the telephone model of everybody having their own private line to the end office? If so, how many one-telephone houses could be hooked up to a single fiber?

21. A cable TV system has 100 commercial channels, all of them alternating programs with advertising. Is this more like TDM or like FDM?

22. Why has the PCM sampling time been set at 125 μsec?

23. What is the percent overhead on a T1 carrier; that is, what percent of the 1.544 Mbps are not delivered to the end user?

24. Compare the maximum data rate of a noiseless 4-kHz channel using
(a) Analog encoding with 2 bits per sample.
(b) The T1 PCM system.

25. If a T1 carrier system slips and loses track of where it is, it tries to resynchronize using the 1st bit in each frame. How many frames will have to be inspected on the average to resynchronize with a probability of 0.001 of being wrong?

26. What is the difference, if any, between the demodulator part of a modem and the coder part of a codec? (After all, both convert analog signals to digital ones.)

27. A signal is transmitted digitally over a 4-kHz noiseless channel with one sample every 125 μsec. How many bits per second are actually sent for each of these encoding methods?
(a) CCITT 2.048 Mbps standard.
(b) DPCM with a 4-bit relative signal value.
(c) Delta modulation.

28. A pure sine wave of amplitude A is encoded using delta modulation, with x samples/sec. An output of +1 corresponds to a signal change of $+A/8$, and an output signal of −1 corresponds to a signal change of $-A/8$. What is the highest frequency that can be tracked without cumulative error?

29. SONET clocks have a drift rate of about 1 part in 10^9. How long does it take for the drift to equal the width of 1 bit? What are the implications of this calculation?

30. In Fig. 2-32, the user data rate for OC-3 is stated to be 148.608 Mbps. Show how this number can be derived from the SONET OC-3 parameters.

31. What is the available user bandwidth in an OC-12c connection?

32. Three packet-switching networks each contain n nodes. The first network has a star topology with a central switch, the second is a (bidirectional) ring, and the third is fully interconnected, with a wire from every node to every other node. What are the best, average, and worst case transmission paths in hops?

33. Compare the delay in sending an x-bit message over a k-hop path in a circuit-switched network and in a (lightly loaded) packet-switched network. The circuit setup time is s sec, the propagation delay is d sec per hop, the packet size is p bits, and the data rate is b bps. Under what conditions does the packet network have a lower delay?

34. Suppose that x bits of user data are to be transmitted over a k-hop path in a packet-switched network as a series of packets, each containing p data bits and h header bits, with $x \gg p + h$. The bit rate of the lines is b bps and the propagation delay is negligible. What value of p minimizes the total delay?

35. How many crosspoints do the switches of Fig. 2-39(a) and Fig. 2-39(b) have? Compare this to a full 16×16 single-stage crossbar switch.

36. In the space division switch of Fig. 2-39(a), what is the smallest number of existing connections that can block a new outgoing call?

37. An alternative design to that of Fig. 2-39(a) is one in which the 16 lines are divided into two blocks of eight, instead of four blocks of four (i.e., $n = 8$ instead of $n = 4$). Such a design would save on hardware costs, since only two concentrators would be needed on the input and output sides. What is the strongest argument against this alternative?

38. How many lines can a time division switch handle if the RAM access time is 50 nsec?

39. How many bits of RAM buffer does a time switch interchanger need if the input line samples are 10 bits and there are 80 input lines?

40. Does time division switching necessarily introduce a minimum delay at each switching stage? If so, what is it?

41. How long does it take to transmit an 8 inch by 10 inch image by facsimile over an ISDN B channel? The facsimile digitizes the image into 300 pixels per inch and assigns 4 bits per pixel. Current FAX machines go faster than this over ordinary telephone lines. How do you think they do it?

42. Give an advantage and a disadvantage of NT12 (as opposed to NT1 and NT2) in an ISDN network.

43. In Fig. 2-50(a) we saw collisions between cells traveling through a banyan switch. These collisions occurred in the first and second stages. Can collisions also occur in the third stage? If so, under what conditions?

44. For this problem you are to route some cells through a Batcher-banyan ATM switch step by step. Four cells are present on input lines 0 through 3, headed for 3, 5, 2, and 1 respectively. For each of the six stages in the Batcher switch and the four steps in the banyan switch (including the input and output), list which cells are there as an eight-tuple (cell on line 0, cell on line 1, and so on). Indicate lines with no cell by –.

45. Now repeat the previous problem starting from $(7, -, 6, -, 5, -4, -)$.

46. An ATM switch has 1024 input lines and 1024 output lines. The lines operate at the SONET rate of 622 Mbps, which gives a user rate of approximately 594 Mbps. What aggregate bandwidth does the switch need to handle the load? How many cells per second must it be able to process?

47. In a typical cellular telephone system with hexagonal cells, it is forbidden to reuse a frequency band in an adjacent cell. If a total of 840 frequencies are available, how many can be used in a given cell?

48. Make a rough estimate of the number of PCS microcells 100 m in diameter it would take to cover San Francisco (120 square km).

49. Sometimes when a cellular user crosses the boundary from one cell to another, the current call is abruptly terminated, even though all transmitters and receivers are functioning perfectly. Why?

50. The 66 low-orbit satellites in the Iridium project are divided into six necklaces around the earth. At the altitude they are using, the period is 90 minutes. What is the average interval for handoffs for a stationary transmitter?

3

THE DATA LINK LAYER

In this chapter we will study the design of layer 2, the data link layer. This study deals with the algorithms for achieving reliable, efficient communication between two adjacent machines at the data link layer. By adjacent, we mean that the two machines are physically connected by a communication channel that acts conceptually like a wire (e.g., a coaxial cable or a telephone line). The essential property of a channel that makes it "wire-like" is that the bits are delivered in exactly the same order in which they are sent.

At first you might think this problem is so trivial that there is no software to study—machine A just puts the bits on the wire, and machine B just takes them off. Unfortunately, communication circuits make errors occasionally. Furthermore, they have only a finite data rate, and there is a nonzero propagation delay between the time a bit is sent and the time it is received. These limitations have important implications for the efficiency of the data transfer. The protocols used for communications must take all these factors into consideration. These protocols are the subject of this chapter.

After an introduction to the key design issues present in the data link layer, we will start our study of its protocols by looking at the nature of errors, their causes, and how they can be detected and corrected. Then we will study a series of increasingly complex protocols, each one solving more and more of the problems present in this layer. Finally, we will conclude with an examination of protocol modeling and correctness and give some examples of data link protocols.

3.1. DATA LINK LAYER DESIGN ISSUES

The data link layer has a number of specific functions to carry out. These functions include providing a well-defined service interface to the network layer, determining how the bits of the physical layer are grouped into frames, dealing with transmission errors, and regulating the flow of frames so that slow receivers are not swamped by fast senders. In the following sections we will examine each of these issues in turn.

3.1.1. Services Provided to the Network Layer

The function of the data link layer is to provide services to the network layer. The principal service is transferring data from the network layer on the source machine to the network layer on the destination machine. On the source machine there is an entity, call it a process, in the network layer that hands some bits to the data link layer for transmission to the destination. The job of the data link layer is to transmit the bits to the destination machine, so they can be handed over to the network layer there, as shown in Fig. 3-1(a). The actual transmission follows the path of Fig. 3-1(b), but it is easier to think in terms of two data link layer processes communicating using a data link protocol. For this reason, we will implicitly use the model of Fig. 3-1(a) throughout this chapter.

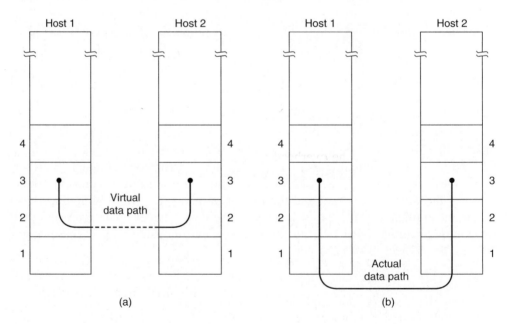

Fig. 3-1. (a) Virtual communication. (b) Actual communication.

The data link layer can be designed to offer various services. The actual services offered can vary from system to system. Three reasonable possibilities that are commonly provided are

1. Unacknowledged connectionless service.

2. Acknowledged connectionless service.

3. Acknowledged connection-oriented service.

Let us consider each of these in turn.

Unacknowledged connectionless service consists of having the source machine send independent frames to the destination machine without having the destination machine acknowledge them. No connection is established beforehand or released afterward. If a frame is lost due to noise on the line, no attempt is made to recover it in the data link layer. This class of service is appropriate when the error rate is very low so recovery is left to higher layers. It is also appropriate for real-time traffic, such as speech, in which late data are worse than bad data. Most LANs use unacknowledged connectionless service in the data link layer.

The next step up in terms of reliability is acknowledged connectionless service. When this service is offered, there are still no connections used, but each frame sent is individually acknowledged. In this way, the sender knows whether or not a frame has arrived safely. If it has not arrived within a specified time interval, it can be sent again. This service is useful over unreliable channels, such as wireless systems.

It is perhaps worth emphasizing that providing acknowledgements in the data link layer is just an optimization, never a requirement. The transport layer can always send a message and wait for it to be acknowledged. If the acknowledgement is not forthcoming before the timer goes off, the sender can just send the entire message again. The trouble with this strategy is that if the average message is broken up into, say, 10 frames, and 20 percent of all frames are lost, it may take a very long time for the message to get through. If individual frames are acknowledged and retransmitted, entire messages get through much faster. On reliable channels, such as fiber, the overhead of a heavyweight data link protocol may be unnecessary, but on wireless channels it is well worth the cost due to their inherent unreliability.

Getting back to our services, the most sophisticated service the data link layer can provide to the network layer is connection-oriented service. With this service, the source and destination machines establish a connection before any data are transferred. Each frame sent over the connection is numbered, and the data link layer guarantees that each frame sent is indeed received. Furthermore, it guarantees that each frame is received exactly once and that all frames are received in the right order. With connectionless service, in contrast, it is conceivable that a lost acknowledgement causes a frame to be sent several times and thus received several times. Connection-oriented service, in contrast, provides the network layer processes with the equivalent of a reliable bit stream.

When connection-oriented service is used, transfers have three distinct phases. In the first phase the connection is established by having both sides initialize variables and counters needed to keep track of which frames have been received and which ones have not. In the second phase, one or more frames are actually transmitted. In the third and final phase, the connection is released, freeing up the variables, buffers, and other resources used to maintain the connection.

Consider a typical example: a WAN subnet consisting of routers connected by point-to-point leased telephone lines. When a frame arrives at a router, the hardware verifies the checksum and passes the frame to the data link layer software (which might be embedded in a chip on the network adaptor board). The data link layer software checks to see if this is the frame expected, and if so, gives the packet contained in the payload field to the routing software. The routing software chooses the appropriate outgoing line and passes the packet back down to the data link layer software, which then transmits it. The flow over two routers is shown in Fig. 3-2.

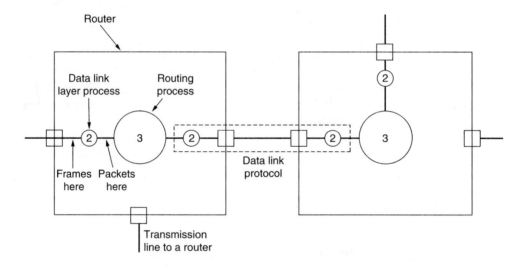

Fig. 3-2. Placement of the data link protocol.

The routing code frequently wants the job done right, that is, reliable, sequenced connections on each of the point-to-point lines. It does not want to be bothered too often with packets that got lost on the way. It is up to the data link protocol, shown in the dotted rectangle, to make unreliable communication lines look perfect, or at least, fairly good. This property is especially important for wireless links, which are inherently very unreliable. As an aside, although we have shown multiple copies of the data link layer software in each router, in fact, one copy handles all the lines, with different tables and data structures for each one.

Although this chapter is explicitly about the data link layer and the data link protocols, many of the principles we will study here, such as error control and flow control, are also found in transport and other protocols as well.

3.1.2. Framing

In order to provide service to the network layer, the data link layer must use the service provided to it by the physical layer. What the physical layer does is accept a raw bit stream and attempt to deliver it to the destination. This bit stream is not guaranteed to be error free. The number of bits received may be less than, equal to, or more than the number of bits transmitted, and they may have different values. It is up to the data link layer to detect, and if necessary, correct errors.

The usual approach is for the data link layer to break the bit stream up into discrete frames and compute the checksum for each frame. (Checksum algorithms will be discussed later in this chapter.) When a frame arrives at the destination, the checksum is recomputed. If the newly computed checksum is different from the one contained in the frame, the data link layer knows that an error has occurred and takes steps to deal with it (e.g., discarding the bad frame and sending back an error report).

Breaking the bit stream up into frames is more difficult than it at first appears. One way to achieve this framing is to insert time gaps between frames, much like the spaces between words in ordinary text. However, networks rarely make any guarantees about timing, so it is possible these gaps might be squeezed out, or other gaps might be inserted during transmission.

Since it is too risky to count on timing to mark the start and end of each frame, other methods have been devised. In this section we will look at four methods:

1. Character count.

2. Starting and ending characters, with character stuffing.

3. Starting and ending flags, with bit stuffing.

4. Physical layer coding violations.

The first framing method uses a field in the header to specify the number of characters in the frame. When the data link layer at the destination sees the character count, it knows how many characters follow, and hence where the end of the frame is. This technique is shown in Fig. 3-3(a) for four frames of sizes 5, 5, 8, and 9 characters respectively.

The trouble with this algorithm is that the count can be garbled by a transmission error. For example, if the character count of 5 in the second frame of Fig. 3-3(b) becomes a 7, the destination will get out of synchronization and will be unable to locate the start of the next frame. Even if the checksum is incorrect so the destination knows that the frame is bad, it still has no way of telling where the

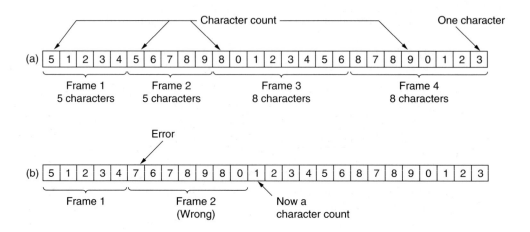

Fig. 3-3. A character stream. (a) Without errors. (b) With one error.

next frame starts. Sending a frame back to the source asking for a retransmission does not help either, since the destination does not know how many characters to skip over to get to the start of the retransmission. For this reason, the character count method is rarely used anymore.

The second framing method gets around the problem of resynchronization after an error by having each frame start with the ASCII character sequence DLE STX and end with the sequence DLE ETX. (DLE is Data Link Escape, STX is Start of TeXt, and ETX is End of TeXt.) In this way, if the destination ever loses track of the frame boundaries, all it has to do is look for DLE STX or DLE ETX characters to figure out where it is.

A serious problem occurs with this method when binary data, such as object programs or floating-point numbers, are being transmitted. It may easily happen that the characters for DLE STX or DLE ETX occur in the data, which will interfere with the framing. One way to solve this problem is to have the sender's data link layer insert an ASCII DLE character just before each "accidental" DLE character in the data. The data link layer on the receiving end removes the DLE before the data are given to the network layer. This technique is called **character stuffing**. Thus a framing DLE STX or DLE ETX can be distinguished from one in the data by the absence or presence of a single DLE. DLEs in the data are always doubled. Figure 3-4 gives an example data stream before stuffing, after stuffing, and after destuffing.

A major disadvantage of using this framing method is that it is closely tied to 8-bit characters in general and the ASCII character code in particular. As networks developed, the disadvantages of embedding the character code in the framing mechanism became more and more obvious so a new technique had to be developed to allow arbitrary sized characters.

The new technique allows data frames to contain an arbitrary number of bits

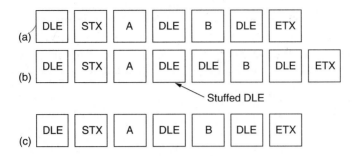

Fig. 3-4. (a) Data sent by the network layer. (b) Data after being character stuffed by the data link layer. (c) Data passed to the network layer on the receiving side.

and allows character codes with an arbitrary number of bits per character. It works like this. Each frame begins and ends with a special bit pattern, 01111110, called a **flag** byte. Whenever the sender's data link layer encounters five consecutive ones in the data, it automatically stuffs a 0 bit into the outgoing bit stream. This **bit stuffing** is analogous to character stuffing, in which a DLE is stuffed into the outgoing character stream before DLE in the data.

When the receiver sees five consecutive incoming 1 bits, followed by a 0 bit, it automatically destuffs (i.e., deletes) the 0 bit. Just as character stuffing is completely transparent to the network layer in both computers, so is bit stuffing. If the user data contain the flag pattern, 01111110, this flag is transmitted as 011111010 but stored in the receiver's memory as 01111110. Figure 3-5 gives an example of bit stuffing.

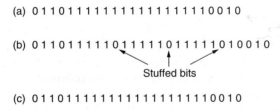

Fig. 3-5. Bit stuffing. (a) The original data. (b) The data as they appear on the line. (c) The data as they are stored in the receiver's memory after destuffing.

With bit stuffing, the boundary between two frames can be unambiguously recognized by the flag pattern. Thus if the receiver loses track of where it is, all it has to do is scan the input for flag sequences, since they can only occur at frame boundaries and never within the data.

The last method of framing is only applicable to networks in which the encoding on the physical medium contains some redundancy. For example, some LANs encode 1 bit of data by using 2 physical bits. Normally, a 1 bit is a high-low pair and a 0 bit is a low-high pair. The combinations high-high and low-low are not used for data. The scheme means that every data bit has a transition in the middle, making it easy for the receiver to locate the bit boundaries. This use of invalid physical codes is part of the 802 LAN standard, which we will study in Chap. 4.

As a final note on framing, many data link protocols use a combination of a character count with one of the other methods for extra safety. When a frame arrives, the count field is used to locate the end of the frame. Only if the appropriate delimiter is present at that position and the checksum is correct, is the frame accepted as valid. Otherwise, the input stream is scanned for the next delimiter.

3.1.3. Error Control

Having solved the problem of marking the start and end of each frame, we come to the next problem: how to make sure all frames are eventually delivered to the network layer at the destination, and in the proper order. Suppose that the sender just kept outputting frames without regard to whether they were arriving properly. This might be fine for unacknowledged connectionless service but would most certainly not be fine for reliable, connection-oriented service.

The usual way to ensure reliable delivery is to provide the sender with some feedback about what is happening at the other end of the line. Typically the protocol calls for the receiver to send back special control frames bearing positive or negative acknowledgements about the incoming frames. If the sender receives a positive acknowledgement about a frame, it knows the frame has arrived safely. On the other hand, a negative acknowledgement means that something has gone wrong, and the frame must be transmitted again.

An additional complication comes from the possibility that hardware troubles may cause a frame to vanish completely (e.g., in a noise burst). In this case, the receiver will not react at all, since it has no reason to react. It should be clear that a protocol in which the sender transmitted a frame and then waited for an acknowledgement, positive or negative, would hang forever if a frame were ever completely lost due to malfunctioning hardware.

This possibility is dealt with by introducing timers into the data link layer. When the sender transmits a frame, it generally also starts a timer. The timer is set to go off after an interval long enough for the frame to reach the destination, be processed there, and have the acknowledgement propagate back to the sender. Normally, the frame will be correctly received and the acknowledgement will get back before the timer runs out, in which case it will be canceled.

However, if either the frame or the acknowledgement is lost, the timer will go off, alerting the sender to a potential problem. The obvious solution is to just transmit the frame again. However, when frames may be transmitted multiple times there is a danger that the receiver will accept the same frame two or more times, and pass it to the network layer more than once. To prevent this from happening, it is generally necessary to assign sequence numbers to outgoing frames, so that the receiver can distinguish retransmissions from originals.

The whole issue of managing the timers and sequence numbers so as to ensure that each frame is ultimately passed to the network layer at the destination exactly once, no more and no less, is an important part of the data link layer's duties. Later in this chapter, we will study in detail how this management is done by looking at a series of increasingly sophisticated examples.

3.1.4. Flow Control

Another important design issue that occurs in the data link layer (and higher layers as well) is what to do with a sender that systematically wants to transmit frames faster than the receiver can accept them. This situation can easily occur when the sender is running on a fast (or lightly loaded) computer and the receiver is running on a slow (or heavily loaded) machine. The sender keeps pumping the frames out at a high rate until the receiver is completely swamped. Even if the transmission is error free, at a certain point the receiver will simply not be able to handle the frames as they arrive and will start to lose some. Clearly, something has to be done to prevent this situation.

The usual solution is to introduce **flow control** to throttle the sender into sending no faster than the receiver can handle the traffic. This throttling generally requires some kind of a feedback mechanism, so the sender can be made aware of whether or not the receiver is able to keep up.

Various flow control schemes are known, but most of them use the same basic principle. The protocol contains well-defined rules about when a sender may transmit the next frame. These rules often prohibit frames from being sent until the receiver has granted permission, either implicitly or explicitly. For example, when a connection is set up, the receiver might say: "You may send me n frames now, but after they have been sent, do not send any more until I have told you to continue." In this chapter, we will study various flow control mechanisms based on this principle. In subsequent chapters, we will study other mechanisms.

3.2. ERROR DETECTION AND CORRECTION

As we saw in Chap. 2, the telephone system has three parts: the switches, the interoffice trunks, and the local loops. The first two are now almost entirely digital in the United States and some other countries. The local loops are still analog twisted copper pairs everywhere and will continue to be so for decades due to the enormous expense of replacing them. While errors are rare on the digital part, they are still common on the local loops. Furthermore, wireless communication is becoming more common, and the error rates here are orders of magnitude worse than on the interoffice fiber trunks. The conclusion is: transmission errors are going to be a fact of life for many years to come.

As a result of the physical processes that generate them, errors on some media (e.g., radio) tend to come in bursts rather than singly. Having the errors come in bursts has both advantages and disadvantages over isolated single-bit errors. On the advantage side, computer data are always sent in blocks of bits. Suppose that the block size is 1000 bits, and the error rate is 0.001 per bit. If errors were independent, most blocks would contain an error. If the errors came in bursts of 100 however, only one or two blocks in 100 would be affected, on the average. The disadvantage of burst errors is that they are much harder to detect and correct than are isolated errors.

3.2.1. Error-Correcting Codes

Network designers have developed two basic strategies for dealing with errors. One way is to include enough redundant information along with each block of data sent to enable the receiver to deduce what the transmitted character must have been. The other way is to include only enough redundancy to allow the receiver to deduce that an error occurred, but not which error, and have it request a retransmission. The former strategy uses **error-correcting codes** and the latter uses **error-detecting codes**.

To understand how errors can be handled, it is necessary to look closely at what an error really is. Normally, a frame consists of m data (i.e., message) bits and r redundant, or check bits. Let the total length be n (i.e., $n = m + r$). An n-bit unit containing data and checkbits is often referred to as an n-bit **codeword**.

Given any two codewords, say, 10001001 and 10110001, it is possible to determine how many corresponding bits differ. In this case, 3 bits differ. To determine how many bits differ, just EXCLUSIVE OR the two codewords, and count the number of 1 bits in the result. The number of bit positions in which two codewords differ is called the **Hamming distance** (Hamming, 1950). Its significance is that if two codewords are a Hamming distance d apart, it will require d single-bit errors to convert one into the other.

In most data transmission applications, all 2^m possible data messages are legal, but due to the way the check bits are computed, not all of the 2^n possible codewords are used. Given the algorithm for computing the check bits, it is possible to construct a complete list of the legal codewords, and from this list find the two codewords whose Hamming distance is minimum. This distance is the Hamming distance of the complete code.

The error-detecting and error-correcting properties of a code depend on its Hamming distance. To detect d errors, you need a distance $d + 1$ code because with such a code there is no way that d single-bit errors can change a valid codeword into another valid codeword. When the receiver sees an invalid codeword, it can tell that a transmission error has occurred. Similarly, to correct d errors, you need a distance $2d + 1$ code because that way the legal codewords are so far apart that even with d changes, the original codeword is still closer than any other codeword, so it can be uniquely determined.

As a simple example of an error-detecting code, consider a code in which a single **parity bit** is appended to the data. The parity bit is chosen so that the number of 1 bits in the codeword is even (or odd). For example, when 10110101 is sent in even parity by adding a bit at the end, it becomes 101101011, whereas 10110001 becomes 101100010 with even parity. A code with a single parity bit has a distance 2, since any single-bit error produces a codeword with the wrong parity. It can be used to detect single errors.

As a simple example of an error-correcting code, consider a code with only four valid codewords:

0000000000, 0000011111, 1111100000, and 1111111111

This code has a distance 5, which means that it can correct double errors. If the codeword 0000000111 arrives, the receiver knows that the original must have been 0000011111. If, however, a triple error changes 0000000000 into 0000000111, the error will not be corrected properly.

Imagine that we want to design a code with m message bits and r check bits that will allow all single errors to be corrected. Each of the 2^m legal messages has n illegal codewords at a distance 1 from it. These are formed by systematically inverting each of the n bits in the n-bit codeword formed from it. Thus each of the 2^m legal messages requires $n + 1$ bit patterns dedicated to it. Since the total number of bit patterns is 2^n, we must have $(n + 1)2^m \leq 2^n$. Using $n = m + r$, this requirement becomes $(m + r + 1) \leq 2^r$. Given m, this puts a lower limit on the number of check bits needed to correct single errors.

This theoretical lower limit can, in fact, be achieved using a method due to Hamming (1950). The bits of the codeword are numbered consecutively, starting with bit 1 at the left end. The bits that are powers of 2 (1, 2, 4, 8, 16, etc.) are check bits. The rest (3, 5, 6, 7, 9, etc.) are filled up with the m data bits. Each check bit forces the parity of some collection of bits, including itself, to be even (or odd). A bit may be included in several parity computations. To see which check bits the data bit in position k contributes to, rewrite k as a sum of powers of 2. For example, $11 = 1 + 2 + 8$ and $29 = 1 + 4 + 8 + 16$. A bit is checked by just those check bits occurring in its expansion (e.g., bit 11 is checked by bits 1, 2, and 8).

When a codeword arrives, the receiver initializes a counter to zero. It then examines each check bit, k ($k = 1, 2, 4, 8, \ldots$) to see if it has the correct parity. If not, it adds k to the counter. If the counter is zero after all the check bits have been examined (i.e., if they were all correct), the codeword is accepted as valid. If the counter is nonzero, it contains the number of the incorrect bit. For example, if check bits 1, 2, and 8 are in error, the inverted bit is 11, because it is the only

Char.	ASCII	Check bits
H	1001000	00110010000
a	1100001	10111001001
m	1101101	11101010101
m	1101101	11101010101
i	1101001	01101011001
n	1101110	01101010110
g	1100111	11111001111
	0100000	10011000000
c	1100011	11111000011
o	1101111	00101011111
d	1100100	11111001100
e	1100101	00111000101

Order of bit transmission

Fig. 3-6. Use of a Hamming code to correct burst errors.

one checked by bits 1, 2, and 8. Figure 3-6 shows some 7-bit ASCII characters encoded as 11-bit codewords using a Hamming code. Remember that the data are found in bit positions 3, 5, 6, 7, 9, 10, and 11.

Hamming codes can only correct single errors. However, there is a trick that can be used to permit Hamming codes to correct burst errors. A sequence of k consecutive codewords are arranged as a matrix, one codeword per row. Normally, the data would be transmitted one codeword at a time, from left to right. To correct burst errors, the data should be transmitted one column at a time, starting with the leftmost column. When all k bits have been sent, the second column is sent, and so on. When the frame arrives at the receiver, the matrix is reconstructed, one column at a time. If a burst error of length k occurs, at most 1 bit in each of the k codewords will have been affected, but the Hamming code can correct one error per codeword, so the entire block can be restored. This method uses kr check bits to make blocks of km data bits immune to a single burst error of length k or less.

3.2.2. Error-Detecting Codes

Error-correcting codes are sometimes used for data transmission, for example, when the channel is simplex, so retransmissions cannot be requested, but most often error detection followed by retransmission is preferred because it is more efficient. As a simple example, consider a channel on which errors are isolated and the error rate is 10^{-6} per bit. Let the block size be 1000 bits. To provide error correction for 1000-bit blocks, 10 check bits are needed; a megabit of data would require 10,000 check bits. To merely detect a block with a single 1-bit error, one parity bit per block will suffice. Once every 1000 blocks an extra block (1001 bits) will have to be transmitted. The total overhead for the error detection +

retransmission method is only 2001 bits per megabit of data, versus 10,000 bits for a Hamming code.

If a single parity bit is added to a block and the block is badly garbled by a long burst error, the probability that the error will be detected is only 0.5, which is hardly acceptable. The odds can be improved considerably by regarding each block to be sent as a rectangular matrix n bits wide and k bits high. A parity bit is computed separately for each column and affixed to the matrix as the last row. The matrix is then transmitted one row at a time. When the block arrives, the receiver checks all the parity bits. If any one of them is wrong, it requests a retransmission of the block.

This method can detect a single burst of length n, since only 1 bit per column will be changed. A burst of length $n + 1$ will pass undetected, however, if the first bit is inverted, the last bit is inverted, and all the other bits are correct. (A burst error does not imply that all the bits are wrong; it just implies that at least the first and last are wrong.) If the block is badly garbled by a long burst or by multiple shorter bursts, the probability that any of the n columns will have the correct parity, by accident, is 0.5, so the probability of a bad block being accepted when it should not be is 2^{-n}.

Although the above scheme may sometimes be adequate, in practice, another method is in widespread use: the **polynomial code** (also known as a **cyclic redundancy code** or CRC code). Polynomial codes are based upon treating bit strings as representations of polynomials with coefficients of 0 and 1 only. A k-bit frame is regarded as the coefficient list for a polynomial with k terms, ranging from x^{k-1} to x^0. Such a polynomial is said to be of degree $k - 1$. The high-order (leftmost) bit is the coefficient of x^{k-1}; the next bit is the coefficient of x^{k-2}, and so on. For example, 110001 has 6 bits and thus represents a six-term polynomial with coefficients 1, 1, 0, 0, 0, and 1: $x^5 + x^4 + x^0$.

Polynomial arithmetic is done modulo 2, according to the rules of algebraic field theory. There are no carries for addition or borrows for subtraction. Both addition and subtraction are identical to EXCLUSIVE OR. For example:

10011011	00110011	11110000	01010101
+ 11001010	+ 11001101	− 10100110	− 10101111
01010001	11111110	01010110	11111010

Long division is carried out the same way as it is in binary except that the subtraction is done modulo 2, as above. A divisor is said "to go into" a dividend if the dividend has as many bits as the divisor.

When the polynomial code method is employed, the sender and receiver must agree upon a **generator polynomial**, $G(x)$, in advance. Both the high- and low-order bits of the generator must be 1. To compute the **checksum** for some frame with m bits, corresponding to the polynomial $M(x)$, the frame must be longer than the generator polynomial. The idea is to append a checksum to the end of the frame in such a way that the polynomial represented by the checksummed frame is divisible by $G(x)$. When the receiver gets the checksummed frame, it tries dividing it by $G(x)$. If there is a remainder, there has been a transmission error.

The algorithm for computing the checksum is as follows:

1. Let r be the degree of $G(x)$. Append r zero bits to the low-order end of the frame, so it now contains $m + r$ bits and corresponds to the polynomial $x^r M(x)$.

2. Divide the bit string corresponding to $G(x)$ into the bit string corresponding to $x^r M(x)$ using modulo 2 division.

3. Subtract the remainder (which is always r or fewer bits) from the bit string corresponding to $x^r M(x)$ using modulo 2 subtraction. The result is the checksummed frame to be transmitted. Call its polynomial $T(x)$.

Figure 3-7 illustrates the calculation for a frame 1101011011 and $G(x) = x^4 + x + 1$.

It should be clear that $T(x)$ is divisible (modulo 2) by $G(x)$. In any division problem, if you diminish the dividend by the remainder, what is left over is divisible by the divisor. For example, in base 10, if you divide 210,278 by 10,941, the remainder is 2399. By subtracting off 2399 from 210,278, what is left over (207,879) is divisible by 10,941.

Now let us analyze the power of this method. What kinds of errors will be detected? Imagine that a transmission error occurs, so that instead of the bit string for $T(x)$ arriving, $T(x) + E(x)$ arrives. Each 1 bit in $E(x)$ corresponds to a bit that has been inverted. If there are k 1 bits in $E(x)$, k single-bit errors have occurred. A single burst error is characterized by an initial 1, a mixture of 0s and 1s, and a final 1, with all other bits being 0.

Upon receiving the checksummed frame, the receiver divides it by $G(x)$; that is, it computes $[T(x) + E(x)]/G(x)$. $T(x)/G(x)$ is 0, so the result of the computation is simply $E(x)/G(x)$. Those errors that happen to correspond to polynomials containing $G(x)$ as a factor will slip by; all other errors will be caught.

If there has been a single-bit error, $E(x) = x^i$, where i determines which bit is in error. If $G(x)$ contains two or more terms, it will never divide $E(x)$, so all single-bit errors will be detected.

If there have been two isolated single-bit errors, $E(x) = x^i + x^j$, where $i > j$. Alternatively, this can be written as $E(x) = x^j(x^{i-j} + 1)$. If we assume that $G(x)$ is not divisible by x, a sufficient condition for all double errors to be detected is that $G(x)$ does not divide $x^k + 1$ for any k up to the maximum value of $i - j$ (i.e., up to the maximum frame length). Simple, low-degree polynomials that give protection to long frames are known. For example, $x^{15} + x^{14} + 1$ will not divide $x^k + 1$ for any value of k below 32,768.

If there are an odd number of bits in error, $E(X)$ contains an odd number of terms (e.g., $x^5 + x^2 + 1$, but not $x^2 + 1$). Interestingly enough, there is no

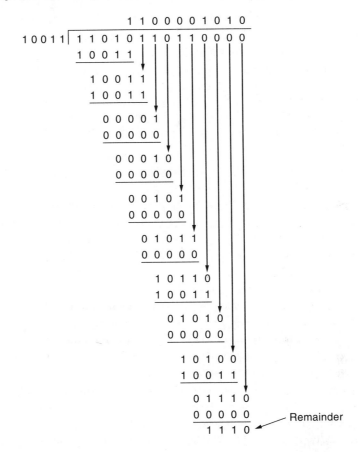

Frame   : 1 1 0 1 0 1 1 0 1 1

Generator: 1 0 0 1 1

Message after appending 4 zero bits: 1 1 0 1 0 1 1 0 1 1 0 0 0 0

Fig. 3-7. Calculation of the polynomial code checksum.

polynomial with an odd number of terms that has $x + 1$ as a factor in the modulo 2 system. By making $x + 1$ a factor of $G(x)$, we can catch all errors consisting of an odd number of inverted bits.

To see that no polynomial with an odd number of terms is divisible by $x + 1$, assume that $E(x)$ has an odd number of terms and is divisible by $x + 1$. Factor $E(x)$ into $(x + 1)\ Q(x)$. Now evaluate $E(1) = (1 + 1)Q(1)$. Since $1 + 1 = 0$ (modulo 2), $E(1)$ must be zero. If $E(x)$ has an odd number of terms, substituting 1 for x everywhere will always yield 1 as result. Thus no polynomial with an odd number of terms is divisible by $x + 1$.

Finally, and most important, a polynomial code with r check bits will detect all burst errors of length $\leq r$. A burst error of length k can be represented by $x^i(x^{k-1} + \ldots + 1)$, where i determines how far from the right-hand end of the received frame the burst is located. If $G(x)$ contains an x^0 term, it will not have x^i as a factor, so if the degree of the parenthesized expression is less than the degree of $G(x)$, the remainder can never be zero.

If the burst length is $r + 1$, the remainder of the division by $G(x)$ will be zero if and only if the burst is identical to $G(x)$. By definition of a burst, the first and last bits must be 1, so whether it matches depends on the $r - 1$ intermediate bits. If all combinations are regarded as equally likely, the probability of such an incorrect frame being accepted as valid is $\frac{1}{2}^{r-1}$.

It can also be shown that when an error burst longer than $r + 1$ bits occurs, or several shorter bursts occur, the probability of a bad frame getting through unnoticed is $\frac{1}{2}^r$ assuming that all bit patterns are equally likely.

Three polynomials have become international standards:

CRC–12 $= x^{12} + x^{11} + x^3 + x^2 + x^1 + 1$
CRC–16 $= x^{16} + x^{15} + x^2 + 1$
CRC–CCITT $= x^{16} + x^{12} + x^5 + 1$

All three contain $x + 1$ as a prime factor. CRC-12 is used when the character length is 6 bits. The other two are used for 8-bit characters. A 16-bit checksum, such as CRC-16 or CRC-CCITT, catches all single and double errors, all errors with an odd number of bits, all burst errors of length 16 or less, 99.997 percent of 17-bit error bursts, and 99.998 percent of 18-bit and longer bursts.

Although the calculation required to compute the checksum may seem complicated, Peterson and Brown (1961) have shown that a simple shift register circuit can be constructed to compute and verify the checksums in hardware. In practice, this hardware is nearly always used.

For decades, it has been assumed that frames to be checksummed contain random bits. All analyses of checksum algorithms have been made under this assumption. More recently inspection of real data has shown this assumption to be quite wrong. As a consequence, under some circumstances, undetected errors are much more common than had been previously thought (Partridge et al., 1995).

3.3. ELEMENTARY DATA LINK PROTOCOLS

To introduce the subject of protocols, we will begin by looking at three protocols of increasing complexity. For interested readers, a simulator for these and subsequent protocols is available via the WWW (see the preface). Before we look at the protocols, it is useful to make explicit some of the assumptions underlying the model of communication. To start with, we are assuming that in the physical layer, data link layer, and network layer are independent processes that communicate by passing messages back and forth. In some cases, the physical and data link layer processes will be running on a processor inside a special network I/O chip and the network layer on the main CPU, but other implementations are also possible (e.g., three processes inside a single I/O chip; the physical and data link layers as procedures called by the network layer process, and so on). In any event, treating the three layers as separate processes makes the discussion conceptually cleaner and also serves to emphasize the independence of the layers.

Another key assumption is that machine A wants to send a long stream of data to machine B using a reliable, connection-oriented service. Later, we will consider the case where B also wants to send data to A simultaneously. A is assumed to have an infinite supply of data ready to send and never has to wait for data to be produced. When A's data link layer asks for data, the network layer is always able to comply immediately. (This restriction, too, will be dropped later.)

As far as the data link layer is concerned, the packet passed across the interface to it from the network layer is pure data, every bit of which is to be delivered to the destination's network layer. The fact that the destination's network layer may interpret part of the packet as a header is of no concern to the data link layer.

When the data link layer accepts a packet, it encapsulates the packet in a frame by adding a data link header and trailer to it (see Fig. 1-11). Thus a frame consists of an embedded packet and some control (header) information. The frame is then transmitted to the other data link layer. We will assume that there exist suitable library procedures *to_physical_layer* to send a frame and *from_physical_layer* to receive a frame. The transmitting hardware computes and appends the checksum, so that the data link layer software need not worry about it. The polynomial algorithm discussed earlier in this chapter might be used, for example.

Initially, the receiver has nothing to do. It just sits around waiting for something to happen. In the example protocols of this chapter we indicate that the data link layer is waiting for something to happen by the procedure call *wait_for_event*(&*event*). This procedure only returns when something has happened (e.g., a frame has arrived). Upon return, the variable *event* tells what happened. The set of possible events differs for the various protocols to be described and will be defined separately for each protocol. Note that in a more realistic situation, the data link layer will not sit in a tight loop waiting for an event, as we have suggested, but will receive an interrupt, which will cause it to stop whatever it was doing and go handle the incoming frame. Nevertheless, for simplicity we will ignore all the details of parallel activity within the data link layer and assume that it is dedicated full time to handling just our one channel.

When a frame arrives at the receiver, the hardware computes the checksum. If the checksum is incorrect (i.e., there was a transmission error), the data link layer is so informed (*event = cksum_err*). If the inbound frame arrived undamaged, the data link layer is also informed (*event = frame_arrival*), so it can acquire the frame for inspection using *from_physical_layer*. As soon as the receiving data link layer has acquired an undamaged frame, it checks the control information in the header, and if everything is all right, the packet portion is passed to the network layer. Under no circumstances is a frame header ever given to a network layer.

There is a good reason why the network layer must never be given any part of the frame header: to keep the network and data link protocols completely separate. As long as the network layer knows nothing at all about the data link protocol or the frame format, these things can be changed without requiring changes to the network layer's software. Providing a rigid interface between network layer and data link layer greatly simplifies the software design, because communication protocols in different layers can evolve independently.

Figure 3-8 shows some declarations (in C) common to many of the protocols to be discussed later. Five data structures are defined there: *boolean*, *seq_nr*, *packet*, *frame_kind*, and *frame*. A *boolean* is an enumerated type and can take on the values *true* and *false*. A *seq_nr* is a small integer used to number the frames, so we can tell them apart. These sequence numbers run from 0 up to and including *MAX_SEQ*, which is defined in each protocol needing it. A *packet* is the unit of information exchanged between the network layer and the data link layer on the same machine, or between network layer peers. In our model it always contains *MAX_PKT* bytes, but more realistically it would be of variable length.

A *frame* is composed of four fields: *kind*, *seq*, *ack*, and *info*, the first three of which contain control information, and the last of which may contain actual data to be transferred. These control fields are collectively called the **frame header**. The *kind* field tells whether or not there are any data in the frame, because some of the protocols distinguish frames containing exclusively control information from those containing data as well. The *seq* and *ack* fields are used for sequence numbers and acknowledgements, respectively; their use will be described in more detail later. The *info* field of a data frame contains a single packet; the *info* field of a control frame is not used. A more realistic implementation would use a variable-length *info* field, omitting it altogether for control frames.

It is important to realize the relationship between a packet and a frame. The network layer builds a packet by taking a message from the transport layer and adding the network layer header to it. This packet is passed to the data link layer for inclusion in the *info* field of an outgoing frame. When the frame arrives at the destination, the data link layer extracts the packet from the frame and passes the packet to the network layer. In this manner, the network layer can act as though machines can exchange packets directly.

A number of procedures are also listed in Fig. 3-8. These are library routines whose details are implementation-dependent and whose inner workings will not concern us further here. The procedure *wait_for_event* sits in a tight loop waiting for something to happen, as mentioned earlier. The procedures *to_network_layer* and *from_network_layer* are used by the data link layer to pass packets to the network layer and accept packets from the network layer, respectively. Note that *from_physical_layer* and *to_physical_layer* are used for passing frames between the data link and physical layers, whereas the procedures *to_network_layer* and *from_network_layer* are used for passing packets between the data link layer and network layer. In other words, *to_network_layer* and *from_network_layer* deal with the interface between layers 2 and 3, whereas *from_physical_layer* and *to_physical_layer* deal with the interface between layers 1 and 2.

In most of the protocols we assume an unreliable channel that loses entire frames upon occasion. To be able to recover from such calamities, the sending data link layer must start an internal timer or clock whenever it sends a frame. If no reply has been received within a certain predetermined time interval, the clock times out and the data link layer receives an interrupt signal.

In our protocols this is handled by allowing the procedure *wait_for_event* to return *event = timeout*. The procedures *start_timer* and *stop_timer* are used to turn the timer on and off, respectively. Timeouts are possible only when the timer is running. It is explicitly permitted to call *start_timer* while the timer is running; such a call simply resets the clock to cause the next timeout after a full timer interval has elapsed (unless it is reset or turned off in the meanwhile).

The procedures *start_ack_timer* and *stop_ack_timer* are used to control an auxiliary timer used to generate acknowledgements under certain conditions.

The procedures *enable_network_layer* and *disable_network_layer* are used in the more sophisticated protocols, where we no longer assume that the network layer always has packets to send. When the data link layer enables the network layer, the network layer is then permitted to interrupt when it has a packet to be sent. We indicate this with *event = network_layer_ready*. When a network layer is disabled, it may not cause such events. By being careful about when it enables and disables its network layer, the data link layer can prevent the network layer from swamping it with packets for which it has no buffer space.

Frame sequence numbers are always in the range 0 to *MAX_SEQ* (inclusive), where *MAX_SEQ* is different for the different protocols. It is frequently necessary to advance a sequence number by 1 circularly (i.e., *MAX_SEQ* is followed by 0). The macro *inc* performs this incrementing. It has been defined as a macro because it is used in-line within the critical path. As we will see later in this book, the factor limiting network performance is often protocol processing, so defining simple operations like this as macros does not affect the readability of the code, but does improve performance. Also, since *MAX_SEQ* will have different values in different protocols, by making it a macro, it becomes possible to include all the protocols in the same binary without conflict. This ability is useful for the simulator.

The declarations of Fig. 3-8 are part of each of the protocols to follow. To save space and to provide a convenient reference, they have been extracted and

```
#define MAX_PKT 1024                     /* determines packet size in bytes */

typedef enum {false, true} boolean;      /* boolean type */
typedef unsigned int seq_nr;             /* sequence or ack numbers */
typedef struct {unsigned char data[MAX_PKT];} packet;/* packet definition */
typedef enum {data, ack, nak} frame_kind;   /* frame_kind definition */

typedef struct {                         /* frames are transported in this layer */
  frame_kind kind;                       /* what kind of a frame is it? */
  seq_nr seq;                            /* sequence number */
  seq_nr ack;                            /* acknowledgement number */
  packet info;                           /* the network layer packet */
} frame;

/* Wait for an event to happen; return its type in event. */
void wait_for_event(event_type *event);

/* Fetch a packet from the network layer for transmission on the channel. */
void from_network_layer(packet *p);

/* Deliver information from an inbound frame to the network layer. */
void to_network_layer(packet *p);

/* Go get an inbound frame from the physical layer and copy it to r. */
void from_physical_layer(frame *r);

/* Pass the frame to the physical layer for transmission. */
void to_physical_layer(frame *s);

/* Start the clock running and enable the timeout event. */
void start_timer(seq_nr k);

/* Stop the clock and disable the timeout event. */
void stop_timer(seq_nr k);

/* Start an auxiliary timer and enable the ack_timeout event. */
void start_ack_timer(void);

/* Stop the auxiliary timer and disable the ack_timeout event. */
void stop_ack_timer(void);

/* Allow the network layer to cause a network_layer_ready event. */
void enable_network_layer(void);

/* Forbid the network layer from causing a network_layer_ready event. */
void disable_network_layer(void);

/* Macro inc is expanded in-line: Increment k circularly. */
#define inc(k) if (k < MAX_SEQ) k = k + 1; else k = 0
```

Fig. 3-8. Some definitions needed in the protocols to follow. These definitions are located in the file *protocol.h*.

listed together, but conceptually they should be merged with the protocols them-selves. In C, this merging is done by putting the definitions in a special header file, in this case *protocol.h*, and using the #include facility of the C preprocessor to include them in the protocol files.

3.3.1. An Unrestricted Simplex Protocol

As an initial example we will consider a protocol that is as simple as can be. Data are transmitted in one direction only. Both the transmitting and receiving network layers are always ready. Processing time can be ignored. Infinite buffer space is available. And best of all, the communication channel between the data link layers never damages or loses frames. This thoroughly unrealistic protocol, which we will nickname "utopia," is shown in Fig. 3-9.

The protocol consists of two distinct procedures, a sender and a receiver. The sender runs in the data link layer of the source machine, and the receiver runs in the data link layer of the destination machine. No sequence numbers or acknowl-edgements are used here, so *MAX_SEQ* is not needed. The only event type possi-ble is *frame_arrival* (i.e., the arrival of an undamaged frame).

The sender is in an infinite while loop just pumping data out onto the line as fast as it can. The body of the loop consists of three actions: go fetch a packet from the (always obliging) network layer, construct an outbound frame using the variable *s*, and send the frame on its way. Only the *info* field of the frame is used by this protocol, because the other fields have to do with error and flow control, and there are no errors or flow control restrictions here.

The receiver is equally simple. Initially, it waits for something to happen, the only possibility being the arrival of an undamaged frame. Eventually, the frame arrives and the procedure *wait_for_event* returns, with *event* set to *frame_arrival* (which is ignored anyway). The call to *from_physical_layer* removes the newly arrived frame from the hardware buffer and puts it in the variable *r*. Finally, the data portion is passed on to the network layer and the data link layer settles back to wait for the next frame, effectively suspending itself until the frame arrives.

3.3.2. A Simplex Stop-and-Wait Protocol

Now we will drop the most unrealistic restriction used in protocol 1: the abil-ity of the receiving network layer to process incoming data infinitely fast (or equivalently, the presence in the receiving data link layer of an infinite amount of buffer space in which to store all incoming frames while they are waiting their respective turns). The communication channel is still assumed to be error free however, and the data traffic is still simplex.

The main problem we have to deal with here is how to prevent the sender from flooding the receiver with data faster than the latter is able to process it. In essence, if the receiver requires a time Δt to execute *from_physical_layer* plus

```
/* Protocol 1 (utopia) provides for data transmission in one direction only, from
   sender to receiver.  The communication channel is assumed to be error free,
   and the receiver is assumed to be able to process all the input infinitely fast.
   Consequently, the sender just sits in a loop pumping data out onto the line as
   fast as it can. */

typedef enum {frame_arrival} event_type;
#include "protocol.h"

void sender1(void)
{
  frame s;                          /* buffer for an outbound frame */
  packet buffer;                    /* buffer for an outbound packet */

  while (true) {
      from_network_layer(&buffer);  /* go get something to send */
      s.info = buffer;              /* copy it into s for transmission */
      to_physical_layer(&s);        /* send it on its way */
  }                                 /* Tomorrow, and tomorrow, and tomorrow,
                                        Creeps in this petty pace from day to day
                                        To the last syllable of recorded time
                                            - Macbeth, V, v */

}

void receiver1(void)
{
  frame r;
  event_type event;                 /* filled in by wait, but not used here */

  while (true) {
      wait_for_event(&event);       /* only possibility is frame_arrival */
      from_physical_layer(&r);      /* go get the inbound frame */
      to_network_layer(&r.info);    /* pass the data to the network layer */
  }
}
```

Fig. 3-9. An unrestricted simplex protocol.

to_network_layer, the sender must transmit at an average rate less than one frame per time Δt. Moreover, if we assume that there is no automatic buffering and queueing done within the receiver's hardware, the sender must never transmit a new frame until the old one has been fetched by *from_physical_layer*, lest the new one overwrite the old one.

In certain restricted circumstances (e.g., synchronous transmission and a receiving data link layer fully dedicated to processing the one input line), it might be possible for the sender to simply insert a delay into protocol 1 to slow it down sufficiently to keep from swamping the receiver. However, more usually, each data link layer will have several lines to attend to, and the time interval between a frame arriving and its being processed may vary considerably. If the network designers can calculate the worst-case behavior of the receiver, they can program the sender to transmit so slowly that even if every frame suffers the maximum delay, there will be no overruns. The trouble with this approach is that it is too conservative. It leads to a bandwidth utilization that is far below the optimum, unless the best and worst cases are almost the same (i.e., the variation in the data link layer's reaction time is small).

A more general solution to this dilemma is to have the receiver provide feedback to the sender. After having passed a packet to its network layer, the receiver sends a little dummy frame back to the sender which, in effect, gives the sender permission to transmit the next frame. After having sent a frame, the sender is required by the protocol to bide its time until the little dummy (i.e., acknowledgement) frame arrives.

Protocols in which the sender sends one frame and then waits for an acknowledgement before proceeding are called **stop-and-wait**. Figure 3-10 gives an example of a simplex stop-and-wait protocol.

As in protocol 1, the sender starts out by fetching a packet from the network layer, using it to construct a frame and sending it on its way. Only now, unlike in protocol 1, the sender must wait until an acknowledgement frame arrives before looping back and fetching the next packet from the network layer. The sending data link layer need not even inspect the incoming frame: there is only one possibility.

The only difference between *receiver1* and *receiver2* is that after delivering a packet to the network layer, *receiver2* sends an acknowledgement frame back to the sender before entering the wait loop again. Because only the arrival of the frame back at the sender is important, not its contents, the receiver need not put any particular information in it.

Although data traffic in this example is simplex, going only from the sender to the receiver, frames do travel in both directions. Consequently, the communication channel between the two data link layers needs to be capable of bidirectional information transfer. However, this protocol entails a strict alternation of flow: first the sender sends a frame, then the receiver sends a frame, then the sender sends another frame, then the receiver sends another one, and so on. A half-duplex physical channel would suffice here.

3.3.3. A Simplex Protocol for a Noisy Channel

Now let us consider the normal situation of a communication channel that makes errors. Frames may be either damaged or lost completely. However, we assume that if a frame is damaged in transit, the receiver hardware will detect this

```
/* Protocol 2 (stop-and-wait) also provides for a one-directional flow of data from
   sender to receiver. The communication channel is once again assumed to be error
   free, as in protocol 1. However, this time, the receiver has only a finite buffer
   capacity and a finite processing speed, so the protocol must explicitly prevent
   the sender from flooding the receiver with data faster than it can be handled. */

typedef enum {frame_arrival} event_type;
#include "protocol.h"

void sender2(void)
{
  frame s;                          /* buffer for an outbound frame */
  packet buffer;                    /* buffer for an outbound packet */
  event_type event;                 /* frame_arrival is the only possibility */

  while (true) {
      from_network_layer(&buffer);  /* go get something to send */
      s.info = buffer;              /* copy it into s for transmission */
      to_physical_layer(&s);        /* bye bye little frame */
      wait_for_event(&event);       /* do not proceed until given the go ahead */
  }
}

void receiver2(void)
{
  frame r, s;                       /* buffers for frames */
  event_type event;                 /* frame_arrival is the only possibility */
  while (true) {
      wait_for_event(&event);       /* only possibility is frame_arrival */
      from_physical_layer(&r);      /* go get the inbound frame */
      to_network_layer(&r.info);    /* pass the data to the network layer */
      to_physical_layer(&s);        /* send a dummy frame to awaken sender */
  }
}
```

Fig. 3-10. A simplex stop-and-wait protocol.

when it computes the checksum. If the frame is damaged in such a way that the checksum is nevertheless correct, an exceedingly unlikely occurrence, this protocol (and all other protocols) can fail (i.e., deliver an incorrect packet to the network layer).

At first glance it might seem that a variation of protocol 2 would work: adding a timer. The sender could send a frame, but the receiver would only send an acknowledgement frame if the data were correctly received. If a damaged frame arrived at the receiver, it would be discarded. After a while the sender would time out and send the frame again. This process would be repeated until the frame finally arrived intact.

The above scheme has a fatal flaw in it. Think about the problem and try to discover what might go wrong before reading further.

To see what might go wrong, remember that it is the task of the data link layer processes to provide error free, transparent communication between network layers processes. The network layer on machine *A* gives a series of packets to its data link layer, which must ensure that an identical series of packets are delivered to the network layer on machine *B* by its data link layer. In particular, the network layer on *B* has no way of knowing that a packet has been lost or duplicated, so the data link layer must guarantee that no combination of transmission errors, no matter how unlikely, can cause a duplicate packet to be delivered to a network layer.

Consider the following scenario:

1. The network layer on *A* gives packet 1 to its data link layer. The packet is correctly received at *B* and passed to the network layer on *B*. *B* sends an acknowledgement frame back to *A*.

2. The acknowledgement frame gets lost completely. It just never arrives at all. Life would be a great deal simpler if the channel only mangled and lost data frames and not control frames, but sad to say, the channel is not very discriminating.

3. The data link layer on *A* eventually times out. Not having received an acknowledgement, it (incorrectly) assumes that its data frame was lost or damaged and sends the frame containing packet 1 again.

4. The duplicate frame also arrives at data link layer on *B* perfectly and is unwittingly passed to the network layer there. If *A* is sending a file to *B*, part of the file will be duplicated (i.e., the copy of the file made by *B* will be incorrect and the error will not have been detected). In other words, the protocol will fail.

Clearly, what is needed is some way for the receiver to be able to distinguish a frame that it is seeing for the first time from a retransmission. The obvious way to achieve this is to have the sender put a sequence number in the header of each frame it sends. Then the receiver can check the sequence number of each arriving frame to see if it is a new frame or a duplicate to be discarded.

Since a small frame header is desirable, the question arises: What is the minimum number of bits needed for the sequence number? The only ambiguity in this protocol is between a frame, m, and its direct successor, $m + 1$. If frame m is lost or damaged, the receiver will not acknowledge it, so the sender will keep trying to send it. Once it has been correctly received, the receiver will send an acknowledgement back to the sender. It is here that the potential trouble crops up. Depending upon whether the acknowledgement frame gets back to the sender correctly or not, the sender may try to send m or $m + 1$.

The event that triggers the sender to start sending $m + 2$ is the arrival of an acknowledgement for $m + 1$. But this implies that m has been correctly received, and furthermore that its acknowledgement has also been correctly received by the sender (otherwise, the sender would not have begun with $m + 1$, let alone $m + 2$). As a consequence, the only ambiguity is between a frame and its immediate predecessor or successor, not between the predecessor and successor themselves.

A 1-bit sequence number (0 or 1) is therefore sufficient. At each instant of time, the receiver expects a particular sequence number next. Any arriving frame containing the wrong sequence number is rejected as a duplicate. When a frame containing the correct sequence number arrives, it is accepted, passed to the network layer, and the expected sequence number is incremented modulo 2 (i.e., 0 becomes 1 and 1 becomes 0).

An example of this kind of protocol is shown in Fig. 3-11. Protocols in which the sender waits for a positive acknowledgement before advancing to the next data item are often called **PAR (Positive Acknowledgement with Retransmission)** or **ARQ (Automatic Repeat reQuest)**. Like protocol 2, this one also transmits data only in one direction. Although it can handle lost frames (by timing out), it requires the timeout interval to be long enough to prevent premature timeouts. If the sender times out too early, while the acknowledgement is still on the way, it will send a duplicate.

When the previous acknowledgement finally does arrive, the sender will mistakenly think that the just-sent frame is the one being acknowledged and will not realize that there is potentially another acknowledgement frame somewhere "in the pipe." If the next frame sent is lost completely but the extra acknowledgement arrives correctly, the sender will not attempt to retransmit the lost frame, and the protocol will fail. In later protocols the acknowledgement frames will contain information to prevent just this sort of trouble. For the time being, the acknowledgement frames will just be dummies, and we will assume a strict alternation of sender and receiver.

Protocol 3 differs from its predecessors in that both sender and receiver have a variable whose value is remembered while the data link layer is in wait state. The sender remembers the sequence number of the next frame to send in *next_frame_to_send*; the receiver remembers the sequence number of the next frame expected in *frame_expected*. Each protocol has a short initialization phase before entering the infinite loop.

After transmitting a frame, the sender starts the timer running. If it was already running, it will be reset to allow another full timer interval. The time interval must be chosen to allow enough time for the frame to get to the receiver, for the receiver to process it in the worst case, and for the acknowledgement frame to propagate back to the sender. Only when that time interval has elapsed

```
/* Protocol 3 (par) allows unidirectional data flow over an unreliable channel. */

#define MAX_SEQ 1                              /* must be 1 for protocol 3 */
typedef enum {frame_arrival, cksum_err, timeout} event_type;
#include "protocol.h"

void sender3(void)
{
  seq_nr next_frame_to_send;                   /* seq number of next outgoing frame */
  frame s;                                     /* scratch variable */
  packet buffer;                               /* buffer for an outbound packet */
  event_type event;

  next_frame_to_send = 0;                      /* initialize outbound sequence numbers */
  from_network_layer(&buffer);                 /* fetch first packet */
  while (true) {
      s.info = buffer;                         /* construct a frame for transmission */
      s.seq = next_frame_to_send;              /* insert sequence number in frame */
      to_physical_layer(&s);                   /* send it on its way */
      start_timer(s.seq);                      /* if answer takes too long, time out */
      wait_for_event(&event);                  /* frame_arrival, cksum_err, timeout */
      if (event == frame_arrival) {
          from_physical_layer(&s);             /* get the acknowledgement */
          if (s.ack == next_frame_to_send) {
              from_network_layer(&buffer);     /* get the next one to send */
              inc(next_frame_to_send);         /* invert next_frame_to_send */
          }
      }
  }
}

void receiver3(void)
{
  seq_nr frame_expected;
  frame r, s;
  event_type event;

  frame_expected = 0;
  while (true) {
      wait_for_event(&event);                  /* possibilities: frame_arrival, cksum_err */
      if (event == frame_arrival) {            /* a valid frame has arrived. */
          from_physical_layer(&r);             /* go get the newly arrived frame */
          if (r.seq == frame_expected) {       /* this is what we have been waiting for. */
              to_network_layer(&r.info);       /* pass the data to the network layer */
              inc(frame_expected);             /* next time expect the other sequence nr */
          }
          s.ack = 1 - frame_expected;          /* tell which frame is being acked */
          to_physical_layer(&s);               /* none of the fields are used */
      }
  }
}
```

Fig. 3-11. A positive acknowledgement with retransmission protocol.

is it safe to assume that either the transmitted frame or its acknowledgement has been lost, and to send a duplicate.

After transmitting a frame and starting the timer, the sender waits for something exciting to happen. There are three possibilities: an acknowledgement frame arrives undamaged, a damaged acknowledgement frame staggers in, or the timer goes off. If a valid acknowledgement comes in, the sender fetches the next packet from its network layer and puts it in the buffer, overwriting the previous packet. It also advances the sequence number. If a damaged frame arrives or no frame at all arrives, neither the buffer nor the sequence number are changed, so that a duplicate can be sent.

When a valid frame arrives at the receiver, its sequence number is checked to see if it is a duplicate. If not, it is accepted, passed to the network layer, and an acknowledgement generated. Duplicates and damaged frames are not passed to the network layer.

3.4. SLIDING WINDOW PROTOCOLS

In the previous protocols, data frames were transmitted in one direction only. In most practical situations, there is a need for transmitting data in both directions. One way of achieving full-duplex data transmission is to have two separate communication channels and use each one for simplex data traffic (in different directions). If this is done, we have two separate physical circuits, each with a "forward" channel (for data) and a "reverse" channel (for acknowledgements). In both cases the bandwidth of the reverse channel is almost entirely wasted. In effect, the user is paying for two circuits but using only the capacity of one.

A better idea is to use the same circuit for data in both directions. After all, in protocols 2 and 3 it was already being used to transmit frames both ways, and the reverse channel has the same capacity as the forward channel. In this model the data frames from A to B are intermixed with the acknowledgement frames from A to B. By looking at the *kind* field in the header of an incoming frame, the receiver can tell whether the frame is data or acknowledgement.

Although interleaving data and control frames on the same circuit is an improvement over having two separate physical circuits, yet another improvement is possible. When a data frame arrives, instead of immediately sending a separate control frame, the receiver restrains itself and waits until the network layer passes it the next packet. The acknowledgement is attached to the outgoing data frame (using the *ack* field in the frame header). In effect, the acknowledgement gets a free ride on the next outgoing data frame. The technique of temporarily delaying outgoing acknowledgements so that they can be hooked onto the next outgoing data frame is known as **piggybacking**.

The principal advantage of using piggybacking over having distinct acknowledgement frames is a better use of the available channel bandwidth. The *ack* field in the frame header costs only a few bits, whereas a separate frame would need a header, the acknowledgement, and a checksum. In addition, fewer frames sent means fewer "frame arrived" interrupts, and perhaps fewer buffers in the receiver, depending on how the receiver's software is organized. In the next protocol to be examined, the piggyback field costs only 1 bit in the frame header. It rarely costs more than a few bits.

However, piggybacking introduces a complication not present with separate acknowledgements. How long should the data link layer wait for a packet onto which to piggyback the acknowledgement? If the data link layer waits longer than the sender's timeout period, the frame will be retransmitted, defeating the whole purpose of having acknowledgements. If the data link layer were an oracle and could foretell the future, it would know when the next network layer packet was going to come in, and could decide either to wait for it or send a separate acknowledgement immediately, depending on how long the projected wait was going to be. Of course, the data link layer cannot foretell the future, so it must resort to some ad hoc scheme, such as waiting a fixed number of milliseconds. If a new packet arrives quickly, the acknowledgement is piggybacked onto it; otherwise, if no new packet has arrived by the end of this time period, the data link layer just sends a separate acknowledgement frame.

In addition to its being only simplex, protocol 3 can fail under some peculiar conditions involving early timeout. It would be nicer to have a protocol that remained synchronized in the face of any combination of garbled frames, lost frames, and premature timeouts. The next three protocols are more robust and continue to function even under pathological conditions. All three belong to a class of protocols called **sliding window** protocols. The three differ among themselves in terms of efficiency, complexity, and buffer requirements, as discussed later.

In all sliding window protocols, each outbound frame contains a sequence number, ranging from 0 up to some maximum. The maximum is usually $2^n - 1$ so the sequence number fits nicely in an n-bit field. The stop-and-wait sliding window protocol uses $n = 1$, restricting the sequence numbers to 0 and 1, but more sophisticated versions can use arbitrary n.

The essence of all sliding window protocols is that at any instant of time, the sender maintains a set of sequence numbers corresponding to frames it is permitted to send. These frames are said to fall within the **sending window**. Similarly, the receiver also maintains a **receiving window** corresponding to the set of frames it is permitted to accept. The sender's window and the receiver's window need not have the same lower and upper limits, or even have the same size. In some protocols they are fixed in size, but in others they can grow or shrink as frames are sent and received.

Although these protocols give the data link layer more freedom about the order in which it may send and receive frames, we have most emphatically not dropped the requirement that the protocol must deliver packets to the destination network layer in the same order that they were passed to the data link layer on the sending machine. Nor have we changed the requirement that the physical communication channel is "wire-like," that is, it must deliver all frames in the order sent.

The sequence numbers within the sender's window represent frames sent but as yet not acknowledged. Whenever a new packet arrives from the network layer, it is given the next highest sequence number, and the upper edge of the window is advanced by one. When an acknowledgement comes in, the lower edge is advanced by one. In this way the window continuously maintains a list of unacknowledged frames.

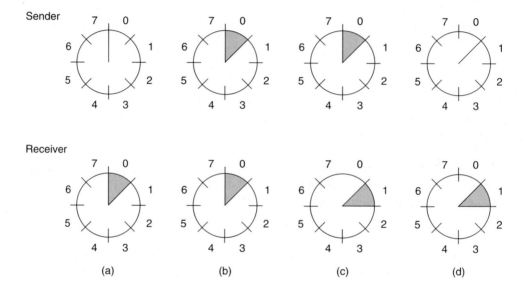

Fig. 3-12. A sliding window of size 1, with a 3-bit sequence number. (a) Initially. (b) After the first frame has been sent. (c) After the first frame has been received. (d) After the first acknowledgement has been received.

Since frames currently within the sender's window may ultimately be lost or damaged in transit, the sender must keep all these frames in its memory for possible retransmission. Thus if the maximum window size is n, the sender needs n buffers to hold the unacknowledged frames. If the window ever grows to its maximum size, the sending data link layer must forcibly shut off the network layer until another buffer becomes free.

The receiving data link layer's window corresponds to the frames it may accept. Any frame falling outside the window is discarded without comment. When a frame whose sequence number is equal to the lower edge of the window is received, it is passed to the network layer, an acknowledgement is generated, and the window is rotated by one. Unlike the sender's window, the receiver's

```
/* Protocol 4 (sliding window) is bidirectional and is more robust than protocol 3. */
#define MAX_SEQ 1                       /* must be 1 for protocol 4 */
typedef enum {frame_arrival, cksum_err, timeout} event_type;
#include "protocol.h"
void protocol4 (void)
{
  seq_nr next_frame_to_send;           /* 0 or 1 only */
  seq_nr frame_expected;               /* 0 or 1 only */
  frame r, s;                          /* scratch variables */
  packet buffer;                       /* current packet being sent */
  event_type event;

  next_frame_to_send = 0;              /* next frame on the outbound stream */
  frame_expected = 0;                  /* number of frame arriving frame expected */
  from_network_layer(&buffer);         /* fetch a packet from the network layer */
  s.info = buffer;                     /* prepare to send the initial frame */
  s.seq = next_frame_to_send;          /* insert sequence number into frame */
  s.ack = 1 − frame_expected;          /* piggybacked ack */
  to_physical_layer(&s);               /* transmit the frame */
  start_timer(s.seq);                  /* start the timer running */
  while (true) {
      wait_for_event(&event);          /* frame_arrival, cksum_err, or timeout */
      if (event == frame_arrival) { /* a frame has arrived undamaged. */
          from_physical_layer(&r);     /* go get it */

          if (r.seq == frame_expected) {
              /* Handle inbound frame stream. */
              to_network_layer(&r.info); /* pass packet to network layer */
              inc(frame_expected);        /* invert sequence number expected next */
          }

          if (r.ack == next_frame_to_send) { /* handle outbound frame stream. */
              from_network_layer(&buffer);      /* fetch new pkt from network layer */
              inc(next_frame_to_send);  /* invert sender's sequence number */
          }
      }
      s.info = buffer;                 /* construct outbound frame */
      s.seq = next_frame_to_send;      /* insert sequence number into it */
      s.ack = 1 − frame_expected;      /* seq number of last received frame */
      to_physical_layer(&s);           /* transmit a frame */
      start_timer(s.seq);              /* start the timer running */
  }
}
```

Fig. 3-13. A 1-bit sliding window protocol.

window always remains at its initial size. Note that a window size of 1 means that the data link layer only accepts frames in order, but for larger windows this is not so. The network layer, in contrast, is always fed data in the proper order, regardless of the data link layer's window size.

Figure 3-12 shows an example with a maximum window size of 1. Initially, no frames are outstanding, so the lower and upper edges of the sender's window are equal, but as time goes on, the situation progresses as shown.

3.4.1. A One Bit Sliding Window Protocol

Before tackling the general case, let us first examine a sliding window protocol with a maximum window size of 1. Such a protocol uses stop-and-wait, since the sender transmits a frame and waits for its acknowledgement before sending the next one.

Figure 3-13 depicts such a protocol. Like the others, it starts out by defining some variables. *Next_frame_to_send* tells which frame the sender is trying to send. Similarly, *frame_expected* tells which frame the receiver is expecting. In both cases, 0 and 1 are the only possibilities.

Normally, one of the two data link layers goes first. In other words, only one of the data link layer programs should contain the *to_physical_layer* and *start_timer* procedure calls outside the main loop. In the event both data link layers start off simultaneously, a peculiar situation arises, which is discussed later. The starting machine fetches the first packet from its network layer, builds a frame from it, and sends it. When this (or any) frame arrives, the receiving data link layer checks to see if it is a duplicate, just as in protocol 3. If the frame is the one expected, it is passed to the network layer and the receiver's window is slid up.

The acknowledgement field contains the number of the last frame received without error. If this number agrees with the sequence number of the frame the sender is trying to send, the sender knows it is done with the frame stored in *buffer* and can fetch the next packet from its network layer. If the sequence number disagrees, it must continue trying to send the same frame. Whenever a frame is received, a frame is also sent back.

Now let us examine protocol 4 to see how resilient it is to pathological scenarios. Assume that A is trying to send its frame 0 to B and that B is trying to send its frame 0 to A. Suppose that A sends a frame to B, but A's timeout interval is a little too short. Consequently, A may time out repeatedly, sending a series of identical frames, all with $seq = 0$ and $ack = 1$.

When the first valid frame arrives at B, it will be accepted, and *frame_expected* will be set to 1. All the subsequent frames will be rejected, because B is now expecting frames with sequence number 1, not 0. Furthermore, since all the duplicates have $ack = 1$ and B is still waiting for an acknowledgement of 0, B will not fetch a new packet from its network layer.

After every rejected duplicate comes in, *B* sends *A* a frame containing *seq* = 0 and *ack* = 0. Eventually, one of these arrives correctly at *A*, causing *A* to begin sending the next packet. No combination of lost frames or premature timeouts can cause the protocol to deliver duplicate packets to either network layer, or to skip a packet, or to get into a deadlock.

However, a peculiar situation arises if both sides simultaneously send an initial packet. This synchronization difficulty is illustrated by Fig. 3-14. In part (a), the normal operation of the protocol is shown. In (b) the peculiarity is illustrated. If *B* waits for *A*'s first frame before sending one of its own, the sequence is as shown in (a), and every frame is accepted. However, if *A* and *B* simultaneously initiate communication, their first frames cross, and the data link layers then get into situation (b). In (a) each frame arrival brings a new packet for the network layer; there are no duplicates. In (b) half of the frames contain duplicates, even though there are no transmission errors. Similar situations can occur as a result of premature timeouts, even when one side clearly starts first. In fact, if multiple premature timeouts occur, frames may be sent three or more times.

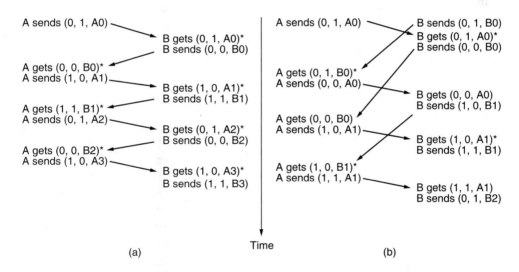

Fig. 3-14. Two scenarios for protocol 4. The notation is (seq, ack, packet number). An asterisk indicates where a network layer accepts a packet.

3.4.2. A Protocol Using Go Back n

Until now we have made the tacit assumption that the transmission time required for a frame to arrive at the receiver plus the transmission time for the acknowledgement to come back is negligible. Sometimes this assumption is clearly false. In these situations the long round-trip time can have important implications for the efficiency of the bandwidth utilization. As an example, consider a 50-kbps satellite channel with a 500-msec round-trip propagation delay. Let us imagine trying to use protocol 4 to send 1000-bit frames via the satellite. At $t = 0$ the sender starts sending the first frame. At $t = 20$ msec the frame has been completely sent. Not until $t = 270$ msec has the frame fully arrived at the receiver, and not until $t = 520$ msec has the acknowledgement arrived back at the sender, under the best of circumstances (no waiting in the receiver and a short acknowledgement frame). This means that the sender was blocked during 500/520 or 96 percent of the time (i.e., only 4 percent of the available bandwidth was used). Clearly, the combination of a long transit time, high bandwidth, and short frame length is disastrous in terms of efficiency.

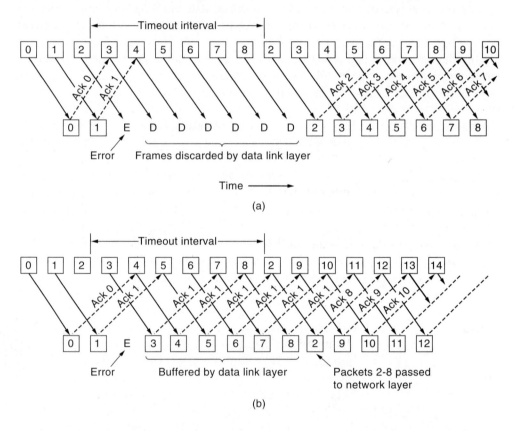

Fig. 3-15. (a) Effect of an error when the receiver window size is 1. (b) Effect of an error when the receiver window size is large.

The problem described above can be viewed as a consequence of the rule requiring a sender to wait for an acknowledgement before sending another frame. If we relax that restriction, much better efficiency can be achieved. Basically the solution lies in allowing the sender to transmit up to w frames before blocking, instead of just 1. With an appropriate choice of w the sender will be able to continuously transmit frames for a time equal to the round-trip transit time without filling up the window. In the example above, w should be at least 26. The sender begins sending frame 0 as before. By the time it has finished sending 26 frames, at $t = 520$, the acknowledgement for frame 0 will have just arrived. Thereafter, acknowledgements will arrive every 20 msec, so the sender always gets permission to continue just when it needs it. At all times, 25 or 26 unacknowledged frames are outstanding. Put in other terms, the sender's maximum window size is 26.

This technique is known as **pipelining**. If the channel capacity is b bits/sec, the frame size l bits, and the round-trip propagation time R sec, the time required to transmit a single frame is l/b sec. After the last bit of a data frame has been sent, there is a delay of $R/2$ before that bit arrives at the receiver, and another delay of at least $R/2$ for the acknowledgement to come back, for a total delay of R. In stop-and-wait the line is busy for l/b and idle for R, giving a line utilization of $l/(l + bR)$. If $l < bR$ the efficiency will be less than 50 percent. Since there is always a nonzero delay for the acknowledgement to propagate back, in principle pipelining can be used to keep the line busy during this interval, but if the interval is small, the additional complexity is not worth the trouble.

Pipelining frames over an unreliable communication channel raises some serious issues. First, what happens if a frame in the middle of a long stream is damaged or lost? Large numbers of succeeding frames will arrive at the receiver before the sender even finds out that anything is wrong. When a damaged frame arrives at the receiver, it obviously should be discarded, but what should the receiver do with all the correct frames following it? Remember that the receiving data link layer is obligated to hand packets to the network layer in sequence.

There are two basic approaches to dealing with errors in the presence of pipelining. One way, called **go back n**, is for the receiver simply to discard all subsequent frames, sending no acknowledgements for the discarded frames. This strategy corresponds to a receive window of size 1. In other words, the data link layer refuses to accept any frame except the next one it must give to the network layer. If the sender's window fills up before the timer runs out, the pipeline will begin to empty. Eventually, the sender will time out and retransmit all unacknowledged frames in order, starting with the damaged or lost one. This approach, shown in Fig. 3-15(a) can waste a lot of bandwidth if the error rate is high.

The other general strategy for handling errors when frames are pipelined, called **selective repeat**, is to have the receiving data link layer store all the correct frames following the bad one. When the sender finally notices that something is wrong, it just retransmits the one bad frame, not all its successors, as shown in Fig. 3-15(b). If the second try succeeds, the receiving data link layer will now have many correct frames in sequence, so they can all be handed off to the network layer quickly and the highest number acknowledged.

This strategy corresponds to a receiver window larger than 1. Any frame within the window may be accepted and buffered until all the preceding ones have

```
/* Protocol 5 (pipelining) allows multiple outstanding frames. The sender may transmit up
   to MAX_SEQ frames without waiting for an ack. In addition, unlike the previous protocols,
   the network layer is not assumed to have a new packet all the time. Instead, the
   network layer causes a network_layer_ready event when there is a packet to send. */

#define MAX_SEQ 7                        /* should be 2^n – 1 */
typedef enum {frame_arrival, cksum_err, timeout, network_layer_ready} event_type;
#include "protocol.h"

static boolean between(seq_nr a, seq_nr b, seq_nr c)
{
/* Return true if (a <=b < c circularly; false otherwise. */
  if (((a <= b) && (b < c)) || ((c < a) && (a <= b)) || ((b < c) && (c < a)))
       return(true);
    else
       return(false);
}

static void send_data(seq_nr frame_nr, seq_nr frame_expected, packet buffer[])
{
/* Construct and send a data frame. */
  frame s;                               /* scratch variable */

  s.info = buffer[frame_nr];            /* insert packet into frame */
  s.seq = frame_nr;                     /* insert sequence number into frame */
  s.ack = (frame_expected + MAX_SEQ) % (MAX_SEQ + 1);/* piggyback ack */
  to_physical_layer(&s);                /* transmit the frame */
  start_timer(frame_nr);                /* start the timer running */
}

void protocol5(void)
{
  seq_nr next_frame_to_send;            /* MAX_SEQ > 1; used for outbound stream */
  seq_nr ack_expected;                  /* oldest frame as yet unacknowledged */
  seq_nr frame_expected;                /* next frame expected on inbound stream */
  frame r;                              /* scratch variable */
  packet buffer[MAX_SEQ + 1];           /* buffers for the outbound stream */
  seq_nr nbuffered;                     /* # output buffers currently in use */
  seq_nr i;                             /* used to index into the buffer array */
  event_type event;

  enable_network_layer();               /* allow network_layer_ready events */
  ack_expected = 0;                     /* next ack expected inbound */
  next_frame_to_send = 0;               /* next frame going out */
  frame_expected = 0;                   /* number of frame expected inbound */
  nbuffered = 0;                        /* initially no packets are buffered */
```

```
while (true) {
    wait_for_event(&event);            /* four possibilities: see event_type above */

    switch(event) {
        case network_layer_ready:      /* the network layer has a packet to send */
            /* Accept, save, and transmit a new frame. */
            from_network_layer(&buffer[next_frame_to_send]); /* fetch new packet */
            nbuffered = nbuffered + 1;  /* expand the sender's window */
            send_data(next_frame_to_send, frame_expected, buffer);/* transmit the frame */
            inc(next_frame_to_send);    /* advance sender's upper window edge */
            break;

        case frame_arrival:            /* a data or control frame has arrived */
            from_physical_layer(&r);   /* get incoming frame from physical layer */

            if (r.seq == frame_expected) {
                /* Frames are accepted only in order. */
                to_network_layer(&r.info);  /* pass packet to network layer */
                inc(frame_expected);    /* advance lower edge of receiver's window */
            }

            /* Ack n implies n − 1, n − 2, etc. Check for this. */
            while (between(ack_expected, r.ack, next_frame_to_send)) {
                /* Handle piggybacked ack. */
                nbuffered = nbuffered − 1; /* one frame fewer buffered */
                stop_timer(ack_expected); /* frame arrived intact; stop timer */
                inc(ack_expected);      /* contract sender's window */
            }
            break;

        case cksum_err: break;         /* just ignore bad frames */

        case timeout:                  /* trouble; retransmit all outstanding frames */
            next_frame_to_send = ack_expected;   /* start retransmitting here */
            for (i = 1; i <= nbuffered; i++) {
                send_data(next_frame_to_send, frame_expected, buffer);/* resend 1 frame */
                inc(next_frame_to_send);  /* prepare to send the next one */
            }
    }

    if (nbuffered < MAX_SEQ)
            enable_network_layer();
    else
            disable_network_layer();
    }
}
```

Fig. 3-16. A sliding window protocol using go back n.

been passed to the network layer. This approach can require large amounts of data link layer memory if the window is large.

These two alternative approaches are trade-offs between bandwidth and data link layer buffer space. Depending on which resource is more valuable, one or the other can be used. Figure 3-16 shows a pipelining protocol in which the receiving data link layer only accepts frames in order; frames following an error are discarded. In this protocol, for the first time, we have now dropped the assumption that the network layer always has an infinite supply of packets to send. When the network layer has a packet it wants to send, it can cause a *network_layer_ready* event to happen. However, in order to enforce the flow control rule of no more than *MAX_SEQ* unacknowledged frames outstanding at any time, the data link layer must be able to prohibit the network layer from bothering it with more work. The library procedures *enable_network_layer* and *disable_network_layer* perform this function.

Note that a maximum of *MAX_SEQ* frames and not *MAX_SEQ* + 1 frames may be outstanding at any instant, even though there are *MAX_SEQ* + 1 distinct sequence numbers: 0, 1, 2, . . . , *MAX_SEQ*. To see why this restriction is needed, consider the following scenario with *MAX_SEQ* = 7.

1. The sender sends frames 0 through 7.

2. A piggybacked acknowledgement for frame 7 eventually comes back to the sender.

3. The sender sends another eight frames, again with sequence numbers 0 through 7.

4. Now another piggybacked acknowledgement for frame 7 comes in.

The question is: Did all eight frames belonging to the second batch arrive successfully, or did all eight get lost (counting discards following an error as lost)? In both cases the receiver would be sending frame 7 as the acknowledgement. The sender has no way of telling. For this reason the maximum number of outstanding frames must be restricted to *MAX_SEQ*.

Although protocol 5 does not buffer the frames arriving after an error, it does not escape the problem of buffering altogether. Since a sender may have to retransmit all the unacknowledged frames at a future time, it must hang on to all transmitted frames until it knows for sure that they have been accepted by the receiver. When an acknowledgement comes in for frame n, frames $n - 1$, $n - 2$, and so on, are also automatically acknowledged. This property is especially important when some of the previous acknowledgement-bearing frames were lost or garbled. Whenever any acknowledgement comes in, the data link layer checks to see if any buffers can now be released. If buffers can be released (i.e., there is some room available in the window), a previously blocked network layer can now be allowed to cause more *network_layer_ready* events.

Because this protocol has multiple outstanding frames, it logically needs multiple timers, one per outstanding frame. Each frame times out independently of all the other ones. All of these timers can easily be simulated in software, using a single hardware clock that causes interrupts periodically. The pending timeouts form a linked list, with each node of the list telling how many clock ticks until the timer goes off, the frame being timed, and a pointer to the next node.

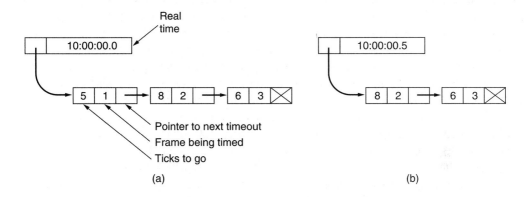

Fig. 3-17. Simulation of multiple timers in software.

As an illustration of how the timers could be implemented, consider the example of Fig. 3-17. Assume that the clock ticks once every 100 msec. Initially the real time is 10:00:00.0 and there are three timeouts pending, at 10:00:00.5, 10:00:01.3, and 10:00:01.9. Every time the hardware clock ticks, the real time is updated and the tick counter at the head of the list is decremented. When the tick counter becomes zero, a timeout is caused and the node removed from the list, as shown in Fig. 3-17(b). Although this organization requires the list to be scanned when *start_timer* or *stop_timer* is called, it does not require much work per tick. In protocol 5, both of these routines have been given a parameter, indicating which frame is to be timed.

3.4.3. A Protocol Using Selective Repeat

Protocol 5 works well if errors are rare, but if the line is poor it wastes a lot of bandwidth on retransmitted frames. An alternative strategy for handling errors is to allow the receiver to accept and buffer the frames following a damaged or lost one. Such a protocol does not discard frames merely because an earlier frame was damaged or lost.

In this protocol, both sender and receiver maintain a window of acceptable sequence numbers. The sender's window size starts out at 0 and grows to some predefined maximum, *MAX_SEQ*. The receiver's window, in contrast, is always fixed in size and equal to *MAX_SEQ*. The receiver has a buffer reserved for each sequence number within its window. Associated with each buffer is a bit (*arrived*) telling whether the buffer is full or empty. Whenever a frame arrives, its sequence number is checked by the function *between* to see if it falls within the window. If so, and if it has not already been received, it is accepted and stored. This action is taken without regard to whether or not it contains the next packet expected by the network layer. Of course, it must be kept within the data link layer and not passed to the network layer until all the lower numbered frames have already been delivered to the network layer in the correct order. A protocol using this algorithm is given in Fig. 3-18.

Nonsequential receive introduces certain problems not present in protocols in which frames are only accepted in order. We can illustrate the trouble most easily with an example. Suppose that we have a 3-bit sequence number, so that the sender is permitted to transmit up to seven frames before being required to wait for an acknowledgement. Initially the sender and receiver's windows are as shown in Fig. 3-19(a). The sender now transmits frames 0 through 6. The receiver's window allows it to accept any frame with sequence number between 0 and 6 inclusive. All seven frames arrive correctly, so the receiver acknowledges them and advance its window to allow receipt of 7, 0, 1, 2, 3, 4, or 5, as shown in Fig. 3-19(b). All seven buffers are marked empty.

It is at this point that disaster strikes in the form of a lightning bolt hitting the telephone pole and wiping out all the acknowledgements. The sender eventually times out and retransmits frame 0. When this frame arrives at the receiver, a check is made to see if it is within the receiver's window. Unfortunately, in Fig. 3-19(b) frame 0 is within the new window, so it will be accepted. The receiver sends a piggybacked acknowledgement for frame 6, since 0 through 6 have been received.

The sender is happy to learn that all its transmitted frames did actually arrive correctly, so it advances its window and immediately sends frames 7, 0, 1, 2, 3, 4, and 5. Frame 7 will be accepted by the receiver and its packet will be passed directly to the network layer. Immediately thereafter, the receiving data link layer checks to see if it has a valid frame 0 already, discovers that it does, and passes the embedded packet to the network layer. Consequently, the network layer gets an incorrect packet, and the protocol fails.

The essence of the problem is that after the receiver advanced its window, the new range of valid sequence numbers overlapped the old one. The following batch of frames might be either duplicates (if all the acknowledgements were lost) or new ones (if all the acknowledgements were received). The poor receiver has no way of distinguishing these two cases.

The way out of this dilemma lies in making sure that after the receiver has advanced its window, there is no overlap with the original window. To ensure that there is no overlap, the maximum window size should be at most half the range of the sequence numbers, as is done in Fig. 3-19(c) and Fig. 3-19(d). For example, if 4 bits are used for sequence numbers, these will range from 0 to 15.

Only eight unacknowledged frames should be outstanding at any instant. That way, if the receiver has just accepted frames 0 through 7 and advanced its window to permit acceptance of frames 8 through 15, it can unambiguously tell if subsequent frames are retransmissions (0 through 7) or new ones (8 through 15). In general, the window size for protocol 6 will be $(MAX\_SEQ + 1)/2$.

An interesting question is: How many buffers must the receiver have? Under no conditions will it ever accept frames whose sequence numbers are below the lower edge of the window or frames whose sequence numbers are above the upper edge of the window. Consequently, the number of buffers needed is equal to the window size, not the range of sequence numbers. In the above example of a 4-bit sequence number, eight buffers, numbered 0 through 7, are needed. When frame i arrives, it is put in buffer i mod 8. Notice that although i and $(i + 8)$ mod 8 are "competing" for the same buffer, they are never within the window at the same time, because that would imply a window size of at least 9.

For the same reason, the number of timers needed is equal to the number of buffers, not the size of the sequence space. Effectively, there is a timer associated with each buffer. When the timer runs out, the contents of the buffer are retransmitted.

In protocol 5, there is an implicit assumption that the channel is heavily loaded. When a frame arrives, no acknowledgement is sent immediately. Instead, the acknowledgement is piggybacked onto the next outgoing data frame. If the reverse traffic is light, the acknowledgement will be held up for a long period of time. If there is a lot of traffic in one direction and no traffic in the other direction, only *MAX_SEQ* packets are sent, and then the protocol blocks.

In protocol 6 this problem is fixed. After an in-sequence data frame arrives, an auxiliary timer is started by *start_ack_timer*. If no reverse traffic has presented itself before this timer goes off, a separate acknowledgement frame is sent. An interrupt due to the auxiliary timer is called an *ack_timeout* event. With this arrangement, one-directional traffic flow is now possible, because the lack of reverse data frames onto which acknowledgements can be piggybacked is no longer an obstacle. Only one auxiliary timer exists, and if *start_ack_timer* is called while the timer is running, it is reset to a full acknowledgement timeout interval.

It is essential that the timeout associated with the auxiliary timer be appreciably shorter than the timer used for timing out data frames. This condition is required to make sure that the acknowledgement for a correctly received frame arrives before the sender times out and retransmits the frame.

Protocol 6 uses a more efficient strategy than protocol 5 for dealing with errors. Whenever the receiver has reason to suspect that an error has occurred, it sends a negative acknowledgement (NAK) frame back to the sender. Such a frame is a request for retransmission of the frame specified in the NAK. There are two cases when the receiver should be suspicious: a damaged frame has arrived or a frame other than the expected one arrived (potential lost frame). To avoid making

```
/* Protocol 6 (nonsequential receive) accepts frames out of order, but passes packets to the
   network layer in order. Associated with each outstanding frame is a timer. When the timer
   goes off, only that frame is retransmitted, not all the outstanding frames, as in protocol 5. */

#define MAX_SEQ 7                               /* should be 2^n − 1 */
#define NR_BUFS ((MAX_SEQ + 1)/2)
typedef enum {frame_arrival, cksum_err, timeout, network_layer_ready, ack_timeout} event_type;
#include "protocol.h"
boolean no_nak = true;                          /* no nak has been sent yet */
seq_nr oldest_frame = MAX_SEQ + 1;             /* initial value is only for the simulator */

static boolean between(seq_nr a, seq_nr b, seq_nr c)
{
/* Same as between in protocol5, but shorter and more obscure. */
  return ((a <= b) && (b < c)) || ((c < a) && (a <= b)) || ((b < c) && (c < a));
}

static void send_frame(frame_kind fk, seq_nr frame_nr, seq_nr frame_expected, packet buffer[])
{
/* Construct and send a data, ack, or nak frame. */
  frame s;                                      /* scratch variable */

  s.kind = fk;                                  /* kind == data, ack, or nak */
  if (fk == data) s.info = buffer[frame_nr % NR_BUFS];
  s.seq = frame_nr;                             /* only meaningful for data frames */
  s.ack = (frame_expected + MAX_SEQ) % (MAX_SEQ + 1);
  if (fk == nak) no_nak = false;                /* one nak per frame, please */
  to_physical_layer(&s);                        /* transmit the frame */
  if (fk == data) start_timer(frame_nr % NR_BUFS);
  stop_ack_timer();                             /* no need for separate ack frame */
}

void protocol6(void)
{
  seq_nr ack_expected;                          /* lower edge of sender's window */
  seq_nr next_frame_to_send;                    /* upper edge of sender's window + 1 */
  seq_nr frame_expected;                        /* lower edge of receiver's window */
  seq_nr too_far;                               /* upper edge of receiver's window + 1 */
  int i;                                        /* index into buffer pool */
  frame r;                                      /* scratch variable */
  packet out_buf[NR_BUFS];                      /* buffers for the outbound stream */
  packet in_buf[NR_BUFS];                       /* buffers for the inbound stream */
  boolean arrived[NR_BUFS];                     /* inbound bit map */
  seq_nr nbuffered;                             /* how many output buffers currently used */
  event_type event;

  enable_network_layer();                       /* initialize */
  ack_expected = 0;                             /* next ack expected on the inbound stream */
  next_frame_to_send = 0;                       /* number of next outgoing frame */
  frame_expected = 0;
  too_far = NR_BUFS;
  nbuffered = 0;                                /* initially no packets are buffered */

  for (i = 0; i < NR_BUFS; i++) arrived[i] = false;
```

```
     wait_for_event(&event);                    /* five possibilities: see event_type above */
     switch(event) {
       case network_layer_ready:                /* accept, save, and transmit a new frame */
             nbuffered = nbuffered + 1;          /* expand the window */
             from_network_layer(&out_buf[next_frame_to_send % NR_BUFS]); /* fetch new packet */
             send_frame(data, next_frame_to_send, frame_expected, out_buf);/* transmit the frame */
             inc(next_frame_to_send);            /* advance upper window edge */
             break;

       case frame_arrival:                      /* a data or control frame has arrived */
             from_physical_layer(&r);            /* fetch incoming frame from physical layer */
             if (r.kind == data) {
                 /* An undamaged frame has arrived. */
                 if ((r.seq != frame_expected) && no_nak)
                     send_frame(nak, 0, frame_expected, out_buf); else start_ack_timer();
                 if (between(frame_expected, r.seq, too_far) && (arrived[r.seq%NR_BUFS] == false)) {
                     /* Frames may be accepted in any order. */
                     arrived[r.seq % NR_BUFS] = true;     /* mark buffer as full */
                     in_buf[r.seq % NR_BUFS] = r.info;    /* insert data into buffer */
                     while (arrived[frame_expected % NR_BUFS]) {
                         /* Pass frames and advance window. */
                         to_network_layer(&in_buf[frame_expected % NR_BUFS]);
                         no_nak = true;
                         arrived[frame_expected % NR_BUFS] = false;
                         inc(frame_expected);    /* advance lower edge of receiver's window */
                         inc(too_far);           /* advance upper edge of receiver's window */
                         start_ack_timer();      /* to see if a separate ack is needed */
                     }
                 }
             }
             if((r.kind==nak) && between(ack_expected,(r.ack+1)%(MAX_SEQ+1),next_frame_to_send))
                 send_frame(data, (r.ack+1) % (MAX_SEQ + 1), frame_expected, out_buf);

             while (between(ack_expected, r.ack, next_frame_to_send)) {
                 nbuffered = nbuffered − 1;       /* handle piggybacked ack */
                 stop_timer(ack_expected % NR_BUFS);    /* frame arrived intact */
                 inc(ack_expected);              /* advance lower edge of sender's window */
             }
             break;

       case cksum_err:
             if (no_nak) send_frame(nak, 0, frame_expected, out_buf);/* damaged frame */
             break;

       case timeout:
             send_frame(data, oldest_frame, frame_expected, out_buf);/* we timed out */
             break;

       case ack_timeout:
             send_frame(ack,0,frame_expected, out_buf);       /* ack timer expired; send ack */
     }
     if (nbuffered < NR_BUFS) enable_network_layer(); else disable_network_layer();
   }
 }
```

Fig. 3-18. A sliding window protocol using selective repeat.

multiple requests for retransmission of the same lost frame, the receiver should keep track of whether a NAK has already been sent for a given frame. The variable *no_nak* in protocol 6 is true if no NAK has been sent yet for *frame_expected*. If the NAK gets mangled or lost, no real harm is done, since the sender will eventually time out and retransmit the missing frame anyway. If the wrong frame arrives after a NAK has been sent and lost, *no_nak* will be true and the auxiliary timer will be started. When it goes off, an ACK will be sent to resynchronize the sender to the receiver's current status.

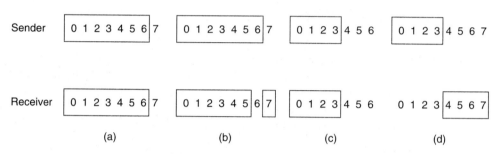

Fig. 3-19. (a) Initial situation with a window of size seven. (b) After seven frames have been sent and received but not acknowledged. (c) Initial situation with a window size of four. (d) After four frames have been sent and received but not acknowledged.

In some situations, the time required for a frame to propagate to the destination, be processed there, and have the acknowledgement come back is (nearly) constant. In these situations, the sender can adjust its timer to be just slightly larger than the normal time interval expected between sending a frame and receiving its acknowledgement. However, if this time is highly variable, the sender is faced with the choice of either setting the interval to a small value and risking unnecessary retransmissions, thus wasting bandwidth, or setting it to a large value, going idle for a long period after an error, thus also wasting bandwidth. If the reverse traffic is sporadic, the time before acknowledgement will be irregular, being shorter when there is reverse traffic and longer when there is not. Variable processing time within the receiver can also be a problem here. In general, whenever the standard deviation of the acknowledgement interval is small compared to the interval itself, the timer can be set "tight" and NAKs are not useful. Otherwise, the timer must be set "loose," and NAKs can appreciably speed up retransmission of lost or damaged frames.

Closely related to the matter of timeouts and NAKs is the question of determining which frame caused a timeout. In protocol 5 it is always *ack_expected*, because it is always the oldest. In protocol 6, there is no trivial way to determine who timed out. Suppose that frames 0 through 4 have been transmitted, meaning that the list of outstanding frames is 01234, in order from oldest to youngest. Now imagine that 0 times out, 5 (a new frame) is transmitted, 1 times out, 2 times out, and 6 (another new frame) is transmitted. At this point the list of outstanding frames is 3405126, from oldest to youngest. If all inbound traffic is lost for a while, the seven outstanding frames will time out in that order. To keep the example from getting even more complicated than it already is, we have not shown the timer administration. Instead, we just assume that the variable *oldest_frame* is set upon timeout to indicate which frame timed out.

3.5. PROTOCOL SPECIFICATION AND VERIFICATION

Realistic protocols, and the programs that implement them, are often quite complicated. Consequently, much research has been done trying to find formal, mathematical techniques for specifying and verifying protocols. In the following sections we will look at some models and techniques. Although we are looking at them in the context of the data link layer, they are also applicable to other layers.

3.5.1. Finite State Machine Models

A key concept used in many protocol models is the **finite state machine**. With this technique, each **protocol machine** (i.e., sender or receiver) is always in a specific state at every instant of time. Its state consists of all the values of its variables, including the program counter.

In most cases, a large number of states can be grouped together for purposes of analysis. For example, considering the receiver in protocol 3, we could abstract out from all the possible states two important ones: waiting for frame 0 or waiting for frame 1. All other states can be thought of as transient, just steps on the way to one of the main states. Typically, the states are chosen to be those instants that the protocol machine is waiting for the next event to happen [i.e., executing the procedure call *wait(event)* in our examples]. At this point the state of the protocol machine is completely determined by the states of its variables. The number of states is then 2^n, where n is the number of bits needed to represent all the variables combined.

The state of the complete system is the combination of all the states of the two protocol machines and the channel. The state of the channel is determined by its contents. Using protocol 3 again as an example, the channel has four possible states: a zero frame or a one frame moving from sender to receiver, an acknowledgement frame going the other way, or an empty channel. If we model the sender and receiver as each having two states, the complete system has 16 distinct states.

A word about the channel state is in order. The concept of a frame being "on the channel" is an abstraction, of course. What we really mean is that a frame has been partially transmitted, partially received, but not yet processed at the destination. A frame remains "on the channel" until the protocol machine executes *FromPhysicalLayer* and processes it.

From each state, there are zero or more possible **transitions** to other states. Transitions occur when some event happens. For a protocol machine a transition might occur when a frame is sent, when a frame arrives, when a timer goes off, when an interrupt occurs, etc. For the channel, typical events are insertion of a new frame onto the channel by a protocol machine, delivery of a frame to a protocol machine, or loss of a frame due to a noise burst. Given a complete description of the protocol machines and the channel characteristics, it is possible to draw a directed graph showing all the states as nodes and all the transitions as directed arcs.

One particular state is designated as the **initial state**. This state corresponds to the description of the system when it starts running, or some convenient starting place shortly thereafter. From the initial state, some, perhaps all, of the other states can be reached by a sequence of transitions. Using well-known techniques from graph theory (e.g., computing the transitive closure of a graph), it is possible to determine which states are reachable and which are not. This technique is called **reachability analysis** (Lin et al., 1987). This analysis can be helpful in determining if a protocol is correct or not.

Formally, a finite state machine model of a protocol can be regarded as a quadruple (S, M, I, T) where:

S is the set of states the processes and channel can be in.

M is the set of frames that can be exchanged over the channel.

I is the set of initial states of the processes.

T is the set of transitions between states.

At the beginning of time, all processes are in their initial states. Then events begin to happen, such as frames becoming available for transmission or timers going off. Each event may cause one of the processes or the channel to take an action and switch to a new state. By carefully enumerating each possible successor to each state, one can build the reachability graph and analyze the protocol.

Reachability analysis can be used to detect a variety of errors in the protocol specification. For example, if it is possible for a certain frame to occur in a certain state and the finite state machine does not say what action should be taken, the specification is in error (incompleteness). If there exists a set of states from which there is no exit and from which no progress can be made (correct frames received), we have another error (deadlock). A less serious error is protocol specification that tells how to handle an event in a state in which the event cannot occur (extraneous transition). Other errors can also be detected.

As an example of a finite state machine model, consider Fig. 3-20(a). This graph corresponds to protocol 3 as described above: each protocol machine has two states and the channel has four states. A total of 16 states exist, not all of them reachable from the initial one. The unreachable ones are not shown in the figure. Each state is labeled by three characters, *XYZ*, where *X* is 0 or 1, corresponding to the frame the sender is trying to send; *Y* is also 0 or 1, corresponding to the frame the receiver expects, and *Z* is 0, 1, *A*, or empty (–), corresponding to the state of the channel. In this example the initial state has been chosen as (000). In other words, the sender has just sent frame 0, the receiver expects frame 0, and frame 0 is currently on the channel.

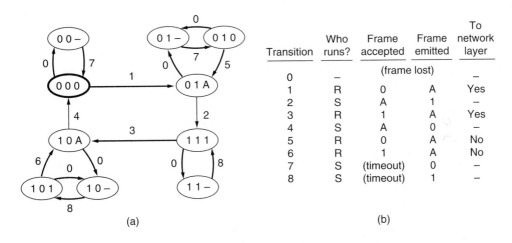

Fig. 3-20. (a) State diagram for protocol 3. (b) Transitions.

Transition	Who runs?	Frame accepted	Frame emitted	To network layer
0		(frame lost)		–
1	R	0	A	Yes
2	S	A	1	–
3	R	1	A	Yes
4	S	A	0	–
5	R	0	A	No
6	R	1	A	No
7	S	(timeout)	0	–
8	S	(timeout)	1	–

Nine kinds of transitions are shown in Fig. 3-20. Transition 0 consists of the channel losing its contents. Transition 1 consists of the channel correctly delivering packet 0 to the receiver, with the receiver then changing its state to expect frame 1 and emitting an acknowledgement. Transition 1 also corresponds to the receiver delivering packet 0 to the network layer. The other transitions are listed in Fig. 3-20(b). The arrival of a frame with a checksum error has not been shown because it does not change the state (in protocol 3).

During normal operation, transitions 1, 2, 3, and 4 are repeated in order over and over. In each cycle, two packets are delivered, bringing the sender back to the initial state of trying to send a new frame with sequence number 0. If the channel loses frame 0, it makes a transition from state (000) to state (00–). Eventually, the sender times out (transition 7) and the system moves back to (000). The loss of an acknowledgement is more complicated, requiring two transitions, 7 and 5, or 8 and 6, to repair the damage.

One of the properties that a protocol with a 1-bit sequence number must have is that no matter what sequence of events happens, the receiver never delivers two odd packets without an intervening even packet, and vice versa. From the graph of Fig. 3-20 we see that this requirement can be stated more formally as "there must not exist any paths from the initial state on which two occurrences of transition 1 occur without an occurrence of transition 3 between them, or vice versa.'' From the figure it can be seen that the protocol is correct in this respect.

Another, similar requirement is that there not be any paths on which the sender changes state twice (e.g., from 0 to 1 and back to 0) while the receiver state remains constant. Were such a path to exist, then in the corresponding sequence of events two frames would be irretrievably lost, without the receiver noticing. The packet sequence delivered would have an undetected gap of two packets in it.

Yet another important property of a protocol is the absence of deadlocks. A **deadlock** is a situation in which the protocol can make no more forward progress (i.e., deliver packets to the network layer) no matter what sequence of events happen. In terms of the graph model, a deadlock is characterized by the existence of a subset of states that is reachable from the initial state and which has two properties:

1. There is no transition out of the subset.

2. There are no transitions in the subset that cause forward progress.

Once in the deadlock situation, the protocol remains there forever. Again, it is easy to see from the graph that protocol 3 does not suffer from deadlocks.

Now let us consider a variation of protocol 3, one in which the half-duplex channel is replaced by a full-duplex channel. In Fig. 3-21 we show the states as the product of the states of the two protocol machines and the states of the two channels. Note that the forward channel now has three states: frame 0, frame 1, or empty, and the reverse channel has two states, A or empty. The transitions are the same as in Fig. 3-20(b), except that when a data frame and an acknowledgement are on the channel simultaneously, there is a slight peculiarity. The receiver cannot remove the data frame by itself, because that would entail having two acknowledgements on the channel at the same time, something not permitted in our model (although it is easy to devise a model that does allow it). Similarly, the sender cannot remove the acknowledgement, because that would entail emitting a second data frame before the first had been accepted. Consequently, both events must occur together, for example, the transition between state (000A) and state (111A), labeled as 1 + 2 in the figure.

In Fig. 3-21(a) there exist paths that cause the protocol to fail. In particular, there are paths in which the sender repeatedly fetches new packets, even though the previous ones have not been delivered correctly. The problem arises because it is now possible for the sender to time out and send a new frame without disturbing the acknowledgement on the reverse channel. When this acknowledgement arrives, it will be mistakenly regarded as referring to the current transmission and not the previous one.

One state sequence causing the protocol to fail is shown in Fig. 3-21(b). In

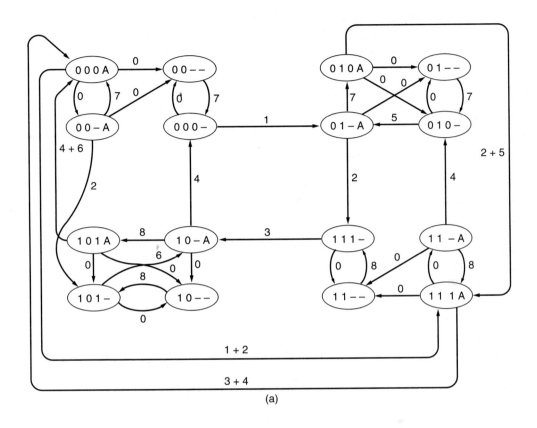

(0 0 0 −), (0 1 − A), (0 1 0 A), (1 1 1 A), (1 1 − A), (0 1 0 −), (0 1 − A), (1 1 1 −)

(b)

Fig. 3-21. (a) State graph for protocol 3 and a full-duplex channel. (b) Sequence of states causing the protocol to fail.

the fourth and sixth states of this sequence, the sender changes state, indicating that it fetches a new packet from the network layer, while the receiver does not change state, that is, does not deliver any packets to the network layer.

3.5.2. Petri Net Models

The finite state machine is not the only technique for formally specifying protocols. In this section we will describe another technique, the **Petri Net** (Danthine, 1980). A Petri net has four basic elements: places, transitions, arcs, and tokens. A **place** represents a state which (part of) the system may be in. Figure 3-22 shows a Petri net with two places, *A* and *B*, both shown as circles. The system is currently in state *A*, indicated by the **token** (heavy dot) in place *A*. A **transition** is indicated by a horizontal or vertical bar. Each transition has zero or more **input arcs**, coming from its input places, and zero or more **output arcs**, going to its output places.

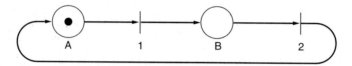

Fig. 3-22. A Petri net with two places and two transitions.

A transition is **enabled** if there is at least one input token in each of its input places. Any enabled transition may **fire** at will, removing one token from each input place and depositing a token in each output place. If the number of input arcs and output arcs differ, tokens will not be conserved. If two or more transitions are enabled, any one of them may fire. The choice of a transition to fire is indeterminate, which is why Petri nets are useful for modeling protocols. The Petri net of Fig. 3-22 is deterministic and can be used to model any two-phase process (e.g., the behavior of a baby: eat, sleep, eat, sleep, and so on). As with all modeling tools, unnecessary detail is suppressed.

Figure 3-23 gives the Petri net model of Fig. 3-21. Unlike the finite state machine model, there are no composite states here; the sender's state, channel state, and receiver's state are represented separately. Transitions 1 and 2 correspond to transmission of frame 0 by the sender, normally, and on a timeout respectively. Transitions 3 and 4 are analogous for frame 1. Transitions 5, 6, and 7 correspond to the loss of frame 0, an acknowledgement, and frame 1, respectively. Transitions 8 and 9 occur when a data frame with the wrong sequence number arrives at the receiver. Transitions 10 and 11 represent the arrival at the receiver of the next frame in sequence and its delivery to the network layer.

Petri nets can be used to detect protocol failures in a way similar to the use of finite state machines. For example, if some firing sequence included transition 10 twice without transition 11 intervening, the protocol would be incorrect. The concept of a deadlock in a Petri net is also similar to its finite state machine counterpart.

Petri nets can be represented in convenient algebraic form resembling a grammar. Each transition contributes one rule to the grammar. Each rule specifies the input and output places of the transition, for example, transition 1 in Fig. 3-23 is *BD → AC*. The current state of the Petri net is represented as an unordered collection of places, each place represented in the collection as many times as it has tokens. Any rule all of whose left-hand side places are present, can be fired, removing those places from the current state, and adding its output places to the current state. The marking of Fig. 3-23 is *ACG*, so rule 10 (*CG → DF*) can be applied but rule 3 (*AD → BE*) cannot be applied.

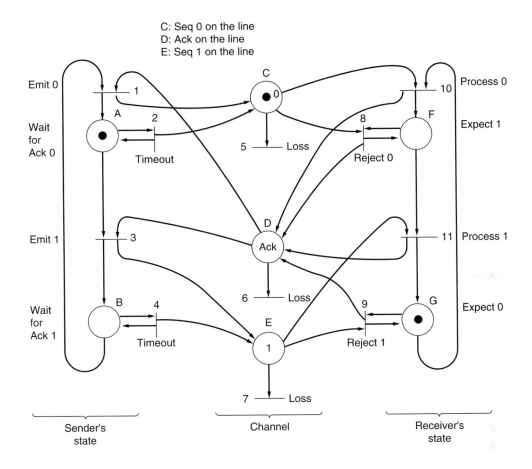

Fig. 3-23. A Petri net model for protocol 3.

3.6. EXAMPLE DATA LINK PROTOCOLS

In the following sections we will examine several widely-used data link protocols. The first one, HDLC, is common in X.25 and many other networks. After that, we will examine data link protocols used in the Internet and ATM networks, respectively. In subsequent chapters, we will also use the Internet and ATM as running examples as well.

3.6.1. HDLC—High-level Data Link Control

In this section we will examine a group of closely related protocols that are a bit old but are still heavily used in networks throughout the world. They are all derived from the data link protocol used in IBM's SNA, called **SDLC**

(**Synchronous Data Link Control**) protocol. After developing SDLC, IBM submitted it to ANSI and ISO for acceptance as U.S. and international standards, respectively. ANSI modified it to become **ADCCP** (**Advanced Data Communication Control Procedure**), and ISO modified it to become **HDLC** (**High-level Data Link Control**). CCITT then adopted and modified HDLC for its **LAP** (**Link Access Procedure**) as part of the X.25 network interface standard but later modified it again to **LAPB**, to make it more compatible with a later version of HDLC. The nice thing about standards is that you have so many to choose from. Furthermore, if you do not like any of them, you can just wait for next year's model.

All of these protocols are based on the same principles. All are bit-oriented, and all use bit stuffing for data transparency. They differ only in minor, but nevertheless irritating, ways. The discussion of bit-oriented protocols that follows is intended as a general introduction. For the specific details of any one protocol, please consult the appropriate definition.

All the bit-oriented protocols use the frame structure shown in Fig. 3-24. The *Address* field is primarily of importance on lines with multiple terminals, where it is used to identify one of the terminals. For point-to-point lines, it is sometimes used to distinguish commands from responses.

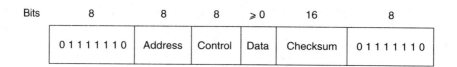

Fig. 3-24. Frame format for bit-oriented protocols.

The *Control* field is used for sequence numbers, acknowledgements, and other purposes, as discussed below.

The *Data* field may contain arbitrary information. It may be arbitrarily long, although the efficiency of the checksum falls off with increasing frame length due to the greater probability of multiple burst errors.

The *Checksum* field is a minor variation on the well-known cyclic redundancy code, using CRC-CCITT as the generator polynomial. The variation is to allow lost flag bytes to be detected.

The frame is delimited with another flag sequence (01111110). On idle point-to-point lines, flag sequences are transmitted continuously. The minimum frame contains three fields and totals 32 bits, excluding the flags on either end.

There are three kinds of frames: **Information, Supervisory**, and **Unnumbered**. The contents of the *Control* field for these three kinds are shown in Fig. 3-25. The protocol uses a sliding window, with a 3-bit sequence number. Up to seven unacknowledged frames may be outstanding at any instant. The *Seq* field in Fig. 3-25(a) is the frame sequence number. The *Next* field is a piggybacked acknowledgement. However, all the protocols adhere to the convention that instead of piggybacking the number of the last frame received correctly, they use the number of the first frame not received (i.e., the next frame expected). The choice of using the last frame received or the next frame expected is arbitrary; it does not matter which convention is used, provided that it is used consistently.

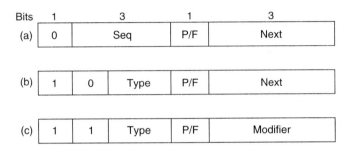

Fig. 3-25. Control field of (a) an information frame, (b) a supervisory frame, (c) an unnumbered frame.

The *P/F* bit stands for *Poll/Final*. It is used when a computer (or concentrator) is polling a group of terminals. When used as *P*, the computer is inviting the terminal to send data. All the frames sent by the terminal, except the final one, have the *P/F* bit set to *P*. The final one is set to *F*.

In some of the protocols, the *P/F* bit is used to force the other machine to send a Supervisory frame immediately rather than waiting for reverse traffic onto which to piggyback the window information. The bit also has some minor uses in connection with the Unnumbered frames.

The various kinds of Supervisory frames are distinguished by the *Type* field. Type 0 is an acknowledgement frame (officially called RECEIVE READY) used to indicate the next frame expected. This frame is used when there is no reverse traffic to use for piggybacking.

Type 1 is a negative acknowledgement frame (officially called REJECT). It is used to indicate that a transmission error has been detected. The *Next* field indicates the first frame in sequence not received correctly (i.e., the frame to be retransmitted). The sender is required to retransmit all outstanding frames starting at *Next*. This strategy is similar to our protocol 5 rather than our protocol 6.

Type 2 is RECEIVE NOT READY. It acknowledges all frames up to but not including *Next*, just as RECEIVE READY, but it tells the sender to stop sending. RECEIVE NOT READY is intended to signal certain temporary problems with the receiver, such as a shortage of buffers, and not as an alternative to the sliding window flow control. When the condition has been repaired, the receiver sends a RECEIVE READY, REJECT, or certain control frames.

Type 3 is the SELECTIVE REJECT. It calls for retransmission of only the frame specified. In this sense it is like our protocol 6 rather than 5 and is therefore most useful when the sender's window size is half the sequence space size, or less. Thus if a receiver wishes to buffer out of sequence frames for potential future use, it can force the retransmission of any specific frame using Selective Reject. HDLC and ADCCP allow this frame type, but SDLC and LAPB do not allow it (i.e., there is no Selective Reject), and type 3 frames are undefined.

The third class of frame is the Unnumbered frame. It is sometimes used for control purposes but can also be used to carry data when unreliable connectionless service is called for. The various bit-oriented protocols differ considerably here, in contrast with the other two kinds, where they are nearly identical. Five bits are available to indicate the frame type, but not all 32 possibilities are used.

All the protocols provide a command, DISC (DISConnect), that allows a machine to announce that it is going down (e.g., for preventive maintenance). They also have a command that allows a machine that has just come back on-line to announce its presence and force all the sequence numbers back to zero. This command is called SNRM (Set Normal Response Mode). Unfortunately, "Normal Response Mode" is anything but normal. It is an unbalanced (i.e., asymmetric) mode in which one end of the line is the master and the other the slave. SNRM dates from a time when data communication meant a dumb terminal talking to a computer, which clearly is asymmetric. To make the protocol more suitable when the two partners are equals, HDLC and LAPB have an additional command, SABM (Set Asynchronous Balanced Mode), which resets the line and declares both parties to be equals. They also have commands SABME and SNRME, which are the same as SABM and SNRM, respectively, except that they enable an extended frame format that uses 7-bit sequence numbers instead of 3-bit sequence numbers.

A third command provided by all the protocols is FRMR (FRaMe Reject), used to indicate that a frame with a correct checksum but impossible semantics arrived. Examples of impossible semantics are a type 3 Supervisory frame in LAPB, a frame shorter than 32 bits, an illegal control frame, and an acknowledgement of a frame that was outside the window, etc. FRMR frames contain a 24-bit data field telling what was wrong with the frame. The data include the control field of the bad frame, the window parameters, and a collection of bits used to signal specific errors.

Control frames may be lost or damaged, just like data frames, so they must be acknowledged too. A special control frame is provided for this purpose, called UA (Unnumbered Acknowledgement). Since only one control frame may be outstanding, there is never any ambiguity about which control frame is being acknowledged.

The remaining control frames deal with initialization, polling, and status reporting. There is also a control frame that may contain arbitrary information, UI (Unnumbered Information). These data are not passed to the network layer but are for the receiving data link layer itself.

Despite its widespread use, HDLC is far from perfect. A discussion of a variety of problems associated with it can be found in (Fiorini et al., 1995).

3.6.2. The Data Link Layer in the Internet

The Internet consists of individual machines (hosts and routers), and the communication infrastructure that connects them. Within a single building, LANs are widely used for interconnection, but most of the wide area infrastructure is built up from point-to-point leased lines. In Chap. 4, we will look at LANs; here we will examine the data link protocols used on point-to-point lines in the Internet.

In practice, point-to-point communication is primarily used in two situations. First, thousands of organizations have one or more LANs, each with some number of hosts (personal computers, user workstations, servers, and so on) along with a router (or a bridge, which is functionally similar). Often, the routers are interconnected by a backbone LAN. Typically, all connections to the outside world go through one or two routers that have point-to-point leased lines to distant routers. It is these routers and their leased lines that make up the communication subnets on which the Internet is built.

The second situation where point-to-point lines play a major role in the Internet is the millions of individuals who have home connections to the Internet using modems and dial-up telephone lines. Usually, what happens is that the user's home PC calls up an **Internet provider**, which includes commercial companies like America Online, CompuServe, and the Microsoft Network, but also many universities and companies that provide home Internet connectivity to their students and employees. Sometimes the home PC just functions as a character-oriented terminal logged into the Internet service provider's timesharing system. In this mode, the user can type commands and run programs, but the graphical Internet services, such as the World Wide Web, are not available. This way of working is called having a **shell account**.

Alternatively, the home PC can call an Internet service provider's router and then act like a full-blown Internet host. This method of operation is no different than having a leased line between the PC and the router, except that the connection is terminated when the user ends the session. With this approach, all Internet services, including the graphical ones, become available. A home PC calling an Internet service provider is illustrated in Fig. 3-26.

For both the router-router leased line connection and the dial-up host-router connection, some point-to-point data link protocol is required on the line for framing, error control, and the other data link layer functions we have studied in this chapter. Two such protocols are widely used in the Internet, SLIP and PPP. We will now examine each of these in turn.

SLIP—Serial Line IP

SLIP is the older of the two protocols. It was devised by Rick Adams in 1984 to connect Sun workstations to the Internet over a dial-up line using a modem. The protocol, which is described in RFC 1055, is very simple. The workstation

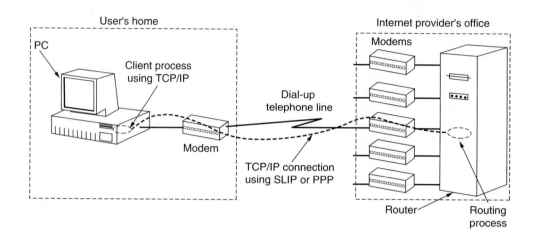

Fig. 3-26. A home personal computer acting as an Internet host.

just sends raw IP packets over the line, with a special flag byte (0xC0) at the end for framing. If the flag byte occurs inside the IP packet, a form of character stuffing is used, and the two byte sequence (0xDB, 0xDC) is sent in its place. If 0xDB occurs inside the IP packet, it, too, is stuffed. Some SLIP implementations attach a flag byte to both the front and back of each IP packet sent.

More recent versions of SLIP do some TCP and IP header compression. What they do is take advantage of the fact that consecutive packets often have many header fields in common. These are compressed by omitting those fields that are the same as the corresponding fields in the previous IP packet. Furthermore, the fields that do differ are not sent in their entirety, but as increments to the previous value. These optimizations are described in RFC 1144.

Although it is still widely used, SLIP has some serious problems. First, it does not do any error detection or correction, so it is up to higher layers to detect and recover from lost, damaged, or merged frames.

Second, SLIP supports only IP. With the growth of the Internet to encompass networks that do not use IP as their native language (e.g., Novell LANs), this restriction is becoming increasingly serious.

Third, each side must know the other's IP address in advance; neither address can be dynamically assigned during setup. Given the current shortage of IP addresses, this limitation is a major issue as it is impossible to give each home Internet user a unique IP address.

Fourth, SLIP does not provide any form of authentication, so neither party knows whom it is really talking to. With leased lines, this is not an issue, but with dial-up lines it is.

Fifth, SLIP is not an approved Internet Standard, so many different (and incompatible) versions exist. This situation does not make interworking easier.

PPP—Point-to-Point Protocol

To improve the situation, the IETF set up a group to devise a data link proto-col for point-to-point lines that solved all these problems and that could become an official Internet Standard. This work culminated in **PPP (Point-to-Point Pro-tocol)**, which is defined in RFC 1661 and further elaborated on in several other RFCs (e.g., RFCs 1662 and 1663). PPP handles error detection, supports multiple protocols, allows IP addresses to be negotiated at connection time, permits authentication, and has many other improvements over SLIP. While many Inter-net service providers still support both SLIP and PPP, the future clearly lies with PPP, not only for dial-up lines, but also for leased router-router lines.

PPP provides three things:

1. A framing method that unambiguously delineates the end of one frame and the start of the next one. The frame format also handles error detection.

2. A link control protocol for bringing lines up, testing them, negotiat-ing options, and bringing them down again gracefully when they are no longer needed. This protocol is called **LCP (Link Control Pro-tocol)**.

3. A way to negotiate network-layer options in a way that is indepen-dent of the network layer protocol to be used. The method chosen is to have a different **NCP (Network Control Protocol)** for each net-work layer supported.

To see how these pieces fit together, let us consider the typical scenario of a home user calling up an Internet service provider to make a home PC a temporary Internet host. The PC first calls the provider's router via a modem. After the router's modem has answered the phone and established a physical connection, the PC sends the router a series of LCP packets in the payload field of one or more PPP frames. These packets, and their responses, select the PPP parameters to be used.

Once these have been agreed upon, a series of NCP packets are sent to config-ure the network layer. Typically, the PC wants to run a TCP/IP protocol stack, so it needs an IP address. There are not enough IP addresses to go around, so nor-mally each Internet provider gets a block of them and then dynamically assigns one to each newly attached PC for the duration of its login session. If a provider owns n IP addresses, it can have up to n machines logged in simultaneously, but its total customer base may be many times that. The NCP for IP is used to do the IP address assignment.

At this point, the PC is now an Internet host and can send and receive IP pack-ets, just as hardwired hosts can. When the user is finished, NCP is used to tear down the network layer connection and free up the IP address. Then LCP is used to shut down the data link layer connection. Finally, the computer tells the modem to hang up the phone, releasing the physical layer connection.

The PPP frame format was chosen to closely resemble the HDLC frame format, since there was no reason to reinvent the wheel. The major difference between PPP and HDLC is that the former is character oriented rather than bit oriented. In particular, PPP, like, SLIP, uses character stuffing on dial-up modem lines, so all frames are an integral number of bytes. It is not possible to send a frame consisting of 30.25 bytes, as it is with HDLC. Not only can PPP frames be sent over dial-up telephone lines, but they can also be sent over SONET or true bit-oriented HDLC lines (e.g., for router-router connections). The PPP frame format is shown in Fig. 3-27.

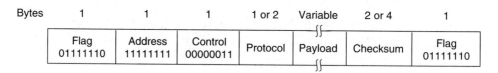

Fig. 3-27. The PPP full frame format for unnumbered mode operation.

All PPP frames begin with the standard HDLC flag byte (01111110), which is character stuffed if it occurs within the payload field. Next comes the *Address* field, which is always set to the binary value 11111111 to indicate that all stations are to accept the frame. Using this value avoids the issue of having to assign data link addresses.

The *Address* field is followed by the *Control* field, the default value of which is 00000011. This value indicates an unnumbered frame. In other words, PPP does not provide reliable transmission using sequence numbers and acknowledgements as the default. In noisy environments, such as wireless networks, reliable transmission using numbered mode can be used. The exact details are defined in RFC 1663.

Since the *Address* and *Control* fields are always constant in the default configuration, LCP provides the necessary mechanism for the two parties to negotiate an option to just omit them altogether and save 2 bytes per frame.

The fourth PPP field is the *Protocol* field. Its job is to tell what kind of packet is in the *Payload* field. Codes are defined for LCP, NCP, IP, IPX, AppleTalk, and other protocols. Protocols starting with a 0 bit are network layer protocols such as IP, IPX, OSI CLNP, XNS. Those starting with a 1 bit are used to negotiate other protocols. These include LCP and a different NCP for each network layer protocol supported. The default size of the *Protocol* field is 2 bytes, but it can be negotiated down to 1 byte using LCP.

The *Payload* field is variable length, up to some negotiated maximum. If the length is not negotiated using LCP during line setup, a default length of 1500 bytes is used. Padding may follow the payload if need be.

After the *Payload* field comes the *Checksum* field, which is normally 2 bytes, but a 4-byte checksum can be negotiated.

In summary, PPP is a multiprotocol framing mechanism suitable for use over modems, HDLC bit-serial lines, SONET, and other physical layers. It supports error detection, option negotiation, header compression, and optionally, reliable transmission using HDLC framing.

Let us now turn from the PPP frame format to the way lines are brought up and down. The (simplified) diagram of Fig. 3-28 shows the phases that a line goes through when it is brought up, used, and taken down again. This sequence applies both to modem connections and to router-router connections.

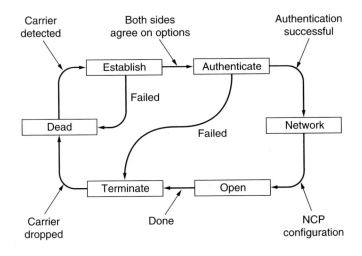

Fig. 3-28. A simplified phase diagram for bringing a line up and down.

When the line is *DEAD*, no physical layer carrier is present and no physical layer connection exists. After physical connection is established, the line moves to *ESTABLISHED*. At that point LCP option negotiation begins, which, if successful, leads to *AUTHENTICATE*. Now the two parties can check on each other's identities, if desired. When the *NETWORK* phase is entered, the appropriate NCP protocol is invoked to configure the network layer. If the configuration is successful, *OPEN* is reached and data transport can take place. When data transport is finished, the line moves into the *TERMINATE* phase, and from there, back to *DEAD* when the carrier is dropped.

LCP is used to negotiate data link protocol options during the *ESTABLISH* phase. The LCP protocol is not actually concerned with the options themselves, but with the mechanism for negotiation. It provides a way for the initiating process to make a proposal and for the responding process to accept or reject it, in whole or in part. It also provides a way for the two processes to test the line quality, to see if they consider it good enough to set up a connection. Finally, the LCP protocol also allows lines to be taken down when they are no longer needed.

Eleven types of LCP packets are defined in RFC 1661. These are listed in Fig. 3-29. The four *Configure-* types allow the initiator (I) to propose option values and the responder (R) to accept or reject them. In the latter case, the responder can make an alternative proposal or announce that it is not willing to negotiate certain options at all. The options being negotiated and their proposed values are part of the LCP packets.

Name	Direction	Description
Configure-request	I → R	List of proposed options and values
Configure-ack	I ← R	All options are accepted
Configure-nak	I ← R	Some options are not accepted
Configure-reject	I ← R	Some options are not negotiable
Terminate-request	I → R	Request to shut the line down
Terminate-ack	I ← R	OK, line shut down
Code-reject	I ← R	Unknown request received
Protocol-reject	I ← R	Unknown protocol requested
Echo-request	I → R	Please send this frame back
Echo-reply	I ← R	Here is the frame back
Discard-request	I → R	Just discard this frame (for testing)

Fig. 3-29. The LCP packet types.

The *Terminate-* codes are used to shut a line down when it is no longer needed. The *Code-reject* and *Protocol-reject* codes are used by the responder to indicate that it got something that it does not understand. This situation could mean that an undetected transmission error has occurred, but more likely it means that the initiator and responder are running different versions of the LCP protocol. The *Echo-* types are used to test the line quality. Finally, *Discard-request* is used for debugging. If either end is having trouble getting bits onto the wire, the programmer can use this type for testing. If it manages to get through, the receiver just throws it away, rather than taking some other action, which might confuse the person doing the testing.

The options that can be negotiated include setting the maximum payload size for data frames, enabling authentication and choosing a protocol to use, enabling line quality monitoring during normal operation, and selecting various header compression options.

There is little to say about the NCP protocols in a general way. Each one is specific to some network layer protocol and allows configuration requests to be made that are specific to that protocol. For IP, for example, dynamic address assignment is the most important possibility.

3.6.3. The Data Link Layer in ATM

It is now time to begin our journey up through the ATM protocol layers of Fig. 1-30. The ATM physical layer covers roughly the OSI physical and data link layers, with the physical medium dependent sublayer being functionally like the OSI physical layer and the transmission convergence (TC) sublayer having data link functionality. There are no physical layer characteristics specific to ATM. Instead, ATM cells are carried by SONET, FDDI, and other transmission systems. Therefore we will concentrate here on the data link functionality of the TC sublayer, but we will discuss some aspects of the interface with the lower sublayer later on.

When an application program produces a message to be sent, that message works its way down the ATM protocol stack, having headers and trailers added and undergoing segmentation into cells. Eventually, the cells reach the TC sublayer for transmission. Let us see what happens to them on the way out the door.

Cell Transmission

The first step is header checksumming. Each cell contains a 5-byte header consisting of 4 bytes of virtual circuit and control information followed by a 1-byte checksum. Although the contents of the header are not relevant to the TC sublayer, curious readers wishing a sneak preview should turn to Fig. 5-62. The checksum only covers the first four header bytes, not the payload field. It consists of the remainder after the 32 header bits have been divided by the polynomial $x^8 + x^2 + x + 1$. To this the constant 01010101 is added, to provide robustness in the face of headers containing mostly 0 bits.

The decision to checksum only the header was made to reduce the probability of cells being delivered incorrectly due to a header error, but to avoid paying the price of checksumming the much larger payload field. It is up to higher layers to perform this function, if they so desire. For many real-time applications, such as voice and video, losing a few bits once in a while is acceptable (although for some compression schemes, all frames are equal but some frames are more equal). Because it covers only the header, the 8-bit checksum field is called the **HEC (Header Error Control)**.

A factor that played a major role in this checksumming scheme is the fact that ATM was designed for use over fiber, and fiber is highly reliable. Furthermore, a major study of the U.S. telephone network has shown that during normal operation 99.64 percent of all errors on fiber optic lines are single-bit errors (AT&T and Bellcore, 1989). The HEC scheme corrects all single-bit errors and detects many multibit errors as well. If we assume that the probability of a single-bit error is 10^{-8}, then the probability of a cell containing a detectable multibit header error is about 10^{-13}. The probability of a cell slipping through with an undetected header error is about 10^{-20}, which means that at OC-3 speed, one bad cell header will get through every 90,000 years. Although this may sound like a long time, once the earth has, say, 1 billion ATM telephones, each used 10 percent of the time, over 1000 bad cell headers per year will go undetected.

For applications that need reliable transmission in the data link layer, Shacham and McKenney (1990) have developed a scheme in which a sequence of consecutive cells are EXCLUSIVE ORed together. The result, an entire cell, is appended to the sequence. If one cell is lost or badly garbled, it can be reconstructed from the available information.

Once the HEC has been generated and inserted into the cell header, the cell is ready for transmission. Transmission media come in two categories: asynchronous and synchronous. When an asynchronous medium is used, a cell can be sent whenever it is ready to go. No timing restrictions exist.

With a synchronous medium, cells must be transmitted according to a predefined timing pattern. If no data cell is available when needed, the TC sublayer must invent one. These are called **idle cells**.

Another kind of nondata cell is the **OAM (Operation And Maintenance)** cell. OAM cells are also used by the ATM switches for exchanging control and other information necessary for keeping the system running. OAM cells also have some other special functions. For example, the 155.52-Mbps OC-3 speed matches the gross data rate of SONET, but an STM-1 frame has a total of 10 columns of overhead out of 270, so the SONET payload is only $260/270 \times 155.52$ Mbps or 149.76 Mbps. To keep from swamping SONET, an ATM source using SONET would normally put out an OAM cell as every 27th cell, to slow the data rate down to 26/27 of 155.52 Mbps and thus match SONET exactly. The job of matching the ATM output rate to the rate of the underlying transmission system is an important task of the TC sublayer.

On the receiver's side, idle cells are processed in the TC sublayer, but OAM cells are given to the ATM layer. OAM cells are distinguished from data cells by having the first three header bytes be all zeros, something not allowed for data cells. The fourth byte describes the nature of the OAM cell.

Another important task of the TC sublayer is generating the framing information for the underlying transmission system, if any. For example, an ATM video camera might just produce a sequence of cells on the wire, but it might also produce SONET frames with the ATM cells embedded inside the SONET payload. In the latter case, the TC sublayer would generate the SONET framing and pack the ATM cells inside, not entirely a trivial business since a SONET payload does not hold an integral number of 53-byte cells.

Although the telephone companies clearly intend to use SONET as the underlying transmission system for ATM, mappings from ATM onto the payload fields of other systems have also been defined, and new ones are being worked on. In particular, mappings onto T1, T3, and FDDI also exist.

Cell Reception

On output, the job of the TC sublayer is to take a sequence of cells, add a HEC to each one, convert the result to a bit stream, and match the bit stream to the speed of the underlying physical transmission system by inserting OAM cells as filler. On input, the TC sublayer does exactly the reverse. It takes an incoming bit stream, locates the cell boundaries, verifies the headers (discarding cells with invalid headers), processes the OAM cells, and passes the data cells up to the ATM layer.

The hardest part is locating the cell boundaries in the incoming bit stream. At the bit level, a cell is just a sequence of $53 \times 8 = 424$ bits. No 01111110 flag bytes are present to mark the start and end of a cell, as they are in HDLC. In fact, there are no markers at all. How can cell boundaries be recognized under these circumstances?

In some case, the underlying physical layer provides help. With SONET, for example, cells can be aligned with the synchronous payload envelope, so the SPE pointer in the SONET header points to the start of the first full cell. However, sometimes the physical layer provides no assistance in framing. What then?

The trick is to use the HEC. As the bits come in, the TC sublayer maintains a 40-bit shift register, with bits entering on the left and exiting on the right. The TC sublayer then inspects the 40 bits to see if it is potentially a valid cell header. If it is, the rightmost 8 bits will be valid HEC over the leftmost 32 bits. If this condition does not hold, the buffer does not hold a valid cell, in which case all the bits in the buffer are shifted right one bit, causing one bit to fall off the end, and a new input bit is inserted at the left end. This process is repeated until a valid HEC is located. At that point, the cell boundary is known because the shift register contains a valid header.

The trouble with this heuristic is that the HEC is only 8 bits wide. For any given shift register, even one containing random bits, the probability of finding a valid HEC is 1/256, a moderately large value. Used by itself, this procedure would incorrectly detect cell headers far too often.

To improve the accuracy of the recognition algorithm, the finite state machine of Fig. 3-30 is used. Three states are used: *HUNT*, *PRESYNCH*, and *SYNCH*. In the *HUNT* state, the TC sublayer is shifting bits into the shift registers one at a time looking for a valid HEC. As soon as one is found, the finite state machine switches to *PRESYNCH* state, meaning that it has tentatively located a cell boundary. It now shifts in the next 424 bits (53 bytes) without examining them. If its guess about the cell boundary was correct, the shift register should now contain another valid cell header, so it once again runs the HEC algorithm. If the HEC is incorrect, the TC goes back to the *HUNT* state and continues to search bit-by-bit for a header whose HEC is correct.

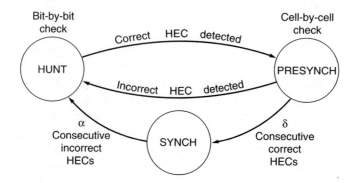

Fig. 3-30. The cell delineation heuristic.

On the other hand, if the second HEC is also correct, the TC may be onto something, so it shifts in another 424 bits and tries again. It continues inspecting headers in this fashion until it has found δ correct headers in a row, at which time it assumes that it is synchronized and moves into the *SYNCH* state to start normal operation. Note that the probability of getting into *SYNCH* state by accident with a purely random bit stream is $2^{-8\delta}$, which can be made arbitrarily small by choosing a large enough δ. The price paid for a large δ, however, is a longer time to synchronize.

In addition to resynchronizing after losing synchronization (or at startup), the TC sublayer needs a heuristic to determine when it has lost synchronization, for example after a bit has been inserted or deleted from the bit stream. It would be unwise to give up if just one HEC was incorrect, since most errors are bit inversions, not insertions or deletions. The wisest course here is just to discard the cell with the bad header and hope the next one is good. However, if α HECs in a row are bad, the TC sublayer has to conclude that it has lost synchronization and must return to the *HUNT* state.

Although unlikely, it is conceivable that a malicious user could try to spoof the TC sublayer by inserting a data pattern into the payload field of many consecutive cells that imitates the HEC algorithm. Then, if synchronization were ever lost, it might be regained in the wrong place. To make this trick much harder, the payload bits are scrambled on transmission and descrambled on reception.

Before leaving the TC sublayer, one comment is in order. The mechanism chosen for cell delineation requires the TC sublayer to understand and use the header of the ATM layer above it. Having one layer make use of the header of a higher layer is in complete violation of the basic rules of protocol engineering. The idea of having layered protocols is to make each layer be independent of the ones above it. It should be possible, for example, to change the header format of the ATM layer without affecting the TC sublayer. However due to the way cell delineation is accomplished, making such a change is not possible.

3.7. SUMMARY

The task of the data link layer is to convert the raw bit stream offered by the physical layer into a stream of frames for use by the network layer. Various framing methods are used, including character count, character stuffing, and bit stuffing. Data link protocols can provide error control to retransmit damaged or lost frames. To prevent a fast sender from overrunning a slow receiver, the data link protocol can also provide flow control. The sliding window mechanism is widely used to integrate error control and flow control in a convenient way.

Sliding window protocols can be categorized by the size of the sender's window and the size of the receiver's window. When both are equal to 1, the protocol is stop-and-wait. When the sender's window is greater than 1, for example to prevent the sender from blocking on a circuit with a long propagation delay, the receiver can be programmed either to discard all frames other than the next one in sequence (protocol 5) or buffer out of order frames until they are needed (protocol 6).

Protocols can be modeled using various techniques to help demonstrate their correctness (or lack thereof). Finite state machine models and Petri net models are commonly used for this purpose.

Many networks use one of the bit-oriented protocols—SDLC, HDLC, ADCCP, or LAPB—at the data link level. All of these protocols use flag bytes to delimit frames, and bit stuffing to prevent flag bytes from occurring in the data. All of them also use a sliding window for flow control. The Internet uses SLIP and PPP as data link protocols. ATM systems have their own simple protocol, which does a bare minimum of error checking and no flow control.

PROBLEMS

1. An upper layer message is split into 10 frames, each of which has an 80 percent chance of arriving undamaged. If no error control is done by the data link protocol, how many times must the message be sent on the average to get the entire thing through?

2. The following data fragment occurs in the middle of a data stream for which the character-stuffing algorithm described in the text is used: DLE, STX, A, DLE, B, DLE, ETX. What is the output after stuffing?

3. If the bit string 0111101111101111110 is bit stuffed, what is the output string?

4. When bit stuffing is used, is it possible for the loss, insertion, or modification of a single bit to cause an error not detected by the checksum? If not, why not? If so, how? Does the checksum length play a role here?

5. Can you think of any circumstances under which an open-loop protocol, (e.g., a Hamming code) might be preferable to the feedback type protocols discussed throughout this chapter?

6. To provide more reliability than a single parity bit can give, an error-detecting coding scheme uses one parity bit for checking all the odd numbered bits and a second parity bit for all the even numbered bits. What is the Hamming distance of this code?

7. One way of detecting errors is to transmit data as a block of n rows of k bits per row and adding parity bits to each row and each column. Will this scheme detect all single errors? Double errors? Triple errors?

8. A block of bits with n rows and k columns uses horizontal and vertical parity bits for error detection. Suppose that exactly 4 bits are inverted due to transmission errors. Derive an expression for the probability that the error will be undetected.

9. What is the remainder obtained by dividing $x^7 + x^5 + 1$ by the generator polynomial $x^3 + 1$?

10. Data link protocols almost always put the CRC in a trailer, rather than in a header. Why?

11. A channel has a bit rate of 4 kbps and a propagation delay of 20 msec. For what range of frame sizes does stop-and-wait give an efficiency of at least 50 percent?

12. A 3000-km long T1 trunk is used to transmit 64-byte frames using protocol 5. If the propagation speed is 6 μsec/km, how many bits should the sequence numbers be?

13. Imagine a sliding window protocol using so many bits for sequence numbers that wraparound never occurs. What relations must hold among the four window edges and the window size?

14. If the procedure *between* in protocol 5 checked for the condition $a \le b \le c$ instead of the condition $a \le b < c$, would that have any effect on the protocol's correctness or efficiency? Explain your answer.

15. In protocol 6, when a data frame arrives, a check is made to see if the sequence number differs from the one expected and *NoNak* is true. If both conditions hold, a NAK is sent. Otherwise, the auxiliary timer is started. Suppose that the else clause were omitted. Would this change affect the protocol's correctness?

16. Suppose that the three-statement while loop near the end of protocol 6 were removed from the code. Would this affect the correctness of the protocol or just the performance? Explain your answer.

17. Suppose that the case for checksum errors were removed from the switch statement of protocol 6. How would this change affect the operation of the protocol?

18. In protocol 6 the code for *FrameArrival* has a section used for NAKs. This section is invoked if the incoming frame is a NAK and another condition is met. Give a scenario where the presence of this other condition is essential.

19. Imagine that you are writing the data link layer software for a line used to send data to you, but not from you. The other end uses HDLC, with a 3-bit sequence number and a window size of seven frames. You would like to buffer as many out of sequence frames as possible to enhance efficiency, but you are not allowed to modify the software on the sending side. Is it possible to have a receiver window greater than one, and still guarantee that the protocol will never fail? If so, what is the largest window that can be safely used?

20. Consider the operation of protocol 6 over a 1-Mbps error-free line. The maximum frame size is 1000 bits. New packets are generated about 1 second apart. The timeout interval is 10 msec. If the special acknowledgement timer were eliminated, unnecessary timeouts would occur. How many times would the average message be transmitted?

21. In protocol 6 $MaxSeq = 2^n - 1$. While this condition is obviously desirable to make efficient use of header bits, we have not demonstrated that it is essential. Does the protocol work correctly for $MaxSeq = 4$, for example?

22. Frames of 1000 bits are sent over a 1-Mbps satellite channel. Acknowledgements are always piggybacked onto data frames. The headers are very short. Three-bit sequence numbers are used. What is the maximum achievable channel utilization for
(a) Stop-and-wait.
(b) Protocol 5.
(c) Protocol 6.

23. Compute the fraction of the bandwidth that is wasted on overhead (headers and retransmissions) for protocol 6 on a heavily loaded 50-kbps satellite channel with data frames consisting of 40 header and 3960 data bits. ACK frames never occur. NAK frames are 40 bits. The error rate for data frames is 1 percent, and the error rate for NAK frames is negligible. The sequence numbers are 8 bits.

24. Consider an error-free 64-kbps satellite channel used to send 512-byte data frames in one direction, with very short acknowledgements coming back the other way. What is the maximum throughput for window sizes of 1, 7, 15, and 127?

25. A 100 km long cable runs at the T1 data rate. The propagation speed in the cable is 2/3 the speed of light. How many bits fit in the cable?

26. Redraw Fig. 3-21 for a full-duplex channel that never loses frames. Is the protocol failure still possible?

27. Give the firing sequence for the Petri net of Fig. 3-23 corresponding to the state sequence (000), (01A), (01—), (010), (01A) in Fig. 3-20. Explain in words what the sequence represents.

28. Given the transition rules $AC \rightarrow B$, $B \rightarrow AC$, $CD \rightarrow E$, and $E \rightarrow CD$, draw the Petri net described. From the Petri net, draw the finite state graph reachable from the initial state ACD. What well-known computer science concept do these transition rules model?

29. PPP is based closely on HDLC, which uses bit stuffing to prevent accidental flag bytes within the payload from causing confusion. Give at least one reason why PPP uses character stuffing instead.

30. What is the minimum overhead in sending an IP packet using PPP? Count only the overhead introduced by PPP itself, not the IP header overhead.

31. Consider the ATM cell delineation heuristic with $\alpha = 5$, $\delta = 6$, and a per-bit error rate of 10^{-5}. Once the system is synchronized, how long will it remain so, despite occasional header bit errors? Assume the line is running at OC-3.

32. Write a program to stochastically simulate the behavior of a Petri net. The program should read in the transition rules as well as a list of states corresponding to the network link layer issuing a new packet or the accepting a new packet. From the initial state, also read in, the program should pick enabled transitions at random and fire them, checking to see if a host ever accepts two messages without the other host emitting a new one in between.

4

THE MEDIUM ACCESS SUBLAYER

As we pointed out in Chap. 1, networks can be divided into two categories: those using point-to-point connections and those using broadcast channels. This chapter deals with broadcast networks and their protocols.

In any broadcast network, the key issue is how to determine who gets to use the channel when there is competition for it. To make this point clearer, consider a conference call in which six people, on six different telephones, are all connected together so that each one can hear and talk to all the others. It is very likely that when one of them stops speaking, two or more will start talking at once, leading to chaos. In a face-to-face meeting, chaos is avoided by external means, for example, at a meeting, people raise their hands to request permission to speak. When only a single channel is available, determining who should go next is much harder. Many protocols for solving the problem are known and form the contents of this chapter. In the literature, broadcast channels are sometimes referred to as **multiaccess channels** or **random access channels**.

The protocols used to determine who goes next on a multiaccess channel belong to a sublayer of the data link layer called the **MAC** (**Medium Access Control**) sublayer. The MAC sublayer is especially important in LANs, nearly all of which use a multiaccess channel as the basis of their communication. WANs, in contrast, use point-to-point links, except for satellite networks. Because multiaccess channels and LANs are so closely related, in this chapter we will discuss LANs in general, as well as satellite and some other broadcast networks.

Technically, the MAC sublayer is the bottom part of the data link layer, so logically we should have studied it before examining all the point-to-point protocols in Chap. 3. Nevertheless, for most people, understanding protocols involving multiple parties is easier after two-party protocols are well understood. For that reason we have deviated slightly from a strict bottom-up order of presentation.

4.1. THE CHANNEL ALLOCATION PROBLEM

The central theme of this chapter is how to allocate a single broadcast channel among competing users. We will first look at static and dynamic schemes in general. Then we will examine a number of specific algorithms.

4.1.1. Static Channel Allocation in LANs and MANs

The traditional way of allocating a single channel, such as a telephone trunk, among multiple competing users is Frequency Division Multiplexing (FDM). If there are N users, the bandwidth is divided into N equal sized portions (see Fig. 2-24), each user being assigned one portion. Since each user has a private frequency band, there is no interference between users. When there is only a small and fixed number of users, each of which has a heavy (buffered) load of traffic (e.g., carriers' switching offices), FDM is a simple and efficient allocation mechanism.

However, when the number of senders is large and continuously varying, or the traffic is bursty, FDM presents some problems. If the spectrum is cut up into N regions, and fewer than N users are currently interested in communicating, a large piece of valuable spectrum will be wasted. If more than N users want to communicate, some of them will be denied permission, for lack of bandwidth, even if some of the users who have been assigned a frequency band hardly ever transmit or receive anything.

However, even assuming that the number of users could somehow be held constant at N, dividing the single available channel into static subchannels is inherently inefficient. The basic problem is that when some users are quiescent, their bandwidth is simply lost. They are not using it, and no one else is allowed to use it either. Furthermore, in most computer systems, data traffic is extremely bursty (peak traffic to mean traffic ratios of 1000:1 are common). Consequently, most of the channels will be idle most of the time.

The poor performance of static FDM can easily be seen from a simple queueing theory calculation. Let us start with the mean time delay, T, for a channel of capacity C bps, with an arrival rate of λ frames/sec, each frame having a length drawn from an exponential probability density function with mean $1/\mu$ bits/frame:

$$T = \frac{1}{\mu C - \lambda}$$

Now let us divide the single channel up into N independent subchannels, each with capacity C/N bps. The mean input rate on each of the subchannels will now be λ/N. Recomputing T we get

$$T_{FDM} = \frac{1}{\mu(C/N) - (\lambda/N)} = \frac{N}{\mu C - \lambda} = NT \qquad (4\text{-}1)$$

The mean delay using FDM is N times worse than if all the frames were somehow magically arranged orderly in a big central queue.

Precisely the same arguments that apply to FDM also apply to time division multiplexing (TDM). Each user is statically allocated every Nth time slot. If a user does not use the allocated slot, it just lies fallow. Since none of the traditional static channel allocation methods work well with bursty traffic, we will now explore dynamic methods.

4.1.2. Dynamic Channel Allocation in LANs and MANs

Before we get into the first of the many channel allocation methods to be discussed in this chapter, it is worthwhile carefully formulating the allocation problem. Underlying all the work done in this area are five key assumptions, described below.

1. **Station model**. The model consists of N independent **stations** (computers, telephones, personal communicators, etc.), each with a program or user that generates frames for transmission. The probability of a frame being generated in an interval of length Δt is $\lambda \Delta t$, where λ is a constant (the arrival rate of new frames). Once a frame has been generated, the station is blocked and does nothing until the frame has been successfully transmitted.

2. **Single Channel Assumption**. A single channel is available for all communication. All stations can transmit on it and all can receive from it. As far as the hardware is concerned, all stations are equivalent, although protocol software may assign priorities to them.

3. **Collision Assumption**. If two frames are transmitted simultaneously, they overlap in time and the resulting signal is garbled. This event is called a **collision**. All stations can detect collisions. A collided frame must be transmitted again later. There are no errors other than those generated by collisions.

4a. **Continuous Time**. Frame transmission can begin at any instant. There is no master clock dividing time into discrete intervals.

4b. **Slotted Time**. Time is divided into discrete intervals (slots). Frame transmissions always begin at the start of a slot. A slot may contain 0, 1, or more frames, corresponding to an idle slot, a successful transmission, or a collision, respectively.

5a. **Carrier Sense**. Stations can tell if the channel is in use before trying to use it. If the channel is sensed as busy, no station will attempt to use it until it goes idle.

5b. **No Carrier Sense**. Stations cannot sense the channel before trying to use it. They just go ahead and transmit. Only later can they determine whether or not the transmission was successful.

Some discussion of these assumptions is in order. The first one says that stations are independent, and that work is generated at a constant rate. It also implicitly assumes that each station only has one program or user, so while the station is blocked, no new work is generated. More sophisticated models allow multiprogrammed stations that can generate work while a station is blocked, but the analysis of these stations is much more complex.

The single channel assumption is the heart of the matter. There are no external ways to communicate. Stations cannot raise their hands to request that the teacher call on them.

The collision assumption is also basic, although in some systems (notably spread spectrum), this assumption is relaxed, with surprising results. Also, some LANs, such as token rings, use a mechanism for contention elimination that eliminates collisions.

There are two alternative assumptions about time. Either it is continuous or it is slotted. Some systems use one and some systems use the other, so we will discuss and analyze both. Obviously, for a given system, only one of them holds.

Similarly, a network can either have carrier sensing or not have it. LANs generally have carrier sense, but satellite networks do not (due to the long propagation delay). Stations on carrier sense networks can terminate their transmission prematurely if they discover that it is colliding with another transmission. Note that the word "carrier" in this sense refers to an electrical signal on the cable and has nothing to do with the common carriers (e.g., telephone companies) that date back to the Pony Express days.

4.2. MULTIPLE ACCESS PROTOCOLS

Many algorithms for allocating a multiple access channel are known. In the following sections we will study a representative sample of the more interesting ones and give some examples of their use.

4.2.1. ALOHA

In the 1970s, Norman Abramson and his colleagues at the University of Hawaii devised a new and elegant method to solve the channel allocation problem. Their work has been extended by many researchers since then (Abramson,

1985). Although Abramson's work, called the ALOHA system, used ground-based radio broadcasting, the basic idea is applicable to any system in which uncoordinated users are competing for the use of a single shared channel.

We will discuss two versions of ALOHA here: pure and slotted. They differ with respect to whether or not time is divided up into discrete slots into which all frames must fit. Pure ALOHA does not require global time synchronization; slotted ALOHA does.

Pure ALOHA

The basic idea of an ALOHA system is simple: let users transmit whenever they have data to be sent. There will be collisions, of course, and the colliding frames will be destroyed. However, due to the feedback property of broadcasting, a sender can always find out whether or not its frame was destroyed by listening to the channel, the same way other users do. With a LAN, the feedback is immediate; with a satellite, there is a delay of 270 msec before the sender knows if the transmission was successful. If the frame was destroyed, the sender just waits a random amount of time and sends it again. The waiting time must be random or the same frames will collide over and over, in lockstep. Systems in which multiple users share a common channel in a way that can lead to conflicts are widely known as **contention** systems.

A sketch of frame generation in an ALOHA system is given in Fig. 4-1. We have made the frames all the same length because the throughput of ALOHA systems is maximized by having a uniform frame size rather than allowing variable length frames.

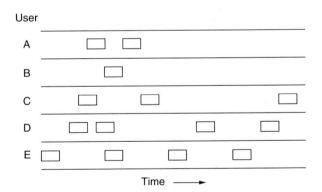

Fig. 4-1. In pure ALOHA, frames are transmitted at completely arbitrary times.

Whenever two frames try to occupy the channel at the same time, there will be a collision and both will be garbled. If the first bit of a new frame overlaps with just the last bit of a frame almost finished, both frames will be totally destroyed, and both will have to be retransmitted later. The checksum cannot (and should not) distinguish between a total loss and a near miss. Bad is bad.

A most interesting question is: What is the efficiency of an ALOHA channel? That is, what fraction of all transmitted frames escape collisions under these chaotic circumstances? Let us first consider an infinite collection of interactive users sitting at their computers (stations). A user is always in one of two states: typing or waiting. Initially, all users are in the typing state. When a line is finished, the user stops typing, waiting for a response. The station then transmits a frame containing the line and checks the channel to see if it was successful. If so, the user sees the reply and goes back to typing. If not, the user continues to wait and the frame is retransmitted over and over until it has been successfully sent.

Let the "frame time" denote the amount of time needed to transmit the standard, fixed-length frame (i.e., the frame length divided by the bit rate). At this point we assume that the infinite population of users generates new frames according to a Poisson distribution with mean S frames per frame time. (The infinite-population assumption is needed to ensure that S does not decrease as users become blocked.) If $S > 1$, the user community is generating frames at a higher rate than the channel can handle, and nearly every frame will suffer a collision. For reasonable throughput we would expect $0 < S < 1$.

In addition to the new frames, the stations also generate retransmissions of frames that previously suffered collisions. Let us further assume that the probability of k transmission attempts per frame time, old and new combined, is also Poisson, with mean G per frame time. Clearly, $G \geq S$. At low load (i.e., $S \approx 0$), there will be few collisions, hence few retransmissions, so $G \approx S$. At high load there will be many collisions, so $G > S$. Under all loads, the throughput is just the offered load, G, times the probability of a transmission being successful—that is, $S = GP_0$, where P_0 is the probability that a frame does not suffer a collision.

A frame will not suffer a collision if no other frames are sent within one frame time of its start, as shown in Fig. 4-2. Under what conditions will the shaded frame arrive undamaged? Let t be the time required to send a frame. If any other user has generated a frame between time t_0 and $t_0 + t$, the end of that frame will collide with the beginning of the shaded one. In fact, the shaded frame's fate was already sealed even before the first bit was sent, but since in pure ALOHA a station does not listen to the channel before transmitting, it has no way of knowing that another frame was already underway. Similarly, any other frame started between $t_0 + t$ and $t_0 + 2t$ will bump into the end of the shaded frame.

The probability that k frames are generated during a given frame time is given by the Poisson distribution:

$$\Pr[k] = \frac{G^k e^{-G}}{k!} \tag{4-2}$$

so the probability of zero frames is just e^{-G}. In an interval two frame times long, the mean number of frames generated is $2G$. The probability of no other traffic

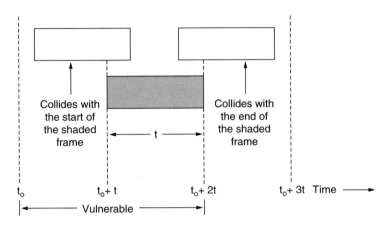

Fig. 4-2. Vulnerable period for the shaded frame.

being initiated during the entire vulnerable period is thus given by $P_0 = e^{-2G}$. Using $S = GP_0$, we get

$$S = Ge^{-2G}$$

The relation between the offered traffic and the throughput is shown in Fig. 4-3. The maximum throughput occurs at $G = 0.5$, with $S = 1/2e$, which is about 0.184. In other words, the best we can hope for is a channel utilization of 18 percent. This result is not very encouraging, but with everyone transmitting at will, we could hardly have expected a 100 percent success rate.

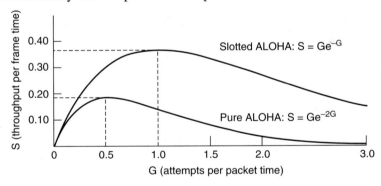

Fig. 4-3. Throughput versus offered traffic for ALOHA systems.

Slotted ALOHA

In 1972, Roberts published a method for doubling the capacity of an ALOHA system (Roberts, 1972). His proposal was to divide time up into discrete intervals, each interval corresponding to one frame. This approach requires the users to agree of slot boundaries. One way to achieve synchronization would be to have one special station emit a pip at the start of each interval, like a clock.

In Roberts' method, which has come to be known as **slotted ALOHA**, in contrast to Abramson's **pure ALOHA**, a computer is not permitted to send whenever a carriage return is typed. Instead, it is required to wait for the beginning of the next slot. Thus the continuous pure ALOHA is turned into a discrete one. Since the vulnerable period is now halved, the probability of no other traffic during the same slot as our test frame is e^{-G} which leads to

$$S = Ge^{-G} \qquad (4\text{-}3)$$

As you can see from Fig. 4-3, slotted ALOHA peaks at $G = 1$, with a throughput of $S = 1/e$ or about 0.368, twice that of pure ALOHA. If the system is operating at $G = 1$, the probability of an empty slot is 0.368 (from Eq. 4-2). The best we can hope for using slotted ALOHA is 37 percent of the slots empty, 37 percent successes, and 26 percent collisions. Operating at higher values of G reduces the number of empties but increases the number of collisions exponentially. To see how this rapid growth of collisions with G comes about, consider the transmission of a test frame. The probability that it will avoid a collision is e^{-G}, the probability that all the other users are silent in that slot. The probability of a collision is then just $1 - e^{-G}$. The probability of a transmission requiring exactly k attempts, (i.e., $k - 1$ collisions followed by one success) is

$$P_k = e^{-G}(1 - e^{-G})^{k-1}$$

The expected number of transmissions, E, per carriage return typed is then

$$E = \sum_{k=1}^{\infty} kP_k = \sum_{k=1}^{\infty} ke^{-G}(1 - e^{-G})^{k-1} = e^G$$

As a result of the exponential dependence of E upon G, small increases in the channel load can drastically reduce its performance.

4.2.2. Carrier Sense Multiple Access Protocols

With slotted ALOHA the best channel utilization that can be achieved is $1/e$. This is hardly surprising, since with stations transmitting at will, without paying attention to what the other stations are doing, there are bound to be many collisions. In local area networks, however it is possible for stations to detect what other stations are doing, and adapt their behavior accordingly. These networks can achieve a much better utilization than $1/e$. In this section we will discuss some protocols for improving performance.

Protocols in which stations listen for a carrier (i.e., a transmission) and act accordingly are called **carrier sense protocols**. A number of them have been proposed. Kleinrock and Tobagi (1975) have analyzed several such protocols in detail. Below we will mention several versions of the carrier sense protocols.

Persistent and Nonpersistent CSMA

The first carrier sense protocol that we will study here is called **1-persistent CSMA** (Carrier Sense Multiple Access). When a station has data to send, it first listens to the channel to see if anyone else is transmitting at that moment. If the channel is busy, the station waits until it becomes idle. When the station detects an idle channel, it transmits a frame. If a collision occurs, the station waits a random amount of time and starts all over again. The protocol is called 1-persistent because the station transmits with a probability of 1 whenever it finds the channel idle.

The propagation delay has an important effect on the performance of the protocol. There is a small chance that just after a station begins sending, another station will become ready to send and sense the channel. If the first station's signal has not yet reached the second one, the latter will sense an idle channel and will also begin sending, resulting in a collision. The longer the propagation delay, the more important this effect becomes, and the worse the performance of the protocol.

Even if the propagation delay is zero, there will still be collisions. If two stations become ready in the middle of a third station's transmission, both will wait politely until the transmission ends and then both will begin transmitting exactly simultaneously, resulting in a collision. If they were not so impatient, there would be fewer collisions. Even so, this protocol is far better than pure ALOHA, because both stations have the decency to desist from interfering with the third station's frame. Intuitively, this will lead to a higher performance than pure ALOHA. Exactly the same holds for slotted ALOHA.

A second carrier sense protocol is **nonpersistent CSMA**. In this protocol, a conscious attempt is made to be less greedy than in the previous one. Before sending, a station senses the channel. If no one else is sending, the station begins doing so itself. However, if the channel is already in use, the station does not continually sense it for the purpose of seizing it immediately upon detecting the end of the previous transmission. Instead, it waits a random period of time and then repeats the algorithm. Intuitively this algorithm should lead to better channel utilization and longer delays than 1-persistent CSMA.

The last protocol is **p-persistent CSMA**. It applies to slotted channels and works as follows. When a station becomes ready to send, it senses the channel. If it is idle, it transmits with a probability p. With a probability $q = 1 - p$ it defers until the next slot. If that slot is also idle, it either transmits or defers again, with probabilities p and q. This process is repeated until either the frame has been transmitted or another station has begun transmitting. In the latter case, it acts as if there had been a collision (i.e., it waits a random time and starts again). If the station initially senses the channel busy, it waits until the next slot and applies the above algorithm. Figure 4-4 shows the throughput versus offered traffic for all three protocols, as well as pure and slotted ALOHA.

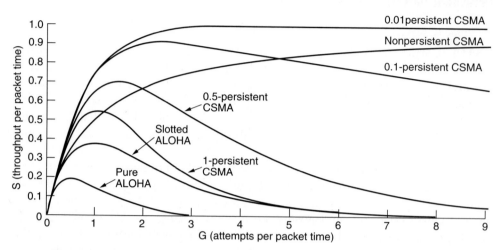

Fig. 4-4. Comparison of the channel utilization versus load for various random access protocols.

CSMA with Collision Detection

Persistent and nonpersistent CSMA protocols are clearly an improvement over ALOHA because they ensure that no station begins to transmit when it senses the channel busy. Another improvement is for stations to abort their transmissions as soon as they detect a collision. In other words, if two stations sense the channel to be idle and begin transmitting simultaneously, they will both detect the collision almost immediately. Rather than finish transmitting their frames, which are irretrievably garbled anyway, they should abruptly stop transmitting as soon as the collision is detected. Quickly terminating damaged frames saves time and bandwidth. This protocol, known as **CSMA/CD** (**Carrier Sense Multiple Access with Collision Detection**), is widely used on LANs in the MAC sublayer.

CSMA/CD, as well as many other LAN protocols, uses the conceptual model of Fig. 4-5. At the point marked t_0, a station has finished transmitting its frame. Any other station having a frame to send may now attempt to do so. If two or more stations decide to transmit simultaneously, there will be a collision. Collisions can be detected by looking at the power or pulse width of the received signal and comparing it to the transmitted signal.

After a station detects a collision, it aborts its transmission, waits a random period of time, and then tries again, assuming that no other station has started transmitting in the meantime. Therefore, our model for CSMA/CD will consist of alternating contention and transmission periods, with idle periods occurring when all stations are quiet (e.g., for lack of work).

Now let us look closely at the details of the contention algorithm. Suppose

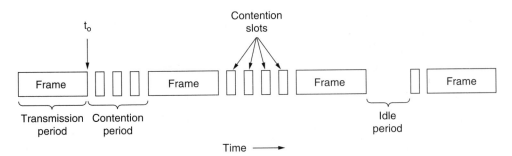

Fig. 4-5. CSMA/CD can be in one of three states: contention, transmission, or idle.

that two stations both begin transmitting at exactly time t_0. How long will it take them to realize that there has been a collision? The answer to this question is vital to determining the length of the contention period, and hence what the delay and throughput will be. The minimum time to detect the collision is then just the time it takes the signal to propagate from one station to the other.

Based on this reasoning, you might think that a station not hearing a collision for a time equal to the full cable propagation time after starting its transmission could be sure it had seized the cable. By "seized," we mean that all other stations knew it was transmitting and would not interfere. This conclusion is wrong. Consider the following worst-case scenario. Let the time for a signal to propagate between the two farthest stations be τ. At t_0, one station begins transmitting. At $\tau - \varepsilon$, an instant before the signal arrives at the most distant station, that station also begins transmitting. Of course, it detects the collision almost instantly and stops, but the little noise burst caused by the collision does not get back to the original station until time $2\tau - \varepsilon$. In other words, in the worst case a station cannot be sure that it has seized the channel until it has transmitted for 2τ without hearing a collision. For this reason we will model the contention interval as a slotted ALOHA system with slot width 2τ. On a 1-km long coaxial cable, $\tau \approx 5$ μsec. For simplicity we will assume that each slot contains just 1 bit. Once the channel has been seized, a station can transmit at any rate it wants to, of course, not just at 1 bit per 2τ sec.

It is important to realize that collision detection is an *analog* process. The station's hardware must listen to the cable while it is transmitting. If what it reads back is different from what it is putting out, it knows a collision is occurring. The implication is that the signal encoding must allow collisions to be detected (e.g., a collision of two 0-volt signals may well be impossible to detect). For this reason, special encoding is commonly used.

CSMA/CD is an important protocol. Later in this chapter we will study one version of it, IEEE 802.3 (Ethernet), which is an international standard.

To avoid any misunderstanding, it is worth noting that no MAC-sublayer protocol guarantees reliable delivery. Even in the absence of collisions, the receiver may not have copied the frame correctly due to various reasons (e.g., lack of buffer space or a missed interrupt).

4.2.3. Collision-Free Protocols

Although collisions do not occur with CSMA/CD once a station has unambiguously seized the channel, they can still occur during the contention period. These collisions adversely affect the system performance, especially when the cable is long (i.e., large τ) and the frames short. As very long, high-bandwidth fiber optic networks come into use, the combination of large τ and short frames will become an increasingly serious problem. In this section, we will examine some protocols that resolve the contention for the channel without any collisions at all, not even during the contention period.

In the protocols to be described, we make the assumption that there are N stations, each with a unique address from 0 to $N - 1$ "wired" into it. That some stations may be inactive part of the time does not matter. The basic question remains: Which station gets the channel after a successful transmission? We continue using the model of Fig. 4-5 with its discrete contention slots.

A Bit-Map Protocol

In our first collision-free protocol, the **basic bit-map method**, each contention period consists of exactly N slots. If station 0 has a frame to send, it transmits a 1 bit during the zeroth slot. No other station is allowed to transmit during this slot. Regardless of what station 0 does, station 1 gets the opportunity to transmit a 1 during slot 1, but only if it has a frame queued. In general, station j may announce the fact that it has a frame to send by inserting a 1 bit into slot j. After all N slots have passed by, each station has complete knowledge of which stations wish to transmit. At that point, they begin transmitting in numerical order (see Fig. 4-6).

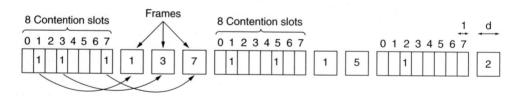

Fig. 4-6. The basic bit-map protocol.

Since everyone agrees on who goes next, there will never be any collisions. After the last ready station has transmitted its frame, an event all stations can easily monitor, another N bit contention period is begun. If a station becomes ready just after its bit slot has passed by, it is out of luck and must remain silent until every station has had a chance and the bit map has come around again. Protocols like this in which the desire to transmit is broadcast before the actual transmission are called **reservation protocols**.

Let us briefly analyze the performance of this protocol. For convenience, we will measure time in units of the contention bit slot, with data frames consisting of d time units. Under conditions of low load, the bit map will simply be repeated over and over, for lack of data frames.

Consider the situation from the point of view of a low-numbered station, such as 0 or 1. Typically, when it becomes ready to send, the "current" slot will be somewhere in the middle of the bit map. On the average, the station will have to wait $N/2$ slots for the current scan to finish and another full N slots for the following scan to run to completion before it may begin transmitting.

The prospects for high-numbered stations are brighter. Generally, these will only have to wait half a scan ($N/2$ bit slots) before starting to transmit. High-numbered stations rarely have to wait for the next scan. Since low-numbered stations must wait on the average $1.5N$ slots and high-numbered stations must wait on the average $0.5N$ slots, the mean for all stations is N slots. The channel efficiency at low load is easy to compute. The overhead per frame is N bits, and the amount of data is d bits, for an efficiency of $d/(N + d)$.

At high load, when all the stations have something to send all the time, the N bit contention period is prorated over N frames, yielding an overhead of only 1 bit per frame, or an efficiency of $d/(d + 1)$. The mean delay for a frame is equal to the sum of the time it queues inside its station, plus an additional $N(d + 1)/2$ once it gets to the head of its internal queue.

Binary Countdown

A problem with the basic bit-map protocol is that the overhead is 1 bit per station. We can do better than that by using binary station addresses. A station wanting to use the channel now broadcasts its address as a binary bit string, starting with the high-order bit. All addresses are assumed to be the same length. The bits in each address position from different stations are BOOLEAN ORed together. We will call this protocol **binary countdown**. It is used in Datakit (Fraser, 1987).

To avoid conflicts, an arbitration rule must be applied: as soon as a station sees that a high-order bit position that is 0 in its address has been overwritten with a 1, it gives up. For example, if stations 0010, 0100, 1001, and 1010 are all trying to get the channel, in the first bit time the stations transmit 0, 0, 1, and 1, respectively. These are ORed together to form a 1. Stations 0010 and 0100 see the 1 and know that a higher-numbered station is competing for the channel, so they give up for the current round. Stations 1001 and 1010 continue.

The next bit is 0, and both stations continue. The next bit is 1, so station 1001 gives up. The winner is station 1010, because it has the highest address. After winning the bidding, it may now transmit a frame, after which another bidding cycle starts. The protocol is illustrated in Fig. 4-7.

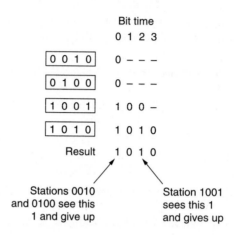

Fig. 4-7. The binary countdown protocol. A dash indicates silence.

The channel efficiency of this method is $d/(d + \ln N)$. If, however, the frame format has been cleverly chosen so that the sender's address is the first field in the frame, even these $\ln N$ bits are not wasted, and the efficiency is 100 percent.

Mok and Ward (1979) have described a variation of binary countdown using a parallel rather than a serial interface. They also suggest using virtual station numbers, with the virtual station numbers from 0 up to and including the successful station being circularly permuted after each transmission, in order to give higher priority to stations that have been silent unusually long. For example, if stations C, H, D, A, G, B, E, F have priorities 7, 6, 5, 4, 3, 2, 1, and 0, respectively, then a successful transmission by D puts it at the end of the list, giving a priority order of C, H, A, G, B, E, F, D. Thus C remains virtual station 7, but A moves up from 4 to 5 and D drops from 5 to 0. Station D will now only be able to acquire the channel if no other station wants it.

4.2.4. Limited-Contention Protocols

We have now considered two basic strategies for channel acquisition in a cable network: contention, as in CSMA, and collision-free methods. Each strategy can be rated as to how well it does with respect to the two important performance measures, delay at low load and channel efficiency at high load. Under conditions of light load, contention (i.e., pure or slotted ALOHA) is preferable due to its low delay. As the load increases, contention becomes increasingly less attractive, because the overhead associated with channel arbitration becomes greater. Just the reverse is true for the collision-free protocols. At low load, they have high delay, but as the load increases, the channel efficiency improves rather than gets worse as it does for contention protocols.

Obviously, it would be nice if we could combine the best properties of the contention and collision-free protocols, arriving at a new protocol that used contention at low loads to provide low delay, but used a collision-free technique at high load to provide good channel efficiency. Such protocols, which we will call **limited contention protocols**, do, in fact, exist, and will conclude our study of carrier sense networks.

Up until now the only contention protocols we have studied have been symmetric, that is, each station attempts to acquire the channel with some probability, p, with all stations using the same p. Interestingly enough, the overall system performance can sometimes be improved by using a protocol that assigns different probabilities to different stations.

Before looking at the asymmetric protocols, let us quickly review the performance of the symmetric case. Suppose that k stations are contending for channel access. Each has a probability p of transmitting during each slot. The probability that some station successfully acquires the channel during a given slot is then $kp(1 - p)^{k-1}$. To find the optimal value of p, we differentiate with respect to p, set the result to zero, and solve for p. Doing so, we find that the best value of p is $1/k$. Substituting $p = 1/k$ we get

$$\text{Pr[success with optimal } p] = \left[\frac{k - 1}{k} \right]^{k-1} \tag{4-4}$$

This probability is plotted in Fig. 4-8. For small numbers of stations, the chances of success are good, but as soon as the number of stations reaches even five, the probability has dropped close to its asymptotic value of $1/e$.

From Fig. 4-8, it is fairly obvious that the probability of some station acquiring the channel can be increased only by decreasing the amount of competition. The limited-contention protocols do precisely that. They first divide the stations up into (not necessarily disjoint) groups. Only the members of group 0 are permitted to compete for slot 0. If one of them succeeds, it acquires the channel and transmits its frame. If the slot lies fallow or if there is a collision, the members of group 1 contend for slot 1, etc. By making an appropriate division of stations into groups, the amount of contention for each slot can be reduced, thus operating each slot near the left end of Fig. 4-8.

The trick is how to assign stations to slots. Before looking at the general case, let us consider some special cases. At one extreme, each group has but one member. Such an assignment guarantees that there will never be collisions, because at most one station is contending per slot. We have seen such protocols before (e.g., binary countdown). The next special case is to assign two stations per group. The probability that both will try to transmit during a slot is p^2, which

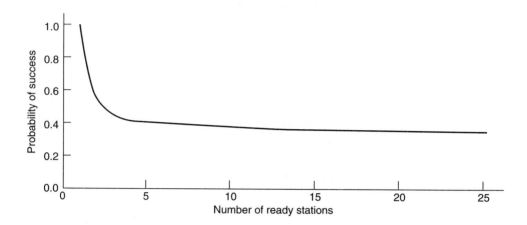

Fig. 4-8. Acquisition probability for a symmetric contention channel.

for small p is negligible. As more and more stations are assigned to the same slot, the probability of a collision grows, but the length of the bit-map scan needed to give everyone a chance shrinks. The limiting case is a single group containing all stations (i.e., slotted ALOHA). What we need is a way to assign stations to slots dynamically, with many stations per slot when the load is low and few (or even just one) station per slot when the load is high.

The Adaptive Tree Walk Protocol

One particularly simple way of performing the necessary assignment is to use the algorithm devised by the U.S. Army for testing soldiers for syphilis during World War II (Dorfman, 1943). In short, the Army took a blood sample from N soldiers. A portion of each sample was poured into a single test tube. This mixed sample was then tested for antibodies. If none were found, all the soldiers in the group were declared healthy. If antibodies were present, two new mixed samples were prepared, one from soldiers 1 through $N/2$ and one from the rest. The process was repeated recursively until the infected soldiers were determined.

For the computer version of this algorithm (Capetanakis, 1979) it is convenient to think of the stations as the leaves of a binary tree, as illustrated in Fig. 4-9. In the first contention slot following a successful frame transmission, slot 0, all stations are permitted to try to acquire the channel. If one of them does so, fine. If there is a collision, then during slot 1 only those stations falling under node 2 in the tree may compete. If one of them acquires the channel, the slot following the frame is reserved for those stations under node 3. If, on the other hand, two or more stations under node 2 want to transmit, there will be a collision during slot 1, in which case it is node 4's turn during slot 2.

In essence, if a collision occurs during slot 0, the entire tree is searched, depth

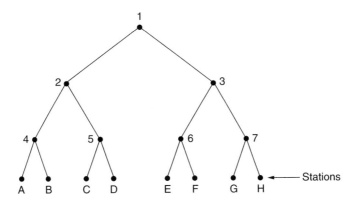

Fig. 4-9. The tree for eight stations.

first, to locate all ready stations. Each bit slot is associated with some particular node in the tree. If a collision occurs, the search continues recursively with the node's left and right children. If a bit slot is idle or if there is only one station that transmits in it, the searching of its node can stop, because all ready stations have been located. (Were there more than one, there would have been a collision.)

When the load on the system is heavy, it is hardly worth the effort to dedicate slot 0 to node 1, because that makes sense only in the unlikely event that precisely one station has a frame to send. Similarly, one could argue that nodes 2 and 3 should be skipped as well for the same reason. Put in more general terms, at what level in the tree should the search begin? Clearly, the heavier the load, the farther down the tree the search should begin. We will assume that each station has a good estimate of the number of ready stations, q, for example, from monitoring recent traffic.

To proceed, let us number the levels of the tree from the top, with node 1 in Fig. 4-9 at level 0, nodes 2 and 3 at level 1, etc. Notice that each node at level i has a fraction 2^{-i} of the stations below it. If the q ready stations are uniformly distributed, the expected number of them below a specific node at level i is just $2^{-i}q$. Intuitively, we would expect the optimal level to begin searching the tree as the one at which the mean number of contending stations per slot is 1, that is, the level at which $2^{-i}q = 1$. Solving this equation we find that $i = \log_2 q$.

Numerous improvements to the basic algorithm have been discovered and are discussed in some detail by Bertsekas and Gallager (1992). For example, consider the case of stations G and H being the only ones wanting to transmit. At node 1 a collision will occur, so 2 will be tried and discovered idle. It is pointless to probe node 3 since it is guaranteed to have a collision (we know that two or more stations under 1 are ready and none of them are under 2 so they must all be under 3). The probe of 3 can be skipped and 6 tried next. When this probe also turns up nothing, 7 can be skipped and node G tried next.

4.2.5. Wavelength Division Multiple Access Protocols

A different approach to channel allocation is to divide the channel into sub-channels using FDM, TDM, or both, and dynamically allocate them as needed. Schemes like this are commonly used on fiber optic LANs in order to permit different conversations to use different wavelengths (i.e., frequencies) at the same time. In this section we will examine one such protocol (Humblet et al., 1992).

A simple way to build an all-optical LAN is to use a passive star coupler (see Fig. 2-10). In effect, two fibers from each station are fused to a glass cylinder. One fiber is for output to the cylinder and one is for input from the cylinder. Light output by any station illuminates the cylinder and can be detected by all the other stations. Passive stars can handle hundreds of stations.

To allow multiple transmissions at the same time, the spectrum is divided up into channels (wavelength bands), as shown in Fig. 2-24. In this protocol, **WDMA (Wavelength Division Multiple Access)**, each station is assigned two channels. A narrow channel is provided as a control channel to signal the station, and a wide channel is provided so the station can output data frames.

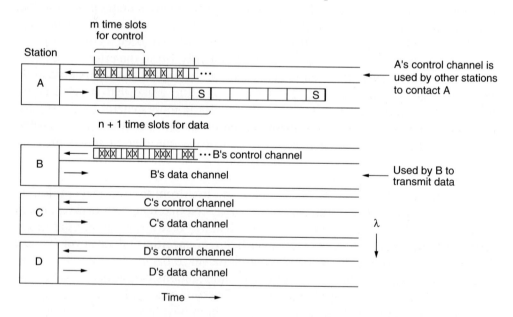

Fig. 4-10. Wavelength division multiple access.

Each channel is divided up into groups of time slots, as depicted in Fig. 4-10. Let us call the number of slots in the control channel m and the number of slots in the data channel $n + 1$, where n of these are for data and the last one is used by the station to report on its status (mainly, which slots on both channels are free). On both channels, the sequence of slots repeats endlessly, with slot 0 being marked in a special way so latecomers can detect it. All channels are synchronized by a single global clock.

The protocol supports three classes of traffic: (1) constant data rate connection-oriented traffic, such as uncompressed video, (2) variable data rate connection-oriented traffic, such as file transfer, and (3) datagram traffic, such as UDP packets. For the two connection-oriented protocols, the idea is that for A to communicate with B, it must first insert a CONNECTION REQUEST frame in a free slot on B's control channel. If B accepts, communication can take place on A's data channel.

Each station has two transmitters and two receivers, as follows:

1. A fixed-wavelength receiver for listening to its own control channel.

2. A tunable transmitter for sending on other station's control channel.

3. A fixed-wavelength transmitter for outputting data frames.

4. A tunable receiver for selecting a data transmitter to listen to.

In other words, every station listens to its own control channel for incoming requests but has to tune to the transmitter's wavelength to get the data. Wavelength tuning is done by a Fabry-Perot or Mach-Zehnder interferometer that filters out all wavelengths except the desired wavelength band.

Let us now consider how station A sets up a class 2 communication channel with station B for, say, file transfer. First, A tunes its data receiver to B's data channel and waits for the status slot. This slot tells which control slots are currently assigned and which are free. In Fig. 4-10, for example, we see that of B's eight control slots, 0, 4, and 5 are free. The rest are occupied (indicated by crosses).

A picks one of the free control slots, say, 4, and inserts its CONNECTION REQUEST message there. Since B constantly monitors its control channel, it sees the request and grants it by assigning slot 4 to A. This assignment is announced in the status slot of the control channel. When A sees the announcement, it knows it has a unidirectional connection. If A asked for a two-way connection, B now repeats the same algorithm with A.

It is possible that at the same time A tried to grab B's control slot 4, C did the same thing. Neither will get it, and both will notice the failure by monitoring the status slot in B's control channel. They now each wait a random amount of time and try again later.

At this point, each party has a conflict-free way to send short control messages to the other one. To perform the file transfer, A now sends B a control message saying, for example, "Please watch my next data output slot 3. There is a data frame for you in it." When B gets the control message, it tunes its receiver to A's output channel to read the data frame. Depending on the higher-layer protocol, B can use the same mechanism to send back an acknowledgement if it wishes.

Note that a problem arises if both *A* and *C* have connections to *B* and each of them suddenly tells *B* to look at slot 3. *B* will pick one of these at random, and the other transmission will be lost.

For constant rate traffic, a variation of this protocol is used. When *A* asks for a connection, it simultaneously says something like: Is it all right if I send you a frame in every occurrence of slot 3? If *B* is able to accept (i.e., has no previous commitment for slot 3), a guaranteed bandwidth connection is established. If not, *A* can try again with a different proposal, depending on which output slots it has free.

Class 3 (datagram) traffic uses yet another variation. Instead of writing a CONNECTION REQUEST message into the control slot it just found (4), it writes a DATA FOR YOU IN SLOT 3 message. If *B* is free during the next data slot 3, the transmission will succeed. Otherwise, the data frame is lost. In this manner, no connections are ever needed.

Several variants of the entire protocol are possible. For example, instead of giving each station its own control channel, a single control channel can be shared by all stations. Each station is assigned a block of slots in each group, effectively multiplexing multiple virtual channels onto one physical one.

It is also possible to make do with a single tunable transmitter and a single tunable receiver per station by having each station's channel be divided up into *m* control slots followed by *n* + 1 data slots. The disadvantage here is that senders have to wait longer to capture a control slot and consecutive data frames are further apart because some control information is in the way.

Numerous other WDMA protocols have been proposed, differing in the details. Some have one control channel, some have multiple control channels. Some take propagation delay into account, others do not; some make tuning time an explicit part of the model, others ignore it. The protocols also differ in terms of processing complexity, throughput and scalability. For more information see (Bogineni et al., 1993; Chen, 1994; Chen and Yum, 1991; Jia and Mukherjee, 1993; Levine and Akyildiz, 1995; and Williams et al., 1993).

4.2.6. Wireless LAN Protocols

As the number of portable computing and communication devices grows, so does the demand to connect them to the outside world. Even the very first portable telephones had the ability to connect to other telephones. The first portable computers did not have this capability, but soon afterward, modems became commonplace. To go on-line, these computers had to be plugged into a telephone wall socket. Requiring a wired connection to the fixed network meant that the computers were portable, but not mobile.

To achieve true mobility, portable computers need to use radio (or infrared) signals for communication. In this manner, dedicated users can read and send email while driving or boating. A system of portable computers that communicate by radio can be regarded as a wireless LAN. These LANs have somewhat different properties than conventional LANs and require special MAC sublayer protocols. In this section we will examine some of these protocols. More information about wireless LANs can be found in (Davis and McGuffin, 1995; and Nemzow, 1995).

A common configuration for a wireless LAN is an office building with base stations strategically placed around the building. All the base stations are wired together using copper or fiber. If the transmission power of the base stations and portables is adjusted to have a range of 3 or 4 meters, then each room becomes a single cell, and the entire building becomes a large cellular system, as in the traditional cellular telephony systems we studied in Chap. 2. Unlike cellular telephone systems, each cell has only one channel, covering the entire available bandwidth. Typically its bandwidth is 1 to 2 Mbps.

In our discussions below, we will make the simplifying assumption that all radio transmitters have some fixed range. When a receiver is within range of two active transmitters, the resulting signal will generally be garbled and useless (but with certain exceptions to be discussed later). It is important to realize that in some wireless LANs, not all stations are within range of one another, which leads to a variety of complications. Furthermore, for indoor wireless LANs, the presence of walls between stations can have a major impact on the effective range of each station.

A naive approach to using a wireless LAN might be to try CSMA: just listen for other transmissions and only transmit if no one else is doing so. The trouble is, this protocol is not really appropriate because what matters is interference at the receiver, not at the sender. To see the nature of the problem, consider Fig. 4-11, where four wireless stations are illustrated. For our purposes, it does not matter which are base stations and which are portables. The radio range is such that A and B are within each other's range and can potentially interfere with one another. C can also potentially interfere with both B and D, but not with A.

Fig. 4-11. A wireless LAN. (a) A transmitting. (b) B transmitting.

First consider what happens when A is transmitting to B, as depicted in Fig. 4-11(a). If C senses the medium, it will not hear A because A is out of range, and thus falsely conclude that it can transmit. If C does start transmitting, it will interfere at B, wiping out the frame from A. The problem of a station not being able to detect a potential competitor for the medium because the competitor is too far away is sometimes called the **hidden station problem**.

Now let us consider the reverse situation: *B* transmitting to *A*, as shown in Fig. 4-11(b). If *C* senses the medium, it will hear an ongoing transmission and falsely conclude that it may not send to *D*, when in fact such a transmission would cause bad reception only in the zone between *B* and *C*, where neither of the intended receivers is located. This situation is sometimes called the **exposed station problem**.

The problem is that before starting a transmission, a station really wants to know whether or not there is activity around the receiver. CSMA merely tells it whether or not there is activity around the station sensing the carrier. With a wire, all signals propagate to all stations so only one transmission can take place at once anywhere in the system. In a system based on short-range radio waves, multiple transmissions can occur simultaneously if they all have different destinations and these destinations are out of range of one another.

Another way to think about this problem is to imagine an office building in which every employee has a wireless portable computer. Suppose that Linda wants to send a message to Milton. Linda's computer senses the local environment and, detecting no activity, starts sending. However, there may still be a collision in Milton's office because a third party may currently be sending to him from a location so far from Linda that her computer could not detect it.

MACA and MACAW

An early protocol designed for wireless LANs is **MACA (Multiple Access with Collision Avoidance)** (Karn, 1990). It was used as the basis for the IEEE 802.11 wireless LAN standard. The basic idea behind it is for the sender to stimulate the receiver into outputting a short frame, so stations nearby can detect this transmission and avoid transmitting themselves for the duration of the upcoming (large) data frame. MACA is illustrated in Fig. 4-12.

Let us consider how *A* sends a frame to *B*. *A* starts by sending an RTS (Request To Send) frame to *B*, as shown in Fig. 4-12(a). This short frame (30 bytes) contains the length of the data frame that will eventually follow. Then *B* replies with a CTS (Clear To Send) frame, as shown in Fig. 4-12(b). The CTS frame contains the data length (copied from the RTS frame). Upon receipt of the CTS frame, *A* begins transmission.

Now let us see how stations overhearing either of these frames react. Any station hearing the RTS is clearly close to *A* and must remain silent long enough for the CTS to be transmitted back to *A* without conflict. Any station hearing the CTS is clearly close to *B* and must remain silent during the upcoming data transmission, whose length it can tell by examining the CTS frame.

In Fig. 4-12, *C* is within range of *A* but not within range of *B*. Therefore it hears the RTS from *A* but not the CTS from *B*. As long as it does not interfere with

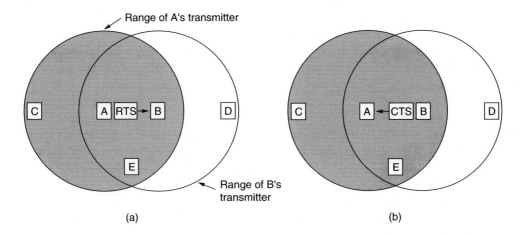

Fig. 4-12. The MACA protocol. (a) *A* sending an RTS to *B*. (b) *B* responding with a CTS to *A*.

the CTS, it is free to transmit while the data frame is being sent. In contrast, *D* is within range of *B* but not *A*. It does not hear the RTS but does hear the CTS. Hearing the CTS tips it off that it is close to a station that is about to receive a frame, so it defers from sending anything until that frame is expected to be finished. Station *E* hears both control messages, and like *D*, must be silent until the data frame is complete.

Despite these precautions, collisions can still occur. For example, *B* and *C* could both send RTS frames to *A* at the same time. These will collide and be lost. In the event of a collision, an unsuccessful transmitter (i.e., one that does not hear a CTS within the expected time interval) waits a random amount of time and tries again later. The algorithm used is binary exponential backoff, which we will study when we come to the IEEE 802.3 LAN.

Based on simulation studies of MACA, Bharghavan et al. (1994) fine tuned MACA to improve its performance and renamed their new protocol **MACAW**. To start with, they noticed that without data link layer acknowledgements, lost frames were not retransmitted until the transport layer noticed their absence, much later. They solved this problem by introducing an ACK frame after each successful data frame. They also observed that CSMA has some utility—namely to keep a station from transmitting an RTS at the same time another nearby station is also doing so to the same destination, so carrier sensing was added. In addition, they decided to run the backoff algorithm separately for each data stream (source-destination pair), rather than for each station. This change improves the fairness of the protocol. Finally, they added a mechanism for stations to exchange information about congestion, and a way to make the backoff algorithm react less violently to temporary problems, to improve system performance.

4.2.7. Digital Cellular Radio

A second form of wireless networking is digital cellular radio, the successor to the AMPS system we studied in Chap. 2. Digital cellular radio presents a somewhat different environment than do wireless LANs and uses different protocols. In particular, it is oriented toward telephony, which requires connections lasting for minutes, rather than milliseconds, so it is more efficient to do channel allocation per call rather than per frame. Nevertheless, the techniques are equally valid for data traffic. In this section we will look at three radically different approaches to channel allocation for wireless digital radio systems, GSM, CDPD, and CDMA.

GSM—Global System for Mobile Communications

The first generation of cellular phones were analog, as described in Chap. 2, but the current generation is digital, using packet radio. Digital transmission has several advantages over analog for mobile communication. First, voice, data, and fax, can be integrated into a single system. Second, as better speech compression algorithms are discovered, less bandwidth will be needed per channel. Third, error-correcting codes can be used to improve transmission quality. Finally, digital signals can be encrypted for security.

Although it might have been nice if the whole world had adopted the same digital standard, such is not the case. The U.S. system, IS-54, and the Japanese system, JDC, have been designed to be compatible with each country's existing analog system, so each AMPS channel could be used either for analog or digital communication.

In contrast, the European digital system, **GSM (Global System for Mobile communications)**, has been designed from scratch as a fully digital system, without any compromises for the sake of backward compatibility (e.g., having to use the existing frequency slots). Since GSM is also further along than the U.S. system and is currently in use in over 50 countries, inside and outside of Europe, we will use it as an example of digital cellular radio.

GSM was originally designed for use in the 900-MHz band. Later, frequencies were allocated at 1800 MHz, and a second system, closely patterned on GSM, was set up there. The latter is called **DCS 1800**, but it is essentially GSM.

The GSM standard is over 5000 [sic] pages long. A large fraction of this material relates to engineering aspects of the system, especially the design of receivers to handle multipath signal propagation, and synchronizing transmitters and receivers.

A GSM system has up to a maximum of 200 full-duplex channels per cell. Each channel consists of a downlink frequency (from the base station to the mobile stations) and an uplink frequency (from the mobile stations to the base station). Each frequency band is 200 kHz wide as shown in Fig. 4-13.

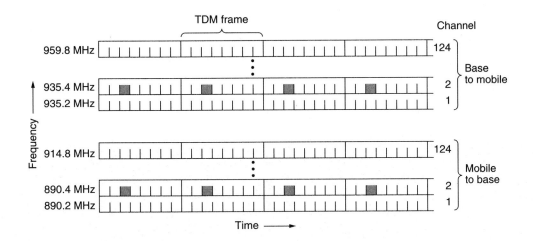

Fig. 4-13. GSM uses 124 frequency channels, each of which use an eight-slot TDM system.

Each of the 124 frequency channels supports eight separate connections using time division multiplexing. Each currently active station is assigned one time slot on one channel. Theoretically, 992 channels can be supported in each cell, but many of them are not available, to avoid frequency conflicts with neighboring cells. In Fig. 4-13, the eight shaded time slots all belong to the same channel, four of them in each direction. If the mobile station assigned to 890.4/935.4 MHz and slot 2 wanted to transmit to the base station, it would use the lower four shaded slots (and the ones following them in time), putting some data in each slot until all the data had been sent.

The TDM slots shown in Fig. 4-13 are part of a complex framing hierarchy. Each TDM slot has a specific structure, and groups of TDM slots form multiframes, also with a specific structure. A simplified version of this hierarchy is shown in Fig. 4-14. Here we can see that each TDM slot consists of a 148-bit data frame. Each data frame starts and ends with three 0 bits, for frame delineation purposes. It also contains two 57-bit *Information* fields, each one having a control bit that indicates whether the following *Information* field is for voice or data. Between the *Information* fields is a 26-bit *Sync* (training) field that is used by the receiver to synchronize to the sender's frame boundaries. A data frame is transmitted in 547 µsec, but a transmitter is only allowed to send one data frame every 4.615 msec, since it is sharing the channel with seven other stations. The gross rate of each channel is 270,833 bps, divided among eight users. Discounting all the overhead, each connection can send one compressed voice signal or 9600 bps of data.

As can be seen from Fig. 4-14, eight data frames make up a TDM frame, and 26 TDM frames make up a 120-msec multiframe. Of the 26 TDM frames in a

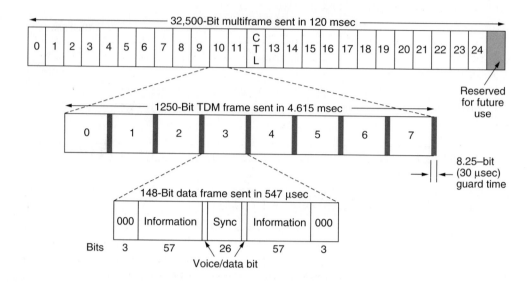

Fig. 4-14. A portion of the GSM framing structure.

multiframe, slot 12 is used for control and slot 25 is reserved for future use, so only 24 are available for user traffic.

However, in addition to the 26-slot multiframe shown in Fig. 4-14, a 51-slot multiframe (not shown) is also used. Some of these slots are used to hold several control channels used to manage the system. The **broadcast control channel** is a continuous stream of output from the base station containing its identity and the channel status. All mobile stations monitor its signal strength to see when they have moved into a new cell.

The **dedicated control channel** is used for location updating, registration, and call setup. In particular, each base station maintains a database of mobile stations currently under its jurisdiction. Information needed to maintain this database is sent on the dedicated control channel.

Finally, there is the **common control channel**, which is split up into three logical subchannels. The first of these subchannels is the **paging channel**, which the base station uses to announce incoming calls. Each mobile station monitors it continuously to watch for calls it should answer. The second is the **random access channel**, which runs a slotted ALOHA system to allow a mobile station to request a slot on the dedicated control channel. Using this slot, the station can set up a call. The assigned slot is announced on the third subchannel, the **access grant channel**.

All in all, GSM is a fairly complex system. It handles channel access using a combination of slotted ALOHA, FDM and TDM. For more information about GSM, including aspects of the system that we have not discussed, for example, the protocol layering architecture, see (Rahnema, 1993).

CDPD—Cellular Digital Packet Data

GSM is basically circuit switched. A mobile computer with a special modem can place a call using a GSM telephone the same way it would place one on a hardwired telephone. However, using this strategy is not without problems. For one, handoffs between base stations are frequent, sometimes even with stationary users (base stations can shuffle users around for load balancing), and each handoff results in losing ca. 300 msec of data. For another, GSM can suffer from a high error rate. Typing an "a" and having it echoed as an "m" gets tiresome quickly. Finally, wireless calls are expensive, and costs mount quickly because the charge is per minute of connect time, not per byte sent.

One approach to solving these problems is a packet-switched digital datagram service called **CDPD** (**Cellular Digital Packet Data**). It is built on top of AMPS (see Chap. 2) and entirely compatible with AMPS. Basically, any idle 30-kHz channel can be temporarily grabbed for sending data frames at a gross rate of 19.2 kbps. Because CDPD involves quite a bit of overhead, the net data rate is closer to 9600 bps. Still, a connectionless, wireless datagram system for sending, for example, IP packets, using the existing cellular phone system is an interesting proposition for many users, so its use is growing rapidly.

CDPD follows the OSI model closely. The physical layer deals with the details of modulation and radio transmission, which do not concern us here. Data link, network, and transport protocols also exist but are not of special interest to us either. Instead, we will give a general description of the system and then describe the medium access protocol. For more information about the full CDPD system, see (Quick and Balachandran, 1993).

A CDPD system consists of three kinds of stations: mobile hosts, base stations, and base interface stations (in CDPD jargon: mobile end systems, mobile data base systems, and mobile data intermediate systems, respectively). These stations interact with stationary hosts and standard routers, of the kind found in any WAN. The mobile hosts are the users' portable computers. The base stations are the transmitters that talk to the mobile hosts. The base interface stations are special nodes that interface all the base stations in a CDPD provider's area to a standard (fixed) router for further transmission through the Internet or other WAN. This arrangement is shown in Fig. 4-15.

Three kinds of interfaces are defined in CDPD. The **E-interface** (external to the CDPD provider) connects a CDPD area to a fixed network. This interface must be well defined to allow CDPD to connect to a variety of networks. The **I-interface** (internal to the CDPD provider) connects two CDPD areas together. It must be standardized to allow users to roam between areas. The third one is the **A-interface**, (air interface) between the base station and mobile hosts. This is the most interesting one, so we will now examine it more closely.

Data over the air interface are sent using compression, encryption, and error correction. Units of 274 compressed, encrypted data bits are wrapped in 378-bit

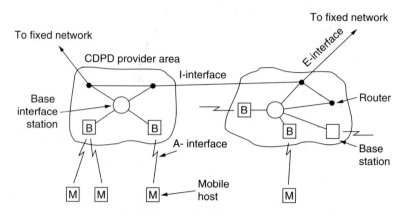

Fig. 4-15. An example CDPD system.

blocks using a Reed-Solomon error correcting code. To each RS block is added seven 6-bit flag words, to form a total of 420-bit blocks. Each 420-bit block is divided up into seven 60-bit microblocks, which are sent consecutively. Each microblock has its own 6-bit flag word, used for indicating channel status. These microblocks go over a 19.2-kbps downlink channel (from the base) or over a second 19.2-kbps uplink channel (to the base), in full-duplex mode. In effect, both the downlink and uplink channel are slotted in time, as a sequence of 60-bit microblocks. Each microblock lasts for 3.125 msec.

Each CDPD cell has only one downlink/uplink pair available for data. The downlink channel is easy to manage since there is only one sender per cell: the base station. All frames sent on it are broadcast, with each mobile host selecting out those destined for it or for everyone.

The tricky part is the uplink channel, for which all mobile hosts wishing to send must contend. When a mobile host has a frame to send, it watches the down-link channel for a flag bit telling whether the current uplink slot is busy or idle. If it is busy, instead of just waiting for the next time slot, it skips a random number of slots and tries again. If it again sees that the uplink channel is busy, it waits a longer random time, and repeats the procedure. The statistically average waiting time doubles with each unsuccessful attempt. When it finally finds the channel supposedly idle, it begins transmitting its microblock.

The point of this algorithm, called **DSMA (Digital Sense Multiple Access)**, is to prevent all the mobile hosts from jumping on the uplink channel as soon it goes idle. It somewhat resembles the slotted p-persistent CSMA protocol we mentioned earlier, since it, too, uses discrete time slots on both channels.

The trouble is, despite DSMA, a collision with another mobile host is still possible, since two or more of them may pick the same time slot to starting send-ing. To allow mobile hosts to discover whether or not they have suffered a colli-sion, a flag bit in each microblock tells whether a previous microblock on the uplink channel was received correctly. Unfortunately, the base station cannot make the determination instantly after a microblock terminates, so the correct/incorrect reception of microblock n is delayed until microblock $n + 2$.

Since it cannot tell if its transmission was successful, if a sender has more microblocks to send, it just goes ahead, without having to reacquire the channel. If in the *following* time slot it sees that its *previous* transmission failed, it stops. Otherwise it continues transmitting, up to a certain maximum number of Reed-Solomon blocks, or until the base station sets a flag bit on the downlink channel to indicate that it has heard enough from this particular sender for the moment.

An additional property of CDPD is that data users are second-class citizens. When a new voice call is about to be assigned to a channel currently in use for CDPD, the base station sends a special signal on the downlink, closing down the channel. If the base station already knows the number of the new CDPD channel, it announces it. Otherwise, mobile hosts have to hunt around among a designated set of potential CDPD channels to find it. In this way, CDPD can suck up any idle capacity in a cell, without interfering with the big cash cow, voice.

It should be clear from this description that CDPD was added to the voice system after the latter was already operational, and that its design was subject to the constraint that no changes could be made to the existing voice system. Consequently, when channel selection for voice calls occurs, the algorithm is not aware of the existence of CDPD. This is the reason that the CDPD channel is sometimes suddenly preempted. However, nothing in the design prevents having dedicated CDPD channels. As CDPD grows in popularity, providers are likely to reserve channels exclusively for it.

CDMA—Code Division Multiple Access

GSM might be described as a brute force solution to channel allocation. It uses a combination of practically every known technique (ALOHA, TDM, FDM) intertwined in complex ways. CDPD for single-frame transmissions is fundamentally nonpersistent CSMA. Now we will examine yet another method for allocating a wireless channel, **CDMA (Code Division Multiple Access)**.

CDMA is completely different from all the other allocation techniques we have studied so far. Some of these have been based on dividing the channel into frequency bands and assigning those statically (FDM) or on demand (wavelength division multiplexing), with the owner using the band indefinitely. Others allocate the channel in bursts, giving stations the entire channel statically (TDM with fixed time slots) or dynamically (ALOHA). CDMA allows each station to transmit over the entire frequency spectrum all the time. Multiple simultaneous transmissions are separated using coding theory. CDMA also relaxes the assumption that colliding frames are totally garbled. Instead, it assumes that multiple signals add linearly.

Before getting into the algorithm, let us consider the cocktail party theory of channel access. In a large room, many pairs of people are conversing. TDM is when all the people are in the middle of the room, but they take turns speaking, first one then another. FDM is when the people group into widely separated clumps, each clump holding its own conversation at the same time as, but still independent of, the others. CDMA is when they are all in the middle of the room talking at once, but with each pair in a different language. The French-speaking couple just hones in on the French, rejecting everything else as noise. Thus the key to CDMA is to be able to extract the desired signal while rejecting everything else as random noise.

In CDMA each bit time is subdivided into m short intervals called **chips**. Typically there are 64 or 128 chips per bit, but in the example given below we will use 8 chips/bit for simplicity.

Each station is assigned a unique m-bit code or **chip sequence**. To transmit a 1 bit, a station sends its chip sequence. To transmit a 0 bit, it sends the one's complement of its chip sequence. No other patterns are permitted. Thus for $m = 8$, if station A is assigned the chip sequence 00011011, it sends a 1 bit by sending 00011011 and a 0 bit by sending 11100100.

Increasing the amount of information to be sent from b bits/sec to mb chips/sec can only be done if the bandwidth available is increased by a factor of m, making CDMA a form of spread spectrum communication (assuming no changes in the modulation or encoding techniques). If we have a 1-MHz band available for 100 stations, with FDM each one would have 10 kHz and could send at 10 kbps (assuming 1 bit per Hz). With CDMA, each station uses the full 1 MHz, so the chip rate is 1 megachip per second. With fewer than 100 chips per bit, the effective bandwidth per station is higher for CDMA than FDM, and the channel allocation problem is also solved, as we will see shortly.

For pedagogical purposes, it is more convenient to use a bipolar notation, with binary 0 being -1 and binary 1 being $+1$. We will show chip sequences in parentheses, so a 1 bit for station A now becomes $(-1\ -1\ -1\ +1\ +1\ -1\ +1\ +1)$. In Fig. 4-16(a) we show the binary chip sequences assigned to four example stations. In Fig. 4-16(b) we show them in our bipolar notation.

Each station has its own unique chip sequence. Let us use the symbol **S** to indicate the m-chip vector for station S, and $\bar{\mathbf{S}}$ for its negation. All chip sequences are pairwise **orthogonal**, by which we mean that the normalized inner product of any two distinct chip sequences, **S** and **T** (written as **S•T**) is 0. In mathematical terms,

$$\mathbf{S}\bullet\mathbf{T} \equiv \frac{1}{m} \sum_{i=1}^{m} S_i T_i = 0 \qquad (4\text{-}5)$$

In plain English, as many pairs are the same as are different. This orthogonality property will prove crucial later on. Note that if $\mathbf{S}\bullet\mathbf{T} = 0$ then $\mathbf{S}\bullet\bar{\mathbf{T}}$ is also 0. The normalized inner product of any chip sequence with itself is 1:

$$\mathbf{S}\bullet\mathbf{S} = \frac{1}{m} \sum_{i=1}^{m} S_i S_i = \frac{1}{m} \sum_{i=1}^{m} S_i^2 = \frac{1}{m} \sum_{i=1}^{m} (\pm1)^2 = 1$$

A: 0 0 0 1 1 0 1 1   A: (−1 −1 −1 +1 +1 −1 +1 +1)
B: 0 0 1 0 1 1 1 0   B: (−1 −1 +1 −1 +1 +1 +1 −1)
C: 0 1 0 1 1 1 0 0   C: (−1 +1 −1 +1 +1 +1 −1 −1)
D: 0 1 0 0 0 0 1 0   D: (−1 +1 −1 −1 −1 −1 +1 −1)

(a)   (b)

Six examples:

$$
\begin{array}{ll}
-\,-\,1\,-\quad \mathbf{C} & S_1 = (-1\ +1\ -1\ +1\ +1\ +1\ -1\ -1) \\
-\,1\,1\,-\quad \mathbf{B} + \mathbf{C} & S_2 = (-2\ \ 0\ \ 0\ \ 0\ +2\ +2\ \ 0\ -2) \\
1\,0\,-\,-\quad \mathbf{A} + \overline{\mathbf{B}} & S_3 = (\ 0\ \ 0\ -2\ +2\ \ 0\ -2\ \ 0\ +2) \\
1\,0\,1\,-\quad \mathbf{A} + \mathbf{B} + \mathbf{C} & S_4 = (-1\ +1\ -3\ +3\ -1\ -1\ -1\ +1) \\
1\,1\,1\,1\quad \mathbf{A} + \mathbf{B} + \mathbf{C} + \mathbf{D} & S_5 = (-4\ \ 0\ -2\ \ 0\ +2\ \ 0\ +2\ -2) \\
1\,1\,0\,1\quad \mathbf{A} + \mathbf{B} + \overline{\mathbf{C}} + \mathbf{D} & S_6 = (-2\ -2\ \ 0\ -2\ \ 0\ -2\ +4\ \ 0)
\end{array}
$$

(c)

$S_1 \bullet C = (1\ +1\ +1\ +1\ +1\ +1\ +1\ +1)/8 = 1$
$S_2 \bullet C = (2\ +0\ +0\ +0\ +2\ +2\ +0\ +2)/8 = 1$
$S_3 \bullet C = (0\ +0\ +2\ +2\ +0\ -2\ +0\ -2)/8 = 0$
$S_4 \bullet C = (1\ +1\ +3\ +3\ +1\ -1\ +1\ -1)/8 = 1$
$S_5 \bullet C = (4\ +0\ +2\ +0\ +2\ +0\ -2\ +2)/8 = 1$
$S_6 \bullet C = (2\ -2\ +0\ -2\ +0\ -2\ -4\ +0)/8 = -1$

(d)

Fig. 4-16. (a) Binary chip sequences for four stations. (b) Bipolar chip sequences. (c) Six examples of transmissions. (d) Recovery of station C's signal.

This follows because each of the m terms in the inner product is 1, so the sum is m. Also note that $\mathbf{S} \bullet \overline{\mathbf{S}} = -1$.

During each bit time, a station can transmit a 1 by sending its chip sequence, it can transmit a 0 by sending the negative of its chip sequence, or it can be silent and transmit nothing. For the moment, we assume that all stations are synchronized in time, so all chip sequences begin at the same instant.

When two or more stations transmit simultaneously, their bipolar signals add linearly. For example, if in one chip period three stations output +1 and one station outputs −1, the result is +2. One can think of this as adding voltages: three stations outputting +1 volts and 1 station outputting −1 volts gives 2 volts.

In Fig. 4-16(c) we see six examples of one or more stations transmitting at the same time. In the first example, C transmits a 1 bit, so we just get C's chip sequence. In the second example, both B and C transmit 1 bits, so we get the sum of their bipolar chip sequences, namely:

$$(-1\ -1\ +1\ -1\ +1\ +1\ +1\ -1) + (-1\ +1\ -1\ +1\ +1\ +1\ -1\ -1) = (-2\ \ 0\ \ 0\ \ 0\ +2\ +2\ \ 0\ -2)$$

In the third example, station A sends a 1 and station B sends a 0. The others are silent. In the fourth example, A and C send a 1 bit while B sends a 0 bit. In the fifth example, all four stations send a 1 bit. Finally, in the last example, A, B, and

D send a 1 bit, while C sends a 0 bit. Note that each of the six sequences S_1 through S_6 given in Fig. 4-16(c) represents only one bit time.

To recover the bit stream of an individual station, the receiver must know that station's chip sequences in advance. It does the recovery by computing the normalized inner product of the received chip sequence (the linear sum of all the stations that transmitted) and the chip sequence of the station whose bit stream it is trying to recover. If the received chip sequence is $\mathbf{S}$ and the receiver is trying to listen to a station whose chip sequence is $\mathbf{C}$, it just computes the normalized inner product, $\mathbf{S} \bullet \mathbf{C}$.

To see why this works, imagine that two stations, A and C, both transmit a 1 bit at the same time that B transmits a 0 bit. The receiver sees the sum: $\mathbf{S} = \mathbf{A} + \overline{\mathbf{B}} + \mathbf{C}$ and computes

$$\mathbf{S} \bullet \mathbf{C} = (\mathbf{A} + \overline{\mathbf{B}} + \mathbf{C}) \bullet \mathbf{C} = \mathbf{A} \bullet \mathbf{C} + \overline{\mathbf{B}} \bullet \mathbf{C} + \mathbf{C} \bullet \mathbf{C} = 0 + 0 + 1 = 1$$

The first two terms vanish because all pairs of chip sequences have been carefully chosen to be orthogonal, as shown in Eq. (4-5). Now it should be clear why this property must be imposed on the chip sequences.

An alternative way of thinking about this situation is to imagine that the three chip sequences all came in separately, rather than summed. Then the receiver would compute the inner product with each one separately and add the results. Due to the orthogonality property, all the inner products except $\mathbf{C} \bullet \mathbf{C}$ would be 0. Adding them and then doing the inner product is in fact the same as doing the inner products and then adding those.

To make the decoding process more concrete, let us consider the six examples of Fig. 4-16(d) again. Suppose that the receiver is interested in extracting the bit sent by station C from each of the six sums S_1 through S_6. It calculates the bit by summing the pairwise products of the received $\mathbf{S}$ and the $\mathbf{C}$ vector of Fig. 4-16(b), and then taking 1/8 of the result (since $m = 8$ here). As shown, each time the correct bit is decoded. It is just like speaking French.

In an ideal, noiseless CDMA system, the capacity (i.e., number of stations) can be made arbitrarily large, just as the capacity of a noiseless Nyquist channel can be made arbitrarily large by using more and more bits per sample. In practice, physical limitations reduce the capacity considerably. First, we have assumed that all the chips are synchronized in time. In reality, doing so is impossible. What can be done is that the sender and receiver synchronize by having the sender transmit a long enough known chip sequence that the receiver can lock onto. All the other (unsynchronized) transmissions are then seen as random noise. If there are not too many of them, however, the basic decoding algorithm still works fairly well. A large body of theory exists relating the superposition of chip sequences to noise level (Pickholtz et al., 1982). As one might expect, the longer the chip sequence, the higher the probability of detecting it correctly in the presence of noise. For extra security, the bit sequence can use an error correcting code. Chip sequences never use error correcting codes.

An implicit assumption in the above discussion is that the power levels of all stations are the same as perceived by the receiver. CDMA is typically used for wireless systems with a fixed base station and many mobile stations at varying distances from it. The power levels received at the base station depend on how far away the transmitters are. A good heuristic here is for each mobile station to transmit to the base station at the inverse of the power level it receives from the base station, so a mobile station receiving a weak signal from the base will use more power than one getting a strong signal. The base station can also give explicit commands to the mobile stations to increase or decrease their transmission power.

We have also assumed that the receiver knows who the sender is. In principle, given enough computing capacity, the receiver can listen to all the senders at once by running the decoding algorithm for each of them in parallel. In real life, suffice it to say that this is easier said than done. CDMA also has many other complicating factors that have been glossed over in this brief introduction. Nevertheless, CDMA is a clever scheme that is being rapidly introduced for wireless mobile communication.

Readers with a solid electrical engineering background who want to gain a deeper understanding of CDMA should read (Viterbi, 1995). An alternative spreading scheme, in which the spreading is over time rather than frequency, is described in (Crespo et al., 1995).

4.3. IEEE STANDARD 802 FOR LANS AND MANS

We have now finished our general discussion of abstract channel allocation protocols, so it is time to see how these principles apply to real systems, in particular, LANs. As discussed in Sec. 1.7.2, IEEE has produced several standards for LANs. These standards, collectively known as **IEEE 802**, include CSMA/CD, token bus, and token ring. The various standards differ at the physical layer and MAC sublayer but are compatible at the data link layer. The IEEE 802 standards have been adopted by ANSI as American National Standards, by NIST as government standards, and by ISO as international standards (known as ISO 8802). They are surprisingly readable (as standards go).

The standards are divided into parts, each published as a separate book. The 802.1 standard gives an introduction to the set of standards and defines the interface primitives. The 802.2 standard describes the upper part of the data link layer, which uses the **LLC** (**Logical Link Control**) protocol. Parts 802.3 through 802.5 describe the three LAN standards, the CSMA/CD, token bus, and token ring standards, respectively. Each standard covers the physical layer and MAC sublayer protocol. The next three sections cover these three systems. Additional information can be found in (Stallings, 1993b).

4.3.1. IEEE Standard 802.3 and Ethernet

The IEEE 802.3 standard is for a 1-persistent CSMA/CD LAN. To review the idea, when a station wants to transmit, it listens to the cable. If the cable is busy, the station waits until it goes idle; otherwise it transmits immediately. If two or more stations simultaneously begin transmitting on an idle cable, they will collide. All colliding stations then terminate their transmission, wait a random time, and repeat the whole process all over again.

The 802.3 standard has an interesting history. The real beginning was the ALOHA system constructed to allow radio communication between machines scattered over the Hawaiian Islands. Later, carrier sensing was added, and Xerox PARC built a 2.94-Mbps CSMA/CD system to connect over 100 personal work-stations on a 1-km cable (Metcalfe and Boggs, 1976). This system was called **Ethernet** after the *luminiferous ether*, through which electromagnetic radiation was once thought to propagate. (When the Nineteenth Century British physicist James Clerk Maxwell discovered that electromagnetic radiation could be described by a wave equation, scientists assumed that space must be filled with some ethereal medium in which the radiation was propagating. Only after the famous Michelson-Morley experiment in 1887, did physicists discover that electromagnetic radiation could propagate in a vacuum.)

The Xerox Ethernet was so successful that Xerox, DEC, and Intel drew up a standard for a 10-Mbps Ethernet. This standard formed the basis for 802.3. The published 802.3 standard differs from the Ethernet specification in that it describes a whole family of 1-persistent CSMA/CD systems, running at speeds from 1 to 10-Mbps on various media. Also, the one header field differs between the two (the 802.3 length field is used for packet type in Ethernet). The initial standard also gives the parameters for a 10 Mbps baseband system using 50-ohm coaxial cable. Parameter sets for other media and speeds came later.

Many people (incorrectly) use the name "Ethernet" in a generic sense to refer to all CSMA/CD protocols, even though it really refers to a specific product that almost implements 802.3. We will use the terms "802.3" and "CSMA/CD" except when specifically referring to the Ethernet product in the next few paragraphs.

802.3 Cabling

Since the name "Ethernet" refers to the cable (the ether), let us start our discussion there. Four types of cabling are commonly used, as shown in Fig. 4-17. Historically, **10Base5** cabling, popularly called **thick Ethernet,** came first. It resembles a yellow garden hose, with markings every 2.5 meters to show where the taps go. (The 802.3 standard does not actually *require* the cable to be yellow, but it does *suggest* it.) Connections to it are generally made using **vampire taps**, in which a pin is carefully forced halfway into the coaxial cable's core. The notation 10Base5 means that it operates at 10 Mbps, uses baseband signaling, and can support segments of up to 500 meters.

Name	Cable	Max. segment	Nodes/seg.	Advantages
10Base5	Thick coax	500 m	100	Good for backbones
10Base2	Thin coax	200 m	30	Cheapest system
10Base-T	Twisted pair	100 m	1024	Easy maintenance
10Base-F	Fiber optics	2000 m	1024	Best between buildings

Fig. 4-17. The most common kinds of baseband 802.3 LANs.

Historically, the second cable type was **10Base2** or **thin Ethernet,** which, in contrast to the garden-hose-like thick Ethernet, bends easily. Connections to it are made using industry standard BNC connectors to form T junctions, rather than using vampire taps. These are easier to use and more reliable. Thin Ethernet is much cheaper and easier to install, but it can run for only 200 meters and can handle only 30 machines per cable segment.

Detecting cable breaks, bad taps, or loose connectors can be a major problem with both media. For this reason, techniques have been developed to track them down. Basically, a pulse of known shape is injected into the cable. If the pulse hits an obstacle or the end of the cable, an echo will be generated and sent back. By carefully timing the interval between sending the pulse and receiving the echo, it is possible to localize the origin of the echo. This technique is called **time domain reflectometry**.

The problems associated with finding cable breaks have driven systems toward a different kind of wiring pattern, in which all stations have a cable running to a central **hub**. Usually, these wires are telephone company twisted pairs, since most office buildings are already wired this way, and there are normally plenty of spare pairs available. This scheme is called **10Base-T**.

These three wiring schemes are illustrated in Fig. 4-18. For 10Base5, a **transceiver** is clamped securely around the cable so that its tap makes contact with the inner core. The transceiver contains the electronics that handle carrier detection and collision detection. When a collision is detected, the transceiver also puts a special invalid signal on the cable to ensure that all other transceivers also realize that a collision has occurred.

With 10Base5, a **transceiver cable** connects the transceiver to an interface board in the computer. The transceiver cable may be up to 50 meters long and contains five individually shielded twisted pairs. Two of the pairs are for data in and data out, respectively. Two more are for control signals in and out. The fifth pair, which is not always used, allows the computer to power the transceiver electronics. Some transceivers allow up to eight nearby computers to be attached to them, to reduce the number of transceivers needed.

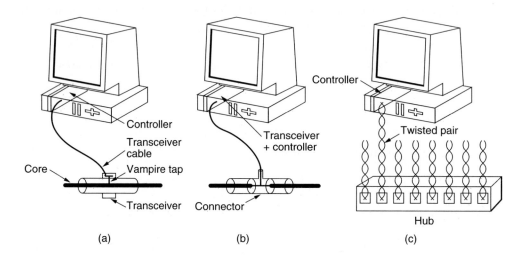

Fig. 4-18. Three kinds of 802.3 cabling. (a) 10Base5. (b) 10Base2. (c) 10Base-T.

The transceiver cable terminates on an interface board inside the computer. The interface board contains a controller chip that transmits frames to, and receives frames from, the transceiver. The controller is responsible for assembling the data into the proper frame format, as well as computing checksums on outgoing frames and verifying them on incoming frames. Some controller chips also manage a pool of buffers for incoming frames, a queue of buffers to be transmitted, DMA transfers with the host computers, and other aspects of network management.

With 10Base2, the connection to the cable is just a passive BNC T-junction connector. The transceiver electronics are on the controller board, and each station always has its own transceiver.

With 10Base-T, there is no cable at all, just the hub (a box full of electronics). Adding or removing a station is simpler in this configuration, and cable breaks can be detected easily. The disadvantage of 10Base-T is that the maximum cable run from the hub is only 100 meters, maybe 150 meters if high-quality (category 5) twisted pairs are used. Also, a large hub costs thousands of dollars. Still, 10Base-T is becoming steadily more popular due to the ease of maintenance that it offers. A faster version of 10Base-T (100Base-T) will be discussed later in this chapter.

A fourth cabling option for 802.3 is **10Base-F**, which uses fiber optics. This alternative is expensive due to the cost of the connectors and terminators, but it has excellent noise immunity and is the method of choice when running between buildings or widely separated hubs.

Figure 4-19 shows different ways of wiring up a building. In Fig. 4-19(a), a single cable is snaked from room to room, with each station tapping onto it at the nearest point. In Fig. 4-19(b), a vertical spine runs from the basement to the roof, with horizontal cables on each floor connected to it by special amplifiers (repeaters). In some buildings the horizontal cables are thin, and the backbone is thick. The most general topology is the tree, as in Fig. 4-19(c), because a network with two paths between some pairs of stations would suffer from interference between the two signals.

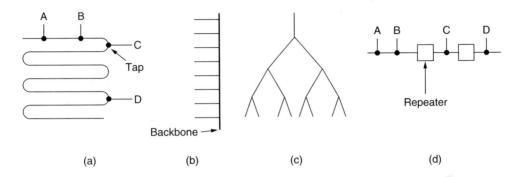

Fig. 4-19. Cable topologies. (a) Linear. (b) Spine. (c) Tree. (d) Segmented.

Each version of 802.3 has a maximum cable length per segment. To allow larger networks, multiple cables can be connected by **repeaters**, as shown in Fig. 4-19(d). A repeater is a physical layer device. It receives, amplifies, and retransmits signals in both directions. As far as the software is concerned, a series of cable segments connected by repeaters is no different than a single cable (except for some delay introduced by the repeaters). A system may contain multiple cable segments and multiple repeaters, but no two transceivers may be more than 2.5 km apart and no path between any two transceivers may traverse more than four repeaters.

Manchester Encoding

None of the versions of 802.3 use straight binary encoding with 0 volts for a 0 bit and 5 volts for a 1 bit because it leads to ambiguities. If one station sends the bit string 0001000, others might falsely interpret it as 10000000 or 01000000 because they cannot tell the difference between an idle sender (0 volts) and a 0 bit (0 volts).

What is needed is a way for receivers to unambiguously determine the start, end, or middle of each bit without reference to an external clock. Two such approaches are called **Manchester encoding** and **differential Manchester encoding**. With Manchester encoding, each bit period is divided into two equal intervals. A binary 1 bit is sent by having the voltage set high during the first interval and low in the second one. A binary 0 is just the reverse: first low and then high. This scheme ensures that every bit period has a transition in the middle, making it easy for the receiver to synchronize with the sender. A disadvantage of Manchester encoding is that it requires twice as much bandwidth as straight binary encoding, because the pulses are half the width. Manchester encoding is shown in Fig. 4-20(b).

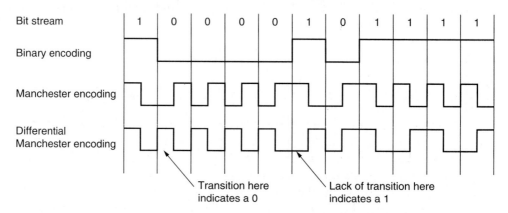

Fig. 4-20. (a) Binary encoding. (b) Manchester encoding. (c) Differential Manchester encoding.

Differential Manchester encoding, shown in Fig. 4-20(c), is a variation of basic Manchester encoding. In it, a 1 bit is indicated by the absence of a transition at the start of the interval. A 0 bit is indicated by the presence of a transition at the start of the interval. In both cases, there is a transition in the middle as well. The differential scheme requires more complex equipment but offers better noise immunity. All 802.3 baseband systems use Manchester encoding due to its simplicity. The high signal is $+0.85$ volts and the low signal is -0.85 volts, giving a DC value of 0 volts.

The 802.3 MAC Sublayer Protocol

The 802.3 (IEEE, 1985a) frame structure is shown in Fig. 4-21. Each frame starts with a *Preamble* of 7 bytes, each containing the bit pattern 10101010. The Manchester encoding of this pattern produces a 10-MHz square wave for 5.6 µsec to allow the receiver's clock to synchronize with the sender's. Next comes a *Start of frame* byte containing 10101011 to denote the start of the frame itself.

The frame contains two addresses, one for the destination and one for the source. The standard allows 2-byte and 6-byte addresses, but the parameters defined for the 10-Mbps baseband standard use only the 6-byte addresses. The high-order bit of the destination address is a 0 for ordinary addresses and 1 for group addresses. Group addresses allow multiple stations to listen to a single address. When a frame is sent to a group address, all the stations in the group receive it. Sending to a group of stations is called **multicast**. The address consisting of all 1 bits is reserved for **broadcast**. A frame containing all 1s in the destination field is delivered to all stations on the network.

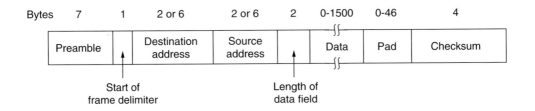

Fig. 4-21. The 802.3 frame format.

Another interesting feature of the addressing is the use of bit 46 (adjacent to the high-order bit) to distinguish local from global addresses. Local addresses are assigned by each network administrator and have no significance outside the local network. Global addresses, in contrast, are assigned by IEEE to ensure that no two stations anywhere in the world have the same global address. With $48 - 2 = 46$ bits available, there are about 7×10^{13} global addresses. The idea is that any station can uniquely address any other station by just giving the right 48-bit number. It is up to the network layer to figure out how to locate the destination.

The *Length* field tells how many bytes are present in the data field, from a minimum of 0 to a maximum of 1500. While a data field of 0 bytes is legal, it causes a problem. When a transceiver detects a collision, it truncates the current frame, which means that stray bits and pieces of frames appear on the cable all the time. To make it easier to distinguish valid frames from garbage, 802.3 states that valid frames must be at least 64 bytes long, from destination address to checksum. If the data portion of a frame is less than 46 bytes, the pad field is used to fill out the frame to the minimum size.

Another (and more important) reason for having a minimum length frame is to prevent a station from completing the transmission of a short frame before the first bit has even reached the far end of the cable, where it may collide with another frame. This problem is illustrated in Fig. 4-22. At time 0, station A, at one end of the network, sends off a frame. Let us call the propagation time for this frame to reach the other end τ. Just before the frame gets to the other end (i.e., at time $\tau - \varepsilon$) the most distant station, B, starts transmitting. When B detects that it is receiving more power than it is putting out, it knows that a collision has occurred, so it aborts its transmission and generates a 48-bit noise burst to warn all other stations. At about time 2τ, the sender sees the noise burst and aborts its transmission, too. It then waits a random time before trying again.

If a station tries to transmit a very short frame, it is conceivable that a collision occurs, but the transmission completes before the noise burst gets back at 2τ. The sender will then incorrectly conclude that the frame was successfully sent. To prevent this situation from occurring, all frames must take more than 2τ to send. For a 10-Mbps LAN with a maximum length of 2500 meters and four

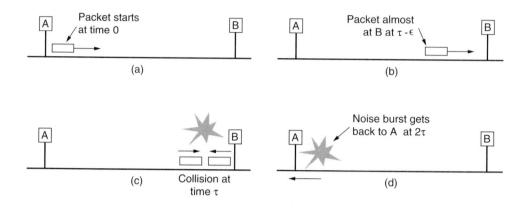

Fig. 4-22. Collision detection can take as long as 2τ.

repeaters (from the 802.3 specification), the minimum allowed frame must take 51.2 μsec. This time corresponds to 64 bytes. Frames with fewer bytes are padded out to 64 bytes.

As the network speed goes up, the minimum frame length must go up or the maximum cable length must come down, proportionally. For a 2500-meter LAN operating at 1 Gbps, the minimum frame size would have to be 6400 bytes. Alternatively, the minimum frame size could be 640 bytes and the maximum distance between any two stations 250 meters. These restrictions are becoming increasingly painful as we move toward gigabit networks.

The final 802.3 field is the *Checksum*. It is effectively a 32-bit hash code of the data. If some data bits are erroneously received (due to noise on the cable), the checksum will almost certainly be wrong, and the error will be detected. The checksum algorithm is a cyclic redundancy check of the kind discussed in Chap. 3.

The Binary Exponential Backoff Algorithm

Let us now see how randomization is done when a collision occurs. The model is that of Fig. 4-5. After a collision, time is divided up into discrete slots whose length is equal to the worst case round-trip propagation time on the ether (2τ). To accommodate the longest path allowed by 802.3 (2.5 km and four repeaters), the slot time has been set to 512 bit times, or 51.2 μsec.

After the first collision, each station waits either 0 or 1 slot times before trying again. If two stations collide and each one picks the same random number, they will collide again. After the second collision, each one picks either 0, 1, 2, or 3 at random and waits that number of slot times. If a third collision occurs (the probability of this happening is 0.25), then the next time the number of slots to wait is chosen at random from the interval 0 to $2^3 - 1$.

In general, after i collisions, a random number between 0 and $2^i - 1$ is chosen, and that number of slots is skipped. However, after ten collisions have been reached, the randomization interval is frozen at a maximum of 1023 slots. After 16 collisions, the controller throws in the towel and reports failure back to the computer. Further recovery is up to higher layers.

This algorithm, called **binary exponential backoff**, was chosen to dynamically adapt to the number of stations trying to send. If the randomization interval for all collisions was 1023, the chance of two stations colliding for a second time would be negligible, but the average wait after a collision would be hundreds of slot times, introducing significant delay. On the other hand, if each station always delayed for either zero or one slots, then if 100 stations ever tried to send at once, they would collide over and over until 99 of them picked 0 and the remaining station picked 1, or vice versa. This might take years. By having the randomization interval grow exponentially as more and more consecutive collisions occur, the algorithm ensures a low delay when only a few stations collide but also ensures that the collision is resolved in a reasonable interval when many stations collide.

As described so far, CSMA/CD provides no acknowledgements. Since the mere absence of collisions does not guarantee that bits were not garbled by noise spikes on the cable, for reliable communication the destination must verify the checksum, and if correct, send back an acknowledgement frame to the source. Normally, this acknowledgement would be just another frame as far as the protocol is concerned and would have to fight for channel time just like a data frame. However, a simple modification to the contention algorithm would allow speedy confirmation of frame receipt (Tokoro and Tamaru, 1977). All that would be needed is to reserve the first contention slot following successful transmission for the destination station.

802.3 Performance

Now let us briefly examine the performance of 802.3 under conditions of heavy and constant load, that is, k stations always ready to transmit. A rigorous analysis of the binary exponential backoff algorithm is complicated. Instead we will follow Metcalfe and Boggs (1976) and assume a constant retransmission probability in each slot. If each station transmits during a contention slot with probability p, the probability A that some station acquires the channel in that slot is

$$A = kp(1-p)^{k-1} \tag{4-6}$$

A is maximized when $p = 1/k$, with $A \to 1/e$ as $k \to \infty$. The probability that the contention interval has exactly j slots in it is $A(1-A)^{j-1}$, so the mean number of slots per contention is given by

$$\sum_{j=0}^{\infty} jA(1-A)^{j-1} = \frac{1}{A}$$

Since each slot has a duration 2τ, the mean contention interval, w, is $2\tau/A$.

Assuming optimal p, the mean number of contention slots is never more than e, so w is at most $2\tau e \approx 5.4\tau$.

If the mean frame takes P sec to transmit, when many stations have frames to send,

$$\text{Channel efficiency} = \frac{P}{P + 2\tau/A} \tag{4-7}$$

Here we see where the maximum cable distance between any two stations enters into the performance figures, giving rise to topologies other than that of Fig. 4-19(a). The longer the cable, the longer the contention interval. By allowing no more than 2.5 km of cable and four repeaters between any two transceivers, the round-trip time can be bounded to 51.2 μsec, which at 10 Mbps corresponds to 512 bits or 64 bytes, the minimum frame size.

It is instructive to formulate Eq. (4-7) in terms of the frame length, F, the network bandwidth, B, the cable length, L, and the speed of signal propagation, c, for the optimal case of e contention slots per frame. With $P = F/B$, Eq. (4-7) becomes

$$\text{Channel efficiency} = \frac{1}{1 + 2BLe/cF} \tag{4-8}$$

When the second term in the denominator is large, network efficiency will be low. More specifically, increasing network bandwidth or distance (the BL product) reduces efficiency for a given frame size. Unfortunately, much research on network hardware is aimed precisely at increasing this product. People want high bandwidth over long distances (fiber optic MANs, for example), which suggests that 802.3 may not be the best system for these applications.

In Fig. 4-23, the channel efficiency is plotted versus number of ready stations for $2\tau = 51.2$ μsec and a data rate of 10 Mbps using Eq. (4-8). With a 64-byte slot time, it is not surprising that 64-byte frames are not efficient. On the other hand, with 1024-byte frames and an asymptotic value of e 64-byte slots per contention interval, the contention period is 174 bytes long and the efficiency is 0.85.

To determine the mean number of stations ready to transmit under conditions of high load, we can use the following (crude) observation. Each frame ties up the channel for one contention period and one frame transmission time, for a total of $P + w$ sec. The number of frames per second is therefore $1/(P + w)$. If each station generates frames at a mean rate of λ frames/sec, when the system is in state k the total input rate of all unblocked stations combined is $k\lambda$ frames/sec. Since in equilibrium the input and output rates must be identical, we can equate these two expressions and solve for k. (Notice that w is a function of k.) A more sophisticated analysis is given in (Bertsekas and Gallager, 1992).

It is probably worth mentioning that there has been a large amount of theoretical performance analysis of 802.3 (and other networks). Virtually all of this work has assumed that traffic is Poisson. As researchers have begun looking at real

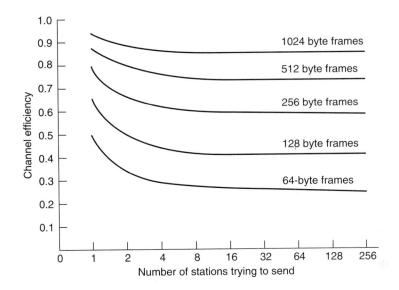

Fig. 4-23. Efficiency of 802.3 at 10 Mbps with 512-bit slot times.

data, it now appears that network traffic is rarely Poisson, but self-similar (Paxson and Floyd, 1994; and Willinger et al., 1995). What this means is that averaging over long periods of time does not smooth out the traffic. The average number of packets in each minute of an hour has as much variance as the average number of packets in each second of a minute. The consequence of this discovery is that most models of network traffic do not apply to the real world and should be taken with a grain (or better yet, a metric ton) of salt.

Switched 802.3 LANs

As more and more stations are added to an 802.3 LAN, the traffic will go up. Eventually, the LAN will saturate. One way out is to go to a higher speed, say from 10 Mbps to 100 Mbps. This solution requires throwing out all the 10 Mbps adaptor cards and buying new ones, which is expensive. If the 802.3 chips are on the computers' main circuit boards, it may not even be possible to replace them.

Fortunately, a different, less drastic solution is possible: a switched 802.3 LAN, as shown in Fig. 4-24. The heart of this system is a switch containing a high-speed backplane and room for typically 4 to 32 plug-in line cards, each containing one to eight connectors. Most often, each connector has a 10Base-T twisted pair connection to a single host computer.

When a station wants to transmit an 802.3 frame, it outputs a standard frame to the switch. The plug-in card getting the frame checks to see if it is destined for one of the other stations connected to the same card. If so, the frame is copied

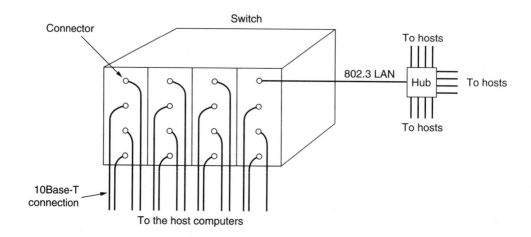

Fig. 4-24. A switched 802.3 LAN.

there. If not, the frame is sent over the high-speed backplane to the destination station's card. The backplane typically runs at over 1 Gbps using a proprietary protocol.

What happens if two machines attached to the same plug-in card transmit frames at the same time? It depends on how the card has been constructed. One possibility is for all the ports on the card to be wired together to form a local on-card LAN. Collisions on this on-card LAN will be detected and handled the same as any other collisions on a CSMA/CD network—with retransmissions using the binary backoff algorithm. With this kind of plug-in card, only one transmission per card is possible at any instant, but all the cards can be transmitting in parallel. With this design, each card forms its own **collision domain**, independent of the others.

With the other kind of plug-in card, each input port is buffered, so incoming frames are stored in the card's on-board RAM as they arrive. This design allows all input ports to receive (and transmit) frames at the same time, for parallel, full-duplex operation. Once a frame has been completely received, the card can then check to see if the frame is destined for another port on the same card, or for a distant port. In the former case it can be transmitted directly to the destination. In the latter case, it must be transmitted over the backplane to the proper card. With this design, each port is a separate collision domain, so collisions do not occur. The total system throughput can often be increased by an order of magnitude over 10Base-5, which has a single collision domain for the entire system.

Since the switch just expects standard 802.3 frames on each input port, it is possible use some of the ports as concentrators. In Fig. 4-24, the port in the upper right-hand corner is connected not to a single station, but to a 12-port hub. As frames arrive at the hub, they contend for the 802.3 LAN in the usual way, including collisions and binary backoff. Successful frames make it to the switch, and are treated there like any other incoming frames: they are switched to the correct output line over the high-speed backplane. If all the input ports are connected to hubs, rather than to individual stations, the switch just becomes an 802.3 to 802.3 bridge. We will study bridges later in this chapter.

4.3.2. IEEE Standard 802.4: Token Bus

Although 802.3 is widely used in offices, during the development of the 802 standard, people from General Motors and other companies interested in factory automation had serious reservations about it. For one thing, due to the probabilistic MAC protocol, with a little bad luck a station might have to wait arbitrarily long to send a frame (i.e., the worst case is unbounded). For another, 802.3 frames do not have priorities, making them unsuited for real-time systems in which important frames should not be held up waiting for unimportant frames.

A simple system with a known worst case is a ring in which the stations take turns sending frames. If there are n stations and it takes T sec to send a frame, no frame will ever have to wait more than nT sec to be sent. The factory automation people in the 802 committee liked the conceptual idea of a ring but did not like the physical implementation because a break in the ring cable would bring the whole network down. Furthermore, they noted that a ring is a poor fit to the linear topology of most assembly lines. As a result, a new standard was developed, having the robustness of the 802.3 broadcast cable, but the known worst-case behavior of a ring.

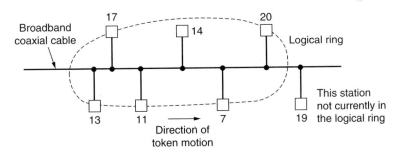

Fig. 4-25. A token bus.

This standard, 802.4 (Dirvin and Miller, 1986; and IEEE, 1985b), describes a LAN called a **token bus**. Physically, the token bus is a linear or tree-shaped cable onto which the stations are attached. Logically, the stations are organized into a ring (see Fig. 4-25), with each station knowing the address of the station to its "left" and "right." When the logical ring is initialized, the highest numbered station may send the first frame. After it is done, it passes permission to its immediate neighbor by sending the neighbor a special control frame called a **token**. The token propagates around the logical ring, with only the token holder being permitted to transmit frames. Since only one station at a time holds the token, collisions do not occur.

An important point to realize is that the physical order in which the stations are connected to the cable is not important. Since the cable is inherently a broadcast medium, each station receives each frame, discarding those not addressed to it. When a station passes the token, it sends a token frame specifically addressed to its logical neighbor in the ring, irrespective of where that station is physically located on the cable. It is also worth noting that when stations are first powered on, they will not be in the ring (e.g., stations 14 and 19 in Fig. 4-25), so the MAC protocol has provisions for adding stations to, and deleting stations from, the ring.

The 802.4 MAC protocol is very complex, with each station having to maintain ten different timers and more than two dozen internal state variables. The 802.4 standard is much longer than 802.3, filling more than 200 pages. The two standards are also quite different in style, with 802.3 giving the protocols as Pascal procedures, whereas 802.4 gives them as finite state machines, with the actions written in Ada[®].

For the physical layer, the token bus uses the 75-ohm broadband coaxial cable used for cable television. Both single- and dual-cable systems are allowed, with or without head-ends. Three different analog modulation schemes are permitted: phase continuous frequency shift keying, phase coherent frequency shift keying, and multilevel duobinary amplitude modulated phase shift keying. Speeds of 1, 5, and 10 Mbps are possible. Furthermore, the modulation schemes not only provide ways to represent 0, 1, and idle on the cable, but also three other symbols used for network control. All in all, the physical layer is totally incompatible with 802.3, and a lot more complicated.

The Token Bus MAC Sublayer Protocol

When the ring is initialized, stations are inserted into it in order of station address, from highest to lowest. Token passing is also done from high to low addresses. Each time a station acquires the token, it can transmit frames for a certain amount of time; then it must pass the token on. If the frames are short enough, several consecutive frames may be sent. If a station has no data, it passes the token immediately upon receiving it.

The token bus defines four priority classes, 0, 2, 4, and 6 for traffic, with 0 the lowest and 6 the highest. It is easiest to think of each station internally being divided into four substations, one at each priority level. As input comes in to the MAC sublayer from above, the data are checked for priority and routed to one of the four substations. Thus each substation maintains its own queue of frames to be transmitted.

When the token comes into the station over the cable, it is passed internally to the priority 6 substation, which may begin transmitting frames, if it has any.

When it is done (or when its timer expires), the token is passed internally to the priority 4 substation, which may then transmit frames until its timer expires, at which point the token is passed internally to the priority 2 substation. This process is repeated until either the priority 0 substation has sent all its frames or its timer has expired. Either way, at this point the token is sent to the next station in the ring.

Without getting into all the details of how the various timers are managed, it should be clear that by setting the timers properly, we can ensure that a guaranteed fraction of the total token-holding time can be allocated to priority 6 traffic. The lower priorities will have to live with what is left over. If the higher priority substations do not need all of their allocated time, the lower priority substations can have the unused portion, so it is not wasted.

This priority scheme, which guarantees priority 6 traffic a known fraction of the network bandwidth, can be used to implement real-time traffic. For example, suppose the parameters of a 50-station network running at 10 Mbps have been adjusted to give priority 6 traffic 1/3 of the bandwidth. Then each station has a guaranteed 67 kbps for priority 6 traffic. This bandwidth could be used to synchronize robots on an assembly line or carry one digital voice channel per station, with a little left over for control information.

The token bus frame format is shown in Fig. 4-26. It is unfortunately different from the 802.3 frame format. The preamble is used to synchronize the receiver's clock, as in 802.3, except that here it may be as short as 1 byte. The *Starting delimiter* and *Ending delimiter* fields are used to mark the frame boundaries. Both of these fields contain analog encoding of symbols other than 0s and 1s, so that they cannot occur accidentally in the user data. As a result, no length field is needed.

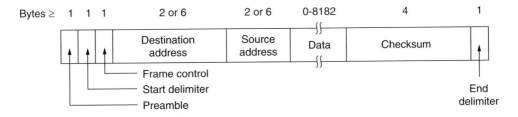

Fig. 4-26. The 802.4 frame format.

The *Frame control* field is used to distinguish data frames from control frames. For data frames, it carries the frame's priority. It can also carry an indicator requiring the destination station to acknowledge correct or incorrect receipt of the frame. Without this indicator, the destination would not be allowed to send anything because it does not have the token. This indicator turns the token bus into something resembling the acknowledgement scheme of Tokoro and Tamaru.

For control frames, the *Frame control* field is used to specify the frame type.

The allowed types include token passing and various ring maintenance frames, including the mechanism for letting new stations enter the ring, the mechanism for allowing stations to leave the ring, and so on. Note that the 802.3 protocol does not have any control frames. All the MAC layer does there is provide a way to get frames onto the cable; it does not care what is in them.

The *Destination address* and *Source address* fields are the same as in 802.3 (yes, the two groups did talk to each other; no, they did not agree on very much). As in 802.3, a given network must use all 2-byte addresses or all 6-byte addresses, not a mixture on the same cable. The initial 802.4 standard allows either size. The individual and group addressing and the local and global address assignments are identical to 802.3.

The *Data* field may be up to 8182 bytes long when 2-byte addresses are used, and up to 8174 bytes long when 6-byte addresses are used. This is more than five times as long as the maximum 802.3 frame, which was made short to prevent one station from hogging the channel too long. With the token bus, the timers can be used as an antihogging measure, but it is nice to be able to send long frames when real-time traffic is not an issue. The *Checksum* is used to detect transmission errors. It uses the same algorithm and polynomial as 802.3.

The token bus control frames are shown in Fig. 4-27. They will be discussed below. The only one we have seen so far is the *token* frame, used to pass the token from station to station. Most of the rest relate to adding and deleting stations from the logical ring.

Frame control field	Name	Meaning
00000000	Claim_token	Claim token during ring initialization
00000001	Solicit_successor_1	Allow stations to enter the ring
00000010	Solicit_successor_2	Allow stations to enter the ring
00000011	Who_follows	Recover from lost token
00000100	Resolve_contention	Used when multiple stations want to enter
00001000	Token	Pass the token
00001100	Set_successor	Allow station to leave the ring

Fig. 4-27. The token bus control frames.

Logical Ring Maintenance

From time to time, stations are powered on and want to join the ring. Other are turned off and want to leave. The MAC sublayer protocol provides a detailed specification of exactly how this is done while maintaining the known worst case bound on token rotation. Below we will just briefly sketch the mechanisms used.

Once the ring has been established, each station's interface maintains the addresses of the predecessor and successor stations internally. Periodically, the token holder sends one of the SOLICIT_SUCCESSOR frames shown in Fig. 4-27 to solicit bids from stations that wish to join the ring. The frame gives the sender's address and the successor's address. Stations inside that range may bid to enter (to keep the ring sorted in descending order of station address).

If no station bids to enter within a slot time (2τ, as in 802.3), the **response window** is closed and the token holder continues with its normal business. If exactly one station bids to enter, it is inserted into the ring and becomes the token holder's successor.

If two or more stations bid to enter, their frames will collide and be garbled, as in 802.3. The token holder then runs an arbitration algorithm, starting with the broadcast of a RESOLVE_CONTENTION frame. The algorithm is a variation of binary countdown, using two bits at a time.

Furthermore, all station interfaces maintain two random bits inside. These bits are used to delay all bids by 0, 1, 2, or 3 slot times, to further reduce contention. In other words, two stations only collide on a bid if the current two address bits being used are the same and they happen to have the same two random bits. To prevent stations that must wait 3 slot times from being at a permanent disadvantage, the random bits are regenerated every time they are used or periodically every 50 msec.

The solicitation of new stations may not interfere with the guaranteed worst case for token rotation. Each station has a timer that is reset whenever it acquires the token. When the token comes in, the old value of this timer (i.e., the previous token rotation time) is inspected just before the timer is reset. If it exceeds a certain threshold value, there has been too much traffic recently, so no bids may be solicited this time around. In any event, only one station may enter at each solicitation, to put a bound on how much time can be consumed in ring maintenance. No guarantee is provided for how long a station may have to wait to join the ring when traffic is heavy, but in practice it should not be more than a few seconds. This uncertainty is unfortunate, making 802.4 less suitable for real-time systems than its supporters often claim.

Leaving the ring is easy. A station, X, with successor S, and predecessor P, leaves the ring, by sending P a SET_SUCCESSOR frame telling it that henceforth its successor is S instead of X. Then X just stops transmitting.

Ring initialization is a special case of adding new stations. Consider an idle system with all stations powered off. When the first station comes on-line, it notices that there is no traffic for a certain period. Then it sends a CLAIM_TOKEN frame. Not hearing any competitors contending for the token, it creates a token and sets up a ring containing only itself. Periodically, it solicits bids for new stations to join. As new stations are powered on, they will respond to these bids and join the ring using the contention algorithm described above. Eventually, every station that wants to join the ring will be able to do so. If the first two stations are powered on simultaneously, the protocol deals with this by letting them bid for the token using the standard modified binary countdown algorithm and the two random bits.

Due to transmission errors or hardware failures, problems can arise with the logical ring or the token. For example, if a station tries to pass the token to a station that has gone down, what happens? The solution is straightforward. After passing the token, a station listens to see if its successor either transmits a frame or passes the token. If it does neither, the token is passed a second time.

If that also fails, the station transmits a WHO_FOLLOWS frame specifying the address of its successor. When the failed station's successor sees a WHO_FOLLOWS frame naming its predecessor, it responds by sending a SET_SUCCESSOR frame to the station whose successor failed, naming itself as the new successor. In this way, the failed station is removed from the ring.

Now suppose that a station fails to pass the token to its successor and also fails to locate the successor's successor, which may also be down. It adopts a new strategy by sending a SOLICIT_SUCCESSOR_2 frame to see if *anyone* else is still alive. Once again the standard contention protocol is run, with all stations that want to be in the ring now bidding for a place. Eventually, the ring is re-established.

Another kind of problem occurs if the token holder goes down and takes the token with it. This problem is solved using the ring initialization algorithm. Each station has a timer that is reset whenever a frame appears on the network. When this timer hits a threshold value, the station issues a CLAIM_TOKEN frame, and the modified binary countdown algorithm with random bits determines who gets the token.

Still another problem is multiple tokens. If a station holding the token notices a transmission from another station, it discards its token. If there were two, there would now be one. If there were more than two, this process would be repeated sooner or later until all but one were discarded. If, by accident, all the tokens are discarded, then the lack of activity will cause one or more stations to try to claim the token.

4.3.3. IEEE Standard 802.5: Token Ring

Ring networks have been around for many years (Pierce, 1972) and have long been used for both local and wide area networks. Among their many attractive features is the fact that a ring is not really a broadcast medium, but a collection of individual point-to-point links that happen to form a circle. Point-to-point links involve a well-understood and field-proven technology and can run on twisted pair, coaxial cable, or fiber optics. Ring engineering is also almost entirely digital, whereas 802.3, for example, has a substantial analog component for collision detection. A ring is also fair and has a known upper bound on channel access.

For these reasons, IBM chose the ring as its LAN and IEEE has included the **token ring** standard as 802.5 (IEEE, 1985c; Latif et al., 1992).

A major issue in the design and analysis of any ring network is the "physical length" of a bit. If the data rate of the ring is R Mbps, a bit is emitted every $1/R$ μsec. With a typical signal propagation speed of about 200 m/μsec, each bit occupies $200/R$ meters on the ring. This means, for example, that a 1-Mbps ring whose circumference is 1000 meters can contain only 5 bits on it at once. The implications of the number of bits on the ring will become clearer later.

As mentioned above, a ring really consists of a collection of ring interfaces connected by point-to-point lines. Each bit arriving at an interface is copied into a 1-bit buffer and then copied out onto the ring again. While in the buffer, the bit can be inspected and possibly modified before being written out. This copying step introduces a 1-bit delay at each interface. A ring and its interfaces are shown in Fig. 4-28.

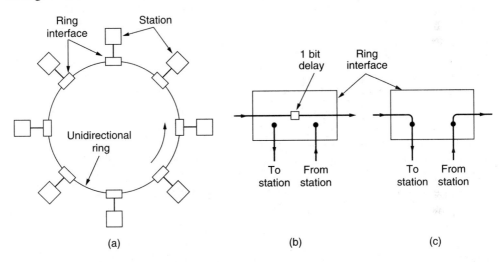

Fig. 4-28. (a) A ring network. (b) Listen mode. (c) Transmit mode.

In a token ring a special bit pattern, called the **token**, circulates around the ring whenever all stations are idle. When a station wants to transmit a frame, it is required to seize the token and remove it from the ring before transmitting. This action is done by inverting a single bit in the 3-byte token, which instantly changes it into the first 3 bytes of a normal data frame. Because there is only one token, only one station can transmit at a given instant, thus solving the channel access problem the same way the token bus solves it.

An implication of the token ring design is that the ring itself must have a sufficient delay to contain a complete token to circulate when all stations are idle. The delay has two components: the 1-bit delay introduced by each station, and the signal propagation delay. In almost all rings, the designers must assume that stations may be powered down at various times, especially at night. If the interfaces are powered from the ring, shutting down the station has no effect on the interface, but if the interfaces are powered externally, they must be designed to connect the input to the output when power goes down, thus removing the 1-bit delay. The point here is that on a short ring an artificial delay may have to be inserted into the ring at night to ensure that a token can be contained on it.

Ring interfaces have two operating modes, listen and transmit. In listen mode, the input bits are simply copied to output, with a delay of 1 bit time, as shown in Fig. 4-28(b). In transmit mode, which is entered only after the token has been seized, the interface breaks the connection between input and output, entering its own data onto the ring. To be able to switch from listen to transmit mode in 1 bit time, the interface usually needs to buffer one or more frames itself rather than having to fetch them from the station on such short notice.

As bits that have propagated around the ring come back, they are removed from the ring by the sender. The sending station can either save them, to compare with the original data to monitor ring reliability, or discard them. Because the entire frame never appears on the ring at one instant, this ring architecture puts no limit on the size of the frames. After a station has finished transmitting the last bit of its last frame, it must regenerate the token. When the last bit of the frame has gone around and come back, it must be removed, and the interface must switch back into listen mode immediately, to avoid removing the token that might follow if no other station has removed it.

It is straightforward to handle acknowledgements on a token ring. The frame format need only include a 1-bit field for acknowledgements, initially zero. When the destination station has received a frame, it sets the bit. Of course, if the acknowledgement means that the checksum has been verified, the bit must follow the checksum, and the ring interface must be able to verify the checksum as soon as its last bit has arrived. When a frame is broadcast to multiple stations, a more complicated acknowledgement mechanism must be used (if any is used at all).

When traffic is light, the token will spend most of its time idly circulating around the ring. Occasionally a station will seize it, transmit a frame, and then output a new token. However, when the traffic is heavy, so that there is a queue at each station, as soon as a station finishes its transmission and regenerates the token, the next station downstream will see and remove the token. In this manner the permission to send rotates smoothly around the ring, in round-robin fashion. The network efficiency can begin to approach 100 percent under conditions of heavy load.

Now let us turn from token rings in general to the 802.5 standard in particular. At the physical layer, 802.5 calls for shielded twisted pairs running at 1 or 4 Mbps, although IBM later introduced a 16-Mbps version. Signals are encoded using differential Manchester encoding [see Fig. 4-20(c)] with high and low being positive and negative signals of absolute magnitude 3.0 to 4.5 volts. Normally, differential Manchester encoding uses high-low or low-high for each bit, but

802.5 also uses high-high and low-low in certain control bytes (e.g., to mark the start and end of a frame). These nondata signals always occur in consecutive pairs so as not to introduce a DC component into the ring voltage.

One problem with a ring network is that if the cable breaks somewhere, the ring dies. This problem can be solved very elegantly by the use of a **wire center**, as shown in Fig. 4-29. While logically still a ring, physically each station is connected to the wire center by a cable containing (at least) two twisted pairs, one for data to the station and one for data from the station.

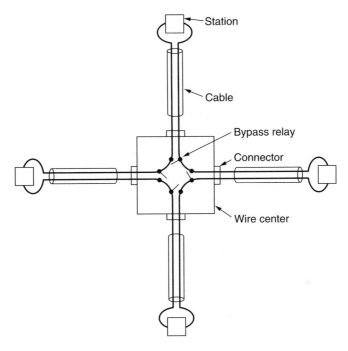

Fig. 4-29. Four stations connected via a wire center.

Inside the wire center are bypass relays that are energized by current from the stations. If the ring breaks or a station goes down, loss of the drive current will release the relay and bypass the station. The relays can also be operated by software to permit diagnostic programs to remove stations one at a time to find faulty stations and ring segments. The ring can then continue operation with the bad segment bypassed. Although the 802.5 standard does not formally require this kind of ring, often called a **star-shaped ring** (Saltzer et al., 1983), most 802.5 LANs, in fact, do use wire centers to improve their reliability and maintainability.

When a network consists of many clusters of stations far apart, a topology with multiple wire centers can be used. Just imagine that the cable to one of the stations in Fig. 4-29 were replaced by a cable to a distant wire center. Although logically all the stations are on the same ring, the wiring requirements are greatly reduced. An 802.5 ring using a wire center has a similar topology to an 802.3 10Base-T hub-based network, but the formats and protocols are different.

The Token Ring MAC Sublayer Protocol

The basic operation of the MAC protocol is straightforward. When there is no traffic on the ring, a 3-byte token circulates endlessly, waiting for a station to seize it by setting a specific 0 bit to a 1 bit, thus converting the token into the start-of-frame sequence. The station then outputs the rest of a normal data frame, as shown in Fig. 4-30.

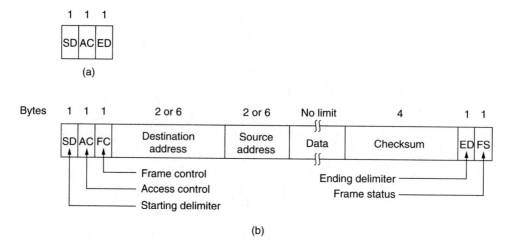

Fig. 4-30. (a) Token format. (b) Data frame format.

Under normal conditions, the first bit of the frame will go around the ring and return to the sender before the full frame has been transmitted. Only a very long ring will be able to hold even a short frame. Consequently, the transmitting station must drain the ring while it continues to transmit. As shown in Fig. 4-28(c), this means that the bits that have completed the trip around the ring come back to the sender and are removed.

A station may hold the token for the **token-holding time**, which is 10 msec unless an installation sets a different value. If there is enough time left after the first frame has been transmitted to send more frames, these may be sent as well. After all pending frames have been transmitted or the transmission of another frame would exceed the token-holding time, the station regenerates the 3-byte token frame and puts it out onto the ring.

The *Starting delimiter* and *Ending delimiter* fields of Fig. 4-30(b) mark the beginning and ending of the frame. Each contains invalid differential Manchester patterns (HH and LL) to distinguish them from data bytes. The *Access control* byte contains the token bit, and also the *Monitor bit*, *Priority bits*, and *Reservation bits* (described below). The *Frame control* byte distinguishes data frames from various possible control frames.

Next come the *Destination address* and *Source address* fields, which are the same as in 802.3 and 802.4. These are followed by the data, which may be as long as necessary, provided that the frame can still be transmitted within the token-holding time. The *Checksum* field, like the destination and source addresses, is also the same as 802.3 and 802.4.

An interesting byte not present in the other two protocols is the *Frame status* byte. It contains the *A* and *C* bits. When a frame arrives at the interface of a station with the destination address, the interface turns on the *A* bit as it passes through. If the interface copies the frame to the station, it also turns on the *C* bit. A station might fail to copy a frame due to lack of buffer space or other reasons.

When the sending station drains the frame from the ring, it examines the *A* and *C* bits. Three combinations are possible:

1. $A = 0$ and $C = 0$: destination not present or not powered up.

2. $A = 1$ and $C = 0$: destination present but frame not accepted.

3. $A = 1$ and $C = 1$: destination present and frame copied.

This arrangement provides an automatic acknowledgement for each frame. If a frame is rejected but the station is present, the sender has the option of trying again in a little while. The *A* and *C* bits are present twice in the *Frame status* to increase reliability inasmuch as they are not covered by the checksum.

The *Ending delimiter* contains an *E* bit which is set if any interface detects an error (e.g., a non-Manchester pattern where that is not permitted). It also contains a bit that can be used to mark the last frame in a logical sequence, sort of like an end-of-file bit.

The 802.5 protocol has an elaborate scheme for handling multiple priority frames. The 3-byte token frame contains a field in the middle byte giving the priority of the token. When a station wants to transmit a priority *n* frame, it must wait until it can capture a token whose priority is less than or equal to *n*. Furthermore, when a data frame goes by, a station can try to reserve the next token by writing the priority of the frame it wants to send into the frame's *Reservation bits*. However, if a higher priority has already been reserved there, the station may not make a reservation. When the current frame is finished, the next token is generated at the priority that has been reserved.

A little thought will show that this mechanism acts like a ratchet, always jacking the reservation priority higher and higher. To eliminate this problem, the protocol contains some complex rules. The essence of the idea is that the station raising the priority is responsible for lowering the priority again when it is done.

Notice that this priority scheme is substantially different from the token bus scheme, in which each station always gets its fair share of the bandwidth, no matter what other stations are doing. In the token ring, a station with only low priority frames may starve to death waiting for a low priority token to appear. Clearly, the two committees had different taste when trading off good service for high priority traffic versus fairness to all stations.

Ring Maintenance

The token bus protocol goes to considerable lengths to do ring maintenance in a fully decentralized way. The token ring protocol handles maintenance quite differently. Each token ring has a **monitor station** that oversees the ring. If the monitor goes down, a contention protocol ensures that another station is quickly elected as monitor. (Every station has the capability of becoming the monitor.) While the monitor is functioning properly, it alone is responsible for seeing that the ring operates correctly.

When the ring comes up or any station notices that there is no monitor, it can transmit a CLAIM TOKEN control frame. If this frame circumnavigates the ring before any other CLAIM TOKEN frames are sent, the sender becomes the new monitor (each station has monitor capability built in). The token ring control frames are shown in Fig. 4-31.

Control field	Name	Meaning
00000000	Duplicate address test	Test if two stations have the same address
00000010	Beacon	Used to locate breaks in the ring
00000011	Claim token	Attempt to become monitor
00000100	Purge	Reinitialize the ring
00000101	Active monitor present	Issued periodically by the monitor
00000110	Standby monitor present	Announces the presence of potential monitors

Fig. 4-31. Token ring control frames.

Among the monitor's responsibilities are seeing that the token is not lost, taking action when the ring breaks, cleaning the ring up when garbled frames appear, and watching out for orphan frames. An orphan frame occurs when a station transmits a short frame in its entirety onto a long ring and then crashes or is powered down before the frame can be drained. If nothing is done, the frame will circulate forever.

To check for lost tokens, the monitor has a timer that is set to the longest possible tokenless interval: each station transmitting for the full token-holding time. If this timer goes off, the monitor drains the ring and issues a new token.

When a garbled frame appears, the monitor can detect it by its invalid format or checksum, open the ring to drain it, and issue a new token when the ring has been cleaned up. Finally, the monitor detects orphan frames by setting the *monitor* bit in the *Access control* byte whenever it passes through. If an incoming frame has this bit set, something is wrong since the same frame has passed the monitor twice without having been drained, so the monitor drains it.

One last monitor function concerns the length of the ring. The token is 24 bits long, which means that the ring must be big enough to hold 24 bits. If the 1-bit delays in the stations plus the cable length add up to less than 24 bits, the monitor inserts extra delay bits so that a token can circulate.

One maintenance function that cannot be handled by the monitor is locating breaks in the ring. When a station notices that either of its neighbors appears to be dead, it transmits a BEACON frame giving the address of the presumably dead station. When the beacon has propagated around as far as it can, it is then possible to see how many stations are down and delete them from the ring using the bypass relays in the wire center, all without human intervention.

It is instructive to compare the approaches taken to controlling the token bus and the token ring. The 802.4 committee was scared to death of having any centralized component that could fail in some unexpected way and take the system down with it. Therefore they designed a system in which the current token holder had special powers (e.g., soliciting bids to join the ring), but no station was otherwise different from the others (e.g., currently assigned administrative responsibility for maintenance).

The 802.5 committee, on the other hand, felt that having a centralized monitor made handling lost tokens, orphan frames and so on much easier. Furthermore, in a normal system, stations hardly ever crash, so occasionally having to put up with contention for a new monitor is not a great hardship. The price paid is that if the monitor ever really goes berserk but continues to issue ACTIVE MONITOR PRESENT control frames periodically, no station will ever challenge it. Monitors cannot be impeached.

This difference in approach comes from the different application areas the two committees had in mind. The 802.4 committee was thinking in terms of factories with large masses of metal moving around under computer control. Network failures could result in severe damage and had to be prevented at all costs. The 802.5 committee was interested in office automation, where a failure once in a rare while could be tolerated as the price for a simpler system. Whether 802.4 is, in fact, more reliable than 802.5 is a matter of some controversy.

4.3.4. Comparison of 802.3, 802.4, and 802.5

With three different and incompatible LANs available, each with different properties, many organizations are faced with the question: Which one should we install? In this section we will look at all three of the 802 LAN standards, pointing out their strengths and weaknesses, comparing and contrasting them.

To start with, it is worth noting that the three LAN standards use roughly similar technology and get roughly similar performance. While computer scientists and engineers can discuss the merits of coax versus twisted pair for hours on end if given half a chance, the people in the marketing, personnel, or accounting departments probably do not really care that much one way or the other.

Let us start with the advantages of 802.3. It is far and away the most widely used type at present, with a huge installed base and considerable operational experience. The protocol is simple. Stations can be installed on the fly, without taking the network down. A passive cable is used and modems are not required. Furthermore, the delay at low load is practically zero (stations do not have to wait for a token; they just transmit immediately).

On the other hand, 802.3 has a substantial analog component. Each station has to be able to detect the signal of the weakest other station, even when it itself is transmitting, and all of the collision detect circuitry in the transceiver is analog. Due to the possibility of having frames aborted by collisions, the minimum valid frame is 64 bytes, which represents substantial overhead when the data consist of just a single character from a terminal.

Furthermore, 802.3 is nondeterministic, which is often inappropriate for real-time work [although some real-time work is possible by simulating a token ring in software (Venkatramani and Chiueh, 1995)]. It also has no priorities. The cable length is limited to 2.5 km (at 10 Mbps) because the round-trip cable length determines the slot time, hence the performance. As the speed increases, the efficiency drops because the frame transmission times drop but the contention interval does not (the slot width is 2τ no matter what the data rate is). Alternatively, the cable has to be made shorter. Also, at high load, the presence of collisions becomes a major problem and can seriously affect the throughput.

Now let us consider 802.4, the token bus. It uses highly reliable cable television equipment, which is available off-the-shelf from numerous vendors. It is more deterministic than 802.3, although repeated losses of the token at critical moments can introduce more uncertainty than its supporters like to admit. It can handle short minimum frames.

Token bus also supports priorities and can be configured to provide a guaranteed fraction of the bandwidth to high-priority traffic, such as digitized voice. It also has excellent throughput and efficiency at high load, effectively becoming TDM. Finally, broadband cable can support multiple channels, not only for data, but also for voice and television.

On the down side, broadband systems use a lot of analog engineering and include modems and wideband amplifiers. The protocol is extremely complex and has substantial delay at low load (stations must always wait for the token, even in an otherwise idle system). Finally, it is poorly suited for fiber optic implementations and has a small installed base of users.

Now consider the token ring. It uses point-to-point connections, meaning that the engineering is easy and can be fully digital. Rings can be built using virtually any transmission medium from carrier pigeon to fiber optics. The standard twisted pair is cheap and simple to install. The use of wire centers make the token ring the only LAN that can detect and eliminate cable failures automatically.

Like the token bus, priorities are possible, although the scheme is not as fair. Also like the token bus, short frames are possible, but unlike the token bus, so are arbitrarily large ones, limited only by the token-holding time. Finally, the throughput and efficiency at high load are excellent, like the token bus and unlike 802.3.

The major minus is the presence of a centralized monitor function, which introduces a critical component. Even though a dead monitor can be replaced, a sick one can cause headaches. Furthermore, like all token passing schemes, there is always delay at low load because the sender must wait for the token.

It is also worth pointing out that there have been numerous studies of all three LANs. The principal conclusion we can draw from these studies is that we can draw no conclusions from them. One can always find a set of parameters that makes one of the LANs look better than the others. Under most circumstances, all three perform well, so that factors other than the performance are probably more important when making a choice.

4.3.5. IEEE Standard 802.6: Distributed Queue Dual Bus

None of the 802 LANs we have studied so far are suitable for use as a MAN. Cable length limitations and performance problems when thousands of stations are connected limits them to campus-sized areas. For networks covering an entire city, IEEE defined one MAN, called **DQDB (Distributed Queue Dual Bus)**, as standard 802.6. In this section we will examine how it works. For additional information, see (Kessler and Train, 1992). A bibliography listing 171 papers about DQDB is given in (Sadiku and Arvind, 1994).

The basic geometry of 802.6 is illustrated in Fig. 1-4. Two parallel, unidirectional buses snake through the city, with stations attached to both buses in parallel. Each bus has a head-end, which generates a steady stream of 53-byte cells. Each cell travels downstream from the head-end. When it reaches the end, it falls off the bus.

Each cell carries a 44-byte payload field, making it compatible with some AAL modes. Each cell also holds two protocol bits, *Busy*, set to indicate that a cell is occupied, and *Request*, which can be set when a station wants to make a request.

To transmit a cell, a station has to know whether the destination is to the left of it or to the right of it. If the destination is to the right, the sender uses bus *A*. Otherwise, it uses bus *B*. Data are inserted onto either bus using a wired-OR circuit, so failure of a station does not take down the network.

Unlike all the other 802 LAN protocols, 802.6 is not greedy. In all the others, if a station gets the chance to send, it will. Here, stations queue up in the order they became ready to send and transmit in FIFO order. The interesting part about the protocol is how it achieves FIFO order without having a central queue.

The basic rule is that stations are polite: they defer to stations downstream from them. This politeness is needed to prevent a situation in which the station nearest the head-end simply grabs all the empty cells as they come by and fills them up, starving everyone downstream. For simplicity, we will only examine transmission on bus A, but the same story holds for bus B as well.

To simulate the FIFO queue, each station maintains two counters, RC and CD. RC (*Request Counter*) counts the number of downstream requests pending until the station itself has a frame to send. At that point, RC is copied to CD, RC is reset to 0, and now counts the number of requests made after the station became ready. For example, if $CD = 3$ and $RC = 2$ for station k, the next three empty cells that pass by station k are reserved for downstream stations, then station k may send, then two more cells are reserved for downstream stations. For simplicity, we assume a station can have only one cell ready for transmission at a time.

To send a cell, a station must first make a reservation by setting the *Request* bit in some cell on the reverse bus (i.e., on bus B for a transmission that will later take place on bus A). As this cell propagates down the reverse bus, every station along the way notes it and increments its RC. To illustrate this concept, we will use an example. Initially, all the RC counters are 0, and no cells are queued up, as shown in Fig. 4-32(a). Then station D makes a request, which causes stations, C, B, and A, to increment their RC counters, as shown in Fig. 4-32(b). After that, B makes a request, copying its current RC value into CD, leading to the situation of Fig. 4-32(c).

At this point, the head-end on bus A generates an empty cell. As it passes by B, that station sees that its $CD > 0$, so it may not use the empty cell. (When a station has a cell queued, CD represents its position in the queue, with 0 being the front of the queue.) Instead it decrements CD. When the still-empty cell gets to D, that station sees that $CD = 0$, meaning that no one is ahead of it on the queue, so it ORs its data into the cell and sets the *Busy* bit. After the transmissions are done, we have the situation of Fig. 4-32(d).

When the next empty cell is generated, station B sees that it is now at the head of the queue, and seizes the cell (by setting 1 bit), as illustrated in Fig. 4-32(e). In this way, stations queue up to take turns, without a centralized queue manager.

DQDB systems are now being installed by many carriers throughout entire cities. Typically they run for up to 160 km at speeds of 44.736 Mbps (T3).

4.3.6. IEEE Standard 802.2: Logical Link Control

It is now perhaps time to step back and compare what we have learned in this chapter with what we studied in the previous one. In Chap. 3, we saw how two machines could communicate reliably over an unreliable line by using various

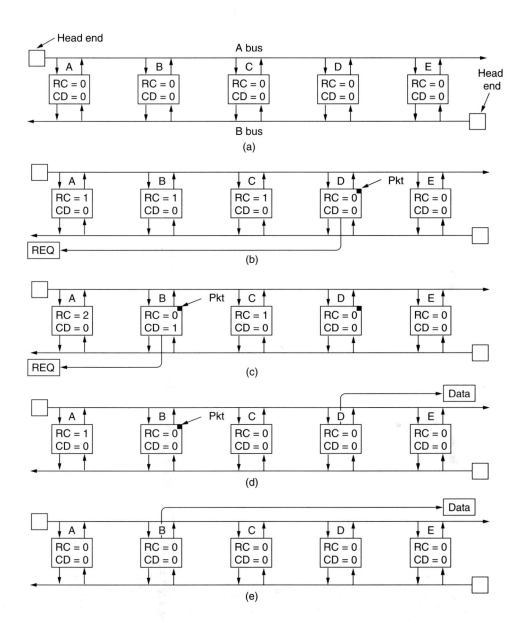

Fig. 4-32. (a) Initially the MAN is idle. (b) After *D* makes a request. (c) After *B* makes a request. (d) After *D* transmits. (e) After *B* transmits.

data link protocols. These protocols provided error control (using acknowledgements) and flow control (using a sliding window).

In contrast, in this chapter, we have not said a word about reliable communication. All that the 802 LANs and MAN offer is a best-efforts datagram service.

Sometimes, this service is adequate. For example, for transporting IP packets, no guarantees are required or even expected. An IP packet can just be inserted into an 802 payload field and sent on its way. If it gets lost, so be it.

Nevertheless, there are also systems in which an error-controlled, flow-controlled data link protocol is desired. IEEE has defined one that can run on top of all the 802 LAN and MAN protocols. In addition, this protocol, called **LLC** (**Logical Link Control**), hides the differences between the various kinds of 802 networks by providing a single format and interface to the network layer. This format, interface, and protocol are all closely based on OSI. LLC forms the upper half of the data link layer, with the MAC sublayer below it, as shown in Fig. 4-33.

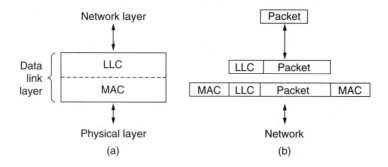

Fig. 4-33. (a) Position of LLC. (b) Protocol formats.

Typical usage of LLC is as follows. The network layer on the sending machine passes a packet to LLC using the LLC access primitives. The LLC sublayer then adds an LLC header, containing sequence and acknowledgement numbers. The resulting structure is then inserted into the payload field of an 802.x frame and transmitted. At the receiver, the reverse process takes place.

LLC provides three service options: unreliable datagram service, acknowledged datagram service, and reliable connection-oriented service. The LLC header is based on the older HDLC protocol. A variety of different formats are used for data and control. For acknowledged datagram or connection-oriented service, the data frames contain a source address, a destination address, a sequence number, an acknowledgement number, and a few miscellaneous bits. For unreliable datagram service, the sequence number and acknowledgement number are omitted.

4.4. BRIDGES

Many organizations have multiple LANs and wish to connect them. LANs can be connected by devices called **bridges**, which operate in the data link layer. This statement means that bridges do not examine the network layer header and can thus copy IP, IPX, and OSI packets equally well. In contrast, a pure IP, IPX, or OSI router can handle only its own native packets.

In the following sections we will look at bridge design, especially for connecting 802.3, 802.4, and 802.5 LANs. For a comprehensive treatment of bridges and related topics, see (Perlman, 1992). Before getting into the technology of bridges, it is worthwhile taking a look at some common situations in which bridges are used. We will mention six reasons why a single organization may end up with multiple LANs. First, many university and corporate departments have their own LANs, primarily to connect their own personal computers, workstations, and servers. Since the goals of the various departments differ, different departments choose different LANs, without regard to what other departments are doing. Sooner or later, there is a need for interaction, so bridges are needed. In this example, multiple LANs came into existence due to the autonomy of their owners.

Second, the organization may be geographically spread over several buildings separated by considerable distances. It may be cheaper to have separate LANs in each building and connect them with bridges and infrared links than to run a single coaxial cable over the entire site.

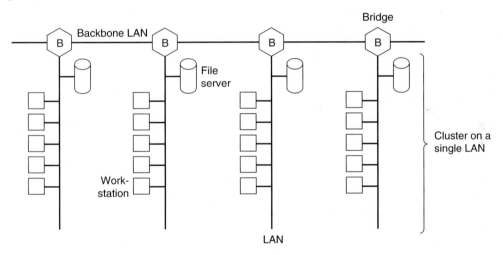

Fig. 4-34. Multiple LANs connected by a backbone to handle a total load higher than the capacity of a single LAN.

Third, it may be necessary to split what is logically a single LAN into separate LANs to accommodate the load. At many universities, for example, thousands of workstations are available for student and faculty computing. Files are normally kept on file server machines, and are downloaded to users' machines upon request. The enormous scale of this system precludes putting all the workstations on a single LAN—the total bandwidth needed is far too high. Instead multiple LANs connected by bridges are used, as shown in Fig. 4-34. Each LAN contains a cluster of workstations with its own file server, so that most traffic is restricted to a single LAN and does not add load to the backbone.

Fourth, in some situations, a single LAN would be adequate in terms of the load, but the physical distance between the most distant machines is too great (e.g., more than 2.5 km for 802.3). Even if laying the cable is easy to do, the network would not work due to the excessively long round-trip delay. The only solution is to partition the LAN and install bridges between the segments. Using bridges, the total physical distance covered can be increased.

Fifth, there is the matter of reliability. On a single LAN, a defective node that keeps outputting a continuous stream of garbage will cripple the LAN. Bridges can be inserted at critical places, like fire doors in a building, to prevent a single node which has gone berserk from bringing down the entire system. Unlike a repeater, which just copies whatever it sees, a bridge can be programmed to exercise some discretion about what it forwards and what it does not forward.

Sixth, and last, bridges can contribute to the organization's security. Most LAN interfaces have a **promiscuous mode**, in which *all* frames are given to the computer, not just those addressed to it. Spies and busybodies love this feature. By inserting bridges at various places and being careful not to forward sensitive traffic, it is possible to isolate parts of the network so that its traffic cannot escape and fall into the wrong hands.

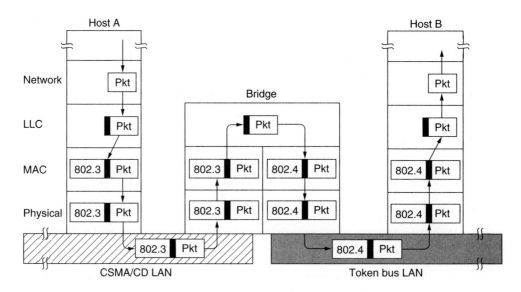

Fig. 4-35. Operation of a LAN bridge from 802.3 to 802.4.

Having seen why bridges are needed, let us now turn to the question of how they work. Figure 4-35 illustrates the operation of a simple two-port bridge. Host *A* has a packet to send. The packet descends into the LLC sublayer and acquires an LLC header. Then it passes into the MAC sublayer and an 802.3 header is prepended to it (also a trailer, not shown in the figure). This unit goes out onto the cable and eventually is passed up to the MAC sublayer in the bridge, where the 802.3 header is stripped off. The bare packet (with LLC header) is then handed off to the LLC sublayer in the bridge. In this example, the packet is destined for an 802.4 subnet connected to the bridge, so it works its way down the 802.4 side of the bridge and off it goes. Note that a bridge connecting k different LANs will have k different MAC sublayers and k different physical layers, one for each type.

4.4.1. Bridges from 802.x to 802.y

You might naively think that a bridge from one 802 LAN to another one would be completely trivial. Such is not the case. In the remainder of this section we will point out some of the difficulties that will be encountered when trying to build a bridge between the various 802 LANs.

Each of the nine combinations of 802.x to 802.y has its own unique set of problems. However, before dealing with these one at a time, let us look at some general problems common to all the bridges. To start with, each of the LANs uses a different frame format (see Fig. 4-36). There is no valid technical reason for this incompatibility. It is just that none of the corporations supporting the three standards (Xerox, GM, and IBM) wanted to change *theirs*. As a result, any copying between different LANs requires reformatting, which takes CPU time, requires a new checksum calculation, and introduces the possibility of undetected errors due to bad bits in the bridge's memory. None of this would have been necessary if the three committees had been able to agree on a single format.

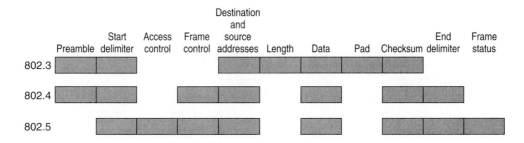

Fig. 4-36. The IEEE 802 frame formats.

A second problem is that interconnected LANs do not necessarily run at the same data rate. When forwarding a long run of back-to-back frames from a fast LAN to a slower one, the bridge will not be able to get rid of the frames as fast as they come in. It will have to buffer them, hoping not to run out of memory. The problem also exists from 802.4 to 802.3 at 10 Mbps to some extent because some of 802.3's bandwidth is lost to collisions. It does not really have 10 Mbps, whereas 802.4 really does (well, almost). Bridges that connect three or more LANs have a similar problem when several LANs are trying to feed the same output LAN at the same time.

A subtle, but important problem related to the bridge-as-bottleneck problem is the value of timers in the higher layers. Suppose that the network layer on an 802.4 LAN is trying to send a very long message as a sequence of frames. After sending the last one it starts a timer to wait for an acknowledgement. If the message has to transit a bridge to a slower 802.5 LAN, there is a danger that the timer will go off before the last frame has been forwarded onto the slower LAN. The network layer will assume the problem is due to a lost frame and just retransmit the entire sequence again. After n failed attempts it may give up and tell the transport layer that the destination is dead.

A third, and potentially most serious problem of all, is that all three 802 LANs have a different maximum frame length. For 802.3 it depends on the parameters of the configuration, but for the standard 10-Mbps system the payload is a maximum of 1500 bytes. For 802.4 it is fixed at 8191 bytes. For 802.5 there is no upper limit, except that a station may not transmit longer than the token-holding time. With the default value of 10 msec, the maximum frame length is 5000 bytes.

An obvious problem arises when a long frame must be forwarded onto a LAN that cannot accept it. Splitting the frame into pieces is out of the question in this layer. All the protocols assume that frames either arrive or they do not. There is no provision for reassembling frames out of smaller units. This is not to say that such protocols could not be devised. They could be and have been. It is just that 802 does not provide this feature. Basically, there is no solution. Frames that are too large to be forwarded must be discarded. So much for transparency.

Now let us briefly consider each of the nine cases of 802.x to 802.y bridges to see what other problems are lurking in the shadows. From 802.3 to 802.3 is easy. The only thing that can go wrong is that the destination LAN is so heavily loaded that frames keep pouring into the bridge, but the bridge cannot get rid of them. If this situation persists long enough, the bridge might run out of buffer space and begin dropping frames. Since this problem is always potentially present when forwarding onto an 802.3 LAN, we will not mention it further. With the other two LANs, each station, including the bridge is guaranteed to acquire the token periodically and cannot be shut out for long intervals.

From 802.4 to 802.3 two problems exist. First, 802.4 frames carry priority bits that 802.3 frames do not have. As a result, if two 802.4 LANs communicate via an 802.3 LAN, the priority will be lost by the intermediate LAN.

The second problem is caused by a specific feature in 802.4: temporary token handoff. It is possible for an 802.4 frame to have a header bit set to 1 to temporarily pass the token to the destination, to let it send an acknowledgement frame. However, if such a frame is forwarded by a bridge, what should the bridge do? If it sends an acknowledgement frame itself, it is lying because the frame really has not been delivered yet. In fact, the destination may be dead.

On the other hand, if it does not generate the acknowledgement, the sender will almost assuredly conclude that the destination is dead and report back failure to its superiors. There does not seem to be any way to solve this problem.

From 802.5 to 802.3 we have a similar problem. The 802.5 frame format has *A* and *C* bits in the frame status byte. These bits are set by the destination to tell the sender whether the station addressed saw the frame, and whether it copied it. Here again, the bridge can lie and say the frame has been copied, but if it later turns out that the destination is down, serious problems may arise. In essence, the insertion of a bridge into the network has changed the semantics of the bits. It is hard to imagine a proper solution to this problem.

From 802.3 to 802.4 we have the problem of what to put in the priority bits. A good case can be made for having the bridge retransmit all frames at the highest priority, because they have probably suffered enough delay already.

From 802.4 to 802.4 the only problem is what to do with the temporary token handoff. At least here we have the possibility of the bridge managing to forward the frame fast enough to get the response before the timer runs out. Still it is a gamble. By forwarding the frame at the highest priority, the bridge is telling a little white lie, but it thereby increases the probability of getting the response in time.

From 802.5 to 802.4 we have the same problem with the *A* and *C* bits as before. Also, the definition of the priority bits is different for the two LANs, but beggars can't be choosers. At least the two LANs have the same number of priority bits. All the bridge can do is copy the priority bits across and hope for the best.

From 802.3 to 802.5 the bridge must generate priority bits, but there are no other special problems. From 802.4 to 802.5 there is a potential problem with frames that are too long and the token handoff problem is present again. Finally, from 802.5 to 802.5 the problem is what to do with the *A* and *C* bits again. Figure 4-37 summarizes the various problems we have been discussing.

When the IEEE 802 committee set out to come up with a LAN standard, it was unable to agree on a single standard, so it produced *three* incompatible standards, as we have just seen in some detail. For this failure, it has been roundly criticized. When it was later assigned the job of designing a standard for bridges to interconnect its three incompatible LANs, it resolved to do better. It did. It came up with *two* incompatible bridge designs. So far nobody has asked it to design a gateway standard to connect its two incompatible bridges, but at least the trend is in the right direction.

This section has dealt with the problems encountered in connecting two IEEE 802 LANs via a single bridge. The next two sections deal with the problems of connecting large internetworks containing many LANs and many bridges and the two IEEE approaches to designing these bridges.

Destination LAN

	802.3 (CSMA/CD)	802.4 (Token bus)	802.4 (Token ring)
802.3		1, 4	1, 2, 4, 8
Source LAN 802.4	1, 5, 8, 9, 10	9	1, 2, 3, 8, 9, 10
802.5	1, 2, 5, 6, 7, 10	1, 2, 3, 6, 7	6, 7

Actions:
1. Reformat the frame and compute new checksum
2. Reverse the bit order.
3. Copy the priority, meaningful or not.
4. Generate a ficticious priority.
5. Discard priority.
6. Drain the ring (somehow).
7. Set A and C bits (by lying).
8. Worry about congestion (fast LAN to slow LAN).
9. Worry about token handoff ACK being delayed or impossible.
10. Panic if frame is too long for destination LAN.

Parameters assumed:
802.3: 1500-byte frames, 10 Mbps (minus collisions)
802.4: 8191-byte frames 10 Mbps
802.5: 5000-byte frames 4 Mbps

Fig. 4-37. Problems encountered in building bridges from 802.x to 802.y.

4.4.2. Transparent Bridges

The first 802 bridge is a **transparent bridge** or **spanning tree bridge** (Perlman, 1992). The overriding concern of the people who supported this design was complete transparency. In their view, a site with multiple LANs should be able to go out and buy bridges designed to the IEEE standard, plug the connectors into the bridges, and everything should work perfectly, instantly. There should be no hardware changes required, no software changes required, no setting of address switches, no downloading of routing tables or parameters, nothing. Just plug in the cables and walk away. Furthermore, the operation of the existing LANs should not be affected by the bridges at all. Surprisingly enough, they actually succeeded.

A transparent bridge operates in promiscuous mode, accepting every frame transmitted on all the LANs to which it is attached. As an example, consider the configuration of Fig. 4-38. Bridge B1 is connected to LANs 1 and 2, and bridge B2 is connected to LANs 2, 3, and 4. A frame arriving at bridge B1 on LAN 1 destined for A can be discarded immediately, because it is already on the right LAN, but a frame arriving on LAN 1 for C or F must be forwarded.

When a frame arrives, a bridge must decide whether to discard or forward it,

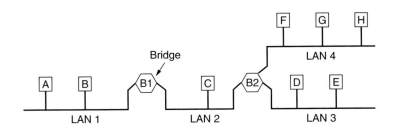

Fig. 4-38. A configuration with four LANs and two bridges.

and if the latter, on which LAN to put the frame. This decision is made by looking up the destination address in a big (hash) table inside the bridge. The table can list each possible destination and tell which output line (LAN) it belongs on. For example, B2's table would list A as belonging to LAN 2, since all B2 has to know is which LAN to put frames for A on. That, in fact, more forwarding happens later is not of interest to it.

When the bridges are first plugged in, all the hash tables are empty. None of the bridges know where any of the destinations are, so they use the flooding algorithm: every incoming frame for an unknown destination is output on all the LANs to which the bridge is connected except the one it arrived on. As time goes on, the bridges learn where destinations are, as described below. Once a destination is known, frames destined for it are put on only the proper LAN and are not flooded.

The algorithm used by the transparent bridges is **backward learning**. As mentioned above, the bridges operate in promiscuous mode, so they see every frame sent on any of their LANs. By looking at the source address, they can tell which machine is accessible on which LAN. For example, if bridge B1 in Fig. 4-38 sees a frame on LAN 2 coming from C, it knows that C must be reachable via LAN 2, so it makes an entry in its hash table noting that frames going to C should use LAN 2. Any subsequent frame addressed to C coming in on LAN 1 will be forwarded, but a frame for C coming in on LAN 2 will be discarded.

The topology can change as machines and bridges are powered up and down and moved around. To handle dynamic topologies, whenever a hash table entry is made, the arrival time of the frame is noted in the entry. Whenever a frame whose destination is already in the table arrives, its entry is updated with the current time. Thus the time associated with every entry tells the last time a frame from that machine was seen.

Periodically, a process in the bridge scans the hash table and purges all entries more than a few minutes old. In this way, if a computer is unplugged from its LAN, moved around the building, and replugged in somewhere else, within a few minutes it will be back in normal operation, without any manual intervention. This algorithm also means that if a machine is quiet for a few minutes, any traffic sent to it will have to be flooded, until it next sends a frame itself.

The routing procedure for an incoming frame depends on the LAN it arrives on (the source LAN) and the LAN its destination is on (the destination LAN), as follows:

1. If destination and source LANs are the same, discard the frame.

2. If the destination and source LANs are different, forward the frame.

3. If the destination LAN is unknown, use flooding.

As each frame arrives, this algorithm must be applied. Special purpose VLSI chips exist to do the lookup and update the table entry, all in a few microseconds.

To increase reliability, some sites use two or more bridges in parallel between pairs of LANs, as shown in Fig. 4-39. This arrangement, however, also introduces some additional problems because it creates loops in the topology.

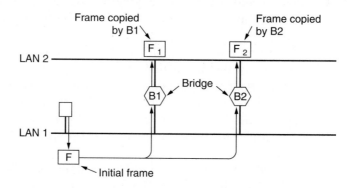

Fig. 4-39. Two parallel transparent bridges.

A simple example of these problems can be seen by observing how a frame, F, with unknown destination is handled in Fig. 4-39. Each bridge, following the normal rules for handling unknown destinations, uses flooding, which in this example, just means copying it to LAN 2. Shortly thereafter, bridge 1 sees F_2, a frame with an unknown destination, which it copies to LAN 1, generating F_3 (not shown). Similarly, bridge 2 copies F_1 to LAN 1 generating F_4 (also not shown). Bridge 1 now forwards F_4 and bridge 2 copies F_3. This cycle goes on forever.

Spanning Tree Bridges

The solution to this difficulty is for the bridges to communicate with each other and overlay the actual topology with a spanning tree that reaches every LAN. In effect, some potential connections between LANs are ignored in the interest of constructing a fictitious loop-free topology. For example, in Fig. 4-40(a) we see nine LANs interconnected by ten bridges. This configuration can be abstracted into a graph with the LANs as the nodes. An arc connects any two LANs that are connected by a bridge. The graph can be reduced to a spanning tree by dropping the arcs shown as dotted lines in Fig. 4-40(b). Using this spanning tree, there is exactly one path from every LAN to every other LAN. Once the bridges have agreed on the spanning tree, all forwarding between LANs follows the spanning tree. Since there is a unique path from each source to each destination, loops are impossible.

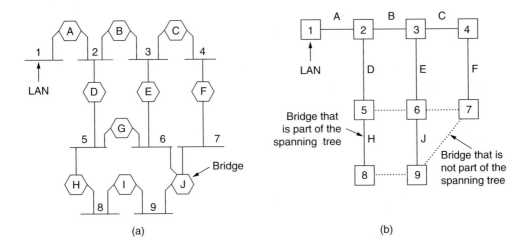

(a)   (b)

Fig. 4-40. (a) Interconnected LANs. (b) A spanning tree covering the LANs. The dotted lines are not part of the spanning tree.

To build the spanning tree, first the bridges have to choose one bridge to be the root of the tree. They make this choice by having each one broadcast its serial number, installed by the manufacturer, and guaranteed to be unique worldwide. The bridge with the lowest serial number becomes the root. Next, a tree of shortest paths from the root to every bridge and LAN is constructed. This tree is the spanning tree. If a bridge or LAN fails, a new one is computed.

The result of this algorithm is that a unique path is established from every LAN to the root, and thus to every other LAN. Although the tree spans all the LANs, not all the bridges are necessarily present in the tree (to prevent loops). Even after the spanning tree has been established, the algorithm continues to run in order to automatically detect topology changes and update the tree. The distributed algorithm used for constructing the spanning tree was invented by Perlman and is described in detail in (Perlman, 1992).

Bridges can also be used to connect LANs that are widely separated. In this model, each site consists of a collection of LANs and bridges, one of which has a connection to a WAN. Frames for remote LANs travel over the WAN. The basic spanning tree algorithm can be used, preferably with certain optimizations to select a tree that minimizes the amount of WAN traffic.

4.4.3. Source Routing Bridges

Transparent bridges have the advantage of being easy to install. You just plug them in and walk away. On the other hand, they do not make optimal use of the bandwidth, since they only use a subset of the topology (the spanning tree). The relative importance of these two (and other) factors led to a split within the 802 committees (Pitt, 1988). The CSMA/CD and token bus people chose the transparent bridge. The ring people (with encouragement from IBM) preferred a scheme called **source routing**, which we will now describe. For additional details, see (Dixon, 1987).

Reduced to its barest essentials, source routing assumes that the sender of each frame knows whether or not the destination is on its own LAN. When sending a frame to a different LAN, the source machine sets the high-order bit of the source address to 1, to mark it. Furthermore, it includes in the frame header the exact path that the frame will follow.

This path is constructed as follows. Each LAN has a unique 12-bit number, and each bridge has a 4-bit number that uniquely identifies it in the context of its LANs. Thus, two bridges far apart may both have number 3, but two bridges between the same two LANs must have different bridge numbers. A route is then a sequence of bridge, LAN, bridge, LAN, ... numbers. Referring to Fig. 4-38, the route from A to D would be (L1, B1, L2, B2, L3).

A source routing bridge is only interested in those frames with the high-order bit of the destination set to 1. For each such frame that it sees, it scans the route looking for the number of the LAN on which the frame arrived. If this LAN number is followed by its own bridge number, the bridge forwards the frame onto the LAN whose number follows its bridge number in the route. If the incoming LAN number is followed by the number of some other bridge, it does not forward the frame.

This algorithm lends itself to three possible implementations:

1. Software: the bridge runs in promiscuous mode, copying all frames to its memory to see if they have the high-order destination bit set to 1. If so, the frame is inspected further; otherwise it is not.

2. Hybrid: the bridge's LAN interface inspects the high-order destination bit and only accepts frames with the bit set. This interface is easy to build into hardware and greatly reduces the number of frames the bridge must inspect.

3. Hardware: the bridge's LAN interface not only checks the high-order destination bit, but it also scans the route to see if this bridge must do forwarding. Only frames that must actually be forwarded are given to the bridge. This implementation requires the most complex hardware but wastes no bridge CPU cycles because all irrelevant frames are screened out.

These three implementations vary in their cost and performance. The first one has no additional hardware cost for the interface but may require a very fast CPU to handle all the frames. The last one requires a special VLSI chip but offloads much of the processing from the bridge to the chip, so that a slower CPU can be used, or alternatively, the bridge can handle more LANs.

Implicit in the design of source routing is that every machine in the internetwork knows, or can find, the best path to every other machine. How these routes are discovered is an important part of the source routing algorithm. The basic idea is that if a destination is unknown, the source issues a broadcast frame asking where it is. This **discovery frame** is forwarded by every bridge so that it reaches every LAN on the internetwork. When the reply comes back, the bridges record their identity in it, so that the original sender can see the exact route taken and ultimately choose the best route.

While this algorithm clearly finds the best route (it finds *all* routes), it suffers from a frame explosion. Consider the configuration of Fig. 4-41, with N LANs linearly connected by triple bridges. Each discovery frame sent by station 1 is copied by each of the three bridges on LAN 1, yielding three discovery frames on LAN 2. Each of these is copied by each of the bridges on LAN 2, resulting in nine frames on LAN 3. By the time we reach LAN N, 3^{N-1} frames are circulating. If a dozen sets of bridges are traversed, more than half a million discovery frames will have to be injected into the last LAN, causing severe congestion.

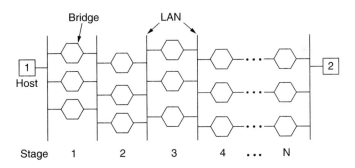

Fig. 4-41. A series of LANs connected by triple bridges.

A somewhat analogous process happens with the transparent bridge, only it is not nearly so severe. When an unknown frame arrives, it is flooded, but only along the spanning tree, so the total volume of frames sent is linear with the size of the network, not exponential.

Once a host has discovered a route to a certain destination, it stores the route in a cache, so that the discovery process will not have to be run next time. While this approach greatly limits the impact of the frame explosion, it does put some administrative burden on all the hosts, and the whole algorithm is definitely not transparent, which was one of the original goals, as we mentioned above.

4.4.4. Comparison of 802 Bridges

The transparent and source routing bridges each have advantages and disadvantages. In this section we will discuss some of the major ones. They are summarized in Fig. 4-42 and covered in more detail in (Soha and Perlman, 1988; and Zhang, 1988). Be warned, however, that every one of the points is highly contested.

Issue	Transparent bridge	Source routing bridge
Orientation	Connectionless	Connection-oriented
Transparency	Fully transparent	Not transparent
Configuration	Automatic	Manual
Routing	Suboptimal	Optimal
Locating	Backward learning	Discovery frames
Failures	Handled by the bridges	Handled by the hosts
Complexity	In the bridges	In the hosts

Fig. 4-42. Comparison of transparent and source routing bridges.

At the heart of the difference between the two bridge types is the distinction between connectionless and connection-oriented networking. The transparent bridges have no concept of a virtual circuit at all and route each frame independently from all the others. The source routing bridges, in contrast, determine a route using discovery frames and then use that route thereafter.

The transparent bridges are completely invisible to the hosts and are fully compatible with all existing 802 products. The source routing bridges are neither transparent nor compatible. To use source routing, hosts must be fully aware of the bridging scheme and must actively participate in it. Splitting an existing LAN into two LANs connected by a source routing bridge requires making changes to the host software.

When using transparent bridges, no network management is needed. The bridges configure themselves to the topology automatically. With source routing bridges, the network manager must manually install the LAN and bridge numbers. Mistakes, such as duplicating a LAN or bridge number, can be very difficult to detect, as they may cause some frames to loop, but not others on different routes. Furthermore, when connecting two previously disjoint internetworks, with transparent bridges there is nothing to do except connect them, whereas with source routing, it may be necessary to manually change many LAN numbers to make them unique in the combined internetwork.

One of the few advantages of source routing is that, in theory, it can use optimal routing, whereas transparent bridging is restricted to the spanning tree.

Furthermore, source routing can also make good use of parallel bridges between two LANs to split the load. Whether actual bridges will be clever enough to make use of these theoretical advantages is questionable.

Locating destinations is done using backward learning in the transparent bridge and using discovery frames in source routing bridges. The disadvantage of backward learning is that the bridges have to wait until a frame from a particular machine happens to come along in order to learn where that machine is. The disadvantage of discovery frames is the exponential explosion in moderate to large internetworks with parallel bridges.

Failure handling is quite different in the two schemes. Transparent bridges learn about bridge and LAN failures and other topology changes quickly and automatically, just from listening to each other's control frames. Hosts do not notice these changes at all.

With source routing, the situation is quite different. When a bridge fails, machines that are routing over it initially notice that their frames are no longer being acknowledged, so they time out and try over and over. Finally, they conclude that something is wrong, but they still do not know if the problem is with the destination itself, or with the current route. Only by sending another discovery frame can they see if the destination is available. Unfortunately, when a major bridge fails, a large number of hosts will have to experience timeouts and send new discovery frames before the problem is resolved, even if an alternative route is available. This greater vulnerability to failures is one of the major weaknesses of all connection-oriented systems.

Finally, we come to complexity and cost, a very controversial topic. If source routing bridges have a VLSI chip that reads in only those frames that must be forwarded, these bridges will experience a lighter frame processing load and deliver a better performance for a given investment in hardware. Without this chip they will do worse because the amount of processing per frame (searching the route in the frame header) is substantially more.

In addition, source routing puts extra complexity in the hosts: they must store routes, send discovery frames, and copy route information into each frame. All of these things require memory and CPU cycles. Since there are typically one to two orders of magnitude more hosts than bridges, it may be better to put the extra cost and complexity into a few bridges, rather than in all the hosts.

4.4.5. Remote Bridges

A common use of bridges is to connect two (or more) distant LANs. For example, a company might have plants in several cities, each with its own LAN. Ideally, all the LANs should be interconnected, so the complete system acts like one large LAN.

This goal can be achieved by putting a bridge on each LAN and connecting the bridges pairwise with point-to-point lines (e.g., lines leased from a telephone company). A simple system, with three LANs, is illustrated in Fig. 4-43. The usual routing algorithms apply here. The simplest way to see this is to regard the three point-to-point lines as hostless LANs. Then we have a normal system of six LANS interconnected by four bridges. Nothing in what we have studied so far says that a LAN must have hosts on it.

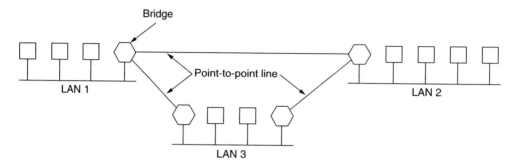

Fig. 4-43. Remote bridges can be used to interconnect distant LANs.

Various protocols can be used on the point-to-point lines. One possibility is to choose some standard point-to-point data link protocol, putting complete MAC frames in the payload field. This strategy works best if all the LANs are identical, and the only problem is getting frames to the right LAN. Another option is to strip off the MAC header and trailer at the source bridge and put what is left in the payload field of the point-to-point protocol. A new MAC header and trailer can then be generated at the destination bridge. A disadvantage of this approach is that the checksum that arrives at the destination host is not the one computed by the source host, so errors caused by bad bits in a bridge's memory may not be detected.

4.5. HIGH-SPEED LANS

The 802 LANs and MAN we have just studied are all based on one copper wire (two copper wires for 802.6). For low speeds and short distances, this will do just fine, but for high speeds and longer distances LANs must be based on fiber optics or highly parallel copper networks. Fiber has high bandwidth, is thin and lightweight, is not affected by electromagnetic interference from heavy machinery (important when cabling runs through elevator shafts), power surges, or lightning, and has excellent security because it is nearly impossible to wiretap without detection. Consequently, fast LANs often use fiber. In the following sections we will look at some local area networks that use fiber optics, as well as one extremely high-speed LAN that uses old fashioned copper wire (but lots of it).

4.5.1. FDDI

FDDI (Fiber Distributed Data Interface) is a high-performance fiber optic token ring LAN running at 100 Mbps over distances up to 200 km with up to 1000 stations connected (Black, 1994; Jain, 1994; Mirchandani and Khanna, 1993; Ross and Hamstra, 1993; Shah and Ramakrishnan, 1994; and Wolter, 1990). It can be used in the same way as any of the 802 LANs, but with its high bandwidth, another common use is as a backbone to connect copper LANs, as shown in Fig. 4-44. FDDI-II is the successor to FDDI, modified to handle synchronous circuit-switched PCM data for voice or ISDN traffic, in addition to ordinary data. We will refer to both of them as just FDDI. This section deals with both the physical layer and the MAC sublayer of FDDI.

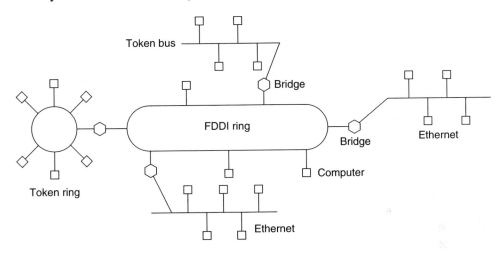

Fig. 4-44. An FDDI ring being used as a backbone to connect LANs and computers.

FDDI uses multimode fibers because the additional expense of single mode fibers is not needed for networks running at only 100 Mbps. It also uses LEDs rather than lasers, not only due to their lower cost, but also because FDDI may sometimes be used to connect directly to user workstations. There is a danger that curious users may occasionally unplug the fiber connector and look directly into it to watch the bits go by at 100 Mbps. With a laser the curious user might end up with a hole in his retina. LEDs are too weak to do any eye damage but are strong enough to transfer data accurately at 100 Mbps. The FDDI design specification calls for no more than 1 error in 2.5×10^{10} bits. Many implementations do much better.

The FDDI cabling consists of two fiber rings, one transmitting clockwise and the other transmitting counterclockwise, as illustrated in Fig. 4-45(a). If either one breaks, the other can be used as a backup. If both break at the same point, for example, due to a fire or other accident in the cable duct, the two rings can be joined into a single ring approximately twice as long, as shown in Fig. 4-45(b). Each station contains relays that can be used to join the two rings or bypass the station in the event of station problems. Wire centers can also be used, as in 802.5.

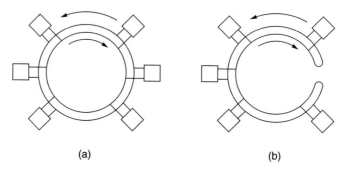

(a)   (b)

Fig. 4-45. (a) FDDI consists of two counterrotating rings. (b) In the event of failure of both rings at one point, the two rings can be joined together to form a single long ring.

FDDI defines two classes of stations, *A* and *B*. Class *A* stations connect to both rings. The cheaper class *B* stations only connect to one of the rings. Depending on how important fault tolerance is, an installation can choose class *A* or class *B* stations, or some of each.

The physical layer does not use Manchester encoding because 100-Mbps Manchester encoding requires 200 megabaud, which was deemed too expensive. Instead a scheme called **4 out of 5** encoding is used. Each group of 4 MAC symbols (0s, 1s, and certain nondata symbols such as start-of-frame) are encoded as a group of 5 bits on the medium. Sixteen of the 32 combinations are for data, 3 are for delimiters, 2 are for control, 3 are for hardware signaling, and 8 are unused (i.e., reserved for future versions of the protocol).

The advantage of this scheme is that it saves bandwidth, but the disadvantage is the loss of the self-clocking property of Manchester encoding. To compensate for this loss, a long preamble is used to synchronize the receiver to the sender's clock. Furthermore, all clocks are required to be stable to at least 0.005 percent. With this stability, frames up to 4500 bytes can be sent without danger of the receiver's clock drifting too far out of sync with the data stream.

The basic FDDI protocols are closely modeled on the 802.5 protocols. To transmit data, a station must first capture the token. Then it transmits a frame and removes it when it comes around again. One difference between FDDI and 802.5 is that in 802.5, a station may not generate a new token until its frame has gone all the way around and come back. In FDDI, with potentially 1000 stations and 200 km of fiber, the amount of time wasted waiting for the frame to circumnavigate the ring could be substantial. For this reason, it was decided to allow a station to put a new token back onto the ring as soon as it has finished transmitting its frames. In a large ring, several frames might be on the ring at the same time.

FDDI data frames are similar to 802.5 data frames. The FDDI format is shown in Fig. 4-46. The *Start delimiter* and *End delimiter* fields mark the frame boundaries. The *Frame control* field tells what kind of frame this is (data, control, etc.). The *Frame status* byte holds acknowledgement bits, similar to those of 802.5. The other fields are analogous to 802.5.

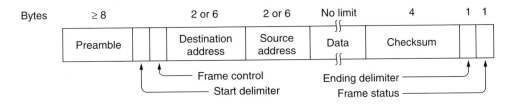

Fig. 4-46. FDDI frame format.

In addition to the regular (asynchronous) frames, FDDI also permits special synchronous frames for circuit-switched PCM or ISDN data. The synchronous frames are generated every 125 μsec by a master station to provide the 8000 samples/sec needed by PCM systems. Each of these frames has a header, 16 bytes of noncircuit-switched data, and up to 96 bytes of circuit-switched data (i.e., up to 96 PCM channels per frame).

The number 96 was chosen because it allows four T1 channels (4×24) at 1.544 Mbps or three CCITT E1 channels (3×32) at 2.048 Mbps to fit in a frame, thus making it suitable for use anywhere in the world. One synchronous frame every 125 μsec consumes 6.144 Mbps of bandwidth for the 96 circuit-switched channels. A maximum of 16 synchronous frames every 125 μsec allows up to 1536 PCM channels and eats up 98.3 Mbps.

Once a station has acquired one or more time slots in a synchronous frame, those slots are reserved for it until they are explicitly released. The total bandwidth not used by the synchronous frames is allocated on demand. A bit mask is present in each of these frames to indicate which slots are available for demand assignment. The nonsynchronous traffic is divided into priority classes, with the higher priorities getting first shot at the leftover bandwidth.

The FDDI MAC protocol uses three timers. The **token holding timer** determines how long a station may continue to transmit once it has acquired the token. This timer prevents a station from hogging the ring forever. The **token rotation timer** is restarted every time the token is seen. If this timer expires, it means that the token has not been sighted for too long an interval. Probably it has been lost, so the token recovery procedure is initiated. Finally, the **valid transmission timer** is used to time out and recover from certain transient ring errors.

FDDI also has a priority algorithm similar to 802.4. It determines which priority classes may transmit on a given token pass. If the token is ahead of schedule, all priorities may transmit, but if it is behind schedule, only the highest ones may send.

4.5.2. Fast Ethernet

FDDI was supposed to be the next generation LAN, but it never really caught on much beyond the backbone market (where it continues to do fine). The station management was too complicated, which led to complex chips and high prices. The substantial cost of FDDI chips made workstation manufacturers unwilling to make FDDI the standard network, so volume production never happened and FDDI never broke through to the mass market. The lesson that should have been learned here was KISS (Keep It Simple, Stupid).

In any event, the failure of FDDI to catch fire left a gap for a garden-variety LAN at speeds above 10 Mbps. Many installations needed more bandwidth and thus had numerous 10-Mbps LANs connected by a maze of repeaters, bridges, routers, and gateways, although to the network managers it sometimes felt that they were being held together by bubble gum and chicken wire.

It was in this environment that IEEE reconvened the 802.3 committee in 1992 with instructions to come up with a faster LAN. One proposal was to keep 802.3 exactly as it was, but just make it go faster. Another proposal was to redo it totally, to give it lots of new features, such as real-time traffic and digitized voice, but just keep the old name (for marketing reasons). After some wrangling, the committee decided to keep 802.3 the way it was, but just make it go faster. The people behind the losing proposal did what any computer-industry people would have done under these circumstances—they formed their own committee and standardized their LAN anyway (eventually as 802.12).

The three primary reasons that the 802.3 committee decided to go with a souped-up 802.3 LAN were:

1. The need to be backward compatible with thousands of existing LANs.

2. The fear that a new protocol might have unforeseen problems.

3. The desire to get the job done before the technology changed.

The work was done quickly (by standards committees' norms), and the result, **802.3u**, was officially approved by IEEE in June 1995. Technically, 802.3u is not a new standard, but an addendum to the existing 802.3 standard (to emphasize its backward compatibility). Since everyone calls it **fast Ethernet**, rather than 802.3u, we will do that, too.

The basic idea behind fast Ethernet was simple: keep all the old packet formats, interfaces, and procedural rules, but just reduce the bit time from 100 nsec to 10 nsec. Technically, it would have been possible to copy 10Base-5 or 10Base-2 and still detect collisions on time by just reducing the maximum cable length by a factor of ten. However, the advantages of 10Base-T wiring were so overwhelming, that fast Ethernet is based entirely on this design. Thus all fast Ethernet systems use hubs; multidrop cables with vampire taps or BNC connectors are not permitted.

Nevertheless, some choices still had to be made, the most important of which was which wire types to support. One contender was category 3 twisted pair. The argument for it was that practically every office in the Western world has at least four category 3 (or better) twisted pairs running from it to a telephone wiring closet within 100 meters. Sometimes two such cables exist. Thus using category 3 twisted pair would make it possible to wire up desktop computers using fast Ethernet without having to rewire the building, an enormous advantage for many organizations.

The main disadvantage of category 3 twisted pair is its inability to carry 200 megabaud signals (100 Mbps with Manchester encoding) 100 meters, the maximum computer-to-hub distance specified for 10Base-T (see Fig. 4-17). In contrast, category 5 twisted pair wiring can handle 100 meters easily, and fiber can go much further. The compromise chosen was to allow all three possibilities, as shown in Fig. 4-47, but to pep up the category 3 solution to give it the additional carrying capacity needed.

Name	Cable	Max. segment	Advantages
100Base-T4	Twisted pair	100 m	Uses category 3 UTP
100Base-TX	Twisted pair	100 m	Full duplex at 100 Mbps
100Base-FX	Fiber optics	2000 m	Full duplex at 100 Mbps; long runs

Fig. 4-47. Fast Ethernet cabling.

The category 3 UTP scheme, called **100Base-T4**, uses a signaling speed of 25 MHz, only 25 percent faster than standard 802.3's 20 MHz (remember that Manchester encoding, as shown in Fig. 4-20, requires two clock periods for each of the 10 million bits each second). To achieve the necessary bandwidth, 100Base-T4 requires four twisted pairs. Since standard telephone wiring for decades has had four twisted pairs per cable, most offices are able to handle this. Of course, it means giving up your office telephone, but that is surely a small price to pay for faster email.

Of the four twisted pairs, one is always to the hub, one is always from the hub, and other two are switchable to the current transmission direction. To get the necessary bandwidth, Manchester encoding is not used, but with modern clocks and such short distances, it is no longer needed. In addition, ternary signals are sent, so that during a single clock period the wire can contain a 0, a 1, or a 2. With three twisted pairs going in the forward direction and ternary signaling, any one of 27 possible symbols can be transmitted, making it possible to send 4 bits with some redundancy. Transmitting 4 bits in each of the 25 million clock cycles per second gives the necessary 100 Mbps. In addition, there is always a 33.3 Mbps reverse channel using the remaining twisted pair. This scheme, known as **8B6T**, (8 bits map to 6 trits) is not likely to win any prizes for elegance, but it works with the existing wiring plant.

For category 5 wiring, the design, **100Base-TX**, is simpler because the wires can handle clock rates up to 125 MHz and beyond. Only two twisted pairs per station are used, one to the hub and one from it. Rather than just use straight binary coding, a scheme called **4B5B** is used at 125 MHz. Every group of five clock periods is used to send 4 bits in order to give some redundancy, provide enough transitions to allow easy clock synchronization, create unique patterns for frame delimiting, and be compatible with FDDI in the physical layer. Consequently, 100Base-TX is a full-duplex system; stations can transmit at 100 Mbps and receive at 100 Mbps at the same time. In addition, you can have two telephones in your office for real communication in case the computer is fully occupied with surfing the Web.

The last option, **100Base-FX**, uses two strands of multimode fiber, one for each direction, so it, too, is full duplex with 100 Mbps in each direction. In addition, the distance between a station and the hub can be up to 2 km.

Two kinds of hubs are possible with 100Base-T4 and 100Base-TX, collectively known as **100Base-T**. In a shared hub, all the incoming lines (or at least all the lines arriving at one plug-in card) are logically connected, forming a single collision domain. All the standard rules, including the binary backoff algorithm, apply, so the system works just like old-fashioned 802.3. In particular, only one station at a time can be transmitting.

In a switched hub, each incoming frame is buffered on a plug-in line card. Although this feature makes the hub and cards more expensive, it also means that all stations can transmit (and receive) at the same time, greatly improving the total bandwidth of the system, often by an order of magnitude or more. Buffered frames are passed over a high-speed backplane from the source card to the destination card. The backplane has not been standardized, nor does it need to be, since it is entirely hidden deep inside the switch. If past experience is any guide, switch vendors will compete vigorously to produce ever faster backplanes in order to improve system throughput. Because 100Base-FX cables are too long for the normal Ethernet collision algorithm, they must be connected to buffered, switched hubs, so each one is a collision domain unto itself.

As a final note, virtually all switches can handle a mix of 10-Mbps and 100-Mbps stations, to make upgrading easier. As a site acquires more and more 100-Mbps workstations, all it has to do is buy the necessary number of new line cards and insert them into the switch.

More information about Fast Ethernet can be found in (Johnson, 1996). For a comparison of high-speed local area networks, in particular, FDDI, fast Ethernet, ATM, and VG-AnyLAN, see (Cronin et al., 1994).

4.5.3. HIPPI—High-Performance Parallel Interface

During the Cold War, Los Alamos National Laboratory, the U.S. government's nuclear weapons design center, routinely bought one of every supercomputer offered for sale. Los Alamos also collected fancy peripherals, such as massive storage devices and special graphics workstations for scientific visualization. At that time, each manufacturer had a different interface for connecting peripherals to its supercomputer, so it was not possible to share peripherals among machines or to connect two supercomputers together.

In 1987, researchers at Los Alamos began work on a standard supercomputer interface, with the intention of getting it standardized and then talking all the vendors into using it. (Given the size of Los Alamos' computing budget, when it talked, vendors listened.) The goal for the interface was an interface that everyone could implement quickly and efficiently. The guiding principle was KISS: Keep It Simple, Stupid. It was to have no options, not require any new chips to be designed, and have the performance of a fire hose.

The initial specification called for a data rate of 800 Mbps, because watching movies of bombs going off required frames of 1024×1024 pixels with 24 bits per pixel and 30 frames/sec, for an aggregate data rate of 750 Mbps. Later, one option crept in: a second data rate of 1600 Mbps. When this proposal, called **HIPPI (HIgh Performance Parallel Interface)** was later offered to ANSI for standardization, the proposers were regarded as the lunatic fringe because LANs in the 1980s meant 10-Mbps Ethernets.

HIPPI was originally designed to be a data channel rather than a LAN. Data channels operate point-to-point, from one master (a computer) to one slave (a peripheral), with dedicated wires and no switching. No contention is present and the environment is entirely predictable. Later, the need to be able to switch a peripheral from one supercomputer to another became apparent, and a crossbar switch was added to the HIPPI design, as illustrated in Fig. 4-48.

In order to achieve such enormous performance using only off-the-shelf chips, the basic interface was made 50 bits wide, 32 bits of data and 18 bits of control, so the HIPPI cable contains 50 twisted pairs. Every 40 nsec, a word is transferred in parallel across the interface. To achieve 1600 Mbps, two cables are used and two words are transferred per cycle. All transfers are simplex. To get two-way communication, two (or four) cables are needed. At these speeds, the maximum cable length is 25 meters.

After it got over some initial shock, the ANSI X3T9.3 committee produced a HIPPI standard based on the Los Alamos input. The standard covers the physical and data link layers. Everything above that is up to the users. The basic protocol is that to communicate, a host first asks the crossbar switch to set up a connection. Then it (usually) sends a single message and releases the connection.

Messages are structured with a control word, a header of up to 1016 bytes, and a data part of up to $2^{32} - 2$ bytes. For flow control reasons, messages are

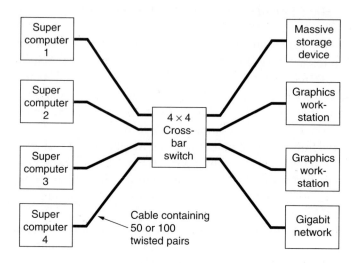

Fig. 4-48. HIPPI using a crossbar switch.

broken up into frames of 256 words. When the receiver is able to accept a frame, it signals the sender, which then sends a frame. Receivers can also ask for multiple frames at once. Error control consists of a horizontal parity bit per word and a vertical parity word at the end of each frame. Traditional checksums were regarded as unnecessary and too slow.

HIPPI was quickly implemented by dozens of vendors and has been the supercomputer interconnect standard for years. For more information about it, see (Hughes and Franta, 1994; Tolmie, 1992; and Tolmie and Renwick, 1993).

4.5.4. Fibre Channel

At the time HIPPI was designed, fiber optics was too expensive and not considered reliable enough, so the fastest LAN ever built was constructed from low-grade telephone wire. As time went on, fiber became cheaper and more reliable, so it was natural that there would eventually be an attempt to redo HIPPI using a single fiber instead of 50 or 100 twisted pairs. Unfortunately, the discipline that Los Alamos had in beating down proposed new features every time one reared its ugly head was lost along the way. The successor to HIPPI, called **fibre channel**, is far more complicated and more expensive to implement. Whether it will enjoy HIPPI's commercial success remains to be seen.

Fibre channel handles both data channel and network connections. In particular, it can be used to carry data channels including HIPPI, SCSI, and the multiplexor channel used on IBM mainframes. It can also carry network packets, including IEEE 802, IP, and ATM. Like HIPPI, the basic structure of fibre channel is a crossbar switch that connects inputs to outputs. Connections can be established for a single packet or for a much longer interval.

Fibre channel supports three service classes. The first class is pure circuit switching, with guaranteed delivery in order. The data channel modes use this service class. The second class is packet switching with guaranteed delivery. The third class is packet switching without guaranteed delivery.

Fibre channel has an elaborate protocol structure, as shown in Fig. 4-49. Here we see five layers, which together cover the physical and data link layers. The bottom layer deals with the physical medium. So far, it supports data rates of 100, 200, 400, and 800 Mbps. The second layer handles the bit encoding. The system used is somewhat like FDDI, but instead of 5 bits being used to encode 16 valid symbols, 10 bits are used to encode 256 valid symbols, providing a small amount of redundancy. Together, these two layers are functionally equivalent to the OSI physical layer.

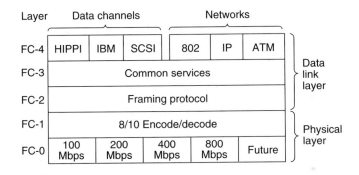

Fig. 4-49. The fibre channel protocol layers.

The middle layer defines the frame layout and header formats. Data are transmitted in frames whose payloads can be up to 2048 bytes. The next layer allows common services to be provided to the top layer in the future, as required. Finally, the top layer provides the interfaces to the various kinds of computers and peripherals supported.

As an aside, although fibre channel was designed in the United States, the spelling of the name was chosen by the editor of the standard, who was British. Additional information about fibre channel can be found in (Tolmie, 1992). A comparison of it with HIPPI and ATM is in (Tolmie, 1995).

4.6. SATELLITE NETWORKS

Although most multiple access channels are found in LANs, one kind of WAN also uses multiple access channels: communication satellite based WANs. In the following sections we will briefly study some of the problems that occur

with satellite-based wide area networks. We will also look at some of the protocols that have been devised to deal with them.

Communication satellites generally have up to a dozen or so transponders.
Each transponder has a beam that covers some portion of the earth below it, ranging from a wide beam 10,000 km across to a spot beam only 250 km across. Stations within the beam area can send frames to the satellite on the uplink frequency. The satellite then rebroadcasts them on the downlink frequency. Different frequencies are used for uplink and downlink to keep the transponder from
going into oscillation. Satellites that do no on-board processing, but just echo
whatever they hear (most of them), are often called **bent pipe** satellites.

Each antenna can aim itself at some area, transmit some frames, and then aim
at a new area. Aiming is done electronically, but still takes some number of
microseconds. The amount of time a beam is pointed to a given area is called the
dwell time. For maximum efficiency, it should not be too short or too much time
will be wasted moving the beam.

Just as with LANs, one of the key design issues is how to allocate the transponder channels. However, unlike LANs, carrier sensing is impossible due to
the 270-msec propagation delay. When a station senses the state of a downlink
channel, it hears what was going on 270 msec ago. Sensing the uplink channel is
generally impossible. As a result, the CSMA/CD protocols (which assume that a
transmitting station can detect collisions within the first few bit times, and then
pull back if one is occurring) cannot be used with satellites. Hence the need for
other protocols.

Five classes of protocols are used on the multiple access (uplink) channel:
polling, ALOHA, FDM, TDM, and CDMA. Although we have studied each of
these already, satellite operation sometimes adds new twists. The main problem
is with the uplink channel, since the downlink channel has only a single sender
(the satellite) and thus has no channel allocation problem.

4.6.1. Polling

The traditional way to allocate a single channel among competing users is for
somebody to poll them. Having the satellite poll each station in turn to see if it
has a frame is prohibitively expensive, given the 270-msec time required for each
poll/response sequence.

However, if all the ground stations are also tied to a (typically low-bandwidth)
packet-switching network, a minor variation of this idea is conceivable. The idea
is to arrange all the stations in a logical ring, so each station knows its successor.
Around this terrestrial ring circulates a token. The satellite never sees the token.
A station is allowed to transmit on the uplink only when it has captured the token.
If the number of stations is small and constant, the token transmission time is
short, and the bursts sent on the uplink channel are much longer than the token
rotation time, the scheme is moderately efficient.

4.6.2. ALOHA

Pure ALOHA is easy to implement: every station just sends whenever it wants to. The trouble is that the channel efficiency is only about 18 percent. Generally, such a low utilization factor is unacceptable for satellites that costs tens of millions of dollars each.

Using slotted ALOHA doubles the efficiency but introduces the problem of how to synchronize all the stations so they all know when each time slot begins. Fortunately, the satellite itself holds the answer, since it is inherently a broadcast medium. One ground station, the **reference station**, periodically transmits a special signal whose rebroadcast is used by all the ground stations as the time origin. If the time slots all have length ΔT, each station now knows that time slot k begins at a time $k\Delta T$ after the time origin. Since clocks run at slightly different rates, periodic resynchronization is necessary to keep everyone in phase. An additional complication is that the propagation time from the satellite is different for each ground station, but this effect can be corrected for.

To increase the utilization of the uplink channel above $1/e$, we could go from the single uplink channel of Fig. 4-50(a), to the dual uplink scheme of Fig. 4-50(b). A station with a frame to transmit chooses one of the two uplink channels at random and sends the frame in the next slot. Each uplink then operates an independent slotted ALOHA channel.

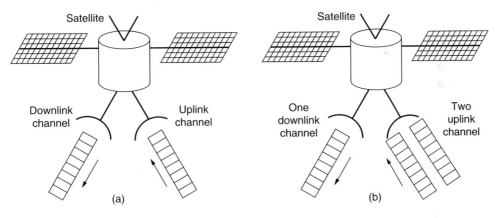

Fig. 4-50. (a) A standard ALOHA system. (b) Adding a second uplink channel.

If one of the uplink channels contains a single frame, it is just transmitted in the corresponding downlink slot later. If both channels are successful, the satellite can buffer one of the frames and transmit it during an idle slot later on. Working out the probabilities, it can be shown that given an infinite amount of buffer space, the downlink utilization can be gotten up to 0.736 at a cost of increasing the bandwidth requirements by one half.

4.6.3. FDM

Frequency division multiplexing is the oldest and probably still the most widely used channel allocation scheme. A typical 36-Mbps transponder might be divided statically into 500 or so 64,000-bps PCM channels, each one operating at its own unique frequency to avoid interfering with the others.

Although simple, FDM also has some drawbacks. First, guard bands are needed between the channels to keep the stations separated. This requirement exists because it is not possible to build transmitters that output all their energy in the main band and nothing in the side bands. The amount of bandwidth wasted in the guard bands can be a substantial fraction of the total.

Second, the stations must be carefully power controlled. If a station puts out too much power in the main band, it will also automatically put out too much power in the side bands, spilling over into adjacent channels and causing interference. Finally, FDM is entirely an analog technique and does not lend itself well to implementation in software.

If the number of stations is small and fixed, the frequency channels can be allocated statically in advance. However, if the number of stations, or the load on each one can fluctuate rapidly, some form of dynamic allocation of the frequency bands is needed. One such mechanism is the **SPADE** system used on some early Intelsat satellites. Each SPADE transponder was divided into 794 simplex (64-kbps) PCM voice channels, along with a 128-kbps common signaling channel. The PCM channels were used in pairs to provide full duplex service. The total transponder bandwidth used was 50 Mbps for the uplink portion and another 50 Mbps for the downlink.

The common signaling channel was divided into units of 50 msec. A unit contained 50 slots of 1 msec (128 bits). Each slot was "owned" by one of (not more than) 50 ground stations. When a ground station had data to send, it picked a currently unused channel at random and wrote the number of that channel in its next 128-bit slot. If the selected channel was still unused when the request was seen on the downlink, the channel was considered allocated and all other stations refrained from trying to acquire it. If two or more stations tried to allocate the same channel in the same frame, a collision occurred and they had to try again later. When a station was finished using its channel, it sent a deallocation message in its slot on the common channel.

4.6.4. TDM

Like FDM, TDM is well understood and widely used in practice. It requires time synchronization for the slots, but this can be provided by a reference station, as described for slotted ALOHA above. Similarly to FDM, for a small and unvarying number of stations, the slot assignment can be set up in advance and never changed, but for a varying number of stations, or a fixed number of stations with time-varying loads, time slots must be assigned dynamically.

Slot assignment can be done in a centralized or a decentralized way. As an example of centralized slot assignment, let us consider the experimental **ACTS** (**Advanced Communication Technology Satellite**), which was designed for a few dozen stations (Palmer and White, 1990). ACTS was launched in 1992 and has four independent 110-Mbps TDM channels, two uplink and two downlink. Each channel is organized as a sequence of 1-msec frames, each frame containing 1728 time slots. Each time slot has a 64-bit payload, allowing each one to hold a 64-kbps voice channel.

The beams can be switched from one geographical area to another, but since moving the beam takes several slot times, channels originating or terminating in the same geographic area are normally assigned to contiguous time slots to increase dwell time and minimize time lost to beam motion. Thus time slot management requires a thorough knowledge of station geography to minimize the number of wasted time slots. For this and other reasons, time slot management is done by one of the ground stations, the **MCS (Master Control Station)**.

The basic operation of ACTS is a continuous three-step process, each step taking 1 msec. In step 1, the satellite receives a frame and stores it in a 1728-entry onboard RAM. In step 2, an onboard computer copies each input entry to the corresponding output entry (possibly for the other antenna). In step 3, the output frame is transmitted on the downlink.

Initially, each station is assigned at least one time slot. To acquire additional channels (for new voice calls), a station sends a short request message to the MCS. Similarly, it can release an existing channel with a message to the MCS. These messages make use of a small number of overhead bits and provide a special control channel to the MCS with a capacity of about 13 messages/sec per station. The channels are dedicated; there is no contention for them.

Dynamic TDM slot allocation is also possible. Below we will discuss three schemes. In each of these, TDM frames are divided into time slots, with each slot having a (temporary) owner. Only the owner may use a time slot.

The first scheme assumes that there are more slots than stations, so each station can be assigned a home slot (Binder, 1975). If there are more slots than stations, the extra slots are not assigned to anyone. If the owner of a slot does not want it during the current group, it goes idle. An empty slot is a signal to everyone else that the owner has no traffic. During the next frame, the slot becomes available to anyone who wants it, on a contention (ALOHA) basis.

If the owner wants to retrieve "his" home slot, he transmits a frame, thus forcing a collision (if there was other traffic). After a collision, everyone except the owner must desist from using the slot in the next frame. Thus the owner can always begin transmitting within two frame times in the worst case. At low channel utilization the system does not perform as well as normal slotted ALOHA, since after each collision, the collidees must abstain for one frame to see if the owner wants the slot back. Fig. 4-51(a) shows a frame with eight slots, seven of which are owned by *G*, *A*, *F*, *E*, *B*, *C*, and *D*, respectively. The eighth slot is not owned by anyone and can be fought over.

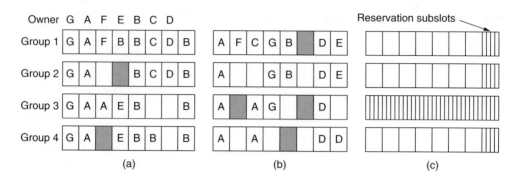

Fig. 4-51. Reservation schemes. (a) Binder. (b) Crowther. (c) Roberts. The shaded boxes indicate collisions. For each of the three schemes, four consecutive groups of slots are shown.

A second scheme is applicable even when the number of stations is unknown and varying (Crowther et al., 1973). In this method, slots do not have permanent owners, as in Binder's. Instead, stations compete for slots using slotted ALOHA. Whenever a transmission is successful, the station making the successful transmission is entitled to that slot in the next frame as well. Thus, as long as a station has data to send, it can continue doing so indefinitely (subject to some "Please-do-not-be-a-pig" rules). In essence the proposal allows a dynamic mix of slotted ALOHA and TDM, with the number of slots devoted to each varying with demand. Fig. 4-51(b) also shows a frame with eight slots. Initially, *E* is using the last slot, but after two frames, it no longer needs it. It lies idle for one frame, and then *D* picks it up and keeps it until it is done.

A third scheme, due to Roberts (1973), requires stations to make advance requests before transmitting. Each frame contains, say, one special slot [the last one in Fig. 4-51(c)] which is divided into *V* smaller subslots used to make reservations. When a station wants to send data, it broadcasts a short request frame in a randomly-chosen reservation subslot. If the reservation is successful (i.e., no collision), then the next regular slot (or slots) is reserved. At all times everyone must keep track of the queue length (number of slots reserved), so that when any station makes a successful reservation it will know how many data slots to skip before transmitting. Stations need not keep track of *who* is queued up; they merely need to know how long the queue is. When the queue length drops to zero, all slots revert to reservation subslots, to speed up the reservation process.

Although TDM is widely used, both with and without reservation schemes, it, too, has some shortcomings. For one, it requires all stations to synchronize in time, which is not entirely trivial in practice because satellites tend to drift in orbit, which changes the propagation time to each ground station. It also requires each ground station to be capable of extremely high burst speeds. For example, even though an ACTS station may have only one 64-kbps channel, it must be capable of putting out a 64-bit burst in a 578-nsec time slot. In other words, it must actually operate at 110 Mbps. In contrast, a 64-kbps FDM station really operates at 64 kbps.

4.6.5. CDMA

The final scheme is CDMA. CDMA avoids the time synchronization problem and also the channel allocation problem. It is completely decentralized and fully dynamic.

However, it has three main disadvantages. First, the capacity of a CDMA channel in the presence of noise and uncoordinated stations is typically lower than what TDM can achieve. Second, with 128 chips/bit (a common value), although the bit rate may not be high, the chip rate will be, necessitating a fast (read: expensive) transmitter. Third, few practicing engineers actually understand CDMA, which generally does not increase the chances of their using it, even if it is the best method for a particular application. Nevertheless, CDMA has been used by the military for decades and is now becoming more common in commercial applications as well.

4.7. SUMMARY

Some networks have a single channel that is used for all communication. In these networks, the key design issue is the allocation of this channel among the competing stations wishing to use it. Numerous channel allocation algorithms have been devised. A summary of some of the more important channel allocation methods is given in Fig. 4-52.

The simplest allocation schemes are FDM and TDM. These are efficient when the number of stations is small and the traffic is continuous. Both are widely used under these circumstances, for example, for dividing up the bandwidth in satellite links used as telephone trunks.

When the number of stations is large and variable or the traffic bursty, FDM and TDM are poor choices. The ALOHA protocol, with and without slotting and control, has been proposed as an alternative. ALOHA and its many variants and derivatives have been widely discussed, analyzed, and used in real systems.

When the state of the channel can be sensed, stations can avoid starting a transmission while another station is transmitting. This technique, carrier sensing, has led to a variety of protocols that can be used on LANs and MANs.

A class of protocols that eliminate contention altogether, or at least reduce it considerably, is known. Binary countdown completely eliminates contention.

Method	Description
FDM	Dedicate a frequency band to each station
TDM	Dedicate a time slot to each station
Pure ALOHA	Unsynchronized transmission at any instant
Slotted ALOHA	Random transmission in well-defined time slots
1-persistent CSMA	Standard carrier sense multiple access
Nonpersistent CSMA	Random delay when channel is sensed busy
P-persistent CSMA	CSMA, but with a probability of p of persisting
CSMA/CD	CSMA, but abort on detecting a collision
Bit map	Round robin scheduling using a bit map
Binary countdown	Highest numbered ready station goes next
Tree walk	Reduced contention by selective enabling
Wavelength division	A dynamic FDM scheme for fiber
MACA, MACAW	Wireless LAN protocols
GSM	FDM plus TDM for cellular radio
CDPD	Packet radio within an AMPS channel
CDMA	Everybody speak at once but in a different language
Ethernet	CSMA/CD with binary exponential backoff
Token bus	Logical ring on a physical bus
Token ring	Capture the token to send a frame
DQDB	Distributed queuing on a two-bus MAN
FDDI	Fiber-optic token ring
HIPPI	Crossbar using 50-100 twisted pairs
Fibre channel	Crossbar using fiber optics
SPADE	FDM with dynamic channel allocation
ACTS	TDM with centralized slot allocation
Binder	TDM with ALOHA when slot owner is not interested
Crowther	ALOHA with slot owner getting to keep it
Roberts	Channel time reserved in advance by ALOHA

Fig. 4-52. Channel allocation methods and systems for a common channel.

The tree walk protocol reduces it by dynamically dividing the stations into two disjoint groups, one of which is permitted to transmit and one of which is not. It tries to make the division in such a way that only one station that is ready to send is permitted to do so.

Wireless LANs have their own problems and solutions. The biggest problem is caused by hidden stations, so CSMA does not work. One class of solutions, typified by MACA, attempts to stimulate transmissions around the destination, to make CSMA work better.

For mobile computers and telephones, cellular radio is the up-and-coming technology. GSM, CDPD, and CDMA are widely used.

The IEEE 802 LANs are: CSMA/CD, token bus, and token ring. Each of these has its own unique advantages and disadvantages, and each has found its own user community and will probably continue to serve that community for years to come. Convergence to a single LAN standard is an unlikely event. A new addition to this family is DQDB, being sold as a MAN in many cities.

An organization with multiple LANs often connects them with bridges. When a bridge connects two or more different kinds of LANs, new problems arise, some of them insoluble.

While the 802 LANs are the work horses of the day, the race horses are FDDI, fast Ethernet, HIPPI, and fibre channel. All of these offer bandwidth in the 100 Mbps range and up.

Finally, satellite networks also use multiple access channels (for the uplink). Various channel allocation methods are used here, including ALOHA, FDM, TDM, and CDMA.

PROBLEMS

1. A group of N stations share a 56-kbps pure ALOHA channel. Each station outputs a 1000-bit frame on an average of once every 100 sec, even if the previous one has not yet been sent (e.g., the stations are buffered). What is the maximum value of N?

2. Consider the delay of pure ALOHA versus slotted ALOHA at low load. Which one is less? Explain your answer.

3. Ten thousand airline reservation stations are competing for the use of a single slotted ALOHA channel. The average station makes 18 requests/hour. A slot is 125 μsec. What is the approximate total channel load?

4. A large population of ALOHA users manages to generate 50 requests/sec, including both originals and retransmissions. Time is slotted in units of 40 msec.
   (a) What is the chance of success on the first attempt?
   (b) What is the probability of exactly k collisions and then a success?
   (c) What is the expected number of transmission attempts needed?

5. Measurements of a slotted ALOHA channel with an infinite number of users show that 10 percent of the slots are idle.
   (a) What is the channel load, G?
   (b) What is the throughput?
   (c) Is the channel underloaded or overloaded?

6. In an infinite-population slotted ALOHA system, the mean number of slots a station waits between a collision and its retransmission is 4. Plot the delay versus throughput curve for this system.

7. A LAN uses Mok and Ward's version of binary countdown. At a certain instant, the ten stations have the virtual station numbers 8, 2, 4, 5, 1, 7, 3, 6, 9, and 0. The next three stations to send are 4, 3, and 9, in that order. What are the new virtual station numbers after all three have finished their transmissions?

8. Sixteen stations are contending for the use of a shared channel using the adaptive tree walk protocol. If all the stations whose addresses are prime numbers suddenly become ready at once, how many bit slots are needed to resolve the contention?

9. A collection of 2^n stations uses the adaptive tree walk protocol to arbitrate access to a shared cable. At a certain instant two of them become ready. What are the minimum, maximum, and mean number of slots to walk the tree if $2^n \gg 1$?

10. The wireless LANs that we studied used protocols such as MACA instead of CSMA/CD. Under what conditions would it be possible to use CSMA/CD instead?

11. What properties do the WDMA and GSM channel access protocols have in common?

12. Using the GSM framing structure as given in Fig. 4-14, determine how often any given user may send a data frame.

13. Suppose that A, B, and C are simultaneously transmitting 0 bits using a CDMA system with the chip sequences of Fig. 4-16(b). What is the resulting chip sequence?

14. In the discussion about orthogonality of CDMA chip sequences, it was stated that if $\mathbf{S} \bullet \mathbf{T} = 0$ then $\mathbf{S} \bullet \overline{\mathbf{T}}$ is also 0. Prove this.

15. Consider a different way of looking at the orthogonality property of CDMA chip sequences. Each bit in a pair of sequence can match or not match. Express the orthogonality property in terms of matches and mismatches.

16. A CDMA receiver gets the following chips: $(-1 +1 -3 +1 -1 -3 +1 +1)$. Assuming the chip sequences defined in Fig. 4-16(b), which stations transmitted, and which bits did each one send?

17. A seven-story office building has 15 adjacent offices per floor. Each office contains a wall socket for a terminal in the front wall, so the sockets form a rectangular grid in the vertical plane, with a separation of 4 m between sockets, both horizontally and vertically. Assuming that it is feasible to run a straight cable between any pair of sockets, horizontally, vertically, or diagonally, how many meters of cable are needed to connect all sockets using
    (a) a star configuration with a single router in middle?
    (b) an 802.3 LAN?
    (c) a ring net (without a wire center)?

18. What is the baud rate of the standard 10-Mbps 802.3 LAN?

19. A 1-km-long, 10-Mbps CSMA/CD LAN (not 802.3) has a propagation speed of 200 m/μsec. Data frames are 256 bits long, including 32 bits of header, checksum, and other overhead. The first bit slot after a successful transmission is reserved for the receiver to capture the channel to send a 32-bit acknowledgement frame. What is the effective data rate, excluding overhead, assuming that there are no collisions?

20. Two CSMA/CD stations are each trying to transmit long (multiframe) files. After each frame is sent, they contend for the channel using the binary exponential backoff algorithm. What is the probability that the contention ends on round k, and what is the mean number of rounds per contention period?

21. Consider building a CSMA/CD network running at 1 Gbps over a 1-km cable with no repeaters. The signal speed in the cable is 200,000 km/sec. What is the minimum frame size?

22. Sketch the Manchester encoding for the bit stream: 0001110101.

23. Sketch the differential Manchester encoding for the bit stream of the previous problem. Assume the line is initially in the low state.

24. A token bus system works like this. When the token arrives at a station, a timer is reset to 0. The station then begins transmitting priority 6 frames until the timer reaches $T6$. Then it switches over to priority 4 frames until the timer reaches $T4$. This algorithm is then repeated with priority 2 and priority 0. If all stations have timer values of 40, 80, 90, and 100 msec for $T6$ through $T0$, respectively, what fraction of the total bandwidth is reserved for each priority class?

25. What happens in a token bus if a station accepts the token and then crashes immediately? How does the protocol described in the text handle this case?

26. At a transmission rate of 5 Mbps and a propagation speed of 200 m/μsec, to how many meters of cable is the 1-bit delay in a token ring interface equivalent?

27. The delay around a token ring must be enough to contain the entire token. If the wire is not long enough, some artificial delay must be introduced. Explain why this extra delay is necessary in the content of a 24-bit token and a ring with only 16 bits of delay.

28. A very heavily loaded 1-km-long, 10-Mbps token ring has a propagation speed of 200 m/μsec. Fifty stations are uniformly spaced around the ring. Data frames are 256 bits, including 32 bits of overhead. Acknowledgements are piggybacked onto the data frames and are thus included as spare bits within the data frames and are effectively free. The token is 8 bits. Is the effective data rate of this ring higher or lower than the effective data rate of a 10-Mbps CSMA/CD network?

29. In a token ring the sender removes the frame. What modifications to the system would be needed to have the receiver remove the frame instead, and what would the consequences be?

30. A 4-Mbps token ring has a token-holding timer value of 10 msec. What is the longest frame that can be sent on this ring?

31. Does the use of a wire center have any influence on the performance of a token ring?

32. A fiber optic token ring used as a MAN is 200 km long and runs at 100 Mbps. After sending a frame, a station drains the frame from the ring before regenerating the token. The signal propagation speed in the fiber is 200,000 km/sec and the maximum frame size is 1K bytes. What is the maximum efficiency of the ring (ignoring all other sources of overhead)?

33. In Fig. 4-32, station D wants to send a cell. To which station does it want to send it?

34. The system of Fig. 4-32 is idle. A little later, stations C, A, and B become ready to send, in that order and in rapid succession. Assuming that no data frames are transmitted until all three have sent a request upstream, show the RC and CD values after each request and after the three data frames.

35. Ethernet is sometimes said to be inappropriate for real-time computing because the worst case retransmission interval is not bounded. Under what circumstances can the same argument be leveled at the token ring? Under what circumstances does the token ring have a known worst case? Assume the number of stations on the token ring is fixed and known.

36. Ethernet frames must be at least 64 bytes long to ensure that the transmitter is still going in the event of a collision at the far end of the cable. Fast Ethernet has the same 64 byte minimum frame size, but can get the bits out ten times faster. How is it possible to maintain the same minimum frame size?

37. Imagine two LAN bridges, both connecting a pair of 802.4 networks. The first bridge is faced with 1000 512-byte frames per second that must be forwarded. The second is faced with 200 4096-byte frames per second. Which bridge do you think will need the faster CPU? Discuss.

38. Suppose that the two bridges of the previous problem each connected an 802.4 LAN to an 802.5 LAN. Would that change have any influence on the previous answer?

39. A bridge between an 802.3 LAN and an 802.4 LAN has a problem with intermittent memory errors. Can this problem cause undetected errors with transmitted frames, or will these all be caught by the frame checksums?

40. A university computer science department has 3 Ethernet segments, connected by two transparent bridges into a linear network. One day the network administrator quits and is hastily replaced by someone from the computer center, which is an IBM token ring shop. The new administrator, noticing that the ends of the network are not connected, quickly orders a new transparent bridge and connects both loose ends to it, making a closed ring. What happens next?

41. A large FDDI ring has 100 stations and a token rotation time of 40 msec. The token-holding time is 10 msec. What is the maximum achievable efficiency of the ring?

42. Consider building a supercomputer interconnect using the HIPPI approach, but modern technology. The data path is now 64 bits wide, and a word can be sent every 10 nsec. What is the bandwidth of the channel?

43. In the text it was stated that a satellite with two uplink and one downlink slotted ALOHA channels can achieve a downlink utilization of 0.736, given an infinite amount of buffer space. Show how this result can be obtained.

5

THE NETWORK LAYER

The network layer is concerned with getting packets from the source all the way to the destination. Getting to the destination may require making many hops at intermediate routers along the way. This function clearly contrasts with that of the data link layer, which has the more modest goal of just moving frames from one end of a wire to the other. Thus the network layer is the lowest layer that deals with end-to-end transmission. For more information about it, see (Huitema, 1995; and Perlman, 1992).

To achieve its goals, the network layer must know about the topology of the communication subnet (i.e., the set of all routers) and choose appropriate paths through it. It must also take care to choose routes to avoid overloading some of the communication lines and routers while leaving others idle. Finally, when the source and destination are in different networks, it is up to the network layer to deal with these differences and solve the problems that result from them. In this chapter we will study all these issues and illustrate them with our two running examples, the Internet and ATM.

5.1. NETWORK LAYER DESIGN ISSUES

In the following sections we will provide an introduction to some of the issues that the designers of the network layer must grapple with. These issues include the service provided to the transport layer and the internal design of the subnet.

5.1.1. Services Provided to the Transport Layer

The network layer provides services to the transport layer at the network layer/transport layer interface. This interface is often especially important for another reason: it frequently is the interface between the carrier and the customer, that is, the boundary of the subnet. The carrier often has control of the protocols and interfaces up to and including the network layer. Its job is to deliver packets given to it by its customers. For this reason, this interface must be especially well defined.

The network layer services have been designed with the following goals in mind.

1. The services should be independent of the subnet technology.

2. The transport layer should be shielded from the number, type, and topology of the subnets present.

3. The network addresses made available to the transport layer should use a uniform numbering plan, even across LANs and WANs.

Given these goals, the designers of the network layer have a lot of freedom in writing detailed specifications of the services to be offered to the transport layer. This freedom often degenerates into a raging battle between two warring factions. The discussion centers on the question of whether the network layer should provide connection-oriented service or connectionless service.

One camp (represented by the Internet community) argues that the subnet's job is moving bits around and nothing else. In their view (based on nearly 30 years of actual experience with a real, working computer network), the subnet is inherently unreliable, no matter how it is designed. Therefore, the hosts should accept the fact that it is unreliable and do error control (i.e., error detection and correction) and flow control themselves.

This viewpoint leads quickly to the conclusion that the network service should be connectionless, with primitives SEND PACKET and RECEIVE PACKET, and little else. In particular, no packet ordering and flow control should be done, because the hosts are going to do that anyway, and there is probably little to be gained by doing it twice. Furthermore, each packet must carry the full destination address, because each packet sent is carried independently of its predecessors, if any.

The other camp (represented by the telephone companies) argues that the subnet should provide a (reasonably) reliable, connection-oriented service. They claim 100 years of successful experience with the worldwide telephone system is a good guide. In this view, connections should have the following properties:

1. Before sending data, a network layer process on the sending side must set up a connection to its peer on the receiving side. This connection, which is given a special identifier, is then used until all the data have been sent, at which time it is explicitly released.

2. When a connection is set up, the two processes can enter into a nego-
    tiation about the parameters, quality, and cost of the service to be
    provided.

3. Communication is in both directions, and packets are delivered in
    sequence.

4. Flow control is provided automatically to prevent a fast sender from
    dumping packets into the pipe at a higher rate than the receiver can
    take them out, thus leading to overflow.

Other properties, such as guaranteed delivery, explicit confirmation of delivery,
and high priority packets are optional. As we pointed out in Chap. 1, connectionless service is like the postal system, and connection-oriented service is like the
telephone system.

The argument between connection-oriented and connectionless service really
has to do with where to put the complexity. In the connection-oriented service, it
is in the network layer (subnet); in the connectionless service, it is in the transport
layer (hosts). Supporters of connectionless service say that user computing power
has become cheap, so that there is no reason not to put the complexity in the hosts.
Furthermore, they argue that the subnet is a major (inter)national investment that
will last for decades, so it should not be cluttered up with features that may
become obsolete quickly but will have to be calculated into the price structure for
many years. Furthermore, some applications, such as digitized voice and real-
time data collection may regard *speedy* delivery as much more important than
accurate delivery.

On the other hand, supporters of connection-oriented service say that most
users are not interested in running complex transport layer protocols in their
machines. What they want is reliable, trouble-free service, and this service can be
best provided with network layer connections. Furthermore, some services, such
as real time audio and video are much easier to provide on top of a connection-
oriented network layer than on top of a connectionless network layer.

Although it is rarely discussed in these terms, two separate issues are involved
here. First, whether the network is connection-oriented (setup required) or connectionless (no setup required). Second, whether it is reliable (no lost, duplicated,
or garbled packets) or unreliable (packets can be lost, duplicated, or garbled). In
theory, all four combinations exist, but the dominant combinations are reliable
connection-oriented and unreliable connectionless, so the other two tend to get
lost in the noise.

These two camps are represented by our two running examples. The Internet
has a connectionless network layer, and ATM networks have a connection-
oriented network layer. An obvious question arises about how the Internet works
when it runs over an ATM-based, carrier-provided subnet. The answer is that the
source host first establishes an ATM network layer connection to the destination

host and then sends independent (IP) packets over it, as shown in Fig. 5-1. Although this approach works, it is inefficient because certain functionality is in both layers. For example, the ATM network layer guarantees that packets are always delivered in order, but the TCP code still contains the full mechanism for managing and reordering out-of-order packets. For more information about how to run IP over ATM, see RFC 1577 and (Armitage and Adams, 1995).

Email	FTP	. . .
TCP		
IP		
ATM		
Data link		
Physical		

Fig. 5-1. Running TCP/IP over an ATM subnet.

5.1.2. Internal Organization of the Network Layer

Having looked at the two classes of service the network layer can provide to its users, it is time to see how it works inside. There are basically two different philosophies for organizing the subnet, one using connections and the other working connectionless. In the context of the *internal* operation of the subnet, a connection is usually called a **virtual circuit**, in analogy with the physical circuits set up by the telephone system. The independent packets of the connectionless organization are called **datagrams**, in analogy with telegrams.

Virtual circuits are generally used in subnets whose primary service is connection-oriented, so we will describe them in that context. The idea behind virtual circuits is to avoid having to choose a new route for every packet or cell sent. Instead, when a connection is established, a route from the source machine to the destination machine is chosen as part of the connection setup and remembered. That route is used for all traffic flowing over the connection, exactly the same way that the telephone system works. When the connection is released, the virtual circuit is also terminated.

In contrast, with a datagram subnet no routes are worked out in advance, even if the service is connection-oriented. Each packet sent is routed independently of its predecessors. Successive packets may follow different routes. While datagram subnets have to do more work, they are also generally more robust and adapt to failures and congestion more easily than virtual circuit subnets. We will discuss the pros and cons of the two approaches later.

If packets flowing over a given virtual circuit always take the same route through the subnet, each router must remember where to forward packets for each of the currently open virtual circuits passing through it. Every router must maintain a table with one entry per open virtual circuit passing through it. Each packet traveling through the subnet must contain a virtual circuit number field in its header, in addition to sequence numbers, checksums, and the like. When a packet arrives at a router, the router knows on which line it arrived and what the virtual circuit number is. Based on only this information, the packet must be forwarded on the correct output line.

When a network connection is set up, a virtual circuit number not already in use on that machine is chosen as the connection identifier. Since each machine chooses virtual circuit numbers independently, these numbers have only local significance. If they were globally significant over the whole network, it is likely that two virtual circuits bearing the same global virtual circuit number might pass through some intermediate router, leading to ambiguities.

Because virtual circuits can be initiated from either end, a problem occurs when call setups are propagating in both directions at once along a chain of routers. At some point they have arrived at adjacent routers. Each router must now pick a virtual circuit number to use for the (full-duplex) circuit it is trying to establish. If they have been programmed to choose the lowest number not already in use on the link, they will pick the same number, causing two unrelated virtual circuits over the same physical line to have the same number. When a data packet arrives later, the receiving router has no way of telling whether it is a forward packet on one circuit or a reverse packet on the other. If circuits are simplex, there is no ambiguity.

Note that every process must be required to indicate when it is through using a virtual circuit, so that the virtual circuit can be purged from the router tables to recover the space. In public networks, the motivation is the stick rather than the carrot: users are invariably charged for connect time as well as for data transported. In addition, some provision must be made for dealing with machines that terminate their virtual circuits by crashing rather than politely releasing them when done.

So much for the use of virtual circuits internal to the subnet. The other possibility is to use datagrams internally, in which case the routers do not have a table with one entry for each open virtual circuit. Instead, they have a table telling which outgoing line to use for each possible destination router. These tables are also needed when virtual circuits are used internally, to determine the route for a setup packet.

Each datagram must contain the full destination address. For a large network, these addresses can be quite long (e.g., a dozen bytes or more). When a packet comes in, the router looks up the outgoing line to use and sends the packet on its way. Also, the establishment and release of network or transport layer connections do not require any special work on the part of the routers.

5.1.3. Comparison of Virtual Circuit and Datagram Subnets

Both virtual circuits and datagrams have their supporters and their detractors. We will now attempt to summarize the arguments both ways. The major issues are listed in Fig. 5-2, although purists could probably find a counterexample for everything in the figure.

Issue	Datagram subnet	VC subnet
Circuit setup	Not needed	Required
Addressing	Each packet contains the full source and destination address	Each packet contains a short VC number
State information	Subnet does not hold state information	Each VC requires subnet table space
Routing	Each packet is routed independently	Route chosen when VC is set up; all packets follow this route
Effect of router failures	None, except for packets lost during the crash	All VCs that passed through the failed router are terminated
Congestion control	Difficult	Easy if enough buffers can be allocated in advance for each VC

Fig. 5-2. Comparison of datagram and virtual circuit subnets.

Inside the subnet, several trade-offs exist between virtual circuits and datagrams. One trade-off is between router memory space and bandwidth. Virtual circuits allow packets to contain circuit numbers instead of full destination addresses. If the packets tend to be fairly short, a full destination address in every packet may represent a significant amount of overhead, and hence wasted bandwidth. The price paid for using virtual circuits internally is the table space within the routers. Depending upon the relative cost of communication circuits versus router memory, one or the other may be cheaper.

Another trade-off is setup time versus address parsing time. Using virtual circuits requires a setup phase, which takes time and consumes resources. However, figuring out what to do with a data packet in a virtual circuit subnet is easy: the router just uses the circuit number to index into a table to find out where the packet goes. In a datagram subnet, a more complicated procedure is required to determine where the packet goes.

Virtual circuits have some advantages in avoiding congestion within the subnet because resources can be reserved in advance, when the connection is established. Once the packets start arriving, the necessary bandwidth and router capacity will be there. With a datagram subnet, congestion avoidance is more difficult.

For transaction processing systems (e.g., stores calling up to verify credit card purchases), the overhead required to set up and clear a virtual circuit may easily dwarf the use of the circuit. If the majority of the traffic is expected to be of this kind, the use of switched virtual circuits inside the subnet makes little sense. On the other hand, permanent virtual circuits, which are set up manually and last for months or years, may be useful here.

Virtual circuits also have a vulnerability problem. If a router crashes and loses its memory, even if it comes back up a second later, all the virtual circuits passing through it will have to be aborted. In contrast, if a datagram router goes down, only those users whose packets were queued up in the router at the time will suffer, and maybe not even all those, depending upon whether they have already been acknowledged or not. The loss of a communication line is fatal to virtual circuits using it but can be easily compensated for if datagrams are used. Datagrams also allow the routers to balance the traffic throughout the subnet, since routes can be changed halfway through a connection.

It is worth explicitly pointing out that the service offered (connection-oriented or connectionless) is a separate issue from the subnet structure (virtual circuit or datagram). In theory, all four combinations are possible. Obviously, a virtual circuit implementation of a connection-oriented service and a datagram implementation of a connectionless service are reasonable. Implementing connections using datagrams also makes sense when the subnet is trying to provide a highly robust service.

The fourth possibility, a connectionless service on top of a virtual circuit subnet, seems strange but certainly occurs. The obvious example is running IP over an ATM subnet. Here it is desired to run an existing connectionless protocol over a new connection-oriented network layer. As mentioned earlier, this is more of an ad hoc solution to a problem than a good design. In a new system designed to run over an ATM subnet, one would not normally put a connectionless protocol like IP over a connection-oriented network layer like ATM and then layer a connection-oriented transport protocol on top of the connectionless protocol. Examples of all four cases are shown in Fig. 5-3.

5.2. ROUTING ALGORITHMS

The main function of the network layer is routing packets from the source machine to the destination machine. In most subnets, packets will require multiple hops to make the journey. The only notable exception is for broadcast

Upper layer	Type of subnet	
	Datagram	Virtual circuit
Connectionless	UDP over IP	UDP over IP over ATM
Connection-oriented	TCP over IP	ATM AAL1 over ATM

Fig. 5-3. Examples of different combinations of service and subnet structure.

networks, but even here routing is an issue if the source and destination are not on the same network. The algorithms that choose the routes and the data structures that they use are a major area of network layer design.

The **routing algorithm** is that part of the network layer software responsible for deciding which output line an incoming packet should be transmitted on. If the subnet uses datagrams internally, this decision must be made anew for every arriving data packet since the best route may have changed since last time. If the subnet uses virtual circuits internally, routing decisions are made only when a new virtual circuit is being set up. Thereafter, data packets just follow the previously established route. The latter case is sometimes called **session routing**, because a route remains in force for an entire user session (e.g., a login session at a terminal or a file transfer).

Regardless of whether routes are chosen independently for each packet or only when new connections are established, there are certain properties that are desirable in a routing algorithm: correctness, simplicity, robustness, stability, fairness, and optimality. Correctness and simplicity hardly require comment, but the need for robustness may be less obvious at first. Once a major network comes on the air, it may be expected to run continuously for years without systemwide failures. During that period there will be hardware and software failures of all kinds. Hosts, routers, and lines will go up and down repeatedly, and the topology will change many times. The routing algorithm should be able to cope with changes in the topology and traffic without requiring all jobs in all hosts to be aborted and the network to be rebooted every time some router crashes.

Stability is also an important goal for the routing algorithm. There exist routing algorithms that never converge to equilibrium, no matter how long they run. Fairness and optimality may sound obvious—surely no one would oppose them—but as it turns out, they are often contradictory goals. As a simple example of this conflict, look at Fig. 5-4. Suppose that there is enough traffic between A and A', between B and B', and between C and C' to saturate the horizontal links. To maximize the total flow, the X to X' traffic should be shut off altogether.

Unfortunately, *X* and *X'* may not see it that way. Evidently, some compromise between global efficiency and fairness to individual connections is needed.

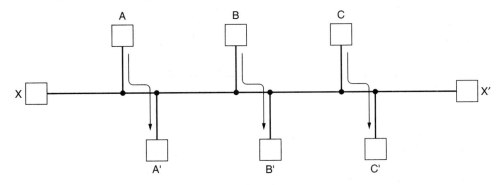

Fig. 5-4. Conflict between fairness and optimality.

Before we can even attempt to find trade-offs between fairness and optimality, we must decide what it is we seek to optimize. Minimizing mean packet delay is an obvious candidate, but so is maximizing total network throughput. Furthermore, these two goals are also in conflict, since operating any queueing system near capacity implies a long queueing delay. As a compromise, many networks attempt to minimize the number of hops a packet must make, because reducing the number of hops tends to improve the delay and also reduce the amount of bandwidth consumed, which tends to improve the throughput as well.

Routing algorithms can be grouped into two major classes: nonadaptive and adaptive. **Nonadaptive algorithms** do not base their routing decisions on measurements or estimates of the current traffic and topology. Instead, the choice of the route to use to get from *I* to *J* (for all *I* and *J*) is computed in advance, off-line, and downloaded to the routers when the network is booted. This procedure is sometimes called **static routing**.

Adaptive algorithms, in contrast, change their routing decisions to reflect changes in the topology, and usually the traffic as well. Adaptive algorithms differ in where they get their information (e.g., locally, from adjacent routers, or from all routers), when they change the routes (e.g., every Δ*T* sec, when the load changes, or when the topology changes), and what metric is used for optimization (e.g., distance, number of hops, or estimated transit time). In the following sections we will discuss a variety of routing algorithms, both static and dynamic.

5.2.1. The Optimality Principle

Before getting into specific algorithms, it may be helpful to note that one can make a general statement about optimal routes without regard to network topology or traffic. This statement is known as the **optimality principle**. It states that if router *J* is on the optimal path from router *I* to router *K*, then the optimal path from J to K also falls along the same route. To see this, call the part of the route from I to J r_1 and the rest of the route r_2. If a route better than r_2 existed from J to K, it could be concatenated with r_1 to improve the route from I to K, contradicting our statement that $r_1 r_2$ is optimal.

As a direct consequence of the optimality principle, we can see that the set of optimal routes from all sources to a given destination form a tree rooted at the destination. Such a tree is called a **sink tree** and is illustrated in Fig. 5-5 where the distance metric is the number of hops. Note that a sink tree is not necessarily unique; other trees with the same path lengths may exist. The goal of all routing algorithms is to discover and use the sink trees for all routers.

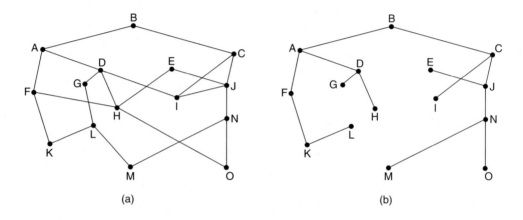

Fig. 5-5. (a) A subnet. (b) A sink tree for router B.

Since a sink tree is indeed a tree, it does not contain any loops, so each packet will be delivered within a finite and bounded number of hops. In practice, life is not quite this easy. Links and routers can go down and come back up during operation, so different routers may have different ideas about the current topology. Also, we have quietly finessed the issue of whether each router has to individually acquire the information on which to base its sink tree computation, or whether this information is collected by some other means. We will come back to these issues shortly. Nevertheless, the optimality principle and the sink tree provide a benchmark against which other routing algorithms can be measured.

In the next three sections, we will look at three different static routing algorithms. After that we will move on to adaptive ones.

5.2.2. Shortest Path Routing

Let us begin our study of routing algorithms with a technique that is widely used in many forms because it is simple and easy to understand. The idea is to build a graph of the subnet, with each node of the graph representing a router and each arc of the graph representing a communication line (often called a link). To choose a route between a given pair of routers, the algorithm just finds the shortest path between them on the graph.

The concept of a **shortest path** deserves some explanation. One way of measuring path length is the number of hops. Using this metric, the paths *ABC* and *ABE* in Fig. 5-6 are equally long. Another metric is the geographic distance in kilometers, in which case *ABC* is clearly much longer than *ABE* (assuming the figure is drawn to scale).

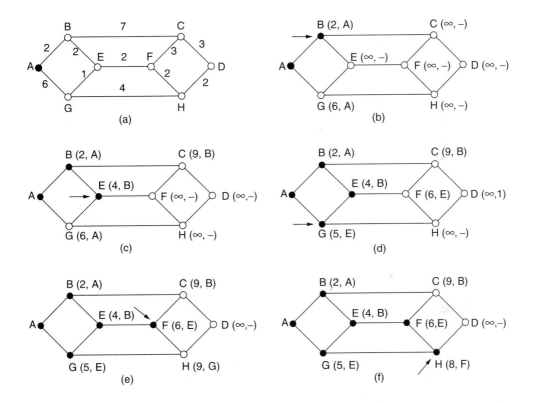

Fig. 5-6. The first five steps used in computing the shortest path from *A* to *D*. The arrows indicate the working node.

However, many other metrics are also possible besides hops and physical distance. For example, each arc could be labeled with the mean queueing and transmission delay for some standard test packet as determined by hourly test runs. With this graph labeling, the shortest path is the fastest path, rather than the path with the fewest arcs or kilometers.

In the most general case, the labels on the arcs could be computed as a function of the distance, bandwidth, average traffic, communication cost, mean queue length, measured delay, and other factors. By changing the weighting function, the algorithm would then compute the "shortest" path measured according to any one of a number of criteria, or a combination of criteria.

Several algorithms for computing the shortest path between two nodes of a graph are known. This one is due to Dijkstra (1959). Each node is labeled (in parentheses) with its distance from the source node along the best known path. Initially, no paths are known, so all nodes are labeled with infinity. As the algorithm proceeds and paths are found, the labels may change, reflecting better paths. A label may be either tentative or permanent. Initially, all labels are tentative. When it is discovered that a label represents the shortest possible path from the source to that node, it is made permanent and never changed thereafter.

To illustrate how the labeling algorithm works, look at the weighted, undirected graph of Fig. 5-6(a), where the weights represent, for example, distance. We want to find the shortest path from A to D. We start out by marking node A as permanent, indicated by a filled in circle. Then we examine, in turn, each of the nodes adjacent to A (the working node), relabeling each one with the distance to A. Whenever a node is relabeled, we also label it with the node from which the probe was made, so we can reconstruct the final path later. Having examined each of the nodes adjacent to A, we examine all the tentatively labeled nodes in the whole graph and make the one with the smallest label permanent, as shown in Fig. 5-6(b). This one becomes the new working node.

We now start at B, and examine all nodes adjacent to it. If the sum of the label on B and the distance from B to the node being considered is less than the label on that node, we have a shorter path, so the node is relabeled.

After all the nodes adjacent to the working node have been inspected and the tentative labels changed if possible, the entire graph is searched for the tentatively labeled node with the smallest value. This node is made permanent and becomes the working node for the next round. Figure 5-6 shows the first five steps of the algorithm.

To see why the algorithm works, look at Fig. 5-6(c). At that point we have just made E permanent. Suppose that there were a shorter path than ABE, say $AXYZE$. There are two possibilities: either node Z has already been made permanent, or it has not been. If it has, then E has already been probed (on the round following the one when Z was made permanent), so the $AXYZE$ path has not escaped our attention.

Now consider the case where Z is still tentatively labeled. Either the label at Z is greater than or equal to that at E, in which case $AXYZE$ cannot be a shorter path than ABE, or it is less than that of E, in which case Z and not E will become permanent first, allowing E to be probed from Z.

This algorithm is given in Fig. 5-7. The only difference between the program and the algorithm described above is that in Fig. 5-7, we compute the shortest path starting at the terminal node, t, rather than at the source node, s. Since the shortest path from t to s in an undirected graph is the same as the shortest path from s to t, it does not matter at which end we begin (unless there are several shortest paths, in which case reversing the search might discover a different one). The reason for searching backward is that each node is labeled with its predecessor rather than its successor. When copying the final path into the output variable, *path*, the path is thus reversed. By reversing the search, the two effects cancel, and the answer is produced in the correct order.

5.2.3. Flooding

Another static algorithm is **flooding**, in which every incoming packet is sent out on every outgoing line except the one it arrived on. Flooding obviously generates vast numbers of duplicate packets, in fact, an infinite number unless some measures are taken to damp the process. One such measure is to have a hop counter contained in the header of each packet, which is decremented at each hop, with the packet being discarded when the counter reaches zero. Ideally, the hop counter should be initialized to the length of the path from source to destination. If the sender does not know how long the path is, it can initialize the counter to the worst case, namely, the full diameter of the subnet.

An alternative technique for damming the flood is to keep track of which packets have been flooded, to avoid sending them out a second time. One way to achieve this goal is to have the source router put a sequence number in each packet it receives from its hosts. Each router then needs a list per source router telling which sequence numbers originating at that source have already been seen. If an incoming packet is on the list, it is not flooded.

To prevent the list from growing without bound, each list should be augmented by a counter, k, meaning that all sequence numbers through k have been seen. When a packet comes in, it is easy to check if the packet is a duplicate; if so, it is discarded. Furthermore, the full list below k is not needed, since k effectively summarizes it.

A variation of flooding that is slightly more practical is **selective flooding**. In this algorithm the routers do not send every incoming packet out on every line, only on those lines that are going approximately in the right direction. There is usually little point in sending a westbound packet on an eastbound line unless the topology is extremely peculiar.

Flooding is not practical in most applications, but it does have some uses. For example, in military applications, where large numbers of routers may be blown to bits at any instant, the tremendous robustness of flooding is highly desirable. In distributed database applications, it is sometimes necessary to update all the databases concurrently, in which case flooding can be useful. A third possible use of flooding is as a metric against which other routing algorithms can be compared. Flooding always chooses the shortest path, because it chooses every possible path in parallel. Consequently, no other algorithm can produce a shorter delay (if we ignore the overhead generated by the flooding process itself).

```
#define MAX_NODES 1024              /* maximum number of nodes */
#define INFINITY 1000000000         /* a number larger than every maximum path */
int n, dist[MAX_NODES][MAX_NODES];/* dist[i][j] is the distance from i to j */

void shortest_path(int s, int t, int path[])
{ struct state {                    /* the path being worked on */
      int predecessor;              /* previous node */
      int length;                   /* length from source to this node */
      enum {permanent, tentative} label; /* label state */
  } state[MAX_NODES];

  int i, k, min;
  struct state *
            p;
  for (p = &state[0]; p < &state[n]; p++) { /* initialize state */
      p->predecessor = -1;
      p->length = INFINITY;
      p->label = tentative;
  }
  state[t].length = 0;  state[t].label = permanent;
  k = t;                            /* k is the initial working node */
  do {                              /* Is there a better path from k? */
      for (i = 0; i < n; i++)       /* this graph has n nodes */
          if (dist[k][i] != 0 && state[i].label == tentative) {
              if (state[k].length + dist[k][i] < state[i].length) {
                  state[i].predecessor = k;
                  state[i].length = state[k].length + dist[k][i];
              }
          }

      /* Find the tentatively labeled node with the smallest label. */
      k = 0; min = INFINITY;
      for (i = 0; i < n; i++)
          if (state[i].label == tentative && state[i].length < min) {
              min = state[i].length;
              k = i;
          }
      state[k].label = permanent;
  } while (k != s);

  /* Copy the path into the output array. */
  i = 0;  k = s;
  do {path[i++] = k; k = state[k].predecessor; } while (k >= 0);
}
```

Fig. 5-7. Dijkstra's algorithm to compute the shortest path through a graph.

5.2.4. Flow-Based Routing

The algorithms studied so far take only the topology into account. They do not consider the load. If, for example, there is always a huge amount of traffic from A to B, in Fig. 5-6, then it may be better to route traffic from A to C via AGEFC, even though this path is much longer than ABC. In this section we will study a static algorithm that uses both topology and load for routing. It is called **flow-based routing**.

In some networks, the mean data flow between each pair of nodes is relatively stable and predictable. For example, in a corporate network for a retail store chain, each store might send orders, sales reports, inventory updates, and other well-defined types of messages to known sites in a predefined pattern, so that the total volume of traffic varies little from day to day. Under conditions in which the average traffic from i to j is known in advance and, to a reasonable approximation, constant in time, it is possible to analyze the flows mathematically to optimize the routing.

The basic idea behind the analysis is that for a given line, if the capacity and average flow are known, it is possible to compute the mean packet delay on that line from queueing theory. From the mean delays on all the lines, it is straightforward to calculate a flow-weighted average to get the mean packet delay for the whole subnet. The routing problem then reduces to finding the routing algorithm that produces the minimum average delay for the subnet. Fig. 5-8.

To use this technique, certain information must be known in advance. First the subnet topology must be known. Second, the traffic matrix, F_{ij}, must be given. Third, the line capacity matrix, C_{ij}, specifying the capacity of each line in bps must be available. Finally, a (possibly tentative) routing algorithm must be chosen.

As an example of this method, consider the full-duplex subnet of Fig. 5-8(a). The weights on the arcs give the capacities, C_{ij}, in each direction measured in kbps. The matrix of Fig. 5-8(b) has an entry for each source-destination pair. The entry for source i to destination j shows the route to be used for i-j traffic, and also the number of packets/sec to be sent from source i to destination j. For example, 3 packets/sec go from B to D, and they use route BFD to get there. Notice that some routing algorithm has already been applied to derive the routes shown in the matrix.

Given this information, it is straightforward to calculate the total in line i, λ_i. For example, the B-D traffic contributes 3 packets/sec to the BF line and also 3 packets/sec to the FD line. Similarly, the A-D traffic contributes 1 packet/sec to each of three lines. The total traffic in each eastbound line is shown in the λ_i column of Fig. 5-9. In this example, all the traffic is symmetric, that is, the XY traffic is identical to the YX traffic, for all X and Y. In real networks this condition does not always hold. The figure also shows the mean number of packets/sec on each line, μC_i assuming a mean packet size of $1/\mu = 800$ bits.

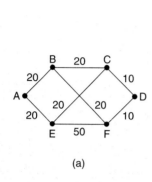

| | Destination | | | | | |
	A	B	C	D	E	F
A		9 AB	4 ABC	1 ABFD	7 AE	4 AEF
B	9 BA		8 BC	3 BFD	2 BFE	4 BF
C	4 CBA	8 CB		3 CD	3 CE	2 CEF
D	1 DFBA	3 DFB	3 DC		3 DCE	4 DF
E	7 EA	2 EFB	3 EC	3 ECD		5 EF
F	4 FEA	4 FB	2 FEC	4 FD	5 FE	

(Source)

(b)

Fig. 5-8. (a) A subnet with line capacities shown in kbps. (b) The traffic in packets/sec and the routing matrix.

The next-to-last column of Fig. 5-9 gives the mean delay for each line derived from the queueing theory formula

$$T = \frac{1}{\mu C - \lambda}$$

where $1/\mu$ is the mean packet size in bits, C is the capacity in bps, and λ is the mean flow in packets/sec. For example, with a capacity $\mu C = 25$ packets/sec and an actual flow $\lambda = 14$ packets/sec, the mean delay is 91 msec. Note that with $\lambda = 0$, the mean delay is still 40 msec, because the capacity is 25 packets/sec. In other words, the "delay" includes both queueing and service time.

To compute the mean delay time for the entire subnet, we take the weighted sum of each of the eight lines, with the weight being the fraction of the total traffic using that line. In this example, the mean turns out to be 86 msec.

To evaluate a different routing algorithm, we can repeat the entire process, only with different flows to get a new average delay. If we restrict ourselves to only single path routing algorithms, as we have done so far, there are only a finite number of ways to route packets from each source to each destination. It is always possible to write a program to simply try them all, one after another, and find out which one has the smallest mean delay. Since this calculation can be done off-line in advance, the fact that it may be time consuming is not necessarily a serious problem. This one is then the best routing algorithm. Bertsekas and Gallager (1992) discuss flow-based routing in detail.

i	Line	λ_i (pkts/sec)	C_i (kbps)	μC_i (pkts/sec)	T_i (msec)	Weight
1	AB	14	20	25	91	0.171
2	BC	12	20	25	77	0.146
3	CD	6	10	12.5	154	0.073
4	AE	11	20	25	71	0.134
5	EF	13	50	62.5	20	0.159
6	FD	8	10	12.5	222	0.098
7	BF	10	20	25	67	0.122
8	EC	8	20	25	59	0.098

Fig. 5-9. Analysis of the subnet of Fig. 5-8 using a mean packet size of 800 bits. The reverse traffic (*BA*, *CB*, etc.) is the same as the forward traffic.

5.2.5. Distance Vector Routing

Modern computer networks generally use dynamic routing algorithms rather than the static ones described above. Two dynamic algorithms in particular, distance vector routing and link state routing, are the most popular. In this section we will look at the former algorithm. In the following one we will study the latter one.

Distance vector routing algorithms operate by having each router maintain a table (i.e, a vector) giving the best known distance to each destination and which line to use to get there. These tables are updated by exchanging information with the neighbors.

The distance vector routing algorithm is sometimes called by other names, including the distributed **Bellman-Ford** routing algorithm and the **Ford-Fulkerson** algorithm, after the researchers who developed it (Bellman, 1957; and Ford and Fulkerson, 1962). It was the original ARPANET routing algorithm and was also used in the Internet under the name RIP and in early versions of DECnet and Novell's IPX. AppleTalk and Cisco routers use improved distance vector protocols.

In distance vector routing, each router maintains a routing table indexed by, and containing one entry for, each router in the subnet. This entry contains two parts: the preferred outgoing line to use for that destination, and an estimate of the time or distance to that destination. The metric used might be number of hops, time delay in milliseconds, total number of packets queued along the path, or something similar.

The router is assumed to know the "distance" to each of its neighbors. If the metric is hops, the distance is just one hop. If the metric is queue length, the router simply examines each queue. If the metric is delay, the router can measure it directly with special ECHO packets that the receiver just timestamps and sends back as fast as it can.

As an example, assume that delay is used as a metric and that the router knows the delay to each of its neighbors. Once every T msec each router sends to each neighbor a list of its estimated delays to each destination. It also receives a similar list from each neighbor. Imagine that one of these tables has just come in from neighbor X, with X_i being X's estimate of how long it takes to get to router i. If the router knows that the delay to X is m msec, it also knows that it can reach router i via X in $X_i + m$ msec via X. By performing this calculation for each neighbor, a router can find out which estimate seems the best and use that estimate and the corresponding line in its new routing table. Note that the old routing table is not used in the calculation.

This updating process is illustrated in Fig. 5-10. Part (a) shows a subnet. The first four columns of part (b) show the delay vectors received from the neighbors of router J. A claims to have a 12-msec delay to B, a 25-msec delay to C, a 40-msec delay to D, etc. Suppose that J has measured or estimated its delay to its neighbors, A, I, H, and K as 8, 10, 12, and 6 msec, respectively.

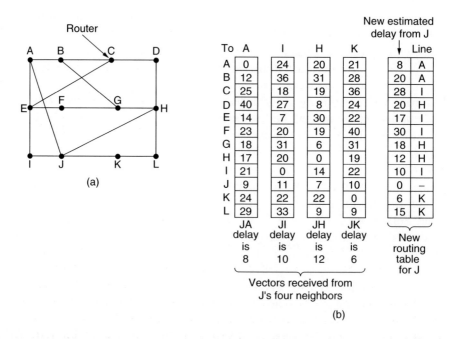

Fig. 5-10. (a) A subnet. (b) Input from A, I, H, K, and the new routing table for J.

Consider how J computes its new route to router G. It knows that it can get to A in 8 msec, and A claims to be able to get to G in 18 msec, so J knows it can count on a delay of 26 msec to G if it forwards packets bound for G to A.

Similarly, it computes the delay to G via I, H, and K as 41 (31 + 10), 18 (6 + 12), and 37 (31 + 6) msec respectively. The best of these values is 18, so it makes an entry in its routing table that the delay to G is 18 msec, and that the route to use is via H. The same calculation is performed for all the other destinations, with the new routing table shown in the last column of the figure.

The Count-to-Infinity Problem

Distance vector routing works in theory but has a serious drawback in practice: although it converges to the correct answer, it may do so slowly. In particular, it reacts rapidly to good news, but leisurely to bad news. Consider a router whose best route to destination X is large. If on the next exchange neighbor A suddenly reports a short delay to X, the router just switches over to using the line to A to send traffic to X. In one vector exchange, the good news is processed.

To see how fast good news propagates, consider the five-node (linear) subnet of Fig. 5-11, where the delay metric is the number of hops. Suppose A is down initially and all the other routers know this. In other words, they have all recorded the delay to A as infinity.

A	B	C	D	E	
	∞	∞	∞	∞	Initially
	1	∞	∞	∞	After 1 exchange
	1	2	∞	∞	After 2 exchanges
	1	2	3	∞	After 3 exchanges
	1	2	3	4	After 4 exchanges

(a)

A	B	C	D	E	
	1	2	3	4	Initially
	3	2	3	4	After 1 exchange
	3	4	3	4	After 2 exchanges
	5	4	5	4	After 3 exchanges
	5	6	5	6	After 4 exchanges
	7	6	7	6	After 5 exchanges
	7	8	7	8	After 6 exchanges
	⋮				
	∞	∞	∞	∞	

(b)

Fig. 5-11. The count-to-infinity problem.

When A comes up, the other routers learn about it via the vector exchanges. For simplicity we will assume that there is a gigantic gong somewhere that is struck periodically to initiate a vector exchange at all routers simultaneously. At the time of the first exchange, B learns that its left neighbor has zero delay to A. B now makes an entry in its routing table that A is one hop away to the left. All the other routers still think that A is down. At this point, the routing table entries for A are as shown in the second row of Fig. 5-11(a). On the next exchange, C learns that B has a path of length 1 to A, so it updates its routing table to indicate a path of length 2, but D and E do not hear the good news until later. Clearly, the good news is spreading at the rate of one hop per exchange. In a subnet whose longest path is of length N hops, within N exchanges everyone will know about newly revived lines and routers.

Now let us consider the situation of Fig. 5-11(b), in which all the lines and routers are initially up. Routers B, C, D, and E have distances to A of 1, 2, 3, and 4, respectively. Suddenly A goes down, or alternatively, the line between A and B is cut, which is effectively the same thing from B's point of view.

At the first packet exchange, B does not hear anything from A. Fortunately, C says "Do not worry. I have a path to A of length 2." Little does B know that C's path runs through B itself. For all B knows, C might have ten outgoing lines all with independent paths to A of length 2. As a result, B now thinks it can reach A via C, with a path length of 3. D and E do not update their entries for A on the first exchange.

On the second exchange, C notices that each of its neighbors claims to have a path to A of length 3. It picks one of the them at random and makes its new distance to A 4, as shown in the third row of Fig. 5-11(b). Subsequent exchanges produce the history shown in the rest of Fig. 5-11(b).

From this figure, its should be clear why bad news travels slowly: no router ever has a value more than one higher than the minimum of all its neighbors. Gradually, all the routers work their way up to infinity, but the number of exchanges required depends on the numerical value used for infinity. For this reason, it is wise to set infinity to the longest path plus 1. If the metric is time delay, there is no well-defined upper bound, so a high value is needed to prevent a path with a long delay from being treated as down. Not entirely surprisingly, this problem is known as the **count-to-infinity** problem.

The Split Horizon Hack

Many ad hoc solutions to the count-to-infinity problem have been proposed in the literature, each one more complicated and less useful than the one before it. We will describe just one of them here and then tell why it, too, fails. The **split horizon** algorithm works the same way as distance vector routing, except that the distance to X is not reported on the line that packets for X are sent on (actually, it is reported as infinity). In the initial state of Fig. 5-11(b), for example, C tells D the truth about the distance to A, but C tells B that its distance to A is infinite. Similarly, D tells the truth to E but lies to C.

Now let us see what happens when A goes down. On the first exchange, B discovers that the direct line is gone, and C is reporting an infinite distance to A as well. Since neither of its neighbors can get to A, B sets its distance to infinity as well. On the next exchange, C hears that A is unreachable from both of its neighbors, so it marks A as unreachable too. Using split horizon, the bad news propagates one hop per exchange. This rate is much better than without split horizon.

The real bad news is that split horizon, although widely used, sometimes fails.

Consider, for example, the four-node subnet of Fig. 5-12. Initially, both *A* and *B* have a distance 2 to *D*, and *C* has a distance 1 there.

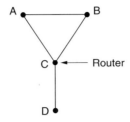

Fig. 5-12. An example where split horizon fails.

Now suppose that the *CD* line goes down. Using split horizon, both *A* and *B* tell *C* that they cannot get to *D*. Thus *C* immediately concludes that *D* is unreachable and reports this to both *A* and *B*. Unfortunately, *A* hears that *B* has a path of length 2 to *D*, so it assumes it can get to *D* via *B* in 3 hops. Similarly, *B* concludes it can get to *D* via *A* in 3 hops. On the next exchange, they each set their distance to *D* to 4. Both of them gradually count to infinity, precisely the behavior we were trying to avoid.

5.2.6. Link State Routing

Distance vector routing was used in the ARPANET until 1979, when it was replaced by link state routing. Two primary problems caused its demise. First, since the delay metric was queue length, it did not take line bandwidth into account when choosing routes. Initially, all the lines were 56 kbps, so line bandwidth was not an issue, but after some lines had been upgraded to 230 kbps and others to 1.544 Mbps, not taking bandwidth into account was a major problem. Of course, it would have been possible to change the delay metric to factor in line bandwidth, but a second problem also existed, namely, the algorithm often took too long to converge, even with tricks like split horizon. For these reasons, it was replaced by an entirely new algorithm now called **link state routing**. Variants of link state routing are now widely used.

The idea behind link state routing is simple and can be stated as five parts. Each router must

1. Discover its neighbors and learn their network addresses.

2. Measure the delay or cost to each of its neighbors.

3. Construct a packet telling all it has just learned.

4. Send this packet to all other routers.

5. Compute the shortest path to every other router.

In effect, the complete topology and all delays are experimentally measured and distributed to every router. Then Dijkstra's algorithm can be used to find the shortest path to every other router. Below we will consider each of these five steps in more detail.

Learning about the Neighbors

When a router is booted, its first task is to learn who its neighbors are. It accomplishes this goal by sending a special HELLO packet on each point-to-point line. The router on the other end is expected to send back a reply telling who it is. These names must be globally unique because when a distant router later hears that three routers are all connected to F, it is essential that it can determine whether or not all three mean the same F.

When two or more routers are connected by a LAN, the situation is slightly more complicated. Fig. 5-13(a) illustrates a LAN to which three routers, A, C, and F, are directly connected. Each of these routers is connected to one or more additional routers, as shown.

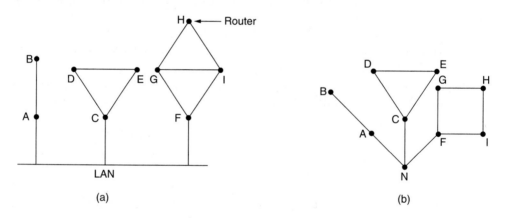

Fig. 5-13. (a) Nine routers and a LAN. (b) A graph model of (a).

One way to model the LAN is to consider it as a node itself, as shown in Fig. 5-13(b). Here we have introduced a new, artificial node, N, to which A, C, and F are connected. The fact that it is possible to go from A to C on the LAN is represented by the path ANC here.

Measuring Line Cost

The link state routing algorithm requires each router to know, or at least have a reasonable estimate, of the delay to each of its neighbors. The most direct way to determine this delay is to send a special ECHO packet over the line that the other side is required to send back immediately. By measuring the round-trip time and dividing it by two, the sending router can get a reasonable estimate of the delay. For even better results, the test can be conducted several times, and the average used.

An interesting issue is whether or not to take the load into account when measuring the delay. To factor the load in, the round-trip timer must be started when the ECHO packet is queued. To ignore the load, the timer should be started when the ECHO packet reaches the front of the queue.

Arguments can be made both ways. Including traffic-induced delays in the measurements means that when a router has a choice between two lines with the same bandwidth, one of which is heavily loaded all the time and one of which is not, it will regard the route over the unloaded line as a shorter path. This choice will result in better performance.

Unfortunately, there is also an argument against including the load in the delay calculation. Consider the subnet of Fig. 5-14, which is divided up into two parts, East and West, connected by two lines, *CF* and *EI*. Suppose that most of the traffic between East and West is using line *CF*, and as a result, this line is heavily loaded with long delays. Including queueing delay in the shortest path calculation will make *EI* more attractive. After the new routing tables have been installed, most of the East-West traffic will now go over *EI*, overloading this line. Consequently, in the next update, *CF* will appear to be the shortest path. As a result, the routing tables may oscillate wildly, leading to erratic routing and many potential problems. If load is ignored and only bandwidth is considered, this problem does not occur. Alternatively, the load can be spread over both lines, but this solution does not fully utilize the best path.

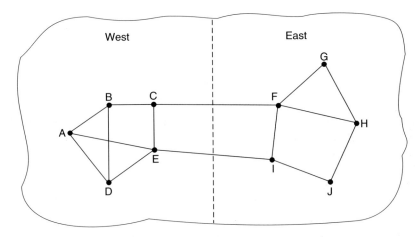

Fig. 5-14. A subnet in which the East and West parts are connected by two lines.

Building Link State Packets

Once the information needed for the exchange has been collected, the next step is for each router to build a packet containing all the data. The packet starts with the identity of the sender, followed by a sequence number and age (to be described later), and a list of neighbors. For each neighbor, the delay to that neighbor is given. An example subnet is given in Fig. 5-15(a) with delays shown in the lines. The corresponding link state packets for all six routers are shown in Fig. 5-15(b).

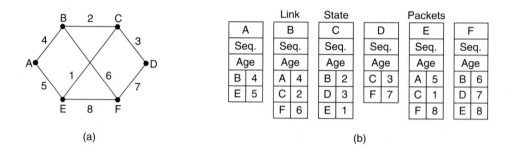

(a)   (b)

Fig. 5-15. (a) A subnet. (b) The link state packets for this subnet.

Building the link state packets is easy. The hard part is determining when to build them. One possibility is to build them periodically, that is, at regular intervals. Another possibility is when some significant event occurs, such as a line or neighbor going down or coming back up again, or changing its properties appreciably.

Distributing the Link State Packets

The trickiest part of the algorithm is distributing the link state packets reliably. As the packets are distributed and installed, the routers getting the first ones will change their routes. Consequently, the different routers may be using different versions of the topology, which can lead to inconsistencies, loops, unreachable machines, and other problems.

First we will describe the basic distribution algorithm. Later we will give some refinements. The fundamental idea is to use flooding to distribute the link state packets. To keep the flood in check, each packet contains a sequence number that is incremented for each new packet sent. Routers keep track of all the (source router, sequence) pairs they see. When a new link state packet comes in, it is checked against the list of packets already seen. If it is new, it is forwarded on all lines except the one it arrived on. If it is a duplicate, it is discarded.

If a packet with a sequence number lower than the highest one seen so far ever arrives, it is rejected as being obsolete.

This algorithm has a few problems, but they are manageable. First, if the sequence numbers wrap around, confusion will reign. The solution here is to use a 32-bit sequence number. With one link state packet per second, it would take 137 years to wrap around, so this possibility can be ignored.

Second, if a router ever crashes, it will lose track of its sequence number. If it starts again at 0, the next packet will be rejected as a duplicate.

Third, if a sequence number is ever corrupted and 65,540 is received instead of 4 (a 1-bit error), packets 5 through 65,540 will be rejected as obsolete, since the current sequence number is thought to be 65,540.

The solution to all these problems is to include the age of each packet after the sequence number and decrement it once per second. When the age hits zero, the information from that router is discarded. Normally, a new packet comes in, say, every 10 minutes, so router information only times out when a router is down (or six consecutive packets have been lost, an unlikely event). The age field is also decremented by each router during the initial flooding process, to make sure no packet can get lost and live for an indefinite period of time (a packet whose age is zero is discarded).

Some refinements to this algorithm make it more robust. When a link state packet comes in to a router for flooding, it is not queued for transmission immediately. Instead it is put in a holding area to wait a short while first. If another link state packet from the same source comes in before it is transmitted, their sequence numbers are compared. If they are equal, the duplicate is discarded. If they are different, the older one is thrown out. To guard against errors on the router-router lines, all link state packets are acknowledged. When a line goes idle, the holding area is scanned in round robin order to select a packet or acknowledgement to send.

The data structure used by router B for the subnet shown in Fig. 5-15(a) is depicted in Fig. 5-16. Each row here corresponds to a recently arrived, but as yet not fully processed, link state packet. The table records where the packet originated, its sequence number and age, and the data. In addition, there are send and acknowledgement flags for each of B's three lines (to A, C, and F, respectively). The send flags mean that the packet must be sent on the indicated line. The acknowledgement flags mean that it must be acknowledged there.

In Fig. 5-16, the link state packet from A arrived directly, so it must be sent to C and F and acknowledged to A, as indicated by the flag bits. Similarly, the packet from F has to be forwarded to A and C and acknowledged to F.

However, the situation with the third packet, from E, is different. It arrived twice, once via EAB and once via EFB. Consequently, it has to be sent only to C, but acknowledged to both A and F, as indicated by the bits.

If a duplicate arrives while the original is still in the buffer, bits have to be changed. For example, if a copy of C's state arrives from F before the fourth

			Send flags			ACK flags			
Source	Seq.	Age	A	C	F	A	C	F	Data
A	21	60	0	1	1	1	0	0	
F	21	60	1	1	0	0	0	1	
E	21	59	0	1	0	1	0	1	
C	20	60	1	0	1	0	1	0	
D	21	59	1	0	0	0	1	1	

Fig. 5-16. The packet buffer for router *B* in Fig. 5-15.

entry in the table has been forwarded, the six bits will be changed to 100011 to indicate that the packet must be acknowledged to *F* but not sent there.

Computing the New Routes

Once a router has accumulated a full set of link state packets, it can construct the entire subnet graph because every link is represented. Every link is, in fact, represented twice, once for each direction. The two values can be averaged or used separately.

Now Dijkstra's algorithm can be run locally to construct the shortest path to all possible destinations. The results of this algorithm can be installed in the routing tables, and normal operation resumed.

For a subnet with *n* routers, each of which has *k* neighbors, the memory required to store the input data is proportional to *kn*. For large subnets, this can be a problem. Also, the computation time can be an issue. Nevertheless, in many practical situations, link state routing works well.

However, problems with the hardware or software can wreak havoc with this algorithm (also with other ones). For example, if a router claims to have a line it does not have, or forgets a line it does have, the subnet graph will be incorrect. If a router fails to forward packets, or corrupts them while forwarding them, trouble will arise. Finally, if it runs out of memory or does the routing calculation wrong, bad things will happen. As the subnet grows into the range of tens or hundreds of thousands of nodes, the probability of some router failing occasionally becomes nonnegligible. The trick is to try to arrange to limit the damage when the inevitable happens. Perlman (1988) discusses these problems and their solutions in detail.

Link state routing is widely used in actual networks, so a few words about some example protocols using it are in order. The OSPF protocol, which is increasingly being used in the Internet, uses a link state algorithm. We will describe OSPF in Sec. 5.5.5.

Another important link state protocol is **IS-IS (Intermediate System-Intermediate System**), which was designed for DECnet and later adopted by ISO for use with its connectionless network layer protocol, CLNP. Since then it has been modified to handle other protocols as well, most notably, IP. IS-IS is used in numerous Internet backbones (including the old NSFNET backbone), and in some digital cellular systems such as CDPD. Novell NetWare uses a minor variant of IS-IS (NLSP) for routing IPX packets.

Basically IS-IS distributes a picture of the router topology, from which the shortest paths are computed. Each router announces, in its link state information, which network layer addresses it can reach directly. These addresses can be IP, IPX, AppleTalk, or any other addresses. IS-IS can even support multiple network layer protocols at the same time.

Many of the innovations designed for IS-IS were adopted by OSPF (OSPF was designed several years after IS-IS). These include a self-stabilizing method of flooding link state updates, the concept of a designated router on a LAN, and the method of computing and supporting path splitting and multiple metrics. As a consequence, there is very little difference between IS-IS and OSPF. The most important difference is that IS-IS is encoded in such a way that it is easy and natural to simultaneously carry information about multiple network layer protocols, a feature OSPF does not have. This advantage is especially valuable in large multiprotocol environments.

5.2.7. Hierarchical Routing

As networks grow in size, the router routing tables grow proportionally. Not only is router memory consumed by ever increasing tables, but more CPU time is needed to scan them and more bandwidth is needed to send status reports about them. At a certain point the network may grow to the point where it is no longer feasible for every router to have an entry for every other router, so the routing will have to be done hierarchically, as it is in the telephone network.

When hierarchical routing is used, the routers are divided into what we will call **regions**, with each router knowing all the details about how to route packets to destinations within its own region, but knowing nothing about the internal structure of other regions. When different networks are connected together, it is natural to regard each one as a separate region in order to free the routers in one network from having to know the topological structure of the other ones.

For huge networks, a two-level hierarchy may be insufficient; it may be necessary to group the regions into clusters, the clusters into zones, the zones into groups, and so on, until we run out of names for aggregations. As an example of a multilevel hierarchy, consider how a packet might be routed from Berkeley, California to Malindi, Kenya. The Berkeley router would know the detailed topology within California but would send all out-of-state traffic to the Los Angeles router. The Los Angeles router would be able to route traffic to other domestic routers, but would send foreign traffic to New York. The New York router would be programmed to direct all traffic to the router in the destination country responsible for handling foreign traffic, say in Nairobi. Finally, the packet would work its way down the tree in Kenya until it got to Malindi.

Figure 5-17 gives a quantitative example of routing in a two-level hierarchy with five regions. The full routing table for router 1A has 17 entries, as shown in Fig. 5-17(b). When routing is done hierarchically, as in Fig. 5-17(c), there are entries for all the local routers as before, but all other regions have been condensed into a single router, so all traffic for region 2 goes via the $1B-2A$ line, but the rest of the remote traffic goes via the $1C-3B$ line. Hierarchical routing has reduced the table from 17 to 7 entries. As the ratio of the number of regions to the number of routers per region grows, the savings in table space increase.

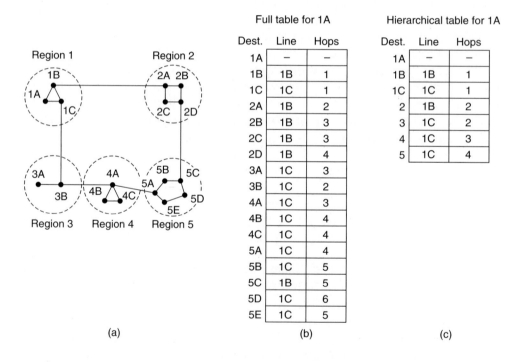

Full table for 1A

Dest.	Line	Hops
1A	–	–
1B	1B	1
1C	1C	1
2A	1B	2
2B	1B	3
2C	1B	3
2D	1B	4
3A	1C	3
3B	1C	2
4A	1C	3
4B	1C	4
4C	1C	4
5A	1C	4
5B	1C	5
5C	1B	5
5D	1C	6
5E	1C	5

Hierarchical table for 1A

Dest.	Line	Hops
1A	–	–
1B	1B	1
1C	1C	1
2	1B	2
3	1C	2
4	1C	3
5	1C	4

(a)   (b)   (c)

Fig. 5-17. Hierarchical routing.

Unfortunately, these gains in space are not free. There is a penalty to be paid, and this penalty is in the form of increased path length. For example, the best route from 1A to 5C is via region 2, but with hierarchical routing all traffic to region 5 goes via region 3, because that is better for most destinations in region 5.

When a single network becomes very large, an interesting question is: How many levels should the hierarchy have? For example, consider a subnet with 720 routers. If there is no hierarchy, each router needs 720 routing table entries. If the subnet is partitioned into 24 regions of 30 routers each, each router needs 30 local entries plus 23 remote entries for a total of 53 entries. If a three-level hierarchy is chosen, with eight clusters, each containing 9 regions of 10 routers, each router needs 10 entries for local routers, 8 entries for routing to other regions within its own cluster, and 7 entries for distant clusters, for a total of 25 entries. Kamoun and Kleinrock (1979) have discovered that the optimal number of levels for an N router subnet is $\ln N$, requiring a total of $e \ln N$ entries per router. They have also shown that the increase in effective mean path length caused by hierarchical routing is sufficiently small that it is usually acceptable.

5.2.8. Routing for Mobile Hosts

Millions of people have portable computers nowadays, and they generally want to read their email and access their normal file systems wherever in the world they may be. These mobile hosts introduce a new complication: to route a packet to a mobile host, the network first has to find it. The subject of incorporating mobile hosts into a network is very young, but in this section we will sketch some of the issues here and give a possible solution.

The model of the world that network designers typically use is shown in Fig. 5-18. Here we have a WAN consisting of routers and hosts. Connected to the WAN are LANs, MANs, and wireless cells of the type we studied in Chap. 2.

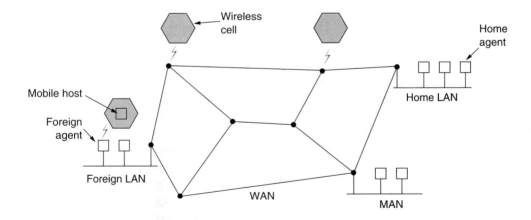

Fig. 5-18. A WAN to which LANs, MANs, and wireless cells are attached.

Users who never move are said to be stationary. They are connected to the network by copper wires or fiber optics. In contrast, we can distinguish two other kinds of users. Migratory users are basically stationary users who move from one fixed site to another from time to time but use the network only when they are physically connected to it. Roaming users actually compute on the run and want to maintain their connections as they move around. We will use the term **mobile users** to mean either of the latter two categories, that is, all users who are away from home.

All users are assumed to have a permanent **home location** that never changes. Users also have a permanent home address that can be used to determine their home locations, analogous to the way the telephone number 1-212-5551212 indicates the United States (country code 1) and Manhattan (212). The routing goal in systems with mobile users is to make it possible to send packets to mobile users using their home addresses, and have the packets efficiently reach them wherever they may be. The trick, of course, is to find them.

In the model of Fig. 5-18, the world is divided up (geographically) into small units. Let us call them areas, where an area is typically a LAN or wireless cell. Each area has one or more **foreign agents**, which keep track of all mobile users visiting the area. In addition, each area has a **home agent**, which keeps track of users whose home is in the area, but who are currently visiting another area.

When a new user enters an area, either by connecting to it (e.g., plugging into the LAN), or just wandering into the cell, his computer must register itself with the foreign agent there. The registration procedure typically works like this:

1. Periodically, each foreign agent broadcasts a packet announcing its existence and address. A newly arrived mobile host may wait for one of these messages, but if none arrives quickly enough, the mobile host can broadcast a packet saying: "Are there any foreign agents around?"

2. The mobile host registers with the foreign agent, giving its home address, current data link layer address, and some security information.

3. The foreign agent contacts the mobile host's home agent and says: "One of your hosts is over here." The message from the foreign agent to the home agent contains the foreign agent's network address. It also includes the security information, to convince the home agent that the mobile host is really there.

4. The home agent examines the security information, which contains a timestamp, to prove that it was generated within the past few seconds. If it is happy, it tells the foreign agent to proceed.

5. When the foreign agent gets the acknowledgement from the home agent, it makes an entry in its tables and informs the mobile host that it is now registered.

Ideally, when a user leaves an area, that, too, should be announced to allow deregistration, but many users abruptly turn off their computers when done.

When a packet is sent to a mobile user, it is routed to the user's home LAN because that is what the address says should be done, as illustrated in step 1 of Fig. 5-19. Packets sent to the mobile user on its home LAN are intercepted by the home agent. The home agent then looks up the mobile user's new (temporary) location and finds the address of the foreign agent handling the mobile user. The home agent then does two things. First, it encapsulates the packet in the payload field of an outer packet and sends the latter to the foreign agent (step 2 in Fig. 5-19). This mechanism is called tunneling; we will look at it in more detail later. After getting the encapsulated packet, the foreign agent removes the original packet from the payload field and sends it to the mobile user as a data link frame.

Second, the home agent tells the sender to henceforth send packets to the mobile host by encapsulating them in the payload of packets explicitly addressed to the foreign agent, instead of just sending them to the mobile user's home address (step 3). Subsequent packets can now be routed directly to the user via the foreign agent (step 4), bypassing the home location entirely.

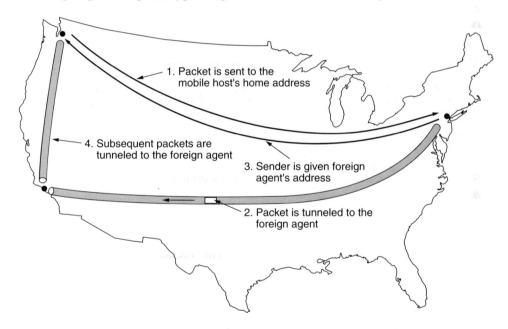

Fig. 5-19. Packet routing for mobile users.

The various schemes that have been proposed differ in several ways. First, there is the issue of how much of this protocol is carried out by the routers and how much by the hosts, and in the latter case, by which layer in the hosts. Second, a few schemes, routers along the way record mapped addresses so they can intercept and redirect traffic even before it gets to the home location. Third, in some schemes each visitor is given a unique temporary address; in others, the temporary address refers to an agent that handles traffic for all visitors.

Fourth, the schemes differ in how they actually manage to arrange for packets that are addressed to one destination to be delivered to a different one. One choice is changing the destination address and just retransmitting the modified packet. Alternatively, the whole packet, home address and all, can be encapsulated inside the payload of another packet sent to the temporary address. Finally, the schemes differ in their security aspects. In general, when a host or router gets a message of the form "Starting right now, please send all of Cayla's mail to me," it might have a couple of questions about whom it was talking to and whether or not this is a good idea. Several mobile host protocols are discussed and compared in (Ioannidis and Maguire, 1993; Myles and Skellern, 1993; Perkins, 1993; Teraoka et al., 1993; and Wada et al., 1993).

5.2.9. Broadcast Routing

For some applications, hosts need to send messages to many or all other hosts. For example, a service distributing weather reports, stock market updates, or live radio programs might work best by broadcasting to all machines and letting those that are interested read the data. Sending a packet to all destinations simultaneously is called **broadcasting**; various methods have been proposed for doing it.

One broadcasting method that requires no special features from the subnet is for the source to simply send a distinct packet to each destination. Not only is the method wasteful of bandwidth, but it also requires the source to have a complete list of all destinations. In practice this may be the only possibility, but it is the least desirable of the methods.

Flooding is another obvious candidate. Although flooding is ill-suited for ordinary point-to-point communication, for broadcasting it might rate serious consideration, especially if none of the methods described below are applicable. The problem with flooding as a broadcast technique is the same problem it has as a point-to-point routing algorithm: it generates too many packets and consumes too much bandwidth.

A third algorithm is **multidestination routing**. If this method is used, each packet contains either a list of destinations or a bit map indicating the desired destinations. When a packet arrives at a router, the router checks all the destinations to determine the set of output lines that will be needed. (An output line is needed if it is the best route to at least one of the destinations.) The router generates a new copy of the packet for each output line to be used and includes in each packet only those destinations that are to use the line. In effect, the destination set is partitioned among the output lines. After a sufficient number of hops, each packet will carry only one destination and can be treated as a normal packet. Multidestination routing is like separately addressed packets, except that when several packets must follow the same route, one of them pays full fare and the rest ride free.

A fourth broadcast algorithm makes explicit use of the sink tree for the router initiating the broadcast, or any other convenient spanning tree for that matter. A

spanning tree is a subset of the subnet that includes all the routers but contains no loops. If each router knows which of its lines belong to the spanning tree, it can copy an incoming broadcast packet onto all the spanning tree lines except the one it arrived on. This method makes excellent use of bandwidth, generating the absolute minimum number of packets necessary to do the job. The only problem is that each router must have knowledge of some spanning tree for it to be applicable. Sometimes this information is available (e.g., with link state routing) but sometimes it is not (e.g., with distance vector routing).

Our last broadcast algorithm is an attempt to approximate the behavior of the previous one, even when the routers do not know anything at all about spanning trees. The idea is remarkably simple once it has been pointed out. When a broadcast packet arrives at a router, the router checks to see if the packet arrived on the line that is normally used for sending packets *to* the source of the broadcast. If so, there is an excellent chance that the broadcast packet itself followed the best route from the router and is therefore the first copy to arrive at the router. This being the case, the router forwards copies of it onto all lines except the one it arrived on. If, however, the broadcast packet arrived on a line other than the preferred one for reaching the source, the packet is discarded as a likely duplicate.

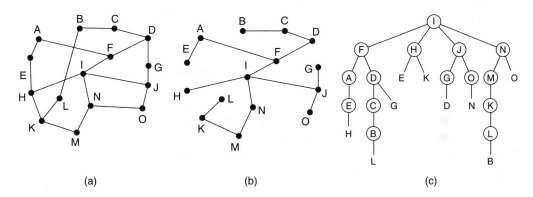

Fig. 5-20. Reverse path forwarding. (a) A subnet. (b) A spanning tree. (c) The tree built by reverse path forwarding.

An example of the algorithm, called **reverse path forwarding**, is shown in Fig. 5-20. Part (a) shows a subnet, part (b) shows a sink tree for router *I* of that subnet, and part (c) shows how the reverse path algorithm works. On the first hop, *I* sends packets to *F*, *H*, *J*, and *N*, as indicated by the second row of the tree. Each of these packets arrives on the preferred path to *I* (assuming that the preferred path falls along the sink tree) and is so indicated by a circle around the letter. On the second hop, eight packets are generated, two by each of the routers that received a packet on the first hop. As it turns out, all eight of these arrive at previously unvisited routers, and five of these arrive along the preferred line. Of the six packets generated on the third hop, only three arrive on the preferred path (at *C*, *E*, and *K*); the others are duplicates. After five hops and 23 packets, the broadcasting terminates, compared with four hops and 14 packets had the sink tree been followed exactly.

The principal advantage of reverse path forwarding is that it is both reasonably efficient and easy to implement. It does not require routers to know about spanning trees, nor does it have the overhead of a destination list or bit map in each broadcast packet as does multidestination addressing. Nor does it require any special mechanism to stop the process, as flooding does (either a hop counter in each packet and a priori knowledge of the subnet diameter, or a list of packets already seen per source).

5.2.10. Multicast Routing

For some applications, widely-separated processes work together in groups, for example, a group of processes implementing a distributed database system. It frequently is necessary for one process to send a message to all the other members of the group. If the group is small, it can just send each other member a point-to-point message. If the group is large, this strategy is expensive. Sometimes broadcasting can be used, but using broadcasting to inform 1000 machines on a million-node network is inefficient because most receivers are not interested in the message (or worse yet, they are definitely interested but are not supposed to see it). Thus we need a way to send messages to well-defined groups that are numerically large in size but small compared to the network as a whole.

Sending a message to such a group is called **multicasting**, and its routing algorithm is called **multicast routing**. In this section we will describe one way of doing multicast routing. For additional information, see (Deering and Cheriton, 1990; Deering et al., 1994; and Rajagopalan, 1992).

To do multicasting, group management is required. Some way is needed to create and destroy groups, and for processes to join and leave groups. How these tasks are accomplished is not of concern to the routing algorithm. What is of concern is that when a process joins a group, it informs its host of this fact. It is important that routers know which of their hosts belong to which groups. Either hosts must inform their routers about changes in group membership, or routers must query their hosts periodically. Either way, routers learn about which of their hosts are in which groups. Routers tell their neighbors, so the information propagates through the subnet.

To do multicast routing, each router computes a spanning tree covering all other routers in the subnet. For example, in Fig. 5-21(a) we have a subnet with two groups, 1 and 2. Some routers are attached to hosts that belong to one or both of these groups, as indicated in the figure. A spanning tree for the leftmost router is shown in Fig. 5-21(b).

When a process sends a multicast packet to a group, the first router examines its spanning tree and prunes it, removing all lines that do not lead to hosts that are

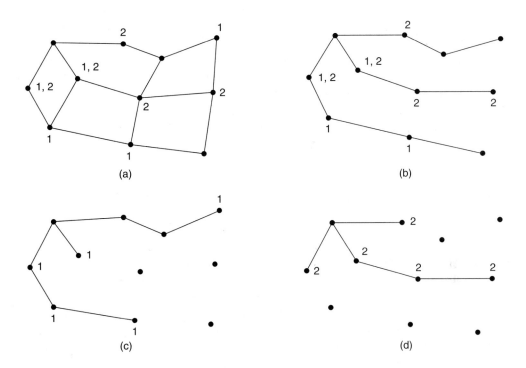

Fig. 5-21. (a) A subnet. (b) A spanning tree for the leftmost router. (c) A multi-cast tree for group 1. (d) A multicast tree for group 2.

members of the group. In our example, Fig. 5-21(c) shows the pruned spanning tree for group 1. Similarly, Fig. 5-21(d) shows the pruned spanning tree for group 2. Multicast packets are forwarded only along the appropriate spanning tree.

Various ways of pruning the spanning tree are possible. The simplest one can be used if link state routing is used, and each router is aware of the complete sub-net topology, including which hosts belong to which groups. Then the spanning tree can be pruned by starting at the end of each path and working toward the root, removing all routers that do not belong to the group in question.

With distance vector routing, a different pruning strategy can be followed. The basic algorithm is reverse path forwarding. However, whenever a router with no hosts interested in a particular group and no connections to other routers receives a multicast message for that group, it responds with a PRUNE message, telling the sender not to send it any more multicasts for that group. When a router with no group members among its own hosts has received such messages on all its lines, it, too, can respond with a PRUNE message. In this way, the subnet is recursively pruned.

One potential disadvantage of this algorithm is that it scales poorly to large networks. Suppose that a network has n groups, each with an average of m

members. For each group, m pruned spanning trees must be stored, for a total of mn trees. When many large groups exist, considerable storage is needed to store all the trees.

An alternative design uses **core-base trees** (Ballardie et al., 1993). Here, a single spanning tree per group is computed, with the root (the core) near the middle of the group. To send a multicast message, a host sends it to the core, which then does the multicast along the spanning tree. Although this tree will not be optimal for all sources, the reduction in storage costs from m trees to one tree per group is a major saving.

5.3. CONGESTION CONTROL ALGORITHMS

When too many packets are present in (a part of) the subnet, performance degrades. This situation is called **congestion**. Figure 5-22 depicts the symptom. When the number of packets dumped into the subnet by the hosts is within its carrying capacity, they are all delivered (except for a few that are afflicted with transmission errors), and the number delivered is proportional to the number sent. However, as traffic increases too far, the routers are no longer able to cope, and they begin losing packets. This tends to make matters worse. At very high traffic, performance collapses completely, and almost no packets are delivered.

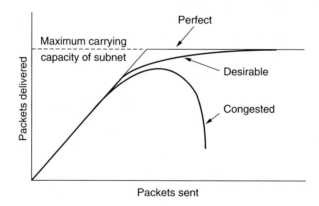

Fig. 5-22. When too much traffic is offered, congestion sets in and performance degrades sharply.

Congestion can be brought about by several factors. If all of a sudden, streams of packets begin arriving on three or four input lines and all need the same output line, a queue will build up. If there is insufficient memory to hold all of them, packets will be lost. Adding more memory may help up to a point, but Nagle (1987) discovered that if routers have an infinite amount of memory, congestion gets worse, not better, because by the time packets get to the front of the queue, they have already timed out (repeatedly), and duplicates have been sent. All these packets will be dutifully forwarded to the next router, increasing the load all the way to the destination.

Slow processors can also cause congestion. If the routers' CPUs are slow at performing the bookkeeping tasks required of them (queueing buffers, updating tables, etc.), queues can build up, even though there is excess line capacity. Similarly, low-bandwidth lines can also cause congestion. Upgrading the lines but not changing the processors, or vice versa, often helps a little, but frequently just shifts the bottleneck. Also, upgrading part, but not all, of the system, often just moves the bottleneck somewhere else. The real problem is frequently a mismatch between parts of the system. This problem will persist until all the components are in balance.

Congestion tends to feed upon itself and become worse. If a router has no free buffers, it must ignore newly arriving packets. When a packet is discarded, the sending router (a neighbor) may time out and retransmit it, perhaps ultimately many times. Since it cannot discard the packet until it has been acknowledged, congestion at the receiver's end forces the sender to refrain from releasing a buffer it would have normally freed. In this manner, congestion backs up, like cars approaching a toll booth.

It is worth explicitly pointing out the difference between congestion control and flow control, as the relationship is subtle. Congestion control has to do with making sure the subnet is able to carry the offered traffic. It is a global issue, involving the behavior of all the hosts, all the routers, the store-and-forwarding processing within the routers, and all the other factors that tend to diminish the carrying capacity of the subnet.

Flow control, in contrast, relates to the point-to-point traffic between a given sender and a given receiver. Its job is to make sure that a fast sender cannot continually transmit data faster than the receiver can absorb it. Flow control nearly always involves some direct feedback from the receiver to the sender to tell the sender how things are doing at the other end.

To see the difference between these two concepts, consider a fiber optic network with a capacity of 1000 gigabits/sec on which a supercomputer is trying to transfer a file to a personal computer at 1 Gbps. Although there is no congestion (the network itself is not in trouble), flow control is needed to force the supercomputer to stop frequently to give the personal computer a chance to breathe.

At the other extreme, consider a store-and-forward network with 1-Mbps lines and 1000 large computers, half of which are trying to transfer files at 100 kbps to the other half. Here the problem is not that of fast senders overpowering slow receivers, but simply that the total offered traffic exceeds what the network can handle.

The reason congestion control and flow control are often confused is that some congestion control algorithms operate by sending messages back to the various sources telling them to slow down when the network gets into trouble. Thus a host can get a "slow down" message either because the receiver cannot handle the load, or because the network cannot handle it. We will come back to this point later.

We will start our study of congestion control by looking at a general model for dealing with it. Then we will look at broad approaches to preventing it in the first place. After that, we will look at various dynamic algorithms for coping with it once it has set in.

5.3.1. General Principles of Congestion Control

Many problems in complex systems, such as computer networks, can be viewed from a control theory point of view. This approach leads to dividing all solutions into two groups: open loop and closed loop. Open loop solutions attempt to solve the problem by good design, in essence, to make sure it does not occur in the first place. Once the system is up and running, midcourse corrections are not made.

Tools for doing open-loop control include deciding when to accept new traffic, deciding when to discard packets and which ones, and making scheduling decisions at various points in the network. All of these have in common the fact that they make decisions without regard to the current state of the network.

In contrast, closed loop solutions are based on the concept of a feedback loop. This approach has three parts when applied to congestion control:

1. Monitor the system to detect when and where congestion occurs.

2. Pass this information to places where action can be taken.

3. Adjust system operation to correct the problem.

Various metrics can be used to monitor the subnet for congestion. Chief among these are the percentage of all packets discarded for lack of buffer space, the average queue lengths, the number of packets that time out and are retransmitted, the average packet delay, and the standard deviation of packet delay. In all cases, rising numbers indicate growing congestion.

The second step in the feedback loop is to transfer the information about the congestion from the point where it is detected to the point where something can be done about it. The obvious way is for the router detecting the congestion to send a packet to the traffic source or sources, announcing the problem. Of course, these extra packets increase the load at precisely the moment that more load is not needed, namely, when the subnet is congested.

However, other possibilities also exist. For example, a bit or field can be reserved in every packet for routers to fill in whenever congestion gets above some threshold level. When a router detects this congested state, it fills in the field in all outgoing packets, to warn the neighbors.

Still another approach is to have hosts or routers send probe packets out periodically to explicitly ask about congestion. This information can then be used to route traffic around problem areas. Some radio stations have helicopters flying around their cities to report on road congestion in the hope that their listeners will route their packets (cars) around hot spots.

In all feedback schemes, the hope is that knowledge of congestion will cause the hosts to take appropriate action to reduce the congestion. To work correctly, the time scale must be adjusted carefully. If every time two packets arrive in a row, a router yells STOP, and every time a router is idle for 20 µsec it yells GO, the system will oscillate wildly and never converge. On the other hand, if it waits 30 minutes to make sure before saying anything, the congestion control mechanism will react too sluggishly to be of any real use. To work well, some kind of averaging is needed, but getting the time constant right is a nontrivial matter.

Many congestion control algorithms are known. To provide a way to organize them in a sensible way, Yang and Reddy (1995) have developed a taxonomy for congestion control algorithms. They begin by dividing all algorithms into open loop or closed loop, as described above. They further divide the open loop algorithms into ones that act at the source versus ones that act at the destination. The closed loop algorithms are also divided into two subcategories: explicit feedback versus implicit feedback. In explicit feedback algorithms, packets are sent back from the point of congestion to warn the source. In implicit algorithms, the source deduces the existence of congestion by making local observations, such as the time needed for acknowledgements to come back.

The presence of congestion means that the load is (temporarily) greater than the resources (in part of the system) can handle. Two solutions come to mind: increase the resources or decrease the load. For example, the subnet may start using dial-up telephone lines to temporarily increase the bandwidth between certain points. In systems like SMDS (see Chap. 1), it may ask the carrier for additional bandwidth for a while. On satellite systems, increasing transmission power often gives higher bandwidth. Splitting traffic over multiple routes instead of always using the best one may also effectively increase the bandwidth. Finally, spare routers that are normally used only as backups (to make the system fault tolerant) can be put on-line to give more capacity when serious congestion appears.

However, sometimes it is not possible to increase the capacity, or it has already been increased to the limit. The only way then to beat back the congestion is to decrease the load. Several ways exist to reduce the load, including denying service to some users, degrading service to some or all users, and having users schedule their demands in a more predictable way.

Some of these methods, which we will study shortly, can best be applied to virtual circuits. For subnets that use virtual circuits internally, these methods can be used at the network layer. For datagram subnets, they can nevertheless sometimes be used on transport layer connections. In this chapter, we will focus on their use in the network layer. In the next one, we will see what can be done at the transport layer to manage congestion.

5.3.2. Congestion Prevention Policies

Let us begin our study of methods to control congestion by looking at open loop systems. These systems are designed to minimize congestion in the first place, rather than letting it happen and reacting after the fact. They try to achieve their goal by using appropriate policies at various levels. In Fig. 5-23 we see different data link, network, and transport policies that can affect congestion (Jain, 1990).

Layer	Policies
Transport	• Retransmission policy • Out-of-order caching policy • Acknowledgement policy • Flow control policy • Timeout determination
Network	• Virtual circuits versus datagram inside the subnet • Packet queueing and service policy • Packet discard policy • Routing algorithm • Packet lifetime management
Data link	• Retransmission policy • Out-of-order caching policy • Acknowledgement policy • Flow control policy

Fig. 5-23. Policies that affect congestion.

Let us start at the data link layer and work our way upward. The retransmission policy deals with how fast a sender times out and what it transmits upon timeout. A jumpy sender that times out quickly and retransmits all outstanding packets using go back n will put a heavier load on the system than a leisurely sender that uses selective repeat. Closely related to this is caching policy. If receivers routinely discard all out-of-order packets, these packets will have to be transmitted again later, creating extra load.

Acknowledgement policy also affects congestion. If each packet is acknowledged immediately, the acknowledgement packets generate extra traffic. However, if acknowledgements are saved up to piggyback onto reverse traffic, extra timeouts and retransmissions may result. A tight flow control scheme (e.g., a small window) reduces the data rate and thus helps fight congestion.

At the network layer, the choice between virtual circuits and datagrams affects congestion, since many congestion control algorithms work only with virtual circuit subnets. Packet queueing and service policy relates to whether routers have one queue per input line, one queue per output line, or both. It also relates to the order packets are processed (e.g., round robin, or priority based). Discard policy is the rule telling which packet is dropped when there is no space. A good policy can help alleviate congestion and a bad one can make it worse.

The routing algorithm can help avoid congestion by spreading the traffic over all the lines, whereas a bad one can send too much traffic over already congested lines. Finally, packet lifetime management deals with how long a packet may live before being discarded. If it is too long, lost packets may clog up the works for a long time, but if it is too short, packets may sometimes time out before reaching their destination, thus inducing retransmissions.

In the transport layer, the same issues occur as in the data link layer, but in addition, determining the timeout interval is harder because the transit time across the network is less predictable than the transit time over a wire between two routers. If it is too short, extra packets will be sent unnecessarily. If it is too long, congestion will be reduced, but the response time will suffer whenever a packet is lost.

5.3.3. Traffic Shaping

One of the main causes of congestion is that traffic is often bursty. If hosts could be made to transmit at a uniform rate, congestion would be less common. Another open loop method to help manage congestion is forcing the packets to be transmitted at a more predictable rate. This approach to congestion management is widely used in ATM networks and is called **traffic shaping**.

Traffic shaping is about regulating the average *rate* (and burstiness) of data transmission. In contrast, the sliding window protocols we studied earlier limit the amount of data in transit at once, not the rate at which it is sent. When a virtual circuit is set up, the user and the subnet (i.e., the customer and the carrier) agree on a certain traffic pattern (i.e., shape) for that circuit. As long as the customer fulfills her part of the bargain and only sends packets according to the agreed upon contract, the carrier promises to deliver them all in a timely fashion. Traffic shaping reduces congestion and thus helps the carrier live up to its promise. Such agreements are not so important for file transfers but are of great importance for real-time data, such as audio and video connections, which do not tolerate congestion well.

In effect, with traffic shaping the customer says to the carrier: "My transmission pattern will look like this. Can you handle it?" If the carrier agrees, the issue arises of how the carrier can tell if the customer is following the agreement, and what to do if the customer is not. Monitoring a traffic flow is called **traffic policing**. Agreeing to a traffic shape and policing it afterward are easier with virtual circuit subnets than with datagram subnets. However, even with datagram subnets, the same ideas can be applied to transport layer connections.

The Leaky Bucket Algorithm

Imagine a bucket with a small hole in the bottom, as illustrated in Fig. 5-24(a). No matter at what rate water enters the bucket, the outflow is at a constant rate, ρ, when there is any water in the bucket, and zero when the bucket is empty. Also, once the bucket is full, any additional water entering it spills over the sides and is lost (i.e., does not appear in the output stream under the hole).

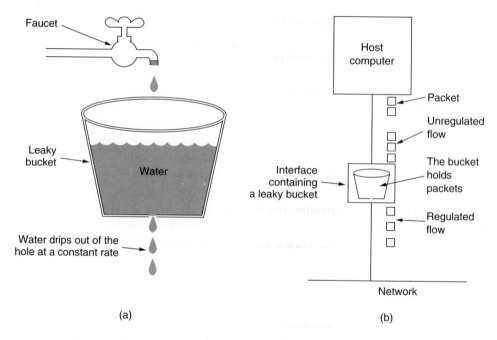

(a) (b)

Fig. 5-24. (a) A leaky bucket with water. (b) A leaky bucket with packets.

The same idea can be applied to packets, as shown in Fig. 5-24(b). Conceptually, each host is connected to the network by an interface containing a leaky bucket, that is, a finite internal queue. If a packet arrives at the queue when it is full, the packet is discarded. In other words, if one or more processes within the host try to send a packet when the maximum number are already queued, the new packet is unceremoniously discarded. This arrangement can be built into the hardware interface or simulated by the host operating system. It was first proposed by Turner (1986) and is called the **leaky bucket algorithm**. In fact, it is nothing other than a single-server queueing system with constant service time.

The host is allowed to put one packet per clock tick onto the network. Again, this can be enforced by the interface card or by the operating system. This mechanism turns an uneven flow of packets from the user processes inside the host into an even flow of packets onto the network, smoothing out bursts and greatly reducing the chances of congestion.

When the packets are all the same size (e.g., ATM cells), this algorithm can be used as described. However, when variable-sized packets are being used, it is often better to allow a fixed number of bytes per tick, rather than just one packet. Thus if the rule is 1024 bytes per tick, a single 1024-byte packet can be admitted on a tick, two 512-byte packets, four 256-byte packets, and so on. If the residual byte count is too low, the next packet must wait until the next tick.

Implementing the original leaky bucket algorithm is easy. The leaky bucket consists of a finite queue. When a packet arrives, if there is room on the queue it is appended to the queue; otherwise, it is discarded. At every clock tick, one packet is transmitted (unless the queue is empty).

The byte-counting leaky bucket is implemented almost the same way. At each tick, a counter is initialized to n. If the first packet on the queue has fewer bytes than the current value of the counter, it is transmitted, and the counter is decremented by that number of bytes. Additional packets may also be sent, as long as the counter is high enough. When the counter drops below the length of the next packet on the queue, transmission stops until the next tick, at which time the residual byte count is overwritten and lost.

As an example of a leaky bucket, imagine that a computer can produce data at 25 million bytes/sec (200 Mbps) and that the network also runs at this speed. However, the routers can handle this data rate only for short intervals. For long intervals, they work best at rates not exceeding 2 million bytes/sec. Now suppose data comes in 1-million-byte bursts, one 40-msec burst every second. To reduce the average rate to 2 MB/sec, we could use a leaky bucket with $\rho = 2$ MB/sec and a capacity, C, of 1 MB. This means that bursts of up to 1 MB can be handled without data loss, and that such bursts are spread out over 500 msec, no matter how fast they come in.

In Fig. 5-25(a) we see the input to the leaky bucket running at 25 MB/sec for 40 msec. In Fig. 5-25(b) we see the output draining out at a uniform rate of 2 MB/sec for 500 msec.

The Token Bucket Algorithm

The leaky bucket algorithm enforces a rigid output pattern at the average rate, no matter how bursty the traffic is. For many applications, it is better to allow the output to speed up somewhat when large bursts arrive, so a more flexible algorithm is needed, preferably one that never loses data. One such algorithm is the **token bucket algorithm**. In this algorithm, the leaky bucket holds tokens, generated by a clock at the rate of one token every ΔT sec. In Fig. 5-26(a) we see a bucket holding three tokens, with five packets waiting to be transmitted. For a packet to be transmitted, it must capture and destroy one token. In Fig. 5-26(b)

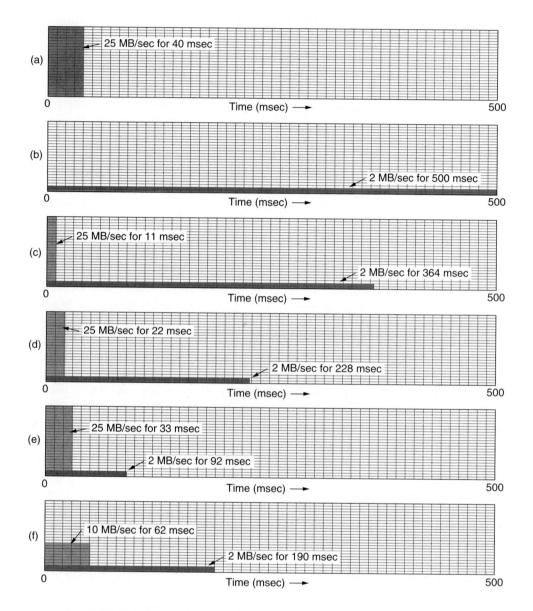

Fig. 5-25. (a) Input to a leaky bucket. (b) Output from a leaky bucket. (c) - (e) Output from a token bucket with capacities of 250KB, 500KB, and 750KB. (f) Output from a 500KB token bucket feeding a 10 MB/sec leaky bucket.

we see that three of the five packets have gotten through, but the other two are stuck waiting for two more tokens to be generated.

The token bucket algorithm provides a different kind of traffic shaping than the leaky bucket algorithm. The leaky bucket algorithm does not allow idle hosts

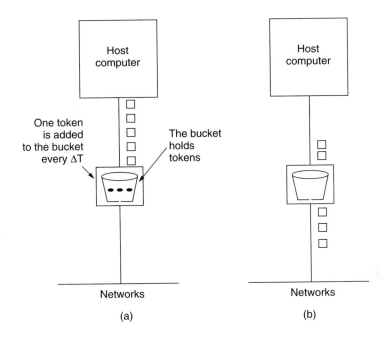

Fig. 5-26. The token bucket algorithm. (a) Before. (b) After.

to save up permission to send large bursts later. The token bucket algorithm does allow saving, up to the maximum size of the bucket, n. This property means that bursts of up to n packets can be sent at once, allowing some burstiness in the output stream and giving faster response to sudden bursts of input.

Another difference between the two algorithms is that the token bucket algorithm throws away tokens when the bucket fills up but never discards packets. In contrast, the leaky bucket algorithm discards packets when the bucket fills up.

Here too, a minor variant is possible, in which each token represents the right to send not one packet, but k bytes. A packet can only be transmitted if enough tokens are available to cover its length in bytes. Fractional tokens are kept for future use.

The leaky bucket and token bucket algorithms can also be used to smooth traffic between routers, as well as being used to regulate host output as in our examples. However, one clear difference is that a token bucket regulating a host can make the host stop sending when the rules say it must. Telling a router to stop sending while its input keeps pouring in may result in lost data.

The implementation of the basic token bucket algorithm is just a variable that counts tokens. The counter is incremented by one every ΔT and decremented by one whenever a packet is sent. When the counter hits zero, no packets may be sent. In the byte-count variant, the counter is increment by k bytes every ΔT and decremented by the length of each packet sent.

Essentially what the token bucket does is allow bursts, but up to a regulated maximum length. Look at Fig. 5-25(c) for example. Here we have a token bucket with a capacity of 250 KB. Tokens arrive at a rate allowing output at 2 MB/sec. Assuming the token bucket is full when the 1-MB burst arrives, the bucket can drain at the full 25 MB/sec for about 11 msec. Then it has to cut back to 2 MB/sec until the entire input burst has been sent.

Calculating the length of the maximum rate burst is slightly tricky. It is not just 1 MB divided by 25 MB/sec because while the burst is being output, more tokens arrive. If we call the burst length S sec, the token bucket capacity C bytes, the token arrival rate ρ bytes/sec, and the maximum output rate M bytes/sec, we see that an output burst contains a maximum of $C + \rho S$ bytes. We also know that the number of bytes in a maximum-speed burst of length S seconds is MS. Hence we have

$$C + \rho S = MS$$

We can solve this equation to get $S = C/(M - \rho)$. For our parameters of $C = 250$ KB, $M = 25$ MB/sec, and $\rho = 2$ MB/sec, we get a burst time of about 11 msec. Figure 5-25(d) and Fig. 5-25(e) show the token bucket for capacities of 500-KB and 750 KB, respectively.

A potential problem with the token bucket algorithm is that it allows large bursts again, even though the maximum burst interval can be regulated by careful selection of ρ and M. Frequently it is desirable to reduce the peak rate, but without going back to the low value of the original leaky bucket.

One way to get smoother traffic is to put a leaky bucket after the token bucket. The rate of the leaky bucket should be higher than the token bucket's ρ but lower than the maximum rate of the network. Figure 5-25(f) shows the output for a 500 KB token bucket followed by a 10-MB/sec leaky bucket.

Policing all these schemes can be a bit tricky. Essentially, the network has to simulate the algorithm and make sure that no more packets or bytes are being sent than are permitted. Excess packets are then discarded or downgraded, as discussed later.

5.3.4. Flow Specifications

Traffic shaping is most effective when the sender, receiver, and subnet all agree to it. To get agreement, it is necessary to specify the traffic pattern in a precise way. Such an agreement is called a **flow specification**. It consists of a data structure that describes both the pattern of the injected traffic and the quality of service desired by the applications. A flow specification can apply either to the packets sent on a virtual circuit, or to a sequence of datagrams sent between a source and a destination (or even to multiple destinations).

In this section we will describe an example flow specification designed by Partridge (1992). It is shown in Fig. 5-27. The idea is that before a connection is established or before a sequence of datagrams are sent, the source gives the flow specification to the subnet for approval. The subnet can either accept it, reject it, or come back with a counterproposal ("I cannot give you 100 msec average delay; can you live with 150 msec?"). Once the sender and subnet have struck a deal, the sender can ask the receiver if it, too, agrees.

Characteristics of the Input	Service Desired
Maximum packet size (bytes)	Loss sensitivity (bytes)
Token bucket rate (bytes/sec)	Loss interval (μsec)
Token bucket size (bytes)	Burst loss sensitivity (packets)
Maximum transmission rate (bytes/sec)	Minimum delay noticed (μsec)
	Maximum delay variation (μsec)
	Quality of guarantee

Fig. 5-27. An example flow specification.

Let us now examine the parameters of our example flow specification starting with the traffic specification. The *Maximum packet size* tells how big packets may be. The next two parameters implicitly assume that traffic will be shaped by the token bucket algorithm working in bytes. They tell how many bytes are put into the token bucket per second, and how big the bucket is. If the rate is r bytes/sec and the bucket size is b bytes, then in any arbitrary time interval Δt, the maximum number of bytes that may be sent is $b + r\Delta t$. Here the first term represents the maximum possible contents of the bucket at the start of the interval and the second one represents the new credits that come in during the interval. The *Maximum transmission rate* is the top rate the host is capable of producing under any conditions and implicitly specifies the shortest time interval in which the token bucket could be emptied.

The second column specifies what the application wants from the subnet. The first and second parameters represent the numerator and denominator of a fraction giving the maximum acceptable loss rate (e.g., 1 byte per hour). Alternatively, they can indicate that the flow is insensitive to packet loss. The *Burst loss sensitivity* tells how many consecutive lost packets can be tolerated.

The next two service parameters deal with delay. The *Minimum delay noticed* says how long a packet can be delayed without the application noticing. For a file transfer, it might be a second, but for an audio stream 3 msec might be the limit. The *Maximum delay variation* tries to quantify the fact that some applications are not sensitive to the actual delay but are highly sensitive to the **jitter**, that is, the amount of variation in the end-to-end packet transit time. It is two times the number of microseconds a packet's delay may vary from the average. Thus a value of 2000 means that a packet may be up to 1 msec early or late, but no more.

Finally, the *Quality of guarantee* indicates whether or not the application really means it. On the one hand, the loss and delay characteristics might be ideal goals, but no harm is done if they are not met. On the other hand, they might be so important that if they cannot be met, the application simply terminates. Intermediate positions are also possible.

Although we have looked at the flow specification as a request from the application to the subnet, it can also be a return value telling what the subnet can do. Thus it can potentially be used for an extended negotiation about the service level.

A problem inherent with any flow specification is that the application may not know what it really wants. For example, an application program running in New York might be quite happy with a delay of 200 msec to Sydney, but most unhappy with the same 200-msec delay to Boston. Here the "minimum service" is clearly a function of what is thought to be possible.

5.3.5. Congestion Control in Virtual Circuit Subnets

The congestion control methods described above are basically open loop: they try to prevent congestion from occurring in the first place, rather than dealing with it after the fact. In this section we will describe some approaches to dynamically controlling congestion in virtual circuit subnets. In the next two, we will look at techniques that can be used in any subnet.

One technique that is widely used to keep congestion that has already started from getting worse is **admission control**. The idea is simple: once congestion has been signaled, no more virtual circuits are set up until the problem has gone away. Thus, attempts to set up new transport layer connections fail. Letting more people in just makes matters worse. While this approach is crude, it is simple and easy to carry out. In the telephone system, when a switch gets overloaded, it also practices admission control, by not giving dial tones.

An alternative approach is to allow new virtual circuits but carefully route all new virtual circuits around problem areas. For example, consider the subnet of Fig. 5-28(a), in which two routers are congested, as indicated.

Suppose that a host attached to router *A* wants to set up a connection to a host attached to router *B*. Normally, this connection would pass through one of the congested routers. To avoid this situation, we can redraw the subnet as shown in Fig. 5-28(b), omitting the congested routers and all of their lines. The dashed line shows a possible route for the virtual circuit that avoids the congested routers.

Another strategy relating to virtual circuits is to negotiate an agreement between the host and subnet when a virtual circuit is set up. This agreement normally specifies the volume and shape of the traffic, quality of service required, and other parameters. To keep its part of the agreement, the subnet will typically reserve resources along the path when the circuit is set up. These resources can include table and buffer space in the routers and bandwidth on the lines. In this

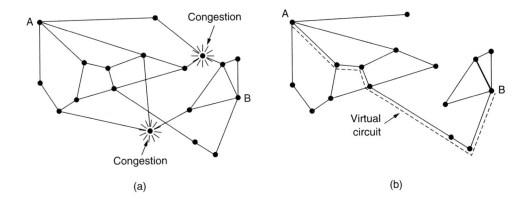

Fig. 5-28. (a) A congested subnet. (b) A redrawn subnet that eliminates the congestion and a virtual circuit from *A* to *B*.

way, congestion is unlikely to occur on the new virtual circuits because all the necessary resources are guaranteed to be available.

This kind of reservation can be done all the time as standard operating procedure, or only when the subnet is congested. A disadvantage of doing it all the time is that it tends to waste resources. If six virtual circuits that might use 1 Mbps all pass through the same physical 6-Mbps line, the line has to be marked as full, even though it may rarely happen that all six virtual circuits are transmitting at the same time. Consequently, the price of the congestion control is unused bandwidth.

5.3.6. Choke Packets

Let us now turn to an approach that can be used in both virtual circuit and datagram subnets. Each router can easily monitor the utilization of its output lines and other resources. For example, it can associate with each line a real variable, u, whose value, between 0.0 and 1.0, reflects the recent utilization of that line. To maintain a good estimate of u, a sample of the instantaneous line utilization, f (either 0 or 1), can be made periodically and u updated according to

$$u_{new} = au_{old} + (1 - a)f$$

where the constant a determines how fast the router forgets recent history.

Whenever u moves above the threshold, the output line enters a "warning" state. Each newly arriving packet is checked to see if its output line is in warning state. If so, the router sends a **choke packet** back to the source host, giving it the destination found in the packet. The original packet is tagged (a header bit is turned on) so that it will not generate any more choke packets further along the path and is then forwarded in the usual way.

When the source host gets the choke packet, it is required to reduce the traffic sent to the specified destination by X percent. Since other packets aimed at the same destination are probably already under way and will generate yet more choke packets, the host should ignore choke packets referring to that destination for a fixed time interval. After that period has expired, the host listens for more choke packets for another interval. If one arrives, the line is still congested, so the host reduces the flow still more and begins ignoring choke packets again. If no choke packets arrive during the listening period, the host may increase the flow again. The feedback implicit in this protocol can help prevent congestion yet not throttle any flow unless trouble occurs.

Hosts can reduce traffic by adjusting their policy parameters, for example, window size or leaky bucket output rate. Typically, the first choke packet causes the data rate to be reduced to 0.50 of its previous rate, the next one causes a reduction to 0.25, and so on. Increases are done in smaller increments to prevent congestion from reoccurring quickly.

Several variations on this congestion control algorithm have been proposed. For one, the routers can maintain several thresholds. Depending on which threshold has been crossed, the choke packet can contain a mild warning, a stern warning, or an ultimatum.

Another variation is to use queue lengths or buffer utilization instead of line utilization as the trigger signal. The same exponential weighting can be used with this metric as with u, of course.

Weighted Fair Queueing

A problem with using choke packets is that the action to be taken by the source hosts is voluntary. Suppose that a router is being swamped by packets from four sources, and it sends choke packets to all of them. One of them cuts back, as it is supposed to, but the other three just keep blasting away. The result is that the honest host gets an even smaller share of the bandwidth than it had before.

To get around this problem, and thus make compliance more attractive, Nagle (1987) proposed a **fair queueing** algorithm. The essence of the algorithm is that routers have multiple queues for each output line, one for each source. When a line becomes idle, the router scans the queues round robin, taking the first packet on the next queue. In this way, with n hosts competing for a given output line, each host gets to send one out of every n packets. Sending more packets will not improve this fraction. Some ATM switches use this algorithm.

Although a start, the algorithm has a problem: it gives more bandwidth to hosts that use large packets than to hosts that use small packets. Demers et al. (1990) suggested an improvement in which the round robin is done in such a way as to simulate a byte-by-byte round robin, instead of a packet-by-packet round robin. In effect, it scans the queues repeatedly, byte-for-byte, until it finds the tick on which each packet will be finished. The packets are then sorted in order of their finishing and sent in that order. The algorithm is illustrated in Fig. 5-29.

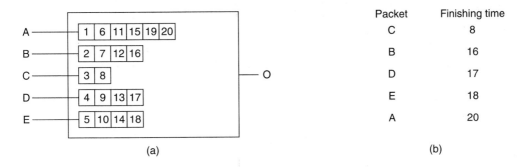

Packet	Finishing time
C	8
B	16
D	17
E	18
A	20

(a)   (b)

Fig. 5-29. (a) A router with five packets queued for line O. (b) Finishing times for the five packets.

In Fig. 5-29(a) we see packets of length 2 to 6 bytes. At (virtual) clock tick 1, the first byte of the packet on line A is sent. Then goes the first byte of the packet on line B, and so on. The first packet to finish is C, after eight ticks. The sorted order is given in Fig. 5-29(b). In the absence of new arrivals, the packets will be sent in the order listed, from C to A.

One problem with this algorithm is that it gives all hosts the same priority. In many situations, it is desirable to give the file and other servers more bandwidth than clients, so they can be given two or more bytes per tick. This modified algorithm is called **weighted fair queueing** and is widely used. Sometimes the weight is equal to the number of virtual circuits or flows coming out of a machine, so each process gets equal bandwidth. An efficient implementation of the algorithm is discussed in (Shreedhar and Varghese, 1995).

Hop-by-Hop Choke Packets

At high speeds and over long distances, sending a choke packet to the source hosts does not work well because the reaction is so slow. Consider, for example, a host in San Francisco (router A in Fig. 5-30) that is sending traffic to a host in New York (router D in Fig. 5-30) at 155 Mbps. If the New York host begins to run out of buffers, it will take about 30 msec for a choke packet to get back to San Francisco to tell it to slow down. The choke packet propagation is shown as the second, third, and fourth steps in Fig. 5-30(a). In those 30 msec, another 4.6 megabits (e.g., over 10,000 ATM cells) will have been sent. Even if the host in San Francisco completely shuts down immediately, the 4.6 megabits in the pipe will continue to pour in and have to be dealt with. Only in the seventh diagram in Fig. 5-30(a) will the New York router notice a slower flow.

An alternative approach is to have the choke packet take effect at every hop it passes through, as shown in the sequence of Fig. 5-30(b). Here, as soon as the choke packet reaches F, F is required to reduce the flow to D. Doing so will require F to devote more buffers to the flow, since the source is still sending away at full blast, but it gives D immediate relief, like a headache remedy in a television commercial. In the next step, the choke packet reaches E, which tells E to reduce the flow to F. This action puts a greater demand on E's buffers but gives F immediate relief. Finally, the choke packet reaches A and the flow genuinely slows down.

The net effect of this hop-by-hop scheme is to provide quick relief at the point of congestion at the price of using up more buffers upstream. In this way congestion can be nipped in the bud without losing any packets. The idea is discussed in more detail and simulation results are given in (Mishra and Kanakia, 1992).

5.3.7. Load Shedding

When none of the above methods make the congestion disappear, routers can bring out the heavy artillery: load shedding. **Load shedding** is a fancy way of saying that when routers are being inundated by packets that they cannot handle, they just throw them away. The term comes from the world of electrical power generation where it refers to the practice of utilities intentionally blacking out certain areas to save the entire grid from collapsing on hot summer days when the demand for electricity greatly exceeds the supply.

A router drowning in packets can just pick packets at random to drop, but usually it can do better than that. Which packet to discard may depend on the applications running. For file transfer, an old packet is worth more than a new one because dropping packet 6 and keeping packets 7 through 10 will cause a gap at the receiver that may force packets 6 through 10 to be retransmitted (if the receiver routinely discards out-of-order packets). In a 12-packet file, dropping 6 may require 7 through 12 to be retransmitted, whereas dropping 10 may require only 10 through 12 to be retransmitted. In contrast, for multimedia, a new packet is more important than an old one. The former policy (old is better than new) is often called **wine** and the latter (new is better than old) is often called **milk**.

A step above this in intelligence requires cooperation from the senders. For many applications, some packets are more important than others. For example, certain algorithms for compressing video periodically transmit an entire frame and then send subsequent frames as differences from the last full frame. In this case, dropping a packet that is part of a difference is preferable to dropping one that is part of a full frame. As another example, consider transmitting a document containing ASCII text and pictures. Losing a line of pixels in some image is far less damaging than losing a line of readable text.

To implement an intelligent discard policy, applications must mark their packets in priority classes to indicate how important they are. If they do this, when

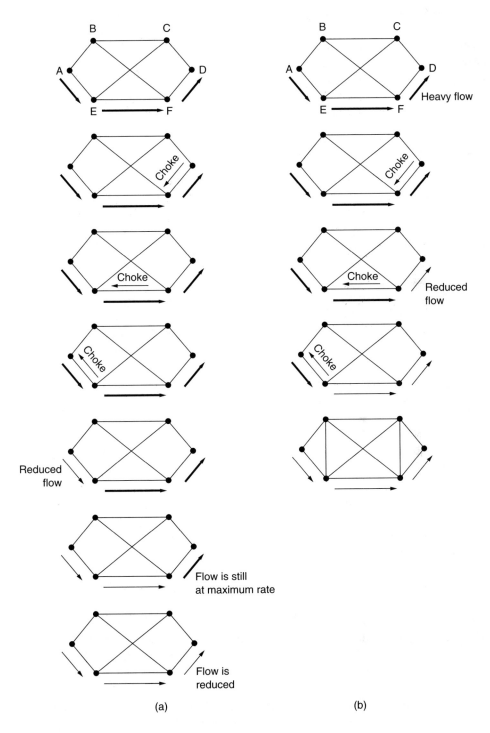

Fig. 5-30. (a) A choke packet that affects only the source. (b) A choke packet that affects each hop it passes through.

packets have to be discarded, routers can first drop packets from the lowest class, then the next lowest class, and so on. Of course, unless there is some significant incentive to mark packets as anything other than VERY IMPORTANT—NEVER, EVER DISCARD, nobody will do it.

The incentive might be in the form of money, with the low-priority packets being cheaper to send than the high-priority ones. Alternatively, priority classes could be coupled with traffic shaping. For example, there might be a rule saying that when the token bucket algorithm is being used and a packet arrives at a moment when no token is available, it may still be sent, provided that it is marked as the lowest possible priority, and thus subject to discard the instant trouble appears. Under conditions of light load, users might be happy to operate in this way, but as the load increases and packets actually begin to be discarded, they might cut back and only send packets when tokens are available.

Another option is to allow hosts to exceed the limits specified in the agreement negotiated when the virtual circuit was set up (e.g., use a higher bandwidth than allowed), but subject to the condition that all excess traffic be marked as low priority. Such a strategy is actually not a bad idea, because it makes more efficient use of idle resources, allowing hosts to use them as long as nobody else is interested, but without establishing a right to them when times get tough.

Marking packets by class requires one or more header bits in which to put the priority. ATM cells have 1 bit reserved in the header for this purpose, so every ATM cell is labeled either as low priority or high priority. ATM switches indeed use this bit when making discard decisions.

In some networks, packets are grouped together into larger units that are used for retransmission purposes. For example, in ATM networks, what we have been calling "packets" are fixed-length cells. These cells are just fragments of "messages." When a cell is dropped, ultimately the entire "message" will be retransmitted, not just the missing cell. Under these conditions, a router that drops a cell might as well drop all the rest of the cells in that message, since transmitting them costs bandwidth and wins nothing—even if they get through they will still be retransmitted later.

Simulation results show that when a router senses trouble on the horizon, it is better off starting to discard packets early, rather than wait until it becomes completely clogged up (Floyd and Jacobson, 1993; Romanow and Floyd, 1994). Doing so may prevent the congestion from getting a foothold.

5.3.8. Jitter Control

For applications such as audio and video transmission, it does not matter much if the packets take 20 msec or 30 msec to be delivered, as long as the transit time is constant. Having some packets taking 20 msec and others taking 30 msec will give an uneven quality to the sound or image. Thus the agreement might be that 99 percent of the packets be delivered with a delay in the range of 24.5 msec to 25.5 msec. The mean value chosen must be feasible, of course. In other words, an average amount of congestion must be calculated in.

The jitter can be bounded by computing the expected transit time for each hop along the path. When a packet arrives at a router, the router checks to see how much the packet is behind or ahead of its schedule. This information is stored in the packet and updated at each hop. If the packet is ahead of schedule, it is held just long enough to get it back on schedule. If it is behind schedule, the router tries to get it out the door quickly. In fact, the algorithm for determining which of several packets competing for an output line should go next can always choose the packet furthest behind in its schedule. In this way, packets that are ahead of schedule get slowed down and packets that are behind schedule get speeded up, in both cases reducing the amount of jitter.

5.3.9. Congestion Control for Multicasting

All of the congestion control algorithms discussed so far deal with messages from a single source to a single destination. In this section we will describe a way of managing multicast flows from multiple sources to multiple destinations. For example, imagine several closed-circuit television stations transmitting audio and video streams to a group of receivers, each of whom can view one or more stations at once and are free to switch from station to station at will. An application of this technology might be a video conference, in which each participant could focus on the current speaker or on the boss' expression, as desired.

In many multicast applications, groups can change membership dynamically, for example, as people enter a video conference or get bored and switch to a soap opera. Under these conditions, the approach of having the senders reserve bandwidth in advance does not work well, as it would require each sender to track all entries and exits of its audience and regenerate the spanning tree at each change. For a system designed to transmit cable television, with millions of subscribers, it would not work at all.

RSVP—Resource reSerVation Protocol

One interesting solution that can handle this environment is the **RSVP** protocol (Zhang et al., 1993). It allows multiple senders to transmit to multiple groups of receivers, permits individual receivers to switch channels freely, and optimizes bandwidth use while at the same time eliminating congestion.

In its simplest form, the protocol uses multicast routing using spanning trees, as discussed earlier. Each group is assigned a group address. To send to a group, a sender puts the group's address in its packets. The standard multicast routing algorithm then builds a spanning tree covering all group members. The routing algorithm is not part of RSVP. The only difference with normal multicasting is a little extra information that is multicast to the group periodically to tell the routers along the tree to maintain certain data structures in their memories.

As an example, consider the network of Fig. 5-31(a). Hosts 1 and 2 are multicast senders, and hosts 3, 4, and 5 are multicast receivers. In this example, the senders and receivers are disjoint, but in general, the two sets may overlap. The multicast trees for hosts 1 and 2 are shown in Fig. 5-31(b) and Fig. 5-31(c), respectively.

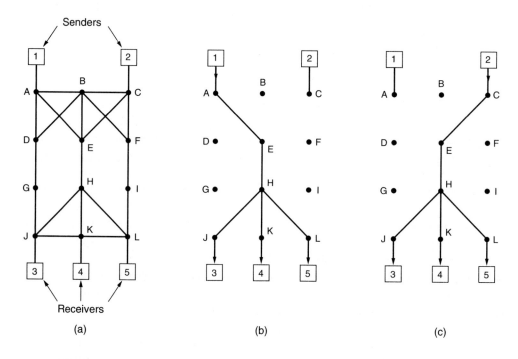

Fig. 5-31. (a) A network. (b) The multicast spanning tree for host 1. (c) The multicast spanning tree for host 2.

To get better reception and eliminate congestion, any of the receivers in a group can send a reservation message up the tree to the sender. The message is propagated using the reverse path forwarding algorithm discussed earlier. At each hop, the router notes the reservation and reserves the necessary bandwidth. If insufficient bandwidth is available, it reports back failure. By the time the message gets back to the source, bandwidth has been reserved all the way from the sender to the receiver making the reservation request along the spanning tree.

An example of such a reservation is shown in Fig. 5-32(a). Here host 3 has requested a channel to host 1. Once it has been established, packets can flow from 1 to 3 without congestion. Now consider what happens if host 3 next reserves a channel to the other sender, host 2, so the user can watch two television programs at once. A second path is reserved, as illustrated in Fig. 5-32(b). Note that two separate channels are needed from host 3 to router E because two independent streams are being transmitted.

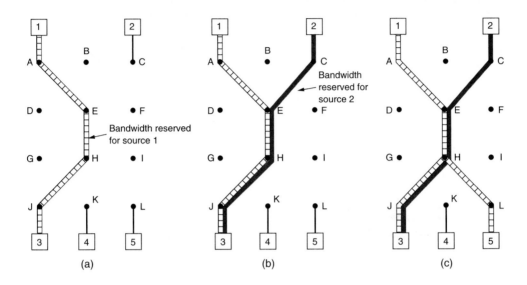

Fig. 5-32. (a) Host 3 requests a channel to host 1. (b) Host 3 then requests a second channel, to host 2. (c) Host 5 requests a channel to host 1.

Finally, in Fig. 5-32(c), host 5 decides to watch the program being transmitted by host 1 and also makes a reservation. First, dedicated bandwidth is reserved as far as router H. However, this router sees that it already has a feed from host 1, so if the necessary bandwidth has already been reserved, it does not have to reserve any more. Note that hosts 3 and 5 might have asked for different amounts of bandwidth (e.g., 3 has a black-and-white television set, so it does not want the color information), so the capacity reserved must be large enough to satisfy the greediest receiver.

When making a reservation, a receiver can (optionally) specify one or more sources that it wants to receive from. It can also specify whether these choices are fixed for the duration of the reservation, or whether the receiver wants to keep open the option of changing sources later. The routers use this information to optimize bandwidth planning. In particular, two receivers are only set up to share a path if they both agree not to change sources later on.

The reason for this strategy in the fully dynamic case is that reserved bandwidth is decoupled from the choice of source. Once a receiver has reserved bandwidth, it can switch to another source and keep that portion of the existing path that is valid for the new source. If host 2 is transmitting several video streams, for example, host 3 may switch between them at will without changing its reservation: the routers do not care what program the receiver is watching.

5.4. INTERNETWORKING

Up until now, we have implicitly assumed that there is a single homogeneous network, with each machine using the same protocol in each layer. Unfortunately, this assumption is wildly optimistic. Many different networks exist, including LANs, MANs, and WANs. Numerous protocols are in widespread use in every layer. In the following sections we will take a careful look at the issues that arise when two or more networks are together to form an **internet**.

Considerable controversy exists about the question of whether today's abundance of network types is a temporary condition that will go away as soon as everyone realizes how wonderful [fill in your favorite network] is, or whether it is an inevitable, but permanent feature of the world that is here to stay. Having different networks invariably means having different protocols.

We believe that a variety of different networks (and thus protocols) will always be around, for the following reasons. First of all, the installed base of different networks is large and growing. Nearly all UNIX shops run TCP/IP. Many large businesses still have mainframes running SNA. DEC is still developing DECnet. Personal computer LANs often use Novell NCP/IPX or AppleTalk. ATM systems are starting to be widespread. Finally, specialized protocols are often used on satellite, cellular, and infrared networks. This trend will continue for years due to the large number of existing networks and because not all vendors perceive it in their interest for their customers to be able to easily migrate to another vendor's system.

Second, as computers and networks get cheaper, the place where decisions get made moves downward. Many companies have a policy to the effect that purchases costing over a million dollars have to be approved by top management, purchases costing over 100,000 dollars have to be approved by middle management, but purchases under 100,000 dollars can be made by department heads without any higher approval. This can easily lead to the accounting department installing an Ethernet, the engineering department installing a token bus, and the personnel department installing a token ring.

Third, different networks (e.g., ATM and wireless) have radically different technology, so it should not be surprising that as new hardware developments occur, new software will be created to fit the new hardware. For example, the average home now is like the average office ten years ago: it is full of computers that do not talk to one another. In the future, it may be commonplace for the telephone, the television set, and other appliances all to be networked together, so they can be controlled remotely. This new technology will undoubtedly bring new protocols.

As an example of how different networks interact, consider the following example. At most universities, the computer science and electrical engineering departments have their own LANs, often different. In addition, the university computer center often has a mainframe and supercomputer, the former for faculty members in the humanities who do not wish to get into the computer maintenance business, and the latter for physicists who want to crunch numbers. As a consequence of these various networks and facilities, the following scenarios are easy to imagine:

1. LAN-LAN: A computer scientist downloading a file to engineering.

2. LAN-WAN: A computer scientist sending mail to a distant physicist.

3. WAN-WAN: Two poets exchanging sonnets.

4. LAN-WAN-LAN: Engineers at different universities communicating.

Figure 5-33 illustrates these four types of connections as dotted lines. In each case, it is necessary to insert a "black box" at the junction between two networks, to handle the necessary conversions as packets move from one network to the other.

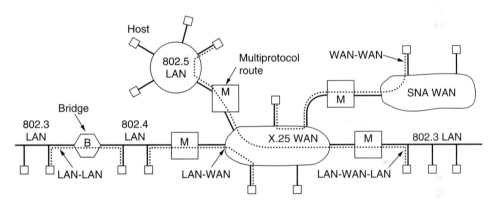

Fig. 5-33. Network interconnection.

The name used for the black box connecting two networks depends on the layer that does the work. Some common names are given below (although there is not much agreement on terminology in this area).

Layer 1: Repeaters copy individual bits between cable segments.

Layer 2: Bridges store and forward data link frames between LANs.

Layer 3: Multiprotocol routers forward packets between dissimilar networks.

Layer 4: Transport gateways connect byte streams in the transport layer.

Above 4: Application gateways allow interworking above layer 4.

For convenience, we will sometimes use the term "gateway" to mean any device that connects two or more dissimilar networks.

Repeaters are low-level devices that just amplify or regenerate weak signals. They are needed to provide current to drive long cables. In 802.3, for example, the timing properties of the MAC protocol (the value of τ chosen) allow cables up to 2.5 km, but the transceiver chips can only provide enough power to drive 500 meters. The solution is to use repeaters to extend the cable length where that is desired.

Unlike repeaters, which copy the bits as they arrive, **bridges** are store-and-forward devices. A bridge accepts an entire frame and passes it up to the data link layer where the checksum is verified. Then the frame is sent down to the physical layer for forwarding on a different network. Bridges can make minor changes to the frame before forwarding it, such as adding or deleting some fields from the frame header. Since they are data link layer devices, they do not deal with headers at layer 3 and above and cannot make changes or decisions that depend on them.

Multiprotocol routers are conceptually similar to bridges, except that they are found in the network layer. They just take incoming packets from one line and forward them on another, just as all routers do, but the lines may belong to different networks and use different protocols (e.g., IP, IPX, and the OSI connectionless packet protocol, CLNP). Like all routers, multiprotocol routers operate at the level of the network layer.

Transport gateways make a connection between two networks at the transport layer. We will discuss this possibility later when we come to concatenated virtual circuits.

Finally, **application gateways** connect two parts of an application in the application layer. For example, to send mail from an Internet machine using the Internet mail format to an ISO MOTIS mailbox, one could send the message to a mail gateway. The mail gateway would unpack the message, convert it to MOTIS format, and then forward it on the second network using the network and transport protocols used there.

When a gateway is between two WANs run by different organizations, possibly in different countries, the joint operation of one workstation-class machine can lead to a lot of finger pointing. To eliminate these problems, a slightly different approach can be taken. The gateway is effectively ripped apart in the middle and the two parts are connected with a wire. Each of the halves is called a **half-gateway** and each one is owned and operated by one of the network operators. The whole problem of gatewaying then reduces to agreeing to a common protocol to use on the wire, one that is neutral and does not favor either party. Figure 5-34 shows both full and half-gateways. Either kind can be used in any layer (e.g., half-bridges also exist).

That all said, the situation is murkier in practice than it is in theory. Many devices on the market combine bridge and router functionality. The key property of a pure bridge is that it examines data link layer frame headers and does not inspect or modify the network layer packets inside the frames. A bridge cannot

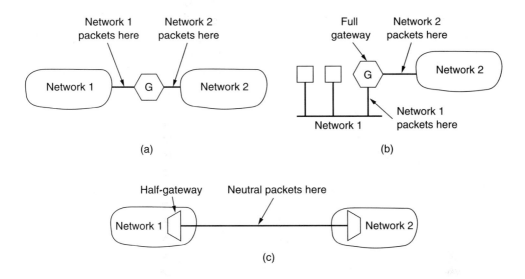

Fig. 5-34. (a) A full gateway between two WANs. (b) A full gateway between a LAN and a WAN. (c) Two half-gateways.

tell and does not care whether the frame it is forwarding from an 802.x LAN to an 802.y contains an IP, IPX, or CLNP packet in the payload field.

A router, in contrast, knows very well whether it is an IP router, an IPX router, a CLNP router, or all three combined. It examines these headers and makes decisions based on the addresses found there. On the other hand, when a pure router hands off a packet to the data link layer, it does not know or care whether it will be carried in an Ethernet frame or a token ring frame. That is the data link layer's responsibility.

The confusion in the industry comes from two sources. First, functionally, bridges and routers are not all that different. They each accept incoming PDUs (Protocol Data Units), examine some header fields, and make decisions about where to send the PDUs based on header information and internal tables.

Second, many commercial products are sold under the wrong label or combine the functionality of both bridges and routers. For example, source routing bridges are not really bridges at all, since they involve a protocol layer above the data link layer to do their job. For an illuminating discussion of bridges versus routers, see Chap. 12 of (Perlman, 1992).

5.4.1. How Networks Differ

Networks can differ in many ways. In Fig. 5-35 we list some of the differences that can occur in the network layer. It is papering over these differences that makes internetworking more difficult than operating within a single network.

Item	Some Possibilities
Service offered	Connection-oriented versus connectionless
Protocols	IP, IPX, CLNP, AppleTalk, DECnet, etc.
Addressing	Flat (802) versus hierarchical (IP)
Multicasting	Present or absent (also broadcasting)
Packet size	Every network has its own maximum
Quality of service	May be present or absent; many different kinds
Error handling	Reliable, ordered, and unordered delivery
Flow control	Sliding window, rate control, other, or none
Congestion control	Leaky bucket, choke packets, etc.
Security	Privacy rules, encryption, etc.
Parameters	Different timeouts, flow specifications, etc.
Accounting	By connect time, by packet, by byte, or not at all

Fig. 5-35. Some of the many ways networks can differ.

When packets sent by a source on one network must transit one or more foreign networks before reaching the destination network (which also may be different from the source network), many problems can occur at the interfaces between networks. To start with, when packets from a connection-oriented network must transit a connectionless one, they may be reordered, something the sender does not expect and the receiver is not prepared to deal with. Protocol conversions will often be needed, which can be difficult if the required functionality cannot be expressed. Address conversions will also be needed, which may require some kind of directory system. Passing multicast packets through a network that does not support multicasting requires generating separate packets for each destination.

The differing maximum packet sizes used by different networks is a major headache. How do you pass an 8000-byte packet through a network whose maximum size is 1500 bytes? Differing qualities of service is an issue when a packet that has real-time delivery constraints passes through a network that does offer any real-time guarantees.

Error, flow, and congestion control frequently differ among different networks. If the source and destination both expect all packets to be delivered in sequence without error, yet an intermediate network just discards packets whenever it smells congestion on the horizon, or packets can wander around aimlessly for a while and then suddenly emerge and be delivered, many applications will break. Different security mechanisms, parameter settings, and accounting rules, and even national privacy laws also can cause problems.

5.4.2. Concatenated Virtual Circuits

Two styles of internetworking are common: a connection-oriented concatenation of virtual circuit subnets, and a datagram internet style. We will now examine these in turn. In the concatenated virtual circuit model, shown in Fig. 5-36, a connection to a host in a distant network is set up in a way similar to the way connections are normally established. The subnet sees that the destination is remote and builds a virtual circuit to the router nearest the destination network. Then it constructs a virtual circuit from that router to an external "gateway" (multiprotocol router). This gateway records the existence of the virtual circuit in its tables and proceeds to build another virtual circuit to a router in the next subnet. This process continues until the destination host has been reached.

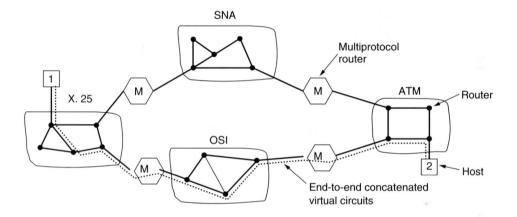

Fig. 5-36. Internetworking using concatenated virtual circuits.

Once data packets begin flowing along the path, each gateway relays incoming packets, converting between packet formats and virtual circuit numbers as needed. Clearly, all data packets must traverse the same sequence of gateways, and thus arrive in order.

The essential feature of this approach is that a sequence of virtual circuits is set up from the source through one or more gateways to the destination. Each gateway maintains tables telling which virtual circuits pass through it, where they are to be routed, and what the new virtual circuit number is.

Although Fig. 5-36 shows the connection made with a full gateway, it could equally well be done with half-gateways.

This scheme works best when all the networks have roughly the same properties. For example, if all of them guarantee reliable delivery of network layer packets, then barring a crash somewhere along the route, the flow from source to destination will also be reliable. Similarly, if none of them guarantee reliable delivery, then the concatenation of the virtual circuits is not reliable either. On the other hand, if the source machine is on a network that does guarantee reliable delivery, but one of the intermediate networks can lose packets, the concatenation has fundamentally changed the nature of the service.

Concatenated virtual circuits are also common in the transport layer. In particular, it is possible to build a bit pipe using, say, OSI, which terminates in a gateway, and have a TCP connection go from the gateway to the next gateway. In this manner, an end-to-end virtual circuit can be built spanning different networks and protocols.

5.4.3. Connectionless Internetworking

The alternative internetwork model is the datagram model, shown in Fig. 5-37. In this model, the only service the network layer offers to the transport layer is the ability to inject datagrams into the subnet and hope for the best. There is no notion of a virtual circuit at all in the network layer, let alone a concatenation of them. This model does not require all packets belonging to one connection to traverse the same sequence of gateways. In Fig. 5-37 datagrams from host 1 to host 2 are shown taking different routes through the internetwork. A routing decision is made separately for each packet, possibly depending on the traffic at the moment the packet is sent. This strategy can use multiple routes and thus achieve a higher bandwidth than the concatenated virtual circuit model. On the other hand, there is no guarantee that the packets arrive at the destination in order, assuming that they arrive at all.

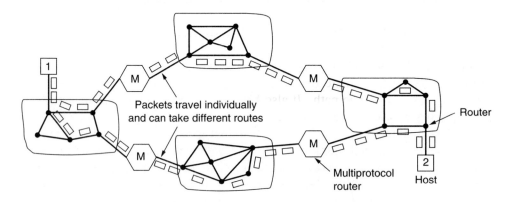

Fig. 5-37. A connectionless internet.

The model of Fig. 5-37 is not quite as simple as it looks. For one thing, if each network has its own network layer protocol, it is not possible for a packet from one network to transit another one. One could imagine the multiprotocol routers actually trying to translate from one format to another, but unless the two formats are close relatives with the same information fields, such conversions will always be incomplete and often doomed to failure. For this reason, conversion is rarely attempted.

A second, and more serious problem, is addressing. Imagine a simple case: a host on the Internet is trying to send an IP packet to a host on an adjoining OSI host. The OSI datagram protocol, CLNP, was based on IP and is close enough to it that a conversion might well work. The trouble is that IP packets all carry the 32-bit Internet address of the destination host in a header field. OSI hosts do not have 32-bit Internet addresses. They use decimal addresses similar to telephone numbers.

To make it possible for the multiprotocol router to convert between formats, someone would have to assign a 32-bit Internet address to each OSI host. Taken to the limit, this approach would mean assigning an Internet address to every machine in the world that an Internet host might want to talk to. It would also mean assigning an OSI address to every machine in the world that an OSI host might want to talk to. The same problem occurs with every other address space (SNA, AppleTalk, etc.). The problems here are insurmountable. In addition, someone would have to maintain a database mapping everything to everything.

Another idea is to design a universal "internet" packet and have all routers recognize it. This approach is, in fact, what IP is—a packet designed to be carried through many networks. The only problem is that IPX, CLNP, and other "universal" packets exist too, making all of them less than universal. Getting everybody to agree to a single format is just not possible.

Let us now briefly recap the two ways internetworking can be attacked. The concatenated virtual circuit model has essentially the same advantages as using virtual circuits within a single subnet: buffers can be reserved in advance, sequencing can be guaranteed, short headers can be used, and the troubles caused by delayed duplicate packets can be avoided.

It also has the same disadvantages: table space required in the routers for each open connection, no alternate routing to avoid congested areas, and vulnerability to router failures along the path. It also has the disadvantage of being difficult, if not impossible, to implement if one of the networks involved is an unreliable datagram network.

The properties of the datagram approach to internetworking are the same as those of datagram subnets: more potential for congestion, but also more potential for adapting to it, robustness in the face of router failures, and longer headers needed. Various adaptive routing algorithms are possible in an internet, just as they are within a single datagram network.

A major advantage of the datagram approach to internetworking is that it can be used over subnets that do not use virtual circuits inside. Many LANs, mobile networks (e.g., aircraft and naval fleets), and even some WANs fall into this category. When an internet includes one of these, serious problems occur if the internetworking strategy is based on virtual circuits.

5.4.4. Tunneling

Handling the general case of making two different networks interwork is exceedingly difficult. However, there is a common special case that is manageable. This case is where the source and destination hosts are on the same type of network, but there is a different network in between. As an example, think of an international bank with a TCP/IP based Ethernet in Paris, a TCP/IP based Ethernet in London, and a PTT WAN in between, as shown in Fig. 5-38.

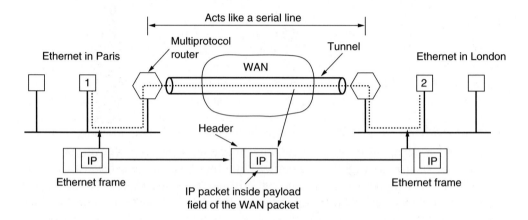

Fig. 5-38. Tunneling a packet from Paris to London.

The solution to this problem is a technique called **tunneling**. To send an IP packet to host 2, host 1 constructs the packet containing the IP address of host 2, inserts it into an Ethernet frame addressed to the Paris multiprotocol router, and puts it on the Ethernet. When the multiprotocol router gets the frame, it removes the IP packet, inserts it in the payload field of the WAN network layer packet, and addresses the latter to the WAN address of the London multiprotocol router. When it gets there, the London router removes the IP packet and sends it to host 2 inside an Ethernet frame.

The WAN can be seen as a big tunnel extending from one multiprotocol router to the other. The IP packet just travels from one end of the tunnel to the other, snug in its nice box. It does not have to worry about dealing with the WAN at all. Neither do the hosts on either Ethernet. Only the multiprotocol router has to understand IP and WAN packets. In effect, the entire distance from the middle of one multiprotocol router to the middle of the other acts like a serial line.

An analogy may make tunneling clearer. Consider a person driving her car from Paris to London. Within France, the car moves under its own power, but when it hits the English Channel, it is loaded into a high-speed train and transported to England through the Chunnel (cars are not permitted to drive through the Chunnel). Effectively, the car is being carried as freight, as depicted in Fig. 5-39.

At the far end, the car is let loose on the English roads and once again continues to move under its own power. Tunneling of packets through a foreign network works the same way.

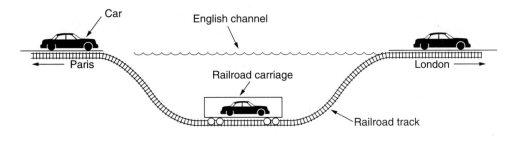

Fig. 5-39. Tunneling a car from France to England.

5.4.5. Internetwork Routing

Routing through an internetwork is similar to routing within a single subnet, but with some added complications. Consider, for example, the internetwork of Fig. 5-40(a) in which five networks are connected by six multiprotocol routers. Making a graph model of this situation is complicated by the fact that every multiprotocol router can directly access (i.e., send packets to) every other router connected to any network to which it is connected. For example, *B* in Fig. 5-40(a) can directly access *A* and *C* via network 2 and also *D* via network 3. This leads to the graph of Fig. 5-40(b).

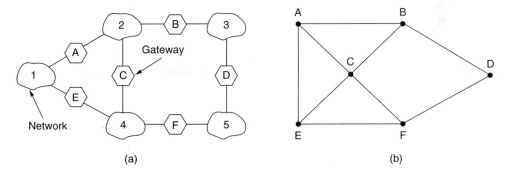

Fig. 5-40. (a) An internetwork. (b) A graph of the internetwork.

Once the graph has been constructed, known routing algorithms, such as the distance vector and link state algorithms, can be applied to the set of multiprotocol routers. This gives a two-level routing algorithm: within each network an **interior gateway protocol** is used, but between the networks, an **exterior gateway protocol** is used ("gateway" is an older term for "router"). In fact, since each network is independent, they may all use different algorithms. Because each network in an internetwork is independent of all the others, it is often referred to as an **Autonomous System (AS)**.

A typical internet packet starts out on its LAN addressed to the local multiprotocol router (in the MAC layer header). After it gets there, the network layer code decides which multiprotocol router to forward the packet to, using its own routing tables. If that router can be reached using the packet's native network protocol, it is forwarded there directly. Otherwise it is tunneled there, encapsulated in the protocol required by the intervening network. This process is repeated until the packet reaches the destination network.

One of the differences between internetwork routing and intranetwork routing is that internetwork routing often requires crossing international boundaries. Various laws suddenly come into play, such as Sweden's strict privacy laws about exporting personal data about Swedish citizens from Sweden. Another example is the Canadian law saying that data traffic originating in Canada and ending in Canada may not leave the country. This law means that traffic from Windsor, Ontario to Vancouver may not be routed via nearby Detroit.

Another difference between interior and exterior routing is the cost. Within a single network, a single charging algorithm normally applies. However, different networks may be under different managements, and one route may be less expensive than another. Similarly, the quality of service offered by different networks may be different, and this may be a reason to choose one route over another.

In a large internetwork, choosing the best route may be a time-consuming operation. Estrin et al. (1992) have proposed dealing with this problem by precomputing routes for popular (source, destination) pairs and storing them in a database to be consulted at route selection time.

5.4.6. Fragmentation

Each network imposes some maximum size on its packets. These limits have various causes, among them:

1. Hardware (e.g., the width of a TDM transmission slot).

2. Operating system (e.g., all buffers are 512 bytes).

3. Protocols (e.g., the number of bits in the packet length field).

4. Compliance with some (inter)national standard.

5. Desire to reduce error induced retransmissions to some level.

6. Desire to prevent one packet from occupying the channel too long.

The result of all these factors is that the network designers are not free to choose any maximum packet size they wish. Maximum payloads range from 48 bytes

(ATM cells) to 65,515 bytes (IP packets), although the payload size in higher layers is often larger.

An obvious problem appears when a large packet wants to travel through a network whose maximum packet size is too small. One solution is to make sure the problem does not occur in the first place. In other words, the internet should use a routing algorithm that avoids sending packets through networks that cannot handle them. However, this solution is no solution at all. What happens if the original source packet is too large to be handled by the destination network? The routing algorithm can hardly bypass the destination.

Basically, the only solution to the problem is to allow gateways to break packets up into **fragments**, sending each fragment as a separate internet packet. However, as every parent of a small child knows, converting a large object into small fragments is considerably easier than the reverse process. (Physicists have even given this effect a name: the second law of thermodynamics.) Packet-switching networks, too, have trouble putting the fragments back together again.

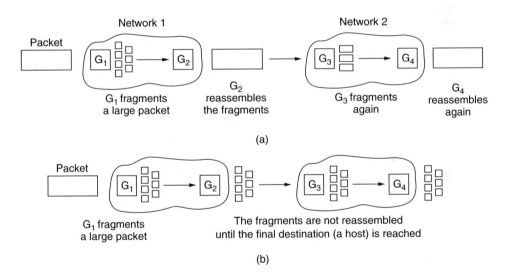

Fig. 5-41. (a) Transparent fragmentation. (b) Nontransparent fragmentation.

Two opposing strategies exist for recombining the fragments back into the original packet. The first strategy is to make fragmentation caused by a "small-packet" network transparent to any subsequent networks through which the packet must pass on its way to the ultimate destination. This option is shown in Fig. 5-41(a). When an oversized packet arrives at a gateway, the gateway breaks it up into fragments. Each fragment is addressed to the same exit gateway, where the pieces are recombined. In this way passage through the small-packet network has been made transparent. Subsequent networks are not even aware that fragmentation has occurred. ATM networks, for example, have special hardware to provide transparent fragmentation of packets into cells and then reassembly of cells into packets. In the ATM world, fragmentation is called segmentation; the concept is the same, but some of the details are different.

Transparent fragmentation is simple but has some problems. For one thing, the exit gateway must know when it has received all the pieces, so that either a count field or an "end of packet" bit must be included in each packet. For another thing, all packets must exit via the same gateway. By not allowing some fragments to follow one route to the ultimate destination, and other fragments a disjoint route, some performance may be lost. A last problem is the overhead required to repeatedly reassemble and then refragment a large packet passing through a series of small-packet networks.

The other fragmentation strategy is to refrain from recombining fragments at any intermediate gateways. Once a packet has been fragmented, each fragment is treated as though it were an original packet. All fragments are passed through the exit gateway (or gateways), as shown in Fig. 5-41(b). Recombination occurs only at the destination host.

Nontransparent fragmentation also has some problems. For example, it requires *every* host to be able to do reassembly. Yet another problem is that when a large packet is fragmented the total overhead increases, because each fragment must have a header. Whereas in the first method this overhead disappears as soon as the small-packet network is exited, in this method the overhead remains for the rest of the journey. An advantage of this method, however, is that multiple exit gateways can now be used and higher performance can be achieved. Of course, if the concatenated virtual circuit model is being used, this advantage is of no use.

When a packet is fragmented, the fragments must be numbered in such a way that the original data stream can be reconstructed. One way of numbering the fragments is to use a tree. If packet 0 must be split up, the pieces are called 0.0, 0.1, 0.2, etc. If these fragments themselves must be fragmented later on, the pieces are numbered 0.0.0, 0.0.1, 0.0.2, . . . , 0.1.0, 0.1.1, 0.1.2, etc. If enough fields have been reserved in the header for the worst case and no duplicates are generated anywhere, this scheme is sufficient to ensure that all the pieces can be correctly reassembled at the destination, no matter what order they arrive in.

However, if even one network loses or discards packets, there is a need for end-to-end retransmissions, with unfortunate effects for the numbering system. Suppose that a 1024-bit packet is initially fragmented into four equal-sized fragments, 0.0, 0.1, 0.2, and 0.3. Fragment 0.1 is lost, but the other parts arrive at the destination. Eventually, the source times out and retransmits the original packet again. Only this time the route taken passes through a network with a 512-bit limit, so two fragments are generated. When the new fragment 0.1 arrives at the destination, the receiver will think that all four pieces are now accounted for and reconstruct the packet incorrectly.

A completely different (and better) numbering system is for the internetwork protocol to define an elementary fragment size small enough that the elementary fragment can pass through every network. When a packet is fragmented, all the pieces are equal to the elementary fragment size except the last one, which may be shorter. An internet packet may contain several fragments, for efficiency reasons. The internet header must provide the original packet number, and the number of the (first) elementary fragment contained in the packet. As usual, there must also be a bit indicating that the last elementary fragment contained within the internet packet is the last one of the original packet.

This approach requires two sequence fields in the internet header: the original packet number, and the fragment number. There is clearly a trade-off between the size of the elementary fragment and the number of bits in the fragment number. Because the elementary fragment size is presumed to be acceptable to every network, subsequent fragmentation of an internet packet containing several fragments causes no problem. The ultimate limit here is to have the elementary fragment be a single bit or byte, with the fragment number then being the bit or byte offset within the original packet, as shown in Fig. 5-42.

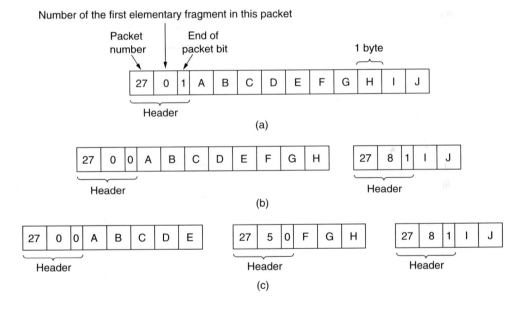

Fig. 5-42. Fragmentation when the elementary data size is 1 byte. (a) Original packet, containing 10 data bytes. (b) Fragments after passing through a network with maximum packet size of 8 bytes. (c) Fragments after passing through a size 5 gateway.

Some internet protocols take this method even further and consider the entire transmission on a virtual circuit to be one giant packet, so that each fragment contains the absolute byte number of the first byte within the fragment. Some other issues relating to fragmentation are discussed in (Kent and Mogul, 1987).

5.4.7. Firewalls

The ability to connect any computer, anywhere, to any other computer, any-where, is a mixed blessing. For individuals at home, wandering around the Internet is lots of fun. For corporate security managers, it is a nightmare. Most companies have large amounts of confidential information on-line—trade secrets, product development plans, marketing strategies, financial analyses, etc. Disclosure of this information to a competitor could have dire consequences.

In addition to the danger of information leaking out, there is also a danger of information leaking in. In particular, viruses, worms, and other digital pests (Kaufman et al., 1995) can breach security, destroy valuable data, and waste large amounts of administrators' time trying to clean up the mess they leave. Often they are imported by careless employees who want to play some nifty new game.

Consequently, mechanisms are needed to keep "good" bits in and "bad" bits out. One method is to use encryption. This approach protects data in transit between secure sites. We will study it in Chap. 7. However, encryption does nothing to keep digital pests and hackers out. To accomplish this goal, we need to look at firewalls (Chapman and Zwicky, 1995; and Cheswick and Bellovin, 1994).

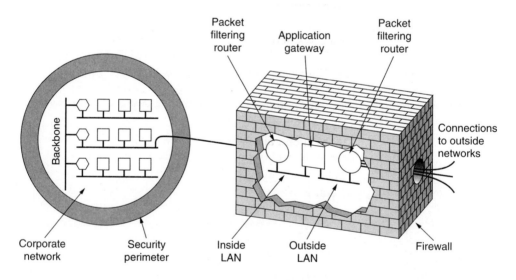

Fig. 5-43. A firewall consisting of two packet filters and an application gateway.

Firewalls are just a modern adaptation of that old medieval security standby: digging a deep moat around your castle. This design forced everyone entering or leaving the castle to pass over a single drawbridge, where they could be inspected by the I/O police. With networks, the same trick is possible: a company can have many LANs connected in arbitrary ways, but all traffic to or from the company is forced through an electronic drawbridge (firewall), as shown in Fig. 5-43.

The firewall in this configuration has two components: two routers that do packet filtering and an application gateway. Simpler configurations also exist, but the advantage of this design is that every packet must transit two filters and an application gateway to go in or out. No other route exists. Readers who think that one security checkpoint is enough clearly have not made an international flight on a scheduled airline recently.

Each **packet filter** is a standard router equipped with some extra functionality. The extra functionality allows every incoming or outgoing packet to be inspected. Packets meeting some criterion are forwarded normally. Those that fail the test are dropped.

In Fig. 5-43, most likely the packet filter on the inside LAN checks outgoing packets and the one on the outside LAN checks incoming packets. Packets crossing the first hurdle go to the application gateway for further examination. The point of putting the two packet filters on different LANs is to ensure that no packet gets in or out without having to pass through the application gateway: there is no path around it.

Packet filters are typically driven by tables configured by the system administrator. These tables list sources and destinations that are acceptable, sources and destinations that are blocked, and default rules about what to do with packets coming from or going to other machines.

In the common case of a UNIX setting, a source or destination consists of an IP address and a port. Ports indicate which service is desired. For example, port 23 is for Telnet, port 79 is for Finger, and port 119 is for USENET news. A company could block incoming packets for all IP addresses combined with one of these ports. In this way, no one outside the company could log in via Telnet, or look up people using the Finger daemon. Furthermore, the company would be spared from having employees spend all day reading USENET news.

Blocking outgoing packets is trickier because although most sites stick to the standard port naming conventions, they are not forced to do so. Furthermore, for some important services, such as FTP (File Transfer Protocol), port numbers are assigned dynamically. In addition, although blocking TCP connections is difficult, blocking UDP packets is even harder because so little is known a priori about what they will do. Many packet filters simply ban UDP traffic altogether.

The second half of the firewall mechanism is the **application gateway**. Rather than just looking at raw packets, the gateway operates at the application level. A mail gateway, for example, can be set up to examine each message going in or coming out. For each one it makes a decision to transmit or discard it based on header fields, message size, or even the content (e.g., at a military installation, the presence of words like "nuclear" or "bomb" might cause some special action to be taken).

Installations are free to set up one or more application gateways for specific applications, but it is not uncommon for suspicious organizations to permit email in and out, and perhaps use of the World Wide Web, but ban everything else as too dicey. Combined with encryption and packet filtering, this arrangement offers a limited amount of security at the cost of some inconvenience.

One final note concerns wireless communication and firewalls. It is easy to design a system that is logically completely secure, but which, in practice, leaks like a sieve. This situation can occur if some of the machines are wireless and use radio communication, which passes right over the firewall in both directions.

5.5. THE NETWORK LAYER IN THE INTERNET

At the network layer, the Internet can be viewed as a collection of subnetworks or **Autonomous Systems (ASes)** that are connected together. There is no real structure, but several major backbones exist. These are constructed from high-bandwidth lines and fast routers. Attached to the backbones are regional (midlevel) networks, and attached to these regional networks are the LANs at many universities, companies, and Internet service providers. A sketch of this quasihierarchical organization is given in Fig. 5-44.

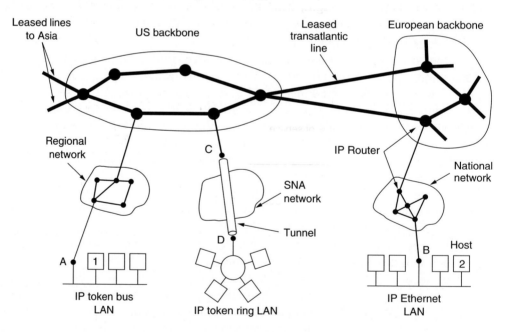

Fig. 5-44. The Internet is an interconnected collection of many networks.

The glue that holds the Internet together is the network layer protocol, **IP (Internet Protocol)**. Unlike most older network layer protocols, it was designed from the beginning with internetworking in mind. A good way to think of the network layer is this. Its job is to provide a best-efforts way to transport datagrams from source to destination, without regard to whether or not these machines are on the same network, or whether or not there are other networks in between them.

Communication in the Internet works as follows. The transport layer takes data streams and breaks them up into datagrams. In theory, datagrams can be up to 64 Kbytes each, but in practice they are usually around 1500 bytes. Each datagram is transmitted through the Internet, possibly being fragmented into smaller units as it goes. When all the pieces finally get to the destination machine, they are reassembled by the network layer into the original datagram. This datagram is then handed to the transport layer, which inserts it into the receiving process' input stream.

5.5.1. The IP Protocol

An appropriate place to start our study of the network layer in the Internet is the format of the IP datagrams themselves. An IP datagram consists of a header part and a text part. The header has a 20-byte fixed part and a variable length optional part. The header format is shown in Fig. 5-45. It is transmitted in big endian order: from left to right, with the high-order bit of the *Version* field going first. (The SPARC is big endian; the Pentium is little endian.) On little endian machines, software conversion is required on both transmission and reception.

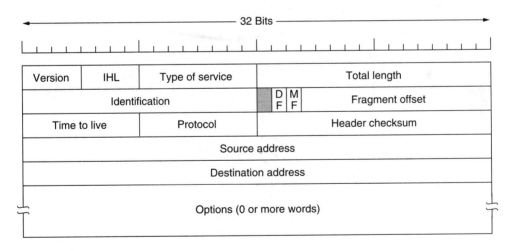

Fig. 5-45. The IP (Internet Protocol) header.

The *Version* field keeps track of which version of the protocol the datagram belongs to. By including the version in each datagram, it becomes possible to have the transition between versions take months, or even years, with some machines running the old version and others running the new one.

Since the header length is not constant, a field in the header, *IHL*, is provided to tell how long the header is, in 32-bit words. The minimum value is 5, which applies when no options are present. The maximum value of this 4-bit field is 15, which limits the header to 60 bytes, and thus the options field to 40 bytes. For some options, such as one that records the route a packet has taken, 40 bytes is far too small, making the option useless.

The *Type of service* field allows the host to tell the subnet what kind of service it wants. Various combinations of reliability and speed are possible. For digitized voice, fast delivery beats accurate delivery. For file transfer, error-free transmission is more important than fast transmission.

The field itself contains (from left to right), a three-bit *Precedence* field, three flags, *D*, *T*, and *R*, and 2 unused bits. The *Precedence* field is a priority, from 0 (normal) to 7 (network control packet). The three flag bits allow the host to specify what it cares most about from the set {Delay, Throughput, Reliability}. In theory, these fields allow routers to make choices between, for example, a satellite link with high throughput and high delay or a leased line with low throughput and low delay. In practice, current routers ignore the *Type of Service* field altogether.

The *Total length* includes everything in the datagram—both header and data. The maximum length is 65,535 bytes. At present, this upper limit is tolerable, but with future gigabit networks larger datagrams will be needed.

The *Identification* field is needed to allow the destination host to determine which datagram a newly arrived fragment belongs to. All the fragments of a datagram contain the same *Identification* value.

Next comes an unused bit and then two 1-bit fields. *DF* stands for Don't Fragment. It is an order to the routers not to fragment the datagram because the destination is incapable of putting the pieces back together again. For example, when a computer boots, its ROM might ask for a memory image to be sent to it as a single datagram. By marking the datagram with the *DF* bit, the sender knows it will arrive in one piece, even if this means that the datagram must avoid a small-packet network on the best path and take a suboptimal route. All machines are required to accept fragments of 576 bytes or less.

MF stands for More Fragments. All fragments except the last one have this bit set. It is needed to know when all fragments of a datagram have arrived.

The *Fragment offset* tells where in the current datagram this fragment belongs. All fragments except the last one in a datagram must be a multiple of 8 bytes, the elementary fragment unit. Since 13 bits are provided, there is a maximum of 8192 fragments per datagram, giving a maximum datagram length of 65,536 bytes, one more than the *Total length* field.

The *Time to live* field is a counter used to limit packet lifetimes. It is supposed to count time in seconds, allowing a maximum lifetime of 255 sec. It must be decremented on each hop and is supposed to be decremented multiple times when queued for a long time in a router. In practice, it just counts hops. When it hits zero, the packet is discarded and a warning packet is sent back to the source host. This feature prevents datagrams for wandering around forever, something that otherwise might happen if the routing tables ever become corrupted.

When the network layer has assembled a complete datagram, it needs to know what to do with it. The *Protocol* field tells it which transport process to give it to. TCP is one possibility, but so are UDP and some others. The numbering of protocols is global across the entire Internet and is defined in RFC 1700.

The *Header checksum* verifies the header only. Such a checksum is useful for detecting errors generated by bad memory words inside a router. The algorithm is to add up all the 16-bit halfwords as they arrive, using one's complement arithmetic and then take the one's complement of the result. For purposes of this algorithm, the *Header checksum* is assumed to be zero upon arrival. This algorithm is more robust than using a normal add. Note that the *Header checksum* must be recomputed at each hop, because at least one field always changes (the *Time to live* field), but tricks can be used to speed up the computation.

The *Source address* and *Destination address* indicate the network number and host number. We will discuss Internet addresses in the next section. The *Options* field was designed to provide an escape to allow subsequent versions of the protocol to include information not present in the original design, to permit experimenters to try out new ideas, and to avoid allocating header bits to information that is rarely needed. The options are variable length. Each begins with a 1-byte code identifying the option. Some options are followed by a 1-byte option length field, and then one or more data bytes. The *Options* field is padded out to a multiple of four bytes. Currently five options are defined, as listed in Fig. 5-46, but not all routers support all of them.

Option	Description
Security	Specifies how secret the datagram is
Strict source routing	Gives the complete path to be followed
Loose source routing	Gives a list of routers not to be missed
Record route	Makes each router append its IP address
Timestamp	Makes each router append its address and timestamp

Fig. 5-46. IP options.

The *Security* option tells how secret the information is. In theory, a military router might use this field to specify not to route through certain countries the military considers to be "bad guys." In practice, all routers ignore it, so its only practical function is to help spies find the good stuff more easily.

The *Strict source routing* option gives the complete path from source to destination as a sequence of IP addresses. The datagram is required to follow that exact route. It is most useful for system managers to send emergency packets when the routing tables are corrupted, or for making timing measurements.

The *Loose source routing* option requires the packet to traverse the list of routers specified, and in the order specified, but it is allowed to pass through other routers on the way. Normally, this option would only provide a few routers, to force a particular path. For example, to force a packet from London to Sydney to go west instead of east, this option might specify routers in New York, Los Angeles, and Honolulu. This option is most useful when political or economic considerations dictate passing through or avoiding certain countries.

The *Record route* option tells the routers along the path to append their IP address to the option field. This allows system managers to track down bugs in the routing algorithms ("Why are packets from Houston to Dallas all visiting Tokyo first?") When the ARPANET was first set up, no packet ever passed through more than nine routers, so 40 bytes of option was ample. As mentioned above, now it is too small.

Finally, the *Timestamp* option is like the *Record route* option, except that in addition to recording its 32-bit IP address, each router also records a 32-bit time-stamp. This option, too, is mostly for debugging routing algorithms.

5.5.2. IP Addresses

Every host and router on the Internet has an IP address, which encodes its network number and host number. The combination is unique: no two machines have the same IP address. All IP addresses are 32 bits long and are used in the *Source address* and *Destination address* fields of IP packets. The formats used for IP address are shown in Fig. 5-47. Those machines connected to multiple networks have a different IP address on each network.

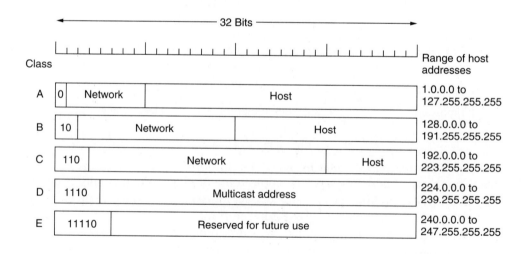

Fig. 5-47. IP address formats.

The class A, B, C, and D formats allow for up to 126 networks with 16 million hosts each, 16,382 networks with up to 64K hosts, 2 million networks, (e.g.,

LANs), with up to 254 hosts each, and multicast, in which a datagram is directed to multiple hosts. Addresses beginning with 11110 are reserved for future use. Tens of thousands of networks are now connected to the Internet, and the number doubles every year. Network numbers are assigned by the **NIC** (**Network Information Center**) to avoid conflicts.

Network addresses, which are 32-bit numbers, are usually written in **dotted decimal notation**. In this format, each of the 4 bytes is written in decimal, from 0 to 255. For example, the hexadecimal address C0290614 is written as 192.41.6.20. The lowest IP address is 0.0.0.0 and the highest is 255.255.255.255.

The values 0 and −1 have special meanings, as shown in Fig. 5-48. The value 0 means this network or this host. The value of −1 is used as a broadcast address to mean all hosts on the indicated network.

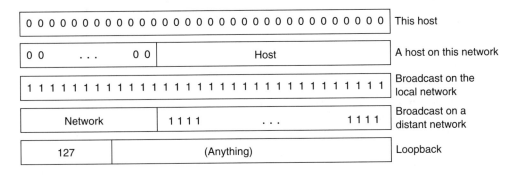

Fig. 5-48. Special IP addresses.

The IP address 0.0.0.0 is used by hosts when they are being booted but is not used afterward. IP addresses with 0 as network number refer to the current network. These addresses allow machines to refer to their own network without knowing its number (but they have to know its class to know how many 0s to include). The address consisting of all 1s allows broadcasting on the local network, typically a LAN. The addresses with a proper network number and all 1s in the host field allow machines to send broadcast packets to distant LANs anywhere in the Internet. Finally, all addresses of the form 127.xx.yy.zz are reserved for loopback testing. Packets sent to that address are not put out onto the wire; they are processed locally and treated as incoming packets. This allows packets to be sent to the local network without the sender knowing its number. This feature is also used for debugging network software.

5.5.3. Subnets

As we have seen, all the hosts in a network must have the same network number. This property of IP addressing can cause problems as networks grow. For example, consider a company that starts out with one class C LAN on the

Internet. As time goes on, it might acquire more than 254 machines, and thus need a second class C address. Alternatively, it might acquire a second LAN of a different type and want a separate IP address for it (the LANs could be bridged to form a single IP network, but bridges have their own problems). Eventually, it might end up with many LANs, each with its own router and each with its own class C network number.

As the number of distinct local networks grows, managing them can become a serious headache. Every time a new network is installed the system administrator has to contact NIC to get a new network number. Then this number must be announced worldwide. Furthermore, moving a machine from one LAN to another requires it to change its IP address, which in turn may mean modifying its configuration files and also announcing the new IP address to the world. If some other machine is given the newly-released IP address, that machine will get email and other data intended for the original machine until the address has propagated all over the world.

The solution to these problems is to allow a network to be split into several parts for internal use but still act like a single network to the outside world. In the Internet literature, these parts are called **subnets**. As we mentioned in Chap. 1, this usage conflicts with "subnet" to mean the set of all routers and communication lines in a network. Hopefully it will be clear from the context which meaning is intended. In this section, the new definition will be the one used. If our growing company started up with a class B address instead of a class C address, it could start out just numbering the hosts from 1 to 254. When the second LAN arrived, it could decide, for example, to split the 16-bit host number into a 6-bit subnet number and a 10-bit host number, as shown in Fig. 5-49. This split allows 62 LANs (0 and −1 are reserved), each with up to 1022 hosts.

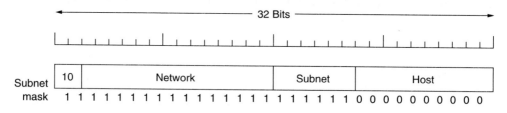

Fig. 5-49. One of the ways to subnet a class B network.

Outside the network, the subnetting is not visible, so allocating a new subnet does not require contacting NIC or changing any external databases. In this example, the first subnet might use IP addresses starting at 130.50.4.1, the second subnet might start at 130.50.8.1, and so on.

To see how subnets work, it is necessary to explain how IP packets are processed at a router. Each router has a table listing some number of (network, 0) IP addresses and some number of (this-network, host) IP addresses. The first kind tells how to get to distant networks. The second kind tells how to get to local hosts. Associated with each table is the network interface to use to reach the destination, and certain other information.

When an IP packet arrives, its destination address is looked up in the routing table. If the packet is for a distant network, it is forwarded to the next router on the interface given in the table. If it is a local host (e.g., on the router's LAN), it is sent directly to the destination. If the network is not present, the packet is forwarded to a default router with more extensive tables. This algorithm means that each router only has to keep track of other networks and local hosts, not (network, host) pairs, greatly reducing the size of the routing table.

When subnetting is introduced, the routing tables are changed, adding entries of the form (this-network, subnet, 0) and (this-network, this-subnet, host). Thus a router on subnet k knows how to get to all the other subnets and also how to get to all the hosts on subnet k. It does not have to know the details about hosts on other subnets. In fact, all that needs to be changed is to have each router do a Boolean AND with the network's **subnet mask** (see Fig. 5-49) to get rid of the host number and look up the resulting address in its tables (after determining which network class it is). For example, a packet addressed to 130.50.15.6 and arriving at a router on subnet 5 is ANDed with the subnet mask of Fig. 5-49 to give the address 130.50.12.0. This address is looked up in the routing tables to find out how to get to hosts on subnet 3. The router on subnet 5 is thus spared the work of keeping track of the data link addresses of hosts other than those on subnet 5. Subnetting thus reduces router table space by creating a three-level hierarchy.

5.5.4. Internet Control Protocols

In addition to IP, which is used for data transfer, the Internet has several control protocols used in the network layer, including ICMP, ARP, RARP, and BOOTP. In this section we will look at each of these in turn.

The Internet Control Message Protocol

The operation of the Internet is monitored closely by the routers. When something unexpected occurs, the event is reported by the **ICMP** (**Internet Control Message Protocol**), which is also used to test the Internet. About a dozen types of ICMP messages are defined. The most important ones are listed in Fig. 5-50. Each ICMP message type is encapsulated in an IP packet.

The DESTINATION UNREACHABLE message is used when the subnet or a router cannot locate the destination, or a packet with the DF bit cannot be delivered because a "small-packet" network stands in the way.

The TIME EXCEEDED message is sent when a packet is dropped due to its counter reaching zero. This event is a symptom that packets are looping, that there is enormous congestion, or that the timer values are being set too low.

Message type	Description
Destination unreachable	Packet could not be delivered
Time exceeded	Time to live field hit 0
Parameter problem	Invalid header field
Source quench	Choke packet
Redirect	Teach a router about geography
Echo request	Ask a machine if it is alive
Echo reply	Yes, I am alive
Timestamp request	Same as Echo request, but with timestamp
Timestamp reply	Same as Echo reply, but with timestamp

Fig. 5-50. The principal ICMP message types.

The PARAMETER PROBLEM message indicates that an illegal value has been detected in a header field. This problem indicates a bug in the sending host's IP software, or possibly in the software of a router transited.

The SOURCE QUENCH message was formerly used to throttle hosts that were sending too many packets. When a host received this message, it was expected to slow down. It is rarely used any more because when congestion occurs, these packets tend to add more fuel to the fire. Congestion control in the Internet is now done largely in the transport layer and will be studied in detail in Chap. 6.

The REDIRECT message is used when a router notices that a packet seems to be routed wrong. It is used by the router to tell the sending host about the probable error.

The ECHO REQUEST and ECHO REPLY messages are used to see if a given destination is reachable and alive. Upon receiving the ECHO message, the destination is expected to send an ECHO REPLY message back. The TIMESTAMP REQUEST and TIMESTAMP REPLY messages are similar, except that the arrival time of the message and the departure time of the reply are recorded in the reply. This facility is used to measure network performance.

In addition to these messages, there are four others that deal with Internet addressing, to allow hosts to discover their network numbers and to handle the case of multiple LANs sharing a single IP address. ICMP is defined in RFC 792.

The Address Resolution Protocol

Although every machine on the Internet has one (or more) IP addresses, these cannot actually be used for sending packets because the data link layer hardware does not understand Internet addresses. Nowadays, most hosts are attached to a

LAN by an interface board that only understands LAN addresses. For example, every Ethernet board ever manufactured comes equipped with a 48-bit Ethernet address. Manufacturers of Ethernet boards request a block of addresses from a central authority to ensure that no two boards have the same address (to avoid conflicts should the two boards ever appear on the same LAN). The boards send and receive frames based on 48-bit Ethernet addresses. They know nothing at all about 32-bit IP addresses.

The question now arises: How do IP addresses get mapped onto data link layer addresses, such as Ethernet? To explain how this works, let us use the example of Fig. 5-51, in which a small university with several class C networks is illustrated. Here we have two Ethernets, one in the Computer Science department, with IP address 192.31.65.0 and one in Electrical Engineering, with IP address 192.31.63.0. These are connected by a campus FDDI ring with IP address 192.31.60.0. Each machine on an Ethernet has a unique Ethernet address, labeled *E1* through *E6*, and each machine on the FDDI ring has an FDDI address, labeled *F1* through *F3*.

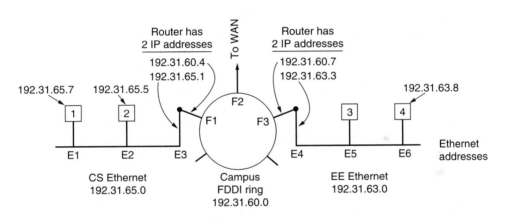

Fig. 5-51. Three interconnected class C networks: two Ethernets and an FDDI ring.

Let us start out by seeing how a user on host 1 sends a packet to a user on host 2. Let us assume the sender knows the name of the intended receiver, possibly something like *mary@eagle.cs.uni.edu*. The first step is to find the IP address for host 2, known as *eagle.cs.uni.edu*. This lookup is performed by the Domain Name System, which we will study in Chap. 7. For the moment, we will just assume that DNS returns the IP address for host 2 (192.31.65.5).

The upper layer software on host 1 now builds a packet with 192.31.65.5 in the *Destination address* field and gives it to the IP software to transmit. The IP software can look at the address and see that the destination is on its own network, but it needs a way to find the destination's Ethernet address. One solution is to have a configuration file somewhere in the system that maps IP addresses onto

Ethernet addresses. This solution is certainly possible, but for organizations with thousands of machines, keeping these files up to date is an error-prone, time-consuming job.

A better solution is for host 1 to output a broadcast packet onto the Ethernet asking: "Who owns IP address 192.31.65.5?" The broadcast will arrive at every machine on Ethernet 192.31.65.0, and each one will check its IP address. Host 2 alone will respond with its Ethernet address (*E2*). In this way host 1 learns that IP address 192.31.65.5 is on the host with Ethernet address *E2*. The protocol for asking this question and getting the reply is called **ARP (Address Resolution Protocol)**. Almost every machine on the Internet runs it. It is defined in RFC 826.

The advantage of using ARP over configuration files is the simplicity. The system manager does not have to do much except assign each machine an IP address and decide about subnet masks. ARP does the rest.

At this point, the IP software on host 1 builds an Ethernet frame addressed to *E2*, puts the IP packet (addressed to 192.31.65.5) in the payload field, and dumps it onto the Ethernet. The Ethernet board of host 2 detects this frame, recognizes it as a frame for itself, scoops it up, and causes an interrupt. The Ethernet driver extracts the IP packet from the payload and passes it to the IP software, which sees that it is correctly addressed, and processes it.

Various optimizations are possible to make ARP more efficient. To start with, once a machine has run ARP, it caches the result in case it needs to contact the same machine shortly. Next time it will find the mapping in its own cache, thus eliminating the need for a second broadcast. In many cases host 2 will need to send back a reply, forcing it, too, to run ARP to determine the sender's Ethernet address. This ARP broadcast can be avoided by having host 1 include its IP to Ethernet mapping in the ARP packet. When ARP broadcast arrives at host 2, the pair (192.31.65.7, E1) is entered into host 2's ARP cache for future use. In fact, all machines on the Ethernet can enter this mapping into their ARP caches.

Yet another optimization is to have every machine broadcast its mapping when it boots. This broadcast is generally done in the form of an ARP looking for its own IP address. There should not be a response, but a side effect of the broadcast is to make any entry in everyone's ARP cache. If a response does arrive, two machines have been assigned the same IP address. The new one should inform the system manager and not boot.

To allow mappings to change, for example, when an Ethernet board breaks and is replaced with a new one (and thus a new Ethernet address), entries in the ARP cache should time out after a few minutes.

Now let us look at Fig. 5-51 again, only this time host 1 wants to send a packet to host 6 (192.31.63.8). Using ARP will fail because host 4 will not see the broadcast (routers do not forward Ethernet-level broadcasts). There are two solutions. First, the CS router could be configured to respond to ARP requests for network 192.31.63.0 (and possibly other local networks). In this case, host 1 will make an ARP cache entry of (192.31.63.8, E3) and happily send all traffic for host

4 to the local router. This solution is called **proxy ARP**. The second solution is to have host 1 immediately see that the destination is on a remote network and just send all such traffic to a default Ethernet address that handles all remote traffic, in this case *E3*. This solution does not require having the CS router know which remote networks it is serving.

Either way, what happens is that host 1 packs the IP packet into the payload field of an Ethernet frame addressed to *E3*. When the CS router gets the Ethernet frame, it removes the IP packet from the payload field and looks up the IP address in its routing tables. It discovers that packets for network 192.31.63.0 are supposed to go to router 192.31.60.7. If it does not already know the FDDI address of 192.31.60.7, it broadcasts an ARP packet onto the ring and learns that its ring address is *F3*. It then inserts the packet into the payload field of an FDDI frame addressed to *F3* and puts it on the ring.

At the EE router, the FDDI driver removes the packet from the payload field and gives it to the IP software, which sees that it needs to send the packet to 192.31.63.8. If this IP address is not in its ARP cache, it broadcasts an ARP request on the EE Ethernet and learns that the destination address is *E6* so it builds an Ethernet frame addressed to *E6*, puts the packet in the payload field, and sends it over the Ethernet. When the Ethernet frame arrives at host 4, the packet is extracted from the frame and passed to the IP software for processing.

Going from host 1 to a distant network over a WAN works essentially the same way, except that this time the CS router's tables tell it to use the WAN router whose FDDI address is *F2*.

The Reverse Address Resolution Protocol

ARP solves the problem of finding out which Ethernet address corresponds to a given IP address. Sometimes the reverse problem has to solved: Given an Ethernet address, what is the corresponding IP address? In particular, this problem occurs when booting a diskless workstation. Such a machine will normally get the binary image of its operating system from a remote file server. But how does it learn its IP address?

The solution is to use the **RARP (Reverse Address Resolution Protocol)** (defined in RFC 903). This protocol allows a newly-booted workstation to broadcast its Ethernet address and say: "My 48-bit Ethernet address is 14.04.05.18.01.25. Does anyone out there know my IP address?" The RARP server sees this request, looks up the Ethernet address in its configuration files, and sends back the corresponding IP address.

Using RARP is better than embedding an IP address in the memory image because it allows the same image to be used on all machines. If the IP address were buried inside the image, each workstation would need its own image.

A disadvantage of RARP is that it uses a destination address of all 1s (limited broadcasting) to reach the RARP server. However, such broadcasts are not forwarded by routers, so a RARP server is needed on each network. To get around this problem, an alternative bootstrap protocol called **BOOTP** has been invented (see RFCs 951, 1048, and 1084). Unlike RARP, it uses UDP messages, which are forwarded over routers. It also provides a diskless workstation with additional information, including the IP address of the file server holding the memory image, the IP address of the default router, and the subnet mask to use. BOOTP is described in RFC 951.

5.5.5. The Interior Gateway Routing Protocol: OSPF

As we mentioned earlier, the Internet is made up of a large number of autonomous systems. Each AS is operated by a different organization and can use its own routing algorithm inside. For example, the internal networks of companies *X*, *Y*, and *Z* would usually be seen as three ASes if all three were on the Internet. All three may use different routing algorithms internally. Nevertheless, having standards, even for internal routing, simplifies the implementation at the boundaries between ASes and allows reuse of code. In this section we will study routing within an AS. In the next one, we will look at routing between ASes. A routing algorithm within an AS is called an **interior gateway protocol**; an algorithm for routing between ASes is called an **exterior gateway protocol**.

The original Internet interior gateway protocol was a distance vector protocol (RIP) based on the Bellman-Ford algorithm. It worked well in small systems, but less well as ASes got larger. It also suffered from the count-to-infinity problem and generally slow convergence, so it was replaced in May 1979 by a link state protocol. In 1988, the Internet Engineering Task Force began work on a successor. That successor, called **OSPF (Open Shortest Path First)** became a standard in 1990. Many router vendors are now supporting it, and it will become the main interior gateway protocol in the near future. Below we will give a sketch of how OSPF works. For the complete story, see RFC 1247.

Given the long experience with other routing protocols, the group designing the new protocol had a long list of requirements that had to be met. First, the algorithm had to be published in the open literature, hence the "O" in OSPF. A proprietary solution owned by one company would not do. Second, the new protocol had to support a variety of distance metrics, including physical distance, delay, and so on. Third, it had to be a dynamic algorithm, one that adapted to changes in the topology automatically and quickly.

Fourth, and new for OSPF, it had to support routing based on type of service. The new protocol had to be able to route real-time traffic one way and other traffic a different way. The IP protocol has a *Type of Service* field, but no existing routing protocol used it.

Fifth, and related to the above, the new protocol had to do load balancing, splitting the load over multiple lines. Most previous protocols sent all packets over the best route. The second-best route was not used at all. In many cases, splitting the load over multiple lines gives better performance.

Sixth, support for hierarchical systems was needed. By 1988, the Internet had grown so large that no router could be expected to know the entire topology. The new routing protocol had to be designed so that no router would have to.

Seventh, some modicum of security was required to prevent fun-loving students from spoofing routers by sending them false routing information. Finally, provision was needed for dealing with routers that were connected to the Internet via a tunnel. Previous protocols did not handle this well.

OSPF supports three kinds of connections and networks:

1. Point-to-point lines between exactly two routers.

2. Multiaccess networks with broadcasting (e.g., most LANs).

3. Multiaccess networks without broadcasting (e.g., most packet-switched WANs).

A **multiaccess** network is one that can have multiple routers on it, each of which can directly communicate with all the others. All LANs and WANs have this property. Figure 5-52(a) shows an AS containing all three kinds of networks. Note that hosts do not generally play a role in OSPF.

OSPF works by abstracting the collection of actual networks, routers, and lines into a directed graph in which each arc is assigned a cost (distance, delay, etc.). It then computes the shortest path based on the weights on the arcs. A serial connection between two routers is represented by a pair of arcs, one in each direction. Their weights may be different. A multiaccess network is represented by a node for the network itself plus a node for each router. The arcs from the network node to the routers have weight 0 and are omitted from the graph.

Figure 5-52(b) shows the graph representation of the network of Fig. 5-52(a). What OSPF fundamentally does is represent the actual network as a graph like this and then compute the shortest path from every router to every other router.

Many of the ASes in the Internet are themselves large and nontrivial to manage. OSPF allows them to be divided up into numbered **areas**, where an area is a network or a set of contiguous networks. Areas do not overlap but need not be exhaustive, that is, some routers may belong to no area. An area is a generalization of a subnet. Outside an area, its topology and details are not visible.

Every AS has a **backbone** area, called area 0. All areas are connected to the backbone, possibly by tunnels, so it is possible to go from any area in the AS to any other area in the AS via the backbone. A tunnel is represented in the graph as an arc and has a cost. Each router that is connected to two or more areas is part of the backbone. As with other areas, the topology of the backbone is not visible outside the backbone.

Within an area, each router has the same link state database and runs the same shortest path algorithm. Its main job is to calculate the shortest path from itself to

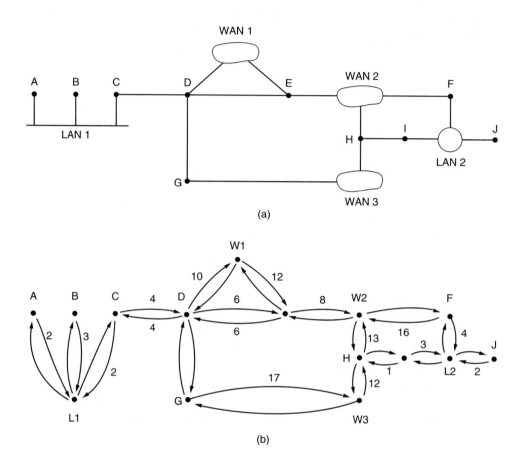

Fig. 5-52. (a) An autonomous system. (b) A graph representation of (a).

every other router in the area, including the router that is connected to the backbone, of which there must be at least one. A router that connects to two areas needs the databases for both areas and must run the shortest path algorithm for each one separately.

The way OSPF handles type of service routing is to have multiple graphs, one labeled with the costs when delay is the metric, one labeled with the costs when throughput is the metric, and one labeled with the costs when reliability is the metric. Although this triples the computation needed, it allows separate routes for optimizing delay, throughput, and reliability.

During normal operation, three kinds of routes may be needed: intra-area, interarea, and interAS. Intra-area routes are the easiest, since the source router already knows the shortest path to the destination router. Interarea routing always proceeds in three steps: go from the source to the backbone; go across the backbone to the destination area; go to the destination. This algorithm forces a star configuration on OSPF with the backbone being the hub and the other areas being spokes. Packets are routed from source to destination "as is." They are not encapsulated or tunneled, unless going to an area whose only connection to the backbone is a tunnel. Figure 5-53 shows part of the Internet with ASes and areas.

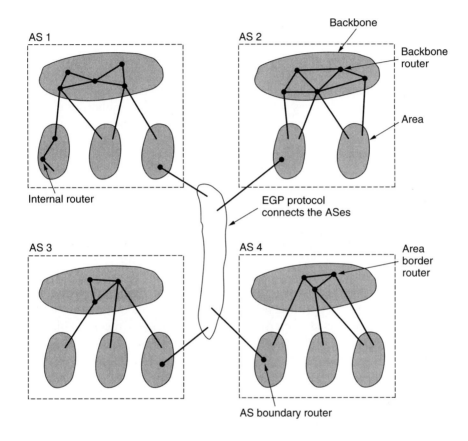

Fig. 5-53. The relation between ASes, backbones, and areas in OSPF.

OSPF distinguishes four classes of routers:

1. Internal routers are wholly within one area.

2. Area border routers connect two or more areas.

3. Backbone routers are on the backbone.

4. AS boundary routers talk to routers in other ASes.

These classes are allowed to overlap. For example, all the border routers are automatically part of the backbone. In addition, a router that is in the backbone but not part of any other area is also an internal router. Examples of all four classes of routers are illustrated in Fig. 5-53.

When a router boots, it sends HELLO messages on all of its point-to-point lines and multicasts them on LANs to the group consisting of all the other routers. On WANs, it needs some configuration information to know who to contact. From the responses, each router learns who its neighbors are.

OSPF works by exchanging information between **adjacent** routers, which is not the same as between neighboring routers. In particular, it is inefficient to have every router on a LAN talk to every other router on the LAN. To avoid this situation, one router is elected as the **designated router**. It is said to be adjacent to all the other routers, and exchanges information with them. Neighboring routers that are not adjacent do not exchange information with each other. A backup designated router is always kept up to date to ease the transition should the primary designated router crash.

During normal operation, each router periodically floods LINK STATE UPDATE messages to each of its adjacent routers. This message gives its state and provides the costs used in the topological database. The flooding messages are acknowledged, to make them reliable. Each message has a sequence number, so a router can see whether an incoming LINK STATE UPDATE is older or newer than what it currently has. Routers also send these messages when a line goes up or down or its cost changes.

DATABASE DESCRIPTION messages give the sequence numbers of all the link state entries currently held by the sender. By comparing its own values with those of the sender, the receiver can determine who has the most recent values. These messages are used when a line is brought up.

Either partner can request link state information from the other one using LINK STATE REQUEST messages. The net result of this algorithm is that each pair of adjacent routers checks to see who has the most recent data, and new information is spread throughout the area this way. All these messages are sent as raw IP packets. The five kinds of messages are summarized in Fig. 5-54.

Message type	Description
Hello	Used to discover who the neighbors are
Link state update	Provides the sender's costs to its neighbors
Link state ack	Acknowledges link state update
Database description	Announces which updates the sender has
Link state request	Requests information from the partner

Fig. 5-54. The five types of OSPF messages.

Finally, we can put all the pieces together. Using flooding, each router informs all the other routers in its area of its neighbors and costs. This information allows each router to construct the graph for its area(s) and compute the shortest path. The backbone area does this too. In addition, the backbone routers accept information from the area border routers in order to compute the best route from each backbone router to every other router. This information is propagated back to the area border routers, which advertise it within their areas. Using this information, a router about to send an interarea packet can select the best exit router to the backbone.

5.5.6. The Exterior Gateway Routing Protocol: BGP

Within a single AS, the recommended routing protocol on the Internet is OSPF (although it is certainly not the only one in use). Between ASes, a different protocol, **BGP** (**Border Gateway Protocol**), is used. A different protocol is needed between ASes because the goals of an interior gateway protocol and an exterior gateway protocol are not the same. All an interior gateway protocol has to do is move packets as efficiently as possible from the source to the destination. It does not have to worry about politics.

Exterior gateway protocol routers have to worry about politics a great deal. For example, a corporate AS might want the ability to send packets to any Internet site and receive packets from any Internet site. However, it might be unwilling to carry transit packets originating in a foreign AS and ending in a different foreign AS, even if its own AS was on the shortest path between the two foreign ASes ("That's their problem, not ours"). On the other hand, it might be willing to carry transit traffic for its neighbors, or even for specific other ASes that paid it for this service. Telephone companies, for example, might be happy to act as a carrier for their customers, but not for others. Exterior gateway protocols in general, and BGP in particular, have been designed to allow many kinds of routing policies to be enforced in the interAS traffic.

Typical policies involve political, security, or economic considerations. A few examples of routing constraints are

1. No transit traffic through certain ASes.

2. Never put Iraq on a route starting at the Pentagon.

3. Do not use the United States to get from British Columbia to Ontario.

4. Only transit Albania if there is no alternative to the destination.

5. Traffic starting or ending at IBM® should not transit Microsoft®.

Policies are manually configured into each BGP router. They are not part of the protocol itself.

From the point of view of a BGP router, the world consists of other BGP routers and the lines connecting them. Two BGP routers are considered connected if they share a common network. Given BGP's special interest in transit traffic, networks are grouped into one of three categories. The first category is the **stub networks**, which have only one connection to the BGP graph. These cannot be used for transit traffic because there is no one on the other side. Then come the **multiconnected networks**. These could be used for transit traffic, except that they refuse. Finally, there are the **transit networks**, such as backbones, which are willing to handle third-party packets, possibly with some restrictions.

Pairs of BGP routers communicate with each other by establishing TCP connections. Operating this way provides reliable communication and hides all the details of the network being passed through.

BGP is fundamentally a distance vector protocol, but quite different from most others such as RIP. Instead of maintaining just the cost to each destination, each BGP router keeps track of the exact path used. Similarly, instead of periodically giving each neighbor its estimated cost to each possible destination, each BGP router tells its neighbors the exact path it is using.

As an example, consider the BGP routers shown in Fig. 5-55(a). In particular, consider F's routing table. Suppose that it uses the path $FGCD$ to get to D. When the neighbors give it routing information, they provide their complete paths, as shown in Fig. 5-55(b) (for simplicity, only destination D is shown here).

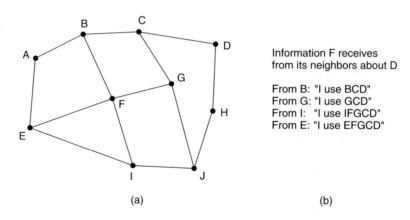

Information F receives
from its neighbors about D

From B: "I use BCD"
From G: "I use GCD"
From I: "I use IFGCD"
From E: "I use EFGCD"

(a)   (b)

Fig. 5-55. (a) A set of BGP routers. (b) Information sent to F.

After all the paths come in from the neighbors, F examines them to see which is the best. It quickly discards the paths from I and E, since these paths pass through F itself. The choice is then between using B and G. Every BGP router contains a module that examines routes to a given destination and scores them, returning a number for the "distance" to that destination for each route. Any route violating a policy constraint automatically gets a score of infinity. The router then adopts the route with the shortest distance. The scoring function is not part of the BGP protocol and can be any function the system managers want.

BGP easily solves the count-to-infinity problem that plagues other distance vector routing algorithms. For example, suppose G crashes or the line FG goes down. *F* then receives routes from its three remaining neighbors. These routes are *BCD*, *IFGCD*, and *EFGCD*. It can immediately see that the two latter routes are pointless, since they pass through *F* itself, so it chooses *FBCD* as its new route. Other distance vector algorithms often make the wrong choice because they cannot tell which of their neighbors have independent routes to the destination, and which do not. The current definition of BGP is in RFC 1654. Additional useful information can be found in RFC 1268.

5.5.7. Internet Multicasting

Normal IP communication is between one sender and one receiver. However, for some applications it is useful for a process to be able to send to a large number of receivers simultaneously. Examples are updating replicated, distributed databases, transmitting stock quotes to multiple brokers, and handling digital conference (i.e., multiparty) telephone calls.

IP supports multicasting, using class D addresses. Each class D address identifies a group of hosts. Twenty-eight bits are available for identifying groups, so over 250 million groups can exist at the same time. When a process sends a packet to a class D address, a best-efforts attempt is made to deliver it to all the members of the group addressed, but no guarantees are given. Some members may not get the packet.

Two kinds of group addresses are supported: permanent addresses and temporary ones. A permanent group is always there and does not have to be set up. Each permanent group has a permanent group address. Some examples of permanent group addresses are

224.0.0.1 All systems on a LAN
224.0.0.2 All routers on a LAN
224.0.0.5 All OSPF routers on a LAN
224.0.0.6 All designated OSPF routers on a LAN

Temporary groups must be created before they can be used. A process can ask its host to join a specific group. It can also ask its host to leave the group. When the last process on a host leaves a group, that group is no longer present on the host. Each host keeps track of which groups its processes currently belong to.

Multicasting is implemented by special multicast routers, which may or may not be colocated with the standard routers. About once a minute, each multicast router sends a hardware (i.e., data link layer) multicast to the hosts on its LAN (address 224.0.0.1) asking them to report back on the groups their processes currently belong to. Each host sends back responses for all the class D addresses it is interested in.

These query and response packets use a protocol called **IGMP (Internet Group Management Protocol**), which is vaguely analogous to ICMP. It has only two kinds of packets: query and response, each with a simple fixed format containing some control information in the first word of the payload field and a class D address in the second word. It is described in RFC 1112.

Multicast routing is done using spanning trees. Each multicast router exchanges information with its neighbors using a modified distance vector protocol in order for each one to construct a spanning tree per group covering all group members. Various optimizations are used to prune the tree to eliminate routers and networks not interested in particular groups. The protocol makes heavy use of tunneling to avoid bothering nodes not in a spanning tree.

5.5.8. Mobile IP

Many users of the Internet have portable computers and want to stay connected to the Internet when they visit a distant Internet site and even on the road in between. Unfortunately, the IP addressing system makes working far from home easier said than done. In this section we will examine the problem and the solution. A more detailed description is given in (Johnson, 1995).

The real villain is the addressing scheme itself. Every IP address contains three fields: the class, the network number, and the host number. For example, consider the machine with IP address 160.80.40.20. The 160.80 gives the class (B) and network number (8272); the 40.20 is the host number (10260). Routers all over the world have routing tables telling which line to use to get to network 160.80. Whenever a packet comes in with a destination IP address of the form 160.80.xxx.yyy, it goes out on that line.

If all of a sudden, the machine with that address is carted off to some distant site, the packets for it will continue to be routed to its home LAN (or router). The owner will no longer get email, and so on. Giving the machine a new IP address corresponding to its new location is unattractive because large numbers of people, programs, and databases would have to be informed of the change.

Another approach is to have the routers use complete IP addresses for routing, instead of just the class and network. However, this strategy would require each router to have millions of table entries, at astronomical cost to the Internet.

When people began demanding the ability to have mobile hosts, the IETF set up a Working Group to find a solution. The Working Group quickly formulated a number of goals considered desirable in any solution. The major ones were

1. Each mobile host must be able to use its home IP address anywhere.

2. Software changes to the fixed hosts were not permitted.

3. Changes to the router software and tables were not permitted.

4. Most packets for mobile hosts should not make detours on the way.

5. No overhead should be incurred when a mobile host is at home.

The solution chosen was the one described in Sec. 5.2.8. To review it briefly, every site that wants to allow its users to roam has to create a home agent. Every site that wants to allow visitors has to create a foreign agent. When a mobile host shows up at a foreign site, it contacts the foreign host there and registers. The foreign host then contacts the user's home agent and gives it a **care-of address**, normally the foreign agent's own IP address.

When a packet arrives at the user's home LAN, it comes in at some router attached to the LAN. The router then tries to locate the host in the usual way, by broadcasting an ARP packet asking, for example: "What is the Ethernet address of 160.80.40.20?" The home agent responds to this query by giving its own Ethernet address. The router then sends packets for 160.80.40.20 to the home agent. It, in turn, tunnels them to the care-of address by encapsulating them in the payload field of an IP packet addressed to the foreign agent. The foreign agent then decapsulates and delivers them to the data link address of the mobile host. In addition, the home agent gives the care-of address to the sender, so future packets can be tunnelled directly to the foreign agent. This solution meets all the requirements stated above.

One small detail is probably worth mentioning. At the time the mobile host moves, the router probably has its (soon-to-be-invalid) Ethernet address cached. To replace that Ethernet address with the home agent's, a trick called **gratuitous ARP** is used. This is a special, unsolicited message to the router that causes it to replace a specific cache entry, in this case, that of the mobile host about to leave. When the mobile host returns later, the same trick is used to update the router's cache again.

Nothing in the design prevents a mobile host from being its own foreign agent, but that approach only works if the mobile host (in its capacity as foreign agent) is logically connected to the Internet at its current site. Also, it must be able to acquire a (temporary) care-of IP address to use. That IP address must belong to the LAN to which it is currently attached.

The IETF solution for mobile hosts solves a number of other problems not mentioned so far. For example, how are agents located? The solution is for each agent to periodically broadcast its address and the type of services it is willing to provide (e.g., home, foreign, or both). When a mobile host arrives somewhere, it can just listen for these broadcasts, called **advertisements**. Alternatively, it can broadcast a packet announcing its arrival and hope that the local foreign agent responds to it.

Another problem that had to be solved is what to do about impolite mobile hosts that leave without saying goodbye. The solution is to make registration valid only for a fixed time interval. If it is not refreshed periodically, it times out, so the foreign host can clear its tables.

Yet another issue is security. When a home agent gets a message asking it to please forward all of Nora's packets to some IP address, it had better not comply unless it is convinced that Nora is the source of this request, and not somebody trying to impersonate her. Cryptographic authentication protocols are used for this purpose. We will study such protocols in Chap. 7.

A final point addressed by the Working Group relates to levels of mobility. Imagine an airplane with an on-board Ethernet used by the navigation and avionics computers. On this Ethernet is a standard router that talks to the wired Internet on the ground over a radio link. One fine day, some clever marketing executive gets the idea to install Ethernet connectors in all the arm rests so passengers with mobile computers can also plug in.

Now we have two levels of mobility: the aircraft's own computers, which are stationary with respect to the Ethernet, and the passengers' computers, which are mobile with respect to it. In addition, the on-board router is mobile with respect to routers on the ground. Being mobile with respect to a system that is itself mobile can be handled using recursive tunneling.

5.5.9. CIDR—Classless InterDomain Routing

IP has been in heavy use for over a decade. It has worked extremely well, as demonstrated by the exponential growth of the Internet. Unfortunately, IP is rapidly becoming a victim of its own popularity: it is running out of addresses. This looming disaster has sparked a great deal of discussion and controversy within the Internet community about what to do about it. In this section we will describe both the problem and several proposed solutions. A more complete description is given in (Huitema, 1996).

Back in 1987, a few visionaries predicted that some day the Internet might grow to 100,000 networks. Most experts pooh-poohed this as being decades in the future, if ever. The 100,000th network was connected in 1996. The problem, simply stated, is that the Internet is rapidly running out of IP addresses. In principle, over 2 billion addresses exist, but the practice of organizing the address space by classes (see Fig. 5-47), wastes millions of them. In particular, the real villain is the class B network. For most organizations, a class A network, with 16 million addresses is too big, and a class C network, with 256 addresses is too small. A class B network, with 65,536, is just right. In Internet folklore, this situation is known as the **three bears problem** (as in *Goldilocks and the Three Bears*).

In reality, a class B address is far too large for most organizations. Studies have shown that more than half of all class B networks have fewer than 50 hosts. A class C network would have done the job, but no doubt every organization that asked for a class B address thought that one day it would outgrow the 8-bit host field. In retrospect, it might have been better to have had class C networks use 10 bits instead of eight for the host number, allowing 1022 hosts per network. Had this been the case, most organizations would have probably settled for a class C network, and there would have been half a million of them (versus only 16,384 class B networks).

However, then another problem would have emerged more quickly: the routing table explosion. From the point of view of the routers, the IP address space is a two-level hierarchy, with network numbers and host numbers. Routers do not have to know about all the hosts, but they do have to know about all the networks. If half a million class C networks were in use, every router in the entire Internet would need a table with half a million entries, one per network, telling which line to use to get to that network, as well as other information.

The actual physical storage of half a million entry tables is probably doable, although expensive for critical routers that keep the tables in static RAM on I/O boards. A more serious problem is that the complexity of various algorithms relating to management of the tables grows faster than linear. Worse yet, much of the existing router software and firmware was designed at a time when the Internet had 1000 connected networks and 10,000 networks seemed decades away. Design choices made then often are far from optimal now.

In addition, various routing algorithms require each router to transmit its tables periodically. The larger the tables, the more likely some parts will get lost underway, leading to incomplete data at the other end and possibly routing instabilities.

The routing table problem could have been solved by going to a deeper hierarchy. For example, having each IP address contain a country, state, city, network, and host field might work. Then each router would only need to know how to get to each country, the states or provinces in its own country, the cities in its state or province, and the networks in its city. Unfortunately, this solution would require considerably more than 32 bits for IP addresses and would use addresses inefficiently (Liechtenstein would have as many bits as the United States).

In short, most solutions solve one problem but create a new one. One solution that is now being implemented and which will give the Internet a bit of extra breathing room is **CIDR** (**Classless InterDomain Routing**). The basic idea behind CIDR, which is described in RFC 1519, is to allocate the remaining class C networks, of which there are almost two million, in variable-sized blocks. If a site needs, say, 2000 addresses, it is given a block of 2048 addresses (eight contiguous class C networks), and not a full class B address. Similarly, a site needing 8000 addresses gets 8192 addresses (32 contiguous class C networks).

In addition to using blocks of contiguous class C networks as units, the allocation rules for the class C addresses were also changed in RFC 1519. The world was partitioned into four zones, and each one given a portion of the class C address space. The allocation was as follows:

Addresses 194.0.0.0 to 195.255.255.255 are for Europe
Addresses 198.0.0.0 to 199.255.255.255 are for North America
Addresses 200.0.0.0 to 201.255.255.255 are for Central and South America
Addresses 202.0.0.0 to 203.255.255.255 are for Asia and the Pacific

In this way, each region was given about 32 million addresses to allocate, with another 320 million class C addresses from 204.0.0.0 through 223.255.255.255

held in reserve for the future. The advantage of this allocation is that now any router outside of Europe that gets a packet addressed to 194.xx.yy.zz or 195.xx.yy.zz can just send it to its standard European gateway. In effect 32 million addresses have now been compressed into one routing table entry. Similarly for the other regions.

Of course, once a 194.xx.yy.zz packet gets to Europe, more detailed routing tables are needed. One possibility is to have 131,072 entries for networks 194.0.0.xx through 195.255.255.xx, but this is precisely this routing table explosion that we are trying to avoid. Instead, each routing table entry is extended by giving it a 32-bit mask. When a packet comes in, its destination address is first extracted. Then (conceptually) the routing table is scanned entry by entry, masking the destination address and comparing it to the table entry looking for a match.

To make this comparison process clearer, let us consider an example. Suppose that Cambridge University needs 2048 addresses and is assigned the addresses 194.24.0.0 through 194.24.7.255, along with mask 255.255.248.0. Next, Oxford University asks for 4096 addresses. Since a block of 4096 addresses must lie on a 4096-byte boundary, they cannot be given addresses starting at 194.8.0.0. Instead they get 194.24.16.0 through 194.24.31.255 along with mask 255.255.240.0. Now the University of Edinburgh asks for 1024 addresses and is assigned addresses 194.24.8.0 through 194.24.11.255 and mask 255.255.252.0.

The routing tables all over Europe are now updated with three entries, each one containing a base address and a mask. These entries (in binary) are:

Address	Mask
11000010 00011000 00000000 00000000	11111111 11111111 11111000 00000000
11000010 00011000 00010000 00000000	11111111 11111111 11110000 00000000
11000010 00011000 00001000 00000000	11111111 11111111 11111100 00000000

Now consider what happens when a packet comes in addressed to 194.24.17.4, which in binary is

11000010 00011000 00010001 00000100

First it is Boolean ANDed with the Cambridge mask to get

11000010 00011000 00010000 00000000

This value does not match the Cambridge base address, so the original address is next ANDed with the Oxford mask to get

11000010 00011000 00010000 00000000

This value does match the Oxford mask, so the packet is sent to the Oxford router. In practice, the router entries are not tried sequentially; indexing tricks are used to speed up the search. Also, it is possible for two entries to match, in which case the one whose mask has the most 1 bits wins. Finally, the same idea can be applied to all addresses, not just the new class C addresses, so with CIDR, the old class A, B, and C networks are no longer used for routing. This is why CIDR is called classless routing. CIDR is described in more detail in (Ford et al., 1993; and Huitema, 1995).

5.5.10. IPv6

While CIDR may buy a few more years' time, everyone realizes that the days of IP in its current form (IPv4) are numbered. In addition to these technical problems, there is another issue looming in the background. Up until recently, the Internet has been used largely by universities, high-tech industry, and the government (especially the Dept. of Defense). With the explosion of interest in the Internet starting in the mid 1990s, it is likely that in the next millenium, it will be used by a much larger group of people, especially people with different requirements. For one thing, millions of people with wireless portables may use it to keep in contact with their home bases. For another, with the impending convergence of the computer, communication, and entertainment industries, it may not be long before every television set in the world is an Internet node, producing a billion machines being used for video on demand. Under these circumstances, it became apparent that IP had to evolve and become more flexible.

Seeing these problems on the horizon, in 1990, IETF started work on a new version of IP, one which would never run out of addresses, would solve a variety of other problems, and be more flexible and efficient as well. Its major goals were to

1. Support billions of hosts, even with inefficient address space allocation.

2. Reduce the size of the routing tables.

3. Simplify the protocol, to allow routers to process packets faster.

4. Provide better security (authentication and privacy) than current IP.

5. Pay more attention to type of service, particularly for real-time data.

6. Aid multicasting by allowing scopes to be specified.

7. Make it possible for a host to roam without changing its address.

8. Allow the protocol to evolve in the future.

9. Permit the old and new protocols to coexist for years.

To find a protocol that met all these requirements, IETF issued a call for proposals and discussion in RFC 1550. Twenty-one responses were received, not all of them full proposals. By December 1992, seven serious proposals were on the table. They ranged from making minor patches to IP, to throwing it out altogether and replacing with a completely different protocol.

One proposal was to run TCP over CLNP, which, with its 160-bit addresses would have provided enough address space forever and would have unified two major network layer protocols. However, many people felt that this would have been an admission that something in the OSI world was actually done right, a statement considered Politically Incorrect in Internet circles. CLNP was patterned closely on IP, so the two are not really that different. In fact, the protocol ultimately chosen differs from IP far more than CLNP does. Another strike against CLNP was its poor support for service types, something required to transmit multimedia efficiently.

Three of the better proposals were published in *IEEE Network* (Deering, 1993; Francis, 1993; and Katz and Ford, 1993). After much discussion, revision, and jockeying for position, a modified combined version of the Deering and Francis proposals, by now called **SIPP** (**Simple Internet Protocol Plus**) was selected and given the designation **IPv6** (IPv5 was already in use for an experimental real-time stream protocol).

IPv6 meets the goals fairly well. It maintains the good features of IP, discards or deemphasizes the bad ones, and adds new ones where needed. In general, IPv6 is not compatible with IPv4, but it is compatible with all the other Internet protocols, including TCP, UDP, ICMP, IGMP, OSPF, BGP, and DNS, sometimes with small modifications being required (mostly to deal with longer addresses). The main features of IPv6 are discussed below. More information about it can be found in RFC 1883 through RFC 1887.

First and foremost, IPv6 has longer addresses than IPv4. They are 16 bytes long, which solves the problem that IPv6 was set out to solve: provide an effectively unlimited supply of Internet addresses. We will have more to say about addresses shortly.

The second major improvement of IPv6 is the simplification of the header. It contains only 7 fields (versus 13 in IPv4). This change allows routers to process packets faster and thus improve throughout. We will discuss the header shortly, too.

The third major improvement was better support for options. This change was essential with the new header because fields that previously were required are now optional. In addition, the way options are represented is different, making it simple for routers to skip over options not intended for them. This feature speeds up packet processing time.

A fourth area in which IPv6 represents a big advance is in security. IETF had its fill of newspaper stories about precocious 12-year-olds using their personal computers to break into banks and military bases all over the Internet. There was a strong feeling that something had to be done to improve security. Authentication and privacy are key features of the new IP.

Finally, more attention has been paid to type of service than in the past. IPv4 actually has an 8-bit field devoted to this matter, but with the expected growth in multimedia traffic in the future, much more is needed.

The Main IPv6 Header

The IPv6 header is shown in Fig. 5-56. The *Version* field is always 6 for IPv6 (and 4 for IPv4). During the transition period from IPv4, which will probably take a decade, routers will be able to examine this field to tell what kind of packet they have. As an aside, making this test wastes a few instructions in the critical path, so many implementations are likely to try to avoid it by using some field in the data link header to distinguish IPv4 packets from IPv6 packets. In this way, packets can be passed to the correct network layer handler directly. However, having the data link layer be aware of network packet types completely violates the design principle that each layer should not be aware of the meaning of the bits given to it from the layer above. The discussions between the "Do it right" and "Make it fast" camps will no doubt be lengthy and vigorous.

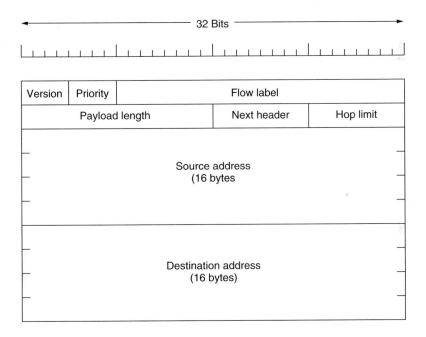

Fig. 5-56. The IPv6 fixed header (required).

The *Priority* field is used to distinguish between packets whose sources can be flow controlled and those that cannot. Values 0 through 7 are for transmissions that are capable of slowing down in the event of congestion. Values 8 through 15 are for real-time traffic whose sending rate is constant, even if all the packets are being lost. Audio and video fall into the latter category. This distinction allows routers to deal with packets better in the event of congestion. Within each group, lower-numbered packets are less important than higher-numbered ones. The IPv6 standard suggests, for example, to use 1 for news, 4 for FTP, and 6 for Telnet connections, since delaying a news packet for a few seconds is not noticeable, but delaying a Telnet packet certainly is.

The *Flow label* field is still experimental but will be used to allow a source and destination to set up a pseudoconnection with particular properties and requirements. For example, a stream of packets from one process on a certain source host to a certain process on a certain destination host might have stringent delay requirements and thus need reserved bandwidth. The flow can be set up in advance and given an identifier. When a packet with a nonzero *Flow label* shows up, all the routers can look it up in internal tables to see what kind of special treatment it requires. In effect, flows are an attempt to have it both ways: the flexibility of a datagram subnet and the guarantees of a virtual circuit subnet.

Each flow is designated by the source address, destination address, and flow number, so many flows may be active at the same time between a given pair of IP addresses. Also, in this way, even if two flows coming from different hosts but with the same flow number pass through the same router, the router will be able to tell them apart using the source and destination addresses. It is expected that flow numbers will be chosen randomly, rather than assigned sequentially starting at 1, to make it easy for routers to hash them.

The *Payload length* field tells how many bytes follow the 40-byte header of Fig. 5-56. The name was changed from the IPv4 *Total length* field because the meaning was changed slightly: the 40 header bytes are no longer counted as part of the length as they used to be.

The *Next header* field lets the cat out of the bag. The reason the header could be simplified is that there can be additional (optional) extension headers. This field tells which of the (currently) six extension headers, if any, follows this one. If this header is the last IP header, the *Next header* field tells which transport protocol handler (e.g., TCP, UDP) to pass the packet to.

The *Hop limit* field is used to keep packets from living forever. It is, in practice, the same as the *Time to live* field in IPv4, namely, a field that is decremented on each hop. In theory, in IPv4 it was a time in seconds, but no router used it that way, so the name was changed to reflect the way it is actually used.

Next come the *Source address* and *Destination address* fields. Deering's original proposal, SIP, used 8-byte addresses, but during the review process many people felt that with 8-byte addresses IPv6 would run out of addresses within a few decades, whereas with 16-byte addresses it would never run out. Other people argued that 16 bytes was overkill, whereas still others favored using 20-byte addresses to be compatible with the OSI datagram protocol. Another faction wanted variable-sized addresses. After much discussion, it was decided that fixed-length 16-byte addresses were the best compromise.

The IPv6 address space is divided up as shown in Fig. 5-57. Addresses beginning with 80 zeros are reserved for IPv4 addresses. Two variants are supported, distinguished by the next 16 bits. These variants relate to how IPv6 packets will be tunneled over the existing IPv4 infrastructure.

Prefix (binary)	Usage	Fraction
0000 0000	Reserved (including IPv4)	1/256
0000 0001	Unassigned	1/256
0000 001	OSI NSAP addresses	1/128
0000 010	Novell NetWare IPX addresses	1/128
0000 011	Unassigned	1/128
0000 1	Unassigned	1/32
0001	Unassigned	1/16
001	Unassigned	1/8
010	Provider-based addresses	1/8
011	Unassigned	1/8
100	Geographic-based addresses	1/8
101	Unassigned	1/8
110	Unassigned	1/8
1110	Unassigned	1/16
1111 0	Unassigned	1/32
1111 10	Unassigned	1/64
1111 110	Unassigned	1/128
1111 1110 0	Unassigned	1/512
1111 1110 10	Link local use addresses	1/1024
1111 1110 11	Site local use addresses	1/1024
1111 1111	Multicast	1/256

Fig. 5-57. IPv6 addresses

The use of separate prefixes for provider-based and geographic-based addresses is a compromise between two different visions of the future of the Internet. Provider-based addresses make sense if you think that in the future there will be some number of companies providing Internet service to customers, analogous to AT&T, MCI, Sprint, British Telecom, and so on providing telephone service now. Each of these companies will be given some fraction of the address space. The first 5 bits following the 010 prefix are used to indicate which registry to look the provider up in. Currently three registries are operating, for North America, Europe, and Asia. Up to 29 new registries can be added later.

Each registry is free to divide up the remaining 15 bytes as it sees fit. It is expected that many of them will use a 3-byte provider number, giving about 16 million providers, in order to allow large companies to act as their own provider. Another possibility is to use 1 byte to indicate national providers and let them do further allocation. In this manner, additional levels of hierarchy can be introduced as needed.

The geographic model is the same as the current Internet, in which providers do not play a large role. In this way, IPv6 can handle both kinds of addresses.

The link and site local addresses have only a local significance. They can be reused at each organization without conflict. They cannot be propagated outside organizational boundaries, making them well suited to organizations that currently use firewalls to wall themselves off from the rest of the Internet.

Multicast addresses have a 4-bit flag field and a 4-bit scope field following the prefix, then a 112-bit group identifier. One of the flag bits distinguishes permanent from transient groups. The scope field allows a multicast to be limited to the current link, site, organization, or planet. These four scopes are spread out over the 16 values to allow new scopes to be added later. For example, the planetary scope is 14, so code 15 is available to allow future expansion of the Internet to other planets, solar systems, and galaxies.

In addition to supporting the standard unicast (point-to-point) and multicast addresses, IPv6 also supports a new kind of addressing: anycast. **Anycasting** is like multicasting in that the destination is a group of addresses, but instead of trying to deliver the packet to all of them, it tries to deliver it to just one, usually the nearest one. For example, when contacting a group of cooperating file servers, a client can use anycast to reach the nearest one, without having to know which one that is. Anycasting uses regular unicast addresses. It is up to the routing system to choose the lucky host that gets the packet.

A new notation has been devised for writing 16-byte addresses. They are written as eight groups of four hexadecimal digits with colons between the groups, like this:

8000:0000:0000:0000:0123:4567:89AB:CDEF

Since many addresses will have many zeros inside them, three optimizations have been authorized. First, leading zeros within a group can be omitted, so 0123 can be written as 123. Second, one or more groups of 16 zeros can be replaced by a pair of colons. Thus the above address now becomes

8000::123:4567:89AB:CDEF

Finally, IPv4 addresses can be written as a pair of colons and an old dotted decimal number, for example

::192.31.20.46

Perhaps it is unnecessary to be so explicit about it, but there are a lot of 16-byte addresses. Specifically, there are 2^{128} of them, which is approximately

3×10^{38}. If the entire earth, land and water, were covered with computers, IPv6 would allow 7×10^{23} IP addresses per square meter. Students of chemistry will notice that this number is larger than Avogadro's number. While it was not the intention to give every molecule on the surface of the earth its own IP address, we are not that far off.

In practice, the address space will not be used efficiently, just as the telephone number address space is not (the area code for Manhattan, 212, is nearly full, but that for Wyoming, 307, is nearly empty). In RFC 1715, Huitema calculated that using the allocation of telephone numbers as a guide, even in the most pessimistic scenario, there will still be well over 1000 IP addresses per square meter of the earth's surface (land and water). In any likely scenario, there will be trillions of them per square meter. In short, it seems unlikely that we will run out in the foreseeable future. It is also worth noting that only 28 percent of the address space has been allocated so far. The other 72 percent is available for future purposes not yet thought of.

It is instructive to compare the IPv4 header (Fig. 5-45) with the IPv6 header (Fig. 5-56) to see what has been left out in IPv6. The *IHL* field is gone because the IPv6 header has a fixed length. The *Protocol* field was taken out because the *Next header* field tells what follows the last IP header (e.g., a UDP or TCP segment).

All the fields relating to fragmentation were removed because IPv6 takes a different approach to fragmentation. To start with, all IPv6 conformant hosts and routers must support packets of 576 bytes. This rule makes fragmentation less likely to occur in the first place. In addition, when a host sends an IPv6 packet that is too large, instead of fragmenting it, the router that is unable to forward it sends back an error message. This message tells the host to break up all future packets to that destination. Having the host send packets that are the right size in the first place is ultimately much more efficient than having the routers fragment them on the fly.

Finally, the *Checksum* field is gone because calculating it greatly reduces performance. With the reliable networks now used, combined with the fact that the data link layer and transport layers normally have their own checksums, the value of yet another checksum was not worth the performance price it extracted. Removing all these features has resulted in a lean and mean network layer protocol. Thus the goal of IPv6—a fast, yet flexible, protocol with plenty of address space—has been met by this design.

Extension Headers

Nevertheless, some of the missing fields are occasionally still needed so IPv6 has introduced the concept of an (optional) **extension header**. These headers can be supplied to provide extra information, but encoded in an efficient way. Six kinds of extension headers are defined at present, as listed in Fig. 5-58. Each one is optional, but if more than one is present, they must appear directly after the fixed header, and preferably in the order listed.

Extension header	Description
Hop-by-hop options	Miscellaneous information for routers
Routing	Full or partial route to follow
Fragmentation	Management of datagram fragments
Authentication	Verification of the sender's identity
Encrypted security payload	Information about the encrypted contents
Destination options	Additional information for the destination

Fig. 5-58. IPv6 extension headers.

Some of the headers have a fixed format; others contain a variable number of variable-length fields. For these, each item is encoded as a (Type, Length, Value) tuple. The *Type* is a 1-byte field telling which option this is. The *Type* values have been chosen so that the first 2 bits tell routers that do not know how to process the option what to do. The choices are: skip the option, discard the packet, discard the packet and send back an ICMP packet, and the same as the previous one, except do not send ICMP packets for multicast addresses (to prevent one bad multicast packet from generating millions of ICMP reports).

The *Length* is also a 1-byte field. It tells how long the value is (0 to 255 bytes). The *Value* is any information required, up to 255 bytes.

The hop-by-hop header is used for information that all routers along the path must examine. So far, one option has been defined: support of datagrams exceeding 64K. The format of this header is shown in Fig. 5-59.

Next header	0	194	0
Jumbo payload length			

Fig. 5-59. The hop-by-hop extension header for large datagrams (jumbograms).

As with all extension headers, this one starts out with a byte telling what kind of header comes next. This byte is followed by one telling how long the hop-by-hop header is in bytes, excluding the first 8 bytes, which are mandatory. The next 2 bytes indicate that this option defines the datagram size (code 194) as a 4-byte number. The last 4 bytes give the size of the datagram. Sizes less than 65,536 are not permitted and will result in the first router discarding the packet and sending back an ICMP error message. Datagrams using this header extension are called

jumbograms. The use of jumbograms is important for supercomputer applications that must transfer gigabytes of data efficiently across the Internet.

The routing header lists one or more routers that must be visited on the way to the destination. Both strict routing (the full path is supplied) and loose routing (only selected routers are supplied) are available, but they are combined. The format of the routing header is shown in Fig. 5-60.

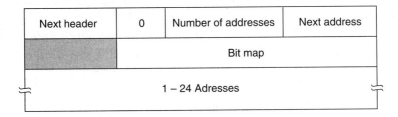

Fig. 5-60. The extension header for routing.

The first 4 bytes of the routing extension header contain four 1-byte integers: the next header type, the routing type (currently 0), the number of addresses present in this header (1 to 24), and the index of the next address to visit. The latter field starts at 0 and is incremented as each address is visited.

Then comes a reserved byte followed by a bit map with bits for each of the 24 potential IPv6 addresses following it. These bits tell whether each address must be visited directly after the one before it (strict source routing), or whether other routers may come in between (loose source routing).

The fragment header deals with fragmentation similarly to the way IPv4 does. The header holds the datagram identifier, fragment number, and a bit telling whether more fragments will follow. In IPv6, unlike in IPv4, only the source host can fragment a packet. Routers along the way may not do this. Although this change is a major philosophical break with the past, it simplifies the routers' work and makes routing go faster. As mentioned above, if a router is confronted with a packet that is too big, it discards the packet and sends an ICMP packet back to the source. This information allows the source host to fragment the packet into smaller pieces using this header and try again.

The authentication header provides a mechanism by which the receiver of a packet can be sure of who sent it. With IPv4, no such guarantee is present. The encrypted security payload makes it possible to encrypt the contents of a packet so that only the intended recipient can read it. These headers use cryptographic techniques to accomplish their missions. We will give brief descriptions below, but readers not already familiar with modern cryptography may not understand the full description now. They should come back after having read Chap. 7 (in particular, Sec. 7.1), which treats cryptographic protocols.

When a sender and receiver wish to communicate securely, they must first agree on one or more secret keys that only they know. How they do this is outside the scope of IPv6. Each of these keys is assigned a unique 32-bit key number. The key numbers are global, so that if Alice is using key 4 to talk to Bob, she cannot also have a key 4 to talk to Carol. Associated with each key number are other parameters, such as key lifetime, and so on.

To send an authenticated message, the sender first constructs a packet consisting of all the IP headers and the payload and then replaces the fields that change underway (e.g., *Hop limit*) with zeros. The packet is then padded out with zeros to a multiple of 16 bytes. Similarly, the secret key to be used is also padded out with zeros to a multiple of 16 bytes. Now a cryptographic checksum is computed on the concatenation of the padded secret key, the padded packet, and the padded secret key again. Users may define their own cryptographic checksum algorithms, but cryptographically unsophisticated users should use the default algorithm, MD5.

Now we come to the role of the authentication header. Basically, it contains three parts. The first part consists of 4 bytes holding the next header number, the length of the authentication header, and 16 zero bits. Then comes the 32-bit key number. Finally, the MD5 (or other) checksum is included.

The receiver then uses the key number to find the secret key. The padded version of it is then prepended and appended to the padded payload, the variable header fields are zeroed out, and the checksum computed. If it agrees with the checksum included in the authentication header, the receiver can be sure that the packet came from the sender with whom the secret key is shared and also be sure that the packet was not tampered with underway. The properties of MD5 make it computationally infeasible for an intruder to forge the sender's identity or modify the packet in a way that escapes detection.

It is important to note that the payload of an authenticated packet is sent unencrypted. Any router along the way can read what it says. For many applications, secrecy is not really important, just authentication. For example, if a user instructs his bank to pay his telephone bill, there is probably no real need for secrecy, but there is a very real need for the bank to be absolutely sure it knows who sent the packet containing the payment order.

For packets that must be sent secretly, the encrypted security payload extension header is used. It starts out with a 32-bit key number, followed by the encrypted payload. The encryption algorithm is up to the sender and receiver, but DES in cipher block chaining mode is the default. When DES-CBC is used, the payload field starts out with the initialization vector (a multiple of 4 bytes), then the payload, then padding out to multiple of 8 bytes. If both encryption and authentication are desired, both headers are needed.

The destination options header is intended for fields that need only be interpreted at the destination host. In the initial version of IPv6, the only options defined are null options for padding this header out to a multiple of 8 bytes, so initially it will not be used. It was included to make sure that new routing and host software can handle it, in case someone thinks of a destination option some day.

Controversies

Given the open design process and the strongly-held opinions of many of the people involved, it should come as no surprise that many choices made for IPv6 were highly controversial. We will summarize a few of these below. For all the gory details, see (Huitema, 1996).

We have already mentioned the argument about the address length. The result was a compromise: 16-byte fixed-length addresses.

Another fight developed over the length of the *Hop limit* field. One camp felt strongly that limiting the maximum number of hops to 255 (implicit in using an 8-bit field) was a gross mistake. After all, paths of 32 hops are common now, and 10 years from now much longer paths may be common. These people argued that using a huge address size was farsighted but using a tiny hop count was short-sighted. In their view, the greatest sin a computer scientist can commit is to provide too few bits somewhere.

The response was that arguments could be made to increase every field, leading to a bloated header. Also, the function of the *Hop limit* field is to keep packets from wandering around for a long time and 65,535 hops is far too long. Finally, as the Internet grows, more and more long-distance links will be built, making it possible to get from any country to any other country in half a dozen hops at most. If it takes more than 125 hops to get from the source and destination to their respective international gateways, something is wrong with the national backbones. The 8-bitters won this one.

Another hot potato was the maximum packet size. The supercomputer community wanted packets in excess of 64 KB. When a supercomputer gets started transferring, it really means business and does not want to be interrupted every 64 KB. The argument against large packets is that if a 1-MB packet hits a 1.5-Mbps T1 line, that packet will tie the line up for over 5 seconds, producing a very noticeable delay for interactive users sharing the line. A compromise was reached here: normal packets are limited to 64 KB, but the hop-by-hop extension header can be used to permit jumbograms.

A third hot topic was removing the IPv4 checksum. Some people likened this move to removing the brakes from a car. Doing so makes the car lighter so it can go faster, but if an unexpected event happens, you have a problem.

The argument against checksums was that any application that really cares about data integrity has to have a transport layer checksum anyway, so having another one in IP (in addition to the data link layer checksum) is overkill. Furthermore, experience showed that computing the IP checksum was a major expense in IPv4. The antichecksum camp won this one, and IPv6 does not have a checksum.

Mobile hosts were also a point of contention. If a portable computer flies halfway around the world, can it continue operating at the destination with the same IPv6 address, or does it have to use a scheme with home agents and foreign agents? Mobile hosts also introduce asymmetries into the routing system. It may well be the case that a small mobile computer can easily hear the powerful signal put out by a large stationary router, but the stationary router cannot hear the feeble signal put out by the mobile host. Consequently, some people wanted to build explicit support for mobile hosts into IPv6. That effort failed when no consensus could be found for any specific proposal.

Probably the biggest battle was about security. Everyone agreed it was needed. The war was about where and how. First where. The argument for putting it in the network layer is that it then becomes a standard service that all applications can use without any advance planning. The argument against it is that really secure applications generally want nothing less than end-to-end encryption, where the source application does the encryption and the destination application undoes it. With anything less, the user is at the mercy of potentially buggy network layer implementations over which he has no control. The response to this argument is that these applications can just refrain from using the IP security features and do the job themselves. The rejoinder to that is that the people who do not trust the network to do it right, do not want to have to pay the price of slow, bulky IP implementations that have this capability, even if it is disabled.

Another aspect of where to put security relates to the fact that many (but not all) countries have stringent export laws concerning cryptography. Some, notably France and Iraq, also greatly restrict its use domestically, so that people cannot have secrets from the police. As a result, any IP implementation that used a cryptographic system strong enough to be of much value could not be exported from the United States (and many other countries) to customers worldwide. Having to maintain two sets of software, one for domestic use and one for export, is something most computer vendors vigorously oppose.

One potential solution is for all vendors to move their cryptography shops to a country that does not regulate cryptography, such as Finland or Switzerland. Strong cryptographic software could be designed and manufactured there and then shipped legally to all countries except France and Iraq. The problem with this approach is that designing part of the router software in one country and part in another can lead to integration problems.

The final controversy concerning security relates to the choice of the default algorithms that all implementations must support. While MD5 was thought to be relatively secure, recent advances in cryptography may weaken it. No serious cryptographer believes that DES is secure against attacks by major governments, but it is probably good enough to foil even the most precocious 12-year-olds for the time being. The compromise was thus to mandate security in IPv6, use a state-of-the-art checksum algorithm for good authentication and a weakish algorithm for secrecy but give users the option of replacing these algorithms with their own.

One point on which there was no controversy is that no one expects the IPv4 Internet to be turned off on a Sunday morning and come back up as an IPv6

Internet Monday morning. Instead, isolated "islands" of IPv6 will be converted, initially communicating via tunnels. As the IPv6 islands grow, they will merge into bigger islands. Eventually, all the islands will merge, and the Internet will be fully converted. Given the massive investment in IPv4 routers currently deployed, the conversion process will probably take a decade. For this reason, an enormous amount of effort has gone into making sure that this transition will be as painless as possible.

5.6. THE NETWORK LAYER IN ATM NETWORKS

The layers of the ATM model (see Fig. 1-30) do not map onto the OSI layers especially well, which leads to ambiguities. The OSI data link layer deals with framing and transfer protocols between two machines on the same physical wire (or fiber). Data link layer protocols are single-hop protocols. They do not deal with end-to-end connections because switching and routing do not occur in the data link layer. About this there is no doubt.

The lowest layer that goes from source to destination, and thus involves routing and switching (i.e., is multihop), is the network layer. The ATM layer deals with moving cells from source to destination and definitely involves routing algorithms and protocols within the ATM switches. It also deals with global addressing. Thus functionally, the ATM layer performs the work expected of the network layer. The ATM layer is not guaranteed to be 100 percent reliable, but that is not required for a network layer protocol.

Also, the ATM layer resembles layer 3 of X.25, which everyone agrees is a network layer protocol. Depending on bit settings, the X.25 network layer protocol may or may not be reliable, but most implementations treat it as unreliable. Because the ATM layer has the functionality expected of the network layer, does not have the functionality expected of the data link layer, and is quite similar to existing network layer protocols, we will discuss the ATM layer in this chapter.

Confusion arises because many people in the ATM community regard the ATM layer as a data link layer, or when doing LAN emulation, even a physical layer. Many people in the Internet community also regard it as a data link layer because they want to put IP on top of it, and making the ATM layer a data link layer fits well with this idea. (Although following through with this line of reasoning, to the Internet community, *all* networks operate at the data link layer, no matter what their physical characteristics are.)

The only problem is that the ATM layer does not have the characteristics of a data link layer protocol: a single-hop protocol used by machines at the opposite ends of a wire, such as protocols 1 through 6 in Chap. 3. It has the characteristics of a network layer protocol: end-to-end virtual circuits, switching, and routing.

The author is reminded of an old riddle:

Q: How many legs would a mule have if you called the tail a leg?
A: Four. *Calling* the tail a leg does not *make* it a leg.

Suffice it to say, the reader is warned of controversy here, combined with a major dose of raw emotion.

The ATM layer is connection oriented, both in terms of the service it offers and the way it operates internally. The basic element of the ATM layer is the virtual circuit (officially called a **virtual channel**). A virtual circuit is normally a connection from one source to one destination, although multicast connections are also permitted. Virtual circuits are unidirectional, but a pair of circuits can be created at the same time. Both parts of the pair are addressed by the same identifier, so effectively a virtual circuit is full duplex. However, the channel capacity and other properties may be different in the two directions and may even be zero for one of them.

The ATM layer is unusual for a connection-oriented protocol in that it does not provide any acknowledgements. The reason for this design is that ATM was designed for use on fiber optic networks, which are highly reliable. It was thought adequate to leave error control to higher layers. After all, sending acknowledgements in the data link or network layer is really only an optimization. It is always sufficient for the transport layer to send a message and then send the entire message again if it is not acknowledged on time.

Furthermore, ATM networks are often used for real-time traffic, such as audio and video. For this kind of traffic, retransmitting an occasional bad cell is worse than just ignoring it.

Despite its lack of acknowledgements, the ATM layer does provide one hard guarantee: cells sent along a virtual circuit will never arrive out of order. The ATM subnet is permitted to discard cells if congestion occurs but under no conditions may it reorder the cells sent on a single virtual circuit. No ordering guarantees are given about cells sent on *different* virtual circuits, however. For example, if a host sends a cell on virtual circuit 10 and later sends a cell on virtual circuit 20 to the same destination, the second cell may arrive first. If the two cells had been sent on the same virtual circuit, the first one sent would always be the first one to arrive.

The ATM layer supports a two-level connection hierarchy that is visible to the transport layer. Along any transmission path from a given source to a given destination, a group of virtual circuits can be grouped together into what is called a **virtual path**, as depicted in Fig. 5-61. Conceptually, a virtual path is like a bundle of twisted copper pairs: when it is rerouted, all the pairs (virtual circuits) are rerouted together. We will consider the implications of this two-level design in detail later.

5.6.1. Cell Formats

In the ATM layer, two interfaces are distinguished: the **UNI (User-Network Interface)** and the **NNI (Network-Network Interface)**. The former defines the boundary between a host and an ATM network (in many cases, between the

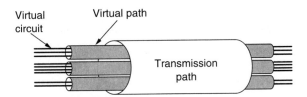

Fig. 5-61. A transmission path can hold multiple virtual paths, each of which can hold multiple virtual circuits.

customer and the carrier). The latter applies to the line between two ATM switches (the ATM term for routers).

In both cases the cells consist of a 5-byte header followed by a 48-byte payload, but the two headers are slightly different. The headers, as defined by the ATM Forum, are illustrated in Fig. 5-62. Cells are transmitted leftmost byte first and leftmost bit within a byte first.

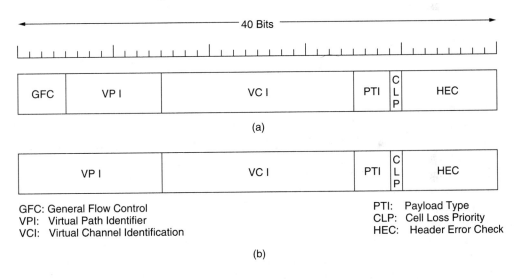

Fig. 5-62. (a) The ATM layer header at the UNI. (b) The ATM layer header at the NNI.

The *GFC* field is present only in cells between a host and the network. It is overwritten by the first switch it reaches, so it does not have end-to-end significance and is not delivered to the destination. It was originally conceived as perhaps having some utility for flow control or priority between hosts and the networks, but no values are defined for it and the network ignores it. The best way to think of it is as a bug in the standard.

The *VPI* field is a small integer selecting a particular virtual path (see Fig. 5-61). Similarly, the *VCI* field selects a particular virtual circuit within the chosen virtual path. Since the *VPI* field has 8 bits (at the UNI) and the *VCI* field has 16 bits, theoretically, a host could have up to 256 VC bundles, each containing up to 65,536 virtual circuits. Actually, slightly fewer of each are available because some *VCIs* are reserved for control functions, such as setting up virtual circuits.

The *PTI* field defines the type of payload the cell contains in accordance with the values given in Fig. 5-63. Here the cell types are user supplied, but the congestion information is network supplied. In other words, a cell sent with *PTI* 000 might arrive with 010 to warn the destination of problems underway.

Payload type	Meaning
000	User data cell, no congestion, cell type 0
001	User data cell, no congestion, cell type 1
010	User data cell, congestion experienced, cell type 0
011	User data cell, congestion experienced, cell type 1
100	Maintenance information between adjacent switches
101	Maintenance information between source and destination switches
110	Resource Management cell (used for ABR congestion control)
111	Reserved for future function

Fig. 5-63. Values of the *PTI* field.

The *CLP* bit can be set by a host to differentiate between high-priority traffic and low-priority traffic. If congestion occurs and cells must be discarded, switches first attempt to discard cells with *CLP* set to 1 before throwing out any set to 0.

Finally, the *HEC* field is a checksum over the header. It does not check the payload. A Hamming code on a 40-bit number only requires 5 bits, so with 8 bits a more sophisticated code can be used. The one chosen can correct all single-bit errors and can detect about 90 percent of all multibit errors. Various studies have shown that the vast majority of errors on optical links are single-bit errors.

Following the header comes 48 bytes of payload. Not all 48 bytes are available to the user, however, since some of the AAL protocols put their headers and trailers inside the payload.

The NNI format is the same as the UNI format, except that the *GFC* field is not present and those 4 bits are used to make the *VPI* field 12 bits instead of 8.

5.6.2. Connection Setup

ATM supports both permanent virtual circuits and switched virtual circuits. The former are always present and can be used at will, like leased lines. The latter have to be established each time they are used, like making phone calls. In this section we will describe how switched virtual circuits are established.

Technically, connection setup is not part of the ATM layer but is handled by the control plane (see Fig. 1-30) using a highly-complex ITU protocol called **Q.2931** (Stiller, 1995). Nevertheless, the logical place to handle setting up a network layer connection is in the network layer, and similar network layer protocols do connection setup here, so we will discuss it here.

Several ways are provided for setting up a connection. The normal way is to first acquire a virtual circuit for signaling and use it. To establish such a circuit, cells containing a request are sent on virtual path 0, virtual circuit 5. If successful, a new virtual circuit is opened on which connection setup requests and replies can be sent and received.

The reason for this two-step setup procedure is that this way the bandwidth reserved for virtual circuit 5 (which is barely used at all) can be kept extremely low. Also, an alternative way is provided to set up virtual circuits. Some carriers may allow users to have permanent virtual paths between predefined destinations, or allow them to set these up dynamically. Once a host has a virtual path to some other host, it can allocate virtual circuits on it itself, without the switches being involved.

Virtual circuit establishment uses the six message types listed in Fig. 5-64. Each message occupies one or more cells and contains the message type, length, and parameters. The messages can be sent by a host to the network or can be sent by the network (usually in response to a message from another host) to a host. Various other status and error reporting messages also exist but are not shown here.

Message	Meaning when sent by host	Meaning when sent by network
SETUP	Please establish a circuit	Incoming call
CALL PROCEEDING	I saw the incoming call	Your call request will be attempted
CONNECT	I accept the incoming call	Your call request was accepted
CONNECT ACK	Thanks for accepting	Thanks for making the call
RELEASE	Please terminate the call	The other side has had enough
RELEASE COMPLETE	Ack for RELEASE	Ack for RELEASE

Fig. 5-64. Messages used for connection establishment and release.

The normal procedure for establishing a call is for a host to send a SETUP message on a special virtual circuit. The network then responds with CALL PROCEEDING to acknowledge receipt of the request. As the SETUP message propagates toward the destination, it is acknowledged at each hop by CALL PROCEEDING.

When the SETUP message finally arrives, the destination host can respond with CONNECT to accept the call. The network then sends a CONNECT ACK message to indicate that it has received the CONNECT message. As the CONNECT message propagates back toward the originator, each switch receiving it acknowledges it with a CONNECT ACK message. This sequence of events is shown in Fig. 5-65(a).

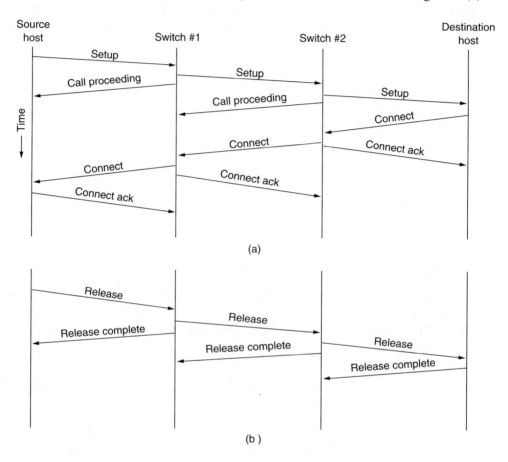

Fig. 5-65. (a) Connection setup in an ATM network. (b) Connection release.

The sequence for terminating a virtual circuit is simple. The host wishing to hang up just sends a RELEASE message, which propagates to the other end and causes the circuit to be released. Each hop along the way, the message is acknowledged, as shown in Fig. 5-65(b).

ATM networks allow multicast channels to be set up. A multicast channel has one sender and more than one receiver. These are constructed by setting up a connection to one of the destinations in the usual way. Then the ADD PARTY message is sent to attach a second destination to the virtual circuit returned by the previous call. Additional ADD PARTY messages can be sent afterward to increase the size of the multicast group.

In order to set up a connection to a destination, it is necessary to specify which destination, by including its address in the SETUP message. ATM addresses come in three forms. The first is 20 bytes long and is based on OSI addresses. The first byte indicates which of three formats the address is in. In the first format, bytes 2 and 3 specify a country, and byte 4 gives the format of the rest of the address, which contains a 3-byte authority, a 2-byte domain, a 2-byte area, and a 6-byte address, plus some other items. In the second format, bytes 2 and 3 designate an international organization instead of a country. The rest of the address is the same as in format 1. Alternatively, a older form of addressing (CCITT E.164) using 15-digit decimal ISDN telephone numbers is also permitted.

5.6.3. Routing and Switching

When a virtual circuit is set up, the SETUP message wends its way through the network from source to destination. The routing algorithm determines the path taken by this message, and thus by the virtual circuit. The ATM standard does not specify any particular routing algorithm, so the carrier is free to choose among the algorithms discussed earlier in this chapter, or to use a different one.

Experience with previous connection-oriented networks, such as X.25, have shown that a considerable amount of computing power in the switches can be expended determining how to convert the virtual circuit information in each cell to the choice of output line. The ATM designers wanted to avoid this fate, so the ATM layer has been designed to make efficient routing possible. In particular, the idea was to route on the *VPI* field, but not the *VCI* field, except at the final hop in each direction, when cells are sent between a switch and a host. Between two switches, only the virtual path was to be used.

Using only the *VPI*s between interior switches has several advantages. To start with, once a virtual path has been established from a source to a destination, any additional virtual circuits along that path can just follow the existing path. No new routing decisions have to be made. It is as though a bundle of twisted pairs has already been pulled from the source to the destination. Setting up a new connection merely requires allocating one of the unused pairs.

Second, routing of individual cells is easier when all virtual circuits for a given path are always in the same bundle. The routing decision only involves looking at a 12-bit number, not a 12-bit number and a 16-bit number. We will describe how cell switching is done below, but even without going into the details, it should be clear that indexing into a table of 2^{12} entries is feasible whereas indexing into a table of 2^{28} entries is not.

Third, basing all routing on virtual paths makes it easier to switch a whole group of virtual circuits. Consider, for example, the hypothetical U.S. ATM backbone illustrated in Fig. 5-66. Normally, virtual circuits from NY to SF pass through Omaha and Denver. However, suppose a disturbance occurs on the Omaha-Denver line. By rerouting the Omaha-Denver virtual path to LA and then SF, all the virtual circuits (potentially up to 65,535 of them) can be switched in one operation instead of potentially thousands of operations.

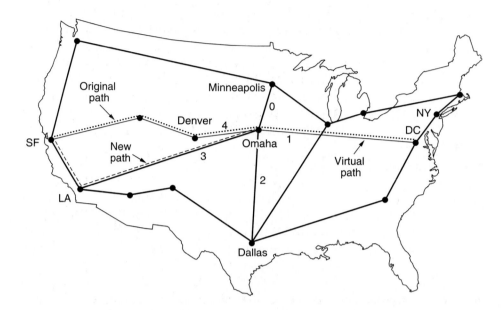

Fig. 5-66. Rerouting a virtual path reroutes all of its virtual circuits.

Finally, virtual paths make it easier for carriers to offer closed user groups (private networks) to corporate customers. A company can set up a network of permanent virtual paths among its various offices, and then allocate virtual circuits within these paths on demand. No calls can come into the private network from outside and no calls can leave the private network, except via special gateways. Many companies like this kind of security.

Whether switches will actually use the *VPI* field for routing as planned, or will, in fact, use the combination of the *VPI* and *VCI* fields (thus negating all the advantages just discussed) remains to be seen. Initial evidence from the field is not encouraging.

Let us now see how cells could be routed within an interior switch (one that is attached only to other switches and not to hosts). To make matters concrete, let us consider the Omaha switch of Fig. 5-66. For each of its five incoming lines, it has a table, *vpi_table*, indexed by incoming *VPI* that tells which of the five outgoing lines to use and what VPI to put in outgoing cells. Let us assume the five lines are numbered from 0 to 4, clockwise starting at Minneapolis. For each outgoing line, the switch maintains a bit map telling which *VPI*s are currently in use on that line.

When the switch is booted, all the entries in all the *vpi_table* structures are marked as not in use. Similarly, all the bit maps are marked to indicate that all *VPI*s are available (except the reserved ones). Now suppose calls come as shown in Fig. 5-67.

As each virtual path (and virtual circuit) is set up, entries are made in the tables. We will assume the virtual circuits are full duplex, so that each one set up

Source	Incoming line	Incoming VPI	Destination	Outgoing line	Outgoing VPI	Path:
NY	1	1	SF	4	1	New
NY	1	2	Denver	4	2	New
LA	3	1	Minneapolis	0	1	New
DC	1	3	LA	3	2	New
NY	1	1	SF	4	1	Old
SF	4	3	DC	1	4	New
DC	1	5	SF	4	4	New
NY	1	2	Denver	4	2	Old
SF	4	5	Minneapolis	0	2	New
NY	1	1	SF	4	1	Old

Fig. 5-67. Some routes through the Omaha switch of Fig. 5-66.

results in two entries, one for the forward traffic from the source and one for the reverse traffic from the destination.

The tables corresponding to the routes of Fig. 5-67 are shown in Fig. 5-68. For example, the first call generates the (4, 1) entry for *VPI* 1 in the DC table because it refers to cells coming in on line 1 with *VPI* 1 and going to SF. However, an entry is also made in the Denver table for *VPI* 1 showing that cells coming in from Denver with *VPI* 1 should go out on line 1 with *VPI* 1. These are cells traveling the other way (from SF to NY) on this virtual path. Note that in some cases two or three virtual circuits are sharing a common path. No new table entries are needed for additional virtual circuits connecting a source and destination that already have a path assigned.

Now we can explain how cells are processed inside a switch. Suppose that a cell arrives on line 1 (DC) with *VPI* 3. The switch hardware or software uses the 3 as an index into the table for line 1 and sees that the cell should go out on line 3 (LA) with *VPI* 2. It overwrites the *VPI* field with a 2 and puts the outgoing line number, 3, somewhere in the cell, for example, in the *HEC* field, since that has to be recomputed later anyway.

Now the question is how to get the cell from its current input buffer to line 3. However, this issue (routing within a switch) was discussed in detail in Chap. 2, and we saw how it was done in knockout and Batcher-banyan switches.

At this point it is straightforward to see how an entire bundle of virtual circuits can be rerouted, as is done in Fig. 5-66. By changing the entry for *VPI* 1 in the DC table from (4, 1) to (3, 3), cells from NY headed for SF will be diverted to LA. Of course, the LA switch has to be informed of this event, so the switch has

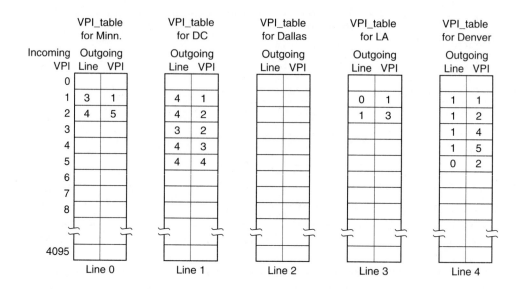

Fig. 5-68. The table entries for the routes of Fig. 5-67.

to generate and send a SETUP message to LA to establish the new path with *VPI* 3. Once this path has been set up, all the virtual circuits from NY to SF are now rerouted via LA, even if there are thousands of them. If virtual paths did not exist, each virtual circuit would have its own table entry and would have to be rerouted separately.

It is worth pointing out explicitly that the discussion above is about ATM in WANs. In a LAN, matters are much simpler. For example, a single virtual path can be used for all virtual circuits.

5.6.4. Service Categories

After a fair amount of trial and error, by version 4.0 of the ATM specification, it was becoming clear what kinds of traffic ATM networks were carrying and what kind of services their customers wanted. Consequently, the standard was modified to explicitly list the service categories commonly used, in order to allow equipment vendors to optimize their adaptor boards and switches for some or all of these categories. The service categories chosen as being important are listed in Fig. 5-69.

The **CBR (Constant Bit Rate)** class is intended to emulate a copper wire or optical fiber (only at much greater expense). Bits are put on one end and they come off the other end. No error checking, flow control, or other processing is done. Nevertheless, this class is essential to making a smooth transition between

Class	Description	Example
CBR	Constant bit rate	T1 circuit
RT-VBR	Variable bit rate: real time	Real-time videoconferencing
NRT-VBR	Variable bit rate: non-real time	Multimedia email
ABR	Available bit rate	Browsing the Web
UBR	Unspecified bit rate	Background file transfer

Fig. 5-69. The ATM service categories.

the current telephone system and future B-ISDN systems, since voice-grade PCM channels, T1 circuits, and most of the rest of the telephone system use constant-rate, synchronous bit transmission. With the CBR class, all of this traffic can be carried directly by an ATM system. CBR is also suited to all other interactive (i.e., real-time) audio and video streams.

The next class, **VBR (Variable Bit Rate)**, is divided into two subclasses, for real time and non-real time, respectively. RT-VBR is intended for services that have variable bit rates combined with stringent real-time requirements, such as interactive compressed video (e.g., videoconferencing). Due to the way MPEG and other compression schemes work, with a complete base frame followed by a series of differences between the current frame and the base frame, the transmission rate varies strongly in time (Pancha and El Zarki, 1994). Despite this variation, it is essential that the ATM network not introduce any jitter in the cell arrival pattern, as this will cause the display to appear jerky. In other words, both the average cell delay and the variation in cell delay must be tightly controlled. On the other hand, an occasional lost bit or cell here is tolerable and is best just ignored.

The other VBR subclass is for traffic where timely delivery is important but a certain amount of jitter can be tolerated by the application. For example, multimedia email is typically spooled to the receiver's local disk before being displayed, so any variation in cell delivery times will be eliminated before the email is viewed.

The **ABR (Available Bit Rate)** service category is designed for bursty traffic whose bandwidth range is known roughly. A typical example might be for use in a company that currently connects its offices by a collection of leased lines. Typically, the company has a choice of putting in enough capacity to handle the peak load, which means that some lines are idle part of the day, or putting in just enough capacity for the minimum load, which leads to congestion during the busiest part of the day.

Using ABR service avoids having to make a long term commitment to a fixed bandwidth. With ABR it is possible to say, for example, that the capacity between two points must always be 5 Mbps, but might have peaks up to 10 Mbps.

The system will then guarantee 5 Mbps all the time, and do its best to provide 10 Mbps when needed, but with no promises.

ABR is the only service category in which the network provides rate feedback to the sender, asking it to slow down when congestion occurs. Assuming that the sender complies with such requests, cell loss for ABR traffic is expected to be low. Traveling ABR is a little like flying standby: if there are seats left over (excess capacity), standby passengers are transported without delay. If there is insufficient capacity, they have to wait (unless some of the minimum bandwidth is available).

Finally, we come to **UBR** (**Unspecified Bit Rate**), which makes no promises and gives no feedback about congestion. This category is well suited to sending IP packets, since IP also makes no promises about delivery. All UBR cells are accepted, and if there is capacity left over, they will also be delivered. If congestion occurs, UBR cells will be discarded, with no feedback to the sender and no expectation that the sender slows down.

To continue our standby analogy, with UBR, all standby passengers get to board, but if halfway to the destination the pilot sees that fuel is running low, standby passengers are unceremoniously pushed through the emergency exit. To make UBR attractive, carriers are likely to make it cheaper than the other classes. For applications that have no delivery constraints and want to do their own error control and flow control anyway, UBR is a perfectly reasonably choice. File transfer, email, and USENET news are all potential candidates for UBR service because none of these applications have real-time characteristics.

The properties of the various service categories are summarized in Fig. 5-70.

Service characteristic	CBR	RT-VBR	NRT-VBR	ABR	UBR
Bandwidth guarantee	Yes	Yes	Yes	Optional	No
Suitable for real-time traffic	Yes	Yes	No	No	No
Suitable for bursty traffic	No	No	Yes	Yes	Yes
Feedback about congestion	No	No	No	Yes	No

Fig. 5-70. Characteristics of the ATM service categories.

5.6.5. Quality of Service

Quality of service is an important issue for ATM networks, in part because they are used for real-time traffic, such as audio and video. When a virtual circuit is established, both the transport layer (typically a process in the host machine, the "customer") and the ATM network layer (e.g., a network operator, the "carrier") must agree on a contract defining the service. In the case of a public network, this contract may have legal implications. For example, if the carrier agrees not to lose more than one cell per billion and it loses two cells per billion, the customer's legal staff may get all excited and start running around yelling "breach of contract."

The contract between the customer and the network has three parts:

1. The traffic to be offered.

2. The service agreed upon.

3. The compliance requirements.

It is worth noting that the contract may be different for each direction. For a video-on-demand application, the required bandwidth from the user's remote control to the video server might be 1200 bps. In the other direction it might be 5 Mbps. It should be noted that if the customer and the carrier cannot agree on terms, or the carrier is unable to provide the service desired, the virtual circuit will not be set up.

The first part of the contract is the **traffic descriptor**. It characterizes the load to be offered. The second part of the contract specifies the quality of service desired by the customer and accepted by the carrier. Both the load and the service must be formulated in terms of measurable quantities, so compliance can be objectively determined. Merely saying "moderate load" or "good service" will not do.

To make it possible to have concrete traffic contracts, the ATM standard defines a number of **QoS (Quality of Service)** parameters whose values the customer and carrier can negotiate. For each quality of service parameter, the worst case performance for each parameter is specified, and the carrier is required to meet or exceed it. In some cases, the parameter is a minimum; in others it is a maximum. Again here, the quality of service is specified separately for each direction. Some of the more important ones are listed in Fig. 5-71, but not all of them are applicable to all service categories.

The first three parameters specify how fast the user wants to send. **PCR (Peak Cell Rate)** is the maximum rate at which the sender is planning to send cells. This parameter may be lower than what the bandwidth of the line permits. If the sender is planning to push out a cell every 4 μsec, its *PCR* is 250,000 cells/sec, even though the actual cell transmission time may be 2.7 μsec.

SCR (Sustained Cell Rate) is the expected or required cell rate averaged over a long time interval. For CBR traffic, *SCR* will be equal to *PCR*, but for all the other service categories, it will be substantially lower. The *PCR/SCR* ratio is one measure of the burstiness of the traffic.

MCR (Minimum Cell Rate) is the minimum number of cells/sec that the customer considers acceptable. If the carrier is unable to guarantee to provide this much bandwidth it must reject the connection. When ABR service is requested, then the actual bandwidth used must lie between *MCR* and *PCR*, but it may vary

Parameter	Acronym	Meaning
Peak cell rate	PCR	Maximum rate at which cells will be sent
Sustained cell rate	SCR	The long-term average cell rate
Minimum cell rate	MCR	The minimum acceptable cell rate
Cell delay variation tolerance	CDVT	The maximum acceptable cell jitter
Cell loss ratio	CLR	Fraction of cells lost or delivered too late
Cell transfer delay	CTD	How long delivery takes (mean and maximum)
Cell delay variation	CDV	The variance in cell delivery times
Cell error rate	CER	Fraction of cells delivered without error
Severely-errored cell block ratio	SECBR	Fraction of blocks garbled
Cell misinsertion rate	CMR	Fraction of cells delivered to wrong destination

Fig. 5-71. Some of the quality of service parameters.

dynamically during the lifetime of the connection. If the customer and carrier agree to setting MCR to 0, then ABR service becomes similar to UBR service.

CVDT (Cell Variation Delay Tolerance) tells how much variation will be present in cell transmission times. It is specified independently for *PCR* and *SCR*. For a perfect source operating at *PCR*, every cell will appear *exactly* $1/PCR$ after the previous one. No cell will ever be early and no cell will ever be late, not even by a picosecond. For a real source operating at *PCR*, some variation will occur in cell transmission times. The question is: How much variation is acceptable? Can a cell be 1 nsec early? How about 30 seconds? *CDVT* controls the amount of variability acceptable using a leaky bucket algorithm to be described shortly.

The next three parameters describe characteristics of the network and are measured at the receiver. All three are negotiable. **CLR (Cell Loss Ratio)** is straightforward. It measures the fraction of the transmitted cells that are not delivered at all or are delivered so late as to be useless (e.g., for real-time traffic). **CTD (Cell Transfer Delay)** is the average transit time from source to destination. **CDV (Cell Delay Variation)** measures how uniformly the cells are delivered.

The model for *CDT* and *CDV* is shown in Fig. 5-72. Here we see the probability of a cell taking time *t* to arrive, as a function of *t*. For a given source, destination, and route through the intermediate switches, some minimum delay always exists due to propagation and switching time. However, not all cells make it in the minimum time; the probability density function usually has a long tail. By choosing a value of *CDT*, the customer and the carrier are, in effect, agreeing, on how late a cell can be delivered and still count as a correctly delivered cell. Normally, *CDV* will be chosen so that, α, the fraction of cells that are rejected for being too late will be on the order of 10^{-10} or less. *CDV* measures the spread in arrival times. For real-time traffic, this parameter is often more important than *CDT*.

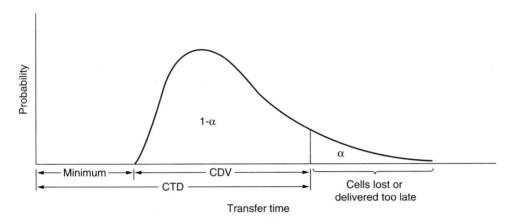

Fig. 5-72. The probability density function for cell arrival times.

The last three QoS parameters specify characteristics of the network. They are generally not negotiable. **CER (Cell Error Ratio)** is the fraction of cells that are delivered with one or more bits wrong. **SECBR (Severely-Errored Cell Block Ratio)** is the fraction of N-cell blocks of which M or more cells contain an error. Finally, **CMR (Cell Misinsertion Rate)** is the number of cells/sec that are delivered to the wrong destination on account of an undetected error in the header.

The third part of the traffic contract tells what constitutes obeying the rules. If the customer sends one cell too early, does this void the contract? If the carrier fails to meet one of its quality targets for a period of 1 msec, can the customer sue? Effectively, this part of the contract is negotiated between the parties and says how strictly the first two parts will be enforced.

The ATM and Internet quality of service models differ somewhat, which impacts their respective implementations. The ATM model is based strictly on connections, whereas the Internet model uses datagrams plus flows (e.g., RSVP). A comparison of these two models is given in (Crowcroft et al., 1995).

5.6.6. Traffic Shaping and Policing

The mechanism for using and enforcing the quality of service parameters is based (in part) on a specific algorithm, the **Generic Cell Rate Algorithm (GCRA)**, and is illustrated in Fig. 5-73. It works by checking every cell to see if it conforms to the parameters for its virtual circuit.

GCRA has two parameters. These specify the maximum allowed arrival rate (*PCR*) and the amount of variation herein that is tolerable (*CDVT*). The

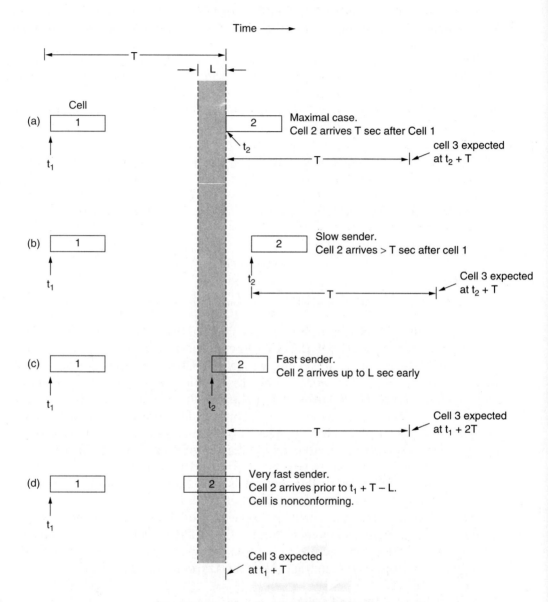

Fig. 5-73. The generic cell rate algorithm.

reciprocal of *PCR*, $T = 1/PCR$, is the minimum cell interarrival time, as shown in Fig. 5-73(a). If the customer agrees not to send more than 100,000 cells/sec, then $T = 10$ μsec. In the maximal case, one cell arrives promptly every 10 μsec. To avoid tiny numbers, we will work in microseconds, but since all the parameters are real numbers, the unit of time does not matter.

A sender is always permitted to space consecutive cells more widely than T, as shown in Fig. 5-73(b). Any cell arriving more than T μsec after the previous one is conforming.

The problem arises with senders that tend to jump the gun, as in Fig. 5-73(c) and (d). If a cell arrives a little early (at or later than $t_1 + T - L$), it is conforming, but the next cell is still expected at $t_1 + 2T$, (not at $t_2 + T$), to prevent the sender from transmitting every cell L μsec early, and thus increasing the peak cell rate.

If a cell arrives more than L μsec early, it is declared as nonconforming. The treatment of nonconforming cells is up to the carrier. Some carriers may simply discard them; others may keep them, but set the *CLP* bit, to mark them as low priority to allow switches to drop nonconforming cells first in the event of congestion. The use of the *CLP* bit may also be different for the different service categories of Fig. 5-69.

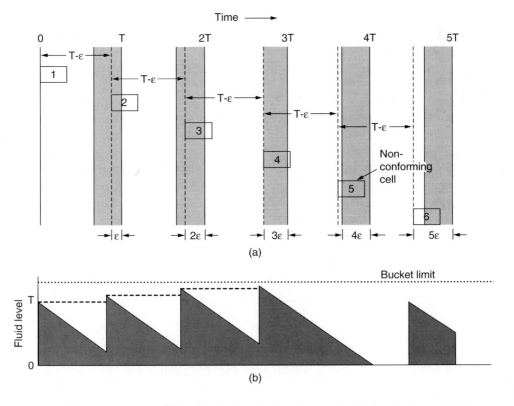

Fig. 5-74. (a) A sender trying to cheat. (b) The same cell arrival pattern, but now viewed in terms of a leaky bucket.

Now let us consider what happens if a sender tries to cheat a little bit, as shown in Fig. 5-74(a). Instead of waiting until time T to send cell 2, the sender transmits it a wee bit early, at $T - \varepsilon$, where, say, $\varepsilon = 0.3L$. This cell is accepted without problems.

Now the sender transmits cell 3, again at $T - \varepsilon$ after the previous cell, that is, at $T - 2\varepsilon$. Again it is accepted. However, every successive cell inches closer and closer to the fatal $T - L$ boundary. In this case, cell 5 arrives at $T - 4\varepsilon$ ($T - 1.2L$) which is too early, so cell 5 is declared nonconforming and is discarded by the network interface.

When viewed in these terms, the GCRA algorithm is called a **virtual scheduling algorithm**. However, viewed differently, it is equivalent to a leaky bucket algorithm, as depicted in Fig. 5-74(b). Imagine that each conforming cell that arrives pours T units of fluid into a leaky bucket. The bucket leaks fluid at a rate of 1 unit/µsec, so that after T µsec it is all gone. If cells arrive precisely every T µsec, each arriving cell will find the bucket (just) emptied, and will refill it with T units of fluid. Thus the fluid level is raised to T when a cell arrives and is reduced linearly until it gets to zero. This situation is illustrated in Fig. 5-74(b) between 0 and T.

Since fluid drains out linearly in time, at a time t after a cell arrives, the amount of its fluid left is $T - t$. At the time cell 2 arrives, at $T - \varepsilon$, there are still ε units of fluid in the bucket. The addition of the new cell raises this value to $T + \varepsilon$. Similarly, at the time cell 3 arrives, 2ε units are left in the bucket so the new cell raises the fluid level to $T + 2\varepsilon$. When cell 4 arrives, it is raised to $T + 3\varepsilon$.

If this goes on indefinitely, some cell is going to raise the level to above the bucket capacity and thus be rejected. To see which one it is, let us now compute what the bucket capacity is. We want the leaky bucket algorithm to give the same result as Fig. 5-74(a), so we want overflow to occur when a cell arrives L µsec early. If the fluid left requires L µsec to drain out, the amount of fluid must be L, since the drain rate is 1 unit/µsec. Thus we want the bucket capacity to be $L + T$ so that any cell arriving more than L µsec early will be rejected due to bucket overflow. In Fig. 5-74(b), when cell 5 arrives, the addition of T units to the 4ε units of fluid already present raises the bucket level to $T + 4\varepsilon$. Since we are using $\varepsilon = 0.3L$ in this example, the bucket would be raised to $T + 1.2L$ by the addition of cell 5, so the cell is rejected, no new fluid is added, and the bucket eventually empties.

For a given T, if we set L very small, the capacity of the bucket will be hardly more than T, so all cells will have to be sent with a very uniform spacing. However, if we now raise L to a value much greater than T, the bucket can hold multiple cells because $T + L \gg T$. This means that the sender can transmit a burst of cells back-to-back at the peak rate and have them still accepted.

We can easily compute the number of conforming cells, N, that can be transmitted back-to-back at the peak cell rate ($PCR = 1/T$). During a burst of N cells, the total amount of fluid added to the bucket is NT because each cell adds T. However, during the maximum burst, fluid drains out of the bucket at a rate of 1 unit per time interval. Let us call the cell transmission time δ time units. Note that $\delta \leq T$ because it is entirely possible for a sender on a 155.52 Mbps line to agree to send no more than 100,000 cells/sec, in which case $\delta = 2.73$ μsec and $T = 10$ μsec. During the burst of N cells, the amount of drainage is $(N - 1)\delta$ because drainage does not start until the first cell has been entirely transmitted.

From these observations, we set that the net increase in fluid in the bucket during the maximum burst is $NT - (N - 1)\delta$. The bucket capacity is $T + L$. Equating these two quantities we get

$$NT - (N - 1)\delta = T + L$$

Solving this equation for N we get

$$N = 1 + \frac{L}{T - \delta}$$

However, if this number is not an integer, it must be rounded downward to an integer to prevent bucket overflow. For example, with $PCR = 100,000$ cells/sec, $\delta = 2.73$ μsec, and $L = 50$ μsec, seven cells may be sent back-to-back at the 155.52 Mbps rate without filling the bucket. An eighth cell would be nonconforming.

The GCRA is normally specified by giving the parameters T and L. T is just the reciprocal of PCR; L is $CDVT$. The GCRA is also used to make sure the mean cell rate does not exceed SCR for any substantial period.

In this example we assumed that cells arrive uniformly. In reality, they do not. Nevertheless, the leaky bucket algorithm can also be used here, too. At every cell arrival, a check is made to see if there is room in the bucket for an additional T units of fluid. If there is, the cell is conforming; otherwise it is not.

In addition to providing a rule about which cells are conforming and which ones are not, the GCRA also shapes the traffic to remove some of the burstiness. The smaller $CDVT$ is, the greater the smoothing effect, but the greater the chance that cells will be discarded as nonconforming. Some implementations combine the GCRA leaky bucket with a token bucket, to provide additional smoothing.

5.6.7. Congestion Control

Even with traffic shaping, ATM networks do not automatically meet the performance requirements set forth in the traffic contract. For example, congestion at intermediate switches is always a potential problem, especially when over 350,000 cells/sec are pouring in on each line, and a switch can have 100 lines. Consequently, a great deal of thought has gone into the subject of performance and congestion in ATM networks. In this section, we will discuss some of the approaches used. For additional information, see (Eckberg, 1992; Eckberg et al., 1991; Hong and Suda, 1991; Jain, 1995; and Newman, 1994).

ATM networks must deal with both long-term congestion, caused by more traffic coming in than the system can handle, and short-term congestion, caused by burstiness in the traffic. As a result, several different strategies are used together. The most important of these fall into three categories:

1. Admission control.

2. Resource reservation.

3. Rate-based congestion control.

We will now discuss each of these strategies in turn.

Admission Control

In low-speed networks, it is usually adequate to wait for congestion to occur and then react to it by telling the source of the packets to slow down. In high-speed networks, this approach often works poorly, because in the interval between sending the notification and notification arriving at the source, thousands of additional packets may arrive.

Furthermore, many ATM networks have real-time traffic sources that produce data at an intrinsic rate. Telling such a source to slow down may not work (imagine a new digital telephone with a red light on it; when congestion is signaled, the red line comes on and the speaker is required to talk 25 percent slower).

Consequently, ATM networks emphasize preventing congestion from occurring in the first place. However, for CBR, VBR, and UBR traffic, no dynamic congestion control is present at all, so here an ounce of prevention is worth a pound (actually, more like a metric ton) of cure. A major tool for preventing congestion is admission control. When a host wants a new virtual circuit, it must describe the traffic to be offered and the service expected. The network can then check to see if it is possible to handle this connection without adversely affecting existing connections. Multiple potential routes may have to be examined to find one which can do the job. If no route can be located, the call is rejected.

Denying admission should be done fairly. Is it fair that one couch potato zapping through dozens of television programs can wipe out 100 busy beavers trying to read their email? If no controls are applied, a small number of high-bandwidth users can severely affect many low-bandwidth users. To prevent this, users should be divided into classes based on usage. The probability of service denial should be roughly the same for all classes (possibly by giving each class its own resource pool).

Resource Reservation

Closely related to admission control is the technique of reserving resources in advance, usually at call setup time. Since the traffic descriptor gives the peak cell rate, the network has the possibility of reserving enough bandwidth along the path to handle that rate. Bandwidth can be reserved by having the SETUP message ear-mark bandwidth along each line it traverses, making sure, of course, that the total bandwidth earmarked along a line is less than the capacity of that line. If the SETUP message hits a line that is full, it must backtrack and look for an alternative path.

The traffic descriptor can contain not only the peak bandwidth, but also the average bandwidth. If a host wants, for example, a peak bandwidth of 100,000 cells/sec, but an average bandwidth of only 20,000 cells/sec, in principle, five such circuits could be multiplexed onto the same physical trunk. The trouble is that all five connections could be idle for half an hour, then start blasting away at the peak rate, causing massive cell loss. Since VBR traffic can be statistically multiplexed, problems can occur with this service category. Possible solutions are being studied.

Rate-Based Congestion Control

With CBR and VBR traffic, it is generally not possible for the sender to slow down, even in the event of congestion, due to the inherent real-time or semi-real-time nature of the information source. With UBR, nobody cares; if there are too many cells, the extra ones are just dropped.

However, with ABR traffic, it is possible and reasonable for the network to signal one or more senders and ask them to slow down temporarily until the net-work can recover. It is in the interest of a sender to comply, since the network can always punish it by throwing out its (excess) cells.

How congestion should be detected, signaled, and controlled for ABR traffic was a hot topic during the development of the ATM standard, with vigorous argu-ments for various proposed solutions. Let us now briefly look at some of the solu-tions that were quickly rejected before examining the winner.

In one proposal, whenever a sender wished to send a burst of data, it first had to send a special cell reserving the necessary bandwidth. After the acknowledge-ment came back, the burst could begin. The advantage here is that congestion never occurs because the required bandwidth is always there when it is needed. The ATM Forum rejected this solution due to the potentially long delay before a host may begin to send.

A second proposal had switches sending back choke cells whenever conges-tion began to occur. Upon receipt of such a cell, a sender was expected to cut back to half its current cell transmission rate. Various schemes were proposed for getting the rate back up again later when the congestion cleared up. This scheme was rejected because choke cells might get lost in the congestion, and because the scheme seemed unfair to small users. For example, consider a switch getting 100-Mbps streams from each of five users, and one 100-kbps stream from another user. Many committee members felt it was inappropriate to tell the 100 kbps user to give up 50 kbps because he was causing too much congestion.

A third proposal used the fact that packet boundaries are marked by a bit in the last cell. The idea here was to discard cells to relieve the congestion but to do this highly selectively. The switch was to scan the incoming cell stream for the end of a packet and then throw out all the cells in the next packet. Of course, this one packet would be transmitted later, but dropping all k cells in one packet ultimately leads to one packet retransmission, which is far better than dropping k random cells, which might lead to k packet retransmissions. This scheme was rejected on fairness grounds because the next end-of-packet mark seen might not belong to the sender overloading the switch. Also the scheme did not need to be standardized. Any switch vendor is free to pick which cells to discard when congestion occurs.

After much discussion, the battle focused on two contenders, a credit-based solution (Kung and Morris, 1995) and rate-based solution (Bonomi and Fendick, 1995). The credit-based solution was essentially a dynamic sliding window protocol. It required each switch to maintain, per virtual circuit, a credit—effectively the number of buffers reserved for that circuit. As long as each transmitted cell had a buffer waiting for it, congestion could never arise.

The argument against it came from the switch vendors. They did not want to do all the accounting to keep track of the credits and did not want to reserve so many buffers in advance. The amount of overhead and waste required was thought to be too much, so ultimately, the rate-based congestion control scheme was adopted. It works like this.

The basic model is that after every k data cells, each sender transmits a special **RM** (**Resource Management**) cell. This cell travels along the same path as the data cells, but is treated specially by the switches along the way. When it gets to the destination, it is examined, updated, and sent back to the sender. The full path for RM cells is shown in Fig. 5-75.

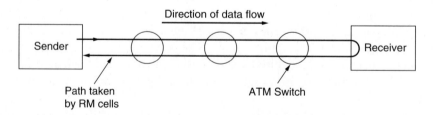

Fig. 5-75. The path taken by RM cells.

In addition, two other congestion control mechanisms are provided. First, overloaded switches can spontaneously generate RM cells and ship them back to the sender. Second, overloaded switches can set the middle *PTI* bit on data cells traveling from the sender to the receiver. Neither of these methods are fully reliable however, since these cells may be lost in the congestion without anyone noticing. In contrast, a lost RM cell will be noticed by the sender when it fails to return within the expected time interval. As an aside, the *CLP* bit is not used for ABR congestion control.

ABR congestion control is based on the idea that each sender has a current rate, **ACR** (**Actual Cell Rate**) that falls between *MCR* and *PCR*. When congestion occurs, *ACR* is reduced (but not below *MCR*). When congestion is absent, *ACR* is increased (but not above *PCR*). Each RM cell sent contains the rate at which the sender would currently like to transmit, possibly *PCR*, possibly lower. This value is called **ER** (**Explicit Rate**). As the RM cell passes through various switches on the way to the receiver, those that are congested may reduce *ER*. No switch may increase it. Reduction can occur either in the forward direction or in the reverse direction. When the sender gets the RM cell back, it can then see what the minimum acceptable rate is according to all the switches along the path. It can then adjust *ACR*, if need be, to bring it into line with what the slowest switch can handle.

The congestion mechanism using the middle *PTI* bit is integrated into the RM cells by having the receiver include this bit (taken from the last data cell) in each RM cell sent back. The bit cannot be taken from the RM cell itself because all RM cells have this bit set all the time, as shown in Fig. 5-63.

The ATM layer is quite complicated. In this chapter, we have highlighted only a portion of the issues. For additional information, see (De Prycker, 1993; McDysan and Spohn, 1995; Minoli and Vitella, 1994; and La Porta et al., 1994). However, the reader should be warned that all these references discuss the ATM 3 standard, not the ATM 4 standard, which was not finalized until 1996.

5.6.8. ATM LANs

As it becomes increasingly obvious that ITU's original goal of replacing the public switched telephone network by an ATM network is going to take a very long time, attention is shifting to the use of ATM technology to connect existing LANs together. In this approach, an ATM network can function either as a LAN, connecting individual hosts, or as a bridge, connecting multiple LANs. Although both concepts are interesting, they raise some challenging issues that we will discuss below. Additional information about ATM LANs can be found in (Chao et al., 1994; Newman, 1994; Truong et al., 1995).

The major problem that must be solved is how to provide connectionless LAN service over a connection-oriented ATM network. One possible solution is to introduce a connectionless server into the network. Every host initially sets up a connection to this server, and sends all packets to it for forwarding. While simple, this solution does not use the full bandwidth of the ATM network, and the connectionless server can easily become a bottleneck.

An alternative approach, proposed by the ATM Forum, is shown in Fig. 5-76. Here every host has a (potential) ATM virtual circuit to every other host. These virtual circuits can be established and released dynamically as needed, or they can be permanent virtual circuits. To send a frame, the source host first encapsulates the packet in the payload field of an ATM AAL message and sends it to the destination, the same way frames are shipped over Ethernets, token rings, and other LANs.

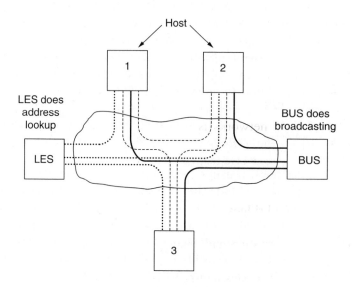

Fig. 5-76. ATM LAN emulation.

The main problem introduced by this scheme is how to tell which IP (or other network layer address) belongs to which virtual circuit. In an 802 LAN, this problem is solved by the ARP protocol, in which a host can broadcast a request such as: "Who has IP address 192.31.20.47?" The host using that address then sends back a point-to-point response, which is cached for later use.

With an ATM LAN, this solution does not work because ATM LANs do not support broadcasting. This problem is solved by introducing a new server, the **LES** (**LAN Emulation Server**). To look up a network layer address (e.g., an IP address), a host sends a packet (e.g., an ARP request) to the LES, which then looks up the corresponding ATM address and returns it to the machine requesting it. This address can then be used to send encapsulated packets to the destination.

However, this solution only solves the host location problem. Some programs use broadcasting or multicasting as an essential part of the application. For these applications, the **BUS** (**Broadcast/Unknown Server**) is introduced. It has connections to all hosts and can simulate broadcasting by sending a packet to all of them, one at a time. Hosts can also speed up delivery of a packet to an unknown host by sending the packet to the BUS for broadcasting and then (in parallel) looking up the address (for future use) using the LES.

A model similar to this one has been adopted by the IETF as the official Internet way to use an ATM network for transporting IP packets. In this model the

LES server is called the **ATMARP** server, but the functionality is essentially the same. Broadcasting and multicasting are not supported in the IETF proposal. The model is described in RFC 1483 and RFC 1577. Another good source of information is (Comer, 1995).

In the IETF method, a set of ATM hosts can be grouped together to form a **logical IP subnet**. Each LIS has its own ATMARP server. In effect, a LIS acts like a virtual LAN. Hosts on the same LIS may exchange IP packets directly, but hosts on different ones are required to go through a router. The reason for having LISes is that every host on a LIS must (potentially) have an open virtual circuit to every other host on its LIS. By restricting the number of hosts per LIS, the number of open virtual circuits can be reduced to a manageable number.

Another use of ATM networks is to use them as bridges to connect existing LANs. In this configuration, only one machine on each LAN needs an ATM connection. Like all transparent bridges, the ATM bridge must listen promiscuously to all LANs to which it is attached, forwarding frames where needed. Since bridges use only MAC addresses (not IP addresses), ATM bridges must build a spanning tree, just as 802 bridges.

In short, while ATM LAN emulation is an interesting idea, there are serious questions about its performance and price, and there is certainly heavy competition from existing LANs and bridges, which are well established and highly optimized. Whether ATM LANs and bridges ever replace 802 LANs and bridges remains to be seen.

5.7. SUMMARY

The network layer provides services to the transport layer. It can be based on either virtual circuits or datagrams. In both cases, its main job is routing packets from the source to the destination. In virtual circuit subnets, a routing decision is made when the virtual circuit is set up. In datagram subnets, it is made on every packet.

Many routing algorithms are used in computer networks. Static algorithms include shortest path routing, flooding, and flow-based routing. Dynamic algorithms include distance vector routing and link state routing. Most actual networks use one of these. Other important routing topics are hierarchical routing, routing for mobile hosts, broadcast routing, and multicast routing.

Subnets can become congested, increasing the delay and lowering the throughput for packets. Network designers attempt to avoid congestion by proper design. Techniques include traffic shaping, flow specifications, and bandwidth reservation. If congestion does occur, it must be dealt with. Choke packets can be sent back, load can be shed, and other methods applied.

Networks differ in various ways, so when multiple networks are connected together problems can occur. Sometimes the problems can be finessed by tunneling a packet through a hostile network, but if the source and destination networks are different, this approach fails. When different networks have different maximum packet sizes, fragmentation may be called for.

The Internet has a rich variety of protocols related to the network layer. These include the data transport protocol, IP, but also the control protocols ICMP, ARP, and RARP, and the routing protocols OSPF and BGP. The Internet is rapidly running out of IP addresses, so a new version of IP, IPv6, has been developed.

Unlike the datagram-based Internet, ATM networks use virtual circuits inside. These must be set up before data can be transferred and torn down after transmission is completed. Quality of service and congestion control are major issues with ATM networks.

PROBLEMS

1. Give two example applications for which connection-oriented service is appropriate. Now give two examples for which connectionless service is best.

2. Are there any circumstances when a virtual circuit service will (or at least should) deliver packets out of order? Explain.

3. Datagram subnets route each packet as a separate unit, independent of all others. Virtual circuit subnets do not have to do this, since each data packet follows a predetermined route. Does this observation mean that virtual circuit subnets do not need the capability to route isolated packets from an arbitrary source to an arbitrary destination? Explain your answer.

4. Give three examples of protocol parameters that might be negotiated when a connection is set up.

5. Consider the following design problem concerning implementation of virtual circuit service. If virtual circuits are used internal to the subnet, each data packet must have a 3-byte header, and each router must tie up 8 bytes of storage for circuit identification. If datagrams are used internally, 15-byte headers are needed, but no router table space is required. Transmission capacity costs 1 cent per 10^6 bytes, per hop. Router memory can be purchased for 1 cent per byte and is depreciated over two years (business hours only). The statistically average session runs for 1000 sec, in which time 200 packets are transmitted. The mean packet requires four hops. Which implementation is cheaper, and by how much?

6. Assuming that all routers and hosts are working properly and that all software in both is free of all errors, is there any chance, however small, that a packet will be delivered to the wrong destination?

7. Give a simple heuristic for finding two paths through a network from a given source to a given destination that can survive the loss of any communication line (assuming two such paths exist). The routers are considered reliable enough, so it is not necessary to worry about the possibility of router crashes.

8. Consider the subnet of Fig. 5-15(a). Distance vector routing is used, and the following vectors have just come in to router C: from B: (5, 0, 8, 12, 6, 2); from D: (16, 12, 6, 0, 9, 10); and from E: (7, 6, 3, 9, 0, 4). The measured delays to B, D, and E, are 6, 3, and 5, respectively. What is C's new routing table? Give both the outgoing line to use and the expected delay.

9. If delays are recorded as 8-bit numbers in a 50-router network, and delay vectors are exchanged twice a second, how much bandwidth per (full-duplex) line is chewed up by the distributed routing algorithm? Assume that each router has three lines to other routers.

10. In Fig. 5-16 the Boolean OR of the two sets of ACF bits are 111 in every row. Is this just an accident here, or does it hold for all subnets under all circumstances?

11. For hierarchical routing with 4800 routers, what region and cluster sizes should be chosen to minimize the size of the routing table for a three-layer hierarchy?

12. In the text it was stated that when a mobile host is not at home, packets sent to its home LAN are intercepted by its home agent. For an IP network on an 802.3 LAN, how does the home agent accomplish this interception?

13. Looking at the subnet of Fig. 5-5, how many packets are generated by a broadcast from B, using
    (a) reverse path forwarding?
    (b) the sink tree?

14. Compute a multicast spanning tree for router C in the subnet below for a group with members at routers A, B, C, D, E, F, I, and K.

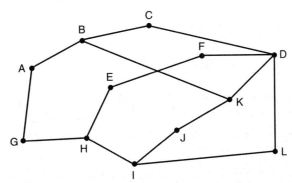

15. As a possible congestion control mechanism in a subnet using virtual circuits internally, a router could refrain from acknowledging a received packet until (1) it knows its last transmission along the virtual circuit was received successfully and (2) it has a free buffer. For simplicity, assume that the routers use a stop-and-wait protocol and that each virtual circuit has one buffer dedicated to it for each direction of traffic. If it

takes T sec to transmit a packet (data or acknowledgement) and there are n routers on the path, what is the rate at which packets are delivered to the destination host? Assume that transmission errors are rare, and that the host-router connection is infinitely fast.

16. A datagram subnet allows routers to drop packets whenever they need to. The probability of a router discarding a packet is p. Consider the case of a source host connected to the source router, which is connected to the destination router, and then to the destination host. If either of the routers discards a packet, the source host eventually times out and tries again. If both host-router and router-router lines are counted as hops, what is the mean number of
    (a) hops a packet makes per transmission?
    (b) transmissions a packet makes?
    (c) hops required per received packet?

17. Give an argument why the leaky bucket algorithm should allow just one packet per tick, independent of how large the packet is.

18. The byte-counting variant of the leaky bucket algorithm is used in a particular system. The rule is that one 1024-byte packet, two 512-byte packets, etc. may be sent on each tick. Give a serious restriction of this system that was not mentioned in the text.

19. An ATM network uses a token bucket scheme for traffic shaping. A new token is put into the bucket every 5 μsec. What is the maximum sustainable net data rate (i.e., excluding header bits)?

20. A computer on a 6-Mbps network is regulated by a token bucket. The token bucket is filled at a rate of 1 Mbps. It is initially filled to capacity with 8 megabits. How long can the computer transmit at the full 6 Mbps?

21. Figure 5-27 shows four input characteristics for a proposed flow specification. Imagine that the maximum packet size is 1000 bytes, the token bucket rate is 10 million bytes/sec, the token bucket size is 1 million bytes, and the maximum transmission rate is 50 million bytes/sec. How long can a burst at maximum speed last?

22. A device accepts frames from the Ethernet to which it is attached. It removes the packet inside each frame, adds framing information around it, and transmits it over a leased telephone line (its only connection to the outside world) to an identical device at the other end. This device removes the framing, inserts the packet into a token ring frame, and transmits it to a local host over a token ring LAN. What would you call the device?

23. Is fragmentation needed in concatenated virtual circuit internets, or only in datagram systems?

24. Tunneling through a concatenated virtual circuit subnet is straightforward: the multiprotocol router at one end just sets up a virtual circuit to the other end and passes packets through it. Can tunneling also be used in datagram subnets? If so, how?

25. An IP datagram using the *Strict source routing* option has to be fragmented. Do you think the option is copied into each fragment, or is it sufficient to just put it in the first fragment? Explain your answer.

26. Suppose that instead of using 16 bits for the network part of a class B address, 20 bits had been used. How many class B networks would there have been?

27. Convert the IP address whose hexadecimal representation is C22F1582 to dotted decimal notation.

28. A class B network on the Internet has a subnet mask of 255.255.240.0. What is the maximum number of hosts per subnet?

29. You have just explained the ARP protocol to a friend. When you are all done, he says: "I've got it. ARP provides a service to the network layer, so it is part of the data link layer." What do you say to him?

30. ARP and RARP both map addresses from one space to another. In this respect, they are similar. However, their implementations are fundamentally different. In what major way do they differ?

31. Describe a way to do reassembly of IP fragments at the destination.

32. Most IP datagram reassembly algorithms have a timer to avoid having a lost fragment tie up reassembly buffers forever. Suppose a datagram is fragmented into four fragments. The first three fragments arrrive, but the last one is delayed. Eventually the timer goes off and the three fragments in the receiver's memory are discarded. A little later, the last fragment stumbles in. What should be done with it?

33. Most IP routing protocols use number of hops as the metric to be minimized when doing routing computations. For ATM networks, number of hops is not terribly important. Why not? *Hint*: Take a look at Chap. 2. to see how ATM switches work. Do they use store-and-forward?

34. In both IP and ATM, the checksum covers only the header and not the data. Why do you suppose this design was chosen?

35. A person who lives in Boston travels to Minneapolis, taking her portable computer with her. To her surprise, the LAN at her destination in Minneapolis is a wireless IP LAN, so she does not have to plug in. Is it still necessary to go through the entire business with home agents and foreign agents to make email and other traffic arrive correctly?

36. IPv6 uses 16-byte addresses. If a block of 1 million addresses is allocated every picosecond, how long will the addresses last?

37. The *Protocol* field used in the IPv4 header is not present in the fixed IPv6 header. Why not?

38. When the IPv6 protocol is introduced, does the ARP protocol have to be changed? If so, are the changes conceptual or technical?

39. In Chap. 1, we classified interactions between the network and the hosts using four classes of primitives: *request*, *indication*, *response*, and *confirm*. Classify the SETUP and CONNECT messages of Fig. 5-65 into these categories.

40. A new virtual circuit is being set up in an ATM network. Between the source and destination hosts lie three ATM switches. How many messages (including acknowledgements) will be sent to establish the circuit?

41. The logic used to construct the table of Fig. 5-67 is simple: the lowest unused *VPI* is always assigned to a connection. If a new virtual circuit is requested between NY and Denver, which *VPI* will be assigned to it?

42. In Fig. 5-73(c), if a cell arrives early, the next one is still due at $t_1 + 2T$. Suppose that the rule were different, namely that the next cell was expected at $t_2 + T$, and the sender made maximum use of this rule. What maximum peak cell rate could then be achieved? For $T = 10$ μsec and $L = 2$ μsec, give the original and new peak cell rates, respectively.

43. What is the maximum burst length on an 155.52 Mbps ATM ABR connection whose *PCR* value is 200,000 and whose *L* value is 25 μsec?

44. Write a program to simulate routing using flooding. Each packet should contain a counter that is decremented on each hop. When the counter gets to zero, the packet is discarded. Time is discrete, with each line handling one packet per time interval. Make three versions of the program: all lines are flooded, all lines except the input line are flooded, and only the (statically chosen) best *k* lines are flooded. Compare flooding with deterministic routing ($k = 1$) in terms of delay and bandwidth used.

45. Write a program that simulates a computer network using discrete time. The first packet on each router queue makes one hop per time interval. Each router has only a finite number of buffers. If a packet arrives and there is no room for it, it is discarded and not retransmitted. Instead, there is an end-to-end protocol, complete with timeouts and acknowledgement packets, that eventually regenerates the packet from the source router. Plot the throughput of the network as a function of the end-to-end timeout interval, parametrized by error rate.

6

THE TRANSPORT LAYER

The transport layer is not just another layer. It is the heart of the whole protocol hierarchy. Its task is to provide reliable, cost-effective data transport from the source machine to the destination machine, independent of the physical network or networks currently in use. Without the transport layer, the whole concept of layered protocols would make little sense. In this chapter we will study the transport layer in detail, including its services, design, protocols, and performance.

6.1. THE TRANSPORT SERVICE

In the following sections we will provide an introduction to the transport service. We look at what kind of service is provided to the application layer (or session layer, if one exists), and especially how one can characterize the quality of service. Then we will look at how applications access the transport service, that is, what the interface is like.

6.1.1. Services Provided to the Upper Layers

The ultimate goal of the transport layer is to provide efficient, reliable, and cost-effective service to its users, normally processes in the application layer. To achieve this goal, the transport layer makes use of the services provided by the network layer. The hardware and/or software within the transport layer that does the work is called the **transport entity**. The transport entity can be in the operating system kernel, in a separate user process, in a library package bound into network applications, or on the network interface card. In some cases, the carrier may even provide reliable transport service, in which case the transport entity lives on special interface machines at the edge of the subnet to which hosts connect. The (logical) relationship of the network, transport, and application layers is illustrated in Fig. 6-1.

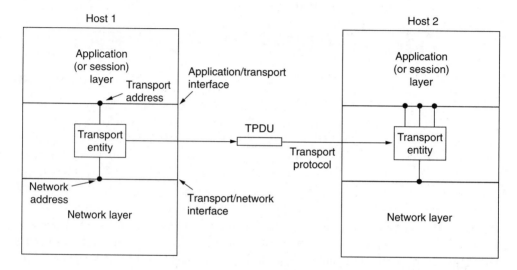

Fig. 6-1. The network, transport, and application layers.

Just as there are two types of network service, connection-oriented and connectionless, there are also the same two types of transport service. The connection-oriented transport service is similar to the connection-oriented network service in many ways. In both cases, connections have three phases: establishment, data transfer, and release. Addressing and flow control are also similar in both layers. Furthermore, the connectionless transport service is also very similar to the connectionless network service.

The obvious question is then: If the transport layer service is so similar to the network layer service, why are there two distinct layers? Why is one layer not adequate? The answer is subtle, but crucial, and goes back to Fig. 1-16. In this figure we can see that the network layer is part of the communication subnet and is run by the carrier (at least for WANs). What happens if the network layer offers connection-oriented service but is unreliable? Suppose that it frequently loses packets? What happens if routers crash from time to time?

Problems occur, that's what. The users have no control over the subnet, so they cannot solve the problem of poor service by using better routers or putting more error handling in the data link layer. The only possibility is to put another layer on top of the network layer that improves the quality of the service. If a transport entity is informed halfway through a long transmission that its network connection has been abruptly terminated, with no indication of what has happened to the data currently in transit, it can set up a new network connection to the remote transport entity. Using this new network connection, it can send a query to its peer asking which data arrived and which did not, and then pick up from where it left off.

In essence, the existence of the transport layer makes it possible for the transport service to be more reliable than the underlying network service. Lost packets and mangled data can be detected and compensated for by the transport layer. Furthermore, the transport service primitives can be designed to be independent of the network service primitives which may vary considerably from network to network (e.g., connectionless LAN service may be quite different than connection-oriented WAN service).

Thanks to the transport layer, it is possible for application programs to be written using a standard set of primitives, and to have these programs work on a wide variety of networks, without having to worry about dealing with different subnet interfaces and unreliable transmission. If all real networks were flawless and all had the same service primitives, the transport layer would probably not be needed. However, in the real world it fulfills the key function of isolating the upper layers from the technology, design, and imperfections of the subnet.

For this reason, many people have made a distinction between layers 1 through 4 on the one hand, and layer(s) above 4 on the other. The bottom four layers can be seen as the **transport service provider**, whereas the upper layer(s) are the **transport service user**. This distinction of provider versus user has a considerable impact on the design of the layers and puts the transport layer in a key position, since it forms the major boundary between the provider and user of the reliable data transmission service.

6.1.2. Quality of Service

Another way of looking at the transport layer is to regard its primary function as enhancing the **QoS** (**Quality of Service**) provided by the network layer. If the network service is impeccable, the transport layer has an easy job. If, however, the network service is poor, the transport layer has to bridge the gap between what the transport users want and what the network layer provides.

While at first glance, quality of service might seem like a vague concept (getting everyone to agree what constitutes "good" service is a nontrivial exercise), QoS can be characterized by a number of specific parameters, as we saw in Chap. 5. The transport service may allow the user to specify preferred, acceptable, and minimum values for various service parameters at the time a connection is set up. Some of the parameters also apply to connectionless transport. It is up to the transport layer to examine these parameters, and depending on the kind of network service or services available to it, determine whether it can provide the required service. In the remainder of this section we will discuss some possible QoS parameters. They are summarized in Fig. 6-2. Note that few networks or protocols provide all of these parameters. Many just try their best to reduce the residual error rate and leave it at that. Others have elaborate QoS architectures (Campbell et al., 1994).

Connection establishment delay
Connection establishment failure probability
Throughput
Transit delay
Residual error ratio
Protection
Priority
Resilience

Fig. 6-2. Typical transport layer quality of service parameters.

The *Connection establishment delay* is the amount of time elapsing between a transport connection being requested and the confirmation being received by the user of the transport service. It includes the processing delay in the remote transport entity. As with all parameters measuring a delay, the shorter the delay, the better the service.

The *Connection establishment failure probability* is the chance of a connection not being established within the maximum establishment delay time, for example, due to network congestion, lack of table space somewhere, or other internal problems.

The *Throughput* parameter measures the number of bytes of user data transferred per second, measured over some time interval. The throughput is measured separately for each direction.

The *Transit delay* measures the time between a message being sent by the transport user on the source machine and its being received by the transport user on the destination machine. As with throughput, each direction is handled separately.

The *Residual error ratio* measures the number of lost or garbled messages as a fraction of the total sent. In theory, the residual error rate should be zero, since it is the job of the transport layer to hide all network layer errors. In practice it may have some (small) finite value.

The *Protection* parameter provides a way for the transport user to specify interest in having the transport layer provide protection against unauthorized third parties (wiretappers) reading or modifying the transmitted data.

The *Priority* parameter provides a way for a transport user to indicate that some of its connections are more important than other ones, and in the event of congestion, to make sure that the high-priority connections get serviced before the low-priority ones.

Finally, the *Resilience* parameter gives the probability of the transport layer itself spontaneously terminating a connection due to internal problems or congestion.

The QoS parameters are specified by the transport user when a connection is requested. Both the desired and minimum acceptable values can be given. In some cases, upon seeing the QoS parameters, the transport layer may immediately realize that some of them are unachievable, in which case it tells the caller that the connection attempt failed, without even bothering to contact the destination. The failure report specifies the reason for the failure.

In other cases, the transport layer knows it cannot achieve the desired goal (e.g., 600 Mbps throughput), but it can achieve a lower, but still acceptable rate (e.g., 150 Mbps). It then sends the lower rate and the minimum acceptable rate to the remote machine, asking to establish a connection. If the remote machine cannot handle the proposed value, but it can handle a value above the minimum, it may make a counteroffer. If it cannot handle any value above the minimum, it rejects the connection attempt. Finally, the originating transport user is informed of whether the connection was established or rejected, and if it was established, the values of the parameters agreed upon.

This process is called **option negotiation**. Once the options have been negotiated, they remain that way throughout the life of the connection. To keep customers from being too greedy, most carriers have the tendency to charge more money for better quality service.

6.1.3. Transport Service Primitives

The transport service primitives allow transport users (e.g., application programs) to access the transport service. Each transport service has its own access primitives. In this section, we will first examine a simple (hypothetical) transport service and then look at a real example.

The transport service is similar to the network service, but there are also some important differences. The main difference is that the network service is intended to model the service offered by real networks, warts and all. Real networks can lose packets, so the network service is generally unreliable.

The (connection-oriented) transport service, in contrast, is reliable. Of course, real networks are not error-free, but that is precisely the purpose of the transport layer—to provide a reliable service on top of an unreliable network.

As an example, consider two processes connected by pipes in UNIX. They assume the connection between them is perfect. They do not want to know about acknowledgements, lost packets, congestion, or anything like that. What they want is a 100 percent reliable connection. Process *A* puts data into one end of the pipe, and process *B* takes it out of the other. This is what the connection-oriented transport service is all about—hiding the imperfections of the network service so that user processes can just assume the existence of an error-free bit stream.

As an aside, the transport layer can also provide unreliable (datagram) service, but there is relatively little to say about that, so we will concentrate on the connection-oriented transport service in this chapter.

A second difference between the network service and transport service is whom the services are intended for. The network service is used only by the transport entities. Few users write their own transport entities, and thus few users or programs ever see the bare network service. In contrast, many programs (and thus programmers) see the transport primitives. Consequently, the transport service must be convenient and easy to use.

To get an idea of what a transport service might be like, consider the five primitives listed in Fig. 6-3. This transport interface is truly bare bones but it gives the essential flavor of what a connection-oriented transport interface has to do. It allows application programs to establish, use, and release connections, which is sufficient for many applications.

Primitive	TPDU sent	Meaning
LISTEN	(none)	Block until some process tries to connect
CONNECT	CONNECTION REQ.	Actively attempt to establish a connection
SEND	DATA	Send information
RECEIVE	(none)	Block until a DATA TPDU arrives
DISCONNECT	DISCONNECTION REQ.	This side wants to release the connection

Fig. 6-3. The primitives for a simple transport service.

To see how these primitives might be used, consider an application with a server and a number of remote clients. To start with, the server executes a LISTEN primitive, typically by calling a library procedure that makes a system call to block the server until a client turns up. When a client wants to talk to the server, it executes a CONNECT primitive. The transport entity carries out this primitive by blocking the caller and sending a packet to the server. Encapsulated in the payload of this packet is a transport layer message for the server's transport entity.

A quick note on terminology is now in order. For lack of a better term, we will reluctantly use the somewhat ungainly acronym **TPDU** (**Transport Protocol Data Unit**) for messages sent from transport entity to transport entity. Thus TPDUs (exchanged by the transport layer) are contained in packets (exchanged by the network layer). In turn, packets are contained in frames (exchanged by the data link layer). When a frame arrives, the data link layer processes the frame header and passes the contents of the frame payload field up to the network entity.

The network entity processes the packet header and passes the contents of the packet payload up to the transport entity. This nesting is illustrated in Fig. 6-4.

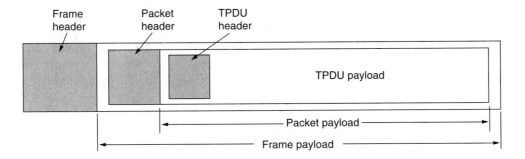

Fig. 6-4. Nesting of TPDUs, packets, and frames.

Getting back to our client-server example, the client's CONNECT call causes a CONNECTION REQUEST TPDU to be sent to the server. When it arrives, the transport entity checks to see that the server is blocked on a LISTEN (i.e., is interested in handling requests). It then unblocks the server and sends a CONNECTION ACCEPTED TPDU back to the client. When this TPDU arrives, the client is unblocked and the connection is established.

Data can now be exchanged using the SEND and RECEIVE primitives. In the simplest form, either party can do a (blocking) RECEIVE to wait for the other party to do a SEND. When the TPDU arrives, the receiver is unblocked. It can then process the TPDU and send a reply. As long as both sides can keep track of whose turn it is to send, this scheme works fine.

Note that at the network layer, even a simple unidirectional data exchange is more complicated than at the transport layer. Every data packet sent will also be acknowledged (eventually). The packets bearing control TPDUs are also acknowledged, implicitly or explicitly. These acknowledgements are managed by the transport entities using the network layer protocol and are not visible to the transport users. Similarly, the transport entities will need to worry about timers and retransmissions. None of this machinery is seen by the transport users. To the transport users, a connection is a reliable bit pipe: one user stuffs bits in and they magically appear at the other end. This ability to hide complexity is the reason that layered protocols are such a powerful tool.

When a connection is no longer needed, it must be released to free up table space within the two transport entities. Disconnection has two variants: asymmetric and symmetric. In the asymmetric variant, either transport user can issue a DISCONNECT primitive, which results in a DISCONNECT TPDU being sent to the remote transport entity. Upon arrival, the connection is released.

In the symmetric variant, each direction is closed separately, independently of the other one. When one side does a DISCONNECT, that means it has no more data to send, but it is still willing to accept data from its partner. In this model, a connection is released when both sides have done a DISCONNECT.

A state diagram for connection establishment and release for these simple primitives is given in Fig. 6-5. Each transition is triggered by some event, either a primitive executed by the local transport user or an incoming packet. For simplicity, we assume here that each TPDU is separately acknowledged. We also assume that a symmetric disconnection model is used, with the client going first. Please note that this model is quite unsophisticated. We will look at more realistic models later on.

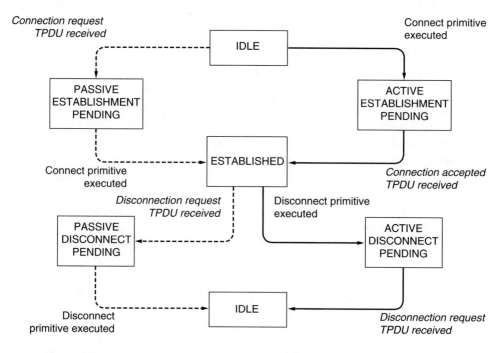

Fig. 6-5. A state diagram for a simple connection management scheme. Transitions labeled in italics are caused by packet arrivals. The solid lines show the client's state sequence. The dashed lines show the server's state sequence.

Berkeley Sockets

Let us now briefly inspect another set of transport primitives, the socket primitives used in Berkeley UNIX for TCP. They are listed in Fig. 6-6. Roughly speaking, they follow the model of our first example but offer more features and flexibility. We will not look at the corresponding TPDUs here. That discussion will have to wait until we study TCP later in this chapter.

The first four primitives in the list are executed in that order by servers. The SOCKET primitive creates a new end point and allocates table space for it within

Primitive	Meaning
SOCKET	Create a new communication end point
BIND	Attach a local address to a socket
LISTEN	Announce willingness to accept connections; give queue size
ACCEPT	Block the caller until a connection attempt arrives
CONNECT	Actively attempt to establish a connection
SEND	Send some data over the connection
RECEIVE	Receive some data from the connection
CLOSE	Release the connection

Fig. 6-6. The socket primitives for TCP.

the transport entity. The parameters of the call specify the addressing format to be used, the type of service desired (e.g., reliable byte stream), and the protocol. A successful SOCKET call returns an ordinary file descriptor for use in succeeding calls, the same way an OPEN call does.

Newly created sockets do not have addresses. These are assigned using the BIND primitive. Once a server has bound an address to a socket, remote clients can connect to it. The reason for not having the SOCKET call create an address directly is that some processes care about their address (e.g., they have been using the same address for years and everyone knows this address), whereas others do not care.

Next comes the LISTEN call, which allocates space to queue incoming calls for the case that several clients try to connect at the same time. In contrast to LISTEN in our first example, in the socket model LISTEN is not a blocking call.

To block waiting for an incoming connection, the server executes an ACCEPT primitive. When a TPDU asking for a connection arrives, the transport entity creates a new socket with the same properties as the original one and returns a file descriptor for it. The server can then fork off a process or thread to handle the connection on the new socket and go back to waiting for the next connection on the original socket.

Now let us look at the client side. Here, too, a socket must first be created using the SOCKET primitive, but BIND is not required since the address used does not matter to the server. The CONNECT primitive blocks the caller and actively starts the connection process. When it completes (i.e., when the appropriate TPDU is received from the server), the client process is unblocked and the connection is established. Both sides can now use SEND and RECEIVE to transmit and receive data over the full-duplex connection.

Connection release with sockets is symmetric. When both sides have executed a CLOSE primitive, the connection is released.

6.2. ELEMENTS OF TRANSPORT PROTOCOLS

The transport service is implemented by a **transport protocol** used between the two transport entities. In some ways, transport protocols resemble the data link protocols we studied in detail in Chap. 3. Both have to deal with error control, sequencing, and flow control, among other issues.

However, significant differences between the two also exist. These differences are due to major dissimilarities between the environments in which the two protocols operate, as shown in Fig. 6-7. At the data link layer, two routers communicate directly via a physical channel, whereas at the transport layer, this physical channel is replaced by the entire subnet. This difference has many important implications for the protocols.

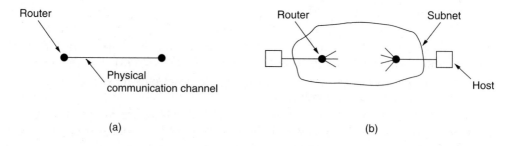

(a)   (b)

Fig. 6-7. (a) Environment of the data link layer. (b) Environment of the transport layer.

For one thing, in the data link layer, it is not necessary for a router to specify which router it wants to talk to—each outgoing line uniquely specifies a particular router. In the transport layer, explicit addressing of destinations is required.

For another thing, the process of establishing a connection over the wire of Fig. 6-7(a) is simple: the other end is always there (unless it has crashed, in which case it is not there). Either way, there is not much to do. In the transport layer, initial connection establishment is more complicated, as we will see.

Another, exceedingly annoying, difference between the data link layer and the transport layer is the potential existence of storage capacity in the subnet. When a router sends a frame, it may arrive or be lost, but it cannot bounce around for a while, go into hiding in a far corner of the world, and then suddenly emerge at an inopportune moment 30 sec later. If the subnet uses datagrams and adaptive routing inside, there is a nonnegligible probability that a packet may be stored for a number of seconds and then delivered later. The consequences of this ability of the subnet to store packets can sometimes be disastrous and require the use of special protocols.

A final difference between the data link and transport layers is one of amount rather than of kind. Buffering and flow control are needed in both layers, but the presence of a large and dynamically varying number of connections in the transport layer may require a different approach than we used in the data link layer. In Chap. 3, some of the protocols allocate a fixed number of buffers to each line, so that when a frame arrives there is always a buffer available. In the transport layer, the larger number of connections that must be managed make the idea of dedicating many buffers to each one less attractive. In the following sections, we will examine all of these important issues and others.

6.2.1. Addressing

When an application process wishes to set up a connection to a remote application process, it must specify which one to connect to. (Connectionless transport has the same problem: To whom should each message be sent?) The method normally used is to define transport addresses to which processes can listen for connection requests. In the Internet, these end points are (IP address, local port) pairs. In ATM networks, they are AAL-SAPs. We will use the neutral term **TSAP** (**Transport Service Access Point**). The analogous end points in the network layer (i.e., network layer addresses) are then called **NSAPs**. IP addresses are examples of NSAPs.

Figure 6-8 illustrates the relationship between the NSAP, TSAP, network connection, and transport connection for a connection-oriented subnet (e.g., ATM). Note that a transport entity normally supports multiple TSAPs. On some networks, multiple NSAPs also exist, but on others each machine has only one NSAP (e.g., one IP address). A possible connection scenario for a transport connection over a connection-oriented network layer is as follows.

1. A time-of-day server process on host 2 attaches itself to TSAP 122 to wait for an incoming call. How a process attaches itself to a TSAP is outside the networking model and depends entirely on the local operating system. A call such as our LISTEN might be used, for example.

2. An application process on host 1 wants to find out the time-of-day, so it issues a CONNECT request specifying TSAP 6 as the source and TSAP 122 as the destination.

3. The transport entity on host 1 selects a network address on its machine (if it has more than one) and sets up a network connection between them. (With a connectionless subnet, establishing this network layer connection would not be done.) Using this network connection, host 1's transport entity can talk to the transport entity on host 2.

4. The first thing the transport entity on 1 says to its peer on 2 is: "Good morning. I would like to establish a transport connection between my TSAP 6 and your TSAP 122. What do you say?"

5. The transport entity on 2 then asks the time-of-day server at TSAP 122 if it is willing to accept a new connection. If it agrees, the transport connection is established.

Note that the transport connection goes from TSAP to TSAP, whereas the network connection only goes part way, from NSAP to NSAP.

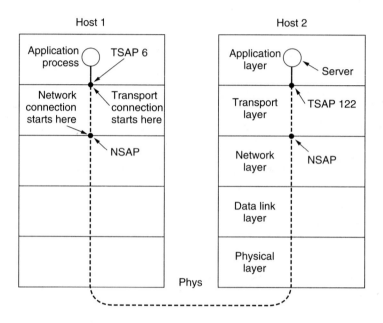

Fig. 6-8. TSAPs, NSAPs, and connections.

The picture painted above is fine, except we have swept one little problem under the rug: How does the user process on host 1 know that the time-of-day server is attached to TSAP 122? One possibility is that the time-of-day server has been attaching itself to TSAP 122 for years, and gradually all the network users have learned this. In this model, services have stable TSAP addresses which can be printed on paper and given to new users when they join the network.

While stable TSAP addresses might work for a small number of key services that never change, in general, user processes often want to talk to other user processes that only exist for a short time and do not have a TSAP address that is known in advance. Furthermore, if there are potentially many server processes, most of which are rarely used, it is wasteful to have each of them active and listening to a stable TSAP address all day long. In short, a better scheme is needed.

One such scheme, used by UNIX hosts on the Internet, is shown in Fig. 6-9 in a simplified form. It is known as the **initial connection protocol**. Instead of every conceivable server listening at a well-known TSAP, each machine that wishes to offer service to remote users has a special **process server** that acts as a proxy for less-heavily used servers. It listens to a set of ports at the same time, waiting for a TCP connection request. Potential users of a service begin by doing a CONNECT request, specifying the TSAP address (TCP port) of the service they want. If no server is waiting for them, they get a connection to the process server, as shown in Fig. 6-9(a).

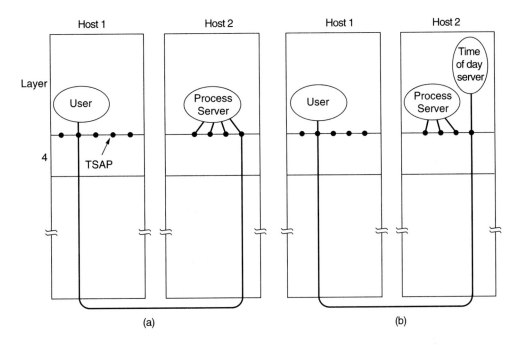

Fig. 6-9. How a user process in host 1 establishes a connection with a time-of-day server in host 2.

After it gets the incoming request, the process server spawns off the requested server, allowing it to inherit the existing connection with the user. The new server then does the requested work, while the process server goes back to listening for new requests, as shown in Fig. 6-9(b).

While the initial connection protocol works fine for those servers that can be created as they are needed, there are many situations in which services do exist independently of the process server. A file server, for example, needs to run on special hardware (a machine with a disk) and cannot just be created on-the-fly when someone wants to talk to it.

To handle this situation, an alternative scheme is often used. In this model, there exists a special process called a **name server** or sometimes a **directory server**. To find the TSAP address corresponding to a given service name, such as "time-of-day," a user sets up a connection to the name server (which listens to a well-known TSAP). The user then sends a message specifying the service name, and the name server sends back the TSAP address. Then the user releases the connection with the name server and establishes a new one with the desired service.

In this model, when a new service is created, it must register itself with the name server, giving both its service name (typically an ASCII string) and the address of its TSAP. The name server records this information in its internal database, so that when queries come in later, it will know the answers.

The function of the name server is analogous to the directory assistance operator in the telephone system—it provides a mapping of names onto numbers. Just as in the telephone system, it is essential that the address of the well-known TSAP used by the name server (or the process server in the initial connection protocol) is indeed well known. If you do not know the number of the information operator, you cannot call the information operator to find it out. If you think the number you dial for information is obvious, try it in a foreign country some time.

Now let us suppose that the user has successfully located the address of the TSAP to be connected to. Another interesting question is how does the local transport entity know on which machine that TSAP is located? More specifically, how does the transport entity know which network layer address to use to set up a network connection to the remote transport entity that manages the TSAP requested?

The answer depends on the structure of TSAP addresses. One possible structure is that TSAP addresses are **hierarchical addresses**. With hierarchical addresses, the address consists of a sequence of fields used to disjointly partition the address space. For example, a truly universal TSAP address might have the following structure:

address = <galaxy> <star> <planet> <country> <network> <host> <port>

With this scheme, it is straightforward to locate a TSAP anywhere in the known universe. Equivalently, if a TSAP address is a concatenation of an NSAP address and a port (a local identifier specifying one of the local TSAPs), then when a transport entity is given a TSAP address to connect to, it uses the NSAP address contained in the TSAP address to reach the proper remote transport entity.

As a simple example of a hierarchical address, consider the telephone number 19076543210. This number can be parsed as 1-907-654-3210, where 1 is a country code (United States + Canada), 907 is an area code (Alaska), 654 is an end office in Alaska, and 3210 is one of the "ports" (subscriber lines) in that end office.

The alternative to a hierarchical address space is a **flat address space**. If the TSAP addresses are not hierarchical, a second level of mapping is needed to locate the proper machine. There would have to be a name server that took transport addresses as input and returned network addresses as output. Alternatively, in some situations (e.g., on a LAN), it is possible to broadcast a query asking the destination machine to please identify itself by sending a packet.

6.2.2. Establishing a Connection

Establishing a connection sounds easy, but it is actually surprisingly tricky. At first glance, it would seem sufficient for one transport entity to just send a CONNECTION REQUEST TPDU to the destination and wait for a CONNECTION ACCEPTED reply. The problem occurs when the network can lose, store, and duplicate packets.

Imagine a subnet that is so congested that acknowledgements hardly ever get back in time, and each packet times out and is retransmitted two or three times. Suppose that the subnet uses datagrams inside, and every packet follows a different route. Some of the packets might get stuck in a traffic jam inside the subnet and take a long time to arrive, that is, they are stored in the subnet and pop out much later.

The worst possible nightmare is as follows. A user establishes a connection with a bank, sends messages telling the bank to transfer a large amount of money to the account of a not-entirely-trustworthy person, and then releases the connection. Unfortunately, each packet in the scenario is duplicated and stored in the subnet. After the connection has been released, all the packets pop out of the subnet and arrive at the destination in order, asking the bank to establish a new connection, transfer money (again), and release the connection. The bank has no way of telling that these are duplicates. It must assume that this is a second, independent transaction, and transfers the money again. For the remainder of this section we will study the problem of delayed duplicates, with special emphasis on algorithms for establishing connections in a reliable way, so that nightmares like the one above cannot happen.

The crux of the problem is the existence of delayed duplicates. It can be attacked in various ways, none of them very satisfactory. One way is to use throwaway transport addresses. In this approach, each time a transport address is needed, a new one is generated. When a connection is released, the address is discarded. This strategy makes the process server model of Fig. 6-9 impossible.

Another possibility is to give each connection a connection identifier (i.e., a sequence number incremented for each connection established), chosen by the initiating party, and put in each TPDU, including the one requesting the connection. After each connection is released, each transport entity could update a table listing obsolete connections as (peer transport entity, connection identifier) pairs. Whenever a connection request came in, it could be checked against the table, to see if it belonged to a previously released connection.

Unfortunately, this scheme has a basic flaw: it requires each transport entity to maintain a certain amount of history information indefinitely. If a machine crashes and loses its memory, it will no longer know which connection identifiers have already been used.

Instead, we need to take a different tack. Rather than allowing packets to live forever within the subnet, we must devise a mechanism to kill off aged packets that are still wandering about. If we can ensure that no packet lives longer than some known time, the problem becomes somewhat more manageable.

Packet lifetime can be restricted to a known maximum using one of the following techniques:

1. Restricted subnet design.

2. Putting a hop counter in each packet.

3. Timestamping each packet.

The first method includes any method that prevents packets from looping, combined with some way of bounding congestion delay over the (now known) longest possible path. The second method consists of having the hop count incremented each time the packet is forwarded. The data link protocol simply discards any packet whose hop counter has exceeded a certain value. The third method requires each packet to bear the time it was created, with the routers agreeing to discard any packet older than some agreed upon time. This latter method requires the router clocks to be synchronized, which itself is a nontrivial task unless synchronization is achieved external to the network, for example by listening to WWV or some other radio station that broadcasts the precise time periodically.

In practice, we will need to guarantee not only that a packet is dead, but also that all acknowledgements to it are also dead, so we will now introduce T, which is some small multiple of the true maximum packet lifetime. The multiple is protocol-dependent and simply has the effect of making T longer. If we wait a time T after a packet has been sent, we can be sure that all traces of it are now gone and that neither it nor its acknowledgements will suddenly appear out of the blue to complicate matters.

With packet lifetimes bounded, it is possible to devise a foolproof way to establish connections safely. The method described below is due to Tomlinson (1975). It solves the problem but introduces some peculiarities of its own. The method was further refined by Sunshine and Dalal (1978). Variants of it are widely used in practice.

To get around the problem of a machine losing all memory of where it was after a crash, Tomlinson proposed equipping each host with a time-of-day clock. The clocks at different hosts need not be synchronized. Each clock is assumed to take the form of a binary counter that increments itself at uniform intervals. Furthermore, the number of bits in the counter must equal or exceed the number of bits in the sequence numbers. Last, and most important, the clock is assumed to continue running even if the host goes down.

The basic idea is to ensure that two identically numbered TPDUs are never outstanding at the same time. When a connection is set up, the low-order k bits of the clock are used as the initial sequence number (also k bits). Thus, unlike our protocols of Chap. 3, each connection starts numbering its TPDUs with a different sequence number. The sequence space should be so large that by the time sequence numbers wrap around, old TPDUs with the same sequence number are long gone. This linear relation between time and initial sequence numbers is shown in Fig. 6-10.

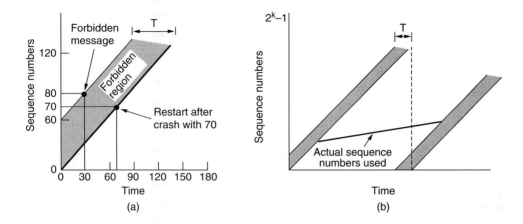

Fig. 6-10. (a) TPDUs may not enter the forbidden region. (b) The resynchronization problem.

Once both transport entities have agreed on the initial sequence number, any sliding window protocol can be used for data flow control. In reality, the initial sequence number curve (shown by the heavy line) is not really linear, but a staircase, since the clock advances in discrete steps. For simplicity we will ignore this detail.

A problem occurs when a host crashes. When it comes up again, its transport entity does not know where it was in the sequence space. One solution is to require transport entities to be idle for T sec after a recovery to let all old TPDUs die off. However, in a complex internetwork, T may be large, so this strategy is unattractive.

To avoid requiring T sec of dead time after a crash, it is necessary to introduce a new restriction on the use of sequence numbers. We can best see the need for this restriction by means of an example. Let T, the maximum packet lifetime, be 60 sec and let the clock tick once per second. As shown in Fig. 6-10, the initial sequence number for a connection opened at time x will be x. Imagine that at $t = 30$ sec, an ordinary data TPDU being sent on (a previously opened) connection 5 is given sequence number 80. Call this TPDU X. Immediately after sending TPDU X, the host crashes and then quickly restarts. At $t = 60$, it begins reopening connections 0 through 4. At $t = 70$, it reopens connection 5, using initial sequence number 70 as required. Within the next 15 sec it sends data TPDUs 70 through 80. Thus at $t = 85$, a new TPDU with sequence number 80 and connection 5 has been injected into the subnet. Unfortunately, TPDU X still exists. If it should arrive at the receiver before the new TPDU 80, TPDU X will be accepted and the correct TPDU 80 will be rejected as a duplicate.

To prevent such problems, we must prevent sequence numbers from being used (i.e., assigned to new TPDUs) for a time T before their potential use as initial sequence numbers. The illegal combinations of time and sequence number are shown as the **forbidden region** in Fig. 6-10(a). Before sending any TPDU on any connection, the transport entity must read the clock and check to see that it is not in the forbidden region.

The protocol can get itself into trouble in two different ways. If a host sends too much data too fast on a newly opened connection, the actual sequence number versus time curve may rise more steeply than the initial sequence number versus time curve. This means that the maximum data rate on any connection is one TPDU per clock tick. It also means that the transport entity must wait until the clock ticks before opening a new connection after a crash restart, lest the same number be used twice. Both of these points argue for a short clock tick (a few milliseconds).

Unfortunately, entering the forbidden region from underneath by sending too fast is not the only way to get into trouble. From Fig. 6-10(b), it should be clear that at any data rate less than the clock rate, the curve of actual sequence numbers used versus time will eventually run into the forbidden region from the left. The greater the slope of the actual sequence number curve, the longer this event will be delayed. As we stated above, just before sending every TPDU, the transport entity must check to see if it is about to enter the forbidden region, and if so, either delay the TPDU for T sec or resynchronize the sequence numbers.

The clock-based method solves the delayed duplicate problem for data TPDUs, but for this method to be useful, a connection must first be established. Since control TPDUs may also be delayed, there is a potential problem in getting both sides to agree on the initial sequence number. Suppose, for example, that connections are established by having host 1 send a CONNECTION REQUEST TPDU containing the proposed initial sequence number and destination port number to a remote peer, host 2. The receiver, host 2, then acknowledges this request by sending a CONNECTION ACCEPTED TPDU back. If the CONNECTION REQUEST TPDU is lost but a delayed duplicate CONNECTION REQUEST suddenly shows up at host 2, the connection will be established incorrectly.

To solve this problem, Tomlinson (1975) introduced the **three-way handshake**. This establishment protocol does not require both sides to begin sending with the same sequence number, so it can be used with synchronization methods other than the global clock method. The normal setup procedure when host 1 initiates is shown in Fig. 6-11(a). Host 1 chooses a sequence number, x, and sends a CONNECTION REQUEST TPDU containing it to host 2. Host 2 replies with a CONNECTION ACCEPTED TPDU acknowledging x and announcing its own initial sequence number, y. Finally, host 1 acknowledges host 2's choice of an initial sequence number in the first data TPDU that it sends.

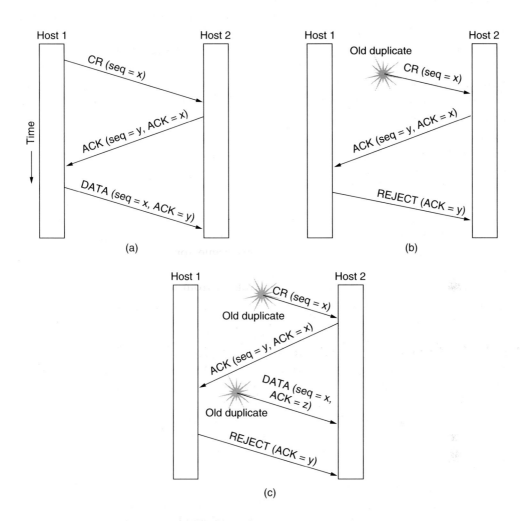

Fig. 6-11. Three protocol scenarios for establishing a connection using a three-way handshake. CR and ACC denote CONNECTION REQUEST and CONNECTION ACCEPTED, respectively. (a) Normal operation. (b) Old duplicate CONNECTION REQUEST appearing out of nowhere. (c) Duplicate CONNECTION REQUEST and duplicate ACK.

Now let us see how the three-way handshake works in the presence of delayed duplicate control TPDUs. In Fig. 6-12(b), the first TPDU is a delayed duplicate CONNECTION REQUEST from an old connection. This TPDU arrives at host 2 without host 1's knowledge. Host 2 reacts to this TPDU by sending host 1 a CONNECTION ACCEPTED TPDU, in effect asking for verification that host 1 was indeed trying to set up a new connection. When host 1 rejects host 2's attempt to establish, host 2 realizes that it was tricked by a delayed duplicate and abandons the connection. In this way, a delayed duplicate does no damage.

The worst case is when both a delayed CONNECTION REQUEST and an acknowledgement to a CONNECTION ACCEPTED are floating around in the subnet. This case is shown in Fig. 6-11(c). As in the previous example, host 2 gets a delayed CONNECTION REQUEST and replies to it. At this point it is crucial to realize that host 2 has proposed using y as the initial sequence number for host 2 to host 1 traffic, knowing full well that no TPDUs containing sequence number y or acknowledgements to y are still in existence. When the second delayed TPDU arrives at host 2, the fact that z has been acknowledged rather than y tells host 2 that this, too, is an old duplicate. The important thing to realize here is that there is no combination of old CONNECTION REQUEST, CONNECTION ACCEPTED, or other TPDUs that can cause the protocol to fail and have a connection set up by accident when no one wants it.

An alternative scheme for establishing connections reliably in the face of delayed duplicates is described in (Watson, 1981). It uses multiple timers to exclude undesired events.

6.2.3. Releasing a Connection

Releasing a connection is easier than establishing one. Nevertheless, there are more pitfalls than one might expect. As we mentioned earlier, there are two styles of terminating a connection: asymmetric release and symmetric release. Asymmetric release is the way the telephone system works: when one party hangs up, the connection is broken. Symmetric release treats the connection as two separate unidirectional connections and requires each one to be released separately.

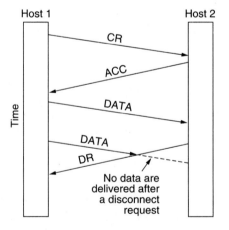

Fig. 6-12. Abrupt disconnection with loss of data.

Asymmetric release is abrupt and may result in data loss. Consider the scenario of Fig. 6-12. After the connection is established, host 1 sends a TPDU that arrives properly at host 2. Then host 1 sends another TPDU. Unfortunately, host 2 issues a DISCONNECT before the second TPDU arrives. The result is that the connection is released and data are lost.

Clearly, a more sophisticated release protocol is required to avoid data loss. One way is to use symmetric release, in which each direction is released independently of the other one. Here, a host can continue to receive data even after it has sent a DISCONNECT TPDU.

Symmetric release does the job when each process has a fixed amount of data to send and clearly knows when it has sent it. In other situations, determining that all the work has been done and the connection should be terminated is not so obvious. One can envision a protocol in which host 1 says: "I am done. Are you done too?" If host 2 responds: "I am done too. Goodbye." the connection can be safely released.

Unfortunately, this protocol does not always work. There is a famous problem that deals with this issue. It is called the **two-army problem**. Imagine that a white army is encamped in a valley, as shown in Fig. 6-13. On both of the surrounding hillsides are blue armies. The white army is larger than either of the blue armies alone, but together they are larger than the white army. If either blue army attacks by itself, it will be defeated, but if the two blue armies attack simultaneously, they will be victorious.

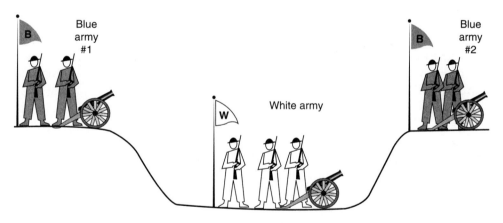

Fig. 6-13. The two-army problem.

The blue armies want to synchronize their attacks. However, their only communication medium is to send messengers on foot down into the valley, where they might be captured and the message lost (i.e., they have to use an unreliable communication channel). The question is: Does a protocol exist that allows the blue armies to win?

Suppose that the commander of blue army #1 sends a message reading: "I propose we attack at dawn on March 29. How about it?" Now suppose that the message arrives, and the commander of blue army #2 agrees, and that his reply gets safely back to blue army #1. Will the attack happen? Probably not, because commander #2 does not know if his reply got through. If it did not, blue army #1 will not attack, so it would be foolish for him to charge into battle.

Now let us improve the protocol by making it a three-way handshake. The initiator of the original proposal must acknowledge the response. Assuming no messages are lost, blue army #2 will get the acknowledgement, but the commander of blue army #1 will now hesitate. After all, he does not know if his acknowledgement got through, and if it did not, he knows that blue army #2 will not attack. We could now make a four-way handshake protocol, but that does not help either.

In fact, it can be proven that no protocol exists that works. Suppose that some protocol did exist. Either the last message of the protocol is essential or it is not. If it is not, remove it (and any other unessential messages) until we are left with a protocol in which every message is essential. What happens if the final message does not get through? We just said that it was essential, so if it is lost, the attack does not take place. Since the sender of the final message can never be sure of its arrival, he will not risk attacking. Worse yet, the other blue army knows this, so it will not attack either.

To see the relevance of the two-army problem to releasing connections, just substitute "disconnect" for "attack." If neither side is prepared to disconnect until it is convinced that the other side is prepared to disconnect too, the disconnection will never happen.

In practice, one is usually prepared to take more risks when releasing connections than when attacking white armies, so the situation is not entirely hopeless. Figure 6-14 illustrates four scenarios of releasing using a three-way handshake. While this protocol is not infallible, it is usually adequate.

In Fig. 6-14(a), we see the normal case in which one of the users sends a DR (DISCONNECTION REQUEST) TPDU in order to initiate the connection release. When it arrives, the recipient sends back a DR TPDU, too, and starts a timer, just in case its DR is lost. When this DR arrives, the original sender sends back an ACK TPDU and releases the connection. Finally, when the ACK TPDU arrives, the receiver also releases the connection. Releasing a connection means that the transport entity removes the information about the connection from its table of open connections and signals the connection's owner (the transport user) somehow. This action is different from a transport user issuing a DISCONNECT primitive.

If the final ACK TPDU is lost, as shown in Fig. 6-14(b), the situation is saved by the timer. When the timer expires, the connection is released anyway.

Now consider the case of the second DR being lost. The user initiating the disconnection will not receive the expected response, will time out, and will start all over again. In Fig. 6-14(c) we see how this works, assuming that the second time no TPDUs are lost and all TPDUs are delivered correctly and on time.

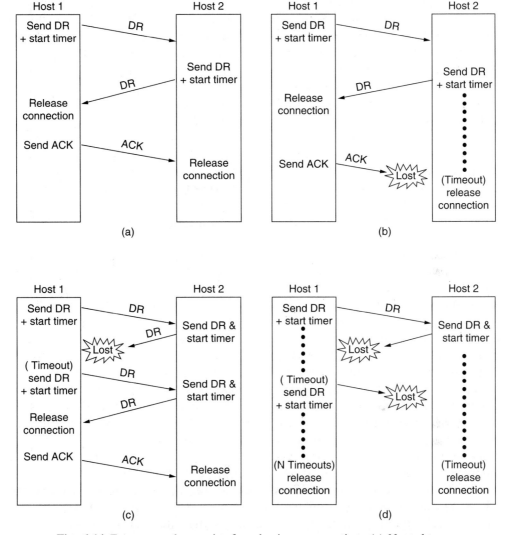

Fig. 6-14. Four protocol scenarios for releasing a connection. (a) Normal case of three-way handshake. (b) Final ACK lost. (c) Response lost. (d) Response lost and subsequent DRs lost.

Our last scenario, Fig. 6-14(d), is the same as Fig. 6-14(c) except that now we assume all the repeated attempts to retransmit the DR also fail due to lost TPDUs. After N retries, the sender just gives up and releases the connection. Meanwhile, the receiver times out and also exits.

While this protocol usually suffices, in theory it can fail if the initial DR and N retransmissions are all lost. The sender will give up and release the connection, while the other side knows nothing at all about the attempts to disconnect and is still fully active. This situation results in a half-open connection.

We could have avoided this problem by not allowing the sender to give up after *N* retries but forcing it to go on forever until it gets a response. However, if the other side is allowed to time out, then the sender will indeed go on forever, because no response will ever be forthcoming. If we do not allow the receiving side to time out, then the protocol hangs in Fig. 6-14(b).

One way to kill off half-open connections is to have a rule saying that if no TPDUs have arrived for a certain number of seconds, the connection is automatically disconnected. That way, if one side ever disconnects, the other side will detect the lack of activity and also disconnect. Of course, if this rule is introduced, it is necessary for each transport entity to have a timer that is stopped and then restarted whenever a TPDU is sent. If this timer expires, a dummy TPDU is transmitted, just to keep the other side from disconnecting. On the other hand, if the automatic disconnect rule is used and too many dummy TPDUs in a row are lost on an otherwise idle connection, first one side, then the other side will automatically disconnect.

We will not belabor this point any more, but by now it should be clear that releasing a connection is not nearly as simple as it at first appears.

6.2.4. Flow Control and Buffering

Having examined connection establishment and release in some detail, let us now look at how connections are managed while they are in use. One of the key issues has come up before: flow control. In some ways the flow control problem in the transport layer is the same as in the data link layer, but in other ways it is different. The basic similarity is that in both layers a sliding window or other scheme is needed on each connection to keep a fast transmitter from overrunning a slow receiver. The main difference is that a router usually has relatively few lines whereas a host may have numerous connections. This difference makes it impractical to implement the data link buffering strategy in the transport layer.

In the data link protocols of Chap. 3, frames were buffered at both the sending router and at the receiving router. In protocol 6, for example, both sender and receiver are required to dedicate $MaxSeq + 1$ buffers to each line, half for input and half for output. For a host with a maximum of, say, 64 connections, and a 4-bit sequence number, this protocol would require 1024 buffers.

In the data link layer, the sending side must buffer outgoing frames because they might have to be retransmitted. If the subnet provides datagram service, the sending transport entity must also buffer, and for the same reason. If the receiver knows that the sender buffers all TPDUs until they are acknowledged, the receiver may or may not dedicate specific buffers to specific connections, as it sees fit. The receiver may, for example, maintain a single buffer pool shared by all connections. When a TPDU comes in, an attempt is made to dynamically acquire a new buffer. If one is available, the TPDU is accepted; otherwise, it is discarded. Since the sender is prepared to retransmit TPDUs lost by the subnet, no harm is done by having the receiver drop TPDUs, although some resources are wasted. The sender just keeps trying until it gets an acknowledgement.

In summary, if the network service is unreliable, the sender must buffer all TPDUs sent, just as in the data link layer. However, with reliable network service, other trade-offs become possible. In particular, if the sender knows that the receiver always has buffer space, it need not retain copies of the TPDUs it sends. However, if the receiver cannot guarantee that every incoming TPDU will be accepted, the sender will have to buffer anyway. In the latter case, the sender cannot trust the network layer's acknowledgement, because the acknowledgement means only that the TPDU arrived, not that it was accepted. We will come back to this important point later.

Even if the receiver has agreed to do the buffering, there still remains the question of the buffer size. If most TPDUs are nearly the same size, it is natural to organize the buffers as a pool of identical size buffers, with one TPDU per buffer, as in Fig. 6-15(a). However, if there is wide variation in TPDU size, from a few characters typed at a terminal to thousands of characters from file transfers, a pool of fixed-sized buffers presents problems. If the buffer size is chosen equal to the largest possible TPDU, space will be wasted whenever a short TPDU arrives. If the buffer size is chosen less than the maximum TPDU size, multiple buffers will be needed for long TPDUs, with the attendant complexity.

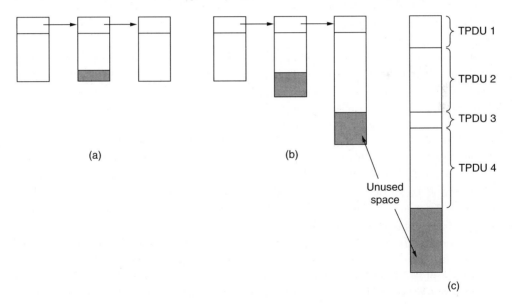

Fig. 6-15. (a) Chained fixed-size buffers. (b) Chained variable-size buffers. (c) One large circular buffer per connection.

Another approach to the buffer size problem is to use variable-size buffers, as in Fig. 6-15(b). The advantage here is better memory utilization, at the price of more complicated buffer management. A third possibility is to dedicate a single large circular buffer per connection, as in Fig. 6-15(c). This system also makes good use of memory, provided that all connections are heavily loaded but is poor if some connections are lightly loaded.

The optimum trade-off between source buffering and destination buffering depends on the type of traffic carried by the connection. For low-bandwidth bursty traffic, such as that produced by an interactive terminal, it is better not to dedicate any buffers, but rather to acquire them dynamically at both ends. Since the sender cannot be sure the receiver will be able to acquire a buffer, the sender must retain a copy of the TPDU until it is acknowledged. On the other hand, for file transfer and other high-bandwidth traffic, it is better if the receiver does dedicate a full window of buffers, to allow the data to flow at maximum speed. Thus for low-bandwidth bursty traffic, it is better to buffer at the sender, and for high-bandwidth, smooth traffic, it is better to buffer at the receiver.

As connections are opened and closed, and as the traffic pattern changes, the sender and receiver need to dynamically adjust their buffer allocations. Consequently, the transport protocol should allow a sending host to request buffer space at the other end. Buffers could be allocated per connection, or collectively, for all the connections running between the two hosts. Alternatively, the receiver, knowing its buffer situation (but not knowing the offered traffic) could tell the sender "I have reserved X buffers for you." If the number of open connections should increase, it may be necessary for an allocation to be reduced, so the protocol should provide for this possibility.

A reasonably general way to manage dynamic buffer allocation is to decouple the buffering from the acknowledgements, in contrast to the sliding window protocols of Chap. 3. Dynamic buffer management means, in effect, a variable-sized window. Initially, the sender requests a certain number of buffers, based on its perceived needs. The receiver then grants as many of these as it can afford. Every time the sender transmits a TPDU, it must decrement its allocation, stopping altogether when the allocation reaches zero. The receiver then separately piggybacks both acknowledgements and buffer allocations onto the reverse traffic.

Figure 6-16 shows an example of how dynamic window management might work in a datagram subnet with 4-bit sequence numbers. Assume that buffer allocation information travels in separate TPDUs, as shown, and is not piggybacked onto reverse traffic. Initially, A wants eight buffers, but is granted only four of these. It then sends three TPDUs, of which the third is lost. TPDU 6 acknowledges receipt of all TPDUs up to and including sequence number 1, thus allowing A to release those buffers, and furthermore informs A that it has permission to send three more TPDUs starting beyond 1 (i.e., TPDUs 2, 3, and 4). A knows that it has already sent number 2, so it thinks that it may send TPDUs 3 and 4, which it proceeds to do. At this point it is blocked and must wait for more buffer allocation. Timeout induced retransmissions (line 9), however, may occur while blocked, since they use buffers that have already been allocated. In line 10, B

acknowledges receipt of all TPDUs up to and including 4, but refuses to let *A* continue. Such a situation is impossible with the fixed window protocols of Chap. 3. The next TPDU from *B* to *A* allocates another buffer and allows *A* to continue.

	A	Message	B	Comments
1	→	< request 8 buffers>	→	A wants 8 buffers
2	←	<ack = 15, buf = 4>	←	B grants messages 0-3 only
3	→	<seq = 0, data = m0>	→	A has 3 buffers left now
4	→	<seq = 1, data = m1>	→	A has 2 buffers left now
5	→	<seq = 2, data = m2>	•••	Message lost but A thinks it has 1 left
6	←	<ack = 1, buf = 3>	←	B acknowledges 0 and 1, permits 2-4
7	→	<seq = 3, data = m3>	→	A has buffer left
8	→	<seq = 4, data = m4>	→	A has 0 buffers left, and must stop
9	→	<seq = 2, data = m2>	→	A times out and retransmits
10	←	<ack = 4, buf = 0>	←	Everything acknowledged, but A still blocked
11	←	<ack = 4, buf = 1>	←	A may now send 5
12	←	<ack = 4, buf = 2>	←	B found a new buffer somewhere
13	→	<seq = 5, data = m5>	→	A has 1 buffer left
14	→	<seq = 6, data = m6>	→	A is now blocked again
15	←	<ack = 6, buf = 0>	←	A is still blocked
16	•••	<ack = 6, buf = 4>	←	Potential deadlock

Fig. 6-16. Dynamic buffer allocation. The arrows show the direction of transmission. An ellipsis (...) indicates a lost TPDU.

Potential problems with buffer allocation schemes of this kind can arise in datagram networks if control TPDUs can get lost. Look at line 16. *B* has now allocated more buffers to *A*, but the allocation TPDU was lost. Since control TPDUs are not sequenced or timed out, *A* is now deadlocked. To prevent this situation, each host should periodically send control TPDUs giving the acknowledgement and buffer status on each connection. That way, the deadlock will be broken, sooner or later.

Up until now we have tacitly assumed that the only limit imposed on the sender's data rate is the amount of buffer space available in the receiver. As memory prices continue to fall dramatically, it may become feasible to equip hosts with so much memory that lack of buffers is rarely, if ever, a problem.

When buffer space no longer limits the maximum flow, another bottleneck will appear: the carrying capacity of the subnet. If adjacent routers can exchange at most *x* frames/sec and there are *k* disjoint paths between a pair of hosts, there is no way that those hosts can exchange more than *kx* TPDUs/sec, no matter how much buffer space is available at each end. If the sender pushes too hard (i.e., sends more than *kx* TPDUs/sec), the subnet will become congested, because it will be unable to deliver TPDUs as fast as they are coming in.

What is needed is a mechanism based on the subnet's carrying capacity rather than on the receiver's buffering capacity. Clearly, the flow control mechanism must be applied at the sender to prevent it from having too many unacknowledged TPDUs outstanding at once. Belsnes (1975) proposed using a sliding window flow control scheme in which the sender dynamically adjusts the window size to match the network's carrying capacity. If the network can handle c TPDUs/sec and the cycle time (including transmission, propagation, queueing, processing at the receiver, and return of the acknowledgement) is r, then the sender's window should be cr. With a window of this size the sender normally operates with the pipeline full. Any small decrease in network performance will cause it to block.

In order to adjust the window size periodically, the sender could monitor both parameters and then compute the desired window size. The carrying capacity can be determined by simply counting the number of TPDUs acknowledged during some time period and then dividing by the time period. During the measurement, the sender should send as fast as it can, to make sure that the network's carrying capacity, and not the low input rate, is the factor limiting the acknowledgement rate. The time required for a transmitted TPDU to be acknowledged can be measured exactly and a running mean maintained. Since the capacity of the network depends on the amount of traffic in it, the window size should be adjusted frequently, to track changes in the carrying capacity. As we will see later, the Internet uses a similar scheme.

6.2.5. Multiplexing

Multiplexing several conversations onto connections, virtual circuits, and physical links plays a role in several layers of the network architecture. In the transport layer the need for multiplexing can arise in a number of ways. For example, in networks that use virtual circuits within the subnet, each open connection consumes some table space in the routers for the entire duration of the connection. If buffers are dedicated to the virtual circuit in each router as well, a user who left a terminal logged into a remote machine during a coffee break is nevertheless consuming expensive resources. Although this implementation of packet switching defeats one of the main reasons for having packet switching in the first place—to bill the user based on the amount of data sent, not the connect time—many carriers have chosen this approach because it so closely resembles the circuit switching model to which they have grown accustomed over the decades.

The consequence of a price structure that heavily penalizes installations for having many virtual circuits open for long periods of time is to make multiplexing of different transport connections onto the same network connection attractive. This form of multiplexing, called **upward multiplexing**, is shown in Fig. 6-17(a). In this figure, four distinct transport connections all use the same network connection (e.g., ATM virtual circuit) to the remote host. When connect time forms the major component of the carrier's bill, it is up to the transport layer to group trans-port connections according to their destination and map each group onto the minimum number of network connections. If too many transport connections are mapped onto one network connection, the performance will be poor, because the window will usually be full, and users will have to wait their turn to send one message. If too few transport connections are mapped onto one network connec-tion, the service will be expensive. When upward multiplexing is used with ATM, we have the ironic (tragic?) situation of having to identify the connection using a field in the transport header, even though ATM provides more than 4000 virtual circuit numbers per virtual path expressly for that purpose.

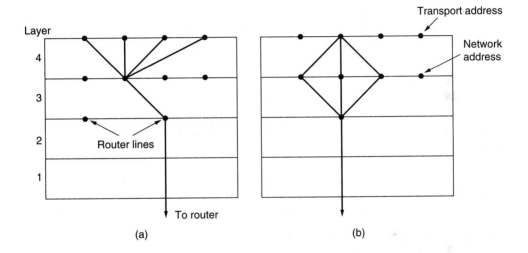

Fig. 6-17. (a) Upward multiplexing. (b) Downward multiplexing.

Multiplexing can also be useful in the transport layer for another reason, related to carrier technical decisions rather than carrier pricing decisions. Sup-pose, for example, that a certain important user needs a high-bandwidth connec-tion from time to time. If the subnet enforces a sliding window flow control with an n-bit sequence number, the user must stop sending as soon as $2^n - 1$ packets are outstanding and must wait for the packets to propagate to the remote host and be acknowledged. If the physical connection is via a satellite, the user is effec-tively limited to $2^n - 1$ packets every 540 msec. With, for example, $n = 8$ and 128-byte packets, the usable bandwidth is about 484 kbps, even though the physi-cal channel bandwidth is more than 100 times higher.

One possible solution is to have the transport layer open multiple network connections and distribute the traffic among them on a round-robin basis, as indi-cated in Fig. 6-17(b). This modus operandi is called **downward multiplexing**. With k network connections open, the effective bandwidth is increased by a factor of k. With 4095 virtual circuits, 128-byte packets, and an 8-bit sequence number, it is theoretically possible to achieve data rates in excess of 1.6 Gbps. Of course, this performance can be achieved only if the output line can support 1.6 Gbps, because all 4095 virtual circuits are still being sent out over one physical line, at least in Fig. 6-17(b). If multiple output lines are available, downward multiplexing can also be used to increase the performance even more.

6.2.6. Crash Recovery

If hosts and routers are subject to crashes, recovery from these crashes becomes an issue. If the transport entity is entirely within the hosts, recovery from network and router crashes is straightforward. If the network layer provides datagram service, the transport entities expect lost TPDUs all the time and know how to cope with them. If the network layer provides connection-oriented service, then loss of a virtual circuit is handled by establishing a new one and then probing the remote transport entity to ask it which TPDUs it has received and which ones it has not received. The latter ones can be retransmitted.

A more troublesome problem is how to recover from host crashes. In particular, it may be desirable for clients to be able to continue working when servers crash and then quickly reboot. To illustrate the difficulty, let us assume that one host, the client, is sending a long file to another host, the file server, using a simple stop-and-wait protocol. The transport layer on the server simply passes the incoming TPDUs to the transport user, one by one. Part way through the transmission, the server crashes. When it comes back up, its tables are reinitialized, so it no longer knows precisely where it was.

In an attempt to recover its previous status, the server might send a broadcast TPDU to all other hosts, announcing that it had just crashed and requesting that its clients inform it of the status of all open connections. Each client can be in one of two states: one TPDU outstanding, *S1*, or no TPDUs outstanding, *S0*. Based on only this state information, the client must decide whether or not to retransmit the most recent TPDU.

At first glance it would seem obvious: the client should retransmit only if it has an unacknowledged TPDU outstanding (i.e., is in state *S1*) when it learns of the crash. However, a closer inspection reveals difficulties with this naive approach. Consider, for example, the situation when the server's transport entity first sends an acknowledgement, and then, when the acknowledgement has been sent, performs the write up to the application process. Writing a TPDU onto the output stream and sending an acknowledgement are two distinct indivisible events that cannot be done simultaneously. If a crash occurs after the acknowledgement has been sent but before the write has been done, the client will receive the acknowledgement and thus be in state *S0* when the crash recovery announcement arrives. The client will therefore not retransmit, (incorrectly) thinking that the TPDU has arrived. This decision by the client leads to a missing TPDU.

At this point you may be thinking: "That problem can be solved easily. All you have to do is reprogram the transport entity to first do the write and then send the acknowledgement." Try again. Imagine that the write has been done but the crash occurs before the acknowledgement can be sent. The client will be in state *S1* and thus retransmit, leading to an undetected duplicate TPDU in the output stream to the server application process.

No matter how the sender and receiver are programmed, there are always situations where the protocol fails to recover properly. The server can be programmed in one of two ways: acknowledge first or write first. The client can be programmed in one of four ways: always retransmit the last TPDU, never retransmit the last TPDU, retransmit only in state *S0*, or retransmit only in state *S1*. This gives eight combinations, but as we shall see, for each combination there is some set of events that makes the protocol fail.

Three events are possible at the server: sending an acknowledgement (*A*), writing to the output process (*W*), and crashing (*C*). The three events can occur in six different orderings: *AC(W)*, *AWC*, *C(AW)*, *C(WA)*, *WAC*, and *WC(A)*, where the parentheses are used to indicate that neither *A* nor *W* may follow *C* (i.e., once it has crashed, it has crashed). Figure 6-18 shows all eight combinations of client and server strategy and the valid event sequences for each one. Notice that for each strategy there is some sequence of events that causes the protocol to fail. For example, if the client always retransmits, the *AWC* event will generate an undetected duplicate, even though the other two events work properly.

Strategy used by receiving host

Strategy used by sending host	First ACK, then write			First write, then ACK		
	AC(W)	AWC	C(AW)	C(WA)	W AC	WC(A)
Always retransmit	OK	DUP	OK	OK	DUP	DUP
Never retransmit	LOST	OK	LOST	LOST	OK	OK
Retransmit in S0	OK	DUP	LOST	LOST	DUP	OK
Retransmit in S1	LOST	OK	OK	OK	OK	DUP

OK   = Protocol functions correctly
DUP = Protocol generates a duplicate message
LOST = Protocol loses a message

Fig. 6-18. Different combinations of client and server strategy.

Making the protocol more elaborate does not help. Even if the client and server exchange several TPDUs before the server attempts to write, so that the client knows exactly what is about to happen, the client has no way of knowing whether a crash occurred just before or just after the write. The conclusion is inescapable: under our ground rules of no simultaneous events, host crash and recovery cannot be made transparent to higher layers.

Put in more general terms, this result can be restated as recovery from a layer N crash can only be done by layer $N + 1$, and then only if the higher layer retains enough status information. As mentioned above, the transport layer can recover from failures in the network layer, provided that each end of a connection keeps track of where it is.

This problem gets us into the issue of what a so-called end-to-end acknowledgement really means. In principle, the transport protocol is end-to-end and not chained like the lower layers. Now consider the case of a user entering requests for transactions against a remote database. Suppose that the remote transport entity is programmed to first pass TPDUs to the next layer up and then acknowledge. Even in this case, the receipt of an acknowledgement back at the user's machine does not necessarily mean that the remote host stayed up long enough to actually update the database. A truly end-to-end acknowledgement, whose receipt means that the work has actually been done, and lack thereof means that it has not, is probably impossible to achieve. This point is discussed in more detail by Saltzer et al. (1984).

6.3. A SIMPLE TRANSPORT PROTOCOL

To make the ideas discussed so far more concrete, in this section we will study an example transport layer in detail. The example has been carefully chosen to be reasonably realistic, yet still simple enough to be easy to understand. The abstract service primitives we will use are the connection-oriented primitives of Fig. 6-3.

6.3.1. The Example Service Primitives

Our first problem is how to express these transport primitives concretely. CONNECT is easy: we will just have a library procedure *connect* that can be called with the appropriate parameters necessary to establish a connection. The parameters are the local and remote TSAPs. During the call, the caller is blocked (i.e., suspended) while the transport entity tries to set up the connection. If the connection succeeds, the caller is unblocked, and can start transmitting data.

When a process wants to be able to accept incoming calls, it calls *listen*, specifying a particular TSAP to listen to. The process then blocks until some remote process attempts to establish a connection to its TSAP.

Note that this model is highly asymmetric. One side is passive, executing a *listen* and waiting until something happens. The other side is active and initiates the connection. An interesting question arises of what to do if the active side begins first. One strategy is to have the connection attempt fail if there is no listener at the remote TSAP. Another strategy is to have the initiator block (possibly forever) until a listener appears.

A compromise, used in our example, is to hold the connection request at the receiving end for a certain time interval. If a process on that host calls *listen* before the timer goes off, the connection is established; otherwise, it is rejected and the caller is unblocked and given an error return.

To release a connection, we will use a procedure *disconnect*. When both sides have disconnected, the connection is released. In other words, we are using a symmetric disconnection model.

Data transmission has precisely the same problem as connection establishment: sending is active but receiving is passive. We will use the same solution for data transmission as for connection establishment, an active call *send* that transmits data, and a passive call *receive* that blocks until a TPDU arrives.

Our concrete service definition thus consists of five primitives: CONNECT, LISTEN, DISCONNECT, SEND, and RECEIVE. Each primitive corresponds exactly with a library procedure that executes the primitive. The parameters for the service primitives and library procedures are as follows:

```
connum   = LISTEN(local)
connum   = CONNECT(local, remote)
status   = SEND(connum, buffer, bytes)
status   = RECEIVE(connum, buffer, bytes)
status   = DISCONNECT(connum)
```

The LISTEN primitive announces the caller's willingness to accept connection requests directed at the indicated TSAP. The user of the primitive is blocked until an attempt is made to connect to it. There is no timeout.

The CONNECT primitive takes two parameters, a local TSAP (i.e., transport address), *local*, and a remote TSAP, *remote*, and tries to establish a transport connection between the two. If it succeeds, it returns in *connum* a nonnegative number used to identify the connection on subsequent calls. If it fails, the reason for failure is put in *connum* as a negative number. In our simple model, each TSAP may participate in only one transport connection, so a possible reason for failure is that one of the transport addresses is currently in use. Some other reasons are: remote host down, illegal local address, and illegal remote address.

The SEND primitive transmits the contents of the buffer as a message on the indicated transport connection, possibly in several units if it is too big. Possible errors, returned in *status*, are no connection, illegal buffer address, or negative count.

The RECEIVE primitive indicates the caller's desire to accept data. The size of the incoming message is placed in *bytes*. If the remote process has released the connection or the buffer address is illegal (e.g., outside the user's program), *status* is set to an error code indicating the nature of the problem.

The DISCONNECT primitive terminates a transport connection. The parameter *connum* tells which one. Possible errors are *connum* belongs to another process, or *connum* is not a valid connection identifier. The error code, or 0 for success, is returned in *status*.

6.3.2. The Example Transport Entity

Before looking at the code of the example transport entity, please be sure you realize that this example is analogous to the early examples presented in Chap. 3: it is more for pedagogical purposes than a serious proposal. Many of the technical details (such as extensive error checking) that would be needed in a production system have been omitted here for the sake of simplicity.

The transport layer makes use of the network service primitives to send and receive TPDUs. For this example, we need to choose network service primitives to use. One choice would have been unreliable datagram service. We have not made that choice to keep the example simple. With unreliable datagram service, the transport code would have been large and complex, mostly dealing with lost and delayed packets. Furthermore, most of these ideas have already been discussed at length in Chap. 3.

Instead, we have chosen to use a connection-oriented reliable network service. This way we can focus on transport issues that do not occur in the lower layers. These include connection establishment, connection release, and credit management, among others. A simple transport service built on top of an ATM network might look something like this.

In general, the transport entity may be part of the host's operating system or it may be a package of library routines running within the user's address space. It may also be contained on a coprocessor chip or network board plugged into the host's backplane. For simplicity, our example has been programmed as though it were a library package, but the changes needed to make it part of the operating system are minimal (primarily how user buffers are accessed).

It is worth noting, however, that in this example, the "transport entity" is not really a separate entity at all, but part of the user process. In particular, when the user executes a primitive that blocks, such as LISTEN, the entire transport entity blocks as well. While this design is fine for a host with only a single user process, on a host with multiple users, it would be more natural to have the transport entity be a separate process, distinct from all the user processes.

The interface to the network layer is via the procedures *to_net* and *from_net* (not shown). Each has six parameters. First comes the connection identifier, which maps one-to-one onto network virtual circuits. Next come the Q and M bits, which, when set to 1, indicate control message and more data from this message follows in the next packet, respectively. After that we have the packet type, chosen from the set of six packet types listed in Fig. 6-19. Finally, we have a pointer to the data itself, and an integer giving the number of bytes of data.

Network packet	Meaning
CALL REQUEST	Sent to establish a connection
CALL ACCEPTED	Response to CALL REQUEST
CLEAR REQUEST	Sent to release a connection
CLEAR CONFIRMATION	Response to CLEAR REQUEST
DATA	Used to transport data
CREDIT	Control packet for managing the window

Fig. 6-19. The network layer packets used in our example.

On calls to *to_net*, the transport entity fills in all the parameters for the network layer to read; on calls to *from_net*, the network layer dismembers an incoming packet for the transport entity. By passing information as procedure parameters rather than passing the actual outgoing or incoming packet itself, the transport layer is shielded from the details of the network layer protocol. If the transport entity should attempt to send a packet when the underlying virtual circuit's sliding window is full, it is suspended within *to_net* until there is room in the window. This mechanism is transparent to the transport entity and is controlled by the network layer using commands like *enable_transport_layer* and *disable_transport_layer* analogous to those described in the protocols of Chap. 3. The management of the packet layer window is also done by the network layer.

In addition to this transparent suspension mechanism, there are also explicit *sleep* and *wakeup* procedures (not shown) called by the transport entity. The procedure *sleep* is called when the transport entity is logically blocked waiting for an external event to happen, generally the arrival of a packet. After *sleep* has been called, the transport entity (and the user process, of course) stop executing.

The actual code of the transport entity is shown in Fig. 6-20. Each connection is always in one of seven states, as follows:

1. IDLE—Connection not established yet.

2. WAITING—CONNECT has been executed and CALL REQUEST sent.

3. QUEUED—A CALL REQUEST has arrived; no LISTEN yet.

4. ESTABLISHED—The connection has been established.

5. SENDING—The user is waiting for permission to send a packet.

6. RECEIVING—A RECEIVE has been done.

7. DISCONNECTING—A DISCONNECT has been done locally.

Transitions between states can occur when any of the following events occur: a primitive is executed, a packet arrives, or the timer expires.

```
#define MAX_CONN 32              /* maximum number of simultaneous connections */
#define MAX_MSG_SIZE 8192        /* largest message in bytes */
#define MAX_PKT_SIZE 512         /* largest packet in bytes */
#define TIMEOUT 20
#define CRED 1
#define OK 0

#define ERR_FULL -1
#define ERR_REJECT -2
#define ERR_CLOSED -3
#define LOW_ERR -3

typedef int transport_address;
typedef enum {CALL_REQ,CALL_ACC,CLEAR_REQ,CLEAR_CONF,DATA_PKT,CREDIT} pkt_type;
typedef enum {IDLE,WAITING,QUEUED,ESTABLISHED,SENDING,RECEIVING,DISCONN} cstate;

/* Global variables. */
transport_address listen_address;    /* local address being listened to */
int listen_conn;                     /* connection identifier for listen */
unsigned char data[MAX_PKT_SIZE];    /* scratch area for packet data */

struct conn {
  transport_address local_address, remote_address;
  cstate state;                      /* state of this connection */
  unsigned char *user_buf_addr;      /* pointer to receive buffer */
  int byte_count;                    /* send/receive count */
  int clr_req_received;              /* set when CLEAR_REQ packet received */
  int timer;                         /* used to time out CALL_REQ packets */
  int credits;                       /* number of messages that may be sent */
} conn[MAX_CONN];

void sleep(void);                    /* prototypes */
void wakeup(void);
void to_net(int cid, int q, int m, pkt_type pt, unsigned char *p, int bytes);
void from_net(int *cid, int *q, int *m, pkt_type *pt, unsigned char *p, int *bytes);

int listen(transport_address t)
{ /* User wants to listen for a connection. See if CALL_REQ has already arrived. */
  int i = 1, found = 0;

  for (i = 1; i <= MAX_CONN; i++)        /* search the table for CALL_REQ */
    if (conn[i].state == QUEUED && conn[i].local_address == t) {
        found = i;
        break;
    }

  if (found == 0) {
      /* No CALL_REQ is waiting.  Go to sleep until arrival or timeout. */
      listen_address = t;  sleep();  i = listen_conn ;
  }
  conn[i].state = ESTABLISHED;           /* connection is ESTABLISHED */
  conn[i].timer = 0;                     /* timer is not used */
```

```
    listen_conn = 0;                          /* 0 is assumed to be an invalid address */
    to_net(i, 0, 0, CALL_ACC, data, 0);      /* tell net to accept connection */
    return(i);                                /* return connection identifier */
}

int connect(transport_address l, transport_address r)
{ /* User wants to connect to a remote process;  send CALL_REQ packet. */
  int i;
  struct conn *cptr;

  data[0] = r;   data[1] = l;                /* CALL_REQ packet needs these */
  i = MAX_CONN;                              /* search table backward */
  while (conn[i].state != IDLE && i > 1) i = i − 1;
  if (conn[i].state == IDLE) {
      /* Make a table entry that CALL_REQ has been sent. */
      cptr = &conn[i];
      cptr->local_address = l; cptr->remote_address = r;
      cptr->state = WAITING; cptr->clr_req_received = 0;
      cptr->credits = 0; cptr->timer = 0;
      to_net(i, 0, 0, CALL_REQ, data, 2);
      sleep();                               /* wait for CALL_ACC or CLEAR_REQ */
      if (cptr->state == ESTABLISHED) return(i);
      if (cptr->clr_req_received) {
          /* Other side refused call. */
          cptr->state = IDLE;                /* back to IDLE state */
          to_net(i, 0, 0, CLEAR_CONF, data, 0);
          return(ERR_REJECT);
      }
  } else return(ERR_FULL);                   /* reject CONNECT: no table space */
}

int send(int cid, unsigned char bufptr[], int bytes)
{ /* User wants to send a message. */
  int i, count, m;
  struct conn *cptr = &conn[cid];

  /* Enter SENDING state. */
  cptr->state = SENDING;
  cptr->byte_count = 0;                      /* # bytes sent so far this message */
  if (cptr->clr_req_received == 0 && cptr->credits == 0) sleep();
  if (cptr->clr_req_received == 0) {
      /* Credit available; split message into packets if need be. */
      do {
          if (bytes − cptr->byte_count > MAX_PKT_SIZE) {/* multipacket message */
              count = MAX_PKT_SIZE; m = 1;  /* more packets later */
          } else {                          /* single packet message */
              count = bytes − cptr->byte_count; m = 0;   /* last pkt of this message */
          }
          for (i = 0; i < count; i++) data[i] = bufptr[cptr->byte_count + i];
          to_net(cid, 0, m, DATA_PKT, data, count);  /* send 1 packet */
          cptr->byte_count = cptr->byte_count + count;     /* increment bytes sent so far */
      } while (cptr->byte_count < bytes);    /* loop until whole message sent */
```

```
        cptr->credits−−;                        /* each message uses up one credit */
        cptr->state = ESTABLISHED;
        return(OK);
  } else {
        cptr->state = ESTABLISHED;
        return(ERR_CLOSED);                      /* send failed: peer wants to disconnect */
  }
}

int receive(int cid, unsigned char bufptr[], int *bytes)
{ /* User is prepared to receive a message. */
  struct conn *cptr = &conn[cid];

  if (cptr->clr_req_received == 0) {
        /* Connection still established; try to receive. */
        cptr->state = RECEIVING;
        cptr->user_buf_addr = bufptr;
        cptr->byte_count = 0;
        data[0] = CRED;
        data[1] = 1;
        to_net(cid, 1, 0, CREDIT, data, 2);      /* send credit */
        sleep();                                 /* block awaiting data */
        *bytes = cptr->byte_count;
  }
  cptr->state = ESTABLISHED;
  return(cptr->clr_req_received ? ERR_CLOSED : OK);
}

int disconnect(int cid)
{ /* User wants to release a connection. */
  struct conn *cptr = &conn[cid];

  if (cptr->clr_req_received) {                  /* other side initiated termination */
        cptr->state = IDLE;                      /* connection is now released */
        to_net(cid, 0, 0, CLEAR_CONF, data, 0);
  } else {                                       /* we initiated termination */
        cptr->state = DISCONN;                   /* not released until other side agrees */
        to_net(cid, 0, 0, CLEAR_REQ, data, 0);
  }
  return(OK);
}

void packet_arrival(void)
{ /* A packet has arrived, get and process it. */
  int cid;                                       /* connection on which packet arrived */
  int count, i, q, m;
  pkt_type ptype;       /* CALL_REQ, CALL_ACC, CLEAR_REQ, CLEAR_CONF, DATA_PKT, CREDIT */
  unsigned char data[MAX_PKT_SIZE];              /* data portion of the incoming packet */
  struct conn *cptr;

  from_net(&cid, &q, &m, &ptype, data, &count);  /* go get it */
  cptr = &conn[cid];
```

```
switch (ptype) {
    case CALL_REQ:                              /* remote user wants to establish connection */
        cptr->local_address = data[0]; cptr->remote_address = data[1];
        if (cptr->local_address == listen_address) {
            listen_conn = cid; cptr->state = ESTABLISHED; wakeup();
        } else {
            cptr->state = QUEUED; cptr->timer = TIMEOUT;
        }
        cptr->clr_req_received = 0;  cptr->credits = 0;
        break;

    case CALL_ACC:                              /* remote user has accepted our CALL_REQ */
        cptr->state = ESTABLISHED;
        wakeup();
        break;

    case CLEAR_REQ:                             /* remote user wants to disconnect or reject call */
        cptr->clr_req_received = 1;
        if (cptr->state == DISCONN) cptr->state = IDLE; /* clear collision */
        if (cptr->state == WAITING || cptr->state == RECEIVING || cptr->state == SENDING) wakeup();
        break;

    case CLEAR_CONF:                            /* remote user agrees to disconnect */
        cptr->state = IDLE;
        break;

    case CREDIT:                                /* remote user is waiting for data */
        cptr->credits += data[1];
        if (cptr->state == SENDING) wakeup();
        break;

    case DATA_PKT:                              /* remote user has sent data */
        for (i = 0; i < count; i++) cptr->user_buf_addr[cptr->byte_count + i] = data[i];
        cptr->byte_count += count;
        if (m == 0 ) wakeup();
    }
}

void clock(void)
{ /* The clock has ticked, check for timeouts of queued connect requests. */
    int i;
    struct conn *cptr;

    for (i = 1; i <= MAX_CONN; i++) {
        cptr = &conn[i];
        if (cptr->timer > 0) {                  /* timer was running */
            cptr->timer--;
            if (cptr->timer == 0) {             /* timer has now expired */
                cptr->state = IDLE;
                to_net(i, 0, 0, CLEAR_REQ, data, 0);
            }
        }
    }
}
```

Fig. 6-20. An example transport entity.

The procedures shown in Fig. 6-20 are of two types. Most are directly callable by user programs. *packet_arrival* and *clock* are different, however. They are spontaneously triggered by external events: the arrival of a packet and the clock ticking, respectively. In effect, they are interrupt routines. We will assume that they are never invoked while a transport entity procedure is running. Only when the user process is sleeping or executing outside the transport entity may they be called. This property is crucial to the correct functioning of the transport entity.

The existence of the Q (Qualifier) bit in the packet header allows us to avoid the overhead of a transport protocol header. Ordinary data messages are sent as data packets with $Q = 0$. Transport protocol control messages, of which there is only one (CREDIT) in our example, are sent as data packets with $Q = 1$. These control messages are detected and processed by the receiving transport entity.

The main data structure used by the transport entity is the array *conn*, which has one record for each potential connection. The record maintains the state of the connection, including the transport addresses at either end, the number of messages sent and received on the connection, the current state, the user buffer pointer, the number of bytes of the current messages sent or received so far, a bit indicating that the remote user has issued a DISCONNECT, a timer, and a permission counter used to enable sending of messages. Not all of these fields are used in our simple example, but a complete transport entity would need all of them, and perhaps more. Each *conn* entry is assumed initialized to the *IDLE* state.

When the user calls CONNECT, the network layer is instructed to send a CALL REQUEST packet to the remote machine, and the user is put to sleep. When the CALL REQUEST packet arrives at the other side, the transport entity is interrupted to run *packet_arrival* to check if the local user is listening on the specified address. If so, a CALL ACCEPTED packet is sent back and the remote user is awakened; if not, the CALL REQUEST is queued for *TIMEOUT* clock ticks. If a LISTEN is done within this period, the connection is established; otherwise, it times out and is rejected with a CLEAR REQUEST packet. This mechanism is needed to prevent the initiator from blocking forever in the event that the remote process does not want to connect to it.

Although we have eliminated the transport protocol header, we still need a way to keep track of which packet belongs to which transport connection, since multiple connections may exist simultaneously. The simplest approach is to use the network layer virtual circuit number as the transport connection number as well. Furthermore, the virtual circuit number can also be used as the index into the *conn* array. When a packet comes in on network layer virtual circuit k, it belongs to transport connection k, whose state is in the record *conn*[k]. For connections initiated at a host, the connection number is chosen by the originating transport entity. For incoming calls, the network layer makes the choice, choosing any unused virtual circuit number.

To avoid having to provide and manage buffers within the transport entity, a flow control mechanism different from the traditional sliding window is used here. Instead, when a user calls RECEIVE, a special **credit message** is sent to the transport entity on the sending machine and is recorded in the *conn* array. When SEND is called, the transport entity checks to see if a credit has arrived on the specified connection. If so, the message is sent (in multiple packets if need be) and the credit decremented; if not, the transport entity puts itself to sleep until a credit arrives. This mechanism guarantees that no message is ever sent unless the other side has already done a RECEIVE. As a result, whenever a message arrives there is guaranteed to be a buffer available into which it can be put. The scheme can easily be generalized to allow receivers to provide multiple buffers and request multiple messages.

You should keep the simplicity of Fig. 6-20 in mind. A realistic transport entity would normally check all user supplied parameters for validity, handle recovery from network layer crashes, deal with call collisions, and support a more general transport service including such facilities as interrupts, datagrams, and nonblocking versions of the SEND and RECEIVE primitives.

6.3.3. The Example as a Finite State Machine

Writing a transport entity is difficult and exacting work, especially for more realistic protocols. To reduce the chance of making an error, it is often useful to represent the state of the protocol as a finite state machine.

We have already seen that our example protocol has seven states per connection. It is also possible to isolate 12 events that can happen to move a connection from one state to another. Five of these events are the five service primitives. Another six are the arrivals of the six legal packet types. The last one is the expiration of the timer. Figure 6-21 shows the main protocol actions in matrix form. The columns are the states and the rows are the 12 events.

Each entry in the matrix (i.e., the finite state machine) of Fig. 6-21 has up to three fields: a predicate, an action, and a new state. The predicate indicates under what conditions the action is taken. For example, in the upper left-hand entry, if a LISTEN is executed and there is no more table space (predicate *P1*), the LISTEN fails and the state does not change. On the other hand, if a CALL REQUEST packet has already arrived for the transport address being listened to (predicate *P2*), the connection is established immediately. Another possibility is that *P2* is false, that is, no CALL REQUEST has come in, in which case the connection remains in the *IDLE* state, awaiting a CALL REQUEST packet.

It is worth pointing out that the choice of states to use in the matrix is not entirely fixed by the protocol itself. In this example, there is no state *LISTENING*, which might have been a reasonable thing to have following a LISTEN. There is no *LISTENING* state because a state is associated with a connection record entry, and no connection record is created by LISTEN. Why not? Because we have decided to use the network layer virtual circuit numbers as the connection

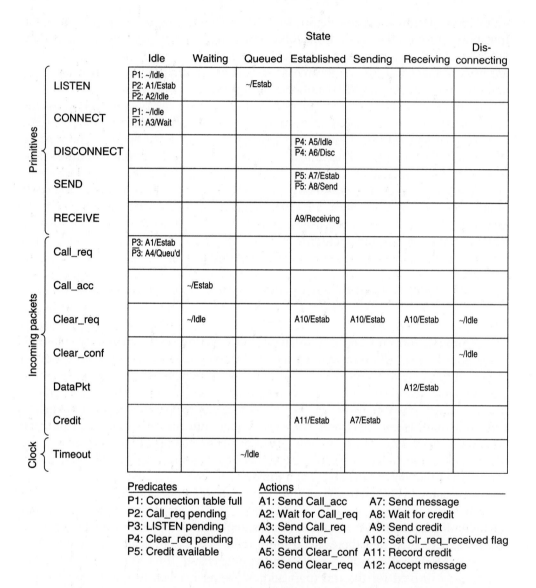

			State				
	Idle	**Waiting**	**Queued**	**Established**	**Sending**	**Receiving**	**Dis-connecting**
LISTEN	P1: ~/Idle P2: A1/Estab P̄2: A2/Idle		~/Estab				
CONNECT	P1: ~/Idle P̄1: A3/Wait						
DISCONNECT				P4: A5/Idle P̄4: A6/Disc			
SEND				P5: A7/Estab P̄5: A8/Send			
RECEIVE				A9/Receiving			
Call_req	P3: A1/Estab P̄3: A4/Queu'd						
Call_acc		~/Estab					
Clear_req		~/Idle		A10/Estab	A10/Estab	A10/Estab	~/Idle
Clear_conf							~/Idle
DataPkt						A12/Estab	
Credit				A11/Estab	A7/Estab		
Timeout		~/Idle					

(Row groups at left: "Primitives" covers LISTEN, CONNECT, DISCONNECT, SEND, RECEIVE; "Incoming packets" covers Call_req, Call_acc, Clear_req, Clear_conf, DataPkt, Credit; "Clock" covers Timeout.)

Predicates	Actions	
P1: Connection table full	A1: Send Call_acc	A7: Send message
P2: Call_req pending	A2: Wait for Call_req	A8: Wait for credit
P3: LISTEN pending	A3: Send Call_req	A9: Send credit
P4: Clear_req pending	A4: Start timer	A10: Set Clr_req_received flag
P5: Credit available	A5: Send Clear_conf	A11: Record credit
	A6: Send Clear_req	A12: Accept message

Fig. 6-21. The example protocol as a finite state machine. Each entry has an optional predicate, an optional action, and the new state. The tilde indicates that no major action is taken. An overbar above a predicate indicates the negation of the predicate. Blank entries correspond to impossible or invalid events.

identifiers, and for a LISTEN, the virtual circuit number is ultimately chosen by the network layer when the CALL REQUEST packet arrives.

The actions *A1* through *A12* are the major actions, such as sending packets and starting timers. Not all the minor actions, such as initializing the fields of a connection record, are listed. If an action involves waking up a sleeping process, the actions following the wakeup also count. For example, if a CALL REQUEST packet comes in and a process was asleep waiting for it, the transmission of the CALL ACCEPT packet following the wakeup counts as part of the action for CALL REQUEST. After each action is performed, the connection may move to a new state, as shown in Fig. 6-21.

The advantage of representing the protocol as a matrix is threefold. First, in this form it is much easier for the programmer to systematically check each combination of state and event to see if an action is required. In production implementations, some of the combinations would be used for error handling. In Fig. 6-21 no distinction is made between impossible situations and illegal ones. For example, if a connection is in *waiting* state, the DISCONNECT event is impossible because the user is blocked and cannot execute any primitives at all. On the other hand, in *sending* state, data packets are not expected because no credit has been issued. The arrival of a data packet is a protocol error.

The second advantage of the matrix representation of the protocol is in implementing it. One could envision a two-dimensional array in which element $a[i][j]$ was a pointer or index to the procedure that handled the occurrence of event i when in state j. One possible implementation is to write the transport entity as a short loop, waiting for an event at the top of the loop. When an event happens, the relevant connection is located and its state is extracted. With the event and state now known, the transport entity just indexes into the array a and calls the proper procedure. This approach gives a much more regular and systematic design than our transport entity.

The third advantage of the finite state machine approach is for protocol description. In some standards documents, the protocols are given as finite state machines of the type of Fig. 6-21. Going from this kind of description to a working transport entity is much easier if the transport entity is also driven by a finite state machine based on the one in the standard.

The primary disadvantage of the finite state machine approach is that it may be more difficult to understand than the straight programming example we used initially. However, this problem may be partially solved by drawing the finite state machine as a graph, as is done in Fig. 6-22.

6.4. THE INTERNET TRANSPORT PROTOCOLS (TCP AND UDP)

The Internet has two main protocols in the transport layer, a connection-oriented protocol and a connectionless one. In the following sections we will study both of them. The connection-oriented protocol is TCP. The connectionless protocol is UDP. Because UDP is basically just IP with a short header added, we will focus on TCP.

TCP (Transmission Control Protocol) was specifically designed to provide a reliable end-to-end byte stream over an unreliable internetwork. An

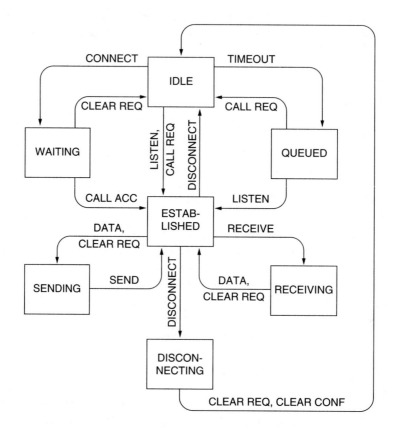

Fig. 6-22. The example protocol in graphical form. Transitions that leave the connection state unchanged have been omitted for simplicity.

internetwork differs from a single network because different parts may have wildly different topologies, bandwidths, delays, packet sizes, and other parameters. TCP was designed to dynamically adapt to properties of the internetwork and to be robust in the face of many kinds of failures.

TCP was formally defined in RFC 793. As time went on, various errors and inconsistencies were detected, and the requirements were changed in some areas. These clarifications and some bug fixes are detailed in RFC 1122. Extensions are given in RFC 1323.

Each machine supporting TCP has a TCP transport entity, either a user process or part of the kernel that manages TCP streams and interfaces to the IP layer. A TCP entity accepts user data streams from local processes, breaks them up into pieces not exceeding 64K bytes (in practice, usually about 1500 bytes), and sends each piece as a separate IP datagram. When IP datagrams containing TCP data arrive at a machine, they are given to the TCP entity, which reconstructs the original byte streams. For simplicity, we will sometimes use just "TCP" to mean the

TCP transport entity (a piece of software) or the TCP protocol (a set of rules). From the context it will be clear which is meant. For example, in "The user gives TCP the data," the TCP transport entity is clearly intended.

The IP layer gives no guarantee that datagrams will be delivered properly, so it is up to TCP to time out and retransmit them as need be. Datagrams that do arrive may well do so in the wrong order; it is also up to TCP to reassemble them into messages in the proper sequence. In short, TCP must furnish the reliability that most users want and that IP does not provide.

6.4.1. The TCP Service Model

TCP service is obtained by having both the sender and receiver create end points, called sockets, as discussed in Sec. 6.1.3. Each socket has a socket number (address) consisting of the IP address of the host and a 16-bit number local to that host, called a **port**. A port is the TCP name for a TSAP. To obtain TCP service, a connection must be explicitly established between a socket on the sending machine and a socket on the receiving machine. The socket calls are listed in Fig. 6-6.

A socket may be used for multiple connections at the same time. In other words, two or more connections may terminate at the same socket. Connections are identified by the socket identifiers at both ends, that is, (*socket1, socket2*). No virtual circuit numbers or other identifiers are used.

Port numbers below 256 are called **well-known ports** and are reserved for standard services. For example, any process wishing to establish a connection to a host to transfer a file using FTP can connect to the destination host's port 21 to contact its FTP daemon. Similarly, to establish a remote login session using TEL-NET, port 23 is used. The list of well-known ports is given in RFC 1700.

All TCP connections are full-duplex and point-to-point. Full duplex means that traffic can go in both directions at the same time. Point-to-point means that each connection has exactly two end points. TCP does not support multicasting or broadcasting.

A TCP connection is a byte stream, not a message stream. Message boundaries are not preserved end to end. For example, if the sending process does four 512-byte writes to a TCP stream, these data may be delivered to the receiving process as four 512-byte chunks, two 1024-byte chunks, one 2048-byte chunk (see Fig. 6-23), or some other way. There is no way for the receiver to detect the unit(s) in which the data were written.

Files in UNIX have this property too. The reader of a file cannot tell whether the file was written a block at a time, a byte at a time, or all in one blow. As with a UNIX file, the TCP software has no idea of what the bytes mean and no interest in finding out. A byte is just a byte.

When an application passes data to TCP, TCP may send it immediately or buffer it (in order to collect a larger amount to send at once), at its discretion.

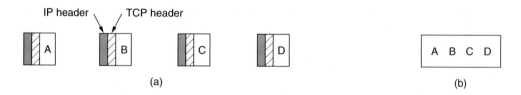

Fig. 6-23. (a) Four 512-byte segments sent as separate IP datagrams. (b) The 2048 bytes of data delivered to the application in a single READ call.

However, sometimes, the application really wants the data to be sent immediately. For example, suppose a user is logged into a remote machine. After a command line has been finished and the carriage return typed, it is essential that the line be shipped off to the remote machine immediately and not buffered until the next line comes in. To force data out, applications can use the PUSH flag, which tells TCP not to delay the transmission.

Some early applications used the PUSH flag as a kind of marker to delineate messages boundaries. While this trick sometimes works, it sometimes fails since not all implementations of TCP pass the PUSH flag to the application on the receiving side. Furthermore, if additional PUSHes come in before the first one has been transmitted (e.g., because the output line is busy), TCP is free to collect all the PUSHed data into a single IP datagram, with no separation between the various pieces.

One last feature of the TCP service that is worth mentioning here is **urgent data**. When an interactive user hits the DEL or CTRL-C key to break off a remote computation that has already begun, the sending application puts some control information in the data stream and gives it to TCP along with the URGENT flag. This event causes TCP to stop accumulating data and transmit everything it has for that connection immediately.

When the urgent data are received at the destination, the receiving application is interrupted (e.g., given a signal in UNIX terms), so it can stop whatever it was doing and read the data stream to find the urgent data. The end of the urgent data is marked, so the application knows when it is over. The start of the urgent data is not marked. It is up to the application to figure that out. This scheme basically provides a crude signaling mechanism and leaves everything else up to the application.

6.4.2. The TCP Protocol

In this section we will give a general overview of the TCP protocol. In the next one we will go over the protocol header, field by field. Every byte on a TCP connection has its own 32-bit sequence number. For a host blasting away at full speed on a 10-Mbps LAN, theoretically the sequence numbers could wrap around in an hour, but in practice it takes much longer. The sequence numbers are used both for acknowledgements and for the window mechanism, which use separate 32-bit header fields.

The sending and receiving TCP entities exchange data in the form of segments. A **segment** consists of a fixed 20-byte header (plus an optional part) followed by zero or more data bytes. The TCP software decides how big segments should be. It can accumulate data from several writes into one segment or split data from one write over multiple segments. Two limits restrict the segment size. First, each segment, including the TCP header, must fit in the 65,535 byte IP payload. Second, each network has a **maximum transfer unit** or **MTU**, and each segment must fit in the MTU. In practice, the MTU is generally a few thousand bytes and thus defines the upper bound on segment size. If a segment passes through a sequence of networks without being fragmented and then hits one whose MTU is smaller than the segment, the router at the boundary fragments the segment into two or more smaller segments.

A segment that is too large for a network that it must transit can be broken up into multiple segments by a router. Each new segment gets its own IP header, so fragmentation by routers increases the total overhead (because each additional segment adds 20 bytes of extra header information in the form of an IP header).

The basic protocol used by TCP entities is the sliding window protocol. When a sender transmits a segment, it also starts a timer. When the segment arrives at the destination, the receiving TCP entity sends back a segment (with data if any exists, otherwise without data) bearing an acknowledgement number equal to the next sequence number it expects to receive. If the sender's timer goes off before the acknowledgement is received, the sender transmits the segment again.

Although this protocol sounds simple, there are many ins and outs that we will cover below. For example, since segments can be fragmented, it is possible that part of a transmitted segment arrives and is acknowledged by the receiving TCP entity, but the rest is lost. Segments can also arrive out of order, so bytes 3072–4095 can arrive but cannot be acknowledged because bytes 2048–3071 have not turned up yet. Segments can also be delayed so long in transit that the sender times out and retransmits them. If a retransmitted segment takes a different route than the original, and is fragmented differently, bits and pieces of both the original and the duplicate can arrive sporadically, requiring a careful administration to achieve a reliable byte stream. Finally, with so many networks making up the Internet, it is possible that a segment may occasionally hit a congested (or broken) network along its path.

TCP must be prepared to deal with these problems and solve them in an efficient way. A considerable amount of effort has gone into optimizing the performance of TCP streams, even in the face of network problems. A number of the algorithms used by many TCP implementations will be discussed below.

6.4.3. The TCP Segment Header

Figure 6-24 shows the layout of a TCP segment. Every segment begins with a fixed-format 20-byte header. The fixed header may be followed by header options. After the options, if any, up to $65,535 - 20 - 20 = 65,515$ data bytes may follow, where the first 20 refers to the IP header and the second to the TCP header. Segments without any data are legal and are commonly used for acknowledgements and control messages.

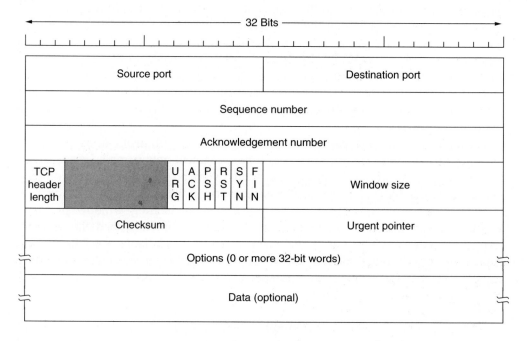

Fig. 6-24. The TCP header.

Let us dissect the TCP header field by field. The *Source port* and *Destination port* fields identify the local end points of the connection. Each host may decide for itself how to allocate its own ports starting at 256. A port plus its host's IP address forms a 48-bit unique TSAP. The source and destination socket numbers together identify the connection.

The *Sequence number* and *Acknowledgement number* fields perform their usual functions. Note that the latter specifies the next byte expected, not the last byte correctly received. Both are 32 bits long because every byte of data is numbered in a TCP stream.

The *TCP header length* tells how many 32-bit words are contained in the TCP header. This information is needed because the *Options* field is of variable length, so the header is too. Technically, this field really indicates the start of the data within the segment, measured in 32-bit words, but that number is just the header length in words, so the effect is the same.

Next comes a 6-bit field that is not used. The fact that this field has survived intact for over a decade is testimony to how well thought out TCP is. Lesser protocols would have needed it to fix bugs in the original design.

Now come six 1-bit flags. *URG* is set to 1 if the *Urgent pointer* is in use. The *Urgent pointer* is used to indicate a byte offset from the current sequence number at which urgent data are to be found. This facility is in lieu of interrupt messages. As we mentioned above, this facility is a bare bones way of allowing the sender to signal the receiver without getting TCP itself involved in the reason for the interrupt.

The *ACK* bit is set to 1 to indicate that the *Acknowledgement number* is valid. If *ACK* is 0, the segment does not contain an acknowledgement so the *Acknowledgement number* field is ignored.

The *PSH* bit indicates PUSHed data. The receiver is hereby kindly requested to deliver the data to the application upon arrival and not buffer it until a full buffer has been received (which it might otherwise do for efficiency reasons).

The *RST* bit is used to reset a connection that has become confused due to a host crash or some other reason. It is also used to reject an invalid segment or refuse an attempt to open a connection. In general, if you get a segment with the *RST* bit on, you have a problem on your hands.

The *SYN* bit is used to establish connections. The connection request has *SYN* = 1 and *ACK* = 0 to indicate that the piggyback acknowledgement field is not in use. The connection reply does bear an acknowledgement, so it has *SYN* = 1 and *ACK* = 1. In essence the *SYN* bit is used to denote CONNECTION REQUEST and CONNECTION ACCEPTED, with the *ACK* bit used to distinguish between those two possibilities.

The *FIN* bit is used to release a connection. It specifies that the sender has no more data to transmit. However, after closing a connection, a process may continue to receive data indefinitely. Both *SYN* and *FIN* segments have sequence numbers and are thus guaranteed to be processed in the correct order.

Flow control in TCP is handled using a variable-size sliding window. The *Window* field tells how many bytes may be sent starting at the byte acknowledged. A *Window* field of 0 is legal and says that the bytes up to and including *Acknowledgement number* − 1 have been received, but that the receiver is currently badly in need of a rest and would like no more data for the moment, thank you. Permission to send can be granted later by sending a segment with the same *Acknowledgement number* and a nonzero *Window* field.

A *Checksum* is also provided for extreme reliability. It checksums the header, the data, and the conceptual pseudoheader shown in Fig. 6-25. When performing this computation, the TCP *Checksum* field is set to zero, and the data field is padded out with an additional zero byte if its length is an odd number. The checksum algorithm is simply to add up all the 16-bit words in 1's complement and then to take the 1's complement of the sum. As a consequence, when the receiver performs the calculation on the entire segment, including the *Checksum* field, the result should be 0.

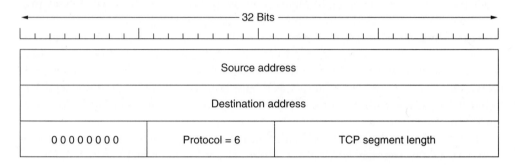

Fig. 6-25. The pseudoheader included in the TCP checksum.

The pseudoheader contains the 32-bit IP addresses of the source and destination machines, the protocol number for TCP (6), and the byte count for the TCP segment (including the header). Including the pseudoheader in the TCP checksum computation helps detect misdelivered packets, but doing so violates the protocol hierarchy since the IP addresses in it belong to the IP layer, not the TCP layer.

The *Options* field was designed to provide a way to add extra facilities not covered by the regular header. The most important option is the one that allows each host to specify the maximum TCP payload it is willing to accept. Using large segments is more efficient than using small ones because the 20-byte header can then be amortized over more data, but small hosts may not be able to handle very large segments. During connection setup, each side can announce its maximum and see its partner's. The smaller of the two numbers wins. If a host does not use this option, it defaults to a 536-byte payload. All Internet hosts are required to accept TCP segments of $536 + 20 = 556$ bytes.

For lines with high bandwidth, high delay, or both, the 64 KB window is often a problem. On a T3 line (44.736 Mbps), it takes only 12 msec to output a full 64 KB window. If the round trip propagation delay is 50 msec (typical for a transcontinental fiber), the sender will be idle 3/4 of the time waiting for acknowledgements. On a satellite connection, the situation is even worse. A larger window size would allow the sender to keep pumping data out, but using the 16-bit *Window size* field, there is no way to express such a size. In RFC 1323, a *Window scale* option was proposed, allowing the sender and receiver to negotiate a window scale factor. This number allows both sides to shift the *Window size* field up to 16 bits to the left, thus allowing windows of up to 2^{32} bytes. Most TCP implementations now support this option.

Another option proposed by RFC 1106 and now widely implemented is the use of the selective repeat instead of go back n protocol. If the receiver gets one bad segment and then a large number of good ones, the normal TCP protocol will eventually time out and retransmit all the unacknowledged segments, including all those that were received correctly. RFC 1106 introduced NAKs, to allow the receiver to ask for a specific segment (or segments). After it gets these, it can acknowledge all the buffered data, thus reducing the amount of data retransmitted.

6.4.4. TCP Connection Management

Connections are established in TCP using the three-way handshake discussed in Sec. 6.2.2. To establish a connection, one side, say the server, passively waits for an incoming connection by executing the LISTEN and ACCEPT primitives, either specifying a specific source or nobody in particular.

The other side, say the client, executes a CONNECT primitive, specifying the IP address and port to which it wants to connect, the maximum TCP segment size it is willing to accept, and optionally some user data (e.g., a password). The CONNECT primitive sends a TCP segment with the *SYN* bit on and *ACK* bit off and waits for a response.

When this segment arrives at the destination, the TCP entity there checks to see if there is a process that has done a LISTEN on the port given in the *Destination port* field. If not, it sends a reply with the *RST* bit on to reject the connection.

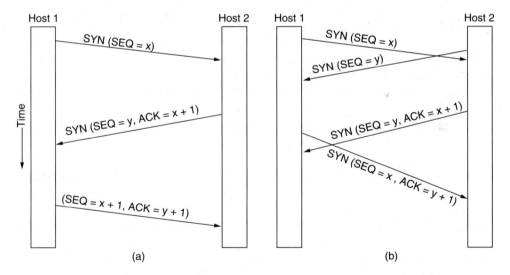

Fig. 6-26. (a) TCP connection establishment in the normal case. (b) Call collision.

If some process is listening to the port, that process is given the incoming TCP segment. It can then either accept or reject the connection. If it accepts, an acknowledgement segment is sent back. The sequence of TCP segments sent in the normal case is shown in Fig. 6-26(a). Note that a *SYN* segment consumes 1 byte of sequence space so it can be acknowledged unambiguously.

In the event that two hosts simultaneously attempt to establish a connection between the same two sockets, the sequence of events is as illustrated in Fig. 6-26(b). The result of these events is that just one connection is established, not two because connections are identified by their end points. If the first setup results in a connection identified by (x, y) and the second one does too, only one table entry is made, namely, for (x, y).

The initial sequence number on a connection is not 0 for the reasons we discussed earlier. A clock-based scheme is used, with a clock tick every 4 μsec. For additional safety, when a host crashes, it may not reboot for the maximum packet lifetime (120 sec) to make sure that no packets from previous connections are still roaming around the Internet somewhere.

Although TCP connections are full duplex, to understand how connections are released it is best to think of them as a pair of simplex connections. Each simplex connection is released independently of its sibling. To release a connection, either party can send a TCP segment with the *FIN* bit set, which means that it has no more data to transmit. When the *FIN* is acknowledged, that direction is shut down for new data. Data may continue to flow indefinitely in the other direction, however. When both directions have been shut down, the connection is released. Normally, four TCP segments are needed to release a connection, one *FIN* and one *ACK* for each direction. However, it is possible for the first *ACK* and the second *FIN* to be contained in the same segment, reducing the total count to three.

Just as with telephone calls in which both people say goodbye and hang up the phone simultaneously, both ends of a TCP connection may send *FIN* segments at the same time. These are each acknowledged in the usual way, and the connection shut down. There is, in fact, no essential difference between the two hosts releasing sequentially or simultaneously.

To avoid the two-army problem, timers are used. If a response to a *FIN* is not forthcoming within two maximum packet lifetimes, the sender of the *FIN* releases the connection. The other side will eventually notice that nobody seems to be listening to it any more, and time out as well. While this solution is not perfect, given the fact that a perfect solution is theoretically impossible, it will have to do. In practice, problems rarely arise.

The steps required to establish and release connections can be represented in a finite state machine with the 11 states listed in Fig. 6-27. In each state, certain events are legal. When a legal event happens, some action may be taken. If some other event happens, an error is reported.

Each connection starts in the *CLOSED* state. It leaves that state when it does either a passive open (LISTEN), or an active open (CONNECT). If the other side does the opposite one, a connection is established and the state becomes *ESTABLISHED*. Connection release can be initiated by either side. When it is complete, the state returns to *CLOSED*.

The finite state machine itself is shown in Fig. 6-28. The common case of a client actively connecting to a passive server is shown with heavy lines—solid for

State	Description
CLOSED	No connection is active or pending
LISTEN	The server is waiting for an incoming call
SYN RCVD	A connection request has arrived; wait for ACK
SYN SENT	The application has started to open a connection
ESTABLISHED	The normal data transfer state
FIN WAIT 1	The application has said it is finished
FIN WAIT 2	The other side has agreed to release
TIMED WAIT	Wait for all packets to die off
CLOSING	Both sides have tried to close simultaneously
CLOSE WAIT	The other side has initiated a release
LAST ACK	Wait for all packets to die off

Fig. 6-27. The states used in the TCP connection management finite state machine.

the client, dotted for the server. The lightface lines are unusual event sequences. Each line in Fig. 6-28 is marked by an *event/action* pair. The event can either be a user-initiated system call (CONNECT, LISTEN, SEND, or CLOSE), a segment arrival (*SYN*, *FIN*, *ACK*, or *RST*), or in one case, a timeout of twice the maximum packet lifetime. The action is the sending of a control segment (*SYN*, *FIN*, or *RST*) or nothing, indicated by —. Comments are shown in parentheses.

The diagram can best be understood by first following the path of a client (the heavy solid line) then later the path of a server (the heavy dashed line). When an application on the client machine issues a CONNECT request, the local TCP entity creates a connection record, marks it as being in the *SYN SENT* state, and sends a *SYN* segment. Note that many connections may be open (or being opened) at the same time on behalf of multiple applications, so the state is per connection and recorded in the connection record. When the *SYN+ACK* arrives, TCP sends the final *ACK* of the three-way handshake and switches into the *ESTABLISHED* state. Data can now be sent and received.

When an application is finished, it executes a CLOSE primitive, which causes the local TCP entity to send a *FIN* segment and wait for the corresponding *ACK* (dashed box marked active close). When the *ACK* arrives, a transition is made to state *FIN WAIT 2* and one direction of the connection is now closed. When the other side closes, too, a *FIN* comes in, which is acknowledged. Now both sides are closed, but TCP waits a time equal to the maximum packet lifetime to guarantee that all packets from the connection have died off, just in case the acknowledgement was lost. When the timer goes off, TCP deletes the connection record.

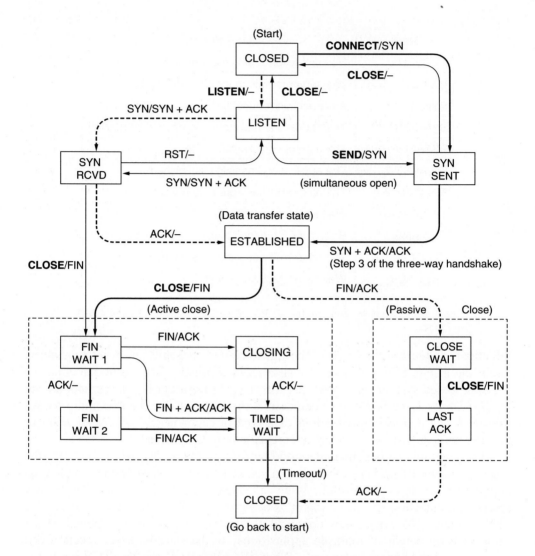

Fig. 6-28. TCP connection management finite state machine. The heavy solid line is the normal path for a client. The heavy dashed line is the normal path for a server. The light lines are unusual events.

Now let us examine connection management from the server's viewpoint. The server does a LISTEN and settles down to see who turns up. When a *SYN* comes in, it is acknowledged and the server goes to the *SYN RCVD* state. When the server's *SYN* is itself acknowledged, the three-way handshake is complete and the server goes to the *ESTABLISHED* state. Data transfer can now occur.

When the client has had enough, it does a CLOSE, which causes a *FIN* to arrive at the server (dashed box marked passive close). The server is then signaled. When it, too, does a CLOSE, a *FIN* is sent to the client. When the client's acknowledgement shows up, the server releases the connection and deletes the connection record.

6.4.5. TCP Transmission Policy

Window management in TCP is not directly tied to acknowledgements as it is in most data link protocols. For example, suppose the receiver has a 4096-byte buffer as shown in Fig. 6-29. If the sender transmits a 2048-byte segment that is correctly received, the receiver will acknowledge the segment. However, since it now has only 2048 of buffer space (until the application removes some data from the buffer), it will advertise a window of 2048 starting at the next byte expected.

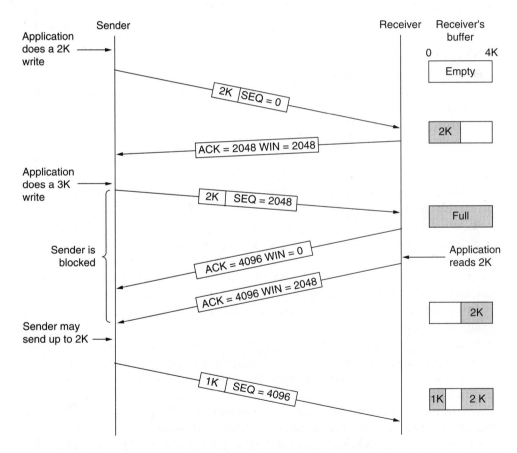

Fig. 6-29. Window management in TCP.

Now the sender transmits another 2048 bytes, which are acknowledged, but the advertised window is 0. The sender must stop until the application process on the receiving host has removed some data from the buffer, at which time TCP can advertise a larger window.

When the window is 0, the sender may not normally send segments, with two exceptions. First, urgent data may be sent, for example, to allow the user to kill the process running on the remote machine. Second, the sender may send a 1-byte segment to make the receiver reannounce the next byte expected and window size. The TCP standard explicitly provides this option to prevent deadlock if a window announcement ever gets lost.

Senders are not required to transmit data as soon as they come in from the application. Neither are receivers required to send acknowledgements as soon as possible. For example, in Fig. 6-29, When the first 2 KB of data came in, TCP, knowing that it had a 4-KB window available, would have been completely correct in just buffering the data until another 2 KB came in, to be able to transmit a segment with a 4-KB payload. This freedom can be exploited to improve performance.

Consider a TELNET connection to an interactive editor that reacts on every keystroke. In the worst case, when a character arrives at the sending TCP entity, TCP creates a 21-byte TCP segment, which it gives to IP to send as a 41-byte IP datagram. At the receiving side, TCP immediately sends a 40-byte acknowledgement (20 bytes of TCP header and 20 bytes of IP header). Later, when the editor has read the byte, TCP sends a window update, moving the window 1 byte to the right. This packet is also 40 bytes. Finally, when the editor has processed the character, it echoes it as a 41-byte packet. In all, 162 bytes of bandwidth are used and four segments are sent for each character typed. When bandwidth is scarce, this method of doing business is not desirable.

One approach that many TCP implementations use to optimize this situation is to delay acknowledgements and window updates for 500 msec in the hope of acquiring some data on which to hitch a free ride. Assuming the editor echoes within 500 msec, only one 41-byte packet now need be sent back to the remote user, cutting the packet count and bandwidth usage in half.

Although this rule reduces the load placed on the network by the receiver, the sender is still operating inefficiently by sending 41-byte packets containing 1 byte of data. A way to reduce this usage is known as **Nagle's algorithm** (Nagle, 1984). What Nagle suggested is simple: when data come into the sender one byte at a time, just send the first byte and buffer all the rest until the outstanding byte is acknowledged. Then send all the buffered characters in one TCP segment and start buffering again until they are all acknowledged. If the user is typing quickly and the network is slow, a substantial number of characters may go in each segment, greatly reducing the bandwidth used. The algorithm additionally allows a new packet to be sent if enough data have trickled in to fill half the window or a maximum segment.

Nagle's algorithm is widely used by TCP implementations, but there are times when it is better to disable it. In particular, when an X-Windows application is being run over the Internet, mouse movements have to be sent to the remote computer. Gathering them up to send in bursts makes the mouse cursor move erratically, which makes for unhappy users.

Another problem that can ruin TCP performance is the **silly window syndrome** (Clark, 1982). This problem occurs when data are passed to the sending TCP entity in large blocks, but an interactive application on the receiving side reads data 1 byte at a time. To see the problem, look at Fig. 6-30. Initially, the TCP buffer on the receiving side is full and the sender knows this (i.e., has a window of size 0). Then the interactive application reads one character from the TCP stream. This action makes the receiving TCP happy, so it sends a window update to the sender saying that it is all right to send 1 byte. The sender obliges and sends 1 byte. The buffer is now full, so the receiver acknowledges the 1-byte segment but sets the window to 0. This behavior can go on forever.

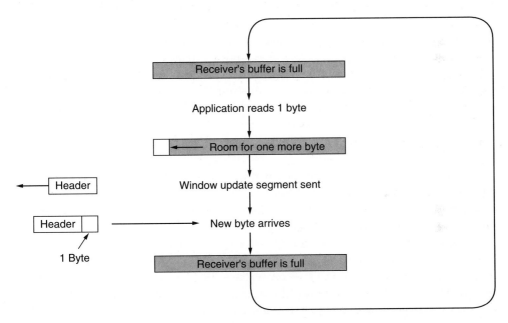

Fig. 6-30. Silly window syndrome.

Clark's solution is to prevent the receiver from sending a window update for 1 byte. Instead it is forced to wait until it has a decent amount of space available and advertise that instead. Specifically, the receiver should not send a window update until it can handle the maximum segment size it advertised when the connection was established, or its buffer is half empty, whichever is smaller.

Furthermore, the sender can also help by not sending tiny segments. Instead, it should try to wait until it has accumulated enough space in the window to send a full segment or at least one containing half of the receiver's buffer size (which it must estimate from the pattern of window updates it has received in the past).

Nagle's algorithm and Clark's solution to the silly window syndrome are complementary. Nagle was trying to solve the problem caused by the sending application delivering data to TCP a byte at a time. Clark was trying to solve the problem of the receiving application sucking the data up from TCP a byte at a time. Both solutions are valid and can work together. The goal is for the sender not to send small segments and the receiver not to ask for them.

The receiving TCP can go further in improving performance than just doing window updates in large units. Like the sending TCP, it also has the ability to buffer data, so it can block a READ request from the application until it has a large chunk of data to provide. Doing this reduces the number of calls to TCP, and hence the overhead. Of course, it also increases the response time, but for noninteractive applications like file transfer, efficiency may outweigh response time to individual requests.

Another receiver issue is what to do with out of order segments. They can be kept or discarded, at the receiver's discretion. Of course, acknowledgements can be sent only when all the data up to the byte acknowledged have been received. If the receiver gets segments 0, 1, 2, 4, 5, 6, and 7, it can acknowledge everything up to and including the last byte in segment 2. When the sender times out, it then retransmits segment 3. If the receiver has buffered segments 4 through 7, upon receipt of segment 3 it can acknowledge all bytes up to the end of segment 7.

6.4.6. TCP Congestion Control

When the load offered to any network is more than it can handle, congestion builds up. The Internet is no exception. In this section we will discuss algorithms that have been developed over the past decade to deal with congestion. Although the network layer also tries to manage congestion, most of the heavy lifting is done by TCP because the real solution to congestion is to slow down the data rate.

In theory, congestion can be dealt with by employing a principle borrowed from physics: the law of conservation of packets. The idea is not to inject a new packet into the network until an old one leaves (i.e., is delivered). TCP attempts to achieve this goal by dynamically manipulating the window size.

The first step in managing congestion is detecting it. In the old days, detecting congestion was difficult. A timeout caused by a lost packet could have been caused by either (1) noise on a transmission line or (2) packet discard at a congested router. Telling the difference was difficult.

Nowadays, packet loss due to transmission errors is relatively rare because most long-haul trunks are fiber (although wireless networks are a different story). Consequently, most transmission timeouts on the Internet are due to congestion. All the Internet TCP algorithms assume that timeouts are caused by congestion and monitor timeouts for signs of trouble the way miners watch their canaries.

Before discussing how TCP reacts to congestion, let us first describe what it does to try to prevent it from occurring in the first place. When a connection is established, a suitable window size has to be chosen. The receiver can specify a window based on its buffer size. If the sender sticks to this window size, problems will not occur due to buffer overflow at the receiving end, but they may still occur due to internal congestion within the network.

In Fig. 6-31, we see this problem illustrated hydraulically. In Fig. 6-31(a), we see a thick pipe leading to a small-capacity receiver. As long as the sender does not send more water than the bucket can contain, no water will be lost. In Fig. 6-31(b), the limiting factor is not the bucket capacity, but the internal carrying capacity of the network. If too much water comes in too fast, it will back up and some will be lost (in this case by overflowing the funnel).

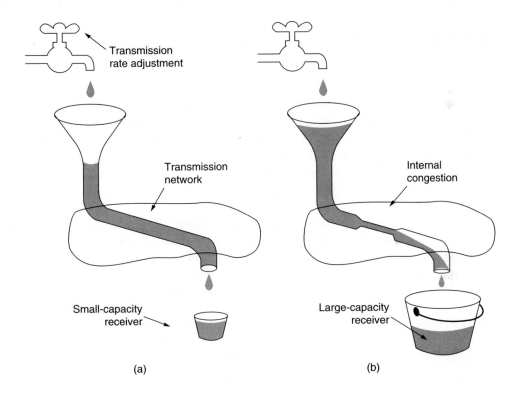

Fig. 6-31. (a) A fast network feeding a low-capacity receiver. (b) A slow network feeding a high-capacity receiver.

The Internet solution is to realize that two potential problems exist—network capacity and receiver capacity—and to deal with each of them separately. To do so, each sender maintains two windows: the window the receiver has granted and a second window, the **congestion window**. Each reflects the number of bytes the sender may transmit. The number of bytes that may be sent is the minimum of the two windows. Thus the effective window is the minimum of what the sender thinks is all right and what the receiver thinks is all right. If the receiver says "Send 8K" but the sender knows that bursts of more than 4K clog the network up, it sends 4K. On the other hand, if the receiver says "Send 8K" and the sender knows that bursts of up to 32K get through effortlessly, it sends the full 8K requested.

When a connection is established, the sender initializes the congestion window to the size of the maximum segment in use on the connection. It then sends one maximum segment. If this segment is acknowledged before the timer goes off, it adds one segment's worth of bytes to the congestion window to make it two maximum size segments and sends two segments. As each of these segments is acknowledged, the congestion window is increased by one maximum segment size. When the congestion window is n segments, if all n are acknowledged on time, the congestion window is increased by the byte count corresponding to n segments. In effect, each burst successfully acknowledged doubles the congestion window.

The congestion window keeps growing exponentially until either a timeout occurs or the receiver's window is reached. The idea is that if bursts of size, say, 1024, 2048, and 4096 bytes work fine, but a burst of 8192 bytes gives a timeout, the congestion window should be set to 4096 to avoid congestion. As long as the congestion window remains at 4096, no bursts longer than that will be sent, no matter how much window space the receiver grants. This algorithm is called **slow start**, but it is not slow at all (Jacobson, 1988). It is exponential. All TCP implementations are required to support it.

Now let us look at the Internet congestion control algorithm. It uses a third parameter, the **threshold**, initially 64K, in addition to the receiver and congestion windows. When a timeout occurs, the threshold is set to half of the current congestion window, and the congestion window is reset to one maximum segment. Slow start is then used to determine what the network can handle, except that exponential growth stops when the threshold is hit. From that point on, successful transmissions grow the congestion window linearly (by one maximum segment for each burst) instead of one per segment. In effect, this algorithm is guessing that it is probably acceptable to cut the congestion window in half, and then it gradually works its way up from there.

As an illustration of how the congestion algorithm works, see Fig. 6-32. The maximum segment size here is 1024 bytes. Initially the congestion window was 64K, but a timeout occurred, so the threshold is set to 32K and the congestion window to 1K for transmission 0 here. The congestion window then grows exponentially until it hits the threshold (32K). Starting then it grows linearly.

Transmission 13 is unlucky (it should have known) and a timeout occurs. The threshold is set to half the current window (by now 40K, so half is 20K) and slow start initiated all over again. When the acknowledgements from transmission 18 start coming in, the first four each increment the congestion window by one segment, but after that, growth becomes linear again.

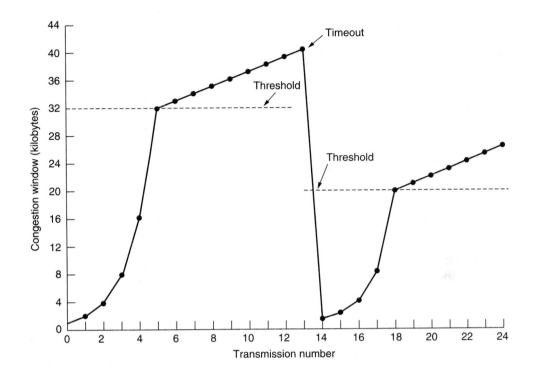

Fig. 6-32. An example of the Internet congestion algorithm.

If no more timeouts occur, the congestion window will continue to grow up to the size of the receiver's window. At that point, it will stop growing and remain constant as long as there are no more timeouts and the receiver's window does not change size. As an aside, if an ICMP SOURCE QUENCH packet comes in and is passed to TCP, this event is treated the same way as a timeout.

Work on improving the congestion control mechanism is continuing. For example, Brakmo et al. (1994) have reported improving TCP throughput by 40 percent to 70 percent by managing the clock more accurately, predicting congestion before timeouts occur, and using this early warning system to improve the slow start algorithm.

6.4.7. TCP Timer Management

TCP uses multiple timers (at least conceptually) to do its work. The most important of these is the **retransmission timer**. When a segment is sent, a retransmission timer is started. If the segment is acknowledged before the timer expires, the timer is stopped. If, on the other hand, the timer goes off before the acknowledgement comes in, the segment is retransmitted (and the timer started again). The question that arises is: How long should the timeout interval be?

This problem is much more difficult in the Internet transport layer than in the generic data link protocols of Chap. 3. In the latter case, the expected delay is highly predictable (i.e., has a low variance), so the timer can be set to go off just slightly after the acknowledgement is expected, as shown in Fig. 6-33(a). Since acknowledgements are rarely delayed in the data link layer, the absence of an acknowledgement at the expected time generally means the frame or the acknowledgement has been lost.

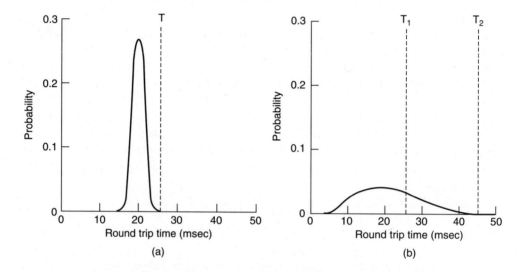

Fig. 6-33. (a) Probability density of acknowledgement arrival times in the data link layer. (b) Probability density of acknowledgement arrival times for TCP.

TCP is faced with a radically different environment. The probability density function for the time it takes for a TCP acknowledgement to come back looks more like Fig. 6-33(b) than Fig. 6-33(a). Determining the round-trip time to the destination is tricky. Even when it is known, deciding on the timeout interval is also difficult. If the timeout is set too short, say T_1 in Fig. 6-33(b), unnecessary retransmissions will occur, clogging the Internet with useless packets. If it is set too long, (T_2), performance will suffer due to the long retransmission delay whenever a packet is lost. Furthermore, the mean and variance of the acknowledgement arrival distribution can change rapidly within a few seconds as congestion builds up or is resolved.

The solution is to use a highly dynamic algorithm that constantly adjusts the timeout interval, based on continuous measurements of network performance. The algorithm generally used by TCP is due to Jacobson (1988) and works as follows. For each connection, TCP maintains a variable, *RTT*, that is the best current estimate of the round-trip time to the destination in question. When a segment is sent, a timer is started, both to see how long the acknowledgement takes and to trigger a retransmission if it takes too long. If the acknowledgement gets back before the timer expires, TCP measures how long the acknowledgement took, say, M. It then updates RTT according to the formula

$$RTT = \alpha RTT + (1 - \alpha)M$$

where α is a smoothing factor that determines how much weight is given to the old value. Typically $\alpha = 7/8$.

Even given a good value of RTT, choosing a suitable retransmission timeout is a nontrivial matter. Normally, TCP uses βRTT, but the trick is choosing β. In the initial implementations, β was always 2, but experience showed that a constant value was inflexible because it failed to respond when the variance went up.

In 1988, Jacobson proposed making β roughly proportional to the standard deviation of the acknowledgement arrival time probability density function so a large variance means a large β and vice versa. In particular, he suggested using the *mean deviation* as a cheap estimator of the *standard deviation*. His algorithm requires keeping track of another smoothed variable, D, the deviation. Whenever an acknowledgement comes in, the difference between the expected and observed values, $|RTT - M|$ is computed. A smoothed value of this is maintained in D by the formula

$$D = \alpha D + (1 - \alpha)\,|RTT - M|$$

where α may or may not be the same value used to smooth RTT. While D is not exactly the same as the standard deviation, it is good enough and Jacobson showed how it could be computed using only integer adds, subtracts, and shifts, a big plus. Most TCP implementations now use this algorithm and set the timeout interval to

$$\text{Timeout} = RTT + 4{*}D$$

The choice of the factor 4 is somewhat arbitrary, but it has two advantages. First, multiplication by 4 can be done with a single shift. Second, it minimizes unnecessary timeouts and retransmissions because less than one percent of all packets come in more than four standard deviations late. (Actually, Jacobson initially said to use 2, but later work has shown that 4 gives better performance.)

One problem that occurs with the dynamic estimation of RTT is what to do when a segment times out and is sent again. When the acknowledgement comes in, it is unclear whether the acknowledgement refers to the first transmission or a later one. Guessing wrong can seriously contaminate the estimate of RTT. Phil Karn discovered this problem the hard way. He is an amateur radio enthusiast interested in transmitting TCP/IP packets by ham radio, a notoriously unreliable medium (on a good day, half the packets get through). He made a simple proposal: do not update RTT on any segments that have been retransmitted. Instead, the timeout is doubled on each failure until the segments get through the first time. This fix is called **Karn's algorithm**. Most TCP implementations use it.

The retransmission timer is not the only one TCP uses. A second timer is the **persistence timer**. It is designed to prevent the following deadlock. The receiver sends an acknowledgement with a window size of 0, telling the sender to wait. Later, the receiver updates the window, but the packet with the update is lost. Now both the sender and the receiver are waiting for each other to do something. When the persistence timer goes off, the sender transmits a probe to the receiver. The response to the probe gives the window size. If it is still zero, the persistence timer is set again and the cycle repeats. If it is nonzero, data can now be sent.

A third timer that some implementations use is the **keepalive timer**. When a connection has been idle for a long time, the keepalive timer may go off to cause one side to check if the other side is still there. If it fails to respond, the connection is terminated. This feature is controversial because it adds overhead and may terminate an otherwise healthy connection due to a transient network partition.

The last timer used on each TCP connection is the one used in the *TIMED WAIT* state while closing. It runs for twice the maximum packet lifetime to make sure that when a connection is closed, all packets created by it have died off.

6.4.8. UDP

The Internet protocol suite also supports a connectionless transport protocol, **UDP (User Data Protocol)**. UDP provides a way for applications to send encapsulated raw IP datagrams and send them without having to establish a connection. Many client-server applications that have one request and one response use UDP rather than go to the trouble of establishing and later releasing a connection. UDP is described in RFC 768.

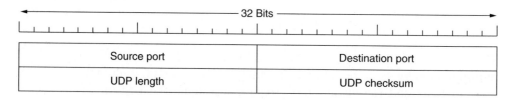

Fig. 6-34. The UDP header.

A UDP segment consists of an 8-byte header followed by the data. The header is shown in Fig. 6-34. The two ports serve the same function as they do in TCP: to identify the end points within the source and destination machines. The *UDP length* field includes the 8-byte header and the data. The *UDP checksum* includes the same format pseudoheader shown in Fig. 6-25, the UDP header, and the UDP data, padded out to an even number of bytes if need be. It is optional and stored as 0 if not computed (a true computed 0 is stored as all 1s, which is the same in 1's complement). Turning it off is foolish unless the quality of the data does not matter (e.g., digitized speech).

6.4.9. Wireless TCP and UDP

In theory, transport protocols should be independent of the technology of the underlying network layer. In particular, TCP should not care whether IP is running over fiber or over radio. In practice, it does matter because most TCP implementations have been carefully optimized based on assumptions that are true for wired networks but which fail for wireless networks. Ignoring the properties of wireless transmission can lead to a TCP implementation that is logically correct but has horrendous performance.

The principal problem is the congestion control algorithm. Nearly all TCP implementations nowadays assume that timeouts are caused by congestion, not by lost packets. Consequently, when a timer goes off, TCP slows down and sends less vigorously (e.g., Jacobson's slow start algorithm). The idea behind this approach is to reduce the network load and thus alleviate the congestion.

Unfortunately, wireless transmission links are highly unreliable. They lose packets all the time. The proper approach to dealing with lost packets is to send them again, and as quickly as possible. Slowing down just makes matters worse. If, say, 20 percent of all packets are lost, then when the sender transmits 100 packets/sec, the throughput is 80 packets/sec. If the sender slows down to 50 packets/sec, the throughput drops to 40 packets/sec.

In effect, when a packet is lost on a wired network, the sender should slow down. When one is lost on a wireless network, the sender should try harder. When the sender does not know what the network is, it is difficult to make the correct decision.

Frequently, the path from sender to receiver is inhomogeneous. The first 1000 km might be over a wired network, but the last 1 km might be wireless. Now making the correct decision on a timeout is even harder, since it matters where the problem occurred. A solution proposed by Bakne and Badrinath (1995), **indirect TCP**, is to split the TCP connection into two separate connections, as shown in Fig. 6-35. The first connection goes from the sender to the base station. The second one goes from the base station to the receiver. The base station simply copies packets between the connections in both directions.

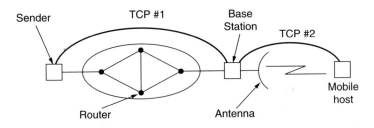

Fig. 6-35. Splitting a TCP connection into two connections.

The advantage of this scheme is that both connections are now homogeneous. Timeouts on the first connection can slow the sender down, whereas timeouts on the second one can speed it up. Other parameters can also be tuned separately for the two connections. The disadvantage is that it violates the semantics of TCP. Since each part of the connection is a full TCP connection, the base station acknowledges each TCP segment in the usual way. Only now, receipt of an acknowledgement by the sender does not mean that the receiver got the segment, only that the base station got it.

A different solution, due to Balakrishnan et al. (1995), does not break the semantics of TCP. It works by making several small modifications to the network layer code in the base station. One of the changes is the addition of a snooping agent that observes and caches TCP segments going out to the mobile host, and acknowledgements coming back from it. When the snooping agent sees a TCP segment going out to the mobile host but does not see an acknowledgement coming back before its (relatively short) timer goes off, it just retransmits that segment, without telling the source that it is doing so. It also generates a retransmission when it sees duplicate acknowledgements from the mobile host go by, invariably meaning that the mobile host has missed something. Duplicate acknowledgements are discarded on the spot, to avoid having the source misinterpret them as a sign of congestion.

One disadvantage of this transparency, however, is that if the wireless link is very lossy, the source may time out waiting for an acknowledgement and invoke the congestion control algorithm. With indirect TCP, the congestion control algorithm will never be started unless there really is congestion in the wired part of the network.

The Balakrishnan et al. paper also has a solution to the problem of lost segments originating at the mobile host. When the base station notices a gap in the inbound sequence numbers, it generates a request for a selective repeat of the missing bytes using a TCP option. Using these two fixes, the wireless link is made more reliable in both directions, without the source knowing about it, and without changing the semantics of TCP.

While UDP does not suffer from the same problems as TCP, wireless communication also introduces difficulties for it. The main trouble is that programs use UDP expecting it to be highly reliable. They know that no guarantees are given, but they still expect it to be near perfect. In a wireless environment, it will be far from perfect. For programs that are able to recover from lost UDP messages, but only at considerable cost, suddenly going from an environment where messages theoretically can be lost but rarely are, to one in which they are constantly being lost can result in a performance disaster.

Wireless communication also affects areas other than just performance. For example, how does a mobile host find a local printer to connect to, rather than use its home printer? Somewhat related to this is how to get the WWW page for the local cell, even if its name is not known. Also, WWW page designers tend to assume lots of bandwidth is available. Putting a large logo on every page becomes counterproductive if it is going to take 30 sec to transmit at 9600 bps every time the page is referenced, irritating the users no end.

6.5. THE ATM AAL LAYER PROTOCOLS

It is not really clear whether or not ATM has a transport layer. On the one hand, the ATM layer has the functionality of a network layer, and there is another layer on top of it (AAL), which sort of makes AAL a transport layer. Some experts agree with this view (e.g., De Prycker, 1993, page 112). One of the protocols used here (AAL 5) is functionally similar to UDP, which is unquestionably a transport protocol.

On the other hand, none of the AAL protocols provide a reliable end-to-end connection, as TCP does (although with only very minor changes they could). Also, in most applications another transport layer is used on top of AAL. Rather than split hairs, we will discuss the AAL layer and its protocols in this chapter without making a claim that it is a true transport layer.

The AAL layer in ATM networks is radically different than TCP, largely because the designers were primarily interested in transmitting voice and video streams, in which rapid delivery is more important than accurate delivery. Remember that the ATM layer just outputs 53-byte cells one after another. It has no error control, no flow control, and no other control. Consequently, it is not well matched to the requirements that most applications need.

To bridge this gap, in Recommendation I.363, ITU has defined an end-to-end layer on top of the ATM layer. This layer, called **AAL** (**ATM Adaptation Layer**) has a tortuous history, full of mistakes, revisions, and unfinished business. In the following sections we will look at it and its design.

The goal of AAL is to provide useful services to application programs and to shield them from the mechanics of chopping data up into cells at the source and reassembling them at the destination. When ITU began defining AAL, it realized that different applications had different requirements, so it organized the service space along three axes:

1. Real-time service versus nonreal-time service.

2. Constant bit rate service versus variable bit rate service.

3. Connection-oriented service versus connectionless service.

In principle, with three axes and two values on each axis, eight distinct services can be defined, as shown in Fig. 6-36. ITU felt that only four of these were of any use, and named them classes A, B, C, and D, as noted. The others were not supported. Starting with ATM 4.0, Fig. 6-36 is somewhat obsolete, so it has been presented here mostly as background information to help understand why the

AAL protocols have been designed as they have been. Instead of these service classes, the major distinction now is between the traffic classes we studied in Chap. 5 (ABR, CBR, NRT-VBR, RT-VBR, and UBR).

	A		B	C				D	
Timing	Real time	None	Real time	None	Real time	None		Real time	None
Bit rate	Constant		Variable		Constant			Variable	
Mode	Connection orientated				Connectionless				

Fig. 6-36. Original service classes supported by AAL (now obsolete).

To handle these four classes of service, ITU defined four protocols, AAL 1 through AAL 4, respectively. However, later it discovered that the technical requirements for classes C and D were so similar that AAL 3 and AAL 4 were combined into AAL 3/4. Then the computer industry, which had been asleep at the switch, realized that none of them were any good. It solved this problem by the simple expedient of defining another protocol, AAL 5. We will look at all four of these shortly. We will also look at an interesting control protocol used on ATM systems.

6.5.1. Structure of the ATM Adaptation Layer

The ATM adaptation layer is divided into two major parts, one of which is often further subdivided, as illustrated in Fig. 6-37.

The upper part of the ATM adaptation layer is called the **convergence sublayer**. Its job is to provide the interface to the application. It consists of a subpart that is common to all applications (for a given AAL protocol) and an application specific subpart. The functions of each of these parts are protocol dependent but can include message framing and error detection.

In addition, at the source, the convergence sublayer is responsible for accepting bit streams or arbitrary length messages from the applications and breaking them up into units of 44 to 48 bytes for transmission. The exact size is protocol dependent, since some protocols use part of the 48-byte ATM payload for their own headers. At the destination, this sublayer reassembles the cells into the original messages. In general, message boundaries are preserved, when present. In other words, if the source sends four 512-byte messages, they will arrive as four 512-byte messages, not one 2048-byte message. For data streams, no message boundaries exist, so they are not preserved.

The lower part of the AAL is called the **SAR (Segmentation And Reassembly)** sublayer. It can add headers and trailers to the data units given to it by the

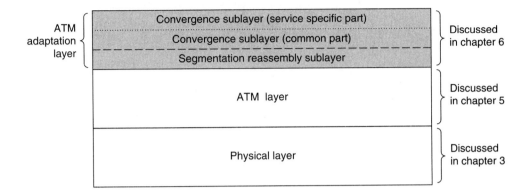

Fig. 6-37. The ATM model showing the ATM adaptation layer and its sublayers.

convergence sublayer to form cell payloads. These payloads are then given to the ATM layer for transmission. At the destination, the SAR sublayer reassembles the cells into messages. The SAR sublayer is basically concerned with cells, whereas the convergence sublayer is concerned with messages.

The generic operation of the convergence and SAR sublayers is shown in Fig. 6-38. When a message comes in to the AAL from the application, the convergence sublayer may give it a header and/or trailer. The message is then broken up into 44- to 48-byte units, which are passed to the SAR sublayer. The SAR sublayer may add its own header and trailer to each piece and pass them down to the ATM layer for transmission as independent cells. Note that the figure shows the most general case because some of the AAL protocols have null headers and/or trailers.

The SAR sublayer also has some additional functions for some (but not all) service classes. In particular, it sometimes handles error detection and multiplexing. The SAR sublayer is present for all service classes but does more or less work, depending on the specific protocol.

The communication between the application and AAL layer uses the standard OSI *request* and *indication* primitives that we discussed in Chap. 1. The communication between the sublayers uses different primitives.

6.5.2. AAL 1

AAL 1 is the protocol used for transmitting class A traffic, that is, real-time, constant bit rate, connection-oriented traffic, such as uncompressed audio and video. Bits are fed in by the application at a constant rate and must be delivered at the far end at the same constant rate, with a minimum of delay, jitter, and overhead. The input is a stream of bits, with no message boundaries. For this traffic, error detecting protocols such as stop-and-wait are not used because the delays that are introduced by timeouts and retransmissions are unacceptable. However,

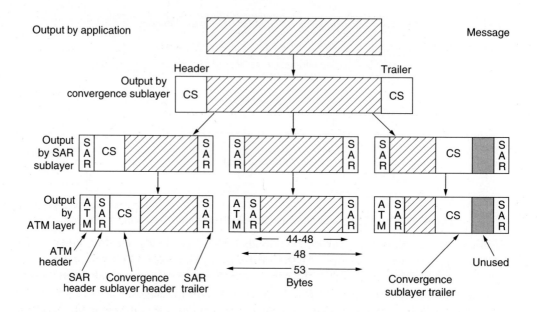

Fig. 6-38. The headers and trailers that can be added to a message in an ATM network.

missing cells are reported to the application, which must then take its own action (if any) to recover from them.

AAL 1 uses a convergence sublayer and a SAR sublayer. The convergence sublayer detects lost and misinserted cells. (A misinserted cell is one that is delivered to the wrong destination as a result of an undetected error in its virtual circuit or virtual path identifiers.) It also smoothes out incoming traffic to provide delivery of cells at a constant rate. Finally, the convergence sublayer breaks up the input messages or stream into 46- or 47-byte units that are given to the SAR sublayer for transmission. At the other end it extracts these and reconstructs the original input. The AAL 1 convergence sublayer does not have any protocol headers of its own.

In contrast, the AAL 1 SAR sublayer does have a protocol. The formats of its cells are given in Fig. 6-39. Both formats begin with a 1-byte header containing a 3-bit cell sequence number, *SN*, (to detect missing or misinserted cells). This field is followed by a 3-bit sequence number protection, *SNP*, (i.e., checksum) over the sequence number to allow correction of single errors and detection of double errors in the sequence field. It uses a cyclic redundancy check with the polynomial $x^3 + x + 1$. An even parity bit covering the header byte further reduces the likelihood of a bad sequence number sneaking in unnoticed. AAL 1 cells need not be filled with a full 47 bytes. For example, to transmit digitized voice arriving at a rate of 1 byte every 125 μsec, filling a cell with 47 bytes means collecting samples for 5.875 msec. If this delay before transmission is

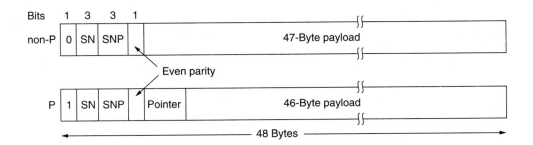

Fig. 6-39. The AAL 1 cell format.

unacceptable, partial cells can be sent. In this case, the number of actual data bytes per cell is the same for all cells and agreed on in advance.

The *P* cells are used when message boundaries must be preserved. The *Pointer* field is used to give the offset of the start of the next message. Only cells with an even sequence number may be *P* cells, so the pointer is in the range 0 to 92, to put it within the payload of either its own cell or the one following it. Note that this scheme allows messages to be an arbitrary number of bytes long, so messages can be run continuously and need not align on cell boundaries.

The high-order bit of the *Pointer* field is reserved for future use. The initial header bit of all the odd-numbered cells forms a data stream used for clock synchronization.

6.5.3. AAL 2

AAL 1 is designed for simple, connection-oriented, real-time data streams without error detection, except for missing and misinserted cells. For pure uncompressed audio or video, or any other data stream in which having a few garbled bits once in a while is not a problem, AAL 1 is adequate.

For compressed audio or video, the rate can vary strongly in time. For example, many compression schemes transmit a full video frame periodically and then send only the differences between subsequent frames and the last full frame for several frames. When the camera is stationary and nothing is moving, the difference frames are small, but when the camera is panning rapidly, they are large. Also, message boundaries must be preserved so that the start of the next full frame can be recognized, even in the presence of lost cells or bad data. For these reasons, a fancier protocol is needed. AAL 2 has been designed for this purpose.

As in AAL 1, the CS sublayer does not have a protocol but the SAR sublayer does. The SAR cell format is shown in Fig. 6-40. It has a 1-byte header and a 2-byte trailer, leaving room for up to 45 data bytes per cell.

The *SN* field (*Sequence Number*) is used for numbering cells in order to detect missing or misinserted cells. The *IT* field (*Information Type*) is used to indicate

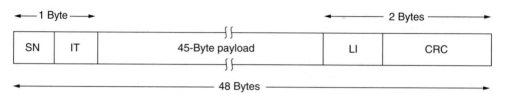

Fig. 6-40. The AAL 2 cell format.

that the cell is the start, middle, or end of a message. The *LI* (*Length indicator*) field tells how big the payload is, in bytes (it might be less than 45 bytes). Finally, the *CRC* field is a checksum over the entire cell, so errors can be detected.

Strange as it may sound, the field sizes are not included in the standard. According to one insider, at the very end of the standardization process the committee realized that AAL 2 had so many problems that it should not be used. Unfortunately, it was too late to stop the standardization process. They had a deadline to meet. In a last ditch effort, the committee removed all the field sizes so that the formal standard could be issued on time, but in such a way that nobody could actually use it. Such is life in the world of standardization.

6.5.4. AAL 3/4

Originally, ITU had different protocols for classes C and D, connection-oriented service and connectionless service for data transport that is sensitive to loss or errors but is not time dependent. Then ITU discovered that there was no real need for two protocols, so they were combined into a single protocol, AAL 3/4.

AAL 3/4 can operate in two modes: stream or message. In message mode, each call from the application to AAL 3/4 injects one message into the network. The message is delivered as such, that is, message boundaries are preserved. In stream mode the boundaries are not preserved. The discussion below will concentrate on message mode. Reliable and unreliable (i.e., no guarantee) transport are available in each mode.

A feature of AAL 3/4 not present in any of the other protocols is multiplexing. This aspect of AAL 3/4 allows multiple sessions (e.g., remote logins) from a single host to travel along the same virtual circuit and be separated at the destination, as illustrated in Fig. 6-41.

The reason that this facility is desirable is that carriers often charge for each connection setup and for each second that a connection is open. If a pair of hosts have several sessions open simultaneously, giving each one its own virtual circuit will be more expensive than multiplexing all of them onto the same virtual circuit. If one virtual circuit has sufficient bandwidth to handle the job, there is no need

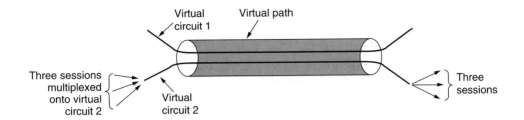

Fig. 6-41. Multiplexing of several sessions onto one virtual circuit.

for more than one. All sessions using a single virtual circuit get the same quality of service, since this is negotiated per virtual circuit.

This issue is the real reason that there were originally separate AAL 3 and AAL 4 formats: the Americans wanted multiplexing and the Europeans did not. So each group went off and made its own standard. Eventually, the Europeans decided that saving 10 bits in the header was not worth the price of having the United States and Europe not be able to communicate. For the same money, they could have stuck to their guns and we would have had four incompatible AAL standards (of which one is broken) instead of three.

Unlike AAL 1 and AAL 2, AAL 3/4 has both a convergence sublayer protocol and a SAR sublayer protocol. Messages as large as 65,535 bytes come into the convergence sublayer from the application. These are first padded out to a multiple of 4 bytes. Then a header and a trailer are attached, as shown in Fig. 6-42.

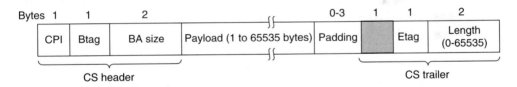

Fig. 6-42. AAL 3/4 convergence sublayer message format.

The *CPI* field (*Common Part Indicator*) gives the message type and the counting unit for the *BA size* and *Length* fields. The *Btag* and *Etag* fields are used to frame messages. The two bytes must be the same and are incremented by one on every new message sent. This mechanism checks for lost or misinserted cells. The *BA size* field is used for buffer allocation. It tells the receiver how much buffer space to allocate for the message in advance of its arrival. The *Length* field gives the payload length again. In message mode, it must be equal to *BA size*, but in stream mode it may be different. The trailer also contains 1 unused byte.

After the convergence sublayer has constructed and added a header and trailer to the message, as shown in Fig. 6-42, it passes the message to the SAR sublayer, which chops the message up into 44-byte chunks. Note that to support multiplexing, the convergence sublayer may have several messages constructed internally at once and may pass 44-byte chunks to the SAR sublayer first from one message, then from another, in any order.

The SAR sublayer inserts each 44-byte chunk into the payload of a cell whose format is shown in Fig. 6-43. These cells are then transmitted to the destination for reassembly, after which checksum verification is performed and action taken if need be.

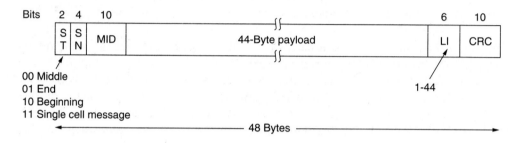

Fig. 6-43. The AAL 3/4 cell format.

The fields in the AAL 3/4 cell are as follows. The *ST* (*Segment Type*) field is used for message framing. It indicates whether the cell begins a message, is in the middle of a message, is the last cell of a message, or is a small (i.e., single cell) message. Next comes a 4-bit sequence number, *SN*, for detecting missing and misinserted cells. The *MID* (*Multiplexing ID*) field is used to keep track of which cell belongs to which session. Remember that the convergence sublayer may have several messages, belonging to different sessions, buffered at once, and it may send pieces of these messages in whatever order it wishes. All the pieces from messages belonging to session i carry i in the *MID* field, so they can be correctly reassembled at the destination. The trailer contains the payload length and cell checksum.

Notice that AAL 3/4 has two layers of protocol overhead: 8 bytes are added to every message and 4 bytes are added to every cell. All in all, it is a heavyweight mechanism, especially for short messages.

6.5.5. AAL 5

The AAL 1 through AAL 3/4 protocols were largely designed by the telecommunications industry and standardized by ITU without a lot of input from the computer industry. When the computer industry finally woke up and began to understand the implications of Fig. 6-43, a sense of panic set in. The complexity and inefficiency generated by two layers of protocol, coupled with the surprisingly short checksum (only 10 bits), caused some researchers to invent a new adaptation protocol. It was called **SEAL (Simple Efficient Adaptation Layer)**, which suggests what the designers thought of the old ones. After some discussion, the ATM Forum accepted SEAL and assigned it the name AAL 5. For more information about AAL 5 and how it differs from AAL 3/4, see (Suzuki, 1994).

AAL 5 offers several kinds of service to its applications. One choice is reliable service (i.e., guaranteed delivery with flow control to prevent overruns). Another choice is unreliable service (i.e., no guaranteed delivery), with options to have cells with checksum errors either discarded or passed to the application anyway (but reported as bad). Both unicast and multicast are supported, but multicast does not provide guaranteed delivery.

Like AAL 3/4, AAL 5 supports both message mode and stream mode. In message mode, an application can pass a datagram of length 1 to 65,535 bytes to the AAL layer and have it delivered to the destination, either on a guaranteed or a best efforts basis. Upon arrival in the convergence sublayer, a message is padded out and a trailer added, as shown in Fig. 6-44. The amount of padding (0 to 47 bytes) is chosen to make the entire message, including the padding and trailer, be a multiple of 48 bytes. AAL 5 does not have a convergence sublayer header, just an 8-byte trailer.

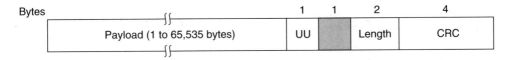

Fig. 6-44. AAL 5 convergence sublayer message format.

The *UU* (*User to User*) field is not used by the AAL layer itself. Instead, it is available for a higher layer for its own purposes, for example, sequencing or multiplexing. The higher layer in question may be the service-specific subpart of the convergence sublayer. The *Length* field tells how long the true payload is, in bytes, not counting the padding. A value of 0 is used to abort the current message in midstream. The *CRC* field is the standard 32-bit checksum over the entire message, including the padding and the trailer (with the *CRC* field set to 0). One 8-bit field in the trailer is reserved for future use.

The message is transmitted by passing it to the SAR sublayer, which does not add any headers or trailers. Instead, it breaks the message into 48-byte units and passes each of these to the ATM layer for transmission. It also tells the ATM layer to set a bit in the *PTI* field on the last cell, so message boundaries are preserved. A case can be made that this is an incorrect mixing of protocol layers because the AAL layer should not be using bits in the ATM layer's header. Doing so violates the most basic principle of protocol engineering, and suggests the layering should have perhaps been done differently.

The principal advantage of AAL 5 over AAL 3/4 is the much greater efficiency. While AAL 3/4 adds only 4 bytes per message, it also adds 4 bytes per cell, reducing the payload capacity to 44 bytes, a loss of 8 percent on long messages. AAL 5 has a slightly large trailer per message (8 bytes) but has no overhead in each cell. The lack of sequence numbers in the cells is compensated for by the longer checksum, which can detect lost, misinserted, or missing cells without using sequence numbers.

Within the Internet community, it is expected that the normal way of interfacing to ATM networks will be to transport IP packets with the AAL 5 payload field. Various issues relating to this approach are discussed in RFC 1483 and RFC 1577.

6.5.6. Comparison of AAL Protocols

The reader is hereby forgiven if he or she thinks that the various AAL protocols seem unnecessarily similar to one another and poorly thought out. The value of having distinct convergence and SAR sublayers is also questionable, especially since AAL 5 does not have anything in the SAR sublayer. A slightly enhanced ATM layer header could have provided for sequencing, multiplexing, and framing quite adequately.

Some of the differences between the various AAL protocols are summarized in Fig. 6-45. These relate to efficiency, error handling, multiplexing, and the relation between the AAL sublayers.

Item	AAL 1	AAL 2	AAL 3/4	AAL 5
Service class	A	B	C/D	C/D
Multiplexing	No	No	Yes	No
Message delimiting	None	None	Btag/Etag	Bit in PTI
Advance buffer allocation	No	No	Yes	No
User bytes available	0	0	0	1
CS padding	0	0	32-Bit word	0–47 bytes
CS protocol overhead (bytes)	0	0	8	8
CS checksum	None	None	None	32 Bits
SAR payload bytes	46–47	45	44	48
SAR protocol overhead (bytes)	1–2	3	4	0
SAR checksum	None	None	10 Bits	None

Fig. 6-45. Some differences between the various AAL protocols.

The overall impression that AAL gives is of too many variants with too many minor differences and a job half done. The original four service classes, A, B, C, D, have been effectively abandoned. AAL 1 is probably not really necessary;

AAL 2 is broken; AAL 3 and AAL 4 never saw the light of day; and AAL 3/4 is inefficient and has too short a checksum.

The future lies with AAL 5, but even here there is room for improvement. AAL 5 messages should have had a sequence number and a bit to distinguish data from control messages, so it could have been used as a reliable transport protocol. Unused space in the trailer was even available for them. As it stands, for reliable transport, the additional overhead of a transport layer is required on top of it, when it could have been avoided. If the full AAL committee had turned its work in as a class project, the professor would probably have given it back with instructions to fix it and turn it in again when it was finished. More criticism of ATM can be found in (Sterbenz et al., 1995).

6.5.7. SSCOP—Service Specific Connection-Oriented Protocol

Despite all these different AAL protocols, none of them provides for simple end-to-end reliable transport connections. For applications where that is required, another AAL protocol exists: **SSCOP (Service Specific Connection Oriented Protocol**). However, SSCOP is only used for control, not for data transmission.

SSCOP users send messages, each of which is assigned a 24-bit sequence number. Messages can be up to 64K bytes and are not fragmented. They must be delivered in order. Unlike some other reliable transport protocols, missing messages are always retransmitted using selective repeat rather than go back n.

SSCOP is fundamentally a dynamic sliding window protocol. For each connection, the receiver maintains a window of message sequence numbers that it is prepared to receive, and a bit map marking the ones it already has. This window can change size during protocol operation.

What makes SSCOP unusual is the way acknowledgements are handled: there is no piggybacking. Instead, periodically, the sender polls the receiver and asks it to send back the bit map giving the window status. Based on the result, the sender discards messages that have been accepted and updates its window. SSCOP is described in detail in (Henderson, 1995).

6.6. PERFORMANCE ISSUES

Performance issues are very important in computer networks. When hundreds or thousands of computers are connected together, complex interactions, with unforeseen consequences, are common. Frequently, this complexity leads to poor performance and no one knows why. In the following sections, we will examine many issues related to network performance to see what kinds of problems exist and what can be done about them.

Unfortunately, understanding network performance is more of an art than a science. There is little underlying theory that is actually of any use in practice.

The best we can do is give rules of thumb gained from hard experience and present examples taken from the real world. We have intentionally delayed this discussion until after studying the transport layer in TCP and ATM networks in order to be able to point out places where they have done things right or done things wrong.

The transport layer is not the only place performance issues arise. We saw some of them in the network layer in the previous chapter. Nevertheless, the network layer tends to be largely concerned with routing and congestion control. The broader, system-oriented issues tend to be transport related, so this chapter is an appropriate place to examine them.

In the next five sections, we will look at five aspects of network performance:

1. Performance problems.

2. Measuring network performance.

3. System design for better performance.

4. Fast TPDU processing.

5. Protocols for future high-performance networks.

As an aside, we need a name for the units exchanged by transport entities. The TCP term, segment, is confusing at best and is never used outside the TCP world in this context. The proper ATM terms, CS-PDU, SAR-PDU, and CPCS-PDU, are specific to ATM. Packets clearly refer to the network layer and messages belong to the application layer. For lack of a standard term, we will go back to calling the units exchanged by transport entities TPDUs. When we mean both TPDU and packet together, we will use packet as the collective term, as in "The CPU must be fast enough to process incoming packets in real time." By this we mean both the network layer packet and the TPDU encapsulated in it.

6.6.1. Performance Problems in Computer Networks

Some performance problems, such as congestion, are caused by temporary resource overloads. If more traffic suddenly arrives at a router than the router can handle, congestion will build up and performance will suffer. We studied congestion in detail in the previous chapter.

Performance also degrades when there is a structural resource imbalance. For example, if a gigabit communication line is attached to a low-end PC, the poor CPU will not be able to process the incoming packets fast enough, and some will be lost. These packets will eventually be retransmitted, adding delay, wasting bandwidth, and generally reducing performance.

Overloads can also be synchronously triggered. For example, if a TPDU contains a bad parameter (e.g., the port or process for which it is destined), in many cases the receiver will thoughtfully send back an error notification. Now consider what could happen if a bad TPDU is broadcast to 10,000 machines: each one might send back an error message. The resulting **broadcast storm** could cripple the network. UDP suffered from this problem until the protocol was changed to cause hosts to refrain from responding to errors in UDP TPDUs sent to broadcast addresses.

A second example of synchronous overload is what happens after an electrical power failure. When the power comes back on, all the machines simultaneously jump to their ROMs to start rebooting. A typical reboot sequence might require first going to some (RARP) server to learn one's true identity, and then to some file server to get a copy of the operating system. If hundreds of machines all do this at once, the server will probably collapse under the load.

Even in the absence of synchronous overloads and when there are sufficient resources available, poor performance can occur due to lack of system tuning. For example, if a machine has plenty of CPU power and memory, but not enough of the memory has been allocated for buffer space, overruns will occur and TPDUs will be lost. Similarly, if the scheduling algorithm does not give a high enough priority to processing incoming TPDUs, some of them may be lost.

Another tuning issue is setting timeouts correctly. When a TPDU is sent, a timer is typically set to guard against its loss. If the timeout is set too short, unnecessary retransmissions will occur, clogging the wires. If the timeout is set too long, unnecessary delays will occur after a TPDU is lost. Other tunable parameters include how long to wait for data to piggyback onto before sending a separate acknowledgement and the number of retransmissions before giving up.

Gigabit networks bring with them new performance problems. Consider, for example, sending data from San Diego to Boston when the receiver's buffer is 64K bytes. Suppose that the link is 1 Gbps and the one-way speed-of-light-in-fiber delay is 20 msec. Initially, at $t = 0$, the pipe is empty, as illustrated in Fig. 6-46(a). Only 500 μsec later, in Fig. 6-46(b), all the TPDUs are out on the fiber. The lead TPDU will now be somewhere in the vicinity of Brawley, still deep in Southern California. However, the transmitter must stop until it gets a window update.

After 20 msec, the lead TPDU hits Boston, as shown in Fig. 6-46(c) and is acknowledged. Finally, 40 msec after starting, the first acknowledgement gets back to the sender and the second burst can be transmitted. Since the transmission line was used for 0.5 msec out of 40, the efficiency is about 1.25 percent. This situation is typical of running older protocols over gigabit lines.

A useful quantity to keep in mind when analyzing network performance is the **bandwidth-delay product**. It is obtained by multiplying the bandwidth (in bits/sec) by the round-trip delay time (in sec). The product is the capacity of the pipe from the sender to the receiver and back (in bits).

For the example of Fig. 6-46 the bandwidth-delay product is 40 million bits. In other words, the sender would have to transmit a burst of 40 million bits to be

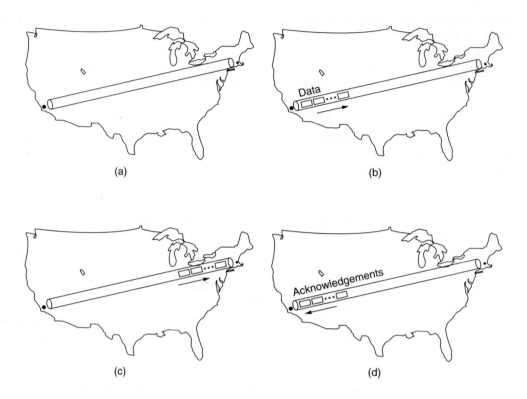

Fig. 6-46. The state of transmitting one megabit from San Diego to Boston. (a) At $t = 0$. (b) After 500 μsec. (c) After 20 msec. (d) After 40 msec.

able to keep going full speed until the first acknowledgement came back. It takes this many bits to fill the pipe (in both directions). This is why a burst of half a million bits only achieves a 1.25 percent efficiency: it is only 1.25 percent of the pipe capacity.

The conclusion to be drawn here is that to achieve good performance, the receiver's window must be at least as large as the bandwidth-delay product, preferably somewhat larger since the receiver may not respond instantly. For a transcontinental gigabit line, at least 5 megabytes are required for each connection.

If the efficiency is terrible for sending a megabit, imagine what it is like when sending a few hundred bytes for a remote procedure call. Unless some other use can be found for the line while the first client is waiting for its reply, a gigabit line is no better than a megabit line, just more expensive.

Another performance problem that occurs with time-critical applications like audio and video is jitter. Having a short mean transmission time is not enough. A small standard deviation is also required. Achieving a short mean transmission time along with a small standard deviation demands a serious engineering effort.

6.6.2. Measuring Network Performance

When a network performs poorly, its users often complain to the folks running it, demanding improvements. To improve the performance, the operators must first determine exactly what is going on. To find out what is really happening, the operators must make measurements. In this section we will look at network performance measurements. The discussion below is based on the work of Mogul (1993). For a more thorough discussion of the measurement process, see (Jain, 1991; and Villamizan and Song, 1995).

The basic loop used to improve network performance contains the following steps:

1. Measure the relevant network parameters and performance.

2. Try to understand what is going on.

3. Change one parameter.

These steps are repeated until the performance is good enough or it is clear that the last drop of improvement has been squeezed out.

Measurements can be made in many ways and at many locations (both physically and in the protocol stack). The most basic kind of measurement is to start a timer when beginning some activity and use it to see how long that activity takes. For example, knowing how long it takes for a TPDU to be acknowledged is a key measurement. Other measurements are made with counters that record how often some event has happened (e.g., number of lost TPDUs). Finally, one is often interested in knowing the amount of something, such as the number of bytes processed in a certain time interval.

Measuring network performance and parameters has many potential pitfalls. Below we list a few of them. Any systematic attempt to measure network performance should be careful to avoid these.

Make Sure that the Sample Size Is Large Enough

Do not measure the time to send one TPDU, but repeat the measurement, say, one million times and take the average. Having a large sample will reduce the uncertainty in the measured mean and standard deviation. This uncertainty can be computed using standard statistical formulas.

Make Sure that the Samples Are Representative

Ideally, the whole sequence of one million measurements should be repeated at different times of the day and the week to see the effect of different system loads on the measured quantity. Measurements of congestion, for example, are of little use if they are made at a moment when there is no congestion. Sometimes the results may be counterintuitive at first, such as heavy congestion at 10, 11, 1, and 2 o'clock, but no congestion at noon (when all the users are away at lunch).

Be Careful When Using a Coarse-Grained Clock

Computer clocks work by adding one to some counter at regular intervals. For example, a millisecond timer adds one to a counter every 1 msec. Using such a timer to measure an event that takes less than 1 msec is not impossible, but requires some care.

To measure the time to send a TPDU, for example, the system clock (say, in milliseconds) should be read out when the transport layer code is entered, and again when it is exited. If the true TPDU send time is 300 μsec, the difference between the two readings will be either 0 or 1, both wrong. However, if the measurement is repeated one million times and the total of all measurements added up and divided by one million, the mean time will be accurate to better than 1 μsec.

Be Sure that Nothing Unexpected Is Going On during Your Tests

Making measurements on a university system the day some major lab project has to be turned in may give different results than if made the next day. Likewise, if some researcher has decided to run a video conference over your network during your tests, you may get a biased result. It is best to run tests on an idle system and create the entire workload yourself. Even this approach has pitfalls though. While you might think nobody will be using the network at 3 A.M., that might be precisely when the automatic backup program begins copying all the disks to videotape. Furthermore, there might be heavy traffic for your wonderful World Wide Web pages from distant time zones.

Caching Can Wreak Havoc with Measurements

To measure file transfer times, the obvious way to do it is to open a large file, read the whole thing, close it, and see how long it takes. Then repeat the measurement many more times to get a good average. The trouble is, the system may cache the file, so that only the first measurement actually involves network traffic. The rest are just reads from the local cache. The results from such a measurement are essentially worthless (unless you want to measure cache performance).

Often you can get around caching by simply overflowing the cache. For example, if the cache is 10 MB, the test loop could open, read, and close two 10-MB files on each pass, in an attempt to force the cache hit rate to 0. Still, caution is advised unless you are absolutely sure you understand the caching algorithm.

Buffering can have a similar effect. One popular TCP/IP performance utility program has been known to report that UDP can achieve a performance substantially higher than the physical line allows. How does this occur? A call to UDP normally returns control as soon as the message has been accepted by the kernel and added to the transmission queue. If there is sufficient buffer space, timing 1000 UDP calls does not mean that all the data have been sent. Most of them may still be in the kernel, but the performance utility thinks they have all been transmitted.

Understand What You Are Measuring

When you measure the time to read a remote file, your measurements depend on the network, the operating systems on both the client and server, the particular hardware interface boards used, their drivers, and other factors. If done carefully, you will ultimately discover the file transfer time for the configuration you are using. If your goal is to tune this particular configuration, these measurements are fine.

However, if you are making similar measurements on three different systems in order to choose which network interface board to buy, your results could be thrown off completely by the fact that one of the network drivers is truly awful and is only getting 10 percent of the performance of the board.

Be Careful about Extrapolating the Results

Suppose that you make measurements of something with simulated network loads running from 0 (idle) to 0.4 (40 percent of capacity), as shown by the data points and solid line through them in Fig. 6-47. It may be tempting to extrapolate linearly, as shown by the dotted line. However, many queueing results involve a factor of $1/(1 - \rho)$, wher ρ is the load, so the true values may look more like the dashed line.

6.6.3. System Design for Better Performance

Measuring and tinkering can often improve performance considerably, but they cannot substitute for good design in the first place. A poorly designed network can be improved only so much. Beyond that, it has to be redone from scratch.

In this section, we will present some rules of thumb based on experience with many networks. These rules relate to system design, not just network design, since the software and operating system are often more important than the routers and interface boards. Most of these ideas have been common knowledge to network designers for years and have been passed on from generation to generation by word of mouth. They were first stated explicitly by Mogul (1993); our treatment largely parallels his. Another relevant source is (Metcalfe, 1993).

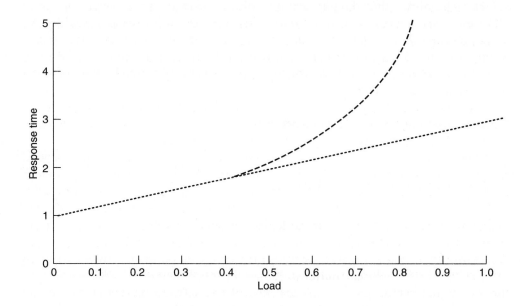

Fig. 6-47. Response as a function of load.

Rule #1: CPU Speed Is More Important than Network Speed

Long experience has shown that in nearly all networks, operating system and protocol overhead dominates actual time on the wire. For example, in theory, the minimum RPC time on an Ethernet is 102 μsec, corresponding to a minimum (64-byte) request followed by a minimum (64-byte) reply. In practice, getting the RPC time down to 1500 μsec is a considerable achievement (Van Renesse et al., 1988). Note that 1500 μsec is 15 times worse than the theoretical minimum. Nearly all the overhead is in the software.

Similarly, the biggest problem in running at 1 Gbps is getting the bits from the user's buffer out onto the fiber fast enough and having the receiving CPU process them as fast as they come in. In short, if you double the CPU speed, you often can come close to doubling the throughput. Doubling the network capacity often has no effect since the bottleneck is generally in the hosts.

Rule #2: Reduce Packet Count to Reduce Software Overhead

Processing a TPDU has a certain amount of overhead per TPDU (e.g., header processing) and a certain amount of processing per byte (e.g., doing the checksum). When sending 1 million bytes, the per-byte overhead is the same no matter what the TPDU size is. However, using 128-byte TPDUs means 32 times as much per-TPDU overhead as using 4K TPDUs. This overhead adds up fast.

In addition to the TPDU overhead, there is overhead in the lower layers to consider. Each arriving packet causes an interrupt. On a modern RISC processor, each interrupt breaks the CPU pipeline, interferes with the cache, requires a change to the memory management context, and forces a substantial number of CPU registers to be saved. An n-fold reduction in TPDUs sent thus reduces the interrupt and packet overhead by a factor of n.

This observation argues for collecting a substantial amount of data before transmission in order to reduce interrupts at the other side. Nagle's algorithm and Clark's solution to the silly window syndrome are attempts to do precisely this.

Rule #3: Minimize Context Switches

Context switches (e.g., from kernel mode to user mode) are deadly. They have the same bad properties as interrupts, the worst being a long series of initial cache misses. Context switches can be reduced by having the library procedure that sends data do internal buffering until it has a substantial amount of them. Similarly, on the receiving side, small incoming TPDUs should be collected together and passed to the user in one fell swoop instead of individually to minimize context switches.

In the best case, an incoming packet causes a context switch from the current user to the kernel, and then a switch to the receiving process to give it the newly-arrived data. Unfortunately, with many operating systems, additional context switches happen. For example, if the network manager runs as a special process in user space, a packet arrival is likely to cause a context switch from the current user to the kernel, then another one from the kernel to the network manager followed by another one back to the kernel, and finally one from the kernel to the receiving process. This sequence is shown in Fig. 6-48. All these context switches on each packet are very wasteful of CPU time and will have a devastating effect on network performance.

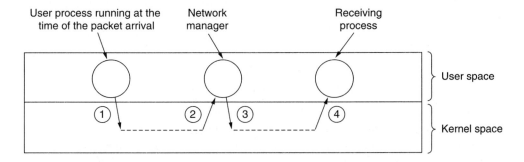

Fig. 6-48. Four context switches to handle one packet with a user-space network manager.

Rule #4: Minimize Copying

Even worse than multiple context switches is making multiple copies. It is not unusual for an incoming packet to be copied three or four times before the TPDU enclosed in it is delivered. After a packet is received by the network interface in a special on-board hardware buffer, it is typically copied to a kernel buffer. From there it is copied to a network layer buffer, then to a transport layer buffer, and finally to the receiving application process.

A clever operating system will copy a word at a time, but it is not unusual to require about five instructions per word (a load, a store, incrementing an index register, a test for end-of-data, and a conditional branch). On a 50-MIPS machine, making three copies of each packet at five instructions per 32-bit word copied requires 75 nsec per incoming byte. Such a machine can thus accept data at a maximum rate of about 107 Mbps. When overhead for header processing, interrupt handling, and context switches is factored in, 50 Mbps might be achievable, and we have not even considered the actual processing of the data. Clearly, handling a 1-Gbps line is out of the question.

In fact, probably a 50-Mbps line is out of the question, too. In the computation above, we have assumed that a 50-MIPS machine can execute any 50 million instructions/sec. In reality, machines can only run at such speeds if they are not referencing memory. Memory operations are often a factor of three slower than register-register instructions, so actually getting 16 Mbps out of the 1 Gbps line might be considered pretty good. Note that hardware assistance will not help here. The problem is too much copying by the operating system.

Rule #5: You Can Buy More Bandwidth but Not Lower Delay

The next three rules deal with communication, rather than protocol processing. The first rule states that if you want more bandwidth, you can just buy it. Putting a second fiber next to the first one doubles the bandwidth but does nothing to reduce the delay. Making the delay shorter requires improving the protocol software, the operating system, or the network interface. Even if all of these are done, the delay will not be reduced if the bottleneck is the transmission time.

Rule #6: Avoiding Congestion Is Better than Recovering from It

The old maxim that an ounce of prevention is worth a pound of cure certainly holds for network congestion. When a network is congested, packets are lost, bandwidth is wasted, useless delays are introduced, and more. Recovering from it takes time and patience. Not having it occur in the first place is better. Congestion avoidance is like getting your DTP vaccination: it hurts a little at the time you get it, but it prevents something that would hurt a lot more.

Rule #7: Avoid Timeouts

Timers are necessary in networks, but they should be used sparingly and timeouts should be minimized. When a timer goes off, some action is generally repeated. If it is truly necessary to repeat the action, so be it, but repeating it unnecessarily is wasteful.

The way to avoid extra work is to be careful that timers are set a little bit on the conservative side. A timer that takes too long to expire adds a small amount of extra delay to one connection in the (unlikely) event of a TPDU being lost. A timer that goes off when it should not have uses up scarce CPU time, wastes bandwidth, and puts extra load on perhaps dozens of routers for no good reason.

6.6.4. Fast TPDU Processing

The moral of the story above is that the main obstacle to fast networking is protocol software. In this section we will look at some ways to speed up this software. For more information, see (Clark et al., 1989; Edwards and Muir, 1995; and Chandranmenon and Varghese, 1995).

TPDU processing overhead has two components: overhead per TPDU and overhead per byte. Both must be attacked. The key to fast TPDU processing is to separate out the normal case (one-way data transfer) and handle it specially. Although a sequence of special TPDUs are needed to get into the *ESTABLISHED* state, once there, TPDU processing is straightforward until one side starts to close the connection.

Let us begin by examining the sending side in the *ESTABLISHED* state when there are data to be transmitted. For the sake of clarity, we assume here that the transport entity is in the kernel, although the same ideas apply if it is a user-space process or a library inside the sending process. In Fig. 6-49, the sending process traps into the kernel to do the SEND. The first thing the transport entity does is make a test to see if this is the normal case: the state is *ESTABLISHED*, neither side is trying to close the connection, a regular (i.e., not an out-of-band) full TPDU is being sent, and there is enough window space available at the receiver. If all conditions are met, no further tests are needed and the fast path through the sending transport entity can be taken.

In the normal case, the headers of consecutive data TPDUs are almost the same. To take advantage of this fact, a prototype header is stored within the transport entity. At the start of the fast path, it is copied as fast as possible to a scratch buffer, word by word. Those fields that change from TPDU to TPDU are then overwritten in the buffer. Frequently, these fields are easily derived from state variables, such as the next sequence number. A pointer to the full TPDU header plus a pointer to the user data are then passed to the network layer. Here the same strategy can be followed (not shown in Fig. 6-49). Finally, the network layer gives the resulting packet to the data link layer for transmission.

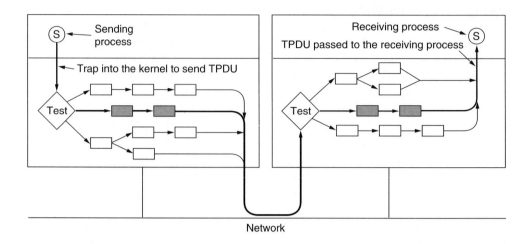

Fig. 6-49. The fast path from sender to receiver is shown with a heavy line. The processing steps on this path are shaded.

As an example of how this principle works in practice, let us consider TCP/IP. Fig. 6-50(a) shows the TCP header. The fields that are the same between consecutive TPDUs on a one-way flow are shaded. All the sending transport entity has to do is copy the five words from the prototype header into the output buffer, fill in the next sequence number (by copying it from a word in memory), compute the checksum, and increment the sequence number in memory. It can then hand the header and data to a special IP procedure for sending a regular, maximum TPDU. IP then copies its five-word prototype header [see Fig. 6-50(b)] into the buffer, fills in the *Identification* field, and computes its checksum. The packet is now ready for transmission.

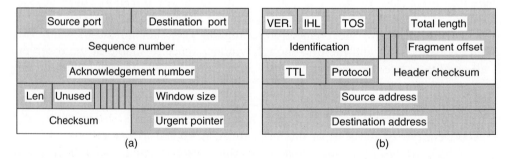

Fig. 6-50. (a) TCP header. (b) IP header. In both cases, the shaded fields are taken from the prototype without change.

Now let us look at fast path processing on the receiving side of Fig. 6-49. Step 1 is locating the connection record for the incoming TPDU. For ATM, finding the connection record is easy: the *VPI* field can be used as an index into the path table to find the virtual circuit table for that path and the *VCI* can be used as an index to find the connection record. For TCP, the connection record can be stored in a hash table for which some simple function of the two IP addresses and two ports is the key. Once the connection record has been located, both addresses and both ports must be compared to verify that the correct record has been found.

An optimization that often speeds up connection record lookup even more is just to maintain a pointer to the last one used and try that one first. Clark et al. (1989) tried this and observed a hit rate exceeding 90 percent. Other lookup heuristics are described in (McKenney and Dove, 1992).

The TPDU is then checked to see if it is a normal one: the state is *ESTAB-LISHED*, neither side is trying to close the connection, the TPDU is a full one, no special flags are set, and the sequence number is the one expected. These tests take just a handful of instructions. If all conditions are met, a special fast path TCP procedure is called.

The fast path updates the connection record and copies the data to the user. While it is copying, it also computes the checksum, eliminating an extra pass over the data. If the checksum is correct, the connection record is updated and an acknowledgement is sent back. The general scheme of first making a quick check to see if the header is what is expected, and having a special procedure to handle that case, is called **header prediction**. Many TCP implementations use it. When this optimization and all the other ones discussed in this chapter are used together, it is possible to get TCP to run at 90 percent of the speed of a local memory-to-memory copy, assuming the network itself is fast enough.

Two other areas where major performance gains are possible are buffer management and timer management. The issue in buffer management is avoiding unnecessary copying, as we mentioned above. Timer management is important because nearly all timers set do not expire. They are set to guard against TPDU loss, but most TPDUs arrive correctly and their acknowledgements also arrive correctly. Hence it is important to optimize timer management for the case of timers rarely expiring.

A common scheme is to use a linked list of timer events sorted by expiry time. The head entry contains a counter telling how many ticks away from expiry it is. Each successive entry contains a counter telling how many ticks after the previous entry it is. Thus if timers expire in 3, 10, and 12 ticks, respectively, the three counters are 3, 7, and 2, respectively.

At every clock tick, the counter in the head entry is decremented. When it hits zero, its event is processed and the next item on the list becomes the head. Its counter does not have to be changed. In this scheme, inserting and deleting timers are expensive operations, with execution times proportional to the length of the list.

A more efficient approach can be used if the maximum timer interval is bounded and known in advance. Here an array, called a **timing wheel**, can be used, as shown in Fig. 6-51. Each slot corresponds to one clock tick. The current time shown is $T = 4$. Timers are scheduled to expire at 3, 10, and 12 ticks from now. If a new timer suddenly is set to expire in seven ticks, an entry is just made in slot 11. Similarly, if the timer set for $T + 10$ has to be canceled, the list starting in slot 14 has to be searched and the required entry removed. Note that the array of Fig. 6-51 cannot accommodate timers beyond $T + 15$.

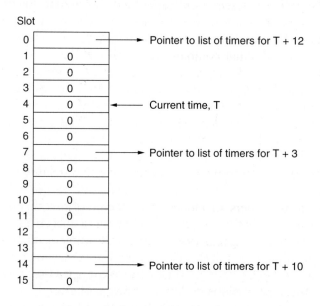

Fig. 6-51. A timing wheel.

When the clock ticks, the current time pointer is advanced by one slot (circularly). If the entry now pointed to is nonzero, all of its timers are processed. Many variations on the basic idea are discussed in (Varghese and Lauck, 1987).

6.6.5. Protocols for Gigabit Networks

At the start of the 1990s, gigabit networks began to appear. People's first reaction was to use the old protocols on them, but various problems quickly arose. In this section we will discuss some of these problems and the directions new protocols are taking to solve them. Other information can be found in (Baransel et al., 1995; and Partridge, 1994).

The first problem is that many protocols use 16-bit or 32-bit sequence numbers. In the old days, 2^{32} was a pretty good approximation to infinity. It no longer is. At a data rate of 1 Gbps, it takes about 32 sec to send 2^{32} bytes. If sequence numbers refer to bytes, as they do in TCP, then a sender can start transmitting byte 0, blast away, and 32 sec later be back at byte 0. Even assuming that all bytes have been acknowledged, the sender cannot safely transmit new data labeled starting at 0 because the old packets may still be floating around some-where. In the Internet, for example, packets can live for 120 sec. If packets are numbered instead of bytes, the problem is less severe, unless the sequence numbers are 16 bits, in which case the problem is even worse.

The problem is that many protocol designers simply assumed, without stating it, that the time to use up the entire sequence space would greatly exceed the max-imum packet lifetime. Consequently there was no need to even worry about the problem of old duplicates still existing when the sequence numbers wrapped around. At gigabit speeds, that unstated assumption fails.

A second problem is that communication speeds have improved much faster than computing speeds. (Note to computer engineers: Go out and beat those com-munication engineers! We are counting on you.) In the 1970s, the ARPANET ran at 56 kbps and had computers that ran at about 1 MIPS. Packets were 1008 bits, so the ARPANET was capable of delivering about 56 packets/sec. With almost 18 msec available per packet, a host could afford to spend 18,000 instruc-tions processing a packet. Of course, doing so would soak up the entire CPU, but it could devote 9000 instructions per packet and still have half the CPU left over to do real work.

Compare these numbers to modern 100-MIPS computers exchanging 4-KB packets over a gigabit line. Packets can flow in at a rate of over 30,000 per second, so packet processing must be completed in 15 μsec if we want to reserve half the CPU for applications. In 15 μsec, a 100-MIPS computer can execute 1500 instructions, only 1/6 of what the ARPANET hosts had available. Further-more, modern RISC instructions do less per instruction than the old CISC instruc-tions did, so the problem is even worse than it appears. The conclusion is: there is less time available for protocol processing than there used to be, so protocols must become simpler.

A third problem is that the go back n protocol performs poorly on lines with a large bandwidth-delay product. Consider, for example, a 4000-km line operating at 1 Gbps. The round-trip transmission time is 40 msec, in which time a sender can transmit 5 megabytes. If an error is detected, it will be 40 msec before the sender is told about it. If go back n is used, the sender will have to retransmit not just the bad packet, but also the 5 megabytes worth of packets that came after-ward. Clearly, this is a massive waste of resources.

A fourth problem is that gigabit lines are fundamentally different from mega-bit lines in that long ones are delay limited rather than bandwidth limited. In Fig. 6-52 we show the time it takes to transfer a 1-megabit file 4000 km at various transmission speeds. At speeds up to 1 Mbps, the transmission time is dominated by the rate at which the bits can be sent. By 1 Gbps, the 40-msec round-trip delay dominates the 1 msec it takes to put the bits on the fiber. Further increases in bandwidth have hardly any effect at all.

Figure 6-52 has unfortunate implications for network protocols. It says that stop-and-wait protocols, such as RPC, have an inherent upper bound on their

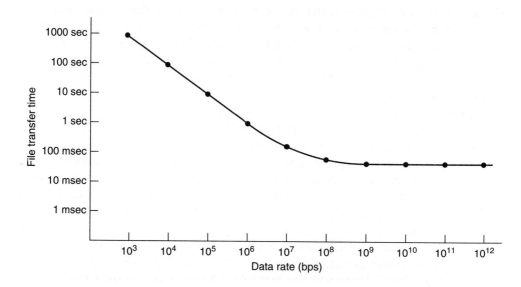

Fig. 6-52. Time to transfer and acknowledge a 1-megabit file over a 4000-km line.

performance. This limit is dictated by the speed of light. No amount of techno-logical progress in optics will improve matters (new laws of physics would help, though).

A fifth problem that is worth mentioning is not a technological or protocol one like the others, but a result of new applications. Simply stated, it is that for many gigabit applications, such as multimedia, the variance in the packet arrival times is as important as the mean delay itself. A slow-but-uniform delivery rate, is often preferable to a fast-but-jumpy one.

Let us now turn from the problems to ways of dealing with them. We will first make some general remarks, then look at protocol mechanisms, packet lay-out, and protocol software.

The basic principle that all gigabit network designers should learn by heart is:

Design for speed, not for bandwidth optimization.

Old protocols were often designed to minimize the number of bits on the wire, frequently by using small fields and packing them together into bytes and words. Nowadays, there is plenty of bandwidth. Protocol processing is the problem, so protocols should be designed to minimize it.

A tempting way to go fast is to build fast network interfaces in hardware. The difficulty with this strategy is that unless the protocol is exceedingly simple, hardware just means a plug-in board with a second CPU and its own program. To avoid having the network coprocessor be as expensive as the main CPU, it is often a slower chip. The consequence of this design is that much of the time the main (fast) CPU is idle waiting for the second (slow) CPU to do the critical work. It is a myth to think that the main CPU has other work to do while waiting. Furthermore, when two general-purpose CPUs communicate, race conditions can occur, so elaborate protocols are needed between the two processors to synchronize them correctly. Usually, the best approach is to make the protocols simple and have the main CPU do the work.

Let us now look at the issue of feedback in high-speed protocols. Due to the (relatively) long delay loop, feedback should be avoided: it takes too long for the receiver to signal the sender. One example of feedback is governing the transmission rate using a sliding window protocol. To avoid the (long) delays inherent in the receiver sending window updates to the sender, it is better to use a rate-based protocol. In such a protocol, the sender can send all it wants to, provided it does not send faster than some rate the sender and receiver have agreed upon in advance.

A second example of feedback is Jacobson's slow start algorithm. This algorithm makes multiple probes to see how much the network can handle. With high-speed networks, making half a dozen or so small probes to see how the network responds wastes a huge amount of bandwidth. A more efficient scheme is to have the sender, receiver, and network all reserve the necessary resources at connection setup time. Reserving resources in advance also has the advantage of making it easier to reduce jitter. In short, going to high speeds inexorably pushes the design toward connection-oriented operation, or something fairly close to it.

Packet layout is an important consideration in gigabit networks. The header should contain as few fields as possible, to reduce processing time, and these fields should be big enough to do the job and be word aligned for ease of processing. In this context, "big enough" means that problems such as sequence numbers wrapping around while old packets still exist, receivers being unable to advertise enough window space because the window field is too small, and so on, do not occur.

The header and data should be separately checksummed, for two reasons. First, to make it possible to checksum the header but not the data. Second, to verify that the header is correct before starting to copy the data into user space. It is desirable to do the data checksum at the time the data are copied to user space, but if the header is incorrect, the copy may be to the wrong process. To avoid an incorrect copy but to allow the data checksum to be done during copying, it is essential that the two checksums be separate.

The maximum data size should be large, to permit efficient operation even in the face of long delays. Also, the larger the data block, the smaller the fraction of the total bandwidth devoted to headers.

Another valuable feature is the ability to send a normal amount of data along with the connection request. In this way, one round-trip time can be saved.

Finally, a few words about the protocol software are appropriate. A key thought is concentrating on the successful case. Many older protocols tend to emphasize what to do when something goes wrong (e.g., a packet getting lost). To make the protocols run fast, the designer should aim for minimizing processing time when everything goes right. Minimizing processing time when an error occurs is secondary.

A second software issue is minimizing copying time. As we saw earlier, copying data is often the main source of overhead. Ideally, the hardware should dump each incoming packet into memory as a contiguous block of data. The software should then copy this packet to the user buffer with a single block copy. Depending on how the cache works, it may even be desirable to avoid a copy loop. In other words, to copy 1024 words, the fastest way may be to have 1024 back-to-back MOVE instructions (or 1024 load-store pairs). The copy routine is so critical it should be carefully handcrafted in assembly code, unless there is a way to trick the compiler into producing precisely the optimal code.

In the late 1980s, there was a brief flurry of interest in fast special-purpose protocols such as NETBLT (Clark et al., 1987), VTMP (Cheriton and Williamson, 1989), and XTP (Chesson, 1989). A survey is given in (Doeringer et al., 1990). However, the trend now is toward simplifying general-purpose protocols to make them fast, too. ATM exhibits many of the features discussed above, and IPv6 does too.

6.7. SUMMARY

The transport layer is the key to understanding layered protocols. It provides various services, the most important of which is an end-to-end, reliable, connection-oriented byte stream from sender to receiver. It is accessed through service primitives that permit the establishment, use and release of connections.

Transport protocols must be able to do connection management over unreliable networks. Connection establishment is complicated by the existence of delayed duplicate packets that can reappear at inopportune moments. To deal with them, three-way handshakes are needed to establish connections. Releasing a connection is easier than establishing one but is still far from trivial due to the two-army problem.

Even when the network layer is completely reliable, the transport layer has plenty of work to do, as we saw in our example. It must handle all the service primitives, manage connections and timers, and allocate and utilize credits.

The main Internet transport protocol is TCP. It uses a 20-byte header on all segments. Segments can be fragmented by routers within the Internet, so hosts must be prepared to do reassembly. A great deal of work has gone into optimizing TCP performance, using algorithms from Nagle, Clark, Jacobson, Karn, and others.

ATM has four protocols in the AAL layer. All of them break messages into cells at the source and reassemble the cells into messages at the destination. The

CS and SAR sublayers add their own headers and trailers in various ways, leaving from 44 to 48 bytes of cell payload.

Network performance is typically dominated by protocol and TPDU processing overhead, and this situation gets worse at higher speeds. Protocols should be designed to minimize the number of TPDUs, context switches, and times each TPDU is copied. For gigabit networks, simple protocols using rate, rather than credit, flow control are called for.

PROBLEMS

1. In our example transport primitives of Fig. 6-3, LISTEN is a blocking call. Is this strictly necessary? If not, explain how a nonblocking primitive could be used. What advantage would this have over the scheme described in the text?

2. In the model underlying Fig. 6-5, it is assumed that packets may be lost by the network layer and thus must be individually acknowledged. Suppose that the network layer is 100 percent reliable and never loses packets. What changes, if any, are needed to Fig. 6-5?

3. Imagine a generalized n-army problem, in which the agreement of any two of the armies is sufficient for victory. Does a protocol exist that allows blue to win?

4. Suppose that the clock-driven scheme for generating initial sequence numbers is used with a 15-bit wide clock counter. The clock ticks once every 100 msec, and the maximum packet lifetime is 60 sec. How often need resynchronization take place
   (a) in the worst case?
   (b) when the data consumes 240 sequence numbers/min?

5. Why does the maximum packet lifetime, T, have to be large enough to ensure that not only the packet, but also its acknowledgements, have vanished?

6. Imagine that a two-way handshake rather than a three-way handshake were used to set up connections. In other words, the third message was not required. Are deadlocks now possible? Give an example or show that none exist.

7. Consider the problem of recovering from host crashes (i.e., Fig. 6-18). If the interval between writing and sending an acknowledgement, or vice versa, can be made relatively small, what are the two best sender-receiver strategies for minimizing the chance of a protocol failure?

8. Are deadlocks possible with the transport entity described in the text?

9. Out of curiosity, the implementer of the transport entity of Fig. 6-20 has decided to put counters inside the *sleep* procedure to collect statistics about the *conn* array. Among these are the number of connections in each of the seven possible states, n_i ($i = 1, \ldots, 7$). After writing a massive FORTRAN program to analyze the data, our implementer discovered that the relation $\sum n_i = MAX\_CONN$ appears to always be true. Are there any other invariants involving only these seven variables?

10. What happens when the user of the transport entity given in Fig. 6-20 sends a zero length message? Discuss the significance of your answer.

11. For each event that can potentially occur in the transport entity of Fig. 6-20, tell whether it is legal or not when the user is sleeping in *sending* state.

12. Discuss the advantages and disadvantages of credits versus sliding window protocols.

13. Datagram fragmentation and reassembly are handled by IP and are invisible to TCP. Does this mean that TCP does not have to worry about data arriving in the wrong order?

14. A process on host 1 has been assigned port p and a process on host 2 has been assigned port q. Is it possible for there to be two or more TCP connections between these two ports at the same time?

15. The maximum payload of a TCP segment is 65,515 bytes. Why was such a strange number chosen?

16. Describe two ways to get into the *SYN RCVD* state of Fig. 6-28.

17. Give a potential disadvantage when Nagle's algorithm is used on a badly congested network.

18. Consider the effect of using slow start on a line with a 10-msec round-trip time and no congestion. The receive window is 24 KB and the maximum segment size is 2 KB. How long does it take before the first full window can be sent?

19. Suppose that the TCP congestion window is set to 18K bytes and a timeout occurs. How big will the window be if the next four transmission bursts are all successful? Assume that the maximum segment size is 1 KB.

20. If the TCP round-trip time, *RTT*, is currently 30 msec and the following acknowledgements come in after 26, 32, and 24 msec, respectively, what is the new *RTT* estimate? Use $\alpha = 0.9$.

21. A TCP machine is sending windows of 65,535 bytes over a 1-Gbps channel that has a 10-msec one-way delay. What is the maximum throughput achievable? What is the line efficiency?

22. In a network that has a maximum TPDU size of 128 bytes, a maximum TPDU lifetime of 30 sec, and an 8-bit sequence number, what is the maximum data rate per connection?

23. Why does UDP exist? Would it not have been enough to just let user processes send raw IP packets?

24. A group of N users located in the same building are all using the same remote computer via an ATM network. The average user generates L lines of traffic (input + output) per hour, on the average, with the mean line length being P bytes, excluding the ATM headers. The packet carrier charges C cents per byte of user data transported, plus X cents per hour for each ATM virtual circuit open. Under what conditions is it cost effective to multiplex all N transport connections onto the same ATM virtual circuit, if such multiplexing adds 2 bytes of data to each packet? Assume that even one ATM virtual circuit has enough bandwidth for all the users.

25. Can AAL 1 handle messages shorter than 40 bytes using the scheme with the *Pointer* field? Explain your answer.

26. Make a guess at what the field sizes for AAL 2 were before they were pulled from the standard.

27. AAL 3/4 allows multiple sessions to be multiplexed onto a single virtual circuit. Give an example of a situation in which that has no value. Assume that one virtual circuit has sufficient bandwidth to carry all the traffic. *Hint*: Think about virtual paths.

28. What is the payload size of the maximum length message that fits in a single AAL 3/4 cell?

29. When a 1024-byte message is sent with AAL 3/4, what is the efficiency obtained? In other words, what fraction of the bits transmitted are useful data bits? Repeat the problem for AAL 5.

30. An ATM device is transmitting single-cell messages at 600 Mbps. One cell in 100 is totally scrambled due to random noise. How many undetected errors per week can be expected with the 32-bit AAL 5 checksum?

31. A client sends a 128-byte request to a server located 100 km away over a 1-gigabit optical fiber. What is the efficiency of the line during the remote procedure call?

32. Consider the situation of the previous problem again. Compute the minimum possible response time both for the given 1-Gbps line and for a 1-Mbps line. What conclusion can you draw?

33. Suppose that you are measuring the time to receive a TPDU. When an interrupt occurs, you read out the system clock in milliseconds. When the TPDU is fully processed, you read out the clock again. You measure 0 msec 270,000 times and 1 msec 730,000 times. How long does it take to receive a TPDU?

34. A CPU executes instructions at the rate of 100 MIPS. Data can be copied 64 bits at a time, with each word copied costing six instructions. If an coming packet has to be copied twice, can this system handle a 1-Gbps line? For simplicity, assume that all instructions, even those instructions that read or write memory, run at the full 100-MIPS rate.

35. To get around the problem of sequence numbers wrapping around while old packets still exist, one could use 64-bit sequence numbers. However, theoretically, an optical fiber can run at 75 Tbps. What maximum packet lifetime is required to make sure that future 75 Tbps networks do not have wraparound problems even with 64-bit sequence numbers? Assume that each byte has its own sequence number, as TCP does.

36. In the text we calculated that a gigabit line dumps 30,000 packets/sec on the host, giving it only 1500 instructions to process it and leaving half the CPU time for applications. This calculation assumed a 4-KB packet. Redo the calculation for an ARPANET-sized packet (128 bytes).

37. For a 1-Gbps network operating over 4000 km, the delay is the limiting factor, not the bandwidth. Consider a MAN with the average source and destination 20 km apart. At what data rate does the round-trip delay due to the speed of light equal the transmission delay for a 1-KB packet?

38. Modify the program of Fig. 6-20 to do error recovery. Add a new packet type, *reset*, that can arrive after a connection has been opened by both sides but closed by neither. This event, which happens simultaneously on both ends of the connection, means that any packets that were in transit have either been delivered or destroyed, but in either case are no longer in the subnet.

39. Write a program that simulates buffer management in a transport entity using a sliding window for flow control rather than the credit system of Fig. 6-20. Let higher-layer processes randomly open connections, send data, and close connections. To keep it simple, have all the data travel from machine *A* to machine *B*, and none the other way. Experiment with different buffer allocation strategies at *B*, such as dedicating buffers to specific connections versus a common buffer pool, and measure the total throughput achieved by each one.

7

THE APPLICATION LAYER

Having finished all the preliminaries, we now come to the application layer, where all the interesting applications can be found. The layers below the application layer are there to provide reliable transport, but they do not do any real work for users. In this chapter we will study some real applications.

However, even in the application layer there is a need for support protocols to allow the real applications to function. Accordingly, we will look at three of these before starting with the applications themselves. The first area is security, which is not a single protocol, but a large number of concepts and protocols that can be used to ensure privacy where needed. The second is DNS, which handles naming within the Internet. The third support protocol is for network management. After that, we will examine four real applications: electronic mail, USENET (net news), the World Wide Web, and finally, multimedia.

7.1. NETWORK SECURITY

For the first few decades of their existence, computer networks were primarily used by university researchers for sending email, and by corporate employees for sharing printers. Under these conditions, security did not get a lot of attention. But now, as millions of ordinary citizens are using networks for banking, shopping, and filing their tax returns, network security is looming on the horizon as a potentially massive problem. In the following sections, we will study network security from several angles, point out numerous pitfalls, and discuss many algorithms and protocols for making networks more secure.

Security is a broad topic and covers a multitude of sins. In its simplest form, it is concerned with making sure that nosy people cannot read, or worse yet, modify messages intended for other recipients. It is concerned with people trying to access remote services that they are not authorized to use. It also deals with how to tell whether that message purportedly from the IRS saying: "Pay by Friday or else" is really from the IRS or from the Mafia. Security also deals with the problems of legitimate messages being captured and replayed, and with people trying to deny that they sent certain messages.

Most security problems are intentionally caused by malicious people trying to gain some benefit or harm someone. A few of the most common perpetrators are listed in Fig. 7-1. It should be clear from this list that making a network secure involves a lot more than just keeping it free of programming errors. It involves outsmarting often intelligent, dedicated, and sometimes well-funded adversaries. It should also be clear that measures that will stop casual adversaries will have little impact on the serious ones.

Adversary	Goal
Student	To have fun snooping on people's email
Hacker	To test out someone's security system; steal data
Sales rep	To claim to represent all of Europe, not just Andorra
Businessman	To discover a competitor's strategic marketing plan
Ex-employee	To get revenge for being fired
Accountant	To embezzle money from a company
Stockbroker	To deny a promise made to a customer by email
Con man	To steal credit card numbers for sale
Spy	To learn an enemy's military strength
Terrorist	To steal germ warfare secrets

Fig. 7-1. Some people who cause security problems and why.

Network security problems can be divided roughly into four intertwined areas: secrecy, authentication, nonrepudiation, and integrity control. Secrecy has to do with keeping information out of the hands of unauthorized users. This is what usually comes to mind when people think about network security. Authentication deals with determining whom you are talking to before revealing sensitive information or entering into a business deal. Nonrepudiation deals with signatures:

How do you prove that your customer really placed an electronic order for ten million left-handed doohickeys at 89 cents each when he later claims the price was 69 cents? Finally, how can you be sure that a message you received was really the one sent and not something that a malicious adversary modified in transit or concocted?

All these issues (secrecy, authentication, nonrepudiation, and integrity control) occur in traditional systems, too, but with some significant differences. Secrecy and integrity are achieved by using registered mail and locking documents up. Robbing the mail train is harder than it was in Jesse James' day.

Also, people can usually tell the difference between an original paper document and a photocopy, and it often matters to them. As a test, make a photocopy of a valid check. Try cashing the original check at your bank on Monday. Now try cashing the photocopy of the check on Tuesday. Observe the difference in the bank's behavior. With electronic checks, the original and the copy are indistinguishable. It may take a while for banks to get used to this.

People authenticate other people by recognizing their faces, voices, and handwriting. Proof of signing is handled by signatures on letterhead paper, raised seals, and so on. Tampering can usually be detected by handwriting, paper, and ink experts. None of these options are available electronically. Clearly, other solutions are needed.

Before getting into the solutions themselves, it is worth spending a few moments considering where in the protocol stack network security belongs. There is probably no one single place. Every layer has something to contribute. In the physical layer, wiretapping can be foiled by enclosing transmission lines in sealed tubes containing argon gas at high pressure. Any attempt to drill into a tube will release some gas, reducing the pressure and triggering an alarm. Some military systems use this technique.

In the data link layer, packets on a point-to-point line can be encoded as they leave one machine and decoded as they enter another. All the details can be handled in the data link layer, with higher layers oblivious to what is going on. This solution breaks down when packets have to traverse multiple routers, however, because packets have to be decrypted at each router, leaving them vulnerable to attacks from within the router. Also, it does not allow some sessions to be protected (e.g., those involving on-line purchases by credit card) and others not. Nevertheless, **link encryption**, as this method is called, can be added to any network easily and is often useful.

In the network layer, firewalls can be installed to keep packets in or keep packets out. We looked at firewalls in Chap. 5. In the transport layer, entire connections can be encrypted, end to end, that is, process to process. Although these solutions help with secrecy issues and many people are working hard to improve them, none of them solve the authentication or nonrepudiation problem in a sufficiently general way. To tackle these problems, the solutions must be in the application layer, which is why they are being studied in this chapter.

7.1.1. Traditional Cryptography

Cryptography has a long and colorful history. In this section we will just sketch some of the highlights, as background information for what follows. For a complete history, Kahn's (1967) book is still recommended reading. For a comprehensive treatment of the current state-of-the-art, see (Kaufman et al., 1995; Schneier, 1996; and Stinson, 1995).

Historically, four groups of people have used and contributed to the art of cryptography: the military, the diplomatic corps, diarists, and lovers. Of these, the military has had the most important role and has shaped the field. Within military organizations, the messages to be encrypted have traditionally been given to poorly paid code clerks for encryption and transmission. The sheer volume of messages prevented this work from being done by a few elite specialists.

Until the advent of computers, one of the main constraints on cryptography had been the ability of the code clerk to perform the necessary transformations, often on a battlefield with little equipment. An additional constraint has been the difficulty in switching over quickly from one cryptographic method to another one, since this entails retraining a large number of people. However, the danger of a code clerk being captured by the enemy has made it essential to be able to change the cryptographic method instantly, if need be. These conflicting requirements have given rise to the model of Fig. 7-2.

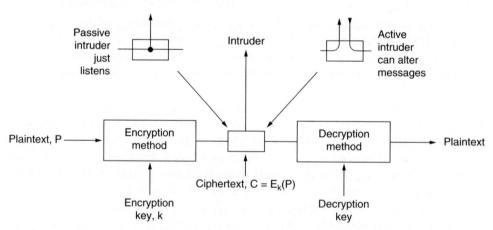

Fig. 7-2. The encryption model.

The messages to be encrypted, known as the **plaintext**, are transformed by a function that is parametrized by a **key**. The output of the encryption process, known as the **ciphertext**, is then transmitted, often by messenger or radio. We assume that the enemy, or **intruder**, hears and accurately copies down the complete ciphertext. However, unlike the intended recipient, he does not know what the decryption key is and so cannot decrypt the ciphertext easily. Sometimes the intruder can not only listen to the communication channel (passive intruder) but can also record messages and play them back later, inject his own messages, or modify legitimate messages before they get to the receiver (active intruder). The art of breaking ciphers is called **cryptanalysis**. The art of devising ciphers (cryptography) and breaking them (cryptanalysis) is collectively known as **cryptology**.

It will often be useful to have a notation for relating plaintext, ciphertext, and keys. We will use $C = E_K(P)$ to mean that the encryption of the plaintext P using key K gives the ciphertext C. Similarly, $P = D_K(C)$ represents of decryption of C to get the plaintext again. It then follows that

$$D_K(E_K(P)) = P$$

This notation suggests that E and D are just mathematical functions, which they are. The only tricky part is that both are functions of two parameters, and we have written one of the parameters (the key) as a subscript, rather than as an argument, to distinguish it from the message.

A fundamental rule of cryptography is that one must assume that the cryptanalyst knows the general method of encryption used. In other words, the cryptanalyst knows how the encryption method, E, of Fig. 7-2 works. The amount of effort necessary to invent, test, and install a new method every time the old method is compromised or thought to be compromised has always made it impractical to keep this secret, and thinking it is secret when it is not does more harm than good.

This is where the key enters. The key consists of a (relatively) short string that selects one of many potential encryptions. In contrast to the general method, which may only be changed every few years, the key can be changed as often as required. Thus our basic model is a stable and publicly known general method parametrized by a secret and easily changed key.

The nonsecrecy of the algorithm cannot be emphasized enough. By publicizing the algorithm, the cryptographer gets free consulting from a large number of academic cryptologists eager to break the system so they can publish papers demonstrating how smart they are. If many experts have tried to break the algorithm for 5 years after its publication and no one has succeeded, it is probably pretty solid.

The real secrecy is in the key, and its length is a major design issue. Consider a simple combination lock. The general principle is that you enter digits in sequence. Everyone knows this, but the key is secret. A key length of two digits means that there are 100 possibilities. A key length of three digits means 1000 possibilities, and a key length of six digits means a million. The longer the key, the higher the **work factor** the cryptanalyst has to deal with. The work factor for breaking the system by exhaustive search of the key space is exponential in the key length. Secrecy comes from having a strong (but public) algorithm and a long key. To prevent your kid brother from reading your email, 64-bit keys will do. To keep major governments at bay, keys of at least 256 bits are needed.

From the cryptanalyst's point of view, the cryptanalysis problem has three principal variations. When he has a quantity of ciphertext and no plaintext, he is confronted with the **ciphertext only** problem. The cryptograms that appear in the puzzle section of newspapers pose this kind of problem. When he has some matched ciphertext and plaintext, the problem becomes known as the **known plaintext** problem. Finally, when the cryptanalyst has the ability to encrypt pieces of plaintext of his own choosing, we have the **chosen plaintext** problem. Newspaper cryptograms could be broken trivially if the cryptanalyst were allowed to ask such questions as: What is the encryption of ABCDE?

Novices in the cryptography business often assume that if a cipher can withstand a ciphertext only attack, it is secure. This assumption is very naive. In many cases the cryptanalyst can make a good guess at parts of the plaintext. For example, the first thing many timesharing systems say when you call them up is "PLEASE LOGIN." Equipped with some matched plaintext-ciphertext pairs, the cryptanalyst's job becomes much easier. To achieve security, the cryptographer should be conservative and make sure that the system is unbreakable even if his opponent can encrypt arbitrary amounts of chosen plaintext.

Encryption methods have historically been divided into two categories: substitution ciphers and transposition ciphers. We will now deal with each of these briefly as background information for modern cryptography.

Substitution Ciphers

In a **substitution cipher** each letter or group of letters is replaced by another letter or group of letters to disguise it. One of the oldest known ciphers is the **Caesar cipher**, attributed to Julius Caesar. In this method, a becomes D, b becomes E, c becomes $F, \ldots$, and z becomes C. For example, *attack* becomes *DWWDFN*. In examples, plaintext will be given in lowercase letters, and ciphertext in uppercase letters.

A slight generalization of the Caesar cipher allows the ciphertext alphabet to be shifted by k letters, instead of always 3. In this case k becomes a key to the general method of circularly shifted alphabets. The Caesar cipher may have fooled the Carthaginians, but it has not fooled anyone since.

The next improvement is to have each of the symbols in the plaintext, say the 26 letters for simplicity, map onto some other letter. For example,

    plaintext: a b c d e f g h i j k l m n o p q r s t u v w x y z
    ciphertext: Q W E R T Y U I O P A S D F G H J K L Z X C V B N M

This general system is called a **monoalphabetic substitution**, with the key being the 26-letter string corresponding to the full alphabet. For the key above, the plaintext *attack* would be transformed into the ciphertext *QZZQEA*.

At first glance this might appear to be a safe system because although the cryptanalyst knows the general system (letter for letter substitution), he does not know which of the $26! \simeq 4 \times 10^{26}$ possible keys is in use. In contrast with the Caesar cipher, trying all of them is not a promising approach. Even at 1 μsec per solution, a computer would take 10^{13} years to try all the keys.

Nevertheless, given a surprisingly small amount of ciphertext, the cipher can be broken easily. The basic attack takes advantage of the statistical properties of natural languages. In English, for example, *e* is the most common letter, followed by *t, o, a, n, i,* etc. The most common two letter combinations, or **digrams**, are *th, in, er, re,* and *an*. The most common three letter combinations, or **trigrams**, are *the, ing, and,* and *ion*.

A cryptanalyst trying to break a monoalphabetic cipher would start out by counting the relative frequencies of all letters in the ciphertext. Then he might tentatively assign the most common one to *e* and the next most common one to *t*. He would then look at trigrams to find a common one of the form *tXe*, which strongly suggests that *X* is *h*. Similarly, if the pattern *thYt* occurs frequently, the *Y* probably stands for *a*. With this information, he can look for a frequently occurring trigram of the form *aZW*, which is most likely *and*. By making guesses at common letters, digrams, and trigrams, and knowing about likely patterns of vowels and consonants, the cryptanalyst builds up a tentative plaintext, letter by letter.

Another approach is to guess a probable word or phrase. For example, consider the following ciphertext from an accounting firm (blocked into groups of five characters):

CTBMN BYCTC BTJDS QXBNS GSTJC BTSWX CTQTZ CQVUJ
QJSGS TJQZZ MNQJS VLNSX VSZJU JDSTS JQUUS JUBXJ
DSKSU JSNTK BGAQJ ZBGYQ TLCTZ BNYBN QJSW

A likely word in a message from an accounting firm is *financial*. Using our knowledge that *financial* has a repeated letter (*i*), with four other letters between their occurrences, we look for repeated letters in the ciphertext at this spacing. We find 12 hits, at positions 6, 15, 27, 31, 42, 48, 56, 66, 70, 71, 76, and 82. However, only two of these, 31 and 42, have the next letter (corresponding to *n* in the plaintext) repeated in the proper place. Of these two, only 31 also has the *a* correctly positioned, so we know that *financial* begins at position 30. From this point on, deducing the key is easy by using the frequency statistics for English text.

Transposition Ciphers

Substitution ciphers preserve the order of the plaintext symbols but disguise them. **Transposition ciphers**, in contrast, reorder the letters but do not disguise them. Figure 7-3 depicts a common transposition cipher, the columnar transposition. The cipher is keyed by a word or phrase not containing any repeated letters. In this example, MEGABUCK is the key. The purpose of the key is to number the columns, column 1 being under the key letter closest to the start of the alphabet, and so on. The plaintext is written horizontally, in rows. The ciphertext is read out by columns, starting with the column whose key letter is the lowest.

```
M  E  G  A  B  U  C  K
7  4  5  1  2  8  3  6
p  l  e  a  s  e  t  r        Plaintext
a  n  s  f  e  r  o  n
e  m  i  l  l  i  o  n        pleasetransferonemilliondollarsto
d  o  l  l  a  r  s  t        myswissbankaccountsixtwotwo
o  m  y  s  w  i  s  s        Ciphertext
b  a  n  k  a  c  c  o
u  n  t  s  i  x  t  w        AFLLSKSOSELAWAIATOOSSCTCLNMOMANT
o  t  w  o  a  b  c  d        ESILYNTWRNNTSOWDPAEDOBUOERIRICXB
```

Fig. 7-3. A transposition cipher.

To break a transposition cipher, the cryptanalyst must first be aware that he is dealing with a transposition cipher. By looking at the frequency of *E*, *T*, *A*, *O*, *I*, *N*, etc., it is easy to see if they fit the normal pattern for plaintext. If so, the cipher is clearly a transposition cipher, because in such a cipher every letter represents itself.

The next step is to make a guess at the number of columns. In many cases a probable word or phrase may be guessed at from the context of the message. For example, suppose that our cryptanalyst suspected the plaintext phrase *milliondollars* to occur somewhere in the message. Observe that digrams *MO*, *IL*, *LL*, *LA*, *IR* and *OS* occur in the ciphertext as a result of this phrase wrapping around. The ciphertext letter *O* follows the ciphertext letter *M* (i.e., they are vertically adjacent in column 4) because they are separated in the probable phrase by a distance equal to the key length. If a key of length seven had been used, the digrams *MD*, *IO*, *LL*, *LL*, *IA*, *OR*, and *NS* would have occurred instead. In fact, for each key length, a different set of digrams is produced in the ciphertext. By hunting for the various possibilities, the cryptanalyst can often easily determine the key length.

The remaining step is to order the columns. When the number of columns, k, is small, each of the $k(k - 1)$ column pairs can be examined to see if its digram frequencies match those for English plaintext. The pair with the best match is assumed to be correctly positioned. Now each remaining column is tentatively tried as the successor to this pair. The column whose digram and trigram frequencies give the best match is tentatively assumed to be correct. The predecessor column is found in the same way. The entire process is continued until a potential ordering is found. Chances are that the plaintext will be recognizable at this point (e.g., if *milloin* occurs, it is clear what the error is).

Some transposition ciphers accept a fixed-length block of input and produce a fixed-length block of output. These ciphers can be completely described by just giving a list telling the order in which the characters are to be output. For example, the cipher of Fig. 7-3 can be seen as a 64 character block cipher. Its output is 4, 12, 20, 28, 36, 44, 52, 60, 5, 13 , . . . , 62. In other words, the fourth input character, *a*, is the first to be output, followed by the twelfth, *f*, and so on.

One-Time Pads

Constructing an unbreakable cipher is actually quite easy; the technique has been known for decades. First choose a random bit string as the key. Then convert the plaintext into a bit string, for example by using its ASCII representation. Finally, compute the EXCLUSIVE OR of these two strings, bit by bit. The resulting ciphertext cannot be broken, because every possible plaintext is an equally probable candidate. The ciphertext gives the cryptanalyst no information at all. In a sufficiently large sample of ciphertext, each letter will occur equally often, as will every digram and every trigram.

This method, known as the **one-time pad**, has a number of practical disadvantages, unfortunately. To start with, the key cannot be memorized, so both sender and receiver must carry a written copy with them. If either one is subject to capture, written keys are clearly undesirable. Additionally, the total amount of data that can be transmitted is limited by the amount of key available. If the spy strikes it rich and discovers a wealth of data, he may find himself unable to transmit it back to headquarters because the key has been used up. Another problem is the sensitivity of the method to lost or inserted characters. If the sender and receiver get out of synchronization, all data from then on will appear garbled.

With the advent of computers, the one-time pad might potentially become practical for some applications. The source of the key could be a special CD that contains several gigabits of information, and if transported in a music CD box and prefixed by a few songs, would not even be suspicious. Of course, at gigabit network speeds, having to insert a new CD every 5 sec could become tedious. For this reason, we will now start looking at modern encryption algorithms that can process arbitrarily large amounts of plaintext.

7.1.2. Two Fundamental Cryptographic Principles

Although we will study many different cryptographic systems in the pages ahead, there are two principles underlying all of them that are important to understand. The first principle is that all encrypted messages must contain some redundancy, that is, information not needed to understand the message. An example may make it clear why this is needed. Consider a mail-order company, The Couch Potato (TCP), with 60,000 products. Thinking they are being very efficient, TCP's programmers decide that ordering messages should consist of a 16-byte customer name followed by a 3-byte data field (1 byte for the quantity and 2 bytes for the product number). The last 3 bytes are to be encrypted using a very long key known only by the customer and TCP.

At first this might seem secure, and in a sense it is because passive intruders cannot decrypt the messages. Unfortunately, it also has a fatal flaw that renders it useless. Suppose that a recently-fired employee wants to punish TCP for firing her. Just before leaving, she takes (part of) the customer list with her. She works through the night writing a program to generate fictitious orders using real customer names. Since she does not have the list of keys, she just puts random numbers in the last 3 bytes, and sends hundreds of orders off to TCP.

When these messages arrive, TCP's computer uses the customer's name to locate the key and decrypt the message. Unfortunately for TCP, almost every 3-byte message is valid, so the computer begins printing out shipping instructions. While it might seem odd for a customer to order 137 sets of children's swings, or 240 sandboxes, for all the computer knows, the customer might be planning to open a chain of franchised playgrounds. In this way an active intruder (the ex-employee) can cause a massive amount of trouble, even though she cannot understand the messages her computer is generating.

This problem can be solved by adding redundancy to all messages. For example, if order messages are extended to 12 bytes, the first 9 of which must be zeros, then this attack no longer works because the ex-employee no longer can generate a large stream of valid messages. The moral of the story is that all messages must contain considerable redundancy so that active intruders cannot send random junk and have it be interpreted as a valid message.

However, adding redundancy also makes it much easier for cryptanalysts to break messages. Suppose that the mail order business is highly competitive, and The Couch Potato's main competitor, The Sofa Tuber, would dearly love to know how many sandboxes TCP is selling. Consequently, they have tapped TCP's telephone line. In the original scheme with 3-byte messages, cryptanalysis was nearly impossible, because after guessing a key, the cryptanalyst had no way of telling whether the guess was right. After all, almost every message is technically legal. With the new 12-byte scheme, it is easy for the cryptanalyst to tell a valid message from an invalid one.

Thus cryptographic principle number one is that all messages must contain redundancy to prevent active intruders from tricking the receiver into acting on a false message. However, this same redundancy makes it much easier for passive intruders to break the system, so there is some tension here. Furthermore, the redundancy should never be in the form of n zeros at the start or end of a message, since running such messages through some cryptographic algorithms gives more predictable results, making the cryptanalysts' job easier. A random string of English words would be a much better choice for the redundancy.

The second cryptographic principle is that some measures must be taken to prevent active intruders from playing back old messages. If no such measures were taken, our ex-employee could tap TCP's phone line and just keep repeating previously sent valid messages. One such measure is including in every message a timestamp valid only for, say, 5 minutes. The receiver can then just keep messages around for 5 minutes, to compare newly arrived messages to previous ones to filter out duplicates. Messages older than 5 minutes can be thrown out, since any replays sent more than 5 minutes later will be rejected as too old. Measures other than timestamps will be discussed later.

7.1.3. Secret-Key Algorithms

Modern cryptography uses the same basic ideas as traditional cryptography, transposition and substitution, but its emphasis is different. Traditionally, cryptographers have used simple algorithms and relied on very long keys for their security. Nowadays the reverse is true: the object is to make the encryption algorithm so complex and involuted that even if the cryptanalyst acquires vast mounds of enciphered text of his own choosing, he will not be able to make any sense of it at all.

Transpositions and substitutions can be implemented with simple circuits. Figure 7-4(a) shows a device, known as a **P-box** (P stands for permutation), used to effect a transposition on an 8-bit input. If the 8 bits are designated from top to bottom as 01234567, the output of this particular P-box is 36071245. By appropriate internal wiring, a P-box can be made to perform any transposition, and do it at practically the speed of light.

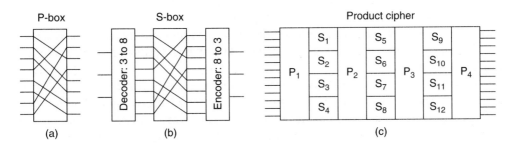

Fig. 7-4. Basic elements of product ciphers. (a) P-box. (b) S-box. (c) Product.

Substitutions are performed by **S-boxes**, as shown in Fig. 7-4(b). In this example a 3-bit plaintext is entered and a 3-bit ciphertext is output. The 3-bit input selects one of the eight lines exiting from the first stage and sets it to 1; all the other lines are 0. The second stage is a P-box. The third stage encodes the selected input line in binary again. With the wiring shown, if the eight octal numbers 01234567 were input one after another, the output sequence would be 24506713. In other words, 0 has been replaced by 2, 1 has been replaced by 4, etc. Again, by appropriate wiring of the P-box inside the S-box, any substitution can be accomplished.

The real power of these basic elements only becomes apparent when we cascade a whole series of boxes to form a **product cipher**, as shown in Fig. 7-4(c). In this example, 12 input lines are transposed by the first stage. Theoretically, it would be possible to have the second stage be an S-box that mapped a 12-bit number onto another 12-bit number. However, such a device would need $2^{12} = 4096$ crossed wires in its middle stage. Instead, the input is broken up into four groups of 3 bits, each of which is substituted independently of the others. Although this method is less general, it is still powerful. By including a sufficiently large number of stages in the product cipher, the output can be made to be an exceedingly complicated function of the input.

DES

In January 1977, the U.S. government adopted a product cipher developed by IBM as its official standard for unclassified information. This cipher, **DES (Data Encryption Standard)**, was widely adopted by the industry for use in security products. It is no longer secure in its original form (Wayner, 1995), but in a modified form it is still useful. We will now explain how DES works.

An outline of DES is shown in Fig. 7-5(a). Plaintext is encrypted in blocks of 64 bits, yielding 64 bits of ciphertext. The algorithm, which is parametrized by a 56-bit key, has 19 distinct stages. The first stage is a key independent transposition on the 64-bit plaintext. The last stage is the exact inverse of this transposition. The stage prior to the last one exchanges the leftmost 32 bits with the rightmost 32 bits. The remaining 16 stages are functionally identical but are parametrized by different functions of the key. The algorithm has been designed to allow decryption to be done with the same key as encryption. The steps are just run in the reverse order.

The operation of one of these intermediate stages is illustrated in Fig. 7-5(b). Each stage takes two 32-bit inputs and produces two 32-bit outputs. The left output is simply a copy of the right input. The right output is the bitwise EXCLUSIVE OR of the left input and a function of the right input and the key for this stage, K_i. All the complexity lies in this function.

The function consists of four steps, carried out in sequence. First, a 48-bit number, E, is constructed by expanding the 32-bit R_{i-1} according to a fixed transposition and duplication rule. Second, E and K_i are EXCLUSIVE ORed together. This output is then partitioned into eight groups of 6 bits each, each of which is fed into a different S-box. Each of the 64 possible inputs to an S-box is mapped onto a 4-bit output. Finally, these 8×4 bits are passed through a P-box.

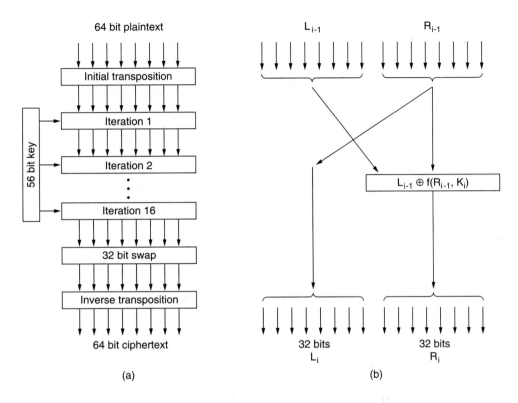

Fig. 7-5. The data encryption standard. (a) General outline. (b) Detail of one iteration.

In each of the 16 iterations, a different key is used. Before the algorithm starts, a 56-bit transposition is applied to the key. Just before each iteration, the key is partitioned into two 28-bit units, each of which is rotated left by a number of bits dependent on the iteration number. K_i is derived from this rotated key by applying yet another 56-bit transposition to it. A different 48-bit subset of the 56 bits is extracted and permuted on each round.

DES Chaining

Despite all this complexity, DES is basically a monoalphabetic substitution cipher using a 64-bit character. Whenever the same 64-bit plaintext block goes in the front end, the same 64-bit ciphertext block comes out the back end. A cryptanalyst can exploit this property to help break DES.

To see how this monoalphabetic substitution cipher property can be used to subvert DES, let us consider encrypting a long message the obvious way: by breaking it up into consecutive 8-byte (64-bit) blocks and encrypting them one after another with the same key. The last block is padded out to 64 bits, if need be. This technique is known as **electronic code book mode**.

In Fig. 7-6 we have the start of a computer file listing the annual bonuses a company has decided to award to its employees. This file consists of consecutive 32-byte records, one per employee, in the format shown: 16 bytes for the name, 8 bytes for the position, and 8 bytes for the bonus. Each of the sixteen 8-byte blocks (numbered from 0 to 15) is encrypted by DES.

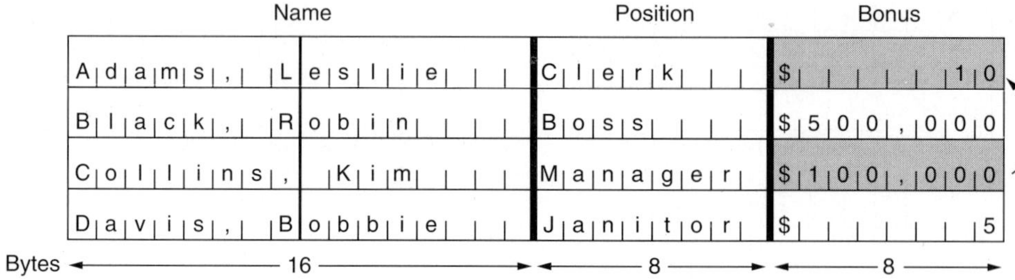

Name		Position	Bonus
A d a m s , L e s l i e	C l e r k	$ 1 0
B l a c k , R o b i n	B o s s	$ 5 0 0 , 0 0 0
C o l l i n s , K i m	M a n a g e r	$ 1 0 0 , 0 0 0
D a v i s , B o b b i e	J a n i t o r	$ 5

Bytes ◄——————— 16 ———————► ◄——— 8 ———► ◄——— 8 ———►

Fig. 7-6. The plaintext of a file encrypted as 16 DES blocks.

Leslie just had a fight with the boss and is not expecting much of a bonus. Kim, in contrast is the boss' favorite, and everyone knows this. Leslie can get access to the file after it is encrypted but before it is sent to the bank. Can Leslie rectify this unfair situation, given only the encrypted file?

No problem at all. All Leslie has to do is make a copy of ciphertext block 11 (which contains Kim's bonus) and use it to replace ciphertext block 3 (which contains Leslie's bonus). Even without knowing what block 11 says, Leslie can expect to have a much merrier Christmas this year. (Copying ciphertext block 7 is also a possibility, but is more likely to be detected; besides, Leslie is not a greedy person.)

To thwart this type of attack, DES (and all block ciphers) can be chained in various ways so that replacing a block the way Leslie did will cause the plaintext decrypted starting at the replaced block to be garbage. One way of chaining is **cipher block chaining**. In this method, shown in Fig. 7-7, each plaintext block is EXCLUSIVE ORed (#) with the previous ciphertext block before being encrypted. Consequently, the same plaintext block no longer maps onto the same ciphertext block, and the encryption is no longer a big monoalphabetic substitution cipher. The first block is EXCLUSIVE ORed with a randomly chosen **initialization vector**, **IV**, that is transmitted along with the ciphertext.

We can see how cipher block chaining works by examining the example of Fig. 7-7. We start out by computing $C_0 = E(P_0 \text{ XOR } IV)$. Then we compute $C_1 = E(P_1 \text{ XOR } C_0)$, and so on. Decryption works the other way, with $P_0 = IV \text{ XOR } D(C_0)$, and so on. Note that the encryption of block i is a function

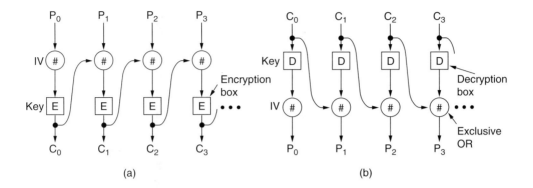

Fig. 7-7. Cipher block chaining

of all the plaintext in blocks 0 through $i - 1$, so the same plaintext generates different ciphertext depending on where it occurs. A transformation of the type Leslie made will result in nonsense for two blocks starting at Leslie's bonus field. To an astute security officer, this peculiarity might suggest where to start the ensuing investigation.

Cipher block chaining also has the advantage that the same plaintext block will not result in the same ciphertext block, making cryptanalysis more difficult. In fact, this is the main reason it is used.

However, cipher block chaining has the disadvantage of requiring an entire 64-bit block to arrive before decryption can begin. For use with interactive terminals, where people can type lines shorter than eight characters and then stop, waiting for a response, this mode is unsuitable. For byte-by-byte encryption, **cipher feedback mode**, shown in Fig. 7-8, can be used. In this figure, the state of the encryption machine is shown after bytes 0 through 9 have been encrypted and sent. When plaintext byte 10 arrives, as illustrated in Fig. 7-8(a), the DES algorithm operates on the 64-bit shift register to generate a 64-bit ciphertext. The leftmost byte of that ciphertext is extracted and EXCLUSIVE ORed with P_{10}. That byte is transmitted on the transmission line. In addition, the shift register is shifted left 8 bits, causing C_2 to fall off the left end, and C_{10} is inserted in the position just vacated at the right end by C_9. Note that the contents of the shift register depend on the entire previous history of the plaintext, so a pattern that repeats multiple times in the plaintext will be encrypted differently each time in the ciphertext. As with cipher block chaining, an initialization vector is needed to start the ball rolling.

Decryption with cipher feedback mode just does the same thing as encryption. In particular, the contents of the shift register is *encrypted*, not *decrypted*, so the selected byte that is EXCLUSIVE ORed with C_{10} to get P_{10} is the same one that was EXCLUSIVE ORed with P_{10} to generate C_{10} in the first place. As long as the two shift registers remain identical, decryption works correctly.

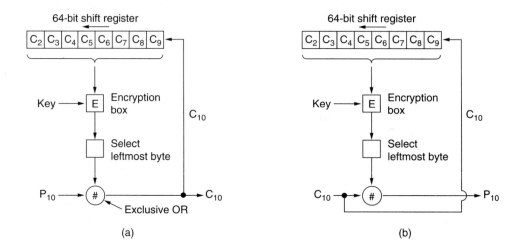

Fig. 7-8. Cipher feedback mode.

As an aside, it should be noted that if one bit of the ciphertext is accidentally inverted during transmission, the 8 bytes that are decrypted while the bad byte is in the shift register will be corrupted. Once the bad byte is pushed out of the shift register, correct plaintext will once again be generated. Thus the effects of a single inverted bit are relatively localized and do not ruin the rest of the message.

Nevertheless, there exist applications in which having a 1-bit transmission error mess up 64 bits of plaintext is too large an effect. For these applications, a fourth option, **output feedback mode**, exists. It is identical to cipher feedback mode, except that the byte fed back into the right end of the shift register is taken from just before the EXCLUSIVE OR box, not just after it.

Output feedback mode has the property that a 1-bit error in the ciphertext causes only a 1-bit error in the resulting plaintext. On the other hand, it is less secure than the other modes, and should be avoided for general-purpose use. Electronic code book mode should also be avoided except under special circumstances (e.g., encrypting a single random number, such as a session key). For normal operation, cipher block chaining should be used when the input arrives in 8-byte units (e.g., for encrypting disk files) and cipher feedback mode should be used for irregular input streams, such as keyboard input.

Breaking DES

DES has been enveloped in controversy from the day it was launched. It was based on a cipher developed and patented by IBM, called Lucifer, except that IBM's cipher used a 128-bit key instead of a 56-bit key. When the U.S. federal government wanted to standardize on one cipher for unclassified use, it "invited"

IBM to "discuss" the matter with NSA, the government's code-breaking arm, which is the world's largest employer of mathematicians and cryptologists. NSA is so secret that an industry joke goes:

Q: What does NSA stand for?
A: No Such Agency.

Actually, NSA stands for National Security Agency.

After these discussions took place, IBM reduced the key from 128 bits to 56 bits and decided to keep secret the process by which DES was designed. Many people suspected that the key length was reduced to make sure that NSA could just break DES, but no organization with a smaller budget could. The point of the secret design was supposedly to hide a trapdoor that could make it even easier for NSA to break DES. When an NSA employee discreetly told IEEE to cancel a planned conference on cryptography, that did not make people any more comfortable.

In 1977, two Stanford cryptography researchers, Diffie and Hellman (1977), designed a machine to break DES and estimated that it could be built for 20 million dollars. Given a small piece of plaintext and matched ciphertext, this machine could find the key by exhaustive search of the 2^{56}-entry key space in under 1 day. Nowadays, such a machine would cost perhaps 1 million dollars. A detailed design for a machine that can break DES by exhaustive search in about four hours is presented in (Wiener, 1994).

Here is another strategy. Although software encryption is 1000 times slower than hardware encryption, a high-end home computer can still do about 250,000 encryptions/sec in software and is probably idle 2 million seconds/month. This idle time could be put to use breaking DES. If someone posted a message to one of the popular Internet newsgroups, it should not be hard to sign up the necessary 140,000 people to check all 7×10^{16} keys in a month.

Probably the most innovative idea for breaking DES is the **Chinese Lottery** (Quisquater and Girault, 1991). In this design, every radio and television has to be equipped with a cheap DES chip capable of performing 1 million encryptions/sec in hardware. Assuming that every one of the 1.2 billion people in China owns a radio or television, whenever the Chinese government wants to decrypt a message encrypted by DES, it just broadcasts the plaintext/ciphertext pair, and each of the 1.2 billion chips begins searching its preassigned section of the key space. Within 60 seconds, one (or more) hits will be found. To ensure that they are reported, the chips could be programmed to display or announce the message:

CONGRATULATIONS! YOU HAVE JUST WON THE CHINESE LOTTERY.
TO COLLECT, PLEASE CALL 1-800-BIG-PRIZE

The conclusion that one can draw from these arguments is that DES should no longer be used for anything important. However, although 2^{56} is a paltry

7×10^{16}, 2^{112} is a magnificent 5×10^{33}. Even with a billion DES chips doing a billion operations per second, it would take 100 million years to exhaustively search a 112-bit key space. Thus the thought arises of just running DES twice, with two different 56-bit keys.

Unfortunately, Merkle and Hellman (1981) have developed a method that makes double encryption suspect. It is called the **meet-in-the-middle** attack and works like this (Hellman, 1980). Suppose that someone has doubly encrypted a series of plaintext blocks, using electronic code book mode. For a few values of i, the cryptanalyst has matched pairs (P_i, C_i) where

$$C_i = E_{K2}(E_{K1}(P_i))$$

If we now apply the decryption function, D_{K2} to each side of this equation, we get

$$D_{K2}(C_i) = E_{K1}(P_i) \tag{7-1}$$

because encrypting x and then decrypting it with the same key gives back x.

The meet-in-the-middle attack uses this equation to find the DES keys, $K1$ and $K2$, as follows:

1. Compute $R_i = E_i(P_1)$ for all 2^{56} values of i, where E is the DES encryption function. Sort this table in ascending order of R_i.

2. Compute $S_j = D_j(C_1)$ for all 2^{56} values of j, where D is the DES decryption function. Sort this table in ascending order of S_j.

3. Scan the first table looking for an R_i that matches some S_j in the second table. When a match is found, we then have a key pair (i,j) such that $D_j(C_1) = E_i(P_1)$. Potentially, i is $K1$ and j is $K2$.

4. Check to see if $E_j(E_i(P_2))$ is equal to C_2. If it is, try all the other (plaintext, ciphertext) pairs. If it is not, continue searching the two tables looking for matches.

Many false alarms will certainly occur before the real keys are located, but eventually they will be found. This attack requires only 2^{57} encryption or decryption operations (to construct the two tables), far less than 2^{112}. However it also requires a total of 2^{60} bytes of storage for the two tables, so it is not currently feasible in this basic form, but Merkle and Hellman have shown various optimizations and trade-offs that permit less storage at the expense of more computing. All in all, double encryption using DES is probably not much more secure than single encryption.

Triple encryption is another matter. As early as 1979, IBM realized that the DES key length was too short and devised a way to effectively increase it using triple encryption (Tuchman, 1979). The method chosen, which has since been incorporated in International Standard 8732, is illustrated in Fig. 7-9. Here two keys and three stages are used. In the first stage, the plaintext is encrypted with K_1. In the second stage, DES is run in decryption mode, using K_2 as the key. Finally, another encryption is done with K_1.

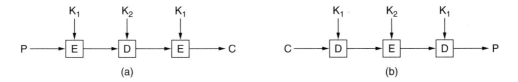

Fig. 7-9. Triple encryption using DES.

This design immediately gives rise to two questions. First, why are only two keys used, instead of three? Second, why is EDE used, instead of EEE? The reason that two keys are used is that even the most paranoid cryptographers concede that 112 bits is sufficient for commercial applications for the time being. Going to 168 bits would just add the unnecessary overhead of managing and transporting another key.

The reason for encrypting, decrypting, and then encrypting again is backward compatibility with existing single-key DES systems. Both the encryption and decryption functions are mappings between sets of 64-bit numbers. From a cryptographic point of view, the two mappings are equally strong. By using EDE, however, instead of EEE, a computer using triple encryption can speak to one using single encryption by just setting $K_1 = K_2$. This property allows triple encryption to be phased in gradually, something of no concern to academic cryptographers, but of considerable import to IBM and its customers.

No method is known for breaking triple DES in EDE mode. Van Oorschot and Wiener (1988) have presented a method to speed up the search of EDE by a factor of 16, but even with their attack, EDE is highly secure. For anyone wishing nothing less than the very best, EEE with three distinct 56-bit keys (168 bits in all) is recommended.

Before leaving the subject of DES, it is worth at least mentioning two recent developments in cryptanalysis. The first development is **differential cryptanalysis** (Biham and Shamir, 1993). This technique can be used to attack any block cipher. It works by beginning with a pair of plaintext blocks that differ in only a small number of bits and watching carefully what happens on each internal iteration as the encryption proceeds. In many cases, some patterns are much more common than other patterns, and this observation leads to a probabilistic attack.

The other development worth noting is **linear cryptanalysis** (Matsui, 1994). It can break DES with only 2^{43} known plaintexts. It works by EXCLUSIVE ORing certain plaintext and ciphertext bits together to generate 1 bit. When done repeatedly, half the bits should be 0s and half should be 1s. Often, however, ciphers introduce a bias in one direction or the other, and this bias, however small, can be exploited to reduce the work factor. For the details, see Matsui's paper.

IDEA

Perhaps all this hammering on why DES is insecure is like beating a dead horse, but the reality is that singly-encrypted DES is still widely used for secure applications, such as banking using automated teller machines. While this choice was probably appropriate when it was made, a decade or more ago, it is no longer adequate.

At this point, the reader is probably legitimately wondering: "If DES is so weak, why hasn't anyone invented a better block cipher?" The fact is, many other block ciphers have been proposed, including BLOWFISH (Schneier, 1994), Crab (Kaliski and Robshaw, 1994), FEAL (Shimizu and Miyaguchi, 1988), KHAFRE (Merkle, 1991), LOKI91 (Brown et al., 1991), NEWDES (Scott, 1985), REDOC-II (Cusick and Wood, 1991), and SAFER K64 (Massey, 1994). Schneier (1996) discusses all of these and innumerable others. Probably the most interesting and important of the post-DES block ciphers is **IDEA** the (**International Data Encryption Algorithm**) (Lai and Massey, 1990; and Lai, 1992). Let us now study IDEA in more detail.

IDEA was designed by two researchers in Switzerland, so it is probably free of any NSA "guidance" that might have introduced a secret trapdoor. It uses a 128-bit key, which will make it immune to brute force, Chinese lottery, and meet-in-the-middle attacks for decades to come. It was also designed to withstand differential cryptanalysis. No currently known technique or machine is thought to be able to break IDEA.

The basic structure of the algorithm resembles DES in that 64-bit plaintext input blocks are mangled in a sequence of parameterized iterations to produce 64-bit ciphertext output blocks, as shown in Fig. 7-10(a). Given the extensive bit mangling (for every iteration, every output bit depends on every input bit), eight iterations are sufficient. As with all block ciphers, IDEA can also be used in cipher feedback mode and the other DES modes.

The details of one iteration are depicted in Fig. 7-10(b). Three operations are used, all on unsigned 16-bit numbers. These operations are EXCLUSIVE OR, addition modulo 2^{16}, and multiplication modulo $2^{16} + 1$. All three of these can easily be done on a 16-bit microcomputer by ignoring the high-order parts of results. The operations have the property that no two pairs obey the associative law or distributive law, making cryptanalysis more difficult. The 128-bit key is used to generate 52 subkeys of 16 bits each, 6 for each of eight iterations and 4 for the final transformation. Decryption uses the same algorithm as encryption, only with different subkeys.

Both software and hardware implementations of IDEA have been constructed. The first software implementation ran on a 33-MHz 386 and achieved an encryption rate of 0.88 Mbps. On a modern machine running ten times as fast, 9 Mbps should be achievable in software. An experimental 25-MHz VLSI chip was built at ETH Zurich and encrypted at a rate of 177 Mbps.

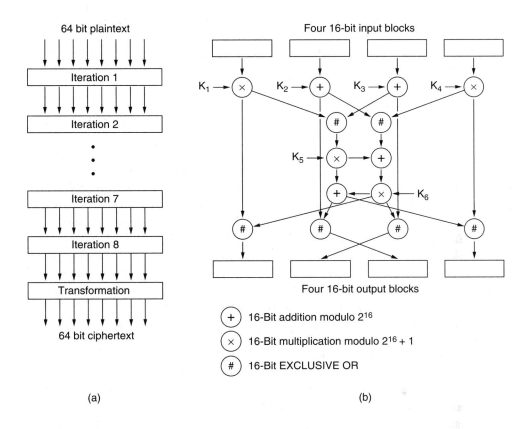

Fig. 7-10. (a) IDEA. (b) Detail of one iteration.

7.1.4. Public-Key Algorithms

Historically the key distribution problem has always been the weak link in most cryptosystems. No matter how strong a cryptosystem was, if an intruder could steal the key, the system was worthless. Since all cryptologists always took for granted that the encryption key and decryption key were the same (or easily derived from one another) and the key had to be distributed to all users of the system, it seemed as if there was an inherent built-in problem: keys had to protected from theft, but they also had to be distributed, so they could not just be locked up in a bank vault.

In 1976, two researchers at Stanford University, Diffie and Hellman (1976), proposed a radically new kind of cryptosystem, one in which the encryption and decryption keys were different, and the decryption key could not be derived from the encryption key. In their proposal, the (keyed) encryption algorithm, E, and the (keyed) decryption algorithm, D, had to meet the following three requirements. These requirements can be stated simply as follows:

1. $D(E(P)) = P$.

2. It is exceedingly difficult to deduce D from E.

3. E cannot be broken by a chosen plaintext attack.

The first requirement says that if we apply D to an encrypted message, $E(P)$, we get the original plaintext message, P, back. The second requirement speaks for itself. The third requirement is needed because, as we shall see in a moment, intruders may experiment with the algorithm to their hearts' content. Under these conditions, there is no reason that the encryption key cannot be made public.

The method works like this. A person, say, Alice, wanting to receive secret messages, first devises two algorithms, E_A and D_A, meeting the above requirements. The encryption algorithm and key, E_A, is then made public, hence the name **public-key cryptography** (to contrast it with traditional secret-key cryptography). This might be done by putting it in a file that anyone who wanted to could read. Alice publishes the decryption algorithm (to get the free consulting), but keeps the decryption key secret. Thus, E_A is public, but D_A is private.

Now let us see if we can solve the problem of establishing a secure channel between Alice and Bob, who have never had any previous contact. Both Alice's encryption key, E_A, and Bob's encryption key, E_B, are assumed to be in a publicly readable file. (Basically, all users of the network are expected to publish their encryption keys as soon as they become network users.) Now Alice takes her first message, P, computes $E_B(P)$, and sends it to Bob. Bob then decrypts it by applying his secret key D_B [i.e., he computes $D_B(E_B(P)) = P$]. No one else can read the encrypted message, $E_B(P)$, because the encryption system is assumed strong and because it is too difficult to derive D_B from the publicly known E_B. Alice and Bob can now communicate securely.

A note on terminology is perhaps useful here. Public-key cryptography requires each user to have two keys: a public key, used by the entire world for encrypting messages to be sent to that user, and a private key, which the user needs for decrypting messages. We will consistently refer to these keys as the *public* and *private* keys, respectively, and distinguish them from the *secret* keys used for both encryption and decryption in conventional (also called **symmetric key**) cryptography.

The RSA Algorithm

The only catch is that we need to find algorithms that indeed satisfy all three requirements. Due to the potential advantages of public-key cryptography, many researchers are hard at work, and some algorithms have already been published. One good method was discovered by a group at M.I.T. (Rivest et al., 1978). It is known by the initials of the three discoverers (Rivest, Shamir, Adleman): **RSA**. Their method is based on some principles from number theory. We will now summarize how to use the method below; for details, consult the paper.

1. Choose two large primes, p and q, (typically greater than 10^{100}).

2. Compute $n = p \times q$ and $z = (p - 1) \times (q - 1)$.

3. Choose a number relatively prime to z and call it d.

4. Find e such that $e \times d = 1 \bmod z$.

With these parameters computed in advance, we are ready to begin encryption. Divide the plaintext (regarded as a bit string) into blocks, so that each plaintext message, P, falls in the interval $0 \le P < n$. This can be done by grouping the plaintext into blocks of k bits, where k is the largest integer for which $2^k < n$ is true.

To encrypt a message, P, compute $C = P^e \pmod{n}$. To decrypt C, compute $P = C^d \pmod{n}$. It can be proven that for all P in the specified range, the encryption and decryption functions are inverses. To perform the encryption, you need e and n. To perform the decryption, you need d and n. Therefore, the public key consists of the pair (e, n) and the private key consists of (d, n).

The security of the method is based on the difficulty of factoring large numbers. If the cryptanalyst could factor the (publicly known) n, he could then find p and q, and from these z. Equipped with knowledge of z and e, d can be found using Euclid's algorithm. Fortunately, mathematicians have been trying to factor large numbers for at least 300 years, and the accumulated evidence suggests that it is an exceedingly difficult problem.

According to Rivest and colleagues, factoring a 200-digit number requires 4 billion years of computer time; factoring a 500-digit number requires 10^{25} years. In both cases, they assume the best known algorithm and a computer with a 1–μsec instruction time. Even if computers continue to get faster by an order of magnitude per decade, it will be centuries before factoring a 500-digit number becomes feasible, at which time our descendants can simply choose p and q still larger.

A trivial pedagogical example of the RSA algorithm is given in Fig. 7-11. For this example we have chosen $p = 3$ and $q = 11$, giving $n = 33$ and $z = 20$. A suitable value for d is $d = 7$, since 7 and 20 have no common factors. With these choices, e can be found by solving the equation $7e = 1 \pmod{20}$, which yields $e = 3$. The ciphertext, C, for a plaintext message, P, is given by $C = P^3 \pmod{33}$. The ciphertext is decrypted by the receiver according to the rule $P = C^7 \pmod{33}$. The figure shows the encryption of the plaintext "SUZANNE" as an example.

Because the primes chosen for this example are so small, P must be less than 33, so each plaintext block can contain only a single character. The result is a

Plaintext (P)			Ciphertext (C)		After decryption	
Symbolic	Numeric	P³	P³ (mod 33)	C⁷	C⁷ (mod 33)	Symbolic
S	19	6859	28	13492928512	19	S
U	21	9261	21	1801088541	21	U
Z	26	17576	20	1280000000	26	Z
A	01	1	1	1	1	A
N	14	2744	5	78125	14	N
N	14	2744	5	78125	14	N
E	05	125	26	8031810176	5	E

Sender's computation   Receiver's computation

Fig. 7-11. An example of the RSA algorithm.

monoalphabetic substitution cipher, not very impressive. If instead we had chosen p and $q \approx 10^{100}$, we would have $n \approx 10^{200}$, so each block could be up to 664 bits ($2^{664} \approx 10^{200}$) or 83 8-bit characters, versus 8 characters for DES.

It should be pointed out that using RSA as we have described is similar to using DES in ECB mode—the same input block gives the same output block. Therefore some form of chaining is needed for data encryption. However, in practice, most RSA-based systems use public-key cryptography primarily for distributing one-time session keys for use with DES, IDEA, or similar algorithms. RSA is too slow for actually encrypting large volumes of data.

Other Public-Key Algorithms

Although RSA is widely used, it is by no means the only public-key algorithm known. The first public-key algorithm was the knapsack algorithm (Merkle and Hellman, 1978). The idea here is that someone owns a large number of objects, each with a different weight. The owner encodes the message by secretly selecting a subset of the objects and placing them in the knapsack. The total weight of the objects in the knapsack is made public, as is the list of all possible objects. The list of objects in the knapsack is kept secret. With certain additional restrictions, the problem of figuring out a possible list of objects with the given weight was thought to be computationally infeasible, and formed the basis of the public-key algorithm.

The algorithm's inventor, Ralph Merkle, was quite sure that this algorithm could not be broken, so he offered a 100-dollar reward to anyone who could break it. Adi Shamir (the "S" in RSA) promptly broke it and collected the reward. Undeterred, Merkle strengthened the algorithm and offered a 1000-dollar reward to anyone who could break the new one. Ron Rivest (the "R" in RSA) promptly broke the new one and collected the reward. Merkle did not dare offer 10,000 dollars for the next version, so "A" (Leonard Adleman) was out of luck. Although it has been patched up again, the knapsack algorithm is not considered secure and is rarely used.

Other public-key schemes are based on the difficulty of computing discrete logarithms (Rabin, 1979). Algorithms that use this principle have been invented by El Gamal (1985) and Schnorr (1991).

A few other schemes exist, such as those based on elliptic curves (Menezes and Vanstone, 1993), but the three major categories are those based on the difficulty of factoring large numbers, computing discrete logarithms, and determining the contents of a knapsack from its weight. These problems are thought to be genuinely difficult to solve because mathematicians have been working on them for many years without any great breakthroughs.

7.1.5. Authentication Protocols

Authentication is the technique by which a process verifies that its communication partner is who it is supposed to be and not an imposter. Verifying the identity of a remote process in the face of a malicious, active intruder is surprisingly difficult and requires complex protocols based on cryptography. In this section, we will study some of the many authentication protocols that are used on insecure computer networks.

As an aside, some people confuse authorization with authentication. Authentication deals with the question of whether or not you are actually communicating with a specific process. Authorization is concerned with what that process is permitted to do. For example, a client process contacts a file server and says: "I am Scott's process and I want to delete the file *cookbook.old*." From the file server's point of view, two questions must be answered:

1. Is this actually Scott's process (authentication)?

2. Is Scott allowed to delete *cookbook.old* (authorization)?

Only after both questions have been unambiguously answered in the affirmative can the requested action take place. The former question is really the key one. Once the file server knows whom it is talking to, checking authorization is just a matter of looking up entries in local tables. For this reason, we will concentrate on authentication in this section.

The general model that all authentication protocols use is this. An initiating user (really a process), say, Alice, wants to establish a secure connection with a second user, Bob. Alice and Bob are sometimes called **principals**, the main characters in our story. Bob is a banker with whom Alice would like to do business. Alice starts out by sending a message either to Bob, or to a trusted **key distribution center** (**KDC**), which is always honest. Several other message exchanges follow in various directions. As these message are being sent, a nasty intruder, Trudy,[†] may intercept, modify, or replay them in order to trick Alice and Bob or just to gum up the works.

Nevertheless, when the protocol has been completed, Alice is sure she is talking to Bob and Bob is sure he is talking to Alice. Furthermore, in most of the protocols, the two of them will also have established a secret **session key** for use in the upcoming conversation. In practice, for performance reasons, all data traffic is encrypted using secret-key cryptography, although public-key cryptography is widely used for the authentication protocols themselves and for establishing the session key.

The point of using a new, randomly-chosen session key for each new connection is to minimize the amount of traffic that gets sent with the users' secret keys or public keys, to reduce the amount of ciphertext an intruder can obtain, and to minimize the damage done if a process crashes and its core dump falls into the wrong hands. Hopefully, the only key present then will be the session key. All the permanent keys should have been carefully zeroed out after the session was established.

Authentication Based on a Shared Secret Key

For our first authentication protocol, we will assume that Alice and Bob already share a secret key, K_{AB} (In the formal protocols, we will abbreviate Alice as A and Bob as B, respectively.) This shared key might have been agreed upon on the telephone, or in person, but, in any event, not on the (insecure) network.

This protocol is based on a principle found in many authentication protocols: one party sends a random number to the other, who then transforms it in a special way and then returns the result. Such protocols are called **challenge-response** protocols. In this and subsequent authentication protocols, the following notation will be used:

A, B are the identities of Alice and Bob
R_i's are the challenges, where the subscript identifies the challenger
K_i are keys, where i indicates the owner; K_S is the session key

The message sequence for our first shared-key authentication protocol is shown in Fig. 7-12. In message 1, Alice sends her identity, A, to Bob in a way that Bob understands. Bob, of course, has no way of knowing whether this message came from Alice or from Trudy, so he chooses a challenge, a large random number, R_B, and sends it back to "Alice" as message 2, in plaintext. Alice then encrypts the message with the key she shares with Bob and sends the ciphertext, $K_{AB}(R_B)$, back in message 3. When Bob sees this message, he immediately knows that it came from Alice because Trudy does not know K_{AB} and thus could

---

† I thank Kaufman[1] et al.[23] (1995) for revealing her name.

not have generated it. Furthermore, since R_B was chosen randomly from a large space (say, 128-bit random numbers), it is very unlikely that Trudy would have seen R_B and its response from an earlier session.

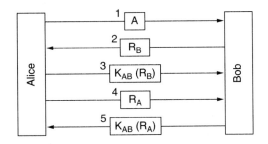

Fig. 7-12. Two-way authentication using a challenge-response protocol.

At this point, Bob is sure he is talking to Alice, but Alice is not sure of anything. For all Alice knows, Trudy might have intercepted message 1 and sent back R_B in response. Maybe Bob died last night. To find out whom she is talking to, Alice picks a random number, R_A and sends it to Bob as plaintext, in message 4. When Bob responds with $K_{AB}(R_A)$, Alice knows she is talking to Bob. If they wish to establish a session key now, Alice can pick one, K_S, and send it to Bob encrypted with K_{AB}.

Although the protocol of Fig. 7-12 works, it contains extra messages. These can be eliminated by combining information, as illustrated in Fig. 7-13. Here Alice initiates the challenge-response protocol instead of waiting for Bob to do it. Similarly, while he is responding to Alice's challenge, Bob sends his own. The entire protocol can be reduced to three messages instead of five.

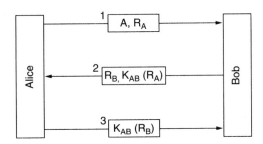

Fig. 7-13. A shortened two-way authentication protocol.

Is this new protocol an improvement over the original one? In one sense it is: it is shorter. Unfortunately, it is also wrong. Under certain circumstances, Trudy can defeat this protocol by using what is known as a **reflection attack**. In particular, Trudy can break it if it is possible to open multiple sessions with Bob at once. This situation would be true, for example, if Bob is a bank and is prepared to accept many simultaneous connections from teller machines at once.

Trudy's reflection attack is shown in Fig. 7-14. It starts out with Trudy claiming she is Alice and sending R_T. Bob responds, as usual, with his own challenge, R_B. Now Trudy is stuck. What can she do? She does not know $K_{AB}(R_B)$.

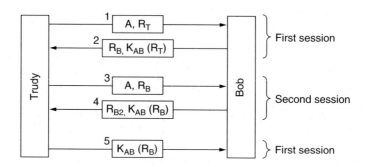

Fig. 7-14. The reflection attack.

She can open a second session with message 3, supplying the R_B taken from message 2 as her challenge. Bob calmly encrypts it and sends back $K_{AB}(R_B)$ in message 4. Now Trudy has the missing information, so she can complete the first session and abort the second one. Bob is now convinced that Trudy is Alice, so when she asks for her bank account balance, he gives it to her without question. Then when she asks him to transfer it all to a secret bank account in Switzerland, he does so without a moment's hesitation.

The moral of this story is:

> *Designing a correct authentication protocol is harder than it looks.*

Three general rules that often help are as follows:

1. Have the initiator prove who she is before the responder has to. In this case, Bob gives away valuable information before Trudy has to give any evidence of who she is.

2. Have the initiator and responder use different keys for proof, even if this means having two shared keys, K_{AB} and K'_{AB}.

3. Have the initiator and responder draw their challenges from different sets. For example, the initiator must use even numbers and the responder must use odd numbers.

All three rules were violated here, with disastrous results. Note that our first (five-message) authentication protocol requires Alice to prove her identity first, so that protocol is not subject to the reflection attack.

Establishing a Shared Key: The Diffie-Hellman Key Exchange

So far we have assumed that Alice and Bob share a secret key. Suppose that they do not? How can they establish one? One way would be for Alice to call Bob and give him her key on the phone, but he would probably start out by saying: "How do I know you are Alice and not Trudy?" They could try to arrange a meeting, with each one bringing a passport, a drivers' license, and three major credit cards, but being busy people, they might not be able to find a mutually acceptable date for months. Fortunately, incredible as it may sound, there is a way for total strangers to establish a shared secret key in broad daylight, even with Trudy carefully recording every message.

The protocol that allows strangers to establish a shared secret key is called the **Diffie-Hellman key exchange** (Diffie and Hellman, 1976) and works as follows. Alice and Bob have to agree on two large prime numbers, n, and g, where $(n - 1)/2$ is also a prime and certain conditions apply to g. These numbers may be public, so either one of them can just pick n and g and tell the other openly. Now Alice picks a large (say, 512-bit) number, x, and keeps it secret. Similarly, Bob picks a large secret number, y.

Alice initiates the key exchange protocol by sending Bob a message containing $(n, g, g^x \bmod n)$, as shown in Fig. 7-15. Bob responds by sending Alice a message containing $g^y \bmod n$. Now Alice takes the number Bob sent her and raises it to the xth power to get $(g^y \bmod n)^x$. Bob performs a similar operation to get $(g^x \bmod n)^y$. By the laws of modular arithmetic, both calculations yield $g^{xy} \bmod n$. Lo and behold, Alice and Bob now share a secret key, $g^{xy} \bmod n$.

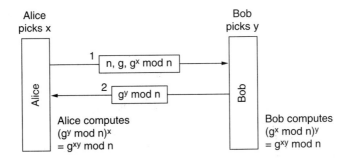

Fig. 7-15. The Diffie-Hellman key exchange.

Trudy, of course, has seen both messages. She knows g and n from message 1. If she could compute x and y, she could figure out the secret key. The trouble is, given only $g^x \bmod n$, she cannot find x. No practical algorithm for computing discrete logarithms modulo a very large prime number is known.

To make the above example more concrete, we will use the (completely unrealistic) values of $n = 47$ and $g = 3$. Alice picks $x = 8$ and Bob picks $y = 10$.

Both of these are kept secret. Alice's message to Bob is (47, 3, 28) because 3^8 mod 47 is 28. Bob's message to Alice is (17). Alice computes 17^8 mod 47, which is 4. Bob computes 28^{10} mod 47, which is 4. Alice and Bob have independently determined that the secret key is now 4. Trudy has to solve the equation 3^x mod 47 = 28, which can be done by exhaustive search for small numbers like this, but not when all the numbers are hundreds of bits long. All currently-known algorithms simply take too long, even using a massively parallel supercomputer.

Despite the elegance of the Diffie-Hellman algorithm, there is a problem: when Bob gets the triple (47, 3, 28), how does he know it is from Alice and not from Trudy? There is no way he can know. Unfortunately, Trudy can exploit this fact to deceive both Alice and Bob, as illustrated in Fig. 7-16. Here, while Alice and Bob are choosing x and y, respectively, Trudy picks her own random number, z. Alice sends message 1 intended for Bob. Trudy intercepts it and sends message 2 to Bob, using the correct g and n (which are public anyway) but with her own z instead of x. She also sends message 3 back to Alice. Later Bob sends message 4 to Alice, which Trudy again intercepts and keeps.

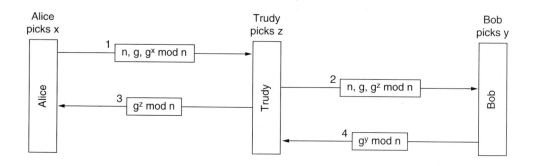

Fig. 7-16. The bucket brigade attack.

Now everybody does the modular arithmetic. Alice computes the secret key as g^{xz} mod n, and so does Trudy (for messages to Alice). Bob computes g^{yz} mod n and so does Trudy (for messages to Bob). Alice thinks she is talking to Bob so she establishes a session key (with Trudy). So does Bob. Every message that Alice sends on the encrypted session is captured by Trudy, stored, modified if desired, and then (optionally) passed on to Bob. Similarly in the other direction. Trudy sees everything and can modify all messages at will, while both Alice and Bob are under the illusion that they have a secure channel to one another. This attack is known as the **bucket brigade attack**, because it vaguely resembles an old-time volunteer fire department passing buckets along the line from the fire truck to the fire. It is also called the **(wo)man-in-the-middle attack**, which should not be confused with the meet-in-the-middle attack on block ciphers. Fortunately, more complex algorithms can defeat this attack.

Authentication Using a Key Distribution Center

Setting up a shared secret with a stranger almost worked, but not quite. On the other hand, it probably was not worth doing in the first place (sour grapes attack). To talk to n people this way, you would need n keys. For popular people, key management would become a real burden, especially if each key had to be stored on a separate plastic chip card.

A different approach is to introduce a trusted key distribution center (KDC). In this model, each user has a single key shared with the KDC. Authentication and session key management now goes through the KDC. The simplest known KDC authentication protocol involving two parties and a trusted KDC is depicted in Fig. 7-17.

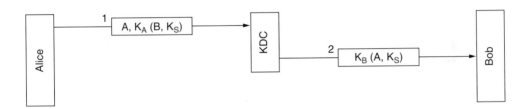

Fig. 7-17. A first attempt at an authentication protocol using a KDC.

The idea behind this protocol is simple: Alice picks a session key, K_S, and tells the KDC that she wants to talk to Bob using K_S. This message is encrypted with the secret key Alice shares (only) with the KDC, K_A. The KDC decrypts this message, extracting Bob's identity and the session key. It then constructs a new message containing Alice's identity and the session key and sends this message to Bob. This encryption is done with K_B, the secret key Bob shares with the KDC. When Bob decrypts the message, he learns that Alice wants to talk to him, and which key she wants to use.

The authentication here happens for free. The KDC knows that message 1 must have come from Alice, since no one else would have been able to encrypt it with Alice's secret key. Similarly, Bob knows that message 2 must have come from the KDC, whom he trusts, since no one else knows his secret key.

Unfortunately, this protocol has a serious flaw. Trudy needs some money, so she figures out some legitimate service she can perform for Alice, makes an attractive offer, and gets the job. After doing the work, Trudy then politely requests Alice to pay by bank transfer. Alice then establishes a session key with her banker, Bob. Then she sends Bob a message requesting money to be transferred to Trudy's account.

Meanwhile, Trudy is back to her old ways, snooping on the network. She copies both message 2 in Fig. 7-17, and the money-transfer request that follows it.

Later, she replays both of them to Bob. Bob gets them and thinks: "Alice must have hired Trudy again. She clearly does good work." Bob then transfers an equal amount of money from Alice's account to Trudy's. Some time after the 50th message pair, Bob runs out of the office to find Trudy to offer her a big loan so she can expand her obviously successful business. This problem is called the **replay attack**.

Several solutions to the replay attack are possible. The first one is to include a timestamp in each message. Then if anyone receives an obsolete message, it can be discarded. The trouble with this approach is that clocks are never exactly synchronized over a network, so there has to be some interval during which a timestamp is valid. Trudy can replay the message during this interval and get away with it.

The second solution is to put a one-time, unique message number, usually called a **nonce**, in each message. Each party then has to remember all previous nonces and reject any message containing a previously used nonce. But nonces have to be remembered forever, lest Trudy try replaying a 5-year-old message. Also, if some machine crashes and it loses its nonce list, it is again vulnerable to a replay attack. Timestamps and nonces can be combined to limit how long nonces have to be remembered, but clearly the protocol is going to get a lot more complicated.

A more sophisticated approach to authentication is to use a multiway challenge-response protocol. A well-known example of such a protocol is the **Needham-Schroeder authentication** protocol (Needham and Schroeder, 1978), one variant of which is shown in Fig. 7-18.

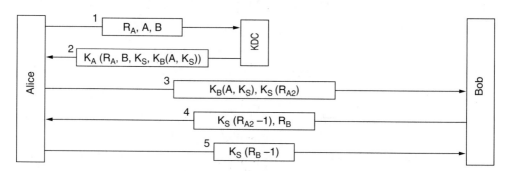

Fig. 7-18. The Needham-Schroeder authentication protocol.

The protocol begins with Alice telling the KDC that she wants to talk to Bob. This message contains a large random number, R_A, as a nonce. The KDC sends back message 2 containing Alice's random number, a session key, and a ticket that she can send to Bob. The point of the random number, R_A, is to assure Alice that message 2 is fresh, and not a replay. Bob's identity is also enclosed in case Trudy gets any funny ideas about replacing B in message 1 with her own identity so the KDC will encrypt the ticket at the end of message 2 with K_T instead of K_B. The ticket encrypted with K_B is included inside the encrypted message to prevent Trudy from replacing it with something else on the way back to Alice.

Alice now sends the ticket to Bob, along with a new random number, R_{A2}, encrypted with the session key, K_S. In message 4, Bob sends back $K_S(R_{A2} - 1)$ to prove to Alice that she is talking to the real Bob. Sending back $K_S(R_{A2})$ would not have worked, since Trudy could just have stolen it from message 3.

After receiving message 4, Alice is now convinced that she is talking to Bob, and that no replays could have been used so far. After all, she just generated R_{A2} a few milliseconds ago. The purpose of message 5 is to convince Bob that it is indeed Alice he is talking to, and no replays are being used here either. By having each party both generate a challenge and respond to one, the possibility of any kind of replay attack is eliminated.

Although this protocol seems pretty solid, it does have a slight weakness. If Trudy ever manages to obtain an old session key in plaintext, she can initiate a new session with Bob replaying the message 3 corresponding to the compromised key and convince him that she is Alice (Denning and Sacco, 1981). This time she can plunder Alice's bank account without having to perform the legitimate service even once.

Needham and Schroeder later published a protocol that corrects this problem (Needham and Schroeder, 1987). In the same issue of the same journal, Otway and Rees (1987) also published a protocol that solves the problem in a shorter way. Figure 7-19 shows a slightly modified Otway-Rees protocol.

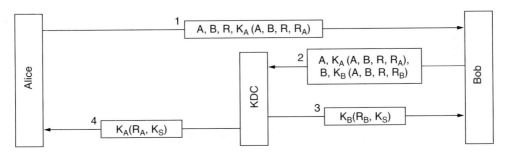

Fig. 7-19. The Otway-Rees authentication protocol (slightly simplified).

In the Otway-Rees protocol, Alice starts out by generating a pair of random numbers, R, which will be used as a common identifier, and R_A which Alice will use to challenge Bob. When Bob gets this message, he constructs a new message from the encrypted part of Alice's message, and an analogous one of his own. Both the parts encrypted with K_A and K_B identify Alice and Bob, contain the common identifier, and contain a challenge.

The KDC checks to see if the R in both parts is the same. It might not be because Trudy tampered with R in message 1 or replaced part of message 2. If the two Rs match, the KDC believes that the request message from Bob is valid. It then generates a session key and encrypts it twice, once for Alice and once for Bob. Each message contains the receiver's random number, as proof that the KDC, and not Trudy, generated the message. At this point both Alice and Bob are in possession of the same session key and can start communicating. The first time they exchange data messages, each one can see that the other one has an identical copy of K_S, so the authentication is then complete.

Authentication Using Kerberos

An authentication protocol used in many real systems is **Kerberos**, which is based on a variant of Needham-Schroeder. It is named for a multiheaded dog in Greek Mythology that used to guard the entrance to Hades (presumably to keep undesirables out). Kerberos was designed at M.I.T. to allow workstation users to access network resources in a secure way. Its biggest difference with Needham-Schroeder is its assumption that all clocks are fairly-well synchronized. The protocol has gone through several iterations. V4 is the version most widely used in industry, so we will describe it. Afterward, we will say a few words about its successor, V5. For more information, see (Neuman and Ts'o, 1994; and Steiner et al., 1988).

Kerberos involves three servers in addition to Alice (a client workstation):

Authentication Server (AS): verifies users during login
Ticket-Granting Server (TGS): issues "proof of identity tickets"
Bob the server: actually does the work Alice wants performed

AS is similar to a KDC in that it shares a secret password with every user. The TGS's job is to issue tickets that can convince the real servers that the bearer of a TGS ticket really is who he or she claims to be.

To start a session, Alice sits down at a arbitrary public workstation and types her name. The workstation sends her name to the AS in plaintext, as shown in Fig. 7-20. What comes back is a session key and a ticket, $K_{TGS}(A, K_S)$, intended for the TGS. These items are packaged together and encrypted using Alice's secret key, so that only Alice can decrypt them. Only when message 2 arrives, does the workstation ask for Alice's password. The password is then used to generate K_A, in order to decrypt message 2 and obtain the session key and TGS ticket inside it. At this point, the workstation overwrites Alice's password, to make sure that it is only inside the workstation for a few milliseconds at most. If Trudy tries logging in as Alice, the password she types will be wrong and the workstation will detect this because the standard part of message 2 will be incorrect.

After she logs in, Alice may tell the workstation that she wants to contact Bob the file server. The workstation then sends message 3 to the TGS asking for a ticket to use with Bob. The key element in this request is $K_{TGS}(A, K_S)$, which is

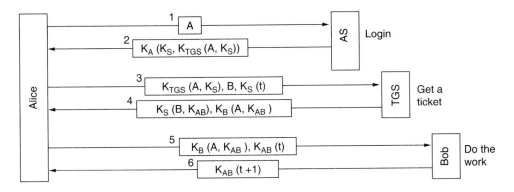

Fig. 7-20. The operation of Kerberos V4.

encrypted with the TGS's secret key and is used as proof that the sender really is Alice. The TGS responds by creating a session key, K_{AB}, for Alice to use with Bob. Two versions of it are sent back. The first is encrypted with only K_S, so Alice can read it. The second is encrypted with Bob's key, K_B, so Bob can read it.

Trudy can copy message 3 and try to use it again, but she will be foiled by the encrypted timestamp, t, sent along with it. Trudy cannot replace the timestamp with a more recent one, because she does not know K_S, the session key Alice uses to talk to the TGS. Even if Trudy replays message 3 quickly, all she will get is another copy of message 4, which she could not decrypt the first time and will not be able to decrypt the second time either.

Now Alice can send K_{AB} to Bob to establish a session with him. This exchange is also timestamped. The response is proof to Alice that she is actually talking to Bob, not to Trudy.

After this series of exchanges, Alice can communicate with Bob under cover of K_{AB}. If she later decides she needs to talk to another server, Carol, she just repeats message 3 to the TGS, only now specifying C instead of B. The TGS will promptly respond with a ticket encrypted with K_C that Alice can send to Carol and that Carol will accept as proof that it came from Alice.

The point of all this work is that now Alice can access servers all over the network in a secure way, and her password never has to go over the network. In fact, it only had to be in her own workstation for a few milliseconds. However, note that each server does its own authorization. When Alice presents her ticket to Bob, this merely proves to Bob who sent it. Precisely what Alice is allowed to do is up to Bob.

Since the Kerberos designers did not expect the entire world to trust a single authentication server, they made provision for having multiple **realms**, each with its own AS and TGS. To get a ticket for a server in a distant realm, Alice would ask her own TGS for a ticket accepted by the TGS in the distant realm. If the distant TGS has registered with the local TGS (the same way local servers do), the local TGS will give Alice a ticket valid at the distant TGS. She can then do business over there, such as getting tickets for servers in that realm. Note, however, that for parties in two realms to do business, each one must trust the other's TGS.

Kerberos V5 is fancier than V4 and has more overhead. It also uses OSI ASN.1 (Abstract Syntax Notation 1) for describing data types and has small changes in the protocols. Furthermore, it has longer ticket lifetimes, allows tickets to be renewed, and will issue postdated tickets. In addition, at least in theory, it is not DES dependent, as V4 is, and supports multiple realms.

Authentication Using Public-Key Cryptography

Mutual authentication can also be done using public-key cryptography. To start with, let us assume Alice and Bob already know each other's public keys (a nontrivial issue). They want to establish a session, and then use secret-key cryptography on that session, since it is typically 100 to 1000 times faster than public-key cryptography. The purpose of the initial exchange then is to authenticate each other and agree on a secret shared session key.

This setup can be done is various ways. A typical one is shown in Fig. 7-21. Here Alice starts by encrypting her identity and a random number, R_A, using Bob's public (or encryption) key, E_B. When Bob receives this message, he has no idea of whether it came from Alice or from Trudy, but he plays along and sends Alice back a message containing Alice's R_A, his own random number, R_B, and a proposed session key, K_S.

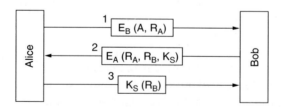

Fig. 7-21. Mutual authentication using public-key cryptography.

When Alice gets message 2, she decrypts it using her private key. She sees R_A in it, which gives her a warm feeling inside. The message must have come from Bob, since Trudy has no way of determining R_A. Furthermore, it must be fresh and not a replay, since she just sent Bob R_A. Alice agrees to the session by sending back message 3. When Bob sees R_B encrypted with the session key he just generated, he knows Alice got message 2 and verified R_A.

What can Trudy do to try to subvert this protocol? She can fabricate message 1 and trick Bob into probing Alice, but Alice will see an R_A that she did not send and will not proceed further. Trudy cannot forge message 3 convincingly because she does not know R_B or K_S and cannot determine them without Alice's private key. She is out of luck.

However, the protocol does have a weakness: it assumes that Alice and Bob already know each other's public keys. Suppose that they do not. Alice could just send Bob her public key in the first message and ask Bob to send his back in the next one. The trouble with this approach is that it is subject to a bucket brigade attack. Trudy can capture Alice's message to Bob and send her own public key back to Alice. Alice will think she has a key for talking to Bob, when, in fact, she has a key for talking to Trudy. Now Trudy can read all the messages encrypted with what Alice thinks is Bob's public key.

The initial public-key exchange can be avoided by having all the public keys stored in a public database. Then Alice and Bob can fetch each other's public keys from the database. Unfortunately, Trudy can still pull off the bucket brigade attack by intercepting the requests to the database and sending simulated replies containing her own public key. After all, how do Alice and Bob know that the replies came from the real data base and not from Trudy?

Rivest and Shamir (1984) have devised a protocol that foils Trudy's bucket brigade attack. In their **interlock protocol**, after the public key exchange, Alice sends only half of her message to Bob, say, only the even bits (after encryption). Bob then responds with his even bits. After getting Bob's even bits, Alice sends her odd bits, then Bob does too.

The trick here is that when Trudy gets Alice's even bits, she cannot decrypt the message, even though Trudy has the private key. Consequently, she is unable to reencrypt the even bits using Bob's public key. If she sends junk to Bob, the protocol will continue, but Bob will shortly discover that the fully assembled message makes no sense and realized that he has been spoofed.

7.1.6. Digital Signatures

The authenticity of many legal, financial, and other documents is determined by the presence or absence of an authorized handwritten signature. And photocopies do not count. For computerized message systems to replace the physical transport of paper and ink documents, a solution must be found to these problems.

The problem of devising a replacement for handwritten signatures is a difficult one. Basically, what is needed is a system by which one party can send a "signed" message to another party in such a way that

1. The receiver can verify the claimed identity of the sender.

2. The sender cannot later repudiate the contents of the message.

3. The receiver cannot possibly have concocted the message himself.

The first requirement is needed, for example, in financial systems. When a customer's computer orders a bank's computer to buy a ton of gold, the bank's computer needs to be able to make sure that the computer giving the order really belongs to the company whose account is to be debited.

The second requirement is needed to protect the bank against fraud. Suppose that the bank buys the ton of gold, and immediately thereafter the price of gold drops sharply. A dishonest customer might sue the bank, claiming that he never issued any order to buy gold. When the bank produces the message in court, the customer denies having sent it.

The third requirement is needed to protect the customer in the event that the price of gold shoots up and the bank tries to construct a signed message in which the customer asked for one bar of gold instead of one ton.

Secret-Key Signatures

One approach to digital signatures is to have a central authority that knows everything and whom everyone trusts, say Big Brother (*BB*). Each user then chooses a secret key and carries it by hand to *BB*'s office. Thus only Alice and *BB* know Alice's secret, K_A, and so on.

When Alice wants to send a signed plaintext message, P, to her banker, Bob, she generates $K_A(B, R_A, t, P)$ and sends it as depicted in Fig. 7-22. *BB* sees that the message is from Alice, decrypts it, and sends a message to Bob as shown. The message to Bob contains the plaintext of Alice's message and also the signed message $K_{BB}(A, t, P)$, where t is a timestamp. Bob now carries out Alice's request.

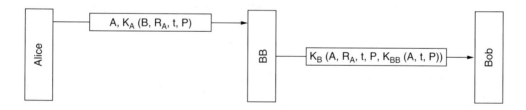

Fig. 7-22. Digital signatures with Big Brother.

What happens if Alice later denies sending the message? Step 1 is that everyone sues everyone (at least, in the United States). Finally, when the case comes to court and Alice vigorously denies sending Bob the disputed message, the judge will ask Bob how he can be sure that the disputed message came from Alice and not from Trudy. Bob first points out that *BB* will not accept a message from Alice unless it is encrypted with K_A, so there is no possibility of Trudy sending *BB* a false message from Alice.

Bob then dramatically produces Exhibit A, $K_{BB}(A, t, P)$. Bob says that this is a message signed by *BB* which proves Alice sent P to Bob. The judge then asks

BB (whom everyone trusts) to decrypt Exhibit A. When *BB* testifies that Bob is telling the truth, the judge decides in favor of Bob. Case dismissed.

One potential problem with the signature protocol of Fig. 7-22 is Trudy replaying either message. To minimize this problem, timestamps are used throughout. Furthermore, Bob can check all recent messages to see if R_A was used in any of them. If so, the message is discarded as a replay. Note that Bob will reject very old messages based on the timestamp. To guard against instant replay attacks, Bob just checks the R_A of every incoming message to see if such a message has been received from Alice in the past hour. If not, Bob can safely assume this is a new request.

Public-Key Signatures

A structural problem with using secret-key cryptography for digital signatures is that everyone has to agree to trust Big Brother. Furthermore, Big Brother gets to read all signed messages. The most logical candidates for running the Big Brother server are the government, the banks, or the lawyers. These organizations do not inspire total confidence in all citizens. Hence, it would be nice if signing documents did not require a trusted authority.

Fortunately, public-key cryptography can make an important contribution here. Let us assume that the public-key encryption and decryption algorithms have the property that $E(D(P)) = P$ in addition to the usual property that $D(E(P)) = P$. (RSA has this property, so the assumption is not unreasonable.) Assuming that this is the case, Alice can send a signed plaintext message, P, to Bob by transmitting $E_B(D_A(P))$. Note carefully that Alice knows her own (private) decryption key, D_A, as well as Bob's public key, E_B, so constructing this message is something Alice can do.

When Bob receives the message, he transforms it using his private key, as usual, yielding $D_A(P)$, as shown in Fig. 7-23. He stores this text in a safe place and then decrypts it using E_A to get the original plaintext.

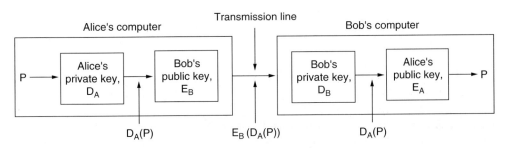

Fig. 7-23. Digital signatures using public-key cryptography.

To see how the signature property works, suppose that Alice subsequently denies having sent the message P to Bob. When the case comes up in court, Bob can produce both P and $D_A(P)$. The judge can easily verify that Bob indeed has a valid message encrypted by D_A by simply applying E_A to it. Since Bob does not know what Alice's private key is, the only way Bob could have acquired a message encrypted by it is if Alice did indeed send it. While in jail for perjury and fraud, Alice will have plenty of time to devise interesting new public-key algorithms.

Although using public-key cryptography for digital signatures is an elegant scheme, there are problems that are related to the environment in which they operate rather than with the basic algorithm. For one thing, Bob can prove that a message was sent by Alice only as long as D_A remains secret. If Alice discloses her secret key, the argument no longer holds, because anyone could have sent the message, including Bob himself.

The problem might arise, for example, if Bob is Alice's stockbroker. Alice tells Bob to buy a certain stock or bond. Immediately thereafter, the price drops sharply. To repudiate her message to Bob, Alice runs to the police claiming that her home was burglarized and her key was stolen. Depending on the laws in her state or country, she may or may not be legally liable, especially if she claims not to have discovered the break-in until getting home from work, several hours later.

Another problem with the signature scheme is what happens if Alice decides to change her key. Doing so is clearly legal, and it is probably a good idea to do so periodically. If a court case later arises, as described above, the judge will apply the *current* E_A to $D_A(P)$ and discover that it does not produce P. Bob will look pretty stupid at this point. Consequently, it appears that some authority is probably needed to record all key changes and their dates.

In principle, any public-key algorithm can be used for digital signatures. The de facto industry standard is the RSA algorithm. Many security products use it. However, in 1991, NIST (National Institute of Standards and Technology) proposed using a variant of the El Gamal public-key algorithm for their new **Digital Signature Standard** (**DSS**). El Gamal gets its security from the difficulty of computing discrete logarithms, rather than the difficulty of factoring large numbers.

As usual when the government tries to dictate cryptographic standards, there was an uproar. DSS was criticized for being

1. Too secret (NSA designed the protocol for using El Gamal).

2. Too new (El Gamal has not yet been thoroughly analyzed).

3. Too slow (10 to 40 times slower than RSA for checking signatures).

4. Too insecure (fixed 512-bit key).

In a subsequent revision, the fourth point was rendered moot when keys up to 1024 bits were allowed. It is not yet clear whether DSS will catch on. For more details, see (Kaufman et al., 1995; Schneier, 1996; and Stinson, 1995).

Message Digests

One criticism of signature methods is that they often couple two distinct functions: authentication and secrecy. Often, authentication is needed but secrecy is not. Since cryptography is slow, it is frequently desirable to be able to send signed plaintext documents. Below we will describe an authentication scheme that does not require encrypting the entire message (De Jonge and Chaum, 1987).

This scheme is based on the idea of a one-way hash function that takes an arbitrarily long piece of plaintext and from it computes a fixed-length bit string. This hash function, often called a **message digest**, has three important properties:

1. Given P, it is easy to compute $MD(P)$.

2. Given $MD(P)$, it is effectively impossible to find P.

3. No one can generate two messages that have the same message digest.

To meet criterion 3, the hash should be at least 128 bits long, preferably more.

Computing a message digest from a piece of plaintext is much faster than encrypting that plaintext with a public-key algorithm, so message digests can be used to speed up digital signature algorithms. To see how this works, consider the signature protocol of Fig. 7-22 again. Instead of signing P with $K_{BB}(A, t, P)$, BB now computes the message digest by applying MD to P, yielding $MD(P)$. BB then encloses $K_{BB}(A, t, MD(P))$ as the fifth item in the list encrypted with K_B that is sent to Bob, instead of $K_{BB}(A, t, P)$.

If a dispute arises, Bob can produce both P and $K_{BB}(A, t, MD(P))$. After Big Brother has decrypted it for the judge, Bob has $MD(P)$, which is guaranteed to be genuine, and the alleged P. However, since it is effectively impossible for Bob to find any other message that gives this hash, the judge will easily be convinced that Bob is telling the truth. Using message digests in this way saves both encryption time and message transport and storage costs.

Message digests work in public-key cryptosystems, too, as shown in Fig. 7-24. Here, Alice first computes the message digest of her plaintext. She then signs the message digest and sends both the signed digest and the plaintext to Bob. If Trudy replaces P underway, Bob will see this when he computes $MD(P)$ himself.

Fig. 7-24. Digital signatures using message digests.

A variety of message digest functions have been proposed. The most widely used ones are MD5 (Rivest, 1992) and SHA (NIST, 1993). **MD5** is the fifth in a series of hash functions designed by Ron Rivest. It operates by mangling bits in a sufficiently complicated way that every output bit is affected by every input bit. Very briefly, it starts out by padding the message to a length of 448 bits (modulo 512). Then the original length of the message is appended as a 64-bit integer to give a total input whose length is a multiple of 512 bits. The last precomputation step is initializing a 128-bit buffer to a fixed value.

Now the computation starts. Each round takes a 512-bit block of input and mixes it thoroughly with the 128-bit buffer. For good measure, a table constructed from the sine function is also thrown in. The point of using a known function like the sine is not because it is more random than a random number generator, but to avoid any suspicion that the designer built in a clever trapdoor through which only he can enter. IBM's refusal to disclose the principles behind the design of the S-boxes in DES led to a great deal of speculation about trapdoors. Four rounds are performed per input block. This process continues until all the input blocks have been consumed. The contents of the 128-bit buffer form the message digest. The algorithm has been optimized for software implementation on 32-bit machines. As a consequence, it may not be fast enough for future high-speed networks (Touch, 1995).

The other major message digest function is **SHA (Secure Hash Algorithm)**, developed by NSA and blessed by NIST. Like MD5, it processes input data in 512-bit blocks, only unlike MD5, it generates a 160-bit message digest. It starts out by padding the message, then adding a 64-bit length to get a multiple of 512 bits. Then it initializes its 160-bit output buffer.

For each input block, the output buffer is updated using the 512-bit input block. No table of random numbers (or sine function values) is used, but for each block 80 rounds are computed, resulting in a thorough mixing. Each group of 20 rounds uses different mixing functions.

Since SHA's hash code is 32 bits longer than MD5's, all other things being equal, it is a factor of 2^{32} more secure than MD5. However, it is also slower than MD5, and having a hash code that is not a power of two might sometimes be an inconvenience. Otherwise, the two are roughly similar technically. Politically, MD5 is defined in an RFC and used heavily on the Internet. SHA is a government standard, and used by companies that have to use it because the government tells them to, or by those that want the extra security. A revised version, SHA-1, has been approved as a standard by NIST.

The Birthday Attack

In the world of crypto, nothing is ever what it seems to be. One might think that it would take on the order of 2^m operations to subvert an m-bit message digest. In fact, $2^{m/2}$ operations will often do using the **birthday attack,** an approach published by Yuval (1979) in his now-classic paper "How to Swindle Rabin."

The idea for this attack comes from a technique that math professors often use in their probability courses. The question is: How many students do you need in a class before the probability of having two people with the same birthday exceeds 1/2? Most students expect the answer to be way over 100. In fact, probability theory says it is just 23. Without giving a rigorous analysis, intuitively, with 23 people, we can form $(23 \times 22)/2 = 253$ different pairs, each of which has a probability of 1/365 of being a hit. In this light, it is not really so surprising any more.

More generally, if there is some mapping between inputs and outputs with n inputs (people, messages, etc.) and k possible outputs (birthdays, message digests, etc.), there are $n(n - 1)/2$ input pairs. If $n(n - 1)/2 > k$, the chance of having at least one match is pretty good. Thus, approximately, a match is likely for $n > \sqrt{k}$. This result means that a 64-bit message digest can probably be broken by generating about 2^{32} messages and looking for two with the same message digest.

Let us look at a practical example. The Dept. of Computer Science at State University has one position for a tenured faculty member and two candidates, Tom and Dick. Tom was hired two years before Dick, so he goes up for review first. If he gets it, Dick is out of luck. Tom knows that the department chairperson, Marilyn, thinks highly of his work, so he asks her to write him a letter of recommendation to the Dean, who will decide on Tom's case. Once sent, all letters become confidential.

Marilyn tells her secretary, Ellen, to write the Dean a letter, outlining what she wants in it. When it is ready, Marilyn will review it, compute and sign the 64-bit digest, and send it to the Dean. Ellen can send the letter later by email.

Unfortunately for Tom, Ellen is romantically involved with Dick and would like to do Tom in, so she writes the letter below with the 32 bracketed options.

Dear Dean Smith,

This [*letter* | *message*] is to give my [*honest* | *frank*] opinion of Prof. Tom Wilson, who is [*a candidate* | *up*] for tenure [*now* | *this year*]. I have [*known* | *worked with*] Prof. Wilson for [*about* | *almost*] six years. He is an [*outstanding* | *excellent*] researcher of great [*talent* | *ability*] known [*worldwide* | *internationally*] for his [*brilliant* | *creative*] insights into [*many* | *a wide variety of*] [*difficult* | *challenging*] problems.

He is also a [*highly* | *greatly*] [*respected* | *admired*] [*teacher* | *educator*]. His students give his [*classes* | *courses*] [*rave* | *spectacular*] reviews. He is [*our* | *the Department's*] [*most popular* | *best-loved*] [*teacher* | *instructor*].

[*In addition* | *Additionally*] Prof. Wilson is a [*gifted* | *effective*] fund raiser. His [*grants* | *contracts*] have brought a [*large* | *substantial*] amount of money into [*the* | *our*] Department. [*This money has* | *These funds have*] [*enabled* | *permitted*] us to [*pursue* | *carry out*] many [*special* | *important*] programs, [*such as* | *for example*] your State 2000 program. Without these funds we would [*be unable* | *not be able*] to continue this program, which is so [*important* | *essential*] to both of us. I strongly urge you to grant him tenure.

Unfortunately for Tom, as soon as Ellen finishes composing and typing in this letter, she also writes a second one:

Dear Dean Smith,

This [*letter* | *message*] is to give my [*honest* | *frank*] opinion of Prof. Tom Wilson, who is [*a candidate* | *up*] for tenure [*now* | *this year*]. I have [*known* | *worked with*] Tom for [*about* | *almost*] six years. He is a [*poor* | *weak*] researcher not well known in his [*field* | *area*]. His research [*hardly ever* | *rarely*] shows [*insight in* | *understanding of*] the [*key* | *major*] problems of [*the* | *our*] day.

Furthermore, he is not a [*respected* | *admired*] [*teacher* | *educator*]. His students give his [*classes* | *courses*] [*poor* | *bad*] reviews. He is [*our* | *the Department's*] least popular [*teacher* | *instructor*], known [*mostly* | *primarily*] within [*the* | *our*] Department for his [*tendency* | *propensity*] to [*ridicule* | *embarrass*] students [*foolish* | *imprudent*] enough to ask questions in his classes.

[*In addition* | *Additionally*] Tom is a [*poor* | *marginal*] fund raiser. His [*grants* | *contracts*] have brought only a [*meager* | *insignificant*] amount of money into [*the* | *our*] Department. Unless new [*money is* | *funds are*] quickly located, we may have to cancel some essential programs, such as your State 2000 program. Unfortunately, under these [*conditions* | *circumstances*] I cannot in good [*conscience* | *faith*] recommend him to you for [*tenure* | *a permanent position*].

Now Ellen sets up her computer to compute the 2^{32} message digests of each letter overnight. Chances are, one digest of the first letter will match one digest of the second letter. If not, she can add a few more options and try again during the weekend. Suppose that she finds a match. Call the "good" letter A and the "bad" one B.

Ellen now emails letter A to Marilyn for her approval. Marilyn, of course, approves, computes her 64-bit message digest, signs the digest, and emails the signed digest off to Dean Smith. Independently, Ellen emails letter B to the Dean.

After getting the letter and signed message digest, the Dean runs the message digest algorithm on letter B, sees that it agrees with what Marilyn sent him, and fires Tom. (Optional ending: Ellen tells Dick what she did. Dick is appalled and breaks off with her. Ellen is furious and confesses to Marilyn. Marilyn calls the Dean. Tom gets tenure after all.) With MD5 the birthday attack is infeasible because even at 1 billion digests per second, it would take over 500 years to compute all 2^{64} digests of two letters with 64 variants each, and even then a match is not guaranteed.

7.1.7. Social Issues

The implications of network security for individual privacy and society in general are staggering. Below we will just mention a few of the salient issues.

Governments do not like citizens keeping secrets from them. In some countries (e.g., France) all nongovernmental cryptography is simply forbidden unless the government is given all the keys being used. As Kahn (1980) and Selfridge and Schwartz (1980) point out, government eavesdropping has been practiced on a far more massive scale than most people could dream of, and governments want more than just a pile of indecipherable bits for their efforts.

The U.S. government has proposed an encryption scheme for future digital telephones that includes a special feature to allow the police to tap and decrypt all telephone calls made in the United States. The government promises not to use this feature without a court order, but many people still remember how former FBI Director J. Edgar Hoover illegally tapped the telephones of Martin Luther King, Jr. and other people in an attempt to neutralize them. The police say they need this power to catch criminals. The debate on both sides is vehement, to put it mildly. A discussion of the technology involved (Clipper) is given in (Kaufman et al., 1995). A way to circumvent this technology and send messages that the government cannot read is described in (Blaze, 1994; and Schneier, 1996). Position statements on all sides are given in (Hoffman, 1995).

The United States has a law (22 U.S.C. 2778) that prohibits citizens from exporting munitions (war materiel), such as tanks and jet fighters, without authorization from the DoD. For purposes of this law, cryptographic software is classified as a munition. Phil Zimmermann, who wrote PGP (Pretty Good Privacy), an email protection program, has been accused of violating this law, even though the government admits that he did not export it (but he did give it to a friend who put it on the Internet where foreigners could obtain it). Many people regarded this widely-publicized incident as a gross violation of the rights of an American citizen working to enhance people's privacy.

Not being an American does not help. On July 9, 1986, three Israeli researchers working at the Weizmann Institute in Israel filed a U.S. patent application for a new digital signature scheme that they had invented. They spent the next 6 months discussing their research at conferences all over the world. On Jan. 6, 1987, the U.S. patent office told them to notify all Americans who knew about their results that disclosure of the research would subject them to two years in prison, a 10,000-dollar fine, or both. The patent office also wanted a list of all foreign nationals who knew about the research. To find out how this story turned out, see (Landau, 1988).

Patents are another hot topic. Nearly all public-key algorithms are patented. Patent protection lasts for 17 years. The RSA patent, for example, expires on Sept. 20, 2000.

Network security is politicized to an extent few other technical issues are, and rightly so, since it relates to the difference between a democracy and a police state in the digital era. The March 1993 and November 1994 issues of *Communications of the ACM* have long sections on telephone and network security, respectively, with vigorous arguments explaining and defending many points of view. Chapter 25 of Schneier's security book deals with the politics of cryptography

(Schneier, 1996). Chapter 8 of his email book does too (Schneier, 1995). Privacy and computers are also discussed in (Adam, 1995). These references are highly recommended for readers who wish to pursue their study of this subject.

7.2. DNS—Domain Name System

Programs rarely refer to hosts, mailboxes, and other resources by their binary network addresses. Instead of binary numbers, they use ASCII strings, such as *tana@art.ucsb.edu*. Nevertheless, the network itself only understands binary addresses, so some mechanism is required to convert the ASCII strings to network addresses. In the following sections we will study how this mapping is accomplished in the Internet.

Way back in the ARPANET, there was simply a file, *hosts.txt*, that listed all the hosts and their IP addresses. Every night, all the hosts would fetch it from the site at which it was maintained. For a network of a few hundred large timesharing machines, this approach worked reasonably well.

However, when thousands of workstations were connected to the net, everyone realized that this approach could not continue to work forever. For one thing, the size of the file would become too large. However, even more important, host name conflicts would occur constantly unless names were centrally managed, something unthinkable in a huge international network. To solve these problems, **DNS** (the **Domain Name System**) was invented.

The essence of DNS is the invention of a hierarchical, domain-based naming scheme and a distributed database system for implementing this naming scheme. It is primarily used for mapping host names and email destinations to IP addresses but can also be used for other purposes. DNS is defined in RFCs 1034 and 1035.

Very briefly, the way DNS is used is as follows. To map a name onto an IP address, an application program calls a library procedure called the **resolver**, passing it the name as a parameter. The resolver sends a UDP packet to a local DNS server, which then looks up the name and returns the IP address to the resolver, which then returns it to the caller. Armed with the IP address, the program can then establish a TCP connection with the destination, or send it UDP packets.

7.2.1. The DNS Name Space

Managing a large and constantly changing set of names is a nontrivial problem. In the postal system, name management is done by requiring letters to specify (implicitly or explicitly) the country, state or province, city, and street address of the addressee. By using this kind of hierarchical addressing, there is no confusion between the Marvin Anderson on Main St. in White Plains, N.Y. and the Marvin Anderson on Main St. in Austin, Texas. DNS works the same way.

Conceptually, the Internet is divided into several hundred top-level **domains**, where each domain covers many hosts. Each domain is partitioned into sub-domains, and these are further partitioned, and so on. All these domains can be represented by a tree, as shown in Fig. 7-25. The leaves of the tree represent domains that have no subdomains (but do contain machines, of course) A leaf domain may contain a single host, or it may represent a company and contains thousands of hosts.

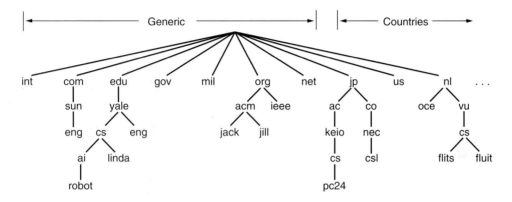

Fig. 7-25. A portion of the Internet domain name space.

The top-level domains come in two flavors: generic and countries. The generic domains are *com (commercial), edu* (educational institutions), *gov* (the U.S. federal government), *int* (certain international organizations), *mil* (the U.S. armed forces), *net* (network providers), and *org* (nonprofit organizations). The country domains include one entry for every country, as defined in ISO 3166.

Each domain is named by the path upward from it to the (unnamed) root. The components are separated by periods (pronounced "dot"). Thus Sun Microsystems engineering department might be *eng.sun.com.*, rather than a UNIX-style name such as */com/sun/eng*. Notice that this hierarchical naming means that *eng.sun.com.* does not conflict with a potential use of *eng* in *eng.yale.edu.*, which might be used by the Yale English department.

Domain names can be either absolute or relative. An absolute domain name ends with a period (e.g., *eng.sun.com.*), whereas a relative one does not. Relative names have to be interpreted in some context to uniquely determine their true meaning. In both cases, a named domain refers to a specific node in the tree and all the nodes under it.

Domain names are case insensitive, so *edu* and *EDU* mean the same thing. Component names can be up to 63 characters long, and full path names must not exceed 255 characters.

In principle, domains can be inserted into the tree in two different ways. For example, *cs.yale.edu* could equally well be listed under the *us* country domain as *cs.yale.ct.us*. In practice, however, nearly all organizations in the United States are under a generic domain, and nearly all outside the United States are under the domain of their country. There is no rule against registering under two top-level domains, but doing so might be confusing, so few organizations do it.

Each domain controls how it allocates the domains under it. For example, Japan has domains *ac.jp* and *co.jp* that mirror *edu* and *com*. The Netherlands does not make this distinction and puts all organizations directly under *nl*. Thus all three of the following are university computer science departments:

1. *cs.yale.edu* (Yale University, in the United States)

2. *cs.vu.nl* (Vrije Universiteit, in The Netherlands)

3. *cs.keio.ac.jp* (Keio University, in Japan)

To create a new domain, permission is required of the domain in which it will be included. For example, if a VLSI group is started at Yale and wants to be known as *vlsi.cs.yale.edu*, it needs permission from whomever manages *cs.yale.edu*. Similarly, if a new university is chartered, say, the University of Northern South Dakota, it must ask the manager of the *edu* domain to assign it *unsd.edu*. In this way, name conflicts are avoided and each domain can keep track of all its subdomains. Once a new domain has been created and registered, it can create subdomains, such as *cs.unsd.edu*, without getting permission from anybody higher up the tree.

Naming follows organizational boundaries, not physical networks. For example, if the computer science and electrical engineering departments are located in the same building and share the same LAN, they can nevertheless have distinct domains. Similarly, even if computer science is split over Babbage Hall and Turing Hall, all the hosts in both buildings will normally belong to the same domain.

7.2.2. Resource Records

Every domain, whether it is a single host or a top-level domain, can have a set of **resource records** associated with it. For a single host, the most common resource record is just its IP address, but many other kinds of resource records also exist. When a resolver gives a domain name to DNS, what it gets back are the resource records associated with that name. Thus the real function of DNS is to map domain names onto resource records.

A resource record is a five-tuple. Although they are encoded in binary for efficiency, in most expositions resource records are presented as ASCII text, one line per resource record. The format we will use is as follows:

Domain_name   Time_to_live   Type   Class   Value

The *Domain_name* tells the domain to which this record applies. Normally, many records exist for each domain and each copy of the database holds information about multiple domains. This field is thus the primary search key used to satisfy queries. The order of the records in the database is not significant. When a query is made about a domain, all the matching records of the class requested are returned.

The *Time_to_live* field gives an indication of how stable the record is. Information that is highly stable is assigned a large value, such as 86400 (the number of seconds in 1 day). Information that is highly volatile is assigned a small value, such as 60 (1 minute). We will come back to this point later when we have discussed caching.

The *Type* field tells what kind of record this is. The most important types are listed in Fig. 7-26.

Type	Meaning	Value
SOA	Start of Authority	Parameters for this zone
A	IP address of a host	32-Bit integer
MX	Mail exchange	Priority, domain willing to accept email
NS	Name Server	Name of a server for this domain
CNAME	Canonical name	Domain name
PTR	Pointer	Alias for an IP address
HINFO	Host description	CPU and OS in ASCII
TXT	Text	Uninterpreted ASCII text

Fig. 7-26. The principal DNS resource record types.

An *SOA* record provides the name of the primary source of information about the name server's zone (described below), the email address of its administrator, a unique serial number, and various flags and timeouts.

The most important record type is the *A* (Address) record. It holds a 32-bit IP address for some host. Every Internet host must have at least one IP address, so other machines can communicate with it. Some hosts have two or more network connections, in which case they will have one type *A* resource record per network connection (and thus per IP address).

The next most important record type is the *MX* record. It specifies the name of the domain prepared to accept email for the specified domain. A common use of this record is to allow a machine that is not on the Internet to receive email from Internet sites. Delivery is accomplished by having the non-Internet site make an arrangement with some Internet site to accept email for it and forward it using whatever protocol the two of them agree on.

For example, suppose that Cathy is a computer science graduate student at UCLA. After she gets her degree in AI, she sets up a company, Electrobrain

Corporation, to commercialize her ideas. She cannot afford an Internet connection yet, so she makes an arrangement with UCLA to allow her to have her email sent there. A few times a day she will call up and collect it.

Next, she registers her company with the *com* domain and is assigned the domain *electrobrain.com*. She might then ask the administrator of the *com* domain to add an *MX* record to the *com* database as follows:

electrobrain.com   86400   IN   MX   1   mailserver.cs.ucla.edu

In this way, mail will be forwarded to UCLA where she can pick it up by logging in. Alternatively, UCLA could call her and transfer the email by any protocol they mutually agree on.

The *NS* records specify name servers. For example, every DNS database normally has an *NS* record for each of the top-level domains, so email can be sent to distant parts of the naming tree. We will come back to this point later.

CNAME records allow aliases to be created. For example, a person familiar with Internet naming in general wanting to send a message to someone whose login name is *paul* in the computer science department at M.I.T. might guess that *paul@cs.mit.edu* will work. Actually this address will not work, because the domain for M.I.T.'s computer science department is *lcs.mit.edu*. However, as a service to people who do not know this, M.I.T. could create a *CNAME* entry to point people and programs in the right direction. An entry like this one might do the job:

cs.mit.edu   86400   IN   CNAME   lcs.mit.edu

Like *CNAME*, *PTR* points to another name. However, unlike *CNAME*, which is really just a macro definition, *PTR* is a regular DNS datatype whose interpretation depends on the context in which it is found. In practice, it is nearly always used to associate a name with an IP address to allow lookups of the IP address and return the name of the corresponding machine.

HINFO records allow people to find out what kind of machine and operating system a domain corresponds to. Finally, *TXT* records allow domains to identify themselves in arbitrary ways. Both of these record types are for user convenience. Neither is required, so programs cannot count on getting them (and probably cannot deal with them if they do get them).

Getting back to the general structure of resource records, the fourth field of every resource record is the *Class*. For Internet information, it is always *IN*. For non-Internet information, other codes can be used.

Finally, we come to the *Value* field. This field can be a number, a domain name, or an ASCII string. The semantics depend on the record type. A short description of the *Value* fields for each of the principal records types is given in Fig. 7-26.

As an example of the kind of information one might find in the DNS database of a domain, see Fig. 7-27. This figure depicts part of a (semihypothetical) database for the *cs.vu.nl* domain shown in Fig. 7-25. The database contains seven types of resource records.

```
; Authoritative data for cs.vu.nl
cs.vu.nl.          86400   IN   SOA     star boss (952771,7200,7200,2419200,86400)
cs.vu.nl.          86400   IN   TXT     "Faculteit Wiskunde en Informatica."
cs.vu.nl.          86400   IN   TXT     "Vrije Universiteit Amsterdam."
cs.vu.nl.          86400   IN   MX      1 zephyr.cs.vu.nl.
cs.vu.nl.          86400   IN   MX      2 top.cs.vu.nl.

flits.cs.vu.nl.    86400   IN   HINFO   Sun Unix
flits.cs.vu.nl.    86400   IN   A       130.37.16.112
flits.cs.vu.nl.    86400   IN   A       192.31.231.165
flits.cs.vu.nl.    86400   IN   MX      1 flits.cs.vu.nl.
flits.cs.vu.nl.    86400   IN   MX      2 zephyr.cs.vu.nl.
flits.cs.vu.nl.    86400   IN   MX      3 top.cs.vu.nl.
www.cs.vu.nl.      86400   IN   CNAME   star.cs.vu.nl
ftp.cs.vu.nl.      86400   IN   CNAME   zephyr.cs.vu.nl

rowboat                    IN   A       130.37.56.201
                           IN   MX      1 rowboat
                           IN   MX      2 zephyr
                           IN   HINFO   Sun Unix

little-sister              IN   A       130.37.62.23
                           IN   HINFO   Mac MacOS

laserjet                   IN   A       192.31.231.216
                           IN   HINFO   "HP Laserjet IIISi" Proprietary
```

Fig. 7-27. A portion of a possible DNS database for *cs.vu.nl*

The first noncomment line of Fig. 7-27 gives some basic information about the domain, which will not concern us further. The next two lines give textual information about where the domain is located. Then come two entries giving the first and second places to try to deliver email sent to *person@cs.vu.nl*. The *zephyr* (a specific machine) should be tried first. If that fails, the *top* should be tried next.

After the blank line, added for readability, come lines telling that the *flits* is a Sun workstation running UNIX and giving both of its IP addresses. Then three choices are given for handling email sent to *flits.cs.vu.nl*. First choice is naturally the *flits* itself, but if it is down, the *zephyr* and *top* are the second and third choices. Next comes an alias, *www.cs.vu.nl*, so that this address can be used without designating a specific machine. Creating this alias allows *cs.vu.nl* to change its World Wide Web server without invalidating the address people use to get to it. A similar argument holds for *ftp.cs.vu.nl*.

The next four lines contain a typical entry for a workstation, in this case, *rowboat.cs.vu.nl*. The information provided contains the IP address, the primary and secondary mail drops, and information about the machine. Then comes an entry for a non-UNIX system that is not capable of receiving mail itself, followed by an entry for a laser printer.

What is not shown (and is not in this file), are the IP addresses to use to look up the top level domains. These are needed to look up distant hosts, but since they are not part of the *cs.vu.nl* domain, they are not in this file. They are supplied by the root servers, whose IP addresses are present in a system configuration file and loaded into the DNS cache when the DNS server is booted. They have very long timeouts, so once loaded, they are never purged from the cache.

7.2.3. Name Servers

In theory at least, a single name server could contain the entire DNS database and respond to all queries about it. In practice, this server would be so overloaded as to be useless. Furthermore, if it ever went down, the entire Internet would be crippled.

To avoid the problems associated with having only a single source of information, the DNS name space is divided up into nonoverlapping **zones**. One possible way to divide up the name space of Fig. 7-25 is shown in Fig. 7-28. Each zone contains some part of the tree and also contains name servers holding the authoritative information about that zone. Normally, a zone will have one primary name server, which gets its information from a file on its disk, and one or more secondary name servers, which get their information from the primary name server. To improve reliability, some servers for a zone can be located outside the zone.

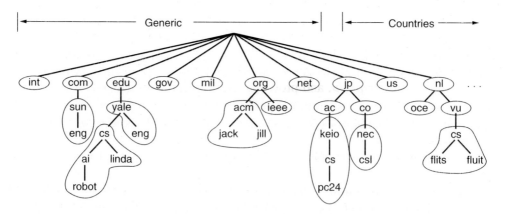

Fig. 7-28. Part of the DNS name space showing the division into zones.

Where the zone boundaries are placed within a zone is up to that zone's administrator. This decision is made in large part based on how many name servers are desired, and where. For example, in Fig. 7-28, Yale has a server for *yale.edu* that handles *eng.yale.edu* but not *cs.yale.edu*, which is a separate zone with its own name servers. Such a decision might be made when a department such as English does not wish to run its own name server, but a department such as computer science does. Consequently, *cs.yale.edu* is a separate zone but *eng.yale.edu* is not.

When a resolver has a query about a domain name, it passes the query to one of the local name servers. If the domain being sought falls under the jurisdiction of the name server, such as *ai.cs.yale.edu* falling under *cs.yale.edu*, it returns the authoritative resource records. An **authoritative record** is one that comes from the authority that manages the record, and is thus always correct. Authoritative records are in contrast to cached records, which may be out of date.

If, however, the domain is remote and no information about the requested domain is available locally, the name server sends a query message to the top-level name server for the domain requested. To make this process clearer, con-sider the example of Fig. 7-29. Here, a resolver on *flits.cs.vu.nl* wants to know the IP address of the host *linda.cs.yale.edu*. In step 1, it sends a query to the local name server, *cs.vu.nl*. This query contains the domain name sought, the type (*A*) and the class (*IN*).

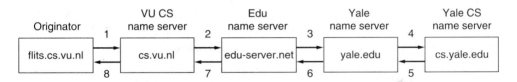

Fig. 7-29. How a resolver looks up a remote name in eight steps.

Let us suppose the local name server has never had a query for this domain before and knows nothing about it. It may ask a few other nearby name servers, but if none of them know, it sends a UDP packet to the server for *edu* given in its database (see Fig. 7-29), *edu-server.net*. It is unlikely that this server knows the address of *linda.cs.yale.edu*, and probably does not know *cs.yale.edu* either, but it must know all of its own children, so it forwards the request to the name server for *yale.edu* (step 3). In turn, this one forwards the request to *cs.yale.edu* (step 4), which must have the authoritative resource records. Since each request is from a client to a server, the resource record requested works its way back in steps 5 through 8.

Once these records get back to the *cs.vu.nl* name server, they will be entered into a cache there, in case they are needed later. However, this information is not authoritative, since changes made at *cs.yale.edu* will not be propagated to all the caches in the world that may know about it. For this reason, cache entries should not live too long. This is the reason that the *Time_to_live* field is included in each resource record. It tells remote name servers how long to cache records. If a certain machine has had the same IP address for years, it may be safe to cache that information for 1 day. For more volatile information, it might be safer to purge the records after a few seconds or a minute.

It is worth mentioning that the query method described here is known as a **recursive query**, since each server that does not have the requested information goes and finds it somewhere, then reports back. An alternative form is also possible. In this form, when a query cannot be satisfied locally, the query fails, but the name of the next server along the line to try is returned. This procedure gives the client more control over the search process. Some servers do not implement recursive queries and always return the name of the next server to try.

It is also worth pointing out that when a DNS client fails to get a response before its timer goes off, it normally will try another server next time. The assumption here is that the server is probably down, rather than the request or reply got lost.

7.3. SNMP—SIMPLE NETWORK MANAGEMENT PROTOCOL

In the early days of the ARPANET, if the delay to some host became unexpectedly large, the person detecting the problem would just run the Ping program to bounce a packet off the destination. By looking at the timestamps in the header of the packet returned, the location of the problem could usually be pinpointed and some appropriate action taken. In addition, the number of routers was so small, that it was feasible to ping each one to see if it was sick.

When the ARPANET turned into the worldwide Internet, with multiple backbones and multiple operators, this solution ceased to be adequate, so better tools for network management were needed. Two early attempts were defined in RFC 1028 and RFC 1067, but these were short lived. In May 1990, RFC 1157 was published, defining version 1 of **SNMP** (**Simple Network Management Protocol**). Along with a companion document (RFC 1155) on management information, SNMP provided a systematic way of monitoring and managing a computer network. This framework and protocol were widely implemented in commercial products and became the de facto standards for network management.

As experience was gained, shortcomings in SNMP came to light, so an enhanced version of SNMP (SNMPv2) was defined (in RFCs 1441 to 1452) and started along the road to become an Internet standard. In the sections to follow, we will give a brief discussion of the SNMP (meaning SNMPv2) model and protocol.

Although SNMP was designed with the idea of its being simple, at least one author has managed to produce a 600-page book on it (Stallings, 1993a). For more compact descriptions (450-550 pages), see the books by Rose (1994) and Rose and McCloghrie (1995), both of whom were among the designers of SNMP. Other references are (Feit, 1995; and Hein and Griffiths, 1995).

7.3.1. The SNMP Model

The SNMP model of a managed network consists of four components:

1. Managed nodes.

2. Management stations.

3. Management information.

4. A management protocol.

These pieces are illustrated in Fig. 7-30 and discussed below.

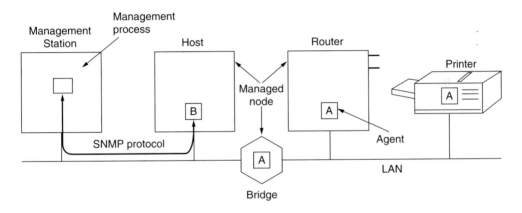

Fig. 7-30. Components of the SNMP management model.

The managed nodes can be hosts, routers, bridges, printers, or any other devices capable of communicating status information to the outside world. To be managed directly by SNMP, a node must be capable of running an SNMP management process, called an **SNMP agent**. All computers meet this requirement, as do increasingly many bridges, routers, and peripheral devices designed for network use. Each agent maintains a local database of variables that describe its state and history and affect its operation.

Network management is done from **management stations**, which are, in fact, general-purpose computers running special management software. The management stations contain one or more processes that communicate with the agents over the network, issuing commands and getting responses. In this design, all the intelligence is in the management stations, in order to keep the agents as simple as possible and minimize their impact on the devices they are running on. Many management stations have a graphical user interface to allow the network manager to inspect the status of the network and take action when required.

Most real networks are multivendor, with hosts from one or more manufacturers, bridges and routers from other companies, and printers from still other ones.

In order to allow a management station (potentially from yet another supplier) to talk to all these diverse components, the nature of the information maintained by all the devices must be rigidly specified. Having the management station ask a router what its packet loss rate is of no use if the router does not keep track of its loss rate. Therefore, SNMP describes (in excruciating detail) the exact information each kind of agent has to maintain and the format it has to supply it in. The largest portion of the SNMP model is the definition of who has to keep track of what and how this information is communicated.

Very briefly, each device maintains one or more variables that describe its state. In the SNMP literature, these variables are called **objects**, but the term is misleading because they are not objects in the sense of an object-oriented system because they just have state and no methods (other than reading and writing their values). Nevertheless, the term is so ingrained (e.g., used in various reserved words in the specification language used) that we will use it here. The collection of all possible objects in a network is given in a data structure called the **MIB** (**Management Information Base**).

The management station interacts with the agents using the SNMP protocol. This protocol allows the management station to query the state of an agent's local objects, and change them if necessary. Most of SNMP consists of this query-response type communication.

However, sometimes events happen that are not planned. Managed nodes can crash and reboot, lines can go down and come back up, congestion can occur, and so on. Each significant event is defined in a MIB module. When an agent notices that a significant event has occurred, it immediately reports the event to all management stations in its configuration list. This report is called an SNMP **trap** (for historical reasons). The report usually just states that some event has occurred. It is up to the management station to then issue queries to find out all the gory details. Because communication from managed nodes to the management station is not reliable (i.e., is not acknowledged), it is wise for the management station to poll each managed node occasionally anyway, checking for unusual events, just in case. The model of polling at long intervals with acceleration on receipt of a trap is called **trap directed polling**.

This model assumes that each managed node is capable of running an SNMP agent internally. Older devices or devices not originally intended for use on a network may not have this capability. To handle them, SNMP defines what is called a **proxy agent**, namely an agent that watches over one or more nonSNMP devices and communicates with the management station on their behalf, possibly communicating with the devices themselves using some nonstandard protocol.

Finally, security and authentication play a major role in SNMP. A management station has the capability of learning a great deal about every node under its control and also has the capability of shutting them all down. Hence it is of great importance that agents be convinced that queries allegedly coming from the management station, in fact, come from the management station. In SNMPv1, the management station proved who it was by putting a (plaintext) password in each message. In SNMPv2, security was improved considerably using modern crypto-graphic techniques of the type we have already studied. However, this addition made an already bulky protocol every bulkier, and it was later thrown out.

7.3.2. ASN.1—Abstract Syntax Notation 1

The heart of the SNMP model is the set of objects managed by the agents and read and written by the management station. To make multivendor communication possible, it is essential that these objects be defined in a standard and vendor-neutral way. Furthermore, a standard way is needed to encode them for transfer over a network. While definitions in C would satisfy the first require-ment, such definitions do not define a bit encoding on the wire in such a way that a 32-bit two's complement little endian management station can exchange infor-mation unambiguously with an agent on a 16-bit one's complement big endian CPU.

For this reason, a standard object definition language, along with encoding rules, is needed. The one used by SNMP is taken from OSI and called **ASN.1** (**Abstract Syntax Notation One**). Like much of OSI, it is large, complex, and not especially efficient. (The author is tempted to say that by calling it ASN.1 instead of just ASN, the designers implicitly admitted that it would soon be replaced by ASN.2, but he will politely refrain from saying this.) The one alleged strength of ASN.1 (the existence of unambiguous bit encoding rules) is now really a weakness, because the encoding rules are optimized to minimize the number of bits on the wire, at the cost of wasting CPU time at both ends encoding and decoding them. A simpler scheme, using 32-bit integers aligned on 4-byte boun-daries would probably have been better. Nevertheless, for better or worse, SNMP is drenched in ASN.1, (albeit a simplified subset of it), so anyone wishing to truly understand SNMP must become fluent in ASN.1. Hence the following explana-tion.

Let us start with the data description language, described in International Standard 8824. After that we will discuss the encoding rules, described in Inter-national Standard 8825. The ASN.1 abstract syntax is essentially a primitive data declaration language. It allows the user to define primitive objects and then com-bine them into more complex ones. A series of declarations in ASN.1 is function-ally similar to the declarations found in the header files associated with many C programs.

SNMP has some lexical conventions that we will follow. These are not entirely the same as pure ASN.1 uses, however. Built-in data types are written in uppercase (e.g., *INTEGER*). User-defined types begin with an uppercase letter but must contain at least one character other than an uppercase letter. Identifiers may contain upper and lowercase letters, digits, and hyphens, but must begin with a lowercase letter (e.g., *counter*). White space (tabs, carriage returns, etc.) is not significant. Finally, comments start with -- and continue until the end of the line or the next occurrence of --.

The ASN.1 basic data types allowed in SNMP are shown in Fig. 7-31. (We will generally ignore features of ASN.1, such as *BOOLEAN* and *REAL* types, not permitted in SNMP.) The use of the codes will be described later.

Primitive type	Meaning	Code
INTEGER	Arbitrary length integer	2
BIT STRING	A string of 0 or more bits	3
OCTET STRING	A string of 0 of more unsigned bytes	4
NULL	A place holder	5
OBJECT IDENTIFIER	An officially defined data type	6

Fig. 7-31. The ASN.1 primitive data types permitted in SNMP.

A variable of type *INTEGER* may, in theory, take on any integral value, but other SNMP rules limit the range. As an example of how types are used, consider how a variable, *count*, of type *INTEGER* would be declared and (optionally) initialized to 100 in ASN.1:

count INTEGER ::= 100

Often a subtype whose variables are restricted to specific values or to a specific range is required. These can be declared as follows:

Status ::= INTEGER { up(1), down(2), unknown(3) }

PacketSize ::= INTEGER (0..1023)

Variables of type *BIT STRING* and *OCTET STRING* contain zero or more bits and bytes, respectively. A bit is either 0 or 1. A byte falls in the range 0 to 255, inclusive. For both types, a string length and an initial value may be given.

*OBJECT IDENTIFIER*s provide a way of identifying objects. In principle, every object defined in every official standard can be uniquely identified. The mechanism that is used is to define a standards tree, and place every object in every standard at a unique location in the tree. The portion of the tree that includes the SNMP MIB is shown in Fig. 7-32.

The top level of the tree lists all the important standards organizations in the world (in ISO's view), namely ISO and CCITT (now ITU), plus the combination of the two. From the *iso* node, four arcs are defined, one of which is for *identified-organization*, which is ISO's concession that maybe some other folks are vaguely involved with standards, too. The U.S. Dept. of Defense has been assigned a place in this subtree, and DoD has assigned the Internet number 1 in its hierarchy. Under the Internet hierarchy, the SNMP MIB has code 1.

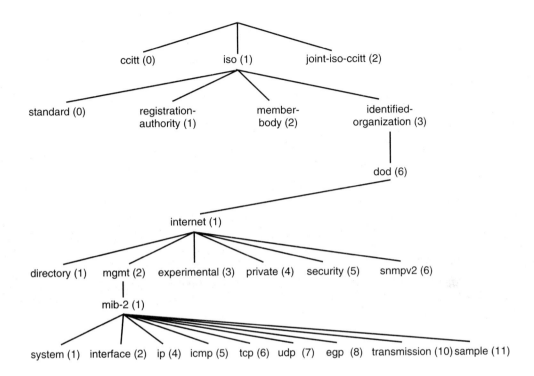

Fig. 7-32. Part of the ASN.1 object naming tree.

Every arc in Fig. 7-32 has both a label and a number, so nodes can be identified by a list of arcs, using label(number) or numbers. Thus all SNMP MIB objects are identified by a label of the form

{iso identified-organization(3) dod(6) internet(1) mgmt(2) mib-2(1) ...}

or alternatively {1 3 6 1 2 1 ...}. Mixed forms are also permitted. For example, the above identification can also be written as

{internet(1) 2 1 ...}

In this way, every object in every standard can be represented as an *OBJECT IDENTIFIER*.

ASN.1 defines five ways to construct new types from the basic ones. *SEQUENCE* is an ordered list of types, similar to a structure in C and a record in Pascal. *SEQUENCE OF* is a one-dimensional array of a single type. *SET* and *SET OF* are analogous, but unordered. *CHOICE* creates a union from a given list of types. The two set constructors are not used in any of the SNMP documents.

Another way to create new types is to tag old ones. Tagging a type is somewhat similar to the practice in C of defining new types, say *time_t* and *size_t*, both of which are longs, but which are used in different contexts. Tags come in four categories: universal, application-wide, context-specific and private. Each tag consists of a label and an integer identifying the tag. For example,

Counter32 ::= [APPLICATION 1] INTEGER (0..4294967295)

Gauge32   ::= [APPLICATION 2] INTEGER (0..4294967295)

define two different application-wide types, both of which are implemented by 32-bit unsigned integers, but which are conceptually different. The former might, for example, wrap around when it gets to the maximum value, whereas the latter might just continue to return the maximum value until its is decreased or reset.

A tagged type can have the keyword *IMPLICIT* after the closing square bracket when the type of what follows is obvious from the context (not true in a *CHOICE*, for example). Doing so allows a more efficient bit encoding since the tag does not have to be transmitted. In a type involving a *CHOICE* between two different types, a tag must be transmitted to tell the receiver which type is present.

ASN.1 defines a complex macro mechanism, which is heavily used in SNMP. A macro can be used as a kind of prototype to generate a set of new types and values, each with its own syntax. Each macro defines some (possibly optional) keywords, that are used in the call to identify which parameter is which (i.e., the macro parameters are identified by keyword, not by position). The details of how ASN.1 macros work is beyond the scope of this book. Suffice it to say that a macro is invoked by giving its name and then listing (some of) its keywords and their values for this invocation. Macros are expanded at compile time, not at run time. Some examples of macros will be cited below.

ASN.1 Transfer Syntax

An ASN.1 **transfer syntax** defines how values of ASN.1 types are unambiguously converted to a sequence of bytes for transmission (and unambiguously decoded at the other end). The transfer syntax used by ASN.1 is called **BER** (**Basic Encoding Rules**). ASN.1 has other transfer syntaxes that SNMP does not use. The rules are recursive, so the encoding of a structured object is just the concatenation of the encodings of the component objects. In this way, all object encodings can be reduced to a well-defined sequence of encoded primitive objects. The encoding of these objects, in turn, is defined by the BER.

The guiding principle behind the basic encoding rules is that every value transmitted, both primitive and constructed ones, consists of up to four fields:

1. The identifier (type or tag).

2. The length of the data field, in bytes.

3. The data field.

4. The end-of-contents flag, if the data length is unknown.

The last one is permitted by ASN.1, but specifically forbidden by SNMP, so we will assume the data length is always known.

The first field identifies the item that follows. It, itself, has three subfields, as shown in Fig. 7-33. The high-order 2 bits identify the tag type. The next bit tells whether the value is primitive (0) or not (1). The tag bits are 00, 01, 10, and 11, for *UNIVERSAL*, *APPLICATION*, context-specific, and *PRIVATE*, respectively. The remaining 5 bits can be used to encode the value of the tag if it is in the range 0 through 30. If the tag is 31 or more, the low-order 5 bits contain 11111, with the true value in the next byte or bytes.

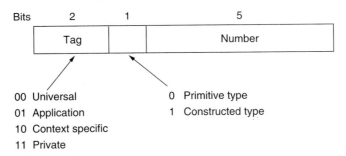

Fig. 7-33. The first byte of each data item sent in the ASN.1 transfer syntax.

The rule used to encode tags greater than 30 has been designed to handle arbitrarily large numbers. Each identifier byte following the first one contains 7 data bits. The high-order bit is set to 0 in all but the last one. Thus tag values up to $2^7 - 1$ can be handled in 2 bytes, and up to $2^{14} - 1$ can be handled in 3 bytes.

The encoding of the *UNIVERSAL* types is straightforward. Each primitive type has been assigned a code, as given in the third column of Fig. 7-31. *SEQUENCE* and *SEQUENCE OF* share code 16. *CHOICE* does not have a code, since any actual value sent always has a specific type. The other codes are for types not used in SNMP.

Following the 1-byte identifier field comes a field telling how many bytes the data occupy. Lengths shorter than 128 bytes are directly encoded in 1 byte whose leftmost bit is 0. Those that are longer use multiple bytes, with first byte containing a 1 in the high-order bit and the length field (up to 127 bytes) in the low-order 7 bits. For example, if the data length is 1000 bytes, the first byte contains 130 to indicate a two byte length field follows. Then come two bytes whose value is 1000, with the high-order byte first.

The encoding of the data field depends on the type of data present. Integers are encoded in two's complement. A positive integer below 128 requires 1 byte, a positive integer below 32,768 requires 2 bytes, and so forth. The most significant byte is transmitted first.

Bit strings are encoded as themselves. The only problem is how to indicate the length. The length field tells how many *bytes* the value has, not how many *bits*. The solution chosen is to transmit 1 byte before the actual bit string telling how many bits (0 through 7) of the final byte are unused. Thus the encoding of the 9-bit string ′010011111′ would be 07, 4F, 80 (hexadecimal).

Octet strings are easy. The bytes of the string are just transmitted in standard big endian style, left to right.

The null value is indicated by setting the length field to 0. No numerical value is actually transmitted.

An *OBJECT IDENTIFIER* is encoded as the sequence of integers it represents. For example, the Internet is {1, 3, 6, 1}. However, since the first number is always 0, 1, or 2, and the second is less than 40 (by definition—ISO simply will not recognize the 41st category to show up on its doorstep), the first two numbers, *a and b*, are encoded as 1 byte having the value $40a + b$. For the Internet, this number is 43. As usual, numbers exceeding 127 are encoded in multiple bytes, the first of which contains the high-order bit set to 1 and a byte count in the other 7 bits.

Both sequence types are transmitted by first sending the type or tag, then the total length of the encoding for all the fields, followed by the fields themselves. The fields are sent in order.

The encoding of a *CHOICE* value is the same as the encoding of the actual data structure being transferred.

An example showing encoding of some values is given in Fig. 7-34. The values encoded are the *INTEGER* 49, the *OCTET STRING* ′110′, ″xy″, the only possible value for *NULL*, the *OBJECT IDENTIFIER* for the Internet {1, 3, 6, 1}, and a *Gauge32* value of 14.

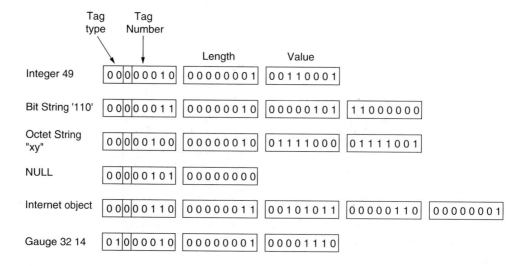

Fig. 7-34. ASN.1 encoding of some example values.

7.3.3. SMI—Structure of Management Information

In the preceding section, we have discussed only those parts of ASN.1 that are used in SNMP. In reality, the SNMP documents are organized differently. RFC 1442 first says that ASN.1 will be used to describe SNMP data structures, then it goes on for 57 pages scratching out parts of the ASN.1 standard that it does not want and adding new definitions (in ASN.1) that are needed. In particular, RFC 1442 defines four key macros and eight new data types that are heavily used throughout SNMP. It is this sub-super-set of ASN.1, which goes by the ungainly name of **SMI (Structure of Management Information)**, that is really used to define the SNMP data structures.

Although this approach is somewhat bureaucratic, some rules and regulations are necessary if products from hundreds of vendors are expected to talk to one another and actually understand what the others are saying. A few words about SMI are therefore now in order.

At the lowest level, SNMP variables are defined as individual objects. Related objects are collected together into groups, and groups are assembled into modules. For example, groups exist for IP objects and TCP objects. A router might support the IP group, since its manager cares about how many packets it has lost. On the other hand, a low-end router might not support the TCP group, since it need not use TCP to perform its routing functions. It is the intention that vendors supporting a group support all the objects in that group. However, a vendor supporting a module need not support all of its groups, since not all may be applicable to the device.

All MIB modules start with an invocation of the *MODULE-IDENTITY* macro. Its parameters provide the name and address of the implementer, the revision history, and other administrative information. Typically, this call is followed by an invocation of the *OBJECT-IDENTITY* macro, which tells where the module fits in the naming tree of Fig. 7-32.

Later on come one or more invocations of the *OBJECT-TYPE* macro, which name the actual variables being managed and specify their properties. Grouping variables into groups is done by convention; there are no *BEGIN-GROUP* and *END-GROUP* statements in ASN.1 or SMI.

The *OBJECT-TYPE* macro has four required parameters and four (sometimes) optional ones. The first required parameter is *SYNTAX* and defines the variable's data type from among the types listed in Fig. 7-35. For the most part, these types should be self explanatory, with the following comments. The suffix 32 is used when the implementer really wants a 32-bit number, even if all the machines in sight have 64-bit CPUs. Gauges differ from counters in that they do not wrap around when they hit their limits. They stick there. If a router has lost exactly 2^{32} packets, it is better to report this as $2^{32} - 1$ than as 0. SMI also supports arrays, but we will not go into those here. For details, see (Rose, 1994).

In addition to requiring a specification of the data type used by the variable

Name	Type	Bytes	Meaning
INTEGER	Numeric	4	Integer (32 bits in current implementations)
Counter32	Numeric	4	Unsigned 32-bit counter that wraps
Gauge32	Numeric	4	Unsigned value that does not wrap
Integer32	Numeric	4	32 Bits, even on a 64-bit CPU
UInteger32	Numeric	4	Like Integer32, but unsigned
Counter64	Numeric	8	A 64-bit counter
TimeTicks	Numeric	4	In hundredths of a second since some epoch
BIT STRING	String	4	Bit map of 1 to 32 bits
OCTET STRING	String	≥ 0	Variable length byte string
Opaque	String	≥ 0	Obsolete; for backward compatibility only
OBJECT IDENTIFIER	String	>0	A list of integers from Fig. 7-32
IpAddress	String	4	A dotted decimal Internet address
NsapAddress	String	< 22	An OSI NSAP address

Fig. 7-35. Data types used for SNMP monitored variables.

being declared, the *OBJECT TYPE* macro also requires three other parameters. *MAX-ACCESS* contains information about the variable's access. The most common values are read-write and read-only. If a variable is read-write, the management station can set it. If it is read-only, the management station can read it but cannot set it.

The *STATUS* has three possible values. A current variable is conformant with the current SNMP specification. An obsolete variable is not conformant but was conformant with an older version. A deprecated variable is in between. It is really obsolete, but the committee that wrote the standard did not dare say this in public for fear of the reaction from vendors whose products use it. Nevertheless, the handwriting is on the wall.

The last required parameter is *DESCRIPTION*, which is an ASCII string telling what the variable does. If a manager buys a nice new shiny device, queries it from the management station, and discovers that it keeps track of *pktCnt*, fetching the *DESCRIPTION* field is supposed to give a clue as to what kind of packets it is counting. This field is intended exclusively for human (as opposed to computer) consumption.

A simple example of an *OBJECT TYPE* declaration is given in Fig. 7-36. The variable is called *lostPackets* and might be useful in a router or other device dealing with packets. The value after the ::= sign places it in the tree.

```
lostPackets OBJECT TYPE
    SYNTAX Counter32          -- use a 32-bit counter
    MAX-ACCESS read-only      -- the management station may not change it
    STATUS current            -- this variable is not obsolete (yet)
    DESCRIPTION
        "The number of packets lost since the last boot"
    ::= {experimental 20}
```

Fig. 7-36. An example SNMP variable.

7.3.4. The MIB—Management Information Base

The collection of objects managed by SNMP is defined in the MIB. For convenience, these objects are (currently) grouped into ten categories, which correspond to the ten nodes under *mib-2* in Fig. 7-32. (Note that *mib-2* corresponds to SNMPv2 and that object 9 is no longer present.) The ten categories are intended to provide a basis of what a management station should understand. New categories and objects will certainly be added in the future, and vendors are free to define additional objects for their products. The ten categories are summarized in Fig. 7-37.

Group	# Objects	Description
System	7	Name, location, and description of the equipment
Interfaces	23	Network interfaces and their measured traffic
AT	3	Address translation (deprecated)
IP	42	IP packet statistics
ICMP	26	Statistics about ICMP messages received
TCP	19	TCP algorithms, parameters, and statistics
UDP	6	UDP traffic statistics
EGP	20	Exterior gateway protocol traffic statistics
Transmission	0	Reserved for media-specific MIBs
SNMP	29	SNMP traffic statistics

Fig. 7-37. The object groups of the Internet MIB-II.

Although space limitations prevent us from delving into the details of all 175 objects defined in MIB-II, a few comments may be helpful. The system group allows the manager to find out what the device is called, who made it, what hardware and software it contains, where it is located, and what it is supposed to do. The time of the last boot and the name and address of the contact person are also provided. This information means that a company can contract out system management to another company in a distant city and have the latter be able to easily figure out what the configuration being managed actually is and who should be contacted if there are problems with various devices.

The interfaces group deals with the network adapters. It keeps track of the number of packets and bytes sent and received from the network, the number of discards, the number of broadcasts, and the current output queue size.

The AT group was present in MIB-I and provided information about address mapping (e.g., Ethernet to IP addresses). This information was moved to protocol-specific MIBs in SNMPv2.

The IP group deals with IP traffic into and out of the node. It is especially rich in counters keeping track of the number of packets discarded for each of a variety of reasons (e.g., no known route to the destination or lack of resources). Statistics about datagram fragmentation and reassembly are also available. All these items are particular important for managing routers.

The ICMP group is about IP error messages. Basically, it has a counter for each ICMP message that records how many of that type have been seen.

The TCP group monitors the current and cumulative number of connections opened, segments sent and received, and various error statistics.

The UDP group logs the number of UDP datagrams sent and received, and how many of the latter were undeliverable due to an unknown port or some other reason.

The EGP group is used for routers that support the exterior gateway protocol. It keeps track of how many packets of what kind went out, came in and were forwarded correctly, and came in and were discarded.

The transmission group is a place holder for media-specific MIBs. For example, Ethernet-specific statistics can be kept here. The purpose of including an empty group in MIB-II is to reserve the identifier {internet 2 1 9} for such purposes.

The last group is for collecting statistics about the operation of SNMP itself. How many messages are being sent, what kinds of messages are they, and so on.

MIB-II is formally defined in RFC 1213. The bulk of RFC 1213 consists of 175 macro calls similar to those of Fig. 7-36, with comments delineating the ten groups. For each of the 175 objects defined, the data type is given along with an English text description of what the variable is used for. For further information about MIB-II, the reader is referred to this RFC.

7.3.5. The SNMP Protocol

We have now seen that the model underlying SNMP is a management station that sends requests to agents in managed nodes, inquiring about the 175 variables just alluded to, and many other vendor-specific variables. Our last topic is the actual protocol that the management station and agents speak. The protocol itself is defined in RFC 1448.

The normal way that SNMP is used is that the management station sends a request to an agent asking it for information or commanding it to update its state in a certain way. Ideally, the agent just replies with the requested information or confirms that it has updated its state as requested. Data are sent using the ASN.1 transfer syntax. However, various errors can also be reported, such as No Such Variable.

SNMP defines seven messages that can be sent. The six messages from an initiator are listed in Fig. 7-38 (the seventh message is the response message). The first three request variable values to be sent back. The first format names the variables it wants explicitly. The second one asks for the next variable, allowing a manager to step through the entire MIB alphabetically (the default is the first variable). The third is for large transfers, such as tables.

Message	Description
Get-request	Requests the value of one or more variables
Get-next-request	Requests the variable following this one
Get-bulk-request	Fetches a large table
Set-request	Updates one or more variables
Inform-request	Manager-to-manager message describing local MIB
SnmpV2-trap	Agent-to-manager trap report

Fig. 7-38. SNMP message types.

Then comes a message that allows the manager to update an agent's variables, to the extent that the object specification permits such updates, of course. Next is an informational request that allows one manager to tell another one which variables it is managing. Finally, comes the message sent from an agent to a manager when a trap has sprung.

7.4. ELECTRONIC MAIL

Having finished looking at some of the support protocols used in the application layer, we finally come to real applications. When asked: "What are you going to do now?" few people will say: "I am going to look up some names with DNS." People do say they are going to read their email or news, surf the Web, or watch a movie over the net. In the remainder of this chapter, we will explain in a fair amount of detail how these four applications work.

Electronic mail, or **email**, as it is known to its many fans, has been around for over two decades. The first email systems simply consisted of file transfer protocols, with the convention that the first line of each message (i.e., file) contained the recipient's address. As time went on, the limitations of this approach became more obvious. Some of the complaints were

1. Sending a message to a group of people was inconvenient. Managers often need this facility to send memos to all their subordinates.

2. Messages had no internal structure, making computer processing difficult. For example, if a forwarded message was included in the body of another message, extracting the forwarded part from the received message was difficult.

3. The originator (sender) never knew if a message arrived or not.

4. If someone was planning to be away on business for several weeks and wanted all incoming email to be handled by his secretary, this was not easy to arrange.

5. The user interface was poorly integrated with the transmission system requiring users first to edit a file, then leave the editor and invoke the file transfer program.

6. It was not possible to create and send messages containing a mixture of text, drawings, facsimile, and voice.

As experience was gained, more elaborate email systems were proposed. In 1982, the ARPANET email proposals were published as RFC 821 (transmission protocol) and RFC 822 (message format). These have since become the de facto Internet standards. Two years later, CCITT drafted its X.400 recommendation, which was later taken over as the basis for OSI's MOTIS. In 1988, CCITT modified X.400 to align it with MOTIS. MOTIS was to be the flagship application for OSI, a system that was to be all things to all people.

After a decade of competition, email systems based on RFC 822 are widely used, whereas those based on X.400 have disappeared under the horizon. How a system hacked together by a handful of computer science graduate students beat an official international standard strongly backed by all the PTTs worldwide, many governments, and a substantial part of the computer industry brings to mind the Biblical story of David and Goliath. The reason for RFC 822's success is not that it is so good, but that X.400 is so poorly designed and so complex that nobody could implement it well. Given a choice between a simple-minded, but working, RFC 822-based email system and a supposedly truly wonderful, but nonworking, X.400 email system, most organizations chose the former. For a long diatribe on what is wrong with X.400, see Appendix C of (Rose, 1993). Consequently, our discussion of email will focus on RFC 821 and RFC 822 as used in the Internet.

7.4.1. Architecture and Services

In this section we will provide an overview of what email systems can do and how they are organized. They normally consist of two subsystems: the **user agents**, which allow people to read and send email, and the **message transfer agents**, which move the messages from the source to the destination. The user agents are local programs that provide a command-based, menu-based, or graphical method for interacting with the email system. The message transfer agents are typically system daemons that run in the background and move email through the system.

Typically, email systems support five basic functions, as described below. **Composition** refers to the process of creating messages and answers. Although any text editor can be used for the body of the message, the system itself can provide assistance with addressing and the numerous header fields attached to each message. For example, when answering a message, the email system can extract the originator's address from the incoming email and automatically insert it into the proper place in the reply.

Transfer refers to moving messages from the originator to the recipient. In large part, this requires establishing a connection to the destination or some intermediate machine, outputting the message, and releasing the connection. The email system should do this automatically, without bothering the user.

Reporting has to do with telling the originator what happened to the message. Was it delivered? Was it rejected? Was it lost? Numerous applications exist in which confirmation of delivery is important and may even have legal significance ("Well, Your Honor, my email system is not very reliable, so I guess the electronic subpoena just got lost somewhere").

Displaying incoming messages is needed so people can read their email. Sometimes conversion is required or a special viewer must be invoked, for example, if the message is a PostScript file or digitized voice. Simple conversions and formatting are sometimes attempted as well.

Disposition is the final step and concerns what the recipient does with the message after receiving it. Possibilities include throwing it away before reading, throwing it away after reading, saving it, and so on. It should also be possible to retrieve and reread saved messages, forward them, or process them in other ways.

In addition to these basic services, most email systems provide a large variety of advanced features. Let us just briefly mention a few of these. When people move, or when they are away for some period of time, they may want their email forwarded, so the system should be able to do this automatically.

Most systems allow users to create **mailboxes** to store incoming email. Commands are needed to create and destroy mailboxes, inspect the contents of mailboxes, insert and delete messages from mailboxes, and so on.

Corporate managers often need to send a message to each of their subordinates, customers, or suppliers. This gives rise to the idea of a **mailing list**, which is a list of email addresses. When a message is sent to the mailing list, identical copies are delivered to everyone on the list.

Registered email is another important idea, to allow the originator to know that his message has arrived. Alternatively, automatic notification of undeliverable email may be desired. In any case, the originator should have some control over reporting what happened.

Other advanced features are carbon copies, high-priority email, secret (encrypted) email, alternative recipients if the primary one is not available, and the ability for secretaries to handle their bosses' email.

Email is now widely used within industry for intracompany communication. It allows far-flung employees to cooperate on complex projects, even over many time zones. By eliminating most cues associated with rank, age, and gender, email debates tend to focus on ideas, not on corporate status. With email, a brilliant idea from a summer student can have more impact than a dumb one from an executive vice president. Some companies have estimated that email has improved their productivity by as much as 30 percent (Perry and Adam, 1992).

A key idea in all modern email systems is the distinction between the **envelope** and its contents. The envelope encapsulates the message. It contains all the information needed for transporting the message, such as the destination address, priority, and security level, all of which are distinct from the message itself. The message transport agents use the envelope for routing, just as the post office does.

The message inside the envelope contains two parts: the **header** and the **body**. The header contains control information for the user agents. The body is entirely for the human recipient. Envelopes and messages are illustrated in Fig. 7-39.

7.4.2. The User Agent

Email systems have two basic parts, as we have seen: the user agents and the message transfer agents. In this section we will look at the user agents. A user agent is normally a program (sometimes called a mail reader) that accepts a variety of commands for composing, receiving, and replying to messages, as well as for manipulating mailboxes. Some user agents have a fancy menu- or icon-driven interface that requires a mouse, while others expect 1-character commands from the keyboard. Functionally, these are the same.

Sending Email

To send an email message, a user must provide the message, the destination address, and possibly some other parameters (e.g., the priority or security level). The message can be produced with a free-standing text editor, a word processing

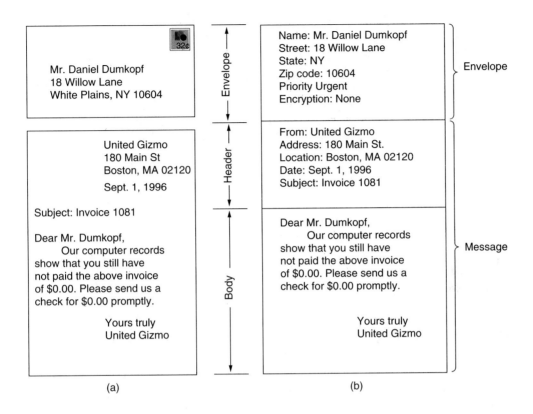

Fig. 7-39. Envelopes and messages. (a) Postal email. (b) Electronic email.

program, or possibly with a text editor built into the user agent. The destination address must be in a format that the user agent can deal with. Many user agents expect DNS addresses of the form *mailbox@location*. Since we have studied these earlier in this chapter, we will not repeat that material here.

However, it is worth noting that other forms of addressing exist. In particular, X.400 addresses look radically different than DNS addresses. They are composed of *attribute* = *value* pairs, for example,

/C=US/SP=MASSACHUSETTS/L=CAMBRIDGE/PA=360 MEMORIAL DR./CN=KEN SMITH/

This address specifies a country, state, locality, personal address and a common name (Tom Smith). Many other attributes are possible, so you can send email to someone whose name you do not know, provided you know enough other attributes (e.g., company and job title). Many people feel that this form of naming is considerably less convenient than DNS names.

In all fairness, however, the X.400 designers assumed that people would use **aliases** (short user-assigned strings) to identify recipients, so that they would never even see the full addresses. However, the necessary software was never widely available, so people sending mail to users with X.400 addresses often had to type in strings like the one above. In contrast, most email systems for the Internet have always allowed users to have alias files.

Most email systems support mailing lists, so that a user can send the same message to a list of people with a single command. If the mailing list is maintained locally, the user agent can just send a separate message to each intended recipient. However, if the list is maintained remotely, then messages will be expanded there. For example, if a group of bird watchers have a mailing list called *birders* installed on *meadowlark.arizona.edu*, then any message sent to *birders@meadowlark.arizona.edu* will be routed to the University of Arizona and expanded there into individual messages to all the mailing list members, wherever in the world they may be. Users of this mailing list cannot tell that it is a mailing list. It could just as well be the personal mailbox of Prof. Gabriel O. Birders.

Reading Email

Typically, when a user agent is started up, it will look at the user's mailbox for incoming email before displaying anything on the screen. Then it may announce the number of messages in the mailbox or display a one-line summary of each one and wait for a command.

As an example of how a user agent works, let us take a look at a typical mail scenario. After starting up the user agent, the user asks for a summary of his email. A display like that of Fig. 7-40 then appears on the screen. Each line refers to one message. In this example, the mailbox contains eight messages.

#	Flags	Bytes	Sender	Subject
1	K	1030	asw	Changes to MINIX
2	KA	6348	radia	Comments on material you sent me
3	K F	4519	Amy N. Wong	Request for information
4		1236	bal	Deadline for grant proposal
5		103610	kaashoek	Text of DCS paper
6		1223	emily E.	Pointer to WWW page
7		3110	saniya	Referee reports for the paper
8		1204	dmr	Re: My student's visit

Fig. 7-40. An example display of the contents of a mailbox.

Each display line contains several fields extracted from the envelope or header of the corresponding message. In a simple email system, the choice of fields displayed is built into the program. In a more sophisticated system, the user can specify which fields are to be displayed by providing a **user profile**, a file describing the display format. In this example, the first field is the message number. The second field, *Flags*, can contain a *K*, meaning that the message is not new but was read previously and kept in the mailbox; an *A*, meaning that the message has already been answered; and/or an *F*, meaning that the message has been forwarded to someone else. Other flags are also possible.

The third field tells how long the message is and the fourth one tells who sent the message. Since this field is simply extracted from the message, this field may contain first names, full names, initials, login names, or whatever else the sender chooses to put there. Finally, the *Subject* field gives a brief summary of what the message is about. People who fail to include a *Subject* field often discover that responses to their email tend not to get the highest priority.

After the headers have been displayed, the user can perform any of the commands available. A typical collection is listed in Fig. 7-41. Some of the commands require a parameter. The # sign means that the number of a message (or perhaps several messages) is expected. Alternatively, the letter *a* can be used to mean all messages.

Command	Parameter	Description
h	#	Display header(s) on the screen
c		Display current header only
t	#	Type message(s) on the screen
s	address	Send a message
f	#	Forward message(s)
a	#	Answer message(s)
d	#	Delete message(s)
u	#	Undelete previously deleted message(s)
m	#	Move message(s) to another mailbox
k	#	Keep message(s) after exiting
r	mailbox	Read a new mailbox
n		Go to the next message and display it
b		Backup to the previous message and display it
g	#	Go to a specific message but do not display it
e		Exit the mail system and update the mailbox

Fig. 7-41. Typical mail handling commands.

Innumerable email programs exist. Our example email program is patterned after the one used by the UNIX Mmdf system, as it is quite straightforward. The *h* command displays one or more headers in the format of Fig. 7-40. The *c* command prints the current message's header. The *t* command types (i.e., displays on the screen) the requested message or messages. Possible commands are *t 3*, to type message 3, *t 4–6*, to type messages 4 through 6, and *t a* to type them all.

The next group of three commands deals with sending messages rather than receiving them. The *s* command sends a message by calling an appropriate editor (e.g., specified in the user's profile) to allow the user to compose the message. Spelling, grammar, and diction checkers can see if the message is syntactically correct. Unfortunately, the current generation of email programs do not have checkers to see if the sender knows what he is talking about. When the message is finished, it is prepared for transmission to the message transfer agent.

The *f* command forwards a message from the mailbox, prompting for an address to send it to. The *a* command extracts the source address from the message to be answered and calls the editor to allow the user to compose the reply.

The next group of commands is for manipulating mailboxes. Users typically have one mailbox for each person with whom they correspond, in addition to the mailbox for incoming email that we have already seen. The *d* command deletes a message from the mailbox, but the *u* command undoes the delete. (The message is not actually deleted until the email program is exited.) The *m* command moves a message to another mailbox. This is the usual way to save important email after reading it. The *k* command keeps the indicated message in the mailbox even after it is read. If a message is read but not explicitly kept, some default action is taken when the email program is exited, such as moving it to a special default mailbox. Finally, the *r* command is used to finish up with the current mailbox and go read another one.

The *n*, *b*, and *g* commands are for moving about in the current mailbox. It is common for a user to read message 1, answer, move, or delete it, and then type *n* to get the next one. The value of this command is that the user does not have to keep track of where he is. It is possible to go backward using *b* or to a given message with *g*.

Finally, the *e* command exits the email program and makes whatever changes are required, such as deleting some messages and marking others as kept. This command overwrites the mailbox, replacing its contents.

In mail systems designed for beginners, each of these commands is typically associated with an on-screen icon, so that the user does not have to remember that *a* stands for *answer*. Instead, she has to remember that the little picture of a person with his mouth open means answer and not display message.

It should be clear from this example that email has come a long way from the days when it was just file transfer. Sophisticated user agents make managing a large volume of email possible. For people such as the author who (reluctantly) receive and send thousands of messages a year, such tools are invaluable.

7.4.3. Message Formats

Let us now turn from the user interface to the format of the email messages themselves. First we will look at basic ASCII email using RFC 822. After that, we will look at multimedia extensions to RFC 822

RFC 822

Messages consist of a primitive envelope (described in RFC 821), some number of header fields, a blank line, and then the message body. Each header field (logically) consists of a single line of ASCII text containing the field name, a colon, and, for most fields, a value. RFC 822 is an old standard, and does not clearly distinguish envelope from header fields, as a new standard would do. In normal usage, the user agent builds a message and passes it to the message transfer agent, which then uses some of the header fields to construct the actual envelope, a somewhat old-fashioned mixing of message and envelope.

The principal header fields related to message transport are listed in Fig. 7-42. The *To:* field gives the DNS address of the primary recipient. Having multiple recipients is also allowed. The *Cc:* field gives the addresses of any secondary recipients. In terms of delivery, there is no distinction between the primary and secondary recipients. It is entirely a psychological difference that may be important to the people involved but is not important to the mail system. The term *Cc:* (Carbon copy) is a bit dated, since computers do not use carbon paper, but it is well established. The *Bcc:* (Blind carbon copy) field is like the *Cc:* field, except that this line is deleted from all the copies sent to the primary and secondary recipients. This feature allows people to send copies to third parties without the primary and secondary recipients knowing this.

Header	Meaning
To:	Email address(es) of primary recipient(s)
Cc:	Email address(es) of secondary recipient(s)
Bcc:	Email address(es) for blind carbon copies
From:	Person or people who created the message
Sender:	Email address of the actual sender
Received:	Line added by each transfer agent along the route
Return-Path:	Can be used to identify a path back to the sender

Fig. 7-42. RFC 822 header fields related to message transport.

The next two fields, *From:* and *Sender:* tell who wrote and sent the message, respectively. These may not be the same. For example, a business executive may write a message, but her secretary may be the one who actually transmits it. In this case, the executive would be listed in the *From:* field and the secretary in the *Sender:* field. The *From:* field is required, but the *Sender:* field may be omitted if it is the same as the *From:* field. These fields are needed in case the message is undeliverable and must be returned to the sender.

A line containing *Received:* is added by each message transfer agent along the way. The line contains the agent's identity, the date and time the message was received, and other information that can be used for finding bugs in the routing system.

The *Return-Path:* field is added by the final message transfer agent and was intended to tell how to get back to the sender. In theory, this information can be gathered from all the *Received:* headers (except for the name of the sender's mailbox), but it is rarely filled in as such and typically just contains the sender's address.

In addition to the fields of Fig. 7-42, RFC 822 messages may also contain a variety of header fields used by the user agents or human recipients. The most common ones are listed in Fig. 7-43. Most of these are self-explanatory, so we will not go into all of them in detail.

Header	Meaning
Date:	The date and time the message was sent
Reply-To:	Email address to which replies should be sent
Message-Id:	Unique number for referencing this message later
In-Reply-To:	Message-Id of the message to which this is a reply
References:	Other relevant Message-Ids
Keywords:	User chosen keywords
Subject:	Short summary of the message for the one-line display

Fig. 7-43. Some fields used in the RFC 822 message header.

The *Reply-To:* field is sometimes used when neither the person composing the message nor the person sending the message wants to see the reply. For example, a marketing manager writes an email message telling customers about a new product. The message is sent by a secretary, but the *Reply-To:* field lists the head of the sales department, who can answer questions and take orders.

The RFC 822 document explicitly says that users are allowed to invent new headers for their own private use, provided that these headers start with the string *X-*. It is guaranteed that no future headers will use names starting with *X-*, to avoid conflicts between official and private headers. Sometimes wiseguy undergraduates include fields like *X-Fruit-of-the-Day:* or *X-Disease-of-the-Week:*, which are legal, although not always illuminating.

After the headers comes the message body. Users can put whatever they want here. Some people terminate their messages with elaborate signatures, including simple ASCII cartoons, quotations from greater and lesser authorities, political statements, and disclaimers of all kinds (e.g., The ABC Corporation is not responsible for my opinions; it cannot even comprehend them).

MIME—Multipurpose Internet Mail Extensions

In the early days of the ARPANET, email consisted exclusively of text messages written in English and expressed in ASCII. For this environment, RFC 822 did the job completely: it specified the headers but left the content entirely up to the users. Nowadays, on the worldwide Internet, this approach is no longer adequate. The problems include sending and receiving

1. Messages in languages with accents (e.g., French and German).

2. Messages in nonLatin alphabets (e.g., Hebrew and Russian).

3. Messages in languages without alphabets (e.g., Chinese and Japanese).

4. Messages not containing text at all (e.g., audio and video).

A solution was proposed in RFC 1341 and updated in RFC 1521. This solution, called **MIME (Multipurpose Internet Mail Extensions)** is now widely used. We will now describe it. For additional information about MIME, see RFC 1521 or (Rose, 1993).

The basic idea of MIME is to continue to use the RFC 822 format, but to add structure to the message body and define encoding rules for non-ASCII messages. By not deviating from 822, MIME messages can be sent using the existing mail programs and protocols. All that has to be changed are the sending and receiving programs, which users can do for themselves.

MIME defines five new message headers, as shown in Fig. 7-44. The first of these simply tells the user agent receiving the message that it is dealing with a MIME message, and which version of MIME it uses. Any message not containing a *MIME-Version:* header is assumed to be an English plaintext message, and is processed as such.

Header	Meaning
MIME-Version:	Identifies the MIME version
Content-Description:	Human-readable string telling what is in the message
Content-Id:	Unique identifier
Content-Transfer-Encoding:	How the body is wrapped for transmission
Content-Type:	Nature of the message

Fig. 7-44. RFC 822 headers added by MIME.

The *Content-Description:* header is an ASCII string telling what is in the message. This header is needed so the recipient will know whether it is worth decoding and reading the message. If the string says: "Photo of Barbara's gerbil" and the person getting the message is not a big gerbil fan, the message will probably be discarded rather than decoded into a high-resolution color photograph.

The *Content-Id:* header identifies the content. It uses the same format as the standard *Message-Id:* header.

The *Content-Transfer-Encoding:* tells how the body is wrapped for transmission through a network that may object to most characters other than letters, numbers, and punctuation marks. Five schemes (plus an escape to new schemes) are provided. The simplest scheme is just ASCII text. ASCII characters use 7 bits, and can be carried directly by the email protocol provided that no line exceeds 1000 characters.

The next simplest scheme is the same thing, but using 8-bit characters, that is, all values from 0 up to and including 255. This encoding scheme violates the (original) Internet email protocol but is used by some parts of the Internet that implement some extensions to the original protocol. While declaring the encoding does not make it legal, having it explicit may at least explain things when something goes wrong. Messages using the 8-bit encoding must still adhere to the standard maximum line length.

Even worse are messages that use binary encoding. These are arbitrary binary files that not only use all 8 bits but also do not even respect the 1000 character line limit. Executable programs fall into this category. No guarantee is given that messages in binary will arrive correctly, but many people send them anyway.

The correct way to encode binary messages is to use **base64 encoding**, sometimes called **ASCII armor**. In this scheme, groups of 24 bits are broken up into four 6-bit units, with each unit being sent as a legal ASCII character. The coding is "A" for 0, "B" for 1, and so on, followed by the 26 lowercase letters, the ten digits, and finally + and / for 62 and 63, respectively. The == and = sequences are used to indicate that the last group contained only 8 or 16 bits, respectively. Carriage returns and line feeds are ignored, so they can be inserted at will to keep the lines short enough. Arbitrary binary text can be sent safely using this scheme.

For messages that are almost entirely ASCII, but with a few non-ASCII characters, base64 encoding is somewhat inefficient. Instead, an encoding known as **quoted-printable encoding** is used. This is just 7-bit ASCII, with all the characters above 127 encoded as an equal sign followed by the character's value as two hexadecimal digits.

In summary, binary data should be sent encoded in base64 or quoted printable form. When there are valid reasons not to use one of these schemes, it is possible to specify a user-defined encoding in the *Content-Transfer-Encoding:* header.

The last header shown in Fig. 7-44 is really the most interesting one. It specifies the nature of the message body. Seven types are defined in RFC 1521, each of which has one or more subtypes. The type and subtype are separated by a slash, as in

Content-Type: video/mpeg

The subtype must be given explicitly in the header; no defaults are provided. The initial list of types and subtypes specified in RFC 1521 is given in Fig. 7-45.

Many new ones have been added since then, and additional entries are being added all the time as the need arises.

Type	Subtype	Description
Text	Plain	Unformatted text
	Richtext	Text including simple formatting commands
Image	Gif	Still picture in GIF format
	Jpeg	Still picture in JPEG format
Audio	Basic	Audible sound
Video	Mpeg	Movie in MPEG format
Application	Octet-stream	An uninterpreted byte sequence
	Postscript	A printable document in PostScript
Message	Rfc822	A MIME RFC 822 message
	Partial	Message has been split for transmission
	External-body	Message itself must be fetched over the net
Multipart	Mixed	Independent parts in the specified order
	Alternative	Same message in different formats
	Parallel	Parts must be viewed simultaneously
	Digest	Each part is a complete RFC 822 message

Fig. 7-45. The MIME types and subtypes defined in RFC 1521.

Let us now go through the list of types. The *text* type is for straight text. The *text/plain* combination is for ordinary messages that can be displayed as received, with no encoding and no further processing. This option allows ordinary messages to be transported in MIME with only a few extra headers.

The *text/richtext* subtype allows a simple markup language to be included in the text. This language provides a system-independent way to express boldface, italics, smaller and larger point sizes, indentation, justification, sub- and super-scripting, and simple page layout. The markup language is based on SGML, the Standard Generalized Markup Language also used as the basis for the World Wide Web's HTML. For example, the message

The <bold> time </bold> has come the <italic> walrus </italic> said ...

would be displayed as

The **time** has come the *walrus* said ...

It is up to the receiving system to choose the appropriate rendition. If boldface and italics are available, they can be used; otherwise, colors, blinking, underlining, reverse video, etc. can be used for emphasis. Different systems can, and do, make different choices.

The next MIME type is *image*, which is used to transmit still pictures. Many formats are widely used for storing and transmitting images nowadays, both with and without compression. Two of these, GIF and JPEG, are official subtypes, but no doubt others will be added later.

The *audio* and *video* types are for sound and moving pictures, respectively. Note that *video* includes only the visual information, not the soundtrack. If a movie with sound is to be transmitted, the video and audio portions may have to be transmitted separately, depending on the encoding system used. The only video format defined so far is the one devised by the modestly-named Moving Picture Experts Group (MPEG).

The *application* type is a catchall for formats that require external processing not covered by one of the other types. An *octet-stream* is just a sequence of uninterpreted bytes. Upon receiving such a stream, a user agent should probably display it by suggesting to the user that it be copied to a file and prompting for a file name. Subsequent processing is then up to the user.

The other defined subtype is *postscript*, which refers to the PostScript language produced by Adobe Systems and widely used for describing printed pages. Many printers have built-in PostScript interpreters. Although a user agent can just call an external PostScript interpreter to display incoming PostScript files, doing so is not without danger. PostScript is a full-blown programming language. Given enough time, a sufficiently masochistic person could write a C compiler or a database management system in PostScript. Displaying an incoming PostScript message is done by executing the PostScript program contained in it. In addition to displaying some text, this program can read, modify, or delete the user's files, and have other nasty side effects.

The *message* type allows one message to be fully encapsulated inside another. This scheme is useful for forwarding email, for example. When a complete RFC 822 message is encapsulated inside an outer message, the *rfc822* subtype should be used.

The *partial* subtype makes it possible to break an encapsulated message up into pieces and send them separately (for example, if the encapsulated message is too long). Parameters make it possible to reassemble all the parts at the destination in the correct order.

Finally, the *external-body* subtype can be used for very long messages (e.g., video films). Instead of including the MPEG file in the message, an FTP address is given and the receiver's user agent can fetch it over the network at the time it is needed. This facility is especially useful when sending a movie to a mailing list of people, only a few of whom are expected to view it (think about electronic junk mail containing advertising videos).

The final type is *multipart*, which allows a message to contain more than one part, with the beginning and end of each part being clearly delimited. The *mixed* subtype allows each part to be different, with no additional structure imposed. In contrast, with the *alternative* subtype, each part must contain the same message but expressed in a different medium or encoding. For example, a message could be sent in plain ASCII, in richtext, and in PostScript. A properly-designed user agent getting such a message would display it in PostScript if possible. Second choice would be richtext. If neither of these were possible, the flat ASCII text would be displayed. The parts should be ordered from simplest to most complex to help recipients with pre-MIME user agents make some sense of the message (e.g., even a pre-MIME user can read flat ASCII text).

The *alternative* subtype can also be used for multiple languages. In this context, the Rosetta Stone can be thought of as an early *multipart/alternative* message.

A multimedia example is shown in Fig. 7-46. Here a birthday greeting is transmitted both as text and as a song. If the receiver has an audio capability, the user agent there will fetch the sound file, *birthday.snd*, and play it. If not, the lyrics are displayed on the screen in stony silence. The parts are delimited by two hyphens followed by the (user-defined) string specified in the *boundary* parameter.

Note that the *Content-Type* header occurs in three positions within this example. At the top level, it indicates that the message has multiple parts. Within each part, it gives the type and subtype of that part. Finally, within the body of the second part, it is required to tell the user agent what kind of an external file it is to fetch. To indicate this slight difference in usage, we have used lowercase letters here, although all headers are case insensitive. The *content-transfer-encoding* is similarly required for any external body that is not encoded as 7-bit ASCII.

Getting back to the subtypes for multipart messages, two more possibilities exist. The *parallel* subtype is used when all parts must be "viewed" simultaneously. For example, movies often have an audio channel and a video channel. Movies are more effective if these two channels are played back in parallel, instead of consecutively.

Finally, the *digest* subtype is used when many messages are packed together into a composite message. For example, some discussion groups on the Internet collect messages from subscribers and then send them out as a single *multipart/digest* message.

7.4.4. Message Transfer

The message transfer system is concerned with relaying messages from originator to the recipient. The simplest way to do this is to establish a transport connection from the source machine to the destination machine and then just transfer the message. After examining how this is normally done, we will examine some situations in which this does not work and what can be done about them.

From: elinor@abc.com
To: carolyn@xyz.com
MIME-Version: 1.0
Message-Id: <0704760941.AA00747@abc.com>
Content-Type: multipart/alternative; boundary=qwertyuiopasdfghjklzxcvbnm
Subject: Earth orbits sun integral number of times

This is the preamble. The user agent ignores it. Have a nice day.

--qwertyuiopasdfghjklzxcvbnm
Content-Type: text/richtext

Happy birthday to you
Happy birthday to you
Happy birthday dear <bold> Carolyn </bold>
Happy birthday to you

--qwertyuiopasdfghjklzxcvbnm
Content-Type: message/external-body;
    access-type="anon-ftp";
    site="bicycle.abc.com";
    directory="pub";
    name="birthday.snd"

content-type: audio/basic
content-transfer-encoding: base64
--qwertyuiopasdfghjklzxcvbnm--

Fig. 7-46. A multipart message containing richtext and audio alternatives.

SMTP—Simple Mail Transfer Protocol

Within the Internet, email is delivered by having the source machine establish a TCP connection to port 25 of the destination machine. Listening to this port is an email daemon that speaks **SMTP (Simple Mail Transfer Protocol)**. This daemon accepts incoming connections and copies messages from them into the appropriate mailboxes. If a message cannot be delivered, an error report containing the first part of the undeliverable message is returned to the sender.

SMTP is a simple ASCII protocol. After establishing the TCP connection to port 25, the sending machine, operating as the client, waits for the receiving machine, operating as the server, to talk first. The server starts by sending a line of text giving its identity and telling whether or not it is prepared to receive mail. If it is not, the client releases the connection and tries again later.

If the server is willing to accept email, the client announces whom the email is coming from and whom it is going too. If such a recipient exists at the destination, the server gives the client the go-ahead to send the message. Then the client sends the message and the server acknowledges it. No checksums are generally needed because TCP provides a reliable byte stream. If there is more email, that is now sent. When all the email has been exchanged in both directions, the connection is released. A sample dialog for sending the message of Fig. 7-46, including the numerical codes used by SMTP, is shown in Fig. 7-47. The lines sent by the client are marked *C:*; those sent by the server are marked *S:*.

A few comments about Fig. 7-47 may be helpful. The first command from the client is indeed *HELO*. Of the two four-character abbreviations for *HELLO*, this one has numerous advantages over its competitor. Why all the commands had to be four characters has been lost in the mists of time.

In Fig. 7-47, the message is sent to only one recipient, so only one *RCPT* command is used. Multiple such commands are allowed to send a single message to multiple receivers. Each one is individually acknowledged or rejected. Even if some recipients are rejected (because they do not exist at the destination), the message can be sent to the remainder.

Finally, although the syntax of the four-character commands from the client is rigidly specified, the syntax of the replies is less rigid. Only the numerical code really counts. Each implementation can put whatever string it wants after the code.

Even though the SMTP protocol is well defined (by RFC 821), a few problems can still arise. One problem relates to message length. Some older implementations cannot handle messages exceeding 64KB. Another problem relates to timeouts. If the client and server have different timeouts, one of them may give up while the other is still busy, unexpectedly terminating the connection. Finally, in rare situations, infinite mailstorms can be triggered. For example, if host 1 holds mailing list *A* and host 2 holds mailing list *B* and each list contains an entry for the other one, then any message sent to either list will generate a never-ending amount of email traffic.

To get around some of these problems, extended STMP (**ESMTP**) has been defined in RFC 1425. Clients wanting to use it should send an *EHLO* message instead of *HELO* initially. If this is rejected, then the server is a regular SMTP server, and the client should proceed in the usual way. If the *EHLO* is accepted, then new commands and parameters are allowed. The standardization of these commands and parameters is an ongoing process.

Email Gateways

Email using SMTP works best when both the sender and the receiver are on the Internet and can support TCP connections between sender and receiver. However, many machines that are not on the Internet still want to send and receive email from Internet sites. For example, many companies intentionally do not

```
            S: 220 xyz.com SMTP service ready
C: HELO abc.com
            S: 250 xyz.com says hello to abc.com
C: MAIL FROM: <elinor@abc.com>
            S: 250 sender ok
C: RCPT TO: <carolyn@xyz.com>
            S: 250 recipient ok
C: DATA
            S: 354 Send mail; end with "." on a line by itself
C: From: elinor@abc.com
C: To: carolyn@xyz.com
C: MIME-Version: 1.0
C: Message-Id: <0704760941.AA00747@abc.com>
C: Content-Type: multipart/alternative; boundary=qwertyuiopasdfghjklzxcvbnm
C: Subject: Earth orbits sun integral number of times
C:
C: This is the preamble. The user agent ignores it. Have a nice day.
C:
C: --qwertyuiopasdfghjklzxcvbnm
C: Content-Type: text/richtext
C:
C: Happy birthday to you
C: Happy birthday to you
C: Happy birthday dear <bold> Carolyn </bold>
C: Happy birthday to you
C:
C: --qwertyuiopasdfghjklzxcvbnm
C: Content-Type: message/external-body;
C:      access-type="anon-ftp";
C:      site="bicycle.abc.com";
C:      directory="pub";
C:      name="birthday.snd"
C:
C: content-type: audio/basic
C: content-transfer-encoding: base64
C: --qwertyuiopasdfghjklzxcvbnm
C: .
            S: 250 message accepted
C: QUIT
            S: 221 xyz.com closing connection
```

Fig. 7-47. Transferring a message from *elinor@abc.com* to *carolyn@xyz.com*.

want to be on the Internet for security reasons. Some of them even remove themselves from the Internet by erecting firewalls between themselves and the Internet.

Another problem occurs when the sender speaks only RFC 822 and the receiver speaks only X.400 or some proprietary vendor-specific mail protocol. Since all these worlds differ in message formats and protocols, direct communication is impossible.

Both of these problems are solved using application layer **email gateways**. In Fig. 7-48 host 1 speaks only TCP/IP and RFC 822, whereas host 2 speaks only OSI TP4 and X.400. Nevertheless, they can exchange email using an email gateway. The procedure is for host 1 to establish a TCP connection to the gateway and then use SMTP to transfer a message (1) there. The daemon on the gateway then puts the message in a buffer of messages destined for host 2. Later, a TP4 connection (the OSI equivalent to TCP) is established with host 2 and the message (2) is transferred using the OSI equivalent of SMTP. All the gateway process has to do is to extract incoming messages from one queue and deposit them in another.

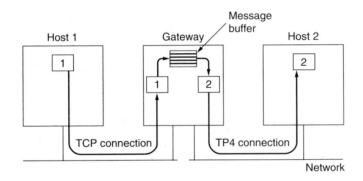

Fig. 7-48. Transferring email using an application layer email gateway.

It looks easy, but it is not. The first problem is that Internet addresses and X.400 addresses are totally different. An elaborate mapping mechanism is needed between them. The second problem is that envelope or header fields that are present in one system may not be present in the other. For example, if one system requires priority classes and the other does not have this concept at all, in one direction valuable information must be dropped and in the other it must be generated out of thin air.

An even worse concept is what to do if body parts are incompatible. What should a gateway do with a message from the Internet whose body holds a reference to an audio file to be obtained by FTP if the destination system does not support this concept? What should it do when an X.400 system tells it to deliver a message to a certain address, but if that fails, to send the contents by fax? Using fax is not part of the RFC 822 model. Clearly, there are no simple solutions here. For simple unstructured text messages in ASCII, gatewaying is a reasonable solution, but for anything fancier, the idea tends to break down.

Final Delivery

Up until now, we have assumed that all users work on machines that are capable of sending and receiving email. Frequently this situation is false. For example, at many companies, users work at desktop PCs that are not on the Internet and are not capable of sending or receiving email from outside the company. Instead, the company has one or more email servers that can send and receive email. To send or receive messages, a PC must talk to an email server using some kind of delivery protocol.

A simple protocol used for fetching email from a remote mailbox is **POP3** (**Post Office Protocol**), which is defined in RFC 1225. It has commands for the user to log in, log out, fetch messages, and delete messages. The protocol itself consists of ASCII text and has something of the flavor of SMTP. The point of POP3 is to fetch email from the remote mailbox and store it on the user's local machine to be read later.

A more sophisticated delivery protocol is **IMAP** (**Interactive Mail Access Protocol**), which is defined in RFC 1064. It was designed to help the user who uses multiple computers, perhaps a workstation in the office, a PC at home, and a laptop on the road. The basic idea behind IMAP is for the email server to maintain a central repository that can be accessed from any machine. Thus unlike POP3, IMAP does not copy email to the user's personal machine because the user may have several.

IMAP has many features, such as the ability to address mail not by arrival number as is done in Fig. 7-40, but by using attributes (e.g., Give me the first message from Sam). In this view, a mailbox is more like a relational database system than a linear sequence of messages.

Yet a third delivery protocol is **DMSP** (**Distributed Mail System Protocol**), which is part of the PCMAIL system and described in RFC 1056. This one does not assume that all email is on one server, as do POP3 and IMAP. Instead, it allows users to download email from the server to a workstation, PC, or laptop and then disconnect. The email can be read and answered while disconnected. When reconnection occurs later, email is transferred and the system is resynchronized.

Independent of whether email is delivered directly to the user's workstation or to a remote server, many systems provide hooks for additional processing of incoming email. An especially valuable tool for many email users is the ability to set up **filters**. These are rules that are checked when email comes in or when the user agent is started. Each rule specifies a condition and an action. For example, a rule could say that any message from Andrew S. Tanenbaum should be displayed in a 24-point flashing red boldface font (or alternatively, be discarded automatically without comment).

Another delivery feature often provided is the ability to (temporarily) forward incoming email to a different address. This address can even be a computer operated by a commercial paging service, which then pages the user by radio or satellite, displaying the *Subject:* line on his beeper.

Still another common feature of final delivery is the ability to install a **vacation daemon**. This is a program that examines each incoming message and sends the sender an insipid reply such as

Hi. I'm on vacation. I'll be back on the 24th of August. Have a nice day.

Such replies can also specify how to handle urgent matters in the interim, other people to contact for specific problems, etc. Most vacation daemons keep track of whom they have sent canned replies to and refrain from sending the same person a second reply. The good ones also check to see if the incoming message was sent to a mailing list, and if so, do not send a canned reply at all. (People who send messages to large mailing lists during the summer probably do not want to get hundreds of replies detailing everyone's vacation plans.)

The author recently ran into a most extreme form of delivery processing when he sent an email message to a person who claims to get 600 messages a day. His identity will not be disclosed here, lest half the readers of this book also send him email. Let us call him John.

John has installed an email robot that checks every incoming message to see if it is from a new correspondent. If so, it sends back a canned reply explaining that John can no longer personally read all his email. Instead he has produced a personal FAQ (Frequently Asked Questions) document that answers many questions he is commonly asked. Normally, newsgroups have FAQs, not people.

John's FAQ gives his address, fax, and telephone numbers and tells how to contact his company. It explains how to get him as a speaker and describes where to get his papers and other documents. It also provides pointers to software he has written, a conference he is running, a standard he is the editor of, and so on. Perhaps this approach is necessary, but maybe a personal FAQ is the ultimate status symbol.

7.4.5. Email Privacy

When an email message is sent between two distant sites, it will generally transit dozens of machines on the way. Any of these can read and record the message for future use. Privacy is nonexistent, despite what many people think (Weisband and Reinig, 1995). Nevertheless, many people would like to be able to send email that can be read by the intended recipient and no one else: not their boss, not hackers, not even the government. This desire has stimulated several people and groups to apply the cryptographic principles we studied earlier to email to produce secure email. In the following sections we will study two widely used secure email systems, PGP and PEM. For additional information, see (Kaufman et al., 1995; Schneier, 1995; Stallings, 1995b; and Stallings, 1995c).

PGP—Pretty Good Privacy

Our first example, **PGP (Pretty Good Privacy)** is essentially the brainchild of one person, Phil Zimmermann (Zimmermann, 1995a, 1995b). It is a complete email security package that provides privacy, authentication, digital signatures, and compression, all in easy-to-use form. Furthermore, the complete package, including all the source code, is distributed free of charge via the Internet, bulletin boards, and commercial networks. Due to its quality, price (zero), and easy availability on MS-DOS/Windows, UNIX, and Macintosh platforms, it is widely used today. A commercial version is also available for those companies requiring support.

It has also been embroiled in various controversies (Levy, 1993). Because it is freely available over the Internet, the U.S. government has claimed the ability of foreigners to obtain it constitutes a violation of the laws concerning the export of munitions. Later versions were produced outside the United States to get around this restriction. Another problem has involved an alleged infringement of the RSA patent, but that problem was settled with releases starting at 2.6. Nevertheless, not everyone likes the idea of people being able to keep secrets from them, so PGP's enemies are always lurking in the shadows, waiting to pounce. Accordingly, Zimmermann's motto is: "If privacy is outlawed, only outlaws will have privacy."

PGP intentionally uses existing cryptographic algorithms rather than inventing new ones. It is largely based on RSA, IDEA, and MD5, all algorithms that have withstood extensive peer review and were not designed or influenced by any government agency trying to weaken them. For people who tend to distrust government, this property is a big plus.

PGP supports text compression, secrecy, and digital signatures and also provides extensive key management facilities. To see how PGP works, let us consider the example of Fig. 7-49. Here, Alice wants to send a signed plaintext message, P, to Bob in a secure way. Both Alice and Bob have private (D_X) and public (E_X) RSA keys. Let us assume that each one knows the other's public key; we will cover key management later.

Alice starts out by invoking the PGP program on her computer. PGP first hashes her message, P, using MD5 and then encrypts the resulting hash using her private RSA key, D_A. When Bob eventually gets the message, he can decrypt the hash with Alice's public key and verify that the hash is correct. Even if someone else (e.g., Trudy) could acquire the hash at this stage and decrypt it with Alice's known public key, the strength of MD5 guarantees that it would be computationally infeasible to produce another message with the same MD5 hash.

The encrypted hash and the original message are now concatenated into a single message, $P1$, and compressed using the ZIP program, which uses the Ziv-Lempel algorithm (Ziv and Lempel, 1977). Call the output of this step $P1.Z$.

Next, PGP prompts Alice for some random input. Both the content and the

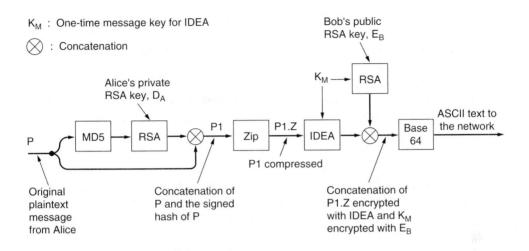

Fig. 7-49. PGP in operation for sending a message.

typing speed are used to generate a 128-bit IDEA message key, K_M (called a session key in the PGP literature, but this is really a misnomer since there is no session). K_M is now used to encrypt *P1.Z* with IDEA in cipher feedback mode. In addition, K_M is encrypted with Bob's public key, E_B. These two components are then concatenated and converted to base64, as we discussed in the section on MIME. The resulting message then contains only letters, digits, and the symbols +, / and =, which means it can be put into an RFC 822 body and be expected to arrive unmodified.

When Bob gets the message, he reverses the base64 encoding and decrypts the IDEA key using his private RSA key. Using this key, he decrypts the message to get *P1.Z*. After decompressing it, Bob separates the plaintext from the encrypted hash and decrypts the hash using Alice's public key. If the plaintext hash agrees with his own MD5 computation, he knows that *P* is the correct message and that it came from Alice.

It is worth noting that RSA is only used in two places here: to encrypt the 128-bit MD5 hash and to encrypt the 128-bit IDEA key. Although RSA is slow, it has to encrypt only 256 bits, not a large volume of data. Furthermore, all 256 plaintext bits are exceedingly random, so a considerable amount of work will be required on Trudy's part just to determine if a guessed key is correct. The heavy-duty encryption is done by IDEA, which is orders of magnitude faster than RSA. Thus PGP provides security, compression, and a digital signature and does so in a much more efficient way than the scheme illustrated in Fig. 7-23.

PGP supports three RSA key lengths. It is up to the user to select the one that is most appropriate. The lengths are

1. Casual (384 bits): can be broken today by folks with large budgets.

2. Commercial (512 bits): might be breakable by three-letter organizations.

3. Military (1024): Not breakable by anyone on earth.

There has been some discussion about a fourth category: alien (2048 bits), which could not be broken by anyone or anything in the universe, but this has not yet been adopted. Since RSA is only used for two small computations, probably everyone should use military strength keys all the time, except perhaps on aged PC-XTs.

The format of a PGP message is shown in Fig. 7-50. The message has three parts, containing the IDEA key, the signature, and the message, respectively. The key part contains not only the key, but also a key identifier, since users are permitted to have multiple public keys.

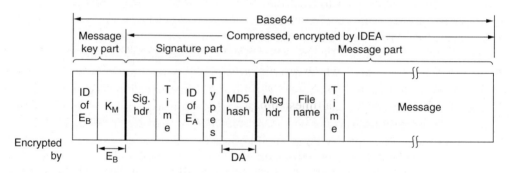

Fig. 7-50. A PGP message.

The signature part contains a header, which will not concern us here. The header is followed by a timestamp, the identifier for the sender's public key that can be used to decrypt the signature hash, some type information that identifies the algorithms used (to allow MD6 and RSA2 to be used when they are invented), and the encrypted hash itself.

The message part also contains a header, the default name of the file to be used if the receiver writes the file to the disk, a message creation timestamp, and, finally, the message itself.

Key management has received a large amount of attention in PGP as it is the Achilles heel of all security systems. Each user maintains two data structures locally: a private key ring and a public key ring. The **private key ring** contains one or more personal private-public key pairs. The reason for supporting multiple pairs per user is to permit users to change their public keys periodically or when one is thought to have been compromised, without invalidating messages currently in preparation or in transit. Each pair has an identifier associated with it, so that a message sender can tell the recipient which public key was used to encrypt it. Message identifiers consist of the low-order 64 bits of the public key. Users are responsible for avoiding conflicts in their public key identifiers. The private keys on disk are encrypted using a special (arbitrarily long) password to protect them against sneak attacks.

The **public key ring** contains public keys of the user's correspondents. These are needed to encrypt the message keys associated with each message. Each entry on the public key ring contains not only the public key, but also its 64-bit identifier and an indication of how strongly the user trusts the key.

The problem being tackled here is the following. Suppose that public keys are maintained on bulletin boards. One way for Trudy to read Bob's secret email is to attack the bulletin board and replace Bob's public key with one of her choice. When Alice later fetches the key so-called belonging to Bob, Trudy can mount a bucket brigade attack on Bob.

To prevent such attacks, or at least minimize the consequences of them, Alice needs to know how much to trust the item called "Bob's key" on her public key ring. If she knows that Bob personally handed her a floppy disk containing the key, she can set the trust value to the highest value.

However, in practice, people often receive public keys by querying a trusted key server, a number of which are already in operation on the Internet. When a key server receives a request for someone's public key, it generates a response containing the public key, a timestamp, and the expiration date of the key. It then hashes this response with MD5 and signs the response with its own private key so the requesting party can verify who sent it. It is up to the user to assign a trust level to keys maintained by the local system administrator, the phone company, ACM, the Bar Association, the government, or whoever else decides to get into the business of maintaining keys.

PEM—Privacy Enhanced Mail

In contrast to PGP, which was initially a one-man show, our second example, **PEM (Privacy Enhanced Mail)**, is an official Internet standard and described in four RFCs: RFC 1421 through RFC 1424. Very roughly, PEM covers the same territory as PGP: privacy and authentication for RFC 822-based email systems. Nevertheless, it also has some differences with PGP in approach and technology. Below we will describe PEM and then compare and contrast it to PGP. For more information about PEM, see (Kent, 1993).

Messages sent using PEM are first converted to a canonical form so they all have the same conventions about white space (e.g., tabs, trailing spaces) and the use of carriage returns and line feeds. This transformation is done to eliminate the effects of message transfer agents that modify messages not to their liking.

Without canonicalization, such modifications might affect hashes made from messages at their destinations.

Next, a message hash is computed using MD2 or MD5. It is not optional, as it is in PGP. Then the concatenation of the hash and the message is encrypted using DES. In light of the known weakness of a 56-bit key, this choice is certainly suspect. The encrypted message can then be encoded with base64 coding and transmitted to the recipient. Mailing lists are explicitly supported.

As in PGP, each message is encrypted with a one-time key that is enclosed along with the message. The key can be protected either with RSA or with triple DES using EDE. In practice, everyone uses RSA, so we will concentrate on that. In fact, we have to: PEM does not tell how to do key management with DES.

Key management is more structured than in PGP. Keys are certified by **certification authorities** in the form of certificates stating a user's name, public key, and the key's expiration date. Each certificate has a unique serial number for identifying it. Certificates include an MD5 hash signed by the certification authority's private key. These certificates conform to the ITU X.509 recommendation for public key certificates, and as such, use X.400 names like the Tom Smith example given earlier.

PGP has a similar scheme (without the use of X.509), but has a problem: Should a user believe a certification authority? PEM solves this problem by certifying the certification authorities using what are called **PCAs** (**Policy Certification Authorities**). These, in turn, are certified by the **IPRA** (**Internet Policy Registration Authority**), the ultimate arbiter of who's naughty and who's nice.

Each PCA must define an official policy on registration and file it with IPRA. These statements are then signed by IPRA and made public. For example, one PCA may insist on having users under its jurisdiction show up in person with a birth certificate, drivers' license, passport, two major credit cards, a live witness, and a public key on floppy disk. Another PCA may accept email registrations from strangers. By making the policy statements public, users have some basis for deciding which authorities to trust. No provision has been made for seeing if the policies are actually enforced.

Three different kinds of certification authorities are planned. An organizational one can issue certificates for its employees. Most companies will run their own. A residential one will operate on behalf of private citizens, much as current Internet service providers will provide service to anyone willing to pay for it. Finally, a scheme is planned for anonymous registration. With all these certification authorities running around, the need for the PCAs to ride herd on them should now be clear.

While rigidly hierarchical and bureaucratic, this scheme has the advantage over PGP of making certificate revocation potentially practical. Revocation is needed if a user wants to change his public key, for example, because it has been compromised or his certification authority has been burglarized (or stolen). Revocation is accomplished by a user telling his certification authority that his public key has been compromised (or possibly vice versa). The certification authority then adds the serial number of the now-invalid certificate to a list of revoked certificates, signs it, and spreads the list far and wide.

Anyone wanting to send a PEM message to a user must therefore first check the most recent revocation list to see if the cached public key is still valid. This process is analogous to a merchant checking the list of stolen credit cards before accepting one. Critics of PEM argue that checking all the time is too much work so nobody will bother. Supporters argue that computers do not get bored; if they are programmed to check all the time, they will check all the time.

Some of the similarities and differences between PGP and PEM are listed in Fig. 7-51. Most of these points have already been covered, but a few are worth commenting on. Authentication seems more important in PEM than in PGP since it is mandatory in PEM and optional in PGP. PEM also carries the authentication information outside the encryption wrapper, which means that the network can verify the origin of every message. As a consequence, eavesdroppers can log who is sending to whom, even if they cannot read the messages.

All these technical differences aside, there is a surprising cultural difference as well. PGP, which is not an official internet standard, has the Internet culture. PEM, which is an official Internet standard, does not. PGP was based on what Dave Clark calls "rough consensus and running code." Somebody (Zimmermann) thought of a solution to a well-known problem, implemented it well, and released the source code for everyone to use. PEM began as a four-part official standard, using ASN.1 to define layouts, X.400 to define names, and X.509 to define certificates. It uses a rigid three-layer organizational hierarchy for multiple kinds of certification authorities, complete with officially certified policy statements and a requirement that everyone trust the IPRA. Implementations came later and are far behind PGP in quality, quantity, and availability on many platforms. In short, PGP looks like a typical Internet package, whereas PEM exhibits most of the characteristics of an OSI standard that Internet people hate and PTTs love. You figure.

7.5. USENET NEWS

One of the more popular applications of computer networking is the worldwide system of newsgroups called **net news**. Often net news is referred to as **USENET**, which harks back to a separate UNIX-to-UNIX physical network that once carried the traffic using a program called **uucp**. Nowadays, much of the traffic is carried on the Internet, but USENET and the Internet are not the same. Some Internet sites do not get net news, and other sites get net news without being on the Internet.

In the follow sections we will describe USENET. First we will look at it from the users' viewpoint. Then we will describe how it is implemented.

Item	PGP	PEM
Supports encryption?	Yes	Yes
Supports authentication?	Yes	Yes
Supports nonrepudiation?	Yes	Yes
Supports compression?	Yes	No
Supports canonicalization?	No	Yes
Supports mailing lists?	No	Yes
Uses base64 coding?	Yes	Yes
Current data encryption algorithm	IDEA	DES
Key length for data encryption (bits)	128	56
Current algorithm for key management	RSA	RSA or DES
Key length for key management (bits)	384/512/1024	Variable
User name space	User defined	X.400
X.509 conformant?	No	Yes
Do you have to trust anyone?	No	Yes (IPRA)
Key certification	Ad hoc	IPRA/PCA/CA hierarchy
Key revocation	Haphazard	Better
Can eavesdroppers read messages?	No	No
Can eavesdroppers read signatures?	No	Yes
Internet Standard?	No	Yes
Designed by	Small team	Standards committee

Fig. 7-51. A comparison of PGP and PEM.

7.5.1. The User View of USENET

A newsgroup is a worldwide discussion forum on some specific topic. People interested in the subject can "subscribe" to the newsgroup. Subscribers can use a special kind of user agent, a news reader, to read all the articles (messages) posted to the newsgroup. People can also post articles to the newsgroup. Each article posted to a newsgroup is automatically delivered to all the subscribers, wherever they may be in the world. Delivery typically takes between a few seconds and a few hours, depending how far off the beaten path the sender and receiver are. In effect, a newsgroup is somewhat like a mailing list, but internally it is implemented differently. It can also be thought of as a kind of high-level multicast.

The number of newsgroups is so large (probably over 10,000) that they are arranged in a hierarchy to make them manageable. Figure 7-52 shows the top levels of the "official" hierarchies. Other hierarchies also exist, but these are typically intended for regional consumption or are in languages other than English. One of the other hierarchies *alt*, is special. *Alt* is to the official groups as a flea market is to a department store. It is a chaotic, unregulated mishmash of newsgroups on all topics, some of which are very popular, and most of which are worldwide.

Name	Topics covered
Comp	Computers, computer science, and the computer industry
Sci	The physical sciences and engineering
Humanities	Literature and the humanities
News	Discussion of USENET itself
Rec	Recreational activities, including sports and music
Misc	Everything that does not fit in somewhere else
Soc	Socializing and social issues
Talk	Diatribes, polemics, debates and arguments galore
Alt	Alternative tree covering virtually everything

Fig. 7-52. USENET hierarchies in order of decreasing signal-to-noise ratio.

The *comp* groups were the original USENET groups. These groups are populated by computer scientists, computer professionals, and computer hobbyists. Each one features technical discussions on a topic related to computer hardware or software.

The *sci* and *humanities* groups are populated by scientists, scholars, and amateurs with an interest in physics, chemistry, biology, Shakespeare, and so on. Not entirely surprisingly, the *sci* hierarchy is much larger than the *humanities* hierarchy because the very concept of instant electronic communication with colleagues all over the world is something most scientists like, and most humanists are at least skeptical about. C.P. Snow was right.

The *news* hierarchy is used to discuss and manage the news system itself. System administrators can get help here, and discussions about whether to create new newsgroups occurs here.

The hierarchies covered so far have a professional, somewhat academic tone. That changes with *rec* which is about recreational activities and hobbies. Nevertheless, many of the people who post here are fairly knowledgeable about their respective interests.

As we drift downward, we come to *soc*, which has many newsgroups concerning, politics, gender, religion, various national cultures, and genealogy. *Talk* covers controversial topics and is populated by people who are strong on opinions, weak on facts. *Alt* is a complete alternative tree which operates under its own rules.

Each of the categories listed in Fig. 7-52 is broken into subcategories, recursively. For example, *rec.sport* is about sports, *rec.sport.basketball* is about basketball, and *rec.sport.basketball.women* is about women's basketball. A sample of some of the newsgroups in each category is given in Fig. 7-53. In many cases, the existence of additional groups can be inferred by changing the obvious parameters. For example, *comp.lang.c* is about the C programming language, but the *.c* can be replaced by just about every other programming language to generate the name of the corresponding newsgroup.

Numerous news readers exist. Like email readers, some are keyboard based; others are mouse based. In nearly all cases, when the news reader is started, it checks a file to see which newsgroups the user subscribes to. It then typically displays a one-line summary of each as-yet-unread article in the first newsgroup and waits for the user to select one or more for reading. The selected articles are then displayed one at a time. After being read, they can be discarded, saved, printed, and so on.

News readers also allow users to subscribe and unsubscribe to newsgroups. Changing a subscription simply means editing the local file listing which newsgroups the user is subscribed to. To make an analogy, subscribing to a newsgroup is like watching a television program. If you want to watch some program every week, you just do it. You do not have to register with some central authority first.

News readers also handle posting. The user composes an article and then gives a command or clicks on a icon to send the article on its way. Within a day, it will reach almost everyone in the world subscribing to the newsgroup to which it was posted. It is possible to **crosspost** an article, that is, to send it to multiple newsgroups with a single command. It is also possible to restrict the geographic distribution of a posting. An announcement of Tuesday's colloquium at Stanford will probably not be of much interest in, say, Hong Kong, so the posting can be restricted to California.

The sociology of USENET is unique, to put it mildly. Never before has it been possible for thousands of people who do not know each other to have world-wide discussions on a vast variety of topics. For example, it is now possible for someone with a problem to post it to the net. The next day, the poster may have 18 solutions, and with a little bit of luck, only 17 of them are wrong.

Unfortunately, some people use their new-found power to communicate to a large group irresponsibly. When someone posts a message saying: "People like you should be shot" tempers flare and a torrent of abusive postings, called a **flamewar**, typically follows.

This situation can be attacked in two ways, one individual and one collective. Individual users can install a **killfile**, which specifies that articles with a certain subject or from a certain person are to discarded upon arrival, prior to being

Name	Topics covered
Comp.ai	Artificial intelligence
Comp.databases	Design and implementation of database systems
Comp.lang.c	The C programming language
Comp.os.minix	Tanenbaum's educational MINIX operating system
Comp.os.ms-windows.video	Video hardware and software for Windows
Sci.bio.entomology.lepidoptera	Research on butterflies and moths
Sci.geo.earthquakes	Geology, seismology, and earthquakes
Sci.med.orthopedics	Orthopedic surgery
Humanities.lit.authors.shakespeare	Shakespeare's plays and poetry
News.groups	Potential new newsgroups
News.lists	Lists relating to USENET
Rec.arts.poems	Free poetry
Rec.food.chocolate	Yum yum
Rec.humor.funny	Did you hear the joke about the farmer who ...
Rec.music.folk	Folks discussing folk music
Misc.jobs.offered	Announcements of positions available
Misc.health.diabetes	Day-to-day living with diabetes
Soc.culture.estonia	Life and culture in Estonia
Soc.singles	Single people and their interests
Soc.couples	Graduates of soc.singles
Talk.abortion	No signal, all noise
Talk.rumors	This is where rumors come from
Alt.alien.visitors	Place to report flying saucer rides
Alt.bermuda.triangle	If you read this, you vanish mysteriously
Alt.sex.voyeurism	Take a peek and see for yourself
Alt.tv.simpsons	Bart et al.

Fig. 7-53. A small selection of the newsgroups.

displayed. Most news readers also allow an individual discussion thread to be killed, too. This feature is useful when a discussion looks like it is starting to get into an infinite loop.

If enough subscribers to a group get annoyed with newsgroup pollution, they can propose having the newsgroup be moderated. A **moderated newsgroup** is one in which only one person, the moderator, can post articles to the newsgroup. All postings to a moderated newsgroup are automatically sent to the moderator, who posts the good ones and discards the bad ones. Some topics have both a moderated newsgroup and an unmoderated one.

Since thousands of people subscribe to USENET for the first time every day, the same beginner's questions tend to be asked over and over. To reduce this traffic, many newsgroups have constructed a **FAQ (Frequently Asked Questions)** document that tries to answer all the questions that beginners have. Some of these are highly authoritative and run to over 100 pages. The maintainer typically posts them once or twice a month.

USENET is full of jargon such as BTW (By The Way), ROFL (Rolling On the Floor Laughing), and IMHO (In My Humble Opinion). Many people also use little ASCII symbols called **smileys** or **emoticons**. A few of the more interesting ones are reproduced in Fig. 7-54. For most, rotating the book 90 degrees clockwise will make them clearer. For a minibook giving over 650 smileys, see (Sanderson and Dougherty, 1993).

Smiley	Meaning	Smiley	Meaning	Smiley	Meaning
:-)	I'm happy	=|:-)	Abe Lincoln	:+)	Big nose
:-(	I'm sad/angry	=):-)	Uncle Sam	:-))	Double chin
:-|	I'm apathetic	*<:-)	Santa Claus	:-{)	Mustache
;-)	I'm winking	<:-(	Dunce	#:-)	Matted hair
:-(O)	I'm yelling	(-:	Australian	8-)	Wears glasses
:-(*)	I'm vomiting	:-)X	Man with bowtie	C:-)	Large brain

Fig. 7-54. Some smileys.

Although most people use their real names in postings, some people wish to remain totally anonymous, especially when posting to controversial newsgroups or when posting personal ads to newsgroups dealing with finding partners. This desire has led to the creation of **anonymous remailers**, which are servers that accept email messages (including postings) and change the *From:*, *Sender:*, and *Reply-To:* fields to make them point to the remailer instead of the sender. Some of the remailers assign a number to each user and forward email addressed to these numbers, so people can send email replies to anonymous postings like "SWF 25 seeks SWM/DWM 20-30 ...." Whether these remailers can keep their secrets when the local police become curious about the identity of some user is doubtful (Barlow, 1995).

As more and more people subscribe to USENET, there is a constant demand for new and more specialized newsgroups. Consequently, a procedure has been established for creating new ones. Suppose that somebody likes cockroaches and wants to talk to other cockroach fans. He posts a message to *news.groups* naming the proposed group, say *rec.animals.wildlife.cockroaches*, and describing why it is so important (cockroaches are fascinating; there are 3500 species of them; they come in red, yellow, green, brown, and black; they appeared on earth long before the first dinosaurs; they were probably the first flying animals, and so on). He also specifies whether or not it should be moderated.

Discussion then ensues. When it settles down, an email vote is taken. The votes are posted, identifying who voted which way (to prevent fraud). If the yeas outnumber the nays by more than 2:1 and there were at least 100 more yeas than nays, the moderator of *news.groups* posts a message accepting the new newsgroup. This message is the signal to system administrators worldwide that the new newsgroup has been blessed by the powers that be and is now official.

New group creation is less formal in the *alt* hierarchy and this is, in fact, the reason *alt* exists. Some of the newsgroups there are so close to the legal and moral edge of what is tolerable that they would never have been accepted in a public vote. In effect, the people who supported them, just bypassed the normal procedure and created their own hierarchy. Nevertheless, much of the *alt* hierarchy is fairly conventional.

7.5.2. How USENET Is Implemented

Some of the smaller news groups are implemented as mailing lists. To post an article to such a mailing list, one sends it to the mailing list address, which causes copies to be sent to each address on the mailing list.

However, if half the undergraduates at a large university subscribed to *alt.sex*, the servers there would collapse under the weight of the incoming email. Consequently, USENET is not generally implemented using mailing lists. Instead each site (campus, company, or Internet service provider) stores incoming mail in a single directory, say, *news*, with subdirectories for *comp*, *sci*, etc. These, in turn have subdirectories such as *news/comp/os/minix*. All incoming news is deposited in the appropriate directory. News readers just fetch the articles from there as they need them. This arrangement means that each site needs only one copy of each news article, no matter how many people subscribe to its newsgroup. After a few days, articles time out and are removed from the disk.

To get on USENET, a site must have a **newsfeed** from another site on USENET. One can think of the set of all sites that get net news as the nodes of a directed graph. The transmission lines connecting pairs of nodes form the arcs of the graph. This graph is USENET. Note that being on the Internet is neither necessary nor sufficient for being on USENET.

Periodically, each site that wants news can poll its newsfeed(s), asking if any new news has arrived since the previous contact. If so, that news is collected and stored in the appropriate subdirectory of *news*. In this manner, news diffuses around the network. It is equally possible for the newsfeed, rather than the receiver, to take the initiative and make contact when there is enough new news. Initially, most sites polled their newsfeeds, but now it is mostly the other way.

Not every site gets all newsgroups. There are several reasons here. First, the total newsfeed exceeds 500 MB per day and is growing rapidly. Storing it all would require a very large amount of disk space. Second, transmission time and cost are issues. At 28.8 kbps, it takes 39 hours and a dedicated telephone line to transmit 24 hours worth of news. Even at 56 kbps, getting everything requires having a dedicated line for almost 20 hours a day. In fact, the total volume has now gotten so large that newsfeeds via satellite have been created.

Third, not every site is interested in every topic. For example, it is unlikely that many people at companies in Finland want to read *rec.arts.manga* (about Japanese comic books). Finally, some newsgroups are a bit too funky for the tastes of many system administrators, who then ban them, despite considerable local interest. In Dec. 1995, the worldwide CompuServe network (temporarily) stopped carrying all newsgroups with "sex" in the name because some minor German official thought this would be a good way to combat pornography. The ensuing uproar was predictable, instantaneous, worldwide, and very loud.

News articles have the same format as RFC 822 email messages, but with the addition of a few extra headers. This property makes them easy to transport and compatible with most of the existing email software. The news headers are defined in RFC 1036 An example article is shown in Fig. 7-55.

```
From: Vogel@nyu.edu
Message-Id: <54731@nyu.edu>
Subject: Bird Sighting
Path: cs.vu.nl!sun4nl!EU.net!news.sprintlink.net!in2.uu.net!pc144.nyu.edu!news
Newsgroups: rec.birds
Followup-To: rec.birds
Distribution: world
Nntp-Posting-host: nuthatch.bio.nyu.edu
References:
Organization: New York University
Lines: 4
Summary: Guess what I saw

I just saw an ostrich on 52nd St. and Fifth Ave. in New York. Is this their migration
season? Did anybody else see it?

Jay Vogel
```

Fig. 7-55. A sample news article.

A few words about the news headers are perhaps in order. The *Path:* header is the list of nodes the message traversed to get from the poster to the recipient. At each hop, the forwarding machine puts its name at the front of the list. This list gives a path back to the poster. The use of exclamation marks (pronounced: bang) go back to USENET addresses, which predate DNS.

The *Newsgroups:* header tells which newsgroups the message belongs to. It may contain more than one newsgroup name. Any message crossposted to multiple newsgroups will contain all of their names. Because multiple names are allowed here, the *Followup-To:* header is needed to tell people where to post comments and reactions to put all of the subsequent discussion in one newsgroup.

The *Distribution:* header tells how far to spread the posting. It may contain one or more state or country codes, the name of a specific site or network, or "world."

The *Nntp-Posting-Host:* header is analogous to the RFC 822 *Sender:* header. It tells which machine actually posted the article, even if it was composed on a different machine (NNTP is the news protocol, described below).

The *References:* header indicates that this article is a response to an earlier article and gives the ID of that article. It is required on all follow-up articles and prohibited when starting a new discussion.

The *Organization:* header can be used to tell what company, university, or agency the poster is affiliated with. Articles that fill in this header often have a disclaimer at the end saying that if the article is goofy, it is not the organization's fault.

The *Lines:* header gives the length of the body. The header lines and the blank line separating the header from the body do not count.

The *Subject:* lines tie discussion threads together. Many news readers have a command to allow the user to see the next article on the current subject, rather than the next article that came in. Also, killfiles and kill commands use this header to know what to reject.

Finally, the *Summary:* is normally used to summarize the follow-up article. On follow-up articles, the *Subject:* header contains "Re: " followed by the original subject.

NNTP—Network News Transfer Protocol

Now let us look at how articles diffuse around the network. The initial algorithm just flooded articles onto every line within USENET. While this worked for a while, eventually the volume of traffic made this scheme impractical, so something better had to be worked out.

Its replacement was a protocol called **NNTP** (**Network News Transfer Protocol**), which is defined in RFC 977. NNTP has something of the same flavor as SMTP, with a client issuing commands in ASCII and a server issuing responses as decimal numbers coded in ASCII. Most USENET machines now use NNTP.

NNTP was designed for two purposes. The first goal was to allow news articles to propagate from one machine to another over a reliable connection (e.g., TCP). The second goal was to allow users whose desktop computers cannot receive news to read news remotely. Both are widely used, but we will concentrate on how news articles spread out over the network using NNTP.

As mentioned above, two general approaches are possible. In the first one, news pull, the client calls one of its newsfeeds and asks for new news. In the second one, news push, the newsfeed calls the client and announces that it has news. The NNTP commands support both of these approaches, as well as having people read news remotely.

To acquire recent articles, a client must first establish a TCP connection with port 119 on one of its newsfeeds. Behind this port is the NNTP daemon, which is either there all the time waiting for clients or is created on the fly as needed. After the connection has been established, the client and server communicate using a sequence of commands and responses. These commands and responses are used to ensure that the client gets all the articles it needs, but no duplicates, no matter how many newsfeeds it uses. The main ones used for moving articles between news daemons are listed in Fig. 7-56.

Command	Meaning
LIST	Give me a list of all newsgroups and articles you have
NEWGROUPS date time	Give me a list of newsgroups created after date/time
GROUP grp	Give me a list of all articles in grp
NEWNEWS grps date time	Give me a list of new articles in specified groups
ARTICLE id	Give me a specific article
POST	I have an article for you that was posted here
IHAVE id	I have article id. Do you want it?
QUIT	Terminate the session

Fig. 7-56. The principal NNTP commands for news diffusion.

The *LIST* and *NEWGROUPS* commands allow the client to find out which groups the server has. The former gives the complete list. The latter gives only those groups created after the date and time specified. If the client knows the list is long, it is more efficient for the client to keep track of what each of its newsfeeds has and just ask for updates. The responses to each of these commands is a list, in ASCII, one newsgroup per line, giving the name of the newsgroup, the number of the last article the server has, the number of the first article the server has, and a flag telling whether posting to this newsgroup is allowed.

Once the client knows which newsgroups the server has, it can begin asking about what articles the server has (e.g., for old newsgroups when *NEWGROUPS* is used). The *GROUP* and *NEWNEWS* commands are used for this purpose. Again, the former gives the full list and the latter gives only updates subsequent to the indicated date and time, normally the time of the last connection to this newsfeed. The first parameter may contain asterisks, meaning all of them. For example, *comp.os.* ∗ means all the newsgroups that start with the string *comp.os*.

After the client has assembled a complete list of which articles exist in which groups (or even before it has the full list), it can begin to ask for the articles it needs using the *ARTICLE* command. Once all the required articles are in, the client can offer articles it has acquired from other newsfeeds using the *IHAVE* command and articles that were posted locally using the *POST* command. The server can accept or decline these, as it wishes. When the client is done, it can terminate the session using *QUIT*. In this way, each machine has complete control over which articles it gets from which newsfeeds, eliminating all duplicate articles.

As an example of how NNTP works, consider an information provider, *wholesome.net* that wants to avoid controversy at all costs, so the only newsgroups it offers are *soc.couples* and *misc.kids*. Nevertheless, management is open minded and willing to carry other newsgroups, provided they contain no material potentially offensive to anyone. Therefore, it wants to be informed of all newly created groups so it can make an informed decision for its customers. A possible scenario between *wholesome.com* acting as the client and its newsfeed, *feeder.com*, acting as the server, is shown in Fig. 7-57. This scenario uses the news pull approach (the client initiates the connection to ask for news). The remarks in parentheses are comments and not part of the NNTP protocol.

In this session, *wholesome.com* first asks if there is any news for *soc.couples*. When it is told there are two articles, it fetches both of them and stores them in *news/soc/couples* as separate files. Each file is named by its article number. Then *wholesome.com* asks about *misc.kids* and is told there is one article. It fetches that one and puts it in *news/misc/kids*.

Having gotten all the news about the groups it carries, it now checks for new groups and is told that two new groups have appeared since the last session. One of them looks promising, so its articles are fetched. The other looks scary, so it is not taken. (*Wholesome.com* has made a big investment in AI software to be able to figure out what to carry just by looking at the names.)

After having acquired all the articles it wants, *wholesome.com* offers *feeder.com* a new article posted by someone at its site. The offer is accepted and the article is transferred. Now *wholesome.com* offers another article, one that came from its other newsfeed. Since *feeder.com* already has this one, it declines. Finally, *wholesome.com* ends the session and releases the TCP connection.

The news push approach is similar. It begins with the newsfeed calling the machine that is to receive the news. The newsfeed normally keeps track of which newsgroups its customers subscribe to and begins by announcing its first article in the first of these newsgroups using the *IHAVE* command. The potential recipient then checks its tables to see whether it already has the article, and can accept or reject it. If the article is accepted, it is transmitted, followed by a line containing a period. Then the newsfeed advertises the second article, and so forth, until all the news has been transferred.

A problem with both news pull and news push is that they use stop and wait. Typically 100 msec are lost waiting for an answer to a question. With 100,000 or more news articles per day, this lost time adds up to a substantial overhead.

```
    S: 200 feeder.com NNTP server at your service (response to new connection)
C: NEWNEWS soc.couples 960901 030000 (any new news in soc.couples?)
    S: 230 List of 2 articles follows
    S: <13281@psyc.berkeley.edu>    (article 1 of 2 in soc.couples is from Berkeley)
    S: <162721@aol.com>          (article 2 of 2 in soc.couples is from AOL)
    S: .                         (end of list)
C: ARTICLE <13281@psyc.berkeley.edu>  (please give me the Berkeley article)
    S: 220 <13281@psyc.berkeley.edu> follows
    S: (entire article <13281@psyc.berkeley.edu> is sent here)
    S: .                         (end of article)
C: ARTICLE <162721@aol.com>    (please give me the AOL article)
    S: 220 <162721@aol.com> follows
    S: (entire article <162721@aol.com> is sent here)
    S: .                         (end of article)
C: NEWNEWS misc.kids 960901 030000    (any new news in misc.kids?)
    S: 230 List of 1 article follows
    S: <43222@bio.rice.edu>      (1 article from Rice)
    S: .                         (end of list)
C: ARTICLE <43222@bio.rice.edu> (please give me the Rice article)
    S: 220 <43222@bio.rice.edu> follows
    S: (entire article <43222@bio.rice.edu> is sent here)
    S: .                         (end of article)
C: NEWGROUPS 960901 030000
    S: 231 2 new groups follow
    S: rec.pets
    S: rec.nude
    S: .
C: NEWNEWS rec.pets 0 0         (list everything you have)
    S: 230 List of 1 article follows
    S: <124@fido.net>           (1 article from fido.net)
    S: .                         (end of list)
C: ARTICLE <124@fido.net>       (please give me the fido.net article)
    S: 220 <124@fido.net> follows
    S: (entire article is sent here)
    S: .
C: POST
    S: 340                       (please send your posting)
C:   (article posted on wholesome.com sent here)
    S: 240                       (article received)
C: IHAVE <5321@foo.com>
    S: 435                       (I already have it, please do not send it)
C: QUIT
    S: 205                       (Have a nice day)
```

Fig. 7-57. How *wholesome.com* might acquire news articles from its newsfeed.

7.6. THE WORLD WIDE WEB

The World Wide Web is an architectural framework for accessing linked documents spread out over thousands of machines all over the Internet. In 5 years, it went from being a way to distribute high-energy physics data to the application that millions of people think of as being "The Internet." Its enormous popularity stems from the fact that it has a colorful graphical interface that is easy for beginners to use, and it provides an enormous wealth of information on almost every conceivable subject, from aboriginals to zoology.

The Web (also known as **WWW**) began in 1989 at CERN, the European center for nuclear research. CERN has several accelerators at which large teams of scientists from the participating European countries carry out research in particle physics. These teams often have members from half a dozen or more countries. Most experiments are highly complex, and require years of advance planning and equipment construction. The Web grew out of the need to have these large teams of internationally dispersed researchers collaborate using a constantly changing collection of reports, blueprints, drawings, photos, and other documents.

The initial proposal for a web of linked documents came from CERN physicist Tim Berners-Lee in March 1989. The first (text-based) prototype was operational 18 months later. In December 1991, a public demonstration was given at the Hypertext '91 conference in San Antonio, Texas. Development continued during the next year, culminating in the release of the first graphical interface, Mosaic, in February 1993 (Vetter et al., 1994).

Mosaic was so popular that a year later, its author, Marc Andreessen left the National Center for Supercomputing Applications, where Mosaic was developed, to form a company, Netscape Communications Corp., whose goal was to develop clients, servers, and other Web software. When Netscape went public in 1995, investors, apparently thinking this was the next Microsoft, paid 1.5 billion dollars for the stock. This record was all the more surprising because the company had only one product, was operating deeply in the red, and had announced in its prospectus that it did not expect to make a profit for the foreseeable future.

In 1994, CERN and M.I.T. signed an agreement setting up the World Wide Web Consortium, an organization devoted to further developing the Web, standardizing protocols, and encouraging interoperability between sites. Berners-Lee became the director. Since then, hundreds of universities and companies have joined the consortium. M.I.T. runs the U.S. part of the consortium and the French research center, INRIA, runs the European part. Although there are more books about the Web than you can shake a stick at, the best place to get up-to-date information about the Web is (naturally) on the Web itself. The consortium's home page can be found at *http://www.w3.org* . Interested readers are referred there for links to pages covering all of the consortium's documents and activities.

In the following sections we will describe how the Web appears to the user, and, especially, how it works inside. Since the Web is basically a client-server system, we will discuss both the client (i.e., user) side and the server side. Then we will examine the language in which Web pages are written (HTML and Java). Finally, comes an examination of how to find information on the Web.

7.6.1. The Client Side

From the users' point of view, the Web consists of a vast, worldwide collection of documents, usually just called **pages** for short. Each page may contain links (pointers) to other, related pages, anywhere in the world. Users can follow a link (e.g., by clicking on it), which then takes them to the page pointed to. This process can be repeated indefinitely, possibly traversing hundreds of linked pages while doing so. Pages that point to other pages are said to use **hypertext.**

Pages are viewed with a program called a **browser**, of which Mosaic and Netscape are two popular ones. The browser fetches the page requested, interprets the text and formatting commands that it contains, and displays the page, properly formatted, on the screen. An example is given in Fig. 7-58(a). Like many Web pages, this one starts with a title, contains some information, and ends with the email address of the page's maintainer. Strings of text that are links to other pages, called **hyperlinks**, are highlighted, either by underlining, displaying them in a special color, or both. To follow a link, the user places the cursor on the highlighted area (using the mouse or the arrow keys) and selects it (by clicking a mouse button or hitting ENTER). Although nongraphical browsers, such as Lynx, exist, they are not as popular as graphical browsers, so we will concentrate on the latter. Voice-based browsers are also being developed.

Users who are curious about the Department of Animal Psychology can learn more about it by clicking on its (underlined) name. The browser then fetches the page to which the name is linked and displays it, as shown in Fig. 7-58(b). The underlined items here can also be clicked on to fetch other pages, and so on. The new page can be on the same machine as the first one, or on a machine halfway around the globe. The user cannot tell. Page fetching is done by the browser, without any help from the user. If the user ever returns to the main page, the links that have already been followed may be shown with a dotted underline (and possibly a different color) to distinguish them from links that have not been followed. Note that clicking on the *Campus Information* line in the main page does nothing. It is not underlined, which means that it is just text and is not linked to another page.

Most browsers have numerous buttons and features to make it easier to navigate the Web. Many have a button for going back to the previous page, a button for going forward to the next page (only operative after the user has gone back from it), and a button for going straight to the user's own home page. Most browsers have a button or menu item to set a bookmark on a given page and another one to display the list of bookmarks, making it possible to revisit any of

---

WELCOME TO THE UNIVERSITY OF EAST PODUNK'S WWW HOME PAGE

- Campus Information
  - ☐ Admissions information
  - ☐ Campus map
  - ☐ Directions to campus
  - ☐ The UEP student body

- Academic Departments
  - ☐ Department of Animal Psychology
  - ☐ Department of Alternative Studies
  - ☐ Department of Microbiotic Cooking
  - ☐ Department of Nontraditional Studies
  - ☐ Department of Traditional Studies

Webmaster@eastpodunk.edu

(a)

THE DEPARTMENT OF ANIMAL PSYCHOLOGY

- Information for prospective majors
- Personnel
  - ☐ Faculty members
  - ☐ Graduate students
  - ☐ Nonacademic staff
- Research Projects
- Positions available
- Our most popular courses
  - ☐ Dealing with herbivores
  - ☐ Horse management
  - ☐ Negotiating with your pet
  - ☐ User-friendly doghouse construction
- Full list of courses

Webmaster@animalpsyc.eastpodunk.edu

(b)

Fig. 7-58. (a) A Web page. (b) The page reached by clicking on Department of Animal Psychology

them with a single mouse click. Pages can also be saved to disk or printed. Numerous options are generally available for controlling the screen layout and setting various user preferences. A comparison of nine browsers is given in (Berghel, 1996).

In addition to having ordinary text (not underlined) and hypertext (underlined), Web pages can also contain icons, line drawings, maps, and photographs. Each of these can (optionally) be linked to another page. Clicking on one of these elements causes the browser to fetch the linked page and display it, the same as clicking on text. With images such as photos and maps, which page is fetched next may depend on what part of the image was clicked on.

Not all pages are viewable in the conventional way. For example, some pages consist of audio tracks, video clips, or both. When hypertext pages are mixed with other media, the result is called **hypermedia**. Some browsers can display all kinds of hypermedia, but others cannot. Instead they check a configuration file to see how to handle the received data. Normally, the configuration file gives the name of a program, called an **external viewer**, or a **helper application**, to be run with the incoming page as input. If no viewer is configured, the browser usually asks the user to choose one. If no viewer exists, the user can tell the browser to save the incoming page to a disk file, or to discard it. Helper applications for producing speech are making it possible for even blind users to access the Web. Other helper applications contain interpreters for special Web languages, making it possible to download and run programs from Web pages. This mechanism makes it possible to extend the functionality of the Web itself.

Many Web pages contain large images, which take a long time to load. For example, fetching an uncompressed 640×480 (VGA) image with 24 bits per pixel (922 KB) takes about 4 minutes over a 28.8-kbps modem line. Some browsers deal with the slow loading of images by first fetching and displaying the text, then getting the images. This strategy gives the user something to read while the images are coming in and also allows the user to kill the load if the page is not sufficiently interesting to warrant waiting. An alternative strategy is to provide an option to disable the automatic fetching and display of images.

Some page writers attempt to placate potentially bored users by displaying images in a special way. First the image quickly appears in a coarse resolution. Then the details are gradually filled in. For the user, seeing the whole image after a few seconds, albeit at low resolution, is often preferable to seeing it built up slowly from the top, scan line by scan line.

Some Web pages contain forms that request the user to enter information. Typical applications of these forms are searching a database for a user-supplied item, ordering a product, or participating in a public opinion survey. Other Web pages contain maps that allow users to click on them to zoom in or get information about some geographical area. Handling forms and active (clickable) maps requires more sophisticated processing than just fetching a known page. We will describe later how these features are implemented.

Some browsers use the local disk to cache pages that they have fetched. Before a page is fetched, a check is made to see if it is in the local cache. If so, it is only necessary to check if the page if still up to date. If so, the page need not be loaded again. As a result, clicking on the BACK button to see the previous page is normally very fast.

To host a Web browser, a machine must be directly on the Internet, or at least have a SLIP or PPP connection to a router or other machine that is directly on the Internet. This requirement exists because the way a browser fetches a page is to establish a TCP connection to the machine where the page is, and then send a message over the connection asking for the page. If it cannot establish a TCP connection to an arbitrary machine on the Internet, a browser will not work.

Sometimes the lengths that people will go to get Web access are amazing. At least one company is offering Web-by-Fax service. A client without Internet access calls up the Web-by-Fax server and logs in using the telephone keypad. He then types in a code identifying the Web page desired and it is faxed to the caller's fax machine.

7.6.2. The Server Side

Every Web site has a server process listening to TCP port 80 for incoming connections from clients (normally browsers). After a connection has been established, the client sends one request and the server sends one reply. Then the connection is released. The protocol that defines the legal requests and replies is called HTTP. We will study it in some detail below, but a simple example using it may provide a reasonable idea of how Web servers work. Figure 7-59 shows how the various parts of the Web model fit together.

For this example, we can imagine that the user has just clicked on some piece of text or perhaps on an icon that points to the page whose name (URL—Uniform Resource Locator) is *http://www.w3.org/hypertext/WWW/TheProject.html*. We will also explain URLs later on in this chapter. For the moment, it is sufficient to know that a URL has three parts: the name of the protocol (*http*), the name of the machine where the page is located (*www.w3.org*), and the name of the file containing the page (*hypertext/WWW/TheProject.html*). The steps that occur between the user's click and the page being displayed are as follows:

1. The browser determines the URL (by seeing what was selected).

2. The browser asks DNS for the IP address of *www.w3.org*.

3. DNS replies with 18.23.0.23.

4. The browser makes a TCP connection to port 80 on 18.23.0.23.

5. It then sends a *GET /hypertext/WWW/TheProject.html* command.

6. The *www.w3.org* server sends the file *TheProject.html*.

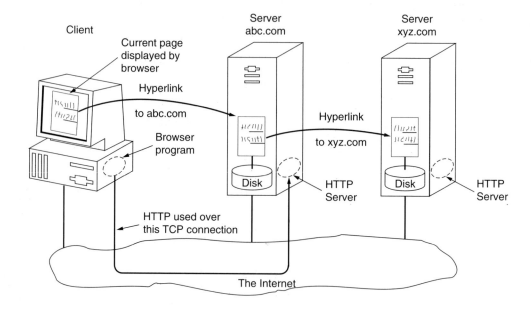

Fig. 7-59. The parts of the Web model.

7. The TCP connection is released.

8. The browser displays all the text in *TheProject.html*.

9. The browser fetches and displays all images in *TheProject.html*.

Many browsers display which step they are currently executing in a status line at the bottom of the screen. In this way, when the performance is poor, the user can see if it is due to DNS not responding, the server not responding, or simply network congestion during page transmission.

It is worth noting that for each in-line image (icon, drawing, photo, etc.) on a page, the browser establishes a new TCP connection to the relevant server to fetch the image. Needless to say, if a page contains many icons, all on the same server, establishing, using, and releasing a new connection for each one is not wildly efficient, but it keeps the implementation simple. Future revisions of the protocol will address the efficiency issue. One proposal is given in (Mogul, 1995).

Because HTTP is an ASCII protocol like SMTP, it is quite easy for a person at a terminal (as opposed to a browser) to directly talk to Web servers. All that is needed is a TCP connection to port 80 on the server. The simplest way to get such a connection is to use the Telnet program. Figure 7-60 shows a scenario of how this can be done. In this example, the lines marked *C:* are typed in by the user (client), the lines marked *T:* are produced by the Telnet program, and the lines marked *S:* are produced by the server at M.I.T.

```
C: telnet  www.w3.org  80
T: Trying 18.23.0.23 ...
T: Connected to www.w3.org.
T: Escape character is '^]'.
C: GET  /hypertext/WWW/TheProject.html  HTTP/1.0
C:
    S: HTTP/1.0 200 Document follows
    S: MIME-Version: 1.0
    S: Server: CERN/3.0
    S: Content-Type: text/html
    S: Content-Length: 8247
    S:
    S: <HEAD> <TITLE> The World Wide Web Consortium (W3C) </TITLE> </HEAD>
    S: <BODY>
    S: <H1> <IMG ALIGN=MIDDLE ALT="W3C" SRC="Icons/WWW/w3c_96x67.gif">
    S: The World Wide Web Consortium </H1> <P>
    S:
    S: The World Wide Web is the universe of network-accessible information.
    S: The <A HREF="Consortium/"> World Wide Web Consortium </A>
    S: exists to realize the full potential of the Web. <P>
    S:
    S: W3C works with the global community to produce
    S: <A HREF="#Specifications"> specifications </A> and
    S: <A HREF="#Reference"> reference software </A> .
    S: W3C is funded by industrial
    S: <A HREF="Consortium/Member/List.html"> members </A>
    S: but its products are freely available to all. <P>
    S:
    S: In this document:
    S: <menu>
    S: <LI> <A HREF="#Specifications"> Web Specifications and Development Areas </A>
    S: <LI> <A HREF="#Reference"> Web Software </A>
    S: <LI> <A HREF="#Community"> The World Wide Web and the Web Community </A>
    S: <LI> <A HREF="#Joining"> Getting involved with the W3C </A>
    S: </menu>
    S: <P> <HR>
    S: <P> W3C is hosted by the
    S: <A HREF="http://www.lcs.mit.edu/"> Laboratory for Computer Science </A> at
    S: <A HREF="http://web.mit.edu/"> MIT </A> , and
    S: in Europe by <A HREF="http://www.inria.fr/"> INRIA </A> .
    S: </BODY>
```

Fig. 7-60. A sample scenario for obtaining a Web page.

Readers are encouraged to try this scenario personally (preferably from a UNIX system, because some other systems do not return the connection status). Be sure to note the spaces and the protocol version on the *GET* line, and the blank line following the *GET* line. As an aside, the actual text that will be received will differ from what is shown in Fig. 7-60 for three reasons. First, the example output here has been abridged and edited to make it fit on one page. Second, it has been cleaned up somewhat to avoid embarrassing the author, who no doubt expected thousands of people to examine the formatted page, but zero people to scrutinize the HTML that produced it. Third, the contents of the page are constantly being revised. Nevertheless, this example should give a reasonable idea of how HTTP works.

What the example shows is the following. The client, in this case a person, but normally a browser, first connects to a particular host and then sends a command asking for a particular page and specifying a particular protocol and version to use (HTTP/1.0). On line 7, the server responds with a status line telling the protocol it is using (the same as the client) and the code 200, meaning OK. This line is followed by an RFC 822 MIME message, of which five of the header lines are shown in the figure (several others have been omitted to save space). Then comes a blank line, followed by the message body. For sending a picture, the *Content-Type* field might be

Content-Type: Image/GIF

In this way, the MIME types allow arbitrary objects to be sent in a standard way. As an aside, the MIME *Content-Transfer-Encoding* header is not needed because TCP allows arbitrary byte streams, even pictures, to be sent without modification. The meaning of the commands within angle brackets used in the sample page will be discussed later in this chapter.

Not all servers speak HTTP. In particular, many older servers use the FTP, Gopher, or other protocols. Since a great deal of useful information is available on FTP and Gopher servers, one of the design goals of the Web was to make this information available to Web users. One solution is to have the browser use these protocols when speaking to an FTP or Gopher server. Some of them, in fact, use this solution, but making browsers understand every possible protocol makes them unnecessarily large.

Instead, a different solution is often used: proxy servers (Luotonen and Altis, 1994). A **proxy server** is a kind of gateway that speaks HTTP to the browser but FTP, Gopher, or some other protocol to the server. It accepts HTTP requests and translates them into, say, FTP requests, so the browser does not have to understand any protocol except HTTP. The proxy server can be a program running on the same machine as the browser, but it can also be on a free-standing machine somewhere in the network serving many browsers. Figure 7-61 shows the difference between a browser that can speak FTP and one that uses a proxy.

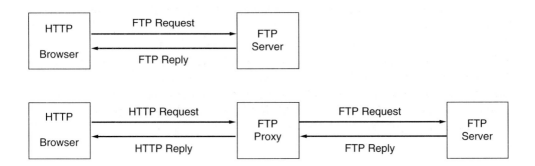

Fig. 7-61. (a) A browser that speaks FTP. (b) A browser that does not.

Often users can configure their browsers with proxies for protocols that the browsers do not speak. In this way, the range of information sources to which the browser has access is increased.

In addition to acting as a go-between for unknown protocols, proxy servers have a number of other important functions, such as caching. A caching proxy server collects and keeps all the pages that pass through it. When a user asks for a page, the proxy server checks to see if it has the page. If so, it can check to see if the page is still current. In the event that the page is still current, it is passed to the user. Otherwise, a new copy is fetched.

Finally, an organization can put a proxy server inside its firewall to allow users to access the Web, but without giving them full Internet access. In this configuration, users can talk to the proxy server, but it is the proxy server that contacts remote sites and fetches pages on behalf of its clients. This mechanism can be used, for example, by high schools, to block access to Web sites the principal feels are inappropriate for tender young minds.

For information about one of the more popular Web servers (NCSA's HTTP daemon) and its performance, see (Katz et al., 1994; and Kwan et al., 1995).

HTTP—HyperText Transfer Protocol

The standard Web transfer protocol is **HTTP (HyperText Transfer Protocol)**. Each interaction consists of one ASCII request, followed by one RFC 822 MIME-like response. Although the use of TCP for the transport connection is very common, it is not formally required by the standard. If ATM networks become reliable enough, the HTTP requests and replies could be carried in AAL 5 messages just as well.

HTTP is constantly evolving. Several versions are in use and others are under development. The material presented below is relatively basic and is unlikely to change in concept, but some details may be a little different in future versions.

The HTTP protocol consists of two fairly distinct items: the set of requests from browsers to servers and the set of responses going back the other way. We will now treat each of these in turn.

All the newer versions of HTTP support two kinds of requests: simple requests and full requests. A simple request is just a single *GET* line naming the page desired, without the protocol version. The response is just the raw page, with no headers, no MIME, and no encoding. To see how this works, try making a Telnet connection to port 80 of *www.w3.org* (as shown in the first line of Fig. 7-60) and then type

GET /hypertext/WWW/TheProject.html

but without the HTTP/1.0 this time. The page will be returned with no indication of its content type. This mechanism is needed for backward compatibility. Its use will decline as browsers and servers based on full requests become standard.

Full requests are indicated by the presence of the protocol version on the *GET* request line, as in Fig. 7-60. Requests may consist of multiple lines, followed by a blank line to indicate the end of the request, which is why the blank line was needed in Fig. 7-60. The first line of a full request contains the command (of which *GET* is but one of the possibilities), the page desired, and the protocol/version. Subsequent lines contain RFC 822 headers.

Although HTTP was designed for use in the Web, it has been intentionally made more general than necessary with an eye to future object-oriented applications. For this reason, the first word on the full request line is simply the name of the **method** (command) to be executed on the Web page (or general object). The built-in methods are listed in Fig. 7-62. When accessing general objects, additional object-specific methods may also be available. The names are case sensitive, so, *GET* is a legal method but *get* is not.

Method	Description
GET	Request to read a Web page
HEAD	Request to read a Web page's header
PUT	Request to store a Web page
POST	Append to a named resource (e.g., a Web page)
DELETE	Remove the Web page
LINK	Connects two existing resources
UNLINK	Breaks an existing connection between two resources

Fig. 7-62. The built-in HTTP request methods.

The *GET* method requests the server to send the page (by which we mean object, in the most general case), suitably encoded in MIME. However, if the

GET request is followed by an *If-Modified-Since* header, the server only sends the data if it has been modified since the date supplied. Using this mechanism, a browser that is asked to display a cached page can conditionally ask for it from the server, giving the modification time associated with the page. If the cache page is still valid, the server just sends back a status line announcing that fact, thus eliminating the overhead of transferring the page again.

The *HEAD* method just asks for the message header, without the actual page. This method can be used to get a page's time of last modification, to collect information for indexing purposes, or just to test a URL for validity. Conditional *HEAD* requests do not exist.

The *PUT* method is the reverse of *GET*: instead of reading the page, it writes the page. This method makes it possible to build a collection of Web pages on a remote server. The body of the request contains the page. It may be encoded using MIME, in which case the lines following the *PUT* might include *Content-Type* and authentication headers, to prove that the caller indeed has permission to perform the requested operation.

Somewhat similar to *PUT* is the *POST* method. It too bears a URL, but instead of replacing the existing data, the new data is "appended" to it in some generalized sense. Posting a message to a news group or adding a file to a bulletin board system are examples of appending in this context. It is clearly the intention here to have the Web take over the functionality of the USENET news system.

DELETE does what you might expect: it removes the page. As with *PUT*, authentication and permission play a major role here. There is no guarantee that *DELETE* succeeds, since even if the remote HTTP server is willing to delete the page, the underlying file may have a mode that forbids the HTTP server from modifying or removing it.

The *LINK* and *UNLINK* methods allow connections to be established between existing pages or other resources.

Every request gets a response consisting of a status line, and possibly additional information (e.g., all or part of a Web page). The status line can bear the code 200 (OK), or any one of a variety of error codes, for example 304 (not modified), 400 (bad request), or 403 (forbidden).

The HTTP standards describe message headers and bodies in considerable detail. Suffice it to say that these are very close to RFC 822 MIME messages, so we will not look at them here.

7.6.3. Writing a Web Page in HTML

Web pages are written in a language called **HTML (HyperText Markup Language)**. HTML allows users to produce Web pages that include text, graphics, and pointers to other Web pages. We will begin our study of HTML with these pointers, since they are the glue that holds the Web together.

URLs—Uniform Resource Locators

We have repeatedly said that Web pages may contain pointers to other Web pages. Now it is time to see how these pointers are implemented. When the Web was first created, it was immediately apparent that having one page point to another Web page required mechanisms for naming and locating pages. In particular, there were three questions that had to be answered before a selected page could be displayed:

1. What is the page called?

2. Where is the page located?

3. How can the page be accessed?

If every page were somehow assigned a unique name, there would not be any ambiguity in identifying pages. Nevertheless, the problem would not be solved. Consider a parallel between people and pages. In the United States, almost everyone has a social security number, which is a unique identifier, as no two people have the same one. Nevertheless, armed only with a social security number, there is no way to find the owner's address, and certainly no way to tell whether you should write to the person in English, Spanish, or Chinese. The Web has basically the same problems.

The solution chosen identifies pages in a way that solves all three problems at once. Each page is assigned a **URL** (**Uniform Resource Locator**) that effectively serves as the page's worldwide name. URLs have three parts: the protocol (also called a scheme), the DNS name of the machine on which the page is located, and a local name uniquely indicating the specific page (usually just a file name on the machine where it resides). For example, the URL for the author's department is

http://www.cs.vu.nl/welcome.html

This URL consists of three parts: the protocol (*http*), the DNS name of the host (*www.cs.vu.nl*), and the file name (*welcome.html*), with certain punctuation separating the pieces.

Many sites have certain shortcuts for file names built in. For example, *~user/* might be mapped onto *user*'s WWW directory, with the convention that a reference to the directory itself implies a certain file, say, *index.html*. Thus the author's home page can be reached at

http://www.cs.vu.nl/~ast/

even though the actual file name is different. At many sites, a null file name defaults to the organization's home page.

Now it should be clear how hypertext works. To make a piece of text clickable, the page writer must provide two items of information: the clickable text to be displayed and the URL of the page to go to if the text is selected. When the text is selected, the browser looks up the host name using DNS. Now armed with the host's IP address, the browser then establishes a TCP connection to the host. Over that connection, it sends the file name using the specified protocol. Bingo. Back comes the page. This is precisely what we saw in Fig. 7-60.

This URL scheme is open-ended in the sense that it is straightforward to have protocols other than HTTP. In fact, URLs for various other common protocols have been defined, and many browsers understand them. Slightly simplified forms of the more common ones are listed in Fig. 7-63.

Name	Used for	Example
http	Hypertext (HTML)	http://www.cs.vu.nl/~ast/
ftp	FTP	ftp://ftp.cs.vu.nl/pub/minix/README
file	Local file	/usr/suzanne/prog.c
news	News group	news:comp.os.minix
news	News article	news:AA0134223112@cs.utah.edu
gopher	Gopher	gopher://gopher.tc.umn.edu/11/Libraries
mailto	Sending email	mailto:kim@acm.org
telnet	Remote login	telnet://www.w3.org:80

Fig. 7-63. Some common URLs.

Let us briefly go over the list. The *http* protocol is the Web's native language, the one spoken by HTTP servers. It supports all the methods of Fig. 7-62, as well as whatever object-specific methods are needed.

The *ftp* protocol is used to access files by FTP, the Internet's file transfer protocol. FTP has been around more than two decades and is well entrenched. Numerous FTP servers all over the world allow people anywhere on the Internet to log in and download whatever files have been placed on the FTP server. The Web does not change this; it just makes obtaining files by FTP easier, as FTP has a somewhat arcane interface. In due course, FTP will probably vanish, as there is no particular advantage for a site to run an FTP server instead of an HTTP server, which can do everything that the FTP server can do, and more (although there are some arguments about efficiency).

It is possible to access a local file as a Web page, either by using the *file* protocol, or more simply, by just naming it. This approach is similar to using FTP but does not require having a server. Of course, it only works for local files.

The *news* protocol allows a Web user to call up a news article as though it were a Web page. This means that a Web browser is simultaneously a news reader. In fact, many browsers have buttons or menu items to make reading USENET news even easier than using standard news readers.

Two formats are supported for the *news* protocol. The first format specifies a newsgroup and can be used to get a list of articles from a preconfigured news site. The second one requires the identifier of a specific news article to be given, in this case *AA0134223112@cs.utah.edu*. The browser then fetches the given article from its preconfigured news site using the NNTP protocol.

The *gopher* protocol is used by the Gopher system, which was designed at the University of Minnesota and named after the school's athletic teams, the Golden Gophers (as well as being a slang expression meaning "go for", i.e., go fetch). Gopher predates the Web by several years. It is an information retrieval scheme, conceptually similar to the Web itself, but supporting only text and no images. When a user logs into a Gopher server, he is presented with a menu of files and directories, any of which can be linked to another Gopher menu anywhere in the world.

Gopher's big advantage over the Web is that it works very well with 25×80 ASCII terminals, of which there are still quite a few around, and because it is text based, it is very fast. Consequently, there are thousands of Gopher servers all over the world. Using the *gopher* protocol, Web users can access Gopher and have each Gopher menu presented as a clickable Web page. If you are not familiar with Gopher, try the example given in Fig. 7-63 or have your favorite Web search engine look for "gopher."

Although the example given does not illustrate it, it is also possible to send a complete query to a Gopher server using the *gopher+* protocol. What is displayed is the result of querying the remote Gopher server.

The last two protocols do not really have the flavor of fetching Web pages, and are not supported by all browsers, but are useful anyway. The *mailto* protocol allows users to send email from a Web browser. The way to do this is to click on the OPEN button and specify a URL consisting of *mailto:* followed by the recipient's email address. Most browsers will respond by popping up a form containing slots for the subject and other header lines and space for typing the message.

The *telnet* protocol is used to establish an on-line connection to a remote machine. It is used the same way as the Telnet program, which is not surprising, since most browsers just call the Telnet program as a helper application. As an exercise, try the scenario of Fig. 7-60 again, but now using a Web browser.

In short, the URLs have been designed to not only allow users to navigate the Web, but to deal with FTP, news, Gopher, email, and telnet as well, making all the specialized user interface programs for those other services unnecessary, and thus integrating nearly all Internet access into a single program, the Web browser. If it were not for the fact that this scheme was designed by a physics researcher, it could easily pass for the output of some software company's advertising department.

Despite all these nice properties, the growing use of the Web has turned up an inherent weakness in the URL scheme. A URL points to one specific host. For pages that are heavily referenced, it is desirable to have multiple copies far apart, to reduce the network traffic. The trouble is that URLs do not provide any way to reference a page without simultaneously telling where it is. There is no way to say: "I want page xyz, but I do not care where you get it." To solve this problem and make it possible to replicate pages, the IETF is working on a system of **URIs** (**Universal Resource Identifiers**). A URI can be thought of as a generalized URL. This topic is the subject of much current research.

Although we have discussed only absolute URLs here, relative URLs also exist. The difference is analogous to the difference between the absolute file name */usr/ast/foobar* and just *foobar* when the context is unambiguously defined.

HTML—HyperText Markup Language

Now that we have a good idea of how URLs work, it is time to look at HTML itself. HTML is an application of ISO standard 8879, **SGML (Standard Generalized Markup Language)**, but specialized to hypertext and adapted to the Web.

As mentioned earlier, HTML is a markup language, a language for describing how documents are to be formatted. The term "markup" comes from the old days when copyeditors actually marked up documents to tell the printer—in those days, a human being—which fonts to use, and so on. Markup languages thus contain explicit commands for formatting. For example, in HTML, <B> **means start boldface mode, and** </B> means leave boldface mode. The advantage of a markup language over one with no explicit markup is that writing a browser for it is straightforward: the browser simply has to understand the markup commands. TeX and troff are other well-known examples of markup languages.

Documents written in a markup language can be contrasted to documents produced with a WYSIWYG (What You See Is What You Get) word processor, such as MS-Word® or WordPerfect®. These systems may store their files with hidden embedded markup so they can reproduce them later, but not all of them work this way. Word processors for the Macintosh, for example, keep the formatting information in separate data structures, not as commands embedded in the user files.

By embedding the markup commands within each HTML file and standardizing them, it becomes possible for any Web browser to read and reformat any Web page. Being able to reformat Web pages after receiving them is crucial because a page may have been produced full screen on a 1024×768 display with 24-bit color but may have to be displayed in a small window on a 640×480 screen with 8-bit color. Proprietary WYSIWYG word processors cannot be used on the Web because their internal markup languages (if any) are not standardized across vendors, machines and operating systems. Also, they do not handle reformatting for different-sized windows and different resolution displays. However, word processing program can offer the option of saving documents in HTML instead of in the vendor's proprietary format, and some of them already do.

Like HTTP, HTML is in a constant state of flux. When Mosaic was the only browser, the language it interpreted, HTML 1.0, was the de facto standard. When new browsers came along, there was a need for a formal Internet standard, so the HTML 2.0 standard was produced. HTML 3.0 was initially created as a research effort to add many new features to HTML 2.0, including tables, toolbars, mathematical formulas, advanced style sheets (for defining page layout and the meaning of symbols), and more.

The official standardization of HTML is being managed by the WWW Consortium, but various browser vendors have added their own ad hoc extensions. These vendors hope to get people to write Web pages using their extensions, so readers of these pages will need the vendor's browser to properly interpret the pages. This tendency does not make HTML standardization any easier.

Below we will give a brief introduction to HTML, just to give an idea of what it is like. While it is certainly possible to write HTML documents with any standard editor, and many people do, it is also possible to use special HTML editors that do most of the work (but correspondingly give the user less control over all the details of the final result).

A proper Web page consists of a head and a body enclosed by <HTML> and </HTML> **tags** (formatting commands), although most browsers do not complain if these tags are missing. As can be seen from Fig. 7-64(a), the head is bracketed by the <HEAD> and </HEAD> tags and the body is bracketed by the <BODY> and </BODY> tags. The commands inside the tags are called **directives**. Most HTML tags have this format, that is, <SOMETHING> to mark the beginning of something and </SOMETHING> to mark its end. Numerous other examples of HTML are easily available. Most browsers have a menu item VIEW SOURCE or something like that. Selecting this item displays the current page's HTML source, instead of its formatted output.

Tags can be in either lowercase or uppercase. Thus <HEAD> and <head> mean the same thing, but the former stands out better for human readers. Actual layout of the HTML document is irrelevant. HTML parsers ignore extra spaces and carriage returns since they have to reformat the text to make it fit the current display area. Consequently, white space can be added at will to make HTML documents more readable, something most of them are badly in need of. As another consequence, blank lines cannot be used to separate paragraphs, as they are simply ignored. An explicit tag is required.

Some tags have (named) parameters. For example

<IMG SRC="abc" ALT="foobar">

is a tag, <IMG>, with parameter *SRC* set equal to *abc* and parameter *ALT* set equal to *foobar*. For each tag, the HTML standard gives a list of what the permitted parameters, if any, are, and what they mean. Because each parameter is named, the order in which the parameters are given is not significant.

```
<HTML> <HEAD> <TITLE> AMALGAMATED WIDGET, INC. </TITLE> </HEAD>
<BODY> <H1> Welcome to AWI's Home Page </H1>
<IMG SRC="http://www.widget.com/images/logo.gif" ALT="AWI Logo"> <BR>
We are so happy that you have chosen to visit <B> Amalgamated Widget's</B>
home page. We hope <I> you </I> will find all the information you need here.
<P>Below we have links to information about our many fine products.
You can order electronically (by WWW), by telephone, or by fax. <HR>
<H2> Product information </H2>
<UL> <LI> <A HREF="http://widget.com/products/big">  Big widgets   </A>
     <LI> <A HREF="http://widget.com/products/little"> Little widgets </A>
</UL>
<H2> Telephone numbers </H2>
<UL> <LI> By telephone: 1-800-WIDGETS
     <LI> By fax: 1-415-765-4321
</UL> </BODY> </HTML>
```

(a)

Welcome to AWI's Home Page

We are so happy that you have chosen to visit **Amalgamated Widget's** home page. We hope *you* will find all the information you need here.

Below we have links to information about our many fine products. You can order electronically (by WWW), by telephone, or by FAX.

Product Information
- Big widgets
- Little widgets

Telephone numbers
- 1-800-WIDGETS
- 1-415-765-4321

(b)

Fig. 7-64. (a) The HTML for a sample Web page. (b) The formatted page.

Technically, HTML documents are written in the ISO 8859-1 Latin-1 character set, but for users whose keyboards only support ASCII, escape sequences are present for the special characters, such as è. The list of special characters is given in the standard. All of them begin with an ampersand and end with a semicolon. For example, è produces è and é produces é. Since <, >, and & have special meanings, they can be expressed only with their escape sequences, < > and & respectively.

The main item in the head is the title, delimited by <TITLE> and </TITLE>, but certain kinds of meta-information may also be present. The title itself is not displayed on the page. Some browsers use it to label the page's window.

Let us now take a look at some of the other features illustrated in Fig. 7-64. All of the tags used in Fig. 7-64 and some others are shown in Fig. 7-65. Headings are generated by an <Hn> tag, where n is a digit in the range 1 to 6. <H1> is the most important heading; <H6> is the least important one. It is up to the browser to render these appropriately on the screen. Typically the lower numbered headings will be displayed in a larger and heavier font. The browser may also choose to use different colors for each level of heading. Typically <H1> headings are large and boldface with at least one blank line above and below. In contrast, <H2> headings are in a smaller font, and with less space above and below.

The tags <B> and <I> are used to enter boldface and italics mode, respectively. If the browser is not capable of displaying boldface and italics, it must use some other method of rendering them, for example, using a different color for each or perhaps reverse video. Instead of specifying physical styles such as boldface and italics, authors can also use logical styles such as <DN> (define), <EM> (weak emphasis), <STRONG> (strong emphasis), and <VAR> (program variables). The logical styles are defined in a document called a **style sheet**. The advantage of the logical styles is that by changing one definition, all the variables can be changed, for example, from italics to a constant width font.

HTML provides various mechanisms for making lists, including nested lists. The <UL> tag starts an unordered list. The individual items, which are marked with the <LI> tag in the source, appear with bullets (•) in front of them. A variant of this mechanism is <OL>, which is for ordered lists. When this tag is used, the <LI> items are numbered by the browser. A third option is <MENU>, which typically produces a more compact list on the screen, with no bullets and no numbers. Other than the use of different starting and ending tags, <UL>, <OL>, and <MENU> have the same syntax and similar results.

In addition to the list mechanisms shown in Fig. 7-65, there are two others that are worth mentioning briefly. <DIR> can be used for making short tables. Also, <DL> and </DL> can make definition lists (glossaries) with two-part entries, whose parts are defined by <DT> and <DD> respectively. The first is for the name, the second for its meaning. These features are largely superseded by the (more general and complex) table mechanism, described below.

Tag	Description
<HTML> ... </HTML>	Declares the Web page to be written in HTML
<HEAD> ... </HEAD>	Delimits the page's head
<TITLE> ... </TITLE>	Defines the title (not displayed on the page)
<BODY> ... </BODY>	Delimits the page's body
<H*n*> ... </H*n*>	Delimits a level *n* heading
<B> ... </B>	Set ... in boldface
<I> ... </I>	Set ... in italics
<UL> ... </UL>	Brackets an unordered (bulleted) list
<OL> ... </OL>	Brackets a numbered list
<MENU> ... </MENU>	Brackets a menu of <LI> items
<LI>	Start of a list item (there is no </LI>)
 	Force a break here
<P>	Start of paragraph
<HR>	Horizontal rule
<PRE> ... </PRE>	Preformatted text; do not reformat
<IMG SRC="...">	Load an image here
<A HREF="..."> ... </A>	Defines a hyperlink

Fig. 7-65. A selection of common HTML tags. Some have additional parameters.

The <BR>, <P>, and <HR> tags all indicate a boundary between sections of text. The precise format can be determined by the style sheet associated with the page. The <BR> tag just forces a line break. Typically, browsers do not insert a blank line after <BR>. In contrast, <P> starts a paragraph, which might, for example, insert a blank line and possibly some indentation. (Theoretically, </P> exists to mark the end of a paragraph, but it is rarely used; most HTML authors do not even know it exists.) Finally, <HR> forces a break and draws a horizontal line across the screen.

HTML 1.0 had no ability to display tables or other formatted information. Worse yet, if the HTML writer carefully formatted a table by judicious use of spaces and carriage returns, browsers would ignore all the layout and display the page as if all the formatted material were unformatted. To prevent browsers from messing up carefully laid out text, the <PRE> and </PRE> tags were provided. They are instructions to the browser to just display everything in between literally, character for character, without changing anything. As the table and other fancy layout features become more widely implemented, the need for <PRE> will diminish, except for program listings, for which most programmers will tolerate no formatting other than their own.

HTML allows images to be included in-line on a Web page. The <IMG> tag specifies that an image is to be loaded at the current position in the page. It can have several parameters. The *SRC* parameter gives the URL (or URI) of the image. The HTML standard does not specify which graphic formats are permitted. In practice, all browsers support GIF files and many support JPEG files as well. Browsers are free to support other formats, but this extension is a two-edged sword. If a user is accustomed to a browser that supports, say, BMP files, he may include these in his Web pages and later be surprised when other browsers just ignore all of his wonderful art.

Other parameters of <IMG> are *ALIGN*, which controls the alignment of the image with respect to the text baseline (*TOP*, *MIDDLE*, *BOTTOM*), *ALT*, which provides text to use instead of the image when the user has disabled images, and *ISMAP*, a flag indicating that the image is an active map.

Finally, we come to hyperlinks, which use the <A> (anchor) and </A> tags. Like <IMG>, <A> has various parameters, including *HREF* (the URL), *NAME* (the hyperlink's name), and *METHODS* (access methods), among others. The text between the <A> and </A> is displayed. If it is selected, the hyperlink is followed to a new page. It is also permitted to put an <IMG> image there, in which case clicking on the image also activates the hyperlink.

As an example, consider the following HTML fragment:

```
<A HREF="http://www.nasa.gov"> NASA's home page </A>
```

When a page with this fragment is displayed, what appears on the screen is

<u>NASA's home page</u>

If the user subsequently clicks on this text, the browser immediately fetches the page whose URL is *http://www.nasa.gov* and displays it.

As a second example, now consider

```
<A HREF="http://www.nasa.gov"> <IMG SRC="shuttle.gif" ALT="NASA"> </A>
```

When displayed, this page shows a picture (e.g., of the space shuttle). Clicking on the picture switches to NASA's home page, just as clicking on the underlined text did in the previous example. If the user has disabled automatic image display, the text NASA will be displayed where the picture belongs.

The <A> tag can take a parameter *NAME* to plant a hyperlink, so it can be referred to from within the page. For example, some Web pages start out with a clickable table of contents. By clicking on an item in the table of contents, the user jumps to the corresponding section of the page.

One feature that HTML 2.0 did not include and which many page authors missed, was the ability to create tables whose entries could be clicked on to active hyperlinks. As a consequence, a large amount of work was done to add tables to

HTML 3.0. Below we give a very brief introduction to tables, just to capture the essential flavor.

An HTML table consists of one or more rows, each consisting of one or more **cells**. Cells can contain a wide range of material, including text, figures, and even other tables. Cells can be merged, so, for example, a heading can span multiple columns. Page authors have limited control over the layout, including alignment, border styles, and cell margins, but the browsers have the final say in rendering tables.

An HTML table definition is listed in Fig. 7-66(a) and a possible rendition is shown in Fig. 7-66(b). This example just shows a few of the basic features of HTML tables. Tables are started by the <TABLE> tag. Additional information can be provided to describe general properties of the table.

The <CAPTION> tag can be used to provide a figure caption. Each row is started with a <TR> (Table Row) tag. The individual cells are marked as <TH> (Table Header) or <TD> (Table Data). The distinction is made to allow browsers to use different renditions for them, as we have done in the example.

Numerous other tags are also allowed in tables. They include ways to specify horizontal and vertical cell alignments, justification within a cell, borders, grouping of cells, units, and more.

Forms

HTML 1.0 was basically one way. Users could call up pages from information providers, but it was difficult to send information back the other way. As more and more commercial organizations began using the Web, there was a large demand for two-way traffic. For example, many companies wanted to be able to take orders for products via their Web pages, software vendors wanted to distribute software via the Web and have customers fill out their registration cards electronically, and companies offering Web searching wanted to have their customers be able to type in search keywords.

These demands led to the inclusion of **forms** starting in HTML 2.0. Forms contain boxes or buttons that allow users to fill in information or make choices and then send the information back to the page's owner. They use the <INPUT> tag for this purpose. It has a variety of parameters for determining the size, nature, and usage of the box displayed. The most common forms are blank fields for accepting user text, boxes that can be checked, active maps, and SUBMIT buttons. The example of Fig. 7-67 illustrates some of these choices.

Let us start our discussion of forms by going over this example. Like all forms, this one is enclosed between the <FORM> and </FORM> tags. Text not enclosed in a tag is just displayed. All the usual tags (e.g., <B>) are allowed in a form. Three kinds of input boxes are used in this form.

The first kind of input box follows the text "Name". The box is 46 characters wide and expects the user to type in a string, which is then stored in the variable

```
<HTML> <HEAD> <TITLE> A sample page with a table </TITLE> </HEAD>
<BODY>
<TABLE BORDER=ALL RULES=ALL>
<CAPTION> Some Differences between HTML Versions </CAPTION>
<COL ALIGN=LEFT>
<COL ALIGN=CENTER>
<COL ALIGN=CENTER>
<COL ALIGN=CENTER>
<TR> <TH>Item  <TH>HTML 1.0  <TH>HTML 2.0  <TH>HTML 3.0
<TR> <TH> Active Maps and Images <TD> <TD> x <TD> x
<TR> <TH> Equations <TD> <TD> <TD> x
<TR> <TH> Forms <TD> <TD> x <TD> x
<TR> <TH> Hyperlinks x <TD> <TD> x <TD> x
<TR> <TH> Images <TD> x <TD> x <TD> x
<TR> <TH> Lists <TD> x <TD> x <TD> x
<TR> <TH> Toolbars <TD> <TD> <TD> x
<TR> <TH> Tables <TD> <TD> <TD> x
</TABLE> </BODY> </HTML>
```

(a)

Some Differences between HTML Versions

Item	HTML 1.0	HTML 2.0	HTML 3.0
Active Maps and Images		x	x
Equations			x
Forms		x	x
Hyperlinks	x	x	x
Images	x	x	x
Lists	x	x	x
Toolbars			x
Tables			x

Fig. 7-66. (a) An HTML table. (b) A possible rendition of this table.

customer for later processing. The <P> tag instructs the browser to display subsequent text and boxes on the next line, even if there is room on the current line. By using <P> and other layout tags, the author of the page can control the look of the form on the screen.

The next line of the form asks for the user's street address, 40 columns wide, also on a line by itself. Then comes a line asking for the city, state, and country. No <P> tags are used between the fields here, so the browser displays them all on one line if they will fit. As far as the browser is concerned, this paragraph just contains six items: three strings alternating with three boxes. It displays them linearly from left to right, going over to a new line whenever the current line

```
<HTML> <HEAD> <TITLE> AWI CUSTOMER ORDERING FORM </TITLE> </HEAD>
<BODY>
<H1> Widget Order Form </H1>
<FORM ACTION="http://widget.com/cgi-bin/widgetorder" METHOD=POST>
Name <INPUT NAME="customer" SIZE=46> <P>
Street Address <INPUT NAME="address" SIZE=40> <P>
City <INPUT NAME="city" SIZE=20> State <INPUT NAME="state" SIZE =4>
Country <INPUT NAME="country" SIZE=10> <P>
Credit card # <INPUT NAME="cardno" SIZE=10>
Expires <INPUT NAME="expires" SIZE=4>
M/C <INPUT NAME="cc" TYPE=RADIO VALUE="mastercard">
VISA <INPUT NAME="cc" TYPE=RADIO VALUE="visacard"> <P>
Widget size Big <INPUT NAME="product" TYPE=RADIO VALUE="expensive">
Little <INPUT NAME="product" TYPE=RADIO VALUE="cheap">
Ship by express courier <INPUT NAME="express" TYPE=CHECKBOX> <P>
<INPUT TYPE=SUBMIT VALUE="Submit order"> <P>
Thank you for ordering an AWI widget, the best widget money can buy!
</FORM> </BODY> </HTML>
```

(a)

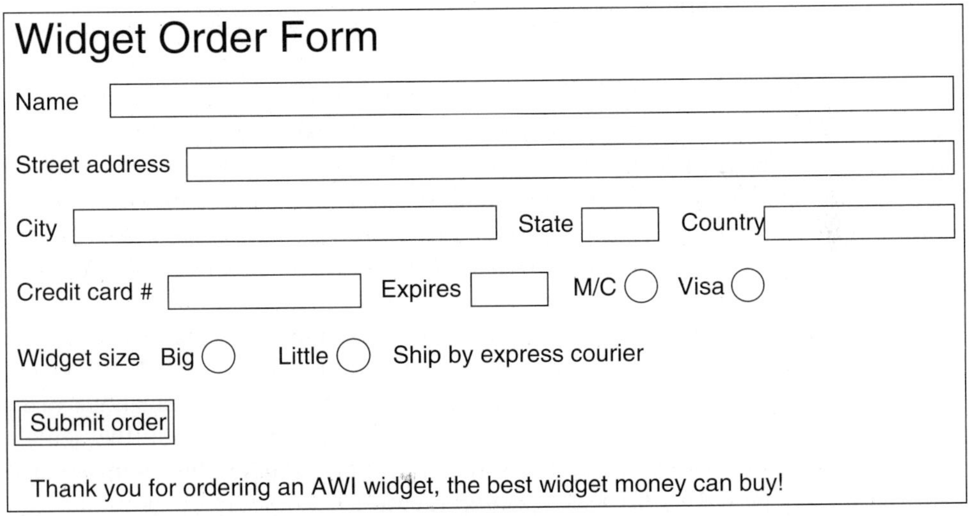

(b)

Fig. 7-67. (a) The HTML for an order form. (b) The formatted page.

cannot hold the next item. Thus it is conceivable that on a 1024×768 screen all three strings and their corresponding boxes will appear on the same line, but on a 640×480 screen they might be split over two lines. In the worst scenario, the word "Country" is at the end of one line and its box is at the beginning of the next line. There is no way to tell the browser to force the box adjacent to the text.

The next line asks for the credit card number and expiration date. Transmitting credit card numbers over the Internet should only be done when adequate security measures have been taken. For example, some, but not all, browsers encrypt information sent by users. Even then, secure communication and key management are complicated matters and are subject to many kinds of attacks, as we saw earlier.

Following the expiration date we encounter a new feature: radio buttons. These are used when a choice must be made among two or more alternatives. The intellectual model here is a car radio with half a dozen buttons for choosing stations. The browser displays these boxes in a form that allows the user to select and deselect them by clicking on them (or using the keyboard). Clicking on one of them turns off all the other ones in the same group. The visual presentation depends on the graphical interface being used. It is up to the browser to choose a form that is consistent with Windows, Motif, OS/2 Warp, or whatever windowing system is being used. The widget size also uses two radio buttons. The two groups are distinguished by their *NAME* field, not by static scoping using something like <RADIOBUTTON> ... </RADIOBUTTON>.

The *VALUE* parameters are used to indicate which radio button was pushed. Depending on which of the credit card options the user has chosen, the variable *cc* will be set to either the string "mastercard" or the string "visacard".

After the two sets of radio buttons, we come to the shipping option, represented by a box of type *CHECKBOX*. It can be either on or off. Unlike radio buttons, where exactly one out of the set must be chosen, each box of type *CHECKBOX* can be on or off, independently of all the others. For example, when ordering a pizza via Electropizza's Web page, the user can choose sardines *and* onions *and* pineapple (if she can stand it), but she cannot choose small *and* medium *and* large for the same pizza. The pizza toppings would be represented by three separate boxes of type *CHECKBOX*, whereas the pizza size would be a set of radio buttons.

As an aside, for very long lists from which a choice must be made, radio buttons are somewhat inconvenient. Therefore, the <SELECT> and </SELECT> tags are provided to bracket a list of alternatives, but with the semantics of radio buttons (unless the *MULTIPLE* parameter is given, in which case the semantics are those of checkable boxes). Some browsers render the items between <SELECT> and </SELECT> as a pop-up menu.

We have now seen two of the built-in types for the <INPUT> tag: *RADIO* and *CHECKBOX*. In fact, we have already seen a third one as well: *TEXT*. Because this type is the default, we did not bother to include the parameter *TYPE = TEXT*, but we could have. Two other types are *PASSWORD* and *TEXTAREA*. A *PASSWORD* box is the same as a *TEXT* box, except that the characters are not displayed as they are typed. A *TEXTAREA* box is also the same as a *TEXT* box, except that it can contain multiple lines.

Getting back to the example of Fig. 7-67, we now come across an example of a *SUBMIT* button. When this is clicked, the user information on the form is sent back to the machine that provided the form. Like all the other types, *SUBMIT* is a reserved word that the browser understands. The *VALUE* string here is the label on the button and is displayed. All boxes can have values; we only needed that feature here. For *TEXT* boxes, the contents of the *VALUE* field are displayed along with the form, but the user can edit or erase it. *CHECKBOX* and *RADIO* boxes can also be initialized, but with a field called *CHECKED* (because *VALUE* just gives the text, but does not indicate a preferred choice).

The browser also understands the *RESET* button. When clicked, it resets the form to its initial state.

Two more types are worth noting. The first is the *HIDDEN* type. This is output only; it cannot be clicked or modified. For example, when working through a series of pages throughout which choices have to be made, previously made choices might be of *HIDDEN* type, to prevent them from being changed.

Our last type is *IMAGE*, which is for active maps (and other clickable images). When the user clicks on the map, the (x, y) coordinates of the pixel selected (i.e., the current mouse position) are stored in variables and the form is automatically returned to the owner for further processing.

Forms can be submitted in three ways: using the submit button, clicking on an active map, or typing ENTER on a one-item *TEXT* form. When a form is submitted, some action must be taken. The action is specified by the parameters of the <FORM> tag. The *ACTION* parameter specifies the URL (or URI) to tell about the submission, and the *METHOD* parameter tells which method to use. The order of these (and all other) parameters is not significant.

The way the form's variables are sent back to the page's owner depends on the value of the *METHOD* parameter. For *GET*, the only way to return values is to cheat: they are appended to the URL, separated by a question mark. This approach can result in URLs that are thousands of characters long. Nevertheless, this method is frequently used because it is simple.

If the *POST* method (see Fig. 7-62) is used, the body of the message contains the form's variables and their values. The & is used to separate fields; the + represents the space character. For example, the response to the widget form might be

```
customer=John+Doe&address=100+Main+St.&city=White+Plains&
state=NY&country=USA&cardno=1234567890&expires=6/98&cc=mastercard&
product=cheap&express=on
```

The string would be sent back to the server as one line, not three. If a *CHECK-BOX* is not selected, it is omitted from the string. It is up to the server to make sense of this string.

Fortunately, a standard for handling forms' data is already available. It is called **CGI (Common Gateway Interface)**. Let us consider a common way of using it. Suppose that someone has an interesting database (e.g., an index of Web pages by keyword and topic) and wants to make it available to Web users. The CGI way to make the database available is to write a script (or program) that interfaces (i.e., gateways) between the database and the Web. This script is given a URL, by convention in the directory *cgi-bin*. HTTP servers know (or can be told) that when they have to invoke a method on a page located in *cgi-bin*, they are to interpret the file name as being an executable script or program and start it up.

Eventually, some user opens the form associated with our widget script and has it displayed. After the form has been filled out, the user clicks on the SUB-MIT button. This action causes the browser to establish a TCP connection to the URL listed in the form's *ACTION* parameter—the script in the *cgi-bin* directory. Then the browser invokes the operation specified by the form's *METHOD*, usually *POST*. The result of this operation is that the script is started and presented (via the TCP connection, on standard input) with the long string given above. In addition, several environment variables are set. For example, the environment variable *CONTENT_LENGTH* tells how long the input string is.

At this point, most scripts need to parse their input to put it in a more convenient form. This goal can be accomplished by calling one of the many libraries or script procedures available. The script can then interact with its database in any way it wishes. For example, active maps normally use CGI scripts to take different actions depending on where the user pointed.

CGI scripts can also produce output and do many other things as well as accepting input from forms. If a hyperlink points to a CGI script, when that link is invoked, the script is started up, with several environment variables set to provide some information about the user. The script then writes a file (e.g. an HTML page) on standard output, which is shipped to the browser and interpreted there. This mechanism makes it possible for the script to generate custom Web pages on the spot.

For better or worse, some Web sites that answer queries have a database of advertisements that can be selectively included in the Web page being constructed, depending on what the user is looking for. If the user is searching for "car" a General Motors ad might be displayed, whereas a search for "vacation" might produce an ad from United Airlines. These ads usually include clickable text and pictures.

7.6.4. Java

HTML makes it possible to describe how static Web pages should appear, including tables and pictures. With the cgi-bin hack, it is also possible to have a limited amount of two-way interaction (forms, etc.). However, rapid interaction with Web pages written in HTML is not possible. To make it possible to have highly interactive Web pages, a different mechanism is needed. In this section we will describe one such mechanism, the Java™ language and interpreter.

Java originated when some people at Sun Microsystems were trying to develop a new language that was suitable for programming information-oriented consumer appliances. Later it was reoriented toward the World Wide Web. Although Java borrows many ideas and some syntax from C and C++, it is a new object-oriented language, compatible with neither. It is sometimes said that in the large, Java is like Smalltalk, but that in the small it is like C or C++.

The main idea of using Java for interactive Web pages is that a Web page can point to a small Java program, called an **applet** (SAT I verbal analogy question: Pig is to piglet as application is to ?). When the browser reaches it, the applet is downloaded to the client machine and executed there in a secure way. It must be structurally impossible for the applet to read or write any files that it is not author- ized to access. It must also be impossible for the applet to introduce viruses or cause any other damage. For these reasons, and to achieve portability across machines, applets are compiled to a bytecode after being written and debugged. It is these bytecode programs that are pointed to by Web pages, similar to the way images are pointed to. When an applet arrives, it is executed interpretively in a secure environment.

Before getting into the details of the Java language, it is worth saying a few words about what the whole Java system is good for and why people want to include Java applets in their Web pages. For one thing, applets allow Web pages to become interactive. For example, a web page can contain a board for tic tac toe, othello, or chess, and play a game with the user. The game-playing program (written in Java) is just downloaded along with its Web page. As a second exam- ple, complex forms (e.g., spreadsheets) can be displayed, with the user filling in items and seeing calculations made instantly.

It is entirely possible that in the long run, the model of people buying pro- grams, installing them, and running them locally will be replaced by a model in which people click on Web pages, get applets downloaded to do work for them, possibly in conjunction with a remote server or data base. Instead of filling out the income tax form by hand or using a special program, people may be able to click on the IRS home page to get a tax applet downloaded. This applet might ask some questions, then contact the person's employer, bank, and stockbroker to col- lect the required salary, interest, and dividend information, fill the tax form in, and then display it for verification and submission.

Another reason for running applets on the client machine is they make it pos- sible to add animation and sound to Web pages without having to spawn external viewers. The sound can be played when the page is loaded, as background music, or when some specific event happens (e.g., clicking on the cat makes it meow). The same is true for animation. Because the applet is running locally, even if it is being interpreted, it can write all over (its portion) of the screen any way it wants to, and at very high speed (compared to a remote cgi-bin shell script).

The Java system has three parts:

1. A Java-to-bytecode compiler.

2. A browser that understands applets.

3. A bytecode interpreter.

The developer writes the applet in Java, then compiles it to bytecode. To include this compiled applet on a Web page, a new HTML tag, <APPLET>, has been invented. A typical use is

<APPLET CODE=game.class WIDTH=100 HEIGHT=200> </APPLET>

When the browser sees the <APPLET> tag, it fetches the compiled applet *game.class* from the current Web page's site (or if another parameter, *CODE-BASE*, is present, from the URL it specifies). The browser than passes the applet to the local bytecode interpreter for execution (or interprets the applet itself, if it has an internal interpreter). The *WIDTH* and *HEIGHT* parameters give the size of the applet's default window, in pixels.

In a sense, the <APPLET> tag is analogous to the <IMG> tag. In both cases, the browser goes and gets a file and then hands it off to a (possibly internal) interpreter for display within a bounded area of the screen. Then it continues processing the Web page.

For applications that need very high performance, some Java interpreters have the ability to compile bytecode programs to actual machine language on-the-fly, as needed.

As a consequence of this model, Java-based browsers are extensible in a way that first-generation browsers are not. First generation browsers are basically HTML interpreters that have built-in modules for speaking the various protocols needed, such as HTTP 1.0, FTP, etc., as well as decoders for various image formats. An example is shown in Fig. 7-68(a). If someone invents or popularizes a new format, such as audio or MPEG-2, these old browsers are not able to read pages containing them. At best, the user has to find, download, and install an appropriate external viewer.

With a Java-based browser, the situation is different. At startup, the browser is effectively an empty Java virtual machine, as shown in Fig. 7-68(b). By loading HTML and HTTP applets, it becomes able to read standard Web pages. However, as new protocols and decoders are required, their classes are loaded dynamically, possibly over the network from sites specified in Web pages. After a while, the browser might look like Fig. 7-68(c).

Thus if someone invents a new format, all that person has to do is include the URL of an applet for handling it in a Web page, and the browser will automatically fetch and load the applet. No first-generation browser is capable of automatically downloading and installing new external viewers on-the-fly. The ability to

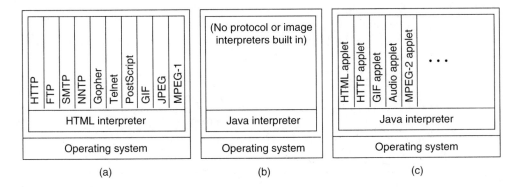

Fig. 7-68. (a) A first generation browser. (b) A Java-based browser at startup. (c) The browser of (b) after running for a while.

load applets dynamically means that people can easily experiment with new formats without first having to have endless standardization meetings to reach a consensus.

This extensibility also applies to protocols. For some applications, special protocols are needed, for example, secure protocols for banking and commerce. With Java, these protocols can be loaded dynamically as needed, and there is no need to achieve universal standardization. To communicate with company X, you just download its protocol applet. To talk to company Y, you get its protocol applet. There is no need for X and Y to agree on a standard protocol.

Introduction to the Java Language

The objectives listed above have led to a type-safe, object-oriented language with built-in multithreading and no undefined or system dependent features. What follows is a highly simplified description of Java, just to give a feel for it. Many features, details, options, and special cases have been omitted for the sake of brevity. The complete language specification, and much more about Java, is available on the Web itself (naturally) at *http://java.sun.com*. For tutorials on Java, see (Campione and Walrath, 1996; and Van der Linden, 1996). For the full story, see (Arnold and Gosling, 1996; and Gosling et al., 1996). For a brief comparison between Java and Microsoft's answer to it (Blackbird), see (Singleton, 1996).

As we mentioned above, in the small, Java is similar to C and C++. The lexical rules, for example, are pretty much the same (e.g., tokens are delimited by white space, and new lines can be inserted between any two tokens). Comments can be inserted using either the C syntax (/* ... */) or the C++ syntax (// ...).

Java has eight primitive data types, as listed in Fig. 7-69. Each type has a specific size, independent of the local implementation. Thus unlike C, where an integer may be 16, 32, or 64 bits, depending on the underlying machine architecture, a Java int is always 32 bits, no more and no less, no matter what kind of machine the interpreter is running on. This consistency is essential since the same applet must run on 16-bit, 32-bit, and 64-bit machines, and give the same result on all of them.

Type	Size	Description
Byte	1 Byte	A signed integer between -128 and $+127$
Short	2 Bytes	A signed 2-byte integer
Int	4 Bytes	A signed 4-byte integer
Long	8 Bytes	A signed 8-byte integer
Float	4 Bytes	A 4-byte IEEE floating-point number
Double	8 Bytes	An 8-byte IEEE floating-point number
Boolean	1 Bit	The only values are true and false
Char	2 Bytes	A character in Unicode

Fig. 7-69. The basic Java data types.

Arithmetic variables (the first 6 types) can be combined using the usual arithmetic operators (including ++ and −−) and compared using the usual relational operators (e.g., <, <=, ==, !=). Conversions between types are permitted where they make sense.

Java uses the 16-bit Unicode instead of ASCII for characters, so character variables are 2 bytes long. The first 127 Unicode characters are the same as ASCII for backward compatibility. Above these are some graphic symbols, and then the characters needed for Russian, Arabic, Hebrew, Japanese (kanji, kata-kana, and hiragana), and virtually every other language. Characters not present in ASCII can be represented with \u followed by four hexadecimal digits. For example, \u0ae6 is the Gujarati zero.

Java allows one dimensional arrays to be declared. For example,

int[] table;

declares an array, *table*, but does not allocate any space for it. That can be done later on, as in C++, for example, by

table = new int [1024];

to allocate an array with 1024 entries. It is not necessary (or even possible) to return arrays that are no longer needed; the garbage collector reclaims them. Thus the highly error-prone *malloc* and *free* library routines are not needed for storage management. Arrays can be initialized, and arrays of arrays can be used to get higher dimensionality, as in C. Strings are available, but they are defined in a class, rather than being simply character arrays ending with a null byte.

The Java control statements are shown in Fig. 7-70. The first nine have essentially the same syntax and semantics as in C, except that where a Boolean expression is required, the language actually insists upon a Boolean expression. Also, the break and continue statements now can take labels indicating which of the labeled loops to exit or repeat.

Statement	Description	Example
Assignment	Assign a value	n = i + j;
If	Boolean choice	if (k < 0) k = 0; else k = 2*k;
Switch	Select a case	switch (b) {case 1: n++; case 2: n—;}
For	Iteration	for (i = 0; i < n; i++) a[i] = b[i];
While	Repetition	while (n < k) n += i;
Do	Repetition	do {n = n + n} while (n < m);
Break	Exit statement	break label;
Return	Return	return n;
Continue	Next iteration	continue label;
Throw	Raise exception	throw new IllegalArgumentException();
Try	Exception scoping	try { ... } catch (Exception e) {return –1};
Synchronized	Mutual exclusion	synchronized void update(int s) { ... }

Fig. 7-70. The Java statements. The notation { ... } indicates a block of code.

The next two statements are in C++ but not in C. The throw and try statements deal with exception handling. Java defines a variety of standard exceptions, such as attempting to divide by zero, and allows programmers to define and raise their own exceptions. Programmers can write handlers to catch exceptions, making it unnecessary to constantly test if something has gone wrong (e.g., when reading from a file). The throw statement raises an exception, and the try statement defines a scope to associate exception handlers with a block of code in which an exception might occur.

The synchronized statement is new to Java and has to do with the fact that Java programs can have multiple threads of control. To avoid race conditions, this statement is used to delimit a block of code (or a whole procedure) that must not have more than one thread active in it at once. Such blocks of code are usually called **critical regions**. When the synchronized statement is executed, the thread executing it must acquire the lock associated with the critical region, execute the code, and then release the lock. If the lock is not available, the thread waits until it is free. By guarding entire procedures this way and using condition variables, programmers have the full power of monitors (Hoare, 1974).

Java programs can be called with arguments. Command-line processing is similar to C, except that the argument array is called *args* instead of *argv* and *args*[0] is the first parameter, not the program name. Figure 7-71 illustrates a small Java program that computes a table of factorials, just to give an idea of what a small Java program looks like.

```java
class Factorial { /* This program consists of a single class with two methods. */

    public static void main (int argc, String args[]) { // main program
    long i, f, lower = 1, upper = 20;          // declarations of four longs

        for (i = lower; i <= upper; i++) {      // loop from lower to upper
            f = factorial(i);                    // f = i!
            System.out.println(i + " " + f);     // print i and f
        }
    }

    static long factorial (long k) {             // recursive factorial function
        if (k == 0)
            return 1;                            // 0! = 1
        else
            return k * factorial(k-1);           // k! = k * (k-1)!
    }
}
```

Fig. 7-71. A Java program for computing and printing 0! to 20!.

Despite both being object-oriented languages based on C, Java and C++ differ in some ways. Some features were removed from Java to make it typesafe or easier to read. These include #define, typedef, enums, unions, structs, operator overloading, explicit pointers, global variables, standalone functions, and friend functions. It almost goes without saying that the goto statement has been sent to that special place reserved for obsolete programming language features. Other features were added to give the language more power. The features added include garbage collection, multithreading, object interfaces, and packages.

Object Orientation in Java

In traditional procedural languages such as Pascal or C, a program consists of a collection of variables and procedures, without any general organizing principle. In contrast in **object-oriented languages**, (almost) everything is an object. An **object** normally contains some internal (i.e., hidden) state variables along with some public procedures, called **methods**, for accessing them. Programs that use the object are expected (and can be forced) to invoke the methods to manipulate the object's state. In this way, the object writer can control how programs use the information inside the object. This principle is called **encapsulation**, and is the basis of all object-oriented programming.

Java tries to capture the best of both worlds. It can be used as a traditional procedural language or as an object-oriented language. The Java example of Fig. 7-71, for example, could equally well have been written in C, and in essentially the same way. In this view, a subset of Java can be regarded as a cleaned-up version of C. However, for writing Web pages, Java is better regarded as an object-oriented language, so we will study its object orientation in this section.

A Java program consists of one or more **packages**, each of which contains some class definitions. Packages can be accessed remotely over a network, so those intended for use by a wide audience must have unique names. Normally, hierarchical names are used, starting with the reverse of their machine's DNS name, for example

EDU.univ.cs.catie.games.chess

A **class** definition is a template for stamping out object instances, each of which contains the same state variables and same methods as all the other object instances of its class. The values of the state variables within different objects are independent, however. Classes are thus like cookie cutters: they are not cookies themselves, but are used to stamp out structurally identical cookies, with each cookie cutter producing a different shape of cookie. Once produced, different cookies (objects) are independent of one another.

Java objects can be produced dynamically during execution, for example by

object = new ClassName()

These objects are stored on the heap and removed by the garbage collector when no longer needed. In this way, storage management in Java is handled by the system, with no need for the dreaded *malloc* and *free* procedures, or even for explicit pointers, for that matter.

Each class is based on another class. A newly defined class is said to be a **subclass** of the class on which it is based, the **superclass**. A (sub)class always **inherits** the methods of its superclass. It may or may not have direct access to the superclass' internal variables, depending on whether or not the superclass wants that. For example, if a superclass, *A*, has methods *M1*, *M2*, and *M3*, and a subclass, *B*, defines a new method, *M4*, then objects created from *B*, will have methods *M1*, *M2*, *M3*, and *M4*. The property of a class automatically acquiring all the methods of its superclass is called **inheritance**, and is an important property of Java. Adding new methods to the superclass' methods is called **extending** the superclass. As an aside, some object-oriented languages allow classes to inherit methods from two or more superclasses (multiple inheritance), but the Java designers thought this property to be too messy and intentionally left it out.

Since every class has exactly one immediate superclass, the set of all classes in a Java program form a tree. The class at the top of the tree is called **Object**.

All other classes inherit its methods. Any class whose superclass is not explicitly mentioned in its definition defaults to being a subclass of the *Object* class. The *Factorial* class of Fig. 7-71, for example, is thus a subclass of *Object*.

Let us now take a look at an example of the object-oriented concepts presented so far. In Fig. 7-72 we have a package defining two classes, *Complex-Number*, for defining and using complex numbers (i.e., numbers with a real part and an imaginary part), and *test*, for showing how *ComplexNumber* can be used.

```
class ComplexNumber {          // Define a subclass of Object called ComplexNumber
    // Hidden data.
    protected double re, im;      // real and imaginary parts

    // Five methods that manage the hidden data.
    public void Complex(double x, double y) {re = x; im = y;}
    public double Real() {return re;}
    public double Imaginary() {return im;}
    public double Magnitude() {return Math.sqrt(re*re + im*im);}
    public double Angle() {return Math.atan(im/re);}
}

class test {                   // A second class, for testing ComplexNumber
    public static void main (String args[]) {
        ComplexNumber c;          // declare an object of class ComplexNumber

        c = new ComplexNumber();  // actually allocate storage for c
        c.Complex(3.0, 4.0);      // invoke the Complex method to initialize c
        System.out.println("The magnitude of c is " + c.Magnitude() );
    }
}
```

Fig. 7-72. A package defining two classes.

Like *Factorial*, the class *ComplexNumber* is based on *Object*, because no other superclass is named in its definition. Each object of class *ComplexNumber* represents one complex number. Each object of this class contains two hidden variables, *re*, and *im*, both 64-bit floating-point numbers, for representing the real and imaginary parts, respectively. They cannot be accessed outside the class definition (and its subclasses), because they have been declared protected. Had they been declared private, then they would have been visible only to *Complex-Number* and not to any subclasses. For the moment, private would have been fine, but we will soon define a subclass. Had they been declared public, they would have been visible everywhere the package was visible, thus destroying much of the value of object-oriented programming. Nevertheless, situations do exist in which having the internal state of an object be public is sometimes needed.

Five methods are defined on objects belonging to class *ComplexNumber*. Users of the class are thus restricted to the operations provided by these five methods, and cannot get at the state directly. An example of how objects of class *ComplexNumber* are created, initialized, and used is given in *test*.

When this package is compiled, the Java compiler produces two binary (bytecode) files, one containing each of the classes and named after its class. Typing the command

java test

results in invoking the Java interpreter with class *test* as parameter. The interpreter then looks for a method called *main*, and upon finding it, executes it. The result of execution is that the line

The magnitude of c is 5

is printed out.

Now let us define a subclass of *ComplexNumber*, just to see how that works. It starts out by importing the original class, to learn what it does and what its methods are. Then it defines an extension of *ComplexNumber*, which we will call *HairyNumber*. The new class automatically inherits the five methods present in the superclass. To make things interesting, we will define a sixth method, *AddTo*, in the subclass, which adds a complex number to the object, increasing its real and imaginary parts.

The subclass definition is shown in Fig. 7-73, along with another test program showing how an object belonging to class *HairyNumber* can be used. When the new test program is run, it will print out

h = (−0.5,6)

Remember that the six methods are usable on the objects *a* and *h*, without regard to which method was defined where. If we now define yet another subclass based on *HairyNumber* and give it, say, three new methods, objects produced from it will have nine valid methods.

In addition to adding new methods to its superclass, a subclass can override (replace) existing methods by simply redefining them. Thus it is possible for a subclass to redefine all the methods inherited from its superclass, so objects belonging to the two classes have nothing in common. Doing so, however, is in poor taste, and should be avoided.

Finally, a Java class may define multiple methods with the same name but different parameters and different definitions. When the compiler sees a method invocation using this name, it has to use the parameter types to determine which method to use. This property is called **overloading** or **polymorphism**. Unlike C++, where operators can also be overloaded, in Java, only methods, not operators, can be overloaded, to make programs easier to understand.

```
import ComplexNumber;           // import the ComplexNumber package


class HairyNumber extends ComplexNumber {   // define a new class
  public void AddTo(ComplexNumber z) {        // with one method
    re = re + z.Real();
    im = im + z.Imaginary();
  }
}


class test2 {                    // test program for HairyNumber
  public static void main(String args[]) {
    HairyNumber a, h;            // declare two HairyNumbers

    a = new HairyNumber();       // allocate storage for a
    h = new HairyNumber();       // allocate storage for h
    a.Complex(1.0, 2.0);         // assign a value to a
    h.Complex(-1.5, 4.0);        // assign a value to h
    h.AddTo(a);                  // invoke the AddTo method on h
    System.out.println("h = (" + h.Real() + "," + h.Imaginary() + ")"  );
  }
}
```

Fig. 7-73. A subclass of *ComplexNumber* defining a new method.

The Application Programmers Interface

In addition to the bare language, the Java designers have defined and implemented about 200 classes with the initial release. The methods contained in these classes form a kind of standard environment for Java program developers. The classes are written in Java, so they are portable to all platforms and operating systems.

While a detailed discussion of all these classes and methods is clearly beyond the scope of this book, a brief description may be of some interest. The 200 classes are grouped into seven packages of uneven size, each of which is focused on some central theme. Applets that need a particular package can include it using the Java import statement. The methods contained within can just be used as needed. This mechanism replaces the need for including header files in C. It also replaces the need for libraries, since the packages are dynamically loaded during execution when they are invoked.

The seven packages are summarized in Fig. 7-74. The *java.lang* package contains classes that can be viewed as part of the language, but are technically not. These include classes for managing the classes themselves, threads, and exception handling. The standard mathematical and string libraries are also here.

Package	Example functionality
Java.lang	Classes, threads, exceptions, math, strings
Java.io	I/O on streams and random access files, printing
Java.net	Sockets, IP addresses, URLs, datagrams
Java.util	Stacks, hash tables, vectors, time, date
Java.applet	Getting and displaying Web pages, audio, Object class
Java.awt	Events, dialog, menus, fonts, graphics, window management
Java.awt.image	Colors, image cropping, filtering, and conversion
Java.awt.peer	Access to the underlying window system

Fig. 7-74. The packages included in the standard API.

Like C, the Java language contains no I/O primitives. I/O is done by loading and using the *java.io* package. It is analogous to the standard I/O library in C. Methods are provided for reading and writing streams, random access files, and doing the formatting needed for printing. In Fig. 7-71 we saw one of these methods, *println*, which does formatted printing.

Closely related to I/O is network transport. Methods that look up and manage IP addresses are located here. Access to sockets is also part of this package. So is datagram preparation. The actual transmission is handled in *java.io*.

The next class is *java.util*. It contains classes and methods for common data structures, such as stacks and hash tables, so programmers do not constantly have to reinvent the wheel. Time and date management is also here.

The *java.applet* package contains some of the basic machinery for applets, including methods for getting Web pages starting from their URLs. It also has methods for displaying Web pages and playing audio clips (e.g., background music). The *java.applet* package also contains the *Object* class. All objects inherit its methods, unless they are overridden. These methods include cloning an object, comparing two objects for equality, converting an object to a string, and various others.

Finally, we come to *java.awt* and its two subpackages. AWT stands for **Abstract Window Toolkit**, and is designed to make applets portable across window systems. For example, how should an applet draw a rectangle on the screen in such a way that the same compiled (bytecode) version of the applet can run on UNIX, Windows, and the Macintosh, even though each one has its own window system? Part of the package deals with drawing on the screen, so there are methods for placing lines, geometric figures, text, menus, buttons, scroll bars, and many other items on the screen. Java programmers call these methods to write on the screen. It is up to the *java.awt* package to make the appropriate calls to the local operating system to get the job done. This strategy means that *java.awt* has to be rewritten for each new platform, but that applets are then platform independent, which is far more important.

Another important task of this class is event management. Most window systems are fundamentally event driven. What this means is that the operating system detects keystrokes, mouse motion, button pushes and releases, and other events, and converts these into calls to user procedures. In the case of Java, a large library of methods for dealing with these events is provided in *java.awt*. Using them makes it easier to write programs that interact with the local window system and still be 100 percent portable to machines with different operating systems and different window systems.

Some of the work of this package is done in *java.awt.image*, such as image management, and in *java.awt.peer*, which allows access to the underlying window system.

Security

One of the most important aspects of Java is its security properties. When a Web page containing an applet is fetched, the applet is automatically executed on the client's machine. Ideally, it should not crash or otherwise bring down the client's machine.

Furthermore, it does not take much imagination to envision some enterprising undergraduate producing a Web page containing some nifty new game, then publicizing its URL widely (e.g., crossposting it to every newsgroup). Not mentioned in the posting is the small detail that the page also contains an applet that upon arrival immediately encrypts all the files on the user's hard disk. When it is finished, the applet announces what it has done and politely mentions that users wishing to purchase the decryption key can do so by sending 1000 dollars in small unmarked bills to a certain post office box in Panama.

In addition to the above get-rich-quick scheme, there are other dangers inherent in letting foreign code run on your machine. An applet could hunt around for interesting information (saved email, the password file, the local environment strings, etc.) and send or email them back over the network. It could also consume resources (e.g., filling up the disk), display naughty pictures or political slogans on the screen, or make an earsplitting racket using the sound card.

The Java designers were well aware of these problems, of course, and erected a series of barriers against them. The first line of defense is a typesafe language. Java has strong typing, true arrays with bounds checking and no pointers. These restrictions make it impossible for a Java program to construct a pointer to read and write arbitrary memory locations.

However, Trudy, who has given up on trying to break cryptographic protocols and gotten into the much more interesting business of writing malicious Java applets, can just write or modify a C compiler to produce Java bytecode, thus bypassing all the safeguards provided by the Java language and compiler.

The second line of defense is that before an incoming applet is executed, it is run through a bytecode verifier. The bytecode verifier looks for attempts to manufacture pointers, execute instructions or call methods with invalid parameters, use variables before they are initialized, and so on. These checks are supposed to guarantee that only legal applets get executed, but Trudy will certainly work hard on finding tricks the verifier does not check for.

The third line of defense is the class loader. Since classes can be loaded on the fly, there is a danger that an applet could load one of its own classes to replace a critical system class, thus bypassing that class' security checks. This Trojan horse attack has been rendered impossible by virtue of giving each class its own name space (like a kind of abstract directory), and carefully searching for system classes before looking for user classes. In other words, if the user loads a malicious version of *println*, it will never be used because the official *println* will always be found first.

The fourth line of defense is that some standard classes have their own security measures built in. For example, the file access class maintains a list of files that may be accessed by applets, and pops up a dialog box any time an applet tries to do something that violates the protection rules.

Despite all these measures, security problems are to be expected. First, there can be bugs in the Java software that clever programmers can exploit to bypass the security. The infamous Internet worm of 1988 used a bug in the UNIX Finger daemon to bring thousands of machines all over the Internet to a grinding halt (Hafner and Markoff, 1991; and Spafford, 1989).

Second, while it may be possible to prevent an applet from doing anything except writing to the screen, many applets will need more power, so when they ask for additional privileges, users may grudgingly (or naively) grant them. For example, applets may need to write temporary files, so users may give them access to the */tmp* directory, thinking that nothing important is there. Unfortunately, most editors keep the temporary versions of documents and email being edited there, so malicious applets can copy them and try to send them over the network. Of course, it may be possible to block applets' access to the network, but many may not work then, so they will have to be granted this power too.

But even in the unlikely event that applets are allowed no network access at all, they may be able to transmit information using **covert channels** (Lampson, 1973). For example, after acquiring some information, an applet can form a bit stream by using the local system's real time clock. To send a 1, it computes very hard for ΔT; to send a 0, it just waits for ΔT.

To acquire this information, the applet's owner can establish a connection to the client's machine to read some of its public Web pages or FTP some of its public files. By carefully monitoring the incoming data rate, the applet owner's can see whether the applet is computing (and thus slowing down the observed output stream) or resting. Of course, this channel is noisy, but that can be handled by standard techniques. The stream can be divided into frames delimited by flag bytes, individual frames can use a strong error-correcting code, and all frames can be sent two or three times. Many other covert channels exist, and it is extremely difficult to discover and block them all. For more information about the security problems in Java see (Dean and Wallach, 1995).

In short, Java introduces many new possibilities and opportunities into the World Wide Web. It allows Web pages to be interactive, and to contain animation and sound. It also permits browsers to be infinitely extensible. However, the Java model of downloading applets also introduces some serious new security problems that have not been entirely solved yet.

7.6.5. Locating Information on the Web

Although the Web contains a vast amount of information, finding the right item is not always easy. To make it easier for people to find pages that are useful to them, several researchers have written programs to index the Web in various ways. Some of these have become so popular that they have gone commercial. Programs that search the Web are sometimes called **search engines**, **spiders**, **crawlers**, **worms**, or **knowbots** (knowledge robots). In this section we will give a brief introduction to this subject. For more information, see (Pinkerton, 1994; and McBryan, 1994).

Although the Web is huge, reduced to its barest essentials, the Web is a big graph, with the pages being the nodes and the hyperlinks being the arcs. Algorithms for visiting all the nodes in a graph are well known. What makes Web indexing difficult is the enormous amount of data that must be managed and the fact that it is constantly changing.

Let us start our discussion with a simple goal: indexing all the keywords in Web pages' titles. For our algorithm, we will need three data structures. First, we need a large, linear array, *url_table*, that contains millions of entries, ultimately one per Web page. It should be kept in virtual memory, so parts not heavily used will automatically be paged to disk. Each entry contains two pointers, one to the page's URL and one to the page's title. Both of these items are variable length strings and can be kept on a heap (a large unstructured chunk of virtual memory to which strings can be appended). The heap is our second data structure.

The third data structure is a hash table of size *n* entries. It is used as follows. Any URL can be run through a hash function to produce a nonnegative integer less than *n*. All URLs that hash to the value *k* are hooked together on a linked list starting at entry *k* of the hash table. Whenever a URL is entered into *url_table*, it is also entered into the hash table. The main use of the hash table is to start with a URL and be able to quickly determine whether it is already present in *url_table*. These three data structures are illustrated in Fig. 7-75.

Building the index requires two phases: searching and indexing. Let us start with a simple engine for doing the searching. The heart of the search engine is a recursive procedure *process_url*, which takes a URL string as input. It operates as

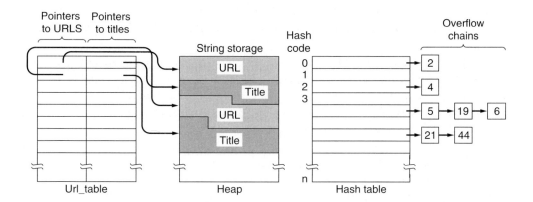

Fig. 7-75. Data structures used in a simple search engine.

follows. First, it hashes the URL to see if it is already present in *url_table*. If so, it is done and returns immediately. Each URL is processed only once.

If the URL is not already known, its page is fetched. The URL and title are then copied to the heap and pointers to these two strings are entered in *url_table*. The URL is also entered into the hash table.

Finally, *process_url* extracts all the hyperlinks from the page and calls *process_url* once per hyperlink, passing the hyperlink's URL as the input parameter.

To run the search engine, *process_url* is called with some starting URL. When it returns, all pages reachable from that URL have been entered into *url_table* and the search phase has been completed.

Although this design is simple and theoretically correct, it has a serious problem in a system as large as the Web. The problem is that this algorithm does a depth-first search, and will ultimately go into recursion as many times as the longest noncyclic path on the Web. No one knows how long this path is, but it is probably thousands of hyperlinks long. As a consequence, any search engine that uses this depth-first search will probably hit stack overflow before finishing the job.

In practice, actual search engines first collect all the hyperlinks on each page they read, remove all the ones that have already been processed, and save the rest. The Web is then searched breadth-first; that is, each link on a page is followed and all the hyperlinks on all the pages pointed to are collected, but they are not traced in the order obtained.

The second phase does the keyword indexing. The indexing procedure goes down *url_table* linearly, processing each entry in turn. For each entry, it examines the title and selects out all words not on the stop list. (The stop list prevents indexing of prepositions, conjunctions, articles, and other words with many hits and little value.) For each word selected, it writes a line consisting of the word followed by the current *url_table* entry number to a file. When the whole table has been scanned, the file is sorted by word.

The index will have to be stored on disk and can be used as follows. The user fills in a form listing one or more keywords and clicks on the SUBMIT button. This action causes a *POST* request to be done to a CGI script on the machine where the index is located. This script (or, more likely, program) then looks up the keywords in the index to find the set of *url_table* indices for each one. If the user wants the BOOLEAN AND of the keywords, the set intersection is computed. If the BOOLEAN OR is desired, the set union is computed.

The script now indexes into *url_table* to find all the titles and URLs. These are then combined to form a Web page and are sent back to the user as the response to the *POST*. The browser now displays the page, allowing the user to click on any items that appear interesting.

Sounds easy? It's not. The following problems have to be solved in any practical system:

1. Some URLs are obsolete (i.e., point to pages that no longer exist).

2. Some machines will be temporarily unreachable.

3. Not all pages may be reachable from the starting URL.

4. Some pages may be reachable only from active maps.

5. Some documents cannot be indexed (e.g., audio clips).

6. Not all documents have (useful) titles.

7. The search engine could run out of memory or disk space.

8. The entire process might take too long.

Obsolete URLs waste time but are mostly a nuisance because the server on which they are supposed to be located replies immediately with an error code. In contrast, when the server is down, all the search engine observes is a long delay in establishing the TCP connection. To prevent it from hanging indefinitely, it must have a timeout. If the timeout is too short, valid URLs will be missed. If it is too long, searching will be slowed down appreciably.

Choosing the starting URL is clearly a major issue. If the search engine starts with the home page of some astrophysicist, it may eventually find everything on astronomy, physics, chemistry and space science, but it may miss pages about veterinary medicine, Middle English, and rock 'n roll completely. These sets may simply be disjoint. One solution is to gather as large a set of URLs as possible, and use each of them as a starting page. Starting URLs can be gathered from USENET news articles and last week's version of the *url_table*, since some of these pages may have changed recently (e.g., one of the astrophysicists married a veterinarian and they solemnly updated their home pages to point to each other).

Indexing works well on text, but increasingly, many pages contain items other than text, including pictures, audio, and video. One approach here is to probe each new-found URL with the *HEAD* method, just to get back its MIME header. Anything not of type *text* is not searched.

About 20 percent of all Web pages have no title, and many of those that do have a title have a quasi-useless one ("Joe's page"). A big improvement to the basic index is to not only include titles, but also all the hypertext. In this approach, when a page is scanned, all the hyperlinks are also recorded, along with the page they came from and the page they point to. After the search phase has been completed, all the hyperwords can be indexed too.

Even more ambitious is to index all the important words in each page. To determine the important words, the occurrence frequency of all words not on the stop list can be computed (per Web page). The top 10 or 20 words are probably worth indexing. After all, if the word "liver" is the most common word on a page, there is a chance that the page will be of interest to biliary surgeons (or to cooks). Some search engines (e.g., Lycos) use this strategy.

Finally, the search engine can run out of memory or time. One attack is to redesign the algorithms more carefully. A completely different approach is to do what Harvest does and offload the work (Bowman et al., 1994, 1996). In particular, Harvest provides a program to run on cooperating servers. This program does all the searching locally and transmits back the finished local index. At the central site, all the local indices are merged into the master index. This approach reduces by orders of magnitude the amount of memory, CPU time, and network bandwidth required but has the major disadvantage of requiring all Web servers to cooperate by running foreign software. Given the potential problems with viruses and worms, when a system administrator is approached with the request: "Will you please run this program on your machine for me?" it should not be surprising if many of them decline.

One small request is in order. Although writing a search engine sounds easy, a buggy one can wreak havoc with the network by generating vast numbers of spurious requests, not only wasting bandwidth but bringing many servers to their knees due to the load. If you cannot resist the temptation to write your own search engine, proper netiquette requires restricting it to your own local DNS domain until it is totally debugged.

7.7. MULTIMEDIA

Multimedia is the holy grail of networking. When the word is mentioned, both the propeller heads and the suits begin salivating as if on cue. The former see immense technical challenges in providing (interactive) video on demand to every home. The latter see equally immense profits in it. No book on networking would be complete without at least an introduction to the subject. Given the length of this one so far, our introduction will of necessity be brief. For additional information about this fascinating and potentially profitable subject, see (Buford, 1994; Deloddere et al., 1994; Dixit and Skelly, 1995; Fluckiger, 1995; Minoli, 1995; and Steinmetz and Nahrstedt, 1995).

Literally, multimedia is just two or more media. If the publisher of this book wanted to join the current hype about multimedia, it could advertise the book as using multimedia technology. After all, it contains two media: text and graphics (the figures). Nevertheless, when most people refer to multimedia, they generally mean the combination of two or more **continuous media**, that is, media that have to be played during some well-defined time interval, usually with some user interaction. In practice, the two media are normally audio and video, that is, sound plus moving pictures. For this reason, we will begin our study with an introduction to audio and video technology. Then we will combine them and move on to true multimedia systems, including video on demand and the Internet's multimedia system, MBone.

7.7.1. Audio

An audio (sound) wave is a one-dimensional acoustic (pressure) wave. When an acoustic wave enters the ear, the eardrum vibrates, causing the tiny bones of the inner ear to vibrate along with it, sending nerve pulses to the brain. These pulses are perceived as sound by the listener. In a similar way, when an acoustic wave strikes a microphone, the microphone generates an electrical signal, representing the sound amplitude as a function of time. The representation, processing, storage, and transmission of such audio signals are a major part of the study of multimedia systems.

The frequency range of the human ear runs from 20 Hz to 20,000 Hz, although some animals, notably dogs, can hear higher frequencies. The ear hears logarithmically, so the ratio of two sounds with amplitudes A and B is conventionally expressed in **dB** (**decibels**) according to the formula

$$dB = 20 \log_{10}(A/B)$$

If we define the lower limit of audibility (a pressure of about 0.0003 dyne/cm^2) for a 1-kHz sine wave as 0 dB, an ordinary conversation is about 50 dB and the pain threshold is about 120 dB, a dynamic range of a factor of 1 million. To avoid any confusion, A and B above are *amplitudes*. If we were to use the power level, which is proportional to the square of the amplitude, the coefficient of the logarithm would be 10, not 20.

The ear is surprisingly sensitive to sound variations lasting only a few milliseconds. The eye, in contrast, does not notice changes in light level that last only a few milliseconds. The result of this observation is that jitter of only a few milliseconds during a multimedia transmission affects the perceived sound quality more than it affects the perceived image quality.

Audio waves can be converted to digital form by an **ADC (Analog Digital Converter)**. An ADC takes an electrical voltage as input and generates a binary number as output. In Fig. 7-76(a) we see an example of a sine wave. To represent this signal digitally, we can sample it every ΔT seconds, as shown by the bar heights in Fig. 7-76(b). If a sound wave is not a pure sine wave, but a linear superposition of sine waves where the highest frequency component present is f, then the Nyquist theorem (see Chap. 2) states that it is sufficient to make samples at a frequency $2f$. Sampling more often is of no value since the higher frequencies that such sampling could detect are not present.

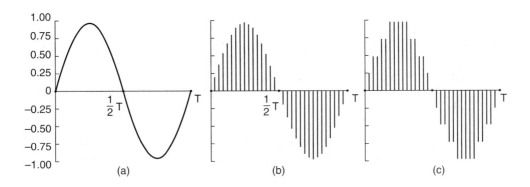

Fig. 7-76. (a) A sine wave. (b) Sampling the sine wave. (c) Quantizing the samples to 3 bits.

Digital samples are never exact. The 3-bit samples of Fig. 7-76(c) allow only eight values, from −1.00 to +1.00 in steps of 0.25. An 8-bit sample would allow 256 distinct values. A 16-bit sample would allow 65,536 distinct values. The error introduced by the finite number of bits per sample is called the **quantization noise**. If it is too large, the ear detects it.

Two well-known examples of sampled sound are the telephone and audio compact discs. Pulse code modulation, as used within the telephone system, uses 7-bit (North America and Japan) or 8-bit (Europe) samples 8000 times per second. This system gives a data rate of 56,000 bps or 64,000 bps. With only 8000 samples/sec, frequencies above 4 kHz are lost.

Audio CDs are digital with a sampling rate of 44,100 samples/sec, enough to capture frequencies up to 22,050 Hz, which is good for people, bad for dogs. The samples are 16 bits each, and are linear over the range of amplitudes. Note that 16-bit samples allow only 65,536 distinct values, even though the dynamic range of the ear is about 1 million when measured in steps of the smallest audible sound. Thus using only 16 bits per sample introduces some quantization noise (although the full dynamic range is not covered—CDs are not supposed to hurt). With 44,100 samples/sec of 16 bits each, an audio CD needs a bandwidth of 705.6 kbps for monaural and 1.411 Mbps for stereo. While this is lower than what video needs (see below), it still takes almost a full T1 channel to transmit uncompressed CD quality stereo sound.

Digitized sound can be easily processed by computers in software. Dozens of programs exist for personal computers to allow users to record, display, edit, mix, and store sound waves from multiple sources. Virtually all professional sound recording and editing are digital nowadays.

Many musical instruments even have a digital interface now. When digital instruments first came out, each one had its own interface, but after a while, a standard, **MIDI (Music Instrument Digital Interface)**, was developed and adopted by virtually the entire music industry. This standard specifies the connector, the cable, and the message format. Each MIDI message consists of a status byte followed by zero or more data bytes. A MIDI message conveys one musically significant event. Typical events are a key being pressed, a slider being moved, or a foot pedal being released. The status byte indicates the event, and the data bytes give parameters, such as which key was depressed and with what velocity it was moved.

Every instrument has a MIDI code assigned to it. For example, a grand piano is 0, a marimba is 12, and a violin is 40. This is needed to avoid having a flute concerto be played back as a tuba concerto. The number of "instruments" defined is 127. However, some of these are not instruments, but special effects such as chirping birds, helicopters, and the canned applause that accompanies many television programs.

The heart of every MIDI system is a synthesizer (often a computer) that accepts messages and generates music from them. The synthesizer understands all 127 instruments, so it generates a different power spectrum for middle C on a trumpet than for a xylophone. The advantage of transmitting music using MIDI compared to sending a digitized waveform is the enormous reduction in bandwidth, often by a factor of 1000. The disadvantage of MIDI is that the receiver needs a MIDI synthesizer to reconstruct the music again, and different ones may give slightly different renditions.

Music, of course, is just a special case of general audio, but an important one. Another important special case is speech. Human speech tends to be in the 600-Hz to 6000-Hz range. Speech is made up of vowels and consonants, which have different properties. Vowels are produced when the vocal tract is unobstructed, producing resonances whose fundamental frequency depends on the size and shape of the vocal system and the position of the speaker's tongue and jaw. These sounds are almost periodic for intervals of about 30 msec. Consonants are produced when the vocal tract is partially blocked. These sounds are less regular than vowels.

Some speech generation and transmission systems make use of models of the vocal system to reduce speech to a few parameters (e.g., the sizes and shapes of various cavities), rather than just sampling the speech waveform.

7.7.2. Video

The human eye has the property that when an image is flashed on the retina, it is retained for some number of milliseconds before decaying. If a sequence of images is flashed at 50 or more images/sec, the eye does not notice that it is looking at discrete images. All video (i.e., television) systems exploit this principle to produce moving pictures.

Analog Systems

To understand video systems, it is best to start with simple, old-fashioned black-and-white television. To represent the two-dimensional image in front of it as a one-dimensional voltage as a function of time, the camera scans an electron beam rapidly across the image and slowly down it, recording the light intensity as it goes. At the end of the scan, called a **frame**, the beam retraces. This intensity as a function of time is broadcast, and receivers repeat the scanning process to reconstruct the image. The scanning pattern used by both the camera and the receiver is shown in Fig. 7-77. (As an aside, CCD cameras integrate rather than scan, but some cameras and all monitors do scan.)

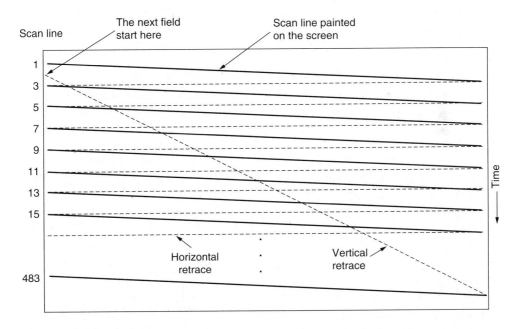

Fig. 7-77. The scanning pattern used for NTSC video and television.

The exact scanning parameters vary from country to country. The system used in North and South America and Japan has 525 scan lines, a horizontal to vertical aspect ratio of 4:3, and 30 frames/sec. The European system has 625 scan lines, the same aspect ratio of 4:3, and 25 frames/sec. In both systems, the top few and bottom few lines are not displayed (to approximate a rectangular image on the original round CRTs). Only 483 of the 525 NTSC scan lines (and 576 of the 625 PAL/SECAM scan lines) are displayed. The beam is turned off during the vertical retrace, so many stations (especially in Europe) use this interval to broadcast TeleText (text pages containing news, weather, sports, stock prices, etc.).

While 25 frames/sec is enough to capture smooth motion, at that frame rate many people, especially older ones, will perceive the image to flicker (because the old image has faded off the retina before the new one appears). Rather than increase the frame rate, which would require using more scarce bandwidth, a different approach is taken. Instead of displaying the scan lines in order, first all the odd scan lines are displayed, then the even ones are displayed. Each of these half frames is called a **field**. Experiments have shown that although people notice flicker at 25 frames/sec, they do not notice it at 50 fields/sec. This technique is called **interlacing**. Noninterlaced television or video is said to be **progressive**.

Color video uses the same scanning pattern as monochrome (black and white), except that instead of displaying the image with one moving beam, three beams moving in unison are used. One beam is used for each of the three additive primary colors: red, green, and blue (RGB). This technique works because any color can be constructed from a linear superposition of red, green, and blue with the appropriate intensities. However, for transmission on a single channel, the three color signals must be combined into a single **composite** signal.

When color television was invented, various methods for displaying color were technically possible, and different countries made different choices, leading to systems that are still incompatible. (Note that these choices have nothing to do with VHS versus Betamax versus P2000, which are recording methods.) In all countries, a political requirement was that programs transmitted in color had to be receivable on existing black-and-white television sets. Consequently, the simplest scheme, just encoding the RGB signals separately, was not acceptable. RGB is also not the most efficient scheme.

The first color system was standardized in the United States by the National Television Standards Committee, which lent its acronym to the standard: **NTSC**. Color television was introduced in Europe several years later, by which time the technology had improved substantially, leading to systems with greater noise immunity and better colors. These are called **SECAM** (**SEquentiel Couleur Avec Memoire**), which is used in France and Eastern Europe, and **PAL** (**Phase Alternating Line**) used in the rest of Europe. The difference in color quality between the NTSC and PAL/SECAM has led to an industry joke that NTSC really stands for Never Twice the Same Color.

To allow color transmissions to be viewed on black-and-white receivers, all three systems linearly combine the RGB signals into a **luminance** (brightness) signal, and two **chrominance** (color) signals, although they all use different coefficients for constructing these signals from the RGB signals. Interestingly enough, the eye is much more sensitive to the luminance signal than to the chrominance signals, so the latter need not be transmitted as accurately. Consequently, the luminance signal can be broadcast at the same frequency as the old black-and-white signal, so it can be received on black-and-white television sets. The two chrominance signals are broadcast in narrow bands at higher frequencies. Some television sets have controls labeled brightness, hue, and saturation (or brightness, tint and color) for controlling these three signals separately. Understanding luminance and chrominance is necessary for understanding how video compression works.

In the past few years, there has been considerable interest in **HDTV** (**High Definition TeleVision**), which produces sharper images by roughly doubling the number of scan lines. The United States, Europe, and Japan have all developed HDTV systems, all different and all mutually incompatible. The basic principles of HDTV in terms of scanning, luminance, chrominance, and so on, are similar to the existing systems. However, all three formats have a common aspect ratio of 16:9 instead of 4:3 to match them better to the format used for movies (which are recorded on 35 mm film).

For an introduction to television technology, see (Buford, 1994).

Digital Systems

The simplest representation of digital video is a sequence of frames, each consisting of a rectangular grid of picture elements, or **pixels**. Each pixel can be a single bit, to represent either black or white. The quality of such a system is similar to what you get by sending a color photograph by fax—awful. (Try it if you can; otherwise photocopy a color photograph on a copying machine that does not rasterize.)

The next step up is to use 8 bits per pixel to represent 256 gray levels. This scheme gives high-quality black-and-white video. For color video, good systems use 8 bits for each of the RGB colors, although nearly all systems mix these into composite video for transmission. While using 24 bits per pixel limits the number of colors to about 16 million, the human eye cannot even distinguish this many colors, let alone more. Digital color images are produced using three scanning beams, one per color. The geometry is the same as for the analog system of Fig. 7-77 except that the continuous scan lines are now replaced by neat rows of discrete pixels.

To produce smooth motion, digital video, like analog video, must display at least 25 frames/sec. However, since good quality computer monitors often rescan the screen from images stored in memory at 75 times per second or more, interlacing is not needed and consequently is not normally used. Just repainting (i.e., redrawing) the same frame three times in a row is enough to eliminate flicker.

In other words, smoothness of motion is determined by the number of *different* images per second, whereas flicker is determined by the number of times the screen is painted per second. These two parameters are different. A still image painted at 20 frames/sec will not show jerky motion but it will flicker because one frame will decay from the retina before the next one appears. A movie with 20 different frames per second, each of which is painted four times in a row, will not flicker, but the motion will appear jerky.

The significance of these two parameters becomes clear when we consider the bandwidth required for transmitting digital video over a network. Current computer monitors all use the 4:3 aspect ratio so they can use inexpensive, mass-produced picture tubes designed for the consumer television market. Common configurations are 640×480 (VGA), 800×600 (SVGA), and 1024×768 (XGA). An XGA display with 24 bits per pixel and 25 frames/sec needs to be fed at 472 Mbps. Even OC-9 is not quite good enough, and running an OC-9 SONET carrier into everyone's house is not exactly on the agenda. Doubling this rate to avoid flicker is even less attractive. A better solution is to transmit 25 frames/sec and have the computer store each one and paint it twice. Broadcast television does not use this strategy because television sets do not have memory, and in any event, analog signals cannot be stored in RAM without first converting them to digital form, which requires extra hardware. As a consequence, interlacing is needed for broadcast television but not for digital video.

7.7.3. Data Compression

It should be obvious by now that transmitting multimedia material in uncompressed form is completely out of the question. The only hope is that massive compression is possible. Fortunately, a large body of research over the past few decades has led to many compression techniques and algorithms that make multimedia transmission feasible. In this section we will study some methods for compressing multimedia data, especially images. For more detail, see (Fluckiger, 1995; and Steinmetz and Nahrstedt, 1995).

All compression systems require two algorithms: one for compressing the data at the source, and another for decompressing it at the destination. In the literature, these algorithms are referred to as the **encoding** and **decoding** algorithms, respectively. We will use this terminology here, too.

These algorithms have certain asymmetries that are important to understand. First, for many applications, a multimedia document, say, a movie will only be encoded once (when it is stored on the multimedia server) but will be decoded thousands of times (when it is viewed by customers). This asymmetry means that it is acceptable for the encoding algorithm to be slow and require expensive hardware provided that the decoding algorithm is fast and does not require expensive hardware. After all, the operator of a multimedia server might be quite willing to rent a parallel supercomputer for a few weeks to encode its entire video library, but requiring consumers to rent a supercomputer for 2 hours to view a video is not likely to be a big success. Many practical compression systems go to great lengths to make decoding fast and simple, even at the price of making encoding slow and complicated.

On the other hand, for real-time multimedia, such as video conferencing, slow encoding is unacceptable. Encoding must happen on-the-fly, in real time. Consequently, real-time multimedia uses different algorithms or parameters than storing videos on disk, often with appreciably less compression.

A second asymmetry is that the encode/decode process need not be invertible. That is, when compressing a file, transmitting it, and then decompressing it, the user expects to get the original back, accurate down to the last bit. With multimedia, this requirement does not exist. It is usually acceptable to have the video signal after encoding and then decoding be slightly different than the original. When the decoded output is not exactly equal to the original input, the system is said to be **lossy**. If the input and output are identical, the system is **lossless**. Lossy systems are important because accepting a small amount of information loss can give a huge payoff in terms of the compression ratio possible.

Entropy Encoding

Compression schemes can be divided into two general categories: entropy encoding and source encoding. We will now discuss each in turn.

Entropy encoding just manipulates bit streams without regard to what the bits mean. It is a general, lossless, fully reversible technique, applicable to all data. We will illustrate it by means of three examples.

Our first example of entropy encoding is **run-length encoding**. In many kinds of data, strings of repeated symbols (bits, numbers, etc.) are common. These can be replaced by a special marker not otherwise allowed in the data, followed by the symbol comprising the run, followed by how many times it occurred. If the special marker itself occurs in the data, it is duplicated (as in character stuffing). For example, consider the following string of decimal digits:

3150000000000000845871111111111111163546740000000000000000000000065

If we now introduce A as the marker and use two-digit numbers for the repetition count, we can encode the above digit string as

315A01284587A11316354674A02265

Here run-length encoding has cut the data string in half.

Runs are common in multimedia. In audio, silence is often represented by runs of zeros. In video, runs of the same color occur in shots of the sky, walls, and many flat surfaces. All of these runs can be greatly compressed.

Our second example of entropy encoding is **statistical encoding**. By this we mean using a short code to represent common symbols and long ones to represent infrequent ones. Morse code uses this principle, with E being • and Q being – – • – and so on. Huffman coding and the Ziv-Lempel algorithm used by the UNIX Compress program also use statistical encoding.

Our third example of entropy encoding is **CLUT (Color Look Up Table)** encoding. Consider an image using RGB encoding with 3 bytes/pixel. In theory, the image might contain as many as 2^{24} different color values. In practice, it will normally contain many fewer values, especially if the image is a cartoon or computer-generated drawing, rather than a photograph. Suppose that only 256 color values are actually used. A factor of almost three compression can be achieved by building a 768-byte table listing the RGB values of the 256 colors actually used, and then representing each pixel by the index of its RGB value in the table. Here we see a clear example where encoding is slower than decoding because encoding requires searching the table whereas decoding can be done with a single indexing operation.

Source Encoding

Now we come to **source encoding**, which takes advantage of properties of the data to produce more (usually lossy) compression. Here, too, we will illustrate the idea with three examples. Our first example is **differential encoding**, in which a sequence of values (e.g., audio samples) are encoded by representing each one as the difference from the previous value. Differential pulse code modulation, which we saw in Chap. 2, is an example of this technique. It is lossy because the signal might jump so much between two consecutive values that the difference does not fit in the field provided for expressing differences, so at least one incorrect value will be recorded and some information lost.

Differential encoding is a kind of source encoding because it takes advantage of the property that large jumps between consecutive data points are unlikely. Not all sequences of numbers have this property. An example lacking this property is a computer-generated list of random telephone numbers to be used by telemarketers for bothering people during dinner. The differences between consecutive telephone numbers in the list will take as many bits to represent as the numbers themselves.

Our second example of source encoding consists of **transformations**. By transforming signals from one domain to another, compression may become much easier. Consider, for example, the Fourier transformation of Fig. 2-1(e). Here a function of time is represented as a list of amplitudes. Given the exact values of all the amplitudes, the original function can be reconstructed perfectly. However, given only the values of the first, say, eight amplitudes rounded off to two decimal places, it may still be possible to reconstruct the signal so well that the listener cannot tell that some information has been lost. The gain is that transmitting eight amplitudes requires many fewer bits than transmitting the sampled waveform.

Transformations are also applicable to two-dimensional image data. Suppose that the 4×4 matrix of Fig. 7-78(a) represents the gray-scale values of a monochrome image. We can transform these data by subtracting the value in the upper left-hand corner from all elements except itself, as shown in Fig. 7-78(b). This transformation might be useful if variable-length encoding is used. For example, values between -7 and $+7$ could be encoded with 4-bit numbers and values between 0 and 255 could be encoded as a special 4-bit code (-8) followed by an 8-bit number.

Pixel value

4 pixels

160	160	161	160
161	165	166	158
160	167	165	161
159	160	160	160

(a)

160	0	1	0
1	5	6	-2
0	7	5	1
-1	0	1	0

(b)

Fig. 7-78. (a) Pixel values for part of an image. (b) A transformation in which the upper left-hand element is subtracted from all elements except itself.

Although this simple transformation is lossless, other, more useful ones are not. An especially important two-dimensional spatial transformation is the **DCT** (**Discrete Cosine Transformation**) (Feig and Winograd, 1992). This transformation has the property that for images without sharp discontinuities, most of the spectral power is in the first few terms, allowing the later ones to be ignored without much information loss. We will come back to DCT shortly.

Our third example of source encoding is **vector quantization**, which is also directly applicable to image data. Here, the image is divided up into fixed-size rectangles. In addition to the image itself, we also need a table of rectangles of the same size as the image rectangles (possibly constructed from the image). This table is called the **code book**. Each rectangle is transmitted by looking it up in the code book and just sending the index instead of the rectangle. If the code book is created dynamically (i.e., per image), it must be transmitted, too. Clearly, if a small number of rectangles dominate the image, large savings in bandwidth are possible here.

An example of vector quantization is shown in Fig. 7-79. In Fig. 7-79(a) we have a grid of rectangles of unspecified size. In Fig. 7-79(b) we have the code book. The output stream is just the list of integers 001022032200400 shown in Fig. 7-79(c). Each one represents an entry from the code book.

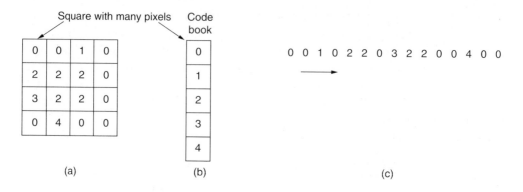

Fig. 7-79. An example of vector quantization. (a) An image divided into squares. (b) A code book for the image. (c) The encoded image.

In a sense, vector quantization is just a two-dimensional generalization of CLUT. The real difference, however, is what happens if no match can be found. Three strategies are possible. The first one is just to use the best match. The second one is to use the best match, and append some information about how to improve the match (e.g., append the true mean value). The third one is use the best match and append whatever is necessary to allow the decoder to reconstruct the data exactly. The first two strategies are lossy but exhibit high compression. The third is lossless but less effective as a compression algorithm. Again, we see that encoding (pattern matching) is far more time consuming than decoding (indexing into a table).

The JPEG Standard

The **JPEG** (**Joint Photographic Experts Group**) standard for compressing continuous-tone still pictures (e.g., photographs) was developed by photographic experts working under the joint auspices of ITU, ISO, and IEC, another standards body. It is important for multimedia because, to a first approximation, the multimedia standard for moving pictures, MPEG, is just the JPEG encoding of each frame separately, plus some extra features for interframe compression and motion detection. JPEG is defined in International Standard 10918.

JPEG has four modes and many options. It is more like a shopping list than a single algorithm. For our purposes, though, only the lossy sequential mode is relevant, and that one is illustrated in Fig. 7-80. Furthermore, we will concentrate on the way JPEG is normally used to encode 24-bit RGB video images and will leave out some of the minor details for the sake of simplicity.

Step 1 of encoding an image with JPEG is block preparation. For the sake of specificity, let us assume that the JPEG input is a 640 × 480 RGB image with 24 bits/pixel, as shown in Fig. 7-81(a). Since using luminance and chrominance

Fig. 7-80. The operation of JPEG in lossy sequential mode.

gives better compression, we first compute the luminance, *Y*, and the two chromi-nances, *I* and *Q* (for NTSC), according to the following formulas:

$$Y = 0.30R + 0.59G + 0.11B$$
$$I = 0.60R - 0.28G - 0.32B$$
$$Q = 0.21R - 0.52G + 0.31B$$

For PAL, the chrominances are called *U* and *V* and the coefficients are different, but the idea is the same. SECAM is different from both NTSC and PAL.

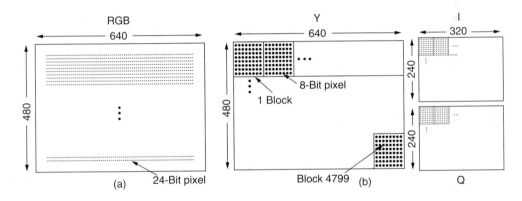

Fig. 7-81. (a) RGB input data. (b) After block preparation.

Separate matrices are constructed for *Y*, *I*, and *Q*, each with elements in the range 0 to 255. Next, square blocks of four pixels are averaged in the *I* and *Q* matrices to reduce them to 320×240. This reduction is lossy, but the eye barely notices it since the eye responds to luminance more than to chrominance. Nevertheless, it compresses the data by a factor of two. Now 128 is subtracted from each element of all three matrices to put 0 in the middle of the range. Finally, each matrix is divided up into 8×8 blocks. The *Y* matrix has 4800 blocks; the other two have 1200 blocks each, as shown in Fig. 7-81(b).

Step 2 of JPEG is to apply a discrete cosine transformation to each of the 7200 blocks separately. The output of each DCT is an 8×8 matrix of DCT coef-ficients. DCT element (0, 0) is the average value of the block. The other ele-ments tell how much spectral power is present at each spatial frequency. In theory, a DCT is lossless, but in practice using floating-point numbers and transcendental functions always introduces some roundoff error that results in a little information loss. Normally, these elements decay rapidly with distance from the origin, (0, 0), as suggested by Fig. 7-82.

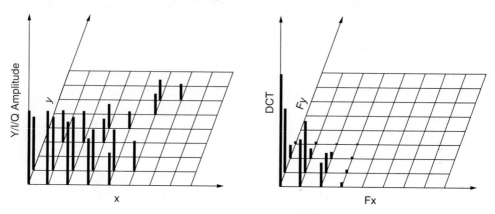

Fig. 7-82. (a) One block of the Y matrix. (b) The DCT coefficients.

Once the DCT is complete, JPEG moves on to step 3, called **quantization**, in which the less important DCT coefficients are wiped out. This (lossy) transformation is done by dividing each of the coefficients in the 8×8 DCT matrix by a weight taken from a table. If all the weights are 1, the transformation does nothing. However, if the weights increase sharply from the origin, higher spatial frequencies are dropped quickly.

An example of this step is given in Fig. 7-83. Here we see the initial DCT matrix, the quantization table, and the result obtained by dividing each DCT element by the corresponding quantization table element. The values in the quantization table are not part of the JPEG standard. Each application must supply its own, allowing it to control the loss-compression trade-off.

Step 4 reduces the (0, 0) value of each block (the one in the upper left-hand corner) by replacing it with the amount it differs from the corresponding element in the previous block. Since these elements are the averages of their respective blocks, they should change slowly, so taking the differential values should reduce most of them to small values. No differentials are computed from the other values. The (0, 0) values are referred to as the DC components; the other values are the AC components.

Step 5 linearizes the 64 elements and applies run-length encoding to the list. Scanning the block from left to right and then top to bottom will not concentrate the zeros together, so a zig zag scanning pattern is used, as shown in Fig. 7-84. In this example, the zig zag pattern ultimate produces 38 consecutive 0s at the end of the matrix. This string can be reduced to a single count saying there are 38 zeros.

Now we have a list of numbers that represent the image (in transform space). Step 6 Huffman encodes the numbers for storage or transmission.

DCT Coefficients

150	80	40	14	4	2	1	0
92	75	36	10	6	1	0	0
52	38	26	8	7	4	0	0
12	8	6	4	2	1	0	0
4	3	2	0	0	0	0	0
2	2	1	1	0	0	0	0
1	1	0	0	0	0	0	0
0	0	0	0	0	0	0	0

Quantized coefficients

150	80	20	4	1	0	0	0
92	75	18	3	1	0	0	0
26	19	13	2	1	0	0	0
3	2	2	1	0	0	0	0
1	0	0	0	0	0	0	0
0	0	0	0	0	0	0	0
0	0	0	0	0	0	0	0
0	0	0	0	0	0	0	0

Quantization table

1	1	2	4	8	16	32	64
1	1	2	4	8	16	32	64
2	2	2	4	8	16	32	64
4	4	4	4	8	16	32	64
8	8	8	8	8	16	32	64
16	16	16	16	16	16	32	64
32	32	32	32	32	32	32	64
64	64	64	64	64	64	64	64

Fig. 7-83. Computation of the quantized DCT coefficients.

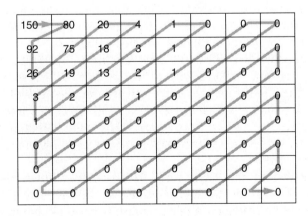

Fig. 7-84. The order in which the quantized values are transmitted.

JPEG may seem complicated, but that is because it *is* complicated. Still, since it often produces a 20:1 compression or better, it is widely used. Decoding a JPEG image requires running the algorithm backward. Unlike some of the other compression algorithms we have seen, JPEG is roughly symmetric: decoding takes as long as encoding.

Interestingly enough, due to the mathematical properties of the DCT, it is possible to perform certain geometric transformations (e.g. image rotation) directly on the transformed matrix, without regenerating the original image. These transformations are discussed in (Shen and Sethi, 1995). Similar properties also apply to MPEG compressed audio (Broadhead and Owen, 1995).

The MPEG Standard

Finally, we come to the heart of the matter: the **MPEG** (**Motion Picture Experts Group**) standards. These are the main algorithms used to compress videos and have been international standards since 1993. Because movies contain both images and sound, MPEG can compress both audio and video, but since video takes up more bandwidth and also contains more redundancy than audio, we will primarily focus on MPEG video compression below.

The first standard to be finalized was MPEG-1 (International Standard 11172). Its goal was to produce video recorder-quality output (352×240 for NTSC) using a bit rate of 1.2 Mbps. Since we saw earlier that uncompressed video alone can run to 472 Mbps, getting it down to 1.2 Mbps is not entirely trivial, even at this lower resolution. MPEG-1 can be transmitted over twisted pair transmission lines for modest distances. MPEG-1 is also used for storing movies on CD-ROM in CD-I and CD-Video format.

The next standard in the MPEG family was MPEG-2 (International Standard 13818), which was originally designed for compressing broadcast quality video into 4 to 6 Mbps, so it could fit in a NTSC or PAL broadcast channel. Later, MPEG-2 was expanded to support higher resolutions, including HDTV. MPEG-4 is for medium-resolution videoconferencing with low frame rates (10 frames/sec) and at low bandwidths (64 kbps). This will permit videoconferences to be held over a single N-ISDN B channel. Given this numbering, one might think that the next standard will be MPEG-8. Actually, ISO is numbering them linearly, not exponentially. Originally MPEG-3 existed. It was intended for HDTV, but that project was later canceled, and HDTV was added to MPEG-2.

The basic principles of MPEG-1 and MPEG-2 are similar, but the details are different. To a first approximation, MPEG-2 is a superset of MPEG-1, with additional features, frame formats and encoding options. It is likely that in the long run MPEG-1 will dominate for CD-ROM movies and MPEG-2 will dominate for long-haul video transmission. We will discuss MPEG-1 first and then MPEG-2.

MPEG-1 has three parts: audio, video, and system, which integrates the other two, as shown in Fig. 7-85. The audio and video encoders work independently, which raises the issue of how the two streams get synchronized at the receiver. This problem is solved by having a 90-kHz system clock that outputs the current time value to both encoders. These values are 33 bits, to allow films to run for 24 hours without wrapping around. These timestamps are included in the encoded output and propagated all the way to the receiver, which can use them to synchronize the audio and video streams.

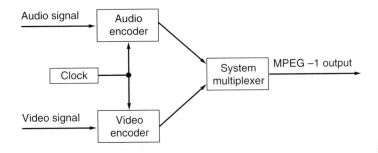

Fig. 7-85. Synchronization of the audio and video streams in MPEG-1.

MPEG audio compression is done by sampling the waveform at 32 kHz 44.1 kHz, or 48 kHz. It can handle monaural, disjoint stereo (each channel compressed separately), or joint stereo (interchannel redundancy exploited). It is organized as three layers, each one applying additional optimizations to get more compression (and at greater cost). Layer 1 is the basic scheme. This layer is used, for example, in the DCC digital tape system. Layer 2 adds advanced bit allocation to the basic scheme. It is used for CD-ROM audio and movie soundtracks. Layer 3 adds hybrid filters, nonuniform quantization, Huffman coding, and other advanced techniques.

MPEG audio can compress a rock 'n roll CD down to 96 kbps with no perceptible loss in quality, even for rock 'n roll fans with no hearing loss. For a piano concert, at least 128 kbps are needed. These differ because the signal-to-noise ratio for rock 'n roll is much higher than for a piano concert (in an engineering sense, anyway).

Audio compression is carried out by performing a fast Fourier transformation on the audio signal to transform it from the time domain to the frequency domain. The resulting spectrum is then divided up into 32 frequency bands, each of which is processed separately. When two stereo channels are present, the redundancy inherent in having two highly overlapping audio sources is also exploited. The resulting MPEG-1 audio stream is adjustable from 32 kbps to 448 kbps. An introduction to the process is given in (Pan, 1995).

Now let us consider MPEG-1 video compression. Two kinds of redundancies exist in movies: spatial and temporal. MPEG-1 uses both. Spatial redundancy can be utilized by simply coding each frame separately with JPEG. This approach is sometimes used, especially when random access to each frame is needed, as in editing video productions. In this mode, a compressed bandwidth in the 8- to 10-Mbps range is achievable.

Additional compression can be achieved by taking advantage of the fact that consecutive frames are often almost identical. This effect is smaller than it might first appear since many movie makers cut between scenes every 3 or 4 seconds (time a movie and count the scenes). Nevertheless, even a run of 75 highly similar frames offers the potential of a major reduction over simply encoding each frame separately with JPEG.

For scenes where the camera and background are stationary and one or two actors are moving around slowly, nearly all the pixels will be identical from frame to frame. Here, just subtracting each frame from the previous one and running JPEG on the difference would do fine. However, for scenes where the camera is panning or zooming, this technique fails badly. What is needed is some way to compensate for this motion. This is precisely what MPEG does; it is the main difference between MPEG and JPEG.

MPEG-1 output consists of four kinds of frames:

1. I (Intracoded) frames: Self-contained JPEG-encoded still pictures.

2. P (Predictive) frames: Block-by-block difference with the last frame.

3. B (Bidirectional) frames: Differences with the last and next frame.

4. D (DC-coded) frames: Block averages used for fast forward.

I-frames are just still pictures coded using JPEG, also using full-resolution luminance and half-resolution chrominance along each axis. It is necessary to have I-frames appear in the output stream periodically for three reasons. First, MPEG-1 can be used for a multicast transmission, with viewers tuning it at will. If all frames depended on their predecessors going back to the first frame, anybody who missed the first frame could never decode any subsequent frames. Second, if any frame were received in error, no further decoding would be possible. Third, without I-frames, while doing a fast forward or rewind, the decoder would have to calculate every frame passed over so it would know the full value of the one it stopped on. For these reasons, I-frames are inserted into the output once or twice per second.

P-frames, in contrast, code interframe differences. They are based on the idea of **macroblocks**, which cover 16×16 pixels in luminance space and 8×8 pixels in chrominance space. A macroblock is encoded by searching the previous frame for it or something only slightly different from it.

An example of where P-frames would be useful is given in Fig. 7-86. Here we see three consecutive frames that have the same background, but differ in the position of one person. The macroblocks containing the background scene will match exactly, but the macroblocks containing the person will be offset in position by some unknown amount and will have to be tracked down.

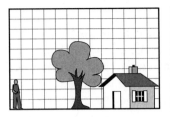

Fig. 7-86. Three consecutive frames.

The MPEG-1 standard does not specify how to search, how far to search, or how good a match has to be to count. This is up to each implementation. For example, an implementation might search for a macroblock at the current position in the previous frame, and all other positions offset $\pm\Delta x$ in the x direction and $\pm\Delta y$ in the y direction. For each position, the number of matches in the luminance matrix could be computed. The position with the highest score would be declared the winner, provided it was above some predefined threshold. Otherwise, the macroblock would be said to be missing. Much more sophisticated algorithms are also possible, of course.

If a macroblock is found, it is encoded by taking the difference with its value in the previous frame (for luminance and both chrominances). These difference matrices are then subject to the discrete cosine transformation, quantization, run-length encoding, and Huffman encoding, just as with JPEG. The value for the macroblock in the output stream is then the motion vector (how far the macroblock moved from its previous position in each direction), followed by the Huffman encoded list of numbers. If the macroblock is not located in the previous frame, the current value is encoded with JPEG, just as in an I-frame.

Clearly, this algorithm is highly asymmetric. An implementation is free to try every plausible position in the previous frame if it wants to, in a desperate attempt to locate every last macroblock. This approach will minimize the encoded MPEG-1 stream at the expense of very slow encoding. This approach might be fine for a one-time encoding of a film library but would be terrible for real-time videoconferencing.

Similarly, each implementation is free to decide what constitutes a "found" macroblock. This freedom allows implementers to compete on the quality and speed of their algorithms, but always produce compliant MPEG-1. No matter what search algorithm is used, the final output is either the JPEG encoding of the current macroblock, or the JPEG encoding of the difference between the current macroblock and one in the previous frame at a specified offset from the current one.

So far, decoding MPEG-1 is straightforward. Decoding I-frames is the same as decoding JPEG images. Decoding P-frames requires the decoder to buffer the previous frame and then build up the new one in a second buffer based on fully encoded macroblocks and macroblocks containing differences with the previous frame. The new frame is assembled macroblock by macroblock.

B-frames are similar to P-frames, except that they allow the reference macroblock to be in either a previous frame or in a succeeding frame. This additional freedom allows improved motion compensation, and is also useful when objects pass in front of, or behind, other objects. To do B-frame encoding, the encoder needs to hold three decoded frames in memory at once: the past one, the current one, and the future one. Although B-frames give the best compression, not all implementations support them.

D-frames are only used to make it possible to display a low-resolution image when doing a rewind or fast forward. Doing the normal MPEG-1 decoding in real time is difficult enough. Expecting the decoder to do it when slewing through the video at ten times normal speed is asking a bit much. Instead, the D-frames are used to produce low-resolution images. Each D-frame entry is just the average value of one block, with no further encoding, making it easy to display in real time. This facility is important to allow people to scan through a video at high speed in search of a particular scene.

Having finished our treatment of MPEG-1, let us move on to MPEG-2. MPEG-2 encoding is fundamentally similar to MPEG-1 encoding, with I-frames, P-frames, and B-frames. D-frames are not supported, however. Also, the discrete cosine transformation is 10×10 instead of 8×8, to give 50 percent more coefficients, hence better quality. Since MPEG-2 is targeted at broadcast television as well as CD-ROM applications, it supports both progressive and interlaced images, whereas MPEG-1 supports only progressive images. Other minor details also differ between the two standards.

Instead of supporting only one resolution level, MPEG-2 supports four: low (352×240), main (720×480), high-1440 (1440×1152), and high (1920×1080). Low resolution is for VCRs and backward compatibility with MPEG-1. Main is the normal one for NTSC broadcasting. The other two are for HDTV.

In addition to having four resolution levels, MPEG-2 also supports five **profiles**. Each profile targets some application area. The main profile is for general-purpose use, and probably most chips will be optimized for the main profile and the main resolution level. The simple profile is similar to the main one, except that it excludes the use of B-frames, to make software encoding and decoding easier. The other profiles deal with scalability and HDTV. The profiles differ in terms of the presence or absence of B-frames, chrominance resolution, and scalability of the encoded bit stream to other formats.

The compressed data rate for each combination of resolution and profile is different. These range from about 3 Mbps up to 100 Mbps for HDTV. The normal case is about 3 to 4 Mbps. Some performance data for MPEG are given in (Pancha and El Zarki, 1994).

MPEG-2 has a more general way of multiplexing audio and video than the MPEG-1 model of Fig. 7-85. It defines an unlimited number of elementary streams, including video and audio, but also including data streams that must be synchronized with the audio and video, for example, subtitles in multiple languages. Each of the streams is first packetized with timestamps. A simple two-stream example is shown in Fig. 7-87.

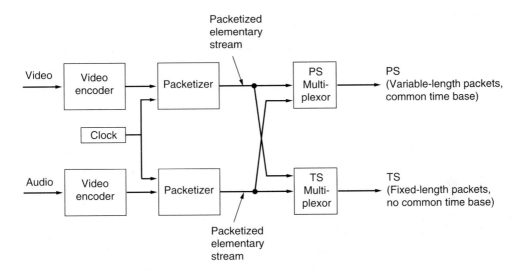

Fig. 7-87. Multiplexing of two streams in MPEG-2.

The output of each packetizer is a **PES** (**Packetized Elementary Stream**). Each PES packet has about 30 header fields and flags, including lengths, stream identifiers, encryption control, copyright status, timestamps, and a CRC.

The PES streams for audio, video, and possibly data are then multiplexed together on a single output stream for transmission. Two types of streams are defined. The MPEG-2 **program stream** is similar to the MPEG-1 systems stream of Fig. 7-85. It is used for multiplexing together elementary streams that have a common time base and have to be displayed in a synchronized way. The program stream uses long variable-length packets.

The other MPEG-2 stream is the **transport stream**. It is used for multiplexing together streams (including program streams) that do not use a common time base. The transport stream packets are fixed length (188 bytes), to make it easier to limit the effect of packets damaged or lost during transmission.

It is worth noting that all the encoding schemes we have discussed are based on the model of lossy encoding followed by lossless transmission. Neither JPEG nor MPEG, for example, can recover from lost or damaged packets in a graceful way. A different approach to image transmission is to transform the images in a way that separates the important information from the less important information (as the DCT does, for example). Then add a considerable amount of redundancy (even duplicate packets) to the important information and none to the less important information. If some packets are lost or garbled, it may still be possible to display reasonable images without retransmission. These ideas are described further in (Danskin et al., 1995). They are especially applicable to multicast transmissions, where feedback from each receiver is impossible anyway.

7.7.4. Video on Demand

Video on demand is sometimes compared to an electronic video rental store. The user (customer) selects any one of a large number of available videos and takes it home to view. Only with video on demand, the selection is made at home using the television set's remote control, and the video starts immediately. No trip to the store is needed. Needless to say, implementing video on demand is a wee bit more complicated than describing it. In this section, we will give an overview of the basic ideas and their implementation. A description of one real implementation can be found in (Nelson and Linton, 1995). A more general treatment of interactive television is in (Hodge, 1995). Other relevant references are (Chang et al., 1994; Hodge et al., 1993; and Little and Venkatesh, 1994).

Is video on demand really like renting a video, or is it more like picking a movie to watch from a 500- or 5000-channel cable system? The answer has important technical implications. In particular, video rental users are used to the idea of being able to stop a video, make a quick trip to the kitchen or bathroom, and then resume from where the video stopped. Television viewers do not expect to put programs on pause.

If video on demand is going to compete successfully with video rental stores, it may be necessary to allow users to stop, start, and rewind videos at will. Giving users this ability virtually forces the video provider to transmit a separate copy to each one.

On the other hand, if video on demand is seen more as advanced television, then it may be sufficient to have the video provider start each popular video, say, every 10 minutes, and run these nonstop. A user wanting to see a popular video may have to wait up to 10 minutes for it to start. Although pause/resume is not possible here, a viewer returning to the living room after a short break can switch to another channel showing the same video but 10 minutes behind. Some material will be repeated, but nothing will be missed. This scheme is called **near video on demand**. It offers the potential for much lower cost, because the same feed from the video server can go to many users at once. The difference between video on demand and near video on demand is similar to the difference between driving your own car and taking the bus.

Watching movies on (near) demand is but one of a vast array of potential new services possible once wideband networking is available. The general model that many people use is illustrated in Fig. 7-88. Here we see a high-bandwidth, (national or international) wide area backbone network at the center of the system. Connected to it are thousands of local distribution networks, such as cable TV or telephone company distribution systems. The local distribution systems reach into people's houses, where they terminate in **set-top boxes**, which are, in fact, powerful, specialized personal computers.

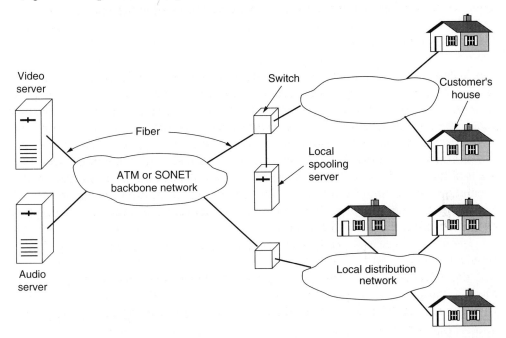

Fig. 7-88. Overview of a video-on-demand system.

Attached to the backbone by high-bandwidth optical fibers are thousands of information providers. Some of these will offer pay-per-view video or pay-per-hear audio CDs. Others will offer specialized services, such as home shopping (with the ability to rotate a can of soup and zoom in on the list of ingredients or view a video clip on how to drive a gasoline-powered lawn mower). Sports, news, reruns of "I Love Lucy," WWW access, and innumerable other possibilities will no doubt quickly become available.

Also included in the system are local spooling servers that allow videos to be prepositioned closer to the users, to save bandwidth during peak hours. How these pieces will fit together and who will own what are matters of vigorous debate within the industry. Below we will examine the design of the main pieces of the system: the video servers, the distribution network, and the set-top boxes.

Video Servers

To have (near) video on demand, we need **video servers** capable of storing and outputting a large number of movies simultaneously. The total number of movies ever made is estimated at 65,000 (Minoli, 1995). When compressed in

MPEG-2, a normal movie occupies roughly 4 GB of storage, so 65,000 of them would require something like 260 terabytes. Add to this all the old television programs ever made, sports films, newsreels, talking shopping catalogs, etc., and it is clear that we have an industrial-strength storage problem on our hands.

The cheapest way to store large volumes of information is on magnetic tape. This has always been the case and probably always will be. A DAT tape can store 8 GB (two movies) at a cost of about 5 dollars/gigabyte. Large mechanical tape servers that hold thousands of tapes and have a robot arm for fetching any tape and inserting it into a tape drive are commercially available now. The problem with these systems is the access time (especially for the second movie on a tape), the transfer rate, and the limited number of tape drives (to serve n movies at once, the unit would need n drives).

Fortunately, experience with video rental stores, public libraries, and other such organizations shows that not all items are equally popular. Experimentally, when there are N movies available, the fraction of all requests being for the kth most popular one is approximately C/k (Chervenak, 1994). Here C is computed to normalize the sum to 1, namely

$$C = 1/(1 + 1/2 + 1/3 + 1/4 + 1/5 + \cdots + 1/N)$$

Thus the most popular movie is seven times as popular as the number seven movie. This result is known as **Zipf's law** (Zipf, 1949).

The fact that some movies are much more popular than others suggests a possible solution in the form of a storage hierarchy, as shown in Fig. 7-89. Here, the performance increases as one moves up the hierarchy.

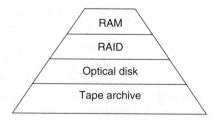

Fig. 7-89. A video server storage hierarchy.

An alternative to tape is optical storage. Current CD-ROMs hold only 650 MB, but the next generation will hold about 4 GB, to make them suitable for distributing MPEG-2 movies. Although seek times are slow compared to magnetic disks (100 msec versus 10 msec), their low cost and high reliability make optical juke boxes containing thousands of CD-ROMs a good alternative to tape for the more heavily used movies.

Next come magnetic disks. These have short access times (10 msec), high transfer rates (10 MB/sec), and substantial capacities (10 GB), which makes them well suited to holding movies that are actually being transmitted (as opposed to just being stored in case somebody ever wants them). Their main drawback is the high cost for storing movies that are rarely accessed.

At the top of the pyramid of Fig. 7-89 is RAM. RAM is the fastest storage medium, but also the most expensive. It is best suited to movies for which different parts are being sent to different destinations at the same time (e.g., true video on demand to 100 users who all started at different times). When RAM prices drop to 10 dollars/megabyte, a 4-GB movie will occupy 40,000 dollars worth of RAM, so having 100 movies in RAM will cost 4 million dollars for the 400 GB of memory. Still, for a 10 million dollar video server, this expense might well be worthwhile if each movie has enough simultaneous paying customers.

Since a video server is really just a massive real-time I/O device, it needs a different hardware and software architecture than a PC or a UNIX workstation. The hardware architecture of a typical video server is illustrated in Fig. 7-90. The server has one or more high-performance RISC CPUs, each with some local memory, a shared main memory, a massive RAM cache for popular movies, a variety of storage devices for holding the movies, and some networking hardware, normally an optical interface to an ATM (or SONET) network at OC-3 or higher. These subsystems are connected by an extremely high-speed bus (at least 1 GB/sec).

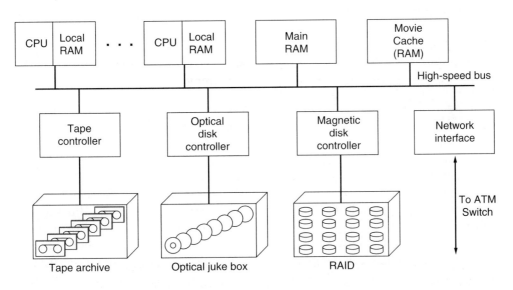

Fig. 7-90. The hardware architecture of a typical video server.

Now let us take a brief look at video server software. The CPUs are used for accepting user requests, locating movies, moving data between devices, customer billing, and many other functions. Some of these are not time critical, but many others are, so some, if not all, the CPUs will have to run a real-time operating system, such as a real-time microkernel. These systems normally break work up into small tasks, each with a known deadline. The scheduler can then run an algorithm such as nearest deadline next or the rate monotonic algorithm (Liu and Layland, 1973).

The CPU software also defines the nature of the interface that the server presents to the clients (spooling servers and set-top boxes). Two designs are popular. The first one is a traditional file system, in which the clients can open, read, write, and close files. Other than the complications introduced by the storage hierarchy and real-time considerations, such a server can have a file system modeled after that of UNIX.

The second kind of interface is based on the video recorder model. The commands to the server request it to open, play, pause, fast forward, and rewind files. The difference with the UNIX model is that once a PLAY command is given, the server just keeps pumping out data at a constant rate, with no new commands required.

The heart of the video server software is the disk management software. It has two main jobs: placing movies on the magnetic disk when they have to be pulled up from optical or tape storage, and handling disk requests for the many output streams. Movie placement is important because it can greatly affect performance.

Two possible ways of organizing disk storage are the disk farm and the disk array. With the **disk farm**, each drive holds a few entire movies. For performance and reliability reasons, each movie should be present on at least two drives, maybe more. The other storage organization is the **disk array** or **RAID (Redundant Array of Inexpensive Disks)**, in which each movie is spread out over multiple drives, for example, block 0 on drive 0, block 1 on drive 1, and so on, with block $n-1$ on drive $n-1$. After that, the cycle repeats, with block n on drive 0, and so forth. This organizing is called **striping**.

A striped disk array has several advantages over a disk farm. First, all n drives can be running in parallel, increasing the performance by a factor of n. Second, it can be made redundant by adding an extra drive to each group of n, where the redundant drive contains the block-by-block EXCLUSIVE OR of the other drives, to allow full data recover in the event one drive fails. Finally, the problem of load balancing is solved (manual placement is not needed to avoid having all the popular movies on the same drive). On the other hand, the disk array organization is more complicated than the disk farm and highly sensitive to multiple failures. It is also ill-suited to video recorder operations such as rewinding or fast forwarding a movie. A simulation study comparing the two organizations is given in (Chervenak et al., 1995).

Closely related to block placement is finding disk blocks. The UNIX scheme of having an unbalanced tree of disk blocks pointed to by the i-node is usually unacceptable because video files are huge, so most blocks can only be located by going through a triple indirect block, which means many extra disk accesses (Tanenbaum, 1992). Instead, it is common to link the blocks together on a singly-

or doubly-linked list. Sometimes a UNIX-style index (i-node) is also used to allow random access.

The other job of the disk software is to service all the real-time output streams and meet their timing constraints. An MPEG-2 video stream at 25 frames/sec needs to fetch and transmit about 14 KB every 40 msec, but the actual amount varies considerably because I-, P-, and B-frames have different compression ratios. Consequently, to maintain a uniform output rate, buffering is needed at both ends of the stream.

In Fig. 7-91 we see a staircase showing the total amount of data fetched from the disk for a given video stream (assuming that the movie is on disk). It moves up in discrete jumps, one jump for each block read. Nevertheless, transmission must occur at a more uniform rate, so the disk reading process must keep ahead of the transmission process. The shaded area in the figure shows data that have been fetched from disk but not yet transmitted.

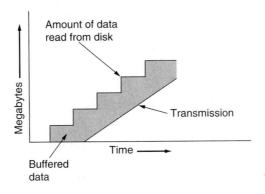

Fig. 7-91. Disk buffering at the server.

Normally, disks are scheduled using the elevator algorithm, which starts the arm moving inward and keeps going until it hits the innermost cylinder, processing all requests it hits in cylinder order. When it gets as far in as it can, the arm reverses and starts moving outward, again processing all pending requests along the way in order. While this algorithm minimizes seek time, it makes no guarantees about real-time performance, so is not useful for a video server.

A better algorithm is to keep track of all video streams and make a list of the next block needed by each one. These block numbers are then sorted and the blocks read in cylinder order. When the last block is read, the next round begins by collecting the number of the block now at the head of each stream. These are also sorted and read in cylinder order, and so on. This algorithm maintains real-time performance for all streams but also minimizes seek time compared to a pure first-come, first-served algorithm.

Another software issue is admission control. If a request for a new stream comes in, can it be accepted without ruining the real-time performance of the existing streams? One algorithm that can be used for making a decision examines the worst case to see if going from k streams to $k + 1$ streams is guaranteed to be possible, based on the known properties of the CPU, RAM, and disk. Another algorithm just looks at the statistical properties.

Another server software issue is how to manage the display during a fast forward or fast backward (so people can search visually). The D-frames provide the necessary information for MPEG-1, but unless they are marked and stored in some special way, the server will not be able to find them without decoding the entire stream, and normally servers do not perform MPEG decoding during transmission. For MPEG-2, some other mechanism will be needed, at the very least to make it easy to find and decode I-frames.

Finally, encryption is an issue. When movies are multicast (e.g., if the local distribution network is a cable TV system), encryption is needed to ensure that only paying customers can watch movies. Two approaches are possible: pre-encryption and encryption on the fly. If movies are stored encrypted, then anyone learning a movie's key may be able to watch it for free because the same key is used every time. Separate encryption for each stream is more secure, but also more costly of computing resources.

Key management is also an issue. The usual approach is to encrypt on the fly with a simple algorithm, but change the key often, so even if an intruder can break the key in 10 minutes, it will be obsolete by then.

The Distribution Network

The distribution network is the set of switches and lines between the source and destination. As we saw in Fig. 7-88, it consists of a SONET or ATM (or ATM over SONET) backbone, connected to a local distribution network. Usually, the backbone is switched and the local distribution network is not.

The main requirements imposed on the backbone are high bandwidth and low jitter. For a pure SONET backbone, these are trivial to achieve—the bandwidth is guaranteed and the jitter is zero because the network is synchronous. For an ATM backbone, or ATM over SONET, the quality of service is very important. It is managed by the leaky bucket algorithm and all the other techniques we studied in great detail in Chap. 5, so we will not repeat that discussion here. For additional information about real-time MPEG over ATM backbones, see (Dixit and Skelly, 1995; and Morales et al., 1995). Below we will focus on the local distribution network, a topic we have barely touched upon so far.

Local distribution is highly chaotic, with different companies trying out different networks in different regions. Telephone companies, cable TV companies, and new entrants are all convinced that whoever gets there first will be the big winner, so we are now seeing a proliferation of technologies being installed. The four main local distribution schemes for video on demand go by the acronyms ADSL, FTTC, FTTH, and HFC. We will now explain each of these in turn.

ADSL (**Asymmetric Digital Subscriber Line**) was the telephone industry's first entrant in the local distribution sweepstakes (Chen and Waring, 1994). The idea is that virtually every house in the United States, Europe, and Japan already has a copper twisted pair going into it (for analog telephone service). If these wires could be used for video on demand, the telephone companies could clean up.

The problem, of course, is that these wires cannot support even MPEG-1 over their typical 10-km length, let alone MPEG-2. The ADSL solution takes advantage of advances in digital signal processing to eliminate echoes and other line noise electronically. As shown in Fig. 7-92, each ADSL subscriber is given an in-house ADSL subscriber unit containing a digital signal processing chip. The telephone and set-top box plug into the ADSL unit. At the other end of the local loop, another ADSL unit is attached. This one may either be in the telephone company end office, or, if the local loop is too long, at the end of an optical fiber in the neighborhood of the house.

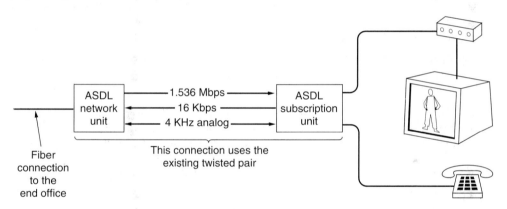

Fig. 7-92. ADSL as the local distribution network.

ADSL-1 offers a 1.536-Mbps downlink channel (T1 minus the 193rd bit), but only a 16-kbps uplink channel. In addition, the old 4-kHz analog telephone channel (or in some cases, two N-ISDN digital channels) is also on there. The idea is that the uplink has enough bandwidth for the user to order movies, and the downlink has enough bandwidth to send them encoded in MPEG-1. ADSL should be regarded more as a quick-and-dirty hack than a long-term solution, but it is being installed in various cities. Improved versions, called ADSL-2 and ADSL-3 are also being worked on. The latter allows MPEG-2 over local loops of up to about 2 km.

The second telephone company design is **FTTC** (**Fiber To The Curb**). We saw this design in Fig. 2-23(a). In FTTC, the telephone company runs optical fiber from the end office into each residential neighborhood, terminating in a device called an **ONU** (**Optical Network Unit**). The ONU is labeled "junction box" in Fig. 2-23(a). On the order of 16 copper local loops can terminate in an ONU. These loops are now so short that it is possible to run full-duplex T1 or T2 over them, allowing MPEG-1 and MPEG-2 movies, respectively. In addition, videoconferencing for home workers and small businesses is now possible because FTTC is symmetric.

The third telephone company solution is to run fiber into everyone's house. It is called **FTTH** (**Fiber To The Home**). In this scheme, everyone can have an OC-1, OC-3, or even higher carrier if that is required. FTTH is very expensive and will not happen for years but clearly will open a vast range of new possibilities when it finally happens.

ADSL, FTTC, and FTTH are all point-to-point local distribution networks, which is not surprising given how the current telephone system is organized. A completely different approach is **HFC** (**Hybrid Fiber Coax**), which is the preferred solution currently being installed by cable TV providers. It is illustrated in Fig. 2-23(b). The story goes something like this. The current 300- to 450-MHz coax cables will be replaced by 750-MHz coax cables, upgrading the capacity from 50 to 75 6-MHz channels to 125 6-MHz channels. Seventy-five of the 125 channels will be used for transmitting analog television.

The 50 new channels will each be modulated using QAM-256, which provides about 40 Mbps per channel, giving a total of 2 Gbps of new bandwidth. The head-ends will be moved deeper into the neighborhoods, so each cable runs past only 500 houses. Simple division show that each house can then be allocated a dedicated 4 Mbps channel, which can be used for some combination of MPEG-1 programs, MPEG-2 programs, upstream data, analog and digital telephony, and so on.

While this sounds wonderful, it does require the cable providers to replace all the existing cables with 750 MHz coax, install new head-ends, and remove all the one-way amplifiers—in short, replace the entire cable TV system. Consequently, the amount of new infrastructure here is comparable to what the telephone companies need for FTTC. In both cases the local network provider has to run fiber into residential neighborhoods. Again, in both cases, the fiber terminates at an optoelectrical converter. In FTTC, the final segment is a point-to-point local loop using twisted pairs. In HFC, the final segment is a shared coaxial cable. Technically, these two systems are not really as different as their respective proponents often make out.

Nevertheless, there is one real difference that is worth pointing out. HFC uses a shared medium without switching and routing. Any information put onto the cable can be removed by any subscriber without further ado. FTTC, which is fully switched, does not have this property. As a result, HFC operators want video servers to send out encrypted streams, so customers who have not paid for a movie cannot see it. FTTC operators do not especially want encryption because it adds complexity, lowers performance, and provides no additional security in their system. From the point of view of the company running a video server, is it a good idea to encrypt or not? A server operated by a telephone company or one of its subsidiaries or partners might intentionally decide not to encrypt its videos, claiming efficiency as the reason but really to cause economic losses to its HFC competitors.

For all these local distribution networks, it is likely that each neighborhood will be outfitted with one or more spooling servers. These are, in fact, just smaller versions of the video servers we discussed above. The big advantage of these local servers is that since the local distribution networks are short and generally not switched, they do not introduce jitter as an ATM backbone network would.

They can be preloaded with movies either dynamically or by reservation. For example, when a user selects a movie, the first minute could be transmitted to the local server in under 2 seconds at OC-3. After 55 seconds, the next minute could be shipped to the local server in 2 seconds, and so on. In this way, the traffic over the ATM backbone no longer has to be jitter free, making it possible to use ABR service instead of the more expensive CBR service.

If people tell the provider which movies they want well in advance, they can be downloaded to the local server during off-peak hours, giving even bigger savings. This observation is likely to lead the network operators to lure away airline executives to do their pricing. One can envision tariffs in which movies ordered 24 to 72 hours in advance for viewing on a Tuesday or Thursday evening before 6 P.M, or after 11 P.M. get a 27 percent discount. Movies ordered on the first Sunday of the month before 8 A.M. for viewing on a Wednesday afternoon on a day whose date is a prime number get a 43 percent discount, and so on.

The choice of the protocol stack to use for video on demand is still up in the air. ATM is clearly the technology of choice, but which adaptation protocol should be used? AAL 1 was designed for video, so it is a strong candidate, but it corresponds to the CBR service category. Dedicating the maximum possible bandwidth needed is expensive, especially since MPEG is inherently VBR traffic so the virtual circuit will have to be overdimensioned.

AAL 2 is not finished (and probably never will be) and AAL 3/4 is too clumsy, so AAL 5 is the only remaining contender. It is not tied to CBR service, and sending a large block of MPEG in each message would be extremely efficient, getting nearly 100 percent of the user bandwidth for the video stream. On the downside, AAL 5 does error detection. Having an entire block discarded due to a 1-bit error is highly unattractive, especially since most errors are single bit errors in the middle of the data. As a consequence, there is some movement toward changing AAL 5 to allow applications to ask for all blocks, along with a bit telling whether or not the checksum was correct.

The video on demand protocol stack we have sketched above is illustrated in Fig. 7-93. Above the AAL layer, we see the MPEG program and transport stream layer. Then come the encoding and decoding of MPEG audio and video, respectively. Finally, we have the application on top.

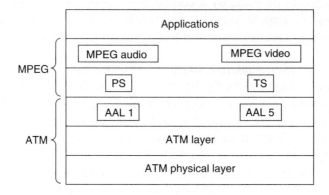

Fig. 7-93. A video-on-demand protocol stack.

Set-Top Boxes

All of the above local distribution methods ultimately bring one or more MPEG streams into the home. To decode and view them, a network interface, MPEG decoder, and other electronic components are needed. Two approaches are possible here.

In approach one, people use their personal computers for decoding and viewing movies. Doing this requires buying a special plug-in board containing a few special chips and a connector for interfacing to the local distribution network. The movies then appear on the computer's monitor, possibly even in a window. One might call this the set-bottom box since with computers, the box is usually under the monitor instead of on top of it. This approach is cheaper (all that is needed is one plug-in board and the software), uses a high-resolution noninterlaced monitor, has a sophisticated mouse-oriented user interface, and can easily be integrated with the WWW and other computer-oriented information and entertainment sources. On the other hand, PCs usually have small screens, are located in studies or dens rather than in living rooms, and are traditionally used by one person at a time. They also emit significantly less light than television sets.

In approach two, the local network operator rents or sells the user a **set-top box** to which the network and television set are connected. This approach has the advantage that everyone has a television but not everyone has a PC, and many of the PCs that people do have are old, peculiar, or otherwise unsuited to MPEG decoding. Furthermore, the television is often located in a room intended for group viewing.

On the down side, the monitor has a low-resolution interlaced display (making it unsuited for text-oriented material, such as the WWW). In addition, it has a dreadful user interface (the remote control), making it virtually impossible for the user to do anything except select items from simple menus. Even typing in the name of a movie is painful, let alone engaging in a dialog asking the server to search for all the films made by a certain actor, director, or production company during a certain time period. Finally, set-top boxes with the required performance are not easy to produce for an acceptable price (thought to be a few hundred dollars).

All these factors considered, most video-on-demand systems have opted for the set-top box model, primarily because mass marketeers hate to exclude any potential customers (people without a PC). Also, there may be money to be made renting or selling set-top boxes. Nevertheless, the PC plug-in board market is large enough so no doubt these boards will be produced, too.

The primary functions of the set-top box are interfacing with the local distribution network, decoding the MPEG signal, synchronizing the audio and video streams, producing a composite NTSC, PAL, or SECAM signal for the television set, listening to the remote control, and handling the user interface. Additional functions might include interfacing with stereos, telephones, and other devices. A major battle is raging within the industry about how much functionality should be put in the set-top box and how much should be in the network. How that turns out remains to be seen.

A possible architecture for a simple set-top box is shown in Fig. 7-94. The device consists of a CPU, ROM, RAM, I/O controller, MPEG decoder, and network interface. Optionally, a security chip can also be added for decryption of incoming movies and encryption of outgoing messages (credit card numbers for home shopping, etc.).

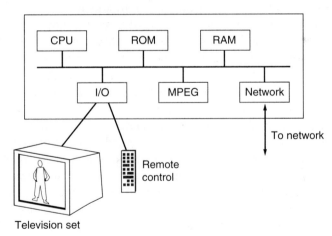

Fig. 7-94. The hardware architecture of a simple set-top box.

An important issue for video on demand is audio/video synchronization and jitter management. Adding an additional 500 KB of RAM allows for 1 second of MPEG-2 buffering, but at additional expense in a device that the manufacturers are hoping to sell for a few hundred dollars, at most.

Since the set-top box is just a computer, it will need software, probably a microkernel-based real-time operating system kept in the ROM. To provide flexibility and adaptability, it is probably a good idea to make it possible to download other software from the network. This possibility then raises the problem of what happens when the owner of a MIPS-based set-top box wants to play a game written for a SPARC-based set-top box? Using an interpreted language such as Java solves the compatibility problem but severely lowers performance in a real-time environment in which high performance is crucial.

Standards

The economics of video on demand cannot be ignored. A large video server can easily cost more than a mainframe, certainly 10 million dollars. Suppose that it serves 100,000 homes, each of which has rented a 300-dollar set-top box. Now throw in 10 million dollars worth of networking equipment and a 4-year depreciation period, and the system has to generate 10 dollars per home per month. At 5 dollars/movie, everyone has to buy two movies a month for the operator to break even (excluding salaries, marketing, and all other costs). Whether this will actually happen is far from obvious.

The numbers given above can be rearranged in many ways (e.g., charging 6 dollars per month rental for the set-top box and 2 dollars per movie), and the costs are changing all the time, but it should be clear that without a mass market, there is no way that video on demand makes economic sense. For a mass market to develop, it is essential that all parts of the system be standardized. If each video provider, network operator, and set-top box manufacturer designs its own interface, nothing will interwork with the rest of the system. So far, the only standard that everyone agrees on is the use of MPEG-2 for video encoding. Everything else is up for grabs. A few of the many questions that have to be answered before a national system can be built are listed in Fig. 7-95.

If all these areas can be standardized, we can easily imagine many vendors producing products consisting of a box with a telephone jack, monitor, keyboard, and mouse that can be used for watching videos, computing, or maybe doing both at once. The much-discussed convergence of the computing, communication, and entertainment industries will then be a reality.

7.7.5. MBone—Multicast Backbone

While all these industries are making great—and highly publicized—plans for future (inter)national digital video on demand, the Internet community has been quietly implementing its own digital multimedia system, **MBone** (**Multicast Backbone**). In this section we will give a brief overview of what it is and how it works. For an entire book on MBone, see (Kumar, 1996). For articles on MBone, see (Eriksson, 1994; and Macedonia and Brutzman, 1994).

What technology will the backbone use (SONET, ATM, SONET + ATM)?
What speed will the backbone run at (OC-3, OC-12)?
How will local distribution be done (HFC, FTTC)?
How much upstream bandwidth will there be (16 kbps, 1.5 Mbps)?
Will movies be encrypted, and if so, how?
Will error correction be present (mandatory, optional, absent)?
Who will own the set-top box (user, network operator)?
Will telephony be part of the system (analog, N-ISDN)?
Will high-resolution hypertext applications be supported (e.g., WWW)?

Fig. 7-95. A few areas in which standards are needed.

MBone can be thought of as Internet radio and television. Unlike video on demand, where the emphasis is on calling up and viewing precompressed movies stored on a server, MBone is used for broadcasting live audio and video in digital form all over the world via the Internet. It has been operational since early 1992. Many scientific conferences, especially IETF meetings, have been broadcast, as well as newsworthy scientific events, such as space shuttle launches. A Rolling Stones concert was once broadcast over MBone. Whether this qualifies as a newsworthy scientific event is arguable. For people who want to digitally record an MBone broadcast, software for accomplishing that is also available (Holfelder, 1995).

Most of the research concerning MBone has been about how to do multicasting efficiently over the (datagram-oriented) Internet. Little has been done on audio or video encoding. MBone sources are free to experiment with MPEG or any other encoding technology they wish. There are no Internet standards on content or encoding.

Technically, MBone is a virtual overlay network on top of the Internet. It consists of multicast-capable islands connected by tunnels, as shown in Fig. 7-96. In this figure, MBone consists of six islands, *A* through *F*, connected by seven tunnels. Each island (typically a LAN or group of interconnected LANs) supports hardware multicast to its hosts. The tunnels propagate MBone packets between the islands. Some day in the future, when all the routers are capable of handling multicast traffic directly, this superstructure will no longer be needed, but for the moment, it does the job.

Each island contains one or more special routers called **mrouters** (**multicast routers**). Some of these are actually normal routers, but most are just UNIX workstations running special user-level software (but as the root). The mrouters are logically connected by tunnels. In the past, MBone packets were tunneled from mrouter to mrouter (usually through one or more routers that did not know

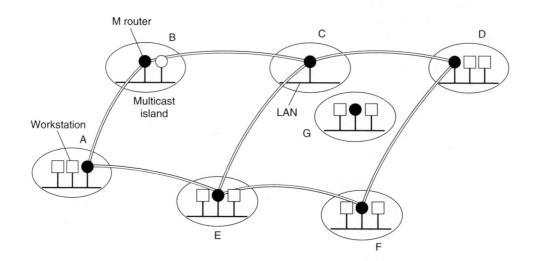

Fig. 7-96. MBone consists of multicast islands connected by tunnels.

about MBone) using loose source routing. Nowadays, MBone packets are encapsulated within IP packets and sent as regular unicast packets to the destination mrouter's IP address. If all the intervening routers support multicast, however, tunneling is not needed.

Tunnels are configured manually. Usually, a tunnel runs above a path for which a physical connection exists, but this is not a requirement. If, by accident, the physical path underlying a tunnel goes down, the mrouters using the tunnel will not even notice it, since the Internet will automatically reroute all the IP traffic between them via other lines.

When a new island appears and wishes to join MBone, such as *G* in Fig. 7-96, its administrator sends a message announcing its existence to the MBone mailing list. The administrators of nearby sites then contact him to arrange to set up tunnels. Sometimes existing tunnels are reshuffled to take advantage of the new island to optimize the topology. After all, tunnels have no physical existence. They are defined by tables in the mrouters and can be added, deleted, or moved simply by changing these tables. Typically, each country on MBone has a backbone, with regional islands attached to it. Normally, MBone is configured with one or two tunnels crossing the Atlantic and Pacific oceans, making MBone global in scale.

Thus at any instant, MBone consists of a specific topology consisting of islands and tunnels, independent of the number of multicast addresses currently in use and who is listening to them or watching them. This situation is very similar to a normal (physical) subnet, so the normal routing algorithms apply to it. Consequently, MBone initially used a routing algorithm, **DVMRP** (**Distance Vector Multicast Routing Protocol**) based on the Bellman-Ford distance vector algorithm. For example, in Fig. 7-96, island C can route to A either via B or via E (or conceivably via D). It makes its choice by taking the values those nodes give it about their respective distances to A and then adding its distance to them. In this way, every island determines the best route to every other island. The routes are not actually used in this way, however, as we will see shortly.

Now let us consider how multicasting actually happens. To multicast an audio or video program, a source must first acquire a class D multicast address, which acts like a station frequency or channel number. Class D addresses are reserved by using a program that looks in a database for free multicast addresses. Many multicasts may be going on at once, and a host can "tune" to the one it is interested in by listening to the appropriate multicast address.

Periodically, each mrouter sends out an IGMP broadcast packet limited to its island asking who is interested in which channel. Hosts wishing to (continue to) receive one or more channels send another IGMP packet back in response. These responses are staggered in time, to avoid overloading the local LAN. Each mrouter keeps a table of which channels it must put out onto its LAN, to avoid wasting bandwidth by multicasting channels that nobody wants.

Multicasts propagate through MBone as follows. When an audio or video source generates a new packet, it multicasts it to its local island using the hardware multicast facility. This packet is picked up by the local mrouter, which then copies it into all the tunnels to which it is connected.

Each mrouter getting such a packet via a tunnel then checks to see if the packet came along the best route, that is, the route that its table says to use to reach the source (as if it were a destination). If the packet came along the best route, the mrouter copies the packet to all its other tunnels. If the packet arrived via a suboptimal route, it is discarded. Thus, for example, in Fig. 7-96, if C's tables tell it to use B to get to A, then when a multicast packet from A reaches C via B, the packet is copied to D and E. However, when a multicast packet from A reaches C via E (not the best path), it is simply discarded. This algorithm is just the reverse path forwarding algorithm that we saw in Chap. 5. While not perfect, it is fairly good and very simple to implement.

In addition to using reverse path forwarding to prevent flooding the Internet, the IP *Time to live* field is also used to limit the scope of multicasting. Each packet starts out with some value (determined by the source). Each tunnel is assigned a weight. A packet is only passed through a tunnel if it has enough weight. Otherwise it is discarded. For example, transoceanic tunnels are normally configured with a weight of 128, so packets can be limited to the continent of origin by giving them an initial *Time to live* of 127 or less. After passing through a tunnel, the *Time to live* field is decremented by the tunnel's weight.

While the MBone routing algorithm works, much research has been devoted to improving it. One proposal keeps the idea of distance vector routing, but makes the algorithm hierarchical by grouping MBone sites into regions and first routing to them (Thyagarajan and Deering, 1995).

Another proposal is to use a modified form of link state routing instead of distance vector routing. In particular, an IETF working group is busy modifying OSPF to make it suitable for multicasting within a single autonomous system. The resulting multicast OSPF is called **MOSPF** (Moy, 1994). What the modifications do is have the full map built by MOSPF keep track of multicast islands and tunnels, in addition to the usual routing information. Armed with the complete topology, it is straightforward to compute the best path from every island to every other island using the tunnels. Dijkstra's algorithm can be used, for example.

A second area of research is inter-AS routing. Here an algorithm called **PIM (Protocol Independent Multicast)** is being developed by another IETF working group (Huitema, 1995). PIM comes in two versions, depending one whether the islands are dense (almost everyone wants to watch) or sparse (almost nobody wants to watch). Both versions use the standard unicast routing tables, instead of creating an overlay topology as DVMRP and MOSPF do.

In PIM-dense, the idea is to prune useless paths. Pruning works as follows. When a multicast packet arrives via the "wrong" tunnel, a prune packet is sent back through the tunnel telling the sender to stop sending it packets from the source in question. When a packet arrives via the "right" tunnel, it is copied to all the other tunnels that have not previously pruned themselves. If all the other tunnels have pruned themselves and there is no interest in the channel within the local island, the mrouter sends a prune message back through the "right" channel. In this way, the multicast adapts automatically and only goes where it is wanted.

PIM-sparse works differently. The idea here is to prevent saturating the Internet because three people in Berkeley want to hold a conference call over a class D address. PIM-sparse works by setting up rendezvous points. Each of the sources in a PIM-sparse multicast group send their packets to the rendezvous points. Any site interested in joining up asks one of the rendezvous points to set up a tunnel to it. In this way, all PIM-sparse traffic is transported by unicast instead of by multicast.

All in all, multimedia is an exciting and rapidly moving field. New technologies and applications are announced daily, but the area as a whole is likely to remain important for decades to come.

7.8. SUMMARY

Computer networks are inherently insecure. To keep information secret, it must be encrypted. Encryption protocols fall into two general classes: secret key (e.g., DES, IDEA), and public key (e.g., RSA). Using these protocols is straightforward; the hard part is key management.

In addition to providing secrecy, cryptographic protocols can also provide authentication, so that when Alice thinks she is communicating with Bob, she really is communicating with Bob, and not with Trudy. Finally, cryptography can also be used to allow messages to be signed in such a way that the sender cannot repudiate them after they have been sent.

Naming in the Internet uses a distributed database system, DNS. DNS holds records with IP addresses, mail exchanges, and other information. By querying a DNS server, a process can map an Internet domain name onto the IP address used to communicate with that domain.

As networks grow larger, they become harder to manage. For this reason, special network management systems and protocols have been devised, the most popular of which is SNMP. This protocol allows managers to communicate with agents inside devices to read out their status and issue commands to them.

Four major network applications are electronic mail, USENET news, the World Wide Web, and multimedia (video on demand and MBone). Most email systems use the mail system defined in RFCs 821 and 822. Messages sent in this system use system ASCII headers to define message properties. These messages are sent using SMTP. Two systems for securing email exist, PGP and PEM.

USENET news consists of thousands of newsgroups on all manner of topics. People can join newsgroups locally, and can then post messages all over the world using the NNTP protocol, which has some resemblence to SMTP.

The World Wide Web is a system for linking up hypertext documents. Each document is a page written in HTML, possible with hyperlinks to other documents. A browser can display a document by establishing a TCP connection to its server, asking for the document, and then closing the connection. When a hyperlink is selected by the user, that document can also be fetched in the same way. In this manner, documents all over the world are linked together in a giant web.

Multimedia is the rising star in the networking firmament. It allows audio and video to be digitized and transported electronically for display. Most multimedia projects use the MPEG standards and transmit the data over ATM connections. The MBone is an experimental worldwide digital radio and television service on the Internet.

PROBLEMS

1. Break the following monoalphabetic cipher. The plaintext, consisting of letters only, is a well-known excerpt from a poem by Lewis Carroll.

   kfd ktbd fzm eubd kfd pzyiom mztx ku kzyg ur bzha kfthcm
   ur mfudm zhx mftnm zhx mdzythc pzq ur ezsszcdm zhx gthcm
   zhx pfa kfd mdz tm sutythc fuk zhx pfdkfdi ntcm fzld pthcm
   sok pztk z stk kfd uamkidm eitdx sdruid pd fzld uoi efzk
   rui mubd ur om zid uok ur sidzkf zhx zyy ur om zid rzk
   hu foiia mztx kfd ezindhkdi kfda kfzhgdx ftb boef rui kfzk

2. Break the following columnar transposition cipher. The plaintext is taken from a popular computer textbook, so "computer" is a probable word. The plaintext consists entirely of letters (no spaces). The ciphertext is broken up into blocks of five characters for readability.

aauan cvlre rurnn dltme aeepb ytust iceat npmey iicgo gorch srsoc
nntii imiha oofpa gsivt tpsit lbolr otoex

3. In Fig. 7-4, the P-boxes and S-boxes alternate. Although this arrangement is esthetically pleasing, is it any more secure than first having all the P-boxes and then all the S-boxes?

4. Suppose that a message has been encrypted using DES in ciphertext block chaining mode. One bit of ciphertext in block C_i is accidentally transformed from a 0 to a 1 during transmission. How much plaintext will be garbled as a result?

5. Now consider ciphertext block chaining again. Instead of a single 0 bit being transformed into a 1 bit, an extra 0 bit is inserted into the ciphertext stream after block C_i. How much plaintext will be garbled as a result?

6. Design an attack on DES based on the knowledge that the plaintext consists exclusively of uppercase ASCII letters, plus space, comma, period, semicolon, carriage return, and line feed. Nothing is known about the plaintext parity bits.

7. Compare cipher block chaining with cipher feedback mode in terms of the number of encryption operations needed to transmit a large file. Which one is more efficient and by how much?

8. Using the RSA public key cryptosystem, with $a = 1$, $b = 2$, etc.,
   (a) If $p = 7$ and $q = 11$, list five legal values for d.
   (b) If $p = 13$, $q = 31$ and $d = 7$, find e.
   (c) Using $p = 5$, $q = 11$, and $d = 27$, find e and encrypt "abcdefghij"

9. The Diffie-Hellman key exchange is being used to establish a secret key between Alice and Bob. Alice sends Bob (719, 3, 191). Bob responds with (543). Alice's secret number, x, is 16. What is the secret key?

10. Change one message in protocol of Fig. 7-14 in a minor way to make it resistant to the reflection attack. Explain why your change works.

11. In the protocol of Fig. 7-17, why is A sent in plaintext along with the encrypted session key?

12. In the protocol of Fig. 7-17, we pointed out that starting each plaintext message with 32 zero bits is a security risk. Suppose that each message begins with a per-user random number, effectively a second secret key known only to its user and the KDC. Does this eliminate the known plaintext attack?

13. In the Needham-Schroeder protocol, Alice generates two challenges, R_A and R_{A2}. This seems like overkill. Would one not have done the job?

14. In the public-key authentication protocol of Fig. 7-21, in message 3, R_B is encrypted with K_S. Is this encryption necessary, or would it have been adequate to send it back in plaintext?

15. The signature protocol of Fig. 7-22 has the following weakness. If Bob crashes, he may lose the contents of his RAM. What problems does this cause and what can he do to prevent them?

16. After Ellen confessed to Marilyn about tricking her in the matter of Tom's tenure, Marilyn resolved to avoid this problem by dictating the contents of future messages into a dictating machine and having her new secretary just type them in. Marilyn then planned to examine the messages on her terminal after they have been typed in to make sure they contain her exact words. Can the new secretary still use the birthday attack to falsify a message, and if so, how? *Hint*: She can.

17. Point-of-sale terminals that use magnetic-stripe cards and PIN codes have a fatal flaw: a malicious merchant can modify his card reader to capture and store all the information on the card as well as the PIN code in order to post additional (fake) transactions in the future. The next generation of point-of-sale terminals will use cards with a complete CPU, keyboard, and tiny display on the card. Devise a protocol for this system that malicious merchants cannot break.

18. According to the information given in Fig. 7-27, is *little-sister.cs.vu.nl* on a class A, B, or C network?

19. In Fig. 7-27, there is no period after *rowboat*? Why not?

20. What is the *OBJECT IDENTIFIER* for the tcp object?

21. An SNMP integer whose value is 200 has to be transmitted. Show the binary representation of the bits sent in the ASN.1 transfer syntax.

22. What is the representation of the 11-bit binary bit string '11100001111' in the ASN.1 transfer syntax?

23. Suppose that you are hired by a bridge vendor to write SNMP-conformant code for one of their bridges. You read all the RFCs and still have questions. You suggest to IAB that a complete, formal grammar of the language used to describe SNMP variables be given in one place. IAB's reaction is to agree and appoint you to do the job. Should the grammar be added to RFC 1442 or RFC 1213? Why? *Hint*: You do not need to fetch the RFCs; enough information is given in the text.

24. Some email systems support a header field *Content Return:*. It specifies whether the body of a message is to be returned in the event of nondelivery. Does this field belong to the envelope or to the header?

25. Electronic mail systems need directories so people's email addresses can be looked up. To build such directories, names should be broken up into standard components (e.g., first name, last name) to make searching possible. Discuss some problems that must be solved for a worldwide standard to be acceptable.

26. A binary file is 3072 bytes long. How long will it be if encoded using base64 encoding, with a CR+LF pair inserted after every 80 bytes sent and at the end?

27. Consider the quoted-printable MIME encoding scheme. Mention a problem not discussed in the text and propose a solution.

28. Give *two* reasons why PGP compresses messages.

29. Suppose that someone sets up a vacation daemon and then sends a message just before logging out. Unfortunately, the recipient has been on vacation for a week and also has a vacation daemon in place. What happens next? Will canned replies go back and forth until somebody returns?

30. Assuming that everyone on the Internet used PGP, could a PGP message be sent to an arbitrary Internet address and be decoded correctly by all concerned? Discuss your answer.

31. PGP does not support canonicalization as does PEM. Why not?

32. Make a guess about what the smiley :-X (sometimes written as :-#) might mean.

33. How long does it take to distribute a days' worth of news over a 50-Mbps satellite channel?

34. Which of the commands listed in Fig. 7-56 are theoretically redundant?

35. A large network consists of an $n \times n$ grid of machines. All the interior nodes have four neighbors; the ones on the edges (corners) have three (two) neighbors. If an m-byte article is posted on some machine using NNTP, how many bytes of bandwidth are consumed getting it to all other machines (ignoring the NNTP overhead and just counting the message bytes)?

36. Repeat the previous problem, but now compute the approximate bandwidth that would be needed to distribute the message using a mailing list. How much more is it than in the previous problem?

37. When Web pages are sent out, they are prefixed by MIME headers. Why?

38. When are external viewers needed? How does a browser know which one to use?

39. Imagine that someone in the CS Department at Stanford has just written a new program that he wants to distribute by FTP. He puts the program in the FTP directory *ftp/pub/freebies/newprog.c*. What is the URL for this program likely to be?

40. In Fig. 7-60, the *ALT* parameter is set in the <IMG> tag. Under what conditions does the browser use it, and how?

41. How do you make an image clickable in HTML? Given an example.

42. Show the <A> tag that is needed to make the string "ACM" be a hyperlink to *http://www.acm.org*.

43. Design a form for a new company, Interburger, that allows hamburgers to be ordered via the Internet. The form should include the customer's name, address, and city, as well as a choice of size (either gigantic or immense) and a cheese option. The burgers are to be paid for in cash upon delivery, so no credit card information is needed.

44. Java does not have structures as in C or records as in Pascal. Is there some other way to achieve the same effect of bundling a group of dissimilar variables together to form a single data type? If so, what is it?

45. Using the data structures of Fig. 7-75, list the exact steps needed to check a new URL to see if it is already in *url_table*.

46. Suppose that in its effort to become more market oriented, the KGB goes commercial and hires an advertising agency that designs a Web page for it. Your company has been hired as an outside consultant to implement it. Write the HTML to produce the Web page below.

WELCOME TO THE KGB'S WWW HOME PAGE

As a consequence of its recent privatization, the KGB is pleased to announce the commercial availability of many fine products and services previously available only to major governments.

Competitive prices! Discreet service ensured!

- Products
  - □ <u>Nuclear weapons</u> (small, medium, large, jumbo)
  - □ <u>Spy satellites</u> (keep tabs on your neighbors)
  - □ <u>Low-radar-profile supersonic aircraft</u> (buzz your friends' houses unseen)

- Services
  - □ <u>Mole placement in the organization of your choice</u>
  - □ <u>Coups</u> (corporate as well as governmental)
  - □ <u>Assistance in setting up your very own germ-warfare laboratory</u>

- Bargain basement specials
  - □ <u>The collected works of Felix Dzerzhinsky</u> (limited edition)
  - □ <u>Aerial photographs of Afghanistan</u> (ca. 1984)
  - □ <u>Quality Bulgarian-made tanks</u> (95 percent discount)

Webmaster@kgb.ru

---

47. In C and C++, the size of an integer is not specified by the language. In Java it is. Give an argument for the C way and one for the Java way.

48. Suppose that the Web contains 10 million pages, each with an average of 10 hyperlinks. Fetching a page averages 100 msec. What is the minimum time to index the entire Web?

49. A compact disc holds 650 MB of data. Is compression used for audio CDs? Explain your reasoning.

50. What is the bit rate for transmitting uncompressed VGA color with 8 bits/pixel at 40 frames/sec?

51. In Fig. 7-76(c) quantization noise occurs due to the use of 3-bit samples. The first sample, at 0, is exact, but the next few are not. What is the percent error for the samples at 1/32, 2/32, and 3/32 of the period?

52. Can a 1-bit error in an MPEG frame affect more than the frame in which the error occurs? Explain your answer.

53. Consider the 100,000 customer video server example given in the text. Suppose that half of all movies are served from 8 P.M to 10 P.M. How many movies does the server have to transmit at once during this time period? If each movie requires 4 Mbps, how many OC-12 connections does the server need to the network?

54. Suppose that Zipf's law holds for accesses to a 10,000-movie video server. If the server holds the most popular 1000 movies on magnetic disk and the remaining 9000 on optical disk, give an expression for the fraction of all references that will be to magnetic disk. Write a little program to evaluate this expression numerically.

55. MPEG PES packets contain a field giving the copyright status of the current transmission. Of what conceivable use is this field?

8

READING LIST AND BIBLIOGRAPHY

We have now finished our study of computer networks, but this is only the beginning. Many interesting topics have not been treated in as much detail as they deserve, and others have been omitted altogether for lack of space. In this chapter we provide some suggestions for further reading and a bibliography, for the benefit of readers who wish to continue their study of computer networks.

8.1. SUGGESTIONS FOR FURTHER READING

There is an extensive literature on all aspects of computer networks and distributed systems. Four journals that frequently publish papers in this area are *IEEE Transactions on Communications*, *IEEE Journal on Selected Areas in Communications*, *Computer Communication Review*, and *Computer Networks and ISDN Systems*. Many other journals also publish occasional papers on the subject.

IEEE also publishes two magazines, *IEEE Network Magazine* and *IEEE Communications Magazine*, that contain surveys, tutorials, and case studies on networking. The former emphasizes architecture, standards, and software, and the latter tends toward communications technology (fiber optics, satellites, and so on).

In addition, there are several annual or biannual conferences that often attract many papers on networks and distributed systems, in particular, *SIGCOMM '9x*, *The International Conference on Distributed Computer Systems*, *The Symposium on Operating Systems Principles* and *The N-th Data Communications Symposium*.

Furthermore, IEEE has published several volumes of network paper reprints in convenient paperback form.

Below we list some suggestions for supplementary reading, keyed to the chapters of this book.

8.1.1. Introduction and General Works

Bell, "Communications"
For an excellent overview of trends in communication, including telephone, ATM, ISDN, wireless LANs, the Internet, and pagers, this article is a must.

Comer, *The Internet Book*
Anyone looking for an easy-going introduction to the Internet should look here. Comer describes the history, growth, technology, protocols, and services of the Internet in terms that novices can understand, but so much material is covered that the book is also of interest to more technical readers as well.

Jabbari et al., "Network Issues for Wireless Communication"
This introduction to cellular radio systems covers call control, routing, signaling, and other aspects of modern mobile communication systems.

Kwok, "A Vision for Residential Broadband Service"
If you want to know how Microsoft thinks video on demand should be organized, this article is for you. In it, Microsoft's chief ATM architect explains his company's vision. Briefly summarized, Microsoft's idea is: ATM to the home is the way to go. Forget all the "realistic" (i.e., ad hoc) solutions, like ADSL and do it right.

Le Boudec, "The Asynchronous Transfer Mode: A tutorial"
ATM is an up-and-coming technology, and this paper gives a thorough introduction to it. The physical layer, ATM layer, and AAL layer are all covered. In addition, the final section discusses the debate about ATM.

Pahlavan et al., "Trends in Local Wireless Networks"
Wireless LANs will no doubt become increasingly important in the future. In this paper, the authors discuss the state of the art and trends in spectrum use and technologies for wireless LANs.

Siu and Jain, "A Brief Overview of ATM"
Many features of ATM systems are covered in this introductory paper, but the focus is on LAN emulation and traffic management. It also serves as the introduction to a special issue of *Computer Communication Review* devoted to ATM technology.

8.1.2. The Physical Layer

Awdeh and Mouftah, "Survey of ATM Switch Architectures"
Anyone interested in learning more about ATM switch design should look here. After introducing switches in general and buffering strategies, the authors discuss many kinds of crossbar, disjoint-path, and banyan switches. The paper also provides over 200 references to other papers.

Bellamy, *Digital Telephony*
Everything you ever wanted to know about the telephone system and more is contained in this authoritative book. Particularly interesting are the chapters on transmission and multiplexing, digital switching, fiber optics, and ISDN.

De Prycker, *Asynchronous Transfer Mode*, 2nd ed.
Chapter 4 contains a wealth of information on ATM switches. The principles are illustrated by numerous example switches, including the knockout, Roxanne, Coprin, and Athena switches.

Held, *The Complete Modem Reference*, 2nd ed.
Everything you might conceivably want to know about modems is here, from the U.S. and Canadian governments' compliance rules, through modulation techniques and standards, to how to troubleshoot a sick modem.

IEEE Communications Mag., Jan. 1995, "Wireless Personal Communications"
This special issue contains seven papers on different aspects of wireless personal communication. Collectively they cover propagation, access methods, receiver principles, system aspects, and network issues.

Metcalfe, "Computer/Network Interface Design: Lessons from Arpanet & Ethernet"
Although engineers have been building network interfaces for decades now, one often wonders if they have learned anything from all this experience. In this paper, the designer of the Ethernet tells how to build a network interface, and what to do with it once you have built it. He pulls no punches, telling what he did wrong as well as what he did right.

Padgett et al., "Overview of Wireless Personal Communications"
An introduction to cellular and cordless communication systems and a comparison of the two. Both the American and European standards are covered.

Palais, *Fiber Optic Communication*, 3rd ed.
Books on fiber optic technology tend to be aimed at the specialist, but this one is more accessible than most. It covers waveguides, light sources, light detectors, couplers, modulation, noise, and many other topics.

Pandya, "Emerging Mobile and Personal Communications Systems"

For a short and sweet introduction to hand-held personal communication systems, this article is worth looking at. One of the nine pages contains a list of 70 acronyms used on the other eight pages.

Partridge, *Gigabit Networking*

In addition to describing several kinds of ATM switches, Chap. 5 also compares input buffering and output buffering and derives formulas for the performance of each.

Spragins et al., *Telecommunications Protocols and Design*

Chapter 2 contains a good introduction to transmission technology, including copper wires, fiber optics, cellular radio, and satellites. It also has extended discussions of the Nyquist and Shannon limits and their implications.

8.1.3. The Data Link Layer

Black, *Data Link Protocols*

Here is an entire book on the data link layer. It has a practical emphasis, with a large amount of material on HDLC, LLC, PPP, and other commercially important protocols.

Holzmann, *Design and Validation of Computer Protocols*

Readers interested in the more formal aspects of data link (and similar) protocols should look here. The specification, modeling, correctness, and testing of such protocols are all covered in this book.

Spragins et al., *Telecommunications Protocols and Design*

Readers interested in learning more about error-detecting and error-correcting codes should look at Chap. 6 of this book. It also covers the principles of elementary data link protocols at about the same level as this book does. Chapter 7 continues the discussion and discusses various data link protocols in detail.

Walrand, *Communication Networks: A First Course*

Chapter 4 covers data link protocols, with an emphasis on performance analysis. The finite state machine and Petri net approaches to protocol correctness are also treated.

8.1.4. The Medium Access Control Sublayer

Abeysundara and Kamal, "High-Speed Local Area Networks and Their Performance"

Since high-speed LANs are of interest due to their high speed, a paper discussing and analyzing the performance is welcome. In this one, the focus is on different kinds of bus, ring, tree, and star LANs, and their delay and utilization characteristics.

Jain, *FDDI Handbook—High-Speed Networking Using Fiber and other Media*
For a thorough treatment of FDDI (including nice tutorials on fiber optics and SONET), this book is a good choice. In addition to long sections on FDDI hardware and software, it has a section on performance and even advice on shopping for fiber optic cables.

Perlman, *Interconnections: Bridges and Routers*
For an authoritative, but entertaining, treatment of bridges (and routers), Perlman's book is the place to look. The author designed the algorithms used in the IEEE 802 spanning tree bridge as well as the DECnet routing algorithms and is clearly an expert on the subject.

Stallings, *Local and Metropolitan Area Networks*, 4th ed.
The three IEEE 802 LANs form the core of this book, but material on other LANs and MANs is also present.

Walrand, *Communication Networks: A First Course*
Like Stallings book above, Chap. 5 of this one covers the basic 802 material, plus FDDI and DQDB. The emphasis is on analyzing protocol performance.

8.1.5. The Network Layer

Comer, *Internetworking with TCP/IP*, Vol. 1, 3rd ed.
Comer has written the definitive work on the TCP/IP protocol suite. Chapters 4 through 11 deal with IP and related protocols in the network layer. The other chapters deal primarily with the higher layers, and are also worth reading.

Huitema, *Routing in the Internet*
If you want to know everything there is to know about routing in the Internet, this is the book for you. Both pronounceable algorithms (e.g., RIP, CIDR, and MBONE) and unpronounceable algorithms (e.g., OSPF, IGRP, EGP, and BGP) are treated in great detail. New features, such as multicast, mobile IP, and resource reservation, are also here.

Perlman, *Interconnections: Bridges and Routers*
In Chap. 9, Perlman describes many of the issues involved in unicast and multicast routing algorithm design, both for WANs and networks of LANs, and their implementation in various devices. The author clearly cares about the subject, having entitled Sec. 9.13.10 "My Opinion on IP-Style Network Layer Multicast."

Sterbenz et al., "Report on the IEEE ComSoc Gigabit Networking Workshop"

Before gigabit networking is usable, a number of basic questions have to be resolved. A key one is whether these networks will use ATM, TCP/IP, or both. To better understand these issues, IEEE organized a workshop in April 1995, a summary of which is presented here. The critique of ATM by Schulzrinne is worth reading by anyone who believes that ATM is the solution to the world's telecommunication problems.

Stevens, *TCP/IP Illustrated*, Vol. 1

Chapters 3-10 provide a comprehensive treatment of IP and related protocols (ARP, RARP, and ICMP) illustrated by examples.

Yang and Reddy, "A Taxonomy for Congestion Control Algorithms in Packet Switching Networks"

The authors have devised a taxonomy for congestion control algorithms. The main categories are open loop with source control, open loop with destination control, closed loop with explicit feedback, and closed loop with implicit feedback. They use this taxonomy to describe and classify 23 existing algorithms.

8.1.6. The Transport Layer

Comer, *Internetworking with TCP/IP*, Vol. 1, 3rd ed.

As mentioned above, Comer has written the definitive work on the TCP/IP protocol suite. Chap. 12 is about UDP; Chap. 13 is about TCP.

Mogul, "IP Network Performance"

Despite the title of this article, it is at least, if not more, about TCP and network performance in general, than about IP performance in particular. It is full of useful guidelines and rules of thumb.

Stallings, *Data and Computer Communications*, 4th ed.

Chapter 12 is about transport protocols and covers services and mechanisms in the abstract, as well as the OSI and TCP transport protocols in detail.

Stevens, *TCP/IP Illustrated*, Vol. 1

Chapters 17-24 provide a comprehensive treatment of TCP illustrated by examples.

8.1.7. The Application Layer

Anderson, R., "Why Cryptosystems Fail"

According to Anderson, security in banking systems is poor, but not due to clever intruders breaking DES on their PCs. The real problems range from dishonest employees (a bank clerk's changing a customer's mailing address to his own to intercept the bank card and PIN number) to programming errors (giving all customers the same PIN code). What is especially interesting is the response banks give when confronted with an error: our systems are perfect and therefore all errors must be due to customer errors or fraud.

Berghel, "The Client Side of the Web"
     An easygoing introduction to Web browsers and the features they (can) support. The main topics are HTML/HTTP compliance, performance, reconfigurability, integration with the desktop, and navigational aids. Nine popular browsers are compared on these issues.

Berners-Lee et al., "The World Wide Web"
     A perspective on the Web and where it is going by the person who invented it. The article focuses on the Web architecture, HTTP, and HTML, as well as future directions.

Carl-Mitchell and Quarterman, *Practical Internetworking with TCP/IP and UNIX*
     Chapter 5 presents a nice introduction to naming and DNS, including naming authorities, the operational architecture, and the DNS database.

Choudbury et al., "Copyright Protection for Electronic Publishing on Computer Networks"
     Although numerous books and articles describe cryptographic algorithms, few describe how they could be used to prevent users from further distributing documents which they are allowed to decrypt. This paper describes a variety of mechanisms that might help protect authors' copyrights in the electronic era.

Furht et al., "Design Issues for Interactive Television Systems"
     Video on demand raises many complex technical issues related to the system architecture, network topology, server design, and set-top box design. In this paper, the authors present a tutorial on some of the key problems and some solutions that are being investigated.

Handley and Crowcroft, *The World Wide Web—Beneath the Surf*
     While 99 percent of WWW books just tell you how to use some browser or list interesting URLs, this one explains how the Web works inside. The client side, the server side, and HTML are all explained in nice bite-sized chunks.

Kaufman et al., *Network Security*
     This authoritative and frequently witty book is the first place to look for more information on network security. Secret and public key algorithms and protocols, message hashes, authentication, Kerberos, and email are all explained at length.

The best parts are the interauthor (and even intra-author) discussions, labeled by subscripts, as in: "I_2 could not get me_1 to be very specific ... "

Kumar, *MBone: Interactive Multimedia on the Internet*

The cover of this book says: "Discover how you can broadcast, advertise, and display your products on the Internet." Fortunately, this subject is not mentioned anywhere else in the book. What is covered is the architecture and implementation of the MBone, including a lot of material about how it works and how to use it.

Nemeth et al., *UNIX System Administration Handbook*

Chapter 16 is a long introduction to DNS. It gets into all the nitty-gritty details, illustrating the various files and resource records with numerous examples. Programs and other tools used for managing a DNS server are also covered in some detail.

Rose, *The Internet Message*

If you like your email served with a dash of iconoclasm, this book is a good bet. The author is not above getting up on a soapbox from time to time to announce what is wrong with the world. When you come right down to it, his taste is not bad.

Schneier, *Applied Cryptography*, 2nd ed.

This monumental compendium is NSA's worst nightmare: a single book that describes every known cryptographic algorithm. To make it worse (or better, depending on your point of view), the book contains most of the algorithms as runnable programs (in C). Furthermore, over 1600 references to the cryptographic literature are provided. If you *really* want to keep your files secret, read this book.

Steinmetz and Nahrstedt, *Multimedia: Computing, Communications and Applications*

Although somewhat chaotic, this book does cover a lot of ground in multimedia. Topics treated at length include audio, still pictures, moving pictures, compression, optical storage, multimedia operating systems, networking, hypertext, synchronization of streams, and multimedia applications.

Van der Linden, *Just Java*

When Chap. 1 of a book is entitled "Come into my parlor, said the spider to the fly," it is a safe bet that it is either a children's fairy tale or about the World Wide Web. This one is about the Web, specifically about the Java language and its environment. For people who want to play with Java, the book comes complete with the full Java system on CD-ROM.

8.2. ALPHABETICAL BIBLIOGRAPHY

ABEYSUNDARA, B.W., and KAMAL, A.E.: "High-Speed Local Area Networks and Their Performance" *Computing Surveys*, vol. 23, pp. 221-264, June 1991.

ABRAMSON, N.: "Development of the ALOHANET," *IEEE Trans. on Information Theory*, vol. IT-31, pp. 119-123, March 1985.

ADAM, J.A.: "Privacy and Computers," *IEEE Spectrum*, vol. 32, pp. 46-52, Dec. 1995.

ADAMS, N., GOLD, R., SCHILIT, B.N., TSO, M.M., and WANT, R.: "An Infrared Network for Mobile Computers," *Proc. USENIX Mobile and Location-Independent Computing Symposium*, USENIX, pp. 41-51, 1993.

ANDERSON, R.J.: "Why Cryptosystems Fail," *Commun. of the ACM*, vol. 37, pp. 32-40, Nov. 1994.

ARMBRUSTER, H.: "The Flexibility of ATM: Supporting Future Multimedia and Mobile Communications," *IEEE Commun. Magazine*, vol. 33, pp. 76-84, Feb. 1995.

ARMITAGE, G.J., and ADAMS, K.M.: "How Efficient is IP over ATM Anyway?" *IEEE Network Magazine*, vol. 9, pp. 18-26, Jan./Feb. 1995.

ARNOLD, K., and GOSLING, J.: *The Java Programming Language*, Reading, MA: Addison-Wesley, 1996.

AT&T and BELLCORE: "Observations of Error Characteristics of Fiber Optic Transmission Systems," CCITT SG XVIII, San Diego, Jan. 1989.

AWDEH, R.Y., and MOUFTAH, H.T.: "Survey of ATM Switch Architectures," *Computer Networks and ISDN Systems*, vol. 27, pp. 1567-1613, Nov. 1995.

BAKNE, A., and BADRINATH, B.R.: "I-TCP: Indirect TCP for Mobile Hosts," *Proc. Fifteenth Int'l. Conf. on Distr. Computer Systems*, IEEE, pp. 136-143, 1995.

BALAKRISHNAN, H., SESHAN, S, and KATZ, R.H.: "Improving Reliable Transport and Handoff Performance in Cellular Wireless Networks," *Proc. ACM Mobile Computing and Networking Conf.*, ACM, pp. 2-11, 1995.

BALLARDIE, T., FRANCIS, P., and CROWCROFT, J.: "Core Based Trees (CBT)," *Proc. SIGCOMM '93 Conf.*, ACM, pp. 85-95, 1993.

BANTZ, D.F., and BAUCHOT, F.J.: "Wireless LAN Design Alternatives," *IEEE Network Magazine*, vol. 8, pp. 43-53, March/April, 1994.

BARANSEL, C., DOBOSIEWICZ, W., and GBURZYNSKI, P.: "Routing in Multihop Packet Switching Networks: Gb/s Challenge," *IEEE Network Magazine*, vol. 9, pp. 38-61, May/June, 1995.

BARLOW, J.P.: "Property and Speech: Who Owns What You Say in Cyberspace," *Commun. of the ACM*, vol. 38, pp. 19-22, Dec. 1995.

BATCHER, K.E.: "Sorting Networks and Their Applications," *Proc. AFIPS Spring Joint Computer Conf.*, vol. 32, pp. 307-315, 1968.

BATES, R.J.: *Wireless Networked Communications*, New York: McGraw-Hill, 1994.

BERGHEL, H.L.: "The Client Side of the Web," *Commun. of the ACM*, vol. 39, pp. 33-40, Jan. 1996.

BELL, T.E. "Communications," *IEEE Spectrum*, vol. 33, pp. 30-41, Jan 1996.

BELLAMY, J.: *Digital Telephony*, New York: John Wiley, 1991.

BELLMAN, R.E.: *Dynamic Programming*, Princeton, NJ: Princeton University Press, 1957.

BELSNES, D.: "Flow Control in the Packet Switching Networks," *Communications Networks*, Uxbridge, England: Online, pp. 349-361, 1975.

BERNERS-LEE, T., CAILLAU, A., LOUTONEN, A., NIELSEN, H.F., and SECRET, A.: "The World Wide Web," *Commun. of the ACM*, vol. 37, pp. 76-82, Aug. 1994.

BERTSEKAS, D., and GALLAGER, R.: *Data Networks*, 2nd ed., Englewood Cliffs, NJ: Prentice Hall, 1992.

BHARGHAVAN, V., DEMERS, A., SHENKER, S., and ZHANG, L.: "MACAW: A Media Access Protocol for Wireless LANs," *Proc. SIGCOMM '94 Conf.*, ACM, pp. 212-225, 1994.

BIHAM, E., and SHAMIR, A.: *Differential Cryptanalysis of the Data Encryption Standard*, New York: Springer-Verlag, 1993.

BINDER, R.: "A Dynamic Packet Switching System for Satellite Broadcast Channels," *Proc. Int'l. Conf. on Commun.*, pp. 41-1 to 41-5a, 1975.

BLACK, U.D.: *TCP/IP and Related Protocols*, New York: McGraw-Hill, 1995.

BLACK, U.D.: *Emerging Commun. Technol.*, Englewood Cliffs, NJ: Prentice Hall, 1994.

BLACK, U.D.: *Data Link Protocols*, Englewood Cliffs, NJ: Prentice Hall, 1993.

BLAZE, M.: "Protocol Failure in the Escrowed Encryption Standard," *Proc. Second ACM Conf. on Computer and Commun. Security*, ACM, pp. 59-67, 1994.

BOGINENI, K., SIVALINGAM, K.M., and DOWD, P.W.: "Low-Complexity Multiple Access Protocols for Wavelength-Division Multiplexed Photonic Networks," *IEEE Journal on Selected Areas in Commun.*, vol. 11, pp. 590-604, May 1993.

BONOMI, F., and FENDICK, K.W.: "The Rate-Based Flow Control Framework for the Available Bit-rate ATM Service," *IEEE Network Magazine*, vol. 9, pp. 25-39, March/April 1995.

BOWMAN, C.M., DANZIG, P.B., HARDY, D.R., MANBER, U., and SCHWARTZ, M.F.: "The Harvest Information Discovery and Access System," *Computer Networks and ISDN Systems*, vol. 28, pp. 119-125, Dec. 1995.

BOWMAN, C.M., DANZIG, P.B., MANBER, U., and SCHWARTZ, M.F.: "Scalable Internet Resource Discovery: Research Problems and Approaches," *Commun. of the ACM*, vol. 37, pp. 98-107, Aug. 1994.

BRAKMO, L.S., O'MALLEY, S.W., and PETERSON, L.L.: "TCP Vegas: New Techn. for Congestion Detection and Avoidance," *Proc. SIGCOMM '94 Conf.*, ACM, pp. 24-35, 1994.

BROADHEAD, M.A. and OWEN, C.B.: "Direct Manipulation of MPEG Compressed Digital Audio," *Proc. of ACM Multimedia '95*, ACM, pp. 499-507, 1995.

BROWN, L., KWAN, M., PIEPRZYK, J., and SEBERRY, J.: "Improving Resistance to Differential Cryptanalysis and the Redesign of LOKI," *ASIACRYPT '91 Abstracts*, pp. 25-30, 1991.

BUFORD, J.F.K. (Ed.): *Multimedia Systems*, Reading, MA: Addison-Wesley, 1994. DEC System Research Center Report, Feb. 1989.

CAMPBELL, A., COULSON, G., and HUTCHISON, D.: "A Quality of Service Architecture," *Computer Commun. Rev.*, vol. 24, pp. 6-27, April 1994.

CAMPIONE, M., and WALRATH, K.: *The Java Language Tutorial: Object-Oriented Programming for the Internet*, Reading, MA: Addison-Wesley, 1996.

CAPETANAKIS, J.I.: "Tree Algorithms for Packet Broadcast Channels," *IEEE Trans. on Information Theory*, vol. IT-25, pp. 505-515, Sept. 1979.

CARL-MITCHELL, S., and QUARTERMAN, J.S.: *Practical Internetworking with TCP/IP and UNIX*, Reading, MA: Addison-Wesley, 1993.

CATLETT, C.E.: "In Search of Gigabit Applications," *IEEE Commun. Magazine*, vol. 30, pp. 42-51, April 1992.

CERF, V., and KAHN, R.: "A Protocol for Packet Network Interconnection," *IEEE Trans. on Commun.*, vol. COM-22, pp. 637-648, May 1974.

CHANDRANMENON, G.P., and VARGHESE, G.: *"Trading Packet Headers for Packet Processing," Proc. SIGCOMM '95 Conf., ACM, pp. 162-173, 1995.*

CHANG, Y.-H., COGGINS, D., PITT, D., SKELLERN, D., THAPAR, M., and VENKATRAMAN, C.: "An Open-System Approach to Video on Demand," *IEEE Commun. Magazine*, vol. 32, pp. 68-80, May 1994.

CHAO, J.J., GHOSAL, D., SAHA, D., and TRIPATHI, S.K.: "IP on ATM Local Area Networks," *IEEE Commun. Magazine*, vol. 32, pp. 52-59, Aug. 1994.

CHAPMAN, D.E., and ZWICKY, E.D.: *Building Internet Firewalls*, Sebastopol, CA: O'Reilly, 1995.

CHEN, K.-C.: "Medium Access Control of Wireless LANs for Mobile Computing," *IEEE Network Magazine*, vol. 8, pp. 50-63, Sept./Oct. 1994.

CHEN, M., and YUM, T.-S.: "A Conflict-Free Protocol for Optical WDMA Networks," *Proc. Globecom '91*, pp. 1276-1281, 1991.

CHEN, W.Y., and WARING, D.L.: "Applicability of ADSL to Support Video Dial Tone in the Copper Loop," *IEEE Commun. Magazine*, vol. 32, pp. 102-106, May 1994.

CHERITON, D., and WILLIAMSON, C.: "VMTP as the Transport Layer for High-Performance Distributed Systems," *IEEE Commun. Magazine*, vol. 27, pp. 37-44, June 1989.

CHERVENAK, A.L.: *Tertiary Storage: An Evaluation of New Applications*, Ph.D. thesis, CSD, Univ. of California at Berkeley, 1994.

CHERVENAK, A.L., PATTERSON, D.A., and KATZ, R.H.: "Choosing the Best Storage System for Video Service," *Proc. of ACM Multimedia '95*, ACM, pp. 109-119, 1995.

CHESSON, G.L.: "XTP/PE Design Considerations," *IFIP Workshop on Protocols for High-Speed Networks*, IFIP, pp. 27-33, 1989.

CHESWICK, W.R. and BELLOVIN, S.M.: *Firewalls and Interwalls—Repelling the Wily Hacker*, Reading, MA: Addison-Wesley, 1994.

CHOUDBURY, A.K., MAXEMCHUK, N.F., PAUL, S., and SCHULZRINNE, H.G.: "Copyright Protection for Electronic Publishing on Computer Networks," *IEEE Network Magazine*, vol. 9, pp. 12-20, May/June, 1995.

CLARK, D.D.: "The Design Philosophy of the DARPA Internet Protocols," *Proc. SIGCOMM '88 Conf.*, ACM, pp. 106-114, 1988.

CLARK, D.D.: "NETBLT: A Bulk Data Transfer Protocol," RFC 998, 1987.

CLARK, D.D.: "Window and Acknowledgement Strategy in TCP," RFC 813, July 1982.

CLARK, D.D., DAVIE, B.S., FARBER, D.J., GOPAL, I.S., KADABA, B.K., SINCOSKIE, W.D., SMITH, J.M., and TENNENHOUSE, D.L.: "The Aurora Gigabit Testbed," *Computer Networks and ISDN Systems*, vol. 25, pp. 599-621, Jan. 1993.

CLARK, D.D., JACOBSON, V., ROMKEY, J., and SALWEN, H.: "An Analysis of TCP Processing Overhead," *IEEE Commun. Magazine*, vol. 27, pp. 23-29, June 1989.

CLARK, D.D., LAMBERT, M., and ZHANG, L.: "NETBLT: A High Throughput Transport Protocol," *Proc. SIGCOMM '87 Conf.*, ACM, pp. 353-359, 1987.

CLOS, C.: "A Study of Non-Blocking Switching Networks," *Bell System Tech. J.*, vol. 32, pp. 406-424, March 1953.

COMER, D.E.: *The Internet Book*, Englewood Cliffs, NJ: Prentice Hall, 1995.

COMER, D.E.: *Internetworking with TCP/IP*, vol. 1, 3rd ed., Englewood Cliffs, NJ: Prentice Hall, 1995.

COOK, A., and STERN, J.: "Optical Fiber Access—Perspectives Toward the 21st Century," *IEEE Commun. Magazine*, vol. 32, pp. 78-86, Feb. 1994.

COOPER, E.: *Broadband Network Technology*, Englewood Cliffs, NJ: Prentice Hall, 1986.

COULOURIS, G.F., DOLLIMORE, J., and KINDBERG, T.: *Distributed Systems Concepts and Design*, 2nd ed. Reading, MA: Addison-Wesley, 1994.

CRESPO, P.M., HONIG, M.L., and SALEHI, J.A.: "Spread-Time Code-Division Multiple Access," *IEEE Trans. on Commun.*, vol. 43, pp. 2139-2148, June 1995.

CRONIN, W.J., HUTCHINSON, J.D., RAMAKRISHNAN, K.K., and YANG, H.: "A Comparison of High Speed LANs," *Proc. Nineteenth Conf. on Local Computer Networks*, IEEE, pp. 40-49, 1994.

CROWCROFT, J., WANG, Z., SMITH, A., and ADAMS, J.: "A Rough Comparison of the IETF and ATM Service Models," *IEEE Network Magazine*, vol. 9, pp. 12-16, Nov./Dec. 1995.

CROWTHER, W., RETTBERG, R., WALDEN, D., ORNSTEIN, S., and HEART, F.: "A System for Broadcast Communication: Reservation-Aloha," *Proc. Sixth Hawaii Int. Conf. System Sci.*, pp. 371-374, 1973.

CUSICK, T.W., and WOOD, M.C.: "The REDOC-II Cryptosystem," *Advances in Cryptology—CRYPTO '90 Proceedings*, NY: Springer-Verlag, pp. 545-563, 1991.

DAGDEVIREN, N., NEWELL, J.A., SPINDEL, L.A., and STEFANICK, M.J.: "Global Networking with ISDN," *IEEE Commun. Magazine*, vol. 32, pp. 26-32, June 1994.

DANSKIN, J.M., DAVIS, G.M., and SONG, X.: "Fast Lossy Internet Image Transmission," *Proc. of ACM Multimedia '95*, ACM, pp. 321-332, 1995.

DANTHINE, A.A.S.: "Protocol Representation with Finite-State Models," *IEEE Trans. on Commun.*, vol. COM-28, pp. 632-643, April 1980.

DAVIS, P.T., and McGUFFIN, C.R.: *Wireless Local Area Networks*, New York: McGraw-Hill, 1995.

DAY, J.D.: "The (Un)Revised OSI Reference Model," *Computer Commun. Rev.*, vol. 25, pp. 39-55, Oct. 1995.

DAY, J.D., and ZIMMERMANN, H.: "The OSI Reference Model," *Proc. of the IEEE*, vol. 71, pp. 1334-1340, Dec. 1983.

DE JONGE, W., and CHAUM, D.: "Some Variations on RSA Signatures and Their Security," in *Advances in Cryptology—CRYPTO '86 Proceedings*, Odlyzko, A.M. (Ed.), New York: Springer Verlag, 1987.

DE PRYCKER, M.: *Asynchronous Transfer Mode*, 2nd. ed., New York: Ellis Horwood, 1993.

DEAN, D., and WALLACH, D.S.: "Security Flaws in the HotJava Web Browser," Technical Report 502, Dept. of Computer Science, Princeton Univ., 1995.

DEERING, S.E.: "SIP: Simple Internet Protocol," *IEEE Network Magazine*, vol. 7, pp. 16-28, May/June 1993.

DEERING, S.E., and CHERITON, D.R.: "Multicast Routing in Datagram Internetworks and Extended LANs," *ACM Trans. on Computer Systems*, vol. 8, pp. 85-110, May 1990.

DEERING, S.E., ESTRIN, D., FARINACCI, D., JACOBSON, V., LIU, C.-G., and WEI, L.: "An Architecture for Wide-Area Multicast Routing," *Proc. SIGCOMM '94 Conf.*, ACM, pp. 126-135, 1994.

DELODDERE, D., VERBIEST, W., and VERHILLE, H.: "Interactive Video on Demand," *IEEE Commun. Magazine*, vol. 32, pp. 82-88, May 1994.

DEMERS, A., KESHAV, S., and SHENKER, S.: "Analysis and Simulation of a Fair Queueing Algorithm," *Internetwork: Research and Experience*, vol. 1, pp. 3-26, Sept. 1990.

DENNING, D.E., and SACCO, G.M.: "Timestamps in Key Distribution Protocols," *Commun. of the ACM*, vol. 24, pp. 533-536, Aug. 1981.

DIFFIE, W., and HELLMAN, M.E.: "Exhaustive Cryptanalysis of the NBS Data Encryption Standard," *IEEE Computer Magazine*, vol. 10, pp. 74-84, June 1977.

DIFFIE, W., and HELLMAN, M.E.: "New Directions in Cryptography," *IEEE Trans. on Information Theory*, vol. IT-22, pp. 644-654, Nov. 1976.

DIJKSTRA, E.W.: "A Note on Two Problems in Connexion with Graphs," *Numer. Math.*, vol. 1, pp. 269-271, Oct. 1959.

DIRVIN, R.A., and MILLER, A.R.: "The MC68824 Token Bus Controller: VLSI for the Factory LAN," *IEEE Micro Magazine*, vol. 6, pp. 15-25, June 1986.

DIXIT, S., and SKELLY, P.: "MPEG-2 over ATM for Video Dial Tone Network," *IEEE Network Magazine*, vol. 9, pp. 30-40, Sept./Oct. 1995.

DIXON, R.C.: "Lore of the Token Ring," *IEEE Network Magazine*, vol. 1, pp. 11-18, Jan./Feb. 1987.

DOERINGER, W.A., DYKEMAN, D., KAISERSWERTH, M., MEISTER, B.W., RUDIN, H., and WILLIAMSON, R.: "A Survey of Light-Weight Transport Protocols for High-Speed Networks," *IEEE Trans. on Commun.*, vol. 38, pp. 2025-2039, Nov. 1990.

DORFMAN, R.: "Detection of Defective Members of a Large Population," *Annals Math. Statistics*, vol. 14, pp. 436-440, 1943.

ECKBERG, A.E.: "B-ISDN/ATM Traffic and Congestion Control," *IEEE Network Magazine*, vol. 6, pp. 28-37, Sept./Oct. 1992.

ECKBERG, A.E., DOSHI, B.T., and ZOCCOLILLO, R.: "Controlling Congestion in B-ISDN/ATM: Issues and Strategies," *IEEE Commun. Magazine*, vol. 29, pp. 64-70, Sept. 1991.

EDWARDS, A., and MUIR, S.: "Experience Implementing a High-Performance TCP in User-Space," *Proc. SIGCOMM '95 Conf.*, ACM, pp. 197-205, 1995.

EL GAMAL, T.: "A Public-Key Cryptosystem and a Signature Scheme Based on Discrete Logarithms," *IEEE Trans. on Information Theory*, vol. IT-31, pp. 469-472, July 1985.

ERIKSSON, H.: "MBone: The Multicast Backbone," *Commun. of the ACM*, vol. 37, pp. 54-60, Aug. 1994.

ESTRIN, D., REKHTER, Y., and HOTZ, S.: "Scalable Inter-Domain Routing Architecture," *Proc. SIGCOMM '92 Conf.*, ACM, pp. 40-52, 1992.

FEIG, E., and WINOGRAD, S.: "Fast Algorithms for Discrete Cosine Transformations," *IEEE Trans. on Signal Processing*, vol. 40, Sept. 1992.

FEIT, S.: *SNMP—A Guide to Network Management*, New York: McGraw-Hill, 1995.

FIORINI, D., CHIANI, M., TRALLI, V., and SALATI., C.: "Problems with HDLC," *Computer Commun. Rev.*, vol. 25, pp. 61-80, Oct. 1995.

FISCHER, W., WALLMEIER, E., WORSTER, T., DAVIS, S.P., HAYTER, A.: "Data Communications Using ATM: Architectures, Protocols, and Resource Management," *IEEE Commun. Magazine*, vol. 32, pp. 24-33, Aug. 1994.

FLOYD, S., and JACOBSON, V.: "Random Early Detection for Congestion Avoidance," *IEEE/ACM Trans. on Networking*, vol. 1, pp. 397-413, Aug. 1993.

FLUCKIGER, F.: *Understanding Networked Multimedia*, Englewood Cliffs, NJ: Prentice Hall, 1995.

FORD, L.R., Jr., and FULKERSON, D.R.: *Flows in Networks*, Princeton, NJ: Princeton University Press, 1962.

FORD, P.S., REKHTER, Y., and BRAUN, H.-W.: "Improving the Routing and Addressing of IP," *IEEE Network Magazine*, vol. 7, pp. 10-15, May/June 1993.

FORMAN, G.H., and ZAHORJAN, J.: "The Challenges of Mobile Computing," *IEEE Computer Magazine*, vol. 27, pp. 38-47, April 1994.

FRANCIS, P.: "A Near-Term Architecture for Deploying Pip," *IEEE Network Magazine*, vol. 7, pp. 30-37, May/June 1993.

FRASER, A.G.: "Early Experiments with Asynchronous Time Division Networks," *IEEE Network Magazine*, vol. 7, pp. 12-27, Jan./Feb. 1993.

FRASER, A.G.: "Towards a Universal Data Transport System," in *Advances in Local Area Networks*, Kummerle, K., Tobagi, F., and Limb, J.O. (Eds.), New York: IEEE Press, 1987.

FURHT, B., KALRA, D., KITSON, F.L., RODRIGUEZ, and WALL, W.E.: "Design Issues for Interactive Televisions Systems," *IEEE Computer Magazine*, vol. 28, pp. 25-39, May 1995.

GARCIA-HARO, J., and JAJSZCZYK, A.: "ATM Shared-Memory Switching Architectures," *IEEE Network Magazine*, vol. 8., pp. 18-26, July/Aug. 1994.

GARG, V., and WILKES, J.E.: *Wireless and Personal Communication Systems*, Englewood Cliffs, NJ: Prentice Hall, 1996.

GASMAN, L.: *Broadband Networking*, New York: Van Nostrand Reinhold, 1994.

GIACOPELLI, J.N., HICKEY, J.J., MARCUS, W.S., SINCOSKIE, W.D., and LITTLEWOOD, M.: "Sunshine: A High-Performance Self-Routing Broadband Packet Switch Architecture," *IEEE Journal on Selected Areas in Commun.*, vol. 9, pp. 1289-1298, Oct. 1991.

GOODMAN, D.J.: "Trends in Cellular and Cordless Communications," *IEEE Commun. Magazine*, vol. 29, pp. 31-40, June 1991.

GORALSKI, W.J.: *Introduction to ATM Networking*, New York: McGraw-Hill, 1995.

GOSLING, J., JOY, B., and STEELE, G.: *The Java Language Specification*, Reading, MA: Addison-Wesley, 1996.

GREEN, P.E., Jr.: *Fiber Optic Networks*, Englewood Cliffs, NJ: Prentice Hall, 1993.

HAC, ANNA: "Wireless and Cellular Architecture and Services," *IEEE Commun. Magazine*, vol. 33, pp. 98-104, Nov. 1995.

HAFNER, K., and MARKOFF, J.: *Cyberpunk*, New York: Simon and Schuster, 1991.

HAMMING, R.W.: "Error Detecting and Error Correcting Codes," *Bell System Tech. J.*, vol. 29, pp. 147-160, April 1950.

HANDEL, R., HUBER, M.N., and SCHRODER, S.: *ATM Concepts, Protocols, and Applications*, 2nd ed., Reading, MA: Addison-Wesley, 1994.

HANDLEY, M., and CROWCROFT, J.: *The World Wide Web—Beneath the Surf*, London: UCL Press, 1994.

HAWLEY, G.T.: "Historical Perspectives on the U.S. Telephone System," *IEEE Commun. Magazine*, vol. 29, pp. 24-28, March 1991.

HEIN, M., and GRIFFITHS, D.: *SNMP*, London: Thompson, 1995.

HELD, G.: *The Complete Modem Reference*, 2nd ed., New York: John Wiley, 1994.

HELLMAN, M.E.: "A Cryptanalytic Time-Memory Tradeoff," *IEEE Trans. on Information Theory*, vol. IT-26, pp. 401-406, July 1980.

HENDERSON, T.R.: "Design Principles and Performance Analysis of SSCOP: A New ATM Adaptation Layer Protocol," *Computer Commun. Review*, vol. 25, pp. 47-59, April 1995.

HOARE, C.A.R.: "Monitors, An Operating System Structuring Concept," *Commun. of the ACM*, vol. 17, pp. 549-557, Oct. 1974; Erratum in *Commun. of the ACM*, vol. 18, p. 95, Feb. 1975.

HODGE, W.W.: *Interactive Television*, New York: McGraw-Hill, 1995.

HODGE, W.W., Martin, S., POWERS, J.T., Jr.: "Video on Demand: Architectures, Systems, and Applications," *Society of Motion Picture and Television Engineers Journal*, vol. 102, pp. 791-803, Sept. 1993.

HOFFMAN, L.J. (ed.): *Building in Big Brother: The Cryptographic Policy Debate*, New York: Springer-Verlag, 1995.

HOLFELDER, W.: "MBone VCR—Video Conference Recording on the MBone," *Proc. of ACM Multimedia '95*, ACM, pp. 237-238, 1995.

HOLZMANN, G.J.: *Design and Validation of Computer Protocols*, Englewood Cliffs, NJ: Prentice Hall, 1991.

HONG, D., and SUDA, T.: "Congestion Control and Prevention in ATM Networks," *IEEE Network Magazine*, vol. 5, pp. 10-16, July/Aug. 1991.

HUANG, A., and KNAUER, S.: "Starlite: A Wideband Digital Switch," *Proc. Globecom '84*, pp. 121-125, 1984.

HUGHES, J.P., and FRANTA, W.R.: "Geographic Extension of HIPPI Channels," *IEEE Network Magazine*, vol. 8, pp. 42-53, May/June 1994.

HUI, J.: "A Broadband Packet Switch for Multi-rate Services," *Proc. Int'l. Conf. on Communications*, IEEE, pp. 782-788, 1987.

HUITEMA, C.: *IPv6: The New Internet Protocol*, Englewood Cliffs, NJ: Prentice Hall, 1996.

HUITEMA, C.: *Routing in the Internet*, Englewood Cliffs, NJ: Prentice Hall, 1995.

HUMBLET, P.A., RAMASWAMI, R., and SIVARAJAN, K.N.: "An Efficient Communication Protocol for High-Speed Packet-Switched Multichannel Networks," *Proc. SIGCOMM '92 Conf.*, ACM, pp. 2-13, 1992.

IEEE: *Communications Magazine*, vol. 33, Jan. 1995.

IEEE: *802.3: Carrier Sense Multiple Access with Collision Detection*, New York: IEEE, 1985a.

IEEE: *802.4: Token-Passing Bus Access Method*, New York: IEEE, 1985b.

IEEE: *802.5: Token Ring Access Method*, New York: IEEE, 1985c.

IOANNIDIS, J., and MAQUIRE, G.Q., Jr.: "The Design and Implementation of a Mobile Internetworking Architecture," *Proc. Winter USENIX Conf.*, USENIX, pp. 491-502, Jan. 1993.

IRMER, T.: "Shaping Future Telecommunications: The Challenge of Global Standardization," *IEEE Commun. Magazine*, vol. 32, pp. 20-28, Jan. 1994.

IVANCIC, W.D., SHALKHAUSER, M.J., and QUINTANA, J.A.: "A Network Architecture for a Geostationary Communication Satellite," *IEEE Commun. Magazine*, vol. 32, pp. 72-84, July 1994.

JABBARI, B., COLOMBO, G., NAKAJIMA, A., and KULKARNI, J. "Network Issues for Wireless Communications," *IEEE Commun. Magazine*, vol. 33, pp. 88-98, Jan. 1995.

JACOBSON, V.: "Congestion Avoidance and Control," *Proc. SIGCOMM '88 Conf.*, ACM, pp. 314-329, 1988.

JAIN, R.: "Congestion Control and Traffic Management in ATM Networks: Recent Advances and a Survey," *Computer Networks and ISDN Systems*, vol. 27, Nov. 1995.

JAIN, R.: *FDDI Handbook—High-Speed Networking Using Fiber and other Media*, Reading, MA: Addison-Wesley, 1994.

JAIN, R.: *The Art of Computer Systems Performance Analysis*, New York: John Wiley, 1991.

JAIN, R.: "Congestion Control in Computer Networks: Issues and Trends," *IEEE Network Magazine*, vol. 4, pp. 24-30, May/June 1990.

JIA, F., and MUKHERJEE, B.: "The Receiver Collision Avoidance (RCA) Protocol for a Single-Hop WDM Lightwave Network," *Journal of Lightwave Technology*, vol. 11, pp. 1053-1065, May/June 1993.

JOHNSON, D.B.: "Scalable Support for Transparent Mobile Host Internetworking," *Wireless Networks*, vol. 1, pp. 311-321, Oct. 1995.

JOHNSON, H.W.: *Fast Ethernet—Dawn of a New Network*, Englewood Cliffs, NJ: Prentice Hall, 1996.

KAHN, D.: "Cryptology Goes Public," *IEEE Commun. Magazine*, vol. 18, pp. 19-28, March 1980.

KAHN, D.: *The Codebreakers*, New York: Macmillan, 1967.

KALISKI, B.S., and ROBSHAW, M.J.B.: "Fast Block Cipher Proposal," *Proc. Cambridge Security Workshop*, Springer-Verlag, pp. 26-39, 1994.

KAMOUN, F., and KLEINROCK, L.: "Stochastic Performance Evaluation of Hierarchical Routing for Large Networks," *Computer Networks*, vol. 3, pp. 337-353, Nov. 1979.

KARN, P.: "MACA—A New Channel Access Protocol for Packet Radio," *ARRL/CRRL Amateur Radio Ninth Computer Networking Conf.*, pp. 134-140, 1990.

KAROL, M.J., HLUCHYJ, M.G., and MORGAN, S.P.: "Input Versus Output Queueing on a Space-Division Packet Switch," *IEEE Trans. on Commun.*, vol. 35, pp. 1347-1356, Dec. 1987.

KARSHMER, A.I., and THOMAS, J.N.: "Computer Networking on Cable TV Plants," *IEEE Commun. Magazine*, vol. 30, pp. 32-40, Nov. 1992.

KATZ, D., and FORD, P.S.: "TUBA: Replacing IP with CLNP," *IEEE Network Magazine*, vol. 7, pp. 38-47, May/June 1993.

KATZ, E.D., BUTLER, M., and McGRATH, R.: "A Scalable HTTP Server: The NCSA Prototype," *Computer Networks and ISDN Systems*, vol. 27, pp. 155-164, Nov. 1994.

KAUFMAN, C., PERLMAN, R., and SPECINER, M.: *Network Security*, Englewood Cliffs, NJ: Prentice Hall, 1995.

KAVAK, N.: "Data Communication in ATM Networks," *IEEE Network Magazine*, vol. 9, pp. 28-37, May/June 1995.

KENT, C.A., and MOGUL, J.C.: "Fragmentation Considered Harmful," *Proc. SIGCOMM '87 Conf.*, ACM, pp. 390-401, 1987.

KENT, S.T.: "Internet Privacy Enhanced Mail," *Commun. of the ACM*, vol. 36, pp. 48-60, Aug. 1993.

KESSLER, G.C.: *ISDN*, 2nd ed., New York: McGraw-Hill, 1993.

KESSLER, G.C., and TRAIN, D.: *Metropolitan Area Networks: Concepts, Standards, and Services*, New York: McGraw-Hill, 1992.

KIM, J.B., SUDA, T., and YOSHIMURA, M.: "International Standardization of B-ISDN," *Computer Networks and ISDN Systems*, vol. 27, pp. 5-27, Oct. 1994.

KLEINROCK, L., and TOBAGI, F.: "Random Access Techniques for Data Transmission over Packet-Switched Radio Channels," *Proc. Nat. Computer Conf.*, pp. 187-201, 1975.

KOHNO, R., MEIDAN, R., and MILSTEIN, L.B.: "Spread Spectrum Access Methods for Wireless Communication," *IEEE Commun. Magazine*, vol. 33, pp. 58-67, Jan. 1995.

KUMAR, V.: *MBone: Interactive Multimedia on the Internet*, Indianapolis, IN: New Riders, 1996.

KUNG, H.T., and MORRIS, R.: "Credit-Based Flow Control for ATM Networks," *IEEE Network Magazine*, vol. 9, pp. 40-48, March/April 1995.

KWAN, T.T., McGRATH, R.E., and REED, D.A.: "NCSA's WWW Server: Design and Performance," *IEEE Computer Magazine*, vol. 28, pp. 68-74, Nov. 1995.

KWOK, T.: "A Vision for Residential Broadband Service: ATM to the Home," *IEEE Network Magazine*, vol. 9, pp. 14-28, Sept./Oct. 1995.

KYAS, O.: *ATM Networks*, London: International Thomson Publishing, 1995.

LAI, X.: *On the Design and Security of Block Ciphers*, Konstanz, Germany: Hartung-Gorre, 1992.

LAI, X., and MASSEY, J.: "A Proposal for a New Block Encryption Standard," *Advances in Cryptology—Eurocrypt '90 Proceedings*, New York: Springer-Verlag, pp. 389-404, 1990.

LAMPSON, B.W.: "A Note on the Confinement Problem," *Commun. of the ACM*, vol. 10, pp. 613-615, Oct. 1973.

LANDAU, S.: "Zero-Knowledge and the Department of Defense," *Notices of the American Mathematical Society*, vol. 35, pp. 5-12, Jan. 1988.

LANGSFORD, A.: "The Open System User's Programming Interfaces," *Computer Networks*, vol. 8, pp. 3-12, 1984.

LA PORTA, T.F., VEERARAGHAVAN, M., AYANOGLU, E., KAROL, M., and GITLIN, R.D.: "B-ISDN: A Technological Discontinuity," *IEEE Commun. Magazine*, vol. 32, pp. 84-97, Oct. 1994.

LATIF, A., ROWLANCE, E.J., and ADAMS, R.H.: "The IBM 8209 LAN Bridge," *IEEE Network Magazine*, vol. 6, pp. 28-37, May/June 1992.

LAUDON, K.C.: "Ethical Concepts and Information Technology," *Commun. of the ACM*, vol. 38, pp. 33-39, Dec. 1995.

LE BOUDEC, J.-Y.: "The Asynchronous Transfer Mode: A Tutorial," *Computer Networks and ISDN Systems*, vol. 24, pp. 279-309, May 1992.

LEINER, B.M., COLE, R., POSTEL, J., and MILLS, D.: "The DARPA Internet Protocol Suite," *IEEE Commun. Magazine*, vol. 23, pp. 29-34, March 1985.

LEVINE, D.A., and AKYILDIZ, I.A.: "PROTON: A Media Access Control Protocol for Optical Networks with Star Topology," *IEEE/ACM Trans. on Networking*, vol. 3, pp. 158-168, April 1995.

LEVY, S.: "Crypto Rebels," *Wired*, pp. 54-61, May/June 1993.

LIN, F., CHU, P., and LIU, M.: "Protocol Verification Using Reachability Analysis: The State Space Explosion Problem and Relief Strategies," *Proc. SIGCOMM '87 Conf.*, ACM, pp. 126-135, 1987.

LIPPER, E.H., and RUMSEWICZ, M.P.: "Teletraffic Considerations for Widespread Deployment of PCS," *IEEE Network Magazine*, vol. 8, pp. 40-49, Sept./Oct. 1994.

LITTLE, T.D.C., and VENKATESH, D.: "Prospects for Interactive Video on Demand," *IEEE Multimedia Magazine*, vol. 1, pp. 14-24, Fall 1994.

LIU, C.L., and LAYLAND, J.W.: "Scheduling Algorithms for Multiprogramming in a Hard Real-Time Environment," *Journal of the ACM*, vol. 20, pp. 46-61, Jan. 1973.

LUOTONEN, A., and ALTIS, K.: "World Wide Web Proxies," *Computer Networks and ISDN Systems*, vol. 27, pp. 147-154, Nov. 1994.

MACARIO, R.C.V.: *Cellular Radio—Principles and Design*, New York: McGraw-Hill, 1993.

MACEDONIA, M.R., and BRUTZMAN, D.P.: "MBone Provides Audio and Video Across the Internet," *IEEE Computer Magazine*, vol. 27, pp. 30-36, April 1994.

MASSEY, J.L.: "SAFER K-64: A Byte-Oriented Block Ciphering Algorithm," *Proc. Cambridge Security Workshop*, Springer-Verlag, pp. 1-17, 1994.

MATSUI, M.: "Linear Cryptanalysis Method for DES Cipher," *Advances in Cryptology—Eurocrypt '93 Proceedings*, New York: Springer-Verlag, pp. 386-397, 1994.

McBRYAN, O.: "GENVL and WWWW: Tools for Taming the Web," *Proc. First Int'l. WWW Conference*, pp. 79-90, 1994.

McDYSAN, D.E., and SPOHN, D.L.: *ATM—Theory and Application*, NY: McGraw-Hill, 1995.

McKENNEY, P.E., and DOVE, K.F.: "Efficient Demultiplexing of Incoming TCP Packets," *Proc. SIGCOMM '92 Conf.*, ACM, pp. 269-279, 1992.

MENEZES, A.J., and VANSTONE, S.A.: "Elliptic Curve Cryptosystems and Their Implementation," *Journal of Cryptology*, vol. 6, pp. 209-224, 1993.

MERKLE, R.C.: "Fast Software Encryption Functions," *Advances in Cryptology—CRYPTO '90 Proceedings*, New York: Springer-Verlag, pp. 476-501, 1991.

MERKLE, R.C., and HELLMAN, M.: "On the Security of Multiple Encryption," *Commun. of the ACM*, vol. 24, pp. 465-467, July 1981.

MERKLE, R.C., and HELLMAN, M.: "Hiding and Signatures in Trapdoor Knapsacks," *IEEE Trans. on Information Theory*, vol. IT-24, pp. 525-530, Sept. 1978.

METCALFE, R.M.: "On Mobile Computing," *Byte*, vol. 20, p. 110, Sept. 1995.

METCALFE, R.M.: "Computer/Network Interface Design: Lessons from Arpanet and Ethernet," *IEEE Journal on Selected Areas in Commun.*, vol. 11, pp. 173-179, Feb. 1993.

METCALFE, R.M., and BOGGS, D.R.: "Ethernet: Distributed Packet Switching for Local Computer Networks," *Commun. of the ACM*, vol. 19, pp. 395-404, July 1976.

MIKI, T.: "The Potential of Photonic Networks," *IEEE Commun. Magazine*, vol. 32, pp. 23-27, Dec. 1994a.

MIKI, T.: "Toward the Service-Rich Era," *IEEE Commun. Magazine*, vol. 32, pp. 34-39, Feb. 1994b.

MINOLI, D.: *Video Dialtone Technology*, New York: McGraw-Hill, 1995

MINOLI, D., and VITELLA, M.: *ATM & Cell Relay for Corporate Environments*, New York: McGraw-Hill, 1994.

MIRCHANDANI, S., and KHANNA, R. (eds): *FDDI Technologies and Applications*, New York: John Wiley, 1993.

MISHRA, P.P. and KANAKIA, H.: "A Hop by Hop Rate-Based Congestion Control Scheme," *Proc. SIGCOMM '92 Conf.*, ACM, pp. 112-123, 1992.

MOCHIDA, Y.: "Technologies for Local-Access Fibering," *IEEE Commun. Magazine*, vol. 32, pp. 64-73, Feb. 1994.

MOGUL, J.C.: "The Case for Persistent-Connection HTTP," *Proc. SIGCOMM '95 Conf.*, ACM, pp. 299-314, 1995.

MOGUL, J.C.: "IP Network Performance," in *Internet System Handbook*, Lynch, D.C. and Rose, M.T. (eds.), Reading, MA: Addison-Wesley, pp. 575-675, 1993.

MOK, A.K., and WARD, S.A.: "Distributed Broadcast Channel Access," *Computer Networks*, vol. 3, pp. 327-335, Nov. 1979.

MORALES, J., PATKA, A., CHOA, P., and KUI, J.: "Video Dial Tone Sessions," *IEEE Network Magazine*, vol. 9, pp. 42-47, Sept./Oct. 1995.

MOY, J.: "Multicast Routing Extensions," *Commun. of the ACM*, vol. 37, pp. 61-66, Aug. 1994.

MULLENDER, S.J. (ed.): *Distributed Systems*, 2nd ed., New York: ACM Press, 1993.

MYLES, A., and SKELLERN, D.: "Comparison of Mobile Host Protocols for IP," *Computer Networks and ISDN Systems*, vol. 26, pp. 349-355, Dec. 1993.

NAGLE, J.: "On Packet Switches with Infinite Storage," *IEEE Trans. on Commun.*, vol. COM-35, pp. 435-438, April 1987.

NAGLE, J.: "Congestion Control in TCP/IP Internetworks," *Computer Commun. Rev.*, vol. 14, pp. 11-17, Oct. 1984.

NEEDHAM, R.M., and SCHROEDER, M.D.: "Authentication Revisited," *Operating Systems Rev.*, vol. 21, p. 7, Jan. 1987.

NEEDHAM, R.M., and SCHROEDER, M.D.: "Using Encryption for Authentication in Large Networks of Computers," *Commun. of the ACM*, vol. 21, pp. 993-999, Dec. 1978.

NELSON, M.N., and LINTON, M.: "A Highly Available, Scalable ITV System," *Proc. Fifteenth Symp. on Operating Systems Prin.*, ACM, pp. 54-67, 1995.

NEMETH, E., SNYDER, G., SEEBASS, S., and HEIN, T.R.: *UNIX System Administration Handbook*, Englewood Cliffs, NJ: Prentice Hall, 1995.

NEMZOW, M.: *Implementing Wireless Networks*, New York: McGraw-Hill, 1995.

NEUMAN, B.C., and TS'O, T.: "Kerberos: An Authentication Service for Computer Networks," *IEEE Commun. Magazine*, vol. 32, pp. 33-38, Sept. 1994.

NEWMAN, P.: "Traffic Management for ATM Local Area Networks," *IEEE Commun. Magazine*, vol. 32, pp. 44-50, Aug. 1994.

NEWMAN, P.: "ATM Local Area Networks," *IEEE Commun. Magazine*, vol. 32, pp. 86-98, March 1994.

NIST: "Secure Hash Algorithm," U.S. Government Federal Information Processing Standard 180, 1993.

OMIDYAR, C.G., and ALDRIDGE, A.: "Introduction to SDH/SONET," *IEEE Commun. Magazine*, vol. 31, pp. 30-33, Sept. 1993.

OTWAY, D., and REES, O.: "Efficient and Timely Mutual Authentication," *Operating Systems Rev.*, pp. 8-10, Jan. 1987.

PADGETT, J.E., GUNTHER, C.G., and HATTORI, T.: "Overview of Wireless Personal Communications," *IEEE Commun. Magazine*, vol. 33, pp. 28-41, Jan. 1995.

PAFF, A.: "Hybrid Fiber/Coax in the Public Telecommunications Infrastructure," *IEEE Commun. Magazine*, vol. 33, pp. 40-45, April 1995.

PAHLAVAN, K., PROBERT, T.H., and CHASE, M.E.: "Trends in Local Wireless Networks," *IEEE Commun. Magazine*, vol. 33, pp. 88-95, March 1995.

PALAIS, J.C.: *Fiber Optic Commun.*, 3rd ed., Englewood Cliffs, NJ: Prentice Hall, 1992.

PALMER, L.C., and WHITE, L.W.: "Demand Assignment in the ACTS LBR System," *IEEE Trans. on Commun.*, vol. 38, pp. 684-692, May 1990.

PAN, D.: "A Tutorial on MPEG/Audio Compression," *IEEE Multimedia Magazine*, vol. 2, pp.60-74, Summer 1995.

PANCHA, P., and EL ZARKI, M.: "MPEG Coding for Variable Bit Rate Video Transmission," *IEEE Commun. Magazine*, vol. 32, pp. 54-66, May 1994.

PANDYA, R.: "Emerging Mobile and Personal Communication Systems," *IEEE Commun. Magazine*, vol. 33, pp. 44-52, June 1995.

PARTRIDGE, C.: *Gigabit Networking*, Reading, MA: Addison-Wesley, 1994.

PARTRIDGE, C.: "A Proposed Flow Specification," Internet RFC 1363, Sept. 1992.

PARTRIDGE, C., HUGHES, J., and STONE, J.: "Performance of Checksums and CRCs over Real Data," *Proc. SIGCOMM '95 Conf.*, ACM, pp. 68-76, 1995.

PARULKAR, G., SCHMIDT, D.C., and TURNER, J.S.: "AITPM: A Strategy for Integrating IP with ATM," *Proc. SIGCOMM '95 Conf.*, ACM, pp. 49-58, 1995.

PAXSON, V.: "Growth Trends in Wide-Area TCP Connections," *IEEE Network Magazine*, vol. 8, pp. 8-17, July/Aug. 1994.

PAXSON, V., and FLOYD, S.: "Wide-Area Traffic: The Failure of Poisson Modeling," *Proc. SIGCOMM '94 Conf.*, ACM, pp. 257-268, 1995.

PERKINS, C.: "Providing Continuous Network Access to Mobile Hosts Using TCP/IP," *Computer Networks and ISDN Systems*, vol. 26, pp. 357-370, Nov. 1993.

PERLMAN, R.: *Interconnections: Bridges and Routers*, Reading, MA: Addison-Wesley, 1992.

PERLMAN, R.: *Network Layer Protocols with Byzantine Robustness*, Ph.D. thesis, M.I.T., 1988.

PERRY, T.S., and ADAM, J.A.: "E-Mail: Pervasive and Persuasive," *IEEE Spectrum*, vol. 29, pp. 22-28, Oct. 1992.

PETERSON, W.W., and BROWN, D.T.: "Cyclic Codes for Error Detection," *Proc. IRE*, vol. 49, pp. 228-235, Jan. 1961.

PICKHOLTZ, R.L., SCHILLING, D.L., and MILSTEIN, L.B.: "Theory of Spread Spectrum Communication—A Tutorial," *IEEE Trans. on Commun.*, vol. COM-30, pp. 855-884, May 1982.

PIERCE, J.: "How Far Can Data Loops Go?" *IEEE Trans. on Commun.*, vol. COM-20, pp. 527-530, June 1972.

PINKERTON, B.: "Finding What People Want: Experiences with the WebCrawler," *Proc. First Int'l. WorldWide Web Conference*, 1994.

PISCITELLO, D.M., and CHAPIN, A.L.: *Open Systems Networking: TCP/IP and OSI*, Reading, MA: Addison-Wesley, 1993.

PITT, D.A.: "Bridging—The Double Standard," *IEEE Network Magazine*, vol. 2, pp. 94-95, Jan. 1988.

QUICK, R. F., Jr., and BALACHANDRAN, K.: "An Overview of the Cellular Digital Packet Data (CDPD) System," *Fourth Int'l. Symp. on Personal, Indoor, and Mobile Radio Commun.*, pp. 338-343, 1993.

QUISQUATER, J.-J., and GIRAULT., M.: "Chinese Lotto as an Exhaustive Code-Breaking Machine," *IEEE Computer Magazine*, vol. 24, pp. 14-22, Nov. 1991.

RABIN, M.O.: "Digital Signatures and Public-Key Functions as Intractable as Factorization," Technical Report LCS-TR-212, M.I.T., Jan 1979.

RAHNEMA, M.: "Overview of the GSM System and Protocol Architecture," *IEEE Commun. Magazine*, vol. 31, pp. 92-100, April 1993.

RAJAGOPALAN, B.: "Reliability and Scaling Issues in Multicast Communication," *Proc. SIGCOMM '92 Conf.*, ACM, pp. 188-198, 1992.

RANSOM, M.N.: "The VISTAnet Gigabit Network Testbed," *Journal of High Speed Networks*, vol. 1, pp. 49-60, 1992.

RAO, S.K., and HATAMIAN, M.: "The ATM Physical Layer," *Computer Commun. Rev.*, vol. 25, pp. 73-81, April 1995.

RIVEST, R.L.: "The MD5 Message-Digest Algorithm," RFC 1320, April 1992.

RIVEST, R.L., and SHAMIR, A.: "How to Expose an Eavesdropper," *Commun. of the ACM*, vol. 27, pp. 393-395, April 1984.

RIVEST, R.L., SHAMIR, A., and ADLEMAN, L.: "On a Method for Obtaining Digital Signatures and Public Key Cryptosystems," *Commun. of the ACM*, vol. 21, pp. 120-126, Feb. 1978.

ROBERTS, L.: "Dynamic Allocation of Satellite Capacity through Packet Reservation," *Proc. NCC*, AFIPS, pp. 711-716, 1973.

ROBERTS, L.: "Extensions of Packet Communication Technology to a Hand Held Personal Terminal," *Proc. Spring Joint Computer Conference*, AFIPS, pp. 295-298, 1972.

ROMANOW, A., and FLOYD, S.: "Dynamics of TCP Traffic over ATM Networks," *Proc. SIGCOMM '84 Conf.*, ACM, pp. 79-88, 1994.

ROSE, M.T.: *The Simple Book*, Englewood Cliffs, NJ: Prentice Hall, 1994.

ROSE, M.T.: *The Internet Message*, Englewood Cliffs, NJ: Prentice Hall, 1993.

ROSE, M.T., and McCLOGHRIE, K.: *How to Manage Your Network Using SNMP*, Englewood Cliffs, NJ: Prentice Hall, 1995.

ROSS, F.E., and HAMSTRA, J.R.: "Forging FDDI," *IEEE Journal on Selected Areas in Commun.*, vol. 11, pp. 181-190, Feb. 1993.

SADIKU, M.N.O., and ARVIND, A.S.: "Annotated Bibliography on Distributed Queue Dual Bus (DQDB)," *Computer Commun. Rev.*, vol. 24, pp. 21-36, Jan. 1994.

SALTZER, J.H., POGRAN, K.T., and CLARK, D.D.: "Why a Ring?" *Computer Networks*, vol. 7, pp. 223-230, Aug. 1983.

SALTZER, J.H., REED, D.P., and CLARK, D.D.: "End-to-End Arguments in System Design," *ACM Trans. on Computer Systems*, vol. 2, pp. 277-288, Nov. 1984.

SANDERSON, D.W., and DOUGHERTY, D.: *Smileys*, Sebastopol, CA: O'Reilly, 1993.

SANTIFALLER, M.: "TCP/IP and ONC/NFS," Reading, MA: Addison-Wesley, 1994.

SCHNEIER, B.: *Applied Cryptography*, 2nd ed., New York: John Wiley, 1996.

SCHNEIER, B.: *E-Mail Security*, New York: John Wiley, 1995.

SCHNEIER, B.: "Description of a New Variable-Length Key, 64-Bit Block Cipher [Blowfish]," *Proc. of the Cambridge Security Workshop*, Springer-Verlag, pp. 191-204, 1994.

SCHNORR, C.P.: "Efficient Signature Generation for Smart Cards," *Journal of Cryptology*, vol. 4, pp. 161-174, 1991.

SCHOLTZ, R.A.: "The Origins of Spread-Spectrum Communications," *IEEE Trans. on Commun.*, vol. COM-30, pp. 822-854, May 1982.

SCOTT, R.: "Wide Open Encryption Design Offers Flexible Implementations," *Cryptologia*, vol. 9, pp. 75-90, Jan. 1985.

SELFRIDGE, O.G., and SCHWARTZ, R.T.: "Telephone Technology and Privacy," *Technology Rev.*, vol. 82, pp. 56-65, May 1980.

SEYBOLD, A.M.: *Using Wireless Communications in Business*, New York: Van Nostrand Reinhold, 1994.

SHACHAM, N., and McKENNEY, P.: "Packet Recovery in High-Speed Networks Using Coding and Buffer Management," *Proc. INFOCOM '90*, IEEE, pp. 124-130, 1990.

SHAH, A., and RAMAKRISHNAN, G.: *FDDI—A High Speed Network*, Englewood Cliffs, NJ: Prentice Hall, 1994.

SHANNON, C.: "A Mathematical Theory of Communication," *Bell System Tech. J.*, vol. 27, pp. 379-423, July 1948; and pp. 623-656, Oct. 1948.

SHEN, B., and SETHI, I.K.: "Inner-Block Operations on Compressed Images," *Proc. of ACM Multimedia '95*, ACM, pp. 489-498, 1995.

SHIMIZU, A., and MIYAGUCHI, S.: "Fast Data Encipherment Algorithm FEAL," *Advances in Cryptology—Eurocrypt '87 Proceedings*, NY: Springer-Verlag, pp. 267-278, 1988.

SHREEDHAR, M., and VARGHESE, G.: "Efficient Fair Queueing Using Deficit Round Robin," *Proc. SIGCOMM '95 Conf.*, ACM, pp. 231-243, 1995.

SINGLETON, A.: "Wired on the Web," *Byte*, vol. 21, pp. 77-80, Jan. 1996.

SIPIOR, J.C., and WARD, B.T.: "The Ethical and Legal Quandary of Email Privacy," *Commun. of the ACM*, vol. 38, pp. 48-54, Dec. 1995.

SIU, K.-Y., and JAIN, R.: "A Brief Overview of ATM: Protocol Layers, LAN Emulation, and Traffic Management," *Computer Commun. Rev.*, vol. 25, pp. 6-20. April 1995.

SMITH, P.: *Frame Relay*, Reading, MA: Addison-Wesley, 1993.

SOHA, M., and PERLMAN, R.: "Comparison of Two LAN Bridge Approaches," *IEEE Network Magazine*, vol. 2, pp. 37-43, Jan./Feb. 1988.

SPAFFORD, E.H.: "The Internet Worm: Crisis and Aftermath," *Commun. of the ACM*, vol. 32, pp. 678-687, June 1989.

SPRAGINS, J.D., with HAMMOND, J.L., and PAWLIKOWSKI, K.: *Telecommunications Protocols and Design*, Reading, MA: Addison-Wesley, 1991.

STALLINGS, W.: *ISDN and Broadband ISDN with Frame Relay and ATM*, Englewood Cliffs, NJ: Prentice Hall, 1995a.

STALLINGS, W.: *Network and Internetwork Security*, Englewood Cliffs, NJ: Prentice Hall, 1995b.

STALLINGS, W.: *Protect Your Privacy: The PGP User's Guide*, Englewood Cliffs, NJ: Prentice Hall, 1995c.

STALLINGS, W.: *Data and Computer Communications*, 4th ed., New York: Macmillan, 1994.

STALLINGS, W.: *SNMP, SNMPv2, and CMIP*, Reading, MA: Addison-Wesley, 1993a

STALLINGS, W.: *Local and Metropolitan Area Networks*, 4th ed., New York: Macmillan, 1993b.

STEELE, R., WHITEHEAD, J., and WONG, W.C.: "System Aspects of Cellular Radio," *IEEE Commun. Magazine*, vol. 33, pp. 80-86, Jan. 1995a.

STEELE, R., WILLIAMS, J., CHANDLER, D., DEHGHAN, S., and COLLARD, A.: "Teletraffic Performance of GSM900/DCS1800 in Street Microcells," *IEEE Commun. Magazine*, vol. 33, pp. 102-108, March 1995b.

STEINER, J.G., NEUMAN, B.C., and SCHILLER, J.I.: "Kerberos: An Authentication Service for Open Network Systems," *Proc. Winter USENIX Conf.*, USENIX, pp. 191-201, 1988.

STEINMETZ, R., and NAHRSTEDT, K.: *Multimedia: Computing, Communications and Applications*, Englewood Cliffs, NJ: Prentice Hall, 1995.

STEPHENS, W.E., and BANWELL, T.C.: "155.52 Mb/s Data Transmission on Category 5 Cable Plant," *IEEE Commun. Magazine*, vol. 33, pp. 62-69, April 1995.

STERBENZ, J.P.G., SCHULZRINNE, H.G., and TOUCH, J.D.: "Report and Discussion of the IEEE ComSoc TCGN Gigabit Networking Workshop 1995," *IEEE Network Magazine*, vol. 9, pp. 9-29, July/Aug. 1995.

STEVENS, W.R.: *TCP/IP Illustrated*, Vol. 1, Reading, MA: Addison-Wesley, 1994.

STILLER, B.: "A Survey of UNI Signaling Systems and Protocols," *Computer Commun. Rev.*, vol. 25, pp. 21-33, April 1995.

STINSON, D.R.: *Cryptography Theory and Practice*, Boca Raton, FL: CRC Press, 1995.

SUNSHINE, C.A., and DALAL, Y.K.: "Connection Management in Transport Protocols," *Computer Networks*, vol. 2, pp. 454-473, 1978.

SUZUKI, T.: "ATM Adaptation Layer Protocol," *IEEE Commun. Magazine*, vol. 32., pp. 80-83, April 1994.

TANENBAUM, A.S.: *Distributed Operating Systems*, Englewood Cliffs, NJ: Prentice Hall, 1995.

TANENBAUM, A.S.: *Modern Operating Systems*, Englewood Cliffs, NJ: Prentice Hall, 1992.

TERAOKA, F., YOKTE, Y., and TOKORO, M.: "Host Migration Transparency in IP Networks," *Computer Commun. Rev.*, vol. 23, pp. 45-65, Jan. 1993.

THYAGARAJAN, A.S., and DEERING, S.E.: "Hierarchical Distance-Vector Multicast Routing for the MBone," *Proc. SIGCOMM '95 Conf.*, ACM, pp. 60-66, 1995.

TOKORO, M., and TAMARU, K.: "Acknowledging Ethernet," *Compcon*, IEEE, pp. 320-325, Fall 1977.

TOLMIE, D.E.: "Gigabit LAN Issues—HIPPI, Fibre Channel, and ATM," in *Proc. High-Performance Computing and Networking*, Hertzberger, B., and Serazzi, G. (Eds.), Berlin: Springer Verlag, pp. 45-53, 1995.

TOLMIE, D.E.: "Gigabit Networking," *IEEE LTS*, vol. 3, pp. 28-36, May 1992.

TOLMIE, D.E., and RENWICK, J.: "HIPPI: Simplicity Yields Success," *IEEE Network Magazine*, vol. 7, pp. 28-32, Jan./Feb. 1993.

TOMLINSON, R.S.: "Selecting Sequence Numbers," *Proc. SIGCOMM/SIGOPS Interprocess Commun. Workshop*, ACM, pp. 11-23, 1975.

TOUCH, J.D.: "Performance Analysis of MD5," *Proc. SIGCOMM '95 Conf.*, ACM, pp. 77-86, 1995.

TRUONG, H.L., ELLINGTON, W.W. Jr., LE BOUDEC, J.-Y., MEIER, A.X., and PACE, J.W.: "LAN Emulation on an ATM Network," *IEEE Commun. Magazine*, vol. 33, pp. 70-85, May 1995.

TUCHMAN, W.: "Hellman Presents No Shortcut Solutions to DES," *IEEE Spectrum*, vol. 16, pp. 40-41, July 1979.

TURNER, J.S.: "New Directions in Communications (or Which Way to the Information Age)," *IEEE Commun. Magazine*, vol. 24, pp. 8-15, Oct. 1986.

VAN DER LINDEN, P.: *Just Java*, Englewood Cliffs, NJ: Prentice Hall, 1996.

VAN OORSCHOT, P.C., and WIENER, M.J.: "A Known-Plaintext Attack on Two-Key Triple Encryption," *Advances in Cryptology—CRYPTO '88 Proceedings*, New York: Springer-Verlag, pp. 119-131, 1988.

VAN RENESSE, R., VAN STAVEREN, H., and TANENBAUM, A.S.: "Performance of the World's Fastest Distributed Operating System," *Operating Systems Rev.*, vol. 22, pp. 25-34, Oct. 1988.

VARGHESE, G., and LAUCK, T.: "Hashed and Hierarchical Timing Wheels: Data Structures for the Efficient Implementation of a Timer Facility," *Proc. Eleventh Symp. on Operating Systems Prin.*, ACM, pp. 25-38, 1987.

VENKATRAMANI, C., and CHIUEH, T.: "Design, Implementation, and Evaluation of a Software-Based Real-Time Ethernet Protocol," *Proc. SIGCOMM '95 Conf.*, ACM, pp. 27-37, 1995.

VETTER, R.J., SPELL, C., and WARD, C.: "Mosaic and the World-Wide Web," *IEEE Computer Magazine*, vol. 27, pp. 49-57, Oct. 1994.

VILLAMIZAN, C., and SONG, C.: "High Performance TCP in ANSNET," *Computer Commun. Rev.*, vol. 25, pp. 45-60, Oct. 1995.

VITERBI, A.J.: *CDMA Principles of Spread Spectrum Communication*, Reading, MA: Addison-Wesley, 1995.

WADA, H., YOZAWA, T., OHNISHI, T., and TANAKA, Y.: "Mobile Computing Environment Based on Internet Packet Forwarding," *Proc. Winter USENIX Conf.*, USENIX, pp. 503-517, Jan. 1993.

WALRAND, J.: *Communication Networks: A First Course*, Homewood, IL: Irwin, 1991.

WATSON, R.W.: "Timer-Based Mechanisms in Reliable Transport Protocol Connection Management," *Computer Networks*, vol. 5, pp. 47-56, Feb. 1981.

WAYNER, P.: "Picking the Crypto Lock," *Byte*, pp. 77,80, Oct. 1995.

WEISBAND, S.P., and REINIG, B.A.: "Managing User Perceptions of Email Privacy," *Commun. of the ACM*, vol. 38, pp. 40-47, Dec. 1995.

WIENER, M.J.: "Efficient DES Key Search," Technical Report TR-244, School of Computer Science, Carleton Univ., Ottawa, 1994.

WILLIAMS, K.A., DAM, T.Q., and DU, D.H.-C.: "A Media Access Protocol for Time and Wavelength-Division Multiplexed Passive Star Networks," *IEEE Journal on Selected Areas in Commun.*, vol. 11, pp. 560-567, May 1993.

WILLINGER, W., TAQQU, M.S., SHERMAN, R., and WILSON, D.V.: "Self-Similarity through High Variability: Statistical Analysis of Ethernet LAN Traffic at the Source Level," *Proc. SIGCOMM '95 Conf.*, ACM, pp. 100-113, 1995.

WOLTER, M.S.: "Fiber Distributed Data Interface—A Tutorial," *ConneXions*, pp. 16-26, Oct. 1990.

YANG, C.-Q., and REDDY, A.V.S.: "A Taxonomy for Congestion Control Algorithms in Packet Switching Networks," *IEEE Network Magazine*, vol. 9, pp. 34-45, July/Aug. 1995.

YEH, Y.-S., HLUCHYJ, M.G., and ACAMPORA, A.S.: "The Knockout Switch: A Simple, Modular Architecture for High-Performance Packet Switching," *IEEE Journal on Selected Areas in Commun.*, vol. 5, pp. 1274-1283, Oct. 1987.

YOUSSEF, A.M., KALMAN, E., BENZONI, L.: "Technico-Economic Methods of Radio Spectrum Assignment," *IEEE Commun. Magazine*, vol. 33, pp. 88-94, June 1995.

YUVAL, G.: "How to Swindle Rabin," *Cryptologia*, vol. 3, pp. 187-190, July 1979.

ZHANG, L.: "Comparison of Two Bridge Routing Approaches," *IEEE Network Magazine*, vol. 2, pp. 44-48, Jan./Feb. 1988.

ZHANG, L.: "RSVP A New Resource ReSerVation Protocol," *IEEE Network Magazine*, vol. 7, pp. 8-18, Sept./Oct. 1993.

ZIMMERMANN, P.R.: *The Official PGP User's Guide*, Cambridge, MA: M.I.T. Press, 1995a.

ZIMMERMANN, P.R.: *PGP: Source Code and Internals*, Cambridge, MA: M.I.T. Press, 1995b.

ZIPF, G.K.: *Human Behavior and the Principle of Least Effort: An Introduction to Human Ecology*, Cambridge, MA: Addison-Wesley, 1949.

ZIV, J., and LEMPEL, Z.: "A Universal Algorithm for Sequential Data Compression," *IEEE Trans. on Information Theory*, vol. IT-23, pp. 337-343, May 1977.

INDEX

Very high frequency band, 95, 97-98
Very low frequency band, 95, 97
Very small aperture terminal, 165
VHF band (*see* Very High Frequency band)
Video, 727-730
    analog, 727-729
    digital, 729-730
    interlaced, 728
    progressive, 728
Video on demand, 744-756
    distribution network, 750-754
    server, 745-750
    set-top box, 754-756
Video server, 745-750
    software, 747-749
Videoconference, 5
Virtual channel, ATM, 450
Virtual circuit, 342-345
    compared to datagram, 344-345
Virtual path, ATM, 450
Virtual scheduling algorithm, 466
VISTAnet, 56
VLF band (*see* Very low frequency band)
Voice-grade line, 79
VSAT (*see* Very Small Aperture Terminal)
VTMP, 572

W

WAN (*see* Wide Area Network)
WARC (*see* World Administrative Radio
    Conference)
Wavelength, 94
Wavelength division multiple access, 260-262
Wavelength division multiplexing, 119-121
WDM (*see* Wavelength Division
    Multiplexing)
WDMA (*see* Wavelength Division Multiple
    Access)
Web (*see* World Wide Web)
Web page, 682, 683, 697
Weighted fair queueing, 388-389
Well-known port, 523
Wide area network, 11-13
Wine policy, 390

Wireless networking, 13-15
    analog radio, 155-163
    digital radio, 266-275
    electromagnetic waves, 94-101
    mobile hosts, 367-370, 432-434
    wireless LANs, 262-265
    wireless TCP, 543-545
Wireline carrier, 160
Wiring closet, 83
Work factor, 581
World administrative radio conference, 95
World Wide Web, 54, 681-723
    browser, 682
    CGI, 705-706
    external viewer
    fetching a page, 685-687
    HTML language, 691-706
    HTTP protocol, 689-691
    hyperlink, 682
    hypermedia, 684
    hypertext, 682
    Java, 706-720
    search engine, 720-723
    server, 685-689
    URL, 692-695
Worm, 720
WWV, 494
WWW (*see* World Wide Web)
WYSIWYG, 695

X

X.3, 60
X.21, 59
X.25, 59-60
X.28, 60
X.29, 60
X.400, 644, 661
X.509, 668-669
XTP, 572

Z

Zipf's law, 746
Zone, DNS, 628

About the Author

Andrew S. Tanenbaum has an S.B. degree from M.I.T. and a Ph.D. from the University of California at Berkeley. He is currently a Professor of Computer Science at the Vrije Universiteit in Amsterdam, The Netherlands, where he heads the Computer Systems Group. He is also Dean of the Advanced School for Computing and Imaging, an interuniversity graduate school doing research on advanced parallel systems, distributed systems, and imaging systems. Nevertheless, he is trying very hard to avoid turning into a bureaucrat.

In the past, he has done research on compilers, operating systems, networking, and local-area distributed systems. His current research focuses primarily on the design of wide-area distributed systems that scale to millions of users. These research projects have led to over 70 refereed papers in journals and conference proceedings. He is also the author of five books (see page ii).

Prof. Tanenbaum has also produced a considerable volume of software. He was the principal architect of the Amsterdam Compiler Kit, a widely-used toolkit for writing portable compilers, and MINIX, a small UNIX-like operating system for operating systems courses. Together with his Ph.D. students and programmers, he helped design the Amoeba distributed operating system, a high-performance microkernel-based distributed operating system. MINIX and Amoeba are now available for free for education and research via the Internet.

His Ph.D. students have gone on to greater glory after getting their degrees. He is very proud of them. In this respect he resembles a mother hen.

Prof. Tanenbaum is a Fellow of the ACM, a Senior Member of the IEEE, a member of the Royal Netherlands Academy of Arts and Sciences, and winner of the 1994 ACM Karl V. Karlstrom Outstanding Educator Award. He is also listed in *Who's Who in the World*. His home page on the World Wide Web is located at *http://www.cs.vu.nl/~ast/* .